With the
compliments
of the
Canada Council

Avec les
hommages
du Conseil des
Arts du Canada

# COLOMBO'S
# CANADIAN
# QUOTATIONS

# COLOMBO'S

# CANADIAN

# QUOTATIONS

### EDITED BY
### JOHN ROBERT COLOMBO

### HURTIG PUBLISHERS
### EDMONTON

Hurtig   Publishers
10560  105  Street
Edmonton, Alberta


ISBN
0-88830-079-4

Printed and bound
in Canada.

# CONTENTS

Preface/*vii*

Acknowledgements/*ix*

Quotations/*1*

Index/*651*

Canada only needs to be known in order to be great.
(J. Castell Hopkins)

Dedicated
To the Honourable Walter L. Gordon

But no one had done more than Walter Gordon to reveal to Canadians
that there is such a thing as the national interest,
and that its defence is a normal act of national self-respect.
(Denis Smith)

A dictionary of quotations is a collective composition incorporating the experiences of a vast range of people. In offering the thoughts and sayings of those who call themselves Canadians, or who have had occasion to observe or think about Canada, *Colombo's Canadian Quotations* is really about human experience. It is a celebration of Canada (though it is not entirely concerned with Canada) through the medium of quotation. It is an immense mosaic and a living collage, a repository and an inventory of lore and learning.

In the words of one of the contributors, I have tried "to chart old landmarks" and "to map new terrain" through the compilation of both a dictionary of familiar quotations and an anthology of memorable passages that should be better known. I have ransacked many hundreds of printed sources, from the double-columned tomes of *Hansard* to slim volumes of forgotten verse, and scanned countless newspapers, magazines and micro-texts with pen and paper in hand. Rudolph Flesch once referred to the research this sort of reference work requires as "determined browsing," and the phrase aptly describes the activity that engaged me for four years. In addition, I have badgered friends at parties and lingered perhaps too long at other gatherings of knowledgeable associates and acquaintances in the hope that they would recall a choice riposte or a revealing image, which many of them at my urging did. The forty-eight months I devoted to "this agreeable pursuit" (the phrase is John Bartlett's) were preceded by fifteen years of professional involvement in the worlds of publishing, education and authorship. Tracing my interest back still further, I realize that the book really began in the early years of elementary school, the day a Grade V student encountered his first Canadian quotation in a school reader:

> We have beside us a mountain of Books, Magazines, Pamphlets and Newspapers, that have been accumulating for the last two months, unopened and unread. Like a Turk, in the dim twilight of his Harem, we scarcely know which to choose. . . .

The image of the literary harem thrilled me as a ten-year-old, and it thrills me today, not quite thirty years later. (The reader who is curious about the source of this passage will find it on page 270.)

When I began to read widely in Canadiana, I noticed that Canadians were seldom taken seriously by the editors of books of quotations that were published in the United States and Great Britain. Wolfe's dying words, Osler's bedside observations, Leacock's hyperbole—these may appear. But one searches in vain for the wise observations of "Calgary Bob" Edwards, Jean-Paul Desbiens, Sir John A. Macdonald, to name but three eminently quotable people who go unquoted outside the country (and, as often as not, inside as well). This nation's contribution to Bartlett's *Familiar Quotations* or *The Oxford Dictionary of Quotations* has been in the neighbourhood of one-half of one per cent. Are Canadians too taciturn, too unimaginative, to originate memorable remarks? A more convincing reason for the universal neglect of Canadian wit and eloquence might be that this country has always lacked lively and wide-ranging collections of quotable material from which native and foreign editors could crib.

*Colombo's Canadian Quotations* presents six thousand quotations by twenty-five hundred contributors—men and women who have some connection with this country, however nominal that may be, and who span the centuries from approximately 400 B.C. to December 31, 1973. It is probably true that fewer than three hundred of the quotations are in the instant-recognition category, but the great majority are notable for being charged with literary power. They dramatize an important incident in the past; they cast new light on a subject close at hand; they make vivid an unusual or a communal point of view; they share an insight with the reader. Across these many pages the famous are juxtaposed with the unknown, as men and women have been throughout history. Canadians are permitted to comment on any subject under the sun; non-Canadians are limited to observations about this country and its people. More than half the passages cited derive from the modern period and more than one-quarter have to do with the contemporary scene. There is also much traditional material, found under the heading "Anonymous." This section has been organized into eleven categories: Eskimo; Indian; Lore; Mottos; Select Epitaphs; One Dozen Limericks; R.C.M.P.; Some Documents; Martial Airs; Songs; Verses and Rhymes. Most of the material included makes its début in a dictionary of quotations.

All along I have thought it better to include rather than to exclude. The result is a big book—the largest dictionary of its kind ever published in Canada, the first to be based for the most part on primary sources, and the only one to follow in the footsteps of Bartlett's *Familiar Quotations* and *The Oxford Dictionary of Quotations* in adopting an author arrangement with an exhaustive index.

Every effort has been made to trace passages of prose and poetry back to their earliest appearances in printed form and to transcribe the originals accurately. Passages are reprinted in the form in which they first appeared. But I have sometimes allowed myself latitude in transcribing those that have minor inconsistencies or that derive from an oral source. Known bibliographical references are given in the notes, with additional information when this is not easily available or when the significance of the passage requires explanation. In writing these notes I have assumed that the reader has a general knowledge of Canadian history and literature.

The index contains twenty thousand keyword and subject entries. Each quotation has been indexed an average of three times—under keyword, subject word, and a combination of the two. To locate "The medium is the message," having forgotten that the author is Marshall McLuhan, one could check either of the two keywords ("medium" or "message") or the subject word ("communications"). The reader should check all possible synonyms for the subject in question. As Canada is the subject of perhaps one-fifth of the book, only substantial references have been indexed under the headings "Canada," "Canadian," "Dominion." References to Great Britain and the United States will be found under these headings and their related forms and also under analytic subheadings included among the "Canada" entries ("Canada and Great Britain," etc.). The book itself is an alphabetical index of 2,500 contributors with numerous cross-references. There are many passing references to contributors in the text; those that have not been cross-referenced may be found in the index.

*Colombo's Canadian Quotations* should be seen as an ongoing endeavour. Readers and users of this volume can help in the preparation of future editions and successors by drawing the editor's attention to errors of omission and commission. I am especially eager to learn of memorable passages and remarks that have been overlooked, and I will try to acknowledge all letters.

JOHN ROBERT COLOMBO

42 Dell Park Avenue
Toronto, Ontario
Canada   M6B 2T6

# ACKNOWLEDGEMENTS

This book would not exist but for the achievements of others. Norah Story's *The Oxford Companion to Canadian History and Literature* (1967) became my *vade mecum*. It was often disheartening, at the first flush of discovering an obscure source, to turn to Miss Story's book to find that she (like the Frenchman in John Buchan's poem) had "done it before." Other works frequently referred to include W. Stewart Wallace's *The Macmillan Dictionary of Canadian Biography* (Third Edition, 1963), William Rose Benét's *The Reader's Encyclopedia: An Encyclopedia of World Literature and the Arts* (1948), Walter S. Avis's *A Dictionary of Canadianisms on Historical Principles* (1967), and the ten-volume set of John E. Robbins' *Encyclopedia Canadiana* (1963 edition). Margaret Fairley's *Spirit of Canadian Democracy: Canadian Writings from the Beginnings to the Present Day* (1945) and William Toye's *A Book of Canada* (1962) were also very useful. *The Oxford Dictionary of Quotations* (Second Edition, 1959) and John Bartlett's *Familiar Quotations* (Fourteenth Edition, Revised and Enlarged, 1968) were consulted from time to time, as was *Canadian Quotations and Phrases: Literary and Historical* (1952) by Robert M. Hamilton, whose pioneering work I am pleased to acknowledge. I know of three other books of Canadian quotations: *Canadian Days: Selections for Every Day in the Year from the Works of Canadian Authors* (1911), compiled by the Toronto Women's Press Club, and *"Quotations" from English Canadian Literature* (1973) and *Dictionnaire de citations de la littérature québécoise* (1974), both edited by David Strickland.

My research was largely conducted at the Metropolitan Toronto Central Library, where I found the "Metro Central" staff unfailingly helpful; one librarian, Cameron Hollyer, encouraged me in numerous ways. The John P. Robarts Research Library of the University of Toronto opened in time to provide new and comfortable quarters for the last months of fact-checking. I borrowed bushels of current books from the Bathurst Heights Area Branch of the North York Library System, where one of the librarians, Philip Singer, was of considerable assistance in checking obscure references and locating hard-to-find books in out-of-the-way parts of the country.

A number of antiquarian book dealers in Toronto extended borrowing privileges. Co-operative bookmen included Martin Ahvenus (of the Village Book Store), Hugh Anson-Cartwright (of Hugh Anson-Cartwright Books), Nelson Ball (of William Nelson Books), David Mason (of David Mason Books) and Jerry Sherlock (of Joseph Patrick Books). But my principal debt is to Asher Joram of Acadia Books. For a period of two years this patient man watched with mounting disbelief as I carted in and out of his store each week at least twenty out-of-print books and rare publications. (I think I have finally returned them all.)

I originally planned to express my gratitude to each person who supplied me with a useable remark or reference or helped me in other ways. But as the quoted material increased in volume, so did the list of my "assistants." When the roster reached three hundred names, it was with reluctance that I decided to mention only a few of them. Robert Fulford and William Kilbourn were enthusiastic from the start. Cyril Greenland and Doug Fetherling supplied me with an endless stream of quotations, well beyond the requirements of friendship. J. Alex. Edmison, Mark Frank, Jack Granatstein, Hugh Hood, Gordon Johnston, R.S. Kenny, S.W. Horrall, Bob Ward, Peter Weinrich and Morris Wolfe directed me to marvellous material that I would never have found on my own. *Weekend Magazine* published two features on my quote-collecting project (on March 17 and August 25, 1973) and these produced a mine of useable items; I am indebted to Don Bell, Jacqui Cole, Frank Lowe and Paul Rush. Helpful in specialized areas were Harald Bohne, Claude X. LaBrecque, Helmut Kallmann, Mavor Moore, Patricia Oliver, I.M. Owen, Pauline E. Rhind, Henry Roxborough and Robert Weaver. Many French and German passages were newly translated by Irène Currie, and Russian passages by Maria Ponomarev.

# Acknowledgements

The task of editing the unwieldy manuscript fell into the capable hands of, first, Diane Mew, and, second, Jan Walter, who saved me from not a few errors. In my work on the proofs I benefitted from the knowledge and advice of William Toye. (In my Latin dictionary the noun *error*, which means "a wandering about," is immediately followed by the verb *erubesco*, which means "to grow red, blush.") The format and design of the book were evolved by David Shaw. From the first Mel Hurtig of Hurtig Publishers wished to publish the book for the same reasons that I wanted to compile it—to help reveal the Canadian spirit through the medium of quotation. Ruth Colombo, my wife, made an immense contribution through her wide reading and moral support, often without being aware of it.

The Canada Council underwrote a portion of the expenses of the project through its Explorations (then called Horizons) Program, and the Ontario Arts Council (then called the Province of Ontario Council for the Arts) made a small personal grant available. I am grateful to the officers and advisers of both bodies for their interest and encouragement.

# A

## Abbott, Francis
In all my wanderings, I have never met with anything in Nature that equals it in sublimity, except perhaps Mount Etna during an eruption.

> Francis Abbott, "the Hermit of Niagara," lived for two years on Goat Island, practised on his violin at the precipice of the falls, and eventually drowned in the Great Whirlpool below the falls, June 10, 1831. Quoted by Edgar Andrew Collard in *Canadian Yesterdays* (1955).

## Abbott, Sir John
Draw on me for ten thousand dollars.

> Sir John Abbott, legal adviser to the CPR which had been granted lucrative contracts by the Conservative government, wired this message to Sir John A. Macdonald a few hours after receiving the prime minister's wire, August 26, 1872: "I must have another ten thousand; will be the last time of calling; do not fail me; answer today." Revelation of such campaign-fund contributions brought about the Pacific Scandal of 1873. See also Sir John A. Macdonald.

## 'Abdu'l-Bahá
. . . again I repeat, that the future of Canada, whether from the standpoint of civilization or from the viewpoint of the virtues of the kingdom, is very great. Day by day civilization and freedom shall increase. Likewise the cloud of the Kingdom will water the seeds of guidance in that Dominion.

> *Tablets of the Divine Plan* (1959), revealed by 'Abdu'l-Bahá in Haifa in 1917. 'Abdu'l-Bahá, the eldest son of Bahá'u'lláh, the prophet and founder of the Bahá'í Faith, visited Montreal in 1912.

## Aberdeen, Lady
. . No one lives here who is not obliged to, & its absolutely flat, arid, treeless surroundings do but typify the life of the place.

> Regina as seen by the wife of Lord Aberdeen, the governor general, July 13, 1898. *The Canadian Journal of Lady Aberdeen: 1893-1898* (1960), edited by John T. Saywell.

## Aberhart, William
Food is rotting in warehouses, being burned and dumped into the sea. It is the money system destroying food to maintain prices. [Memorandum, 1932]

\*

You can't talk religion to a man who has had nothing to eat for three days.

\*

Major Douglas, Fig Tree Court, London: Victorious. When could you come? Aberhart.

> When the Social Credit party assumed power in Alberta, August 22, 1935, William Aberhart sent this cable to Major C.H. Douglas. Although John Gordon Hargrave's Green Shirts marched seven times around the Bank of England, shouting Aberhart's name, the Social Credit theorist did not accept the invitation. Quoted by L.P.V. Johnson and Ola J. MacNutt in *Aberhart of Alberta* (1970).

If we cannot feed, clothe and shelter the people of Alberta, tell me who else is going to do it?

> "Social Credit," September 13, 1935, *Addresses Delivered before the Canadian Club of Toronto: Season of 1935-36* (1936).

If the people have not suffered enough, it is their God-given right to suffer some more.

> Quoted by Jon Whyte in "The Ballad of Twain and Abel" in *The Unfinished Revolt: Some Views on Western Independence* (1971), edited by John Barr and Owen Anderson.

It is the duty of the state through its Government to organize its economic structure in such a way that no bona fide citizen, man, woman, or child, shall be allowed to suffer for lack of the bare necessities of food, clothing, and shelter, in the midst of plenty of abundance. [Opening sentence of *Social Credit Manual* (1935).]

*

Will you tell me how a heart can pump 135 gallons an hour with only four quarts of blood? Well, cannot money circulate the same? [Annual Convention, United Farmers of Alberta, January 16, 1935]

*

Fool-osophy. [Aberhart's term for "philosophy"]

*

The Eyes of the World are on Alberta. [Social Credit slogan in the election of August 22, 1935, which brought Aberhart's reform party to provincial power]

> Quoted by John A. Irving in *The Social Credit Movement in Alberta* (1959). See also Major C.H. Douglas and Hewlett Johnson.

## Acheson, Dean

Americans take Canada for granted, and Canadians are forever saying so. By this they mean that Americans assume Canada to be bestowed as a right and accept this bounty, as they do air, without thought or appreciation. Perhaps they do; and perhaps they should. For, if it were not taken as a bounty of nature, America might not grasp Canada at all for sheer difficulty in figuring out what Canada is.

> Dean Acheson served as secretary of State under President Harry S. Truman from 1949 to 1953. "Canada: 'Stern Daughter of the Voice of God,'" *Neighbors Taken for Granted: Canada and the United States* (1966), edited by Livingston T. Merchant. The address was reprinted in Acheson's *Grapes from Thorns* (1972).

## Acorn, Milton

Without freedom, no one really has a name.

Final line of "Proposed Dedication for a Monument to Lount and Matthews," *More Poems for People* (1972).

## Adam, G. Mercer

In Canada . . . there is, in the ebbing out of national spirit, a growing intellectual callousness, and a deadening of interest in the things that make for the nation's higher life.

> "An Interregnum in Literature," *The Week*, June 10, 1884.

## Adam of Bremen

He told me of yet another land, discovered by many in that ocean, which is called Wineland from the fact that there grow vines, producing the best of wines. Moreover, that grain abounds there without sowing, we have ascertained, not from fabulous conjecture, but from the reliable reports of the Danes.

*

King Swen said that beyond this island [of Wineland, Vineland, Newfoundland?] no habitable land is found in that ocean, but all that is beyond is full of intolerable ice and utter darkness. . . . This was lately tested by the most enterprising Harald, Prince of the Norsemen, who, when exploring with his ships the breadth of the northern ocean, hardly escaped with safety from the awful gulf of the abyss by turning back, when at length the bounds of the earth grew dark before his eyes.

> Adam of Bremen, rector of the Cathedral School of Hamburg, recorded in 1070 details of a conversation with King Swen Estridson of Denmark. The Danish king referred to King Harald the Ruthless of Norway who was a great traveller and had set out "to explore the western sea" about 1050. Quoted by Hjalmar R. Holand in *Explorations in America before Columbus* (1956).

## Adams, Henry

This Canadian business is suddenly found to be serious, and the prospect of Sherman marching down the St. Lawrence and Farragut sailing up it, doesn't just seem agreeable.

> From *A Cycle of Adams Letters, 1861-*

*65* (1920) by the American historian. Quoted by Mason Wade in *The French-Canadian Outlook: A Brief Account of the Unknown North Americans* (1946).

## Adams, Ian
How can they tell us to free ourselves from the pressures they have forced upon us, or to seek our equality when we are only pawns to be used in their game.

*The Poverty Wall* (1970).

To be poor in our society is to suffer the most outrageous kinds of violence perpetuated by human beings on other human beings.

*The Real Poverty Report* (1971), by Ian Adams, William Cameron, Brian Hill, and Peter Penz.

## Adams, Joey
It gets so cold in the northern Canadian woods the women wear mink girdles.

\*

Up in Canada they have an organization called the Royal Canadian Mounted Police. They have the reputation of always getting their man. We got the same thing here in this country. We call it Selective Service.

*The Joey Adams Joke Dictionary* (1961).

## Adams, John
The Unanimous Voice of the Continent is Canada must be ours; Quebec must be taken.

Statement made following the death of Brigadier-General Richard Montgomery who fell trying to take Quebec, New Year's Day, 1776. Adams went on to become the second president of the United States (1796-1800).

## Adams, Lydia
I am afraid the slaveholders will go to a bad place—I am really afraid they will. I don't think any slaveholder can get to the kingdom.

Lydia Adams, a Virginia slave, settled in Windsor. Quoted by Benjamin Drew in *The Refugee: or the Narratives of Fugitive Slaves in Canada* (1856).

## Adams, Martha
The prostitute is never an enemy of the man's wife.

*Martha Adams* (1972), by the woman who calls herself the most famous of Montreal's madams. Ms. Adams ran against Claude Wagner in the federal election of 1972.

## Adario
Ha! Long live the *Hurons*; who without Laws, without Prisons, and without Torture, pass their Life in a State of Sweetness and Tranquility, and enjoy a pitch of Felicity to which the *French* are utter Strangers. We live quietly under the Laws of Instinct and innocent Conduct, which wise Nature has imprinted upon our Minds from our Cradles.

"Adario is believed to have been the prototype of Jean-Jacques Rousseau's 'noble savage,'" according to Norah Story in *The Oxford Companion to Canadian History and Literature* (1967). Adario, an actual Huron chief named The Rat who died in 1701, was used by the traveller Baron de La Hontan in the third volume of his memoirs published in 1703 as a mouthpiece for his own unorthodox opinions. *New Voyages to North America* (1905), translated by Reuben Gold Thwaites. See also Baron de La Hontan.

## Adaskin, Murray
I have often wondered whether an abiding love for a subject wasn't in itself an indication of some talent for it.

Composer interviewed by *Musicanada*, May, 1967.

## Adelman, Howard
To create a community of radical scholars, men and women who recognize that rules and social conventions are arbitrary, but have mastered them nonetheless—a community which shares such a scorn and disrespect for the present society that it can embrace the whole bundle of rules and subvert them thereby—that should be our goal.

"In Search of a University," *The University Game* (1968), edited by Howard Adelman and Dennis Lee.

## Adreon, Franklin

A band of foreign agents who are engineering a mysterious operation in the frozen regions of Canada are the subject of a widespread search by the Canadian Mounted Police.

> Adreon directed for Republic Pictures in 1953 a twelve-part serial called *Canadian Mounties vs. Atomic Invaders.* This first sentence of the plot synopsis comes from *To Be Continued . . .* (1972), by Ken Weiss and Ed Goodgold. See also William Stedman.

## Aitken, Hugh G.J.

Canada's new northern frontier is Canadian only in a geographic and political sense; economically, it is a frontier of United States resource investment. The emerging pattern of resource depletion in the United States is fundamental to an understanding of the forces working to integrate the two nations into a continental economic system.

*

Experience has underlined a principle that could have been stated *a priori.* If Canada wants the United States to do something, she must be able to prove it is in the national interests of the United States to do it.

> *American Capital and Canadian Resources* (1961).

## Aitken, Kate

A good speech should contain a lot of shortening. [Attributed]

On my return [from Germany in 1947] came one of the worst *faux pas* I've ever uttered. I assured our [radio] audience that husbands and sweethearts thought longingly of home, but added, "However there's no doubt that German girls are bending over backwards to please Canadian soldiers."

> *Making Your Living Is Fun* (1959).

## Aitken, Margaret

One little helpful hint that the candidate picked up at about this time as a result of experience was the principle: pass things whenever possible. By doing so, one can circulate smoothly and also appear useful. The thing not to do is pour tea. In doing that, one gets stuck in a corner and a whole afternoon can be wasted. The candidate was learning—pass but don't pour.

*

A speech is like a good piece of fiction or an article. It must have a beginning, a middle and an end. A very fine preacher once said, "The best way to give a sermon is to take one idea and *burn a hole with it.*"

> *Hey Ma! I Did It* (1953), by Margaret Aitken and Byrne Hope Sanders.

## Aitken, Sir Max   See Lord Beaverbrook.

## Aitken, Sir Max

As long as I live there will be only one Lord Beaverbrook.

> When his illustrious father died, the son of Lord Beaverbrook renounced the title but retained the baronetcy. Quoted by A.J.P. Taylor in *Beaverbrook* (1972).

## Alanbrooke, Field Marshal The Viscount

There is an account of the Combined Chiefs of Staff's visit to the Heights of Abraham in Admiral King's *Life.* The battlefield was poorly marked and the guide was unable to answer all the searching questions asked by these formidable visitors. As they were wandering about the field, trying to locate the salient points, they chanced to meet an old French priest who knew the area thoroughly. He spoke no English, but Brooke's French was fluent, and so for some time the heads of the land, naval and air forces of Great Britain and the United States grouped themselves closely around a country priest in shabby cassock, who instructed them in military history, with the Chief of the Imperial General Staff acting as interpreter.

> Arthur Bryant's *The Turn of the Tide 1939-1943: A Study Based on the Diaries and Autobiographical Notes of Field Marshal The Viscount Alanbrooke, K.G.,* (1957), August 18, 1943. The volume referred to is *Fleet Admiral King* (1953), by E.J. King and W.M. Whitehill.

## Albani, Emma

I had always loved beautiful and artistic

things, though before leaving America I had had a very little chance of seeing any.

> *Forty Years of Song* (1911). Madame Albani, born Marie Louise Emma Cécile Lajeunesse at Chambly, Quebec, took her professional name from the city of Albany, New York, where she studied opera in her youth.

## Alcock, Norman Z.
Peace research.

> If Dr. Alcock did not originate this phrase, to parallel "war research," he certainly gave it currency when he founded the Canadian Peace Research Institute in Oakville, Ontario, in 1961.

## Alderson, Sir Edwin Alfred
There is one thing more. My old regiment, the Royal West Kents, has been here since the beginning of the war, and it has never lost a trench. The Army says, "The West Kents never budge." I am proud of the great record of my old regiment. And I think it is a good omen. I now belong to you and you belong to me; and before long the Army will say: "The Canadians never budge." Lads, it can be left there, and there I leave it. The Germans will never turn you out.

> General officer commanding the Canadian Corps before General Arthur Currie assumed command, 1915. *Canada in Flanders* (1916), by Lord Beaverbrook.

## Alexander, Sir James E.
"Come boys and have some grog, I'm what you call a canuck;" (a Canadian).

> Quoting "a lusty fellow," *L'Acadie; or, Seven Years' Explorations in British America* (1849). Perhaps the earliest appearance of "Canuck" for Canadian. By the turn of the century "Johnny Canuck" personified Canada.

## Alexander, Sir William
"James was a king who tried to be a poet and Alexander was a poet who tried to be a king."

> Remark made of King James I of England and Sir William Alexander, Earl of Stirling, Scottish poet and Baronet

of Nova Scotia. Quoted by Thomas B. Costain in *The White and the Gold: The French Regime in Canada* (1954), who adds: "It may be stated at the outset that both failed." See also Charles I.

## Alexander of Tunis, Lord Earl
Canada has fascinated me since childhood. As a boy in Ireland, I was intrigued by the sporting trophies my father brought home from there—moose heads, bear and buffalo rugs, Indian bows and arrows, not to mention three black bear cubs and a young elk stag, all very much alive.

> Foreword by the Right Honourable Field Marshal Earl Alexander of Tunis, Governor General (1946-1952), *The Canadians at War 1939-45* (1969), by the editors of *Reader's Digest*.

## Alinsky, Saul
You've got a patronage set-up here that makes Daley's operation look like a junior league.

> The Chicago reformer addressing the Canadian Union of Postal Workers, Ottawa, July 29, 1971. The reference is to the mayor of Chicago, Richard Daley.

## Allan, Andrew
I'm tired of the gut, but not the heart.

> *

The CBC has never learned how to let an individual make a career of his own talent.

> *The Globe and Mail*, January 16, 1971.

## Allan, Ted
Norman Bethune was the kind of Communist we all should be. He didn't seek power.

> "The Pierre Berton Show," telecast May 29, 1973.

## Allemagne, André d'
Confederation is a genocide without end.

> *

Colonialism reduces the culture of the colonized person to the level of folklore and propaganda.

> *Le colonialisme au Québec* (1966). Quoted by Marcel Rioux in *Quebec in Question* (1971).

## Allen, Ethan

I shall do everything in my power to make this state a British province.

"Ethan Allen," *The Encyclopaedia Britannica* (Eleventh Edition, 1910-11). Between 1779 and 1783, the American revolutionary hero negotiated with Governor-in-Chief Frederick Haldimand to bring Vermont under the British flag. This was the same Allen who, on May 10, 1775, captured Ticonderoga, calling on the British commanding officer to surrender "in the name of the Great Jehovah and the Continental Congress." Captured at Quebec in 1775 and imprisoned for two years, Allen wrote a famous work of prison literature, *A Narrative of Colonel Ethan Allen's Captivity* (1779).

## Allen, Ralph

Suppose Herbert Norman *had been* a Communist.

"For Sake of Argument," *Maclean's Magazine*, May 11, 1957. For the story, see Herbert Norman.

For twenty-seven glorious minutes last Saturday night Canada came close to rediscovering the only unique part of its inheritance. In spite of what they'll say in the commissions on culture and the proliferating expositions and festivals and aids-in-grant to anybody who knows anybody else, the only true Canadian invention is a game called hockey.

*The Toronto Star*, May 3, 1965. From *The Man from Oxbow: The Best of Ralph Allen* (1967), edited by Christina McCall Newman. The reference is to a Stanley Cup playoff.

God bless.

This "was how he said goodbye to friends, and somehow it was a benediction worthy of a poet, although Ralph himself had a Presbyterian conscience and claimed that he was a lapsed Unitarian." Peter C. Newman in "Ralph Allen" (1966), *Home Country: People, Places, and Power Politics* (1973).

## Allen, Robert Thomas

Even when Canadian humour is awful, it just lies there being awful in its own fresh way.

Introduction, *A Treasury of Canadian Humour* (1967).

## Allen, William

Fifty-four Forty, or Fight!

Attributed to William Allen in a speech on the Oregon boundary question in the U.S. Senate, 1844. The rallying cry became the slogan of the Democratic party in the federal election later that year. Allen demanded that the United States extend the American boundary north to 54° 40', to present-day Prince Rupert, but the new Democratic president, James K. Polk, reached a compromise with Great Britain and established the forty-ninth parallel as the boundary between the United States and the British colonies in North America.

## Allinson, Cyril L.C.

I took the mail first to the fire command post that was dug into the bank near McCrae's, then crossed past the little cemetery to a razed farmhouse where the mess was located.

I saw him sitting on the ambulance step, a pad on his knee. He looked up as I approached but continued to write. He was my senior officer, second in command of the brigade, and I did not interrupt. He wrote on for five minutes more, then, as I handed him his mail, he handed me his pad.

His face was very tired but calm as he wrote. He looked around from time to time, his eyes straying to Helmer's grave. The poem was almost an exact description of the scene in front of us both.

Major John McCrae wrote his famous poem "In Flanders Field" on May 3, 1917. Half a century later the inauspicious event was recalled by the soldier-physician-poet's friend, Cyril L. C. Allinson, who was the youngest brigade sergeant-major in the British forces at the time. The grave referred to was the newly turned one of Lieutenant Alexis Helmer, a close friend of McCrae's who was buried the previous night. Quoted by Don Delaplante, *The Globe and Mail*, November 11, 1968. See also John McCrae.

## Almighty Voice
Brothers, we've had a good fight today. We've worked hard and are hungry. You've plenty of grub; send us in some. Tomorrow we'll finish the fight.

The young Cree brave Almighty Voice evaded capture for three years. On May 30, 1897, at a shoot-out near Duck Lake, Almighty Voice and his two accomplices, Little Salteaux and Doubling, were surrounded by almost fifty Mounties and shot to death, but not before Almighty Voice issued the above taunt. Quoted by Captain Ernest J. Chambers in *The Royal North-West Mounted Police: A Corps History* (1906).

## Almond, Paul
Sooner or later my films will reach people. They may change, I may change. Someday we'll connect. I propose a final toast to the day I connect.

Film director and one-time husband of Geneviève Bujold, quoted by John Hofsess in *The Toronto Star*, September 16, 1972.

## Alverstone, Lord
"My decision is that you are entitled to the temporary use of all the air not required for United States' purposes."

Words put into the mouth of Lord Alverstone, chief justice of Great Britain, by the editorial cartoonist of the *Toronto News* to illustrate the betrayal Canadians felt in his decision in the Alaska Boundary Award, 1903. Quoted by W.G. Hardy in *From Sea Unto Sea: Canada 1850 to 1910, The Road to Nationhood* (1960).

## Amherst, Jeffrey
Tell M. de Vaudreuil I have come to take Canada and I will take nothing less.

Spoken by the commander-in-chief of His Majesty's forces in America to Chevalier Louis-Antoine de Bougainville who, on September 7, 1760, approached Amherst at Lachine, on behalf of the Marquis de Vaudreuil, governor of New France, to come to terms. Quoted by J.C. Long in *Lord Jeffrey Amherst, A Soldier of the King* (1933).

## Anahareo
Any interference with nature is damnable. Not only nature but also the people will suffer.

Ojibway wife of Grey Owl, quoted by Robert Martin in *The Globe and Mail*, June 9, 1972. See also Grey Owl.

## Anburey, Thomas
They are seldom or ever found without a pipe in their mouths, a habit which they acquire in their very infancy.

A description of the *habitant*, from *Travels through the Interior Parts of North America* (1789).

## Anderson, Charley
I never had a million dollars. The most I ever had was nine hundred thousand.

The "Lucky Swede" bought a million-dollar claim in the Klondike for eight hundred dollars, then lost his fortune through a series of calamities. He died a labourer in a British Columbia sawmill in 1939, as philosophical as ever. Quoted by Pierre Berton in *Klondike: The Life and Death of the Last Great Gold Rush* (1958).

## Anderson, Patrick
What are you . . . ? they ask.
And she replies: I am the wind that wants a flag.
I am the mirror of your picture
until you make me the marvel of your life.
Yes, I am one and none, pin and pine, snow and slow,
America's attic, an empty room,
a something possible, a chance, a dance
that is not danced. A cold kingdom.

From "Poem on Canada," *The White Centre* (1946).

Gave up his right to pardon. Was ordered hanged as a traitor.

But they say his body made a great
wound in the air,
and God Damn the English judge that
put him there.

> From "The Country Still Unpossessed,"
> *The White Centre* (1946).

All we knew was that, however "young"
the country might be, the landscape
seemed old and violent and sad.

> *Search Me* (1957).

### André, Brother
Old? I am not old. Let me see . . . seven
and five . . . that is twelve . . . yes, I am
twelve years old . . . you might say.
Tired? One is never tired in the service
of the Master.

*

Have I cured them . . . you should not
ask that . . . just say, they have, I hope,
all gone away happy . . . God bless you
all.

> Brother André, Alfred Bessette, inspired
> the building of St. Joseph's Oratory in
> Montreal in 1924. Many cures were
> ascribed to him. Quoted by George H.
> Ham in *The Miracle Man of Montreal*
> (Third Edition, 1922). A characteristic
> remark was: "I am St. Joseph's little
> dog."

### Angell, Norman
God has made Canada one of those nations which cannot be conquered and
cannot be destroyed, except by itself.

*

You know, of course, that we in the Old
Country are coming to take a very lively
interest in Canadian politics, for a very
good reason: you are beginning to dictate ours.

> "Canada's Best Service for British Ide-
> als," June 2, 1913, *Addresses Delivered
> before the Canadian Club of Toronto:
> Season of 1913-14* (1914).

### Anglin, Margaret
Actresses don't have husbands, they have
attendants.

> Quoted by Harding Lemay in *Inside,
> Looking Out: A Personal Memoir*
> (1971). Once North America's leading

dramatic actress, Margaret Anglin was
born in the Speaker's Chambers of the
House of Commons in 1875; her father
was the Speaker of the House. She died
in Toronto in 1958.

### Anka, Paul
Canada is a good country to *be* from. It
has a gentler, slower pace—it lends perspective.

*

The thing is to be able to outlast the
trends.

> Quoted by David Cobb in *The Cana-
> dian Magazine*, January 22, 1972.

### Annett, Philip
I think you was better sell your house
and get a little of the parish and come
to Canada whilst you have a chance. If
you don't come soon it is likely you will
starve, and if you don't your children
will; whilst if you was to come hither
with your family, any one would be glad
to take one or two of them and keep
them as their own children until of age,
and then give them 100 acres of land
and stock besides. I was agreeably surprised when I came here to see what a
fine country it was. It being excellent
land, bearing crops of wheat and other
corn for twenty or thirty years without
any dung. Here you have no rent to pay,
no poor-rates, and scarcely any taxes. No
game-keepers or lords over you. Here you
can go and shoot wild deer, Turkeys,
Pheasants, Quails, Pigeons, any other
sort of game and catch plenty of fish
without molestation whatever; here you
can raise everything of your own that
you want to make use of in your family.
You can make your own soap, candles,
sugar, treacle and vinegar without paying any duty. Clothing is as cheap as in
England. Wages is high . . . a man can
earn enough in three days to last him all
the week. I am satisfied with the country
and so is Luesa, for we are so much respected here as any of our neighbours,
and so would you if you come. . . .

> Letter from the day-labourer, Port Tal-
> bot, Upper Canada, May 24, 1830, *Ex-
> tracts from Letters from Poor Persons
> who Emigrated Last Year to Canada
> and the United States* (1832).

# ANONYMOUS

## Eskimo

And yet, there is only
One great thing,
The only thing:
To live to see, in huts and on journeys
The great day that dawns
And the light that fills the world.

> From "a little nameless Eskimo song" sung at Kent Peninsula, N.W.T. Knud Rasmussen, *The Mackenzie Eskimos: After Knud Rasmussen's Posthumous Notes: Report of the Fifth Thule Expedition, 1921-24* (1942), edited by H. Ostermann.

A man's best friend is his dog, better even than his wife.

*

Luck is better than long legs.

*

Trust the river but do not trust the brook.

*

You do not know who is your friend or who is your enemy until the ice breaks.

*

Love comes after marriage. [Eskimo proverbs]

## Chimo

> A mixed Indian and Eskimo word of salutation, pronounced either "chy-mo" or "chee-mo," according to Walter S. Avis's *A Dictionary of Canadianisms on Historical Principles* (1967). (Fort Chimo, founded in Ungava by the Hudson's Bay Company in 1830, is today called Umingmaqautik.)

## Indian

Father, I love your daughter, will you give her to me, that the small roots of her heart may entangle with mine, so that the strongest wind that blows shall never separate them.

> Chippewa brave addressing his future father-in-law; quoted by J. Long in *Voyages and Travels of an Indian Interpreter and Trader* (1791).

It is not enough for a man to know how to ride, he must know how to fall.

*

He who does not speak is not heard by God.

*

He who tells the truth doesn't sin, but he causes inconvenience.

*

No one gets out of bed to sleep on the floor.

*

A deer, although toothless, may accomplish something.

*

He wants to die with all his teeth in his head.

*

The spirit walking in the sky takes care of us. [Ojibway and other North American Indian proverbs]

## Lore

### Dominion

The word Canada . . . has no official meaning.

> *Reader's Digest Almanac* (1956).

The Fathers of Confederation.

> This sobriquet is applied to those thirty-six delegates from the British North American colonies who attended one or more of the three conferences in Charlottetown (September 1, 1864), Quebec City (October 10-29, 1864), and London, England (December 4, 1866), that led to Confederation (July 1, 1867). The Fathers are listed by Norah Story in *The Oxford Companion to Canadian History and Literature* (1967).

"Miss B. going to Canada? Why, she'll be eaten up by the tigers!" Such was the exclamation of the old family coachman on hearing of my intended marriage and emigration.

> "A Lady's Reflections on Canada," *Chambers's Journal of Popular Literature, Science and Art* (1873).

Made in Canada.

> Unofficial motto of the Canadian Manufacturers' Association during a "Buy Canadian" campaign in 1903.

No Englishmen Need Apply.

> From an advertisement for a "position

vacant" in a Winnipeg newspaper, August, 1909, which coincided with a meeting of the British Association in that city. See also Keir Hardie.

### The North Atlantic Triangle.

"A neat way of summarizing the overall interchange would be to note that Canada normally bought more from the United States than she sold to her and paid the balance with the sterling credits which materialized from selling more to Great Britain than she bought from her." John Bartlet Brebner in *North Atlantic Triangle: The Interplay of Canada, the United States and Great Britain* (1945). Brebner is writing about the triangular trade pattern that had developed by 1935, but the concept of the "middle passage" in Atlantic trade goes back to the eighteenth century.

### Bonne entente.

"The *bonne entente* ('good will' or 'cordial cooperation') movement attempted just after the First World War and through the 1920s to heal some of the widening fissures between English and French Canadians. The movement harboured business men and politicians whose vested interests were fairly obvious in innumerable after-dinner speeches of good will. The term became, and has remained, one of derision in nationalist circles in Quebec." Susan Mann Trofimenkoff in *Abbé Groulx: Variations on a Nationalist Theme* (1973).

### Canada Carries On.

This is the general title given to a series of ten-minute newsreels devoted to the war effort and produced by the National Film Board. Sixty-two short features were released between 1940 and June of 1945. The series survived the war; another ninety-eight, dealing with general subjects, were produced until 1959.

### A mid-Atlantic accent.

The British-Canadian accent is frequently described this way, especially by CBC actors. The phrase "mid-Atlantic" presumably implies a merging of the best of British and American accents, for the phrase has nothing to do with Bermuda. It may date from "the Golden Age of Radio" (1940-1955).

Sentry: 'Alt, who goes there?
Reply: Scots Guards.
Sentry: Pass, Scots Guards.

Sentry: 'Alt, who goes there?
Reply: The Buffs.
Sentry: Pass, The Buffs.

Sentry: 'Alt, who goes there?
Reply: Mind your own God-damn business!
Sentry: Pass, Canadians.

Quoted by Leslie F. Hannon in *Canada at War* (1968).

### Newfoundland

A piece of rock entirely surrounded by fog.

A home entirely surrounded by hospitality.

God made the world in six days, and on the seventh, sailed inshore and hurled rocks at Labrador.

Quoted by Richard Gwyn in *Smallwood: The Unlikely Revolutionary* (1968).

As fine a man as ever broke a cake of the world's bread.

*

An honest man when there are no anchors around.

*

A fisherman is one rogue, a merchant is many.

*

Cape St. Mary's pays for all.

*

Empty vessels loom biggest.

*

Fair weather to you and snow to your heels.

*

Let no man steal your lines.

*

Pigs may fly, but they are very unlikely birds.

*

'Tis not every day that Morris kills a cow.

*
You are as deep as the grave.

Proverbs and folk expressions quoted by L.E.F. English in *Historic Newfoundland* (1960).

## Prince Edward Island

In the hearts and minds of the
delegates who assembled
in this room on September 1, 1864
was born the Dominion of Canada.

Providence being their guide
They builded better than they knew.

Inscription on a bronze plaque erected in 1917 but unveiled July 1, 1927, in the Legislative Chamber, Charlottetown, which marks the place where the basis was established for a confederation of the British North American colonies. The haunting couplet "Providence being their guide / They builded better than they knew" is a powerful pastiche of lines by Milton and Emerson, British and American poets who represent, respectively, reason and idealism. In the final lines of *Paradise Lost* (1667), John Milton described Adam and Eve leaving the Garden of Eden: "The world was all before them, where to choose / Their place of rest, and Providence their guide: / They hand in hand with wand'ring steps and slow / Through Eden took their solitary way." Ralph Waldo Emerson wrote of the need for belief in "The Problem," *Poems* (1847): "The hand that rounded Peter's dome, / And groined the aisles of Christian Rome, / Wrought in a sad sincerity; / Himself from God he could not free; / He builded better than he knew;— / The conscious stone to beauty grew." These passages, uniting the Old World and the New, could not have been better chosen or combined.

I found Charlottetown to be wicked enough for a far larger place. [Early visitor]

Covers the Island like the Dew.

Motto of *The Charlottetown Guardian and Patriot*, the Island's leading newspaper, founded in 1864.

LONG COURTED: WON AT LAST

Inscription on the ceremonial arch in Charlottetown through which the governor general passed when P.E.I. joined Confederation, July 1, 1873.

## Nova Scotia

Nova Scotia is a peninsula entirely surrounded by fish. [Early travel book]

May your road rise with you;
May the wind blow always at your back;
May the good Lord hold you in the hollow of His hand.

Gaelic blessing from Cape Breton, quoted by Edward McCourt in *The Road Across Canada* (1964).

Breathes there the man, with soul so dead,
Who never to himself hath said,
    This is my own, my native land.

The last line was the motto of a series of articles on Nova Scotia in the *Acadian Register* in 1826. The passage comes from Sir Walter Scott's *The Lay of the Last Minstrel* (1805).

They Sacrificed Everything Save Honour

Inscription on a cairn dedicated in 1964 to the United Empire Loyalists who settled the province, Tusket, Yarmouth County.

## New Brunswick

Lord, have compassion upon me, a poor unfortunate sinner, three thousand miles from my own country, and seventy-five from anywhere else.

Irish immigrant's prayer, 1784, quoted by John Murray Gibbon in *Canadian Mosaic: The Making of a Northern Nation* (1938).

How are your potatoes?
Very small.
How do you eat them?
Skins and all!

New Brunswick folk song, quoted by Lord Beaverbrook in *Courage: The Story of Sir James Dunn* (1961).

## Quebec

In this secluded spot lie the mortal remains of 5,424 persons who, fleeing from pestilence and famine in Ireland in the year 1847, found in America but a grave.

> Memorial, Grosse Ile, St. Lawrence River. "Grosse Isle is now an animal quarantine station, and is normally closed to visitors, though there is a suggestive view of it in Montmagny on the southern bank. The fever sheds still stand, and a monument commemorates the Irish who died on the island." James Morris in *Heaven's Command: An Imperial Progress* (1973).

Saint-Louis-du-Ha! Ha!

> Amusingly named Quebec village in Rivière du Loup County on the south shore of the St. Lawrence. On the north shore there is a tributary of the Saguenay River named Ha Ha River which has a Ha Ha Bay.

Jean Mance St.
Esplanade Ave.
Waverley St.
St. Urbain Street

> Adjacent Montreal streets, the initial letters of which spell out the name of a minority group in the area.

After your catechism, your Canadian history textbook should be the most precious of all your books.

> *Mon pays* (1954), a textbook for grades seven and eight by Frères des écoles chrétiennes. Quoted by Marcel Trudel and Geneviève Jain in *Canadian History Textbooks: A Comparative Study* (1970), Studies of the Royal Commission on Bilingualism and Biculturalism.

Cent ans d'injustice.

> "When they said at the time of the Centenary, *cent ans d'injustice*, one hundred years of injustice, I said they should say, one hundred years of ignorance. They don't know what happened." Michel Brunet in *The Craft of History* (1973), edited by Eleanor Cook.

VIVE ELISABETH . . . TAYLOR!
VISIT/EZ EXPO? VISIT/EZ LES SLUMS!

> Graffiti for Queen Elizabeth II's royal visit to Montreal in 1964; graffiti for the opening of Expo in 1967.

## Ontario

They may tak' Montreal, and they may tak' Toronto, and they may tak' Woodstock, but they'll no tak' Zorra!

> The good citizens of East and West Zorra, Oxford county townships, defied the invading Fenians in 1866. Quoted by W.E. Elliott in *Politics is Funny* (1952).

One of the principal thoroughfares, called Yonge Street, extends northwards under that name through a rich and prosperous agricultural district about thirty-six miles; probably the longest *street* in the world, with the exception of the old Roman roads in England.

> *The Canadian Handbook and Tourist's Guide* (1867). See also George Augustus Sala.

We ain't the Waldorf-Astoria. If we were, you wouldn't be here. You ain't Pierpont Morgan. If you were, you wouldn't be here. We know this hotel is on the bum. What about yourself?

> Sign, Stag Hotel, Porcupine, 1920s, quoted by Frank Rasky in *Great Canadian Disasters* (1961).

This stone bears witness to the common purpose of two nations whose frontiers are the frontiers of friendship, whose ways are the ways of freedom, and whose works are the works of peace.

> Inscription, St. Lawrence Seaway, Prescott, June 26, 1959.

They are too near
To be great
But our children
Shall understand
When and how our
Fate was changed
And by whose hand

> Inscription, Memorial Chamber, Peace Tower, Ottawa.

United to Support, Not Combined to Injure.

> Motto of the International Typographical Society, No. 91, since 1844, the old-

est of Canada's printing associations. Noted by H.A. Logan in *Trade Unions in Canada: Their Development and Functioning* (1948).

First prize, one week in Toronto. Second prize, two weeks in Toronto. Third prize, three weeks in Toronto. [Quebec joke, probably 1920s]

## Manitoba

Scotch is the wine of the West. [Winnipeg adage]

The climate of Manitoba consists of seven months of Arctic weather and five months of cold weather.

*Settler's Guide to the North-West* (1882), published in New York by the Northern Pacific Railway Company.

Drive Carefully / You Might Hit / An Anglican. [Sign in front of St. James Anglican Church, Neepawa; the church is located on busy Highway No. 4]

## Saskatchewan

"Moose Jaw! Moose Jaw! Wouldn't that be an odd name for a college town?" "No, not at all. What about Oxford?"

Tisdale / Land of Rape and Honey. [Roadside sign outside town of Tisdale]

NEW YORK IS BIG, BUT THIS IS BIGGAR. [Roadsign outside Biggar, west of Saskatoon]

The Last One Out, Turn Out the Light. [Hastily erected sign on Highway No. 9 at the Saskatchewan-Alberta border meant to be read by those leaving Saskatchewan]

Tuxford hit the Marquis on the Eyebrow with his Elbow and spoiled his Outlook.

Mnemonic device to recall the names of the towns on the CPR branch line between Moose Jaw and Macklin, 1910s.

## Alberta

Drink the Water of the Peace River and You Will Return Again. [Sign outside the Administrative Building, Peace River]

Edmonton is as big as Chicago, but it isn't all built up yet.

Quoted by Lena Newman in *An Historical Almanac of Canada* (1967).

Drive Carefully / Watch for Pedestrians / Killam. [Sign on Highway No. 13, approaching Killam, 100 miles southeast of Edmonton]

Drilling Regulations / Palliser Hotel, Calgary

1. No well shall be drilled before 6:00 A.M. or after 3:00 P.M. Operations at that time are liable to disturb the paying guests while in the midst of beautiful dreams of vast wealth and permanent gushers.

2. No more than one well shall be drilled in each leather chair, or sofa, during one time interval. It is exhausting to the furniture.

3. No well shall be drilled in a tone of voice which is audible within the three-mile zone, and causes the skylight to flutter.

4. No well shall be drilled within one foot from any door, window, or passageway, and no disputes shall be indulged in, or any lease located in such areas.

5. No dry holes will be tolerated in the lobby. All wells brought in must be in the thousand barrel class, or larger.

Reproduced by John Patrick Gillese in *Chinook Arch: A Centennial Anthology of Alberta Writing* (1967).

Mt. Khruschev, alt. 4' 6"

Sign erected along the Trans-Canada Highway, Banff National Park. Instead of pointing up at the Rocky Mountains, the sign pointed down to the ground. Beside it, pointing up, was the regular park sign: Mt. Eisenhower, alt. 8750'. Observed following the Soviet premier's dramatic attendance at the Paris Summit Conference, May 16, 1960, and quickly removed.

It's twenty miles to water and thirty miles to wood;
I'm leaving sunny Alberta and I'm leaving it for good.

"The story was told of a young hopeful over in Alberta who, after some years of continuous drought, abandoned his farm and when leaving nailed a card to the outside of his door bearing the jingle." Quoted by Walter Wiggins in "Hired Man in Saskatchewan," *The Marxist Quarterly*, Winter, 1964.

## British Columbia

All aboard for the Pacific!

"Then the locomotive whistle sounded again and a voice was heard to cry: 'All aboard for the Pacific!' It was the first time that phrase had been used by a conductor from the East," according to Pierre Berton in *The Great Railway: Illustrated* (1972).

No Orientals Need Apply. [Sign common in British Columbia around the turn of the century]

I said [Prince] Rupert was founded mainly on hope. However, it now rests mainly on halibut and halibut is so much a part of Rupert's bread and butter that the children are taught to pray at nights: "Halibut be Thy Name!"

*Cross Roads* (1936), by Austin J. Cross.

The Riot Act / is never / read in Victoria / Households where ladies use / White Swan Cleanser. / Everything is Clean, Neat and Orderly. [Advertisement from *The Victoria Colonist*, May, 1915]

To Cross Pacific / Push Button and Wait / For Walk Signal. [Vancouver street sign, 1972]

## Yukon Territory

There is a Klondike in every man's brain; keep digging.

"There is a saying current in Canada which is extraordinarily characteristic of the place and its people," explained S. Macnaughtan in *My Canadian Memories* (1920).

Of all Klondike proverbs none was more comforting than the enigmatic "Gold is where you find it." The simple geographical truth excused all, explained all.

Merrill Denison in *Klondike Mike: An Alaskan Odyssey* (1943).

The North has got him.

Robert W. Service calls this a Yukonism and quotes it as the subtitle to "The Ballad of Pious Pete," *Ballads of a Cheechako* (1909).

## Northwest Territories

Combine the unknowns with the variables and the imponderables and you have it—the Canadian Arctic. [Traditional]

## Miscellaneous

Few females possess that mental ability and decision of character which are so essential to the successful teacher. The framers of the School Law committed *a grave error* in authorizing females to teach at all.

From the official report of the superintendent of schools, Upper Canada, 1859. Quoted by G. Blair Laing, "Education Today—Are We in Tune with the Times?" *Empire Club of Canada: Addresses Delivered to the Members During the 1950-51 Season* (1951).

Spring forward, / Fall back. [Mnemonic device for adjusting clocks from standard time to daylight saving time and back again; the Daylight Saving Act was passed in 1918]

Live, and let Nelson Eddy live. And if the tourists turn up on Dominion Day with skis, just switch on the artificial snow machines.

*To Know and Be Known: Report of the Task Force on Government Information* (1969), D'Iberville Fortier, chairman.

## Mottos

*Country, Province or Territory: Date of Confederation; Floral Emblem; Motto. Capital; motto.*

Canada: July 1, 1867; Maple Leaf; "A Mari Usque ad Mare" (From Sea to Sea; D'un océan à l'autre). Ottawa: "Advance—Ottawa—*En Avant*."

Alberta: September 1, 1905; Wild Rose; no official motto (unofficially "Next Year Country"). Edmonton; "Industry, Integrity, Progress."

British Columbia: July 20, 1871; Dogwood; *"Splendor Sine Occasu"* (Splendour Undiminished; Splendour Without Diminishment). Victoria; *"Semper Liber"* (Always Free [an allusion to its free-port facilities]).

Manitoba: July 15, 1870; Prairie Crocus; no official motto (unofficially "Home of the [Hudson's] Bay," "The Prairie Province"). Winnipeg; *"Unum cum Virtute Multorum"* (One with the Strength of Many).

New Brunswick: July 1, 1867; Purple Violet; *"Spem Reduxit"* (She [England] Restored Hope). Fredericton; *"Fredericopolis Silvae Filia Nobilis"* (Fredericton, Noble Daughter of the Forest).

Newfoundland: March 31, 1949; Pitcher Plant; *"Quaerite Prime Regnum Dei"* (Seek Ye First the Kingdom of God), unofficially "The Great Island." St. John's; no official motto (unofficially "The Most Easterly City of America").

Nova Scotia: July 1, 1867; Trailing Arbutus; *"Munit Haec et Altera Vincit"* (One Defends and the Other Conquers). Halifax; *"E Mari Merces"* (Wealth from the Sea), unofficially "Warden of the North."

Ontario: July 1, 1867; White Trillium; *"Ut Incepit Fidelis Sic Permanet"* (Loyal She Began, Loyal She Remains [an allusion to the Loyalist settlers]. Toronto; "Industry, Intelligence, Integrity."

Prince Edward Island: July 1, 1873; Lady's Slipper; *"Parva sub Ingenti"* (The Small under the Protection of the Great), unofficially "The Garden of the Gulf." Charlottetown; no official motto (unofficially "Cradle of Confederation").

Quebec: July 1, 1867; White Garden Lily; *"Je me Souviens"* (I Remember), unofficially *"La Belle Province"* (The Beautiful Province). Quebec City; *"Don de Dieu Feray Valoir"* (God's Gift to Make the Most).

Saskatchewan: September 1, 1905; Prairie Lily; no official motto (unofficially "Wheat Province," "Home of the RCMP"). Regina; *"Floreat Regina"* (Let Regina Flourish).

Northwest Territories: July 15, 1870 (the three administrative districts of Mackenzie, Keewatin and Franklin were created July 1, 1920); Mountain Avens; no official motto (unofficially "The New North"). Yellowknife: *"Multum in Parvo"* (Much from Little).

Yukon Territory: June 13, 1898; Purple

Fireweed; no official motto (unofficially "Home of the Klondike"). Whitehorse; no official motto (unofficially "Trail of '98" and "Sourdough City").

## Select Epitaphs

### Newfoundland

John Daws / died / 1650. [Said to be the oldest remaining gravestone in Canada, Ship Cove, Conception Bay]

He's done a catching cod
And gone to meet his God.

Block Island sea captain's epitaph.

To the Memory of / Three Noble Dogs. / Moody. / Watch. / Spy. /Whose Lives Were Given / For Mine on the Ice. / April 21st, 1908. / Wilfred Grenfell, / St. Anthony. [Plaque erected by Sir Wilfred after killing the dogs to use their fur for warmth until he was rescued]

### Nova Scotia

Here lies old twenty-five percent,
The more he had, the more he lent.
The more he had, the more he craved,
Great God, can this poor soul be saved?

Allegedly the epitaph of a Nova Scotia money-lender.

Here Lies / Ezekial Aikle / Age 102. / The Good / Die Young. [East Dalhousie]

### New Brunswick

Tho' Boreas' blast and Neptune's waves
Have tossed me to and fro,
Now I'm escaped from all their rage
And anchored here below.

Epitaph for Abel Judson, drowned seaman, Old Burial Ground, Saint John.

It was by accident I was shot.
To die that death it was my lot.
The gun discharged into my right side,
I lived five hours, then I died.

"Alphias Macks / died October 2, 1875," Albert County.

Born a man—Died a grocer.

Epitaph of John Smith, 1852-1914, "in a certain cemetery in New Brunswick."

## Quebec

As a wife she was a treasure
Virtue did her life adorn
But her health & earthly pleasure
Ended when her twins were born.

"Jane, wife of Sergeant George Baby, of
the 2nd Battalion of the Coldstream
Guards, 1810," Burial Ground, St. Matthew's Anglican Church, Quebec City.

Youth's for an hour,
Beauty's a flower,
But love is the jewel that wins the world.

Epitaph of Dr. W.H. Drummond, who
died on April 6, 1907; said to be written by Moira O'Neill; Mount Royal
Cemetery, Montreal.

## Ontario

This Lark / Taken to Canada by a Poor
/ Emigrant, / Was Shipwrecked in the /
St. Lawrence / and After Singing at /
Toronto for Nine Years / Died There
on the 14th of / March, 1843 / Univer-
sally Regretted. [The lark, named Charley, was bought at an auction by Sir
Francis Bond Head who, after its death,
had the bird stuffed and mounted]

Here Lies / General Bain / Who Died
in his Bist / Clothes, A Rispictable Man
— / A Rayl Ould Irish Protestant. [On
a wooden slab, Sandy Beach, about
1890]

The beauty of this Lake of the Woods
pervades me. [Self-chosen epitaph of
David K. Brown, a journalist who died
at twenty-nine, October 14, 1883, Lake
of the Woods Cemetery, near Kenora]

Ye weak beware, here lies the strong,
A Victim of his strength,
He lifted sixteen hundred pounds,
And here he lies at length.

Daniel MacDonald died October 27,
1871, at the age of thirty-three, after
participating in a strong-man contest
in Montreal—and winning. Little Lake
Cemetery, Peterborough.

Our Little Freddy Has Been Transplanted from This Earthly Flower Garden to Bloom in a Superior Flower Pot

Above. [Little Lake Cemetery, Peter-
borough]

Here I lie between two of the best women in the world: my wives. But I have
requested my relatives to tip me a little
toward Tillie. [Inscribed on the middle
of three tombstones "in a family burial
plot," Niagara Falls]

## Saskatchewan

If we did not as brothers live,
Let us here as brothers lie.

Inscription over the entrance to a graveyard for both Indians and whites at
LaRonge.

Lest We Forget. Murdered, Estevan,
Sept. 29, 1931, by the RCMP.

Inscription on the headstone raised at
Bienfait, near Estevan, by the Mine
Workers of Canada to mark the common grave of three young workers—P.
Markunas, N. Nargan, J. Gryshko—
killed by rifle fire during the Estevan
coal-miner's strike. A short time after
the monument was erected, the words
"the RCMP" were erased.

## Alberta

Good-bye / Jim / Take ker / O' yourself
[Inscription on a headstone, Edmonton,
about 1900, echoing a line from a once-
familiar poem by James Whitcomb
Riley]

### British Columbia

SACRED OF KATIE—IPOO
SAM BOYAN HE DIDE—IPOO
RIP JULIE YECTION—IPOO
JOSEPH'S ROSIE DI—IPOO

West Coast Indian grave markings on
wooden crosses. "Time was marked by
centuries in this cemetery. Years—little
years—what are they? As insignificant as
the fact that reversing the figure nine
turns it into the letter P." Emily Carr
in *Klee Wyck* (1941).

It is a rotten world / Artful politicians
are its bane / Its saving grace is the /
Artlessness of the young / And the wonders of the sky ["In memory of John
Dean. Born Stretton, Cheshire, England,

Dec. 17, 1850. Died Mar. 30, 1943." Ross Bay Cemetery, Victoria]

### Elsewhere and Otherwise

He loved the simple things,
He hated war,
But when his call came,
He gave his all.

> Inscribed on the marker of an unidentified Canadian soldier who died at Normandy, June 6, 1944.

Nearby the world's most famous mystery ship, the *Mary Celeste*, a brigantine, was built and launched in 1861. She was first named the *Amazon*. In 1868 she was driven ashore in a storm and after being repaired was renamed the *Mary Celeste*. In December 1872 she was discovered at sea with all sail set and everything in order—but not a person was on board or ever found. [Plaque, Spencer's Island, Nova Scotia]

And this same thing goes on from week to week, — working, eating, sleeping. Books are scarce for they are too bulky to carry; no newspapers and no news— unless fragments from three to six months old, strangely metamorphosed by Packers and Indians, can be dignified by the name of news. Nothing occurs to break the monotony save rheumatism, festered hands or feet, or a touch of sickness, perhaps scurvy if the campaign has been long: the arrival of the pack-train with supplies, or some such interesting event as the following, which we found duly chronicled on a blazed tree, between Moose Lake and Tête Jaune Cache:—

"BIRTH,
"Monday, 5th August 1872.

"This morning at about 5 o'clock. 'Aunt Polly,' bell-mare to the Nth. Thompson-trail parties pack-train, was safely delivered of a Bay Colt, with three white legs and white star on forehead.
"This wonderful progeny of a C.P.R. Survey's pack-train, is in future to be known, to the racing community of the Pacific slope, as Rocky Mountain Ned."

> George M. Grant in *Ocean to Ocean: Sandford Fleming's Expedition through Canada in 1872* (1873).

### One Dozen Limericks

An Eskimo in Athabasca
Let his igloo to friends from Alaska:
    When they asked if his spouse
    Went along with the house,
He replied, "I don't know, but I'll aska."

A lady from near Lake Louise
Declared she was bothered by fleas.
    She used gasoline
    And later was seen
Sailing over the hills and the trees.

There was a young girl from Montreal
Who wore a newspaper dress to a ball.
    But her dress caught on fire
    And burnt her entire
Front page—sporting section and all.

There was a young man of Moose Jaw
Who wanted to meet Bernard Shaw;
    When they questioned him, "Why?"
    He made no reply,
But sharpened an ax and a saw.

There once was a boy of Quebec
Who was buried in snow to his neck.
    When asked, "Are you frizz?"
    He replied, "Yes, I is.
But we don't call this cold in Quebec."

A tailor, who sailed from Quebec,
In a storm ventured once upon deck;
    But the waves of the sea
    Were as strong as could be,
And he tumbled in up to his neck.

In the turbulent turgid St. Lawrence
Fell a luscious young damsel named
        Florence,
    Where poor famished fish
    made this beautiful dish
An object of utter abhorrence.

A boy at Sault Ste. Marie
Said, "Spelling is all Greek to me,
    Till they learn to spell 'Soo'
    Without any 'u,'
Or an 'a' or an 'l' or a 't'!"

There was a young man of South Bay,
Making fireworks one summer day.
    He dipped his cigar
    In the gunpowder jar . . .
There *was* a young man of South Bay.

The art-loving Bishop of Truro
Kept a nude by Renoir in his bureau;

He said, "It's not smut
That engrosses me but
Nineteenth-century chiaroscuro!"

There was an old maid of Vancouver,
Who captured a man by manoeuver.
　　She jumped on his knee
　　With some rare *eau de vie,*
And nothing on earth could remove her.

One night a young amorous Sioux
Had a date with a maiden he knioux;
　　The coroner found
　　The couple had drowned
Making love in a leaky canioux.

> These are but a few of the many limericks that make use of Canadian place-names. The best-known of all limericks is "There was a young lady named Bright," which was written by a Canadian; see A.H. Reginald Buller. For another version of "There once was a boy of Quebec," see Rudyard Kipling. For a limerick on Gerda Munsinger, see Gillis Purcell. See also Edward Lear.

## R.C.M.P.

Maintiens le droit.

> Official motto of the Mounties—of the North-West Mounted Police (1873-1904), Royal North-West Mounted Police (1904-1920), Royal Canadian Mounted Police (from 1920). The French phrase is officially translated: "Uphold the right." Its use was advocated in 1873 and adopted two years later.

Without fear, favour or affection.

> Oath of office from "An Act respecting the Administration of Justice, and for the establishment of a Police Force in the North West Territories," assented to May 23, 1874. "I, A.B., solemnly swear that I will faithfully, diligently and impartially execute and perform the duties and office of ——— in the Police Force of the North West Territories, and will well and truly obey and perform all lawful orders or instructions which I shall receive as such ———, without fear, favour or affection of or towards any person or party whomsoever. So help me God."

The Pioneers of a Glorious Future.

> Unofficial motto hammered to the primitive log cabin built by the Force for its first headquarters, Fort Macleod, Cypress Hills, December, 1874.

The Old Originals.

> Nickname of the first five hundred recruits, 1873.

They always get their man.

> This expression is popularly associated with the Force. For this unofficial motto, see John J. Healy.

And though we win no praise or fame
　　In the struggle here alone—
To carry out good British law
　　And plant old England's throne;
Yet when our task has been performed,
　　And law with order reigns,
The peaceful settler long will bless
　　The Riders of the Plains.

> Last of seventeen stanzas of "The Riders of the Plains." The verse, which has been attributed to numerous authors and constables, appeared in print in 1878. The entire work was published in Charles Pelham Mulvaney's *The History of the North-West Rebellion of 1885* (1885); a more polished but shortened version appears in *The Oxford Book of Canadian Verse* (1913), edited by Wilfred Campbell.

The American commanding officer looked at them with a surprised air.
"Where's your escort for these Indians?" he asked.
"We're here," answered the corporal.
"Yes, yes, I see. But where is your regiment?"
"I guess it's here all right," said the corporal. "The other fellow's looking after the breakfast things."
"But are there only *four* of you then?"
"That's so, Colonel, but you see we wear the Queen's scarlet."

> Quoted by A.L. Haydon in *The Riders of the Plains: A Record of the Royal Northwest Mounted Police of Canada, 1873-1910* (1910). Haydon explained that the U.S. Cavalry accompanied two hundred Crees with 450 horses to the Montana border and turned the refugee Indian band over to a NWMP detachment consisting of one corporal and

three troopers.

The story, which is too good to be true and cannot be authenticated, might be based on an incident that took place in June of 1896 in which a small detachment of Mounted Policemen did receive a large band of peaceful Crees from the Americans. "Annual Report of Superintendent R.B. Deane, Commanding 'K' Division, 1896."

The Silent Force.

This epithet comes from *The Silent Force: Scenes from the Life of the Mounted Police of Canada* (1927), by the Philadelphia writer T.M. Longstreth.

## Some Documents

It shall be lawful for the Queen, by and with the Advice of Her Majesty's Most Honourable Privy Council, to declare by Proclamation that, on and after a Day therein appointed, not being more than Six Months after the passing of this Act, the Provinces of Canada, of Nova Scotia, and New Brunswick shall form and be One Dominion under the name of Canada; and on and after that Day those Three Provinces shall form and be One Dominion under that Name accordingly. [Article 3]

*

It shall be lawful for the Queen, by and with the Advice and Consent of the Senate and House of Commons, to make Laws for the Peace, Order, and good Government of Canada. . . . [Article 91]

The British North America Act, 1867; commonly called the BNA Act. The full title of the act is "The Confederation Act, 1867; An Act for the Union of Canada, Nova Scotia, and New Brunswick, and the Government thereof; and for purposes connected therewith." The BNA Act was passed March 29, 1867, and became effective July 1, 1867.

"Person" means a male person, including an Indian, and excluding a person of Mongolian or Chinese race.

"An Act Respecting the Electoral Franchise" (short title "The Electoral Franchise Act"), assented to July 20, 1885. *Acts of the Parliament of the United Kingdom and Great Britain and Ireland* (1885). Frequently cited by Nellie McClung as a racist clause.

No woman, idiot, lunatic, or criminal shall vote.

Quoted by Nellie McClung in her book *In Times Like These* (1915) as being "from Election Act of Dominion of Canada." She probably had in mind the "Dominion Elections Act" of 1906 (not revised until 1927) which includes this sidenote: "Disqualified voters. Prisoners, or patients in asylum or persons supported by charity." As the franchise was not extended to women until later, the statute did not specifically exclude them. *The Revised Statutes of Canada, 1906.*

The provisions of sections 6, 10, 11 and 13 of this Act shall be in force during war, invasion, or insurrection, real or apprehended.

Section 3 of the War Measures Act, 1914, assented to August 22, 1914. Reproduced in *Historical Documents of Canada: Volume V: The Arts of War and Peace, 1914-1945* (1972), edited by C.P. Stacey, who notes: "This drastic measure, which gives the Governor in Council virtually unlimited powers in a time of emergency, is (with adjustments) still on the statute books."

They [the Dominions] are autonomous Communities within the British Empire, equal in status, in no way subordinate one to another in any aspect of their domestic or external affairs, though united by a common allegiance to the Crown, and freely associated as members of the British Commonwealth of Nations.

From the "Report of Inter-Imperial Relations Committee," Imperial Conference, November 18, 1926, called "the Balfour Declaration" after A.J. Balfour. Reproduced in *Historical Documents of Canada: Volume V: The Arts of War and Peace, 1914-1945* (1972), edited by C.P. Stacey.

Their Lordships are of opinion that the

word "persons" in s. 24 does include women, and that women are eligible to be summoned to and become members of the Senate of Canada. . . .

> Landmark decision in the "Persons" case, delivered by Lord Sankey, lord chancellor of the Privy Council of Great Britain, October 18, 1929. The case is entitled "Henrietta Muir Edwards and Others *v.* Attorney-General for Canada (1929)." The five women behind this case were all from Alberta: Emily Murphy, Nellie McClung, Louise McKinney, Irene Parlby, Henrietta Edwards. Catherine Lyle Cleverdon discusses the case in *The Woman Suffrage Movement in Canada* (1950). *Historical Documents of Canada: Volume V: The Arts of War and Peace, 1914-1945* (1972), edited by C.P. Stacey.

3. It is hereby declared and enacted that the Parliament of a Dominion has full power to make laws having extra-territorial operation.
4. No Act of Parliament of the United Kingdom passed after the commencement of this Act shall extend or be deemed to extend, to a Dominion as part of the law of that Dominion, unless it is expressly declared in that Act that that Dominion has requested, and consented to, the enactment thereof.

> Historic sections from the "Statute of Westminster, 1931," *British North America Acts and Selected Statutes: 1867-1962* (1962), edited by Maurice Ollivier.

We are fed up with a federalism which classes the Quebec nation among the ethnic minorities of Canada. . . . Repeat after me: "Cheap labour is *main d'oeuvre à bon marché* in French". . . . We are terrorized by the Roman Capitalist Church, though this is less and less true today (who owns the square where the Stock Exchange was built?); terrorized by the payments owing to Household Finance, by the advertising of the grand masters of consumption, Eaton's, Simpson's, Morgan's, Steinberg's, General Motors. . . . There are more and more of us who know and suffer under this terrorist society, and the day is coming

when all the Westmounts of Quebec will disappear from the map.
Long live Free Quebec!
Long live our comrades the political prisoners!
Long live the Quebec Revolution!
Long live the *Front de Libération du Québec!*

> "FLQ Manifesto" (1970), reprinted by Marcel Rioux in *Quebec in Question* (1971).

I, ———, swear that I will be faithful and bear true allegiance to Her Majesty Queen Elizabeth the Second, her Heirs and Successors, according to law, and that I will faithfully observe the laws of Canada and fulfil my duties as a Canadian citizen.
So help me God.

> This is "The Oath of Allegiance" as administered at the citizenship ceremony. *Guide to Canadian Citizenship* (1971), published by the Department of the Secretary of State.

## Martial Airs

Oh, General Wolfe to his men did say,
"Come, come, my boys, come follow me
To yon blue mountain that stands so high,
You lads of honour, you lads of honour,
You lads of honour, come follow me."

> First verse of "General Wolfe," *Canada's Story in Song* (1965), edited by Edith Fowke and Alan Mills.

He raiséd his head
  Where the guns did rattle,
And to his aid he said,
  "How goes the battle?"
"Quebec is all our own,
  They can't prevent it."
He said without a groan,
  "I die contented."

> Final verse of "Brave Wolfe," *Ballads and Sea-Songs of Newfoundland* (1933), edited by E.B. Greenleaf and G.Y. Mansfield.

Oh, we're marching down to Old Quebec
And the fifes and the drums are abeating,
For the British boys have gained the day,

And the Yankees are retreating,
So we'll turn back and we'll come again
To the place where we first started,
And we'll open the ring and we'll take a
couple in,
Since they proved that they are true-
hearted.

"Marching Down to Old Quebec," *Canada's Story in Song* (1965), edited by
Edith Fowke and Alan Mills.

With sword and spear he vows and
swears
That Quebec shall be taken;
But if he'd be advised by me,
He'd fly to save his bacon.

One verse from "A New Song: To the
Tune 'Yankee Doodle'" (1776), ridicul-
ing Benedict Arnold; quoted by Iona
and Peter Opie in *The Oxford Dictionary of Nursery Rhymes* (1951).

Come all you bold Canadians, I'd have
you lend an ear
Concerning a fine ditty that would make
your courage cheer,
Concerning an engagement that we had
at Sandwich town,
The courage of those Yankee boys so
lately we pulled down.

First verse of "Come All You Bold Canadians," *Shantymen and Shantyboys*
(1951), edited by W.M. Doerflinger.

Upon the Heights of Queenston one
dark October day,
Invading foes were marshalled in battle's
dread array.
Brave Brock looked up the rugged steep
and planned a bold attack,
"No foreign flag shall float," said he,
"a--bove the Union Jack."
        *
Each true Canadian soldier laments the
death of Brock;
His country told its sorrow in monumen-
tal rock;
And if a foe should e'er invade our land
in future years,
His dying words will guide us still:
"Push on, brave Volunteers!"

First and last verses of "The Battle of
Queenston Heights," *Canada's Story in
Song* (1965), edited by Edith Fowke and
Alan Mills.

The *Chesapeake* so bold out of Boston
as we're told
Came to take the British frigate neat and
handy O,
And the people in the port all came out
to see the sport
While their bands all played up Yankee
Doodle Dandy O!

First verse of "The *Chesapeake* and the
*Shannon*," *Ballads and Sea-Songs from
Nova Scotia* (1928), edited by Roy W.
Mackenzie.

Lord! o'er our own loved land
Spread thy protecting hand!
        Help! ere we fall!
Free us from Monarchy—
Free us from Hierarchy,
Sabres and *Squirearchy*—
        Lord free us all!

"Lord Free Us All!" (1838) to be sung to
the tune of "God Save the King," reproduced by John S. Moir in *Rhymes of
Rebellion: Being a Selection of Contemporary Verses about the "Recent
Unpleasantness" in Upper Canada,
1837* (1965).

Mackenzie was this hero called,
        From Scotia's land he came,
To sow and reap—if e'er he could—
        The deeds of future fame.
        *
And now that the rebellion's o'er
        Let each true Briton sing,
Long live the Queen in health and
        peace,
        And may each rebel swing.

"New Words to an Old Song; or, John
Gilpin Travestied" (1838), reproduced
by John S. Moir in *Rhymes of Rebellion: Being a Selection of Contemporary
Verses about the "Recent Unpleasantness" in Upper Canada, 1837* (1965).

O master and mistress, don't come after
me,
For I cannot be a slave any more.
I am under British laws, I'm beneath the
lion's paws,
And he's growl if you come near the
shore.

One verse from "The Free Slave" (1851),
*Canada's Story in Song* (1965), edited by
Edith Fowke and Alan Mills.

Farewell, old master, this is enough for me.
I'm going straight to Canada where coloured men are free.

> Couplet from "The Voice of the Fugitive" (1851), *Canada's Story in Song* (1965), edited by Edith Fowke and Alan Mills.

Soon our banners will be streaming,
Soon the eagle will be screaming;
And the lion—see it cowers.
Hurrah boys, the River's ours!

> American gold prospectors' song, Fraser River, 1850s.

When the war breaks out in Mexico,
 I'll be living up in Montreal;
Got a forty-second cousin up in Canada,
 And it's time I paid a friendly call.

> First verse of "When the War Breaks out in Mexico," composed late in the American Civil War when the fighting might have spread into Mexico. This early draft-dodger's ditty, which was sung about 1864, ends: "When the war breaks out in Canada, / I'll be living down in Mexico."

We are a Fenian Brotherhood, skilled in the arts of war,
And we're going to fight for Ireland, the land that we adore.
Many battles we have won, along with the boys in blue,
And we'll go aid capture Canada, for we've nothing else to do.

> "Song of the Fenian Brotherhood" (1866), quoted by John Murray Gibbon in *Canadian Mosaic: The Making of a Northern Nation* (1938).

Tramp, tramp, tramp our boys are marching,
Cheer up, let the Fenians come!
For beneath the Union Jack we'll drive the rabble back,
And we'll fight for our beloved Canadian home.

> "Canadian Militia Song" (1866), quoted by Captain John A. Macdonald in *Troublous Times in Canada: A History of the Fenian Raids of 1866 and 1870* (1910). See also Lachlan McGoun.

Tramp! Tramp! Tramp! the New Dominion
Now is knocking at the door,
So, good-bye dear Uncle Sam,
As we do not care a clam
For your Greenbacks or your bunkum any more.

> Chorus of a Confederation song published in *The Cariboo Sentinel*, June 16, 1869. Quoted by Reginald Eyre Watters, editor, *British Columbia: A Centennial Anthology* (1958).

### Songs

God save our gracious Queen,
Long live our noble Queen,
God save the Queen!
Send her victorious,
Happy and glorious,
Long to reign over us,
God save the Queen!

Dieu sauve notre Reine,
Notre gracieuse Reine,
Vive la Reine!
Qu'elle soit victorieuse,
Heureuse et glorieuse,
Que Dieu protège notre Reine,
Vive la Reine!

> The first of four verses of "God Save the King" in English and French. "This must be the best-known tune in the world," comments Percy A. Scholes in *The Oxford Companion to Music* (Ninth Edition, 1956). "If any attribution is necessary in song-books, the word 'tradition' seems to be the only one possible, or, perhaps, '*Traditional; earliest known version by John Bull, 1563-1628.*'"
>
> Since 1967, "God Save the King" has been Canada's royal anthem, and the music (but not the words) of "O Canada" the national anthem. (For "O Canada," see R. Stanley Weir. For an unofficial favourite of the past, "The Maple Leaf Forever," see Alexander Muir.)
>
> Only the tune (and not the words) of "God Save the King" comprise the national anthem of Great Britain. Over twenty nations at various times have adopted it as the official or semi-official tune. The words and the music were first printed in their present form in

1744. In the United States, the tune is called "America," with these words written by Samuel Francis Smith in 1831: "My country, 'tis of thee, / Sweet land of liberty, / Of thee I sing; / Land where my fathers died, / Land of the pilgrims' pride. / From every mountainside / Let Freedom ring."

O Alouette, gentille Alouette,
Alouette, je t'y plumerai.

Je t'y plumerai la têt',
Je t'y plumerai la têt',

Et la têt', et la têt',
Alouett', Alouett'.

O Alouette, gentille Alouette,
Alouette, je t'y plumerai.

> The lyrics of the famous French-Canadian song "Alouette." To sing it, repeat the above, replacing la têt' (head) with: le bec (beak), le nez (nose), les yeux (eyes), le cou' (neck), les ail's (wings), le dos (back), les patt's (feet), la queue (tail). Loosely translated:

O Alouette, gentle Alouette,
Alouette, I'll pluck your feathers yet.

Pluck your plumage from your head,
Pluck your plumage from your head,

And your head, and your head,
Alouett', Alouett'.

O Alouette, gentle Alouette,
Alouette, I'll pluck your feathers yet.

A Saint-Malo, beau port de mer,
A Saint-Malo, beau port de mer,
Trois gros navir's sont arrivés.

> Opening lines of "A Saint-Malo" (At St. Malo), *Canada's Story in Song* (1965), edited by Edith Fowke and Alan Mills. "At St. Malo beside the sea, / At St. Malo beside the sea, / Floated at anchor vessels three."

Lui y a longtemps que je t'aime,
Jamais je ne t'-oublierai.

> Last lines of the refrain of the popular folk song "A la Claire Fontaine." The lines of "Unto a Fountain Clear" have been translated: "I loved thee from the hour we met, / And never can that love forget." Quoted by Henry James Morgan in *The Tour of HRH the Prince of Wales through British America and the United States* (1860).

T[u] es mon compagnon de voyage!—
Je veux mourir dans mon canot.
Sur le tombeau, près du rivage,
Vous renverserez mon canot.

> From "Mon Canot d'écorce." The song "My Bark Canoe" has been translated by Frank Oliver Call in *The Spell of French Canada* (1926): "And when I must leave the great river, / O bury me close to its wave, / And let my canoe and my paddle / Be the only mark over my grave!"

Behind the Manor lies the mere,
*En roulant ma boulé;*
Three ducks bathe in its waters clear,
*En roulant ma boulé.*

*Rouli, roulant, ma boulé roulant,*
*En roulant ma boulé roulant,*
*En roulant ma boulé.*

> First verse (in English) and refrain (in French) of "En Roulant ma Boulé." Translated by William McLennan, *Canadian Poems and Lays: Selections of Native Verse, Reflecting the Seasons, Legends, and Life of the Dominion* (1893), edited by W.D. Lighthall. Marius Barbeau and Edward Sapir, in *Folk Songs of French Canada* (1925), amusingly translate the refrain: "A-roly pololy, / My bowlie rowlie. / A-roly pololy, / Bowlie rowlie, / Rolling my bowl / For to roll, / A-rolling my bowl."

Then hurrah for our own native isle, Newfoundland!
Not a stranger shall hold one inch of its strand!
Her face turns to Britain, her back to the Gulf.
Come near at your peril, Canadian Wolf!

> Last menacing verse of "An Anti-Confederation Song" (1869), *Old-Time Poetry and Songs of Newfoundland* (1940), edited by Gerald S. Doyle.

Farewell to Nova Scotia, the sea-bound coast!
Let your mountains dark and dreary be,
For when I am far away on the briny ocean tossed

Will you ever heave a sigh and a wish for me?

Refrain from "Nova Scotia," *Folk Songs of Canada* (1954), edited by Edith Fowke and Richard Johnston.

And now the winter's over, it's home-
ward we are bound,
And in this cursed country we'll never
more be found.
Go back to your wives and sweethearts,
tell others not to go
To that God-forsaken country called
Canaday-I-O.

Last verse of "Canaday-I-O," said to be written by Ephraim Braley, New Eng-land lumberjack working in the Mari-times, 1853; *Folk Songs of Canada* (1954), edited by Edith Fowke and Richard Johnston.

On the Old Ontario Strand, my boys,
Where Queen's forever shall stand!
For has she not stood
Since the time of the flood
On the Old Ontario Strand!

Chorus of "On the Old Ontario Strand," the college song of Queen's University. It was first sung at Convocation cere-monies on April 26, 1886. "The song is an historical story in verse of the great incidents at Queen's in the early days," according to Lennox Irving in *The Queen's Alumni Review*, August, 1933. The song is sometimes identified with Victoria University in 1892 when it moved from Cobourg to Toronto. The melody is said to derive from the Amer-ican college song "On the Banks of the Old Raritan."

One by one they all clear out,
Thinking to better themselves, no doubt,
Caring little how far they go
From the poor little girls of Ontario.

Refrain of "The Poor Little Girls of Ontario," *Canada's Story in Song* (1965), edited by Edith Fowke and Alan Mills.

For we'll sing a little sing of Cobalt,
If you don't live there it's your fault.
Oh you Cobalt, where the wintry breezes
blow,
Where all the silver comes from
And you live a life and then some,

Oh you Cobalt, you're the best old town
I know.

First of four verses of "The Cobalt Song," words by the mining engineer L.F. Steenman and music by R.L. Mac-Adam, about 1910; *Canada's Story in Song* (1965), edited by Edith Fowke and Alan Mills.

Rings on my fingers, corns on my toes,
Gold up in Porcupine, everybody knows.
Put on your snowshoes, and hit the trail
with me,
For P-o-r-c-u-p-i-n-e—that's me!

From "The Porcupine Song," *Canada's Story in Song* (1965), edited by Edith Fowke and Alan Mills.

Then come sit here awhile e'er you leave
us,
Do not hasten to bid us adieu,
Just remember the Red River Valley
And the cowboy who loves you so true.

Chorus of "Red River Valley," Ameri-can cowboy song popular in Canada, reprinted by Ralph L. Woods in *A Sec-ond Treasury of the Familiar* (1950).

Saskatchewan, Saskatchewan,
There's no place like Saskatchewan.
We sit and gaze across the plain,
And wonder why it never rains,
And Gabriel blows his trumpet sound;
He says: "The rain, she's gone around."

Refrain from "Saskatchewan," *Canada's Story in Song* (1965), edited by Edith Fowke and Alan Mills.

Alberta Land, Alberta Land,
Oh land of drifting snow and sand,
I gaze across the frozen plain
And wish that I was home again
With all the money in my hand
I've squandered in Alberta Land.

From "Alberta Land," *Canada's Story in Song* (1965), edited by Edith Fowke and Alan Mills.

So farewell to Alberta, farewell to the
west,
It's backwards I'll go to the girl I love
best.
I'll go back to the east and get me a wife
And never eat cornbread the rest of my
life.

Last verse of "The Alberta Home-steader," *Canada's Story in Song* (1965), edited by Edith Fowke and Alan Mills.

## Verses and Rhymes

Lives of farmers all remind us
We must work at every chance,
And departing leave behind us
Extra patches on our pants.

"Quoted in a budget speech of long ago"—F.R. Scott, 1973.

They gave away the forest,
They gave away the land,
They gave away the rivers,
They gave away the sand,

They gave away the silver,
They gave away the gold,
They would have given away the air,
But the air they couldn't hold.

"I would like to see preserved this little jingle . . . it was written of course before radio and TV were invented; now you can hold the air and it is given away. This is an anonymous verse and you will simply have to call it Anon.; after all, Anon. is a distinguished entrant to every good anthology."—F.R. Scott, 1973.

C'est le bon, bon, bon;
C'est le que, que, que;
C'est le bec, bec, bec;
C'est le bon, C'est le que, C'est le bec;
C'est le bon Québec!

Quebec, 1940s.

One, two, three, alora,
Four, five, six, alora,
Seven, eight, nine, alora,
Ten, A-Laura Secord!

Ball bouncing rhyme, traditional.

The twenty-fourth of May
Is the Queen's Birthday;
If you don't give us a holiday,
We'll all run away.

Ball bouncing rhyme, traditional. Quoted by Sara Jeannette Duncan in *The Imperialist* (1904).

Deanna Durbin wears a turban
Red, white, and blue.

Deanna Durbin, she wore a turban
Until she was 2, 4, 6, 8. . . .

Deanna Durbin wore her turban
In-side-out!

Deanna Durbin lost her turban
In a pool of water.

Topical ball-bouncing and rope-skipping rhymes popular in Britain (and to some extent in Canada) in the early fifties. Deanna Durbin wore a turban in *Nice Girl* (1940). Iona and Peter Opie in *The Lore and Language of Schoolchildren* (1959). See also Deanna Durbin.

## Anonymous, Brother
See Jean-Paul Desbiens.

## Apagkaq
He was squatting in the darkness.

He was quite alone on earth, when suddenly he became conscious and discovered himself. He had no idea where he was. Nor did he know how he had come there. But he breathed and there was life in him. He lived!

But who was he? A being—something living. More than that he could not comprehend. All about him was dark, and he could see nothing.

Beginning of an Eskimo creation myth as told by the storyteller Apagkaq. Knud Rasmussen, *The Mackenzie Eskimos: After Knud Rasmussen's Posthumous Notes: Report of the Fifth Thule Expedition, 1921-24* (1942), edited by H. Ostermann.

## Apollinaire, Guillaume
Where the hunters of rats
Skin their furs
Sparkling diamond
Vancouver
Where the train white and the snow nocturnal lights escapes from the winter
O Paris
From the red to the green all the yellow dies
Paris Vancouver Hyères Maintenon New York and the West Indies
The window opens like an orange
The beautiful fruit of light

From "The Windows" (1913), *Calligrammes* (1918). "A. often stated his predilections for 'Les Fenêtres,'" according to Michel Décaudin, editor of *Oeuvres complètes de Guillaume Apollinaire* (1966).

## Aqikhivik

In the olden days, things were very different from what they are now. Everything had a soul, everything was more alive. When a caribou had been eaten, the meat grew again on the bones. Only one had to be careful not to crush or break any of the bones.

> Eskimo legend as told by Aqikhivik. Knud Rasmussen, *Intellectual Culture of the Caribou Eskimos: Igulik and Caribou Eskimo Texts: Report of the Fifth Thule Expedition, 1921-24* (1930).

## Aquin, Hubert

My mission is suicide, everywhere and forever.

> *Prochain Épisode* (1967), translated by Penny Williams.

## Arcand, Adrien

Politics is not a game. It is a battle. There is the difference between us. You English, you *play* politics. But, we French, we *fight* politics.

\*

We don't attack Jews, we simply defend our country against their conspiracy.

> The Quebec fascist, quoted by Frederick Edwards in "Fascism in Canada," *Maclean's Magazine*, April 15, 1938.

## Archer, Dr. A.E.

The face of medicine has indeed changed, but are we primarily concerned with faces? It is the character and spirit of our friends that we love. The spirit of medicine through the ages has been the spirit of service. That remains unchanged.

> Quoted by H.E. MacDermot in *One Hundred Years of Medicine in Canada 1867-1967* (1967).

## Arden, Elizabeth

I'm not interested in age. People who tell their ages are silly. You're as young as you feel.

> Quoted by Lore and Maurice Cowan in *The Wit of Women* (1969).

To be Catholic or Jewish isn't chic. Chic is Episcopalian.

\*

Treat a horse like a woman, and a woman like a horse. And they'll both win for you.

> Quoted by Alfred Allan Lewis and Constance Woodworth in *Miss Elizabeth Arden* (1972). The American cosmetic queen was born Florence Nightingale Graham in 1884 in Woodbridge, Ontario. She chose "Elizabeth" for its regal quality and "Arden" for its poetry (via Tennyson's *Enoch Arden*) and singlehandedly founded the House of Elizabeth Arden in New York. She died in 1966. See also Coco Chanel.

## Arnold, Benedict

The unjust, cruel and tyrannical acts of a venal British Parliament, tending to enslave the American Colonies, have obliged them to appeal to God and the sword of redress. That Being in whose hands are all human events, has hitherto smiled on their virtuous efforts. And as every artifice has been used to make the innocent Canadians instruments of their cruelty by instigating them against the Colonies, and oppressing them in their refusing to enforce every oppressive mandate, the American Congress, induced by motives of humanity, have at their request sent Gen. Schuyler into Canada for their relief. To cooperate with him, I am ordered by His Excellency, Gen. Washington, to take possession of the town of Quebec. I do, therefore, in the name of the United Colonies, demand surrender of the town, fortifications, etc., of Quebec to the forces of the United Colonies under my command; forbidding you to injure any of the inhabitants of the town in their person or property, as you will answer the same at your peril. On surrendering the town the property of every individual shall be secured to him; but if I am obliged to carry the town by storm, you may expect every severity practised on such occasions; and the merchants who may now save their property, will probably be involved in the general ruin.

> Letter from General Arnold, Camp be-

fore Quebec, to Lieutenant-Governor Hector Cramahé of Quebec, November 14, 1775. Quoted by John Codman II in *Arnold's Expedition to Quebec* (1901).

**Arnold, Matthew**
Imagine the face of Philip or Alexander at hearing of a primer of Macedonian Literature! Are we to have a primer of Canadian literature, too, and a primer of Australian?

Quoted by E.K. Brown in *On Canadian Poetry* (Revised Edition, 1944).

Quebec is the most interesting thing by much that I have seen on this Continent, and I think I would sooner be a poor priest in Quebec than a rich hog-merchant in Chicago.

Letter to Walter Arnold, New York, February 28, 1884. *Letters of Matthew Arnold: 1848-1888* (1895), edited by George W.E. Russell.

The Englishman in those parts is apt to be what I call a Philistine, and a Philistine of a hard type.

The British man-of-letter's evaluation of English-speaking Montrealers, February, 1884. Quoted by Edgar Andrew Collard in *Canadian Yesterdays* (1955).

I said that the pretensions of the Catholic Church on the one hand, and the "black Presbyterianism" of the Protestants on the other, hindered the fusion of French and English in Canada; but that I looked to literature for gradually opening and softening men's minds. Some of the Catholics resented this; the Protestants took it much better.

After addressing the Athenaeum Club in Montreal, February 21, 1884. Arnold so infuriated Louis Fréchette, that the Quebec poet, who had written a poem especially for the occasion, stamped out of the hall. Quoted by Edgar Andrew Collard in *Canadian Yesterdays* (1955).

You know the conversation which reigns in the thousands of middle-class families at this hour, about nunneries, teetotalism, the confessional, eternal punishment, ritualism, disestablishment. It goes on wherever the class goes which is

moulded on the Puritan type of life. In the long winter evenings of Toronto Mr. Goldwin Smith has had, probably, abundant experience of it.

"Equality," *Mixed Essays* (1904). Arnold Haultain in *Goldwin Smith: His Life and Opinions* (1913) quotes Arnold as writing: "His absence from the scene, his retirement in Canada, is a loss to his friends, but a still greater loss to his country."

**Arrabal, Fernando**
I adore Rochdale College. It's exactly like Paris was during the riots. Garbage everywhere.

The Moroccan-born, French-Spanish playwright made this observation to Tom Hendry in Toronto, 1970.

**Arthur, Eric**
I believe it will take a thousand years to develop a national style in Canada, but I do see a light in the west over a grain elevator.

"Architecture in Canada," *Yearbook of the Arts in Canada: 1928-29* (1929), edited by Bertram Brooker.

It is possible that millions now living in North America have never seen a barn, let alone been in one.

*The Barn: A Vanishing Landmark in North America* (1972), by Eric Arthur and Dudley Witney.

**Arthur, Sir George**
I do think if Rolph and Mackenzie were here mercy would be shown to them. Two lives were lost at Montgomery's and two must now suffer.

Lieutenant-governor of Upper Canada, Sir George Arthur, to Elizabeth Lount, refusing pardon to her husband Samuel Lount and Peter Mathews who were hanged for treason, April 12, 1838. Recorded by Mrs. Lount in an open letter published in the *Pontiac Herald*, June 12, 1838, and reprinted in *New Frontiers*, Summer, 1954. See also Elizabeth Lount.

**Ashburton, Lord**
I wish the British Government would

give you Canada at once. It is fit for nothing but to breed quarrels.

> Letter from Alexander Baring, Lord Ashburton, to John Quincy Adams, U.S. ambassador to Britain, 1816. See also William IV.

## Asquith, Margot
If I ever return to America, I shall not be surprised if a line of "safe-sailing steamships" has been engineered to go down the Niagara Falls.

> *Places and Persons* (1925).

## Asselin, Olivar
Lie, lie for all you're worth; something will come of it.

> Quebec journalist, quoted by Jacques Hébert in *Trois jours en prison* (1965).

## Astor, John Jacob
Now the fur trade will build me a fortune.

> German-born American fur-trader at the signing of Jay's Treaty in 1794 which permitted trade between the United States and the British colonies in North America.

## Athlone, The Earl of
Never have we shouldered such an immense responsibility, never has so much depended on how we acquit ourselves, let us have "no craven fear of being great" but let us gird ourselves and steel our hearts and clench our fists and prove to mankind, as we are proving every day, that we have never been so great as in this hour of trial, and let us pay the debt we owe to our fathers that begat us by ensuring that each of our children and their children and all those who now suffer humiliation and defeat will be beholden to us for their salvation, their freedom and civilization.

> Address, Joint Meeting of the Canadian and Empire Clubs, Toronto, January 20, 1941. Quoted by John Cowan in *Canada's Governors-General 1867-1952* (1952). The Earl of Athlone, a brother of Queen Mary, was governor general from 1940 to 1946.

## Atholstan, Lord   See Sir Hugh Graham.

## Atkinson, Joseph E.
The *Star* will print what I tell it to.

> Journal of Mrs. Herbert Bruce, August 25, 1937, quoted by Neil McKenty in *Mitch Hepburn* (1967).

Nobody can escape his beginnings, and I despise the man who is untrue to them.

\*

Four things an Executive Should Know
1. What ought to be done
2. How should it be done
3. Who should do it
4. Has it been done
May 1st, 1940   J.E.A.

> Quoted by Ross Harkness in *J.E. Atkinson of the Star* (1963). See also George Drew and Timothy Eaton.

## Atwood, Margaret
If the national mental illness of the United States is megalomania, that of Canada is paranoid schizophrenia. . . . We are all immigrants to this place even if we were born here: the country is too big for anyone to inhabit completely, and in the parts unknown to us we move in fear, exiles and invaders. This country is something that must be chosen—it is so easy to leave—and if we do choose it we are still choosing a violent duality.

> "Afterword" to *The Journals of Susanna Moodie* (1970).

you fit into me
like a hook into an eye

a fish hook
an open eye

> Epigraph to *Power Politics* (1971).

A divorce is like an amputation; you survive, but there's less of you.

> *Time*, March 19, 1973.

Literature is not only a mirror; it is also a map, a geography of the mind.

> *Survival: A Thematic Guide to Canadian Literature* (1972).

People put down Canadian literature and ask us why there isn't a *Moby Dick*. The reason there isn't a *Moby Dick* is that if a Canadian did a *Moby Dick*, it would be done from the point of view of the whale. Nobody ever thought of that.

> Quoted by John Ayre in *Saturday Night*, November, 1972.

I've been described as the Barbra Streisand of Canadian literature. But I think of myself more as the Mary Pickford, spreading joy.

> Address to the Empire Club, reported by William French in *The Globe and Mail*, April 7, 1973.

## Aua

You see, you are equally unable to give any reason when we ask you why life is as it is. And so it must be. All our customs come from life and turn towards life; we explain nothing, we believe nothing, but in what I have just shown you lies our answer to all you ask.

> Eskimo attitudes related by Aua. Knud Rasmussen, *Intellectual Culture of the Iglulik Eskimos: Report of the Fifth Thule Expedition, 1921-24* (1929).

## Auden, W.H.

As Pinder long ago in Greece was proud to hail
Thessalian Hippokleas, even so
It is meet we praise in our days fleet-footed
Bruce Kidd from Toronto.

> "Runner," commentary for a film, directed by Donald Owen and produced by the National Film Board of Canada, in Auden's *City Without Walls* (1969).

The dominions . . . are for me *triefste Provinz*, places which have produced no art and are inhabited by the kind of person with whom I have least in common.

> Attributed to the Anglo-American man-of-letters, 1963. The German phrase translates "deepest hinterlands."

## Audubon, J.J.

*July 2:* A beautiful day for Labrador. Went on shore, and was most pleased with what I saw. The country, so wild and grand, is of itself enough to interest any one in its wonderful dreariness.

> Entry for July 2, 1833, "The Labrador Journal," *Journal of John James Audubon Made while Obtaining Susbscriptions to his Birds of America* (1929).

## Aylmer, Lord

Honneur à Montcalm
Le Destin
En lui dérobant la Victoire
L'a récompensé
Par une Mort glorieuse

> "Honour to Montcalm. Destiny, in robbing him of victory, compensated him with a glorious death." Inscription on Montcalm's monument, Plains of Abraham, composed by the governor of Lower Canada in 1831. S. Macnaughtan in *My Canadian Memories* (1920) and Agnes Repplier in *Mère Marie of the Ursulines: A Study in Adventure* (1931).

> Here Died
> WOLFE
> Victorious
> Sept. 13
> 1759

> Original wording on Wolfe's Monument, Battlement Park, Quebec City, raised at the personal expense of the governor general in 1832. The present monument omits the word "Victorious." See also James Wolfe.

## Ayre, Robert

Conservative critics seem to have a nostalgia for Paradise, a hope of returning to the innocence of Eden, unbiting the bite and hanging the apple once again on the bough of the Tree of Knowledge. They would have us unlearn all that has been learned, forget Cézanne, Braque, and Picasso, the Bauhaus, Freud and Jung, chemistry, photography, electronics and nuclear physics.

> "Painting," *The Arts in Canada: A Stock-Taking at Mid-Century* (1958), edited by Malcolm Ross.

# B

## Bachle, Leo
They had better start making stronger rope—if they want to hold Canadians captive!

> Johnny Canuck, the eponymous strongman hero created by artist Leo Bachle, first appeared in *Dime Comics* in 1941. In Michael Hirsch and Patrick Loubert's *The Great Canadian Comic Books* (1971), what he says is: ". . . hold Canadian captives!"

## Baden-Powell, Lady
We want to offer our thanks to groups and clubs for they have welcomed us as if we belonged and, indeed, I would like to say we do feel definitely that we are at this moment very Canadian.

> Lady Baden-Powell, pinch-hitting for her husband who founded the Boy Scouts. "Girl Guides and Boy Scouts," May 15, 1935, *Addresses Delivered before the Canadian Club of Toronto: Season of 1935-36* (1936).

## Baden-Powell, Lord
Each boy is expected—and we put him on his honour to do it—to carry out some good deed every day to some animal or person. I have today received information of one of your local scouts who woke up in the night to find he had forgotten to do his good turn. He heard a mouse in the trap, so he got up, went to that mouse, tenderly took it out of the trap, and handed it to the cat. [Laughter] Gentlemen, I trust you will excuse that digression.

> "The Boy Scout Movement," August 30, 1910, *Addresses Delivered before the Canadian Club of Toronto: Season of 1910-1911* (1911).

## Baedeker, Karl
Few of the speeches delivered in the House of Commons can be called inspiring. In fact, when not personal, they are prosaic. This can hardly be helped, for a Canadian parliament, like Congress in the United States, deals, as a rule, with matters from which only genius could draw inspiration.

> *Canada: A Guidebook* (1894).

## Baffin, William
And now it may be that som expect I should give my opynion concerning the passadge. To those my answere must be, that doubtles theare is a passadge.

> Conclusion to the Fourth Recorded Voyage, *The Voyages of William Baffin, 1612-1622* (1881), edited by Clements R. Markham. In 1616, the English navigator discovered Baffin Island and predicted the Northwest Passage would be found through Davis Strait.

Now it remayneth for your Worship to know, what hath beene performed this yere: wherefore I entreat you to admit of my custome, and pardon me if I take the plaine highway in relating the particulars, without using any refined phrases and eloquent speeches.

Therefore briefly, and as it were in the forefront, I intend to shew you the whole proceeding of the voyage in a word: as namely, there is no passage, nor hope of passage in the North of Davis Streights, wee having coasted all or neere all the Circumference thereof, and finde it to be no other then a great Bay, as the Map here placed doth truly shew: wherefore I cannot but much admire the worke of the Almightie, when I consider how vaine the best and chiefest hopes of men are in things uncertaine.

> "To the Right Worshipful Master John Wostenholme Esquire" (1615), *Hakluytus Posthumus, or Purchas His Pilgrimes: Contayning a History of the World in Sea Voyages and Lande Travells by Englishmen and Others* (1625), by Samuel Purchas; reproduced from the edition of 1905.

## Bagnold, Enid
Canada, fifty years ago, was naive,

touchy, longing to be praised, young. "What do you think of us?" (said immediately before one had even thought). I was always so nearly saying, "I think you're a bore." I wouldn't have thought it if I hadn't been so disgruntled by the haste of the question. The Daughters of Empire were always asking it and always taking me aside. I could see what a marvellous country it was but I never could get into it. I was chained to Empire and the train.

> *Autobiography* (1969). The English novelist attended an imperial conference in Ottawa with her husband, then chairman of Reuter's.

**Bagot, Sir Charles**
And His Royal Highness agrees, that all other armed vessels, on these lakes shall be forthwith dismantled, and that no other vessels of war shall be there built or armed.

> Historic "arms limitation" clause (which reduced the number of naval vessels on the Great Lakes and Lake Champlain to a total of eight), of the Rush-Bagot Agreement 1817, between Great Britain and the United States, Washington, April 28-29, 1817. Sir Charles was "His Britannic Majesty's Envoy Extraordinary and Minister Plenipotentiary to the U.S." See also Richard Rush.

**Bahá'u'lláh**   See 'Abdu'l-Bahá.

**Bailey, Jacob**
In short, I am convinced that no animal in nature makes so pernicious an improvement of liberty as man; for notwithstanding all his boasted pretences to wisdom, if you place him in a situation of unrestrained licence, it is a thousand to one if he do not ruin both himself and all his intimate connections. But enough of liberty for the present, since I had a sufficient surfeit of it in New England, and have seen from that abused principle all the miseries of licentiousness, anarchy, and tyranny, flowing like so many torrents to deluge that unhappy and devoted land.

> *Journal of a Voyage from Pownalboro to Halifax*, June 18, 1779, reprinted by

A.J.M. Smith in *The Book of Canadian Prose: Volume I, Early Beginnings to Confederation* (1965).

**Bain, George**
No, Agnes, a Bordeaux is not a house of ill-repute.

> *Champagne is for Breakfast* (1972).

If it puckers, he's there.

> Comment on Trudeau's first "kissing campaign," 1968, quoted by Walter Stewart in *Shrug: Trudeau in Power* (1971).

It is a peculiar Canadian trait to be able to spot an inequity better at a distance, especially if facing south, than close up. [Attributed]

If there is one thing that worries Canadians more than economic domination, it is that someone, sometime, will try to do something about it.

> *The Globe and Mail*, November 4, 1969.

**Baker, Eddie**
Part of my job is to open society's eyes.

> Blinded in the war, Edwin Albert Baker founded the Canadian National Institute for the Blind, Toronto, 1918. "The Vision of Eddie Baker" by Frank G.J. McDonagh in *In Search of Canada* (1971), by the editors of *Reader's Digest*.

**Balcer, Léon**
Ninety percent of the Kennedy administration's proposed legislation has been inspired by Canadian legislation of the Diefenbaker government.

> Conservative rally, Quebec City, March 4, 1961. Quoted by Peter C. Newman in *The Distemper of Our Times: Canadian Politics in Transition: 1963-1968* (1968).

**Baldwin, Eugene O.**
We will not be made to forget that in 1837 it was necessary to bore holes in the British Flag in order to breathe the atmosphere of liberty.

> Baldwin, a Quebec customs employee, was fired for making the above remark prior to the general election of 1911.

Quoted by J.H. Sinclair in the House of Commons, January 12, 1912.

## Baldwin, Robert
Responsible Government.

In a memorandum to the colonial secretary in 1836, Robert Baldwin, a moderate reformer in Upper Canada, recommended responsible government (elected rather than appointed cabinet members) in local affairs. The idea was adopted by Lord Durham in his famous report. See also his father William Warren Baldwin.

You must place the Government in advance of public opinion[,] you must give those in whom the people have confidence an interest in preserving the *system* of your Government, and maintaining the connection with the Mother Country, and then you will hear no more grievances because real ones will be redressed[,] imaginary ones will be forgotten. . . .

Letter to Lord Durham, Toronto, August 23, 1828, quoted by P.B. Waite in *Pre-Confederation* (1965).

You all, no doubt, remember the story of little Red Riding Hood, and the poor child's astonishment and alarm as she began to trace the features of the wolf instead of those of her venerable grandmother. Let the people of Canada beware lest when they begin to trace the real outlines of this new-fangled Responsible Government, and are calling out in the simplicity of their hearts, "Oh! Grandmother, what great big eyes you have! Oh! Grandmother, what a great big nose you've got!" it may not, as in the case of poor little Red Riding Hood, be too late, and the reply to the exclamation, "Oh Grandmother, what a great big mouth you have!" be, "That's to gobble you up the better, my child!"

Address to the Reform Association, March 25, 1844, *Builders of the Canadian Commonwealth* (1923), edited by George H. Locke.

It may be well to have the strength of a giant, but it should not be used like a giant.

Letter to Sir Francis Hincks, January 26, 1848. Quoted by George E. Wilson in *The Life of Robert Baldwin* (1933).

## Baldwin, Stanley
We make much today of the difficulties which face the settler. It is almost impossible for us to realize the difficulties that met the first settlers. When Lord Selkirk set out, a friend who heard of his project said to him, "Sir, if you are bent on doing something futile, why do you not sow tares at home in order to reap wheat, or plough the desert of Sahara, which is so much nearer?" Today we can smile at that in the knowledge that the greatest wheat market of the world is almost on the site of Lord Selkirk's settlement.

"The Romance of the West," Winnipeg, August 13, 1927, *Our Inheritance: Speeches and Addresses* (1928).

Sometimes, in these wonderful Canadian evenings, I have looked out at that most beautiful view from my window in the Château Laurier and watched the afterglow over the Laurentian Hills, and the still waters of the Ottawa, and I seem to see passing along towards the hills, to the sunset, the eternal procession of mankind, emerging from the dimness and the darkness of the earliest ages, struggling, raising themselves, falling—empires and kingdoms rising and falling—and I see the procession come to my own time, when I step down and take a humble place in it, and march on with the multitude, little knowing when we came, or whither we are going.

"To a Canadian Audience," Canadian Club of Ottawa, Ottawa Conference, August 15, 1932, *This Torch of Freedom: Speeches and Addresses* (1935). Baldwin was Conservative prime minister of Great Britain on three occasions between 1923 and 1937.

## Baldwin, William Warren
Responsible Government.

The first colonist to suggest the application of the principle of Responsible Government to the colonies was W.W. Baldwin, the Upper Canadian doctor, lawyer and reform leader. The suggestion that the provincial ministry, appointed by the governor, be removed should it lose the support of the elected assembly, was made in a letter to the Duke of Wellington in 1828. See also his son Robert Baldwin.

**Balfour, Arthur J.**
We go away inspired by the consciousness that here on this side of the Atlantic your hearts beat in unison with ours, and separated though we be from you by thousands of miles of stormy ocean, there is no separation of sentiment, of will, of ideal, of effort.

"Farewell Message to Canada," May 30, 1917, *Addresses Delivered before the Canadian Club of Montreal: Season of 1916-17* (1917). Balfour was Conservative prime minister of Great Britain from 1902 to 1905. For the "Balfour Declaration," see Anonymous: Some Documents.

**Ball, George**
Canada, I have long believed, is fighting a rearguard action against the inevitable —substantial integration which will require for its full realization a progressively expanding area of common political decision. . . . I wonder, for example, if the Canadian people will be prepared indefinitely to accept, for the psychic satisfaction of maintaining a separate national and political identity, a per capita income less than three-fourths of ours. The struggle is bound to be a difficult one—and I suspect over the years, a losing one. . . .

*The Discipline of Power* (1968). Ball was U.S. under-secretary of State in the administrations of presidents Kennedy and Johnson.

**Baltimore, Baron**
See Sir George Calvert.

**Band, Charles S.**
Never collect by ear.

Millionaire Toronto art collector, quoted by Pearl McCarthy in *The Globe and Mail*, February 16, 1963, who interprets this as meaning "never buy because others think a picture important."

**Banks, Hal**
I can buy any government.

Former head of the Seafarers' International Union who skipped bail in July of 1964. Quoted by Peter C. Newman in *The Distemper of Our Times: Canadian Politics in Transition: 1963-1968* (1968).

**Bannerman, George**
G.B. and T.G., July 13, 1909.

Prospectors George Bannerman and Tom Geddes staked their first claim, squaring a small spruce on which they marked the above message near Porcupine. This signalled the beginning of gold mining in northern Ontario.

**Bannerman, Lady Margaret**
See Margaret Elizabeth Gordon.

**Bannerman, Margaret**
There's no past; there's no future; only the present.

The "favourite quotation" of the Toronto-born stage actress. *My Favourite Quotation: An Anthology* (1934), edited by H. Vincent Brome.

**Banting, Sir Frederick G.**
I watched every movement of his skilful hands, and in those tense minutes I thought, "The greatest service to man is in the medical profession." From that day on it was my greatest ambition to be a doctor. [The discoverer of insulin dedicated his life to medicine after observing a doctor administering to an accident victim, while a youngster, about 1900]

*

Tie off pancreas ducts of dogs. Wait six or eight weeks. Remove and extract.

Dr. Banting lept out of bed at 2:00 A.M., October 30, 1920, scribbled these words in his medical notebook, and went back to sleep. The procedure led to the isolation of insulin in May of the following year, to the control of diabetes, and to the Nobel Prize for Medicine in 1923 (shared with J.J.R. Macleod). The fourteen most important words in medical research in Canada, scribbled down by the twenty-nine-year-old medical researcher, are sometimes given as seventeen: "Ligate pancreatic ducts of dogs.

Wait six to eight weeks for degeneration. Remove the residue and extract."

*

At any meeting or dinner please read the following: I ascribe to Best equal share in the discovery. Hurt that he is not so acknowledged by Nobel trustees. Will share with him. Banting.

Telegram sent October 26, 1923, to the convener of a medical convention in Boston. Banting felt he should have shared the Nobel Prize with Charles H. Best, his co-worker, not with J.J.R. Macleod, his head of department. Banting shared his prize money with Best; Macleod with another co-worker, J.B. Collip.

*

The one thing I dread is affluence. I have a lovely office now, with pictures on the wall and a swivel chair, and I can't do anything.

Remark to a friend after moving from the cramped Medical Research Department into the spacious new Pathology Building at the University of Toronto.

*

I sometimes wonder if we are helped by too full a knowledge of medical literature. I must frankly confess that, had I read all that was written on diabetes and known all of the conflicting views and theories I would probably never have tackled the problem. [Chicago address, late 1920s]

*

It is not within the power of the properly constructed human mind to be satisfied. Progress would cease if this were the case. The greatest joy of life is to accomplish. It is the getting, not the having. It is the giving, not the keeping. I am a firm believer in the theory that you can do or be anything that you wish in this world, within reason, if you are prepared to make the sacrifices, think and work hard enough and long enough. [Article, 1940]

*

You must begin with an ideal and end with an ideal. And if, by the wayside, you falter, you place commercial gain before higher motives, you should stop your studies right now. Medicine is a profession of inspiration, perpetual and eternal. [Advice to a group of medical students shortly before his death in 1941]

Quoted by Lloyd Stevenson in *Sir Frederick Banting* (1946). See also Captain Joseph Mackey.

No one has ever had an idea in a dress suit. [Attributed]

## Barbeau, Jean

On paper, Quebec is a very rich country. On ice, also . . . .

*Le Maclean*, August, 1973.

## Barbeau, Marius

Our national soul has not grown beyond infancy.

"Canadian Folk Songs as a National Asset," January 10, 1928, *Addresses Delivered before the Canadian Club of Toronto: Season of 1927-28* (1928).

Folk songs, to mean something really vital in the art of a nation, must lead to larger forms—rhapsodies, concertos, quartets, symphonies, cantatas, ballets or operas. Not until these issue freely from the hand of our composers and grace the great auditoriums of the world will our expectation be fulfilled.

"French and Indian Motifs in Our Music," *Yearbook of the Arts in Canada: 1928-29* (1929), edited by Bertram Brooker.

## Barclay, Pat

If there's one phrase in the national vocabulary which stands out as being typically Canadian, that's it. Typically Canadian, I mean. We hear people referring to things, ideas, each other, etc., as "typically Canadian" all the time. But what exactly do they mean? Tone of voice has a lot to do with meaning, and I've noticed there's a sort of rueful pride in most voices when they describe something as "typically Canadian." As if what they were really saying was, "Well, we should have expected as much." That's why our success at Expo was such a shock. It wasn't *typical*. A typical Canadian success would have to contain a basic absurdity, like a boat that wouldn't float, or a prime minister with a lisp.

*The Victoria Times*, April 14, 1973.

**Baring, Alexander**
See Lord Ashburton.

**Barker, Edward John**
I have outlived all my enemies. I have therefore no apologies to make, nor for-giveness to crave.

> In 1872, at the age of seventy-three, Dr. Barker turned the editorship of *The British Whig*, the newspaper he founded in Kingston in 1834, over to his grand-son, E.J. Pense. Quoted by J. Alex. Ed-mison in "Kingston and the Founding of the Canadian Press Association," *Historic Kingston*, November, 1960.

**Barker, Lewellys F.**
After seventy, one's reason tells one that the anticipation of many more years of life is not justifiable; one should count every year after one's seventieth as "vel-vet."

> The Ontario-born doctor succeeded Sir William Osler as head of Johns Hop-kins' medical school. *Time and the Phy-sician: The Autobiography of Lewellys F. Barker* (1942).

**Barkway, Michael**
I sometimes feel that we who are trying to promote greater understanding be-tween peoples by the use of broadcast-ing are like people trying to get drunk on cider—we will get there eventually, but it will take an awful lot of hard work.

> "International Radio in War and Peace" (1945), *Empire Club of Canada: Ad-dresses Delivered to the Members Dur-ing the Year 1945-46* (1946).

**Barnes, LaVerne**
The Canadian superfan comes to the Grey Cup to get out of himself and reach out for all those things he has been promised all week, all the vicarious plastic things. He is there with his ticket waiting for it to happen to him.

> *The Plastic Orgasm* (1971), an exposé of football culture by the wife of a player.

**Barnum, P.T.**
In 1861, I learned that some fishermen at the mouth of the St. Lawrence had succeeded in capturing a living white whale. . . . I chartered a sloop to Elbow Island (Isle aux Coudres), in the St. Lawrence River, and found the place populated by Canadian French people of the most ignorant and dirty descrip-tion. They were hospitable, but fright-fully filthy, and gained their livelihood by farming and fishing. Immense quan-tities of maple-sugar are made there, and in exploring about the island, we saw hundreds of birchbark buckets sus-pended to the trees to catch the sap. After numerous consultations, extend-ing over three whole days, with a party of twenty-four fishermen, whose gibber-ish was almost as untranslatable as it was unbearable, I succeeded in contracting for their services to capture for me, alive and unharmed, a couple of white whales, scores of which could at all times be discovered by their "spouting" within sight of the island.

> *Struggles and Triumphs: or, Forty Years' Recollections of P.T. Barnum, Written by Himself* (1869).

**Barr, Isaac M.**
Canada for the British!

\*

The Project. To organize a large body of British people of the right kind—English, Scotch, and Irish—to form a settlement on Government free grant lands, on the prairies of North-West Canada.

\*

Canada for the British and Why Not!

> From the "Barr Pamphlet," *British Set-tlements in North Western Canada*, issued by the Rev. I.M. Barr, 1902. Re-produced by J. Hanna McCormick in *Lloydminster: Or 5,000 Miles with the Barr Colonists* (1922).

**Barr, Robert**
The bold truth is that Canada has the money, but would rather spend it on whiskey than on books. It prefers to in-flame its stomach, rather than inform its brain.

\*

It is not lack of money that makes Canada about the poorest book market in the world outside of Senegambia.

> "Literature in Canada," *The Canadian Magazine*, November, 1889. Barr spent his youthful years in Canada but did most of his writing in England, where he died in 1912.

## Barrett, David (Dave)

The premier called me a Waffle. Well, I called him a pancake. Then he called me a double Waffle. I called him a stack of pancakes. Knowing the way he feels about Quebec, I warned him if he calls me a Waffle again, I'll call him a crêpe suzette.

> The then leader of the NDP reporting on a conversation with Premier W.A.C. Bennett of British Columbia, August, 1972.

The government fired me. The people hired me.

> Premier-elect of British Columbia, the night of his electoral victory, August 30, 1972. Barrett had been fired by the former Social Credit administration from a social-work position for making controversial statements.

I'm the "socialist hordes."

> Attributed to the new premier, August 30, 1972. For the phrase "socialist hordes," see W.A.C. Bennett.

As socialists, we will be hard-nosed capitalists in business ventures.

> *The Financial Post*, March 17, 1973.

Never underestimate the persuasive powers of a former social worker.

> *The Toronto Star*, April 21, 1973.

This job is just an extension of social work. Social workers have more business in politics than lawyers do.

> Quoted by Allan Fotheringham in *Maclean's Magazine*, June, 1973.

## Barris, Alex

Some years ago, George Burns, commenting on the decline of vaudeville and the young performer's problem of finding a few relatively obscure places to learn his trade, complained: "There's no longer

any place to be lousy." But more recently, reminded of this comment, the veteran comedian reversed himself. "I've changed my mind about that," he said. "If there are places to be lousy, you'll stay lousy."

> *The Pierce-Arrow Showroom Is Leaking: An Insider's View of the CBC* (1969).

## Barron, Sid

"Mild, isn't it?"

> This remark has appeared in all the editorial cartoons drawn by Sid Barron for *The Toronto Star* since the early 1960s. The cartoonist lives in Victoria and thus satirizes the Toronto scene from a distance.

## Bartlett, William

You may dream of Niagara, but words will never describe it to you.

> *Brief Memoir of the Late William Henry Bartlett* (1855), by William Beattie.

## Basile, Jean

An American offshoot of Latin greatness, no nation aimed at universal genius more than the French-Canadian nation. None is more deserving of success.

> "Literature in French," *The Canadians 1867-1967* (1967), edited by J.M.S. Careless and R. Craig Brown.

## Bassett I, John

Death came to Billy Bishop in the early morning. He died at that chill hour before the coming of dawn—an hour when he must often have been making ready for his solitary flights. . . . Perhaps if he had a choice, this would have been the hour he would have preferred. For he had that courage which Napoleon once said was the rarest—the courage of the early morning.

> Quoted by William Arthur Bishop in *The Courage of the Early Morning: The Story of Billy Bishop* (1965). Bassett was the publisher of *The Montreal Gazette* and the father of John Bassett II.

**Bassett II, John**
If you want to write about Eaton's you have to ask me first.

Publisher of *The Toronto Telegram* to his new columnist Ron Haggart, 1960s. The Eatons were part owners of the *Telegram*.

I'm sorry, I couldn't do better.

The closest Bassett came to apologizing when he permitted the *Telegram* to fold, September 17, 1971. Quoted by Jock Carroll in *The Death of the Toronto Telegram and Other Newspaper Stories* (1971). See also Lord Beaverbrook.

**Bassett III, John**
You can't beat winning.

Quoted by John Gault in *Toronto Life*, November, 1965.

It's better to be lucky than smart.

The film-maker and son of the publisher of the *Telegram*, quoted by Pat Annesley in *Canadian Magazine*, June 2, 1973.

**Bates, Dr. Gordon**
If there were enough women in Parliament, the health ministry would become more important than that of finance.

Dr. Bates was director of the Health League of Canada. Paraphrased from a remark made in 1941, quoted by Catherine Lyle Cleverdon in *The Woman Suffrage Movement in Canada* (1950).

**Bates, Ron**
This land is not *quelques arpents de neige* but an infinity of snow. Voltaire's countryman, Pascal, felt the fear of infinite spaces which many of our writers share, faced with Canada and their presence in it.

"Roots," *Maclean's Magazine*, August, 1973.

**Baudelaire, Charles**
Every year they ask the sky to send down as much snow, hail and frost as it can contain. What they really need are Canadian or Russian winters. Their own nests will be all the warmer, all the downier, all the better loved.

The great French poet is talking about dreamers and visionaries. Quoted by Gaston Bachelard in *The Poetics of Space* (1964), translated by Marie Jolas.

**Bauer, Walter**
The arctic expresses the sum total of all wisdom: / Silence. Nothing but silence. The end of time.

"Canada," *The Price of Morning: Selected Poems* (1968), translated from the German by Henry Beissel.

**Baum, Gregory**
You have to learn to speak only when you can be heard.

Quoted by Gilbert Roxburgh in *The Globe and Mail*, February 3, 1973.

**Bawtree, Michael**
Canada and Russia are the largest countries of the world. They lie within the same latitudes. They share a climate of extremes. They share a sense of wind and plain, of airy desolation; and they enclose huddles of people within the harsh rhythms of the north. I've always felt that Canada has this kind of elemental kinship with Russia, a kinship more mysterious and so tougher than that with the sultry United States . . . it was time we shared not only snow but visions.

"The Government Inspector," *The Stratford Scene 1958-1968* (1968), edited by Peter Raby.

**Baxter, Beverley**
It does not matter what the surface civilization may be in Canada; it is from this great country overseas that you got the source of your civilization. There in the little winding lanes which lead around to the Red Lion and the Crown and Anchor; there in the little villages scattered all over, and there along the muddy banks of the Thames lie the germs of our civilization here.

"Behind the Scenes," *Empire Club of Canada: Addresses Delivered to the Members During the Year 1932* (1932).

There is an honesty about the very seasons in Canada. In the winter it is cold. In the summer it is hot.

"From the Heart of Things" (1937), *Empire Club of Canada: Addresses Delivered to the Members During the Year 1937-38* (1938).

Gentlemen, it has been a great experience to come from the Island of infinite shadows, Britain in the North Sea, with the hot breath of war a few miles across the Channel, to leave that Island with its mighty courage and faith, and to come across the seas, and in a few days to cover these great stretches of Canada, where there are no frontiers, where the only walls are the four horizons, where there are the mountains and the two seas between the West and the rest of the world.

"What I Have Seen Over There and Over Here" (1941), *Empire Club of Canada: Addresses Delivered to the Members During the Year 1941-42* (1942).

We grow old by moments and not by years.

\*

There may come a higher citizenship some day, when all frontiers will be abolished and a man shall owe allegiance only to humanity. Until that time arrives it is no mean thing to have been a citizen of the British Empire.

\*

The instinct which warns animals of danger does not apply to human beings. He who takes his place at the banqueting table with the proprietors of London's daily journalism needs a long spoon.

\*

And I have seen all this company with the goodly fellows of the Press, poets who never wrote a poem, sentimentalists who never shed a tear, cynics who never refused a companion in distress, historians who recorded nothing older than a day.

*Strange Street* (1935). The Toronto-born journalist and British M.P. enjoyed a distinguished career on Fleet Street and contributed a fortnightly "London Letter" to *Maclean's Magazine*.

The death penalty degraded society,

glamourized murder, and raised the killer to be an aristocrat among criminals.

Quoted by Louis Blake Duff in *The Country Kerchief* (1949).

## Baxter, Portus

What reciprocal advantages can they [Canadians] return to us? What benefits do they give us for those we confer on them? They tell us that we may go to their markets. Why, sir, they have no markets. We may go there, but what is the use of going there if there are no markets? I know there are no markets there; I was born near there, and I know what I say. Fifty bullocks from Illinois would frighten every butcher out of Montreal!

The House will excuse my homely comparisons. I am, when at home, nothing but a farmer, and I thank God for it.

Representative from Vermont, House of Representatives, Washington, *The Congressional Globe*, May 26, 1864. Being discussed was termination of the Reciprocity Treaty signed in 1854.

## Beatty, Admiral David

When you look at the map and you see a great frontier line, stretching over 3,600 miles, and you scratch your head and say, "Well, what is defending it?" Nothing but the sound common sense, the sound good-will of two practical nations.

"Address," November 28, 1921, *Addresses Delivered before the Canadian Club of Toronto: Season of 1921-22* (1922). Admiral Beatty's title: Earl of the North Sea and of Brooksby.

## Beatty, Sir Edward W.

I often say to my directors that I am almost ashamed to take the salary that they pay me because it is the easiest thing in the world to be a railway president. All you have to do is to satisfy the public.

The president of the CPR is quoting an unnamed American railway president of many years standing with whom he agrees. "Confederation," March 28, 1927, *Addresses Delivered before the Canadian Club of Toronto: Season of 1926-27* (1927). See also David Lewis.

**Beaudoin, René**
These days are not easy ones. . . .

*

Now, the house is master of its own rules and it is my right to submit a matter to the house. I intend at the moment to submit to the house that, in my view, the house should revert to the position where it was yesterday when I was brought back to the chair to receive the chairman's report at 5:15.

*

Mr. Coldwell: Mr. Speaker, this is a demonstration, on the part of all Liberals in the house which shows a great disrespect for authority. I protest against this. Parliament has ceased to function.

*

Mr. Fleming: . . . That ought to be on the record. This is the lowest moment in Canadian parliament; the lowest moment. There has never been anything like it.

Mr. Pearson: I thought that was last night.

Mr. Bell: This is black Friday, boy.

Mr. Lesage: You brought it on; you did it yourself.

Mr. Fleming: How absurd can you get?

Mr. Martin: The minority is not running this parliament.

Mr. Rowe: The majority isn't running it either; nobody is running it. The majority cannot run it, let alone the minority.

Mr. Hodgson: Hitlerism.

Some hon. Members:

There will always be a pipe line,
The pipe line shall be free;
The gas shall flow from west to east
    in each locality.
There'll always be a pipe line,
The pipe line shall be free,
For Fulton means no more to you
    than Fulton means to me.

*

I've been working on the pipe line
    all the day through,
I've been working on the pipe line
    just to make the Tories blue.
Can't you hear the Tories moaning,
    getting up so early in the morn';
Hear the C.C.F.'ers groaning, for the
    pipe line's getting warm.

*

Mr. Rowe: He laughs best who laughs last; go to the country and find out.

An hon. Member: You laughed yourself.

Mr. Rowe: No, I am ashamed of you; that is why I cannot laugh.

House of Commons, June 1, 1956. The Speaker of the House on "Black Friday," René Beaudoin (Liberal — Vaudreuil-Soulanges), was personally defeated in the next general election, and the Liberals were turned out of power. See also Thomas M. Bell.

**Beaver, William**
I tell 'em they must all turn away from sin; that the Great Spirit will give 'em new eyes to see, new ears to hear good things; new heart to understand, and sing, and pray; all new! I tell 'em squaws, they must wash 'em blankets clean, must cook 'em victuals clean, like white women; they must live in peace, worship God, and love one another. Then the Good Spirit make the ground all smooth before you.

The Indian "exhorter" or missionary's translator explaining his message to a group of Mississauga Indians at a camp meeting near Adolphustown, June, 1826. Quoted by William Canniff in *The Settlement of Upper Canada* (1869).

**Beaverbrook, Lord**
Hello, what's the news? [Characteristic telephone greeting]

*

He's a little guy. Owns a lot of little newspapers. [Early opinion of Roy Thomson when the fellow Canadian began to acquire broadcasting and publishing interests in Great Britain]

*

We were so agreeably placed until he came along to disturb the waters of tranquillity. [The Beaver's considered opinion of Roy Thomson who had just become Lord Thomson of Fleet]

*

Here I must say, in my eighty-sixth year, I do not feel greatly different from when I was eighty-five. This is my final word. It is time for me to become an apprentice once more. I have not settled in which direction. But somewhere, some-time soon. [Lord Thomson of Fleet held a gala banquet on May 25, 1964, to cele-brate the Beaver's eighty-fifth birthday. It was the guest's last public appearance and within two weeks Beaverbrook was dead.]

> Quoted by Russell Braddon in *Roy Thomson of Fleet Street* (1965).

I am descended from eight or ten gen-erations of agricultural labourers. There-fore I feel quite equal to the Cecil fam-ily, with this difference, that none of my ancestors stole church funds.

*

Everyone who buys an enamelled iron pan in Canada pays tribute to me.

*

I did not make situations; I turned them to account.

*

I was selling papers when I was six and now I'm sixty I'm still selling them.

*

What a fine title—Lord Thomson of Fleet! How did Northcliffe and Rother-mere, Riddell and Lord Dalziel, and I and some others give him the opportu-nity of taking that title? I cannot make it out. We could have been in before him.

*

I no longer control. I still dominate. [Letter to Henry Luce]

> Quoted by A.J.P. Taylor in *Beaver-brook* (1972).

I was brought up in such extreme pov-erty that I was determined to escape from it at all costs.

*

It's the first £10,000 that counts.

*

When *I* cross the Atlantic, the ship goes straight ahead and lets the icebergs get out of the way.

*

I *always* dispute the umpire's verdict.

*

The man who is consistent must be out of touch with reality. There is no con-sistency in the course of events—in his-tory, in the weather, or in the mental attitude of one's fellow men.

*

"I once asked him [Beaverbrook] if he

ever wanted to be Prime Minister of Britain. 'Yes,' he said, 'but only if I can be Leader of the Opposition at the same time!' "

*

I can conceive and create, but I cannot carry on a routine job.

*

Good-bye to you. [Characteristic tele-phone sign-off which became a by-word on Fleet Street]

> Quoted by Alan Wood in *The True History of Lord Beaverbrook* (1965).

Get me Bonar Law on the telephone, and then ask Arnold Bennett if he will lunch with me here at one o'clock.

*

You and I are to save Mesopotamia for England.

> About 1920, quoted by A. Beverley Bax-ter in *Strange Street* (1935).

Man cannot add an inch to his stature, but by taking thought he can stand erect.

*

I once had youth, and now I have ex-perience.

> *The Three Keys to Success* (1956).

A man must feel those early deals right down to the pit of his stomach if he is going to be a great man of business.

*

When I was a boy, I knew the value in exchange of every marble in my village, and this practice of valuing became a subconscious habit until I always had an intuitive perception of the real and not the face value of any article.

> Quoted by Martin Burrell in *Betwixt Heaven and Charing Cross* (1928).

Many people quote Lord Acton's dictum that "power corrupts" without stopping to examine the possibility that it is a piece of nonsense. Who is likely to be corrupted—he who, by bringing his am-bition to fruition, fulfills himself, or he who is warped and frustrated by defeat?

*

Politics are for the few: they are a game, a fancy or an inheritance.

> *Don't Trust to Luck* (1954).

A wonderful thing. A wonderful story.

> To two survivors of the Springhill mining disaster of 1958. Quoted by Frank Rasky in *Great Canadian Disasters* (1961).

It is quite something to have a woman still interested in you when you are eighty-four. [To Christofor Dunn, widow of his lifelong friend Sir James Dunn, when they were married, June 7, 1963]

Rebel if you must but renegade never— Max.

> Cable allegedly sent to John Bassett II (whose *Toronto Telegram* switched support from the Tories to the Liberals in 1963) by Lord Beaverbrook from Cap d'Ail, Côte d'Azure. Quoted by Peter C. Newman in *The Distemper of Our Times: Canadian Politics in Transition: 1963-1968* (1968).

Young man: How should I invest my money?
Beaverbrook: Buy Old Masters. They fetch a much better price than old mistresses. [Attributed to the puckish Canadian-born British "press lord"]

We lead, let those follow who can.

> Motto of *The Leader,* a four-page newspaper issued from Newcastle, New Brunswick, in 1893. Four issues appeared under the imprint of Max Aitken. The future press lord was fourteen years old at the time.
> See also: Sir Max Aitken, Winston Churchill, Sir James Dunn, Andrew Bonar Law, Malcolm Muggeridge, A.J.P. Taylor, H.G. Wells.

**Beck, Sir Adam**
If I have helped to lessen the cares of the housewife by making electricity her servant, I have my reward. If I have helped the farmer to make life more attractive to the boys and girls on the farm, then I have not laboured nor have you cooperated with me in vain. If I have helped to save the life of any afflicted child, or lengthened the days of any afflicted, I am happy.

> First chairman of Ontario Hydro, 1923, quoted by Robert Saunders in "The Case for the St. Lawrence Power Pro-

ject" (1951), *Empire Club of Canada: Addresses 1951-52* (1952).

**Beckwith, John**
From about age eight I had the idea I wanted to be a composer—mainly, at that time, in order to become very, very famous.

> Composer and teacher interviewed by *Musicanada,* November, 1967.

True, there is no special reason why a Brazilian or an Egyptian might not be as adept at using Eskimo themes or responding to elements of our artistic or political background; but the fact is, no Brazilian has done so and no Egyptian: we wanted to, and did.

> "What Every U.S. Musician Should Know about Contemporary Canadian Music," *Musicanada,* Winter, 1970.

**Beddoes, Dick**
Horses and jockeys mature earlier than people—which is why horses are admitted to race tracks at the age of two, and jockeys before they are old enough to shave.

> Characteristic observation of the sports editor of *The Globe and Mail.*

**Beecher, Henry Ward**
I recollect very well that the term of anger toward Englishmen was, "A d—— Britisher"; I use it without the adjective.

> Montreal address, May 25, 1879, quoted by Edgar Andrew Collard in *Montreal Yesterdays* (1962). Mrs. Harriet Beecher Stowe, the sister of the popular preacher, visited the city ten years later.

**Beecroft, Norma**
I most deplore works which bore. Even anger is a reaction!

> Composer interviewed by *Musicanada,* May, 1969.

**Beef, Joe**
Joe Beef of Montreal, the Son of the People; he cares not for Pope, Priest, Parson or King William of the Boyne; all Joe wants is his Coin. He trusts in God in summer time to keep him from

all harm; when he sees the frost and snow poor old Joe trusts to the Almighty Dollar and good old maple wood to keep his belly warm, for Churches, Chapels, Ranters, Preachers, Beechers and such stuff Montreal has already got enough.

*

All your Clergymen, Captains, Sailors, Bums and Scurvy-Tailors, if you can walk or crawl, when you go on the spree, go and see Joe Beef of Montreal.

*

Joe is every man's countryman. He will take five cents from a rank Orangeman as well as a live Fenian.

> The outspoken proprietor of Joe Beef's Canteen at Common and Callières on the Montreal waterfront during the 1880s was a colourful Irishman named Charles McKiernan. These are some of his mottos, written in rhyming prose.

## Beers, Dr. George

Lacrosse is peculiar to our country and originated here as did snowshoeing and tobogganing. Just as we declare the rivers, lakes and lands, once Indian-owned to be now Canadian, so we claim the Indian field-game of lacrosse to be the national field-game of this Dominion.

> From a petition drawn up in 1867 by Dr. George Beers, a Montreal dental surgeon and noted lacrosse player. Although lacrosse is known as "Canada's national game," there is no record the federal Parliament ever recognized it as such.

## Begbie, Judge Matthew B.

It is not a pleasant duty for me to have to sentence you only to prison for life; your crime was unmitigated murder, you deserve to be hanged. Had the jury done their duty I might now have the painful satisfaction of condemning you to death. . . . You, gentlemen of the jury, permit me to say that it would give me great pleasure to see you hanged, each and every one of you, for bringing in a murderer guilty only of manslaughter. [At the murder trial of an American gunman named Gilchrist, January, 1863]

*

If, gentlemen, you have a reasonable doubt as to the prisoner's guilt, give him the benefit of it; but if the circumstances you have heard related permit of only one solution—that the prisoner is the guilty man—then, "Sock it to him, sock it to him."

> Quoted by Edward Nicolls in "Sir Mat-[t]hew Baillie Begbie, Knight, Later Chief Justice of British Columbia," *The Canadian Magazine*, July, 1898.

I am against prohibition on both grounds. I think it would be inexpedient if it were possible, and it is impossible if it were expedient.

> Quoted by Roy St. George Stubbs in "Matthew Baillie Begbie," *Papers Read Before the Historical and Scientific Society of Manitoba*, No. 25, 1968-69.

The statute books are exceedingly muddled. I seldom look into them. [Before an open court]

*

It will take six months or more for the colonial secretary to deal with the matter and months more before we learn of his decision. But you will not be interested in what he decides, for you are to be hanged Monday morning. [To an American desperado convicted of murder at the assize in the Cariboo when he warned Judge Begbie he would appeal his sentence]

> Quoted by D.A. McGregor in "Sir Matthew Begbie" in *Canadian Portraits: CBC Broadcasts* (1940), edited by R.G. Riddell.

Bury me early in the morning, that only my friends will take the trouble to get up in time to follow me to my grave.

> Request made by "the hanging judge" who died at Victoria, June 11, 1894. Quoted by Arthur Beanlands in "Some Recollections" (1894), reproduced by W. Kaye Lamb in *British Columbia Historical Quarterly*, April, 1941.

## Behaim, Martin

Here one catches white falcons.

> Inscribed by the geographer Martin Behaim on his famous terrestrial globe, constructed in 1492 in Nuremberg where it is still preserved. The site where white

falcons may be found is that of Baffin Island in the eastern Arctic. Quoted by E.G. Ravenstein in *Martin Behaim* (1908), and reproduced by Tryggvi J. Oleson in *Early Voyages and Northern Approaches 1000-1632* (1963). See also Marco Polo.

## Behan, Brendan

A lot of people say I hate Canada. I don't hate any place . . . well, I make certain exceptions. Canada's the only place where I've been accused of being a Dogan. That's an Irish Catholic. I asked them for it in writing so I could show them at home.

*

Montreal is the only place where a good French accent isn't a social asset.

*

I have no desire to bolster the sagging cultural economy of this country. [After being hospitalized in Toronto]

*

Anyone who comes to Canada should bring his own home with him.

> *The Wit of Brendan Behan* (1968), compiled by Sean McCann.

I don't know why people take exception to me. A few weeks ago in Toronto a Canadian said that it was an awful black eye for the Yanks that the Russians has put a spaceman up before the Americans. I said to him, "My friend, Ireland will put a shillelagh into orbit, Israel will put a matzo ball into orbit, and Liechtenstein will put a postage stamp into orbit before you Canadians ever put up a mouse." Do you know, he hit me.

*

Canada is barbaric without being picturesque. Toronto will be a fine town when it is finished. I'm not a Yank and you're not a Russian. You're a Canadian. Stick to your league—Ice Hockey. [To Montreal reporters, December 9, 1960]

> Quoted by Ulick O'Connor in *Brendan* (1970).

That's a piece of impertinence in itself. [Referring to the name of London, Ontario]

Critics are like eunuchs in a harem:

They know how it's done, they've seen it done every day, but they're unable to do it themselves.

> This widely quoted aphorism was uttered by Behan in 1961 on a Toronto TV program after reading a hostile review of *The Hostage* by Nathan Cohen. Quoted by Paul King, "Why Our Critics Scare the CBC," *Toronto Life*, June, 1971.
>
> See also Gilbert Harding.

## Belaney, Archibald    See Grey Owl.

## Belasco, David

Only my dear mother seemed to understand me. My adventures and wanderings ("Wandering Feet," she used to call me) worried her, which I grieve to think of now, but she always took my part. "Davey is all right," she used to say; "leave him alone; he's only curious about life, and wants to see everything with those big, dark eyes of his." She was right; and, if I didn't see everything, I saw a good deal.

> Childhood reminiscence of David Belasco, the leading theatrical producer on Broadway at the turn of the century, quoted by William Winter in *The Life of David Belasco* (1918). Born into a theatrical family in San Francisco in 1853, the child was whisked off to Victoria in the wake of the gold rush of 1858. At the age of five he was carried on stage by Julia Dean; at nine he walked across in *East Lynne*; and at eleven he appeared as the Duke of York in Kean's *King Richard III*. The following year, his parents having made a little money supplying goods to miners, he was taken back to San Francisco. See also Mary Pickford.

## Belcher, Jonathan

By what I heard the government of the petty province of Nova Scotia has been one constant scene of tyranny. God deliver me and mine from the government of soldiers.

> Letter from the governor of Massachusetts Bay to Thomas Coram, October 6, 1733. Quoted by W.S. MacNutt in *The Atlantic Provinces: The Emergence of Colonial Society 1712-1857* (1965).

## Béliveau, Jean

I'm not out there to take stiff checks and fight people. I'm playing to see that we put the puck in their net and that they don't put it in ours. Fast skating, sharp passing, smart clean defensive play, that's hockey.

Quoted by Hugh Hood in *Strength Down Centre: The Jean Béliveau Story* (1970).

## Bell, Alexander Graham

I then shouted into M [the mouthpiece] the following sentence: "Mr. Watson—Come here—I want to see you." To my delight he came and declared that he had heard and understood what I said. I asked him to repeat the words. He answered "You said—'Mr. Watson—come here—I want to see you.'" We then changed places and I listened at S [the reed receiver] while Mr. Watson read a few passages from a book into the mouthpiece M.

This is Alexander Graham Bell's own account of the first intelligible communication by telephone, Boston, March 10, 1876, from an entry in his notebook two days following the historic event. Quoted by Robert V. Bruce in *Bell: Alexander Graham Bell and the Conquest of Solitude* (1973). Bruce noted that the summons to his assistant Thomas B. Watson "has become one of history's best remembered utterances." There is no contemporary evidence for the story that the summons was Bell's cry for help over the spilling of acid.

It is rather a curious thing to me to see the dispute about where the telephone was invented. It was I who invented the telephone and it was invented wherever I happened to be at the time. Of this you may be sure, the telephone was invented in Canada. It was made in the United States. The first transmission of a human voice over a telephone wire, where the speaker and the listener were miles apart, was in Canada. The first transmissions by wire in which the conversation was carried on reciprocally over the same wire was in the United States. It certainly is the case that the telephone was invented in Canada and that the first actual use of telephone lines was in this country.

"Recent Developments in the Science of Aviation," March 27, 1909, *Addresses Delivered before the Canadian Club of Ottawa: 1903-1909* (1910).

When I come to look back upon the history of the telephone, it seems almost like a dream that I was connected with it at all, so long it is since I have had anything to do with telephones—and I do not have a telephone in my own house within reach of my ears. [Laughter] So much of the practical development of the telephone has been in the United States that I think the fact that the telephone was invented in Canada should be more widely known than it is —at least in the United States.

\*

The telephone, devised in Brantford, was not made until 1875, when it appeared in Boston; so that the telephone was conceived in Brantford in 1874, and born in Boston in 1875.

\*

But Canada was also associated with a very important development of the practical telephone in the early days. It was in Brantford that the first transmission of speech to a distance occurred. . . . That was in August, 1876.

\*

Of course, the Wrights had been flying earlier, only we did not know what they had been doing, as it was all done in private. We did not hear very much about the "Red Wing" [an early flying machine with red silk wings which was aloft in March 1908 in Hammondsford, New York] in the United States, because the aviator was a Canadian, Mr. Baldwin. [Applause] He was the first man to get into the air in public in America.

"The Substance of My Latest Research" (1917), *Empire Club of Canada: Addresses Delivered to the Members During the Sessions, 1917-18, and May to December, 1918* (1919). The flier was F. W. (Casey) Baldwin of Toronto.

Died a Citizen of the United States.

"The day of the funeral, August 4, 1922, was gray and misty, the sort of day Bell had loved best," wrote Robert V. Bruce in *Bell: Alexander Graham Bell and the Conquest of Solitude* (1973). Bell's grave bears a tablet with the above statement. He is buried at Beinn Bhreagh (the Gaelic words which he named his estate mean "Beautiful Mountain"), Baddeck, Cape Breton, Nova Scotia.

"The largest telephone users in the world are the people of Canada, with 664.1 calls per person in 1966," according to Norris and Ross McWhirter in the *Guinness Book of World Records* (1968). See also Melville Bell.

## Bell, Don

Montreal is a Saturday city. On Saturdays the whole city begins to tingle. There is celebration in the air, there is frenzy, there is pleasure. Everybody important is out in the streets.

*Saturday Night at the Bagel Factory and Other Montreal Stories* (1972).

## Bell, Hiram

But, sir, there is a country and there is a people competent for self-government, that are prepared to take upon themselves the responsibilities of free men, and which we may find for our interest to receive among us—I mean peaceably—and allow them to become a part and parcel of this country, and I care not how soon. I refer, Mr. Chairman, to the whole British possessions upon the north, containing an area of two millions, two hundred and fifty-two thousand, three hundred and ninety-five square miles. That is something worth looking at. . . . The accomplishment of that object peacefully will strengthen this Union, and add to its power and influence. The annexation of that territory to this Union (to use terms of gentlemen) Destiny has ordained, and it will ere long take place.

Representative Bell of Ohio speaking in the U.S. House of Representatives, January 10, 1853. *Manifest Destiny* (1968), edited by Norman A. Graebner.

## Bell, Dr. J. McIntosh

The steep rocky shores which here pre-

sent themselves to the lake are often stained with cobalt-blue and copper-green.

This description of the rocky shore of Echo Bay on Great Bear Lake appeared in the report of a geological survey undertaken by Dr. J. McIntosh Bell and Dr. Charles Camsell in 1900. It excited a prospector named Gilbert LaBine who prospected the region in 1930 and found there immense quantities of pitchblende. This was the beginning of the largest radium refinery in the world. See also Gilbert LaBine.

## Bell, Dr. Leslie

You make your own success.

Quoted by June Callwood in *Maclean's Magazine*, February 1, 1953.

TV performers for the most part fall into two groups—those who have been dropped and those who are going to be dropped.

*Maclean's Magazine*, April 30, 1955. In the early days of television, the Leslie Bell Singers were popular TV fare.

## Bell, Marilyn

I did? I finished?

Sixteen-year-old Marilyn Bell swam choppy Lake Ontario, September 9, 1954, covering the thirty-two miles from Youngstown, New York, to Toronto's Sunnyside Beach in twenty hours and fifty-nine minutes—the first person to succeed. Quoted by June Callwood in "How Marilyn Swam the Lake," *Maclean's Canada: Portrait of a Country* (1960), edited by Leslie F. Hannon.

I did it for Canada!

Marilyn Bell's reason for swimming Lake Ontario. The motto of the Gus Ryder–Marilyn Bell team was "We'll Win for Canada." Miss Bell is now Mrs. Marilyn DiLascio of New Jersey and a grade two teacher. Quoted by Ron McAllister in *Swim to Glory: The Story of Marilyn Bell and the Lakeshore Swimming Club* (1954). See also Gus Ryder.

## Bell, Max

The only time money is really important to anyone is when a person hasn't any.

Newspaper publisher quoted in his obituary notice, *The Globe and Mail*, July 20, 1972.

## Bell, Melville
New motor; hopeful. Electric speech?

Professor Melville Bell, father of Alexander Bell, made this entry in his journal on July 26, 1874, after listening to his son's ideas for the first telephone. Quoted by Alexander Graham Bell in "The Substance of My Latest Research" (1917), *Empire Club of Canada: Addresses Delivered to the Members During the Sessions, 1917-18, and May to December, 1918* (1919).

Yes, Alec, it is I, your father, speaking.

This is the first message ever carried over a long-distance telephone line. The evening of August 10, 1876, Melville Bell spoke into a primitive transmitter in Brantford. His words were heard by his son Alexander Graham Bell who was huddled over a primitive receiver in a Paris, Ontario, shoe store, eight miles away. The inventor of the telephone telegraphed for a confirmation that his father was at the other end of the line, and the above came back loud and clear. The first long-distance conversation lasted three hours. See also Alexander Graham Bell.

## Bell, Thomas M.
This is black Friday, boy.

The Conservative member for Saint John found the perfect epithet to describe the undemocratic procedures that marked the "pipeline debate" in the House of Commons on Friday, June 1, 1956. See also René Beaudoin.

## Bellow, Saul
It began as a holiday, a short reprieve, last May, when I was sent home because my papers were not in order. I have lived here eighteen years, but I am still a Canadian, a British subject, and although a friendly alien I could not be drafted without an investigation.

Like the Chicago novelist himself, who

was born in Lachine in 1915, the hero of Saul Bellow's first novel, *Dangling Man* (1944), was a Canadian, and an existentialist of sorts.

## Bemelmans, Ludwig
I'm going to open a hotel in Paris. A real hotel. The first thing I'm going to do is get some Canadian telephone operators, bilingual, you know, and trained to talk like human beings; not like these yapping old biddies.

Attributed to the Austrian-born American writer, illustrator and humourist.

## Benchley, Robert
Some people may care to discuss this case from the point of view of England, others from the point of view of the United States, but I shall discuss it from the point of view of the fish.

When the American humourist was a Harvard undergraduate about 1905, this is how he began a paper on the Newfoundland-United States cod fisheries dispute.

## Beneš, Eduard
Where is my home? I have no home. And when I am criss-crossing this friendly Dominion, this free Canadian land, I am thinking in words similar to the words of St. Matthew's Gospel: "The foxes have holes, and the birds of the air have nests. But the sons of the small nations, the son of Czechoslovakia hath not where to lay his head."

"Ten Million Prisoners," March 10, 1941, *Addresses Delivered before the Canadian Club of Toronto: Season of 1938-39* (1939). President of Czechoslovakia before and after the Second World War.

## Bengough, J.W.
These hands are clean!

These words are spoken by Sir John A. Macdonald in the most famous of all Canadian political cartoons. Drawn by J.W. Bengough and published in the Toronto comic weekly *Grip*, August 6, 1873, the cartoon is called "Whither Are We Drifting?" and depicts the prime minister absolving himself of all charges of corruption in connection with the Pacific Scandal. Yet his left hand holds the message "Send me another $10,000" and his right a charter for the "Prorogation and Suppression of the Investigation." Sir John never said, "These hands are clean!" (the words are worthy of Pontius Pilate), but in the House of Commons he did ask the question, "Whither are we drifting?"

\*

I admit I took the money and bribed the electors with it. Is there anything wrong about *that*?

Sir John never made so self-righteous a confession, but J.W. Bengough's cartoon in *Grip*, September 27, 1873, has these words issuing from his lips. Bengough does quote the prime minister's actual words: "We in Canada seem to have lost all idea of justice, honour and integrity" (reported in *The Mail*, September 26, 1873).

\*

There was nothing wrong in the Pacific Scandal. The Indignation of the People was all a Mistake.

This "campaign watchword" is attributed to Sir John A. Macdonald in J.W. Bengough's editorial cartoon in *Grip*, September 8, 1877. J.W. Bengough, *A Caricature History of Canadian Politics: Events from the Union of 1841, As Illustrated by Cartoons from "Grip," and Various Other Sources* (1866).

The gravest beast is the Ass; the gravest bird is the Owl;
The gravest fish is the Oyster; the gravest man is the Fool.

Motto of *Grip: An Independent Journal of Humour and Caricature*, founded and edited by the cartoonist, with Phillips Thompson as associate editor, in 1873.

It is not true, however, that Cartier is French for *cashier*, and time has fully vindicated this gentleman's character, as the banks of New Foundland [sic] are today as sound as ever.

"This Humorous Side of Canadian History," *Canadian Leaves: History, Art, Science, Literature, Commerce: A Series of New Papers Read Before the Cana-*

*dian Club of New York* (1887), edited by G.M. Fairchild, Jr.

## Bengough, Percy
Co-operation, Yes. Domination, No!

Celebrated statement of Canadian labour sovereignty made by the president of the Trades and Labour Congress when an attempt was made by the American Federation of Labour to disenfranchise Canadian members. *Trades and Labour Congress Journal*, March, 1949. Quoted by Charles Lipton in *The Trade Union Movement in Canada: 1827-1959* (1967).

## Ben-Gurion, David
After dinner we go to town. We stroll around the streets or go into the YMCA. Most of the boys in the camp are not Jews. But when you go into the YMCA suddenly it appears as if you are at a Jewish wedding or a Jewish farewell party. The young men dance and shout and sing Jewish songs as if they were in their own father's home. The non-Jewish men sit on the sidelines dumbfounded, and I think even with some anger—watching these noisy and exciting men sing songs in a wild and unknown language. It almost seems as if the non-Jews are in exile among us in their own YMCA.

Ben-Gurion was a lance corporal with the Jewish Legionaires in Windsor, Nova Scotia, when he wrote the above letter to his wife, June 3, 1918. These he translated from the Yiddish into the Hebrew and published as *Letters to Paula* (1968). Translated into English by Stuart E. Rosenberg in *The Jewish Community in Canada: Volume 2: In the Midst of Freedom* (1971).

## Benn, Wedgwood
I have crossed the boundaries of some sixty-three states, always in the daytime and one becomes accustomed to seeing a man with a bayonet on one side, the machine guns and batteries and all the habiliment of war. Here, one crosses the frontier between the two greatest powers in the world, and the first thing I heard this morning—I was hardly wide enough awake to know where I was—

was a voice saying, "So you come from home?"

> "The New British Commonwealth" (1933), *Empire Club of Canada: Addresses to the Members During the Year 1933-34* (1934).

### Bennett, Arnold

Morrice came and dined with me last night. He is an old habitué of the quarter. And though he had not been here for years, the old waiter at the Jouanne tripe shop, where we dined excellently, remembered him and how he liked his tripe. Morrice plays the flute charmingly. He performed Bach, etc. At 11 o'clock he said he must go. But he stayed till 1 o'clock.

I found him a most distinguished person, full of right and beautiful ideas about nearly everything. He said a number of brief things that were like knocking holes into the receptacle of his philosophy and giving glimpses of the treasure within. [April 29, 1905]

*

Morrice dined with me and stayed till 1 A.M. He has the joy of life in a high degree, and he likes living alone. "I enjoy everything," he said. "I got up this morning, and I saw an old woman walking along, and she was the finest old woman I ever did see. She was a magnificent old woman, and I was obliged to make a sketch of her. Then there was the *marchant de quatre saisons*. His cry is so beautiful. I began to enjoy myself almost immediately I got out of bed. It is a privilege to be alive." And so on. [May 16, 1905]

> *The Journal of Arnold Bennett: 1896-1928* (1932), edited by Newman Flower. The British novelist enjoyed the friendship of the Montreal-born painter; see also James Wilson Morrice.

### Bennett, James Gordon

Peaceably if possible, forcibly if necessary.

> The formula the United States should adopt to effect the annexation of Canada, according to the publisher and editor of *The New York Herald*, February, 1865.

### Bennett, R.B.

An Imperialist, to me, means a man who accepts gladly and bears proudly the responsibilities of his race and breed. [Applause] If that be so, what a trust is ours, what a trust is ours!

> Empire Day Address, Empire Club of Toronto, 1914. Quoted by Carl Berger in *The Sense of Power: Studies in the Ideas of Canadian Imperialism: 1867-1914* (1970).

Amalgamation? Never! Competition? Ever! That is the policy for which I stand. [On the continued existence of the CNR]

*

I will end unemployment or perish in the attempt. [What Bennett actually said was: "I propose that any government of which I am the head will at the first session of Parliament initiate whatever action is necessary to that end, or perish in the attempt."]

*

I will blast a way into the markets of the world. [What Bennett actually said was: "You say our tariffs are only for the manufacturers. I will make them fight for you as well. I will use them to blast a way into the markets that have been closed to you."]

> Widely quoted Winnipeg address, June 9, 1930. If the campaign speech sounds uncharacteristically vigorous, it is because these phrases were inserted into the address by Bennett's brother-in-law, W. H. Herridge, ambassador to the United States. They do not appear in *The Globe's* full report on the speech the following day. See also Grant Dexter.

Canada First, then the Empire. [Campaign slogan, 1930]

Mr. Mackenzie King: . . . I take the position that it is not part of the duty or obligation of a leader of a political party to have to do with the organization of political campaigns or to possess an inventory of those who make contributions to party funds. That is my view; does my right hon. friend hold a different view?

Mr. Bennett: I have always held that the receiver of stolen goods was a criminal.

Mr. Mackenzie King: Well, I notice that whenever my right hon. friend is asked a direct question, the reply to which is of some importance, he usually evades it by some very smart remark such as the one to which we have just listened.

Exchange between the prime minister and the leader of the Opposition on Beauharnois Power contributions, House of Commons, July 30, 1931.

The very word conservative means that we conserve all that is good; that we reject all that is bad, and we must use our intelligence, our intellect, our training for the purpose of determining what we shall reject and what we shall conserve and retain.

"Democracy on Trial," *Canadian Problems as Seen by Twenty Outstanding Men of Canada* (1933), edited by W.R. Herridge and Richard B. Coates.

And, to my mind, reform means Government intervention. It means Government control and regulation. It means the end of *laissez faire*. Reform heralds certain recovery. There can be no permanent recovery without reform! Reform or no reform! I raise that issue squarely. I nail the flag of progress to the masthead. I summon the power of the State to its support.

First radio address, January 2, 1935, *The Premier Speaks to the People* (1935). Quoted by J.R.H. Wilbur in *The Bennett New Deal: Fraud or Portent?* (1968).

He is the true Conservative who lops the mouldered branch away.

Characteristic remark based on the couplet from Tennyson's "Hands All Round" which runs: "That man's the true Conservative / Who lops the moulder'd branch away." *Canadian Problems as Seen by Twenty Outstanding Men of Canada* (1933), edited by W.R. Herridge and Richard B. Coates.

Do not let us have any misunderstanding about it. When Britain goes we go. Who stands if freedom fall; who dies if England lives? If it was the last word I ever uttered in this House or with the last breath in my body I would say that no Canadian is worthy of his great heritage and his great traditions and his magnificent hope of the future who would deny to the old partner who established as the right in this country to create those centres which she may not have at home to preserve her life and the ring of every man who enjoys freedom and liberty under the protecting aegis of that flag.

Mr. Lapointe (Quebec East): I knew the flag would be the last word.

Mr. Bennett: Certainly and proudly so.

House of Commons, July 1, 1938.

One of the greatest assets any man or woman can have on entering life's struggle is poverty.

\*

The Americans can fly on their side of the line, but we are quite capable of doing all the flying in or over Canada.

Two remarks attributed to the prime minister, who died in England as Viscount Bennett of Mickleham, Calgary and Hopewell. See also W.L. Mackenzie King, Leonard Brockington and Arthur "Slim" Evans.

## Bennett, W.A.C.

They see in me what Social Credit stands for—it gets things done.

Quoted by Gerald Clark in *Canada: The Uneasy Neighbour* (1965). One of Bennett's campaign slogans was "Social Credit Gets Things Done."

Where your treasury is, there your heart is also.

\*

I believe in certain basic things. My fundamental thing is that the only excuse for people being in public life, the only excuse for government, is to do those things, on a constructive basis, that people cannot do for themselves.

Premier of British Columbia, quoted by Paddy Sherman in *Bennett* (1966).

Temper? I have no temper ... I've never lost my temper. Righteous indignation is another thing!

> Quoted by Ronald B. Worsley in *The Wonderful World of W.A.C. Bennett* (1971).

Those people in Ottawa couldn't run a peanut stand. [Attributed in 1967]

The Socialist hordes are at the gates. . . . Socialist barbarians are coming in through the back door.

> Campaign rhetoric that led to the defeat of the Social Credit Party, August 30, 1972. See also David Barrett.

Why, I used to be a Tory when I was young and uninformed. I was Tory until I could stand no more. They're all lawyers—there's nothing wrong with lawyers, but there were just too many of them. They spend all their time changing commas, changing constitution and changing their leaders.

> Quoted by Pat Moan in *The Vancouver Sun*, March 17, 1973. See also Pat Jordan.

## Benoit, Madame Jehane
I feel a recipe is only a theme, which an intelligent cook can play each time with a variation.

> *Encyclopedia of Canadian Cuisine* (1970).

## Bent, Philip Eric
Come on the Tigers!

> "This very gallant officer was killed whilst leading a charge which he inspired with the call of 'Come on the Tigers!'" *London Gazette*, January 11, 1918. Lieutenant-Colonel Bent of the Leicestershire Regiment was twenty-six at the time of the action described, October 10, 1917. George C. Machum, *Canada's V.C.'s: The Story of Canadians Who Have Been Awarded the Victoria Cross* (1956).

## Beny, Roloff
Having lived on the East River in New York, lived by and overlooked the Aegean from Athens, the Grand Canal in Venice, the Arno in Florence, the Seine in Paris, the Thames in London, the Imperial Moat in Tokyo and finally settled on the most theatrical curve of the Tiber in Rome, it surprised me to find even sophistication in the city of my birth.

> "Medicine Hat, an oasis in a deep valley carved by the serpentine South Saskatchewan," writes Roloff Beny in "Reflections on a Journey Home" in *Maclean's Magazine*, March, 1973, "is where I didn't elect to be born."

## Berger, Carl
Imperialism was a sentiment and an outlook before it became a policy.

&#42;

Imperialism was one form of Canadian nationalism.

> *The Sense of Power: Studies in the Ideas of Canadian Imperialism, 1867-1914* (1970).

## Bergeron, Gérard
One is sometimes mistaken to be *always* right.

> *Ne bougez plus* (1968).

## Bergeron, Léandre
This handbook sets its sights on a repossession, the repossession of our history, the first step in the repossession of ourselves, in order to move on to the next step, the possession of our own future.

> *The History of Quebec: A Patriote's Handbook* (1971), translated by Baila Markus.

## Berlioz, Hector
*Jam proximus ardet Ucalegon!* who knows what resort may be left to me before a few months are over? There is no longer any certain subsistence for myself and my family. Every minute is precious, and before long I may have to imitate the stoical resignation of the Indians of Niagara, who, finding their best efforts against the current useless, measure with steady glance the short distance which separates them from the edge, and disappear over the cataract into the abyss beneath, with a song in their mouths.

> *Memoirs of Hector Berlioz, from 1803 to 1805* (1932).

**Bernard, Henry**
The French language used by everyone else is not the one we French Canadians use.

> Reply to Marcel Dugas's remark made in 1918, "The French language exists; the Canadian does not." Quoted by Jean Basile in "Literature in French" in *The Canadians 1867-1967* (1967), edited by J.M.S. Careless and R. Craig Brown. See also Marcel Dugas.

**Bernardi, Mario**
If this orchestra were in Timbuktu, I wouldn't mind. I would still want to conduct it.

> Conductor of the National Arts Centre Orchestra since its inception, October 7, 1969.

**Berne, Eric**
Games people play.

> ✳

We're born princes and the civilizing process turns us into frogs.

> *Games People Play: The Psychology of Human Relationships* (1964).

What do you say after you say hello?
This childlike question, so apparently artless and free of the profundity expected of scientific inquiry, really contains within itself all the basic questions of human living and all the fundamental problems of the social sciences.

> *What Do You Say After You Say Hello? The Psychology of Human Destiny* (1972). Dr. Eric Berne was born Eric Leonard Bernstein in Montreal in 1910. He graduated from the McGill School of Medicine and practised psychiatry in California where he died in 1970. He originated Transactional Analysis.

**Berneche, Stanley R.**   See Peter Evans.

**Bernhardt, Sarah**
I would have been willing to pay any price for it . . . the little girl with the red top-knot reminded me so much of myself when I was little.

> Madame Sarah bid unsuccessfully for Paul Peel's famous painting "After the Bath." Quoted by Adrian Macdonald in

*Canadian Portraits* (1925). See also Arnold Haultain, Paul Peel, and Arthur Stringer.

**Bernier, Captain J.E.**
I took possession of Baffin Island for Canada in the presence of several Eskimo, and after firing nineteen shots I instructed an Eskimo to fire the twentieth, telling him that he was now a Canadian.

> "Our Northern Heritage," *Empire Club of Canada: Addresses Delivered to the Members During the Year 1926* (1927). Captain Bernier claimed the Arctic archipelago for Canada on July 1, 1909.

**Berrey, Lester V.**
*Canada.* Canuckland, Kanuckland, Jack Canuck's country, Land of the Bing Boys, Land of the Peasouper. *Spec.* Land of the Blue Nose, *esp. the Nova Scotia and New Brunswick district;* Newfie, *New Foundland* [sic]; Jean Baptiste, *Canada personified.*

> *The American Thesaurus of Slang: A Complete Reference Book of Colloquial Speech* (1942), by Lester V. Berrey and Melvin Van den Bark.

**Berrigan, Daniel**
Canada helps make our napalm and then takes in our deserters. Canada has both ends of a dirty stick and ends up with both hands dirty.

> American anti-war Jesuit in Montreal, *The Toronto Star*, December 3, 1973.

**Berryer, Nicolas-René**
How could it happen that the small-pox among the Indians cost the King a million francs? What does this expense mean? Who is answerable for it? Is it the officers who command the posts, or is it the storekeepers? You give me no particulars. What has become of the immense quantity of provisions sent to Canada last year? I am forced to conclude that the King's stores are set down as consumed from the moment they arrive, and then sold to His Majesty at exorbitant prices. Thus the King buys stores in France, and then buys them again in Canada. I no longer wonder at

the immense fortunes made in the colony. It seems, then, that there are no bounds to the expenses of Canada. They double almost every year, when you seem to give yourself no concern except to get them paid.

> Letter from the colonial minister in Paris to the intendant, François Bigot, January 19, 1759. Quoted by Francis Parkman in *Montcalm and Wolfe* (1884). See also Louis-Antoine de Bougainville.

## Berton, Pierre

The Klondike experience had taught all these men that they were capable of a kind of achievement they had never dreamed possible. It was this, perhaps more than anything else, that set them apart from their fellows. In the years that followed, they tended to run their lives as if they were scaling a perpetual Chilkoot, secure in the knowledge that any obstacle, real or imagined, can be conquered by a determined man. For each had come to realize that the great stampede, with all its searchings and its yearnings, with all its bitter surprises, its thorny impediments, and its unexpected fulfillments, was, in a way, a rough approximation to life itself.

> *Klondike: The Life and Death of the Last Great Gold Rush* (1958).

To me, as to most northerners, the country is still an unknown quantity, as elusive as the wolf, howling just beyond the rim of the hills. Perhaps that is why it holds its fascination.

> *The Mysterious North* (1959).

If I have any specific advice ["on how to become a writer, preferably the best-seller type"] it is this: when you begin, begin on a very small scale (six-paragraph essays for the local paper) or on a very large one (the kind of sprawling autobiographical novel that the critics will call "undisciplined but promising"). Do not break your heart on those deceptive pieces that seem so simple but are so difficult—the short story, the long essay, the magazine article. These can wait until later. Ignore the advice of friends and amateurs; work; read and

learn from others; and, above all, try to have a good time.

> "On Writing," *Fast Fast Fast Relief* (1962).

It is the thesis of this book that a violent revolution—violent in the psychological and social rather than the physical sense —is needed to save Christianity.

> *The Comfortable Pew: A Critical Look At Christianity and the Religious Establishment in the New Age* (1965).

One of the important lessons a television interviewer must learn—and it's not an easy one—is to *wait*. The radio medium is terrified of dead air. But there is no dead air on television. The picture is always there to tell the story.

> *The Cool Crazy Committed World of the Sixties: Twenty-One Television Encounters* (1966).

The march of social progress is like a long and straggling parade, with the seers and prophets at its head and a smug minority bringing up the rear.

> *The Smug Minority* (1968).

It is not generally understood that most writing takes place away from the typewriter. When you finally approach the machine, it is really the beginning of the end. Nine-tenths of your work has already been done; it remains to put on paper what you have already created. It is this creative process that takes most of the time.

> *

I think I now understand why men must steal to support a drug habit. There are single sentences in *The National Dream* that cost me as much as $100. The book would be perfectly acceptable without them.

> "Stand Clear! Here Comes a Writer, Writing," *Maclean's Magazine*, October 7, 1971.

The National Dream.

> Pierre Berton has encouraged Canadians to regard the construction of the CPR in 1885 as the realization of "the national dream." *The National Dream* is the general title of his two-volume

history: *The Great Railway: 1871-1881* (1970) and *The Last Spike: 1881-1885* (1971).

A Canadian is somebody who knows how to make love in a canoe.

> Attributed by Dick Brown in *The Canadian Magazine*, December 22, 1973.

**Bessborough, Earl of**
Before I left London, a friend of mine, with a great knowledge of this Dominion, gave me his views on various great cities, and when he came to Toronto he prefaced his remarks, I remember, by saying, "There are two things they understand in Toronto—the British Empire and a good horse."

> Lord Bessborough was governor general from 1931 to 1935. Address, November 24, 1931, *Addresses Delivered before the Canadian Club of Toronto: Season of 1931-32* (1932).

The spirit of a nation, if it is to find full expression, must include a National Drama.

> Unofficial motto of the Dominion Drama Festival from an address, April 24, 1933, delivered by the founding patron, the governor general. Quoted by Betty Lee in *Love and Whisky: The Story of the Dominion Drama Festival* (1973).

**Bessette, Alfred**   See Brother André.

**Best, C.H.**
The physiologist believes as someone has said that the advance of our science is limited not by nature's unwillingness to reveal but by man's inability to comprehend.

> "Recent Advances in Our Knowledge of the Bodily Functions," February 10, 1930, *Addresses Delivered before the Canadian Club of Toronto: Season of 1929-30* (1930). Dr. Best was the co-discoverer of insulin.

There have been 70,000 to 80,000 publications on the subject of insulin since 1921, and many times that on the various other factors involved in diabetes. These fields are still being cultivated vigorously and productively, and to miss a month of reading is to be out of date.

> "Diabetes Since 1920" (1960), *Selected Papers of Charles H. Best* (1963).

**Best, George**
How dangerous it is to attempt new discoveries; either for the length of the voyage, or the ignorance of the language, the want of interpreters, new and unaccustomed elements and airs, strange and unsavoury meats, danger of thieves and robbers, fierceness of wilde beasts and fishes, hugeness of woods, dangerousness of seas, dread of tempests, fear of hidden rocks, steepness of mountains, darkness of sudden falling fogs, continual painstaking without rest, and infinite others.

How pleasant and profitable it is to attempt new discoveries; either for the sundry sights and shapes of strange beasts and fishes, the wonderful works of nature, the different manners and fashions of diverse nations, the sundry sorts of government, the sight of strange trees, fruit, fowls, and beasts, the infinite treasure of pearl, gold, and silver, the news of new found lands, and many others.

> *The Three Voyages of Martin Frobisher, in Search of a Passage to Cathaia and India by the North-West, A.D. 1576-8* (1758). Best sailed with Frobisher.

**Bethune, Norman**
Now I can make your life a misery, but I'll never bore you—it's a promise. [To his wife Frances after their wedding, August 13, 1923; Stewart]

Gentlemen, I welcome the risk! [To doctors at Saranac Lake, New York, where Bethune insisted he undergo an experimental lung operation, 1927; Allan]

This Book Belongs to Norman Bethune and His Friends [Bookplate, 1930s; Allan]

"There is a rich man's tuberculosis and a poor man's tuberculosis." The rich man recovers and the poor man dies. . . . ["A Plea for Early Compression," *Canadian Medical Association Journal*, July, 1932; Stewart]

Did you ever get so bored with a woman that you had to make love to her? [To a startled medical colleague, Montreal, 1933; Allan]

The problem of medical economics is a part of the problem of world economics and is inseparable and indivisible from it. Medicine, as we are practising it, is a luxury trade. *We are selling bread at the price of jewels.* [Montreal Medico-Chirurgical Society, April 17, 1936; Allan]

Let us redefine medical ethics—not as a code of professional etiquette between doctors, but as a code of fundamental morality and justice between Medicine and the people. [Montreal Medico-Chirurgical Society, April 17, 1936; Stewart]

Madrid will be the tomb of fascism. ["Letter from Dr. Bethune," Madrid, January 11, 1937; reprinted in *The Marxist Quarterly,* Summer, 1966]

Madrid is the centre of gravity of the world. [*The Daily Clarion,* February 17, 1937; Stewart]

The function of the artist is to disturb. His duty is to arouse the sleeper, to shake the complacent pillars of the world. He reminds the world of its dark ancestry, shows the world its present, and points the way to its new birth. He is at once the product and preceptor of his time. After his passage we are troubled and made unsure of our too-easily accepted realities. He makes uneasy the static, the set and the still. In a world terrified of change, he preaches revolution—the principle of life. He is an agitator, a disturber of the peace—quick, impatient, positive, restless and disquieting. He is the creative spirit of life working in the soul of men. [Letter to Marian Scott, Madrid, May 5, 1937; Stewart]

Why a *Moscow* hireling? Why not a *British* hireling? The theory of socialism was proclaimed in London sixty years before the Russian Revolution. If Russia disappeared from the face of the earth tomorrow, do you think that would eliminate communism? I am sure that if Christ walked the earth again, preaching the brotherhood of man, He too would

have thrown at Him the label of "Moscow hireling." [To heckler who called him a "Moscow hireling" at a public meeting in western Canada, before Bethune left for China, 1937; Allan]

Spain and China are part of the same battle. I am going to China because I feel that is where the need is greatest; that is where I can be most useful. [Letter to his wife from Hong Kong, en route to China, January, 1938; Allan]

What do these enemies of the human race look like? Do they wear on their foreheads a sign so that they may be told, shunned and condemned as criminals? No. On the contrary, they are the respectable ones. They are honoured. They call themselves, and are called, gentlemen. What a travesty on the name, Gentlemen! . . . These men make the wounds.

*

How beautiful the body is; how perfect its parts; with what precision it moves; how obedient, proud and strong. How terrible when torn. The little flame of life sinks lower and lower, and, with a flicker, goes out. It goes out like a candle goes out. Quietly and gently. It makes its protest at extinction, then submits. It has its say, then is silent. ["Wounds," *The Canadian Tribune,* June 15, 1940; reprinted in *New Frontiers,* Fall, 1952]

I find I can get along and operate as well in a dirty Buddhist temple with a 20 foot high statue of the impassive-faced gilded God staring over my shoulder, as in a modern operating room with running water, nice green glazed walls, electric lamps and a thousand other accessories.

*

I dream of coffee, of rare roast beef, of apple pie and ice cream. Mirages of heavenly food. Books—are books still being written? Is music still being played? Do you dance, drink beer, look at pictures? What do clean white sheets in a soft bed feel like? Do women still loved to be loved? [Letter to John Barnwell, August 15, 1939; Stewart]

Be a leader yourself, though you only lead yourself, *for every leader starts by first leading himself.*

*

Give my everlasting love to . . . all my Canadian and American friends. Tell them I have been very happy. My only regret is that I shall now be unable to do more. [Last letter, written in northern China, November 13, 1939; Allan]

The hero of Mao's China was born in Gravenhurst, Ontario, in 1890, and died in northern China in 1939. His Chinese name, Pai Chu En, could be translated "The white man who seeks grace." The passages marked "Allan" appear in *The Scalpel, the Sword: The Story of Dr. Norman Bethune* (1952), by Ted Allan and Sydney Gordon. Those marked "Stewart" appear in *Bethune* (1973), by Roderick Stewart. Some appear in both. See also: Ted Allan, John Houston, B.K. Sandwell, Mao Tse-tung.

## Biarni
"So, let us give Biarni Heriulfson his due as the earliest, Number One, indubitable European discoverer of America, even if he never landed."

Samuel Eliot Morison in *The European Discovery of America: The Northern Voyages A.D. 500-1600* (1971) has added: "Poor Biarni! . . . He left no posterity, nobody built a saga around him." The Norse trader overshot Greenland about 986 and spied the shores of Labrador and Newfoundland. His name is sometimes given as Herjólfsson Bjarni.

## Bidwell, Marshall Spring
I shall be happy to consult with yourself and Mr. Rolf on the measures to be adopted to relieve this province from the evils which a family compact have bought upon it.

The earliest use of the term "family compact," which describes the ultraconservative Loyalist group that governed Upper Canada in the early nineteenth century, appears in the lawyer's letter to William Warren Baldwin, 1828. Walter S. Avis's *A Dictionary of Canadianisms on Historical Principles* (1967).

BIDWELL, and the glorious minority!
1837, and a good beginning!

Old election banner (with the year up-

dated) found by James FitzGibbon at Montgomery's Tavern, December 7, 1837. On the strength of this Bidwell was forced to leave Upper Canada. Sir Francis Bond Head in *A Narrative* (1839).

FitzGibbon explained: "My Lord, if that flag had, as was expected by its followers, triumphantly entered Toronto, I have no hesitation in saying it would have waved over the corpse of every loyal subject in the city; indeed, we have received evidence that a general massacre of the Queen's loyal subjects would have been attempted." Quoted by his daughter Mary Agnes FitzGibbon in *A Veteran of 1812: The Life of James FitzGibbon* (1894).

## Bierce, Ambrose
Man, *n.* An animal so lost in rapturous contemplation of what he thinks he is as to overlook what he indubitably ought to be. His chief occupation is extermination of other animals and his own species, which, however, multiplies with such insistent rapidity as to infest the whole habitable earth and Canada.

*Devil's Dictionary* (1911).

## Big Bear
We are doomed and will be killed one after another by the whites, but before we die or disappear altogether we must enjoy ourselves as much as we possibly can, and therefore we must plunder the stores and kill as many white people as possible.

*Daily Intelligencer*, June 4, 1885. Reprinted in *The Riel Rebellion 1885* (1972), compiled by Nick and Helma Mika.

## Bigelow, Dr. William G.
One night I woke up and thought: "Cool the heart."

The University of Toronto surgeon made the breakthrough into open-heart surgery using hypothermia. Quoted by Alden Whitman in *The New York Times*, February 24, 1974.

## Bigot, François
"A vessel shall also be appointed for the

passage of M. Bigot, the Intendant, and of his suite, in which vessel the proper accommodation shall be made for him and the persons whom he shall take with him. He shall likewise take on board with him his papers, which shall not be examined, his equipages, plate, and baggage, and those of his suite. This vessel shall be victualled, as before mentioned."

> Article 15, "Articles of the Capitulation of Montreal, 1760," signed September 8, 1760, granting the corrupt Intendant special privileges on his departure from New France after the Conquest. *Documents Illustrative of the Canadian Constitution* (1891), edited by William Houston. See also Nicolas-René Berryer.

**Bill, Canada** See Canada Bill.

**Billings, Josh**
Newfoundland dogs are good to save children from drowning, but you must have a pond of water handy and a child, or else there will be no profit in boarding a Newfoundland.

> Lecture by the popular American humourist, San Francisco, 1885, quoted by Robert M. Hamilton in *Canadian Quotations and Phrases: Literary and Historical* (1952).

**Bing, Rudolf**
When people ask me what I think of opera in Maple Leaf Gardens I reply we only hope ice hockey will look as well in the Metropolitan Opera House.

> "This Business of Opera" (1957), *Empire Club of Canada: Addresses 1956-57* (1957).

**Bini**
You shall not kill, you shall not lie, you shall not steal, you shall not have more than one wife, and you shall observe Sunday.

> This is "The Law of the Five Fingers," a mixture of pagan and Christian morality propounded by Bini, seer of the Kitwancool Indians of Tsimshian country on the West Coast. Quoted by Fraser Symington in *The Canadian Indian:*

*The Illustrated History of the Great Tribes of Canada* (1969).

**Binks, Sarah** See Paul Hiebert.

**Birdwell, Russell**
Birdwell assembled his staff to consider plans for the premiere of *The Prisoner of Zenda*. An assistant provided the information that a town in Ontario had been named Zenda after the Anthony Hope novel. Total population: thirteen.

Publicity man Jackson Parks spoke up: "Why don't we fly the whole town to New York for the premiere at the Radio City Music Hall?"

"Brilliant!" exclaimed Birdwell, and he dispatched an agent to the Ontario hamlet to make arrangements. But the inhabitants were busy with the haying and cheese-making season and had no interest in the crazy proposal by a city slicker. Birdwell flew to Ontario and found to his consternation that the Zenda inhabitants were indifferent to his stunt. All except one. A farmer boy expressed interest in Birdwell's tales of the dazzling females to be found in New York. The boy converted his family, and they convinced the rest of the town to make the trip.

Twelve of the thirteen Zenda residents were flown to New York, where press coverage of their visit was immense. The Zendan left at home was an ancient lady deemed unsafe for travel. Canadian news services visited her and splashed the country with stories and photographs of "The Prisoner of Zenda."

> Bob Thomas's *Selznick* (1970). The movie was produced in 1937 by Selznick and starred Ronald Colman, Madeleine Carroll, Douglas Fairbanks Jr., Raymond Massey, Mary Astor, and David Niven. Birdwell was Selznick's publicity director. For a more modest publicity stunt, see John Kenneth Galbraith.

**Birge, Cyrus A.**
We are not manufacturers merely of articles of wood and stone, and iron and cotton and wool, and so on; we manufacture enthusiasms; we manufacture Canadian sentiment; we manufacture a feeling of pride in our country, and we

manufacture a spirit of independence, a spirit of national pride.

> *Industrial Canada*, October, 1903. Birge was president of the Canadian Manufacturer's Association when its unofficial motto was "Made in Canada."

### Birkenhead, Lord
Sport of historic misfortune.

> Epithet for Newfoundland, widely used at the turn of the century, quoted by Joey Smallwood in *I Chose Canada: The Memoirs of the Honourable Joseph R. "Joey" Smallwood* (1973).

### Birnbaum, Dr. Jack
There is sometimes even an ecstasy in anger.

> *Cry Anger: A Cure for Depression* (1973).

### Birney, Earle
I said that he fell straight to the ice where they found him.
And none but the sun and incurious clouds have lingered
Around the marks of that day on the ledge of the Finger,
That day, the last of my youth, on the last of our mountains.

> Concluding stanza of "David" (1940).

*

Parents unmarried and living apart
relatives keen to bag the estate

schizophrenia not excluded—
will he learn to grow up before it's too late?

> "Canada: Case History" (1945).

*

We French, we English, never lost our civil war,
endure it still, a bloodless civil bore;
no wounded lying about, no Whitman wanted.
It's only by our lack of ghosts we're haunted.

> "Can. Lit." (1962).

*

To be truthful, I did not write them even for them, but out of compulsion to talk to another man within me, an intermittent madman who finds unpredictable emblems of the Whole in the trivia

of my experience, and haunts me with them until I have found a spell of words and rhythms to exorcise them and, for the moment, appease them. [Preface]

> *Selected Poems 1940-1966* (1966).

Education is for the preservation and development of the tribe. And the tribe is now the human race. No one can contribute more to that goal than the creative artist whose function it is to bring inter-human understanding and restore and increase the world's belief in living and in the joy of being alive.

> *The Creative Writer* (1966).

### Bishop, Billy
The air age faces mankind with a sharp choice—the choice between Winged Peace or Winged Death.

> *Winged Peace* (1944).

God speed you. God speed you in the skies, or upon the seas, or across unknown acres where, on the edge of destiny, you may test your strength.

> Speech, Tri-Services Rally, Toronto, November, 1941. Quoted by William Arthur Bishop in *The Courage of the Early Morning: The Story of Billy Bishop* (1965). William Avery ("Billy") Bishop was officially credited with destroying seventy-two enemy aircraft during World War One. The flying ace was air marshal and RCAF director during World War Two. See John Bassett I.

### Bishop, Morris
In reading history one must always be impressed by the fact that our knowledge is only a collection of scraps and fragments that we put together into a pleasing design, and often the discovery of one new fragment would cause us to alter utterly the whole design.

> *Champlain: The Life of Fortitude* (1948).

### Bissell, Claude T.
A good deal of what you say and do here will be ephemeral, and will be caught up and dissolved in the stream of experience. But much else that you do will remain with you and will determine your future. One thinks of the words of

Goethe: "Be careful what you wish for in your youth, for you will get it in your middle age." ["Angular, not Spherical," Address to Staff and Students, September, 1958]

\*

In my remarks last year I took for my theme a questioning of the cultural concept of the ideal of the "well-rounded" student, and I suggested that roundness is a function of middle age; the student years are a time for intensity and concentration, and I would prefer the ideal of lopsidedness and angularity, provided it was based upon a genuine intellectual passion. ["The Right to be Angular," Address to Staff and Students, September, 1959]

\*

Canadians move slowly, but when they are aroused they move with remarkable speed. Someone suggested recently that our way of life is "puritanism touched by orgy." Our history is a record of stolidity broken by bold imaginativeness. ["The University and Canadian-American Relations," January, 1966]

> The Strength of the University: A Selection from the Addresses of Claude T. Bissell (1968), by the past president of the University of Toronto.

**Bjarni, Herjólfsson**  See Biarni.

**Black, Davidson**
Peking Man.

Heading a team of archaeologists digging near Peking, Davidson Black of the Royal Ontario Museum uncovered—and named—Peking Man, *Sinanthropus pekinensis*. The team that discovered this important ancestor of modern man included the famous Jesuit philosopher Pierre Teilhard de Chardin.

The skull and bones were dug up in 1929 at Dragon's Bone Hill, Choukoutien, thirty miles southwest of Peking. The remains, buried almost a million years ago, disappeared in 1941 with the Japanese invasion of China. There are rumours the remains of Peking Man are in the United States.

Yes, *Sinanthropus* is growing like a bally weed. I never realized how great an advertising medium primitive man (or woman) was till this skull turned up. Now everybody is crowding round to gaze that can get the least excuse to do so and it gets embarrassing at times. Being front page stuff is a new sensation and encourages a guarded manner of speech!

> Letter of December 1, 1929, quoted by Dora Hood in *Davidson Black: A Biography* (1964). The New York humourist Will Cuppy wrote in *How to Tell Your Friends from the Apes* (1931): "He was discovered near Peking or Peiping and was named *Sinanthropus pekinensis* to keep certain persons from calling him Peiping Tom." When Black died in 1934, his co-worker, the theologian Père Pierre Teilhard de Chardin, wrote, "He was more than a brother to me."

**Black Hawk**
This was the signal for us to commence the battle, but it did not last long; the Americans answered the shout, returning our fire, and at the first discharge of their guns, I saw Tecumseh stagger forwards over a fallen tree, near which he was standing, letting his rifle drop at his feet. As soon as the Indians discovered that he was killed, a sudden fear came over them, and thinking the Great Spirit was angry, they fought no longer, and were quickly put to flight.

> The famous American warrior Ma'kata-wimesheka'ka (Black Hawk) describing the death of Tecumseh in Benjamin Drake's *Life of Tecumseh* (1841). The account is reproduced by Carl F. Klinck in *Tecumseh: Fact and Fiction in Early Records* (1961).

**Blackburn, Ben**
I was born in Maysville, Ky. I got here last Tuesday evening, and spent the Fourth of July in Canada. I felt as big and free as any man could feel, and I worked part of the day for my own benefit: I guess my master's time is out. Seventeen came away in the same gang that I did.

> Blackburn settled in Windsor. Quoted by Benjamin Drew in *The Refugee:* or

*the Narratives of Fugitive Slaves in Canada* (1856).

**Blackwood, Algernon**
My Canadian experience, anyhow, can be summed up in advice, which is, of course, a bromide now: let any emigrant young Englishman earn his own living for at least five years in any colony before a penny of capital is given to him to invest.

\*

The Muskoka interlude remained for me a sparkling, radiant memory, alight with the sunshine of unclouded skies, with the gleam of stars in a blue-black heaven, swept by forest winds, and set against a background of primeval forests that stretched without a break for six hundred miles of lonely and untrodden beauty.

*Episodes before Thirty* (1950).

On his face was no expression of any kind whatever—fear, welcome, or recognition. He did not seem to know who it was that embraced him, or who it was that fed, warmed and spoke to him the words of comfort and relief. Forlorn and broken beyond all reach of human aid, the little man did meekly as he was bidden. The "something" that had constituted his "individuality" had vanished for ever.

"The Wendigo," *Selected Tales* (1943). The British horror-story writer spent a few years in Toronto at the turn of the century, and used Canadian imagery in a few of his stories.

**Blaine, James G.**
Canada is like an apple on a tree just beyond reach. We may strive to grasp it, but the bough recedes from our hold just in proportion to our effort to catch it. Let it alone, and in due time it will fall into our hands.

U.S. secretary of State, 1889, quoted by W.E. Harris in *Canada's Last Chance* (1970).

**Blake, Edward**
The privileges of Parliament are the privileges of the People, and the rights of Parliament are the rights of the People.

*Three Speeches by the Hon. Edward Blake, Q.C., M.P., on the Pacific Scandal* (1873), London, August 28, 1873.

Until these surveys are thoroughly completed, and until we have found the least impracticable route through that inhospitable country, that "sea of mountains," it is folly to talk of commencing the work of construction.

\*

But how long is this talk in the newspaper and elsewhere, this talk which I find in very high places, of the desirability, aye, of the necessity of fostering a national spirit among the people of Canada, to be mere talk? It is impossible to foster a national spirit unless you have national interests to attend to, or among people who do not choose to understand the responsibilities and to devote themselves to the duties to which national attributes belong.

\*

. . . the time will come when that national spirit which has been spoken of will be truly felt among us, when we shall realize that we are four million Britons who are not free, when we shall be ready to take up that freedom, and to ask what the late prime minister of England assured us we should not be denied—our share of national rights.

\*

The future of Canada, I believe, depends very largely upon the cultivation of a national spirit. . . . We must find some common ground on which to unite, some common aspiration to be shared, and I think it can be found alone in the cultivation of that national spirit to which I have referred. [Cheers]

Excerpts from the celebrated "Aurora Speech" delivered by Edward Blake at Aurora, Ontario, October 3, 1873. The address was published as *"A National Sentiment!" Speech of Hon. Edward Blake, M.P., at Aurora* (1874). W. Stewart Wallace reprinted the scarce work as "Aurora Speech, October 3, 1873" in *Canadian Historical Review*, September, 1921.

I maintain that the principle of the demands of the Métis of the North-West Territories, in consideration of extinction of the Indian title, was recognized at that time; justice must be the same on the banks of the Saskatchewan or of the Qu'Appelle, as on those of the Red River or the Assiniboine.

\*

Had there been no neglect there would have been no rebellion. If no rebellion, then no arrest. If no arrest, then no trial. If no trial, then no condemnation. If no condemnation, then no execution. They therefore who are responsible for the first are responsible for every link in that fatal chain.

> Address of the brilliant leader of the Liberal party on the execution of Louis Riel, 1885.

### Blake, S.H.

It is all very well to talk about reforming the prisoner. My friends, we have to commence away back of reforming the prisoner; we have to reform public opinion, on this question. There is where we have to begin. Next, we have to reform our sheriffs, to reform our jailers, and to reform our jails; and then we shall have a better hope of reforming the prisoners.

> Address, National Prison Congress, Toronto, 1887, by the Honourable S.H. Blake, Q.C. Quoted by J. Alex. Edmison in his address to the Annual Meeting of the John Howard Society of Ontario, Toronto, April 29, 1964.

### Blake, W.H.

The weather for catching fish is that weather, and no other, in which fish are caught.

\*

A man's chief duty towards his neighbour is to be happy. For how can he otherwise hope to communicate happiness to his neighbour? And what does it lie within his power to offer him that is so much needed?

> Brown Waters and Other Sketches: Together with a Fragment and Yarns (1915, 1925).

The spirit of man is the candle of God.

The essayist and translator of *Maria Chapdelaine* died in Victoria in 1924 but was buried in the yard of the Murray Bay Protestant Church, Pointe-au-Pic, Quebec. This is the inscription on his granite headstone. Quoted by Blodwen Davies in *Saguenay: The River of Deep Waters* (1930).

### Blake, William

I see a Serpent in Canada who courts me
to his love,
In Mexico an Eagle, and a Lion in Peru;
I see a Whale in the South-sea, drinking
my soul away.
O what limb rending pains I feel! thy
fire & my frost
Mingle in howling pains, in furrows by
thy lightnings rent.
This eternal death, and this the torment
long fortold.

> *America: A Prophecy* (1793). Geoffrey Keynes's *The Complete Writings of William Blake* (1957). S. Foster Damon explains in *A Blake Dictionary: The Ideas and Symbols of William Blake* (1965): "Canada, the northernmost country in North America, is the twenty-fifth of the thirty-two nations which shall guard liberty and rule the world."

### Bland, Salem G.

God educates peoples as He educates individuals, by putting them in tight places.

\*

Denominationalism in Canada is still a stately tree, but the heart is dust.

\*

The national consciousness of the United States is as exacting as religion. Its first commandment is, Thou shalt have no other country and no other ruler than the United States.

> *The New Christianity, or The Religion of the New Age* (1920).

It may be that the liberty of the nations still free will stand or fall with the liberty of Spain, and if the liberty of Spain falls it will fall not through the courage of its foes only but through the timidity of its friends.

> *New Frontier*, December, 1936. Bland

was a Toronto minister who preached the "social gospel."

### Blavatsky, H.P.
For all those numberless gigantic ruins which are discovered one after the other in our day, all those immense avenues of colossal ruins that cross North America along and beyond the Rocky Mountains, are the work of the Cyclopes, the true and actual Giants of old.

*The Secret Doctrine: The Synthesis of Science, Religion and Philosophy: Volume Two: Anthropogenesis* (1888).

### Blewett, Jean
The trouble with wives is they expect too much. Because their husbands kiss them on Monday they look for the same on Tuesday, Wednesday and every day, whereas the husbands, in their ignorance of women's ways, consider the pleasant duty performed for the whole week.

Quoted in *Canadian Days: Selections for Every Day in the Year from the Works of Canadian Authors, Compiled by the Toronto Women's Press Club* (1911).

### Bliss, Michael
In 1909, the Canadian Manufacturers' Association launched another crusade for the support of Canadian home industries. One of the first companies proudly advertising its product as "Made in Canada" was Coca-Cola. Things went better. . . .

"Canadianizing American Business: The Roots of the Branch Plant," *Close the 49th Parallel, Etc.: The Americanization of Canada* (1970), edited by Ian Lumsden.

### Blondin, "The Prince of Manila"
Do not attempt to do any balancing yourself. If you do we shall both go down to our death.

On August 19, 1859, before one hundred thousand spectators, the great Blondin walked across Niagara Gorge from the American to the Canadian side on a rope three inches thick. On his shoulders he carried his reluctant manager, Henry M. Colcord. Born Jean-François Gravelet in France, the funambulist called himself Blondin on account of his blond hair; P.T. Barnum billed him as "The Prince of Manila" because he used manila rope. He captured the public's imagination from the first, and Barnum called him "the world's greatest rope-walker." On September 8, 1860, he performed the Niagara crossing for the nineteen-year-old Prince of Wales. "Thank God, it is over!" exclaimed the future Edward VII. "Please never attempt it again." Blondin offered to take the young prince across on his shoulders or in a wheelbarrow, but the offer was refused. See also Henry M. Colcord.

### Boas, Franz
I had a council with the Indians, who are really suffering because of the stupid persecution of their customs by the government. I can do nothing about it, but promised to do my best in Ottawa. I am not at all certain what I can do, because the missionaries are behind it all. It goes so far that children in school are not allowed to draw in the traditional style of their people but according to prescribed models.

Fort Rupert, November 18, 1930. *The Ethnology of Franz Boas: Letters and Diaries of Franz Boas written on the Northwest Coast from 1886 to 1931* (1969), edited by Ronald P. Rohner, translated from the German by Hedy Parker. The German-born anthropologist was the first man to do field work in Canada. He once wrote, "There is no fundamental difference in the ways of thinking of primitive and civilized man."

### Bochner, Lloyd
Every actor has to move from time to time to satisfy his need to develop.

The Toronto-born CBC actor explaining his departure for Hollywood. Quoted by Wendy Michener in *The Toronto Star*, October 19, 1961.

### Bochner, Martin   See Woody Guthrie.

### Bodsworth, Fred
If we go on as we are, we will destroy in the next century everything that poets have been singing about for the past two thousand years.

＊

Canada, at least about ninety percent of it, *is* a vast backwoods inhabited mainly by moose, bear, Indians and Eskimos.

"Wilderness Canada: Our Threatened Heritage," *Wilderness Canada* (1970), edited by Borden Spears.

It is no coincidence that our national emblem is not a rising sun, a star, a hammer, a sickle, or a dragon, but a beaver and a maple leaf. Nor is it coincidence that there are more paintings of wilderness lakes, spruce bogs, and pine trees on more Canadian living room walls than in any other nation on earth. We may scoff, we may deny, but the wilderness mystique is still a strong element of the Canadian ethos.

Quoted by Richard C. Bocking in *Canada's Water: For Sale?* (1972).

**Bogart, Humphrey**
There's a Canadian for you. You let them take off their clothes and they're happy.

Lines addressed to Mary Astor, playing a girl from Saskatoon, in the Hollywood film *Across the Pacific* (1942).

**Boggs, Jean Sutherland**
It has never cost the taxpayer as much as five cents per capita a year.

A reference to the National Gallery in Ottawa by its director, in her preface to *The National Gallery of Canada* (1971).

**Boisvert, Abraham-Edmond**
See Edmond de Nevers.

**Boivin, Gilles**
The French-speaking film-makers couldn't be here, but they asked me to thank the English-speaking taxpayers.

Accepting an Etrog for the musical scoring of *Vertige* at the Canadian Film Awards banquet in Toronto. Quoted by Kaspars Dzeguze in *The Globe and Mail*, October 6, 1969.

**Boliska, Al**
Contrary to popular opinion, if you went to Sydney, Nova Scotia, and dug a hole straight through the earth, you would not end up in China. Due to the rotation of the earth on its axis, you would come out in Pefferlaw, Ontario.

*The World's Worst Jokes* (1966).

Airline travel is hours of boredom interrupted by moments of stark terror.

＊

Do you realize if it weren't for Edison, we'd be watching TV by candlelight?

＊

In various stages of her life, a woman resembles the continents of the world. From thirteen to eighteen, she's like Africa—virgin territory, unexplored; from eighteen to thirty, she's like Asia—hot and exotic; from thirty to forty-five she's like America—fully explored and free with her resources; from forty-five to fifty-five, she's like Europe—exhausted, but not without places of interest; after fifty-five, she's like Australia—everybody knows it's down there, but nobody much cares.

*The Mahareeshi Says . . .* (1968).

Have you ever noticed what golf spells backwards?

*Fore-Play: Every Golf Joke Ever Told* (1971).

**Bombardier, Joseph Armand**
Ski-doo.

The Ski-doo, the world-famous motor vehicle that operates on snow, was invented by the Quebec manufacturer Joseph Armand Bombardier. The idea came to him in 1926, and within a decade early models of the motorized toboggan were being produced at his Valcourt plant, near Sherbrooke. The first compact models appeared during the fifties, the famous Ski-doo in 1959.

"In 1934, one of Armand's sons died of appendicitis because deep drifts made it impossible to get medical aid even with the type of machine Bombardier had already developed. He worked on the design continually until he came up with the commercial design in 1936.

"At first Bombardier called his machine the Ski-dog because he thought of it as replacing the dog team for the hunter, trapper and Eskimo. The last letter in the name had been badly printed on one side of his machines and it read like SKI-DOO . . . and soon SKI-DOO the machine was called. Besides, it reminded people of another phrase that had gone down into the language—twenty-three ski-doo—from the dazzling twenties." *Canadian Machinery and Metalworking*, January, 1970.

### Bompas, Bishop William Carpenter

An Indian has great shyness in mentioning his name, and if he wishes you to know it, he will ask his friend to tell you. If you wish to know an Indian's name, it is needful to ask this, not of himself, but of his companion, when you will obtain a ready answer.

"Names," *Northern Lights on the Bible: Drawn from A Bishop's Experience During Twenty-five Years in the Great North-West* (1893).

### Bonaparte, Napoleon

England would be better off without Canada; it keeps her in a prepared state for war at a great expense and constant irritation.

*Diary of Pulteney Malcolm at St. Helena*, January 11, 1817. Quoted by Robert M. Hamilton in *Canadian Quotations: Literary and Historical* (1952).

### Bonenfant, Jean-Charles

The history of French-Canadian nationalism, which still has to be written, appears to us, like the social history of any minority group, as a combative, stubbornly composed, unfinished symphony.

"Cultural and Political Implications of French-Canadian Nationalism" by Jean-Charles Bonenfant and Jean-C. Falardeau, *Canadian Historical Association Report*, 1946. Reprinted by Ramsay Cook in *French-Canadian Nationalism: An Anthology* (1969).

Most nations have been formed, not by people who desired intensely to live together, but rather by people who could not live apart.

"L'Esprit de 1867," *Revue d'histoire de l'Amérique française*, June, 1963. Quoted by Ramsay Cook in *Canada and the French-Canadian Question* (1966).

### Bonner, Robert W.

Capital has no nationality.

\*

As to foreign investment, I can say confidently that we have found in western Canada that we can absorb vast amounts of capital from a number of sources, including the United States, without becoming the less Canadian in our characteristics and without loss of proper control of our own affairs.

"Capital Has No Nationality," December 10, 1970, *The Empire Club of Canada: Addresses 1970-71* (1971). Bonner is chairman of the board of MacMillan Bloedel Limited.

### Bonnycastle, Sir Richard Henry

The public amusements in Toronto are not of a nature to attract much attention.

\*

"The blue hills of old Toronto," so poetically spoken of by Moore, exist only in the imagination of the poet, as the land rises very gently and gradually into the back country, clothed with forest, eternal forest. "Blue hills" are, however, perhaps a good phrase, as the distant view in Upper Canada, in clear weather, is always, whenever there are woods, a blue one, and that blue so soft, so cerulean, and so unattainable even in painting, that it is useless to attempt it in poetry or prose.

*The Canadas in 1841* (1841).

### Booth, General Bramwell

With regard to Canada, I am a stranger among you. I am accustomed to ridicule people who visit a country for a month or so and then attempt to criticize it. But while I am here may I offer one or two suggestions to you in Canada, especially in Ontario? Go ahead and keep your lead with regard to all that encourages the home life of your people.

"The Salvation Army," November 3, 1913, *Address Delivered before the Canadian Club of Toronto: Season of 1913-14* (1914).

### Booth, General Evangeline

I appreciate it very, very deeply, so large

a number coming to meet me, and I take it as evidence of your confidence in the work I am called to represent, and perhaps I might say, take it as an impression of your good will and of your affection towards me personally.

> "The Salvation Army," October 7, 1935, *Addresses Delivered before the Canadian Club of Toronto: Season of 1935-36* (1936).

## Booth, General William

Now, gentlemen of the Canadian Club, what do you say as to the Salvation Army? Will you help it? I don't ask for a portmanteau of money. It is your prayers and your sympathies that I am now particularly in quest of. The Salvation Army has made a beginning, an imperfect beginning I am well aware. But we are only learning how. We shall develop and progress.

> "The Success of the Salvation Army," March 14, 1907, *Addresses Delivered before the Canadian Club of Toronto: Season of 1906-1907* (1907).

## Booth, John Wilkes

By——, I like your Canadian style; I must post myself in Canuck airs, for some of us devils may have to settle here shortly.

> The actor who assassinated Abraham Lincoln in 1865 visited Montreal in October of the previous year and was heard to make the above pronouncement over a game of billiards. "An Evening with the Assassin Booth," *The New York Times*, May 7, 1865. Quoted by Edgar Andrew Collard in *Montreal Yesterdays* (1962).

## Borden, Sir Robert

One Fleet, One Flag, One Throne.

> Slogan of Borden's Conservative party in the general election, September 21, 1911.

Continuous consultation leading to concerted action.

> World War One conscription formula, attributed to Borden.

It can hardly be expected that we shall put 400,000 or 500,000 men in the field and willingly accept the position of having no more voice and receiving no more consideration than if we were toy automata. Any person cherishing such an expectation harbours an unfortunate and even dangerous delusion.

> Letter to Sir George Perley, Canadian high commissioner to the Court of St. James, January 4, 1916. Reproduced in *Historical Documents of Canada: Volume V: The Arts of War and Peace, 1914-1945* (1972), edited by C.P. Stacey.

I look forward to a development in the future along the line of an increasingly equal status between the Dominions and the mother country.

> Statement made at the Imperial War Conference in London, April 16, 1917, presenting a resolution favouring "a full recognition of the Dominions as autonomous nations of an Imperial Conference." With the help of Prime Minister Smuts of the Union of South Africa, the resolution was passed. *Robert Laird Borden: His Memoirs* (1938), edited by Henry Borden. See also Jan Christian Smuts.

Mr. Prime Minister, I want to tell you that, if ever there is a repetition of the battle of Passchendaele, not a Canadian soldier will leave the shores of Canada so long as the Canadian people entrust the government of the country to my hands.

> The prime minister of Canada to Lloyd George, prime minister of Great Britain, a few minutes before an emergency meeting of the Imperial War Cabinet, July, 1918. *Letters to Limbo by the Right Honourable Sir Robert Laird Borden* (1971), edited by Henry Borden.

The world has drifted far from its old anchorage and no man can with certainty prophesy what the outcome will be.

> Diary, November 11, 1918. *Robert Laird Borden: His Memoirs* (1938), edited by Henry Borden.

The British Empire first and, within the British Empire, Canada first.

From an address by Sir Robert on July 25, 1930. Used by R.B. Bennett in his election campaign later that year.

## Borduas, Paul-Emile
You are too far to the right for us.

To a Communist at an important Montreal art show, 1947. Quoted by Terry Kirkman in *The Montreal Star*, December 11, 1971.

We are a small people, who yet grew and multiplied in number, if not in spirit, here in the north of this huge American continent; and our bodies were young and our hearts of gold, but our minds remained primitive, with their sterile obsession about Europe's past glories, while the concrete achievements of our own oppressed people were ignored.
It seemed as if there were no future for us.
But wars and revolutions in the outside world broke the spell, shattered the mental block.
Irreparable cracks began to appear in the fortress walls.

\*

MAKE WAY FOR MAGIC! MAKE WAY FOR OBJECTIVE MYSTERY!
MAKE WAY FOR LOVE!
MAKE WAY FOR WHAT IS NEEDED!

\*

The past must no longer be used as an anvil for beating out the present and the future.

\*

Meanwhile we must work without respite, hand in hand with those who long for a better life; together we must persevere, regardless of praise or persecution, toward the joyful fulfilment of our fierce desire for freedom.

Excerpts from *Refus global*, the famous manifesto issued in Montreal by Borduas and other Quebec artists in 1948. "Global Refusal," *French-Canadian Nationalism: An Anthology* (1969), edited by Ramsay Cook.

At this point I would give Paris and all the blessings of the earth for a small corner were it in Canada. [Letter to his Quebec patroness, Mme. Lortie, December, 1955]

## Borges, Jorge Luis
Following their military defeat in 1763, French agents in Canada spread the word among the Indians that the King of France had fallen into a deep slumber and had slept through the past few years, but that he had just now awakened and that his first words were: "We must immediately expel the English who have invaded the country of my red-skinned children." The word spread throughout the continent and was one of the causes of the famous conspiracy of Pontiac.

*Extraordinary Tales* (1971), by Jorge Luis Borges and Adolfo Bioy Casares, translated by Anthony Kerrigan. The passage is attributed to one H. Desvignes Doolittle, "The King's Awakening," *Rambling Thoughts on World History*, published in Niagara Falls in 1903; but this is likely another of Borges' literary impersonations.

## Borovoy, Alan
In Canada we don't ban demonstrations, we re-route them.

Head of the Canadian Civil Liberties Association, *The Canadian Magazine*, April 29, 1972.

## Borowski, Tadeusz
Part of "Canada" has been liquidated and detailed to a labour Kommando— one of the very toughest—at Harmenz. For there exists in the camp a special brand of justice based on envy: when the rich and mighty fall, their friends see to it that they fall to the very bottom. And Canada, our Canada, which smells not of maple forests but of French perfume, has amassed great fortunes in diamonds and currency from all over Europe.

*This Way for the Gas, Ladies and Gentlemen* (1967), translated from the Polish by Barbara Vedder. A footnote reads: "'Canada' designated wealth and well-being in the camp. More specifically, it referred to the members of the labour gang, or Kommando, who helped to unload the incoming transports of people destined for the gas chambers."

## Botha, General Louis
It is our intention to follow in the footsteps of Canada.

What the Boer War general and South African statesman meant was that the BNA Act, 1867, was studied when the South Africa Act, 1909, was passed by the British Parliament, creating the Union of South Africa. Quoted by W. L. Mackenzie King in "Address at the Unveiling of the Statue of Sir Wilfrid Laurier," August 3, 1927.

## Botkin, B.A.
The king of all monte throwers was known as "Canada Bill." Where he came from or who he was, no one ever knew.

A Treasury of Railroad Folklore (1953), by B.A. Botkin and Alvin F. Harlow.

## Bouchard, Georges
What strokes came my way at school were not stolen.

Other Days, Other Ways: Silhouettes of the Past in French Canada (1928), translated by E.H. Holgate.

## Bouchard, Télésphore-Damien
Duplessis operated the only portable dictatorship in the democratic world.

\*

Let us be thankful for his austere celibacy. This traitorous breed will not be perpetuated.

Mémoires (1960). References to the premier of Quebec, Maurice Duplessis, who died in 1959.

## Boucher, Pierre
We know how to hang in Canada.

Attributed to the governor of Trois-Rivières in the 1650s by Agnes Repplier in Mère Marie of the Ursulines: A Study in Adventure (1931).

## Bouchette, Errol
A people is never safe when it leaves the resources of its country unexploited. If it does not exploit them itself, others will come to exploit them for it, and thus give themselves a pretext for intervening in its affairs. Or yet again an industrial

oligarchy will arise, which is not less to be feared.

Observation made in 1901, quoted by Mason Wade in The French Canadians: 1760-1967 (1968).

## Bougainville, Louis-Antoine de
When V. produces an idea he falls in love with it, as Pygmalion did with his statue. I can forgive Pygmalion, for what he produced was a masterpiece.

Montcalm's aide-de-camp writing in his journal, 1757, about Pierre de Rigaud, Marquis de Vaudreuil-Cavagnal, the last governor of New France. Quoted by Francis Parkman in Montcalm and Wolfe (1884).

Berryer: Eh, Monsieur, when the house is on fire one cannot occupy one's self with the stable.
Bougainville: At least, Monsieur, nobody will say that you talk like a horse.

In February of 1759, Bougainville pleaded with the French colonial minister, Nicolas-René Berryer, to send additional troops to New France and consolidate Montcalm's power. But Berryer was more concerned with the situation in Europe than with the one in America. The remarks are quoted by Francis Parkman in Montcalm and Wolfe (1884).

I do not believe that the English will make an attempt against it; but they may have the madness to do so, and it is well to be prepared against surprise.

Remark made one month before the fall of Quebec, September 13, 1759, quoted by Francis Parkman in Montcalm and Wolfe (1884).

## Bougainville. Bougainvillaea.
The remarkable Comte de Bougainville, after serving Montcalm at the fall of Quebec, joined a three-year scientific voyage that took him around the world. In 1769, the largest of the volcanic Solomon Islands in the Pacific Ocean was named after him. Three years later Diderot wrote his Supplément au Voyage de Bougainville, a tract in defence of sexual freedom. "Today he is perhaps best remembered for having introduced an increasingly popular semi-tropical

plant, the *Bougainvillea* [sic], to other parts of the world," wrote Oliver Warner in *With Wolfe to Quebec: The Path to Glory* (1972). (The bougainvillaea is a tropical plant or vine with small flowers almost concealed by large leafy bracts, quite ornamental, exotic, not unlike its namesake.)

## Boulding, Kenneth
Canada has no cultural unity, no linguistic unity, no religious unity, no economic unity, no geographic unity. All it has is unity.

> Professor of Economics, University of Michigan, addressing a group of Toronto students, November, 1957.

## Bourassa, Henri
The ministerial order which decreed the recruiting and the sending of our troops reserves, it seems, the future and forbids this action from being considered a precedent.
The precedent, Sir, is the fait accompli.
The principle at stake is that prize axiom of English liberalism; it is even the basis of the parliamentary regime: No Taxation without Representation. And the tax in blood constitutes the heaviest form of public contributions.

> Letter of resignation published in *La Patrie*, October 20, 1899, objecting to Laurier's decision to send the militia to South Africa because it establishes a "precedent." Reproduced by Joseph Levitt in *Henri Bourassa on Imperialism and Bi-culturalism, 1900-1918* (1970).

Of course, I am met here by the "no precedent" clause contained in the order in council. I am free to say that this clause is the only thing which I can approve in the whole course of the government; but I am afraid it is a frail barrier to oppose to the current of noisy militarism which is carrying us all over British possessions. It is this fear which I expressed in my letter to the Prime Minister when I said: "The precedent, Sir, is the accomplished fact."

> House of Commons, March 13, 1900.

So long as the majority of Canadians have two countries, one here and one in Europe, national unity will remain a myth and a constant source of internecine quarrels.

*

If the Treaty of Paris had saved us for France, what would have become of us? Assuming we would have escaped the bloody Reign of Terror, it is more than probable that Napoleon would have sold us to the Americans without even consulting us, as he did with Louisiana. If we had survived the Empire, how would we fit into France's present regime?

> "French-Canadian Patriotism: What It Is, and What It Ought To Be," Speech at the Monument National, April 27, 1902. *French-Canadian Nationalism: An Anthology* (1969), edited by Ramsay Cook.

Let us be French, as the Americans are English.

> *Le patriotisme canadien-français, ce qu'il est, ce qu'il doit être* (1902), quoted by André Siegfried in *The Race Question in Canada* (1907).

There is Ontario patriotism, Quebec patriotism, or Western patriotism, each based on the hope that it may swallow up the others, but there is no Canadian patriotism, and we can have no Canadian nation when we have no Canadian patriotism.

*

You must think seriously as to the future. If you do not cling loyally to the deep roots, the deep traditions of your past, you are in a dangerous position alongside of a country of eighty millions with all their forces of absorption. Let the good people of Toronto consider that point of view. The Nationalist movement in Quebec is the greatest guaranty of the permanency of Canada.

> "The Nationalist Movement in Quebec," January 22, 1907, *Addresses Delivered before the Canadian Club of Toronto: Season of 1906-1907* (1907).

A free Anglo-French Confederacy, in the northern part of America, united by bonds of amity and kinship with Great Britain and France, of two great nations from which it had derived its races, its civilization and its thoughts, and offering to the trade and the intellectuality of the world a friendly rival and counterpoise to the expanding civilization of the United States, would become one of the greatest contributions to humanity.

"Imperialism and Nationalism," December 18, 1912, *Addresses Delivered before the Canadian Club of Ottawa: 1911-12* (1912).

The enemies of the French language, of French civilization in Canada, are not the Boches on the shores of the Spree; but the English-Canadian anglicizers, the Orange intriguers, or Irish priests. Above all they are French Canadians weakened and degraded by the conquest and three centuries of colonial servitude.

Let no mistake be made: if we let the Ontario minority be crushed, it will soon be the turn of other French groups in English Canada.

*Le Devoir*, April 20, 1915. Quoted by Mason Wade in *The French Canadians: 1760-1967* (1968).

Those who have undertaken to bleed Canada white to uphold the forces of England and France in Europe tell us occasionally that our first line of defence is in Flanders. I say that our first line of defence is at Ottawa.

*Le Devoir et la guerre* (1916), quoted by Joseph Levitt in *Henri Bourassa on Imperialism and Bi-culturalism, 1900-1918* (1970).

Our special task, as French Canadians, is to insert into America the spirit of Christian France. It is to defend against all comers, perhaps even against France herself, our religious and national heritage. This heritage does not belong to us alone. It belongs to all Catholic America. It is the inspiring and shining hearth of that America. It belongs to the whole Church, and it is the basic foundation of the Church in this part of the world. It belongs to all French civilization of which it is the refuge and anchor amid the immense sea of saxonizing Americanism.

*La langue, gardienne de la foi* (1918). Quoted by George Grant in *Lament for a Nation: The Defeat of Canadian Nationalism* (1965).

There, I say, British, yes, but Canadian first; if necessary secession from Britain rather than sacrifice of Canada; Canada alongside of Britain so long as it is possible, but Canada first and forever.

Quoted by A.G. Dewey in *The Dominions and Diplomacy* (1929).

Pétain, greater at Vichy than at Verdun.

"Does anyone believe that Bourassa got his news from France? And yet he spoke once of 'Pétain greater at Vichy than at Verdun,' which seems singular today . . . the truth was that we felt terribly isolated—we were intoxicated with solitude." *André Laurendeau: Witness for Quebec* (1973), translated by Philip Stratford.

Are there any Christian nations left? There remain Portugal, Spain since the restoration of Franco, France under the regime of Pétain. And, I would add, Italy under the reign of Mussolini.

Montreal address, November 5, 1942, quoted by Stanley B. Ryerson in *French Canada: A Study of Canadian Democracy* (1943).

There is no greater farce than to talk of democracy. To begin with, it is a lie; it has never existed in any great country. [Address at Atwater Market Hall, Montreal, February 10, 1943]

Canadian Liberals believe in the autonomy of the Dominion and the maintenance of the unity of the Empire, whereas Canadian Conservatives believe in the unity of the Empire and the preservation of the autonomy of the Dominions.

Quoted by R. MacGregor Dawson in *The Government of Canada* (1952).

**Bourassa, Robert**
We all want—is it necessary to say it?—Mr. Laporte and Mr. Cross to live. Fate, in a rare example of how cruel it can be, has decided to choose them to be the issue on which maintenance of public order depends.

\*

My dear fellow citizens, a great statesman said once: "To govern is to choose." We have chosen justice—individual and collective.

> Statement on Radio-Canada at the height of the FLQ crisis, October 11, 1970. Quoted by John Sewell in *Quebec 70: A Documentary Narrative* (1971).

We will do our best to spread the wealth of Ontario across our country.

> Quoted by Richard Cleroux in *The Globe and Mail*, May 1, 1972.

There is a clear distinction between being a Liberal contractor and being dishonest.

> Remark made in March of 1973.

**Bourget, Bishop Ignace**
Let each say in his heart, "I hear my *curé*, my *curé* hears the bishop, the bishop hears the Pope, and the Pope hears Our Lord Jesus Christ."

> Circular letter, February 1, 1867, quoted by Mason Wade in *The French Canadians: 1760-1967* (1968).

There reposes a rebel who has been buried by force of arms.

> Pastoral letter, November 16, 1875, quoted by Mason Wade in *The French Canadians: 1760-1967* (1968). The bishop of Montreal objected to the Christian burial of Joseph Guibord, a free-thinking Catholic printer who was not buried in consecrated ground until six years later.

**Bourinot, Sir J.G.**
Descriptions of our meadows, prairies and forests, with their wealth of herbage and foliage, or artistic sketches of pretty bits of lake scenery have their limitations as respects their influence on a people. Great thoughts or deeds are not bred by scenery.

> *

... that great river [St. Lawrence], associated with memories of Cartier, Champlain, LaSalle, Frontenac, Wolfe and Montcalm,—that river already immortalized in history by the pen of Parkman—will be as noted in song and story as the Rhine, and will have its Irving to make it as famous as the lovely Hudson.

> *Our Intellectual Strength and Weakness* (1893).

Bourinot's Rules of Order.

> Sir John, clerk of the House of Commons from 1880 until his death in 1902, was the author of *Parliamentary Procedure and Practice in Canada* (1884). In 1924, there appeared an abridgement, *Rules of Order: Being a Canadian Manual on the Procedure at Meetings*. This is the Canadian equivalent of the American manual *Robert's Rules of Order*.

**Bourne, George**　See Maria Monk.

**Bowell, Sir Mackenzie**
A nest of traitors.

> When half the ministers in his cabinet resigned on January 4, 1896, Prime Minister Mackenzie Bowell referred to them as "a nest of traitors." The "seven bolters," who included Sir George Foster and Sir Charles Tupper, resigned over the Conservative leader's handling of the Manitoba schools issue. Bowell himself joined them by resigning on April 27, 1896.

**Bowering, George**
So I look not for masterpieces because we have no more masters.

> Preface, *The Story So Far* (1971), edited by George Bowering.

As examples I will list ten of my favourite beautiful wholly Canadian things. A Montreal Canadiens sweater. The label on Moose Head Ale. The ceiling of the drugstore in High River, Alberta. The red cliffs on the north shore of P.E.I. Jack Chambers' painting of the Highway 401 interchange near London, Ont. The Manitoba coat of arms. The way people say "Jarge" instead of George in Newfoundland and Cape Breton. The scent of the air when you're driving through the Okanagan during apple-blossom time. The wheat elevators that stick up out of Floral, Sask., as you're driving past a mile away on Highway 14. The brave and beautiful name of Snag, Yukon Territory.

The best thing about Canada is that it is not this. It is this and that.

"Confessions of a Failed American," *Maclean's Magazine*, November, 1972.

**Bowes-Lyon, Lady Elizabeth**
See Elizabeth the Queen Mother.

**Bowman, Scotty**
Statistics are for losers.

This maxim was coined by the coach of the Montreal Canadiens in March of 1973, prior to the Stanley Cup playoffs. Bowman was stressing that a winning club has the power to overcome mathematical comparisons that might suggest its defeat. Quoted by Mark Mulvoy in "A Lot More Where They Come From" in *Sports Illustrated*, April 2, 1973.

**Box, Dr. Harold Keith**
Nine years of study have proved that periodental disease has been a problem since the dawn of man. Four out of five Neolithic men would have had "pink tooth brush" if they had owned one.

American Academy of Periodontology, Cincinnati Convention, February, 1922. "Dr. Box has discovered the cure for 'pyorrhea.' This discovery for dentistry is on an equality with the discovery of insulin by Drs. Banting and Best in medicine." Dr. Forbes Godfrey, Ontario minister of Health, Ontario Legislature, March, 1924.

**Boya, Nathan T.**
I always wanted to make this trip and now I have.

The twenty-year-old Black American made the "trip" over Niagara Falls, July 15, 1961, in a six-foot rubber ball of his own devising. A banner he carried in the ball read mysteriously: "Plung / -O- / Sphere / Step from your Pit of Darkness / into light—Dell." Quoted by Andy O'Brien in *Daredevils of Niagara* (1964).

**Boyd, John**  See Antoine Gérin-Lajoie.

**Boyer, Dr. Raymond**
I felt it was of great importance that the scientific war effort on the two fronts should be coordinated.

This is the reason the brilliant Mon-

treal chemist gave for passing top-secret information on to the Russians in 1946, for which he was sentenced to two years' imprisonment. Quoted by Barbara Moon in "The Gouzenko Spy Case," *Historic Headlines* (1967), edited by Pierre Berton.

**Boyle, Sir Cavendish**
When sun rays crown thy pine-clad hills,
　And Summer spreads her hand,
When silvern voices tune thy rills,
　We love thee, smiling land.

We love thee, we love thee,
We love thee, smiling land.

First of four verses of "Ode to Newfoundland," written between 1901 and 1904 while Boyle served as governor. *The Book of Newfoundland* (1937), edited by J.R. Smallwood.

**Boyle, Harry**
PHYSICAL JERK FROM THE EAST [Headline in *The Whitehorse Star* when Ottawa sent a physical fitness expert to Whitehorse]

*

SPORTING HOUSE OPENS ON MAIN ST. [Headline when a local store opened a sports department]

*

Baths 50 cents. With soap 75 cents. Royal Fambly Free (this week only). [Advertisement (with spelling error) when Queen Elizabeth visited the Yukon]

"This is not a newspaper," explained Harry Boyle, publisher of the biweekly *Whitehorse Star*, "it's a Yukon scrapbook." Quoted by Gerald Clark in *Canada: The Uneasy Neighbour* (1965).

**Boyle, Harry J.**
It may have been the "Roaring Twenties," but to me, growing up on an Ontario farm tucked away in a valley near Lake Huron, it was a time of peace, dominated more or less by God and the Methodists!

*With a Pinch of Sin* (1966).

**Boyle, Joseph**
I have gone to sea. Don't worry about me. Joe.

The Woodstock boy left this note for his parents when he ran away from home in 1894. The seventeen-year-old lad went to Dawson City, where he struck it rich, and then to Jassey, Rumania, where he became an intimate of the Queen and "the uncrowned King."

A man with the heart of a Viking
And the simple faith of a child.

This couplet by Robert Service was chosen by Queen Marie of Rumania for Joseph Boyle's headstone which stands in an English cemetery and bears the cross of her personal order and the name "Marie," 1923.

## Braddock, General Edward
We shall know better how to deal with them next time.

Dying words of General Braddock, commander-in-chief of the British forces in North America. He died on July 13, 1755, after failing to rout the French at Fort Duquesne (present-day Pittsburgh), in the Battle of the Monongahela.

## Braden, Bernie
It's hard to remember what we used to do before television.

Quoted by John Gray in *Maclean's Magazine*, November 7, 1959.

I come on after football.

The reason why ten million Britons watched "Braden's Week" on BBC television. The Vancouver-born performer was quoted by Roy Shields in *The Toronto Telegram*, July 25, 1970.

## Bradley, William Henry
Public sentiment will move mountains of laws.
*
Steam-engines don't work harder than a man's heart and veins, when he starts from his master, and fears being overtaken.
*
If a man could make slaves of mud or block, and have them work for him, it would be wrong,—all men came of the hand of the Almighty; and every man ought to have life, and his own method of pursuing happiness.

Bradley was a Maryland slave who escaped and settled in Buxton, Ontario.

Quoted by Benjamin Drew in *The Refugee: or the Narratives of Fugitive Slaves in Canada* (1856).

## Braley, Ephraim   See Anonymous: Songs.

## Brand, Oscar
From the Vancouver Island to the Alberta Highland,
Cross the prairie, the Lakes to Ontario's towers.
From the sound of Mount Royal's chimes out to the Maritimes,
Something to Sing About this Land of Ours.

Refrain of "Something to Sing About" (sometimes called "This Land of Ours"), written by Oscar Brand in 1963. For "This Land is Our Land," see Woody Guthrie.

## Brant, Joseph
You ask me, then, whether in my opinion civilization is favourable to human happiness? In answer to the question, it may be answered, but there are degrees of civilization, from Cannibals to the most polite of European nations. The question is not, then, whether a degree of refinement is not conducive to happiness; but whether you, or the natives of this land, have obtained this medium. On this subject we are at present, I presume, of very different opinions.
*
In the government you called civilized, the happiness of the people is constantly sacrificed to the splendour of empire.
*
The palaces and prisons among you form a most dreadful contrast. Go to the former places, and you will see perhaps a *deformed piece of earth* assuming airs that become none but the Great Spirit above. Go to one of your prisons; here description utterly fails! . . . Liberty, to a rational creature, as much exceeds property as the light of the sun does that of the most twinkling star. . . . And I seriously declare, I had rather die by the most severe tortures ever inflicted on this continent, than languish in one of your prisons for a single year. Great Spirit of the Universe!—and do you call yourselves Christians? [Letter, 1803]

\*

Have pity on the poor Indians: if you can get any influence with the great, endeavour to do them all the good you can.

> Last recorded words of Chief Joseph Brant to his adopted nephew Teyoninhokârâwen, November 24, 1807. Quoted by William L. Stone in *Life of Joseph Brant—Thayendanegea, Including the Indian Wars of the American Revolution* (1838).

**Brault, Jacques**
One cannot speak of Quebec in the present tense; Quebec is not in the world because Quebec is not itself; yet if it exists somehow, this existence can be only an *existence apart*.

> Quoted by Alain Bosquet in *Poésie du Québec* (1971).

**Brébeuf, Jean de**
Seeing them, therefore, thus gathered together at the beginning of this year, we resolved to preach publicly to all, and to acquaint them with the reason of our coming into their Country, which is not for their furs, but to declare to them the true God and his son, Jesus Christ, the universal Saviour of our souls.

\*

If you ask them who made the sky and its inhabitants, they have no other reply than that they know nothing about it. And when we preach to them of one God, Creator of Heaven and earth, and of all things, and even when we talk of them of Hell and Paradise and of our other mysteries, the headstrong reply that this is good for our Country and not for theirs; that every Country has its own fashions. But having pointed out to them, by means of a little globe that we had brought, that there is only one world, they remain without reply. ["Relation of What Occurred Among the Hurons in the Year 1635"]

\*

Jesus Christ is our true greatness; it is He alone and His cross that should be sought in running after these people, for if you strive for anything else, you will find naught but bodily and spiritual affliction. But having found Jesus Christ in His cross, you have found the roses in the thorns, sweetness in bitterness, all in nothing. ["Instructions for the Fathers of Our Society Who Shall Be Sent to the Hurons," Relation for 1637]

> *The Jesuit Relations and Allied Documents* (1954), edited by Edna Kenton.

Chrétiens, prenez courage,
Jésus Saveur est né!
Du malin les ouvrages
A jamais sont ruinés.
Quand il chante merveille,
A ces troublants appas
Ne prêtez plaus l'oreille:
Jésus est né: In excelsis gloria!

'Twas in the moon of wintertime
When all the birds had fled,
That Mighty Gitchi Manitou
Sent angel choirs instead.
Before their light the stars grew dim,
And wand'ring hunters heard the hymn:
"Jesus, your King, is born;
Jesus is born; in excelsis gloria!"

> The Jesuit missionary is credited with writing the first Canadian Christmas carol. The carol, written in the Huron tongue in 1641, was translated by an unknown Quebec Jesuit before 1800 and first printed in Ernest Myrand's *Noëls anciens de la Nouvelle-France* (1899). The English version is an interpretation by Jesse Edgar Middleton. Only the first verses are given; the tune is reminiscent of "God Rest Ye Merry, Gentlemen" and "Une Jeune Pucelle." Robert E. Oliver's *Jesous Ahatonhia: A Canadian Christmas Carol* (1967).

Once, when he was among the Neutral Nation, in the winter of 1640, he beheld the ominous apparition of a great cross slowly approaching from the quarter where lay the country of the Iroquois. He told the vision to his comrades.

"What was it like? How large was it?" they eagerly demanded. "Large enough," replied the priest, "to crucify us all." To explain such phenomena is the province of psychology, and not of history.

> Francis Parkman in *The Jesuits in North America in the Seventeenth Century* (1867).

I am an ox, and I am fit only to carry loads.

> This pun is attributed to Brébeuf, whose name means *boeuf*, ox. Quoted by Thomas B. Costain in *The White and the Gold: The French Regime in Canada* (1954). For an account of Brébeuf's martyrdom, see Christophe Regnault.

**Brebner, J. Bartlet**
On the whole, however, the most substantial Canadian nationalism in times of peace has been economic nationalism.

> "Canadianism," The Presidential Address, *Report of the Canadian Historical Association, 1940* (1940).

Perhaps the most striking thing about Canada is that it is not part of the United States.

> Opening sentence of *Canada: A Modern History* (1960).

Americans are benevolently ignorant about Canada, while Canadians are malevolently well informed about the United States. [Attributed]

**Bremer, Arthur H.**
Canada had crooked teeth and a moustach. He asked where I was from, where I wanted to go, for how long & if I had anything to declair. (I was prepared for this last question, I was going to say, "I declair its a nice day." But I just asked, "What should I declair?"). . . . I instantly lost all respect for the Big Bad Canadian Customs.

> In 1972, Bremer shot and crippled George Wallace, governor of Alabama. The twenty-one-year-old unemployed busboy was gunning for Richard Nixon, whom he stalked with intent to assassinate during the president's Ottawa visit, April, 1971. *An Assassin's Diary* (1973), edited by Harding Lemay.

**Brendan the Apostle**
An hour later a brilliant light shone round them—their boat had reached the shore. Before them lay open country covered with apple trees laden with fruit. The monks ate as much as they wanted and drank deeply from the springs. . . . They gathered fruit and all kinds of gems . . . and sailed away into the belt of darkness . . . on a direct route from their own monastery.

> *

After many more years have rolled by, this island will be revealed to your successors at the time when Christians will be undergoing persecution. This river divides the island in two. You must be thinking that it is autumn and the fruit has just ripened—it is like this the whole year round; dusk and darkness are unknown, for Christ Himself is our light.

> The semi-legendary St. Brendan the Navigator and Apostle of Ireland is said to have died in his nineties in 577, but not before completing a miraculous seven-year voyage in search of the Earthly Paradise. The imaginative account of that voyage, written some three centuries later by an unknown scribe, was popular reading during the Middle Ages. St. Brendan's Earthly Paradise has been variously located— among the Canary Islands, even as far west as Canada. *Lives of the Saints: The Voyage of St. Brendan, Bede: Life of Cuthbert, Eddius Stephanus: Life of Wilfrid* (1965), translated by J.F. Webb.
>
> "Brendan was a real person, and in my opinion his *Navigatio* is based on a real voyage or voyages, enhanced by Celtic imagination. The whole atmosphere of the story is northern," wrote Samuel Eliot Morison in *The European Discovery of America: The Northern Voyages A.D. 500-1600* (1971). "No, here is not a discovery of a New World, but a captivating tale which led men of later centuries to sail into the unknown, hoping to find Brendan's islands, confident that God would watch over them. In that sense the *Navigatio* may be said to have stimulated oceanic exploration for nigh one thousand years, and to have been a precursor of Columbus."

**Bressani, Francesco Giuseppe**
The letter is badly written and quite soiled, because, in addition to other inconveniences, he who writes it has only one whole finger on his right hand; and it is difficult to avoid staining the paper with the blood which flows from his

wounds, not yet healed; he uses arquebus powder for ink, and the earth for a table.

Letter to the general of the Jesuits from the missionary, written July 15, 1644, while a captive of the Iroquois. Quoted by Albert Tessier, "François-Joseph Bressani," *Dictionary of Canadian Biography: Volume I: 1000-1700* (1965).

## Bréton, Andre
Perhaps, as dramatic as this may sound, a large-scale landing of French Canadians on the coast of Normandy today would promote the re-establishment of a vital contact missing for close to two centuries. Yet those who have remained here have demonstrated by their actions and by their utterances that they have never been able to break out of the stage where their common adventure has become muddled and intertwined, for better or for worse, with another's. If, on their part, resentments probably no longer exist, their integration into the English community is nevertheless entirely illusory.

*Arcane 17* (1971) includes the French surrealist poet's impressions of Quebec and the Gaspé.

## Brezhnev, Leonid
"An apocryphal yarn has it that when a Canadian newsman covering President Nixon's visit to Moscow asked Leonid Brezhnev how many Soviet missiles were aimed at Toronto, the Soviet Communist party chief replied: 'None. I've got nothing against the Italians.' "

*Time*, July 10, 1972.

## Bridle, Augustus
Canada has enough unpublished music manuscripts to make a line of the treble clef from Montreal to Winnipeg.

\*

No, we have no Viennas.

\*

None of our poverty is poetic.

\*

For years I have been yearning for the great Canadian music drama of the fur-post, the York boat and the trail. Yearn again. What a background! It fairly

thumps of the magnum opus. Our prairies are Bach fugues. Our Rockies are colossal symphonies. Our rivers are melodies. Objectively, as programme, we have everything that makes great music as inevitable as weather. But there is nobody with a big enough imagination, plus time and experience, to write the music.

"Composers Among Us," *Yearbook of the Arts in Canada: 1928-29* (1929), edited by Bertram Brooker.

## Briggs, William
We're bringing out a book of poetry for a man who lives in the Yukon. You're going to the West Coast—you may be able to sell some to the trade out there. It's the author's publication and we're printing it for him. Try to sell some for him if you can.

William Briggs, the publisher, giving orders to his salesman, R.B. Bond, concerning his dark horse, Robert Service's *Songs of a Sourdough* (1907). Quoted by R.B. Bond in "I Sold Service to the Public," *The Globe Magazine*, May 28, 1958.

## Bright, John
I have another and a far brighter vision before me. It may be but a vision, but I will cherish it. I see one vast confederation, stretching from the frozen north in unbroken lines to the glowing south, and from the wild billows of the Atlantic westward to the calmer waters of the Pacific main, and I see one people, and one language, and one law, and one faith, and over all that wide continent the home of freedom and the refuge of the oppressed of every race and every clime.

Birmingham address, 1862, by the English orator and member of Parliament.

## Brilliant, Jean
Take me to the rear, that my men might not see me suffer, not that I fear to suffer, but that I fear it might affect and discourage them.

Lieutenant Jean Brilliant of the 22nd Canadian Infantry Battalion was twice wounded but he led his men to capture

150 enemy and fifteen machine guns on August 8-9, 1918, during the Battle of Amiens, France. He died of a third set of wounds and was posthumously awarded the Victoria Cross "for most conspicuous bravery and outstanding devotion to duty." Brilliant's words were quoted by the premier of Quebec, Joseph-Adélard Godbout in "Quebec and Pan-Canadian Unity," *Empire Club of Canada: Addresses Delivered to the Members During the Year 1940-41* (1941). Details of the action were described by George C. Machum in *Canada's V.C.'s: The Story of Canadians Who Have Been Awarded the Victoria Cross* (1956).

## Brine, Harold
He spoke to us at our level—at the thirteen-thousand-foot level, where all men are equal. He wasn't like a royal prince, but like a prince of a man.

Nova Scotian miner's tribute to Philip Mountbatten after the prince visited the Springhill mining disaster site, 1958. Quoted by Frank Rasky in *Great Canadian Disasters* (1961).

## Broadbent, Ed
Well, I'd rather waffle to the left than waffle to the right.

Remark made by the NDP federal member of Parliament when accused at a public meeting in 1969 of waffling on an issue. The word "waffle" has stuck as the name of the unofficial "ginger group" within the NDP which seeks to unite socialism and economic nationalism.

Where there are divisions created by unequal access to wealth and power, then men grow up in conflict. A child born in Canada now has a greater chance of having a mental breakdown than he does of graduating from a university. This is no accident.

*The Liberal Rip-Off: Trudeauism vs. the Politics of Equality* (1970).

## Broadfoot, Barry
A wise man once said that the best way to survive a Depression is to become a politician. He was wrong. The best way to survive was to become a successful politician. Few did.

*Ten Lost Years 1929-1939: Memoirs of Canadians Who Survived the Depression* (1973). See also Henry Jacobson and Mother Melville.

## Broadfoot, Dave
I was in an amateur production of *Rose Marie* and had just stepped outside for a smoke when a detachment of the RCMP came along. That's how I got into the Mounties.

\*

Canadians are concerned about the rape of our country by the Americans. And I say that is not true—how can you rape a prostitute.

Nightclub routine by the popular writer-comedian, about 1964.

Canada is a collection of ten provinces with strong governments loosely connected by fear.

Quoted by Gerald Clark in *Canada: The Uneasy Neighbour* (1965).

## Broadus, E.K.
On a day in June, 1908, the president of a university not yet in being, in a province which I had never heard of, in a country which I have never visited, came to Harvard and offered me the professorship of English.

"Small Beginnings" (1935), *Learning and Society* (1963), edited by J.R. Kidd. The influential teacher went to the University of Alberta in Edmonton in 1908 and taught there until his death in 1936.

## Brock, Sir Isaac
Most of the people have lost all confidence—I however speak loud and look big. . . .

Brigadier General Isaac Brock to Sir George Prevost, July 20, 1812, quoted by J. Mackay Hitsman in *The Incredible War of 1812: A Military History* (1965).

Are you prepared, inhabitants of Upper Canada, to become willing subjects, or rather slaves, to the despot who rules the nations of Europe with a rod of iron?—

if not, arise in a body, exert your energies, cooperate cordially with the King's regular forces, to repel the invader, and do not give cause to your children, when groaning under the oppression of a foreign master, to reproach you with having too easily parted with the richest inheritance of this earth,—a participation in the name, character and freedom of Britons.

> From the "Proclamation" issued by the commander of the British forces in Upper Canada, Fort George, July 22, 1812. (The "despot" is France, as it was maintained that if the Americans conquered the Canadas the country would be added to the French empire.) The proclamation was issued in response to the ultimatum of General Hull. Reproduced by Robert Christie in *A History of the Late Province of Lower Canada, Parliamentary and Political* (1854). See also General William Hull.

We are engaged in an awful and eventful contest. By unanimity and despatch in our councils and by vigour in our operations, we will teach the enemy this lesson: that a country defended by free men, enthusiastically devoted to the cause of their King and constitution, can never be conquered.

> Address, Upper Canada Legislature, July 27, 1812.

Push on, brave York Volunteers!

> This ringing command was once believed to be the dying order of Isaac Brock, issued immediately before he fell in the battle of Queenston Heights, October 13, 1812. It is now believed to be Brock's rallying cry to the York (Toronto) Militia, as he galloped past Brown's Point, more than a mile from where he was mortally wounded. "The newly arrived York men have since become one of the legends of the war. The dying Brock is supposed to have urged those near him to 'Push on the York Volunteers' who were, he knew, coming towards Queenston, and folklore has turned a simple command into the ringing exhortation, 'Push on, brave York Volunteers.'" Quoted by J. Mackay Hitsman in *The Incredible War of 1812:*

*A Military History* (1965). See also Tecumseh.

## Brockington, Leonard

There is a tide in the affairs of men which, taken at the Eddy, leads on to fortune.

> The "orator-general" made this pun when the widow of E.B. Eddy died in 1921 and R.B. Bennett inherited part ownership of the Eddy match company.

If only the newspapers would use more often their strongest weapon, which is silence, and not report to Quebec some of the stupid things said in Ontario, and not report to Ontario some of the stupid things said in Quebec, many of us would feel happier. I was born a Celtic optimist and would not be a cousin of the Bretons if I did not continue to believe that our country will survive the horrors of Hansard.

> Address, Queen's University, April 9, 1964.

All I know is that I try to have a beginning and an end and see that the middle moves logically from one to the other. [On his speeches]

*

Never before have I felt so inclined to strike a happy medium. [On failing to dissuade Mackenzie King's medium from writing her memoirs]

> Quoted by Eric Hutton in ". . . and now, a few words from Mr. Brockington," *Maclean's Magazine*, April 15, 1953. The Welsh-born Brockington was "the premier after-dinner speaker on the continent."

## Brogan, Denis

A uranium-producing country cannot be neutral.

> "An Outsider Looking In," *Canada's Tomorrow: Papers and Discussion* (1954). The British historian addressed the "Canada's Tomorrow Conference" in Quebec City, November, 1953.

## Broke, Sir Philip Bowes Vere

As the *Chesapeake* appears now ready for sea, I request you will do me the favour to meet the *Shannon* with her and try the fortune of our respective flags. Choose your terms but let us meet.

> Message sent by "Brave Broke," captain of the H.M.S. *Shannon,* to Captain James Lawrence of the U.S. *Chesapeake* in Boston harbour. Broke captured the American frigate after a fifteen-minute sea battle, June 1, 1813. Broke was seriously wounded, Lawrence killed. See also Captain James Lawrence.

## Bronfman, Edgar M.
There's a lot of sentiment in Seagram.

> Remark made by the son of Samuel Bronfman who founded Distillers Corporation—Seagram's Ltd.

## Bronfman, Samuel
We who make whiskey say: Drink Moderately.

> Motto adopted during the 1930s and 40s. The founder explained, "The House of Seagram does not want a dollar that should be spent for the necessities of life."

## Brooke, Frances
I must venture to Quebec tomorrow, or have company at home: amusements are here necessary to life; we must be jovial, or the blood will freeze in our veins.

I no longer wonder the elegant arts are unknown here; the rigour of the climate suspends the very powers of the understanding: what then must become of those of the imagination? Those who expect to see

> *"A new Athens rising near the pole,"*

will find themselves extremely disappointed. Genius will never mount high, where the faculties of the mind are benumbed half the year.

> *The History of Emily Montague* (1769). This "may be described as the first Canadian novel, and indeed the first American one," according to Carl F. Klinck in his 1961 edition of Mrs. Brooke's work.

## Brooke, Rupert
And high and grey and serene above the morning lay the citadel of Quebec. Is there any city in the world that stands so nobly as Quebec?

> \*

The outcome of it all was a vague general impression that Montreal consists of banks and churches. The people in this city spend much of their time laying up their riches in this world or the next.

> \*

But what Ottawa leaves in the mind is a certain graciousness—dim, for it expresses a barely materialized national spirit— and the sight of kindly English-looking faces, and the rather lovely sound of the soft Canadian accent in the streets.

> \*

Toronto (pronounce *T'ranto,* please) is difficult to describe. It has an individuality, but an elusive one; yet not through any queerness or difficult shade of eccentricity; a subtly normal, and indefinably obvious personality. It is a healthy, cheerful city (by modern standard); a clean-shaven, pink-faced, respectably dressed, fairly energetic, unintellectual, passably sociable, well-to-do, public-school-and-varsity sort of city.

> \*

But Toronto—Toronto is the subject. One must say something—*what* must one say about Toronto? What can one? What has anybody ever said? It is impossible to give it anything but commendation. It is not squalid like Birmingham, or cramped like Canton, or scattered like Edmonton, or sham like Berlin, or hellish like New York, or tiresome like Nice. It is all right. The only depressing thing is that it will always be what it is, only larger, and that no Canadian city can ever be anything better or different. If they are good they become Toronto.

> \*

Canada is a live country, live, but not, like the States, kicking.

> \*

They told me, casually, that there was nothing but a few villages between me and the North Pole . . . it gives me a thrill to hear it.

> \*

Canadian stars are remote and virginal.

> \*

It is that feeling of fresh loneliness that impresses itself before any detail of the wild. The soul—or the personality—seems to have indefinite room to expand. There is no one else within reach, there never has been anyone; no one else is *thinking* of the lake and hills you see before you. They have no tradition, no names even; they are only pools of water and lumps of earth, some day, perhaps to be clothed with loves and memories and the comings and going of men, but now dumbly waiting their Wordsworth or their Acropolis to give them individuality, and a soul.

> *Letters from America* (1916). The English poet visited North America in 1913. He wrote to Wilfrid Gibson: "The only poet in Canada was very nice to me in Ottawa. Canada's a bloody place for a sensitive real poet like this to live all his life in." The poet was Duncan Campbell Scott.

Lord, Lord—I've not really given the Canadians much chance yet. But my impression *is* that they have all the faults of the Americans, and not their one lovely and redeeming virtue, "hospitality." [Letter to Edward Marsh from Ottawa, July 9, 1913]

＊

It is slightly uncanny; like everything in these great lakes. I have a perpetual feeling that a lake ought not to be this size. A river and a little lake and an ocean are natural; but not these creatures. They are too big, and too smooth, and too sunny; like an American business man. [Letter to Edmund Gosse, July 27, 1913, written while sailing Lake Superior]

＊

You can't think how sick one's heart gets for something old. For weeks I have not seen or touched a town so old as myself. Horrible! Horrible! They gather round me & say, "In 1901 Calgary had 139 inhabitants, now it has 75,000"; & so forth. I reply, "My village is also growing. At the time of Julius Caesar it was a bare 300. Domesday Book gives it 347 and it is now close to 390." Which is ill-mannered of me. [Letter to Edward Marsh from Calgary, August 16, 1913]

＊

You think B.C. means before Christ. But it doesn't.

I'm sitting, wildly surmising, on the edge of the Pacific, gazing at mountains which are changing colour every two minutes in the most surprising way. Nature here is half Japanese. [Postcard to Sybil Pye from Victoria, September 12, 1913]

> *The Letters of Rupert Brooke* (1968), edited by Geoffrey Keynes. See also Samuel Butler.

## Brooker, Bertram

Are there many who realize, for example (especially the enthusiasts for universal standards), that books like those of Henry James, George Meredith and Joseph Conrad simply cannot be written by a man who has just breakfasted with an electric toaster at his elbow and whose morning meditation in the garden has been disturbed by ukulele-music out of the sky?

> "When We Awake!" *Yearbook of the Arts in Canada: 1928-29* (1929), edited by Bertram Brooker.

There lives in Toronto an artist, a native of France and a frequenter of Paris, who has not been long in Canada. I met him one day in a downtown store. He had come looking for a picture of a horse. After a few minutes chat he was accosted by a clerk, who knew him, and he mentioned his quest. In musical broken English he said:

"I want a picture of a 'orse."

When asked what kind of a horse and for what purpose, he very pleasantly explained:

"Tonight I give lecture to Art Students' League. I want to show that animal is beautiful because every part made for function, without ornament. In Paris I would show woman, but in Toronto I show a 'orse."

> "Nudes and Prudes," *Open House* (1931), edited by William Arthur Deacon and Wilfred Reeves.

## Brosnan, Jim

Canada has never had a major civil war. After hockey, Canadians would probably have found it dull.

> Former major league American pitcher,

quoted by Jack Batten in *Champions: Great Figures in Canadian Sport* (1971).

**Brossard, Philippe J.**
Canada has always been somebody's Eldorado.

*Sold American!* (1971).

**Brothers, Richard**
Nephew of the Almighty, Cousin of the Lord Jesus, Rightful King of England, Prince of the Hebrews, Lion of the Tribe of Judah, anointed to lead them to the Land of Canaan.

A few of the titles claimed by the religious fanatic who was born at Admiral's Cove, near Fermeuse, Newfoundland, on Christmas Day, 1757. Brothers believed the British people were descendants of the Ten Lost Tribes. He died in 1824 and so had no connection with the British-Israel-World Federation, founded in 1919. "The only place where Brothers made absolutely no impression on the Anglo-Saxon Israelites was in Newfoundland. At Admiral's Cove, where the Brothers family still lives, you had better not mention the name of Richard. They regard him as a dark stain on the escutcheon." Harold Horwood in *Newfoundland* (1969).

**Brown, A. Roy**
Our best effort was on the 21st when we fought Baron von Richthofen's "Circus" . . . among these was the Baron whom I shot down on our side of the lines. We did not lose anyone in that fight. It is going to have a great effect on the war in the air. . . .

Letter to his father J.M. Brown, written on April 27, 1918, six days after the most famous aerial dogfight of World War I, by its leading participant. Flying a "Sopwith Camel," RAF Captain Arthur Roy Brown, twenty-five, from Carleton Place, Ontario, was unaware that the all-red German plane in front of him was piloted by Captain Manfred von Richthofen himself — the "Red Baron," Germany's leading war hero who claimed victory over eighty Allied planes. Brown was on the tail of the "Fokker Triplane" in an attempt to re-

lieve a new flier, Second Lieutenant W. R. "Wop" May, whom Richthofen was attacking. So the order in the air—sometimes as low as tree-top level—was: May, Richthofen, Brown. Captain Brown fired; the "Fokker Triplane" nosedived and landed upright in British-held territory near Cappy, France. Medical reports later established that Richthofen had died of a single bullet wound from one of Brown's machine guns.

I certainly did try my very best to kill myself and from what they have told me I nearly succeeded. They gave me up for hopeless three or four times.

Letter to his father, August 1, 1918. After downing the "Red Knight," Captain Brown flew for a few more days, then his health broke. In July, he fell asleep while in the air and crashed, with serious injuries. Discharged from hospital a year later, he entered the paint business in Toronto.

**Brown, Dr. Alan**
Everything for the Baby. [Personal motto]

*

Cow's milk is for calves. [Frequent saying]

*

It moves direct from producer to consumer. The cats can't get at it. It doesn't have to be warmed up on a picnic. It comes in such cute containers. [List of reasons why mother's milk is superior to the cow's]

Remarks frequently made by Canada's pioneer pediatrician, quoted by Dorothy Sangster in *Maclean's Magazine*, August 1, 1952.

PABLUM. A palatable mixed cereal food, vitamin and mineral enriched. . . . Formula devised by Pediatric Research Foundation of Toronto to furnish not only high nutritive value, but also the Vitamin B-Complex and the mineral elements Calcium, Phosphorus, Iron and Copper. Requires no cooking. Add milk or water, hot or cold. Serve with milk or cream. Mead Johnson & Co. of Canada Ltd. Belleville, Ontario. Keep in cool dry place.

From the label on an early box of Pablum. The world's first vitamin-enriched cereal was devised by Dr. Frederick Tisdall, Dr. T.G.H. Drake and Dr. Alan Brown at the Hospital for Sick Children, Toronto, during the late 1920s. It was marketed in 1930 as Mead's Cereal by Mead Johnson. The pharmaceutical firm then developed a high-pressure process for precooking the cereal and renamed it Pablum (from the Greek "pabulum," food). Substantial royalties from the world-wide sale of Pablum are paid to the Hospital's Pediatrics Research Foundation.

**Brown, Audrey Alexandra**
Blue eyes, dark brown hair—rather curly—and a dimple in the left cheek. The eyes are very near-sighted and the hair is getting to have a great many white threads in it, but the dimple is still practically as good as new.

> Quoted by Martin Burrell in *Crumbs Are Also Bread* (1934), The Nanaimo-born versifier, then thirty, was supplying a description of herself.

**Brown, E.K.**
Canadian books may occasionally have had a mild impact outside Canada; Canadian literature has had none.

\*

A great art is fostered by artists and audience possessing in common a passionate and peculiar interest in the kind of life that exists in the country where they live.

> *On Canadian Poetry* (Revised Edition, 1944).

The notion that a whole literature can develop out of the happy employment of the odd moments of rather busy men is an unrealistic notion, and one that shows an alarming ignorance of the process by which great works are normally written.

> Quoted by John Gray in "Book Publishing," *Writing in Canada: Proceedings of the Canadian Writers' Conference, Queen's University, July 28-31, 1955* (1956), edited by George Whalley.

**Brown, Eric**
Whatever disturbs us is good, since it sets us thinking and acting to prove it either worthy or wrong. We can hope that Canadian art will always disturb us, because there can be no surer proof of its inherent vitality.

> "The Fine Arts," *Handbook of Canada: Issued by the Local Committee on the Occasion of the Meeting of the British Association for the Advancement of Science at Toronto, August, 1924* (1924).

**Brown, George**
Representation by Population.

> Plank in George Brown's platform in the election of 1851. The demand for "Rep by Pop" came ten years earlier when Upper and Lower Canada was united to form the Province of Canada. Eastern Canada demanded more seats because it had a larger population; ten years later western Canada made the same demand for the same reason. "Rep by Pop" was ultimately achieved with Confederation in 1867.

All right!! Confederation through at six o'clock this evening—constitution adopted—a creditable document—a complete reform of all the abuses and injustices we have complained of! Is it not wonderful? French Canadianism entirely extinguished.

> Letter scribbled to his wife Anne Brown at the conclusion of the Quebec Conference, October 27, 1864. Quoted by Ramsay Cook in *Canada and the French-Canadian Question* (1966).

Look, sir, at the map of the continent of America, and mark that island (Newfoundland) commanding the mouth of the noble river that almost cuts our continent in twain. Well, sir, that island is equal in extent to the kingdom of Portugal. Cross the straits to the main land, and you touch the hospitable shores of Nova Scotia, a country as large as the kingdom of Greece. Then mark the sister province of New Brunswick—equal in extent to Denmark and Switzerland combined. Pass up the river St. Lawrence to Lower Canada—a country as large as France. Pass on to Upper Canada, — twenty thousand square miles larger than Great Britain and Ireland put together. Cross over the continent to the shores of the Pacific, and you are in British Columbia, the land of golden promise,—equal in extent to the Austrian Empire. I speak not now of the vast Indian Territories that lie between —greater in extent than the whole soil of Russia—and that will ere long, I trust, be opened up to civilization under the auspices of the British American Confederation. [Cheers] Well, sir, the bold scheme in your hands is nothing less than to gather all these countries into one— to organize them all under one government, with the protection of the British flag, and in heartiest sympathy and affection with our fellow-subjects in the land that gave us birth. [Cheers] Our scheme is to establish a government that will seek to turn the tide of European emigration into this northern half of the American continent—that will strive to develop its great natural resources—and that will endeavour to maintain liberty, and justice, and Christianity throughout the land.

> Member for South Oxford, Legislative Assembly, Province of Canada, February 8, 1865.

In view of all the grand offices that are now talked of—governorships, premierships, and the like—I would rather be editor of *The Globe* with the hearty confidence of the great mass of the people of Upper Canada than to have the choice of them all.

> Brown retired from politics in 1867, after electoral defeat; six years later he accepted an appointment to the Senate.

**Brown, J.J.**
After some interesting bouncing about and experimentation during the early years, the Canadian automobile industry settled down to being a pale copy of that of the United States. For some reason, Canada has never even developed cars suited to its climate. Sweden, a much smaller country, much less endowed with resources, has developed at least two outstanding automobiles—the Saab and the Volvo—both uniquely de-

signed for the difficult Swedish climate, and both of these have enjoyed a good sale abroad, including Canada. The rigours of the Canadian climate would seem to demand a small, manoeuverable, well-heated automobile driven by an air-cooled engine. Since 1907, Canadian automobile manufacturers have generally provided large, heavy, slow-steering vehicles driven by water-cooled engines. These appear to be designed—if they are designed at all—for use at Palm Springs, California.

> *Ideas in Exile: A History of Canadian Invention* (1967).

The most important question facing Canada today is not bilingualism, nor is it cultural growth: it is the problem of economic backwardness which leaves us increasingly weak in competition with other nations.

> *The Inventors: Great Ideas in Canadian Enterprise* (1967).

**Brown, John**
My Dear Friend,
   I have called a *quiet* Convention in this place of true friends of freedom. Your attendance is earnestly requested on the 10th inst. . . .
   Your friend, John Brown.

> Letter to fellow abolitionists written in Chatham, Ontario, May 5, 1858. Quoted by J.C. Hamilton in "John Brown in Canada," *The Canadian Magazine*, December, 1894.

**Brown, Roza**
Gold has a mind of its own . . . gold is a woman. All the gold in the world is waiting for just one thing, for the right man to find it. . . . Maybe that is why I was never able to get my hands on it.

> "Try Kirkland Lake, east of Swastika," Roza Brown, the Budapest-born prospector - turned - boarding - house-operator advised Sir Harry Oakes, who did precisely that in 1912 and made a fortune. Quoted by Geoffrey Bocca in *The Life and Death of Sir Harry Oakes* (1959).

**Bruce, John**
Whereas, it is admitted by all men, as a fundamental principle, that the public

authority commands the obedience and respect of its subjects. It is also admitted, that a people, when it has no Government, is free to adopt one form of Government, in preference to another, to give or to refuse allegiance to that which is proposed. . . . Now, therefore, first, we, the representatives of the people, in Council assembled in Upper Fort Garry, on the twenty-fourth day of November, 1869, after having invoked the God of Nations, relying on these fundamental moral principles, solemnly declare, in the name of our constituents, and in our own names, before God and man, that, from the day on which the Government we had always respected abandoned us, by transferring to a strange power the sacred authority confined to it, the people of Rupert's Land and the North-West became free and exempt from all allegiance to the said Government. John Bruce, President. Louis Riel, Secretary.

> "Declaration of the People of Rupert's Land and the North-West," December 8, 1869. *Canada Sessional Papers* (1870).

### Bruhn, Erik
Mediocrity is the easiest thing in the world to achieve. Just start attacking the people who have been working like slaves to establish things, make money scarce, concentrate on errors of judgment rather than the successes and you'll get it sure enough. That's not criticism, you know, that's bitching and it's a very effective instrument of destruction.

> Quoted by John Fraser in *The Globe and Mail*, December 2, 1972.

### Brunet, Michel
What is nationalism? It is simply the manifestation of the natural and spontaneous solidarity that exists among members of a human group sharing a historical and cultural tradition from which the group derives its distinctive identity. This manifestation of solidarity is more or less conscious and more or less complete, according to the peculiar circumstances which have influenced and continue to condition the development of each collectivity.

> "The French Canadians' Search for a Fatherland," *Nationalism in Canada* (1966), edited by Peter Russell.

. . . the history of the Frenchman comes from the fact that they are there. It continues because they are there. When they are there no more, there will be no more history of them.

\*

I say that we cannot make a hero of Papineau. He died in his bed. All heroes should die young, and not in bed.

\*

The thing which amazes me is that I know perfectly well, as a historian, that there is corruption in any government—there's always corruption. It's bad when it's more than fifteen percent.

> Interviewed by Ramsay Cook in *The Craft of History* (1973), edited by Eleanor Cook.

### Bryan, William Jennings
You have a great country up here. And a great people, too.

> "Ideals," February 11, 1908, *Addresses Delivered before the Canadian Club of Toronto: Season of 1906-1907* (1908).

### Bryant, Arthur   See Field Marshal The Viscount Alanbrooke.

### Bryce, James
It is more to the advantage both of the United States and of the Canadians, that they should continue to develop independent types of political life and intellectual progress. Each may, in working out its own institutions, have something to teach the other. There is already too little variety on the American continent.

> *The American Commonwealth* (1888). Bryce was Britain's ambassador to the United States from 1907 to 1913.

Party seems to exist for its own sake. In Canada ideas are not needed to make parties, for these can live by heredity, and, like the Guelfs and Ghibellines of mediaeval Italy, by memories of past combats; attachments to leaders of such striking gifts and long careers, as were Sir John Macdonald and Sir Wilfrid Laurier, created a personal loyalty which exposed a man to reproach as a deserter when he voted against his party.

"Canada: An Actual Democracy," *Modern Democracies* (1921).

## Bryden, Ronald
Our trouble was that we wrote on the margins of history, trying to visualize ourselves from history's centre. We wanted to see ourselves with the eye of history, and at the same time this happened to be the eye of an English schoolmaster.

"Margin," *Canada: A Guide to the Peaceable Kingdom* (1970), edited by William Kilbourn.

## Buchan, Anne
It's not blood the Buchans have in their veins, it is ink.

Sister of John Buchan, Lord Tweedsmuir, the popular author who became governor general, quoted by John Cowan in *Canada's Governors-General 1867-1952* (1952).

## Buchan, John
You will be better Canadians for being Ukrainians.

Governor General Lord Tweedsmuir to a Ukrainian group in 1936, quoted by Elizabeth Wangenheim, "The Ukrainians: A Case Study of the 'Third Force,' " *Nationalism in Canada* (1966), edited by Peter Russell.

We can only pay our debt to the past by putting the future in debt to ourselves.

Address to the people of Canada on the coronation of George VI, May 12, 1937.

I need not remind you that there may be as much originality in applying an accepted creed to novel conditions as in inventing a new one.

"Lord Durham," *Canadian Historical Review*, March, 1939.

Man, according to Aristotle, is a political animal, but there is an exception in the case of a Governor-General. His views on public policy can only be the views of his Ministers. If he touches on the

subject he must confine himself to what may be called Governor-Generalities.

\*

A man can never have too many loyalties. [Address, Charlottetown, September, 1937]

*Canadian Occasions: Addresses* (1940).

In September 1939 at Ottawa I was got out of bed in the small hours of a Sunday morning to declare war on Germany on Canada's behalf, and had staying in the house at the time a son of the late Emperor of Austria!

*Memory Hold-the-Door* (1940).

You may trace to its lair the soft Chinook,
And the North Wind trail to the Barrens' floor;
But you'll always find, or I'm much mistook,
That some old Frenchman's done it before.

From "The Forerunners," a verse written in character from *The Long Traverse* (1941).

He must be a dull man indeed whose spirit is not fired by the consideration of the oldest, most populous, and most mature of our Colonies.

\*

Canada is essentially a country of the larger air, where men can still face the old primeval forces of Nature and be braced into vigour, and withal so beautiful that it can readily inspire that romantic patriotism which is one of the most priceless assets of a people. ["Canada," *The Spectator*, July 6, 1901]

\*

A country and a people without much glamour. [Informed he might be asked to become the next governor general, Buchan drew up a list of pros and cons; this is one of the cons, 1935]

\*

Whatever you wear, Mr. Aberhart, will be a social credit to Alberta. [Buchan's reply when William Aberhart inquired of the governor general what he should wear to the Coronation in 1937]

\*

. . . the North is altogether beyond the human scale and it has no cleanness and simplicity. I expected bleak moors and cold ice-gray waters. Instead I found a kind of coarse lushness—immense rivers pouring billions of dirty gallons to the ocean, too much coarse vegetation, an infinity of mud, and everywhere a superfluity of obscene insect life. The impression was not of a Nature beautiful and austere, though cold and hard, but of a Nature as coarsely exuberant as a typical forest.

*

It reminded me of nothing so much as the no-man's land between the trenches in the war—but a colossal no-man's land created in some campaign of demons—pitted and pocked with shell-holes from some infernal artillery.

*

It is impossible to describe the country, for it is built on a scale outside that of humanity. [Reaction to the north country around Great Slave Lake; Fort Providence, September, 1937]

*

One may be a little homesick for Oxfordshire here, but not for Scotland, for Canada is simply Scotland on an extended scale. [Letter to Stanley Baldwin, about 1938]

> Quoted by Janet Adam Smith in *John Buchan: A Biography* (1965). See also: Anne Buchan, Fernand Rinfret, Baron Tweedsmuir.

## Buchanan, Donald W.

The visual order in Canada today is certainly no longer based on simplicity, above all not on classical balance. The pattern is becoming instead one which can best be described as the strident juxtaposition of conflicting objects. It demands a new way of looking at things, an adjustment, an ability to learn to live with such incongruities as automobile factories in peach orchards. The examples are endless: the squat yellow block of a Shell gasoline station beside a graceful old stone mansion in Kingston; the soft-drink sign nailed on a fence before a roadside crucifix in the Gatineau hills; the dismembered bodies of obsolete Buicks, Fords and Chevrolets dumped to rot in a field alongside the vivid autumn foliage of a maple-sugar bush on the Island of Orleans; an expensively mani-

cured park in Toronto surrounded by the badly lettered advertisements of three sprawling commercial parking-lots. But why repeat what we all know?

> *A Nostalgic View of Canada* (1962).

## Buck, Tim

We did not come to the working class from communism. We came to communism from the working class. And we did not come to urge strikers by virtue of membership in the Communist Party. We became Communists because we participated in strikes.

> "An Indictment of Capitalism," Address to the Jury, November 12, 1931, at the trial of eight leaders of the CPC. *Our Fight for Canada: Selected Writings (1923-1959)* (1959).

If it's good enough for Moscow, it's good enough for me.

> Leader of the Communist Party of Canada to Joseph Salsberg who had just returned from the Soviet Union with doubts about the official explanation of the purge of Jewish writers in the 1950s. Quoted by Philip Sykes in *The Toronto Star*, November 10, 1972.

## Bucke, Richard Maurice

Cosmic Consciousness, then, is a higher form of consciousness than that possessed by the ordinary man.

*

The simple truth is, that there has lived on the earth, "appearing at intervals," for thousands of years among ordinary men, the first faint beginnings of another race; walking the earth and breathing the air with us, but at the same time walking another earth and breathing another air of which we know little or nothing, but which is, all the same, our spiritual life, as its absence would be our spiritual death. This new race is in the act of being born from us, and in the near future it will occupy and possess the earth.

> *Cosmic Consciousness: A Study in the Evolution of the Human Mind* (1901). This term for an ecstatic or mystical state of awareness was given currency, if not actually coined, by the superin-

tendent of the Asylum for the Insane, London, Ontario, in "Cosmic Consciousness," a paper read before the American Medico-Psychological Association, Philadelphia, May 18, 1894, and published later that year in *The Conservator*.

## Buckler, Ernest
Who needed books—when all their plots and all their wisdoms might be had, for the looking, in a cloud-burst or a smile? Who needed books, when he had memory?

*Ox Bells and Fireflies: A Memoir* (1968).

All the yachts you could build with your Canadian royalties you could sail in your bath tub.

Quoted by William French in *The Globe and Mail*, June 24, 1972.

It is a dictionary where the seasons look up their own meanings and test them. It is a sea-son where men can make their own helms.

*Nova Scotia: Window on the Sea* (1973), with photographs by Hans Weber.

## Buckley Jr., William F.
He is a dilettante. Now understand, when I say dilettante that as much might be said about Michelangelo. But in government I think he is essentially a dilettante.

The American conservative spokesman's estimate of Prime Minister Trudeau, in an interview with Larry Zolf, *Maclean's Magazine*, April, 1969.

## Buffalo Child Long Lance
See Sylvestre Clarke.

## Buies, Arthur
I enter into open war with all stupidities, all hypocrisies, all infamies; that is, I take upon my back three-quarters of mankind, which is a heavy burden.

*La Lanterne*, September, 1868. Quoted by Mason Wade in *The French Canadians: 1760-1967* (1968).

## Bujold, Geneviève
A diploma can't get you work in the theatre but a part can.

Quoted by Judy Klemesrud in *The Montreal Star*, November 18, 1967.

As soon as they say "Action," I can smell in the first two seconds whether I am going to get on the wave or not. And if you don't get on, you have this disastrous feeling. I can tell you—it's like love without climax.

Quoted by David Steele Turner in *Actors about Acting, Loving, Living, Life* (1972).

In order to be psychologically well, and in order to be fully creative, I think people need a strong political identity, a sense of territory. I don't even think it's a question that can be debated, it's a biological imperative. Quebec would not appear so disruptive to the, shall I say, order of Canada, if the rest of Canada were equally strong and concerned with its future.

*Maclean's Magazine*, August, 1973.

## Bull, William Perkins
*From Medicine Man to Medical Man* (1934)
*From Rattlesnake Hunt to Hockey* (1934)
*Spadunk; or, From Paganism to Davenport United* (1935)
*From Brock to Currie* (1935)
*From the Boyne to Brampton* (1936)
*From Strachan to Owen* (1938)
*From Macdonell to McGuigan* (1939)
*From Oxford to Ontario* (1941)

These are the titles of full-length books published by William Perkins Bull, a wealthy Toronto eccentric, and written by his stable of researchers and writers. The subtitles of these regional histories and historical biographies are even stranger and may be found in Reginald Eyre Watters' *A Checklist of Canadian Literature and Background Materials: 1628-1960* (Second Edition, 1972). Titles of other works, either published or projected, include: *From Penalties to Pedigrees*; *From Adam to Us*; *From Fence to Fireplace*; *Downsview, or From Saddlebags to Radio*; *From Forest to FarmStead*; *From Rebellion to Confederation*; *From Home to High School*; *From Humming Bird to Eagle*; *From Amphibians to Reptiles*.

## Buller, A.H. Reginald

There was a young lady named Bright
Whose speed was far faster than light;
   She set out one day
   In a relative way
And returned on the previous night.

Perhaps the most famous of all limericks is "Relativity." William S. Baring-Gould in *The Lure of the Limerick: An Uninhibited History* (1968) writes: "The late Professor A.H. Reginald Buller, F.R.S., onetime professor of botany at the University of Manitoba and a world-wide authority on fungi, found time to write many limericks, and not a few of his later years were spent in trying to establish his authorship of a famous verse which first appeared, over his signature, in the English comic weekly, *Punch*.

" 'I don't mind the credit going to Bishops, Wits, Established Authors and even that finest of English writers, Anon.,' Dr. Buller once complained, 'but I do wish they'd get the last line right and preserve the alliteration in the second!' Dr. Buller also wrote a sequel to 'Relativity.' "

To her friends said the Bright one in chatter,
"I have learned something new about matter:
   My speed was so great,
   Much increased was my weight,
Yet I failed to become any fatter!"

Baring-Gould is wrong about one point. The limerick was published in *Punch*, December 19, 1923, but it appeared anonymously; nor is Buller's name listed in the annual index to the publication. (The *Punch* version is the one published above; Baring-Gould's version differs in two particulars: in the third line the verb is "went" rather than "set"; in the fifth line the preposition "on" is absent.) For other verses in this genre, see Anonymous: One Dozen Limericks.

There is no more exhilarating sight in the west than the prospect of the binders at work on the sea-wide, sky-skirted prairie, with the golden grain gleaming under the August sun and above and about all the cloudless blue dome of heaven. And when the last sheaf has been cut and the binders are silent, how splendid is the view across the gently rolling stubble fields: stook beyond stook, stook beyond stook, for a quarter of a mile, for half a mile, and still more stooks as far as the eye can see, stooks cresting the distant horizon, ten thousand stooks all waiting to be threshed and each with its promise of bread, the gift of the New World to the Old.

"Wheat in the West," *Handbook of Canada: Issued by the Local Committee on the Occasion of the Meeting of the British Association for the Advancement of Science at Toronto, August, 1924* (1924).

## Buller, Charles

Mr. Mother Country.

With this phrase Charles Buller, the chief secretary of Lord Durham in 1838, ridiculed James Stephen, the permanent under-secretary for the colonial department, and others who felt that responsible government would interfere with British parliamentary government of the colonies. The phrase first appeared in articles Buller wrote for the *Colonial Gazette* in December of 1839 and February of 1840. " 'Mr. Mother Country' became a by-word in speeches and political literature dealing with the 'irresponsible' system of government in the colonies," explained Norah Story in *The Oxford Companion to Canadian History and Literature* (1967).

## Bulwer Lytton, Sir Edward

See Lytton, Sir Edward Bulwer.

## Bunyan, Paul

But it happened Paul was asleep in his cradle when they went to get him, and they had to send for the British navy and it took seven hours of bombardin' to wake him up. And then when Paul stepped out of his cradle it made such a swell it caused a seventy-five foot tide in the Bay of Fundy and several villages was swept away and seven of the invincible English warships was sunk to the bottom of the sea.

Well, Paul got out of his cradle then, and that saved Nova Scotia from becomin' an island, but the tides in the Bay of Fundy is just as high as they ever was.

Esther Shephard's *Paul Bunyan* (1924). Bunyan, the legendary lumberjack of giant stature, and his fabulous blue ox Babe, are said to be of French-Canadian origin.

## Burgess, Anthony
John Kenneth Galbraith and Marshall McLuhan are the two greatest modern Canadians the United States has produced.

> Quoted by Peter C. Newman in "Home Country" (1971), *Home Country: People, Places, and Power Politics* (1973).

## Burke, Edmund
No free country can keep another country in slavery. The price they pay for it will be their own servitude. The constitution proposed is one which men will never, and never ought to bear. . . . By being made perpetual, it is evident that this constitution is meant to be both an instrument of tyranny to the Canadians, and an example to others of what they have to expect; at some time or other it will come home to England. . . . Canadians will become a dangerous instrument in the hands of those who wish to destroy English liberty in every part of our possessions.

> The English statesman was commenting on the Quebec Act of 1774 in the British House of Commons. Quoted by Chester Martin in *Empire and Commonwealth: Studies in Government and Self-Government in Canada* (1929).

The province of Nova Scotia was the youngest and the favourite child of the board. Good God! What sums the nursing of that ill-thriven, hard-visaged, and ill-favoured brat, has cost to this wittol nation! Sir, this colony has stood us in a sum of not less than seven hundred thousand pounds. To this day it has made no repayment. It does not even support those offices of expenses, which are miscalled its government; the whole of that job still lies upon the patient, callous shoulders of the people of England.

> "Speech on Economic Reform," delivered in the British House of Commons,

February 11, 1780. *The Speeches of the Right Hon. Edmund Burke, with Memoir and Historical Introductions* (1853), edited by James Burke. A "wittol" is a contented cuckold.

## Burnett, J.R.  See Gillis Purcell.

## Burns, E.L.M.
I sometimes wonder if there is any other sphere of human activity in which so many fine words have been uttered, and so little achieved as in the pursuit of disarmament and a stable peace.

\*

How can influence be weighted anyway? Has not somebody said that influence is what you think you have, so long as you do not try to use it?

> *A Seat at the Table: The Struggle for Disarmament* (1972), by Lieutenant-General E.L.M. Burns, C.C., D.S.O., O.B.E., M.C.

## Burns, Pat
Call me a rancher.

> When asked what he did, the Calgary millionaire who in 1890 founded P. Burns and Co. Ltd., the largest meat-packing plant in the world, would make this reply. Quoted by Grant MacEwan, "Cattle King Burns," *Fifty Mighty Men* (1958).

## Burns, Robert
To the Right Honourable the Earl of Breadalbane, President of the Right Honourable and Honourable the Highland Society, which met on the 23rd of May last, at the Shakespeare, Covent Garden, to concert ways and means to frustrate the desires of five hundred Highlanders, who, as the Society were informed by Mr. Mackenzie of Applecross, were so audacious as to attempt an escape from their lawful lords and masters, whose property they were, by emigrating from the lands of Mr. M'Donald of Glengarry to the wilds of Canada in search of that fantastic thing—LIBERTY.

> Preface, "Address of Beelzebub to the President of the Highland Society" (1796).

\*

The first I'll name, they ca'd him Caesar,
Was keepit for his Honour's pleasure:
His hair, his size, his mouth, his lugs,
Shew'd he was nane o'Scotland's dogs;
But whalpit some place far abroad,
Whare sailors gang to fish for Cod.

> From "The Two Dogs: A Tale" (1786).
> *The Complete Works of Robert Burns*
> (1868), edited by Alexander Smith.

### Burns, Tommy
In Love you manifest Health, Peace,
Happiness and Abundant Life.

> Tommy Burns's calling card; on the re-
> verse side it read: "Tommy Burns,
> former world's heavyweight boxing
> champion—a demonstrator of Universal
> Love." Burns was born Noah Brusso in
> Hanover, Ontario, and after holding the
> world heavyweight boxing title in 1906
> became a noted evangelist. Quoted by
> W.A. Hewitt in *Down the Stretch* (1958).

### Burpee, Lawrence J.
Canada stands alone among the nations
—well, not quite alone, she ranks with
Siam and Abyssinia. None of the three
has a National Library.

> "A Plea for a Canadian National Li-
> brary," *Canadian Historical Review*,
> June, 1920.

Any Canadian who turns up his nose at
a Canadian book because it is a Canadian book, is a foule byrd.

> "Quotable Quotes," *Canadian Author
> and Bookman*, March, 1943.

### Burr, Aaron
I intend to see the Inside of it if possible.

> The future vice-president of the United
> States, November 22, 1775, while serving
> under Benedict Arnold, before the Cita-
> del of Quebec. Quoted by Herbert S.
> Parmet and Marie B. Hecht in *Aaron
> Burr: Portrait of an Ambitious Man*
> (1967).

### Burr, Raymond
Sure I curl. We all curl in Canada.

> The portrayer of Perry Mason and Iron-
> side on TV was born in New Westmin-

ster, British Columbia, in 1917. He made
his professional début in a Vancouver
stock company at twelve and then
played heavies in Hollywood for years.
Quoted by Jack Miller in *The Toronto
Star*, October 17, 1972.

### Burrell, Martin
A sturdy nationalism, excellent within
bounds, may have the defects of its
qualities, become aggressive, clamant
and even absurd. That Canadian writers
and Canadian artists have made valuable contributions to literature and art
will hardly be disputed. Yet I like better
the term "Literature in Canada" than
"Canadian Literature"; "Art in Canada" better than "Canadian Art." Art is
universal, let us not become narrow or
cramping in our phraseology.

> *Betwixt Heaven and Charing Cross*
> (1928).

### Burton, Dennis
Procrastination has a flag: on it, it says,
"I forgot."

\*

Once I taught in Thunder Bay. Thunder Bay has one of the largest mental
hospitals in all of Canada. It was impossible to buy a 6B soft drawing pencil in
what was Fort William and Port Arthur,
now called Thunder Bay. Somehow
there's a relationship between no pen-
cils but plenty of nuts.

> Remarks made in August, 1973, by the
> Toronto artist and teacher.

### Burton, Richard
I have always had a soft spot for Canada, and particularly Toronto. People
there were very kind to us at that time.
When people ask me where I'd like to
open in a play, I always say Toronto.
I've always been lucky there.

> The Welsh-born actor starred in *Ham-
> let* in Toronto in 1964, and in Montreal
> married Elizabeth Taylor. *The Toronto
> Star*, November 18, 1972.

### Bush, Douglas
Our standards of judgment not only
lead us to worship the small but to
neglect the big.

*
The salvation of Canadian literature would be a nation-wide attack of writer's cramp lasting at least a decade.

"Making Literature Hum," *The Canadian Forum*, December, 1926.

## Butchart, Jenny
Pleace Carve Initials Here.

Sign attached to a tree in Butchart Gardens, Victoria. Quoted by David MacDonald in "Jenny Butchart's Garden of Wonders," *Canada—This Land, These People: A Reader's Digest Collection* (1968).

## Butler, Samuel
I have got some really charming literary pabulum among the French Canadians. I was not prepared to find myself so completely in a French and not an English country. I am to stay with an "habitant" tomorrow, in order that I may go to mass on Sunday and inspire the village with confidence in the company. Madame Vigneau has had so many lodgers since we started, that she has had a four-dollar mass said for the company. This is the best mass that money can buy in these parts; the cheapest is twenty-five cents or one shilling; the average is about half a dollar. I have instructed our agent to have an occasional mass said on our account, about six two-dollar masses a year for each set of week. This I am told will be about the right thing. There are bears and wolves and great cariboo deer in our woods—as big as oxen but I have not seen any. The trip is just what I wanted to set me up in health.

Writing to Miss E.M.A. Savage from St. Lawrence Hall, Montreal, July 10, 1874. *Letters Between Samuel Butler and Miss E.M.A. Savage: 1871-1885* (1935), edited by Geoffrey Keynes and Brian Hill. As Daniel F. Howard explained in *The Correspondence of Samuel Butler with His Sister May* (1962): "Butler was on the first of three unsuccessful trips to Canada as representative of the English stockholders in the Canada Tanning Extract Company. The extract tanned leather cheaply, but to such a nauseous colour that it could not be sold."

A man, a true Montrealer, told me he had a yearning to get away from civilization; I said we were all of us given to discontent, and seldom knew *when we had got* what we wanted. He did not see it, and I did not mean that he should, but I felt better for having said it.

Comment in his notebook, 1875, *The Note-Books of Samuel Butler* (1915), edited by Henry Festing Jones.

. . . and I shall be glad if you succeed, but then you will have to stay in Canada, and be killed by bad cooking and *ennui*.

Letter replying to Miss Savage's intimation that she might join Butler in Montreal, January 21, 1875. *Letters Between Samuel Butler and Miss E.M.A. Savage: 1871-1885* (1935), edited by Geoffrey Keynes and Brian Hill.

The City of Montreal is one of the most rising and, in many respects, most agreeable on the American continent, but its inhabitants are as yet too busy with commerce to care greatly about the masterpieces of old Greek art. In the Montreal Museum of Natural History I came upon two plaster casts, one of the Antinous and the other of the Discobolus—not the good one, but in my poem, of course, I intend the good one—banished from public view to a room where were all manner of skins, plants, snakes, insects, etc., and, in the middle of these, an old man stuffing an owl.

"Ah," said I, "so you have some antiques here; why don't you put them where people can see them?"

"Well, sir," answered the custodian, "you see they are rather vulgar."

He then talked a great deal and said his brother did all Mr. Spurgeon's printing.

The dialogue—perhaps true, perhaps imaginary, perhaps a little of the one and a little of the other—between the writer and this old man gave rise to the lines that follow:

Stowed away in a Montreal lumber room
The Discobolus standeth and turneth
      his face to the wall;
Dusty, cobweb-covered, maimed, and set
      at naught,

Beauty crieth in an attic and no man regardeth:
> O God! O Montreal!

Beautiful by night and day, beautiful in summer and winter,
Whole or maimed, always and alike beautiful—
He preached gospel of grace to the skins of owls
And to one who seasoneth the skins of Canadian owls:
> O God! O Montreal!

When I saw him I was wroth and I said, "O Discobolus!
Beautiful Discobolus, a Prince both among gods and men!
What doest thou there, how camest thou hither, Discobolus,
Preaching gospel in vain to the skins of owls?"
> O God! O Montreal!

And I turned to the man of skins and said unto him, "O thou man of skins,
Wherefore hast thou done thus to shame the beauty of the Discobolus?"
But the Lord had hardened the heart of the man of skins
And he answered, "My brother-in-law is haberdasher to Mr. Spurgeon."
> O God! O Montreal!

"The Discobolus is put here because he is vulgar,
He has neither vest nor pants with which to cover his limbs;
I, Sir, am a person of most respectable connections—
My brother-in-law is haberdasher to Mr. Spurgeon."
> O God! O Montreal!

Then I said, "O brother-in-law to Mr. Spurgeon's haberdasher,
Who seasonest also the skins of Canadian owls,
Thou callest trousers 'pants,' whereas I call them 'trousers,'
Therefore thou art in hell-fire and may the Lord pity thee!"
> O God! O Montreal!

"Preferrest thou the gospel of Montreal to the gospel of Hellas,
The gospel of thy connection with Mr. Spurgeon's haberdashery to the gospel of the Discobolus?"

Yet none the less blasphemed he beauty saying, "The Discobolus hath no gospel,
But my brother-in-law is haberdasher to Mr. Spurgeon."
> O God! O Montreal!

"A Psalm of Montreal" was written in 1875 and first appeared in *The Spectator*, May 18, 1878. "Butler often recited it and gave copies of it to his friends," wrote Henry Festing Jones in his edition of *The Note-Books of Samuel Butler* (1926). Rupert Brooke visited Montreal in 1913 and observed (in *Letters from America* [1916]): "I made my investigations in Montreal. I have to report that the Discobolus is very well, and, nowadays, looks the whole world in the face, almost quite unabashed."

## Butler, Sir William Francis
REMEMBER BUTLER, 69TH REGIMENT.

Butler sent this terse cable to Colonel Garnet Wolseley, who was organizing the Red River Expedition in 1870, then immediately left England for Montreal, where Wolseley agreed to take him on as an intelligence officer. The cable is reproduced in Field-Marshal Viscount Wolseley's *The Story of a Soldier's Life* (1903). Butler reproduces a politer form of the message in *The Great Lone Land* (1872): "PLEASE REMEMBER ME. BUTLER, 69TH FOOT." Cited by Edward McCourt in *Remember Butler: The Story of Sir William Butler* (1967).

Going one morning to the nearest telegraph station, I sent the following message under the Atlantic to America: "To ———, Winnipeg Expedition. Please remember me." When words cost at the rate of four shillings each, conversation and correspondence become of necessity limited. In the present instance I was only allowed the use of ten words to convey address, signature, and substance, and the five words of my message were framed both with a view to economy and politeness, as well as in a manner which by calling for no direct answer still left undecided the great question of success.

*

. . . it needs but little cause to recall

again to the wanderer the image of the immense meadows where, far away at the portals of the setting sun, lies the Great Lone Land.

*The Great Lone Land: A Narrative of Travel and Adventure in the North-West of America* (1872). See also Karkakonias.

Row, my boys, row away,
Cowards behind may stay,
Bend to the strain, man!
Miles, as they rise and sink,
Knock off another link,
From Gordon's chain, man!

Rowing song written by Butler for the Canadian voyageurs recruited to take the British forces up the Nile to rescue General Charles Gordon, "the half-mad hero of Khartoum," 1885. They arrived three days too late. Quoted by James Morris in *Heaven's Command: An Imperial Progress* (1973).

**Byng, Lord**
When I first took command of the Canadian forces, someone said to me, "For goodness sake, never patronize the Canadians," to which I replied, "By Heaven, I would as soon patronize a wasp's nest." [Address by Lord Byng of Vimy soon after assuming duties as governor general, August 11, 1921]

Gentlemen, I never mean to write a book. I promise you that. But if ever I did have to write a book I should rather copy the lines of Thomas Hobbes in his *Leviathan*. He wrote, as you probably well know, about the Divine Right of Kings. I should write about the Divine Right of Byngs. And one of the greatest of their Divine Rights should be that they were exempt from making speeches, because they cannot do it.

"Address," August 29, 1921, *Addresses Delivered before the Canadian Club of Toronto: Season of 1921-22* (1922).

There they stood on Vimy Ridge that 9th day of April, 1917, men from Quebec stood shoulder to shoulder with men from Ontario, men from the Maritimes with men from British Columbia, and there was forged a nation tempered by

the fires of sacrifice and hammered on the anvil of high adventure. [Address at Calgary in tribute to the Canadian Corps, Summer, 1922]

*

You know, the Governor-General cannot escape the word "constitutional." You people may say that the government is all right if it votes to your way of thinking but I must say it is all right no matter how it votes. [Address of the governor general to the Canadian Club of Hamilton, Summer, 1923]

Quoted by John Cowan in *Canada's Governors-General 1867-1952* (1952).

My Prime Minister this morning requested me to grant him dissolution. I refused fully and completely realizing the responsibility I was taking. I was solely guided by what I considered to be the best interests of Canada.

Telegram to the secretary of State for dominion affairs, Ottawa, June 28, 1926. Reproduced by Roger Graham in *The King-Byng Affairs, 1926: A Question of Responsible Government* (1967).

**Byng, Viscountess Marie Evelyn**
I sometimes wonder if the Canadian liking for bright colours isn't the outcome of that prolonged session of white during the winter months.

*Up the Stream of Time* (1946).

**Byron, Lord**
Some thought it was Mount Aetna, some the highlands
Of Canada, Cyprus, Rhodes, or other islands.

*

But words are things, and a small drop of ink,
Falling like dew, upon a thought, produces
That which makes thousands, perhaps millions think. . . .

Third Canto, *Don Juan* (1818-24), *Byron's Poems* (1963), edited by V. de Sola Pinto. Charles A. Bowman, the Ottawa editor, took credit for selecting the last three lines to adorn the fireplace of the Press Gallery Lounge, Parliament Buildings, Ottawa, 1920.

# C

## Cable, Howard
The beaver is a good national symbol for Canada. He's so busy chewing he can't see what's going on.

> Quoted by Barrie Mason in *The Toronto Star*, July 31, 1971.

## Cabot, John
Terra Primum Vista.

> "The first-seen land." The Genoese navigator made his historic landfall at Cape Bonavista, Newfoundland, June 24, 1497. John Quinpool in *First Things in Acadia: The Birthplace of a Continent* (1936) ranks this "three-word account of the discovery of America" with "'veni, vidi, vici' and other gems of brevity."
>
> When Cabot returned with news of his discovery, Henry VII made payment of £10 "to hym that founde the new Isle," August 10-11, 1497. His son was Sebastian Cabot.

## Cabot, Sebastian
I began therefore to saile toward the Northwest, not thinking to finde any other land then that of Cathay, and from thence to turne toward India, but after certaine dayes I found that the land ranne towards the North, which was to mee a great displeasure.

> "A Discourse of Sebastian Cabot" (1508-1509), Richard Hakluyt's *The Principal Navigations, Voyages, Traffiques, and Discoveries of the English Nation* (1589), edited by Edmund Goldsmid in 1889. See also Petrus Martyr.

## Caesar, Irving
Swift as the breeze / Was the race on the skis / I would bet on you / In Saskatoon, Saskatchewan / I'd walk ahead / While you rode on the sled / That I'd fetch you on / In Saskatoon, Saskatchewan.

> A verse of "Saskatchewan" by Irving Caesar, Sammy Lerner, and Gerald Marks, a popular musical number in 1936.

## Cahan, Charles H.
No Navy made in London; no reciprocity made in Washington.

> Slogan coined by Charles H. Cahan for Robert Borden whose Conservatives in the election of September 21, 1911, defeated Laurier's Liberals who favoured establishing a navy and reciprocity with the United States. Quoted by Mason Wade in *The French Canadians: 1760-1967* (1968).

I am not a Progressive Conservative, I am a continuing Conservative.

> Secretary of State from 1930 to 1935 in the R.B. Bennett government, when the Conservative party became the Progressive Conservative party in 1942.

## Cahill, Leo
When the tape is on, and the band is playing, we'll be there.

> Coach of the Toronto Argonauts football team in the 1960s.

It will take an act of God to beat us on Saturday.

> Prediction made at the tail end of the 1969 football season by the Toronto Argonauts coach. (The Argos lost.) *Goodbye Argos* (1973), with Scott Young.

## Calder, Ritchie
To me, the military in the Arctic are just the pioneers of its development; the explorers of its wastelands and the trailblazers of modern communications.

> *Men Against the Frozen North* (1957).

## "Calgary Bob" Edwards
See Bob Edwards.

## Callaghan, Morley
. . . there is no spiritual gratification to be found simply in the sale of any book, no matter what kind of tripe, in Canada,

any more than there is in the sale of a package of tea; and that anyway the problem with Canada is not that Canadians don't buy books as well as the people of other countries—in terms of comparative population Canadians do buy books: the trouble is that there is not much sense of adventure in reading in our people: they go for the books that have a big sale in other countries.

"The Plight of Canadian Fiction," *University of Toronto Quarterly*, January, 1938.

To the professor from St. Louis who asked me why I lived in Toronto, I tried saying casually, "Why, I was born in Toronto." For a moment he was silent and I thought I might have found the right easy answer. "How odd," he said finally. "You're the only writer I know who lives in the place where he was born."

*

If you stay in Toronto, the longing remains deep in the soul, and since it can't be satisfied you can't be wearied, and your mind and your imagination should become like a caged tiger. O Toronto! O my tiger city!

"Why Toronto?" (1947), *Our Sense of Identity* (1954), edited by Malcolm Ross.

No one is compelled by anyone else to be a writer. It is a matter of free choice, and he who makes the choice knows that he is dooming himself to a hand-to-hand existence. I am speaking now of the honest writer. There are two kinds of writers: the one who tries to see the world out of his own eyes and the other one, the commercial writer, who tries to see the world out of the eyes of others.

*

There is only one trait that marks the writer. He is always watching. It's a trick of mind and he is born with it.

*

Let the writer then remember his special function. His job is to be concerned with the spirit and heart of man in these times when the general consensus of opinion seems to be that man has very little spirit at all.

"Novelist," *Writing in Canada: Proceedings of the Canadian Writers' Con-*ference, *Queen's University, 28-31 July, 1955* (1956), edited by George Whalley.

In my candid opinion I was the best writer in America in the Thirties.

Quoted by Barbara Moon in "The Second Coming of Morley Callaghan," *Maclean's Magazine*, December 3, 1960.

My old theme. Nothing more; the wonder of the thing in itself. Right for me.

*

"Whatever you do, don't let anyone around here tell you anything." [Hemingway's advice to Callaghan in Toronto]

*That Summer in Paris: Memoirs of Tangled Friendships with Hemingway, Fitzgerald and Others* (1963).

A country may have great corporations, but if it has no literature it is a country that has no soul. It is a shop keeper's society. The new nationalists, it seems to me, are concerned only with who is minding the store.

Speech accepting the Royal Bank Award, June 15, 1970. Quoted by John Metcalf in *Sixteen by Twelve* (1970).

Yet it is true that this land has a group of cranky losers. Again and again they surface, as they did last year, to complain that Canada is not the British America of their grandfathers' time. Yet how could it be so? If only they would look at the country in all its wild grandeur with all its new people and see that such a land must always be changing and becoming something new, and always with a new beauty in its changing face!

*

Everyone seemed to be happily free from all sense of moral outrage. All over the world imaginative intellectuals who know that the glory of man is in his compassion, his capacity for disinterested goodness and his concern for the human condition, seemed to be saying to each other, "If we could only get another good night's sleep." And while they slept —and who knows but that it was good that they sleep—the hard-hatted intellectuals did business, always, of course, leaving their options open.

The hard heads in Moscow, who smother their Solzhenitsyns, had no trouble understanding their tribal brothers in Washington and making deals. And the Washington pragmatists had no trouble understanding the orthodoxy of the Chinese.

> "Canada: 'Always a New Beauty in Its Changing Face,'" *The Toronto Star*, December 30, 1972.

The real friend of this country is the guy who believes in *excellence,* seeks for it, fights for it, defends it, and tries to produce it.

*

The thing is that you must not have a kind of nationalism which is an insistence on the protection of the third-rate, do you see? All you should say is, I know it's excellent, and the world will discover it *is* excellent. They'll discover it's Canadian, because they'll ask where it came from.

> Interviewed by Donald Cameron in *Conversations with Canadian Novelists* (1973). See also Hugh Garner and Robert Weaver.

**Callières, Louis-Hector, Chevalier de**
I bury the hatchet in a deep hole, and over the hole I place a great rock, and over the rock I turn a river, that the hatchet may never be dug up again.

> The governor of New France during a peace parley with Indian chiefs, Montreal, 1700. Quoted by Francis Parkman in *Count Frontenac and New France Under Louis XIV* (1877).

**Callwood, June**
Maternal dislike is more crippling than clubs.

> "The Needs of the Young," *Probings: A Collection of Essays Contributed to the Canadian Mental Health Association for its Golden Jubilee 1918-1968* (1968).

**Calvert, Sir George**
Pro Patria et Avalonia

> The first Baron Baltimore was granted a royal charter for a plantation called "the province of Avalon" located in present-day Avalon Peninsula, Newfoundland, April 7, 1623. To mark the

occasion, Sir George had a coin struck with the above motto, "For Country and Avalon." His ship was named *The Ark of Avalon.* When he chose the Welsh word for "Isle of Apples," he may have had in mind the western regions to which the dying King Arthur sailed.

**Cameron, Agnes D.**
They wanted English breakfast tea, superior rifles and ammunition, and a special brand of tobacco. Failing any or all of these, it was in vain that the Factor displayed before them the wares of John Bull, Uncle Sam, or Johnny Canuck, or any seductive lure made in Germany.

> An early use of Johnny Canuck as the personification of Canada. *The New North: Being Some Account of a Woman's Journey through Canada and the Arctic* (1909).

**Cameron, Colin**
These young men will not enlist. How can we expect them to go out to defend their destitution?

> Attributed to the M.P. for Nanaimo-The Islands when World War II was declared in 1939.

**Cameron, Donald**
Good things flow from the status quo.

> Meant ironically. "Books," *Maclean's Magazine,* June, 1971.

**Cameron, George Frederick**
The good still moveth towards the good:
  The ill still moveth towards the ill:
  But who affirmeth that we will
Not form a nobler brotherhood

When communists, fanatics, those
  Who howl their *"vives"* to Freedom's name
  And yet betray her unto shame,
Are dead and coffined with her foes.

> Last two stanzas of "In After Days," *Lyrics on Freedom, Love and Death* (1887).

**Cameron, Gordon**
You can't drive a team of horses with reins 4,000 miles long. By the time you

give the signal, you've missed the turn.

> Commissioner of the Yukon, quoted by Don Sawatsky in "The Yukon—Canadians or Colonists?" *Canada Month*, July, 1967.

**Cameron, William**  See Ian Adams.

**Camp, Dalton**
It's time for a Diefenbaker Government.

> Campaign slogan for the 1957 election, devised by the Toronto advertising executive to play down the party and play up the leader.

In the trackless wastes of politics, men lose their purpose, and the stars by which they once steered vanish in the bottomless sky of other men's aspirations. They wander like nomads, from oasis to oasis, quenching their thirst from the wells of power and warming themselves by the abandoned fires of those who have come and gone before.

> *Gentlemen, Players and Politicians* (1970). See also Alvin Hamilton.

**Campbell, Charles**
It is significant that Canada has been traditionally personified as a woman, Miss Canada; while the U.S. has been imaged not only as a male but as a skinny, scheming, obviously tight-sphinctered yankee trader. There is the fear today that the Canadian alternative will be "penetrated" . . . by American capital and thus sufficiently raped of her culture as to leave her permanently barren or, worse, impregnated with the death-oriented American dream of possessive individualism. Miss Canada is seen in this context as a whore, allowing herself to be ravaged by American imperialism. There is no denying that the fear is valid, but Canada's femininity should not be rejected as a result; she must not be made to undergo a reverse Christine Jorgensen-type operation to become a thrusting, over-bearing male like her violator.

> "Canadian Dream," *Amex: The American Expatriates in Canada*, August-September, 1970.

**Campbell, Clarence**
One of my predecessors in my office expressed it very well when an American fan once asked him, "Why do you people have that silly arrangement with two intermissions? Every other sensible game only has one." He said, "We have two to enable the customers to rest up."

*

He who is given an inch and takes a yard should be kicked by the foot.

> "Hockey as a Business and as a Career" (1962), *Empire Club of Canada: Addresses 1962-63* (1963).

You can't take half a bottle of whiskey and fill it with water and have the same drink.

> Longtime president of the National Hockey League explaining the effect of expansion. Quoted by Trent Frayne in *The Toronto Star*, July 22, 1972.

**Campbell, Roy**
Against a regiment I oppose a brain
And a dark horse against an armoured train.

> This couplet by the South African poet inspired Alex Colville's famous canvas "Horse and Train" in 1954. "Dedication to Mary Campbell," *The Collected Poems of Roy Campbell* (1949).

**Campbell, Tom**
People just read headlines. The secret of political success is getting the press—with or against is immaterial as far as I'm concerned.

> Three-time mayor of Vancouver, quoted in *Maclean's Magazine*, June, 1973.

**Campbell, William Wilfred**
Along the line of smoky hills
    The crimson forest stands,
And all the day the blue-jay calls
    Throughout the autumn lands.

> First of three verses of "Indian Summer," *Lake Lyrics and Other Poems* (1889).

The true Imperialist is as good a Canadian as any. I protest against the local Independence man calling himself the only true Canadian. I would retort: "Little he knows of Canada, who only Canada knows."

"Imperialism in Canada" (1904), *Empire Club Speeches: Being Addresses Delivered before the Empire Club of Canada During Its Session of 1904-05* (1906). The "retort" would be stronger were it not an adaptation of Rudyard Kipling's famous line from "The English Flag": "And what should they know of England who only England know?"

It may not be realized abroad, but it is recognized in this country that a great deal of our political corruption has arisen in the first place in the local legislatures. We are

"A people for high dreaming meant,
But damned by too much government."

*Canada* (1907), illustrated by T. Mower Martin, described by Wilfred Campbell.

Vaster Britain.

The conception of Canada as a "Vaster Britain" was expressed perfectly in the title and subtitle to Campbell's *Sagas of Vaster Britain: Poems of the Race, the Empire, and the Divinity of Man* (1914). The poet aspired to become the first poet laureate of the British Empire. For the use of the adjective "vast" in the comparative form, see Sir William Mulock.

**Camsell, Dr. Charles**
See Dr. J. McIntosh Bell.

**Canada, Captain**   See Peter Evans.

**Canada Bill**
Herbert Asbury says it was Canada Bill who originated the story of the gambling partners marooned in a little river town a few years before the Civil War. Bill found a faro game and began to play. His partner urged him to stop. "The game is crooked," he said.
"I know," replied Bill, "but it's the only one in town."

*The Modern Handbook of Humour* (1967), edited by Ralph L. Wood.

**Canuck, Janey**
See Emily Ferguson Murphy.

**Canuck, Johnny**   See Leo Bachle.

**Caouette, Réal**
You don't have to understand Social Credit in order to vote for it.

\*

What have you got to lose?

"Il n'y a rien à perdre?" was the Créditiste slogan in the federal election of 1962 when the party under Caouette took one-third of the Quebec seats.

I'm a One Canada man and I've always been a One Canada man. I say the same thing from coast to coast. When I put my foot on the dog's tail in Halifax, it barks right in Vancouver.

*The Toronto Star*, October 7, 1971.

**Capellis, Sieur de**
I even dare advance that the island of Newfoundland and half of St. Domingue are worth much more than all of Canada; and I do not believe that we should hesitate to give it up entirely to obtain the other two establishments.

French minister of Marine in 1758, quoted by K.A. MacKirdy, J.S. Moir, and Y.F. Zoltvany in *Changing Perspectives in Canadian History: Selected Problems* (1967).

**Capone, Al**
I don't even know what street Canada is on.

Quoted in 1931 by Roy Greenaway in *The News Game* (1966). The Chicago gangster "at this . . . showed all the satisfaction of a wit who had spoken memorably and was gloating over it."

**Captain Canada**   See Peter Evans.

**Cardin, Lucien**
Mr. Cardin: I want the right hon. gentleman to tell the house about his participation in the Monseignor case when he was prime minister of this country.
Some hon. Members: Hear, hear.
Mr. Diefenbaker: I am not worried. Have your commission look into it. Put it on the agenda.
Some hon. Members: Oh, oh.

House of Commons, March 4, 1966. This exchange, sparked by the minister of Justice, ignited Canada's only sex-and-security scandal to date. "It was rumoured the Monseignor in question was a Catholic prelate caught smuggling heroin," Peter C. Newman joked in *The Distemper of Our Times: Canadian Politics in Transition: 1963-1968* (1969). See also Gerda Munsinger and Pierre Sévigny.

## Cardinal, Harold
Before I can be a usefully participating and contributing citizen I must be allowed to further develop a sense of pride and confidence in myself as an Indian. I must be allowed to be a red tile in the mosaic, not forced to become an unseen and misplaced white tile.

Indian spokesman, quoted by Jon Ruddy in *Maclean's Magazine*, December, 1969.

## Careless, J.M.S.
One is tempted to conclude, in fact, that there could not be a Canada without the United States—and may not be a Canada with one.

"Horray for the Scars and Gripes!" in *The New Romans: Candid Canadian Opinions of the U.S.* (1968), edited by Al Purdy.

## Carheil, Etienne de
Finally, the most scandalous Evil of all, and that which needs to be the most strenuously opposed, is that the traders have become so accustomed to have women for their Use in the trading-places, and these have become so necessary to them, that they cannot do without them even on their journeys.

Letter from Father Etienne de Carheil to Louis-Hector de Callières, governor, Michilimakina, August 30, 1702. *The Jesuit Relations and Allied Documents* (1954), edited by Edna Kenton.

## Carleton, Sir Guy
U.E., U.E.L.

Sir Guy Carleton, Lord Dorchester, governor-in-chief of British North America, directed in 1789 that as "a Marke of Honor" families of those 50,000 or so immigrants who had left the Thirteen Colonies between 1776 and 1783 may "be distinguished by the letters U.E. affixed to their names." U.E. is an abbreviation of "Unity of the Empire." Those United Empire Loyalists who immigrated after that date are referred to as "late Loyalists."

Barring Catastrophe shocking to think of, this Country must, to the end of Time, be populated by the Canadian Race.

Letter written in 1767, quoted by W. Stewart Wallace in "The Beginnings of British Rule in Canada," *Canadian Historical Review*, September, 1925.

As to my opinion of the Canadians, I think there is nothing to fear from them, while we are in a state of prosperity, and nothing to hope from when in distress; I speak of the people at large; there are some among them who are guided by sentiments of honour, but the multitude is influenced only by hopes of gain, or fear of punishment.

Letter of 1776 concerning the French in Quebec. *Documents Relating to a Constitutional History of Canada: 1759-1828* (1907-35), edited by Adam Shortt and Sir Arthur Doughty.

## Carling, Sir John
Seventy-five cents a day and all the beer they want to drink.

Terms offered by the Conservative M.P. and London brewer to his workers, 1860s. Quoted by Doris French in *Faith, Sweat and Politics: The Early Trade Union Years in Canada* (1962).

## Carlyle, Thomas
Canada too you will no doubt find a place of difficulties, of drawbacks,—what place on this Earth is not such? But you are nearer hand in all senses; you are among people of your own blood and kin: you know much better what you are about there.

Letter to his brother Alexander Carlyle, May 3, 1844. *The Letters of Thomas Carlyle to His Brother Alexander with Related Family Letters* (1968), edited by Edwin W. Marrs, Jr.

We seem to gather that she was young, hazel-eyed, beautiful, and someone's cousin; high born and of high spirit; but unhappily dependent and insolvent; living, perhaps, on the not too gracious bounty of moneyed relatives.

> Carlyle's description of his "Rose Goddess" Blumine in *Sartor Resartus* (1833-34), and a fair depiction of Margaret Elizabeth Gordon. The Charlottetown beauty whom Carlyle met in 1816 in Kirkcaldy, Scotland, became Lady Bannerman, wife of the lieutenant-governor of Prince Edward Island. See also Margaret Elizabeth Gordon.

One insolent Bishop of Toronto, triumphant Canadian.

> A reference to John Strachan, first bishop of Toronto, in 1839.

There is not a Red Indian hunting by Lake Winnipeg can quarrel with his squaw, but the whole world must smart for it.

> Quoted by John McLean in *The Indians: Their Manners and Customs* (1889).

Shooting Niagara

> Title of an article and the origin of the phrase, *Macmillan's Magazine*, 1867.

## Carmack, G.W.
### TO WHOM IT MAY CONCERN

I do, this day, locate and claim, by right of discovery, five hundred feet, running up stream from this notice. Located this 17th day of August, 1896.

G.W. Carmack

> "Carmack blazed a small spruce tree with his hand ax, and on the upstream side wrote with a pencil. . . ." Quoted by Pierre Berton in *Klondike: The Life and Death of the Last Great Gold Rush* (1958). The prospector who made the first gold strike in the Yukon later said:

I felt as if I had just dealt myself a royal flush in the game of life, and the whole world was a jackpot.

## Carman, Bliss
Was it a year or lives ago
We took the grasses in our hands,
And caught the summer flying low
  Over the waving meadow lands,
  And held it there between our hands?

> From "Low Tide on Grand Pré."

*

Have little care that Life is brief,
And less that art is long.
Success is in the silences,
Though fame is in the song.

> "Envoi," *Bliss Carman's Poems* (1929). These lines appear on the poet's tombstone in Poets' Corner, Fredericton.

## Carman, J.W.
You may or not be aware, that in Canada there is a strong and growing American Party—composed of gentlemen—and of every nationality, whose ultimate object is to carry the province or Dominion into the American Union. Of that Party I have for many years been a leader, and have as editor and publisher been in a position to take a prominent part.

> Letter from the publisher of the *British American*, a Kingston newspaper, addressed to U.S. Senator Zachariah Chandler, and read into *The Congressional Globe*, April 19-22, 1870.

## Carnarvon, Lord
I believe it to be a question of confederation amongst themselves, or of absorption by the U.S.

> Letter from the British colonial secretary to the Earl of Derby, October 11, 1866. *Documents on the Confederation of British North America* (1969), edited by G.P. Browne.

The N. American delegates have expressed a strong wish that the Confederate Province sd. not only have a common name but also a certain rank and they wish that it sd. be known as the "Dominion of Canada." They wd. have preferred to call it a Viceroyalty. This in my opinion wd. be open to grave objection but I see no harm in the concession to them of the term "dominion." It is a tribute on their part to the monarchical principle and if somewhat in opposition to the institutions on the other side of the border, not in any offensive opposition.

Letter to the Earl of Derby, February 6, 1867. Quoted by W.L. Morton in *The Critical Years: The Union of British North America 1857-1873* (1964).

We are laying the foundation of a great State—perhaps one which at a future day may even overshadow this country. But, come what may, we shall rejoice that we have shown neither indifference to their wishes nor jealousy of their aspirations, but that we honestly and sincerely, to the utmost of our power and knowledge, fostered their growth, recognizing in it the conditions of our own greatness.

British House of Lords, on second reading of the BNA Bill, February 19, 1867. *Speeches on Canadian Affairs* (1902), edited by Sir Robert Herbert.

The greatest gift that the Crown and the Parliament of England have bestowed upon you seems to me to be this: that they have given you absolute, unqualified, unstinted freedom in self-government combined with a union with the ancient monarchy of England. In legislation, and in self-government, may you ever remain free as the winds of Heaven, but in loyalty to the Crown may you ever be found in chains of adamant.

Quoted by Stanley Baldwin in "The Position of Canada in the Empire," Address at a dinner given by the Province of Ontario, August 6, 1927, *Our Inheritance: Speeches and Addresses* (1928).

## Carnegie, Andrew
Gentlemen, I read some years ago, it may not be very many, that one of your officers had proposed building a row of forts along your borders. I understand that officer is not now in command. Can you imagine anything so wildly, diabolically damnable as that, as far removed from the policy you have adopted on the lakes as right from wrong. What would you build them against? Your brothers of the English-speaking race down there?

"First Words in Canada," April 27, 1906, *Addresses Delivered before the Canadian Club of Toronto: Session of 1905-06* (1906).

Canada, the Scotland of America, is to play the part of Scotland and annex her southern neighbour as Scotland did, and boss it for its good, both in Church and state, as Scotland also did—I need not speak here in the past tense—as she still does. Canada would take her somewhat strenuous, perhaps one might say obstreperous, brother by one hand and her mother by the other, put the one in the other and re-unite them.

"Anglo-American Relations," April 28, 1906, *Addresses Delivered before the Canadian Club of Ottawa: 1903-1909* (1910).

## Caron, Sir Joseph
Wish you to travel night and day. I want to show what the Canadian militia can do.

Telegram from the minister of Militia in Ottawa to the first detachments heading west to put down the Northwest Rebellion, March 31, 1885. Quoted by Donald Creighton in *John A. Macdonald: The Old Chieftain* (1955).

## Carpenter, Edmund
No word meaning "art" occurs in Aivilik, nor does "artist": there are only people. Nor is any distinction made between utilitarian and decorative objects. The Aivilik say simply, "A man should do all things properly."

*Eskimo* (1959), by Edmund Carpenter, Frederick Varley, and Robert Flaherty.

In Eskimo the word to make poetry is the word to breathe; both are derivatives of *anerca*, the soul, that which is eternal: the breath of life.

*Anerca* (1959), edited by Edmund Carpenter.

In a life where neither reason nor strength prevail, where cunning counts for little and pity least of all, the Eskimo sings of life, for only art avails, and even then, not always.

*Eskimo Realities* (1973).

## Carpenter, J.
I forgot to tell you that Carpenter wrote something in his diary just before start-

ing, which on examination proved to be the following, as near as I can recollect, "Arrived this day at the cañon at 10 A.M., and drowned running the canoe down; God keep my poor wife!" Was it not strange? He was not much of a swimmer and clung to the canoe which I think was sucked down under and held under the rocks, at least we never saw it again.

> Apparently J. Carpenter from Toronto had a premonition he would drown shooting the Grand Rapids of the Upper Fraser River, September 30, 1862. This is how his companion, Richard H. Alexander, who was eighteen at the time, remembered the self-fulfilling prophecy many years later. Quoted by Mark Sweeten Wade in *The Overlanders of '62* (1931).

## Carr, Emily

To return to the term "Creative Art." This is the definition a child once gave it: "I think and then I draw a line round my think." Children grasp these things more quickly than we do. They are more creative than grown-ups. It has not been knocked out of them.

> "Fresh Seeing" (1930), *Fresh Seeing: Two Addresses by Emily Carr* (1972), preface by Doris Shadbolt.

Movement is the essence of being. When a thing stands still and says, "Finished," then it dies. There isn't such a thing as completion in this world, for that would mean Stop! [May 3, 1934]

> *Hundreds and Thousands: The Journals of Emily Carr* (1966).

Indians do not hinder the progress of their dead by embalming or tight coffining. When the spirit has gone they give the body back to the earth. The earth welcomes the body—coaxes new life and beauty from it, hurries over what men shudder at. Lovely tender herbage bursts from the graves, swiftly, exulting over corruption.

> "Century Time," *Klee Wyck* (1941).

## Carré, John le

They're about the only ones left who still believe in it all, the Canadians.

*A Small Town in Germany* (1968).

## Carrel, Alexis

But it is chiefly through intellectual and moral discipline, and the rejection of the habits of the herd, that we can reconstruct ourselves. Sufficiently large groups could lead a still more personal life. The Doukhobors of Canada have demonstrated that those whose will is strong can secure complete independence even in the midst of modern civilization.

> *Man the Unknown* (1935).

## Carroll, Leo G.

It got to the point that once when I touched down in Goose Bay, Newfoundland, on a plane flight, the children there came up and asked me for my autograph. They had seen "Topper" on television.

> *The Globe and Mail*, October 19, 1972. The British-born Hollywood actor died in 1971.

## Carroll, Lewis    See Clive Carruthers.

## Carruthers, Clive

*Alicia in Terra Mirabili*

> Title of Lewis Carroll's *Alice in Wonderland* (1865) in the Latin translation of the McGill classics professor, published in 1964. Two years later his version of *Through the Looking-Glass* (1871) appeared as *Aliciae per Speculum Transitus*.

## Carson, Jack

A fan club is a group of people who tell an actor he's not alone in the way he feels about himself.

> "Beefy American comedy actor" is how Leslie Halliwell in *The Filmgoer's Companion* (Third Edition, 1970) describes John Elmer Carson who was born in Carman, Manitoba, in 1910 and became a U.S. citizen in 1949. Carson, who died in 1963, was "previously in vaudeville; usually played 'smart guys' who were really dumb," according to Robin May in *The Wit of the Theatre* (1969).

## Carter, Kenneth
A buck is a buck.

Fiscal philosophy of the chairman of the Carter Commission on Tax Reform in a nutshell. The Carter Report was released on February 24, 1967, and Carter summed up his recommendations: "If a man obtains increased command over goods and services for his personal satisfaction we do not believe it matters, from the point of view of taxation, whether he earned it through working, gained it through operating a business, received it because he held property, or made it by selling property or was given it by a relative."

## Carter, Wilf
I've always said that a man must have a dream to go forward. He must push on until he has reached it. Only then can he be a better and greater man.

*The Yodelling Cowboy: Montana Slim from Nova Scotia* (1961).

## Cartier, Sir George-Étienne
Comme le dit un vieil adage:
Rien n'est si beau que sons pays;
Et de le chanter, c'est l'usage;
Le mien je chante à mes amis
L'étranger voit avec un oeil d'envie
Du Saint-Laurent le majestueux cours;
A son aspect le Canadien s'écrie:
O Canada! mon pays! mes amours!

First of six verses of "O Canada, mon pays, mes amours" which, according to John Boyd in *Sir George Etienne Cartier, Bart.: His Life and Times* (1914), almost became the national anthem. It was composed by the future Father of Confederation in 1834 while still a student. Boyd included the following verse translation of Cartier's famous song:

"One's own land is best of all,"
So an ancient adage says;
To sing it is the poet's call,
Mine be to sing my fair land's praise.
Strangers behold with envious eyes
St. Lawrence's tide so swift and grand,
But the Canadian proudly cries,
O Canada, my own beloved land!

Souvent de la Grande Bretagne,
On vante de les moeurs et les lois;

Par leurs vins, la France et l'Espagne
A nos éloges ont des droits.
Admirez le ciel d'Italie
Louez l'Europe, c'est fort bien;
Moi, je préfère ma patrie:
Avant tout je suis Canadien.

"Avant tout je suis Canadien" ("Before all I am a Canadian") was the marching song of the Sons of Liberty in the Rebellion of 1837 in Lower Canada. The title is sometimes given as "Avant tout soyons Canadiens" ("Before all be Canadians"). Quoted by John Boyd in *Sir George Etienne Cartier, Bart.: His Life and Times* (1914) who appends the following prose translation:

"Often they boast of the customs and laws of Great Britain; France and Spain, on account of their wines, have a right to our praises; to admire the skies of Italy and to laud Europe is all very well, but for me I prefer my own country. Before all I am a Canadian."

Call in de membres. [Characteristic reply of the Quebec Conservative to Liberal criticism in Parliament, 1850s and 1860s]

*

I am an Englishman who speaks French. [Well-known remark, 1850s]

*

Franc et sans dol ["Frank and Without Deceit." Motto chosen by Cartier when he was made a baronet in 1868]

Quoted by John Boyd in *Sir George Etienne Cartier, Bart.: His Life and Times* (1914).

## Cartier, Jacques
In fine I am rather inclined to believe that this is the land God gave to Cain.

No more haunting an image has ever been applied to Canada than Jacques Cartier's reaction to the bleak shore of the Gulf of St. Lawrence, today's Labrador and Quebec, discovered and described during the summer of 1534. The image, which comes from the navigator's *Prèmiere relation*, is among the earliest connected with Canada. Cartier's exact words are: "Fin, j'estime mieulx que aultrement, que c'est la terre que Dieu donna à Cayn." *The Voyages of Jacques*

*Cartier* (1924), translated by H.P. Biggar.

More than four centuries later Samuel Eliot Morison retraced Cartier's voyage, but by plane rather than by ship. In *The European Discovery of America: The Northern Voyages A.D. 500-1600* (1971), he wrote: "The desolation is the same today: granite hills smoothed by a glacier, stunted spruce in the valleys and the only green, and all extending northwards as far as the eye can see."

Until the twentieth century, the standard version of Cartier's description was Hakluyt's: "To be short, I beleeve that this was the land that God allotted to Caine." "The First relation of Jacques Cartier of S. Malo, of the new land called New France, nearly discovered in the yere of our Lord 1534," reproduced by Richard Hakluyt in *The Principal Navigations, Voyages, Traffiques, and Discoveries of the English Nation* (1589).

Pierre Berton wrote in *The Mysterious North* (1959): "Labrador's moment in history has arrived. Finally, after four centuries, it begins to look as if the land no longer belongs to Cain."

The sayd men did moreover certify unto us, that there was the way and beginning of the great river of Hochelaga and ready way to Canada, which river the further it went the narrower it came, even into Canada, and that there was fresh water, which went so farre upwards, that they had never heard of any man who had gone to the head of it, and that there is no other passage but with small boates.

July 26, 1535, "A Shorte and Briefe Narration" (1535), reproduced by Richard Hakluyt in *The Principal Navigations, Voyages, Traffiques, and Discoveries of the English Nation* (1589). This is the earliest recorded use of the word "Canada." To quote Samuel Eliot Morison: "Thus, almost inadvertently, Canada entered the stream of history."

And amidst these fields is situated the town of Hochelaga, near to and touching a mountain, which is around it, very fertile and cultivated, from the summit of which one can see far off. We called this mountain "le Mount Royal."

In 1535, Cartier explored the site of present-day Montreal. *Jacques Cartier and His Four Voyages to Canada* (1890), edited by Hiram B. Stephens.

And upon that high cliffe wee found a faire fountaine very neere the sayd Forte: adioyning whereunto we found good store of stones, which we esteemed to be Diamants. . . . And in some places we have found stones like Diamants, the most faire, pollished and excellently cut that it is possible for a man to see. When the Sunne shineth upon them, they glister as it were sparkles of fire.

"The Third Voyage of Discovery made by Captaine Jaques Cartier," 1541, *The Voyages of Jacques Cartier* (1924), edited by H.P. Biggar. Out of Cartier's disappointment in August of 1541 came the French proverb: *"Voilà un Diament de Canada!"* The proverb is translated variously: "That is a diamond of Canada," "As false as the diamonds of Canada," etc. Cartier's quarry is known to this day as Cape Diamond.

It needs only the nightingale.

Of Prince Edward Island, quoted by Stephen Leacock in "The Island of the Blest" in *My Discovery of the West* (1937).

## Cartwright, Captain George

These Indians are called *Red*, from their custom of painting themselves, and everything belonging to them, with red ochre, which they find in great plenty in various parts of the island; and *Wild*, because they secret themselves in the woods, keep an unremitting watch, and are seldom seen; a conduct, which their defenceless condition, and the inhuman treatment which they have always experienced from strangers, whether Europeans or other tribes of Indians from the Continent, have compelled them to adopt. [On the Beothucks, July 11, 1770]

*

Although in sailing along this coast, the astonished mariner is insensibly drawn into a conclusion, that this country was the last which God made, and that he had no other view than to throw together there, the refuse of his materials, as of no use to mankind, yet, he no sooner penetrates a few miles into a bay, than the great change, both of the climate and prospects, alter his opinion. The air then becomes soft and warm; bare rocks no longer appear; the land is thick clothed with timber, which reaches down almost to high-water mark, and is generally edged with grass. [On Labrador, October 4, 1786]

> A Journal of Transactions and Events, During a Residence of Nearly Sixteen Years on the Coast of Labrador (1792). Captain Cartwright and His Labrador Journal (1911), edited by Charles Wendell Townsend.

## Cartwright, John Robert
I believe the bench, like the navy, should be a silent service.

> Chief justice of the Supreme Court of Canada, quoted in The Globe and Mail, August 16, 1967.

## Cartwright, Sir Richard
I do not think, Sir, that although we have cherished, I hope we will continue to cherish, the most friendly feeling toward the parent state, I do not think for my part, that we are under any deep debt of gratitude to English statesmen, that we owe them much, unless, perchance, it may be the duty, as Christian men, to forgive them for the atrocious blunders which have marked every treaty, or transaction, or negotiation that they have ever had with the United States where the interest of Canada were concerned, from the days of Benjamin Franklin to this hour, not excepting the first and second Treaty of Washington.

> House of Commons, March 14, 1888.

It is not by any manner of means a trifling thing to say when I say that the value of a Senate is not only in what the Senate does, but in what the Senate prevents other people from doing. These are such things as potential checks.

> Senate Debates, May 17, 1906.

There is much gold amid the mud of politics.

*

Politics honourably practised is one of the noblest vocations; carried on for making money, it is one of the vilest trades.

*

Next to a worthy friend, honour a worthy foe.

*

The Dominion that had begun in Lamentations seemed to be ending in Exodus.

*

The biggest stones are thrown at the best apple trees.

> Attributed to the Liberal spokesman and senator who died in 1912, the last remark being quoted by John W. Dafoe in Clifford Sifton in Relation to His Times (1931).

## Casares, Alolfo Bioy
See Jorge Luis Borges.

## Casgrain, Henri-Raymond
We live at two opposite poles; you at the pole of naturalism; I at that of supernaturalism; but there is one point on which we meet: that is the love of humanity.

> The Quebec abbé and historian thanking Francis Parkman for a copy of his newly published The Jesuits in North America in the Seventeenth Century (1867). Quoted by Howard Doughty in Francis Parkman (1962).

## Casgrain, Madame Thérèse-Forget
There are three sexes. Men and women and husbands' wives.

> Quoted by Lotta Dempsey in The Toronto Star, March 22, 1968.

The true liberation of women cannot take place without the liberation of men.

> A Woman in a Man's World: Memoirs (1972), translated by Joyce Marshall.

## Cashman, Tony
There are few parts of the earth where history is bound so inseparably to the character of the land itself. You can feel the history of western Canada as you travel across it. You can feel the future too.

*An Illustrated History of Western Canada* (1971).

**Casson, Herbert N.**
The spineless worker who wipes his eyes and groans and says, "Thank God it is no worse" is of no more use to the world than a dead rabbit.

> *Toronto Souvenir Labour Day Programme, 1898.* Quoted by Doris French in *Faith, Sweat and Politics: The Early Trade Union Years in Canada* (1962).

**Catanoy, Nicholas**
Truth: lie's lie.

> From "The Second Truth" in *Hic et Nunc: Récit* (1968), by the Rumanian-born literary figure.

**Cather, Willa**
On the opposite shore of the river, just across from the proud rock of Quebec, the black pine forest came down to the water's edge; and on the west, behind the town, the forest stretched no living man knew how far. That was the dead, sealed world of the vegetable kingdom, an uncharted continent with interlocking trees, living, dead, half-dead, their roots in bogs and swamps, strangling each other in a slow agony that had lasted for centuries. The forest was suffocation, annihilation.

> *Shadows on the Rock* (1931). This is the American novelist's evocation of Frontenac's Quebec, and of the forest beyond.

**Cendrars, Blaise**
. . . the scenery is among the most beautiful to be found in North America.

> "The Thousand Islands," *Du monde entier* (1919), *Poésies complètes* (1963). The celebrated French writer travelled across Canada after World War I.

**Chalmers, Floyd S.**
Perhaps my political views can best be described by saying that I am the hyphen in the phrase Liberal-Conservative.

> "The World Economic Crisis and the Canadian Monetary Situation," *The Liberal Way: A Record of Opinion on Canadian Problems as Expressed and*

Discussed at the First Liberal Summer Conference, Port Hope, September 1933 (1933).

Any war that is postponed is a war that may never be fought.

> "Britain's Bid for Peace," October 24, 1938, *Addresses Delivered before the Canadian Club of Toronto: Season of 1938-39* (1939).

**Chalvin, Solange and Michel**
Problem: Jeannine prayed nine minutes at the tomb of Brother André, two minutes in the chapel, and ten minutes in the Basilica. How long did she pray altogether?

> *Comment on abrutit nos enfants* (1962), a textbook in use in Quebec before the Lesage government's educational reform.

**Chamberlain, Joseph**
Practically it seems that the Ministry are going to sell the Colony to a contractor —a rather novel proceeding and a questionable result of self-government. We cannot prevent them—but we might at least wash our hands of the business.

> March 5, 1898, quoted by St. John Chadwick in *Newfoundland: Island into Province* (1967). In 1904, Chamberlain was advising Britishers: "Learn to think Imperially."

**Chamberlain, Neville**
Gentlemen, to us in the old country, three thousand miles away, you seem to be a happy, happy land, where allies cease from troubling and labour is at rest.

> "Britain's Need and Canada's Opportunity," October 18, 1922, *The Canadian Club of Ottawa Year Book: 1922-23; 1923-24* (1925).

Gentlemen, there is another way in which you can help us in that Old Country. Not only can you assist us by taking some of our surplus population but you can do something also to provide for those who remain at home, if you will buy more of our goods.

> "Reflections of an Old Country Man," October 11, 1922, *Addresses Delivered*

*before the Canadian Club of Toronto: Season of 1922-23* (1923).

## Chamberland, Paul
I don't understand the revolutionary who does not take the trouble to make love well.

\*

I thought of myself as one of those guys who write political slogans on walls. A signpainter, a shouting signpainter.

> The Quebec separatist poet explaining the significance of the title of his book *L'afficheur hurle* (1964), which translates "The poster-hanger screams." Quoted by Malcolm Reid in *The Shouting Signpainters: A Literary and Political Account of Quebec Revolutionary Nationalism* (1972).

## Chambers, Ernest J.
"Lost, horse dead. Am trying to push ahead. Have done my best."

> Last message scrawled across his order papers by a young constable before perishing in a blizzard en route between NWMP posts in the North-West, carrying urgent despatches, Pendant d'Oreille, 1890s. Quoted by Captain Ernest J. Chambers in *The Royal North-West Mounted Police: A Corps History* (1906). Chambers concludes: "Truly a pathetic vindication of the honour and sense of duty of a gallant member of this remarkable force of soldier-police."

## Chambers, Jack
The artist is a perceptual window.

> Quoted by Ross Mendes, "Windows and Mirrors," *Artscanada*, October, 1969.

When you are interested in life more than you are in painting, then your paintings can come to life.

> London, Ontario, painter, quoted by William Withrow in *Contemporary Canadian Painting* (1972).

## Champlain, Hélène
Because you are always near my heart!

> "A story told by the nuns of the Hôtel Dieu at Quebec later in the century shows Hélène to have been a gracious lady to the natives. Among her jewels

was a tiny mirror hung from a necklace. The Indians loved to look into it, and when one squaw asked her why she could see her own face so near the lady's breast, Madame answered, 'Because you are always near my heart!' So we may conclude that she played her role tactfully and courageously; but we suspect that she prayed daily that her husband would retire to a neat little farm in France." Samuel Eliot Morison in *Samuel de Champlain: Father of New France* (1972). Champlain's wife arrived in 1620, when she was twenty-two and her husband fifty, and left New France four years later.

## Champlain, Samuel de
They are for the most part a people that has no law, as far as I could see and learn from the said grand Sagamore, who told me that in truth they believe there is a God, who has made all things. Then I said to him, "Since they believe in one God only, how had He brought them into the world, and whence had they come?" He answered me, that after God had made all things, He took a number of arrows, and stuck them in the ground, whence He drew men and women, which have multiplied in the world up to the present, and had their origin in this fashion. I replied to him, that what he said was false; but that in truth there was but one God. . . .

\*

Along the shores of the said Quebec are diamonds in the slate rocks which are better than those of Alençon.

\*

Love, which I have always cherished for the exploration of New France, has made me desirous of extending more and more my travels over the country, in order, by means of its numerous rivers, lakes, and streams, to obtain at last a complete knowledge of it, and also to become acquainted with the inhabitants, with the view of bringing them to the knowledge of God.

> "Of Savages, or Voyages of Samuel Champlain of Brouage" (1603), *The Works of Samuel de Champlain* (1922-36), translated by H.P. Biggar. See also Samuel Eliot Morison. The "diamonds"

encountered by the "Father of New France" near present-day Quebec City, June 22, 1603, were not like those from Alençon in France, for the "Diamonds of Canada" were quartz. See also Jacques Cartier.

**Chandler, John Noel**
Art is the art of making the obvious obvious.

"Notes towards a New Aesthetic," *Arts-canada*, October-November, 1972.

**Chanel, Coco**
There is only one Mademoiselle in the world, and that is I; one Madame, and that is Rubenstein; and one Miss, and that is Arden.

The Paris designer's assessment of three "beauty queens," including Canadian-born Elizabeth Arden, whose reply was: "There is only one Elizabeth like me, and that's the queen." Quoted by Alfred Allan Lewis and Constance Woodworth in *Miss Elizabeth Arden* (1972). See also Elizabeth Arden.

**Chapais, Sir Thomas**
Well, before the ladies sit here with us, I hope a new style of hats will have been introduced.

Quebec legislator and historian, on third reading of the suffrage bill to give Quebec women the vote, April 25, 1940. Quoted by Catherine Lyle Cleverdon in *The Woman Suffrage Movement in Canada* (1950).

**Chapin, Miriam**
If the old scornful question were ever asked in our day, "Who reads an American book?" the answer would be shouted, "Canadians."

*

Toronto is tired of being called stuffy and priggish. After all, it produced Beatrice Lillie!

*Contemporary Canada* (1959).

**Chapleau, Sir Joseph-Adolphe**
I have sent to Sir Alexander a new diagnostic which does not alter my opinion on the fate of the "Sick Man" (the Que-

bec Government, like Turkey, lives on the strength of the great Powers).

Letter from the secretary of State to Sir John A. Macdonald, October 7, 1886. Quoted by J.H. Stewart Reid, Kenneth McNaught and Harry S. Crowe in *A Sourcebook of Canadian History: Selected Documents and Personal Papers* (Revised Edition, 1964).

**Chaplin, Charles**
It was the beginning of September and we passed Newfoundland in a fog. At last we sighted the mainland. It was a drizzling day, and the banks of the St. Lawrence River looked desolate. Quebec from the boat looked like the ramparts where Hamlet's ghost might have walked, and I began to wonder about the States.

The British vaudeville comedian made his maiden voyage to America as part of Fred Karno's acting troupe in 1910. *My Autobiography* (1964).

**Chaput, Marcel**
It is a paradox of French-Canadian life: the more bilingual we become, the less need there is to be bilingual.

*

After establishing facts like these, can we keep from crying out: "Confederation, the graveyard of minorities!"

*

*Epitaph*
Here lies a people which died on the way/For want of knowing where it was going.

*Why I am a Separatist* (1962), translated by Robert A. Taylor.

**Charbonneau, Monseignor Joseph**
The working class is the victim of a conspiracy which seeks its destruction and when there is a conspiracy to crush the working class it is the duty of the Church to intervene. . . . We want social peace but we don't want the crushing of the working class. We are attached to man more than to capital. That's why the clergy has decided to intervene. It wants to have justice and charity respected and desires that there shall cease to be a situation where more attention is paid

to money interests than to the human element.

> Sermon supporting the strikers at Asbestos delivered by the archbishop of Montreal, Notre Dame Cathedral, Sunday, May 2, 1949. Quoted by Charles Lipton in *The Trade Union Movement of Canada: 1827-1959* (1967).

I have been smashed and hurled to the Pacific Coast. . . . It came to me as a bolt out of a blue sky.

> "Mgr. Charbonneau et l'opinion publique dans l'Eglise," *Cité libre*, January-February, 1960. Charbonneau was removed from the archbishopric of Montreal and sent to British Columbia to administer a small parish in Victoria after siding with the workers during the Asbestos strike in 1949. See also F.R. Scott.

**Charlebois, Robert**
Vive l'univers libre.

> Quoted by Ian McDougall in *The Toronto Star*, August 9, 1972.

The interesting thing about me is that I speak French and I breathe American air.

\*

I don't want to separate. I want to invade.

\*

Dylan is the Robert Charlebois of America.

> Quebec rock singer quoted by *Time*, December 18, 1972.

**Charles I**
For his crest, on a wreath argent sable, a beaver proper.

> This is said to be the first use of the beaver in heraldry associated with Canada. Royal letter, Newmarket, 1632, from Charles I, King of Great Britain and Ireland, granting a coat of arms to Sir William Alexander, Earl of Stirling. Eleven years earlier, James I had granted Sir William enormous tracts of land in the Maritimes. Eleven years later, Sir William would be favoured with the title Viscount Canada.

**Charles II**
The Governor and Company of Adventurers of England trading into Hudson's Bay.

> The official title of the Hudson's Bay Company. The letters patent were signed on May 2, 1670, by Charles II, King of Great Britain and Ireland, and granted to Prince Rupert and seventeen other noblemen and gentlemen "the sole trade and commerce of all those seas, straits, bays, rivers, lakes, creeks and sounds, in whatsoever latitude they shall be, that lie within the entrance of the straits commonly called Hudson's Straits, together with all the lands and territories upon the countries, coasts and confines of the seas, bays, &c., aforesaid, that are not already actually possessed by or granted to any of our subjects, or possessed by the subjects of any other Christian prince or state."
>
> This grant was taken to include all lands watered by streams flowing into Hudson Bay. The immense area of the Canadian Northwest was named Rupert's Land, after the first governor. This transfer of authority may well be the largest single commercial transaction ever undertaken. The "rights of government" were returned to Queen Victoria when the monopolistic franchise was withdrawn with the Deed of Surrender, November 19, 1869, which was confirmed by an order-in-council at the Court of Windsor, June 23, 1870, two hundred years after the initial deed.

**Charlesworth, Hector**
Sir John Macdonald I recall as a grim sphinx-like figure in grey top hat and grey frock coat sitting with his hands gripping the top of his cane as his carriage stood to let traffic pass on a Toronto thoroughfare.

> *Candid Chronicles: Leaves from the Note Book of a Canadian Journalist* (1925). See also H.G. Wells.

**Charlevoix, Pierre-François-Xavier de**
'Tis a great Pity, Madam, that none of these wonderful Creatures were found in the *Tyber*, or in the Territories of *Parnassus*; what fine Things would the

*Greek* and *Roman* Poets have said on this Subject!

"On beavers" (1720), *A Voyage to North-America: Undertaken by Command of the Present King of France* (1766).

Let us endeavour, then, rather to improve Old France, than strive to found a New France in the most unpromising regions of the West.

Quoted by François-Xavier Garneau in *History of Canada from the Time of Its Discovery till the Union Year 1840-41* (1862), translated by Andrew Bell.

### Charrier, Reine

Better to mourn a lost love than suffer a mournful love all one's life.

＊

A real woman is one who knows how to be a lady in the parlour, a servant in the kitchen, and a mistress in the bedroom.

*Madame X Confidentiel* (1967), by Reine Charrier, hostess of a popular radio talk show in Montreal.

### Chartier, Paul Joseph

Mr. Speaker, Gentlemen, I might as well give you a blast to wake you up. For one whole year I have thought of nothing but how to exterminate as many of you as possible. . . . The only bills you pass are the ones that line your pockets, while the rest of the country has to eat spaghetti and meat balls.

Fragments from the "if-I-were-president" speech prepared by "the Mad Bomber of Parliament Hill." The clerk of the House of Commons refused Chartier permission to deliver this speech. The unemployed truck driver from Alberta, who planned to throw a bomb into the Commons chamber from the visitor's gallery, was killed when his homemade bomb exploded in the men's room of the Parliament Buildings, May 18, 1966. Quoted by Harry Bruce in "The Mad Bomber of Parliament Hill," *The Canadian Magazine*, September 10 and 17, 1966.

Hon. J.R. Nicholson (Minister of Labour): I presume that technically hon. member may be entitled to communications between other organizations.

[*Editor's note: At this point a loud explosion was heard in the chamber.*]

Mr. Speaker, I was saying that technically some of the communications between other organizations. . . .

＊

Right Hon. J.G. Diefenbaker (Leader of the Opposition): Mr. Speaker, the reason for the conversation in the chamber is the current report that someone has just passed away within the precincts of the House of Commons. I suggest to the Prime Minister, and I do so in the desire the House should not be carrying on under these circumstances, that it might be worth considering that the House should adjourn.

Right Hon. L.B. Pearson (Prime Minister): It appears that there was a bomb explosion in the washroom at this end of the third floor and that a man has been killed, under circumstances which are not yet quite clear. There has been a good deal of damage done to the washroom and a certain amount of confusion is natural. Perhaps my right hon. friend's suggestion should be adopted and the House could adjourn until four o'clock when the situation will be cleared up and we can resume.

Mr. Speaker: Is it agreed that the House suspend its sittings until four o'clock?

Some hon. Members: Agreed.

At 3:05 P.M. the sitting was suspended.

The bomb exploded in the Centre Block at three o'clock, and this passage from *Hansard* gives some sense of the occasion. House of Commons, May 18, 1966.

### Chartrand, Michel

The charge should read "since 1938."

Reply of the leader of the left wing of the Quebec labour movement and, since 1968, president of the Montreal Central Council of the Confederation of National Trade Unions (CNTU), when charged with "seditious conspiracy between 1968 and October 1970," after the imposition of the War Measures Act, October 16, 1970.

We are going to win because there are

more boys ready to shoot members of Parliament than there are police, my friend.

> Shouted to newspapermen in the bar of the Hotel Nelson in Montreal during the October Crisis, following the death of Pierre Laporte. *Time*, October 26, 1970.

I have seen the face of capitalism, and it is fascism!

> Quoted by Ken Sobel, in the *Village Voice*, May 27, 1971.

We can count only on ourselves.

> Title of the manifesto *Ne comptons que sur nos propres moyens*, issued in September, 1971, by the CNTU, advocating the overthrow of capitalism in Quebec.

If we are to have human dignity, then we have to break the law. Jails are made for men. We might as well explore them.

> Toronto address, June 15, 1973.

### Chateaubriand, François-René de
One evening, I lost my way in the forest, not far from the cataract of the Niagara; soon I saw the day extinguish itself around me and I tasted, in my solitude, the superb spectacle of a night in the wastes of the New World.

> *Le Génie du Christianisme* (1802).

Unhappy Indians whom I have seen wandering through the wilderness of the New World, with the ashes of your ancestors, you who gave me hospitality in spite of your wretchedness, I cannot today make any return to you, for I also am a wanderer among men; and less fortunate in my exile, I do not bear the bones of my fathers with me!

> From the epilogue to *Atala* (1802). *Atala and René* (1963), translated by Rayner Heppenstall.

If I had died in the Canadian forest, would my soul have carried to the supreme tribunal the sacrifices, the good works and virtues of Père Joques and Père Lallemant, or empty days and futile fantasies?

\*

The northernmost point of Newfound-land touches the latitude of Cape Charles I in Labrador; a few degrees higher, the polar landscape begins. If we are to believe what travellers tell us, there is a strange magic about these regions: in the evening the sun, when it touches the earth, seems to stand motionless, and then rises once more in the sky instead of sinking beneath the horizon. . . . One cannot tell whether one is watching the creation or the end of the world. A small bird, similar to that which sings in our woods at night, warbles sadly. The love leads the Eskimo to the icy rock where his mate is waiting for him: these nuptials at the farthest boundaries of the earth lack neither dignity nor happiness.

> *Mémoirs d'outre-tome* (1848). *The Memoirs of Chateaubriand* (1961), translated by Robert Baldick.

### Chauveau, Pierre-Joseph-Oliver
In French Canada one must be doctor, priest, notary, or lawyer. Outside of these four professions it seems there is no salvation for the young educated French Canadian. If by chance one of us had an invincible distaste for all four; if it was too painful for him to save souls, mutilate bodies, or lose fortunes, there remained only one course for him to take if he were rich, and two if he were poor; to do nothing at all in the first case, to exile himself or starve to death in the second.

> *Charles Guérin, roman des moeurs canadiennes* (1852).

English and French, we climb by a double flight of stairs toward the destinies reserved for us on this continent, without knowing each other, without meeting each other, and without even seeing each other, except on the landing of politics. In social and literary terms, we are far more foreign to each other than the English and French of Europe.

> *L'Instruction publique au Canada (1876)*, quoted by Mason Wade in the introduction to his *Canadian Dualism: Studies of French-English Relations* (1960). Wade remarks that the first premier of Quebec after Confederation "likened the

Canada of that day to the famous stair-case of the Château de Chambord, so constructed that two persons could mount it without meeting and without seeing each other except at intervals."

## Cheadle, W.B.
Talk not to us of intellectual raptures; the mouth and stomach are the doors by which enter true delight. Mutton chops, potatoes, bread, butter, milk, rice pudding, tea, and sugar: contrast dried horseflesh and water, or martens, or nothing at all, with these luxuries!

*The North-West Passage by Land: Being the Narrative of an Expedition from the Atlantic to the Pacific* (1865), by W. B. Cheadle and Viscount Milton.

## Cheiro
Canada will be the one bright spot in the British Empire. Industry and trade will grow rapidly from East to West. American money will every year more and more develop Canadian industries. A working commercial agreement of far reaching importance will be made between the United States and Canada. Frontier restrictions will be so reduced that travel and trade between the two countries will be enormously increased.

*Cheiro's World Predictions: The Fate of Europe, The Future of the U.S.A., The Coming War of Nations, The Restoration of the Jews* (1927, 1937). The well-known clairvoyant and prophet was born Count Louis Hamon and lived in England and Hollywood.

## Chevrier, Jacques
"He was proud to wear over his heart the wings that he had carried in the Battle of Britain—the wings that one summer night were folded over the waters of the St. Lawrence.

"They were broken then, but God stooped down to pick them up."

Epitaph for a young RCAF pilot killed in a crash in 1942. "Georges Vanier composed his epitaph in words that have the beauty of a Greek *stele* and might have been written about some hero of antiquity lost in the waters of the Aegean," according to Robert Speaight

in *Vanier: Soldier, Diplomat and Governor General: A Biography* (1970).

## Child, Philip
Green, green grows the grass
Behind our tired feet.

Refrain of "Descent for the Lost," *The Victorian House and Other Poems* (1951).

## Chiniquy, Charles-Paschal-Télésphore
More than once I have seen women fainting in the confessional-box, who told me, afterwards, that the necessity of speaking to an unmarried man on certain things, on which the most common laws of decency ought to have for ever sealed their lips, had almost killed them!

\*

The confessional is the modern Sodom.

The controversial Father Chiniquy was ordained in 1833 and excommunicated in 1856. *The Priest, the Woman and the Confessional* (1875) appeared in Montreal in a series called "Books and Tracts on Romanism."

## Chiriaeff, Ludmilla
I wonder if the next generation will share our feeling that it's a privilege to be useful. It's this vision that makes us so strong.

Founder of the Grand Ballets Canadiens, quoted by William Littler in *The Toronto Star*, May 12, 1973.

## Chisholm, Brock
You can only cure retail but you can prevent wholesale.

Remark made in 1936 by the Toronto psychiatrist who, from 1948 to 1953, was the first director-general of the World Health Organization, Geneva.

Your conscience is what your mother told you before you were six years old.

\*

Telling lies to a child does permanent damage to his mind. A child who believes in Santa Claus, who really and literally believes, because his daddy told him so, that Santa comes down all the chimneys in the world on the same night has had his thinking ability permanently impaired if not destroyed.

"Tell Them the Truth," *Maclean's Magazine*, January 15, 1946, as told to Blair Fraser.

In the future no one wins a war. It is true, there are degrees of loss, but no one wins.

"World Health" (1951), *Empire Club of Canada: Addresses 1950-51* (1951).

## Chisholm, Robert F.

An airline company's promotion department suggested in its advertising that executives should take their wives on business trips, and it kept records of which ones did. Subsequently the department asked the market-research department to carry out a survey with three hundred of the wives to get their impressions of this scheme. In due time the research department sent a letter to those wives asking how they enjoyed the trip. From ninety percent of them came back a baffled reply, "What airplane trip?"

*The Darlings: The Mystique of the Supermarket* (1970).

## Choquette, Jérôme

No society can consent to have the decisions of its judicial and government institutions challenged or set aside by the blackmail of a minority, for that signifies the end of all social order.

Quebec minister of Justice, press conference, October 10, 1970. Quoted by Gérard Pelletier in *The October Crisis* (1971), translated by Joyce Marshall.

## Choquette, Robert

Oh, dear land of mine, so great, so new—where one feels on the threshold of things, where hope *matters*—you are the stuff of epic poetry. Homer would have glorified your waves, Virgil your prairies, Dante your Rockies. What do I think of when I think of you?

"My Own Dear Land" in *In Search of Canada* (1971), by the editors of *Reader's Digest*.

## Chotem, Neil

To me an orchestration is the memory of a storehouse of souls. . . . Orchestra-tion is to a composer what colour and brush techniques are to a painter.

Composer and director, *CBC Times*, April 30, 1966.

## Chown, Samuel D.

Corruption and bribery had almost become so widespread and so deeply rooted that it was almost impossible for a man of large ideas, of noble ideas, and of honour to obtain a seat in Parliament.

The Reverend Dr. S.D. Chown, before a meeting of Montreal Methodists, February 11, 1904. Quoted by J. Castell Hopkins in *The Canadian Annual Review of Public Affairs, 1904* (1905).

## Christie, David

We want only men who are *Clear Grit*.

A Grit is a member of the Liberal party; a Clear Grit is "an out-and-out purist, and so a thorough-going radical" (in J.M.S. Careless's phrase). The noun "grit" implies something firm, the adjective "clear" something positive and unspotted. The term was coined in 1849 by David Christie, a farmer who ultimately became Speaker of the Senate, in the Toronto office of William McDougall. George Brown used the term in an editorial in *The Globe* on December 13, 1849, to characterize the reform wing of the Liberal party. Quoted by J.C. Dent in *The Last Forty Years: Canada Since the Union of 1841* (1881).

## Christie, Dinah

I was terribly naive. When anyone asked me what I did at Stratford, I stuck out my chest and replied: "I'm the call girl."

The daughter of actor Robert Christie landed her first job at the age of thirteen at the Stratford Festival in 1956. (Her job was to call out, "Five minutes to curtain time!")

## Chrobok, Marie Louise

What do you think I am? A phony?

When a society woman inquired about her nobility, Mrs. Bronislaw Chrobok made the above reply. (Her Royal Highness Marie Louise of Bulgaria is the wife of a Toronto investment dealer and the daughter of the late King Boris III of Bulgaria; granddaughter of the late King Victor Emmanuel III of Italy; great-granddaughter of King Nicholas I of Montenegro; and a descendant of King Louis XIII and Louis Philippe of France.) Quoted by McKenzie Porter in *Chatelaine*, May, 1972.

**Churchill, Sir Winston**
Thank God, we are once more on British soil. [First words of the British M.P. as he stepped from a Boston train at Windsor Station, Montreal, December 23, 1900, when he was twenty-six]

The French Canadians derived greater pleasure from singing "God Save the King" than from singing "Rule Britannia." [British House of Commons, July 19, 1904]

Canada . . . is a magnet exercising a double attraction drawing both Great Britain and the United States towards herself and thus drawing them closer to each other. She is the only surviving bond which stretches from Europe across the Atlantic Ocean. In fact, no state, no country, no band of men can more truly be described as the linchpin of peace and world progress. [*Saturday Evening Post*, February 15, 1930]

That long frontier from the Atlantic to the Pacific oceans, guarded only by neighbourly respect and honourable obligations, is an example to every country and a pattern for the future of the world. [Speech in honour of R.B. Bennett, Canada Club, London, England, April 20, 1939]

Canada is the linchpin of the English-speaking world. Canada, with those relations of friendly affectionate intimacy with the United States on the one hand and with her unswerving fidelity to the British Commonwealth and the Motherland on the other, is the link which, spanning the oceans, brings the continents into their true relation and will prevent in future generations any growth of division between the proud and happy nations of Europe and the great countries which have come into existence in the New World. [Mansion House, London, England, September 4, 1941]

Canada, Sir, occupies a unique position in the British Empire because of its unbreakable ties with Britain and its ever-growing friendship and intimate association drawing together those in the new world and in the old whose fortunes are now united in a deadly struggle for life and honour against a common foe.

*

We have not journeyed all this way across the centuries, across the oceans, across the mountains, across the prairies, because we are made of sugar candy.

*

. . . and France would have held her place as a nation in the councils of the allies, and not at the conference table of the victors.

But their generals misled them. When I warned them that Britain would fight on alone, whatever they did, their generals told their Prime Minister and his divided cabinet, "In three weeks England will have her neck wrung like a chicken." Some chicken! Some neck! [Address to a Joint Meeting of the Senate and the House of Commons, December 30, 1941; this masterpiece of English understatement was broadcast around the world and attained a modicum of immortality]

Here at the gateway of Canada, in mighty lands which have never known the totalitarian tyrannies of Hitler and Mussolini, the spirit of freedom has found a safe and abiding home. Here that spirit is no wandering phantom. It is enshrined in Parliamentary institutions based on universal suffrage and evolved through the centuries by the English-speaking peoples. It is inspired by the Magna Charta and the Declaration of Independence. It is guarded by resolute and vigilant millions, never so strong or so well armed as today. [London, England, August 31, 1943; a reference to the Quebec Conference]

We all look to you as the link with America. That fraternal association must be kept up, and we look to you above all to keep the two together. Canada is the interpreter.

To W.L. Mackenzie King at a dinner at Chequers, before D-Day, May, 1944. Quoted by Blair Fraser in *The Search for Identity: Canada, 1945-1967* (1967).

There are no limits to the majestic future which lies before the mighty expanse of Canada with its virile, aspiring, cultured and generous-hearted people. Canada is the vital link in the English-speaking world and joins across the Atlantic Ocean the vast American democracy of the United States with our famous old island and the fifty millions who keep the flag flying here. [The Guildhall, London, England, November 19, 1951]

Lord Beaverbrook is at his very best when things are at their very worst.

*

Max is a foul-weather friend. [Churchill appointed Max Aitken, Lord Beaverbrook, minister of Aircraft Production during World War II] See also C.D. Howe.

### Chuvalo, George
There's no way that I'd want my kid to be a fighter. There's nothing as tough as boxing.

Heavyweight boxing champion of Canada and one of the ten top boxers in the world, quoted by John Gault in *The Canadian Magazine*, October 13, 1973.

### Claman, Dolores   See Richard Morris.

### Clancy, Francis "King"
Nothing relaxes the boys like a good fight.

*

Imagine being paid to play the game you love!

"Clancy probably invented the cliché," according to Trent Frayne and Peter Gzowski in *Great Canadian Sports Stories: A Century of Competition* (1965), referring to the former hockey player and referee.

And if they ask me to sum up my feelings toward hockey, I'd say what I've always said about the game, "If you don't have fun—what's the sense of playing?"

Elder statesman of the Toronto Maple Leafs. *Clancy: The King's Story* (1968), as told to Brian McFarlane.

### Clapperton, Jane
What, precisely, is a Canadian? The theory (long cherished by outsiders) that between the 49th parallel and the North Pole there is nothing much but Mounted Police, lumberjacks, and Paul Muni in a fur hat is clearly inadequate. Perhaps if we wait a little while, the Canadians will decide for themselves who, and what they are, and then let us into the secret.

From *Frozen North to Filthy Lucre* (1964), by the British cartoonist Ronald Searle, with commentaries by Jane Clapperton.

### Clark, Champ
I am for it, because I hope to see the day when the American flag will float over every square foot of the British-North American possessions clear to the North Pole. They are people of our blood. They speak our language. Their institutions are much like ours. They are trained in the difficult art of self-government. . . . I do not have any doubt whatever that the day is not far distant when Great Britain will joyfully see all her North American possessions become a part of this Republic. That is the way things are tending now.

*The Congressional Record*, February 14, 1911. The Missouri representative was speaking in Congress in favour of reciprocity.

### Clark, Gerald
It possibly was a typographical error when a newspaper in Halifax, Nova Scotia, appeared in 1861 with a column of American news under the heading: "UNTIED STATES." But the next issue made the malice clear when the heading was corrected to "DISUNITED STATES."

*Canada: The Uneasy Neighbour* (1965).

### Clark, Gregory
You'll never get anywhere with all those damned little short sentences.

To Ernest Hemingway when both worked for the *Star* during the early 1920s. Quoted by Robert Thomas Allen in *A Treasury of Canadian Humour* (1967). Carlos Baker in *Ernest Hemingway: A Life Story* (1969) quotes Hemingway's evaluation of Clark: "There's too much India rubber in him."

Among the porcupines, rape is unknown.

Clark told this to the late Jimmy Frise at Lake Scugog in 1933, who passed it on to Gillis Purcell.

Are bombs the only way of setting fire to the spirit of a people? Is the human will as inert as the past two world-wide wars would indicate?

"With the Prime Minister in Great Britain," (1941), *Empire Club of Canada: Addresses Delivered to the Members During the Year 1941-42* (1942).

You know, I've made a very interesting discovery. You don't change when you grow old. You remain just the same. But everything else changes. Your home. Your friends. Your city. The things you are used to just disappear, one by one. And you are left alone.

Quoted by Jock Carroll in "A Typical Old Newspaper Man" (1965), *The Death of the Toronto Telegram and Other Newspaper Stories* (1971).

In the two wars, and seventy years of peace, I do not recall ever having been uncomfortable in anybody's company.

\*

I tell you what you do, boy. Or girl.

Go and look at the western sky where the new moon, the silver shaving of the moon, hangs.

Look at it over your *left* shoulder, and wish.

Wish that your first love shall be your last love.

And if your wish is granted, you will have put on the whole armour of life.

*May Your First Love Be Your Last* (1969).

## Clark, Susan

I'm a tall, gangly, high-bred Canadian who won't be pushed around.

Sarnia-born, Toronto-raised, Hollywood actress, 1965.

## Clarke, Andy

Asking a woman to tell her age is like buying a used car. You *know* the speedometer's been turned back, but hanged if you know how far!

\*

A slice of a cow's rear is very valuable to a cow, but it is worth only a dime to a farmer, twenty-five cents to a meat packer, fifty-six cents to a retail butcher and one dollar and fifty cents to a restaurant, not counting the tip and the side dishes.

*Andy Clarke and His Neighbourly News* (1949).

Spring has lingered so long in the lap of winter it is getting talked about.

From Clarke's "Neighbourly News" column in *The Toronto Telegram*.

## Clarke, Sylvestre

The new day is here: it is here to stay. And now we must leave it to our old people to sit solidly and dream of the glories of our past. Our job is to fit ourselves into the new scheme of life which the Great Spirit has decreed for North America. And we will do that, keeping always before us the old Blackfoot proverb: Mokokit-ki-ackamimat—Be wise and persevere.

Clarke is better known as Buffalo Child Long Lance. Born in North Carolina, he worked as a reporter in Calgary and even made a film in Hollywood. *Long Lance: Autobiography of a Blackfoot* (1928).

## Clarkson, Adrienne

It is one thing to have an affair with a married man, but it is another to love a married man and to have him love you. Romantics and idealists might say that it is impossible for a happily married man to love anyone other than his wife, but all of us others know that this is simply not true; it is only the happily married man who can afford the chaos that love can bring into an ordered life, can take the excitement of the chaos and let the order eventually consume it.

*Hunger Trace* (1970).

## Clarkson, Stephen
Politicians always create their own reality; during campaigns they create their own unreality.

*City Lib: Parties and Reform* (1972).

Parity with Texas!

"The least that Canadian legislation on foreign control should achieve is parity with Texas." Response of the political scientist when Texasgulf Inc. sought an injunction under the Texas law to stop the Canada Development Corporation's bid to gain control of the American-owned and Houston-based company whose largest Canadian asset is Kidd Creek Mine near Timmins. (Economist Abraham Rotstein joined in: "Parity begins at home.") Quoted in *The Independencer: Magazine of the Committee for an Independent Canada*, September, 1973.

## Claudel, Paul
I have a high work, but always have with me a very unfortunate and sometimes annoying companion, which is a poet, and I am slightly ashamed of such failing . . . but I may say I am less ashamed in Canada than in any other country.

\*

My friend Moline . . . said, "What makes poetry is white paper". . . . I cannot help but think that the same gift of white paper which is given to poets was given also to Canada by the Creator. Canada is a country with big white paper of tremendous possibilities, and I think it is what is most inspiring in your beautiful country. It is not only to think of the past, which is so glorious, and the present, which is so grand and impressive, but also of the future, which is so full of inspiration. I think that Canada is only at the beginning of its glorious and splendid career.

The distinguished French poet and ambassador to the United States was in Toronto to receive an LL.D. from the University of Toronto. "France and Canada," *Empire Club of Canada: Ad-*

*dresses Delivered to the Members During the Year 1928* (1929).

## Claxton, Brooke
The Canada Council has some unique features; but the idea that the state should assist the arts is as old as the state itself.

Address to the First Annual Vancouver International Festival, July 19, 1958. *Second Annual Report of the Canada Council* (1959).

## Clay, Henry
It is absurd to suppose that we will not succeed. We have the Canadians as much under our command as Great Britain has the ocean, and the way to conquer her on the ocean is to drive her from the land. I am not for stopping at Quebec or anywhere else; but I could take the whole Continent from her and ask her no favours. I wish never to see peace till we do. God has given us the power and the means. We are to blame if we do not use them. . . . The conquest of Canada is within your power. I trust I shall not be deemed presumptuous when I state, what I verily believe, that the militia of Kentucky are alone competent to place Montreal and Upper Canada at your feet. Is it nothing to the British nation—is it nothing to the pride of her monarch to have the last of the immense North American possessions held by him in the commencement of his reign, wrested from his dominion? Is it nothing to us to extinguish the torch that lights up savage warfare? Is it nothing to acquire the entire fur trade connected with that country, and to destroy the temptation and opportunity of violating your revenue and other laws?

Senator Henry Clay of Kentucky, speaking in the U.S. Senate in 1810. "One of the chief sources of his popularity was his activity in Congress in promoting the war with Great Britain in 1812, while as one of the peace commissioners he reluctantly signed the Treaty of Ghent on the 24th of December 1814." *The Encyclopaedia Britannica* (Eleventh Edition, 1910-11). And William Kirby in *Annals of Niagara* (1896) noted

a further irony: "It may be just remarked here that this same Clay, the
fiery advocate of war, was the same man
sent to England by Congress in 1814 to
beg for peace on any terms obtainable,
and who concluded articles of peace
without gaining the concession of a single point on which they had declared
war. . . . It may also be mentioned here,
that in the year 1862, James Clay, son
of that same Henry Clay, sought refuge
and protection under the British flag
at Niagara. He was an adherent of the
Southern Confederacy, and the officials
of the United States were seeking to
arrest him for rebellion . . . fortunately
for James Clay, and hundreds of prominent refugee Confederates, Canada had
not been conquered in the War of 1812."

### Clayton-Thomas, David
I'm just a Canadian kid who loves the
blues.

> Lead singer of Blood, Sweat and Tears,
> quoted by Ritchie Yorke in *Axes, Chops
> & Hot Licks: The Canadian Rock Music
> Scene* (1971).

### Clemens, Samuel L.   See Mark Twain.

### Clendenan, May
If democracy is right, women should
have it. If it isn't, men shouldn't.

> *Grain Growers' Guide*, February 24,
> 1915. Quoted by Catherine Lyle Clever-
> don in *The Woman Suffrage Movement
> in Canada* (1950).

### Clery, Val
For Canadian writers, patriotism has
never been enough; nationalism, which
in Canada looks too often like the patriotism of the entrepreneur, may prove
too much.

> *Books in Canada*, June, 1972.

### Cleverdon, Catherine Lyle
"The true woman who would make the
most of her every God-given attribute
asks not for the ballot, but for love and
home, where the carols of babyhood are
sung to the sweetest of babies, where
home is heaven, and where the weary

husband may find rest and aching hearts
sympathy."

> Editorial in *The Victoria Daily Times*,
> February 28, 1891, quoted with disap-
> proval by Catherine Lyle Cleverdon in
> *The Woman Suffrage Movement in
> Canada* (1950).

### Cloutier, Eugène
At certain hours there is no solution:
half the human race scares you, and the
other half bores you.

> *No Passport: A Discovery of Canada*
> (1968), translated by Joyce Marshall.

### Cloutier, Suzanne
"Home" is wherever we happen to be—
Hollywood, New York, Cannes, London,
Paris, Rome, or any place in between.

> "Life with Peter Is Never Dull," *Week-
> end Magazine*, September 12, 1959. The
> Ottawa-born daughter of the Queen's
> Printer became the second Mrs. Peter
> Ustinov in 1954.

### Clutesi, George
"My son, when a man passes in his canoe,
if you are too poor to offer him bread,
call him in anyway to rest, and to share
the warmth of your fire."

> The Nootka author and artist always
> remembered his father's advice. Quoted
> in *Profiles: Canadian Books for Chil-
> dren* (1971), edited by Irma McDonough.

### Coady, M.M.
I'm not a leftist; I'm where the righteous
ought to be.

> Father Moses Michael Coady was, with
> Father James J. Tompkins, a founder of
> the Antigonish movement in Nova Sco-
> tia in the 1920s. Quoted by J.R. Kidd
> in 1973 as a characteristic remark.

Education should be coterminous with
human life.

> "A Philosophy of Progress" (1949),
> *Learning and Society* (1963), edited by
> J.R. Kidd.

We have no desire to create a nation of
shopkeepers, whose only thoughts run
to groceries and to dividends. We want

our people to look into the sun, and into the depths of the sea.

*Adult Education in Canada* (1950).

The man who has ceased to learn ought not to be allowed to wander around loose in these dangerous days.

*

I can always tell a good teacher. All I have to do is to speak to him of some transforming idea and then watch him light up just as an electric bulb does when the current is connected.

Quoted by J.R. Kidd in *How Adults Learn* (1959).

If we are seriously interested in raising the cultural level of the masses of men, we will help in solving the economic problem first so that they may cease to worry about bread and begin to enjoy their Brahms. . . . From the people, raised to new levels, will arise poets, painters and musicians to give expression to the new and eternal truths that beat within their breasts. As in nature, so in man, the lofty mountain peaks shall rise not from the level plain but from the foothills. ["The Common Man Is Capable" (1939)]

*

We talk about the American way, the British way. If we had any sense, we would know that there is no American way, no British way. There is only one way—the scientific way that cuts across racial lines with international boundaries.

*

In the middle of this scientific twentieth century we have the sad spectacle of a great sector of the human race being led astray by an ideology that employs force for the solution of human problems. The dictatorships of our time are the greatest examples of direct actionists that the world has ever seen. They, through their jack-booted and helmeted gestapo, intrude themselves into the sanctums of people's private and public affairs and, at the point of the gun, suspend the natural laws according to which society should normally evolve. This procedure is about as scientific as that of the chemist who, waiting for the chemical reaction of the materials in

his test-tube, should say: "Turn red, or I shoot." ["Education by Indirect Action" (1950)]

*

The one good world that men have always desired will emerge from the consciousness of our common nature, our common destiny and our almost instinctive hope that some day there will be a millennium. ["Summing Up" (1959)]

*The Man from Mangaree: Writings and Speeches of M.M. Coady, Educator, Reformer, Priest* (1971), edited by Alexander F. Laidlaw. See also Father James Tompkins.

## Coaker, Sir William

It is humiliating enough to have to witness the giving up of responsible government, but to be plunged from the status, theoretical though it may have been, of a self-governing Dominion of the Crown to a position below that of the ordinary Crown Colony, is degrading. We would be put on a par with one of the subject races—an intolerable situation to even contemplate.

Letter published in *The Evening Telegram*, St. John's, November 23, 1933. Newfoundland lost dominion status and reverted to crown colony status managed by a special commission, the measure being given royal assent on December 21, 1933.

## Cobbett, William

The *loss* of Canada I should deem a gain, though it is worth to us a thousand empires in the east; that is to say, it is not a thousandth part as mischievous to us.

Letter Five, *Letters on the Late War between the United States and Great Britain together with Other Miscellaneous Writings on the Same Subject* (1815).

## Cobden, Richard

From Glasgow, the sensible Scots are pouring out amain. Those that are poor, and cannot pay their passage, or can rake together only as trifle, are going to a rascally heap of sand, rock and swamp, called Prince Edward Island, in the horrible Gulf of St. Lawrence. . . .

Remark made about 1830, quoted by Duncan Campbell in *History of Prince Edward Island* (1875).

We are told indeed of the "loyalty" of the Canadians; but this is an ironical term to apply to people who neither pay our taxes nor obey our laws, nor hold themselves liable to fight our battles, who would repudiate our right to the sovereignty over an acre of their territory, and who claim the right of imposing their own customs duties, even to the exclusion of our manufactures. We are two peoples to all intents and purposes, and it is a perilous delusion to both parties to attempt to keep up a sham connexion and dependence which will snap asunder if it should ever be put to the strain of stern reality. It is all very well for our Cockney newspapers to talk of defending Canada at all hazards. It would be just as possible for the United States to sustain Yorkshire in a war with England, as for us to enable Canada to contend against the United States. It is simply an impossibility. Nor must we forget that the only serious danger of a quarrel between those two neighbours arises from the connexion of Canada with this country. In my opinion it is for the interest of both that we should as speedily as possible sever the political thread by which we are as communities connected, and leave the individuals on both sides to cultivate the relations of commerce and friendly intercourse as with other nations.

\*

There is also, I think, an inherent weakness in the parody of our old English constitution, which is performed on the miniature scenes of the colonial capitals, with their speeches from the throne, votes of confidence, appeals to the country, changes of ministry, &c., and all about such trumpery issues that the game at last becomes ridiculous in the eyes of both spectators and actors.

Letter from the British M.P. and journalist, March 20, 1865, quoted by John Morley in *The Life of Richard Cobden* (1879).

**Coccola, Raymond de**
The Eskimo, on the other hand, simply accepts things as they are, and lets them go at that. If they do not work out for him, he will dismiss misfortune with one word: *"Ayorama"*—"That's destiny, that's life, there isn't anything I can do about it."

*Ayorama* (1955), by Raymond de Coccola and Paul King.

**Cockburn, Bruce**
How much history can you have in a hundred years?

Singer-composer, born in Ottawa in 1945, quoted by Myrna Kostash in *Saturday Night*, June, 1972.

**Cockloft, Jeremy**
A Frenchman is naturally noisy; but the Canadian Charioteers! Heaven defend me from *them*! I have heard the jackalls in the woods of Hindostan,—I have witnessed the chattering herds of monkeys on the coast of Malay,—but their howlings and chatterings were *music* to the sounds which now assailed my ears.

*Cursory Observations Made in Quebec, Province of Lower Canada, in the Year 1811* (1960), edited by William Toye.

**Coffin, Wilbert**
He'll never break me. He's not man enough.

These were among the last words of the Gaspé woodsman who was hanged on February 10, 1956, for the murder of three American hunters whose bodies were found near Gaspé on July 13, 1953. To the end Coffin maintained his innocence, and he alluded to the attempts of Maurice Duplessis, the premier of Quebec and minister of Justice, to deny him a fair trial. Quoted by Leslie Roberts in *The Chief: A Political Biography of Maurice Duplessis* (1963).

**Coghill, Annie Louisa (Walker)**
Work! for the night is coming;
   Work! through the morning hours;
Work! while the dew is sparkling;
   Work! 'mid the springing flowers;

Work! while the day grows brighter,
  Under the glowing sun;
Work! for the night is coming;
  Night, when man's work is done.

The popular hymn "Work! For the Night Is Coming" is based on the poem "The Night Cometh" which was written by Annie Louisa (Walker) Coghill and published anonymously in Montreal in a book of verses called *Leaves from the Backwoods* (1861).

The above text—the first of three stanzas—is taken from this volume, not from *Oak and Maple: English and Canadian Verses* (1890) where the text is slightly different. When Mrs. Coghill returned to England she discovered her poem was being sung as a hymn in an arrangement made in 1864 by Lowell Mason (who is remembered today for his musical versions of "Nearer, My God, to Thee" and "Mary Had a Little Lamb"). Mrs. Coghill may have been unhappy with the liberties taken by her arranger, but it is his hymn rather than her verse that lives on. In the Preface to *Oak and Maple*, she wrote: "But I returned to England. Cares and anxieties, and the swiftly-accomplished loss of all those who had had pleasure in my doings, had swept the blood and its contents almost out of my mind, when I was startled one day by seeing some verses of my own printed among those to be sung at a great temperance meeting. I asked whence they came, and was told 'from Moody and Sankey's Hymnbook.' I borrowed a copy of Messrs. Moody and Sankey's collection, and there, slightly altered, set to a tune which is not, certainly, strikingly beautiful, and attributed to somebody I never heard of, were my verses, beginning, 'Work, for the night is coming!' . . . The poor little 'hymn' in question was not worth a fuss—yet one has a kind of parental feeling for one's children, even if they are small and shy."

## Cogswell, Fred

The snow has pitied you and made you fair,
O snow-washed city of cold, white Christians,

So white you will not cut a black man's hair.

"Ode to Fredericton," *The Blasted Pine: An Anthology of Satire, Invective, and Disrespectful Verse Chiefly by Canadian Writers* (Revised and Enlarged Edition, 1967), edited by F.R. Scott and A.J.M. Smith.

## Cohen, Dian

Having a little inflation is like being a little pregnant—inflation feeds on itself and quickly passes the "little" mark.

Montreal economist, *The Toronto Star*, October 14, 1972.

## Cohen, Leonard

I shouldn't be in Canada at all. Winter is all wrong for me. I belong beside the Mediterranean. My ancestors made a terrible mistake. But I have to keep coming back to Montreal to renew my neurotic affiliations. Greece has the true philosophic climate—you cannot be dishonest in that light. But it's only in Montreal that you can get beat up for wearing a beard. I love Montreal. I hate the speculators who are tearing down my favourite streets and erecting those prisons built in the habit of boredom and gold.

Remarks made in 1961, on the publication of *The Spice-Box of Earth*.

Some say that no one ever leaves Montreal, for that city, like Canada itself, is designed to preserve the past, a past that happened somewhere else. . . . In Montreal there is no present tense, there is only the past claiming victories.

*The Favourite Game* (1963).

Fox: Now that you've become a singer, are you thinking of changing your name?
Cohen: Yes, I'm thinking of changing my name to September.
Fox (incredulous): Leonard September?
Cohen: No, September Cohen.

Interview with Beryl Fox on "Seven Days," CBC-TV, July, 1965.

God is alive. Magic is afoot. God is alive. Magic is afoot. God is afoot. Magic is alive. Alive is afoot. Magic never died.

> Beautiful Losers (1966).

There are many ways to tell your secrets. I think that a decent man who discovered valuable secrets is under some obligation to share them. But I think that the technique of sharing them is a great study.

> Interviewed by Michael Harris in Duel, Winter, 1969.

Poetry is a verdict.

\*

I want History to jump on Canada's spine with sharp skates. [Attributed to the Montreal poet and singer in the 1960s]

May I respectfully request that my name be withdrawn from the list of recipients of the Governor General's Award. . . . I do sincerely thank all those concerned for their generous intention. Much in me strives for this honour but the poems themselves forbid it absolutely.

> Declining the Governor General's Award for Selected Poems 1956-68 (1968), in the Spring of 1969.

There's no story so fantastic that I cannot imagine myself the hero. And there's no story so evil that I cannot imagine myself the villain.

> Quoted by Paul Saltzman in Maclean's Magazine, June, 1972.

Suzanne takes you down
to her place near the river,
you can hear the boats go by
you can stay the night beside her.
And you know that she's half crazy
but that's why you want to be there
and she feeds you tea and oranges
that come all the way from China.

> Opening lines of "Suzanne."

\*

I do not know if the world has lied
I have lied
I do not know if the world has conspired
  against love
I have conspired against love

From "What I'm Doing Here," Selected Poems 1956-68 (1968).

## Cohen, Nathan

I am, in fact, the only drama critic in Canada. The rest are reviewers.

\*

There are three things wrong with Love in Albania: the play, the direction and the casting.

\*

I preach the importance of the play.

\*

Imagine it. A Jew from Cape Breton talking to Lady Astor. [The occasion was the English lady's appearance on "Fighting Words," the TV panel show which Cohen moderated during the 1960s]

> Quoted by Barbara Moon in Maclean's Magazine, June 18, 1957.

An unmitigated disaster.

> Characteristic phrase, used in a review of an English touring production of School for Scandal in 1965, and now identified with him. Wilfrid Eggleston used the phrase at least eight years earlier to describe Grove's reaction to the sale of his novel Settlers of the Marsh; "Frederick Philip Grove," Our Living Tradition: First Series (1957), edited by Claude T. Bissell. See also Herbert Whittaker.

## Colbert, Jean-Baptiste

His Majesty cannot concur in all the reasons you put forward for the formation of Canada into a great and powerful state finding that there are divers obstacles that could only be surmounted by the passage of many years. Even granting that there were no other concerns and that the resources of the Kingdom . . . could be applied to Canada, it would not be prudent to depopulate his Kingdom . . . to populate Canada.

> Letter to Jean Talon, Versailles, January 5, 1666. Quoted by Cameron Nish in The French Régime (1965).

Always endeavour by every possible means to encourage the clergy . . . to bring up in their communities as many Indian children as possible, so that being educated in the maxims of our religion and in our customs they, along with the settlers, may evolve into a single nation and so strengthen the colony.

> Colbert, Louis XIV's great finance minister, writing in 1671 to Jean Talon, the "Great Intendant." Quoted by W.J. Eccles in *Frontenac: The Courtier Governor* (1959). It was Colbert whom Madame de Sévigné dubbed *le Nord* for his coldness.

## Colborne, Maurice
This is a purely Canadian feature; the scenery is built with Canadian wood; and the posters are made of good Canadian pulp.

> "The Real Bernard Shaw," February 4, 1929, *Addresses Delivered before the Canadian Club of Toronto: Session of 1928-29* (1929). Colborne was a British actor with his own touring company.

## Colclough, Caesar
If you can't be civil, Mr. Dalton, be as civil as you can.

> Chief justice of Newfoundland to a vociferous litigant named Dalton, after swapping judgeships with Thomas Tremlett, September, 1813. Quoted by D.W. Prowse in *A History of Newfoundland from English, Colonial, and Foreign Records* (1895). See also Thomas Tremlett.

## Colcord, Henry M.
I cannot describe it better by saying the first sensation was an overwhelming one in which it was hard to separate awe from fear. Then there came what may best be termed an absolute cessation of all feeling.

Out over that horrible gulf I heard the roar of the water below and the hum which ran through the crowd. As we cleared the brink the hum ceased—the strain had spread to them.

Unable to resist, I stole one glance down at the surging waters. It seemed for an instant as if I were poised above the entire universe. There was a feeling of immensity such as I had never felt before or since. Then I looked up.

Blondin walked on steadily, pausing for one brief moment at each point where the guy ropes joined the main cable. The line was a trifle steadier at these points and gave him a chance to assure himself of his balance. Ahead lay the wide space in the middle to which it had not been possible to attach guy-lines. Blondin halted at the last resting point before the middle span and yelled above the roar of water and wind, "Harry, you are no longer Colcord; you are Blondin. Until I clear this place be a part of me, mind, body and soul. If I sway, sway with me. Do not attempt to do any balancing yourself. If you do we shall both go down to our death."

As Blondin started across the unstable part of the line, I cleared my mind of all feeling save one. I tried to think that instead of being poised in mid-air with nothing but a slender rope between us and destruction, I was shut up with Blondin in a confined space where the thought of a fall was farcical.

> Henry M. Colcord was the Chicago-based business manager of Blondin, "the Prince of Manila." On August 19, 1859, Blondin carried Colcord across the Niagara Gorge on a three-inch manila rope, and many years later Colcord vividly remembered the experience. Quoted by Andy O'Brien in *Daredevils of Niagara* (1964). See also Blondin, "The Prince of Manila."

## Coldwell, M.J.
It is unlikely Canada will ever have a Labour government because every Canadian working man considers himself a potential capitalist.

> Attributed to the national president of the CCF who was asked privately by a newspaperman when Labour would come to power in Canada, following Labour's victory under Clement Attlee in Britain in 1945.

> Mr. M.J. Coldwell (Rosetown-Biggar): Mr. Speaker, I rise on a question of privilege. On page 1 of the Ottawa *Citizen* of Saturday, June 2, the following sentences appear:
> Then, white-faced, but determined, the Speaker moved the next vote. The Opposition could restrain itself no longer. Coldwell, shaking his fist, ad-

vanced on the Speaker. "You bloody fool," he shouted above the bedlam.

Mr. Speaker, I wish to say that never in my life anywhere, at any time, in any place, have I used those words to anyone. Earlier above the din I had sought to be heard on privilege. I advanced toward the table and I said: "You are a dictator, Mr. Speaker," and I repeated "dictator" several times. Again, let me say that I have never in my life used the foul language attributed to me.

> House of Commons, June 4, 1956. The CCF leader is referring to events that took place on "Black Friday," June 1, 1956; see also René Beaudoin.

## Cole, Jack
Coles Notes

> Some thirty million copies of Coles Notes have been published since the series of study and review aids was launched by Coles Publishing Company in 1947. A translation of Prosper Mérimée's Colomba was the initial title Currently in print and being sold wherever English is studied throughout the world are 450 different titles.

## Coleridge, Samuel Taylor
The character of most nations in their colonial dependencies is in an inverse ratio of excellence to their character at home. The best people in the mother-country will generally be the worst in the colonies; the worst at home will be the best abroad. Or, perhaps, I may state it less offensively thus:—The colonists of a well-governed country will degenerate; those of an ill-governed country will improve. [August 14, 1831]

*

A nation, to be great, ought to be compressed in its increment by nations more civilized than itself—as Greece by Persia; and Rome by Etruria, the Italian states, and Carthage. I remember Commodore Decatur saying to me at Malta, that he deplored the occupation of Louisiana by the United States, and wished that province had been possessed by England. He thought that if the United States got hold of Canada by conquest or cession, the last chance of his country

becoming a great compact nation would be lost. [June 9, 1832]

> Table Talk (1835).

And now there came both mist and snow,
And it grew wondrous cold:
And ice, mast-high, came floating by,
As green as emerald.

> "The Rime of the Ancient Mariner," The Poetical Works of Samuel Taylor Coleridge (1900), edited by William B. Scott. For the "Canadian content" of these lines, published in 1798, see Captain Thomas James.

## Colicos, John
I can't bear this psychology-probing Method acting. I prefer to be—methodical.

> Quoted by Antony Ferry in Maclean's Magazine, June 1, 1963.

## Collier, Eric
If your home is in the wilderness you seem to realize the omnipresence of danger to a far greater extent than do those who move forward through life bumped by the elbows of their fellow men. Death is there in the swaying treetop, for who can rightly tell when that tree is likely to crash to earth, snuffing out the life of all on whom it falls? Death is there on the snow-covered lakes, and creeks, and rivers for beneath the snow lurks many a treacherous air hole ready to devour instantly all who might stumble into it. Death rides watchful and expectant with the breath of an arctic wind, for intense cold numbs both the will power and the strength of all who have to face it, breeding within them an almost irresistible temptation to sit down and snatch a moment or two of rest. And if they succumb to that temptation? Instead of a few moments of rest they are likely to sleep the sleep of no awakening.

> Three Against the Wilderness (1959).

## Collin, W.E.
The White Savannahs.

> Somewhat wintery title of a book of critical essays on Canadian writers published in 1936.

## Collins, Edmund

The valley of the Saskatchewan, according to scientific computation, is capable of sustaining 800,000,000 souls.

"The Future of the Dominion of Canada," *Canadian Leaves: History, Art, Science, Leisure, Commerce: A Series of New Papers Read before the Canadian Club of New York* (1887).

## Collins, Mary Lou

In Newfoundland it seems like the rest of Canada is a million miles away.

The Newfoundland-born singer was quoted by Flo Diggins in *That's Showbusiness*, May 16, 1973.

## Collins, Peter

It is no coincidence that Anglo-Saxon cooking is proverbially bad, for bad food and bad architecture both derive from the same philosophical disease.

"The Architectonics of Pure Taste," *Journal of the Royal Architectural Institute of Canada*, 38, 1961.

## Colombo, John Robert

Canada could have enjoyed:
English government,
French culture,
and American know-how.

Instead it ended up with:
English know-how,
French government,
and American culture.

"Oh Canada" (1965), *The New Romans: Candid Canadian Opinions of the U.S.* (1968), edited by Al Purdy.

## Colville, Alex

All real artists are brothers and co-workers in different generations; the "made" things which we call works of art stretch in a continuous series through Old Kingdom Egyptian sculptures, the mosaics of Ravenna, the frescoes of Giotto, the canvasses of Seurat, and on into the future. It's a kind of anti-death league. It is in fact true that life *is* short, art *is* long.

Quoted by Harry Bruce in *Saturday Night*, May, 1972.

I guess my aim as an artist is, in Joseph Conrad's words: "To do the highest possible justice to reality." [Statement made in 1961]

Quoted by Helen J. Dow in *The Art of Alex Colville* (1972).

## Comfort, Charles

Within this total milieu develops the characterful Canadian spirit, essentially northern, displaying much that is characteristic of northern peoples, individualistic, conservative, loyal, independent, virile and industrious; the Canadian, in whom are mobilized the special form of his respect for his Creator, his ideals, his conflicts, his insights, his triumphs and frustrations.

"Painting," *Royal Commission Studies: A Selection of Essays Prepared for the Royal Commission on National Development in the Arts, Letters and Sciences* (1951).

## Compton, Neil

Canada's marginal culture—occupying a middle ground between British and American, English and French, civilization and wilderness—appears to favour the interpretative and critical, rather than the fiercely creative, intelligence. Life in Canada inculcates a respect for the brutal, objective thusness of nature and an awareness (sometimes a wry one) of the validity of opposition to it. Canadians tend to become singers, pianists, actors, critics, and diplomats rather than composers, dramatists, poets, or political geniuses.

This is the ideal temperament for democracy, and the greatest triumphs of Canadian broadcasting, as of Canadian cinema, have been in this field. The CBC's audience has become accustomed to workmanlike documentary programs as part of the regular weekly diet on both radio and television and occasionally these sober factual productions come close to the heights of poetic truth.

Recently, the documentary spirit has been tending toward irony, another mode encouraged by Canada's comparatively helpless proximity to stronger or wealthier neighbours. The basic technique is simple—to juxtapose pictures and commentary (often by the subject himself) in order to achieve almost Swiftian satiric intensities.

"Cancult and the CBC" (1964), *Canada: A Guide to the Peaceable Kingdom* (1970), edited by William Kilbourn.

**Comtois, Ulysee**
The two big tricks of the twentieth century are: technology instead of grace, and information instead of virtue.

Quoted by Beverly Carter in "Conversations with Four Montreal Artists," *Artscanada*, February-March, 1971.

**Conchon, Georges**
If Paris and Versailles were swallowed by an earthquake tomorrow morning, the daily lives of "our" people in Tadoussac, Chicoutimi and Beauceville would go on exactly as before; whereas a slight fall in prices on the Detroit stock market affects it noticeably. Americanization is a reality, the other thing is moonshine.

*Canada: Reflections and Impressions of a Visitor* (1969), translated by Patrick Evans. Conchon won the Prix Goncourt in 1964.

**Connaught, Duke of**
Per angler per day, perdition. My good man, I ask you what is the sense of me being Governor of this widespread, far-flung, sea-to-sea Dominion if I cannot catch all the fish I have a mind to?

To a park warden who advised the governor general, fishing at Consolation Lake near Banff, that the limit was "fifteen fish per angler per day." This occurred between 1911 and 1916; a sport as well as a sportsman, the governor general did not exceed the legal limit. Quoted by Dan McCowan in *Hill-Top Tales* (1948).

**Connell, Charles**
Nobody was more surprised than I.

Half a million five-cent stamps appeared bearing the likeness of Charles Connell, postmaster-general of New Brunswick, in 1860. This came as a complete surprise to Connell, who had as many as could be retrieved destroyed.

**Connolly, Cyril**
Meanwhile Canada is behind Jamaica, which has quite a good novelist within it, and a coloured expatriate outside.

The British critic's evaluation of the Canadian novel, after reading Grove's *Our Daily Bread* and Knister's *White Narcissus* in 1929. Quoted by Desmond Pacey in "The Outlook for Canadian Literature" (1968), *Essays in Canadian Criticism: 1938-1968* (1969).

**Connor, Ralph** See Charles W. Gordon.

**Connors, Stompin' Tom**
My ambition? I guess you could say it's to sing Canada to the world.

Quoted by Alden Nowlan in *Maclean's Magazine*, August, 1972.

The Black Donnellys ride;
Their killers by their side;
Down the Roman Line till the end of time.

Chorus of "Massacre of the Black Donnellys" in which the New Brunswick composer-singer recreates the massacre of the Donnelly family on the Roman Line road, near Lucan, Ontario, the night of February 4, 1880.

**Conrad, Joseph**
It seems to me that the resentful sea gods never do sleep, and as long as men will travel on the water, the sea gods will take their toll.

The worst marine disaster in Canadian history occurred in the Gulf of St. Lawrence when the Norwegian collier *Storstad* rammed and sank the CP ocean liner *Empress of Ireland*, May 29, 1914. More than a thousand drowned, and the *Illustrated London News*, in an issue devoted to the catastrophe, published Conrad's article "The Lesson of the Collision."

**Conway, John**
Official oratory about the undefended frontier is misleading. The frontier has been undefended in large part because

it is undefendable, not because of any profound similarity between the two peoples, who are, in fact, different in their historical experience, their political philosophy, and their view of the world outside North America. They are complementary to each other, but they are not identical.

"What Is Canada?" *Atlantic Monthly*, November, 1964.

## Cook, Dr. Frederick
Why did I desire so ardently to reach the Pole? The attainment of the Pole meant at the time simply the accomplishing of a splendid, unprecedented feat—a feat of brain and muscle in which I should, if successful, signally surpass other men. This imaginary spot held for me the revealing of no great scientific secrets. I never regarded the feat as of any scientific value. The real victory would lie, not in reaching the goal itself, but in overcoming the obstacles which exist in the way of it.

The first person to reach the North Pole was probably the American explorer Dr. Frederick Cook on April 21, 1908. *My Attainment of the Pole: Being a Record of the Expedition that First Reached the Boreal Center, 1907-1909* (1911). The counterclaim of Robert Peary is dismissed by Farley Mowat in *The Polar Passion: The Quest for the North Pole* (1967). See also Robert Peary.

## Cook, Captain James
I, who had the ambition not only to go farther than any man had ever been before, but as far as it was possible for man to go. . . .

From a letter written to the Admiralty, 1768. The celebrated navigator served at the sieges of Louisbourg and Quebec and, two decades later on his last voyage, explored the west coast of North America to the Bering Strait. This inscription appears on the base of Cook's statue in London, England: "He laid the foundations of the British Empire in Australia and New Zealand; he charted the shores of Newfoundland and traversed the Ocean Gates of Canada both East and West."

## Cook, Michael
But you don't have to go back to history books [to find material for plays in Newfoundland]. All you've got to do is have a few beers in the kitchen with old-time Newfoundlanders, and listen to their poetic Irish metaphors and their marvellous stories, and you could fill the stage with epic drama for years.

*Canadian Panorama*, January 13, 1973.

## Cook, Ramsay
Every generation of Canadian nationalist intellectuals seem fated to play the part of Sisyphus. Their permanent task is to push the millstone of Canadian nationalism up a steep mountain, only to find that it rolls back down again to await the labours of the next generation. This means that much of Canadian intellectual history sounds like a broken record. The voices change but the refrain is the same: French-English relations are in crisis, and Canada is a colony dominated by Great Britain or the United States—or both. Only the favoured few—the nationalist intellectuals themselves—are free from that colonial mentality which permanently blinds Canadians to their real status as a colonized people.

*Saturday Night*, April, 1970.

That quest for equality which has characterized so much of French Canada's history will not be concluded by the mere promulgation of a new constitution, for after all, every generation dreams of new forms of equality. *Egalité ou Indépendance?* Independence is easy—how many nations have achieved it since 1945? But equality? How many peoples have achieved that in all of recorded history?

*

The besetting disease of Canadian public life for almost a decade had been Diefenbakerism: the belief that promises were policies, that rhetoric was action, and that the electorate believed in Santa Claus.

*The Maple Leaf Forever: Essays on Nationalism and Politics in Canada* (1971).

## Cooke, Jack Kent
I believe that if one works hard, rewards accrue in the natural order.

> Quoted by Thelma Le Cocq in *Saturday Night*, August 2, 1952. Roy Thomson called Cooke, who renounced his Canadian citizenship in 1961, "a salesman of almost supernatural persuasiveness."

## Coolidge, Calvin
Dear Miss Dressler:
This boy wants to go on the stage.
> Yours truly,
> *Calvin Coolidge.*

> The future president of the United States was a twenty-eight-year-old lawyer in 1900 when he addressed this note to Marie Dressler, then a well-known Broadway actress. The "boy" was a young singer named Michael Sinnott, who would acquire fame as Hollywood's Mack Sennett. Coolidge's note effected a profitable film friendship for the comedienne from Ontario and the producer-director from Quebec. *King of Comedy* (1954), by Mack Sennett as told to Cameron Shipp. See also Marie Dressler and Mack Sennett.

## Cooper, John A.
No country on the face of the globe has produced, proportionately, so many volumes of verse as Canada.

> *Canada Under Victoria* (1901). A highly dubious statement made by a literary magazine editor who became a motion-picture distributor.

## Corbett, E.A.
The crucial test of friendship turns on whether or not we are willing to accept the responsibilities of self-government; whether or not we are willing to do our own thinking about the issues that confront us, and then to take positive, active steps to promote the solutions of those problems through the democratic process. This is perhaps a high standard of citizenship but anything lower than that may prove fatal in the dangerous world we live in.

> "A Brief History of Adult Education in Canada," *Adult Education in Canada* (1950), edited by J.R. Kidd.

## Cornish, John
I don't know what a Canadian is. Even Ottawa doesn't know. But I know what I am. I'm a Scot resisting becoming an American.

> *The Provincials* (1951).

## Corte-Real, Gaspar
They are extremely fitted to endure labour and will probably turn out the best slaves which have been discovered up to this time.

> "Labrador — Laboratoris Terra — is undoubtedly so called from the fact that Corte-Real stole from the country some fifty-seven natives, whom he described in a letter to the Venetian ambassador at Lisbon, as well-fitted for slaves," wrote J.G. Bourinot in "Canadian Historical Names," *Canadian Monthly* (1875).

## Cosette-Trudel, Jacques
I thought about violence for at least a year. I thought about killing a person because of something you believe in, and that you're forced to do it because this person doesn't think like you and there's no other way.

> A kidnapper of James Cross, quoted by Gérard Vallières in "The FLQ Exiles," *Weekend Magazine*, January 22, 1972.

## Costain, Thomas B.
I left to seek my fortune in the United States in the years when it was possible to make a fortune.

> Brantford-born editor of *Maclean's Magazine* turned popular historical novelist. "A Glance at the Future" (1951), *Empire Club of Canada: Addresses 1950-51* (1951).

## Costigan, John
I cannot claim any credit for the great success which attended the carrying through of Confederation. But I claim that my opposition to it was just as sincere as my support is sincere now, and I would be sorry to allow any Canadian to claim that he is more loyal to Canada than I am today. As you all know Confederation carried the day, but I hope the history of how it was carried out will never be written. It was a case of the end justifying the means.

Costigan was minister of Marine and Fisheries in the first Parliament. "Fifth Annual Banquet," April 21, 1909, *Addresses Delivered before the Canadian Club of Ottawa: 1903-1909* (1910).

## Coté, Guy L.
What happens between each frame is much more important than what exists on each frame. Animation is therefore the art of manipulating invisible interstices that lie between frames.

"Animation Films in Canada," *The Journal of the British Film Academy*, Winter, 1956-57.

## Coughlin, Father Charles E.
Capitalism is on the straight road to ruin, not due to the socialists, not due to the communists, but due to itself. It has turned the routine of production into destruction. As to that there is no doubt. The croakings of communists who would like to begin digging its grave are by no means premature in their rejoicings. Like a monk in the Trappist Monastery, capitalism is daily digging its own grave. ["The Suicide of Capitalism," a talk broadcast on February 5, 1933]

*

I ask the prayers of those who hear these words, lest while I preach to others I myself become a castaway.

Appeal made by Father Coughlin on his last broadcast, April 16, 1933, before being silenced by his religious superiors. The Basilian priest, born in Hamilton in 1891, took his social ministry to the air waves in 1926, from his studio in the Shrine of the Little Flower in Detroit. Coughlin was known as "the religious Walter Winchell" and "the Huey Long of the air waves." Louis B. Ward's *Father Charles E. Coughlin: An Authorized Biography* (1933).

## Coughtry, Graham
Every damn pine tree in the country has been painted.

Remark made in 1955 by the Toronto artist whose speciality is abstract figures. Quoted by Barrie Hale in *Toronto Painting: 1953-1965* (1972).

## Coulter, John
In countries such as Canada, still in pro-

cess of colonization by immigrants from various stocks in the old world, a national idiom in the arts can hardly be more than emergent. Music and poetry and painting must speak, as yet in old world voices. In the slow passage of centuries these many voices may at last merge in a Canadian dialect of the universal language of art. But meanwhile, and apart from mere geographic nuances of subject-matter, the art of a Canadian remains, with but little differentiation, the art of the country and of his forbears, and the old world heritage of myth and legend remains his heritage, to be used by him for suitable ends, though the desk on which he write be a Canadian desk in a Canadian house, and though his work be designated Canadian.

Preface, *Deirdre of the Sorrows* (1944).

Canadian theatre? what is it? If only playwrights, actors and producers north of Niagara would turn their eyes from Broadway and look around them at a place called Canada!

*

True comedy can be as serious as tragedy. A hundred grand plays are waiting for Canadians who will write them. But if there were a great Canadian play, would Canadians bother to stage it—any more that they bother now to stage that first Canadian grand opera, Healey Willan's latest and major work, *Deirdre of the Sorrows*? Cover it up, good friends; cover it decently up with Canadian dust and let it lie. Some day the Americans or English will do it and tell us not to be ashamed and then, having their word for it, we will tardily take the duster and disinter a work once made in Canada.

Remarks made in 1947 by the Irish-Canadian playwright, quoted by Betty Lee in *Love and Whisky: The Story of the Dominion Drama Festival* (1973).

## Courchene, Chief Dave
We're not fooling around. We've got the bull by the tail, and we're looking him straight in the eye.

From an interview with Colin Hoath at Island Lake, Manitoba, broadcast on the CBC-TV National News, February 22, 1973.

## Courcy, Alcide
Old priests don't make the best bishops.

Quebec Liberal party organizer, in reference to the candidacy of the youthful Robert Bourassa in the election of April 29, 1970. Quoted by John Saywell in *Quebec 70: A Documentary Narrative* (1971) who called this "perhaps the only folksy comment in the Bourassa campaign."

## Cournoyer, Yvon
Some nights you need a few bodychecks to wake you up.

Right wing player of the Montreal Canadiens, quoted by Jim Proudfoot in *The Toronto Star*, May 11, 1973.

## Coward, Noël
I love travelling, but I'm always too late or too early. I arrive in Japan when the cherry blossoms have fallen. I get to China too early for the next revolution. I reach Canada when the maple leaves have gone. People are always telling me about something I haven't seen. I find it very pleasant.

*The Wit of Noël Coward* (1968), compiled by Dick Richards.

## Cowper, William
They have fall'n
Each in his field of glory: one in arms,
And one in council.—Wolfe upon the lap
Of smiling victory that moment won,
And Chatham, heart-sick of his country's shame.
They made us many soldiers. Chatham still
Consulting England's happiness at home,
Secured it by an unforgiving frown,
If any wrong'd her. Wolfe, where'er he fought,
Put so much of his heart into his act,
That his example had a magnet's force,
And all were sought to follow whom he loved.
Those suns are set. Oh rise some other such!
Or all that we have left, is empty talk
Or old atchievements [*sic*], and despair of new.

*The Task: A Poem in Six Books* (1785), Book III: The Time-Piece. *Cowper: Poetry and Prose* (1968), edited by Brian Spiller.

## Cox, Esther
"Esther Cox, you are mine to kill."

Mysterious message on the wall of the house where Miss Cox lived, Nova Scotia. Quoted by Walter Hubbell in *The Haunted House: A True Ghost Story, Being an Account of the Mysterious Manifestations that Have Taken Place in the Residence of Esther Cox, the Young Girl who Is Possessed of Devils, and Has Become Known Throughout the Entire Dominion as the Great Amherst Mystery* (1879).

## Coyne, James
I can only say with deep respect . . . that the question before you is on your conscience—do you find the defendant guilty of misbehaviour, justifying the decision of the government—or do you find him not guilty? A vote in favour of this bill . . . is a verdict of guilty. There can be no equivocation about that.

Governor of the Bank of Canada before the Senate committee reviewing his activities, July 12, 1961. The Senate voted against the Conservative bill that would declare his office vacant. Feeling himself vindicated, Coyne resigned the following day.

## Cranborne, Lord
Fine chap, Vincent, but he does make one feel a bit of a savage.

Lord Cranborne, Marquess of Salisbury, Winston Churchill's Lord Privy Seal, referring to Vincent Massey, 1951. *In Our Time: Highlights of Fifteen Years of Canadian News as It has Been Reported in the Pages of Time, The Weekly News-Magazine* (1958).

## Crann, Mrs. George
As things are, we are building up American millionaires out of the hard earnings of our Western farmers.

*

A great deal of the literature read in the colony is from the U.S.—a very great deal of it.

*A Woman in Canada* (1910).

## Crawford, Isabella Valancy

The South Wind laid his moccasins
  aside,
Broke his gay calumet of flowers, and
  cast
His useless wampum, beaded with cool
  dews,
Far from him northward. . . .

"Malcolm's Katie: A Love Story" (1884).

\*

Toronto, joy and peace!

"Toronto" (1884), *The Collected Poems
of Isabella Valancy Crawford* (1905),
edited by J.W. Garvin.

## Creighton, Donald

The problem of a separate Quebec had
come to obsess and monopolize the
minds of both English and French Canadians. It had distracted them from other
and more vital tasks. It blinded them to
the peril that threatened their existence
as a separate nation in North America.

\*

On the 7th of November, in Eagle Pass
in the Monashee Mountains, at a place
Stephen had determined would be called
Craigellachie in memory of his clan's
meeting-place and battle slogan, Donald
Smith drove home the last spike in the
completed transcontinental line; and
nine days later Louis Riel dropped to his
death in the prison at Regina.

\*

His verbal currency was invariably ten-
dered in the highest denominations; but
in practical politics he always dealt in
very small change. . . . He made both big
words and small deeds serve his turn.
There was at once more in him than met
the eye, and a great deal less than filled
the ear. [On W.L. Mackenzie King]

\*

Confederation had been a political
union of several provinces, not a cultural compact between two ethnic communities, English and French.

*Canada's First Century: 1867-1967* (1970).

What confronts us is either the breaking-
up of our country or its continuance as
a fragmented, decentralized nation, firmly integrated in the American economic
and military empire, with all its assets,
down to the last treasures of its birthright, freely expendable in the service
of the government and people of the
United States. Our only hope of deliver-
ance from this fate lies in the reassertion
of Canadian nationalism in its first and
integral form. The vain and perilous
pursuit of dualism, which was not an
original object of Confederation and has
nearly brought about its undoing, must
be abandoned. One nation, not two
nations in one, can alone maintain an
effective defence of Canada.

"The Coming Defeat of Canadian Nationalism," November 16, 1970, *The Empire Club of Canada: Addresses 1970-71*
(1971).

I feel that history's closest affiliation is
with literature and not with science.

\*

For a person to live in a country, and to
be ignorant of its history on almost every
issue that comes up, means that he is
really walking around in the dark all
the time. I think that history can give
you a sense of courage in a difficult and
dark world. You can say to yourself: I at
least know something about this world,
I know how it got the way it is, I know
where it's possibly going, not certainly
but possibly. I can stand up against the
world.

Interviewed by Ramsay Cook in *The
Craft of History* (1973), edited by Eleanor Cook.

History is the record of an encounter between character and circumstance . . .
the encounter between character and circumstance is essentially a story.

*Towards the Discovery of Canada* (1972).

Heroism is not a memory of the past. It
is the virtue by which a nation can preserve its identity and fulfill its destiny.

"Heroic Beginnings," CBC-TV, February 21, 1973. See also John F. Kennedy.

## Crémazie, Octave

M.M. Garneau and Ferland have already, it is true, supplied a granite base
for our literary edifice; but if one bird
does not make a spring, two books do
not constitute a literature. All that has

been produced by us, beyond these two great works, seems to me to have no chance of survival. Who will read ——— in fifty years? And if I may speak of myself, who will think of my poor verses in twenty years? . . . The cause of this inferiority lies not in the rarity of men of talent, but in the disastrous environment provided for the writer by the indifference of a population which has as yet no taste for letters, at least for works produced by native sons.

*

The more I reflect on the destiny of Canadian literature, the less chance I find for its leaving a mark in history. Canada lacks its own language. If we spoke Iroquois or Huron, our literature would live. Unfortunately we speak and write, after a sufficiently pitiful fashion, it is true, the language of Bossuet and Racine. Say or do what we will, we will always remain only a simple colony from the literary point of view; and even if Canada became an independent country and made her flag shine in the sun of nations, we should remain nonetheless simple literary colonials. . . . I repeat, if we spoke Huron or Iroquois, the works of our writers would attract the attention of the old world. . . . But what does it matter, after all, that the works of Canadian authors are not destined to cross the Atlantic? Are we not a million Frenchmen forgotten by the mother country on the shores of the St. Lawrence? It is not enough to encourage all those who hold a pen to know that this little people will grow great, and that it will always guard the name and memory of those who aided it to conserve intact the most precious of all treasures, the tongue of its fathers?

*

Rhyme "glory" with "victory" a certain number of times, "ancestors" with "glorious," "France" with "hope"; mingle with these rhymes some sonorous words like "religion," our "fatherland," our "tongue," our "laws," the "blood of our fathers"; warm the whole over the flame of patriotism, and serve hot. Everyone will say that it is magnificent.

*

I have come too soon into too young a country.

> Letter to Abbé H.-R. Casgrain, January 29, 1867, *Les Oeuvres complètes d'Octave Crémazie* (1882), edited by Abbé H.-R. Casgrain. The poet addressed the last remark, "I have come too soon into too young a country," to Louis-Honoré Fréchette for him to use; it is said to paraphrase a similar line by Alfred de Mussset.

For the sake of my flag, I come here to die.

> Line from "Le drapeau de Carillon," a poem written by Crémazie in 1858 to recall the centenary of Montcalm's valiant defence of Fort Carillon. *Les Oeuvres complètes d'Octave Crémazie* (1882), edited by Abbé H.-R. Casgrain.

### Crerar, General H.D.G.
"Each for all" has been the guiding principle of the Canadian army in battle. That same principle is the essential one to which we must adhere if we are to assure the life and growth of democratic government in the world—that community system which has been so eloquently described by Abraham Lincoln as "government of the people, by the people, for the people." Soldiers of Canada have worked to it in war. Citizens of Canada can do no less in peace.

> V-E Day message to the First Canadian Army, May 7, 1945. Quoted by Margaret Fairley in *Spirit of Canadian Democracy: A Collection of Canadian Writings from the Beginnings to the Present Day* (1945).

### Crèvecoeur, J. Hector St. John
Whoever traverses the continent must easily observe those strong differences, which will grow more evident in time. The inhabitants of Canada, Massachusetts, the middle provinces, the southern ones will be as different as their climates; their only points of unity will be those of religion and language.

*

It would be a task worthy of speculative genius, to enter immediately into the situation and characters of the people, from Nova Scotia to West Florida; and surely history cannot possibly present any subject more pleasing to behold.

\*

Most of the merchants and young men of Montreal spend the greatest part of their time in trading with the Indians, at an amazing distance from Canada; and it often happens that they are three years together absent from home.

*Letters from an American Farmer* (1782).

## Croghan, Major George
We will give up the fort when there's not a man left to defend it.

With 160 men, the American major held Fort Stephenson, Lower Sandusky, Ohio, against a thousand British and Indian troops under the British general, Henry A. Proctor, on August 2, 1813.

## Croll, David A.
I have never swerved from a conviction that the working people have a right to form their associations for the purpose of collective bargaining; that they have the privilege of joining the lawful union of their own choice; that if they, in their wisdom and in their knowledge of the conditions under which they work, consider that they should make the final resort to a strike, then that too is their right; and, having struck, that they shall not be molested if they picket peacefully and within the law. These I have considered are the rights which our law ensures to them and which Liberalism throughout the years has upheld.

\*

You know my origins; I have always been with, and one of, the workers, and I have neither the desire nor the ability to swing at this late date to the other side. In my official capacity I have travelled the middle of the road, but now that you have put the extreme alternative to me, my place is marching with the workers rather than riding with General Motors. At this late date I cannot oppose unionism and the workers and labour as a whole.

One of the most celebrated of all Cana-

dian aphorisms—"My place is marching with the workers rather than riding with General Motors"—graced the letter of resignation written by the Honourable David A. Croll, minister of Public Welfare, Labour and Municipal Affairs, addressed to Mitchell Hepburn, premier of Ontario, April 14, 1937. This came at the height of the Oshawa strike, when 3,700 auto workers were fighting for union recognition and the right to join the CIO. *The Toronto Star*, April 15, 1937.

## Crombie, Keith
Absinthe makes the heart grow fonder.

\*

Osculation is the sincerest form of Flappery.

*Sackcloth and Splashes: Fragments from "The Goblin"* (1923), by Keith Crombie and J.E. McDougall.

## Cronyn, Hume
The house I was born in was the same house my father was born in. One of my sisters lives there now. We were fairly prosperous. I was thirteen years younger than the next-youngest child in our family, and I was alone a lot as a child. My loneliness and the whole business of pretending led me into acting, which I decided to do at the age of six or seven.

Hume Cronyn (a "slightly-built Canadian actor, long on American stage and screen," according to Leslie Halliwell in *The Filmgoer's Companion* [Third Edition, 1970]) was born in 1911 in London and attended McGill. *The Player: A Profile of an Art* (1962), by Lillian and Helen Ross.

## Crooks, W.J.
Wanted to purchase a negro girl from 7 to 12, of good disposition; W.J. Crooks.

Classified advertisement, *St. Catharines Journal*, October 4, 1795.

## Crosbie, John S.
A day without a pun is a day without sunshine; there is gloom for improvement.

*Crosbie's Dictionary of Puns* (1972).

## Cross, Austin F.

Not one man in ten living in Montreal knows his own same Montreal has nestled its million population around the slope of an extinct volcano, but that geological phenomenon of aeons ago permeates the life of this great, noisy, lively Brobdingnagianly-broadminded city, and today it's a twenty-four-hour town, with more life on its main street at four in the morning than most American cities have at four in the afternoon. Montreal has a permanent case of whoopee.

\*

Lastly, Toronto is known as Toronto the Good, because of its alleged piety. My guess is that there's more polygamy in Toronto than Baghdad, only it's not called that in Toronto.

*Cross Roads* (1936).

## Cross, James R.

What more can I say? What can I expect? When and how will this bad dream end?

Letter "to whom it may concern," November 15, 1970, dictated by the captors of the British trade commissioner, kidnapped by FLQ terrorists on October 5 and rescued fifty-nine days later on December 3.

There's been a lot of talk about journalistic responsibility. But people have responsibility to the kidnapped, to the chap in there, he's the loneliest man in the world. And speculation about what he's trying to do may cost him his life.

\*

It was a case of six kids trying to make a revolution.

Quoted by Ron Haggart and Aubrey E. Golden in *Rumours of War* (1971). Remarks made after his release, December, 1970. See also James Eayrs.

## Crossman, Richard

I find Canadian politics more interesting, more fruitful, and more creative than the politics of almost any country I have studied, because it is so wonderfully varied, because it is plural. . . . It allows people to be themselves, to be different. Canada allows provincial governments to go off into the most extraordinary heresies, heresies it of course forbids in the federal parliament as far as possible. I therefore find federal government a bit boring, but provincial government is absolutely fascinating.

"Canadian Issues as Seen from Outside," *Order and Good Government* (1964), edited by Gordon Hawkins.

## Crowfoot

The advice given me and my people has proved to be very good. If the police had not come to this country, where would we all be now? Bad men and whiskey were killing us so fast that very few of us would have been alive today. The Mounted Police have protected us as the feathers of the bird protect it from the frosts of winter. I wish them all good, and I trust that all our hearts will increase in goodness from this time forward. I am satisfied! I will sign the treaty.

At the signing of Blackfoot Treaty Number Seven, September 22, 1877, Blackfoot Crossing. Quoted by Alexander Morris in *The Treaties of Canada with the Indians* (1880).

Ah, I did not touch it.

"His name was written in English and Blackfoot, and Crowfoot was asked to touch the pen so that his X could be marked. Suspiciously, he asked the reason for this. He was told that the Indian hands, unaccustomed to holding pens, could not make a proper X, so it was customary for the chief to touch the pen, indicating his willingness to sign. Crowfoot made a motion toward the pen and his mark was inscribed. Crowfoot had signed the treaty—or had he?" Hugh A. Dempsey's *Crowfoot: Chief of the Blackfeet* (1972).

We will be loyal to the Queen whatever happens.

Telegram to Sir John A. Macdonald giving the prime minister assurances that Crowfoot would not join the Northwest Rebellion, April 11, 1885. Three days later Sir John replied: "I have received your good and loyal message by telegraph and I have shown it to the Governor General who is our Great Chief under the Queen. He desires me to thank you for your promise to be a faithful friend of our Great Mother and is sure your words are true." Quoted by Hugh A. Dempsey in *Crowfoot: Chief of the Blackfeet* (1972).

A little while and I will be gone from among you, whither I cannot tell. From nowhere we came, into nowhere we go. What is life? It is a flash of a firefly in the night. It is a breath of a buffalo in the winter time. It is as the little shadow that runs across the grass and loses itself in the sunset.

> Dying words of the great chief, overlooking the Bow River, April 25, 1890. Quoted by John Peter Turner in *The North-West Mounted Police: 1873-1893* (1950). Some early versions of the deathbed utterance conclude: "My children, I have spoken." He died at three-thirty in the afternoon, and an Indian was heard shouting: "He is no more. No one like him will fill his place." For a funeral oration, see Father Albert Lacombe.

## Crowley, Aleister
Vancouver presents no interest to the casual visitor. It is severely Scotch. Its beauties lie in its surroundings.

*

The Rockies have no majesty; they do not elevate the mind to contemplation of Almighty God any more than they warm the heart by seeming sentinels to watch over the habitations of one's fellow men.

*

Toronto as a city carries out the idea of Canada as a country. It is a calculated crime both against the aspirations of the soul and the affection of the heart.

*

Of all the loveless, lifeless lands that writhe beneath the wrath of God, commend me to Canada!

> *The Confessions of Aleister Crowley: An Autohagiography* (1970). The self-styled poet and black magician travelled from British Columbia to Niagara Falls in 1906 and recalled his impressions seventeen years later.

## Culbertson, Ely
The game was called *bridge*. I was urged to join, but after a few sessions I gave up in disgust.
*It's a stupid game,* I thought.

*

At that time, the labour laws in Canada and America, especially for immigrants, were made chiefly for the benefit of the contractors. The country had to be built, and built quickly.

> In Winnipeg in 1911, the young Ely Culbertson was introduced to the game of bridge. That summer he organized Ukrainian labourers on the Grand Trunk in Alberta. *The Strange Lives of One Man: An Autobiography* (1940).

## Cullen, Thomas S.
About teaching I have only one important thing to say; never start a lecture at half past two. Everybody goes to sleep on you.

> Influential Canadian-born head of the Department of Gynaecology, Johns Hopkins, about 1910, quoted by Judith Robinson in *Tom Cullen of Baltimore* (1949).

## Cumming, R.D.
We should try to arrange ourselves so that we will appear as plausible as possible to posterity.

*

We sometimes lost dollars by being too careful with our cents.

*

A dollar looks larger going out than it does coming in.

*

Every dog wonders why the other dog was born.

*

When a man reaches forty he usually settles down to make the best of things.

*

A good book has no ending.

*

Sometimes we are called cranks because we will not be sat upon.

*

The present seems to be a thing of the past.

*

A great many children go to school to learn to read novels.

*

It takes as long to become a man as it does to become a philosopher.

*

The poorer a man the greater his misfortunes.

*

You seldom meet an enthusiast who is not a crank also.

> Skookum Chuck Fables, Bits of History, Through the Microscope by Skookum (1915), by R.D. Cumming.

**Cunard, Sir Samuel**
We are entirely unacquainted with the cost of a steamboat, and would not embark in a business of which we are ignorant.

*

Steamers properly built and manned might start and arrive at their destination with the punctuality of railroad trains.

> Remarks made by the Halifax businessman in 1829, nine years before he founded the company that in 1878 would emerge as the Cunard Steam-Ship Co. Ltd. Sir Samuel's motto on his arms, granted in 1859, was: "By Perseverance."

**Curnoe, Greg**
The University of Western Ontario has recently purchased several manuscripts by John Milton for around $250,000; at the same time urban renewal schemes are in effect which will replace the centre of London (which dates from around 1830-60) with parking lots and large office buildings. Can a sense of place survive the physical destruction of that place?

*

CLOSE DOWN THE 49TH PARALLEL, ETC.

*

LOVE DOESN'T LAST LONG, BUT THINKING ABOUT IT DOES

*

WE ARE REALLY RIEL

> Messages stencilled on his canvasses, quoted by Dennis Reid in Greg Curnoe: Canada X Biennial, São Paulo (1969).

**Curran, J.W.**
A Norseman died in Ontario 900 years ago.

> Title of a talk in 1938, Empire Club of Canada: Addresses Delivered to the Members During the Year 1938-39 (1939). Curran wrote Here Was Vinland (1939) about the Sault Ste. Marie area.

The story of Little Red Riding Hood has laid an unreasoning fear on countless millions of human beings.

*

There are, of course, several things in Ontario that are more dangerous than wolves. For instance, the step-ladder.

*

Any man that says he's been et by a wolf is a liar.

> Wolves Don't Bite (1940). The "et by a wolf" quote, which had quite a vogue, Curran attributes to a hunter, "Old Sam Martin."

Shorthorns stand close. The man behind may be in his bare feet.

> Sign placed in the men's washroom at the Sault Daily Star by its publisher, James W. Curran.

**Currelly, C.T.**
The museum is the working man's university, especially the modern museum of art and history.

> Attributed to the first director of the Royal Ontario Museum in 1932.

I brought the ages home.

> Title of Currelly's autobiography, edited by Northrop Frye, published in 1956.

**Currie, Sir Arthur**
Truly magnificent . . . the sight was awful and wonderful.

> Entry for Easter Monday, April 9, 1917, concerning the Battle of Vimy Ridge. Reproduced in Historical Documents of Canada: Volume V: The Arts of War and Peace, 1914-1945 (1972), edited by C.P. Stacey.

To have gone through what anyone who has been here for three years has had to go through, and to have given the very best that is in one to the service of your country, would almost justify one in hoping that your own countrymen would not refer to you as a murderer.

> Letter to Sir George Perley, December 10, 1917. Quoted by A.J.M. Hyatt in "Arthur Currie and Conscription: A Soldier's View," *Canadian Historical Review*, September, 1969.

Looking back with pride on the unbroken record of your glorious achievements, asking you to realize that today the fate of the British Empire hangs in the balance, I place my trust in the Canadian Corps, knowing that where Canadians are engaged there can be no giving way.

Under the orders of your devoted officers in the coming battle you will advance or fall where you stand facing the enemy.

To those who will fall I say, "You will not die but step into immortality. Your mothers will not lament your fate but will be proud to have borne such sons. Your names will be revered for ever and ever by your grateful country, and God will take you unto Himself."

Canadians: in this fateful hour, I command you, and I trust you to fight as you have ever fought with all your strength, with all your determination, with all your tranquil courage. On many a hard fought field of battle you have overcome this enemy. With God's help you shall achieve victory once more.

> Special order of the day on the eve of the final Battle of the Somme, March 27, 1918. Quoted by John D. Robins in *A Pocketful of Canada* (1946).

I know a battalion whose period of relief came and they would not quit fighting. You cannot understand how sick we all were of the war, nor our anxiety of finishing it as soon as possible, if there was any chance of success. Your sons and brothers wanted to see it out. They wanted to be done with the cursed thing. They never want to see any more war.

> "The Last Hundred Days of the War,"

August 29, 1919, *Addresses Delivered before the Canadian Club of Toronto: Season of 1919-20* (1920).

We must think not of the militia and what it needs from Canada, but of Canada and what she needs from the militia.

> Canadian Club address, 1926, quoted by F.F. Worthington in *Great Canadians: A Century of Achievement* (1965).

China and Canada are joined rather than separated by the Pacific.

> Quoted by Kiang-Kan-Hu, "Prospect of Cultural Relations between China and Canada," *Empire Club of Canada: Addresses Delivered to the Members During the Year 1930* (1931).

"Thine own reproach alone do fear."

> Motto on the Currie crest and the First World War general's personal precept, noted by F.F. Worthington in *Great Canadians: A Century of Achievement* (1965).

## Currie, Don

You don't own the land. In winter, the elements own it, and in summer the mosquitos.

> Toronto business executive, July 18, 1973.

## Curtola, Bobby

As far as the future of the Canadian music business is concerned, we badly need to get together in the artistic ranks. We should brag about each other. The Americans are great at that.

> Rock'n'roll star born in Thunder Bay, quoted by Ritchie Yorke in *Axes, Chops & Hot Licks: The Canadian Rock Music Scene* (1971).

## Curwood, James Oliver

God's country.

> The Michigan novelist applied the epithet "God's Country" to the Canadian Northwest in *The River's End: A New Story of God's Country* (1919). Until that time it was associated with the northwestern United States, and first appeared

in print in R.H. Kellogg's *Rebel Prisons* (1865). The variation "God's Own Country" is said to date from 1921.

**Cushing, Harvey**
This road is now the celebrated Yonge Street, said to be the longest "street" in the world, though for many years after it was projected it scarcely deserved even the name of trail.

*The Life of Sir William Osler* (1925).

**Cyr, Louis**
During my moments of leisure I would scratch away at the violin . . . the moments I had with the violin were among the happiest in my memory.

Quoted by Trent Frayne and Peter Gzowski in *Great Canadian Sports Stories: A Century of Competition* (1965). At the turn of the century, Louis Cyr was famed, not for his violin-playing, but for his weight-lifting. He was billed as "the strongest man in the world."

# D

**Dafoe, Dr. Allan Roy**
Naturally, my chief interest in life for the past two years has been the quintuplets who were born in Callander and these babies we regard as the fairy princesses of Canada. And, without fear of contradiction, I can perhaps say I know more about the quintuplets than anybody in the world, but when they asked me in New York and other places how they make them, that is another matter.

"The Country Doctor in Northern Ontario" (1936), *Empire Club of Canada: Addresses Delivered to the Members During the Year 1936-37* (1937).

**Dafoe, John W.**
The Ukraine is the proper place for Ukrainians. If there is such a country as Canada-Ukraine, we do not know of it. Hyphens should be left at the port of embarkation to be applied for when the immigrant returns for good to the land of his fathers. [November, 1913]
 *

Well, what do the Canadian Clubs expect? Isn't the crop that appears to be ripening the result of the sowing? For forty years we have been teaching in

Canada everything but Canada and Canadianism and if generations are now growing up who are not particularly concerned about Canada, her future, her ideals, her national life and her destiny who is to be blamed? . . . Our teaching of history has been all wrong . . . the trouble in Canada is that the emphasis of national life has never been placed where it should have been placed — at home. We have decided that our own Supreme Court was not good enough for the people of Canada, we have never had enough national spirit to provide ourselves with a distinctive flag; we have people in Canada objecting to standing up when "O Canada" is sung, we have trifled with the question of citizenship and nationality until the young Canadian is never quite sure whether he is a Canadian or a Hottentot because he had a Hottentot grandmother. We have put enthusiasm into every national day but our own. . . . For all this we have ourselves to blame. [Convention of Canadian Clubs, 1921]
 *

How could I accept a knighthood? Good heavens! I shovel off my own sidewalk and stoke my own furnace. [Declining a knighthood in 1919]

\*

A journalist is hardly an authority upon anything—unless perhaps upon the appraisal of the drift of public opinion. [Convocation Address, University of Manitoba, May, 1923]

\*

There are two things that are not desirable for Canada, extreme economic nationalism and abject political colonialism. [Letter to W. C. Griffiths, May 4, 1926, quoted by Ramsay Cook in *The Politics of John W. Dafoe and the Free Press* (1963)]

\*

It would be well to bear in mind that the present of today was the future of yesterday and that it is what it is because of the human actions, the human decisions from yesterday. Therefore the future will be what we make it. [Address, Empire Club of Toronto, January 30, 1936]

\*

*Canada: An American Nation.* [Title of a series of lectures delivered at Columbia University and published in 1935]

\*

I wish I could stick around a while to see how things turn out. [Remark made to a fellow writer at *The Winnipeg Free Press* after finishing one of his last editorials, December 23, 1943. Dafoe died at seventy-eight on January 9, 1944.]

\*

Nationalism is simply a stop on the way to internationalism. [Remark characteristic of his later years]

*Dafoe of the Free Press* (1968), by Murray Donnelly.

"He once remarked, with the sombre wisdom of experience, that there were only two kinds of government, the 'scarcely tolerable' and the 'absolutely unbearable,' and it was in that spirit that he faced the future."

\*

We don't want any more Mintos. We don't want any more Byngs. I sometimes wonder if we want any more of 'em at all, but we really do.

Quoted by George V. Ferguson in *John W. Dafoe* (1948). See also Graham Spry.

**Dair, Carl**
*Ulysses* did not come from the same literary mould as *Uncle Tom's Cabin*; why should it be poured into the same typographic mould? The books are different; they should look different.

*Design with Type* (1967).

Printing was an art, born in excellence, but in decline ever since.

Characteristic remark of the Toronto-based typographer, as recalled by Allan Fleming.

**Dale, H. Fred**
My green thumb came only as a result of the mistakes I made while learning to see things from the plant's point of view.

*Fred Dale's Garden Book* (1972).

**Dali, Salvador**
What's Algoma? A new vegetable?

The surrealist painter asked this of Sir James Dunn, head of Algoma Steel Corporation. Quoted by Lord Beaverbrook in *Courage: The Story of Sir James Dunn* (1961).

**Damnable, Mother**
See Mother Damnable.

**Dandurand, Raoul**
We live in a fire-proof house, far from inflammable materials.

"The heavy sacrifices to which we agreed for the re-establishment of peace in Europe led us to reflect on what the future might hold in store.
"May I be permitted to add that in this association of mutual insurance against fire the risks assumed by the different states are not equal? We live in a fire-proof house, far from inflammable materials. A vast ocean separates us from Europe. Canada therefore believed it to be her duty to seek a precise interpretation of what appeared to her to be the indefinite obligations included in Article 10 of the Covenant."

Address of Raoul Dandurand, Canadian delegate to (and former president of) the League of Nations Assembly, October 2, 1924. Article 10 concerns territorial guarantees; Dandurand was expressing isolationist sentiment. *Documents on Canadian Foreign Policy: 1917-1939* (1962), edited by Walter A. Riddell.

French Canadians raise the Tricolor on holidays as a sign of their origin. I do not find fault with this, although this practice may give a false impression of our sentiments in regard to our own country. The day we acquire a Canadian flag, I will no longer know another.

*Les Mémoires du Sénateur Raoul Dandurand: 1861-1942* (1967), edited by Marcel Hamelin.

**Daniels, Adelaide**
There's one sensible way for everybody to eat; *maximum nutrition with minimum calories.*

Founder of Weight Watchers of Ontario, quoted by Carroll Allen in *Homemaker's Magazine*, May, 1973.

**Daniells, Roy**
No temple or epic or solemn tragedy crowns with its glories our sober landscape. Canadian literature is a plank sidewalk angling up the slope of the mountain whose heights are yet unexplored.

"Literature," *The Culture of Contemporary Canada* (1957), edited by Julian Park.

**Davey, Keith**
*Playboy,* to cite one example, collects about as much money selling its magazine in Canada as do the seventeen largest English-language consumer magazines combined.

*

We wish media owners, as an industry, would think again about the policy of maximizing profits by skimping on the quality of the product. The maximizing is their business. The skimping is everybody's business.

*

Above all, maintain a healthy skepticism vis-à-vis the media. We don't mean cynicism. The media are human institutions, humanly fallible. But in our observation they're in the hands of people pretty generally devoted to doing an honest job of information. Don't expect the moon from them, but don't settle for moonshine either.

*

For many years, the Canadian Association of Broadcasters has been the voice of private broadcasting in Canada, and we were particularly interested in what this organization had to contribute to our study of broadcasting and its place in the fabric of Canada's mass media. With reluctance, we were driven to conclude that the private broadcasters, no matter how sophisticated their individual thought, seem by group interaction to achieve a level perhaps best described as neanderthal.

*

What this country now needs, to achieve the sort of editorial competition that is our best guarantee of a good society, is a journalistic equivalent of the Volkswagen.

*

Privately owned radio has often been successful in its own terms: profitability, stability, unflagging mediocrity.

*

Don't shoot the messenger—he didn't make the bad news, he just delivered it. The media really do reflect the society around them.

*Report of the Special Senate Committee on Mass Media, Volume I: The Uncertain Mirror* (1971), commonly called "The Davey Report."

**Davidson, Joyce**
Like most Canadians I'm indifferent to the visit of the Queen. . . . We're a little annoyed at still being dependent.

When Joyce Davidson made these observations on Dave Garroway's "Today Show," June 18, 1959, the attractive TV personality had no idea she would make headline news from coast to coast. Mayor Nathan Phillips of Toronto "resented the remarks which are not the feelings of the people of Canada" and demanded an apology. Miss Davidson wisely refused to recant.

Where do I stand with Susskind? About three inches shorter.

To a Toronto reporter who asked the CBC-TV personality where she stood in her rumoured romance with David Susskind. On April 22, 1966, she married the Broadway producer. Quoted by *Liberty Magazine*, May, 1962.

## Davies, Robertson

Everybody says Canada is a hard country to govern, but nobody mentions that for some people it is also a hard country to live in. Still, if we all run away it will never be any better. So let the geniuses of easy virtue go southward; I know what they feel too well to blame them. But for some of us there is no choice; let Canada do what she will with us, we must stay.

> Nicholas's speech in the last scene of *Fortune My Foe* (1949). For "a hard country to govern," see Sir John A. Macdonald.

. . . poor Rumball, toiling every spare minute of his time at what he was certain would be the great Canadian prose epic, *The Plain that Broke the Plough.*

> *Leaven of Malice* (1954).

Why do countries have to be have literatures? Why does a country like Canada, so late upon the international scene, feel that it must rapidly acquire the trappings of older countries—music of its own, pictures of its own, books of its own—and why does it fuss and stew, and storm the heavens with its outcries when it does not have them?

> Thoughts of Solly Bridgetower in *Leaven of Malice* (1954).

In the pecking order of literary criticism a Frenchman can humiliate an Englishman just as readily as an Englishman can humiliate an American, and an American a Canadian. One of Canada's most serious literary needs at present is some lesser nation to domineer over and shame by displays of superior taste.

\*

Yet how many people there are who read as though some prize awaited them when they turned the last page! They do not wish *to read* a book; they want *to have read* it—no matter how.

> *A Voice from the Attic* (1960).

To be apt in quotation is a splendid and dangerous gift. Splendid, because it ornaments a man's speech with other men's jewels; dangerous, for the same reason.

> *The Toronto Star*, October 1, 1960.

No ghosts in Canada? The country which too vigorously asserts its normality and rationality is like a man who declares that he is without imagination; suddenly the ghosts he has denied may overcome him, and then his imaginative flights make poets stare. Unfortunately, he also needs the help of the psychiatrist, and there are no psychiatrists who minister to whole nations.

However, nations have a way of whispering the inner truth about themselves, sufficiently disguised to deceive those who would keep the truth hidden . . . this self-appraisal now begins to reveal, among much else, that the Canadian writers of the past must have been much more perceptive, more prophetic and disenchanted, than their readers have guessed. In the land which pretends to have no ghosts, they have seen ghosts; in the country without a mythology, they have heard the ground bass of myth; in a country born not of love and struggle but of politics, they have fought battles; and, with reserve and irony, they have offered their country love.

> "The Northern Muse," *Holiday*, April, 1964.

Wisdom is a variable possession. Every man is wise when pursued by a mad dog; fewer when pursued by a mad woman; only the wisest survive when attacked by a mad notion.

\*

"There is no disputing about tastes," says the old saw. In my experience there is little else.

> *Marchbanks' Almanack* (1967).

I think of an author as somebody who goes into the marketplace and puts down his rug and says, "I will tell you a story" and then passes the hat. And when he's taken up his collection, he tells his story, and just before the dénouement he passes the hat again. If it's worth anything, fine. If not, he ceases to be an author. He does not apply for a Canada Council grant.

\*

Canada demands a great deal from people and is not, as some countries are, quick to offer in return a pleasant atmosphere or easy kind of life. . . . Canada is not really a place where you are encouraged to have large spiritual adventures.

\*

I tell my class of graduate students, "Keep your ears open to the prompting of your destiny and don't worry too much if you and your destiny do not agree about what you should have, and when you should have it. Happiness is always a by-product. It is probably a matter of temperament, and for anything I know it may be glandular. But it is not something that can be demanded from life, and if you are not happy you had better stop worrying about it and see what treasures you can pluck from your own brand of unhappiness."

\*

The world is burdened with young fogeys. Old men with ossified minds are easily dealt with. But men who look young, act young and everlastingly harp on the fact that they are young, but who nevertheless think and act with a degree of caution that would be excessive in their grandfathers, are the curse of the world. Their very conservatism is secondhand, and they don't know what they are conserving.

\*

I just am a Canadian. It is not a thing which you can escape from. It is like having blue eyes.

"The Master's Voice: The Table Talk of Robertson Davies," quoted by Peter Newman in *Maclean's Magazine*, September, 1972.

The two great Canadian dramatists are Chekhov and Ibsen. The Ibsen and Chekhov situations can be paralleled in Canada twenty times over.

Interviewed by Donald Cameron in *Conversations with Canadian Novelists* (1973).

They talk of poor Mary dying with seven swords stuck in her heart: if she'd been a Canadian playwright, she would have known what suffering really was.

Quoted by Urjo Kareda in *The Toronto Star*, October 13, 1973.

## Davies, W.H.

What a kind-hearted race of people are these Canadians! Here was I, an entire stranger among them, and yet every hour people were making enquiries, and interesting themselves on my behalf, bringing and sending books, grapes, bananas, and other delicacies for a sick man. When a second operation was deemed necessary, the leg to be amputated at the knee, the whole town was concerned, and the doctors had to give strict injunctions not to admit such a number of kind-hearted visitors.

*The Autobiography of a Super-Tramp* (1908), with a preface by George Bernard Shaw. The Welsh-born poet was a hobo and peddlar until his early thirties when he lost his right foot by hopping a freight train pulling out of Renfrew, Ontario. The accident on March 20, 1899, drew his wanderings to a halt, and Davies returned to London where he launched a modest literary career which encompassed some three dozen books, including the widely read *Autobiography* and the even better-known "Leisure," a poem that begins: "What is this life if, full of care, / We have no time to stand and stare?"

## Davin, Nicholas Flood

Phipps, if you had a secretary you could govern the universe.

Quoted by Sir John Willison in *Reminiscences Political and Personal* (1919). R.W. Phipps, a Toronto pamphleteer and protectionist who helped formulate Sir John A. Macdonald's National Policy, expected the ministry of Finance. "Mr. Phipps . . . made no secret of his own conviction that neither Sir John nor any of his colleagues really understood the principles of political economy." J.W. Bengough devotes a cartoon to Phipps in *Grip*, October 12, 1878.

There are some to declare that Canada's trade is declining; there are some who maintain that the rich glow of health which at present mantles o'er Canada's virgin cheek will soon be replaced by the pallid hues of the corpse. To such pusillanimous propagandists of a preposterous pessimism, I answer, Mr. Speaker, with all confidence, never, never!

Address supposedly delivered in the House of Commons between 1884 and 1888, as recalled by Lord Frederic Hamilton in *The Days before Yesterday* (1920).

**Davis, Charles**
When someone asked me what it felt like to be outside the Roman Catholic Church, I found myself spontaneously answering: it is as if I had rejoined the human race.

*

What I suggest for all Christians is, to borrow a phrase from Harvey Cox, an attitude of creative disaffiliation. [The reference is to the American theologian's *The Secular City* (1965)]

*A Question of Conscience* (1967).

**Davis, Fred**
I know, we're back to that namby-pamby image again, right? Well, don't get me wrong. I'm not always Mr. Affable. I get mad at my kids and grouch at my wife when I'm down. But on the air—and that's what we're talking about—I think pleasantness is simply part of being professional.

Quoted by Paul King in *The Canadian Magazine*, March 8, 1969.

**Davis, Henry Fuller ("Twelve-Foot")**
H.F. Davis,
Born Vermont, 1820,
Died, Slave Lake, 1893.
Pathfinder, Pioneer, Miner, Trader.
"He was everyman's friend
and never locked his cabin door."

Epitaph of the well-loved pioneer prospector and trader "Twelve-Foot" Davis. The gravestone overlooking the town of Peace River is in the form of a tree-trunk, and friends composed the lines above. As for the nickname, Davis once staked a claim between two others only twelve feet wide, from which he took $15,000 in gold. Hugh A. Dempsey, in *Historic Sites: Alberta* (1964), notes that Davis died in 1900, not 1893.

**Davis, Jefferson**
Gentlemen,—I thank you sincerely for the honour you have this evening shown to me; it shows that true British manhood to which misfortune is always attractive. May peace and prosperity be forever the blessing of Canada, for she has been the asylum to my friends, and she is now an asylum to myself. I hope that Canada may forever remain a part of the British Empire, and may God bless you all, and the British flag never cease to wave over you.

Reception for the leader of the Confederacy, Niagara Falls. Reported by William Kirby in *The Niagara Mail*, June 5, 1867, and quoted by Lorne Pierce in *William Kirby: The Portrait of a Tory Loyalist* (1929).

My trust in earthly powers is lost.

Davis expressed his feelings to a Civil War general on July 20, 1867, in a letter written from Montreal where he and his family were resting while he was awaiting trial for treason. The president of the ill-starred Confederacy was finally amnestied, but not before his mother-in-law visited him in Montreal, died there, and was buried in Mount Royal Cemetery. The evening of July 18, 1867, he attended the Theatre Royal's production of Sheridan's *The Rivals* and was feted lavishly, when someone from the milling crowd handed him a note. Opening it later, he read the single word scratched across it: "Andersonville"—the name of the Confederate prison in Georgia where thirteen thousand Northern soldiers died of hunger, exposure and disease. Quoted by Edgar Andrew Collard in *Montreal Yesterdays* (1962).

**Davis, John**
The lothsome view of the shore, and irksome noyse of the yce was such, as that it bred strange conceits among vs, so that we supposed the place to be wast and voyd of any sensible or vegitable creatures, whereupon I called the same Desolation.

*The Worldes Hydrographical Description* (1595). In the words of Captain Davis's clerk, John Janes, on July 20,

1588, in the eastern Arctic, "we discovered the land, which was the most deformed rockie and mountainous land the ever we saw . . . the true pattern of desolation, and after the same our Capitaine named it, The land of Desolation." Janes's account is reproduced by Richard Hakluyt in *The Principal Navigations, Voyages, Traffiques, and Discoveries of the English Nation* (1589), edited by Edmund Goldsmid in 1889.

## Dawson, Sir John William

Again, British America is not one state. It is a rope of sand, made up of a number of petty provinces, and peopled with dissimilar and often antagonistic races. Here again is small prospect of a great national existence. . . .

*

Canada has two emblems which have often appeared to some to point out its position in these respects,—the *Beaver* and the *Maple*. The beaver in his sagacity, his industry, his ingenuity, and his perseverance, is a most respectable animal; a much better emblem for our country than the rapacious eagle or even the lordly lion; but he is also a type of unvarying instincts and old-world traditions. He does not improve, and becomes extinct rather than change his ways. The maple, on the other hand, is the emblem of the vitality and energy of a new country; vigorous and stately in its growth, changing its hues as the seasons change, equally at home in the forest, in the cultivated field, and stretching its green boughs over the dusty streets, it may well be received as a type of the progressive and versatile spirit of a new and growing people.

Some of our artists have the bad taste to represent the beaver as perched on the maple bough; a most unpleasant position for the poor animal, and suggestive of the thought that he is in the act of gnawing through the trunk of our national tree. Perhaps some more venturous designer may some day reverse the position, and represent the maple branch as fashioned into a club, wherewith to knock the beaver on the head. It is the part of a man of taste to avoid both extremes.

*The Duties of Educated Young Men in British America: Being the Annual University Lecture of McGill University, Montreal, Session of 1863-64* (1863).

## Dawson, Robert MacGregor

The Senate will in all likelihood continue to exist as at present constituted for many years to come, not from any high esteem in which it is held, but largely because of its undoubted convenience to the dominant political party and the general indifference of the Canadian people.

*Democratic Government in Canada* (Revised Edition, 1963), edited by W.F. Dawson.

## Dawson, Simon James

Of the valley of Red River I find it impossible to speak in any other terms than those which may express astonishment and admiration. I entirely concur in the brief but expressive description given to me by an English settler on the Assiniboine, that the valley of Red River, including a large portion belonging to its great affluent, is a "Paradise of fertility."

Quoted by Howard Angus Kennedy in *New Canada and the New Canadians* (1907). The felicitous phrase is also associated with Henry Youle Hind.

## Dayan, Moshe

If I had to choose a non-Israeli army to fight with, it would be the Canadian commandos, because they are all volunteers. Of course, I wouldn't want to spend my evenings with the Canadians. For that, I would choose the Italian commandos.

Israeli general, quoted by Peter C. Newman in "Israel" (1969), *Home Country: People, Places, and Power Politics* (1973).

## Deacon, William Arthur

The only positive test of any work of art is the favour of the cultured man.

*

The ideal review, then, is the truthful record of the impression made by a certain book upon a well-read man, who has been stirred by it. It reflects the personalities of both author and reviewer, and holds the attention of its readers. It is at once a narrative, an exposition and a judgment; and it is, in itself, literature.

"A Theory of Book-Reviewing," *Poteen: A Pot-Pourri of Canadian Essays* (1926).

There has never been a war of Canadian origin, nor for a Canadian cause.

*My Vision of Canada* (1933).

**Dean, H.H.**
Prosperity follows the cow.

"Dairying in Canada," *Handbook of Canada: Issued by the Local Committee on the Occasion of the Meeting of the British Association for the Advancement of Science at Toronto, August, 1924* (1924).

**De Carlo, Yvonne**
Howard Hughes taught me to land a plane and how to take off. But he never taught me anything about flying in between. He thought that I had learned the difficult parts, and that was enough.

The exotically named child star and dancer was born Peggy Yvonne Middleton in 1922 in Vancouver, B.C. As one Hollywood columnist said about Yvonne de Carlo when she appeared in *Salome, Where She Danced* (1945), a movie about a dancing girl in a town named Salome: "She can't sing, she can't dance, she can't act—so we made her the star of the picture."

**De Cosmos, Amor**
I desire not to adopt the name of Amor De Cosmos because it smacks of a foreign title, but because it is an unusual name and its meaning tells what I love most, viz: order, beauty, the world, the universe. [On February 17, 1854, by an act of the California legislature, William Alexander Smith became Amor De Cosmos, "Lover of the Universe"]

*

It is too late in the day to stop men thinking. If allowed to think they will speak. If they speak they will write, and what they write will be printed and published. A newspaper is only a thought-throwing machine, a reflex of the popular mind. If it is not, it cannot live. We are not disposed to send our proof-sheets to any-one to correct. [Editorial in the *British Colonist* in 1859 when the governor of British Columbia, Sir James Douglas, failed in his attempt to suppress the newspaper]

Quoted by Roland Wilde in *Amor de Cosmos* (1958).

I would not object to a little revolution now and again in British Columbia, after Confederation, if we were treated unfairly; for I am one of those who believe that political hatreds attest the vitality of a State.

Speech in Victoria, March 10, 1870, two years before becoming premier. *British Columbia: A Centennial Anthology* (1958), edited by R.A. Watters.

I am one of those who believe that this country should have the right to negotiate its commercial treaties. I go a step further, I believe this country should have the right to negotiate every treaty.

*

I see no reason why the people of Canada should not look forward to Canada becoming a sovereign and independent State. The right hon. gentleman stated that he was born a British subject and hoped to die one. Sir, I was born a British colonist, but do not wish to die a tadpole British colonist. I do not wish to die without having all the rights, privileges and immunities of the citizen of a nation.

House of Commons, April 21, 1882. See also Sir John A. Macdonald.

**Dee, John**
Circa An. 1494. Mr. Robert Thorn his father, and Mr. Eliot of Bristow, discovered Newfound Land.

Queen Elizabeth's instructor in astrology added this inscription to the map of the North Atlantic which he drew in 1580. There is slight evidence that Robert Thorn Sr. and a Bristol merchant named Hugh Eliot discovered new lands or Newfoundland before 1500. As Tryggvi J. Oleson in *Early Voyages and Northern Approaches 1000-1632* (1963) concludes, "We do not know."

The Colleagues of the Fellowship of the New Navigations Atlanticall and Septentrional for the Discoverie of the North-West Passage.

> Name of a company formed by the astrologer Dr. Dee, Adrian Gilbert and John Davis to explore a commercial route through the New World to the Orient, 1583. Quoted by Richard Deacon in *John Dee: Scientist, Geographer, Astrologer and Secret Agent to Elizabeth I* (1968). It is said that Dr. Dee first used the phrase "the British Empire."

**Defoe, Daniel**
And yet I must enter a Caveat here too against being misunderstood in saying the Devil stands in no need of agents; for when I speak so, I am to be taken in a limited Sense; I don't say he needs them no where, but only that he does not need them in those polite Parts of the World which I have been speaking of, and perhaps not much here; but in many remote Countries 'tis otherwise still; the Indians of America are particularly said to have Witches among them, as well in those Countries where the Spaniards and the English, and other Nations have planted themselves, as amongst those where the European Nations seldom come: for Example, the People of Canada, that is, of the Countries under the French Government of Quebeck, the Esquimeaux, and other Northern Climates, have Magicians, Wizards and Witches, who they call Pilloatas or Pillotoas; these pretend they speak intimately and familiarly with the devil. . . .

> *The Political History of the Devil* (Second Edition, 1739).

**Deighton, John ("Gassy Jack")**
I have done well since I came here.

> Inscription on the tombstone of the popular publican, New Westminster, British Columbia. Born in Yorkshire, "Gassy Jack" opened a saloon in Vancouver at the time of Confederation and lent his nickname to its Gastown district.

**Dekanahwideh**
I, Dekanahwideh, and the Confederated Chiefs, now uproot the tallest pine tree, and into the cavity thereby made we cast all weapons of war. Into the depth of the earth, deep down into the underwater currents of water flowing to unknown regions, we cast all weapons of strife. We bury them from sight and we plant again the tree. Thus shall the Great Peace be established.

> Pledge of the Confederacy, quoted by Stanley B. Ryerson in *The Founding of Canada: Beginnings to 1815* (New Edition, 1963).

I am Dekanahwideh, and with the Five Nations' Confederate lords I plant the Tree of the Great Peace. . . . [Traditional words inscribed on the Iroquois statesman's stone monument, Deseronto, Ontario]

*

Call on my name in the bushes and I will return.

> "Several times in the present century the chiefs have seriously debated whether the time had come to call on his name in the bushes," according to Paul A.W. Wallace, "Dekanahwideh," *Dictionary of Canadian Biography: Volume I: 1000-1700* (1965).

Let the others have successors, for others can advise you like them. But I am the founder of your league, and no one else can do what I have done.

> Famous boast of the semi-legendary Iroquois statesman, quoted by Horatio Hale in his edition of *The Iroquois Book of Rites* (1883). Dekanahwideh, or Deganawidah, means "two river currents flowing together." Hale believes that Dekanahwideh, with the help of the Mohawk chief Hiawatha, founded the Great League of the Iroquois, also called the Five (later Six) Nations Confederacy, as early as 1459. The peace lasted more than four centuries.

**De la Roche, Mazo**
*Jalna* was inspired by the traditions of that part of southern Ontario on the fringe of which we had built Trail Cottage. The descendants of the retired military and naval officers who had settled there stoutly clung to British traditions. No house in particular was pictured; no family portrayed. From the very first the

characters created themselves. They leaped from my imagination and from memories of my own family. The grandmother, Adeline Whiteoak, refused to remain a minor character but arrogantly, supported on either side by a son, marched to the centre of the stage.

\*

The name Jalna was suggested to me in this way: a member of the Civil Service, in the same department as Caroline, had spent many years in India. When she told him that I was in search of names of military stations there he sent me a list of quite a number. I poured over them and chose Jalna because it was the shortest; it was easy to remember and looked well in print. When I wrote it at the top of my first page of manuscript, it never entered my head that one day it would become well-known to quite a number of people.

> *Ringing the Changes: An Autobiography* (1957). The country house associated with "Jalna" is an attractive residence north of Clarkson, Ontario, still owned and occupied by descendants of the retired British officer who built it in 1837. The house is named Benares and there is no proof that Mazo de la Roche ever entered it. The present occupant and owner, Mrs. Kathleen Sayers, regards the novelist's interest in her family tree and home as a "damned nuisance," but she has willed Benares to the Ontario Heritage Foundation as a public museum. Once surrounded by lovely woods, Benares today manages to retain a modicum of privacy amid a subdivision that boasts Mazo Crescent and Whiteoak Public School. (The Jalna in India is a nondescript, fruit-producing town in Hyderabad state.)
> Her British editor, Lovat Dickson, explained, as quoted by Ronald Hambleton in *Mazo de la Roche of Jalna* (1966): "The Whiteoak books represent the idealized picture of Canada which all English people have. Life is hardly ever painful at Jalna. It's comfortable, it's exciting, there are domestic dramas going on. I think that Englishmen like to believe that anywhere abroad life goes on as it used to go on in England. We always like to think that life for our parents must have been wonderful and

life for us is horrid. Englishmen reading about the Whiteoaks think that life is lived that way now, and we know that life is not lived that way in England— nor in Canada."

No writing in Canada carries such influence as journalism. People who seldom or never read a book, read the newspapers.

> Introduction, *Northern Lights: A New Collection of Distinguished Writing by Canadian Authors* (1960), edited by George E. Nelson.

I just open the doors of the house, it closes behind me, and there they are, all about me, more living than the outside world. [Letter to her publisher about the characters in her fiction]

> Quoted by Ronald Hambleton in *Mazo de la Roche of Jalna* (1966).

Mon Dieu Est Ma Roche

\*

Death Interrupts All That Is Mortal

> Inscriptions on Mazo de la Roche's headstone in historic St. George's churchyard, where Stephen Leacock also is buried, Sibbald Point, Ontario, 1961. See also Edward Weeks.

## De Lorimier, D.

I die without remorse; in the insurrection I only desired the well-being and independence of my country. . . . Peaceful Canadians will see happiness and liberty born again on the banks of the St. Lawrence. Everything works towards this end, even these very executions; the blood and the tears poured on the altar of liberty are watering the tree which will bear the two-starred flag of the Canadas. I leave behind me children whose only heritage is the memory of my misfortune. Poor orphans, it is you who are to be pitied, you whom the bloody and arbitrary hand of the law strikes through my death. You will have no gentle and affectionate memories of happy days with your father. When you are old enough to reflect, you will see in your father a man who has paid on the scaffold for actions such as have immortalized other happier men. The only crime of your father was his failure.

This moving statement was made in February of 1838 shortly before the Patriote leader was hanged in Montreal for participating in Papineau's uprising. The French original appears in Eve Circé-Côte's *Papineau: Son influence sur la pensée canadienne* (1934); the translation is by Margaret Fairley from her anthology *Spirit of Canadian Democracy: A Collection of Canadian Writings from the Beginnings to the Present Day* (1945).

## De Mille, James

Sweet maiden of Passamaquoddy
Shall we seek for communion of souls
Where the deep Mississippi meanders,
Or the distant Saskatchewan rolls?

Ah no,—for in Maine I will find thee,
A sweetly sequestrated nook,
Where the winding Skoodoowabskooksis
Conjoins with the Skoodoowabskook.
*

Let others sing loudly of Saco,
Of Quoddy, and Tattamagouche,
Of Kenneneccasis, and Quaco,
Of Merigonishe, and Buctouche.

Of Nashwaak, and Magaguadavique,
Or Memmerimammericook,—
There's none like the Skoodoowabskooksis
Excepting the Skoodoowabskook!

Four of twelve stanzas of "Lines to Florence Huntingdon, Passamaquoddy, Maine," from *The New Dominion and True Humorist*, April 16, 1870. The verses, frequently misquoted and usually called after the first line, are part of *The Minnehaha Mines*, a comic novel serialized in the Saint John periodical.

## Demitro, Russel

We are all kings when we die.

Gypsy patriarch, quoted by Don Bell in *Saturday Night at the Bagel Factory and Other Montreal Stories* (1972).

## Dempsey, Hugh A.   See Crowfoot.

## Denechoan, Willie

We are different than we used to be.

The government has us in a little box, with a lid on it. Every now and then they open the lid and do something to us and close it again.

We are a dying race. Not this generation but the next, will die.

Hay Lake medicine man, quoted by Heather Robertson in *Reservations are for Indians* (1970).

## Denison, George Taylor

We would rather be loyal Jingoes than disloyal poltroons. ["Lecture on National Spirit," Toronto, December 17, 1891]

*

Several names were mentioned, and someone said that Edgar had made a suggestion. I walked across the hall into Edgar's office, and asked him what he had suggested. He seemed to have forgotten the exact words, but said, "Canada before all, or Canada first of all." I said, "That will do: Canada First," and went back to my room and proposed it to the others, and after some discussion it was unanimously decided that we should call ourselves the "Canada First" Party, meaning that we should put Canada first, before every other consideration.

The phrase "Canada First" was coined in 1870 by Sir James D. Edgar (later Speaker of the House of Commons) and Colonel George Taylor Denison, as Denison recounts in his book *The Struggle for Imperial Unity: Recollections and Experiences* (1909). It was a year later, on the publication of William Foster's address *Canada First; or, Our New Nationality* (1871), that the phrase acquired currency as a slogan. See also Sir James D. Edgar and William A. Foster.

I never allow a point of law to be raised. This is a court of justice, not a court of law.

The founder of Canada First was senior police magistrate in Toronto from 1877 to 1923. Quoted by John Foster Fraser in *Canada As It Is* (1905).

## Denison, Merrill

I find writing about the Canadian theatre or drama depressingly like discussing the art of dinghy sailing among the Bedouins. There is so little to be said on the subject save to point out why there is none. Depending on one's expository habits this can be done tersely, as in the case of the Bedouins, by saying "there are no dinghys because there is no water," or at appalling and splendid length by re-examining the geology of the Mediterranean basin and recalling all the flood-mythology one can remember.

"Nationalism and Drama," *Yearbook of the Arts in Canada: 1928-29* (1929), edited by Bertram Brooker.

Television? It can but hasten the end of the radio as a source of entertainment and of the newspaper as a purveyor of news.

"Thoughts on Radio," *Open House* (1931), edited by William Arthur Deacon and Wilfred Reeves.

If any other word than "American" could be found to describe the continental culture, Canadians would adopt it enthusiastically.

\*

If the coffee is poorer, the tea is better.

"The Unbridled Frontier: Canada and the United States," *Harper's*, July, 1932. This article includes an early use of the notion of the national "inferiority complex."

Fortunately, I am not only an authority on the [national] inferiority complex but possibly one of the greatest living authorities. I don't claim to be the inventor of the famous cliché—some of the credit must be shared with Sigmund Freud—but I was probably the first to diagnose the symptoms and immortalize them on the printed page. . . . I never expected that it would become part of the national folklore and live to become a tedious and shop-worn cliché. For my sins, I have been doing my best to combat it ever since.

"That Inferiority Complex" (1949), *Empire Club of Canada: Addresses Delivered to the Members During the Year 1948-49* (1949). See also Michael Mahoney.

**Denison, Muriel**
"And what is your name, my dear," asked General Colegrave, later.

Before Sue could answer, Lady Char-lotte's deep voice interrupted:

"Her name is Susannah," she boomed, "and from today on, SUSANNAH OF THE MOUNTIES."

Susannah: A Little Girl with the Mounties (1936). Three years later the "Shirley Temple Edition" was published with the movie's title: *Susannah of the Mounties*.

**Dennis, John**
Canada: a vast Tract Land in Northern America, on the Back of New England and New York.

Locale of *Liberty Asserted* (1704), a hit on the London stage.

**Dennis, L.A.**   See Emmett Hall.

**Dent, John Charles**
The term "Responsible Government" was at least as old as 1828. For more than ten years before Lord Durham's report was published the expression was a household word in Upper Canada, as well as in Nova Scotia. Though not so widely known in Lower Canada, it was not uncommon there.

*The Last Forty Years: Canada Since the Union of 1841* (1881).

**DePoe, Norman**   See Woody Guthrie.

**Derbishire, Stewart**
The ambition of bettering their condition seems never to have visited their minds. Locomotive faculties they seem to have none. Each man seems to desire to dig the same piece of ground, and no more, that his father dug before him, & to dig it with the same spade; for an improvement in the instruments of cultivation or in the mode of culture would almost be regarded as an insult to the memory of the dead. There seems to be no decorative taste in the people, no active spirit of improvement, no ambition beyond the mere supply of the wants of nature.

Quoted by Norah Story in "Report to Lord Durham on Lower Canada, 1838," *Canadian Historical Review*, March, 1937.

## Desbarats, Peter

The First Commandment honoured by the Anglostocracy is "Thou shalt not criticize the French Canadian—publicly."

> *The State of Quebec: A Journalist's View of the Quiet Revolution* (1965).

## Desbiens, Jean-Paul

For primitives, a primitive language is good enough; animals get along with a few grunts. But if you want to attain to human speech, joual is not sufficient. You can make do with a board and some whitewash if you want to paint a barn, but finer tools are necessary for the Mona Lisa.

*

I will only say that I don't give a hoot what they say or don't say in Toronto. (First prize, one week in Toronto; second prize, two weeks in Toronto; third prize three weeks in Toronto.) Do we speak joual, yes or no?

*

No one can ever study language enough, for it is the home of all meanings.

*

I write with an axe.

*

If a man is asleep in a house on fire, the neighbours don't wake him up with Mozart's *Eine Kleine Nachtmusik*. They yell at him, and if he still sleeps soundly, they kick him out of bed.

*

We have invented a sure way to fight caterpillars—cut down trees.

> *The Impertinences of Brother Anonymous* (1962), translated by Miriam Chapin. Desbiens published under the name Frère Untel—Brother Nobody or Brother Anonymous.

Every answer is personal; each of us must answer in a state of uncertainty. Freedom is not a comfortable thing. . . . We are imprisoned in freedom. Most men would like to be freed from their freedom, so long as they could retain it nominally. Hitler used to say: "I have come to free men from their conscience."

*

Education is impossible without love, without loving a few of the great men of the past.

*

Giving importance to insignificant matters means choosing hell. . . . We have anchored ourselves in the insignificant.

*

We want national dignity. But dignity isn't something you can simply reclaim. Dignity isn't a constitution locked up in an English safe.

*

"I felt as though my country was stirring deeply within me, like a great gentle thing which didn't need anyone's death to survive." [Quoting the French philosopher Jean Guéhenno]

*

Intelligence can be used for many things. It seems to me that it should be used especially for living.

*

Living is like navigating. You take the waves, the weight and the wind into consideration. And also the North Star.

> *For Pity's Sake* (1965), translated by Frédéric Côté.

## Desjardins, Alphonse

Much of the poverty we see has its roots in despair.

*

Keep the money working.

> Oft-repeated remarks of the journalist who founded the first credit union (*caisse populaire*) in North America at Lévis in 1900. Quoted by George Boyle in *The Poor Man's Prayer: The Story of Credit Union Beginnings* (1951).

## Desruisseaux, Paul

The Senate is not so much in danger of being abolished as it is of being forgotten.

> Liberal senator, quoted by Jay Walz in *The New York Times*, April 15, 1973.

## Dessaulles, George Casimir

"Senator Dessaulles, dead at St. Hyacinthe, who held a seat in the Senate of Canada since 1907, had a remarkable record. So far as is recalled by those around the Senate since he was there, he never once participated in any debate or gave expression to an opinion; but he followed the discussions closely and was there when the division bells rang. He was a kindly old man, held by all parties in venerable respect because of his great age."

The Liberal senator was born in St. Hyacinthe in 1829. R. MacGregor Dawson quotes from his obituary notice in *The Ottawa Citizen*, April 21, 1930, in *The Government of Canada* (1952) and adds: "Canada has had on at least two occasions the singular distinction of possessing the oldest legislator in the world, Senator Wark, who died in 1905 in his 102nd year, and Senator Dessaulles, who died in 1930 in his 103rd year."

**Dettloff, Claude P.**
"Wait for me, Daddy."

Caption to "one of the most famous photographs of the Second World War. It was taken by Claude P. Dettloff in New Westminster, B.C., while the British Columbia Regiment was leaving for the front. After appearing on the front page of *The Vancouver Province* on October 1, 1940, it was published twice by *Life* and used many times to symbolize the Canadian war effort." The candid shot shows a young lad reaching out for his father who is marching off to war. Reproduced by Christopher Young in *A Century of Reporting: The National Press Club Anthology* (1967).

**Devlin, R.J.**
I have a lot of Grey Goat Sleigh Robes at $6.00 each. They are grey, and they are goat, and they are 6 dollars, and that is about all I can truthfully say for them.

They are probably about the average of such things . . . neither better nor worse. They are lined and trimmed, which is a circumstance, but if there is any worse lining or trimming in the country I should be pleased to see it. Of course, with a raging Protectionist Government in power, people can't expect much for 6 dollars, and in the case I think their expectation will be realized, though they *will* get a good 6 dollars' worth.

In the meantime, I should like to realize 6 dollars a piece for about 75 robes. Terms cash.

Quoted by John Murray Gibbon in

*Canadian Mosaic: The Making of a Northern Nation* (1938).

Re the new government (having carefully perused the press)—it consists of: Anarchists, 17; Horse Thieves, 22; Burglars, 10; Would-be Burglars if they had the pluck, 31; Judas Iscariots, 19; Counterfeiters, 27; Forgers, 19; Highwaymen, 46; Murderers, 29; Arch-fiends, 1.

Under the circumstances it is needless for me to say that I decline to sell my new Spring Hats (by the way, they are just opened) to any Member of the new House of Commons. R. J. Devlin.

Post-election advertisement in an Ottawa paper during the 1870s by a sharp-tongued Sparks Street furrier. Quoted by Doris French in *Faith, Sweat and Politics: The Early Trade Union Years in Canada* (1962).

**Devonshire, Duke of**
I am not going into my family history, or I might tell you all of it, how one of my ancestors having to choose between having his head cut off and being made a duke, had chosen the dukedom.

Address, Canadian Club of Winnipeg, April, 1917, by the governor general, a descendant of the Cavendish family. Quoted by John Cowan in *Canada's Governors-General 1867-1952* (1952).

**Dewart, Edward Hartley**
Our colonial position, whatever may be its political advantages, is not favourable to the growth of an indigenous literature.

Introductory Essay, *Selections from Canadian Poets* (1864), edited by Edward Hartley Dewart.

**Dewart, Leslie**
It is those whom we can hate that we should love; it is those who really threaten us that we are enjoined to forgive; it is those who are dangerous that we are asked to negotiate with.

*

It may be that the only type of defensive war the Christian can wage today is on war itself.

*Christianity and Revolution: The Lesson of Cuba* (1963).

Like human culture as a whole, Christianity in the future may become more of a do-it-yourself affair than at any previous time.

*The Foundations of Belief* (1969).

**Dexter, Grant**
Bennett added that he proposed to deal in generalities whilst speaking texts written for him by Herridge. "You really have no conception of the amount of trouble my friend Bill has got me into," said Mr. Bennett. He went on to say that he had never promised to end unemployment. Mr. Herridge had done this for him in issuing a text of a speech with that phrase included in it—against Bennett's express order. Also, he said, it was Herridge who had put the phrase—"I'll blast my way into foreign markets," into his Winnipeg keynote speech. Herridge had put it in: Bennett had struck it out. Herridge had the page re-typed without Bennett's knowledge with the phrase back in. When delivering the speech Bennett referred to his manuscript, found the phrase and was unable to get by it. "And that phrase, O'Leary, has not done me any good."

Letter to John W. Dafoe, January 4, 1935, reporting a conversation in which R.B. Bennett had told Grattan O'Leary about W.H. Herridge's role in coining two catch-phrases now associated with Bennett's campaign of 1930: "I will end unemployment or perish in the attempt," "I will blast a way into the markets of the world." Quoted by J.R.H. Wilbur in *The Bennett New Deal: Fraud or Portent?* (1968). See also R.B. Bennett.

**Dichter, Ernest**
What Canada could offer to the American traveller is to be able to see through an outsider's eyes his own country; and to learn how uninvolved people view the attempts that are being made by Americans to solve the American problems. This should enable him to come back to the U.S. with a fresh point of view and therefore a more positive attitude that solutions to American problems are possible. It's an inverted form of patriotism. Come to Canada and learn how others see you so that you can be a better American.

Dr. Ernest Dichter, president of the Institute for Motivational Research, Croton-on-Hudson, New York, addressed the annual convention of the Travel Industry Association of Canada, Victoria. *The Globe and Mail*, May 13, 1972.

**Dick, Evelyn**
I like to pick out a good-looking lawyer or juror and concentrate on him until I have an orgasm.

Mrs. Dick was tried and found guilty of a grisly murder in Hamilton in 1947. Adapted from "How Could You, Mrs. Dick," *Intense Pleasure* (1972), by David McFadden.

**Dickens, C.H. "Punch"**
No one who has flown over the North West Territories has been able to do so without marvelling at the courage and inspiration of the men who fought their way to the Arctic practically foot by foot.

Quoted by Frederick B. Watt in *Maclean's Magazine*, July 1, 1929.

I'm proud of the title "bush pilot." It originated in Canada, it relates to men of dedicated interest in flying to the remote regions, and I hope it will never disappear.

Quoted by Grant McConachie in *Great Canadians: A Century of Achievement* (1965). See also Grant McConachie.

**Dickens, Charles**
The country round this town [Toronto], being very flat, is bare of scenic interest; but the town itself is full of life and motion, bustle, business, and improvement. The streets are well paved, and lighted with gas; the houses are large and good; the shops excellent. Many of them have a display of goods in their windows, such as may be seen in thriving county towns in England; and there are some which would do no discredit to the metropolis itself. There is a good stone prison here; and there are, besides, a handsome church, a Court-house, public offices, many commodious private resi-

dences, and a Government Observatory for noting and recording the magnetic variations.

*

Indeed, it may be said of Kingston, that one half of it appears to be burnt down, and the other half not to be built up.

*

There is an admirable gaol here [in Kingston], well and wisely governed, and excellently regulated in every respect. The men were employed as shoemakers, ropemakers, blacksmiths, tailors, carpenters, and stone-cutters; and in building a new prison, which was pretty far advanced towards completion. The female prisoners were occupied in needlework. Among them was a beautiful girl of twenty, who had been there nearly three years. She acted as bearer of secret dispatches for the self-styled Patriots on Navy Island during the Canadian Insurrection: sometimes dressing as a girl, and carrying them in her stays; sometimes attiring herself as a boy, and secreting them in the lining of her hat. In the latter character she always rode as a boy would, which was nothing to her, for she could govern any horse that any man could ride, and could drive four-in-hand with the best whip in those parts. Setting forth on one of her patriotic missions, she appropriated to herself the first horse she could lay her hands on; and this offence had brought her where I saw her. She had quite a lovely face, though, as the reader may suppose from this sketch of her history, there was a lurking devil in her bright eye, which looked out pretty sharply from between her prison bars.

*American Notes for General Circulation and Pictures from Italy* (1905). The British novelist first visited eastern Canada in 1842.

We have been to Toronto, and Kingston; experiencing attentions at each which I should have difficulty in describing. The wild and rabid toryism of Toronto is, I speak seriously, *appalling*. English kindness is very different from American. People send their horses and carriages for your use, but they don't exact as payment the right of being always under your nose. [Undated letter (1842) to John Foster]

*Letters of Charles Dickens* (1880), edited by "His Sister-in-Law and His Eldest Daughter."

## Dickens, Francis Jeffrey

Wednesday, April 15.
Very cold weather. Travelled.

Typically terse entry from the diary of Inspector Francis Jeffrey Dickens of the North-West Mounted Police, 1885. Inspector Dickens, third son of the novelist, surrendered Fort Pitt to the Crees during the Riel Rebellion of 1885. "The Diary of Francis Dickens," edited by Vernon LaChance, *Queen's Quarterly*, Spring, 1930. The inspector had a lake in the LaRonge area of northern Saskatchewan named after him in 1950. He once joked that "a book that would take a man's life to write" would be called "Forty Years Without Beer in the Canadian North-West."

## Dickson, Lovat

. . . the reward that I aimed for: it was to write. Not to teach, not necessarily to be a creative writer, not to write only as a writer who wrests a living from his pen: but to be concerned with writing, to make words, which I loved, which had been my support and my companions through all these difficult years, the means of my livelihood as well as of my constant pleasure.

*The Ante-Room* (1959).

In the House of Words the voices of the young are what one ought to listen for.

*The House of Words* (1963). See also Mazo de la Roche and Grey Owl.

## Dickson, Roy Ward

We owe most of what we know to about one hundred men. We owe most of what we have suffered to another hundred or so.

Called the "king of quiz," Dickson devised the first radio quiz programs in 1935 and hosted over five thousand such shows in Canada, the United Kingdom and the United States.

## Diderot, Dénis

CANADA, *Geography. History.* This immense country of North America, bounded on one side by the Ocean and the Mississippi River, has no known boundaries to the north, where it meets the cold lands where European avarice and curiosity have not yet penetrated. Quebec is its capital.

*

M. de Voltaire did not appear to regret this loss. If the tenth part, said he, of the money swallowed up by this colony had been employed to reclaim our uncultivated land in France, the gain would have been considerable. This is the reflection of a citizen-philosopher. Yet it cannot be denied that the commerce in pelts, inexpensive in itself, failed as a source of riches. The savages attached all the rewards of the hunt and sold the most beautiful skins for crude instruments, to them treasures more precious than our metals and luxurious material which only made for a wealth of opinion.

> From the opening and closing paragraphs of the entry on "Canada," signed by M. de Sacy, in Diderot's *Encyclopédie, ou Dictionnaire raisonné des sciences, des arts et des métiers* (1781).
> Nancy Mitford wrote: "The *Encyclopédie* devoted twelve lines to Canada, 'a country inhabited by bears, beavers and barbarians, and covered eight months of the year, with snow.'" This is an amusing canard. Instead of one dozen lines, Diderot allocated more than one thousand lines to Canada. See also Nancy Mitford.

**Diefenbaker, John G.**
My fellow Canadians. . . . [Characteristic salutation]

At last I understand the meaning of revolution.

> To a friend on "Black Friday," June 1, 1956, when the Liberals under Louis St. Laurent and C.D. Howe pushed the "pipeline bill" through the House of Commons by pressuring René Beaudoin, the Speaker, to reverse his own ruling. This helped bring about the fall of the Liberals and the rise of the Conservatives under their new leader. See also René Beaudoin.

I ask for your prayers. I ask for your assistance and your cooperation. I will make mistakes, but I hope it will be said of me when I give up the highest honour that you can confer on any man, as was said of another in public service: "He wasn't always right; sometimes he was on the wrong side, but never on the side of wrong." That is my dedication; that is my humble declaration. [Conclusion of his acceptance speech, December 10, 1955, succeeding George Drew as leader of the Conservative party]

One Canada, one Canada, where Canadians will have preserved to them the control of their own economic and political destiny. Sir John A. Macdonald gave his life to this party. He opened the West. He saw Canada from east to west. I see a new Canada—*a Canada of the North!* [Winnipeg, February 12, 1958]

Freedom is the right to be wrong, not the right to do wrong. [March 11, 1958]

There we were, the Prime Minister of Canada and a newspaper boy. He told me something of his dreams for Canada and I told him of my youthful ideas.

> When John Diefenbaker was a fourteen-year-old newsboy in Prince Albert, he accidentally met Prime Minister Wilfrid Laurier, July 29, 1910. Laurier himself wrote: "They certainly express themselves clearly and definitely. After I talked to a newsboy this morning, he told me: 'I can't waste any time on you, Prime Minister, I must get about my work.'"

*

I am the first prime minister of this country of neither altogether English nor French origin. So I determined to bring about a Canadian citizenship that knew no hyphenated consideration. . . . Well, I never deviated from this purpose. It's the reason I went into public life. I'm very happy to be able to say that in the House of Commons today in my party we have members of Italian, Dutch, German, Scandinavian, Chinese and Ukrainian origin—and they are all Canadians.

> Interviewed by Jeannine Locke, *Maclean's Magazine*, March 29, 1958. For

"a Canadian citizenship that knew no hyphenated consideration," see John Porter.

Apparently I just can't pronounce French well while talking. An English-speaking friend joked to me, "I love to hear you talk French on television. When you do, every English-speaking person in the audience who doesn't know a word of French can understand every word you say." [*Liberty*, April, 1960]

We in Canada believe that good fences are necessary. [Introducing President John F. Kennedy at a joint sitting of the Senate and the House of Commons, May 17, 1961]

I know there are some who feel a sense of embarrassment in expressing pride in their nation, perhaps because of the fear that they might be considered old-fashioned or parochial. I do not belong to that group. I realize that a warped and twisted nationalism is productive of tyranny. But a healthy loyalty and devotion to one's country constitutes a most fruitful inspiration in life. [House of Commons, July 1, 1961]

We shall be Canadians first, foremost, and always, and our policies will be decided in Canada and not dictated by any other country. [Rimouski, May 8, 1962]

I'd never have been Prime Minister if the Gallup Polls had had their way. [Lethbridge, May 11, 1962]

I can assure you that as long as there is a drop of blood in my body they won't stop me from talking about freedom. [Sudbury, June 3, 1962]

They say I've made mistakes, you know. But they've been mistakes of the heart. [Duck Lake, 1963]

I ask myself, is a thing right, and if it is right, I do it. [Bradford, Ontario, 1963]

We don't intend to use Canada as a dumping ground for nuclear warheads. [Winnipeg, March 4, 1963]

Everyone is against me but the people.

\*

There are great interests against us— national and international — but the people of Canada have an appointment with destiny.

Port Hope, Ontario, March 8, 1963; an echo of Franklin Delano Roosevelt's stirring statement in 1936, "This generation of Americans has a rendezvous with destiny."

My friends, you say "give 'em hell, John!" I never do that. I tell the truth and it sounds like hell. It simply sounds that way to the Grits. [Moncton, March 13, 1963]

As Prince Albert goes, so goes the nation. [Prince Albert, Saskatchewan, April 7, 1963]

The duty of the Opposition is to turn out the government. [Kiwanis Club luncheon, Ottawa, March 13, 1964]

I have always been a House of Commons man. [House of Commons, June 4, 1964]

I haven't practised my French. It's just that you are starting to understand it better. [Press conference, St. Hyacinthe, Quebec, August 23, 1965]

The prime minister announced a war on poverty. I was impressed. He appointed Tom Kent to run his war on poverty . . . that was impressive too. And they raised Kent's salary from $12,000 a year to $25,000. . . . He won *his* war on poverty. [Oakville, Ontario, September 18, 1965]

I never campaign. I just visit with the people. [Campaign picnic, 1965]

They criticized me sometimes for being too much concerned with the average Canadian. I can't help that. I'm just one of them. [Toronto, September 7, 1967]

So to each of you, I say I believe in Canada—a Canada undivided. A Canadian I was born, a Canadian I will die.

"That paraphrases the attitude taken by Macdonald," Diefenbaker continued, in an address to the Progressive Conservative Convention, Toronto, September, 1967. "One Canada, One Nation," *Those Things We Treasure: A Selection of Speeches on Freedom and in Defence of Our Parliamentary Heritage* (1972).

"I'll lay me down and rest a while and then I'll rise and fight again."

Diefenbaker was fighting to retain the leadership and respect of the Conservative Party at the leadership convention, Toronto, November 14, 1967, when he recited a verse of an ancient ballad, which might have been "Sir Andrew Barton" in Percy's *Reliques* (1765), which concludes: "Fight on, my men," Sir Andrew says, / "A little Ime hurt, but yett not slaine; / Ile but lye downe and bleede a while, / And then Ile rise and fight againe."

Nothing I ever do is political. [Ottawa, January 16, 1968]

Have you ever seen him kiss a farmer? [Alluding to Prime Minister Pierre Elliott Trudeau's "kissing campaign" of 1968]

Ah, but don't get me started on history because then you shall know the meaning of eternity.

Quoted by Tom Alderman in *The Canadian Magazine*, May 29, 1971. Sources include: Peter C. Newman's *Renegade in Power: The Diefenbaker Years* (1963) and *Quotations from Chairman Diefenbaker* (1968), edited by Anthony Bond and Brian Shaw. See also: Dalton Camp, John F. Kennedy, Sir John A. Macdonald.

**Dietrich, Marlene**
Canada. What a beautiful country. The air and the sky seem to have been freshly washed and polished, and the people too. Like the Swedes, the Canadians have unnorthern temperaments. Such capacity for enthusiasm!

*Marlene Dietrich's ABC* (1961).

**Dilke, Sir Charles W.**
. . . but I may incidentally remark that, while we speak in England of "Her Majesty's Opposition," the Conservatives of Ontario have attempted to better the phrase, and style themselves "Her Majesty's Loyal Opposition."

*Problems of Greater Britain* (1866-67, 1890).

The first time that I saw Sir John Macdonald was shortly after Lord Beaconsfield's death, and as the clock struck midnight, I was starting from Euston station, and there appeared on the step of the railway carriage, in Privy Councillor's uniform (the right to wear which is confined to so small a number of persons, that one expects to know by sight those who wear it), a figure precisely similar to that of the late Conservative leader, and it required, indeed, a severe exercise of presence of mind to remember that there had been a City banquet, from which the apparition must be coming, and to rapidly arrive by a process of exhaustion at the knowledge that this twin brother of that Lord Beaconsfield, whom shortly before I had seen in the sick room which he was not to leave, must be the Prime Minister of Canada.

Quoted by G. Mercer Adam in *Canada's Patriot Statesman: The Life and Career of the Right Honourable Sir John A. Macdonald* (1891).

**Dingman, Harold**
The normal daily attitude of the Montreal police toward gambling houses is one of the monumental jokes of police history.

Quoted by Pax Plante in *Montréal sous le règne de la pègre* (1950).

**Dionne, Oliva**
I ought to be shot.
*
I'm the kind of fellow they should put in jail.
*
I have been chosen by God for a miracle.
*
People will think we are pigs.

Private and public sentiments of Oliva Dionne of Callander, Ontario, when his wife Elzire gave birth to quintuplets—Annette, Cécile, Emilie, Marie, Yvonne—on May 28, 1934.

**Disraeli, Benjamin**
That our dominion in America should now be brought to a conclusion I sincerely desire, but I desire it should terminate in peace and friendship. Great would be the amicable separation of the two countries, and great would be the honour this country would reap in con-

senting to such a state. [British House of Commons, December 22, 1837]

I am not one of those who believe that the destiny of Canada must inevitably be annexation with the United States. Canada possesses all the elements of a great independent country. It is destined, I sometimes say to myself, to become the Russia of the New World. [British House of Commons, 1846]

These wretched colonies will all be independent, too, in a few years, and are a millstone round our necks.

> Letter to James Howard Harris, Third Earl of Malmesbury, former foreign secretary and Lord Privy Seal, August 13, 1852, concerning the Newfoundland fisheries. *The Life of Benjamin Disraeli, Earl of Beaconsfield* (1910-20), by W.F. Monypenny and G.E. Buckle.

Colonies do not cease to be colonies because they are independent. [British House of Commons, February 5, 1863]

It can never be our pretence or our policy to defend the Canadian frontier against the U.S. . . . What is the use of these colonial deadweights *which we do not govern*?

> Letter written as chancellor of the Exchequer to Prime Minister Lord Derby, 1866, quoted by Glen Frankfurter in *Baneful Domination: The Idea of Canada in the Atlantic World 1581-1971* (1971).

The Prime Minister of Canada arrived yesterday and departed by early train this morning. . . . He is gentlemanlike, agreeable, and very intelligent: a considerable man, with no Yankeeisms except a little sing-song occasionally at the end of a sentence. . . . By the bye the Canadian chief is said to be very like your humble servant, tho' a much younger man. I think there is a resemblance.

> Letter from the elderly Lord Beaconsfield, prime minister of Great Britain, to Lady Bradford after a visit from Sir John A. Macdonald in the early fall of 1879. Quoted by Edgar Andrew Collard in *Canadian Yesterdays* (1955). See also Sir Charles W. Dilke.

## Dixon, Fred J.

As far as fighting goes, I prefer to do mine here, and if I have to shed my blood I prefer to shed it here where I know it will be for freedom. [Anti-conscription address, Winnipeg, May 27, 1917]

From a thousand hills, a thousand rills father into a mighty river which sweeps on to the ocean. An attempt to damn the Niagara, in the hope that it would never reach the sea, would be no more foolish than the attempt to damn labour from its resistless onward sweep towards its natural outlet—co-operative industry.

\*

One might as well tell the full-grown man to resolve himself into a boy again and "be seen and not heard" as tell labour it cannot have a voice in the management of industry through collective bargaining. Grass will grow, the river will reach the sea, the boy will come a man, and labour will come into its own.

> *Strike Bulletin No. 27*, by a leader of the Winnipeg general strike which paralyzed the city from May 15 to June 25, 1919.

What shall the sacrifice profit Canada if she who has helped to destroy Kaiserism in Germany shall allow Kaiserism to be established at home?

\*

There have always been those who imagined that "a whiff of grape shot" would stop the cry of the people for justice.

\*

The Committee of One Thousand has, however, many lessons to learn—among other things the members of that committee must be taught that ideas are more powerful than bullets. The blood of the martyrs is the seed of the church. We shall "carry on," in spite of hell, till the victory is won.

> "Kaiserism in Canada," *Western Labour News*, June 23, 1919.

The reason we enjoy our liberties now is because in the past they let people speak out. The people had brains enough to see what was foolish and what was false, sense enough to reject what was false and hold to the truth, and I submit that should be the basis of our public policy in Canada today.

Accused of writing "seditious libel" during the Winnipeg general strike of 1919, Dixon addressed the jury on February 14, 1920, and was found not guilty.

**Dmytruk, Peter**
"Pierre le Canadien."

This eponymous name was given Peter Dmytruk, a young flier of Ukrainian background from Wynyard, Saskatchewan, who was shot down by the German occupation troops at Martres-de-Veyre. Dmytruk joined the French Resistance in the small village in central France and then was caught and killed, December 10, 1943. His body is buried at Martres-de-Veyre; and the village has been twinned with the town of Wynyard since 1972.

**Dobbs, Fred C.**   See Mike Magee.

**Dobbs, Kildare**
The world around us is quite as senseless and unreadable as the *Encyclopaedia Britannica*. We have to make it up as we go along.

Introduction, *Reading the Time* (1968).

The Shield! The Canadian Shield!
Come, Muse of rockbound nationalists, or whom our stammering typing engine waits smiling with teeth of alphabets. You who inflate the eloquence of Northern laureates, come, let us celebrate the real estate. Sing, learned dame —as so often before—not of men, not of poor flesh and blood, but of rocks, stones, mud, bogs, fens, muskegs, permafrost, tundra!

The Great Fur Opera: Annals of the Hudson's Bay Company 1670-1970 (1970), by Ronald Searle and Kildare Dobbs. See also Joseph Robson and James Wolfe.

**Dodds, E. King**
Every now and then a scare is started about the decadence of the horse. First the bicycle and next the automobile was to drive him off the road. I unhesitatingly assert that any vehicle which costs

$1,000 a year for repairs and supplies will never supplant the horse in public favour.

Canadian Turf Recollections (1910).

**Doern, Russell J.**
The 4-H's of today are hair, hostels, hippies and hash.

An allusion to the 4-H Clubs in a speech in the Manitoba Legislature by the minister without portfolio, May, 1971.

**Dollier de Casson, François**
The whole of this day was passed in devotions, thanksgivings, and hymns of praise to the Creator. There were no lighted lamps before the Holy Sacrament, but there were some fire-flies which shone there very pleasantly day and night, hung by threads in a beautiful and marvellous manner altogether fitting for the honour of the most revered of our mysteries, considering the rudeness of this savage country.

An account of the founding of Montreal, May 18, 1642, by the French officer who wrote A History of Montreal: 1640-1672 (1928), translated by Ralph Flenley.

**Domville, James**
Uncle Lou, Uncle Lou, you know what you can do and Howe!

Perhaps the wittiest line from My Fur Lady, the McGill University satiric revue which opened in Montreal on February 7, 1957, and went on to tour the country. The story, written by James Domville and others, concerns Aurora, the Eskimo princess of Mukluko who must marry before she turns twenty-one or her Arctic principality "somewhere off Baffin Island" will revert to Canada. Along the way she meets the governor general (whom she greets as "Gee Gee"). The hit song of the show was "It's a Great Big Wonderful Country."

**Donne, John**
Licence my roving hands, and let them go,
Before, behind, between, above, below.
O my America! my new-found-land,
My kingdome, safeliest when with one man man'd,

My Myne of precious stones, My
Emperie,
How blest am I in this discovering thee!
To enter in these bonds, is to be free;
Then where my hand is set, my seal shall
be.

This lovely literary conceit—Donne's
comparison of his mistress' body with
"my America! my new-found-land"—
appears in "Elegie XIX: To His Mistris
Going to Bed." "It is impossible to date
the 'Elegies' with any certainty," John
Hayward writes in the Nonesuch Press
edition of *John Donne: Complete Poetry
and Selected Prose* (1932). "Elegy XIX"
was first published in 1633, two years
after the poet's death, but the poem
might have been written as early as
1590, some seven years after Sir Humphrey Gilbert claimed Newfoundland as
an English colony.

**Doran, George H.**
In 1846 my father's family came to the
New World and settled in Toronto, Canada. There I arrived in 1869, when Toronto, with 30,000 inhabitants, was a little
city in a great country. The community
was made up largely of Scottish and Irish,
and just enough English to establish a
sense of class distinction expressed by the
established Church of England, for in
these days Toronto and all Canada—in
fact, the world at large—was intensely religious, probably because of the very
limited number of outlets for enthusiasm
and partisanship.

*Chronicles of Barabbas 1884-1934—Fur-
ther Chronicles and Comment 1952*
(1935, 1952). Doran was a founder of
Doubleday, the largest publishing house
in the United States.

**Dorchester, Lord**   See Sir Guy Carleton.

**Dorion, Sir Antoine-Aimé**
The Honorable Mr. *Dorion* (*Hochelaga*)
moved, in amendment thereto, seconded
by the Honorable Mr. *Laframboise,* That
the words, "But this House deems it a
duty respectfully to express to Your Excellency its firm conviction that the
people of this Province, fully appreciat-
ing the blessings of their existing politi-

cal relations with the Great Empire of
which they form a part, neither wish nor
seek to create a new nationality," be
added at the end thereof.

When Governor General Lord Monck
urged the creation "of a new Nationality" in the throne speech, the leader of
the Opposition and member for Hochelaga moved the above amendment,
which, while popular with the Quebec
members, was defeated sixty-four to
twenty-five, January 23, 1865. *Journals
of the Legislative Assembly of the Province of Canada* (1865).

A million of inhabitants may seem a small
affair to the mind of a philosopher who
sits down to write out a constitution. He
may think it would be better that there
should be but one religion, one language,
and one system of laws, and he goes to
work to frame institutions that will bring
all to that desired state; but I can tell
honourable gentlemen that the history of
every country goes to show that not even
by the power of the sword can such
changes be accomplished.

Address, February 16, 1865, *Parliamentary Debates on the Subject of the Confederation of the British North American Provinces* (1865).

**Dorion, Jean-Baptiste-Eric**
Sir—Be kind enough to have the enclosed
petition signed as soon as possible by
men, women and children. Yours very
truly, J.B.E. Dorion.

To ridicule such opponents of Confederation as J.B.E. Dorion, the member
for Drummond and Arthabaska, George-
Etienne Cartier, read out a personal letter which Dorion had written one of his
agents. House of Assembly, Province of
Canada, March 7, 1865. Quoted by P.B.
Waite in *The Confederation Debates in
the Province of Canada: 1865* (1963).

**Dos Passos, John**
So you've been to Toronto—don't you
think it's a beastly place? Toronto on a
Sunday morning. . . .

Letter of October 26, 1907, *The Fourteenth Chronicle: Letters and Diaries of
John Dos Passos* (1973).

## Doughty, Sir Arthur G.

Of all national assets archives are the most precious; they are the gift of one generation to another and the extent of our care of them marks the extent of our civilization.

> The Canadian Archives and its Activities (1924), quoted in Archives: Mirror of Canada Past (1972), Public Archives of Canada.

## Douglas, Major C.H.

A plus B Theorem.

> The British engineer's phrase (in the words of John A. Irving in The Social Credit Movement in Alberta [1959]) "became part of the everyday vocabulary of nearly all adult Albertans." It was popularized by William Aberhart whose Social Credit party came to power on August 22, 1935.
>
> Douglas claimed his theorem demonstrates the weakness of the financial system, for the price of goods must exceed the power of consumers to buy them. A (wages) and B (production costs) always exceed A (wages or buying power). Therefore, unless the state establishes a "just price" for goods and issues a "basic dividend" to all, consumers are condemned to a life of "poverty in the midst of plenty."

So you have this enormous capacity to produce and this enormous need to be filled, and something stands in between those two. Now, what is it? The thing that stands in between those two is the ticket system, by which the people who want can get from the people who can produce. That is the financial system. That is what stands in between this enormous ability to produce and this enormous need to be filled.

> "An Engineer's Solution of the Finance Problem," April 24, 1923, The Canadian Club of Ottawa Year Book: 1922-23; 1923-24 (1925).

Congratulations. There will be others but only one first. C.H. Douglas.

> Cable of congratulations from Major Douglas, the British theorist of Social Credit, to William Aberhart when the

Social Credit party came to power in Alberta, August 22, 1935. Quoted by L.P.V. Johnson and Ola J. MacNutt in Aberhart of Alberta (1970). See also William Aberhart.

I have all the damn fools on my side and all the clever men against me.

> Quoted by Alan Anderson in "A Passion on the Prairies" in Flamboyant Canadians (1964), edited by Ellen Stafford.

## Douglas, Sir James

To change the conversation, perhaps, Mr. Douglas asked the doctor why so many of the Hudson's Bay officers were bald. His answer was "Pro pelle cutem—they had sent their furs home," at which some laughed, but Mr. Douglas gravely said, "Perhaps, having given us the poetry of the thing, you will give the prose—the cause," which nonplussed the doctor as this was a conundrum too.

> "A Skin for a Skin" is the motto of the Hudson's Bay Company. Douglas, chief factor at Fort Victoria, became governor of Vancouver Island in 1851. Quoted by J.S. Helmcken in "A Reminiscence of 1850," Victoria Daily Colonist, December, 1887.

Alternate rain and sunshine. . . . The Union of Vancouver Island with British Columbia was proclaimed today. The Ships of War fired a salute on the occasion. A funeral procession, with minute guns, would have been more appropriate to the sad melancholy event.

> From the diary of Martha Douglas, young daughter of the ex-governor, Sir James Douglas, Victoria, November 19, 1866. Douglas himself added the last sentence. Quoted by R.E. Watters in British Columbia: A Centennial Anthology (1958).

## Douglas Jr., James

A Colonial publisher knows his own interest too well to give anything worth while for a manuscript which, if he publish it, will be likely not to meet with sale enough to cover cost of printing. . . . A Canadian book is sure, with the stigma of a colonial imprimatur upon it, not to circulate beyond the confines of the Dominion; and, therefore, when a Canadian writes a meritorious book . . . he seeks a publisher abroad.

"The Intellectual Progress of Canada During the Last Fifty Years, and the Present State of its Literature: An Address to the Literary and Historical Society of Quebec," March 3, 1875. Quoted by H. Pearson Gundy in "The Development of Trade Book Publishing in Canada," *Royal Commission on Book Publishing: Background Papers* (1972).

### Douglas, Lloyd C.

While I am a Yankee by birth, and pretty largely by training and residence, I do have a good many Canadian connections. For instance, three young gentlemen have honoured me by becoming my grandsons. They are Canadians over in Montreal, and I find that they still speak to me and consider me approximately the same way they would if I lived up there.

"Impatient Idealists" (1942), *Empire Club of Canada: Addresses Delivered During the Year 1941-42* (1942).

### Douglas, Melvyn

When I was eleven, we moved to Toronto, where my father taught at a conservatory of music, and five years later we moved to Lincoln, Nebraska. . . . At the age of fourteen, in Toronto, I lied about my age and tried to enlist in the Canadian Army, but my father stopped them from taking me. I had no interest in the theatre in those days—no appetite for it.

The suave Hollywood actor was born in the American South in 1901. *The Player: A Profile of an Art* (1962), by Lillian and Helen Ross.

### Douglas, T.C.

I've realized that it's possible to plan an economy without owning it.

\*

If the New Party doesn't succeed, it will mean that for the next twenty-five years there'll be no left-of-centre political party in Canada.

Remarks made at the formation of the New Party in 1960. The following year

Douglas was elected leader of the newly named New Democratic Party.

Gardiner: What do you know about farming—you're not a farmer.
Douglas: I never laid an egg either, but I know more about making an omelette than a hen does.

Exchange with James G. Gardiner, minister of Agriculture, quoted by Robert Tyre in *Douglas in Saskatchewan: The Story of a Socialist Experiment* (1962).

Give us seventy seats and we'll turn Parliament upside down. Give us 170 seats and we'll turn the country right side up. [Campaign promise, 1960s]

A recession is when your neighbour has to tighten his belt. A depression is when you have to tighten your own belt. And a panic is when you have no belt to tighten and your pants fall down.

Remark made in 1968, quoted in *T.C. Douglas: A Biographical Essay* (1971), by the NDP.

It is good that Mr. Trudeau did not consult the cabinet. It would probably have insisted on a study session followed by a task force followed by a white paper about which nothing would be done.

On Prime Minister Trudeau's marriage to Margaret Sinclair, Vancouver, March 4, 1971.

Canadians do not want to escape from the tyranny of big business only to fall into the clutches of big government.

Farewell address as leader of the New Democratic Party, Ottawa Convention, April 21, 1971.

I don't mind someone stealing my pajamas, but he should wear all of them if he doesn't want to appear indecent. [On the appropriation of CCF-NDP programs by the Liberals and Conservatives]

\*

In the 1960s my job was to ensure that Canadians did not fall asleep on their full stomachs.

*Time*, May 3, 1971. "Tommy Douglas doesn't have to kiss babies. Babies kiss him"—Saskatchewan proverb.

## Douglas-Home, Sir Alec

My great grandfather wrote the Canadian constitution. . . . I hold the whip hand because if Britain wants to earn dollars from Canada, I warn you, I shall send the Beatles to Toronto and they will bring back, I think, either Canadian dollars or Ontario silver or whatever it may be.

> Sir Alec was prime minister of Great Britain. "Address" (1964), *Empire Club of Canada: Addresses 1963-64* (1964).

## Downes, P.G.

"Tell me, Father, what is the white man's Heaven?"

"It is the most beautiful place in the world."

"Tell me, Father, is it like the land of the little trees when the ice has left the lakes? Are the great musk oxen there? Are the hills covered with flowers? There will I see the caribou everywhere I look? Are the lakes blue with the sky of summer? Is every net full of great, fat whitefish? Is there room for me in this land, like our land, the Barrens? Can I camp anywhere and not find that someone else has camped? Can I feel the wind and be like the wind? Father, if your Heaven is not all these, leave me alone in my land, the land of the little sticks."

> Conversation between a Dogrib Indian and an Oblate missionary, quoted by P.G. Downes in *Sleeping Island: The Story of One Man's Travels in the Great Barren Lands of the Canadian North* (1943). See also Saltatha.

## Doyle, Sir Arthur Conan

Many a terrible secret is hid by those silent woods, and the fate of Charles de la Noue, seigneur de Sainte Marie, is among them.

> Melodramatic concluding sentence of Sir Arthur's romance of the Huguenots, part of which is set in Canada. *The Refugees: A Tale of Two Continents* (1893).

Stanley Hopkins drew from his pocket a drab-covered notebook. The outside was rough and worn, the leaves were discoloured. On the first page were written the initials "J.H.N." and the date "1883."

Holmes laid it on the table and examined it in his minute way, while Hopkins and I gazed over each shoulder. On the second page were printed the letters "C.P.R.," and then came several sheets of numbers. Another heading was Argentine, another Costa Rica, and another São Paulo, each with pages of signs and figures after it.

"What do you make of these?" asked Holmes.

"They appear to be lists of stock exchange securities. I thought that 'J.H.N.' were the initials of a broker, and that 'C.P.R.' may have been his client."

"Try Canadian Pacific Railway," said Holmes.

Stanley Hopkins swore between his teeth, and struck his thigh with his clenched hand.

"What a fool I have been!" he cried. "Of course it is as you say. Then 'J.H.N.' are the only initials we have to solve. . . ."

> Sherlock Holmes's deduction is made in the story "Black Peter" from *The Return of Sherlock Holmes* (1905). It would not amaze a Canadian. There are two other references to this country in the Holmes canon. In "The Copper Beeches" from *The Adventures of Sherlock Holmes* (1891), a character is given a posting in Halifax. And in *The Hound of the Baskervilles* (1902), Sir Henry, who has spent years farming in the West, is described as "this young stranger from Canada." When his missing boot turns up, it can readily be identified because of the markings: "Meyers, Toronto." More than seventy years later, in 1971, the Canadian equivalent of the Baker Street Irregulars was formed, and called, inevitably, The Bootmakers of Toronto.

Before I sit down I will read a verse or two in which I was able, perhaps, to compress a little more of that feeling which Canada has awakened, than can be done in prose. Poetry is like the pemmican of literature: it is compressed thought, and one can mingle emotion with it, which one cannot always do in prosaic speech. I will read you, if I may, these few lines before I take my seat. I call it "The Athabasca Trail," since Athabasca is the place where we have for some time been living an open air life.

*
Mother of a mighty manhood, land of
glamour and of hope,
From the eastward sea-swept islands to
the sunny western slope,
Ever more my heart is with you, ever
more till life shall fail,
I'll be out with pack and packer on the
Athabasca Trail.

> What was described as "prolonged
> cheers" followed the author's recital of
> "The Athabasca Trail," the last lines
> of which are reproduced here. "Some
> Impressions," July 2, 1914, *Addresses De-
> livered before the Canadian Club of
> Ottawa: 1914-15* (1915). The poem was
> published that day in *The Montreal
> Gazette* with "No rights reserved."

As I approached this great city [of Mont-
real] I recollected the time when only a
line of frail palisades lay between its
population and utter barbarism, and
when a sudden rush of savages might
have driven Europe entirely from these
parts. I assure you that I felt as much
veneration as I know you feel when you
approach the historical centres of
Europe.

*

I feel, gentlemen, here in Canada that I
am standing at a place which must in the
process of time produce a very great literature. When I put it in the future I do
not mean that it has not yet done so, but
what I mean is that it will be a great
volume of literature which in time to
come may well influence the literature of
the world. But I should be sorry to see
Canada turning her whole thoughts towards such matters. It seems to me that
for a strong young country with enormous practical work lying in front of it
there are better things to do than dream.
There is such a call for the virile upbringing of the country that it will be unwise
of it to go back to dreaming. Great
deeds are better than great sonnets, and
Canada's call to her sons is a stirring one
to action; for the poetry of action exists
just as does the poetry of words and the
great deed that is accomplished is more
glorious than the great sonnet.

> "The Future of Canadian Literature,"
> June 4, 1914, *Addresses Delivered before*

*the Canadian Club of Montreal: Season
of 1914-15* (1915).

If I am asked, as I shall be asked, when
I go across, what has struck me most, it
is the wisdom and foresight of the Canadian Government. We in England have
got too much into the habit of regarding
the Government to some extent as our
enemy. . . . The Government of Canada
seems to me like a wise old gardener
going around with its watering-pot,
which contains the most precious water
of Capital, and using it just where it will
do most good, from one side of your great
country to another.

*

To those who have the eyes to see, that
great St. Lawrence is still white with the
sails of forgotten vessels and the banks
still red with the campfires of the dead.
One seems to see much more. . . .

> "Some Impressions," July 2, 1914, *Ad-
> dresses Delivered before the Canadian
> Club of Ottawa: 1914-15* (1915).

## Doyle, Lawrence
There is a band within this land
Who live in pomp and pride;
To swell their stores they rob the poor;
On pleasures' wings they ride.
With dishes fine their tables shine,
They live in princely style.
Those are the knaves who made us slaves,
And sold Prince Edward Isle.

> Second of a dozen stanzas from the bal-
> lad "Prince Edward Isle, Adieu," which
> Edward D. Ives believes was written by
> Doyle who lived "along the Fortune
> Road east of St. Peter's" and died in
> 1907. See Ives's *Lawrence Doyle: The
> Farmer-Poet of Prince Edward Island: A
> Study in Local Songmaking* (1971).

## Drainie, John
When an actor reads a story aloud, he
gets to do all the parts! Surely that is
every actor's ambition. Also, he is alone.
He cannot be upstaged by a smart fellow
actor. But aside from these frivolities, the
reading of prose is a far more rewarding
job in many ways than that of delivering
the lines of dialogue in dramatic writing.

> Preface, *Stories with John Drainie* (1963).

**Drake, T.G.H.**   See Dr. Allan Brown.

**Drapeau, Jean**
I have it on good authority—from the roads department chief, Mr. Arpin—that it will not snow after the fifteenth of March.

Cardinal Léger: It would not surprise me if the Pope tried to move our next Vatican Council to Montreal.
Mayor Drapeau: Your Eminence, that is the last time I shall confide in you! [Exchange said to have taken place during the 1960s]

We practised resistance before it was a word . . . it must be admitted that for hundreds of years we have had no connection with France. Almost five generations had no connection with France. . . . It is because of the virtues which we inherited from our ancestors that challenges have never scared us and that we think it is possible to play a role in Canada which I hope is comparable in terms of North America to that which France plays in Europe. We are attached to this immense country, and whatever be our way of serving it, if we serve our country better because we serve it as Canadians of French origin, then we will be of greater service to France and humanity.

Statement at the lunch for Charles de Gaulle, July 26, 1967, two days after the French president's *"Québec libre!"* address. Quoted by Peter C. Newman in *The Distemper of Our Times: Canadian Politics in Transition: 1963-1968* (1968). See also Charles de Gaulle.

The Montreal Olympics can no more have a deficit than a man can have a baby.

*The Globe and Mail*, February 1, 1973.

**Dreiser, Theodore**
Should Russia go down to defeat I hope the Germans invade England. I would rather see the Germans in England than those damn, aristocratic, horse-riding snobs there now. . . . Churchill has no intention of opening a second front. He's afraid the Communists will rule the world. So he does nothing except send thousands of Canadians to be slaughtered

at Dieppe. He didn't send any English. They stay at home and do nothing.

The author of *An American Tragedy* (1925), in Toronto to address a rally for the second front, spoke too frankly to *The Toronto Telegram* which published the above remarks in an interview on September 21, 1942, a few hours before the rally in Eaton Auditorium. It was hastily cancelled, and Dreiser returned to the United States. Quoted by W.A. Swanberg in *Dreiser* (1965).

**Dressler, Marie**
And as for my birthplace—Cobourg, Canada—I can give you only my word that I was born in a house and had a complete set of parents. Certainly no president could claim a more humble birthplace.

＊

My first appearance on the stage was as Cupid in one of these church affairs in Lindsay, Canada. How carefully mother posed me on my improvised pedestal! Her instructions to me were on no account to move! After this nothing could have induced me to breathe. Suddenly the pedestal began toppling. I strove to hold my pose, keeping my golden bow and arrow aloft, but I might have encountered an untimely end had I not been caught in the crash. This was my first stage fall. (I wonder if that was a premonition that one has to fall to win success on the stage?) At any rate, since then I have fallen on some of the hardest stages in this country and Europe.

*The Life Story of an Ugly Duckling: An Autobiographical Fragment in Seven Parts* (1924).

Never shall I forget those naked, clean-swept little Canadian towns, one just like the other. Before I was twelve years old, I must have lived in fifty of them.

＊

Sometimes I think I have had more trouble and more joy and more fun than any woman alive.

The red-haired stage and film comedienne—who often played opposite Wallace Beery—had an Austrian father (whom she hated) and an Irish-Canadian mother. Born in Cobourg in 1869, she died in Hollywood in 1934. *My Own*

*Story* (1934), as told to Mildred Harrington, foreword by Will Rogers. See also Calvin Coolidge, Norman Reilly Raine and Will Rogers.

## Drew, Captain Andrew

Sir Allan [MacNab] said, "This won't do. I say, Drew, do you think you can cut that vessel out?" "Oh, yes," I said, "nothing easier; but it must be done at night." "Well, then," said he, "go and do it." These were literally all the orders I ever received to take the "Caroline". . . .

*A Narrative of the Capture and Destruction of the Steamer "Caroline" and Her Descent over the Falls of Niagara on the Night of the 29th of December, 1837* (1864).

"Remember the *Caroline*."

Slogan of the Patriots in the Rebellion of 1837 arising out of the "cutting-out" of the *Caroline*. The American steamer was cut adrift and set afire by Captain Drew who claimed that he sent it flaming over Niagara Falls.

## Drew, Benjamin

It is reported throughout the world that coloured people cannot live here; I have been ten years and have seen no one starving yet.

*The Refugee: or the Narratives of Fugitive Slaves in Canada* (1856).

## Drew, George

Drew: You are an evil old man.
Atkinson: I resent being called old.

Adapted from Ross Harkness's *J. E. Atkinson of the Star* (1963).

The Toronto *Star* is the worst influence in Canada.

Quoted by Roy Greenaway in *The News Game* (1966).

"George Drew knows my father,
My father knows George Drew. . . ."

This couplet, although not original—it goes back to David Lloyd George—was sung to the tune of Elgar's "Pomp and Circumstance" at Progressive Conservative gatherings in Ontario when Drew was premier from 1943 to 1948.

## Drummond, William Henry

Johnnie Courteau of de mountain
Johnnie Courteau of de hill
Dat was de boy can shoot de gun
Dat was de boy can jomp an' run
An' it's not very offen you ketch heem still
Johnnie Courteau!

First verse of "Johnny Courteau," a personification of the *habitant* that dates back to 1901.

*

You can't get drown on Lac St. Pierre
So long you stay on shore.

Concluding lines of "The Wreck of the 'Julie Plante'—A Legend of Lac St. Pierre."

*

I've told you many a tale, my child, of the old heroic days
Of Indian wars and massacre, of villages ablaze
With savage torch, from Ville Marie to the Mission of Trois Rivières
But never have I told you yet, of Madeleine Verchères.

First stanza of "Madeleine Verchères." *Dr. W.H. Drummond's Complete Poems* (1926), with an introduction by Louis Fréchette and an appreciation by Neil Munro. See also Anonymous: Epitaphs: Quebec.

## Dubuc, Carl

It is said that Canadians, more precisely Quebeckers, are the greatest telephone-users on earth. It would be false to conclude that because of this we have more to say than anyone else. Quite the contrary.

*

Quebec is one of the ten provinces against which Canada is defending itself.

*

Cartier is probably the only tourist who stopped at Gaspé without bothering to go and see Percé rock.

*Lettre à un Français qui veut émigrer au Québec* (1968).

## Duchesneau, Jacques

Violence, upheld by authority, decides everything.

Intendant of New France from 1675 to 1682, quoted by Gustavus Myers in *A History of Canadian Wealth* (1914).

## Duclos, Intendant

It seems to me that in the choice of girls, good looks should be more considered than virtue.

Letter from the intendant of Louisiana to the French colonial minister in 1717 concerning the "king's girls." Quoted by Francis Parkman in *A Half-Century of Conflict* (1892).

## Dudek, Louis

Getting started is never easy.
We have work to do.
    Europe is behind us.
        America before us.

"Selections from *Europe*," *Collected Poetry* (1971).

The beauty of being a critic
is that one can write as if one were infallible
and be forever wrong.

From "A Coronet for Critics," *Collected Poetry* (1971).

Reading a dead poet
Who complained in his time
Against bad laws, bad manners,
And bad weather in bad rhyme,

I thought how glad he'd be
To be living in our time
To damn worse laws, worse matters,
And worse weather, in worst rhyme.

"The Progress of Satire," *Collected Poetry* (1971).

The problem of Canadian literary development has not been one of growth from primitive roots, but one of sloughing off an imported tradition and of discovering the language, the subject matter, and the form natural and true to Canadian needs.

"Literature in English," *The Canadians 1867-1967* (1967), edited by J.M.S. Careless and R. Craig Brown.

But the liberation from the gods, and the liberation of the individual self, to face alone the great issue of existence—working always for this time and this place, this self, to find the hidden meaning of all things—that is the great adventure. It's not a dark prospect, but an infinite horizon of possibilities, for those who are strong enough to bear it. And for the great majority of modern artists it is still the only road.

"The Everyday Self in Poetry," *The First Person in Literature* (1967).

Fame—the privilege of being pestered by strangers.

\*

If you don't want an enemy to know what you think of him, don't tell your friends.

\*

Revolution is very fine so long as it does not succeed.

\*

The German method is to go to the principle of things, to select the wrong principle, and to build on that.

\*

We all have opinions, but some of us happen to be right.

\*

Reputation is better than fame.

\*

The unexamined poem is not worth reading.

\*

Wit: to indulge in hostilities without having to bear the consequences.

Aphorisms from the unpublished notebook of the Montreal poet-critic-professor, 1972.

## Dufferin, Lady

The hills all round, as seen from our celebrated platform [Dufferin Gate, Quebec Citadel], are of the most lovely autumn colours, and covered, as they are with red and orange trees, they really look like flames in the distance, or like gigantic flower-gardens; for our *trees* are quite as brilliant as your best *flowers*, and if you can imagine your conservatory magnified a million times, and spread over miles and miles of hill and dale, you will begin to understand how we do things in this Canada of ours.

Entry for September 21, 1872, *My Canadian Journal* (1891). *My Canadian Journal: 1872-1878* (1969), edited by Gladys Chantler Walker. The last four words of this passage are famous. The felicitous phrase "This Canada of Ours" is associated with Lady Dufferin, and the use of the word "ours" was widely noted at the time. For an earlier use of the patriotic phrase, see Sir James D. Edgar.

## Dufferin, Lord

It is quite true that after I had been appointed to Canada (1872) Bob Lowe (Lord Sherbrooke) came up to me in a club and said, "Now you ought to make it your business to get rid of the Dominion." To which I replied that I certainly did not intend to be handed down to history as the Governor General who had lost Canada.

> Quoted by George W. Ross in "Shall Canada be Always a Dependency of the Empire," Address before the National Club, Ottawa, October 28, 1908. Lord Dufferin's remark appeared a few years earlier in Herbert Paul's *The Life of Froude* (1905). See also Lord Sherbrooke.

Ladies and gentlemen, it may be doubted whether the inhabitants of the Dominion themselves are as yet fully awake to the magnificent destiny in store for them or have altogether realized the promise of their young and virile nationality. Like a virgin goddess in a primaeval world, Canada still walks in unconscious beauty among her golden woods, and by the margin of her trackless streams, catching but broken glances of her radiant majesty, as mirrored on their surface, and scarcely recks as yet of the glories awaiting her in the Olympus of Nations. [Farewell address in Belfast, June 11-12, 1872, before setting out as governor general]

\*

In the chambers of our hearts there is room and verge for many friends. Their avenues are guarded by no state, no ceremonial; no introduction is needed to gain admission there, and those who once enter need never take their leave. [Quebec City, September 23, 1872]

> Quoted by Gladys Chantler Walker in her edition of Lady Dufferin's *My Canadian Journal: 1872-1878* (1969).

My only guiding star in the conduct and maintenance of my official relations with your public men is the Parliament of Canada, in fact, I suppose I am the only person in the Dominion whose faith in the wisdom and in the infallibility of

Parliament is never shaken. Each of you, gentlemen, only believe in Parliament so long as Parliament votes according to your wishes and convictions. I, gentlemen, believe in Parliament, no matter which way it votes, and to those men alone whom the absolute will of the Confederated Parliament of the Dominion may assign me as my responsible advisers, can I give my confidence.

> Halifax address, August 8, 1873. The governor general was being urged by the Liberals to dismiss the government during the Pacific Scandal. Quoted by George Stewart in *Canada Under the Administration of the Earl of Dufferin* (1878).

I found the Island in a high state of jubilation and quite under the impression that it is the Dominion that has been annexed to Prince Edward; and in alluding to the subject I had adopted the same tone.

> The governor general visited Prince Edward Island three weeks after the colony joined Confederation on July 1, 1873. Letter to Sir John A. Macdonald later that year quoted by D.C. Harvey in "Confederation and Prince Edward Island," *Canadian Historical Review*, June 1933.

A Governor General resembles the humble functionary we see superintending the working of some complicated mass of chain-driven machinery. This personage merely walks about with a little tin vessel of oil in his hand and he pours in a drop here and a drop there, as occasion or the creaking of a joint may require, while his utmost vigilance is directed to no higher aim than the preservation of his wheels and cogs from the intrusion of dust, grits, or other foreign bodies.

> Address to the National Club, Toronto, January 12, 1877.

A constitution nursed upon the oxygen of our bright winter atmosphere makes its owner feel as though he could toss about the pine trees in his glee.

> Quoted by William Leggo in *The History of the Administration of the Right Honourable Frederick Temple, Earl of*

*Dufferin, Late Governor General of Canada* (1878). See also Alfred Lord Tennyson.

**Duffy, Dennis**
If the American takeover of Canada could be drowned in a sea of printer's ink, then Pharaoh and his captains would have floated belly-up long ago. We are the first victims of rape ever to reply, not with blows and screams, but with essays.

*

Maybe the American will be happy to have us. True, we aren't as picturesque as Crackers, ebullient as Californians or greedy as Texans, but we're reliable. We could staff a civil service nicely, we're the kind of folks who could be trusted to make the change in a gas station without knocking down the owner for too much. What more could Canada want?

*The Globe and Mail,* June 10, 1972.

**Dugas, Georges**
One month before fall comes winter.

The curé of St. Boniface, who sang at Riel's funeral mass, is referring to wintering in the Hudson Bay region. *Un Voyageur des pays d'en haut* (1890).

**Dugas, Marcel**
The French language exists; the Canadian does not.

Dugas made this observation in 1918, and Henry Bernard's reply was: "The French language used by everyone else is not the one we French Canadians use." Quoted by Jean Basile in "Literature in French" in *The Canadians 1867-1967* (1967), edited by J.M.S. Careless and R. Craig Brown. See also Henry Bernard.

**Duke, Daryl**
I can still remember noticing, as a child, the quality of the sunlight coming into my grandmother's dining-room.

Television and film director, quoted by Clyde Gilmour in *The Toronto Star,* March 3, 1973.

**Dumont, Fernand**
For my part I believe in the quality of small nations: here is where common values have a chance to sink deep roots.

Quoted by René Lévesque in *An Option for Quebec* (1968).

Like many others of my generation, my choice is made—we have reached the age of jealous loyalties. I shall continue to live, love, dream, and write in French Canada. I don't quite know why; in any case, I shall not betray that obscure ideal which I have inherited from my illiterate ancestors. This ideal, vague though it may ever be, has revived in me that most disgraced of feelings, the sense of honour. Each age offers its own challenge; the task assumed by our ancestors was to survive so that their descendants, now and in the future, might set about building a world to embody their obscure dreams.

*Le Devoir,* June 30, 1967, quoted by Marcel Rioux in *Quebec in Question* (1971).

Anyway, every Canadian may understand that a man of forty, charged with researches and responsibilities, does not take the train for Ottawa in order to play a dubious joke on the governor general.

Fernand Dumont journeyed to Ottawa to attend the Governor General's Reception and Banquet and accept the medal and prize (a $2,500 cheque) for writing the best work of non-fiction published in 1968. In an article in *Le Devoir,* May 24, 1969, the Laval sociologist explained he was turning the sum over to the separatist-minded Parti Québécois. *The Globe and Mail* promptly ridiculed his actions, and Professor Dumont replied with a letter to the editor, "On Living with Divided Loyalties," *The Globe and Mail,* June 7, 1969, from which the above sentence is taken. The full reply is included in *Canada: The Peaceable Kingdom* (1970), edited by William Kilbourn.

If you wish to liberate a people, you must use means that put liberty to work.

Radio-Canada, October 20, 1970. Quoted by Gérard Pelletier in *The October Crisis* (1971), translated by Joyce Marshall.

## Dumont, Gabriel
I confess I was afraid of nothing.

\*

If the enemy captures you and blames you for my actions, you tell them that since the government couldn't manage me, it wasn't easy for you to do so.

\*

Our lands were broken up and stolen from us, and we did not defend them; we were treated with insolence and contempt, and we endured it; but from the moment they threatened our lives, and those of our families and our leader, we have the right to defend them, and we shall defend them unto death.

> Dumont was Riel's adjutant general during the Northwest Rebellion of 1885. The quotations appeared in Adolphe Ouimet's *La Vérité sur la Question Métisse au Nord-Ouest* (1889). The first and second were translated by George F.G. Stanley in "Gabriel Dumont's Account of the North West Rebellion, 1885," *Canadian Historical Review*, September, 1949. (In the second, the Métis leader is addressing his wife Madeleine, before fleeing to Montana following the battle of Batoche.) The third was translated by Stanley B. Ryerson in *French Canada: A Study in Canadian Democracy* (1944).

## Duncan, Chester
Our well-known Canadian laconicism is not always concealed wisdom, but a kind of dumbness, a frustration, a betweenness. We are continually on the verge of something but we don't quite get there. We haven't discovered what we are or where we're going and therefore we haven't much to say.

> Quoted by Hugh Kenner in "The Case of the Missing Face" (1948), *Our Sense of Identity* (1954), edited by Malcolm Ross.

## Duncan, Dorothy
Travels are dreams translated into action.

\*

Ontario is a funny place. It's got everything man could want, and knows it, but it doesn't yet know what to do with such abundance.

\*

Ontario is a state of mind, bounded on the east by a foreign language, on the north by wilderness, on the west by the hungry prairies, and on the south by another country.

> *Here's to Canada!* (1941). See also Richard M. Nixon and Frances Shelley Wees.

## Duncan, Norman
"There's no sin, Davy," she solemnly said, "that a woman can't forgive."

> *Dr. Luke of the Labrador* (1904).

## Duncan, Sara Jeannette
The market for Canadian literary wares of all sorts is self-evidently New York, where the intellectual life of the continent is rapidly centralizing. It is true that it will never become a great or profitable market until some original process of development is applied to the transplanted romance of our North-west, to the somewhat squat and uninteresting life of Ontario, to our treasure trove, Quebec; but when this is done, we may be sure that it will be with an eye upon immediate American appreciation, and in the spirit and methods of American literary production.

> *The Week*, July, 1887.

And so, not by anything unusual that we did or said, but by the rare and beautiful correspondence that is sometimes to be felt between the sentiment of the hour and the hour itself, this afternoon took its place in the dateless calendar of the heart which is so much more valuable a reference than any other.

> *The Crow's Nest* (1891).

In wholesome fear of mistake, one would hesitate to put church matters either before or after politics among the preoccupations of Elgin. It would be safer and more indisputable to say that nothing compared with religion but politics, and nothing compared with politics but religion.

\*

"In the scrolls of the future it is already written that the centre of the Empire must shift—and where, if not to Canada?"

*The Imperialist* (1904).

## Dundonald, Lord
Men of Canada, keep both hands on the Union Jack!

> Address on his departure from Ottawa, July 26, 1904, after being dismissed as general officer commanding the militia when he protested political interference. Quoted by J. Castell Hopkins in *The Canadian Annual Review of Public Affairs, 1904* (1905).

## Dunlop, William "Tiger"
In the name of God. Amen.

I, William Dunlop, of Gairbraid, in the Township of Colborne, County and District of Huron, Western Canada, Esquire, being in sound health of body, and my mind just as usual (which my friends who flatter me say is no great shakes at the best of times), do make this my last Will and Testament as follows, revoking, of course, all former Wills:

I leave the property of Gairbraid, and all other landed property I may die possessed of, to my sisters Helen Boyle Story and Elizabeth Boyle Dunlop; the former because she is married to a minister whom (God help him) she henpecks. The latter because she is married to nobody, nor is she like to be, for she is an old maid, and not market-rife. And also, I leave to them and their heirs my share of the stock and implements on the farm; provided always, that the enclosure round my brother's grave be reserved, and if either should die without issue, then the other to inherit the whole.

I leave to my sister-in-law, Louisa Dunlop, all my share of the household furniture and such traps, with the exceptions hereinafter mentioned.

I leave my silver tankard to the eldest son of old John, as the representative of the family. I would have left it to old John himself, but he would melt it down to make temperance medals, and that would be sacrilege—however, I leave my big horn snuff-box to him: he can only make temperance horn spoons of that.

I leave my sister Jenny my Bible, the property formerly of my great-great-grandmother, Bethia Hamilton, of Woodhall: and when she knows as much

of the spirit of it as she does of the letter, she will be another guise Christian than she is.

I also leave my late brother's watch to my brother Sandy, exhorting him at the same time to give up Whiggery, Radicalism, and all other sins that do most easily beset him.

I leave my brother Alan my big silver snuff-box, as I am informed he is rather a decent Christian, with a swag belly and a jolly face.

I leave Parson Chevasse (Magg's husband), the snuff-box I got from the Sarnia Militia, as a small token of my gratitude for the service he has done the family in taking a sister that no man of taste would have taken.

I leave John Caddle a silver teapot, to the end that he may drink tea therefrom to comfort him under the affliction of a slatternly wife.

I leave my books to my brother Andrew, because he has been so long a Jungley Wallah, that he may learn to read with them.

I give my silver cup, with a sovereign in it, to my sister Janet Graham Dunlop, because she is an old maid and pious, and therefore will necessarily take to horning. And also my Granma's snuff mull, as it looks decent to see an old woman taking snuff.

I do hereby constitute and appoint John Dunlop, Esquire, of Gairbraid; Alexander Dunlop, Esquire, Advocate, Edinburgh; Alan C. Dunlop, Esquire, and William Chalk, of Tuckersmith; William Stewart and William Gooding, Esquires, of Goderich, to be the executors of this my last Will and Testament.

In witness whereof I have hereunto set my hand and seal the thirty-first day of August, in the year of our Lord one thousand eight hundred and forty-two.

W. Dunlop

> This is the infamous last will and testament of Dr. William "Tiger" Dunlop, who died at Lachine, near Montreal, June 29, 1848. ("Jungley Wallah—a Bushman.") Quoted by Robina Kathleen MacFarlane Lizars, *In the Days of the Canada Company: The Story of the Settlement of the Huron Tract and a*

*View of the Social Life of the Period: 1825-1850* (1896).

The climate is infinitely more healthy than most of England. Indeed, it may be pronounced the most healthy country under the sun, considering that whiskey can be procured for about one shilling sterling per gallon.

*Statistical Sketches of Upper Canada, for the Use of Emigrants* (1832).

**Dunn, Sir James**
Don't resign. Wait until you're sacked. Don't retire. Wait until you're dead.

Quoted by Lord Beaverbrook in *Courage: The Story of Sir James Dunn* (1961). Dunn took his own advice and resisted C.D. Howe's pressure to resign from Algoma Steel and died in his eighty-second year planning a twenty-year program. See also Salvador Dali.

**Dunraven, Earl of**
Happiness consists in having few wants and being able to satisfy them, and there is more real comfort to be found in a birch-bark camp than in the most luxuriously furnished and carefully appointed dwelling.

\*

Newfoundland has special claims upon us, for though sentiment is generally out of place in politics, it cannot be forgotten that Newfoundland is England's first-born. That foggy little island, although perhaps somewhat of a rough diamond, is a valuable jewel, and is the first that was set in the imperial crown.

The Irish politician and noted sportsman hunted in Newfoundland in 1879. *Canadian Nights: Being Sketches and Reminiscences of Life and Sport in the Rockies, the Prairies, and the Canadian Woods* (1914).

**Duplessis, Maurice**
L'Union Nationale, c'est moi! [Frequent declaration]

\*

Colleague: I hope you are well.
Duplessis: Je suis dangereusement bien. [I am dangerously well]

\*

I took you out of the gutter. Keep your mouth shut, or I'll put you back where I found you! [To a minister during a cabinet meeting]

\*

Workers have the right to organize and the right *not* to organize. Labour has the right to organize, but not to *dis*organize. [1948 campaign]

\*

As long as I have a breath of life I will not fail at the task. My last word will be "I will never surrender." [Quebec Legislature, February 27, 1959]

Adapted from Leslie Roberts's *The Chief: A Political Biography of Maurice Duplessis* (1963).

The future Premier of Quebec stands before you. [Prophetic boast of the young deputy for Trois-Rivières made in 1927 and fulfilled in 1936]

\*

I have no family. My only responsibility is the welfare of Quebec. I belong to the province.

\*

Do you wish to know what public opinion is? It is the opinion of those who are against us.

\*

Help yourself and heaven will help you. Or help yourself and the Union Nationale will help you. Which comes out the same in the end.

\*

You know, we French Canadians are improved Frenchmen.

\*

Nothing is free. Someone always pays. Therefore, it is ridiculous to speak of *free* education.

\*

The best insurance against disease is health. Only God can give you insurance against illness.

You want roads, schools? You want your riding to make progress? Let us know about it by your votes. We will respect this expression of your desires.

*

My nose isn't too long for nothing!

*

Co-operation is not a one-way street.

*

The bishops eat out of my hand.

Characteristic expressions of the premier of Quebec who served intermittently between 1936 and his death in 1959. Quoted by Pierre Laporte in *The True Face of Duplessis* (1961).

There is no great difficulty in governing Quebec. All one must do is keep the Jesuits and the Dominicans fighting. [Reported by Malcolm Muggeridge]

It cost more when the Liberals were in power.

"On one occasion when a Liberal member of the Assembly stated that tavern keepers in Quebec City had to pay the party $500.00 per year, or risk losing their licences, Duplessis replied, 'It cost more when the Liberals were in power.' *Montreal Star*, March 6, 1947." Quoted by Herbert F. Quinn in *The Union Nationale: A Study in Quebec Nationalism* (1963).

Never yet has the St. Laurent overflowed the St. Maurice.

The Quebec premier's answer to a heckler's question, "What about Louis St. Laurent?" Quoted by Stuart Keate in "Maurice the Magnificent," *Maclean's Magazine*, September 1, 1945.

When I'm gone you'll face the outburst.

To members of the Union Nationale, including a future successor, Daniel Johnson. Quoted by Gerald Clark in *Canada: The Uneasy Neighbour* (1965). See also Télésphore-Damien Bouchard and Dr. Jean Grégoire.

## DuPre, George
You can't have guts without God.

Quoted by Quentin Reynolds in *The Man Who Wouldn't Talk* (1953). The American journalist took George Du-Pre's story on faith—the same faith, apparently, that sustained the Calgary businessman in 1943 when, as an undercover agent for British Intelligence in occupied France, he endured terrible torture rather than talk. When the biography was published, it was discovered that DuPre had never been to France. No one discovered why he perpetrated the hoax, except to demonstrate the power of faith. "I wanted to prove to the young that a man with faith in God can endure anything," DuPre confessed in Frank Rasky's *Gay Canadian Rogues: Swindlers, Gold-diggers and Spies* (1958).

## Durbin, Deanna
I was afraid the other girls might think I was getting stuck-up. I was afraid it might make a difference between us, and we were so happy as things were.

"For bringing to the screen the spirit and personification of youth," seventeen-year-old Deanna Durbin received a special Academy Award in 1938. Edna Mae Durbin was born in St. Vital, in 1921, of Winnipeg parents who settled in California when she was three. At thirteen the singer signed an exclusive contract with MGM and, two years later, talked knowingly about the pitfalls of stardom with Kay Proctor. "It's Lonely Being a Child Prodigy," (1937), *The Talkies: Articles and Illustrations from Photoplay Magazine: 1928-1940* (1971), selected by Richard Griffith. She retired in 1949, married a French director, and lives outside Paris. See also Anonymous: Verses and Rhymes.

## Durham, Lord
I expected to find a contest between a government and a people: I found two nations warring in the bosom of a single state: I found a struggle, not of principles, but of races; and I perceived that it would be idle to attempt any amelioration of laws or institutions until we could first succeed in terminating the deadly animosity that now separates the inhabi-

tants of Lower Canada into the hostile divisions of French and English.

*

Their nationality is, after all, an inheritance; and they must be not too severely punished, because they have dreamed of maintaining on the distant banks of the St. Lawrence, and transmitting to their posterity, the language, the manners, and the institutions of that great nation, that for two centuries gave the tone of thought to the European Continent.

*

In the significant language of one of their own ablest advocates, they assert that "Lower Canada must be *English,* at the expense, if necessary, of being *British."*

*

There can hardly be conceived a nationality more destitute of all that can invigorate and elevate a people, than that which is exhibited by the descendants of the French in Lower Canada, owing to their retaining their peculiar language and manners. They are a people with no history, and no literature.

> *Lord Durham's Report on the Affairs of British North America* (1912), edited by Sir Charles P. Lucas. The *Report* appeared in 1839.

I would fain hope I have not lived altogether in vain. Whatever the Tories may say, the Canadians will one day do justice to my memory.

> Remark made by "Radical Jack" two days before his death on July 28, 1840, Cowes, Isle of Wight. Quoted by John Charles Dent in *The Last Forty Years: Canada Since the Union of 1841* (1881). It has been pointed out that the motto of the statesman's family, *Le Jour Viendra* (The Day Has Come), is singularly appropriate. See also John Buchan and John Stuart Mill.

### Duvernay, Ludger
La Société Saint-Jean-Baptiste

> The Quebec newspaper editor founded the Montreal society in 1834 to promote French-Canadian patriotism. In 1843, a Quebec society was formed for cultural and patriotic purposes and later as a mutual-benefit society.

St. John the Baptist ("the voice of one crying in the wilderness") is the patron saint of Canada; he is especially honoured in Quebec, where his birthday, June 24, is a festive holiday.

### Dwan, Allan
If you get your head above the mob, they try to knock it off. If you stay down, you last forever.

> "The last pioneer" is how Peter Bogdanovich described Allan Dwan who was born in Toronto in 1885 and started with Essanay in 1909 and is "perhaps the most prolific director in the history of the cinema, some estimates of his output being as large as 1,500 films" (*The International Encyclopaedia of Film* [1972], edited by Roger Manvell).

### Dwyer, Peter M.
The spectre of bankruptcy rather than the *spectre de la rose* is what haunts some of our stages.

> *Seventh Annual Report of the Canada Council* (1964).

When I was lunching some months ago with the Treasury Board official responsible for steering the board to approve the expenditures of this Seminar, I asked him in my innocent way how things were progressing. He gave me that cold, beady look, characteristic of all officials concerned with the control of finances, and perhaps best described by P.G. Wodehouse as a look to be seen on the face of a parrot who is offered half a banana by a person in whose *bona fides* it does not have absolute confidence. And he said to me: "Whenever I hear the word culture . . . I reach for my purse."

*

Since money is always a delicate and volatile matter I do not wish to press it too hard. I have simply raised one more trial balloon and in doing so I am reminded of that immortal section of the King's Regulation of 1905 which says: "Officers when entering a balloon need not wear their spurs."

*

The problem of "raise or spread" . . . is still with us. It is set out quite clearly . . .

in these words: "to develop the broader landscape or to cultivate the flower; to judge between quality or quantity; to concentrate or disperse resources."

"Some Present Problems of Subsidy," Address delivered at Seminar '65, Ste. Adèle, January 20, 1965, *Eighth Annual Report of the Canada Council* (1965). When the late director of the Canada Council referred to "raise or spread," he had in mind the thorny problem of whether arts councils should subsidize individuals or institutions or both. This is sometimes condensed into a single sentence, "Do we water the fields or the flower?" Sandra Gwyn asked the question in these words and attributed them to Dwyer in *Maclean's Magazine*, December, 1972.

# E

## Earhart, Amelia
It is always very pleasant for me to receive a bouquet of flowers. You know even when women get into aeroplanes and fly they do not lose their liking for flowers. Very often I get boxes, very interesting looking boxes, and I open them and there is a new gadget to put on the aeroplane, a new type of carburetor or a monkey-wrench. I cannot say I am disappointed when I open those boxes but I do like the flowers, too, in addition to the monkey-wrenches.

The famous aviatrix, whose disappearance remains a mystery to this day, lived in Toronto during the First World War and served as a volunteer nurse. "Address," December 13, 1932, *Addresses Delivered before the Canadian Club of Toronto: Season of 1932-33* (1933).

## Earp, Wyatt
If I'd had a couple of those red-coated fellers behind me, we'd have kept Tombstone clean for sure.

The "red-coated fellers" were the North-West Mounted Police, formed in 1873; attributed to the popular sheriff of Tombstone, Arizona.

## Eaton, Cyrus
Why, good heavens, man! Pugwash is right there between Shinimicas and Tatamagouche!

When asked the location of Pugwash, where Cyrus Eaton held his "thinkers' conferences." The Indian name means "deep water." Quoted by Bruce West in *The Globe and Mail*, July 13, 1972.

"The absurd but unforgettable name is an accident; it has stuck because there is no agreement on anything else," wrote Wayland Young in "Notes on Pugwash," *Encounter*, February, 1963. The British M.P. concluded: "There is no such thing as a communist laser or a capitalist neutron."

I am not one who favours political consolidation of Canada and the United States. As I tell my American friends, the only way that could ever be accomplished would be by repeal of the Declaration of Independence and by the designation of a Canadian city, probably Toronto, as capital of the new nation. But I do believe that the economic destinies of the United States and Canada are interwoven, and I do want to urge the fullest possible interchange of goods between the two countries.

"Canada's Opportunity" (1950), *Empire Club of Canada: Addresses 1950-51* (1951).

### Eaton, Flora

The girls of my age and younger—those still waiting for their first encounter with romance—wondered openly if there was a "Jack *Simpson*" in Toronto too!

> When the former nurse married Sir John Craig Eaton in 1901. *Memory's Wall: The Autobiography of Flora McCrae Eaton* (1956).

### Eaton, John Craig

There is not enough money in the whole world to buy my father's name.

> With this remark Timothy Eaton's son scotched rumours in the late 1950s that the department-store chain would be sold to an American operation. Quoted by William Stephenson in *The Store that Timothy Built* (1969).

### Eaton, John David

Nobody thought about money in those days because they never saw any. You could take your girl to a supper dance at the hotel for ten dollars, and that included the bottle and a room for you and your friends to drink in. I'm glad I grew up then. It was a good time for everybody. People learned what it means to work.

> Timothy Eaton's grandson was born in 1909. Quoted by Alexander Ross in "What's It Like to Live in Toyland," *Maclean's Magazine*, June, 1968. Reprinted by Michiel Horn in *The Dirty Thirties: Canadians in the Great Depression* (1971).

### Eaton, Timothy

Tell your story to [the] public—what you have and what you propose to sell. Promise them not only bargains but that every article will be found just what it is guaranteed to be. Whether you sell a first-rate or a third-rate article, the customer will get what they bargain for. . . . Use no deception in the smallest degree—nothing you cannot defend before God and Man.

> "For years he had written his own advertising; when pressure of expansion necessitated turning this duty over to a department, he passed on the note in his own vigorous, sprawling handwriting (a scrap of paper reverently guarded by managers there for many years)," explained Mary-Etta Macpherson in *Shopkeepers to a Nation: The Eatons* (1963).

The greatest good to the greatest number.

> "What Mr. Eaton really meant . . . has never been recorded. The phrase was used extensively in the store advertising at a time when there was great depression and many smaller stores were closing up. . . . It may have been that the phrase 'The greatest good to the greatest number' was intended to indicate that though all people are consumers and comparatively few are distributors if a certain plan of distribution benefits the customer then it is good even though some distributors suffer." George G. Nasmith in *Timothy Eaton* (1923). The great merchant's phrase is a modification of Jeremy Bentham's utilitarian principle: "The greatest happiness of the greatest number is the foundation of morals and legislation."

I'm going to keep store.

> "At a time when department stores were under severe attack, Atkinson asked Timothy Eaton: 'What do you intend doing about it?'
>
> " 'I'm going to keep store,' was the answer." Quoted by J.H. Cranston in *Ink on My Fingers* (1953). The reply was made to Joseph E. Atkinson of *The Toronto Star* about 1900.

Goods Satisfactory or Money Refunded.

> These must be the five most widely recognized words in Canada, the runners-up being: "The medium is the message," "They always get their man," "I did it for Canada." The generous guarantee of the T. Eaton Co., so quotable, was quickly accepted as a corporate slogan. But it was not the motto of the dry goods establishment in 1869 when it was founded in Toronto. In 1884, Timothy Eaton issued his first mail-order catalogue with the following guarantee: "Any goods bought, and found not suitable, will be exchanged

for other goods or money refunded." During the 1890s, the guarantees grew wordier: "We guarantee to take back or exchange goods at your experience if unsatisfactory, provided they are returned promptly and in good condition." In 1903, a company publication included the following announcement: "We cheerfully refund the money if goods do not exactly suit." The following guarantee appeared in 1907: "Goods right or money back." But it was not until the Eaton's catalogue of 1913 that the precise words appeared in print (with a few extra): "Goods Satisfactory or Money Refunded, including Shipping Charges." With the dropping of the last three words later that year, the guarantee first appeared in its present form. Timothy Eaton died in 1907, having evolved the generous return policy, but not the present-day wording. William Stephenson in *The Store that Timothy Built* (1969) explained the significance of the guarantee: "At one stroke it banished forever the Oriental bazaar, *caveat emptor* atmosphere and changed retailing from something closely akin to burglary, fraud and outright larceny into a respectable profession."

**Eayrs, James**
We must see the world as it is, if we are to have a world at all.

> "Nuclear Dilemmas" (1960), *Northern Approaches: Canada and the Search for Peace* (1961).

Natural frontiers exist between nations, but the border between Canada and the United States is not one of them. Birds fly over it, fish swim through it, ore bodies lie under it, stands of timber straddle it, rivers traverse it. As in the movement of trade, so in the disposition of resources. The continent is an economic unit. Its bisection is political, not geographic. What nature joined together, Canadians have sought to sunder.

> "Sharing a Continent: The Hard Issues," *The United States and Canada: The American Assembly* (1964), edited by John Sloan Dickey.

Fragmentation is the mother of amnesia. [November, 1965]

\*

Before the intellectual are two life-styles, and two alone. One is the life-style of detachment. The other is the life-style of commitment. One has to choose.

My late teacher, Harold Innis, knowing better than anyone else how heavily mined and menaced are the slopes of commitment leading away from the ivory tower, begged the intellectual to remain within its precincts.

I used to think this good advice. Now I think otherwise. It is the intellect of commitment which in spite of all my cautionary tales I must finally commend to you. Not just because it is in short supply—although in Canada, God knows, it *is* in short supply. But rather because it alone enables the intellectual to do his job. A detached mind may keep watch upon itself, but it watches over wasteland. Only a mind ethically anaesthetized, morally lobotomized, remains detached from what statesmen are doing in the world. [November, 1965]

\*

The global village, should it come to that, may only offer greater scope to global village idiots. I would rather hope for global village Hampdens. But that is the expression of a faith, not of social science. [December, 1968]

\*

You may have heard of a move to admit you and your wife to the Companionship of the Order of Canada. All here seem enthusiastic, in the manner of hosts solacing themselves for having been so beastly to their guests. Personally I don't care for the spectacle of committees of senior public servants solemnly bestowing awards of state on one another. What we in this country owe you and yours is not decorations but damages.

As a taxpayer I'd gladly help foot the bill. It's obviously impossible to work out the amount of compensation owing to a person obliged for sixty days to "live each day as if thy last" in the most starkly literal meaning of that line from the old hymn. But £1,000 each day comes close to what the London literary agents are saying your story's worth to them and what the foreign office won't allow you to sell your story for. I'd make them 60,000 guineas, not pounds. Guineas have class. So have you. ["An Open Letter to J.R. Cross" (1970); see James Cross]

> Diplomacy and Its Discontents (1971). See also Nikolai Lenin and Lester B. Pearson.

### Eckel, Mrs. Lizzie St. John
Most Catholics shrink with horror at the very mention of the name of Maria Monk; but God is more merciful than His children;—He judges the intent and not the act.

> Maria Monk's Daughter; an Autobiography (1874). Mrs. Eckel purported to be the daughter of the notorious imposter who wrote The Awful Disclosures of Maria Monk (1836). See also Maria Monk.

### Eddy, E.B.
I'm the greatest matchmaker in the world.

> Attributed to Ezra Butler Eddy who, in 1854, established a matchmaking factory in Hull, Quebec, that became the biggest in the world.

### Edel, Leon
Absence of Canadian individuality or national tone is neither a defeat nor a handicap. We might fashion a paradox and suggest that the Canadian writer who will fashion a work reflecting this lack of identity will have achieved a work of Canadian identity: for it is precisely this as yet national pallor that serves to a degree as an identifying mark. Canadian literature quite simply has not yet achieved its own flavour. As soon ask a young boy to mature. Yet that should not prevent him from being his young self: articulate and full of promise. . . . Let the work seek its own identity and one day it may be discovered to be Canadian as well.

> "The Question of Canadian Identity," Canadian Accent: A Collection of Stories and Poems by Contemporary Writers from Canada (1944), edited by Ralph Gustafson.

### Edgar, James D.
Canada First.

The Canada First movement was named by James D. Edgar in 1870. For an account of its origin and significance, see George Taylor Denison. See also William A. Foster.

This Canada of ours.
Fair Canada,
Dear Canada,
This Canada of ours!

> The felicitous phrase is the refrain from This Canada of Ours and Other Poems (1893). The title poem was published as early as 1870. The phrase is associated with Edgar, a founder of Canada First and future Speaker of the House of Commons, but also with Lady Dufferin, the governor general's wife, who employed the phrase in her journal, September 21, 1872, which was not published until two decades later. See also Lady Dufferin.

### Edgar, Pelham
Literature is an affair less of solitude than of contacts, and meditations in a log hut are rarely written by the man that built it. Conditions are more propitious now, but we still suffer in a literary sense from being a young country born into the old age of the world. All that tradition counts for in the literature of a European country we must forgo. Our literary past is the literary past of England; we have not yet had time to strike roots for ourselves.

> "Anglo-Canadian Literature," Handbook of Canada: Issued by the Local Committee on the Occasion of the Meeting of the British Association for the Advancement of Science at Toronto, August, 1924 (1924).

### Edinborough, Arnold
Provincial politics is like the love-life of elephants: nothing is done without a great deal of trumpeting; any achievement is at the highest level and there is nothing to show for it for at least two years.

> Address to the Young Liberals Association, Presqu'Isle Point, June, 1957.

Any fool can bolster his false courage by laughing at death. Only a very brave man can laugh at life.

*Saturday Night*, October 14, 1961.

Curiosity is the very basis of education and if you tell me that curiosity killed the cat, I say only the cat died nobly.

\*

A university should provide you with one thing at least—a reading list for the rest of your life.

Convocation address, University of Ottawa, October, 1962.

All parents were once children: that is why, when you speak to them about education, speak softly, for you are disturbing their dreams.

Address, Ontario Secondary School Teachers' Federation, 1969.

When the learning of a second language is considered a mere skill instead of a political tool, then this country will be getting somewhere.

Address, Alberta Teachers' Association, Edmonton, October, 1972.

Canada has never been a melting pot; more like a tossed salad.

Address, Chautauqua, New York, August 3, 1973.

**Edinburgh, Duke of**
See Philip Mountbatten.

**Edison, Thomas A.**

Cable Address "Edison, New York"
From the Laboratory of Thomas A. Edison
Orange, N.J., May 1, 1894

Holland Bros., Ottawa, Canada
I am pleased to hear that the first public exhibition of my Kinetoscope has been a success under your management, and hope your firm will continue to be associated with its further exploitation.

Yours
Thomas A. Edison

With this letter the famous inventor of Menlo Park acknowledged that two Canadians—Andrew and George Holland

of Ottawa—were the earliest film exhibitors. Edison's Kinetoscope, "a Broadway sensation," was the cornerstone of the motion-picture industry. As Terry Ramsaye wrote in *A Thousand and One Nights* (1926):
"The first ten of the peep show machines were shipped across the Hudson to Andrew Holland of Holland Brothers, who had come down from Ottawa, Ontario, to be the eastern agents of the Kinetoscope Company. . . . The ten machines reached the Holland brothers on April 6, 1894, and on April 14 their Kinetoscope Parlor, the first of hundreds to be scattered over the world, opened at 1155 Broadway, New York City. . . . Edison had now gone into the motion picture business. The industry of the films began then and there, 1155 Broadway, on April 14, 1894. There is a spot that might well be marked by a tablet of bronze." And a bronze tablet now marks the important site, according to Hye Bossin in *Canadian Motion Picture Industry Year Book* (1951).
Edison's grandfather was a United Empire Loyalist; his father was born in Digby, Nova Scotia, and moved to Upper Canada, where he took part in the Rebellion of 1837 and had to flee to Detroit. Thomas was born a decade later in Ohio; his first job, as a sixteen-year-old, was as night telegrapher for the Grand Trunk Railroad at Stratford, where he devised the automatic report signal.

**Edward Augustus, Duke of Kent**
Let me hear no more of the invidious distinction of French and English. You are all his Britannic Majesty's beloved Canadian subjects.

Address upon the passage of the Constitutional Act in 1791. Robina and Kathleen Macfarlane Lizars quote it more dramatically in *Humours of '37: Grave, Gay and Grim* (1897): "Away with those hateful distinctions of English and Canadian."

She is of very good family and has never been an actress, and I am the first and only person who ever lived with her. Her disinterestedness, too, has been equal to her fidelity.

\*

It is now seven-and-twenty years that Madame de St. Laurent and I have lived together. We are of the same age and have been in all climates and in all difficulties together; I protest I don't know what is to become of her if a marriage is to be forced on me.

> From the letters of the Duke of Kent to Thomas Creevey, his diarist, in 1817. The fourth son of George III, Edward Augustus served in Quebec, Nova Scotia and New Brunswick from 1791 to 1800, and was commander-in-chief of the British forces in North America. Prince Edward Island was named in his honour. He lived openly with Julie de Montgenet, Madame de St. Laurent, in Halifax and Quebec. They had two sons, Robert Wood (who became a Quebec merchant) and Jean de Mestre (who died in Martinique). Edward Augustus concluded the liaison with considerable regret and married Victoria Maria Louisa, widow of Prince Charles of Leiningen; their only child ascended the British throne as Queen Victoria. Madame de St. Laurent retired to a convent. The love of Edward and Julie is the great Canadian romance. See also Madame de St. Laurent.

## Edward VII
Thank God it is all over.

> To Blondin, when the celebrated tightrope walker crossed Niagara Gorge on a seven-inch-thick manilla rope, stretched 260 feet above the water, September 15, 1860. Edward, then the Prince of Wales, was one of ten thousand horrified onlookers. See also Blondin, "The Prince of Manila."

I have already been struck throughout my rapid journey by the promise of greatness and the results of energy and industry which are everywhere perceptible, and I feel the pride of an Englishman in the masculine qualities of my countrymen; in the sanguine and hardy enterprise; in the fertility of conception and boldness of execution which have enabled a youthful country to outstrip many of the ancient nations of the world.

> Toronto address, quoted by J. Castell

Hopkins in "Canada in 1896 and 1897," *Imperial and Asiatic Quarterly Review*, April, 1897. Edward VII reigned as king of Great Britain from the death of his mother, Queen Victoria, in 1901 to his own death in 1910. See also N.A. Woods.

## Edward VIII
And here I would like to say how much I appreciate, and how proud I feel of, the request that the Hog's Back Falls, near Ottawa, should be called Prince of Wales Falls.

> "Address of H.R.H. the Prince of Wales," November 8, 1919, *The Canadian Club Year Book: 1919-20* (1920).

It is only repetition when I say that I hope to be often in Canada again and in Toronto, where I have had such a wonderful time, and I will try never to forget the great kindness which you have shown me this year. As you know, my right hand has been out of action for nearly two months. When asked why I shake hands with my left hand, I always reply that my right hand was "done in" in Toronto. Though painful at the time, I shall always look back on that as a great compliment.

> "Address," November 4, 1919, joint meeting at Massey Hall with the Empire Club of Canada, *Addresses Delivered before the Canadian Club of Toronto: Season of 1919-20* (1920).

What I saw in North America stirred me deeply—most of all the beauty and grandeur of the Canadian Rockies. In Alberta I met an American-born cattleman, George Lane. My imagination was stirred by his tales of the life in the foothills of the Rockies, and on impulse I bought a four-thousand-acre ranch adjoining his, in the valley of the Highwood River, some forty miles south of Calgary. On my return to London, my father [King George V] questioned me closely about this ranch. Mistaking my motive in purchasing it, he warned that I was setting for myself a dangerous precedent. The Australians would now expect me to buy a sheep station when I visited their country; and, if I failed to acquire at least an ostrich farm when I went to South Africa, its people, he pointed out, might construe my neglect as a deliberate slight. The fact is, my impulse in making this investment—the only piece of property that I have ever owned—was far removed from Imperial politics. In the midst of that irresistible countryside I had suddenly been overwhelmed by an irresistible longing to immerse myself, if only momentarily, in the simple life of the western prairies. There, I was sure, I would find occasional escape from the sometimes too-confining, too-well-ordered, island life of Great Britain.

*

Everybody seemed so anxious to shake my hand that I decided it would be ungracious to refuse. This rash decision must have been based upon a fallacious idea that Canada was sparsely populated; either that or I failed to appreciate what a feeble and inadequate mechanism the right hand really is. It all started out with a man in the crowd thrusting an outstretched hand toward me. "Put it right here, Ed," he said. "I shook hands with your granddad." Within a week my right hand was blackened and swollen and extremely painful; and the sight of an advancing stranger so welcome only a few days before, now made me flinch. On the advice of my doctor, Surgeon Commander Newport, who warned me that my right hand might be permanently disabled if I went on using it, I retired it temporarily from Imperial service, and offered the left instead.

And of all the information that I brought back I think what delighted him [King George V] most was the following doggerel picked up in a Canadian border town:

> Four and twenty Yankees, feeling
>     very dry,
> Went across the border to get a drink
>     of rye.
> When the rye was opened, the Yanks
>     began to sing,
> "God bless America, but God save the
>     King!"

*A King's Story: The Memoirs of The Duke of Windsor* (1951). The Duke of Windsor, as Edward VIII, visited Can-

ada in 1919, 1923, 1924 and 1927. These passages refer to his first Canadian tour when he was twenty-five. He renounced the British throne in 1936 and died in 1972.

### Edwards, Bob

I am a Prohibitionist. What I propose to prohibit is the reckless use of water. [March 17, 1904]

*

Man wants but little here below zero. [February 4, 1905]

*

Every man has his favourite bird; ours is the bat. [May 13, 1905]

*

One of the reasons why the *Eye Opener* has so many high ideals is that Calgary is over 3,000 feet above the level of the sea. [August 1, 1908]

*

Men continually study women, and know nothing about them. Women never study men, and know all about them. [October 15, 1910]

*

About the only people who don't quarrel over religion are the people who haven't any. [October 15, 1910]

*

If a man understands one woman he should let it go at that. [January 13, 1912]

*

If your luck isn't what it should be, write a "p" in front of it and try again. [January 13, 1912]

*

People are always ready to admit a man's ability after he gets there. [January 27, 1912]

*

All the speculation in the world never raised a bushel of wheat. [February 10, 1912]

*

Most people who are old enough to know better often wish they were young enough not to. [April 20, 1912]

*

One of the worst stings of defeat is the sympathy that goes with it. [June 8, 1912]

Politics has not ceased to make strange bedfellows; at least, the politicians of both parties continue to share the same bunk. You know the kind of bunk we mean. [October 2, 1912]

*

One can always tell when one is getting old and serious by the way that holidays seem to interfere with one's work. [December 20, 1913]

*

The way of the transgressor is very popular. [May 8, 1915]

*

By the time the average man is old enough to gratify his tastes, he hasn't any. [May 8, 1915]

*

Some men are good because they find it cheaper than being wicked. [May 22, 1915]

*

One trouble with being efficient is that it makes everybody hate you so. [March 18, 1916]

*

Ceremony was invented by a wise man to keep fools at a distance. [May 6, 1916]

*

Meanwhile, the meek are a long time inheriting the earth. [September 16, 1916]

*

A good man who goes wrong is just a bad man who has been found out. [September 22, 1917]

*

A woman is more influenced by what she suspects than by what she knows. [November 3, 1917]

*

Somehow the people who do as they please seem to get along just about as well as those who are always trying to please others. [March 9, 1918]

*

The public will pay more for laughing than for any other privilege. [May 11, 1918]

*

You are only what you are when no one is looking. [May 11, 1918]

*

People always laugh at the fool things you try to do until they discover you are making money out of them. [May 31, 1918]

*

If a girl has a pretty face, no man on earth can tell what kind of clothes she has on. [October 5, 1918]

*

Some men spoil a good story by sticking to the facts. [January 25, 1919]

*

Many a great man's reputation for wit is due to his having been interviewed by a bright reporter. [February 22, 1919]

*

If it's all the same to history, it need not repeat itself any more. [May 31, 1919]

*

The path to success is paved with good intentions that were carried out. [November 22, 1919]

*

Don't meet trouble halfway. It is quite capable of making the entire journey. [July 17, 1920]

*

Fame, from a literary point of view, consists in having people know you have written a lot of stuff they haven't read. [Summer, 1920]

*

Never exaggerate your faults; your friends will attend to that. [February 5, 1921]

*

A little learning is a dangerous thing but a lot of ignorance is just as bad. [August 20, 1921]

*

The difference between a friend and an acquaintance is that a friend helps where an acquaintance merely advises. [August 20, 1921]

*

Most of our tragedies look like comedies to the neighbours. [Summer, 1921]

*

Have you ever noticed how much larger your troubles appear at night? [September 24, 1921]

*

So this is Winnipeg; I can tell it's not Paris. [Arriving in Winnipeg, September 12, 1894]

*

Bankruptcy is when you put your money

in your hip pocket and let your creditors take your coat. [Attributed]

*

A fool is a man who is not addicted to your own brand of folly. [Attributed]

*

Now I know what a statesman is; he's a dead politician. We need more statesmen. [Attributed]

*

Next to man is his underwear. [Attributed]

> "Eye Opener Bob" or "Calgary Bob"—Robert Chambers Edwards—was a scion of the prominent Scottish publishing family ("If my mother had only been a gentleman I should have been head of the firm"). He made Calgary his home base, and from 1902 on he wrote and published the *Calgary Eye Opener* until his death in 1922 at the age of fifty-eight.
> These observations and convictions are taken from numerous sources, including back issues of the *Eye Opener*, Grant MacEwan's *Eye Opener Bob: The Story of Bob Edwards* (1957) and Robert M. Hamilton's *Canadian Quotations and Phrases: Literary and Historical* (1952).

### Edwards, Henrietta
See Anonymous: Some Documents.

### Edwards, Murray D.
It must be remembered that to a farmer or small town dweller in Canada at the turn of the century, melodrama was, in a sense, realism. It dealt with life as he understood it, and the problems that he feared, such as an erring daughter. Such a thing had happened to a neighbour; the disgrace to the family, the outraged parent's reaction, "Out in the snow!" the snow, of course, being for dramatic effect! And then the explanation to show that it wasn't as bad as it seemed to be, or perhaps the reassertion of natural kindness, so that life would become tolerable again, even pleasant! Reconciliation, everything as it should be. Life was like that.

*A Stage in Our Past: English-Language Theatre in Eastern Canada from the 1700s to 1914* (1968).

### Eggleston, Wilfrid
We are told that Professor L.E. Horning of the University of Toronto circulated early in 1894 a questionnaire asking anxiously: "What is wrong with Canadian literature?" Goldwin Smith is alleged to have retorted: "*What* Canadian Literature?" In another place his exact answer is reported to have included the sentence: "No such thing as a literature in the local sense exists or is ever likely to exist."

> *The Frontier and Canadian Letters* (1957).

### Eisendrath, Maurice N.
I firmly believe that this glorious land should be first. But first in what? That's the question.

> "Canada First" (1931), *The Never Failing Stream* (1939).

### Eisenhower, Dwight D.
Of course, each of us possesses a distinctive national character and history. You won your independence by evolution, and the United States by revolution.

*

We must never allow ourselves to become so preoccupied with the differences between our two nations that we lose sight of the transcendent importance of free world co-operation in the winning of the global struggle.

> The president of the United States addressed a joint meeting of the Senate and the House of Commons, July 9, 1958.

### Elgin, Earl of
As the Prince of Wales says, no one can visit Canada without being an optimist, and that is the spirit with which I go back to the Old Country. I am on my way now.

*

I am the son of a Canadian. My father was born in Montreal at a time when there were some distinct troubles in that section. And one of the chief points of interest, one of the things which I cherish as a family heirloom, is a certificate which stands in my sitting room today saying that Victor Alexander, Lord Bruce, was entered as a member of St. Andrew's Society, Toronto, when, I think, he was about a day old.

> "Address," October 29, 1926, *Addresses Delivered before the Canadian Club of Toronto: Season of 1926-27* (1927). The tenth Earl of Elgin's maternal grandfather was Lord Durham.

## Elgin, Lord
Excesses correct themselves, and I have no doubt that the violence of the disaffected will elicit a great counter-demonstration.—At the same time I confess I did not before know how thin is the crust of order which covers the anarchical elements that boil and toss beneath our feet.

> Letter from the governor general, the Earl of Elgin, to Earl Grey, April 30, 1847, when opponents of the Rebellion Losses Act set fire to the Parliament Buildings at Montreal. Quoted by J.M.S. Careless in *The Union of the Canadas: The Growth of Canadian Institutions 1841-1857* (1967).

I must moreover confess that I for one am deeply convinced of the impolicy of all such attempts to denationalize the French. Generally speaking they produce the opposite effect from that intended, causing the flame of national prejudice and animosity to burn more fiercely.—But suppose them to be successful what wd. be the result? You may perhaps *americanise,* but, depend upon it, by methods of this description, you will never *anglicise* the French inhabitants of the Province.—Let them feel on the other hand that their religion, their habits, their prepossessions, their prejudices if you will, are more considered and respected here than in other portions of this vast continent which is being overrun by the most reckless, self-sufficient and dictatorial section of the Anglo Saxon race, and who will venture to say that the last hand which waves the British flag on American ground may not be that of a French Canadian?

> Letter to Earl Grey, May 4, 1848, *The Elgin-Grey Papers: 1846-1852* (1937), edited by A.G. Doughty. James Bruce, the eighth Earl of Elgin, married Lord Durham's daughter.

## Eliot, Charles W.
You have a splendid example of the legitimate, the indispensable, the eminently useful police force in Canada—the Northwest Mounted Police.

> Influential president of Harvard University and guiding spirit behind the "Five-Foot Shelf" of *Harvard Classics.* "The Way of Escape from the Competitive Arming of Nations," February 23, 1907, *Addresses Delivered before the Canadian Club of Ottawa: 1903-1909* (1910).

## Elizabeth I
*Meta Incognita*

> There is a tradition that Queen Elizabeth, who ascended the throne of England and Ireland in 1558 and died in 1603, herself wrote the words "Meta Incognita" across an early map of the eastern Arctic in 1577, in the presence of the explorer Sir Martin Frobisher who discovered Baffin Island. The Latin translates as "beyond the unknown things," but in the sixteenth century the sense might have been "the unknown bourne." When Richard Hakluyt edited Frobisher's account of his voyage of 1576 for publication in *The Principal Navigations, Voyages, Traffiques, and Discoveries of the English Nation* (1589), he appended a side note which runs: "The people of Meta Incognita like vnto Samoeds."

## Elizabeth the Queen Mother
I think that I fell in love with Canada when the King and I came here in 1939. And each time I come back my feeling of affection seems to grow.

> Lady Elizabeth Bowes-Lyon, the mother of Queen Elizabeth II, visited Canada with her husband King George VI in 1939. "Address" (1965), *Empire Club of Canada: Addresses 1965-66* (1966).

## Elizabeth II

Philip: This is Doukhobor country, you know.

Elizabeth: Really?

Philip: Yes, if you look over on the edge of the crowd, I think you'll see one of them.

Elizabeth: Naked?

Calgary, 1951. Quoted by Pierre Berton in *The Royal Family: The Story of the British Monarchy from Victoria to Elizabeth* (1954).

True patriotism doesn't exclude an understanding of the patriotism of others.

*

A dynamic state should not fear to reassess its political philosophy. That an agreement worked out a hundred years ago does not necessarily meet all the needs of the present should not necessarily be surprising. [Address, Legislative Council, Quebec City, October 10, 1964]

It is as Queen of Canada that I am here. Queen of Canada and of all Canadians, not just of one or two ancestral strains. I would like the Crown to be seen as a symbol of national sovereignty belonging to all. It is not only a link between Commonwealth nations, but between Canadian citizens of every national origin and ancestry. [Address, Royal York Hotel, Toronto, June 26, 1973]

NOW KNOW YE that by and with the advice of Our Privy Council for Canada We do by this Our Royal Proclamation establish for Canada Our Royal Style and Titles as follows, namely, in the English language:

Elizabeth the Second, by the Grace of God of the United Kingdom, Canada and Her other Realms and Territories Queen, Head of the Commonwealth, Defender of the Faith

And in the French language:

Elisabeth Deux, par la grâce de Dieu, Reine du Royaume-Uni, du Canada et de ses autres royaumes et territoires, Chef du Commonwealth, Défenseur de la Foi.

"Proclamation of the Queen's Title," May 28, 1953. Reproduced by R.A. Mackay in *Canadian Foreign Policy 1945-1954: Selected Speeches and Documents* (1971).

## Elliott, George

The Land is Strong.

Toronto advertising executive's slogan for the Liberal party in the federal election of 1972 in which the Trudeau government was almost defeated. *Maclean's Magazine*, January, 1973.

". . . to which 8,914 Tory speakers, by rough estimate, replied, 'It had to be, to withstand nine years of Liberal rule,'" according to Walter Stewart in *Divide and Con: Canadian Politics at Work* (1973).

## Ellis, Arthur

"Arthur Ellis."

Until capital punishment was abolished in 1967, the traditional name of the official executioner was Arthur Ellis. The name of the Canadian hangman recalls that of the British executioner, John Ellis, who made annual visits to this country in a professional capacity during his twenty-three years of service. (He took his own life in 1923.) For the man who claimed to be related to John Ellis, the man who "made the gallows Canadian," see Arthur Bartholomew English.

## Ellis, Frank H.

"How Thunder Bird stay up in sky?"

Ellis was asked this question by an elderly Cree who watched him land his Avro biplane at Le Pas, Manitoba, October 18, 1920. This marked the first commercial flight in the Canadian North.

The golden age of bush flying is, perhaps, already fading into the past, to make way for new ages whose nature we may only guess.

*Canada's Flying Heritage* (1954).

How wonderful it must be to be young in an age which stands on the very verge of space travel. Yes, it is thrilling indeed to realize that among the children of today some will become the men and women who will reach out into space in their beautifully built rocket ships to charter many routes to distant points which beckon so enticingly in the vast spread of the universe.

*In Canadian Skies: Fifty Years of Adventure and Progress* (1959).

**Ellul, Jacques**
We in France are still in the preparatory phase of this development, but the organization of police power has been pushed very far in Canada and New Zealand, to take two examples. Technical necessity imposes the national concentration camp (which, I must point out, does not involve the suffering usually associated with it).

*The Technological Society* (1964), translated by John Wilkinson.

**Elson, Robert T.**
Canada—a triumph of politics over geography and economics—and sometimes it seems over common sense.

Quoted by Leonard Louis Levinson in *Webster's Unafraid Dictionary* (1967).

**Emerson, Ralph Waldo**
Americans will not take any definite step; they feel that Canada must come into the Confederation, and will of herself. The American party in Canada is always at work.

Remarks made to William Allingham, November, 1872. Quoted by Robert M. Hamilton in *Canadian Quotations and Phrases: Literary and Historical* (1952). See also Anonymous: Lore: P.E.I.

**Emmanuel, Pierre**
One can experience deserts of the soul in Quebec as well as in Arabia Petraea.

Preface by the French man of letters to Anne Hébert's *The Tomb of the Kings* (1967), translated by Peter Miller.

**Engels, Friedrich**
And a wonderful constitution it is, this gentile [i.e., kinship] constitution, in all its childlike simplicity! No soldiers, no gendarmes or police, no nobles, kings, regents, prefects, or judges, no prisons, or lawsuits—and everything takes its orderly course.

Engels is celebrating the Five (later Six) Nations Confederacy "under which the Iroquois lived for over four hundred years and are still living today." *The Origin of the Family, Private Property and the State* (1942), translated by Alec West, edited by Eleanor Burke Leacock. Engels's work first appeared in 1884.

Montreal, September 10, 1888

Dear Sorge:

We arrived here yesterday, after having had to turn about between Toronto and Kingston because of a storm (it was quite a nasty breeze) and tie up in Port Hope. Thus the two days from Toronto to here turned into *three*. The St. Lawrence and the rapids are very pretty. Canada is richer in ruined houses than any other country but Ireland. We are trying to understand the Canadian French here —that language beats *Yankee English holler* [in English in the original]. This evening we leave for Plattsburg and then into the Adirondacks and possibly to the Catskills, so that we can hardly be back in New York by Sunday. . . .

It is a strange transition from the States to Canada. First one imagines that one is in Europe again, and then one thinks one is in a positively retrogressing and decaying country. Here one sees how necessary the feverish speculative spirit of the Americans is for the rapid development of a new country (presupposing capitalist production as a basis); and in ten years this sleepy Canada will be ripe for annexation—the farmers in Manitoba, etc., will demand it themselves. Besides, the country is half-annexed already socially—hotels, newspapers, advertising, etc., all on the American pattern. And they may tug and resist as much as they like; the economic necessity of an infusion of Yankee blood will have its way and abolish this ridiculous boundary line —and when the time comes, John Bull will say "Yea and Amen" to it.

Yours
F.E.

Letter to Victor Sorge, *Letters to Americans 1848-1895: A Selection* (1953), edited by Alexander Trachtenberg.

## English, Arthur Bartholomew

In carrying out the extreme sentence of the law, I am the last wheel and the smallest wheel. The judge sanctions the execution; I merely perform it. I take it very religiously.

> The official executioner, quoted by Frederick Griffin in *Variety Show: Twenty Years of Watching the News Parade* (1936).

The scaffold at Hamilton is in a state of disrepair. It is a dangerous apparatus and should be demolished.

> Letter to Sheriff J.W. Lawrason of Wentworth County, Hamilton, 1935. Quoted by Frank W. Anderson in *Concise History of Capital Punishment in Canada* (1973). As Louis Blake Duff in *The County Kerchief* (1949) comments on this complaint: "No doubt it had proven extremely dangerous to quite a number of persons. Indeed some are known to have lost their lives on that scaffold."

Hanging belongs to a past age. . . . I am strongly in favour of the electric chair, not only on the ground of Humanity but it is safer in every way and it is instantaneous.

> Letter of December 23, 1935, quoted by J. Alex. Edmison in his appearance before the Joint Committee of the Senate and the House of Commons on Capital and Corporal Punishment and Lotteries, March 9, 1955. As Edmison, "the dean of Canadian Corrections," adds: "We might quarrel with his choice of the word 'safe' in this particular connection. . . ."

I consider it the most sacred calling any man could have, since I am entrusted with carrying out the highest sentence our courts can pass. Detectives prepare the case against the murderer. A jury finds him guilty. A judge sentences him to death. But the vast machine of justice ultimately turns to me for the execution of the sentence.

\*

Ninety percent of them die like cowards.

\*

I had no more compunction about executing a convicted murderer than I would at killing a mad dog.

> Quoted by Andy O'Brien in "My Friend, the Hangman," *My Friend, the Hangman: Dramatic Encounters in Sport, Crime and War* (1970).

Arthur Bartholomew English called himself "Official Executioner to the Dominion of Canada." He assumed the name Arthur Ellis, and claimed kinship with the British executioner John Ellis. English oversaw some six hundred hangings before his own death and the abolishment of the death sentence in 1967. See also Arthur Ellis and Mrs. Arthur Bartholomew English.

## English, Mrs. Arthur Bartholomew

I loved Arthur, there is no doubt about it, and he was always good to me. But there are things too horrible to demand even the loyalty of love. Arthur's business was always vague to me—a lot of Englishmen are like that. He discouraged questions and when he travelled I assumed it had something to do with secret governmental affairs. At least, when I hinted that way Arthur never denied it so I accepted the idea. When the incredible news got to me of his true identity it was a devastating shock. I just could not bear the thought of living with the executioner. The kindly husband was inseparable from the man who had killed so many hundreds of murderers on so many scaffolds. I told him I would leave for a while and try to get used to the idea but I never did. And, typically, Arthur was too proud to beg me to return. The "while" stretched into months, then years. . . .

> Quoted by Andy O'Brien in "My Friend, the Hangman," *My Friend, the Hangman: Dramatic Encounters in Sport, Crime and War* (1970).

## Erickson, Arthur

I'm not interested in repeating things. I'd become bored. The real fascination of architecture lies in the subject, in redefining the purpose of a building a little further forward than I have, then I'm interested in doing it.

> Vancouver architect, quoted in *Time*, February 14, 1972.

**Ericsson, Leif**   See Leif the Lucky.

## Ericsson, Samuel S.
A Canadian may be a Mounted Policeman, an Eskimo, a French-speaking farmer or Rose Marie, but not necessarily.

*Are Canadians Really? And Other Pertinent Questions* (1954), published by the United States Chamber of Commerce.

## Esar, Evan
Canada's climate is nine months winter and three months late in the fall.

*20,000 Quips and Quotes* (1968).

## Esposito, Phil
This was more emotional than winning the Stanley Cup. A Stanley Cup's for your team and your city, but beating Russia is for your country.

High-scoring member of Team Canada in the Canada-Soviet hockey series. *The Globe and Mail*, October 2, 1972. See also Yevgeny Yevtushenko.

## Estaing, Comte d'
You were born and have not ceased to be French.

Proclamation to the French Canadians by the commander of the French fleet, October, 1778. Quoted by Hilda Neatby in *Quebec: The Revolutionary Age 1760-1791* (1966).

## Ethier-Blais, Jean
One day the present conflict in the soul of French Canada may result in great novels—but that day is not yet in sight.

Montreal critic and academic, quoted by Gerald Clark in *Canada: The Uneasy Neighbour* (1965).

The cruel, inhuman, negative splendour of his geographical space has made the French Canadian fundamentally different. By his land he is different. There is not the slightest doubt, for example, that at a certain level, hidden deep within himself, the French Canadian is a better interpreter of Chekhov's plays than of Racine's. He feels the Russian play more naturally, he renders it with greater visceral intensity. He discovers in it a kind of excess and an appeal to sensibility which are familiar to him and which

correspond to a basic need in his nature. The North American soil has thus acted upon and, to a certain extent, has defined his instinctive reactions.

Quoted by André Laurendeau in "We Are a Winter Race" (February, 1966), *André Laurendeau: Witness for Quebec* (1973), translated by Philip Stratford.

## Etrog, Sorel
The Etrog

The Canadian Oscar was created by and named after the Israeli-educated sculptor, Sorel Etrog. The foot-high statuettes are handed out at the annual Canadian Film Awards banquet for outstanding achievement in Canadian film-making. The Etrogs, first presented October 4, 1968, symbolize "man in relation to his art," according to Wendy Michener in *The Globe and Mail*, September 28, 1968.

## Eustis, William
We can take the Canadas without soldiers; we have only to send officers into the provinces, and the people, disaffected towards their own government, will rally round our standard.

Eustis was U.S. secretary of War in 1812 when this boast was made.

## Evans, Arthur "Slim"
"Comrades . . . they won't come to us, so I say, let us go to them. I hereby move that we go to Ottawa, to discuss work and wages with the federal cabinet."

A motion proposed by an unknown striker and seconded by "Slim" Evans at a meeting of the striking Relief Camp Workers Union, May 29, 1935. Thus began the "On to Ottawa" trek which led to Evans, a former carpenter and Communist labour organizer, meeting with the prime minister on June 22, and finally the Regina riot in the Market Square, Dominion Day, 1935.

\*

Mr. Evans: The purpose is to demand from you this programme of work and wages.

Mr. Bennett: And we have made it perfectly clear so far as we are concerned that these camps were not established for that purpose.

Mr. Evans: This is passing the buck. We want work and wages.

Mr. Bennett: Just a moment—

Mr. Evans: You referred to us as not wanting work. Give any of us work and see whether we will work. This is an insidious attempt to propagandize the press on your part, and any body who professes to be premier and uses such despicable tactics is not fit to be premier of a Hottentot village.

Mr. Bennett: I come from Alberta. I remember when you embezzled the funds of your union and were sent to penitentiary.

Mr. Evans: You are a liar . . .

> The famous meeting of the delegation from the striking Relief Camp Workers Union, led by Arthur "Slim" Evans, and R.B. Bennett and members of his cabinet in the prime minister's office, East Block, Parliament Buildings, June 22, 1935. Reproduced by Victor Hoar in his edition of *Recollections of the On to Ottawa Trek* by Ronald Liversedge with *Documents Related to the Vancouver Strike and the On to Ottawa Trek* (1973).

## Evans, James

Don't you agree that land monopoly is the most dangerous monopoly of all, because it can be a perpetual thing, and enslaves the people who depend upon the land for their living? [Letter to his brother, Winter, 1840]

\*

September 28, 1840. For a fortnight I have been endeavouring to cast type to print the Cree language, but every attempt hitherto has failed. I have no proper materials, neither type materials nor any other thing requisite. I hope, however, to conquer the difficulties and begin printing in a few weeks or months at the furthest. [Diary entry]

> Two weeks later the Reverend James Evans, the Wesleyan missionary in the North-West, succeeded in his task: he printed one hundred copies of a sixteen-page birchbark booklet which he then bound in deerskin. This collection of

scriptures and hymns was printed in the Cree syllabics of his own devising, using type cast from bullets and the lining of tea chests, with ink made from soot and fish oil. The Indians called his booklet "the talking birchbark." A difficult achievement to manage without a printing press, it was doubly so in 1840 in remote Norway House on the Nelson River in what is now northern Manitoba.

\*

How can a man reach these people if he doesn't speak their language? To work through an interpreter is like hacking one's way through a forest with a feather.

\*

My Mary, there are no mysteries—only wonders.

> To his wife, about 1846, quoted by Nan Shipley in *The James Evans Story* (1966).

## Evans, Peter

Beavers Up!

> Captain Canada yells "Beavers Up!" and downs his drink of magic muskeg which renders him invincible. The anonymous, antler-capped hero appeared in *Fuddle Duddle: The Hansard of the Common People*, a short-lived Ottawa comic magazine published in 1971. The strip character was devised by Peter Evans and drawn by Stanley R. Berneche. (A different Captain Canada took to the air waves on "The Bruno Gerussi Show" on CBC Radio in 1969.)

## Everson, R.G.

No new graves
Congregation gone
Religion gone
I stare at the chance-taking dead

> Last stanza of "The Chance-Taking Dead," *Selected Poems: 1920-1970* (1970).

## Ewart, John S.

We are plagued with false political phrases. We are supposed to be associated with the British Commonwealth of Nations, although no such thing exists. We are alleged to be part of a third British Empire, although there never was more than one, and we have ceased to be part of it. We are called a dominion, although we have become a kingdom. We are said to be a confederation, although we are a federation. We have ten governments, but not one of them has any governing authority.

"False Political Phrases," *Canadian Historical Review*, June, 1933.

An American gets more respect in London than a colonist. In my opinion, he is entitled to it.

*

Nobody could ever understand anything after Arthur Balfour had explained it.

*

I am afraid that I myself am singular.

Ewart was an Ottawa lawyer and constitutional authority. The witticism about Arthur Balfour, the British statesman, was common during the 1920s. The last remark comes from a letter to Henri Bourassa in which Ewart explains that his own liberal nationalism happened to be unpopular in Canada between the wars. Quoted by David M.L. Farr in *Our Living Tradition: Second and Third Series* (1959), edited by Robert L. McDougall.

# F

## Fackenheim, Emil L.
Jews are not permitted to hand Hitler posthumous victories.

*

Had every Christian in Hitler's Europe followed the example of the king of Denmark and decided to put on the yellow star, there would be today neither despair in the church nor talk of the death of God.

*Quest for Past and Future: Essays in Jewish Theology* (1968).

Let me make but a single observation. There is a good deal of talk these days about the right of Christians to criticize Israeli policies. Some of it is innocent nonsense. Some of it is far from innocent. Of course Christians have the right to criticize Israeli policies. On occasion they may even have the duty. But in view of centuries of anti-Jewish Christian ideology, every criticism of Israel is suspect unless it is accompanied by the passionate determination that the Jewish state shall live. No Christian can stand by the Jewish

survivors of the holocaust and wish the death of Jerusalem.

Statement made by the German-born rabbi and philosopher when he accepted an honorary doctorate from St. Andrew's College, a United Church seminary in Saskatoon, on May 3, 1972.

## Fairbanks Jr., Douglas
It is doubtful if the British can, any more than anyone else, see themselves as others see them. However, it is generally conceded that Canadians can see both Britain and the United States in clearer perspective than either can see the other.

"An American View of Britain" (1965), *Empire Club of Canada: Addresses 1964-65* (1965).

## Fairclough, Ellen L.
So it is probably appropriate that I should quote an unknown source which said: "The battle of the sexes will never be won by either side. There is too much fraternizing with the enemy."

"Canadian Women as Citizens" (1957), *Empire Club of Canada: Addresses 1957-58* (1958).

### Fairley, Barker
More and more we hear people saying "Don't ask me" or "I am afraid of being wrong" or words to that effect, pointing to a complete surrender of judgment. And where there is no judgment the arts perish.

"F.H. Varley," *Our Living Tradition: Second and Third Series* (1959), edited by Robert L. McDougall.

### Fairley, Margaret
For the communist . . . his first moral duty is to recognize the truth: the truth that human differences are not a matter of blood and skin; the truth that private ownership of land and resources has come about through theft; the truth that whether he wills it or not each man is dependent on the past and on the present labour of all men.

"Moral Responsibility of the Communist," *Marxist Quarterly*, Winter, 1965.

### Faith, Percy
They say that eighty cents of the recording dollar is spent by kids between the ages of nine and sixteen.

Toronto-born orchestra leader, quoted in *The Globe and Mail*, August 2, 1967.

### Falardeau, Claude
French Kiss: At the time of the Tower of Babel this was called "the confusion of tongues."

\*

*Armour-propre:* The greatest, the sincerest, the most authentic of loves. Being *propre,* it is devoid of all sensuousness.

\*

Waterloo: Water equals L'eau: Anglo-French confrontation that caused the drowning of Napoleon.

Le *dictionnaire d'un Québecois (ou le maudit mot dit)* (1966).

### Falardeau, Jean-Charles
The daughter of Maria Chapdelaine who was an ammunition-factory worker at Valcartier during the war now lives with her own family of five children in the Rosemount ward of Montreal. Maria's married brothers are employees of the Aluminum Company at Arvida and Shipshaw after having been workers at the Jonquière pulp plant.

"The Changing Social Structures," *Essais sur le Québec contemporain* (1953). Quoted by Ramsay Cook in "Quebec: The Ideology of Survival" in *The Prospect of Change: Proposals for Canada's Future* (1965), edited by Abraham Rotstein.

### Falcon, Pierre
Tell, oh tell me who made up this song?
Why it's our own poet, Pierre Falcon.
Yes, it was written this song of praise
    For the victory
    We won this day.
Yes, it was written, this song of praise—
    Come sing the glory
    Of the Bois-Brûlés.

Final stanza of "The Battle of Seven Oaks" by the famous "troubadour of the North-West," celebrating the battle at present-day Winnipeg, June 19, 1816. Translated by James Reaney in *The Poetry of French Canada in Translation* (1970), edited by John Glassco.

### Falconer, Sir Robert
Liberty is a gift which can only be realized in a regulated universe and an ordered society.

"The Education of National Character," *Idealism in National Character: Essays and Addresses* (1920).

Our west never went through a riotous youth; it has few memories to be forgotten. From the first, life has been held sacred and respect has been paid to the law as rigidly as in the east, some of the credit being undoubtedly due to the Royal North-West Mounted Police force which the Dominion called into existence and has kept in high efficiency.

"The Quality of Canadian Life" (1917), *Builders of the Canadian Commonwealth* (1923), edited by George H. Locke.

In Britain, from an ancient society, there rise from time to time original thinkers who disturb the usual academic conservatism. As might have been expected, however, such are the conditions of the country, no arresting adventure in the realm of the spirit has yet been made in Canada.

> "The Tradition of Liberal Education in Canada," *Canadian Historical Review*, June, 1927. Sir Robert was president of the University of Toronto from 1907 to 1923, during which period its enrolment surpassed that of any university in the Commonwealth.

**Falstaff, Jake** See Dick Johnson.

**Faludy, George**
The politicians of our time might be characterized by their vain attempts to change the world and by their inability to change themselves.

\*

The worst superstition of the nineteenth and twentieth centuries is called progress. It is certain there will be no progress until there is an end to this kind of progress.

\*

The cabbalists thought that they would find the secrets of the universe in the Old Testament. The scientists of NASA want us to believe that these secrets can be found in the rocks of the moon.

\*

Most American television stations reproduce all night long what only a Roman could have seen in the Coliseum during the reign of Nero.

\*

Science presented us first with normative ethics, then with relativistic ethics, and at last with no ethics at all.

> Characteristic remarks of the leading Hungarian-born poet and humanist who lives in Toronto.

**Farber, Manny**
The actors who star in the Canadian films —desultory, lacking in intensity, numbed and ominous—never win awards in the category of either the beautiful or the damned. There is no passion about the casting. It is usually the guy next door, the girl friend, or the family pet who are willing to work free and have an inert boldness in front of a camera.

> "Canadian Underground" (1969), *Negative Space: Manny Farber on the Movies* (1971).

**Faribault, Marcel**
Quebec is at present no longer engaged in soul-searching psychiatry. She is sure of herself and of her mind. Her question is whether she can be sure of Canada when she looks to the future and to the world.

> Speech in Banff, March 15, 1963. Quoted by Frank Scott and Michael Oliver in *Quebec States Her Case: Speeches and Articles from Quebec in the Years of Unrest* (1964).

**Farquharson, Charlie** See Don Harron.

**Farquharson, Robert**
Canada's first nationalist was shot and ever since the Dominion's political leaders have diluted their Canadianism with imperialism. There has been no fear of another assassination; there has been dread of political suicide.

> "Debunking Imperialism," *Open House* (1931), edited by William Arthur Deacon and Wilfred Reeves.

There will be no dearth of televiewers from the very beginning of the first CBC program. The major task is to see that there are telethinkers at both ends of the wondrous process. Thinkers at just one end—no matter which end it is—will be ultimately disastrous.

> Farquharson was editor of *Saturday Night* when this remark appeared, September, 1952.

**Farrar, F.S.**
Had I done it alone by canoe, I might have boasted a little.

> Sergeant Farrar of the RCMP was third mate and photographer aboard the *St. Roch* which became the first vessel to circumnavigate the North American continent on May 29, 1950. On one trip he sailed the Northwest Passage, on another the Panama Canal. Quoted by Nora and William Kelly in *The Royal*

*Canadian Mounted Police: A Century of History* (1973).

## Farthing, John Colborne
Freedom wears a crown.

> Farthing was a political scientist at Bishop's College, Lennoxville, and his father bishop of Montreal. The above phrase is the title of his only book which was published in 1957, edited by Judith Robinson.

## Fátima, Our Lady of
See Lucia dos Santos.

## Fatt, Francis F.
Here we have courted our sweethearts, married and begot children and here built our homes, driving our tent pegs deep into Mother Earth, and are going to remain here to hold up the old British traditions, as long as the good God gives us breath.... Can you help us with a few words of encouragement in combating these heretics? Your influence here is great. If it is shown that you are against this proposition, it will help us materially.

> On November 22, 1910, Francis F. Fatt, the postmaster of Medicine Hat, wrote Rudyard Kipling in England, imploring him "as the Father Confessor of the Empire" to help the townsfolk retain the name which the "sons of Belial" were trying to rename. (Three years earlier Kipling had visited Medicine Hat and coined the Alberta town's nickname: "The city with all hell for a basement," an allusion to its subterranean natural gas.) For the reply, see Rudyard Kipling.

## Faulkner, William
I am well and quite busy, surrounded by snow, dogs, Indians, Red Coats, and Nazi spies.

> Letter written from Hollywood, February, 1943, where the novelist was working on the scenario of Raoul Walsh's *Northern Pursuit*, a movie about Mounties starring Errol Flynn, released later that year. Quoted by Joseph Blotner, "Faulkner in Hollywood," *Man and the Movies* (1967), edited by W.R. Robin-

son. In 1917, Faulkner resided at Knox College, University of Toronto, training with Canadians who had enlisted in the Royal Flying Corps (later RAF). About this time he changed the spelling of his name from "Falkner" to "Faulkner."

## Fauquier, John
A man who wasn't frightened lacked imagination, and without imagination he couldn't be a first class warrior. Let's face it: the good men were frightened. Especially between briefing and take-off. The bravest man I knew used to go to bed right after briefing, and refuse to eat. Sick with fear. Any man that frightened who goes to the target is brave.

> World War II flying ace, dubbed "King of the Pathfinders," quoted by Edmund Cosgrove in *Canada's Flying Pilots: Canadian Portraits* (1965).

## Favreau, Guy
I'm not downhearted. It's my friends who need cheering up.

> Favreau was forced to resign as minister of Justice in the Pearson government on June 29, 1965. Quoted by Richard Gwyn in *The Shape of Scandal: A Study of a Government in Crisis* (1965).

## Feinberg, Abraham L.
My private and public feud with Fascism keeps me alive.

\*

I believe that *all* truth is *very* difficult to come by; therefore I must be sceptical.

\*

I believe in "probably," "perhaps"—and also in "Thus says the Lord."

\*

I believe in heaven and hell—on earth.

\*

I believe in praying as though God were all and then doing as though man were all.

\*

Needing to believe, therefore I may choose.

\*

The cost of living is seeing others die.

> *Storm the Gates of Jericho* (1964).

## Fénelon, François
My crimes exist nowhere but in your head.

> The Sulpician missionary made this reply before the Sovereign Council in Quebec in 1674 when accused by Frontenac of dabbling in politics. Quoted by Francis Parkman in *Count Frontenac and New France under Louis XIV* (1877).

## Fennerty, Charles
The enclosed, which is firm in its texture, as white, and to all appearance, as durable as the common wrapping paper made from hemp, cotton, is actually composed of spruce wood reduced to pulp.

> All paper was produced from rags, straw or cotton waste until 1839, when Charles Fennerty, a Sackville lad of eighteen, manufactured paper from spruce from a mill at nearby Bedford. The letter above, enclosing a specimen of this paper, was written in 1844 and addressed to a mill at Halifax. Quoted in "Pulp and Paper in Canada," *The Book of Canada: Published by the Canadian Medical Association* (1930), edited by Chester Martin, W. Stewart Wallace, and T.C. Routley.

## Ferguson, Emily
See Emily Ferguson Murphy.

## Ferguson, George V.
The only thing you have to set against the spectacular appeal of the totalitarian State is the spectacle of liberty.

> The editor of *The Montreal Star*, quoted by John Grierson in "Searchlight on Democracy," *Grierson on Documentary* (1946), edited by Forsyth Hardy.

The pioneer's present is always so rough that he quickly learns to live for tomorrow.

> *John W. Dafoe* (1948).

## Ferguson, Max
Sail on, O CBC—sail on!

> *And Now Here's Max: A Funny Kind of Autobiography* (1967). During the 1950s, CBC Radio's most popular program was

Max Ferguson's "Rawhide" which announcer Allan McFee would introduce with a rousing "And now, here's Max."

## Ferrara, Martin
Public opinion is too precious a thing to leave in private hands.

> Quoted by Scott Young in *The Globe and Mail*, October 2, 1973.

## Ferron, Jacques
Montreal is only a stop on the way from Belgium to Kentucky.

\*

She was one of those English women, still marked by Europe, who for some strange reason flee their race and feel happy only among French Canadians. The latter in return assimilate them. This is where we get a good many of our red heads. One does one's best to gallicize, usually from the bottom up, while Englishness asserts itself from the top down.

> *Tales from the Uncertain Country* (1972), translated by Betty Bednarski.

## Fessenden, Mrs. Clementina
Empire Day, the Twenty-Fourth of May.

> The notion that a day should be set aside each year to commemorate the British Empire occurred to Mrs. Clementina Fessenden, Hamilton school teacher and mother of Reginald Fessenden, in 1898. She chose Queen Victoria's birthday, May 24. For the implementation of the idea, see George W. Ross. For the aims of Empire Day, see Earl Grey.

## Fessenden, Reginald
This afternoon, here at Cobb Island, intelligible speech by electromagnetic waves has for the first time in the world's history been transmitted.

> With these words the Quebec-born inventor recorded the birth of radio, December 23, 1900. (Cobb Island lies in the Potomac River, near Washington, D.C.)

\*

I am yesterday and I know tomorrow.

> These words appear (in Egyptian hieroglyphics) on the stone memorial in Bermuda to Reginald Fessenden who died

on the island in 1932. Quoted by Or-
mond Raby in *Radio's First Voice: The
Story of Reginald Fessenden* (1970).

**Fetherling, Doug**
Canadians are the only people in the
world psychologically capable of distinguishing Wayne from Shuster.

*Tabloid*, December, 1971.

**Feuer, Lewis S.**
Wherever a set of alternative possible
routes toward achieving a given end presents itself, a student movement will tend
to choose the one which involves a higher
measure of violence or humiliation directed against the older generation.

*The Conflict of Generations: The Char-
acter and Significance of Student Movements* (1969).

**Feyer, George**
When I left Hungary, I lost everything
except my accent.

*

I speak an excellent accent, without the
slightest trace of English.

*

Stephen Vizinczey is a true cosmopolitan
—unhappy everywhere.

Hungarian-born cartoonist, quoted by
Beverley Slopen in *Quill and Quire*,
July, 1972.

**Fidelis** See Agnes Maule Machar.

**Fidler, Peter**
All my money in the funds and other personal property after the youngest child
has attained twenty-one years, to be
placed in the public funds, and the interest annually due to be added to the capital and continue so until August 16th,
1969 (I being born on that day two hundred years before), when the whole
amount of the principal and interest so
accumulated I will and desire to be then
placed at the disposal of the next male
child heir in direct descent from my son
Peter Fidler. . . .

Clause seven of Peter Fidler's will, witnessed August 16, 1821, when "the forgotten surveyor" was fifty-two. He died

sixteen months later but his executors
failed to make provision for the amazing
clause which would have made his descendants fabulously wealthy. "Though
from time to time some of them enquire
or write letters asking how to get on the
track of this hoard, they know they will
never get it. And that knowledge they
bear with scarcely a trace of rancour.
It is just one of the facts of life," explained J.G. MacGregor in *Peter Fidler:
Canada's Forgotten Surveyor 1769-1822*
(1966).

**Fiedler, Arkady**
Canada Smells of Resin.

Title of a widely read travel book written by the Polish literary figure in 1947.

**Fiedler, Leslie**
Still, I myself have been reading Canadian books for a long time and have been
variously amused, dismayed, interested
and bored—not really moved (even
enough to want to register my reactions
in print). . . .

"To the Gentiles: Some Notes on the
Jewish Novel in English" (1969), *Collected Essays of Leslie Fiedler* (1971).

**Fielding, William Stevens**
Millions for Corruption, but not a Cent
for Nova Scotia.

Campaign slogan identified with the
leader of the Liberal Party of Nova
Scotia which, in the election of 1886,
was returned to office on a platform of
secession. This was the only election
ever conducted on an anti-Confederation platform. One resolution favouring
independence was passed but never im-
plemented. Fielding became Laurier's
finance minister.

**Fields, W.C.**
The time of which I speak I'm tending
bar up in Medicine Hat. Now a guy used
to come in there with a glass eye and I
used to wait on him. He used to take this
glass eye out and put it in a tumbler of
water. He comes in one day and forgets
his glass eye and I found it. The next
morning when he comes in I said, "Young
man, here's your glass eye," and I gave it

back to him. Ever since that day I've been known as Honest John.

> The American comedian wrote and delivered these lines in one of his many Hollywood features produced during the 1930s.

## Fiennes, Ranulph
The great elements of Fire and Earth, Air and Water still hold sway, if not untrammelled, in the wild Rocky Mountains and north to the Arctic in the land of Nahanni, "somewhere over there and beyond."

> *The Headless Valley* (1973). The young Britisher led an expedition, during the Summer of 1971, through the interior of British Columbia from the Arctic Circle to Vancouver.

## Filion, Gérard
Pressure on newspapers comes, not from advertisers, but from readers who ask editors, as the Israelites asked Isaiah, to beguile them with pleasant errors. It is rarely that people criticize errors; it is only the truth that they ask us to retract.

> Editor of *Le Devoir*, quoted by Hugh MacLennan in "The Public and the Press," *Thirty and Three* (1954).

On the day when every French Canadian, wherever he may be in the country, enjoys the same advantages and the same privileges as his English-speaking compatriot, the last obstacle to the unity of the country will have disappeared.

> *Saturday Night*, November 24, 1954.

Freedom is not a gift but something that must be won. The only freedom is that which has been torn from authority.

> Quoted by Pierre Elliott Trudeau in "Some Obstacles to Democracy in Quebec" (1958), *Federalism and the French Canadians* (1968).

Quebec is not a province like the others. She is a little more stupid.

> Quoted by Brian Moore in *Canada* (1963).

## Fisher, Douglas M.
Mr. D.M. Fisher (Port Arthur): Mr. Speaker, I should like to ask the Minister of Finance a question regarding the preparation of last night's budget speech. Can the minister assure us that he and his government officials alone prepared the budget speech without the assistance of outside consultants or ghost writers from Toronto?
Some hon. Members: Oh, oh.
Mr. Speaker: Order. The hon. member knows that is not the type of question which we enjoy in this House.

> House of Commons, June 14, 1963. The NDP member's question seriously embarrassed Finance Minister Walter L. Gordon and the Liberal government of Lester B. Pearson.

## Fisher, John
Why is it we have no Canadian jokes—I mean the kind I could tell over the radio? Why is there no joke about the Canadian, much as you hear about the Irishman, the Scotsman, the American?

> "Cobwebs" (1947), *Empire Club of Canada: Addresses Delivered to the Members During the Year 1947-48* (1948).

Instead of being owners ourselves of our resources we will wake up some day to find we are owers . . . the "n" is gone. Owners . . . owers . . . note the difference.

> "John Fisher Reports" (1950), *Empire Club of Canada: Addresses 1950-51* (1951). The broadcaster and speaker was known as "Mr. Canada" throughout the 1940s and 1950s.

## Fisher, John Charlton
MORTEM VIRTUS COMMUNEM
FAMAM HISTORIA
MONUMENTUM POSTERITAS DEDIT

> A competition was held to choose the most fitting inscription for the Wolfe and Montcalm monument which stands in the Governor's Garden, adjoining the Château Frontenac, Quebec City. On September 8, 1828, a medal was awarded the Quebec journalist John Charlton Fisher for the eight Latin words above, which translate: "Valour gave them a common death; history a common fame; posterity a common monument." The official French translation runs: *"Leur*

*courage leur a donné même mort; l'histoire, même renommée; la postérité, même monument."*

### Fitzgerald, F.J.

48° Below          Sunday Feb. 5th

Fine with strong SE wind,
Left camp at 7:15 A.M. moved one hour
and camped about 8 miles further down
Just after noon I broke through the
ice and had to make fire, found one
foot slightly frozen
Killed another dog tonight, have only
five dogs more and can only go a
few miles a day, everybody breaking
out on the body and skin peeling off
8 miles

> Last entry in the diary of Inspector
> Francis J. Fitzgerald, the Royal North-
> West Mounted Police officer who headed
> the so-called Lost Patrol. Inspector
> Fitzgerald and three constables at-
> tempted to cross the Northwest Terri-
> tories by dogsled, but perished of hun-
> ger and cold on February 5, 1911, only
> thirty-five miles from Fort McPherson.
> Inspector Fitzgerald's final words do
> not appear in his diary above but in his
> will below, which was found beside his
> corpse. It was drawn up on a scrap of
> paper and painfully composed, using a
> stick of charred wood for a pencil.

All money in Despatch Bag
and Bank clothes etc I leave
to my dearly beloved Mother
Mrs. John Fitzgerald Halifax
God Bless all
F.J. Fitzgerald
RNWMP

### FitzGibbon, James

York 11th May 1827
I do hereby Certify that on the 22nd day
of June 1813, Mrs. Secord, Wife of James
Secord, Esq., then of St. David's, came to
me at the Beaver Dam after Sunset, having come from his House at St. David's
by a circuitous route a distance of twelve
Miles, and informed me that her Husband had learnt from an American Officer the preceding night that a Detachment from the American Army then in
Fort George would be sent out on the
following Morning (the 23rd) for the

purpose of Surprising and Capturing a
Detachment of the 49th Regt. then at the
Beaver Dam under my Command. In consequence of this information, I placed
the Indians under Norton together with
my own Detachment in a Situation to in-
tercept the American Detachment, and
we occupied it during the night of the
22nd—but the Enemy did not come until
the morning of the 24th when his Detachment was captured.

Colonel Boerstler, their Commander,
in a conversation with me, confirmed
fully the information communicated to
me by Mrs. Secord, and accounted for the
attempt not having been made on the
23rd as at first intended.

The weather on the 22nd was very hot
and Mrs. Secord whose person was slight
and delicate appeared to have been and
no doubt was very much exhausted by
the exertion she made in coming to me,
and I have ever since held myself personally indebted to her for her conduct upon
that occasion, and I consider it an imperative duty on my part humbly and
earnestly to recommend her to the favourable consideration of His Majesty's
Provincial Government.

I beg leave to add that Mrs. Secord
and her Family were entire Strangers to
me as from the 22nd of June 1813, her
exertions therefore could have been made
from public motives only.

James FitzGibbon.

> Lieutenant James FitzGibbon was in
> command of the British forces at Beaver
> Dam in 1813 when Laura Secord ap-
> peared with news of the intended attack
> by the Americans. FitzGibbon's holo-
> graph statement, written fourteen years
> after the event, is reproduced in *Ar-
> chives: Mirror of Canada Past* (1972),
> Public Archives of Canada. For this
> stirring event in Upper Canadian his-
> tory, see Laura Secord. See also Marshall
> Spring Bidwell.

### Flaherty, Robert

I was packed out to "civilization"—to
Upper Canada College—English masters,
Eton suits and collars, and English games,
Rugby and cricket. All of which to me
was even more strange than I, wild and
woolly as I was, must have seemed to the

other boys, who spent a great deal of time plying me with questions. There was one boy from Australia who boasted a cattleman's whip which, I did concede, he could crack like a rifle. But didn't I have gold nuggets and Indian moccasins? And besides, I knew a few pidgin Indian words, quite enough to make everyone believe that I spoke real Indian.

> The well-known documentary film-maker Robert Flaherty was sixteen in 1900 when he was enrolled in Upper Canada College in Toronto. His father was an American prospector in Ungava. Quoted by Richard Griffith in *The World of Robert Flaherty* (1953).

I knew nothing whatsoever about films. I had no one to speak to. But here in the North I discovered primitive man, people in the midst of life who are always so close to death that they live in the moment nobly.

\*

Do it all in and through the camera.

\*

There's a saying among prospectors, "Go out looking for one thing, and that's all you'll ever find."

\*

Sir William [Mackenzie, the railroad builder] said to me casually, "Why don't you get one of these new-fangled things called a motion picture camera?" So I bought one, but with no thought really than of taking notes on our exploration. We were going into interesting country, we'd see interesting people. I had no thought of making a film for the theatres.

\*

First I was an explorer; then I was an artist.

\*

One often has to distort a thing to catch its true spirit.

> Quoted by Arthur Calder-Marshall in *The Innocent Eye: The Life of Robert J. Flaherty* (1963).

A story must come out of the life of a people, not from the actions of individuals.

> Quoted by Arthur Rosenheimer Jr., "They Make Documentaries: Number One—Robert J. Flaherty," *Film News*, April, 1946.

Here were a people with less resources than any other people on earth, and yet they were the happiest people I have ever known.

> Quoted by Frances Flaherty in "Introducing *Man of Aran*," Robert Hughes's *Film: Book 1: The Audience and the Filmmaker* (1959). Flaherty is describing the Eskimo in the Hudson Bay area among whom he lived for ten years while prospecting for iron ore.

Less than two years later, I received word by the once-a-year mail that comes out of the North that Nanook was dead. He had ventured into the interior hoping for deer. The herds did not come his way, and he starved to death. Poor old Nanook! Our "big aggie" become *Nanook of the North* has gone into most of the odd corners of the world—into the desert of the Sahara, India, Burma, Siam, where audiences must be told that white means snow; and more kablunaks than there are stones around the shore of Nanook's home have looked upon Nanook, the kindly, the brave, the simple Eskimo.

> *Aggie* means walrus, *nanook* polar bear, and *kablunaks* white men. Flaherty learned of the death of Nanook, the Indian hunter he immortalized in *Nanook of the North* (1920), in 1922. His account is quoted by Richard Griffith in *The World of Robert Flaherty* (1953). See also Sir William Mackenzie and Nanook of the North.

### Flavelle, Sir Joseph

"Profits!" he exclaimed scornfully. "I have come from the heart of a nation where they are sweating blood to win this war. Profits! I stand before you to say this: in the past we have all had our ideas about profits, but—with men sacrificing their lives for us, to hell with profits!"

> Toronto financier during World War One, quoted by Frederick Griffin in *Variety Show: Twenty Years of Watching the News Parade* (1936).

## Fleming, Allan

The Canadian National Railways officially unveiled its new corporate symbol on December 15, 1960. (This immediately replaced the unilingual letters CNR and the overfamiliar maple leaf insignia.) The comprehensive redesign program was based on a simple flowing graphic line, the bilingual acronym CN. The "new look" met the needs of a company the public connected with trains but which was really in the communications and transportation business. The CN trademark now appears on everything from train tickets and telegram forms to rolling stock and advertising around the world.

The symbol has been called "a bent paper clip," "a tapeworm rampant," "a printed radio circuit," and "a tortured snake." Typographers regard it as among the best corporate symbols in the world today. It is almost as familiar as "Coca-Cola" and "IBM."

The symbol was designed by Allan Fleming, a typographer born in Toronto in 1929, who has also redesigned trademarks for Gray Coach Lines, Hudson's Bay Company, the Liberal Party of Canada, Scotiabank, and the National Design Council. On January 29, 1973, he wrote: "I thought about my father who died when I was sixteen and worked for Canadian National all his life as a time-keeper in the freight yards at Simcoe and Front Street [in Toronto]. So I wanted it to be not just a good symbol, but a great one. Not necessarily for CN but for my father, Allan Stevenson Fleming."

## Fleming, Donald
See René Beaudoin.

## Fleming, Ian
You know, I just couldn't open that door. I couldn't kill a man that way.

In the summer of 1941, Ian Fleming trained as a secret agent in Oshawa and Toronto, in a spy school managed by "the Quiet Canadian," Sir William Stephenson, who tried to persuade Fleming to shoot a spy in "a room in a cheap downtown hotel in Toronto—nothing but a table and a chair and a single light bulb." Fleming apologized but refused. Quoted by John Pearson in *The Life of Ian Fleming* (1966), who explains: "Altogether Fleming struck it rich at Oshawa. The school not only provided him with a lot of tricks which he was to pass on to James Bond, but it helped him to decide, when the time came to decide, just what kind of an agent Bond must be."

There are other Canadian connections with Fleming and Bond. Montreal was included in *Thrilling Cities*. Ottawa is the setting for part of *For Your Eyes Only*, and a section of *The Spy Who Loved Me* takes place in Toronto. The mysterious "M," James Bond's chief, was probably modelled on a Canadian; see Sir William Stephenson. The Bond films were co-produced by a Canadian; see Harry Saltzman. So far Bond enthusiasts have overlooked a possible origin of their hero's name. There is a St. James Bond Church in Toronto which was in existence when Fleming visited the city; but it is United, and Bond would be Anglican.

## Fleming, Sir Sandford
The standard time-keeper is referred to the centre of the earth, in order clearly to bring out the idea that it is equally related to every point on the surface of the globe.

\*

It would farther be expedient to distinguish the proposed new system from sidereal, astronomical, civil or local time. For this purpose either of the designations, "common," "universal," "non-local," "uniform," "absolute," "all world," "terrestrial," or "cosmopolitan," might be employed. For the present it may be convenient to use the latter term.

"Time-Reckoning" (1879), *Proceedings of the Canadian Institute, Toronto* (1884). Sir Sandford has been called "the Father of Standard Time," although he himself did not use the term "Standard Time." At the Washington Meridian Conference, October, 1884, the Canadian engineer had the satisfaction of having his resolutions for fixing a prime meridian (Greenwich) passed and widely endorsed by national governments.

Canada has seven time zones: Newfoundland, Atlantic, Eastern, Central, Mountain, Pacific, Yukon. Daylight Saving Time was first introduced in 1918.

In an address at the Guildhall, London, quite recently, Mr. [Joseph] Chamberlain pointed out that 130 years ago a great statesman of the neighbouring republic—Mr. Alexander Henderson—bequeathed a precious legacy to his countrymen when he said to them, "Learn to think continentally." The late secretary of state for the colonies gave an equally precious message to those whom he addressed, when he said, "Learn to think Imperially." We in Canada will do well to take to heart both messages and "learn to think" at one and the same time "continentally and Imperially."

> "Build Up Canada," February 24, 1904, *Addresses Delivered before the Canadian Club of Toronto: Season of 1903-1904* (1904).

They say it is impractical because it has never been done before, a conclusive reason with governments.

> Letter to Rudyard Kipling concerning Fleming's proposal to section land in western Canada into triangles rather than squares to reduce homesteader isolation. Quoted by Walter Vaughan in *The Life and Work of Sir William Van Horne* (1926).

### Flemming, Hugh John
"Carry On, Hugh John"

> Campaign slogan used by the Conservative party of New Brunswick under Hugh John Flemming. It was successful in 1952 and 1956 but unsuccessful in 1960 when Louis J. Robichaud introduced a successful variation: "So Long, Hugh John."

### Flontin, Professor Josiah Flintabbatey
See J.E. Preston-Muddock.

### Flumerfelt, A.C.
The Landless Man and the Manless Land.

> Title of an address on the underpopulated West. January 22, 1917, *Addresses Delivered before the Canadian Club of Montreal: Seasons 1916-17* (1917). See also Robert Forke.

### Forbes, Kenneth
Recreations: literature, music, theatre; "pet aversion," modernistic art.

> From the entry in *The Canadian Who's Who: 1958-1960* (1960) for the Toronto portrait artist who deplores modern art.

### Forbes-Robertson, Sir Johnston
On the occasion of my farewell to Montreal, I have but one thought,—May all success attend the efforts, which have been so well stated, to have a chain of theatres under Canadian control from Halifax to Victoria. Such an undertaking will be of great value in a hundred ways both to Canada and the Old Country.

> The celebrated British actor was quoted by S. Morgan-Powell in *Memories that Live* (1929).

### Ford, Arthur R.
My own opinion is that the credit for the development of independent political thinking in Canada and the breaking down of party lines—for better or for worse—must largely go to the Canadian Press.

> "The Canadian Press," *Canadian Historical Review*, September, 1942. The editor-in-chief of *The London Free Press* had in mind not the press generally but the Canadian Press news service, formed in 1917, which he headed. Floyd S. Chalmers, in *A Gentleman of the Press* (1969), quotes a tribute paid Ford: "A great editor who never ceased to be a good reporter."

### Ford, Ford Madox
He took his parade, the Canadian troops looking like real soldiers in the sunlight, went round his lines with the new Cana-

dian sergeant-major, who had his appointment, thank goodness, from his own authorities; wrote a report on the extreme undesirability of lecturing his men on the causes of the war, since his men were either graduates of one or other Canadian university and thus knew twice as much about the causes of the war as any lecturer the civilian authorities could provide, or else they were half-breed Micamuc Indians, Esquimaux, Japanese, or Alaskan Russians, none of whom could understand any English lecturer. . . .

> *No More Parades* (1925), from *Parade's End* (1950).

## Ford, Glenn

If they try to rush me, I always say, "I've only got one other speed—and it's slower."

> Quoted by Marci McDonald in *The Toronto Star*, July 3, 1971. The Hollywood star was born Gwyllym Samuel Ford in Quebec City and taken to California at the age of eight. The stockily built leading man specializes in playing tortured heroes.

## Ford, Henry

There are over three thousand of these Canadian honkers right here, in front of us; and I could throw a stone to the farthest one.

> Reaction of the American industrialist to Jack Miner's wild geese on his conservation area in Kingsville, Ontario. Quoted by Jack Miner in *Wild Goose Jack* (1969).

## Ford II, Henry

You might very well interpret anything I might say either as an awkward effort to tell you how to run your business or as a veiled invitation to Canada to become the forty-ninth state of the United States of America.

\*

Now there are realities in the situation in which I find myself this afternoon. One of them is this: from the window of my home I can see Canada across the lake. And it never occurs to me that right over there is a foreign country.

> "Some Impressions" (1952), *Empire Club of Canada: Addresses 1951-52* (1952).

## Forest, Lee de

Point the way to a wiser use of this scientific boon that we have let fall into unworthy keeping. . . . We look to you in Canada to lead radio in North America out of the morass in which it is pitiably sunk. May Canada fulfill my early dream!

> This statement from "the father of broadcasting," the American scientist Dr. Lee de Forest, was read by Allan Spry on behalf of the Radio League of Canada before the Special Committee on Radio Broadcasting, 1932. Quoted by Frank W. Peers in *The Politics of Canadian Broadcasting: 1920-1951* (1969).

## Forke, Robert

The Landless Man to the Manless Land.

> Slogan to encourage immigration to the West, attributed to the minister of Immigration and Colonization from 1926 to 1929. See also A.C. Flumerfelt.

## Forrester, Maureen

How many songs do I know? I never could say I know, oh, 2,000 or 5,000 songs —I know so much music, I don't even *know* what I know.

> Quoted by Mollie Gillen in *Chatelaine*, September, 1972. See also Eugene Kash.

## Forsey, Eugene

To those who object that capitalism is "rooted in human nature," we answer: Possibly, but so was cannibalism. We no longer eat each other. A civilization is within our reach in which we shall no longer exploit each other.

\*

Capitalism is a luxury we can no longer afford.

> "The Nature of the Canadian Economy," *Social Planning for Canada* (1935), by the research committee of the League for Social Reconstruction.

The business leaders who clamour for government to "let business alone" would die of fright if any government took them at their word. For it is not only factory acts, workmen's compensation, old age pensions, minimum wage laws and public utility commissions which would disappear; it is also tariff protection, loans, guarantees, subsidies and bounties and half a hundred other government services and aids to business. Laissez-faire is dead. ["The Economic Problem"]

*

Until Christians learn to understand and apply the lessons of Marxism they cannot enter into the Kingdom of Heaven—nor, probably, can any one else. ["A New Economic Order"]

> *Towards the Christian Revolution* (1936), edited by R.B.Y. Scott and Gregory Vlastos.

I am in favour of equal rights for Canadians of French and English speech throughout Canada, within the limits of the practicable. I am not in favour of insisting that every postal clerk in Vancouver should speak French, or every postal clerk in Chicoutimi English. They don't need to: there are not enough French-speaking people in Vancouver or English-speaking people in Chicoutimi.

> Address to the Congress on Canadian Affairs, Laval University, 1961. *The Canadian Experiment, Success or Failure?* (1962).

The fact is that to talk of "developing something purely Canadian which will be neither British nor French" is literally nonsense: It makes "no sense." It is like the middle western American college which posted a notice: "The following are the traditions of this college. They will go into force at four o'clock tomorrow afternoon." Both the British and French traditions are bone of our bone and flesh of our flesh . . . they have sustained each other. They have preserved each other. Together, they have preserved our national existence. Alone, neither can survive. They must preserve each other still; together they must still preserve our national existence.

> Address by the then research director of the Canadian Labour Congress, University of New Brunswick, May 17, 1962.

The Fathers wrought well, and laid our foundations deep and strong. But the building is still unfinished, and parts of it have suffered some damage through the years. It does not need a bombing squad or a wrecking crew. But it does need alterations, repairs, additions, the expansion of certain rooms; and all of us must be made to feel at home in it.

> "Canada: Two Nations or One?" *Canadian Journal of Economics and Political Science*, November, 1962.

I have long considered it one of God's greatest mercies that the future is hidden from us. If it were not, life would surely be unbearable.

> "Trade Unions in 2020?" *Visions 2020: Fifty Canadians in Search of a Future* (1970), edited by Stephen Clarkson.

By instinct, upbringing and conviction alike, I am a Canadian nationalist . . . I have no special love for the Americans. They drove my ancestors into exile, and I am sometimes inclined to think that the American Revolution was one of the great disasters of history. I don't like American civilization, now. It frightens me even more than other forms of modern civilization. I think that Canada has a distinct identity, that it is different from that of any other country in the world, and that it's worth preserving.

*

It's because I am a John A. Macdonald Conservative that I sit in the Senate as a Pierre Elliott Trudeau Liberal.

> Address to the Ontario Conference on Economic and Cultural Nationalism, Toronto, June 24, 1971.

## Fort, Charles

Upon Dec. 2, 1919, Ambrose Small, of Toronto, Canada, disappeared. He was known to have been in his office, in the Toronto Grand Opera House, of which he was the owner, between five and six o'clock, the evening of December 2nd. Nobody saw him leave his office. Nobody —at least nobody whose testimony can be accepted—saw him, this evening, outside the building. There were stories of a woman in the case. But Ambrose Small disappeared and left more than a million dollars behind.

*Wild Talents* (1932). Reprinted in *The Books of Charles Fort* (1941), introduced by Tiffany Thayer. H. Allen Smith writes in "The Mad Genius of the Bronx" in *Low Man on a Totem Pole* (1941): "He cited in his writings scores of instances in which objects have been swished off the earth to vanish in space. Among these mysterious disappearances were not a few human beings who were standing in the middle of the road one moment and gone forever in the next. He called attention, for example, to the simultaneous disappearance of Ambrose Bierce in Mexico and Ambrose Small in Canada. Was someone collecting Ambroses? He suspected as much."

## Fortier, André
Fortunately figures are bilingual.

*

What do white ties have to do with art?

Former Treasury Board official, now director of the Canada Council, quoted by Marci McDonald in *The Toronto Star*, July 21, 1973.

## Fosdick, Harry Emerson
I have every reason for feeling very much at home in Canada. I was born in Buffalo on the twenty-fourth of May—[Laughter and applause]—and whenever the day came around I always used to cross the river into Canada and let you celebrate my birthday by shooting off firecrackers for the Queen. [Laughter]

"The Challenge of International Relations to North America," *Empire Club of Canada: Addresses Delivered to the Members During the Year 1925* (1926).

## Foster, Sir George E.
Splendid isolation.

"But he [the patriot] would read the signs of the times not aright in these somewhat troublesome days, when the great mother Empire stands splendidly isolated in Europe, with interests stretching over the wide world, with a commerce the greatest of any nation of the world has ever possessed and vulnerable on every quarter of the sea, who did not feel as Britain feels today, and is showing it, that the country's weal,

the country's progress, the country's stability, all of the country's pride and glory must base itself upon the strong arms and willing loyal hearts of the citizenship of that Empire from one end of it to the other. It is the right and duty of Britain herself and of every dependency that belongs to her to be ready, aye, ready as well as steady in its sentiments of loyalty and devotion for the Empire as a whole." House of Commons, January 16, 1896.

In a single speech the prominent Conservative finance minister used two phrases—"splendid isolation," "ready, aye, ready"—of Canadian significance. Sir Wilfrid Laurier would make good use of both, and Arthur Meighen would associate himself with the second of the two, the traditional British affirmation of military preparedness. On February 5, 1896, Sir Wilfrid addressed the House of Commons: "It is true, England was—as the Minister of Finance said on a former occasion, and is yet, isolated—whether splendidly isolated or dangerously isolated, I will not now debate; but for my part, I think splendidly isolated, because this isolation of England comes from her superiority, and her superiority, today, seems to be manifest."

Throughout the British Empire the phrase "splendid isolation" is associated with George Joachim, First Viscount Goschen, who spoke at Lewes, February 26, 1896: "We have stood alone in that which is called isolation—our splendid isolation, as one of our colonial friends was good enough to call it." In *Annals of Niagara* (1898), William Kirby explained: "The phrase 'splendid isolation' was coined by Scott of the St. John *Sun*, St. John, N.B., during the crisis of 1895, and has since circled the globe." Some phrases, like generals, fade away; others, like odours, linger on. "Splendid isolation" lingers on: Eric Partridge found a niche for the phrase in *A Dictionary of Clichés* (1940).

## No Truck Nor Trade with the Yankees!

Slogan of the Conservative party in the anti-reciprocity election of 1911. Attributed to Sir George Foster, North Toronto M.P. who became Borden's minister of Trade and Commerce when the Conservatives defeated the Liberals under Laurier in this election.

I have today signed my warrant of political death. . . . How colourless the Senate —the entering gate to coming extinction.

> Diary entry on Sir George's appointment to the Senate in 1921, quoted by W. Stewart Wallace in *The Memoirs of the Rt. Hon. Sir George Foster* (1933).

## Foster, Hal

Cartooning is the presentation of ideas. The best illustration or the funniest caricature is static unless it is the visual part of an interesting comic idea.

> Quoted by Allen Willette in *Top Cartoonists Tell How They Create America's Favourite Comics* (1964). The cartoonist who created "Prince Valiant in the Days of King Arthur" in 1937 was born in Halifax in 1892.

## Foster, Harry (Red)

If you don't care who gets the credit, you can accomplish anything.

> Red Foster founded Foster Advertising Ltd. and headed the Canadian Association for the Mentally Retarded. Quoted by Maggie Siggins in *The Toronto Telegram*, June 19, 1969.

## Foster, J.T.

There is something wrong with the government of the people, when it can enact legislation in twenty-five minutes to arrest labour leaders; when we cannot in five years secure legislation in the interests of Canadian working men.

> President of the Trades and Labour Council speaking in Montreal, reported by *The Montreal Gazette*, June 20, 1919. Quoted by Charles Lipton in *The Trade Union Movement in Canada: 1827-1959* (1967).

## Foster, Kate A.

"Mosaic is the true painting for eternity." These words of Ghirlandaio set forth one of the outstanding characteristics of Mosaic—its capacity to endure. Is not this a quality essential in nation-building also?

*

Let us native and foreign-born alike, in the spirit of friendliness and good-will strive to execute with meticulous care the pattern as revealed to us by the Master Craftsman so that Our Canadian Mosaic, like that of ancient times, may be "practically indestructible," so that it too, may endure!

> *Our Canadian Mosaic* (1926). This study of the foreign-born in Canada includes an early use of the concept of the national mosaic. See also John Porter.

## Foster, William A.

Now that some of the traditions of the past are gradually losing their hold on the imagination of a new generation, that sentiment which so long found an outlet in declamation over the glories of the Mother Land, will draw a more natural nourishment from native sources.

*

The old Norse mythology, with its Thor hammers and Thor hammerings, appeals to us,—for we are a Northern people,—as the true out-crop of human nature, more manly, more real, than the weak marrowbones superstition of an effeminate South.

*

As between the various Provinces comprising the Dominion, we need some cement more binding than geographical contact; some bond more uniting than a shiftless expediency; some loadstar more potent than a mere community of profit. Temporizing makeshifts may suit a futureless people.

> *Canada First; or, Our New Nationality* (1871). This is the key address in the Canada First movement which, between 1868 and 1874, encouraged pan-Canadianism. See also Colonel Taylor Denison and Sir James D. Edgar.
>
> The American President Woodrow Wilson said in 1915: "Our whole duty, for the present, at any rate, is summed up in the motto: America first." Will Rogers wisecracked: " 'America First' is all right, but it allows someone else to be second. 'America Only' is my movement."

## Foulkes, General Charles
Canada is physically joined to the United States just like the Siamese twins. If one of the twins gets hurt the other one suffers. It is just as impossible to separate the defence of Canada from that of the United States as it would be to separate the Siamese twins and expect them to survive.

"Canadian Defence Policy in a Nuclear Age," *Behind the Headlines*, May, 1961. Former chairman of the Canadian Chiefs of Staff Committee.

## Fournier, Captain Paul
I go where the job calls.

Fournier captained the icebreaker *John A. Macdonald* which accompanied the American oil tanker *Manhattan* on its historic voyage through the Northwest Passage, September, 1969.

## Fowler, Robert M.
The only thing that really matters in broadcasting is program content; all the rest is housekeeping.

First sentence of "The Fowler Report," *Royal Commission Report of the Committee on Broadcasting* (1965), by Robert M. Fowler, Marc Lalonde and G.G.E. Steele.

## Fox, Charles James
It is not right for this country to originate and establish a constitution, in which there is not a spark or semblance of liberty.

Maverick Tory M.P. denouncing the Quebec Act of 1774 in the British House of Commons. (Fox once addressed a toast to "Our Sovereign, the People.")

## Fox, Robin  See Lionel Tiger.

## Foxe, Luke
Gentle Reader, expect not heere any florishing Phrases or Eloquent tearmes; for this Child of mine, begot in the North-west's cold Clime (where they breed no Schollers), is not able to digest the sweet milke of Rethorick, that's food for them.

*

To this was replide, that hee was going to the Emperour of Japon, with letters from his Majestie, and that, if it were a ship of his Majesties of 40 Peeces or Ordnance, hee could not strike his flag. "Keepe it up then," quoth I, "but you are out of the way to Japon, for this is not it."

Captain Foxe encountered Captain Thomas James who was searching for a way to Japan in what is now called James Bay, August, 1631. *North-West Foxe; or Foxe from the North-West Passage* (1635).

## Franca, Celia
There is no possibility of the musician or the dancer becoming a wealthy parasite. Indeed, we have just barely brought these people down from the garret.

"Canada's Artistic Boom" (1959), *Empire Club of Canada: Addresses 1958-59* (1959).

The thing that's really important in life, I've discovered, is to forget bad impressions.

Quoted by William Littler in *The Toronto Star*, April 6, 1968.

## Franck, Albert Jacques
I'm a house painter.

To Queen Julianna of the Netherlands who, in 1967, asked the Dutch-born artist, who specialized in depicting Toronto's red-brick houses, what he painted. "In his way—our way—he is the Utrillo of our Annex, the Canaletto of our slums," wrote Robert Fulford in *The Vanishing City: An Exhibition of Paintings by Albert Jacques Franck* (1963).

## Francks, Don
The only city in the world without slums is Disneyland. They forgot to build any. So I think Hollywood is the slums of Disneyland.

The actor worked in Hollywood in the late 1960s.

## François I
I should very much like to know what clause in the will of Adam excludes me from my share in the world.

The French king protested Pope Alexander VI's division of the New World between Spain and Portugal in 1494. Quoted by Raymond Douville and Jacques Casanova in *Daily Life in Early Canada* (1968), translated by Carola Congreve.

We have decided to again send Cartier to Canada and Hochelaga, and as far as the lands of Saguenay . . . with a goodly number of ships and men of all rank, skills, and trades . . . so that we may better fulfil our intention and to do actions agreeable to God our creator and redeemer.

Jacques Cartier's commission from the king of France for his third voyage, October 17, 1540. *A Collection of Documents Relating to Jacques Cartier and the Sieur de Roberval* (1930), edited by H.P. Biggar.

**Frankfurter, Felix**
Canada emphasizes the professionalism of politics by making the leader of the Opposition a paid officer of the state.

"Politics Is an Art," *The Practical Cogitator, or The Thinker's Anthology* (1945), edited by Charles P. Curtis Jr. and Ferris Greenslet.

**Frankfurter, Glen**
If we do not discover ourselves we shall remain invisible and the world will not miss us.

*Baneful Domination: The Idea of Canada in the Atlantic World 1581-1971* (1971).

**Franklin, Benjamin**
The grand leap of the whale up the Falls of Niagara is esteemed, by all who have seen it, as one of the finest spectacles in nature.

"To the Editor of a London Newspaper, Intending to Chaff the English for Their Ignorance of America," 1765.

**Franklin, Lady Jane**
As to the objects of the expedition and their relative importance, I am sure you know that the rescue of any possible survivor of the *Erebus* and *Terror* would be to me, as it would be to you, the noblest result of our efforts.

Letter of instruction from Sir John Franklin's widow to Captain Francis L. McClintock, Aberdeen, June 29, 1857. The explorer disappeared in the Arctic ten years earlier. Quoted by McClintock in *The Voyage of the "Fox" in the Arctic Seas: A Narrative of the Discovery of the Fate of Sir John Franklin and His Companions* (1859). See also Sir Francis Leopold McClintock.

**Franklin, Sir John**
No, no, my lord, only fifty-nine.

In 1845, when the Arctic explorer was outfitting yet another expedition in search of the Northwest Passage, it was pointed out that he was sixty and too old for that sort of thing. Noted in passing by "Bega" (A.C. Codd) in *Last Words of Famous Men* (1930).

**Fraser, Blair**
Yesterday's news is tomorrow's history.
＊
Without at least a touch of anti-Americanism, Canada would have no reason to exist. Of all general definitions of the Canadians, this is the most nearly valid: twenty million people who, for anything up to twenty million reasons, prefer not to be Americans.

*The Search for Identity: Canada, 1945-1967* (1967).

If the Liberal government is beaten at the next election—a prospect less unlikely now than it has been for twenty-one years—this session of parliament will appear in retrospect as a *Gritterdämmerung*, or Twilight of the Grits. [Written July 7, 1956, eleven months before John Diefenbaker's Conservative landslide]
＊
We all, I'm sure, have many hopes for Canada on this Centennial day—that she may grow, thrive, prosper in all things. To these I would add one hope more: that Canada will not so greatly grow, and not so grossly thrive, as to destroy this heritage of solitude which makes us what we are and which our children will know perhaps better than we how to value. ["A Centennial Sermon," Church of the Messiah, Montreal, July 2, 1967]

*"Blair Fraser Reports": Selections 1944-1968* (1969), edited by John Fraser and Graham Fraser.

## Fraser, Simon

As for the road by land we scarcely could make our way in some parts even with our guns. I have been for a long period among the Rocky Mountains, but have never seen any thing equal to this country, for I cannot find words to describe our situation at times. We had to pass where no human being should venture. Yet in those places there is a regular footpath impressed, or rather indented, by frequent travelling upon the very rocks. And besides this, steps which are formed like a ladder, or the shrouds of a ship, by poles hanging to one another and crossed at certain distances with twigs and withes [tree boughs], suspended from the top to the foot of precipices, and fastened at both ends to stones and trees, furnished a safe and convenient passage to the Natives—but we, who had not the advantages of their experience, were often in imminent danger, who obliged to follow their example.

> *Journal of a Voyage from the Rocky Mountains to the Pacific Ocean performed in the Year 1808.* Entry for June 26, 1808, "in the most difficult and dangerous part of the Fraser Canyon, which centres upon Hell's Gate and the Black Canyon," according to W. Kaye Lamb, editor of *The Letters and Journals of Simon Fraser: 1806-1808* (1960).

## Fraser, Sylvia

Has God put my eyes in backwards so all I can see is the meanness inside my own head?

> *Pandora* (1972).

## Frazer, Sir James

When the Canadian Indians were asked their names, they used to hang their heads in silence or answer that they did not know.

> *The Golden Bough, Volume II: Taboo and the Perils of the Soul* (Third Edition, 1911).

## Freberg, Stan

Doesn't it get a little lonely sometimes out on a limb without Him?

\*

Why try to go it alone? The blessings you lose may be your own.

> "Stan Freberg's widely publicized religious-advertising jingles, used by the Anglican and the United Church on Canadian radio stations in 1964"; quoted by Pierre Berton in *The Comfortable Pew: A Critical Look at Christianity and the Religious Establishment in the New Age* (1965). The Reverend A.C. Forrest, writing in the *United Church Observer* about the commercials which were also used by the Presbyterian Church in the United States, called them "American religiosity at its worst."

## Fréchette, Louis-Honoré

We are French in spite of France.

> *La légende d'un peuple* (1887).

Be Canadians and the future is yours.

> Quoted by G.M. Fairchild, editor of *Canadian Leaves: History, Art, Science, Literature, Commerce: A Series of New Papers Read before the Canadian Club of New York* (1887). Fréchette, a distinguished Quebec poet, was a member of the French Academy.

## Frederick the Great

To see for yourself the absence of taste which to this day holds sway in Germany, all you have to do is to attend its public spectacles. There you will witness the abominable pieces of Shakespeare, translated into our language, and see the entire audience languish while listening to those ridiculous faces worthy of the savages of Canada.

> Remark made by the king of Prussia from 1740 to 1786 in "De la littérature allemande," included by Pierre Oster in his *Nouveau dictionnaire de citations françaises* (1970).

## Freedman, Bill

My philosophy is keep doing what you believe in.

> Quoted by Herbert Whittaker in *The Globe and Mail*, September 14, 1968. The Toronto-born West End producer is married to Toby Robins.

## Freedman, Harry

What I deplore on the contemporary scene is the proliferation and indiscriminate use of recordings, resulting in musical conditions that I think are dangerous if not fatal to the art of music as we have known it. Recordings have made music too common, too easy to get. People are no longer hungry for music the way they used to be. The amount of music they get every day has simply dulled their appetites.

The composer was interviewed by *Musicanada*, January-February, 1968.

## Freedman, Samuel

I've had a long and public love affair with Canada. It represents something of unique value. It is dedicated to the idea of unity without uniformity.

Justice of the Manitoba Court of Appeal and chancellor of the University of Manitoba, quoted by Gerald Clark in *Canada: The Uneasy Neighbour* (1965).

## Frégault, Guy

What I mean, and this is precisely the crux of the debate, is that mere survival is not a good thing. Survival is what remains to someone who has not enough to live on. Mere survival is an affliction. What is of interest is life, and the directing of that life. There is no question of mere survival, of being a helpless looker, simply because one is unable to disappear completely. But this last is precisely our situation.

"Canadianism," *The Report of the Canadian Historical Association, 1956* (1956).

## French, George A.

The Dominion Government requires 150 volunteers for the North-West Mounted Police. The knowledge of English or French is obligatory. Moreover, the candidate must have good antecedents and be a good horseman. For further particulars apply to Colonel Bacon.

Newspaper recruitment notice, April 15, 1874, reproduced by T. Morris Longstreth in *The Silent Force: Scenes from the Life of the Mounted Police of Canada* (1927).

## Frenkel, Vera

Is there a collective term for gifts? Cornucopia?

*

If you gave me your secret I would give you my silence. Exchanges change people.

"Notes on Gifts," *Artscanada*, December-January, 1970-71.

## Freuchen, Peter

Our funds were running low, but we still did not worry. I had a series of lectures in Canada to fall back upon. Montreal was the starting point. I talked on the radio, at a hospital and at a home for the aged, before the public lecture in the evening. From Montreal I continued a hectic schedule throughout Canada, speaking everywhere to Danish organizations. My countrymen assured me that my fees were reasonable and would be paid as soon as the club finances permitted. Every evening I confidently expected a check, but I had to be satisfied with a free dinner and a promise. . . . I proudly produced my last two dollars—all I had to show for my trip to Canada.

*Vagrant Viking: My Life and Adventures* (1953), translated from the Danish by John Hambro. The Arctic explorer is referring to an unprofitable lecture tour made in 1934.

## Friedenberg, Edgar Z.

Emigration does not greatly alter national character; if anything, it turns it to caricature: think of the British in E.M. Forster's India and Ian Smith's Rhodesia—or in Westmount. Living in Canada for two years has already taught me how American I am. . . .

"The View from the Citadel," *The Canadian Forum*, September, 1972.

Nova Scotia is a part of the world which is particularly proud of its ability to select from among the cultural influences that might impinge on it.

Quoted by Harry Bruce in *Saturday Night*, February, 1973.

Following Canadian politics closely is a little like being a devoted reader of *Peanuts* or even *Pogo*; it's the characters that hold your interest, not the story line.

> "Good Manners," *The New York Review of Books*, May 17, 1973. The Louisiana-born educator immigrated to Canada in 1970 at the age of forty-nine and teaches at Dalhousie University.

## Friml, Rudolf

Oh, sweet Rose-Marie,
It's easy to see
Why all who learn to know you love you;
You're gentle and kind,
Divinely designed,
As graceful as the pines above you.
There's an angel's breath beneath your sigh,
There's a little devil in your eye,
Oh, Rose-Marie. I love you!
I'm always dreaming of you.
No matter what I do,
I can't forget you.
Sometimes I wish that I had never met you!
And yet if I should lose you,
'Twould mean my very life to me;
Of all the queens that ever lived I'd choose you
To rule me, my Rose-Marie.

> Rudolf Friml did not write the lyrics to *Rose-Marie* but he did compose the music. The inane but appealing words of the operetta, which was the hit of the 1924 Broadway season, flowed from the pens of Otto Harbach and Oscar Hammerstein II.
>
> The operetta has been thrice filmed: with Joan Crawford in 1928 (a silent version); with Jeanette MacDonald and Nelson Eddy in 1936 (the memorable one); with Anne Blyth and Howard Keel in 1954 (undistinguished). The film's title is *Rose Marie*—the hyphen shifted presumably from the heroine to the principals: Jeanette MacDonald-Nelson Eddy.
>
> Within the ranks of the RCMP, a soft assignment is known to this day as "a Rose Marie posting."

I like a full-blooded libretto with a luscious melody, rousing choruses and romantic passion.

> *The Globe and Mail*, November 14, 1972.

## Frisch, Anthony

Maturity means perhaps another cup of coffee.

> Attributed to the author of *Poems* (1954).

## Frobisher, Sir Martin

The stones of this supposed continent with America be altogether sparkled, and glister in the Sunne like gold: so likewise doth the sand in the bright water, yet they verifie the old Proverb: All is not gold that glistereth.

> "The First Voyages of M. Martine Frobisher. . . . 1576," included by Richard Hakluyt in *The Principal Navigations, Voyages, Traffiques, and Discoveries of the English Nation* (1589), edited by Edmund Goldsmid in 1889. See also Queen Elizabeth I.

## Frontenac, Comte de

I never saw anything more superb than the position of this town. It could not be better situated as the future capital of a great empire.

> On first seeing Quebec, September, 1672, quoted by Francis Parkman in *Count Frontenac and New France under Louis XIV* (1877).

I have no reply to make to your general other than from the mouths of my cannon and muskets. He must learn that it is not in this fashion that one summons a man such as I. Let him do the best he can on his side as I will do on mine.

> To Major Thomas Savage, envoy of Admiral Phips who wanted the surrender of Quebec, October 15, 1690. Quoted by W.J. Eccles in *Canada under Louis XIV 1663-1701* (1964). For the ultimatum, see Sir William Phips.

## Frontenac, Madame de

I never had his heart while he was living. I do not want it now that he is dead.

Frontenac bequeathed his heart to his widow, Anne de la Grange-Trianon, in France. After his death in Quebec in 1698, his heart was sent to her in a small silver case, but she is said to have refused the token with the above remark.

**Frost, Leslie M.**
To remember the old is to add strength and background to the new.

*Fighting Men* (1967).

What you say may be in all them books, all right, but it ain't the Law of Killaloe.

Punch line of the Ontario premier's favourite story about a judge in the small Ontario town of Killaloe Station objecting to the pleas of a big-city lawyer. Quoted by Ron Haggart in *Saturday Night*, January, 1972.

**Frost, Rex**
To me the air waves represent the opportunity of a great Canadian tomorrow, in which the sky's the limit.

*The Passing Show* (1946).

Cheerio, Gentlemen, and happy days.

Characteristic sign-off of the popular broadcaster. "Spotlight on Europe" (1938), *Empire Club of Canada: Addresses Delivered to the Members During the Year 1937-38* (1938).

**Frye, Northrop**
Visionaries, artists, prophets and martyrs all live as though an apocalypse were around the corner, and without this sense of a potentially imminent crisis, imagination loses most of its driving power.

*Fearful Symmetry: A Study of William Blake* (1947).

Literature, then, is not a dream-world: it's two dreams, a wish-fulfilment dream and an anxiety dream, that are focused together, like a pair of glasses, and become a fully conscious vision. Art, according to Plato, is a dream for awakened minds, a work of imagination withdrawn from ordinary life, dominated by the same forces that dominate the dream, and yet giving us a perspective and dimension on reality that we don't get from any other approach to reality.

*
Literature is a human apocalypse, man's revelation to man, and criticism is not a body of adjudications, but the awareness of that revelation, the last judgment of mankind.

"The Keys to Dreamland," *The Educated Imagination* (1963).

One of the derivations proposed for the word Canada is a Portuguese phrase meaning "nobody here." The etymology of the word Utopia is very similar, and perhaps the real Canada is an ideal with nobody in it. The Canada to which we really do owe loyalty is the Canada that we have failed to create . . . our identity, like the real identity of all nations, is the one that we have failed to achieve. It is expressed in our culture, but not attained in our life, just as Blake's new Jerusalem to be built in England's green and pleasant land is no less a genuine ideal for not having been built there . . . the uncreated identity of Canada may be after all not so bad a heritage to take with us.

*The Modern Century: The Whidden Lectures* (1967).

I do not see how America can find its identity, much less avoid chaos, unless a massive citizens' resistance develops which is opposed to exploitation and imperialism on the one hand, and to jack-booted radicalism on the other. It would not be a new movement, but simply the will of the people, the people as a genuine society strong enough to contain and dissolve all mobs. It would be based on a conception of freedom as the social expression of tolerance, and on the understanding that violence and lying cannot produce anything except more violence and more lies. It would be politically active, because democracy has to do with majority rule and not merely with enduring the tyranny of organized minorities. It would not be conservative or radical in its direction, but both at once.

"America: True or False?" in Andy Wainwright's *Notes for a Native Land: A New Encounter with Canada* (1969).

We all know how important the reason is in an irrational world, but the imagination, in a society of perverted imagination, is far more essential in making us understand that the phantasmagoria of current events is not real society, but only the appearance of real society. Real society, the total body of what humanity has done and can do, is revealed to us only by the arts and sciences; nothing but the imagination can apprehend that reality as a whole, and nothing but literature, in a culture as verbal as ours, can train the imagination to fight for the sanity and the dignity of man.

> "Elementary Teaching and Elementary Scholarship" (1964), *The Stubborn Structure: Essays on Criticism and Society* (1970).

Canada, with its empty spaces, its largely unknown lakes and rivers and islands, its division of language, its dependence on immense railways to hold it physically together, has had this peculiar problem of an obliterated environment throughout most of its history. The effects of this are clear in the curiously abortive cultural developments of Canada. . . .They are shown even more clearly in its present lack of will to resist its own disintegration, in the fact that it is practically the only country left in the world which is a pure colony, colonial in psychology as well as in mercantile economics. [Preface]

*

What is resented in Canada about annexation to the United States is not annexation itself, but the feeling that Canada would disappear into a larger entity without having anything of any real distinctiveness to contribute to that entity: that, in short, if the United States did annex Canada it would notice nothing except an increase in natural resources.

*

*Ubi bene, ibi patria:* the centre of reality is wherever one happens to be, and its circumference is whatever one's imagination can make sense of. ["Letters in Canada" (1959)]

*

The forms of literature are autonomous: they exist within literature itself, and cannot be derived from any experience outside literature.

*

Literature is conscious mythology. . . .

*

There is no Canadian writer of whom we can say what we can say of the world's major writers, that their readers can grow up inside their work without ever being aware of a circumference.

*

. . . for Canadian culture, no less than Alberta, has always been "next year country."

*

But Canada has, for all practical purposes, no Atlantic seaboard. . . . To enter the United States is a matter of crossing an ocean; to enter Canada is a matter of being silently swallowed by an alien continent.

*

. . . everything that is central in Canadian writing seems to be marked by the imminence of the natural world.

*

Literature, we said, is conscious mythology: it creates an autonomous world that gives us an imaginative perspective on the actual one. ["Conclusion to a *Literary History of Canada*" (1965)]

> *The Bush Garden: Essays on the Canadian Imagination* (1971).

## Fulford, Robert

I have seen the future and it doesn't work.

> This aphorism is associated with Robert Fulford. Covering the opening of the Hall of Fossil Invertebrates at the Royal Ontario Museum, the Toronto cultural journalist reported in *The Toronto Star*, January 25, 1967: "There are technical hitches, incidentally. In two places, where pictures and sound are synchronized to work together, they are not yet synchronized. This confirms one of my lifelong beliefs—i.e., that the future, when it arrives, usually doesn't work."
>
> Fulford might well have been the first person to give the distopian twist to the celebrated utopian remark, first made by Lincoln Steffens upon his return from the Soviet Union in 1919: "I have seen the future, and it works." (When the American social commentator published his *Autobiography* in 1931, he

offered a different version of his quip: " 'So you've been over into Russia?' said Bernard Baruch, and I answered very literally, 'I have been over into the future, and it works.' ")

My own observation is that there is no Canadian community which is as dull as the newspaper it reads. ["The Press in the Community" (1962)]

*

Art history is the nightmare from which art is struggling to awake. ["Pop Art and Museum Culture" (1966)]

*

The road to literary freedom is paved with the confusions of lawyers. ["The Question of Censorship" (1966)]

*

In Canada we talk a lot about cultural protectionism; we don't do it much. Among Canadians you will find a major difference of opinion as to whether that last sentence amounts to bragging or complaining. ["Pro-Canadians and Anti-Americans" (1966)]

*

A print addict is a man who reads in elevators. People occasionally look at me curiously when they see me standing there, reading a paragraph or two as the elevator goes up. To me, it's curious that there are people who do not read in elevators. What can they be thinking about? ["The Pastimes of a Print Addict" (1966)]

*

I like America and Americans. I admire them. I've always been profoundly grateful that Canada shares this continent with the American people; God bless America, as I think both Frank Underhill and Marshall McLuhan have said, for saving us from the fate of Australia. ["Their America, and Mine" (1968)]

*Crisis at the Victory Burlesk: Culture, Politics and Other Diversions* (1968).

My generation of Canadians grew up believing that, if we were very good or very smart, or both, we would someday *graduate* from Canada.

"Notebook," *Saturday Night*, October, 1970.

### Fuller, Alfred Carl
I started out by trying to be helpful. I would knock on the door and say, "Good morning, madam, if there is anything wrong in your house that a good brush could fix, perhaps I could help you."

*A Foot in the Door* (1960), the autobiography of the Nova Scotia-born founder of the Fuller Brush Company.

### Fuller, Buckminster
Toronto does not have to devote all its energies and resources to seeking remedies for yesterday's problems—slums, ghettoes and unemployment. Free of these major constraints, it can be a truly future-oriented protypic city.

*

Toronto has a unique situation to exploit in establishing world prominence. As Canada's largest heartland city, it is part of the world's greatest technological capability; and it is also, in the context of Canada, free of major restrictions on open discussion and cooperation with all other countries.

*Project Toronto*, a report by the inventor of the geodesic dome, sponsored by *The Toronto Telegram* and CFTO-TV, June, 1968.

### Fulton, E. Davie
I believe that the essential characteristic which identifies the Conservative is his belief that there is and must be an underlying moral and spiritual content to all political philosophy and action if it is to have lasting value.

Address to the Young Progressive Conservatives of Toronto and District, March 19, 1960. Quoted by Peter C. Newman in *Renegade in Power: The Diefenbaker Years* (1963). See also C.D. Howe.

### Furie, Sidney
Despite all the work we did in Toronto, and the hopes we had for it, there's really no more reason for Toronto to have a movie industry than Cleveland.

CBC-TV alumnus and director of *The Ipcress File*, quoted by Gerald Utting in *The Toronto Star*, May 22, 1965.

# G

## Gabor, Zsa Zsa
I met your Trudeau in London. What do you call him, the president?

> Quoted by Jack Batten in *The Globe and Mail*, October 4, 1972.

## Gadsby, H.F.
People from the prairies, who have made their pile, spend their declining years in Vancouver on the road to heaven.

> Quoted in *Canadian Days: Selections for Every Day in the Year from the Works of Canadian Authors* (1911).

All their pictures look pretty much alike, the net result being more like a gargle or a gob of porridge than a work of art . . . the Hot Mush madness. . . .

> "The Hot Mush School, or, Peter and I," *The Toronto Star*, December 12, 1913. An early attack on the Group of Seven by the art critic who coined the term "the Hot Mush School." For a rebuttal, see J.E.H. MacDonald.

## Gaglardi, Phillip A.
When I first became minister, I went over and sat in that cotton-picking chair and from then on I was the boss.

> *

The only time I tell a lie is when I think I am telling the truth.

> *

Those trees weren't put on that mountain by God to be praised, they were put there to be chopped down.

> *

I wasn't driving too fast, I was flying too low.

> "Flying Phil" Gaglardi, who was appointed minister of Public Works and Social Improvement when the Social Credit party assumed power in British Columbia under W.A.C. Bennett on June 31, 1952, made the last remark above to a patrol officer who stopped him for speeding. Except for the second remark, which is traditional, the one-liners come from Paddy Sherman's *Bennett* (1966). "Think of the most colourful of all Canadian politicians, the Rev. 'Flying Phil' Gaglardi, minister of Highways in British Columbia and minister to his Pentecostal flock in Kamloops, a man who drives his own roads with something like the speed of the Holy Spirit that his sect particularly celebrates." Prologue, *Religion in Canada: The Spiritual Development of a Nation* (1968), by William Kilbourn.

## Gailly de Taurines, Charles
What is this great work of which the Canadian people is to be the instrument? The Canadians will answer us with one voice, and alike from pulpit and from tribune we shall hear these words given forth: "Our mission is to fulfil in America, we who are a people of French blood, the part that France herself fulfilled in Europe. . . . There is a divine mission which they must fulfil. A Catholic people, one of those that have remained most faithful to the Church, they must win over the whole of North America to Catholicism."

> *La nation canadienne: Etude historique sur les populations françaises du Nord de l'Amérique* (1894), quoted by André Siegfried in *The Race Question in Canada* (1907).

## Galbraith, John Kenneth
We referred to ourselves as Scotch and not Scots. When, years later, I learned that the usage in Scotland was different it seemed to me rather an affectation.

> *

Yet it would be wrong to think of this as a land without beauty. On the contrary, I remember it, and quite accurately, as having a breathtaking loveliness. The difference is that this country does not flaunt its beauty everywhere and always. It is condensed both as to time and place.

> *

A few years ago a Hollywood press agent

was looking for a family of bachelors to publicize a film called *Seven Brides for Seven Brothers*. After an international search, he found seven unmarried brothers a few miles from Hogg Street toward the Lake. It would have been a logical place to look first. [Elgin County, Ontario; for a more elaborate publicity stunt, see Russell Birdwell]

    \*

Most asked me whether, in my travels, I had found a place as good as this. I said no for this could have been the truth and, when I faced up to it, I found I did not wish to have people think me irresponsible.

> *The Scotch* (1964). The well-known economist was born at Iona Station, Elgin County, Ontario, and is credited with creating, or at least popularizing, such phrases as "the affluent society," "the conventional wisdom," "the managerial élite," "private affluence, public squalor."

If I were still a practising as distinct from an advisory Canadian I would be much more concerned about maintaining the cultural integrity of the broadcasting system and with making sure Canada has an active, independent theatre, book-publishing industry, newspapers, magazines and schools of poets and painters.

    I would be very much concerned that the widest possible support was given by all levels of government to the preservation of the cultural traditions associated with the particular ethnic groups in Canada, and with French Canada. Also, to make sure that Canadian theatre and artists received encouragement. And that people weren't totally dependent on American magazines.

    These are the things that are important for the maintenance of cultural autonomy. I wouldn't worry for a moment about the difference between Canadian or American corporations.

> Interview conducted by Robert McKeown, *Weekend Magazine*, March 25, 1967.

Canada was perhaps the first country to commit itself to a firmly Keynesian economic policy.

> "How Keynes Came to America," *New York Times*, May 16, 1965. Reprinted in Whit Burnett's *This Is My Best In the Third Quarter of the Century* (1970).

As a boy on a farm in Canada, I had to help move great tonnages of this nutrient every spring. Nothing is so nostalgic as that odour—in combination with the knowledge that someone else is doing the shoveling.

> "The Nicest Village in the Country," *A Contemporary Guide to Economics, Peace and Laughter* (1972).

I don't have any very strong nationalistic instincts. I was brought up in southwestern Ontario where we were taught that Canadian patriotism should not withstand anything more than a five-dollar-a-month wage differential. Anything more than that, and you went to Detroit. I've always said that one could have a moral and emotional affiliation with any number of countries. I consider myself as much a Canadian as an American.

> Quoted by Peter C. Newman in "John Kenneth Galbraith" (1970), *Home Country: People, Places, and Power Politics* (1973).

Apud Canadienses paulo carius. [Galbraith once suggested that this phrase, which translates "Slightly higher in Canada," might be the national motto]

    \*

The only way to get away from the influence of the American economy would be to float our half of the continent off somewhere else.

> Attributed to the widely quoted economist. See also Anthony Burgess.

### Gallant, Mavis
When everyone is responsible then nobody is, and that is comfortable, finally.

> Introduction by Mavis Gallant, the Paris-based Montreal short-story writer, to *The Affair of Gabrielle Russier* (1971).

### Galloping Gourmet, The
See Graham Kerr.

## Galt, Alexander Tilloch

If the United States desire to outflank us on the West, we must . . . lay our hand on British Columbia and the Pacific Ocean. This country cannot be surrounded by the United States—we are gone if we allow it. . . . We must have our back to the North.

> Lennoxville address, May 22, 1867. Quoted by P.B. Waite in *The Life and Times of Confederation: 1864-1867* (1962).

I cannot believe that the statesmen who have built up this great empire have not bequeathed ability and talent enough to their successors to hold it together.

> *The Relations of the Colonies to the Empire: Present and Future* (1881). Quoted by O.D. Skelton in *The Life and Times of Sir Alexander Tilloch Galt* (1920).

## Galt, John

Every body who has ever been at Dover knows that it is one of the vilest blue-devil haunts on the face of the earth except Little York in U. Canada, when he has been there one day.

> *An Autobiography of John Galt* (1833). For "Canadian Boat Song," which is often ascribed to Galt, see David Macbeth Moir.

## Ganong, W.F.

Every man tends to write that kind of book which he likes best to read. A history of mine would be coldly scientific, precise, classified, complete; but it would lack the life and form and colour which should distinguish a history for the people.

> "A Plan for a General History of the Province of New Brunswick" (1895), quoted by Kenneth N. Windsor in "Historical Writing in Canada to 1920," *Literary History of Canada: Canadian Literature in English* (1965), edited by Carl F. Klinck.

## Gard, Robert E.

Around the babe was a sea of stones,
A million ton or more,

That slid right off the mountain top
With a horrifying roar,
With a horrifying roar they tore,
There in the shiv'ring morning.

> One verse from "Ballad of the Frank Slide." The disaster occurred in British Columbia on April 29, 1903. *Canada's Story in Song* (1965), edited by Edith Fowke and Alan Mills.

The real test of coffee is when it will float a four-bit piece.

> *Johnny Chinook* (1945).

## Gardner, Martin

Nova Scotia and Prince Edward Island:
Two Canadian Provinces: Lands I Dread!

> Anagram noted by Martin Gardner in the notes to his edition of *Oddities and Curiosities of Words and Literature* (1961), by C.C. Bombaugh.

## Garneau, François-Xavier

When we contemplate the history of Canada as a whole, from the time of Champlain till our own day, we first remark its two great divisions,—the period of French supremacy, and that of British domination. The annals of the former are replete with the incidents of wars against the savages and the people of the coterminous British colonies, since become the United States; the other portion is signalized by parliamentary antagonism of the colonists to all infractions of their nationality and designs against their religion.

> *History of Canada from the Time of Its Discovery till the Union Year 1840-41* (1862), translated by Andrew Bell.

## Garneau, Hector

Lord Dufferin was mistaken in saying that we had no history. But this history has yet to be written. The radical peer was nearer the truth when he denied us any literature, since our literature was just then being born.

> "French Canadian Literature," January 15, 1921, *Addresses Delivered before the Canadian Club of Ottawa: 1920-21* (1921).

**Garneau, Hector de Saint-Denys-**
I am a bird cage
A cage of bone
With a bird

The bird in the cage of bone
Is death building his nest

> Opening lines of "Bird Cage" translated
> by F.R. Scott in *The Poetry of French
> Canada in Translation* (1970), edited by
> John Glassco.

I walk beside a joy
Beside a joy that is not mine
A joy of mine which I cannot take

> Opening lines of "Accompaniment"
> translated by F.R. Scott in *The Poetry
> of French Canada in Translation* (1970),
> edited by John Glassco.

Great art consists of going beyond reality
and not in evading it. One must be able
to say, "That is how it is—and something
more." Art lies in that "more." [April
15, 1935]

\*

Death. It has never repelled me. I have
always looked on it as a liberation. [September, 1935]

\*

Is our capacity for suffering commensurate with our capacity for happiness: *infinite*? [June, 1936]

\*

I have made all my journeys by means of
words. We send our words out to reconnoitre, and they bring back reports on the
countries they have seen. We see from
these reports whether the countries are
real, fairly real, or surreal. [Shrove Tuesday, 1936]

> *The Journal of Saint-Denys-Garneau*
> (1962), translated by John Glassco. The
> French-Canadian poet died in 1939 and
> his *Journal* (1954) was edited for publication by Robert Elie and Jean Le
> Moyne.

**Garner, Hugh**
A short time ago Morley Callaghan and I
were talking typical writers' talk—about
our current work, critics, publishers,
other writers and what they were doing.

Before we parted Callaghan said, "Being
a Canadian writer is tough, isn't it?" I
answered, "Well, it beats working in a
pickle factory."

> "My First Hundred Years as a Writer,"
> *The Canadian Weekly*, December 29,
> 1962.

Cabbagetown had one unique feature
which has amazed some people who
haven't given it any thought. It happened
to be the largest Anglo-Saxon slum in
North America.

> Interviewed by Allan Anderson, *The
> Tamarack Review*, 52 (1969). On another
> occasion the Toronto novelist remarked:
> "Cabbagetown remains to mock the
> social workers and the planners."

Do you want to know something? I don't
think I'd have wanted to miss the Great
Depression for the world.

> "On the Road through the Thirties"
> (1971), quoted by Michiel Horn in *The
> Dirty Thirties: Canadians in the Great
> Depression* (1972).

An article is what *Maclean's* publishes;
an essay is what *Maclean's* turns down
and you later read in *Saturday Night*.

> *One Damn Thing after Another* (1973).

**Garner, Lord**
Away with tunics, cocked hats, swords
In proof of stern endeavour
We'll wear (where Adam wore the fig)
The Maple Leaf for Ever.

> Submitted by the British high commissioner in Ottawa (1956-61) to Lester
> B. Pearson who requested External Affairs officers to refuse all foreign honours. Lord Garner attributes the piece
> of doggerel to (now Sir) Raymond Bell,
> a member of his staff. "Mike: An Englishman's View," *International Journal:
> Canadian Institute of International Affairs*, Winter, 1973-74.

**Garnett, Gale**
I really don't care if some lady up the
street thinks I'm the arch-harlot of the
Western world. As long as I don't think
it myself.

> *Homemaker's Magazine*, Summer, 1973.

## Garvie, William
### The Botheration Scheme.

"An epithet for the plan of federal union of the British North American colonies, it was taken from Barney Rooney's *Letters on Confederation, Botheration and Political Transmogrification* (Halifax, 1865), an amusing satire on the Quebec Conference by William Garvie," according to Norah Story in *The Oxford Companion to Canadian History and Literature* (1967). "The term became popular among anti-confederationists in Nova Scotia and was used by Joseph Howe as the title for twelve anti-confederation letters published in the Halifax *Morning Chronicle*," January 11 to March 2, 1865.

## Gascon, Jean
The dream of all my life was to be in a cowboy movie, to gallop across the plains on my faithful horse and shoot from the saddle. But in the end I didn't do anything like that.

Classical actor quoted by Stephen Franklin in *The Toronto Telegram*, February 15, 1969.

## Gaucher, Yves
The artist is the guy who keeps everyone and everything awake.

*

We don't really change, we just become ourselves, but more so all the time.

Quoted by William Withrow in *Contemporary Canadian Painting* (1972).

I prefer the murmur to the shout, for in silence there is real presence.

Quoted by Normand Thériault in *Arts-canada*, February, 1969.

## Gaulle, Charles de
France had given birth to it four centuries ago and then withdrawn, after two hundred years of praiseworthy effort, on account of European commitments. In our day, by a veritable miracle of fecundity and fidelity, the substance of France remained very much alive there in the form of a population of five million inhabitants concentrated in Quebec and on the shores of the St. Lawrence, and two million others spread over the rest of the territory.

*

On leaving this country I wondered whether the establishment of a State of French origin side by side with another of British origin, the two co-operating with each other in every sphere freely and by choice, uniting their twin nationhoods in order to safeguard them, might not be the only way for Canada eventually to obliterate the historic injustice on which it was based, to develop in conformity with its own true realities, and thus to remain Canadian.

The French president is writing about his third and second-last trip to Canada in 1960. *Memoirs of Hope: Renewal 1958-62; Endeavour 1962-* (1970), translated by Terence Kilmartin.

It is about time that Canada entered history.

The president of the French republic is said to have made this observation to a visiting Canadian cabinet minister who complained of the country's difficulties. Quoted by Gerald Clark in *Canada: The Uneasy Neighbour* (1965).

What we are doing in France, you are doing here. We will do it a little more together. Whatever is French has its role to play, as always. [Quebec City, July 23, 1967]

*

Quebec, alive, is on its way to becoming master of itself. [Donnacona, July 24, 1967]

*

Be masters of your own destiny ... France expects you to do your part. [Trois-Rivières, July 24, 1967]

*

Vive le Québec! Vive le Québec libre! Vive le Canada français! Vive la France!

To a crowd of ten thousand from the balcony of the Montreal City Hall, July 24, 1967, the French president deliberately voiced the separatist slogan "Vive le Québec libre!" Mason Wade, in *The French Canadians: 1760-1967* (1968), quotes Claude Ryan's editorial in *Le Devoir*, July 26: "The worst error English Canadians can commit would be to remember only the words 'Long live a free Quebec' and to forget the rest."

For a reply, see Jean Drapeau. Here is a portion of Lester B. Pearson's official statement on behalf of the government: "However, certain statements by the president tend to encourage a small minority of our population whose aim is to destroy Canada, and, as such, they are unacceptable to the Canadian people and its government.

"The people of Canada are free. Every province of Canada is free. Canadians do not need to be liberated. Indeed, many thousands of Canadians gave their lives in two world wars in the liberation of France and other European countries."

For a distant echo of the "Québec libre" speech, see Pauline Julien.

\*

If I am not acceptable, too bad. [Attributed by an aide after the president learned he would not be received in Ottawa, July 24, 1967]

**Gay, James**
To Dr. C.L. Alfred Tennyson,
Poet Laureate of England, Baron, &c., &c.,

Dear Sir,

Now Longfellow is gone there are only two of us left. There ought to be no rivalry between us.

"A poet's mind is clear and bright,
No room for hatred, malice or spite."

. . . I do not know whether a Baron or a Poet Laureate gets any wages in England. In Canada there is no pay. . . . It is a solemn thing to reflect that I am the link connecting two great countries. I hope when I am gone another may raise up. . . .
Yours alway,
James Gay,
(this day).

Poet Laureate of Canada and Master of All Poets.
Royal City of Guelph, Ontario.

> Letter sent to Tennyson in 1882 by the eccentric Canadian bard. *Canada's Poet: Yours alway, James Gay; Poet Laureate of Canada and Master of All Poets, This Day* (1884).

Hail our great Queen in her regalia;
One foot in Canada, the other in Australia.

> Attributed (probably incorrectly) to the "Royal Poet."

**Geddes, Tom**  See George Bannerman.

**Gehring, Franz**
He was an excellent player, but emigrated to Canada, where he settled at Toronto.

> Dr. Gehring wrote the entry in *Grove's Dictionary of Music and Musicians* (Fifth Edition, 1954) for the violinist Wilhelm Labitzky. ("I like that 'but,' " remarked the musicologist Helmut Kallmann.)

**Geiger-Torel, Herman**
If an opera doesn't cost a lot, frankly it just isn't any good.

> Director of the Canadian Opera Company, quoted by Susan Carson in *Weekend Magazine*, December 15, 1973.

**Gélinas, Gratien**
I must not only give birth to the theatre —I must also fill the stage.

> Quoted by James R. Conant in *The Montrealer*, September, 1957.

The theatre is like fireworks. Look at it, look at it, it may not come again.

> Quoted by Joanne Strong in *The Globe and Mail*, June 11, 1973.

**Genest, Emile**
A tourist is a fellow who drives thousands of miles so he can be photographed standing in front of his car.

> *Parlez-moi d'humour* (1965), edited by Jacques de Roussan.

**Geoffrion, Bernie**
I like scoring goals, and I sure as hell like scoring them against Toronto.

> "Boom Boom" Geoffrion of the Montreal Canadiens scored his fiftieth goal during the 1960-61 hockey season.

**George II**
Mad is he? Then I hope he will bite some others of my generals.

George II, king of Great Britain and Ireland, to the Duke of Newcastle in 1758, when the duke objected to the appointment of James Wolfe to command the expedition against Quebec. Quoted by Francis Parkman in *Montcalm and Wolfe* (1884) who observed: "Appointments made for merit, and not through routine and patronage, shocked the Duke of Newcastle, to whom a man like Wolfe was a hopeless enigma; and he told George II that Pitt's new general was mad." See also the Duke of Newcastle.

## George V
The whole Empire will rejoice at the news of yesterday's successful operations. Canada will be proud that the taking of the coveted Vimy Ridge has fallen to the lot of her troops. I heartily congratulate you and all who have taken part in this splendid achievement. GEORGE R.I.

Vimy Ridge was taken by Canadian troops on April 9, 1917, the casualties numbering 13,477. *The Canada Year Book, 1936* (1936).

## George VI
I would end with a social word of greeting to those of my listeners who are young. It is true—and I deplore it deeply —that the skies are overcast in more than one quarter at the present time. Do not on that account lose heart. Life is a great adventure and every one of you can be a pioneer, blazing by thought and service a trail to better things. [Address at Government House, Winnipeg, May 24, 1939]

*

The more balconies, the better.

"Indeed, balconies meant an opportunity for more people to see their Sovereigns," explained Gustave Lanctot in *The Royal Tour of King George VI and Queen Elizabeth in Canada and the United States of America 1939* (1964). See also Grey Owl and Gerry McGeer.

## George, Chief Dan
When the white man came we had the land and they had the bibles; now they have the land and we have the bibles.

Quoted by Gerald Walsh in *Indians in Transition: An Inquiry Approach* (1971).

I am a Chief, but my power to make war is gone, and the only weapon left to me is my speech. It is only with tongue and speech that I can fight my people's war. . . . You call me Chief and you do well for so I am. The blood of chieftains flows in my veins. I am a chief but you may ask where are my warriors, their feathered heads, their painted faces. I am a chief but my quiver has no arrows and my bow is slack.

*

Oh God! Like the Thunderbird of old I shall rise again out of the sea; I shall grab the instruments of the white man's success—his education, his skills, and with these new tools I shall build my race into the proudest segment of your society. Before I follow the great Chiefs who have gone before us, oh Canada, I shall see these things come to pass.

Chief Dan George, chief of the Coast Salish, recited "A Lament for Confederation" before a crowd of thirty-two thousand in Vancouver's Empire Stadium, July 1, 1967. *Profile of a Nation: Canadian Themes and Styles* (1969), edited by Alan Dawe.

I do not take credit for playing the part of an Indian chief because I *was* an Indian chief for twelve years.

Chief Dan received the New York Critics' Award for the best supporting actor of 1970 for his part in *Little Big Man*. Quoted by Sid Adilman, *The Toronto Telegram*, January 22, 1971.

I was born in an age that loved the things of nature and gave them beautiful names like Tes-wall-u-wit instead of dried-up names like Stanley Park.

"My Very Good Dear Friends. . . ." *The Only Good Indian: Essays by Canadian Indians* (1970), edited by Waubageshig (Harvey McCue).

## George, David Lloyd
See Lloyd George, David.

## Gérin-Lajoie, Antoine
Un Canadien errant,
Banni de ses foyers,

Parcourait en pleurant
Des pays étrangers.

Un jour, triste et pensif,
Assis au bord des flots,
Au courant fugitif
Il adressa ces mots:

"Si tu vois mon pays,
Mon pays malheureux,
Va, dis à mes amis
Que je me souviens d'eux.

"O jours si pleins d'appas,
Vous êtes disparus,
Et ma patrie, hélas!
Je ne la verrai plus.

"Non, mais en expirant,
O mon cher Canada,
Mon regard languissant
Vers toi se portera."

"Un Canadien errant: 1838," a lament for those who fled or were exiled for taking part in the Rebellion of 1837, was written a few years after the event by Antoine Gérin-Lajoie and has remained popular ever since. The text comes from A.J.M. Smith's *The Oxford Book of Canadian Verse in English and French* (1960). Here is the translation called "The Canadian Exile" by the journalist and versifier, John Boyd, from *Canadian Poetry in English* (Revised and Enlarged Edition, 1954), edited by Bliss Carman, Lorne Pierce and V.B. Rhodenizer:

Weeping sorely as he journeyed / Over many a foreign strand, / A Canadian exile wandered, / Banished from his native land.

Sad and pensive, sitting lonely, / By a rushing river's shore, / To the flowing waters spake he / Words that fondest memories bore:

"If you see my own dear country— / Most unhappy is its lot— / Say to all my friends, O river, / That they never are forgot.

"Oh! those days so full of gladness, / Now forever are they o'er, / And alas! my own dear country, / I shall never see it more.

"No, dear Canada, O my homeland! / But upon my dying day, / Fondly shall my last look wander / To thee, beloved, far away."

## Gesner, Abraham

It is in vain to suppose that a free trade system will be beneficial to a new and struggling colony, which has nothing to export but raw materials; it is rather calculated to enrich an old commonwealth, whose people by their skill and labour make such raw materials valuable, and then return them for consumption. The result of the system alluded to has been that the suppliers of the raw material at last become hewers of wood and drawers of water to the manufacturers.

The scientist who devised a method of producing kerosene in Halifax in 1846 was a critic of reciprocity. *The Industrial Resources of Nova Scotia* (1849).

## Gibbon, John Murray

The use of the word "mosaic" in connection with the Canadian people was used for the first time, so far as I know, by an American writer, Victoria Hayward, who used to come every summer to Canada with her friend, Edith Watson, to write about and photograph the country folk, both in the East and in the West. These two collaborated on a book, published in 1922. . . .

*Canadian Mosaic: The Making of a Northern Nation* (1938). For the book in question, see Victoria Hayward. For the concept of the mosaic, see John Porter.

## Gibson, Arthur

The most imperative need of our world is not for more and more speaking, subtler and subtler enunciations. It is for more, much more, *listening*. I am persuaded that listening is indicative of a much greater personal serenity of conviction than stormy and discourteous refusal to allow a divergent opinion to be expressed.

*The Faith of the Atheist* (1968).

## Gibson, James

Team Canada probably did more to create a Canadian identity by defeating Russia by four games to three than did ten years of Canada Council fellowships.

President of Brock University to the

Ontario Committee on Economic and Cultural Nationalism, February 20, 1973.

## Giguère, Roland
And yet, a single night of universal love could save everything.

From "Polar Seasons," a poem translated by F.R. Scott and published in his *Selected Poems* (1966).

## Gilbert, Sir Humphrey
We are as near to heaven by sea as by land!

This is among the most famous of all "last lines," and was uttered by Sir Humphrey Gilbert to his crew on board the *Squirrel* when the ten-ton frigate encountered rough weather and icebergs near the Azores, nine hundred miles from Cape Race, Newfoundland, on September 9, 1583. The *Squirrel* sank without a trace; the words of consolation were overheard by the crew on board the *Golden Hinde*, the *Squirrel's* companion ship. Gilbert was last observed sitting towards the stern with a book in his hands, repeatedly calling out, "We are as near to heaven by sea as by land!"

Gilbert was returning to England where he was to have informed Queen Elizabeth that, on August 5, 1583, he had claimed Newfoundland as England's first colony. Gilbert was the step-brother of Sir Walter Raleigh and the author of *A Discourse of a Discovery for a New Passage to Cataia* (1576) which influenced Martin Frobisher.

Gilbert may have uttered these lines but he did not originate them. The book he was holding in his hands might well have been Sir Thomas More's *Utopia* (1516) in which this sentence may be found: "He that hath no grave is covered with the sky: and, the way to heaven out of all places is of like length and distance." Even earlier, Eleanor of Castile was so eager to accompany her husband Edward I on his crusade in 1270, that she argued: "The way to Heaven is as near in the Holy Land (if not nearer) as in England or Spain." The sentiment has even been ascribed to Pythagoras, but in the popular mind it will remain associated with Gilbert,

thanks perhaps to Henry Wadsworth Longfellow's poem, which dates from the 1840s:

> He sat upon the deck,
> The Book was in his hand;
> "Do not fear! Heaven is as near,"
> He said, "by water as by land."

When the storm abated, the words from the Burial at Sea were read by the captain of the *Golden Hinde*: "In the midst of life we are in death." Curious in this context are the sentiments expressed by Gilbert in a letter he sent to Richard Hakluyt from St. John's, Newfoundland, and quoted by Samuel Eliot Morison in *The European Discovery of America: The Northern Voyages A.D. 500-1600* (1971): "I see nothing but solitude. Inexhaustible supply of fish."

## Gillis, Clairie
Instead of the government taking over industry when the war broke out, industry took over the government.

CCF M.P. for Cape Breton, *Steelworker and Miner*, April 12, 1941. Quoted by David A. Frank, et al., *The People's History of Cape Breton* (1971).

## Gillis, James P.
I was twice in the United States; I do not say so for the sake of boast.

Author's note to *The Cape Breton Giant: A Truthful Memoir* (1898). This is an inadvertently amusing biography of Angus MacAskill, the giant, by James P. Gillis, the teacher.

## Gilmour, Clyde
Cultists say it's old hat to have anything with a beginning, middle, and end. But you know something? Life does.

Quoted by Paul King in "The Agony and Ecstasy of Being a Critic," *Toronto Life*, July, 1971.

He came, he saw, he concurred.

"The Max Ferguson Show," CBC Radio, February 11, 1972.

## Gimbel, Norman
Once I was alone, / So, lonely and then, you came out of nowhere, like the sun up

from the hills. / A weekend in Canada, a change of scene, was the most I'd bargained for. / And then I discovered you and in your eyes I found a love I couldn't ignore.

> From "Canadian Sunset" (1956), lyrics by Norman Gimbel, music by Eddie Heywood. *500 Songs that Made the All-Time Hit Parade* (1964), edited by Lyle Kenyon Engel.

## Gimby, Bobby

CA-NA-DA—We love Thee—
(One little two little three little Canadians)
CA-NA-DA—Proud and Free—
(Now we are Twenty Million)
North, South, East, West,
(Four little five little six little Provinces)
There'll be Happy Times,
(Now we are ten and the Territories Sea to Sea)
Church Bells will Ring, Ring Ring—
(Un petit deux petits trois Canadiens)
It's the Hundredth Anniversary of Confederation,
(Maintenant nos sommes Vingt Millions)
Everybody Sing, Together
(Quatre petites cinq petites six petites Provinces)
CA-NA-DA—Notre pays—
(Et nous sommes dix plus les Territoires Longue vie)
CA-NA-DA—Longue vie.
Hur-rah, Vive le Ca-na-da!
Three cheers, Hip, Hip, Hoo-ray!
Le Centenaire! That's the order of the day.
Frère Jacques, Frère Jacques,
Merrily we roll along
Together, all the way.

> "Canada: A Centennial Song," nicknamed "CA-NA-DA," was the song hit of the Centennial. Bobby Gimby, the West Coast composer and bandleader, wrote the catchy words and tune for *Preview '67*, a feature film produced by the Centennial Commission early in 1966, and crossed and recrossed the country performing it with his band for the next year and a half.
> "There had been no original intention of selecting a popular Centennial song," wrote Judy LaMarsh in *Bird in a*

*Gilded Cage* (1969), "but when 'CA-NA-DA' was put forward, it proved to be so bright and sparkly it was quickly accepted. It was the only thing associated with the Centennial Commission, so far as I am aware, that was not chosen by a committee after a contest."

## Gingras, Dr. Gustave

The key to successful rehabilitation isn't the doctor's skill but the patient's will.

> Quoted by David MacDonald in "The Gift for Inspiring Hope," *In Search of Canada* (1971), by the editors of *Reader's Digest*.

## Gisborne, Frederick Newton

Europe and America are united by telegraphy. Glory to God in the Highest, on earth peace, goodwill toward men.

> First message sent from Trinity Bay, Newfoundland, to Valentia, Ireland, upon the successful laying of the trans-Atlantic submarine cable by Gisborne, August 5, 1858. Quoted by John Quinpool in *First Things in Acadia: The Birthplace of a Continent* (1936).

## Givens, Philip

A government member must vote like a wooden soldier.

> Attributed to the former mayor of Toronto and Liberal member of Parliament from 1968 to 1972.

## Gladstone, James

I'll talk only when I have something important to say. I intend to learn a lot as I go along. [On his appointment to the Senate in 1958]

*

If we had one language among us instead of twenty, we'd have to make those invaders learn our language instead of us learning theirs. [On his eightieth birthday in 1967, commenting on divisions among his people]

> The first treaty Indian to be appointed to the Senate, quoted by J.W. Grant MacEwan in *Portraits from the Plains* (1971).

## Gladstone, William Ewart

I say we cannot lead the destinies of

Canada for good against the errors of our friends.

> By "friends" the future prime minister of Great Britain understood "ministers." Diary entry, June 9, 1840. Quoted by Paul Knaplund in "Extracts from Gladstone's Private Political Diary Touching Canadian Questions in 1840," *Canadian Historical Review*, June, 1939.

One of the most weighty questions I have ever discussed.

> Letter to the Duke of Argyle, May 20, 1865, concerning Confederation. Quoted by W.L. Morton in *The Critical Years: The Union of British North America 1857-1873* (1964).

The objection to a trading company under such circumstances applied with ten-fold force to the Hudson's Bay Company. There never was a case in which the evils of monopoly acquired a more rank development than in the instance of that Company. In the case of the Hudson's Bay Company the monopoly of land and trade was aggravated by absolutism in politics covered by the cloak of impenetrable secrecy.

\*

What was the object which a fur-trading company had in view? Could it be their wish that the country in which they carried on their operations should be reclaimed and cultivated? On the contrary, it must be kept like a desert. They must, to be sure, cultivate a few spots in order to obtain corn for the support of their cattle and their agents—but as respected the country at large, their interest required that it should be kept just as nature had left it.

> When he made this speech in the British House of Commons, August 18, 1848, Gladstone was not yet the leader of the Liberal party.

**Glassco, John**
But I was not, to use the theological phrase, *receptive*. The great obstacle to the influx of grace was my own perfect happiness, and it is well known that God takes no thought for the happy, any more than He does for birds or puppies, perhaps realizing they have no need of Him and mercifully letting them alone.

> *Memoirs of Montparnasse* (1970).

**Glover, Elwood**
Imagine! I've had thirty-five years in the most precarious profession in the world (show business), doing things I love. How lucky can you get?

> Quoted by Jack Miller in *Star Week*, February 17, 1973.

**Glover, Guy**
No individuals, no foundations, no institutions have provided money for creative film-making in this country *with no strings attached*.

> "Film," *The Arts in Canada: A Stock-Taking at Mid-Century* (1958), edited by Malcolm Ross.

**Glyn, Elinor**
It is in the elevation of all mankind to the rank of princes and princesses in a fairy kingdom, and not in the abolition of such romantic ideals, and the degradation of all classes to the level of the sordid, that I still see the future happiness of the world.

> *Romantic Adventure: Being the Autobiography of Elinor Glyn* (1936). The woman who popularized "It" in Hollywood during the twenties was born in England but raised near Guelph, Ontario.

It! Don't you see, that one syllable expresses everything—all the difference there is between people. You either have It or you haven't.

\*

There are few people in the world who possess "It." The only ones in Hollywood who do are Rex the wild stallion star, Spanish actor Tony Moreno, the Ambassador Hotel doorman, and Clara Bow.

\*

To define a man: he must be a creature who makes me feel that I am a woman.

\*

Whatever will bring in the most money will happen.

## Godbout, Jacques

Today, Quebeckers are not free. They live behind the wheels of modern automobiles but under a mediaeval law. *When in our society a person can be born, married, have children, or adopt them, avail himself of social services and of the law, provide his sons and daughters with schooling and employment, then die,* WITHOUT THE COMPULSORY INTERVENTION OF THE CHURCH, *freedom of conscience for believers as well as non-believers will be respected.*

Until then, because the presence of the Church is *compulsory* at every level of civil life, the citizen of Quebec is colonized much more deeply by the grip of Rome than by American dollars.

We demand *a Quebec that is secular* because that is the first step on the road to *a Quebec that is free.*

*Le Mouvement du 8 avril* (1966).

What if Canada were a country in the plural? A country where each ethnic group and every culture could have the autonomy to dream its own dreams?

At least five civilizations are already taking shape on Canadian soil. Of these Quebec is the most in evidence, Ontario the most advanced, the Maritimes the most desperate, the Far North of the greatest concern, and the West the newest.

Ten years from now each one of these civilizations will have acquired an autonomy that will be essential to it in a situation of even greater independence than that which exists today.

"Five Civilizations," *The Toronto Star*, December 30, 1972, translated by Christine Roberts. See also Lucia dos Santos.

## Godbout, Joseph-Adélard

Notre maître, l'avenir.

Godbout, twice premier of Quebec during the 1930s and 1940s, punned on Lionel Groulx's *"Notre maître, le passe"* ("Our master, the past") with his own *"Notre maître, l'avenir"* ("Our master, the future"). See also Canon Lionel Groulx.

I undertake, on my honour, carefully weighing every one of my words, to quit my party and even turn against it, if between now and the end of hostilities in Europe a single French Canadian is mobilized against his will under a Liberal government or even under a provisional government in which ministers presently in Mackenzie King's cabinet might be serving.

Quebec Liberal leader, October, 1939. "I write this text practically from memory from having quoted it so often from 1942 to 1945. One day it would put an end to the career of a politician and to a ministry that deserved better of destiny." André Laurendeau in "The Conscription Crisis, 1942," *André Laurendeau: Witness for Quebec* (1973), translated by Philip Stratford. In January of 1942, Godbout made this widely quoted anti-conscription remark:

If I were under the impression that conscription was the last way to win the war, I would be for conscription.

## Godfrey, Dave

Man *deserves* man, and on our present course that is exactly what he will receive: such crowding of territories as can only result in war and famine. Man *requires* something more than man, some structure within our single technological world that can batter and destroy the problems rather than eradicate man himself. The chances of this arriving are somewhat slimmer than the chances for famine and the sword. The need for this arriving is the great need of our times.

"Doomsday Idealism," *Man Deserves Man: CUSO in Developing Countries* (1968), edited by Bill McWhinney and Dave Godfrey.

Ancestors are the process by which gods get made.

Quoted by Donald Cameron in *Conversations with Canadian Novelists* (1973).

## Godin, Gérald

French is an ideal for the future—slang is the present, without losing sight of the future.

Quoted by Jean Basile in "Literature in French" in *The Canadians 1867-1967*

(1967), edited by J.M.S. Careless and R. Craig Brown.

## Godsell, Jean Walker
I was no lady . . . I followed the call of the wild.

> Title of a book published in 1959 with the subtitle "The Autobiography of a Fur Trader's Wife," by the wife of the Arctic trader Philip Henry Godsell.

## Goebbels, Joseph
I also inspected a bombed-out hospital in Luetzow Street. Several corpses were just being carried out—a touching picture. One of the nurses killed was an air-raid warden. It drives one mad to think that any old Canadian boor, who probably can't even find Europe on the globe, flies to Europe from his super-rich country which his people don't know how to exploit, and here bombards a continent with a crowded population. But let's hope we can soon deliver the proper reply. . . .

> February-March, 1943, *The Goebbels Diaries: 1942-43* (1948), edited and translated by Louis P. Lochner.

## Golden, Aubrey E.   See Ron Haggart.

## Goldenberg, H. Carl
People are inclined to judge a dispute in terms of "right" and "wrong": the fact is that generally neither side is wholly right or wholly wrong.

> "Facing Facts in Labour Relations" (1962), *Empire Club of Canada: Addresses 1962-63* (1963).

## Goldman, Emma
I have never called for the police, but the police have often called for me.

> Reply to friends who advised the anarchist to request police protection for her first Montreal lecture, *The Montreal Star*, October 29, 1926. Quoted by Richard Drinnon in *Rebel in Paradise: A Biography of Emma Goldman* (1961).

Both Catholic and Anglican hold the city by the throat, and mould the habits and opinions of the people of Toronto. No book or lecture can have any success that does not have the stamp of approval of the churches. Perhaps you will understand the whole situation when I tell you that the librarian of the public library . . . declared: "No, we do not censor books, we simply do not get them." He certainly spoke the truth.

> Letter to Ben Capes, January 27, 1928. Quoted by Richard Drinnon in *Rebel in Paradise: A Biography of Emma Goldman* (1961).

The expense of travel in Canada and the great distances between the larger cities decided me to go no farther than Edmonton, Alberta. Winnipeg nearly became my Waterloo. The city was extremely cold and in the throes of a grippe epidemic, to which I succumbed in the first twenty-four hours.

> *

The Public and University libraries in Toronto were lacking in modern works on the social, education, and psychologic problems occupying the best minds. "We do not buy books we consider immoral," a local librarian was reported as saying.

> *Living My Life* (1931).

I'd much rather have roses on my table than diamonds on my neck.

> Quoted by Frederick Griffin in *Variety Show: Twenty Years of Watching the News Parade* (1936). The noted anarchist Emma Goldman died in Toronto on May 14, 1940, and was buried in Chicago.

## Goldsmith, Oliver
Have we not seen, round Britain's peopled shore,
Her useful sons exchang'd for useless ore?

> *

Beheld the duteous son, the sire decay'd,
The modest matron, and the blushing maid,
Forc'd from their homes, a melancholy train,
To traverse climes beyond the western main;
Where wild Oswego spreads her swamps around,
And Niagara stuns with thund'ring sound?

*The Traveller; or, A Prospect of Society* (1764). *The Complete Poetical Works of Oliver Goldsmith* (1906), edited by Austin Dobson.

## Goldsmith, Oliver
Here, nails and blankets, side by side, are seen,
There, horses' collars, and a large tureen;
Buttons and tumblers, fish-hooks, aprons and knives,
Shawls for young damsels, flannel for old wives;
Woolcards and stockings, hats for men and boys,
Mill-saws and fenders, silks and children's toys;
All useful things, and joined with many more,
Compose the well-assorted country store.

*The Rising Village: A Poem* (1825). This Oliver Goldsmith, born in New Brunswick, was the grand-nephew of the Irish poet whom Dr. Samuel Johnson praised.

## Golovin, Ivan
The Canadian side of the fall [at Niagara] is nearly twice as large as the American, the waters of both intermingle only far below. Thus the two rival nations must come at least to an understanding; but will it be for the best or the worst of mankind?

Letter written by the Russian traveller and author, August, 1855, *Stars and Stripes, or American Impressions* (1856).

## Gomez, Avelino
You have to be lucky to be good, but you have to be good to be lucky.

Popular jockey, born in Cuba.

## Gompers, Samuel
Men of Canada, fight on, carry on, and victory will be yours and ours, for the whole world and for the generations yet unborn.

"American Labour and the War," April 27, 1918, *Addresses Delivered before the Canadian Club of Ottawa: 1918-19* (1919). Gompers was president of the American Federation of Labour.

## Goodis, Jerry
We care about the shape you're in.

*

At Speedy you're a somebody.

*

We won't hurry our beer.

*

Get your head into Hush Puppies.

Advertising slogans for Wonder Bra, Speedy Muffler King, Formosa Spring Brewery, Hush Puppies, "created" by Jerry Goodis.

If there is an unresolvable conflict between the communication needs of business and the communication needs of Canadians, guess who's going to have to move over? My stakes are in advertising and in capitalism as well as in Canada. I'd like to see a solution found that suits all parties.

*Have I Ever Lied to You Before?* (1972).

## Gordon, Charles W.
A man to see far must climb to some height.

*Black Rock: A Tale of the Selkirks* (1898).

It is a fine thing to have a country to be made, and it is fine to be a man and have a part in the making of it.

*The Foreigner* (1909).

Men women & things
    as I met them
    as they came to me
    as they touched me

Notes made by Charles W. Gordon who wrote under the pen name of Ralph Connor. Quoted by J. King Gordon in his introduction to his father's *Postscript to Adventure: The Autobiography of Ralph Connor* (1938). Out of these phrases grew Gordon's four-hundred-page autobiography.

## Gordon, Crawford
My job here is to organize, deputize and supervise.

President of Avro Canada, when the contract for the CF-100 was cancelled. Quoted by J.W. Bacque in *Saturday Night*, May 22, 1954.

## Gordon, Donald

The formula for happiness or misery stated by Charles Dickens through the mouth of the inimitable Micawber is as true of a railway as it is of an individual. Revenue simply must exceed expense or misery follows. Without the profit margin there is little incentive to efficiency and no yardstick of its achievement.

"Railway Highlights" (1954), *Empire Club of Canada: Addresses 1954-55* (1955).

I treat each new situation with spontaneous ingenuity.

*

Gentlemen, where I come from, a black-hearted bastard is a term of endearment.

*

Nobody ever did anything by pussy-footing.

Controversial CNR president, quoted by Peter C. Newman in *Flame of Power: Intimate Profiles of Canada's Greatest Businessmen* (1959).

## Gordon, Donald R.

A shouted "Hit him!" in a dark alley in downtown New York at 2:00 A.M. conveys a very different kind of communication from the same shout in Maple Leaf Gardens in Toronto at 8:30 P.M. on a Saturday night.

*The New Literacy* (1971).

## Gordon, Huntley K.

We have our own expressions and names for the features of the countryside ("bush" is as poetic as "grove") and above all we have a characteristic spirit. We must learn to use and purify them, and develop a native tradition, or die to literature.

"Canadian Poetry," *The Canadian Forum*, March, 1921.

## Gordon, Margaret Elizabeth

Genius will render you great. May virtue render you beloved! Remove the awful distance between yourself and ordinary men by kind and gentle manners . . . I give you not my address, because I dare not promise to see you.

Charlottetown-born Margaret Gordon was raised in Kirkcaldy, Scotland, where in 1816 at the age of eighteen she fell in love with a young gangly schoolmaster named Thomas Carlyle. When her relatives objected to the match, she wrote the above letter to Carlyle before moving to London. She eventually married Sir Alexander Bannerman, lieutenant-governor of Prince Edward Island. Was the lovely Margaret Gordon the original "Rose Goddess" Blumine of *Sartor Resartus*? See also Thomas Carlyle.

## Gordon, Pamela Anne

I think it's a marvellous thing. Not for myself, for Canada. For Canada!

To Miss Gordon goes the distinction of being the first Canadian Playmate of the Month. The Vancouver girl's figure (39-23-35) graced *Playboy*'s centrefold in March of 1962.

## Gordon, Walter L.

Canadians are much more likely to be respected in the United States if they fight for their interests and their independence, than if they give in silently and without protest every time Uncle Sam looks cross.

*A Choice for Canada: Independence or Colonial Status* (1966).

Rockefeller: You mean that we'll be coming in at our own peril?

Gordon: I wouldn't use those words, but I certainly don't think you should commit yourself to anything until you know what the rules are going to be.

This exchange occurred in the office of the minister of Finance, July 18, 1966, when Gordon warned James S. Rockefeller, chairman of Citibank, that the future growth of its subsidiary, the Mercantile Bank, would be limited. See also James S. Rockefeller.

The choice is clear. We can do the things that are necessary to regain control of our economy, and thus maintain our independence, or we can acquiesce in becoming a colonial dependency of the United States, with no future except the hope of eventual absorption.

\*

History has taught us that with economic control inevitably goes political control. That is what colonialism is all about. Indeed, it is sadly ironic that in a world torn asunder by countries who are demanding and winning their independence, our free, independent and highly developed country should be haunted by the spectre of a colonial or semi-colonial future.

> July, 1967, quoted by Kari Levitt in *Silent Surrender: The Multinational Corporation in Canada* (1970).

If you have too highly developed a sense of the ridiculous, you can't get through daily political life in Ottawa without laughing, and that's not allowed.

\*

I think in straight lines.

> Quoted by Peter C. Newman in *The Distemper of Our Times: Canadian Politics in Transition: 1963-1968* (1968).

Sooner or later this question of Canada's independence—this question of Canada's future—must be faced squarely by some Canadian government. If it is not—and soon—we can all forget about the great Canadian experiment; an experiment that could have been, and still conceivably might be, an example to our troubled world.

> Former finance minister's reaction to the Trudeau government's unwillingness to act on the Gray Report, May, 1972.

### Gotlieb, Phyllis
You don't go after poetry, you take what comes. Maybe the gods do it through me but I certainly do a hell of a lot of the work.

> Quoted by Merle Shain in *Chatelaine*, October, 1972.

### Gotlieb, Sondra
Fat people are today's lepers.

> *The Gourmet's Canada* (1972).

### Gottschalk, Louis Moreau
We are hardly ten hours in Canada, yet we have already met some specimens of that surly, conceited, egotistic type, of which only the English (fortunately) have the secret. [En route to Montreal, July 4, 1862]

\*

Everything reflects the sacristy in Quebec —dull countenances, sallow complexions, and thin women. The streets, the houses distill ennui. [Quebec City, July 6, 1862]

\*

Arrived at Ottawa. They are building a house of parliament here that, considering the narrowness of the town, and the number of deputies it is required to accommodate, gives it the appearance of Robinson Crusoe's canoe. [Ottawa, July 11, 1862]

\*

I have taken a multitude of notes on Canada. What a frightful country! It is enough to let you know that it is essentially Catholic—Irish and French (what French? Low Normans of the seventeenth century) vying with each other in fervent rage, that is, as to which shall have the most churches, sermons, monks, and of white, black, and gray nuns. [Leaving Lower Canada, May 13, 1864]

> Gottschalk, the leading virtuoso pianist of his day, was born in New Orleans and educated in France. He made these (and other) observations in his travel diary, which was translated from the French by Robert E. Peterson and published in 1881. *Notes of a Pianist: Louis Moreau Gottschalk* (1964), edited by Jeanne Behrend.

### Gould, Glenn
I felt very baroque.

> "The concerto happened to be the Brahms D Minor. Gould gave a very languid interpretation to this pretentious work . . . his rendition established a world's record. It lasted fifteen minutes longer than any previous playing. Afterward Irving Kolodin, the music editor of the *Saturday Review*, asked Gould why he had done it that way. He replied: 'I felt very baroque.'" Oscar Levant's *The Unimportance of Being Oscar* (1968).

The habit of concert-going and concert-giving, both as a social institution and as chief symbol of musical mercantilism, will be . . . dormant in the twenty-first century.

> Quoted by Richard Kostelanetz in "The Glenn Gould Variations," *Master Minds* (1969). Reprinted by William Kilbourn in *Canada: A Guide to the Peaceable Kingdom* (1970).

We have no Sibeliuses around. We have nobody identifiable with the soil in that way. We have no Canadian artists as Canadians.

\*

I don't like live concerts because people come for the wrong reasons.

> Quoted by Alfred Bester in "The Zany Genius of Glenn Gould," *Holiday*, April, 1964.

Q. Why did you make the decision to retire from the concert circuit?
A. Well, I'm not essentially a public person. I don't like performing in front of audiences. As a matter of fact, I don't even approve of concerts and I never go to them. I feel they are dying.

> Quoted by Betty Lee in *The Globe and Mail*, December 1, 1965.

### Gould, Mona
This was my brother
At Dieppe,
Quietly a hero
Who gave his life
Like a gift,
Withholding nothing.

\*

That's what he did at Dieppe;
He was needed.
And even death must have been a little ashamed
At his eagerness!

> "This Was My Brother," *Tasting the Earth* (1943).

### Goulet, Robert
But what I'd really love to do is play Errol Flynn roles. I've seen all his movies, and I think he was a gas in all of them. What a guy! A real man's man! A dare-devil! Yes, boobie, that's the man I'd like to be—Errol Flynn.

> Quoted by Frank Rasky in *The Canadian*, December 2, 1967. The nightclub entertainer was raised in Toronto and Edmonton. See also Carol Lawrence.

### Gourlay, Robert Fleming
When I was first shut up in jail, a man confined there was employed making Indian brooms. I asked him to teach me to make these, and said I should advertise my brooms for *sweeping the province*. The joke went round, and then I gave it a turn by saying, I must first provide *shovels*.

> "To the Resident Landowners of Upper Canada," an address written May 20, 1819, while in Niagara Jail. *General Introduction to Statistical Account of Upper Canada* (1822).

The fancy of giving to Canada the British constitution was a good one: about as rational as to think of cultivating sugar canes in Siberia, or to entertain hope from grafting a fruit twig on an icicle.

\*

The first question in political economy should be, can the mass of the people live comfortably under this or that arrangement? But this most necessary question was forgotten, and many of the people have perished.

> *Statistical Account of Upper Canada, Compiled with a View to a Grand System of Emigration* (1822).

Often has my declaration of 1829 been repeated, that "MAN IS A RECORDING ANIMAL," but never before, was there such happy opportunity for putting records to profitable use.

> *The Banished Briton and Neptunian* (1843-46), April 6, 1843. Quoted by Lois D. Milani in *Robert Gourlay, Gadfly: Forerunner of the Rebellion of Upper Canada, 1837* (1971).

### Gouzenko, Igor
Spies rarely look the part.

> The Ukrainian cipher clerk who defected from the Soviet Embassy, September 5, 1945, taking with him the West's

first proof of widespread Soviet espionage. Quoted by Frank Rasky in *Gay Canadian Rogues: Swindlers, Gold-Diggers and Spies* (1958).

If you, reading this book, happen to be a person of some importance, or happen to be in a position whereby your knowledge might be useful, you are undoubtedly "intimately known" in the files in Moscow.

> *This Was My Choice: Gouzenko's Story* (1948). The title of the American edition, *The Iron Curtain*, became that of the Hollywood movie, starring Dana Andrews as the Ukrainian defector, released in 1948.

Lawyer: Mr. Gouzenko, did you think perhaps there were spies in the Royal Canadian Mounted Police?
Gouzenko: [Gesturing toward Fred Rose, M.P.] Why not? You had one in the House of Parliament.

> Gouzenko was the Crown's star witness during the many trials for treason that followed his defection. See also Louis St. Laurent and Nicolai Zabotin.

### Gouzenko, Svetlana
We live a hundred times better than a commissar. We live in air that is perfumed with freedom.

> Mrs. Igor Gouzenko, quoted by Frank Rasky in *Gay Canadian Rogues: Swindlers, Gold-diggers and Spies* (1958).

### Gowan, Ogle Robert
One School, One Flag, One Language.

> Motto of the Orange Association of British America, founded in Brockville, Ontario, in 1830, by the Irish-born politician and journalist.

### Gowans, Alan
. . . you will not find in Canada much of what is commonly considered Great or Original architecture. No Parthenons, no Christopher Wrens, no Westminster Abbeys.

> Preface to *Building Canada: An Architectural History of Canadian Life* (1966). Professor Gowans does admit: "One thing is certain—there is something in

architecture generally, and Canadian architecture in particular, for everyone to enjoy."

Once objects are saved solely as Art, you may be sure that for all practical purposes they are dead.

> *The Unchanging Arts: New Forms for the Traditional Functions of Art in Society* (1971).

### Graham, Billy
I believe God has blessed and spared Canada because she has been traditionally friendly to minority groups and hospitable to people of many countries. . . . If the Maple Leaf is to wave proudly and freely over a prosperous and great Canada of the future, Canada must have a spiritual awakening from the Pacific to the Atlantic.

> *The Globe and Mail*, July 21, 1973.

### Graham, Gwethalyn
Hampered by racial-religious distinctions to start with, relations between the French, English and Jews of Montreal are still further complicated by the fact that all three groups suffer from an inferiority complex—the French because they are a minority in Canada, the English because they are a minority in Quebec, and the Jews because they are a minority elsewhere.

> *Earth and High Heaven* (1944).

### Graham, Sir Hugh
What I want to see in the *Montreal Star* is the sort of news, or item, or story or article which you would be tempted to read aloud to the person next to you if you saw it in a newspaper or book.

> Advice to John W. Dafoe, then a cub reporter on the *Star*, June, 1883. Sir Hugh founded the paper. Quoted by Murray Donnelly in *Dafoe of the Free Press* (1968). A sharpened version of the above was recalled by Grattan O'Leary in *Maclean's Magazine*, June 7, 1958: "Get news that people will read out loud to their neighbours."

### Granatstein, J.L.
Over the long run, it does not matter

how small the probability of nuclear war is per unit time. It is mathematically demonstrable that, as time goes on, this probability approaches certainty.

"A World without War?" *Visions 2020: Fifty Canadians in Search of a Future* (1970), edited by Stephen Clarkson.

## Grannan, Mary
Sometimes I don't know whether I'm in this world or a world of rabbits.

Mary Grannan wrote and broadcast the *Just Mary* and *Maggie Muggins* stories which were popular with children on CBC Radio during the forties and fifties.

## Grant, Cuthbert
You see we have had but one of our people killed, and how little quarter we have given you. Now, if Fort Douglas is not given up with all the public property instantly and without resistance, men, women and children will be put to death.

Grant's ultimatum to the settlers at Seven Oaks, June 19, 1816, as recalled by James Pritchard. Quoted by George Bryce in *The Romantic Settlement of Lord Selkirk's Colonists* (1909).

## Grant, George Monro
Some men, and all cattle, lack patriotism.

Quoted by William Lawson Grant and Frederick Hamilton in *Principal Grant* (1904).

Make us the half-way house of the Empire.

Letter to Sir Wilfrid Laurier, February 25, 1899, with specific reference to the Pacific cable project.

Those who stay at home will build up the country, and those who go abroad will save us from parochialism.

"Our National Objects and Aims," *Maple Leaves: Being the Papers Read before the National Club of Toronto, at the "National Evenings," During the Winter 1890-91* (1891).

Travel a thousand miles up a great river; more than another thousand along great lakes and a succession of smaller lakes; a thousand miles across rolling prairies; and another thousand through woods and over three great ranges of mountains, and you have travelled from Ocean to Ocean through Canada. All this Country is a single Colony of the British Empire; and this Colony is dreaming magnificent dreams of a future when it shall be the "Greater Britain," and the highway across which the fabrics and products of Asia shall be carried, to the Eastern as well as the Western sides of the Atlantic.

\*

But the greater part of the mainland is, "a sea of mountains"; and the Province will have to depend mainly on its rich grazing resources, its valuable timber, its fisheries, and minerals, for any large increase of population. [An early use of the phrase "a sea of mountains" in reference to British Columbia]

\*

We shall be more than an American Russia, because the separation from Great Britain to which he invites us is not involved in our manifest destiny.

*Ocean to Ocean: Sandford Fleming's Expedition through Canada in 1872* (1873). The first selection is part of the celebrated opening of this influential work by George Monro Grant (sometimes referred to as Principal Grant of Queen's) who was the father of William Lawson Grant and the grandfather of George P. Grant.

"And it came to pass, that the beggar died—"

Principal Grant suggested this for his epitaph. (The verse, Luke 16:22, continues: "And was carried by the angels into Abraham's bosom.") Noted by Robertson Davies in *Great Canadians: A Century of Achievement* (1965).

Get it done more quickly.

Said to be Principal Grant's last words on his deathbed, May 10, 1902. Quoted by P.B. Waite in "Across the Rockies," *Canada: An Historical Magazine*, Autumn, 1973.

## Grant, George P.
North America is the first continent called to bring human excellence to birth

throughout the whole range of technological society.

> "An Ethic of Community," *Social Purpose for Canada* (1961), edited by Michael Oliver.

To think of the U.S. is to think of ourselves—almost.

\*

The old platitude must be repeated once again: the United States is the society with the least history prior to the age of progress.

\*

The forlorn hope of Canada once was that from earlier European traditions, British and French, we would maintain moral roots which would allow us to deal more deeply with existence.

> "From Roosevelt to L.B.J." in *The New Romans: Candid Canadian Opinions of the U.S.* (1968), edited by Al Purdy.

When a man truly despairs, he does not write; he commits suicide.

\*

Modern civilization makes all local cultures anachronistic. Where modern science has achieved its mastery, there is no place for local cultures.

\*

The impossibility of conservatism in our era is the impossibility of Canada. As Canadians we attempted a ridiculous task in trying to build a conservative nation in the age of progress, on a continent we share with the most dynamic nation on earth.

> *Lament for a Nation: The Defeat of Canadian Nationalism* (1965).

Today, the British tradition means that Mr. E.P. Taylor, who has given his life to integrating this country into the capitalist empire, still in the 1970s finds it impossible to pronounce the words "Kentucky Derby" in the proper American fashion.

> Introduction to the Carleton Library Edition (1970), *Lament for a Nation: The Defeat of Canadian Nationalism* (1965).

When truth in science seems to teach us that we are accidental inhabitants of a negligible planet in the endless spaces, men are forced to seek meaning in other ways than through the intellect. If truth leads to meaninglessness, then men in their thirst for meaning turn to art. To hope to find in the products of the imagination that meaning which has been cast out of the intellect may, in the light of Socrates, be known to be a fruitless quest. Nevertheless, it is a thirst which is the enemy of tyranny. ["The University Curriculum"]

\*

Canada's survival has always required the victory of political courage over immediate and individual economic advantage. ["Canadian Fate and Imperialism"]

\*

Only in listening for the intimations of deprival can we live critically in the dynamo. ["A Platitude"]

What is so endearing about the young French Canadians revolting against their tradition is that they sometimes write as if Voltaire's *Candide* had come off the press last week instead of two hundred years ago. ["Canadian Fate and Imperialism"]

> *Technology and Empire: Perspectives on North America* (1969). The author, a professor of Religion at McMaster University, is the son of William Lawson Grant and the grandson of George Monro Grant. He is a leading spokesman for conservatism. See also F.H. Underhill.

## Grant, Maggie

E.P. Taylor—Pale Tory

> An anagram run in her column in *The Canadian Magazine*, September 2, 1972.

There are other facets to fascinate me, but as that dear old teacher of mine used to say, "One need not detail each feather to describe a goose."

> *The Many Lives of Maggie Grant* (1964).

## Grant, William Lawson

The retreat of the ice left Canada much in its present condition except for certain post-glacial changes of level which seem to be still in progress.

"Canada," *The Encyclopaedia Britannica* (Eleventh Edition, 1910-11), Volume V.

When I lived in England, one heard of a certain type of ladies who lived in some parts of London under the protection of certain gentlemen. Theirs was a profession considered to be more lucrative than honourable, and I have no desire that this country of mine should be either the kept woman of the United States, or the harlot of the Empire.

"The Fallacy of Nationalism" (1912), *Empire Club of Canada: Addresses Delivered to the Members During the Session of 1911-12* (1913). William Lawson Grant was headmaster of Upper Canada College.

## Granville-Barker, Harley
The drama is in a happy position in Canada. It has such strong supporters!

The British director, adjudicating the Dominion Drama Festival, Ottawa, April, 1936. The audience included the governor general, the prime minister, the leader of the Opposition and several M.P.s. Quoted by Betty Lee in *Love and Whisky: The Story of the Dominion Drama Festival* (1973).

## Gray, Charles F.
When this thing is over the British flag will still be on the City Hall, and not the Red flag!

The mayor of Winnipeg's address to anti-strike veterans, Winnipeg City Hall, June 4, 1919. *Winnipeg 1919: The Strikers' Own History of the Winnipeg General Strike* (1973), edited by Norman Penner.

Any foreigners who make any threats of any kind or in any way intimidate or worry would-be workers in the slightest degree can expect immediate deportation to Russia or wherever they come from. We intend to purge the city of any lawless element and prosecute to the full rigor of the law.

Controversial clause in the Riot Act as read in Winnipeg on June 23, 1919, by Mayor Charles F. Gray. Reproduced in *The Manitoba Free Press*, June 23, 1919.

## Gray, Herb
The so-called multi-national enterprises are really national enterprises with multi-national operations.

\*

Foreign direct investment can act as a transmission belt for the entry of foreign laws into Canada. It can bring cultural influences which may or may not be desirable. Foreign direct investment could also create difficulties in the formation of both domestic and foreign policy for Canada's image abroad.

"The Gray Report," *Foreign Direct Investment in Canada* (1972).

If you want to be on the ninety-fifth floor, with global horizons, you must go to New York; the highest one can go in Canada is the fifty-fourth floor.

Attributed to the Liberal cabinet minister in 1972, when the tallest building in the country, with fifty-four floors, was the Toronto-Dominion Centre.

## Gray, Hugh
I do not mean to say that they are without the reasoning faculty, but they certainly appear excessively stupid. I understand that their numbers decrease each year,—if they were wholly extinct, I do not think that human nation would be a great sufferer by it. [About the Indian population]

·*Letters from Canada, Written During a Residence There in the Years 1806, 1807, and 1808* (1809).

## Gray, James
When the Depression came, our world stopped and we got off.

Quoted by Barry Broadfoot in *Ten Lost Years 1929-1939: Memoirs of Canadians Who Survived the Depression* (1973).

## Gray, Thomas
The boast of heraldry, the pomp of
    power,
And all that beauty, all that wealth
    e'er gave,
Await alike th' inevitable hour:
    The paths of glory lead but to the
    grave.

"Elegy, Written in a Country Churchyard" was composed by the British poet in 1749 while recovering from the death of a favourite aunt. Gray is buried at Stroke Poges, the very "country churchyard" he immortalized.

As one of Gray's editors noted: "General Wolfe, the night before the glorious victory of Quebec, said of it to his fellow-soldiers, 'Gentlemen, I would rather be the author of that poem than take Quebec.' Its popularity has never waned, and it may possibly live as long as the language it adorns." See also James Wolfe.

## Grealis, Walt
The Juno.

The top award of the Canadian recording industry was nicknamed the "Juno" after the Roman goddess of heaven and Pierre Juneau, chairman of the Canadian Radio-Television Commission. Approximately two dozen Junos have been awarded annually since 1969 by *RPM Magazine*, founded by Walt Grealis, to "honour outstanding Canadian artists and industry figures." The award itself, formally known as the RPM Annual Gold Leaf Award, comes in the form of an elongated metronome, eighteen inches high, of solid walnut adorned with gold plate.

## Greeley, Horace
When the experiment of the "dominion" shall have failed—as fail it must—a process of peaceful absorption will give Canada her proper place in the great North American Republic.

*The New York Tribune*, May 10, 1867. Quoted by P.B. Waite in *The Life and Times of Confederation: 1864-1867* (1962). This is the same Greeley who in 1859 said, "Go West, young man, go West."

## Greeley, Horace
I'M OFF TO THE LAST ROUND-UP

The nephew of the famous New York editor, who counselled his generation to "Go West, young man, go West," instead went Northwest and became a rancher on the prairies and then a member of

Parliament. In his will he requested that a fieldstone inscribed with the above words mark his grave. Gordon Johnston's *It Happened in Canada* (1971).

## Green, Billy
I grabbed his gun with one hand and put my sword to him with the other.

News that the Americans were advancing on Stoney Creek was carried to Lieutenant-Colonel Sir John Harvey by Billy Green, a nineteen-year-old United Empire Loyalist. "Billy the Scout" single-handedly disarmed the sentry who shot at him, and was instrumental in routing the American forces at the Battle of Stoney Creek, June 5, 1813. Quoted by Paul Gresco in *The Canadian Magazine*, May 4, 1972.

## Green, Howard    See C.D. Howe.

## Greenaway, Roy
To become a newspaperman you need the hide of a dinosaur, the stamina of a Chinese coolie, the wakefulness and persistence of a mosquito, the analytic powers of a detective and the digging capacity of a steam shovel.

*The News Game* (1966).

## Greenberg, Clement
Nothing in Canadian landscape painting contributes to the "mainstream," exactly; nothing in it amounts, that is, to major art. But this hardly dilutes my pleasure in its freshness and authenticity, or makes it less valuable. Least of all does it justify condescension. In praising it I make no allowances whatsoever.

"Clement Greenberg's View of Art on the Prairies," *Canadian Art*, March-April, 1963.

## Greene, J.J.
Canada needs hewers of water and haulers of wood.

Attributed to cabinet minister Joe Greene at the Liberal leadership convention, Ottawa, April 5, 1968.

There is a malaise that exists in your land—what appears to many as the sudden and tragic disappearance of the

American dream which, in some ways, has turned to nightmare.

\*

Vietnam and Cambodia; disorder in the streets and on the campus; the disaffection of the poor; the coloured people, and youth—these indicate to many of our people, particularly our young, that we should not seek to make the American dream ours. This faltering will have been part of the cause for the new Canadian determination for a separate identity.

Liberal Energy minister's address in Denver, Colorado, May, 1970. Quoted by Charles Lynch in *Weekend Magazine*, January 15, 1972.

**Greene, Lorne**
Those were the great times of Andrew Allan and Fletcher Markle. The literate days.

\*

I once swore I'd make this Ben Cartwright so important, so necessary, so alive, that they'd never get rid of him.

The CBC-trained actor first appeared in *Bonanza* in 1960. *The Toronto Star*, April 2, 1966.

I don't like to use the word alien. I like to use the word friend. We have such a marvelous interplay between Canada and the United States.

Quoted by Judy Klemesrud in *The New York Times*, October 8, 1972. The Ottawa-born TV personality was asked why "as a resident alien" he was so passionate about U.S. politics.

**Greene, Margaret Lawrence**
Morley Callaghan has two short stories in the July issue of *Scribner's*. That sentence is very important. If I were to write it in a diary, with the date, and the diary were put away for a hundred years, and if, at the end of those years, some historian should come upon my diary and find that sentence, he would, likely as not, be much pleased. Which does not mean that one states prematurely that Morley Callaghan is an immortal. But only that in such a way was he discovered in Canada. . . .

Editorial, *Saturday Night*, July, 1928.

**Greene, Nancy**
Doesn't everyone expect to win?

The British Columbia skier won an Olympic gold medal at Grenoble in 1968 and has been called the best woman racer in the world. Quoted by Rod McKuen in *The Will to Win* (1971).

**Greenglass, Dr. Esther**
Women take it for granted that it's a splendid achievement to have a sparkling toilet bowl.

Quoted by Carroll Allen in *Homemaker's Digest*, May-June, 1972.

**Greenough, William Parker**
The caribou seems to have no idea whatever of personal comfort.

\*

Oh, no, it is not always winter in Canada.

\*

Pope Pius IX was once reported to have said that the French Canadians were the most submissive in matters of faith of any Catholics in the world; but that on some other matters they brought more questions before him than others. These disputes probably related to jurisdiction and the like between the higher clergy, or to quarrels of a more or less secular character between priests and people.

*Canadian Folk-Life and Folk-Lore* (1897).

**Grégoire, Dr. Jean**
It was not healthy to resist the orders of Mr. Duplessis.

This remark was made by the deputy minister of Health in the Union Nationale government after the premier's death in 1959. Quoted by Leslie Roberts in *The Chief: A Political Biography of Maurice Duplessis* (1963).

**Gregory, Aline**
A woman's place is in the House . . . of Commons.

Campaign motto of an independent candidate in the general election of 1972 who was not elected.

**Gregory, Dick**
A lot of people tell me: "We just have a small racial problem in Canada." What I

want to know is how do you say that a woman is a little bit pregnant? I think the acid test to the problem here in Canada will be if every white person would go to bed and imagine waking up tomorrow morning black. I think then they would be aware that there are problems.

*Scan*, November, 1965.

There is absolutely no bias in Vancouver. I know because I just had dinner with your Negro.

Quoted by Jay and Audrey Walz in *Portrait of Canada* (1970).

**Grenfell, Sir Wilfred**
Life is like Labrador, a Labourer's Land.
*
It is courage the world needs, not infallibility . . . courage is always the surest wisdom.
*
The real value of your life can only be gauged by what it gives to the world. Life is redeemed by achievement. All its fun is in doing things.
*
The service we render to others is really the rent we pay for our room on this earth.
*
Which turkey did Scrooge enjoy more—the one he could have eaten alone, or the one Tiny Tim ate and he paid for?
*
Life is undeniably worth living if it is a field of honour. It is not life that is the failure; it is the pessimist.
*
This life is either a tragedy ending in death or a field of honour beginning our real life.

*A Labrador Logbook* (1938). The final aphorism was quoted by J. Lennox Kerr in *Wilfred Grenfell: His Life and Work* (1959). "What the name of Schweitzer meant in the 1950s, the name Grenfell meant forty years earlier." Harold Horwood in *Newfoundland* (1969). See also Anonymous: Select Epitaphs.

**Grey, Earl**
I cannot go, I have no message for you yet.

Upon his appointment as governor general, December 10, 1904, Earl Grey declined an invitation to address the Canadian Club of Toronto.

It is only a question of time before you, the people of Canada, become, because of your numbers, if you remain united, high-souled, public-spirited and incorruptible, the most powerful factor, not only in the British Empire, but in the English-speaking world.

*

When the grown Canada shakes the world with his strength, will it be for evil or for good? The answer to that question depends upon yourselves—upon you, the young men of the Canadian Club, who have it in your power to shape for good or for evil the character of your country.

Address, November 26, 1906, *Addresses Delivered before the Canadian Club of Toronto: Season 1906-1907* (1907).

What has Confederation done for Canada? What has Confederation not done for Canada?

"Fifth Annual Banquet," April 21, 1909, *Addresses Delivered before the Canadian Club of Ottawa: 1903-09* (1910).

I want you boys to remember what Empire Day means. Empire Day is the festival on which every British subject should reverently remember that the British Empire stands out before the whole world as the fearless champion of freedom, fair play and equal rights; that its watchwords are responsibility, duty, sympathy and self-sacrifice; and that a special responsibility rests with you individually to be true to the traditions and to the mission of your race.

Address to Toronto school cadets, *The Globe*, May 22, 1909. Quoted by Robert M. Stamp in "Empire Day in the Schools of Ontario" in *Journal of Canadian Studies*, August, 1973.

For nearly five years I have, quite conscious of my constitutional limitations, walked the tight-rope of platitudinous generalities and I am not aware of having made any serious slip.

Winnipeg address, October 13, 1909. Quoted by R. MacGregor Dawson in *The Government of Canada* (1952).

## The Earl Grey Trophy. The Grey Cup.

Albert, fourth Earl of Grey, governor general of Canada from 1904 to 1911, established the Earl Grey Music and Dramatic Trophy Competition in 1907; two years later he presented the country with the Grey Cup for amateur rugby football.

## Grey Owl

I have been often asked what my work consists of. It begins to be rather ambiguous, I think. It is this . . . I want to arouse in Canadian people a sense of responsibility, the great responsibility they have for that north country and its inhabitants, human and animal.

\*

I have been asked where I got the power to stand and do that confidently and talk to people. It is not me at all. I have behind me that immense north country, I have the power of it standing behind me, greater than you or I. I am only the screen for the picture I wish to show. I am the mouthpiece. I have the unlimited experience of those of my people behind me, besides my own life experience.

"A Plea for the Canadian Northland" (1936), *Empire Club of Canada: Addresses Delivered to the Members During the Year 1936-37* (1937).

Give me a good canoe, a pair of Jibway snowshoes, my beaver, my family and ten thousand square miles of wilderness and I am happy.

Quoted by Hugh Eayrs in his foreword to *Pilgrims of the Wild* (1935).

Goodbye, brother, I'll be seeing you.

"They talked for about ten minutes; then the King held out his hand to say goodbye. Grey Owl took it, and moved by what I thought at the time was native simplicity but which I see now to have been a daring improvisation, he clapped the King on the shoulder, and said, 'Goodbye, brother, I'll be seeing you.'" An audience with King George VI, Buckingham Palace, 1937. Grey Owl was

an Englishman, born Archibald Belaney, but this was discovered only after his death. Lovat Dickson's *The House of Words* (1963). See also Anahareo.

## Grier, Eldon

As a poet I need to experience ecstasy. (English poetry never went crazy, a Frenchman said.
It was not a compliment.)

"An Ecstasy," *Selected Poems 1955-1970* (1971).

## Grierson, John

I like to think that subconscious Canada is even more important than conscious Canada and that there is growing up swiftly in this country, under the surface, the sense of a great future and of a great separate destiny—as Canada. ["The Nature of Propaganda"]

*Grierson on Documentary* (1946), edited by Forsyth Hardy.

What is truth isn't a nasty question at all —it's a question that forever is with you when you're a filmmaker. It's to make your truth as many-faceted and as deep, as various, as exciting as possible that you are an artist.

*McGill Reporter*, February 24, 1969.

Art is not a mirror but a hammer.

\*

TV is an instrument of domestic ease.

\*

All things are beautiful as long as you get them in the proper order.

\*

Make peace as exciting as war.

\*

The real internationalism is the manias we have with each other.

\*

Growing points.

John Grierson founded the National Film Board, the world's largest government film unit, in 1939. He was usually credited with being the first to use the term "documentary" in connection with non-fictional films.

## Griffin, Frederick

Every person, I found, had a story, often of an unexpected turn; this hope made newspaper work a quest of which I never tired.

*Variety Show: Twenty Years of Watching the News Parade* (1936).

## Griffin, Harold

In 458 A.D. a group of Buddhist priests travelled to a country they called Fu Sang, 30,000 li (12,000 miles) to the east of China, which stretched 10,000 li (4,000 miles) to another ocean. In 499 A.D., Hoei Shin, the last of them, returned to China and related his story to the court historian. Whether Hoei Shin actually visited what is now British Columbia is a long-disputed point, but his account of the natives and their customs, particularly their use of the bark of a giant tree for textiles and their extraction of oil from a fish which could only be the oolichan, suggests that he may have.

*British Columbia: The People's Early Story* (1958). See also Hoei Shin.

## Griffin, J.D.

The ordinary man in the street, if he were asked what mental illness is like, would very likely think first of the fascinating portrayal of Boris Karloff or a similar character actor in a picture about some supposedly insane or maniacal individual who sent chills up and down the spines of the audience as he went about committing homicide with fiendish glee and cynical laughter. Or he would recall hearing a radio program in which the crazed heroine shrieks as she throws herself from the tenth-story window. [1947]

\*

A great many people know a great deal about mental illness and mental health. Unfortunately, a great deal of what they know is not true. [1953]

\*

We must remember that no one, not even the psychiatrist or the psychiatric clinical team, cures the patient. In effect, the patient must cure himself. [1959]

\*

Every time I try to define a perfectly stable person, I am appalled by the dullness of that person. [1971]

Dr. Griffin was general director of the Canadian Mental Health Association from 1951 to 1971. *Let Just Praise Be Given: A Book of Tribute to John Douglas Morecroft Griffin* (1971).

## Griffith, D.W.

I wonder how important the motion pictures are? I sometimes think they are vastly more important than anyone has dreamed.

"Movies and Friendship," December 14, 1925, *Addresses Delivered before the Canadian Club of Toronto: Season of 1925-26* (1926).

You in Canada should not be dependent either on the United States or on Great Britain. You should have your own films and exchange them with those of other countries. You can make them just as well in Toronto as in New York City.

Interview with the pioneer movie director, *The Toronto Star*, December 15, 1925.

## Gromyko, Andrei

Greece is a sort of American vassal; the Netherlands is the country of American bases that grow like tulip bulbs; Cuba is the main sugar plantation of the American monopolies; Turkey is prepared to kow-tow before any United States proconsul and Canada is the boring second fiddle in the American symphony.

The Soviet delegate to the United Nations, quoted in *The New York Herald Tribune*, June 30, 1953.

## Groseilliers, Sieur des

"Radishes and Gooseberries"

Sobriquets given by young history students to two seventeenth-century French explorers, Médard Chouart, Sieur des Groseilliers, and Pierre-Esprit Radisson. (Groseilliers came by his nickname legitimately, for his name is French for "gooseberries"; but Radisson does not translate "radishes.") See also Pierre-Esprit Radisson.

## Grossman, Irving

People don't really want mechanical order and precision. They want richness, variety, interest for the eye and a human scale. They don't want to feel overwhelmed.

The imaginative architect, quoted by Arnold Rockman in *The Toronto Star*, November 23, 1964.

## Groulx, Canon Lionel
Notre maître, le passé.

"Our master, the past" could be said to be the personal maxim of Abbé Lionel Groulx, the influential priest and historian who taught history at the University of Montreal until his retirement in 1948. The maxim, which was the slogan of the Association de la Jeunesse, a religious-nationalist group headed by Groulx in the 1910s, was the general title of three volumes of Groulx's writings published between 1924 and 1944. "Je me souviens" (I remember) is the motto of the Province of Quebec; "Notre maître, le passé" applies to all of French Canada.

Our Master, the Past, that is to say, the past, master of the future.

"*L'originalité de notre histoire*," Centenaire de l'histoire du Canada de François-Xavier Garneau (1945). See also Joseph-Adélard Godbout.

Alas! What would the Fathers of Confederation say if they reappeared in our midst? Their descendants have taken less than fifty years to sabotage their great achievement. This work of destruction is now almost complete and our legacy to history will be one of the most striking examples of the dismal bankruptcies that often await federal unions.

"*Ce cinquantenaire*," *Action française*, July, 1917.

To survive one must first live.

*

The "revenge of the cradle" should naturally lead to thinking about "the protection of the cradle."

*

There are so many among us who turn through vanity and ambition towards the stronger side, towards an opulence which they mistake for elegance. Even if it were only to protect these weaklings, Ladies and Gentlemen, let us make it *chic* to be French Canadian.

*

It is thus a supremely important task our artists and writers have of retaining a distinct French life and soul and of daily increasing its power. How we must strengthen our young race, that solitary isle buffeted by the waves of the encircling Protestant and [Anglo-] Saxon sea!

*

One of these days we shall find ourselves speaking the horrible jargon of Torontonians: from that day Quebec and Toronto will speak the same language and will understand each other.

"*Pour L'Action française*," address before the Monument National, Montreal, April 10, 1918, *Dix ans d'Action française* (1926). Reproduced by Susan Mann Trofimenkoff in *Abbé Groulx: Variations on a Nationalist Theme* (1973).

O Commander of the old Fort of Ville-Marie, it is time you were among us! We have such pressing need of a young leader like you, a leader of men. Look, on the frontier where you fell a barbarous throng as menacing as the old threatens our French soul. The work we must now undertake is one of total reconstruction and restoration. Arise, Dollard, and live on your granite pedestal. Summon us, with your virile charm, with a hero's accents. We lift toward you our hands quivering like palm leaves, ardent with ambition to serve. Together we shall work for the reconstruction of our family's house. And should you command it, O Dollard, O powerful leader, we are ready to follow you to the supreme holocaust for the defence of our French tongue and our Catholic faith.

"*Si Dollard revenait*," address at the Monument National, Montreal, January 31, 1919, *Dix ans d'Action française* (1926). "If Dollard Were Alive Today," *French-Canadian Nationalism: An Anthology* (1969), edited by Ramsay Cook.

Without any paradox, I would say boldly that history is the most living of things and that there is nothing so present as the past.

*

We carry in our very bones the mind and marrow of our forbears. No, a nation cannot separate itself from its past any more than a river can separate itself from its source, or sap from the soil whence it arises. No generation is self-sufficient. It can and does happen that a generation forgets its history, or turns its back upon it; such an act is a betrayal of History.

*

Because there is God, because there is our history, because there is our youth, I still have hope. I share my hope with all our ancestors who never despaired, and with all those of our people who do not despair today; and this hope rises above my own time, above all discouragement. Whether one likes it or not, we *shall* have our French state: we shall have a young, strong, beautiful, radiant home, a spiritual, dynamic centre for the whole of French America.

*"L'histoire, gardienne des traditions vivantes,"* address before the Second French Language Congress, Quebec City, June 29, 1937, *Directives* (1959). Reproduced by Susan Mann Trofimenkoff in *Abbé Groulx: Variations on a Nationalist Theme* (1973).

Everything which is French comes to us from France, but everything which comes to us from France is not always French.

*Dix ans d'Action française* (1926).

By history, which maintains the continuity between the generations, which carries from one to the other, like a river, the accumulated flood of virtues of the race, a people remains in constant and present possession of its moral richness.

*Soirées de l'Action française* (1926), edited by A. Perrault, Abbé Lionel Groulx, R.P.J.-Papin Archambault. Quoted by Mason Wade in *The French Canadians: 1760-1967* (1968).

Laurentia

"Abbé Groulx became and remained the idol of the ultranationalists. It is clear that at heart he believed in 'Laurentia,' a separate French and Catholic state, rather than in Canada; and although he was cautious about expressing this view openly, once, at the Second Congress of the French Language at Quebec in 1937, he came so close to advocating it on the radio that he was cut off the air." Mason Wade in *The*

*French-Canadian Outlook: A Brief Account of the Unknown North Americans* (1946).

This French State is due us, and we shall have it.

Statement made in 1937, quoted by Mason Wade in *The French Canadians: 1760-1967* (1968).

Can our brothers in the minority groups really believe that they would be worse off for the establishment of an autonomous French State, a true centre of culture which would radiate life and vigour?

*

We belong to that little group of people . . . destined on the earth for a special role, the tragic role. Their anxiety is not the question of whether they will be prosperous or unfortunate tomorrow, great or small, but whether they will exist at all, whether they will rise to salute the day or retire into nothingness.

*Directives* (1937).

Ce petit peuple.

"He spoke of what he called a 'race,' which was becoming in the vocabulary of that period, a 'nationality,' and is today a nation. But the expression which came most spontaneously to his lips was ce petit peuple, 'this tiny people,' the object of his love, his anxieties, his hope." André Laurendeau, *Le Devoir*, May 24, 1967.

**Grove, Frederick Philip**
Imaginative literature is not primarily concerned with facts; it is concerned with truth. It sees fact only within the web of life, coloured and made vital by what followed. ["Author's Note to the Fourth Edition"]

*

In Europe the poor man is tolerated if he can look upon a great past; in America, if he looks to a future.

*

Was Lincoln an accident? Was there in this America a soil from which he had grown? I had not found it. If there was, to find it should be the task of my life.

*A Search for America: The Odyssey of an Immigrant* (1927).

A work of art . . . must have a beginning and an end and something of an infinitude between the two. ["The Happy Ending"]

\*

What we need is dreamers who will stop and listen into themselves instead of mirroring the insane scrambling which goes on about us; who will go into the wilderness to discover new continents, not in an unexplored or undiscovered ocean, but in the human heart and soul. I have a haunting suspicion that that is the only corner left in this world where undiscovered continents are still abounding. Let us find worlds within the world to which we have not yet reacted. ["The Value of Art"]

*It Needs to be Said* (1929).

I entered his office a farm hand in overalls, and since he was not a tailor I left his office in overalls, but principal of a high school.

You are applauding, gentlemen, but you are applauding the apostasy of my life. [Grove was interviewed by the deputy minister of Education in 1912 and permitted to teach in Manitoba without a licence]

\*

Along our own shores and along the shores of Greenland I have seen shapeless mounds erected by Norsemen driven across the sea by hunger. Erected what for? Well, as a wordless protest against death and the cessation of things, and as an expression of their own desire for some small measure of immortality right here on earth.

"Canada—The Spiritual Awakening of an Individual," April 2, 1928, *Addresses Delivered before the Canadian Club of Toronto: Season of 1927-28* (1928).

Let me add one more thing. In their eyes [those of the men and women of the Canadian West], as they read or speak, I have found a thing which I have never found in the eyes of European peasants. I don't know what it is; a new hopefulness perhaps. I don't know whence it comes; but it must be bred by something peculiar to Canada; whether, as some have asserted, that something be the wider spaces of our plains, the greater height of our mountains, the vaster extent of our indented shore-lines or what. I have sometimes thought that perhaps it arises from the fact that here they stand on soil which they can own; for I take it to be a desire still inherent in man as borne of woman to own that bit of land whence, with tentative mind, he reaches out into the dark mysteries that surround us.

"Nationhood within the Empire," *Empire Club of Canada: Addresses Delivered to the Members During the Year 1929* (1930).

We have a book-shelf reaching from Halifax to Victoria; and on it stands one single book, written by a Frenchman transient in Canada. That, in sober fact, is the situation; and to me it is appalling; for a book is a book only when it is read; otherwise it is a bundle of gathered sheets of soiled paper. [The book is Hémon's *Maria Chapdelaine*]

\*

Under the avalanche of manuscripts the sorrowful conviction was forced upon me, that in my youthful innocence—I was not yet sixty—I had been mistaken all the while: the chief industry of Canada was not agriculture; it was writing; six out of its eight million English-speaking citizens dreamed of literary fame.

\*

The Canadian public is ignorant, cowardly, and snobbish; it is mortally afraid of ideas and considers the discussion of first principles as a betrayal of bad manners.

\*

To how many people in Canada are books the daily companions they ought to be? Shall we say five hundred? Or is that too flattering. I mean, of course, outside of educational institutions.

\*

More appallingly, Canadians are at bottom not interested in their own country; I honestly believe they prefer to read about dukes and lords, or about the civil war in the United States. They are supposed to be born explorers; but they have not yet heard that the human heart and soul are perhaps the only corners of this universe where unexplored and undiscovered continents are still abounding.

This lack of mental aliveness is fundamental. Canada is a non-conductor for any sort of intellectual current.

> "The Plight of Canadian Fiction? A Reply," *University of Toronto Quarterly*, July, 1938.

The lack of an audience? But even the lack of an audience is not the important thing. The important thing is that *you* have such an audience *in mind* when you speak. Whether it is really there does not matter. In case of need you can imagine it.

> *In Search of Myself* (1946).

### Guay, Joseph Albert
Will it hurt? Will I still be conscious when my neck breaks? You do die instantaneously, don't you?

> To kill his wife, the Quebec City jeweller planted a bomb on board a Canadian Pacific DC-3 which exploded in mid-air on September 9, 1949, killing twenty-three people. He asked these questions of the prison doctor before his execution. Quoted by Roger Lemelin in "My Friend Guay, the Murderer" in *Maclean's Canada: Portrait of a Country* (1960), edited by Leslie F. Hannon. Lemelin, who knew Guay personally, maintains he never proclaimed: "I die famous."

### Guedella, Philip
. . . as I travelled eastward across this great Dominion, the one thing that is of tremendously good augury for the unshakable future is the fortitude with which its hardy settlers endure the brutalities of public speaking. This appears to be the one region of the world in which audiences hurl themselves, breasts forward, to the spikes of advancing speakers and ask for more!

> "The Past and the Present" (1933), *Empire Club of Canada: Addresses Delivered to the Members During the Year 1933-34* (1934).

### Guest, Edgar A.
From pole to pole the wildfowl have spread Jack Miner's fame. / The youngest goose in Canada by now has learned his name.

> A couplet by the American versifier from "Jack Miner's Fame," quoted by Miner in *Wild Goose Jack* (1969). Guest felt "Jack Miner is the best-loved Christian in America." See also Jack Miner.

### Guibord, Joseph
Let us do and let our deeds cast long shadows . . . let us remake the soul of our people, let us throw ourselves into the future. I ask of life only one thing, use me.

> Ascribed to Guibord by Herman Buller in *Quebec in Revolt: The Guibord Affair* (1965). The Quebec Church refused to bury the freethinker in consecrated ground. See Bishop Ignace Bourget.

### Guild, Leo
We have been led to believe that Canada is a land of fur trappers, lumbermen and Northwest Mounted Police, but according to statistics Canadians spend a great deal of their time on the telephone. If you were in Canada you would average 250 calls a year. Germany comes in second per capita, the United States third.

> *You Bet Your Life* (1946). The paperback edition by "the Wizard of Odds" is called *What Are the Odds* (1949).

### Guinness, Alec
But there is one person to whom we must pay special tribute. A man of so great genius and such profound humility that we are apt to overlook him. I ask you to rise with me and pay tribute to the man who more than any other has been responsible for the success of the Festival and who belongs to us all—Will Shakespeare.

> When the house lights came up to mark the end of the last performance of *Richard III*, the British actor Alec Guinness stepped out on the makeshift stage of the Stratford Shakespearean Festival, still in costume, and paid tributes to Tom Patterson, Tyrone Guthrie and the other prime movers, and concluded with the above tribute, September, 1953.

### Gunther, John  See John E. Kennedy.

### Gustafson, Ralph
In Europe, you can't move without going

down into history. / Here, all is a beginning.

From "In the Yukon," *Selected Poems* (1972).

We are commonplace. We are falling apart. We have customs barriers that will keep an Ontario chicken from laying a Quebec egg.

*Maclean's Magazine*, March, 1972.

## Guthrie, Tyrone

This trip gave me a glimpse of Canada, an impression of its immensity and diversity, and the chance to meet many kind and congenial people who have become lifelong friends. I left Canada thrilled with what I had seen, eager to return and to be somehow, at some time and in some place, a participant in the adventure of developing this land with its vast possibilities, so many of them still dormant, still undreamed—the romance of Canada.

The Irish director's first visit to Canada was in 1929 to direct a series of live radio broadcasts called "The Romance of Canada." As a bonus, the CNR arranged a trip from Montreal to Prince Rupert and back. *A Life in the Theatre* (1959).

Canada is likely in a surprisingly few years to be the richest and most powerful country in the world. There is a great sentimental urge for Canada to be influenced by Great Britain. There is a great practical urge to be influenced by the United States. Almost every commonsense argument based on geography and economics drives Canada and the U.S. into each other's arms. If we, the British, are as stupid, as tactless and as apathetic about this as we look like being, it's just going to be George III and the Boston Tea Party all over again with disastrous results all round. We—you and I—have in this project an exceedingly conspicuous and therefore potentially useful gesture in favour of Anglo-Canadian co-operation. I have never before felt so convinced of the obvious practical value of anything I have been asked to be connected with.

Guthrie's undated letter to Tom Patterson, who earlier that year, 1952, had proposed establishing the Stratford Shakespearean Festival. The letter convinced Alec Guinness to star in the first season's productions. Quoted by Pierre Berton in "Entrepreneur," *Adventures of a Columnist* (1960).

While we may agree that it is impossible to define what is, or is not, distinctively Canadian, and while we may hope that the theatre in Canada may not develop in too isolationist a manner, yet we must remember that what a creative artist needs almost more than anything else is an attachment to a particular environment, usually that in which he was brought up as a child. Again and again one sees in the work of the greatest artists how their strength is derived from geographical roots. . . . It is important, therefore, that Canadians should be able to express their own environment, not only for the artists themselves, not only for the community now, but for posterity.

Letter written from Ireland to Dora Mavor Moore, May 11, 1952, after encouraging Tom Patterson to proceed with his theatre plans. *The Toronto Star*, May 17, 1971.

I don't know how far it may be possible to interpret a classical play in a distinctively Canadian way. I am not even sure that there is a distinctively Canadian way of doing anything. I am not even sure, despite innumerable legends in support of the idea, that there is a distinctively British, French, Jewish or Chinese way of doing anything.

\*

I can only testify that the ugliest, most raucous and unattractive speaking I have heard in Canada has come from the lips, not of roughnecked, horny-handed sons of toil, but from nicely-come-home, expensively educated, sophisticated ladies in Westmount and Rosedale. It was speech, which, as an expert, I would declare to be thoroughly bad in every important respect. Nevertheless it was perfectly acceptable in a Society which was evidently exclusive.

"A Long View of the Stratford Festival," *Twice Have the Trumpets Sounded: A*

*Record of the Stratford Shakespearean Festival in Canada 1954* (1954), by Tyrone Guthrie, Robertson Davies, and Grant Macdonald.

The emotion aroused by even a half-decent performance of great tragedy cannot be measured in terms of chewed hankies and misted specs. The full impact of great tragedy is not immediate; it takes effect slowly. It lies in wait on the fringe of dreams. It wakes one with a start in the small hours. It can shake the confident and strengthen the weak, stop the clock, roll back the seas. It can give a new meaning to life, and an old meaning to death.

"The Production of *King Oedipus*," *Thrice the Brinded Cat Hath Mew'd: A Record of the Stratford Shakespearean Festival in Canada 1955* (1955), by Robertson Davies, Tyrone Guthrie, Boyd Neel, and Tanya Moiseiwitsch.

## Guthrie, Woody

This land is your land, this land is my land,
From Bona Vista to Vancouver Island,
From the Arctic Islands to the Great Lakes waters;
This land was made for you and me.

The refrain of "This Land Is Your Land" in the Canadian version, an adaptation by Martin Bochner for the Travellers which dates from the late 1950s. The original by Woody Guthrie dates from 1956 and runs: "From California to the New York Island, / From the redwood forest to the Gulfstream waters." There are British, Australian and Spanish versions, not to mention the American one popularized by Pete Seeger.

"One phrase rankled: 'From the Arctic Circle to the Great Lakes waters.' Is there nothing north of 60? Where are Dangerous Dan McGrew and Sam McGee? What were Franklin, Davis and McClure doing trying to open the Northwest Passage? If our folksong northern boundary is to be the Arctic Circle, why is the Government messing around with resource exploitation and research?

"A phrase which would scan equally well would be 'From the northern ocean. . . .' Since we claim sovereignty right up to the Pole, I'm inclined to suggest it should be 'From the Polar ice cap to the Great Lakes waters,' except that I feel a good many soft southerners might not feel that land was 'made for you and me.'" Norman DePoe in *The Globe and Mail*, May 5, 1972.

For "Something to Sing About," see Oscar Brand.

## Guyart, Marie

See Marie de l'Incarnation.

## Gwyn, Richard J.

The common denominator of most scandals is simple enough: someone who should know better is caught doing something stupid.

*The Shape of Scandal: A Study of a Government in Crisis* (1965).

If God, as the saying goes, gave Labrador to Cain, then He must have had Joey Smallwood in mind when He made it.

Gwyn continues: "Another version of the familiar aphorism is: 'God made the world in six days, and on the seventh, sailed inshore and hurled rocks at Labrador.'" *Smallwood: The Unlikely Revolutionary* (1968).

## Gyles, John

"Sold! To a Frenchman!" I could say no more, went into the woods alone and wept till I could scarce see or stand. The word *sold*, and that to a people of that persuasion which my dear mother so much detested and in her last words manifested so great fears of my falling into—these thoughts almost broke my heart.

After six years of Indian captivity, the eighteen-year-old lad was sold to a French seigneur living near the St. John River. *Memoirs of Odd Adventures, Strange Deliverances, etc., in the Captivity of John Gyles, Esq.* (1736).

## Gzowski, Peter

Growing up means never having to say you're perfect.

Writer and host of "This Country in the Morning," CBC Radio, October, 1972.

# H

## Haggard, H. Rider

Keep the people on your rich bounteous land, and ample will be your reward in the future. If you do that this great Dominion of Canada will be the most glorious and enduring link in the girdle of empire which the genius and the might of Britain has fastened round the world.

"Address," April 2, 1905, *Addresses Delivered before the Canadian Club of Toronto: Session 1904-1905* (1905).

Here they give my name to a towering Alp; in Norfolk they would not bestow it upon the smallest pightle.

A "pightle" is a small field or enclosure. The author of *She* wrote this in Calgary in July of 1916 when he learned that Sir Rider, a mountain, and Haggard Glacier had been named in his honour. Quoted by Lilias Rider Haggard in *The Cloak That I Left* (1951).

## Haggart, Ron

Neither the War Measures regulations nor the Public Order Act would improve the investigative quality of the Montreal or the Quebec police forces. Neither act could put more men on the case and neither act would motivate the kidnappers to free their victims. The regulation had, however, one real effect. It created the FLQ as an entity. This was probably the first terrorist organization in legal history to be incorporated by a special act of Parliament.

*Rumours of War* (1971), by Ron Haggart and Aubrey E. Golden.

## Haig-Brown, Roderick

A river is never quite silent; it can never, of its very nature, be quite still; it is never quite the same from one day to the next. It has its own life and its own beauty and the creatures it nourishes are alive and beautiful also. Perhaps fishing is for me only an excuse to be near rivers. If so, I'm glad I thought of it.

*A River Never Sleeps* (1950).

The first almighty fact about British Columbia is mountains.

"With Its Face to the West," *The Face of Canada* (1959).

## Hailey, Arthur

I follow the principle that it is unnecessary to invent, except in a minor way. Much more effective is to dig, dig, and keep on digging, around the general subject matter previously decided on.

\*

Despite the current fad for amateur psychiatry, there are still a reassuring number of citizens whose mental health is excellent, and it seems only fair to give them equal time.

\*

Therefore a good ground rule is: don't leave your message showing.

*Close-Up: On Writing for Television* (1960), by the scriptwriter-turned-novelist.

## Haine, Arthur

HAINE HAINT

The Vancouver atheist ordered that the above inscription be included on his tombstone. Quoted by Robert L. Ripley in *Ripley's Believe It or Not!* (Second Series, 1934).

## Haines, Edson

With every civil right there has to be a corresponding civil obligation.

\*

Law is not justice and a trial is not a scientific inquiry into truth. A trial is the resolution of a dispute.

Judge of the Supreme Court of Ontario addressing the Ontario Psychiatric Association, Toronto, January 27, 1973. *The Toronto Star*, January 29, 1973.

## Hakluyt, Richard

For there is no doubt but that there is a straight and short way open into the West even unto Cathay. Into which kingdome, if they take their course aright, they shall gather the most noble merchandise of all the worlde, and shall make the name of Christe to be known unto many idolaterous and heathen people.

> *Divers Voyages Touching the Discovery of America* (1582). *The Original Writings and Correspondence of the Two Richard Hakluyts* (1935), edited by E.G. R. Taylor.

### Halfdanarson, Thrandr

They came out and over wide expanses, and needing cloth to dry themselves on and food, away towards Wineland, up into the ice in the uninhabited country. Evil can take away luck, so that one dies early.

> "The earliest mention of Vineland [or Wineland] is probably that on a rune stone found at Honen in Ringerike, Norway, about 1817. It has since disappeared but an unsatisfactory copy of the inscription exists. . . . The inscription is believed to be an epitaph on a young man. All it tells us is that Vineland seems to have been well known in Norway about 1050, the date assigned to the inscription," explained Tryggvi J. Oleson in *Early Voyages and Northern Approaches 1000-1632* (1963). Oleson regards as a bold conjecture the suggestion that the epitaph is that of Thrandr Halfdanarson, the nephew of King Harold Hardrada, who died in exile in Greenland. The translation of the runic inscription is by Fridtjof Nansen from his book *In Northern Mists* (1911).

### Haliburton, Robert Grant

Is the northern land which we have chosen, a congenial home for the growth of a free and a dominant race? What is the stock from which we are sprung? Who are the men of the north and what is their place in history? Can the generous flame of national spirit be kindled and blaze in the icy bosom of the frozen north?

> *

Canada then either does not signify anything, or it means *the land of nothing*. What a glorious national cognomen to select! What a destiny—to be a nation of nobodies living in a land of nothing!

> *

Let us then, should we ever become a nation, never forget the land that we live in, and the race from which we have sprung. Let us revive the grand old name of Norland, "the Land of the North"; *We are the Northmen of the New World*. We must claim the name and render ourselves worthy of it.

> Son of Thomas Chandler Haliburton and a founder of the Canada First Movement. *The Men of the North and Their Place in History: A Lecture Delivered before the Montreal Literary Club, March 31, 1869* (1869).

Most Canadian poets should be published with mild *Eau Sucrée* style of names—such as "Midnight Musings," or what is more to the point, "Nocturnal Emissions!"

> Letter to Charlie Mair, August 24, 1870, quoted by Norman Shrive in *Charles Mair: Literary Nationalist* (1965).

### Haliburton, Thomas Chandler

An owl should be their emblem, and the motto "He sleeps all the days of his life." The whole country is like this night; beautiful to look at, but silent as the grave—still as death, asleep, becalmed.

> *

The old folks say the country is too young—our time will come, and so on; and in the mean time the young folks won't wait and run off to the States, where the maxim is "youth is the time for improvement"; a new country is never too young for exertion—push on —keep moving—go ahead.

> *

Politics makes a man as crooked as a pack does a pedlar, not that they are so awful heavy, neither, but it teaches a man to stoop in the long run.

> *

. . . and beside, power has a nateral [*sic*] tendency to corpulency.

> *

. . . for when ladies wear the breeches, their petticoats ought to be long enough to hide them. . . .

*

. . . an intemperate advocate is more dangerous than an open foe.

> *The Clockmaker; or, The Sayings and Doings of Sam Slick, of Slickville* (1836).

A Tory government is the proper government for a monarchy, a suitable one for any country, but it is the only one for England.

*

Mothers can get weaned as well as babies.

*

Now, what are ceremonials but ice-houses that keep affections cold, when the blood is at a high temperature?

*

Friendship is selfishness half the time.

*

. . . and the moment a feller has a woman's secret he is that woman's master.

*

Fashion keeps the stalls, and fools are the purchasers.

> *The Attaché; or, Sam Slick in England* (1843-44).

The Nova Scotian . . . is the gentleman known throughout America as Mr. Blue Nose, a *sobriquet* acquired from a superior potato of that name, for the good qualities of which he is never tired of talking, being anxious, like most men of small property, to exhibit to the best advantage the little he had.

*

Are you going to sell your country for a sheepskin?

> *The Old Judge; or, Life in a Colony* (1849). Joseph Howe replied in 1866: "We are sold for the price of a sheepskin." Sir Clifford Sifton, minister of the Interior from 1896 to 1905, encouraged "peasants in sheepskin coats"— Ukrainians and Doukhobors mainly—to immigrate to western Canada.

The imagination has a shadow as well as the body, that keeps just a little ahead of you, or follows close behind your heels, it don't do to let it frighten you.

*

"I tell you what, President," sais I, "seein' is believin'; but it ain't them that stare the most who see the best always."

*

. . . for when a man is wrong, and won't admit it, he always gets angry.

Wherever there is authority, there is a natural inclination to disobedience.

Hope is a pleasant acquaintance, but an unsafe friend.

A feller with one idea grows rich, while he who calls him a fool dies poor.

*

A beautiful bird seldom sings.

*

Life has a chart as well as a coast, and a little care will keep you clear of rocks, reefs and sandbars.

*

The great secret of life is never to be in the way of others.

*

An artist has more than two eyes, that's a fact.

*

What a pity it is marryin' spoils courtin'.

*

Consait [conceit] grows as nateral [sic] as the hair on one's head, but is longer in comin' out.

*

Matrimony likes contrasts; friendship seeks its own counterparts.

*

To claim superiority is to attempt to pass another on the road, and compel him to take the dust.

*

Modesty is brought forward and made way for. Assumption has the door shut in its face.

*

It is easier to make money than to save it; one is exertion, the other self-denial.

*

Colonists are the pariahs of the Empire.

> *Sam Slick's Wise Saws and Modern Instances; or, What He Said, Did, or Invented* (1853).

Receivers make smugglers.

*

Tell you what, Pilot, love and skill laugh at locks, for them that can't be opened can be picked. The mechanism of the human heart, when you thoroughly understand it, is, like all the other works of nature, very beautiful, very wonderful, but very simple. When it does not work well, the fault is not in the machinery, but in the management.

\*

. . . a mocking bird has no voice of its own.

\*

I never shake the faith of an ignorant person. Suppose they do believe too much, it is safer than believing too little. You may make them give up their creed, but they ain't always quite so willing to take your's. It is easier to make an infidel than a convert.

\*

No, Sir, these provinces should be united, and they from their territorial extent, their commercial enterprise, their mineral wealth, their wonderful agricultural productions, and above all, their intelligent, industrious, and still loyal population, in time form a nation second to none on earth; until then I prefer to be a citizen of the world.

\*

Now, take these facts and see what an empire is here, surely the best in climate, soil, mineral, and other productions in the world, and peopled by such a race, as no other country under heaven can produce. No, Sir, here are *the bundle of sticks* [;] all they want is to be well united.

\*

The decencies of life, when polished, become its brightest ornaments.

*Nature and Human Nature* (1855).

The whole country is covered with snow for several months up to your hips; so that when the melancholy season comes, they say they are "hipt"; and the people are so savage, they make "slaying" parties on the ice, and call this barbarous cruel work quite a diversion.

*The Letter Bag of The Great Western; or, Life in a Steamer* (1840).

Everything has altered its dimensions, except the world we live in. The more we know of that, the smaller it seems. Time and distance have been abridged, remote countries have become accessible, and the antipodes are upon visiting terms. There is a reunion of the human race; and the family likeness, now that we begin to think alike, dress alike, and live alike, is very striking.

*The Season-Ticket* (1860).

The true patriot is one who is neither a sycophant to the government nor a tyrant to the people, but one who will manfully oppose either when they are wrong, who regards what's right, as a minister said to me, and not what is popular; who supports institutions as a whole, but is willin' to mend or repair any part that is defective.

\*

Women forgive injuries, but never forget slights.

\*

The happiness of every country depends upon the character of its people, rather than the form of its government.

\*

Books only weaken your understandin' as water does brandy.

\*

If the sea was always calm, it would poison the universe.

\*

Of all the seventeen senses, I like common sense about as well as any of 'em.

\*

You may change constitutions for ever, but you cannot change man.

\*

Old fellers always think young ones fools; but young fellers sometimes know old ones is fools.

\*

Some books are read in the parlour and some in the kitchen, but the test of a real genuine book is that it is read in both.

\*

There's no tyranny on airth equal to the tyranny of a majority.

> Attributed to the great writer and wit of Nova Scotia. See also Walter Savage Landor.

### Hall, Charles Francis

There, amid the snows of the north, under an Eskimo's hospitable roof, for the first time I shared with them in that cheering, invigorating emblem of civilization—tea!

> *Arctic Researches and Life among the Esquimaux* (1865).

Eternal Honour to the Discoverers of the North West Passage.

> The American Arctic explorer erected this inscription over an explorer's grave on the south shore of King William Island, and shortly thereafter died in the Arctic of arsenic poisoning, November 8, 1871. Quoted by Leslie H. Neatby in *In Quest of the North West Passage* (1958).

**Hall, Emmett**
A new idea is abroad which holds that the opportunity for good health is a right possessed by all and not a privilege to be enjoyed by those who can pay.

> *

The only thing more expensive than good health is inadequate or no health care; and second, the bulk of expenditures to be made on health care will be made even if there are no public programs.

> *Living and Learning: The Ontario Provincial Committee on the Aims and Objectives of Education in the Schools of Ontario* (1968). This is usually called "The Hall-Dennis Report" after its co-chairmen, E.M. Hall and L.A. Dennis.

**Hall, Francis**
York being the seat of government for the upper province, is a place of considerable importance in the eyes of its inhabitants; to a stranger, however, it presents little more than about 100 wooden houses, several of them conveniently, and even elegantly built, and I think one, or perhaps two, of brick. The public buildings were destroyed by the Americans; but as no ruins of them are visible, we must conclude, either, that the destruction exceeded the desolation of Jerusalem, or that the loss to the arts is not quite irreparable. I believe they did not leave one stone upon another, for they did not find one. Before the city, a long flat tongue of land runs into the lake, called Gibraltar Point, probably from being very *unlike* Gibraltar. York wholly

useless, either as a port, or military post, would sink into a village, and the seat of government be transferred to Kingston, but for the influence of those, whose property in the place would be depreciated by the change.

> *Travels in Canada and the United States in 1816 and 1817* (1818). The British traveller is describing Toronto after the American invasion of 1813.

**Hall, Monty**
Actually, I'm an overnight success. But it took twenty years.

> The host of the long-running ABC-TV show "Let's Make a Deal" was born Monty Halparin in Winnipeg. Quoted by Betty Lee in *The Globe and Mail*, March 6, 1971.

**Halton, Matthew**
Can you blame me if I call this fantastic? Paris is free. Paris is happy again.
This is Matthew Halton of the CBC speaking from France.

> Historic CBC Radio broadcast, August 26, 1944.

**Hambourg, Clement**
The mechanization of music has fairly killed its more sensitive possibilities . . . why listen to serious interpretations in concert halls when cheese factories and undertakers' establishments will cram your ears full of something that will do for music.

> *Saturday Night*, March, 1935.

**Hamelin, Jean**
For one French-Canadian millionaire, forty English ones appear.

> *Histoire économique du Québec 1851-1896* (1972), by Jean Hamelin and Yves Roby.

**Hamilton, Alvin**
Dalton Camp's attacks on John Diefenbaker remind me of a prairie slough at dusk; you can hear a million bullfrogs croaking there on the lily pads. You sneak up through the bullrushes and quickly grab one of them, and fifty percent of the noise is gone.

Adapted from *The Party's Over* (1971), by James Johnston.

### Hamilton, Mrs. Christopher
I had rather live in Canada, on one potato a day, than to live in the South with all the wealth they have got.

Mrs. Hamilton, a Mississippi slave, settled in London. Quoted by Benjamin Drew in *The Refugee: or the Narratives of Fugitive Slaves in Canada* (1856).

### Hamilton, Edward P.
One cannot but wonder if the French might not have held Canada if they had only been willing to drink water—certainly they would have held out longer.

*The French and Indian Wars: The Story of Battles and Forts in the Wilderness* (1962).

### Hamilton, Frank
If all the Eskimos in the North did nothing but make Ookpiks for the next twelve months, they still could not meet one quarter of the demand.

Ookpik, which in Eskimo means "happy little Arctic owl," was created by Jeannie Snowball, an Eskimo widow in her sixties living at Fort Chimo. Paging through an art magazine, Frank Hamilton, a designer for the Department of Trade and Commerce, spotted the sealskin owl. Ookpik made its first appearance at the Philadelphia Trade Fair in November of 1963 and was an instant hit. Quoted by Frank Lowe in *Weekend Magazine*, May 30, 1964. See also Jeannie Snowball.

### Hamilton, Lord Frederic
Apropos the Eskimo, I once heard a missionary describe the extraordinary difficulty he had found in translating the Bible into Eskimo. . . . "A land flowing with milk and honey" became "A land flowing with whale's blubber," and throughout the New Testament the words "Lamb of God" had to be translated "little Seal of God," as the nearest possible equivalent.

*The Days before Yesterday* (1920). Lord Hamilton was private secretary to Lord Lansdowne, governor general from 1884 to 1888.

### Hamilton, James Clelland
The Prairie Province.

This term was first used by J.C. Hamilton in his study of Manitoba entitled *The Prairie Province: Sketches of Travel from Lake Ontario to Lake Winnipeg* (1876). When Saskatchewan and Alberta were created in 1905, the term "prairie provinces" was used to refer to all three.

Hard indeed was it at once to realize the vastness of the prairie—a sea of waving grass extending from us to the Missouri —measured by miles not acres, coursed through by numerous rivers, of which the Red River of the North with its tributaries is but one, for ages the home of the red man and the bison; its soil enriched and enriching year by year with the ashes of the prairie grass; its verdant outskirts only yet touched by civilization, destined to be the happy home of millions of the Saxon race.

*The Prairie Province: Sketches of Travel from Lake Ontario to Lake Winnipeg* (1876).

### Hamilton, Robert M.
A book of quotations . . . can never be complete.

Preface, *Canadian Quotations and Phrases: Literary and Historical* (1952). This is the pioneering work in the field of Canadian quote books.

### Hammarskjold, Dag
. . . the United Nations has come to expect in its debates to hear from Canada the voice of reason and enlightenment, rejecting the extreme of partisanship, seeking patiently the common ground for men of good will, yet always standing firm upon the basic principles and purposes of our world organization.

"An Address" (1954), *Empire Club of Canada: Addresses 1953-54* (1954).

### Hammerstein II, Oscar
See Rudolf Friml.

### Hamon, Count Louis    See Cheiro.

## Hanlan, Ned
"Edward Hanlan must be pronounced the Shakespeare, the Napoleon, the Michael Angelo, the Bismarck of all oarsmen. However, he ought to wash his face before starting a race."

> This suggestion was made by the *Buffalo Courier* in 1880 when Ned Hanlan was the world's champion sculler. "The Boy in Blue" from Toronto was so superior to all challengers that during a race he would often drop his oars, dip his hands into the water, mop his brow, then speed on to an easy victory. Quoted by Henry Roxborough in *Great Days in Canadian Sport* (1957).

## Hannon, Leslie F.
. . . I submit, that although the Canadians are not a warlike people, they *are* a fighting people, none better.

> Foreword, *Canada at War* (1968).

By a curious coincidence, all the major discoverers of Canada were men whose names begin with the letter "c"—Cabot, Cartier, Champlain, Cook. By an equally unlikely chance, they were all humble men, men of the people, at a time when the leaders of most expeditions were nobles serving their kings or seeking land and riches for their private treasuries. It is destiny's subtle rejoinder that the nation which grew within these coasts is the egalitarian mirror of its discoverers, reflecting their solid strengths —and, inevitably, their limitations.

> *The Discoverers: An Illustrated History* (1971).

## Hansard, Luke
Hansard

> The official records of speeches and debates in the Canadian Parliament are unofficially known as Hansard. The formal titles are *House of Commons Debates: Official Reports* and *Debates of the Senate: Official Reports*. Luke Hansard was printer to the British House of Commons from 1774 to 1828.

## Harbach, Otto   See Rudolf Friml.

## Hardie, Keir
I assume that most of you are from the Old Country. No? Well, I'm sorry for you if you are not. The majority from Scotland? Ah, then that explains the bounding prosperity of your city and your Dominion.

> "Some Recent Political Developments in the Old Country," July 22, 1907, *Addresses Delivered before the Canadian Club of Toronto: Season of 1907-1908* (1908).

But what, gentlemen, am I to do with a gold-headed walking-stick?

> Leader of the Independent Labour Party of Great Britain, thanking the convention of the Trades and Labour Congress meeting at Halifax in 1908 for this gift. Quoted by Doris French in *Faith, Sweat and Politics: The Early Trade Union Years in Canada* (1962).

I was not long in the country before I ran up against a fact which surprised and startled me: *The English immigrant is not popular in Canada.* This remark applies in a special degree to the Londoner. Professor Mavor has an advertisement cut from a local paper asking for workmen, and which states that no English need apply. Scotsmen, Welshmen and Scandinavians are the favourites, pretty much in the order given. The reason, so far as I could make out, for this strange fact is the Englishman's inveterate habit of grumbling, and his unwillingness to adapt himself to new conditions.

> The British socialist made these remarks in the *Labour Leader*, October 4, 1907, as quoted by Basil Stewart in *The Land of the Maple Leaf; or, Canada, As I Saw It* (1908).

## Harding, Gilbert
This is the second time in the lifetime of most of us that the Germans have forced war upon the world. It is the second time that Canadians have crossed the Atlantic, leaving the fishing boats of British Columbia and Nova Scotia, the farms on the prairies, and the villages and towns of Ontario, and, if it is not the last, I think we shall all have to bear a certain amount of responsibility.

> "Postwar Treatment of Germany" (1944),

*Empire Club of Canada: Addresses Delivered to the Members During the Year 1944-45* (1945).

"The late Gilbert Harding, who was a well-known English television personality, was up in Toronto one time with the Canadian Broadcasting Corporation, and he was asked by a society hostess where he was staying in Toronto. When he told her the address, she said: 'That's not a very good address, Mr. Harding.'
" 'No,' said Gilbert Harding, 'neither is Toronto.' "

Recounted by Brendan Behan in *Brendan Behan's New York* (1964).

**Hardwicke, Sir Cedric**
The hospitality of Canada has been such that I am tempted to remember the story that was told to me yesterday of a farmer who had been chased by his bull and after he had been around the field three times with his knees almost on his chin, he turned around to the bull and said, "Well, you can please yourself but this is my last time around."

"The Theatre as a Desirable Cultural Force" (1937), *Empire Club of Canada: Addresses Delivered to the Members During the Year 1936-37* (1937).

The second day I was in Toronto I was walking down the street and I met a very old friend of mine who had been in the army with me. He said, "Good Heavens, what are you doing in Toronto?" I said, "I am acting at the theatre." He said, "Where is the theatre?" This, to me . . . was another very, very severe shock.

"The Theatre as We Know It" (1938), *Empire Club of Canada: Addresses Delivered to the Members During the Year 1938-39* (1939).

**Harlow, Alvin F.**     See B.A. Botkin.

**Harlow, Robert**
Reality is slightly tilted. The novelists in the East try to smooth it down; we tilt it up even further to see what's underneath.

Quoted by William French in *The Globe and Mail*, June 9, 1973.

**Harnum, E. John A.**
My Ministers will lay Bills before you to lower to eighteen years the statutory legal age in this Province for the making of contracts . . . to make suitable provision for children born out of wedlock under The Fatal Accidents (Lord Campbell's) Act. . . .

Speech from the throne delivered before the General Assembly of Newfoundland by the lieutenant-governor, March 22, 1971.

**Harriman, W. Averell**
I place great emphasis on the importance of close co-operation between Canada and the United States. Our point of view is much the same, unhandicapped by prejudices and hatreds. Our task of closer co-operation is not as difficult as in other parts of the world: a leadership in international co-operation should come from us.

"The American N.R.A. in Operation," *The Liberal Way: A Record of Opinion on Canadian Problems as Expressed and Discussed at the First Liberal Summer Conference, Port Hope, September, 1933* (1933).

**Harrington, Michael**
You have problems here. You have difficulties. But you have no idea how envious an American socialist is . . . I pray to God that we soon have the same problems.

The American socialist addressing the Ontario Waffle in Toronto, quoted by Geoffrey Stevens in *The Globe and Mail*, December 11, 1973.

**Harris, Elmer**
The scene of the play is an island, south of Newfoundland and northwest of Nova Scotia, jutting out into the mystery of the Atlantic, and known among the Maritime Provinces of Canada as the garden spot of the Gulf.

From the stage directions to Harris's popular three-act play *Johnny Belinda* (1940). With other New York theatre people, Harris summered at Bay Fortune, Prince Edward Island. He found his subject in nearby Digwell's Mills. The film, starring Jane Wyman as the deaf mute, was produced in 1948 and set in Cape Breton.

## Harris, Lawren

A picture can become for us a highway between a particular thing and a universal feeling.

*

The real basis and urge of the arts is divine discontent.

*

Art is a stimulus to perception, thought, awareness. This stimulus comes from the creations of men as well as from nature and other humans.

*

There is no finality, no final statement; everything remains to be re-created by every creative artist.

*

My own experience has been that art is a voice of the undying and unquenchable spirit in man.

*

When I laid in the painting, it suddenly struck me that it could express Tom Thomson, and thereafter it was Tom I had in mind—his remoteness, his genius, his reticence. ["In Memoriam to a Canadian Artist" (1950)]

> *Lawren Harris* (1969), edited by Bess Harris and R.C.P. Colgrove.

Art is the common denominator of union between men more than race, creed, history or personality. Art binds us together more than any other human activity in life.

> *Arthur Lismer: Paintings 1913-1949* (1950).

## Harris, Robert

He lived that deep ideal life,
And his rapt spirit knew
The mightiness of things unseen
And looked those shadows through.

> These lines, written by Robert Harris in 1873 as an eulogy to Fra Angelico, were chosen by the painter's wife to appear on his own tombstone in Charlottetown. Harris added immeasurably to the natural iconography with the canvas he

painted in 1884: "Meeting of the Delegates of British North America, to Settle Terms of Confederation, Quebec, October 1864" — better known as "The Fathers of Confederation." Quoted by Moncrieff Williamson in *Robert Harris 1849-1919: An Unconventional Biography* (1970).

## Harrison, Ernest

The idea that there is an élite group in charge, which is entitled to make fundamental moral decisions for the obedient remainder, is one of the maddest ideas to possess mankind, the cause of much cruelty and hardship.

> "What Has Gone Wrong?" *Probings: A Collection of Essays Contributed to the Canadian Mental Health Association for its Golden Jubilee 1918-1968* (1968).

## Harrison, Luke

We do not like the country, nor never shall. The mosquitoes are a terrible plague in this country. You may think that mosquitoes cannot hurt, but if you do you are mistaken, for they will swell your legs and hands so that some persons are both blind and lame for some days. They grow worse every year and they bite the English the worst.

> Letter to William Harrison, June 30, 1774, Fort Cumberland, Nova Scotia. Quoted by Howard Trueman in *The Chignecto Isthmus and its First Settlers* (1902).

## Harrison, Stanley

Remember him.
Somewhere in God's own space
There must be some sweet-pastured place
Where creeks sing on and tall trees grow;
Some Paradise where horses go,
For by the love which guides my pen
I know great horses live again.

> Quoted by Grant MacEwan, "Poet of the Qu'Appelle Valley: Stanley Harrison," *Fifty Mighty Men* (1958). The prairie versifier lived on, despite the loss of his favourite mare, Delia D, during the First World War. Harrison once remarked: "The story of the horse is the story of civilization."

## Harron, Don
Histry is somethin' you can't never finish, so you might jist as well git it started at the beginnin'.

> For *Spring Thaw* of 1952, actor-writer Don Harron created Charlie Farquharson, the crotchety farmer from Parry Sound. *Charlie Farquharson's History of Canada* (1972), by Don Harron.

The government is doing something about unemployment—it's creating it.

## Hartwell, Marten
You are welcome here in the camp of a cannibal.

> First words of greeting to Master Corporal Harvey Copeland who rescued the German-born flier on December 9, 1972, after Hartwell had endured thirty-two days of sub-zero weather. Copeland's reply was, "Don't worry about a thing, it's happened before." Quoted by Colin Smith in *The London Observer*, April 29, 1973.

There was no way out but to eat human flesh and this I did.

> Statement at a news conference in Edmonton, February 27, 1973, by the sole survivor of a mercy flight from Cambridge Bay to Yellowknife which crashed on November 8, 1972. Hartwell quoted from Knud Rasmussen's *Across Arctic America: A Narrative of the Fifth Thule Expedition* (1927): "Many people have eaten human flesh. But never from any desire for it, only to save their lives, and that after so much suffering that in many cases they were not fully sensible of what they did." See also David Kootook.

## Harvey, Gurzon
The public must learn to obey the laws like everyone else.

> Remark made by a Winnipeg alderman, early 1960s.

## Harvey, Sir John Martin-
After Halifax we visited New Glasgow, where I saw a name on a shop window which I had always thought the invention of a wag, "MacIsaacs."

*

The average mental attitude was probably that expressed by a well-known man I met at a club luncheon in Winnipeg, who had seen *Richard III* the night before. He had been mildly interested in the armour, weapons and ceremonial costumes and said: "I suppose you pick up these things in the towns you go to?"!! It was some time before I could put my thoughts, quite paralyzed for the moment, into words.

> The British actor-manager is writing about his Canadian tour of 1923. *The Autobiography of Sir John Martin-Harvey* (1933).

## Harvey, Rupert
I live normally in London, England. I am now in London, Ontario. The only difference I can find is that London, Ontario, is far friendlier than London, England.

> The British adjudicator of the Dominion Drama Festival at the finals in 1934, quoted by Betty Lee in *Love and Whisky: The Story of the Dominion Drama Festival* (1973).

## Harvey, Ruth
"Winnipeg!" the manager said in disbelief and derision. "How do they get there—by dog sled? What do they play in—an igloo?"

> From the famous actress' autobiography, *Curtain Time* (1949).

## Harvey, Père Vincent
It is too easy to say that Pierre Laporte was killed by a handful of terrorists. A handful of terrorists with their finger on the trigger. But who put the gun into their hands? . . . I refuse to pass judgment.

> Separatist Dominican, *Québec-Presse*, October 25, 1970. Quoted by John Saywell in *October 70: A Documentary Narrative* (1971).

## Harvison, C.W.
In one of the African countries I visited as commissioner of the Force, a very bright young African officer was detailed as my aide-de-camp. On the morning of

our first meeting, the young man, obviously trying to say the right thing, hesitated and then came out with: "Sir, I understand that you are the commissioner of the Musical Ride."

*The Horsemen* (1967).

## Haultain, Arnold
Woman is a species of which every woman is a variety.

\*

All women are rivals.

\*

A woman can say more in a sigh than a man can say in a sermon.

\*

A woman's tears are a man's terrors.

\*

The beginning, middle, and end of love is—a sigh.

\*

A man imagines he wins by strenuous assault. The woman knows the victory was due to surrender.

\*

More women are wooed for their complexions than for their characters.

\*

Widows rarely choose unwisely!

*Hints for Lovers* (1909). The aphorist was Goldwin Smith's private secretary.

Madame Bernhardt is reported to have called Canada semi-barbarous, and to have declared that we neglected literature and the arts. I am not sure that the Divine Sarah did not speak more truly than she knew; but it is against Canada's politicians, not against her people, that she should have aimed her gibes. Few people, in their way, are more literary or more artistic.

"Art and the Tariff," *The Canadian Magazine*, June, 1906.

## Hay, John
It is far more to Canada's advantage than ours to be on good terms with us. Lord Salisbury, in a private conversation the other day, compared her to a coquettish girl with two suitors, playing off one against the other. I should think a closer analogy would be to call her a married flirt, ready to betray John Bull on any occasion, but holding him responsible for all her follies.

Letter from the U.S. ambassador to the Court of St. James to General John Watson Foster, December 27, 1897. Quoted by John Bartlet Brebner in "The North Atlantic Triangle," *Canada* (1954), edited by George W. Brown.

## Hayakawa, S.I.
Or again, if a young lady with whom we are strolling says, "The moon is bright tonight," we are able to tell by the tone whether she is making a meteorological observation or indicating that she wants to be kissed.

*Language in Action* (1941). Samuel Ichiye Hayakawa, the Vancouver-born semanticist, was president of San Francisco State College during the 1960s.

## Hayden, Melissa
What concerns me is ballet. When you love something it doesn't die. It just grows in intensity and desire. I'm going to dance as long as I can.

Quoted by Barbara Gail Rowes in *The Globe and Mail*, September 24, 1970. The *prima ballerina*, born Mildred Herman and raised in Toronto, retired three years after the interview.

## Hayman, Robert
The Aire in Newfound-land is wholesome, good;
The Fire, as sweet as any made of wood;
The waters, very rich, both salt and fresh;
The Earth more rich, you know it is no lesse.
Where all are good, *Fire, Water, Earth,* and *Aire,*
What man made of these foure would not live there?

This verse was written by Robert Hayman, governor of the colony at Harbour Grace, Conception Bay, Newfoundland, and included in *Quodlibets, Lately Come Over from New Britaniola, Old Newfound-land* (1628). This publication has been called the first book of original verse written on the North American continent.

## Hayward, Victoria

It is indeed a mosaic of vast dimensions and great breadth, essayed of the Prairie.

John Murray Gibbon has suggested that this is the first use of the word "mosaic" to characterize the ethnic composition of Canada. The passage, describing the contributions of new Canadians to the architecture of the prairies, appears in *Romantic Canada* (1922), written by the American travel-writer Victoria Hayward and illustrated with the photographs of Edith S. Watson. See also John Porter.

## Head, Sir Edmund

On the whole, therefore, I believe that the least objectionable place is the city of Ottawa. Every city is jealous of every other city except Ottawa.

"Confidential Memorandum by Sir E. Head, Containing Reasons for Fixing the Seat of Government for Canada at Ottawa," October, 1857. Reprinted by James A. Gibson in *Canadian Historical Review*, December, 1935.

The country is all frontier.

Sir Edmund was governor general from 1854 to 1861. Quoted by Stephen Leacock in *Canada: The Foundations of Its Future* (1941).

## Head, Sir Francis Bond

If you choose to dispute with me and live on bad terms with the mother country you will quarrel with your own bread and butter.

Address to the Electors of the Newcastle District, March, 1836.

That the two tribes of men, French and English, do not assimilate is no new discovery; it is nothing more than Nature herself did when she deliberately created the British Channel.

"Memorandum on the Present Political State of the Canadas," October 18, 1836.

. . . as I drove into Toronto, I observed the walls placarded in large letters which designated me as

"SIR FRANCIS HEAD, A TRIED REFORMER." [January 23, 1836]

*

BIDWELL, and the glorious minority! 1837, and a good beginning!

*

In the name of every regiment of militia in Upper Canada, I publicly promulgate, *let them come if they dare.* [Address in the House of Assembly prior to the election of June 20, 1837]

*

The people of Upper Canada detest democracy; they revere their Constitutional Charter; and are, consequently, staunch in allegiance to their King. [Declaration circularized prior to the election of June 20, 1837]

*

It appears, then, from Lord Durham's own shewing, that this "FAMILY COMPACT," which his Lordship deems it so advisable that the Queen should destroy, is nothing more nor less than that "social fabric" which characterizes every civilized community in the world. It is that social fabric, or rather fortress, within which the British yeoman, farmer, and manufacturer is enabled to repel the extortionate demands of his labourers; and to preserve from pillage and robbery the harvest of his industry after he has reaped it!

*

The *"family compact"* of Upper Canada is composed of those members of its society who, either by their abilities and character have been honoured by the confidence of the executive government, or who, by their industry and intelligence, have amassed wealth. The party, I owe, is comparatively a small one; but to put the multitude at the top and the few at the bottom is a radical reversion of the pyramid of society which every reflecting man must foresee can end only in its downfall.

*A Narrative* (1839), by "Galloping Head," the ebullient lieutenant-governor of Upper Canada during the Rebellion of 1837. See also Marshall Spring Bidwell.

## Healy, John J.

. . . but the M.P.'s are worse than bloodhounds when they scent the track of a smuggler, and they fetch their men every time.

> Said to be the origin of the phrase "They always get their man." When the Mounted Police closed down Fort Whoop-up, the whisky fort operated in the Cypress Hills by Healy, the enterprising American turned to publishing the *Fort Benton Record*. On April 13, 1877, he referred to the Mounties' action suppressing the liquor traffic. Ronald Atkin in *Maintain the Right: The Early History of the North West Mounted Police, 1873-1900* (1973) writes that the unofficial slogan of the force "makes every Mountie cringe."

### Hearn, John

There are women who offer their bodies as though they were bestowing some inestimable gift upon you.

\*

Part of the truth about people is their illusions.

\*

I know of nothing which spoils a good relationship faster than falling in love.

> *Poor John's Almanac* (1973).

### Hearn, Lafcadio

At immense intervals a farm, a ranch, outlines its buildings and fences against sky and snow. You wonder about the lives of those who dwell there, always ringed in by the naked horizon,—seeing always the same round of land level to the edge of heaven. . . . But this will not endure; for all along this great highway to the Orient, the country is being rapidly settled; and these solitary farms in a few years will have grown into villages and cities.

> "A Winter Journey to Japan," *Harper's*, November, 1890. The American author wrote this article in return for a free trip on the CPR from Montreal to Vancouver, from which port Hearn sailed for Japan where he lived for many years.

### Hearne, Samuel

"Women," added he, "were made for labour; one of them can carry, or haul, as much as two men can do. They also pitch our tents, make and mend our clothing, keep us warm at night; and, in fact, there is no such thing as travelling any considerable distance, or for any length of time, in this country, without their assistance. Women," said he again, "though they do every thing, are maintained at trifling expence; for as they always stand cook, the very licking of their fingers in scarce times, is sufficient for their subsistence." [October, 1770; the speaker is Matonabbee, Hearne's Chipewyan guide, who had eight wives, all with him on this trek across the Barren Lands]

\*

Ask a Northern Indian, what is beauty? he will answer, a broad flat face, small eyes, high cheek-bones, three or four broad black lines a-cross each cheek, a low forehead, a large broad chin, a clumsy hook-nose, a tawny hide, and breasts hanging down to the belt. Those beauties are greatly heightened, or at least rendered more valuable, when the possessor is capable of dressing all kinds of skins, converting them into the different parts of their clothing, and able to carry eight or ten stone in Summer, or haul a much greater weight in Winter. These, and other similar accomplishments, are all that are sought after, or expected, of a Northern Indian woman. [April 18, 1771]

\*

As I was the first whom they had ever seen, and in all probability might be the last; it was curious to see how they flocked about me, and expressed as much desire to examine me from top to toe, as an European Naturalist would a nondescript animal. They, however, found and pronounced me to be a perfect human being, except in the colour of my hair and eyes: the former, they said, was like the stained hair of a buffaloe's tail, and the latter, being light, were like those of a gull. The whiteness of my skin also was, in their opinion, no ornament, as they said it resembled meat which had been sodden in water till all the blood was extracted. On the whole, I was viewed as so great a curiosity in this part of the world, that during my stay there, whenever I combed my hair, some or other of them never failed to ask for the hairs that came off, which they carefully wrapped up, saying, "When I see you again, you shall again see your hair." [Coppermine Indians examine the explorer, June 22, 1771]

> A Journey from Prince of Wales's Fort, in Hudson's Bay, to the Northern Ocean, Undertaken by Order of the Hudson's Bay Company, for the Discovery of Copper Mines, a North West Passage, Etc., in the Years 1769, 1770, 1771, and 1772 (1795). The text is taken from A Journey from Prince of Wales's Fort (1958), edited by Richard Glover. See also William Wordsworth.

**Hébert, Anne**
And I discover
In myself
An infinite number
Of hands that reach
Toward me,
Like strangers
Of whom one is afraid.

> Lines from "The Two Hands," translated by F.R. Scott in The Poetry of French Canada in Translation (1970), edited by John Glassco.

This province is a country within a country. Québec the original heart. The hardest and deepest kernel. The core of first time. All around, nine other provinces form the flesh of this still-bitter fruit called Canada.

> "Quebec: The Proud Province," Century 1867-1967 (1967).

**Hébert, Louis**
I, Louis Hébert of Paris, recognize and confess to having engaged myself by act to the Compagnie du Canada, to live with my family, two daughters, and a son, with a man I am taking with me named Claude Rolet to the said land of Canada, and for the first two years to work at anything asked of me by those in charge of the said Compagnie at Quebec, for the service of the same, and when there is nothing worth doing the said agents of Quebec will give me leave to plough, labour, and improve the land of the said country. . . . Done at Hon-

fleur, 6th March 1617. Signed Thomas Porée, Louis Hébert: Vermule, Boyer.

> This is an English translation of a portion of the deed of indenture of Louis Hébert, the first farming colonist in New France. Father Joseph Caron's Au Roy sur la Nouvelle-France (1626).

**Heeney, A.D.P.**
It is in the abiding interest of both countries that, whenever possible, divergent views between the two governments should be expressed and if possible resolved in private through diplomatic channels. Only a firm mutual resolve and the necessary practical arrangements to keep the totality of the relationship in good and friendly working order can enable our countries to avoid needless frictions and minimize the consequences of disagreement.

> "Canada and the United States: Principles for Partnership," June, 1965, by A.D.P. Heeney and Livingston T. Merchant.

**Hees, George**
Whenever I see a hand sticking out of a sleeve, I shake it.

> Reply when "asked by a friend about his political credo as president of the Progressive Conservative Association," quoted by Peter C. Newman in Renegade in Power: The Diefenbaker Years (1963).

Y.C.D.B.S.O.Y.A.

> Initials on the Conservative cabinet minister's tie-clip. "Hees would fidget with the gadget until visitors asked what it meant, then he'd burst out with 'You Can't Do Business Sitting on Your Ass!' and tell the astounded caller that he'd better get going and hustle up more export orders." Quoted by Peter C. Newman in Renegade in Power: The Diefenbaker Years (1963).

**Hellyer, Paul T.**
There will be a revolution even if I have to lead it myself.

> Agenda: A Plan for Action (1971).

## Hemingway, Ernest

The Swiss make no distinction between Canadians and citizens of the United States. I wondered about this, and asked a hotelkeeper if he didn't notice any difference between the people from the two countries.

"Monsieur," he said, "Canadians speak English and always stay two days longer at any place than Americans do." So there you are.

> "The Hotels in Switzerland," *The Toronto Star Weekly*, March 4, 1922. *By-Line: Ernest Hemingway: Selected Articles and Dispatches of Four Decades* (1967), edited by William White.

It is impossible for me to do any writing of my own . . . a dreadful country . . . like to swing a *crochet* on the *mention* of Canada.

> Letter to Gertrude Stein, November 9, 1923, quoted by Carlos Baker in *Ernest Hemingway: A Life Story* (1969). Hadley Hemingway wrote to Sylvia Beach, November 27, 1923, that coming to Toronto was "the first big mistake."

I am sending you *Three Stories and Ten Poems*. As far as I know it has not been reviewed in the States. Gertrude Stein writes me she has done a review but I don't know whether she has gotten it published yet.

You don't know anything in Canada.

> Letter to Edmund Wilson, November 11, 1923, quoted by Wilson in "Emergence of Ernest Hemingway" in *The Shores of Light* (1952).

"And bring your friend," said Mrs. Braddocks laughing. She was a Canadian and had all their easy social graces.

> *The Sun Also Rises* (1926). See also: Morley Callaghan, Gregory Clark, Harry Hindmarsh, Gertrude Stein.

## Hémon, Louis

Strangers have surrounded us whom it is our pleasure to call foreigners; they have taken into their hands most of the rule, they have gathered to themselves much of the wealth; but in this land of Quebec nothing has changed. Nor shall anything change, for we are the pledge of it. Concerning ourselves and our destiny but one duty have we clearly understood: that we should hold fast—should endure. And we have held fast, so that, it may be, many centuries hence the world will look upon us and say:—These people are a race which knows not how to perish. . . . In this land of Quebec naught shall die and naught change. . . .

> *Maria Chapdelaine: A Tale of the Lake St. John Country* (1921), translated by W.H. Blake.

## Hemsworth, Wade

And the black flies, the little black flies,
Always the black fly no matter where you go.
I'll die with the black fly a-pickin' my bones
In North Ontario, io, in North Ontario.

> Refrain from "The Black Fly Song" written in 1949. *Canada's Story in Song* (1964), edited by Edith Fowke and Alan Mills. ". . . it seemed to me the most authentic song I had ever heard of the Canadian north." Hugh MacLennan in *Seven Rivers of Canada* (1961).

## Henderson, James     See James Wolfe.

## Henderson, Maxwell

The history of my thirteen years in office has been the history of the buck that never stopped.

> "My War with the Government," *Maclean's Magazine*, July, 1973. Henderson retired as auditor general in 1973.

## Henderson, Paul

When I scored that final goal, I finally realized what democracy was all about.

> The left-wing on Team Canada scored the winning goal in Moscow, November 12, 1972. Quoted by Dick Beddoes in *Hockey Night in Minsk* (1972).

A pro is someone who makes it look easy.

> Remark made in a radio commercial, Fall, 1973.

## Hendry, Thomas

Alas, once they have made their names

abroad they are generally lost to us, priced out of our modest market. We get them on the way up and on the way down, and sometimes in between.

Hendry is referring to expatriates like Lorne Greene and Zara Nelsova. "The Performing Arts," *The Canadians 1867-1967* (1967), edited by J.M.S. Careless and R. Craig Brown.

If an actor is depicted as someone who goes about pretending to be someone else, wearing clothes not his own, eating food not his own and in all essential respects cheerfully denying his own existence, then it may be usefully said that Canadians are a race of actors for our styles come from New York, Paris, and London, as do our thoughts and even our dreams. To a race of actors perhaps the theatre has something particularly important to say.

"Theatre in Canada: A Reluctant Citizen," *Policy Paper for Committee for an Independent Canada* (1972).

### Hennepin, Louis
Four leagues from Lake Frontenac there is an incredible Cataract or Waterfall, which has no equal. The Niagara river near this place is only the eighth of a league wide, but it is very deep in places, and so rapid above the great fall, that it hurries down all the animals which try to cross it, without a single one being able to withstand its current. They plunge down a height of more than five hundred feet, and its fall is composed of two sheets of water and a cascade, with an island sloping down. In the middle these waters foam and boil in a fearful manner.

This is the first eyewitness description of the Falls of Niagara, which the Récollet missionary saw on December 6, 1678. *Description de la Louisiane, nouvellement découverte au sud'ouest de la Nouvelle France* (1683). *Description of Louisiana* (1880), translated by John Gilmary Shea.

### Hénon, G.-H.
I say, my country right or wrong, but not fifteen countries.

House of Commons, January 30, 1939. The Independent Conservative backed Canada but not the British Empire.

### Henry VII
... to seeke out, discover, and finde whatsoever isles, countreys, regions or provinces of the heathen and infidels whatsoever they be, and in what. part of the world soever they be, which before this times have been unknowen to all Christians.

From the letters patent to John Cabot who set out from Bristol in the *Matthew*, May 2, 1497.

Item to hym that founde the new Isle   *xli*

Entry for August 10-11, 1497, in the account books of Henry VII, to credit John Cabot with ten pounds sterling for the discovery of Newfoundland.

### Henry, Eileen Cameron
We give you ships and tides and men
Anchors a-weigh and wind-filled sail
We give you back the sea again
In sailors' songs and rousing tale;
And inland where the dark hills rise
Between you and the salt-thick foam
You hear the surf, the sea gulls' cries
And eastward turn your hearts toward
home.

"Harmony Harbour" (1947), from Will R. Bird's *Atlantic Anthology* (1959).

### Henson, Josiah
When I got on the Canadian side, my first impulse was to throw myself on the ground, and giving way to the riotous exultation of my feelings, to execute sundry antics which excited the astonishment of those who were looking on. A gentleman of the neighbourhood, Colonel Warren, who happened to be present, thought I was in a fit, and he enquired what was the matter with the poor fellow. I jumped up and told him —I Was Free! "Oh," said he, with a hearty laugh, "Is that it? I never knew freedom made a man roll in the sand before!"

Reproduced in *The Globe Magazine*, February 15, 1969. The Kentucky slave escaped with his family and settled near

Dresden, Ontario, in 1830. He was visited there by Harriet Beecher Stowe who is said to have based her *Uncle Tom's Cabin* (1852) on Henson's experiences. Henson made the above remarks on October 28, 1830.

It has been spread abroad that " 'Uncle Tom' is coming," and that is what has brought you here. Now allow me to say that my name is not Tom, and never was Tom, and that I do not want to have any other name inserted in the newspapers for me than my own. My name is Josiah Henson, always was, and always will be. I never change my colours.

"In public lectures long after the Civil War, Henson repeatedly was introduced as Uncle Tom, but initially he appears to have been careful not to make the claim explicit himself." Robin W. Winks's *The Blacks in Canada: A History* (1971).

**Hepburn, Doug**
Some day I'm going to be the strongest man in the world.

A fourteen-year-old Vancouver lad expressed this desire to his mother. Overcoming a frail body and a crippled leg, Hepburn grew so powerful through exercise that, in 1953, he won the world's heavyweight weight-lifting championship and was officially recognized as the strongest man in the world. The same year he was voted Canada's most outstanding athlete. Quoted by Henry Roxborough in *Great Days in Canadian Sport* (1957).

**Hepburn, Mitchell**
Far, far better to be a good farmer than a dishonest politician. [Taking an independent but unpopular position before an election, July 28, 1930]

*

There are only two absolute monarchs in the world—Haile Selassie and Howard Ferguson. [October 30, 1930, equating the emperor of Ethiopia with the premier of Ontario]

*

This is the first time in my life that I have spoken from a Tory platform.

[Speaking from a manure spreader to a group of farmers, one of whom roared: "Throw her in high gear, Mitch, she's never had a bigger load on."]

*Mitch Hepburn* (1967), by Neil McKenty. When the Ontario premier resigned in 1942, he explained, "I am returning to my Elgin County, to listen to the grass grow."

**Herbert, A.P.**
Labrador may become another Alaska because it has the largest iron ore deposits in the world waiting to be exploited ... whoever runs them, Labrador will be an old-age pension for Newfoundland for a very long time. [British House of Commons, March 2, 1949]

*

The Newfoundlanders no more "belong" to the American continent, in any sense, than I do. [*Punch*, November 17, 1943]

*

A Frenchman said that Labrador was the country that God gave to Cain. History may say that it was the country that Britain gave to Canada.

*

They are the best-tempered, best-mannered people walking. I do not believe I ever heard a Newfoundlander swear ... they are gay, good-humoured and generous; tolerant, temperate, tough, God-fearing, sabbath-keeping and law-abiding ... they will subscribe the earth for a man who had fallen through the rickety bridge, but do nothing at all about mending the bridge. Every man can build his own house, his own boat: but he won't build a parish council. They have all the crafts except the political. [*Punch*, November 17, 1943]

*

A new province was born to Canada that day—God bless them both! But a Dominion was murdered. [When Newfoundland entered Confederation on April 1, 1949]

*Independent Member* (1950). The British humourist and M.P., who visited the "great island" in 1943, retained a life-long attachment to its people.

## Herbert, John

Oh, if I had the wings of an angel,
And the ass of a big buffalo,
I would fly to the heavens above me,
And crap on the people below.

> *Fortune and Men's Eyes* (1967). See also
> Margaret Laurence.

I'm not trying to prove anything to anybody except that the theatre is my world.

> Playwright quoted by Robert Martin in
> *The Globe and Mail*, December 9, 1972.

## Heriot, George

The advancement of this place to its
present condition, has been effected
within the lapse of six or seven years,
and persons who have formerly travelled
in this part of the country, are impressed
with sentiments of wonder, on beholding
a town which may be termed handsome,
reared as if by enchantment, in the midst
of a wilderness. [York, or Toronto, the
seat of government in Upper Canada]

> *Travels through the Canadas, Contain-*
> *ing a Description of the Picturesque*
> *Scenery* (1807).

## Heriulfson, Biarni    See Biarni.

## Herodotus

Beyond the Argippaei, however, lies a
region of which no one can give an
accurate account, for further progress is
barred by a lofty and impassable range
of mountains. The bald men themselves
tell the improbable tale that the mountains are inhabited by a goat-footed race,
beyond which, still further north, are
men who sleep for six months in the
year—which to my mind is utterly incredible. East of the Argippaei, however, the country is definitely known to
be inhabited by the Issedones; it is the
region north of those two nations which,
apart from the stories they themselves
tell of it, is veiled in mystery. . . . The
whole region I have been describing has
excessively hard winters; for eight
months in the year the cold is intolerable; the ground is frozen iron-hard, so
that to turn earth into mud requires
not water but fire. . . . Even apart from
the eight months' winter, the remaining
four months are cold. . . .

> *Herodotus: The Histories* (1954), trans-
> lated from the Greek by Aubrey de Se-
> lincourt. The above passages, written
> about 430 B.C., come from Book 4, Chap-
> ter 45, and in the opinion of some an-
> thropologists, refer to the Arctic regions
> of Canada.

## Herridge, Herbert

Living in daily and constant fear of the
government dragnet encircling the reputation of members of Parliament, I hereby wish to confess my past misdeeds. In
1932, I was fined two dollars for failure
to have a dog licence. At the time, I was
first vice-president of the British Columbia Liberal Association.

> NDP member for Kootenay, House of
> Commons, March 4, 1965. Quoted by
> Richard Gwyn in *The Shape of Scandal:*
> *A Study of a Government in Crisis*
> (1965).

## Herridge, W.H.

God's going to get into this speech
sooner or later. Might as well put him in
now. [To R.K. Findlayson, who was
helping Herridge write a speech for R.
B. Bennett, about 1931]

*

I will end unemployment or perish in
the attempt. I will blast a way into the
markets of the world. [For the origin of
these phrases, see R.B. Bennett and
Grant Dexter]

*

We need a Pandora's box. We need some
means by which the people can be persuaded that they also have a New Deal,
and that the New Deal will do everything for them *in fact* which the New
Deal here has done *in fancy*. [Memoran-
dum to R.B. Bennett from the Canadian ambassador, Washington, April 12,
1934]

> Quoted by J.R.H. Wilbur in *The Ben-*
> *nett New Deal: Fraud or Portent?* (1968).

If we cared less about wealth, perhaps it
would be easier to effect a more even
distribution of it. Perhaps if we gave a
little more unhurried thought to the
purpose of life, we would better understand the place of the economic system
in it.

Canadian Club of Ottawa address, December 15, 1934, delivered by R.B. Bennett's brother-in-law. Quoted by Michiel Horn in *The Dirty Thirties: Canadians in the Great Depression* (1971).

## Hertel, François

O my valorous athletes
Martyrs for Christ and France,
Your sceptre dwindles into a distaff.
See what we have become,
Observe these notaries and grocers
For whom your blood was shed.
See our pitiless stupidity
And all the fine words in which we drew
    it up,
Look at this shameless city
No longer called Ville-Marie. . . .

Opening lines of "To the Holy Martyrs of Canada," translated by John Glassco in his edition of *The Poetry of French Canada in Translation* (1970).

## Herzberg, Dr. Gerhard

If we want the greatest chance of useful scientific discoveries, we must not concern ourselves with planning but with providing the right atmosphere for research.

German-born Ottawa physicist, awarded the Nobel Prize in Chemistry, at the testimonial dinner, Ontario Science Centre, quoted in *The Toronto Star*, May 18, 1972.

## Hewitt, Foster

Hello Canada! and Hockey fans in United States and Newfoundland!

The veteran sports broadcaster's greeting over CBC Radio until Newfoundland joined Confederation in 1949.

That night a new career was launched; but there were no heroics associated with it. I wasn't that little Dutch boy who put his finger in the dyke and saved the town. Instead, I was just an eighteen-year-old radio announcer who had been commanded to do a chore he neither asked for nor wanted.

Hewitt broadcast his first hockey game on March 22, 1923. His career has been longer than that of any other broad-

caster in the world. Quoted by the announcer in *Foster Hewitt: His Own Story* (1967).

He shoots! He scores!

The Toronto Maple Leafs and the Boston Bruins had been battling it out for five hours. Announcing the game for the radio audience, Hewitt was as weary as the players. Then, at 1:45 A.M., April 4, 1933, Ken Doraty, the smallest player on either team, whipped the puck into the Boston net. "He shoots! He scores!" Hewitt murmured, exhausting the last of his waning strength, but coining a phrase that would soon be known to hockey fans around the world.

## Hewitt, John

Two per cent of our population possess half the wealth. In any community 100 of the leading capitalists possess as much as all the rest put together. Have they contributed more labour, physical, intellectual or moral to the community? A wrong has been committed somewhere in the distribution of production. Labour is the operative source of all wealth. No man can exist independent of labour, but many do exist on the labour of others.

*Ontario Workman*, March 13, 1873. John Hewitt of the Cooper's Union was president of the Toronto Typographical Society when it struck for recognition and the nine-hour day. Quoted by Charles Lipton in *The Trade Union Movement of Canada: 1827-1959* (1967).

## Hibbert, Christopher

The capture of Quebec in 1759 has been described as the most fateful, dramatic and important event in the history of the eighteenth century.

*Wolfe at Quebec* (1959).

## Hicks, Seymour

A very kind friend said to me the other day that you have got no Canadian theatre. I would like to say, and I hope you will say it now, that you have got a Canadian theatre. Britain's theatre is your theatre.

"Humour," *Empire Club of Canada:*

*Addresses Delivered to the Members During the Year 1928* (1929).

**Hiebert, Paul**
The farmer is king, oh, the farmer is king,
And except for his wife and daughter,
Who boss him around, he runs the thing,
Come drought, come hell or high water.

Last stanza of a poem supposedly composed by Sarah Binks. "Sarah Binks, the Sweet Songstress of Saskatchewan, as she is often called, no longer needs any introduction to her ever-growing list of admirers." Paul Hiebert's *Sarah Binks* (1947).

**Hiemstra, Mary**
How could the prairie change? I wondered. I did not realize then what an instrument of change a plough is.

*Gully Farm* (1955).

**Hikmet, Nazim**
Between my country and Canada lie a great sea and a mighty ocean, yet our countries are close to one another, because Turks and Canadians have this in common: the love of life; the desire to live a little better day by day; the hope of the joy of neither killing nor dying for the sake of foul imperialist profits.

Nazim Hikmet was the greatest of modern Turkish poets. "Greetings to New Frontiers" (1951), *New Frontiers*, Winter, 1952.

**Hill, Arthur**
I've never starved in a garret, not even once, and I never would. If I couldn't work steadily, and make a decent living for my family, I'd find another line of work. I love acting, but not enough to starve for it.

Saskatchewan-born stage and TV actor quoted by Margaret McManns in *The Toronto Star*, August 8, 1972.

**Hill, Brian**   See Ian Adams.

**Hill, Joe**
Where the Fraser River flows, each fellow worker knows,

They have bullied and oppressed us, but still our Union grows.
And we're going to find a way, boys, for shorter hours and better pay, boys!
And we're going to win the day, boys; where the River Fraser flows.

Chorus of "Where the Fraser River Flows," composed by Joe Hill to the tune of "Where the River Shannon Flows." This is the best-known of the songs the almost legendary Joe Hill wrote to support the striking construction workers laying track for the Canadian Northern Railroad in British Columbia. The strike broke out on March 27, 1912, and Hill wrote his song at Yale a short while after. The strikers, supported by the Wobblies, won. Quoted by Gibbs M. Smith in *Labour Martyr: Joe Hill* (1969).

**Hill Sr., William ("Red")**
The trip over the falls is a fool's stunt. You'll never catch me doing that.

Although he shot the Lower Rapids and the Great Whirlpool, and performed innumerable dramatic and dangerous rescues, the "Hero of Niagara" always refused "to shoot the Falls." Thus Red Hill Sr. died peacefully in his bed in 1942. Quoted by Andy O'Brien in *Daredevils of Niagara* (1964).

**Hill Jr., William ("Red")**
Somebody give me a beer!

The first words of Red Hill Jr., emerging from the barrel in which he shot the Lower Rapids in the Niagara River, September 6, 1948. "The biggest thrill was when my mother kissed me on the dock," he later confessed. Quoted by Andy O'Brien in *Daredevils of Niagara* (1964).

All the time in the world. Don't get excited. It's a sure thing, boys.

Red Hill Jr.'s assurances to those helping him into his contraption of inner tubes and webbing immediately prior to his fatal trip over Niagara Falls, August 5, 1951. Red Hill Jr. was the only Canadian to take the plunge. Quoted by Andy O'Brien in *Daredevils of Niagara* (1964).

## Hiller, Arthur
You know, I think if you asked most directors what they'd like best to work in they'd pick live TV.

Canadian-born director of *Love Story*, quoted by Cynthia Grenier in *The Village Voice*, September 7, 1972.

## Hillier, James
We have to automate if we're going to continue to do business the way we have been doing it.

Brantford-born physicist and vice-president of RCA Laboratories, Princeton, New Jersey. Quoted in *The U.S. and Us: The 37th Couchiching Conference* (1968), edited by Gordon McCaffrey.

## Hincks, Clarence Meredith
The supreme goal is not the striving for personal mental health but for the other fellow—for mankind generally. By working for others we inevitably gain satisfactions that would elude us if we concentrated on our own welfare. To me this philosophy is particularly attractive because it presents to science an unending series of problems in which scientific endeavour can enrich human living.

Founder of the Canadian Mental Health Association, quoted in 1960.

## Hincks, Sir Francis
Responsible Government and the Voluntary Principle.

Motto of *The Toronto Examiner*, founded as a reform paper, July 3, 1838, by the future governor-in-chief of Barbados. Quoted by John Charles Dent in *The Last Forty Years: Canada Since the Union of 1841* (1881).

## Hind, E. Cora
No one loves the West more than I do. It has been my home for thirty years. I have seen it grow up but very early in my newspaper career, I learned that the West was big enough and strong enough to have the truth told about it on all occasions.

The widely respected agricultural journalist made this reply in 1913 to the suggestion that her annual harvest prediction was too low and would do harm in the West. Quoted by Kennethe Haig in *The Clear Spirit: Twenty Canadian Women and Their Times* (1966), edited by Mary Quayle Innis.

## Hind, Henry Youle
These are some of the scenes which must be witnessed and felt before the mind forms a true conception of the Red River prairies in that unrelieved immensity which belongs to them in common with the ocean, but which, unlike the ever-changing and unstable sea, seems to promise a bountiful recompense to millions of our fellow-men.

*Narrative of the Canadian Red River Exploring Expedition of 1857 and of the Assiniboine and Saskatchewan Exploring Expedition of 1858* (1860).

A paradise of fertility.

This phrase is associated with the geologist's description of the Red River Valley in his report published in 1860. See, however, Simon James Dawson.

## Hindenlang, Charles
From this scaffold erected by English hands I declare that I die convinced that I have done my duty. My sentence is unjust but I freely pardon those who pronounced it. The cause for which I die is noble and great; I am proud of it, and I do not fear to die. The blood shed for this cause shall be redeemed by blood. May the guilty bear the responsibility for this. Canadians, in bidding you goodbye, I bequeath you the device of France, "Liberty forever."

The Swiss Protestant who sympathized with the Patriots was hanged in Montreal, February 15, 1839, for taking part in the invasion of Lower Canada under Robert Nelson. His speech from the gallows is quoted by Selwyn P. Giffin in "A Tragedy of Generous Youth," *Open Secrets: Off the Beaten Track in Canada's History* (1929). See also Chevalier de Lorimier.

## Hindmarsh, Harry Comfort
You should strive for power. Power is the most important thing in the world.

Quoted by Roy Greenaway in *The News Game* (1966).

The trouble with you, Mr. Callaghan, is you've never been broken to harness.

"Callaghan was fired five times from the *Star* but never actually stopped working." Quoted by Pierre Berton, "Hindmarsh of the *Star*," *Maclean's Canada: Portrait of a Country* (1960), edited by Leslie F. Hannon.

They all got too big for their breeches.

When asked why men like Morley Callaghan, Gregory Clark, Jimmy Frise, Ernest Hemingway, Matthew Halton, and Pierre van Paassen all left the *Star*. Hemingway once claimed: "Working under the other fellow [Hindmarsh] was like being in the German army with a poor commander." Quoted by J.H. Cranston in *Ink on My Fingers* (1953).

News is the greatest gamble in the world.

\*

Get me a life of Christ by 5:00 P.M.

\*

Put a punch in every paragraph.

\*

World news is Canadian news.

Characteristic remarks quoted by Ross Harkness in *J. E. Atkinson of the Star* (1963).

### Hind-Smith, Michael

This season we are matching *our* strong U.S. imports against *their* strong U.S. imports.

CTV director commenting on the commercial rivalry between the private TV network and the publicly owned CBC-TV network, 1961.

### Hines, Mimi

Rotsa Ruck!

The Vancouver-born comedienne now living in California made a catch-phrase of the Japanese mispronunciation of "lots of luck." With her then husband Phil Ford, she appeared on the "Jack Parr Show" in 1958 and did a parody of Marlon Brando in the movie *Sayonara*.

### Hiramatus, T.

A long way from home
They have been brought
And yet, these goldfish . . .
Already seem to enjoy
Swimming in Canadian waters.

"The Fish," a waka translated from the Japanese by Robert Y. Kadoguchi, was selected from some fifteen thousand entries to be read by its author before Emperor Hirohito in the mid-1960s. *Volvox: Poetry from the Unofficial Languages of Canada . . . in English Translation* (1971), edited by J. Michael Yates.

### Hirsch, John

In Winnipeg most things are still possible. There are people to talk to at the top. People here still listen. Ideas can be seen through. *They* are not quite the same *they* as elsewhere.

The theatre director founded the Manitoba Theatre Centre in Winnipeg in 1959. "Adoption by a Cold Land," *Maclean's Magazine*, April, 1973.

### Hitler, Adolf

In Canada, for example, there are 2.6 persons per square mile; in other countries perhaps 16, 18, 20, or 26 persons. Well, no matter how stupidly one managed one's affairs in such a country, a decent living would still be possible. [Berlin address, December 10, 1940]

\*

From Britain I now hear only a single cry—the cry not of the people but of the politicians, that the war must go on! I do not know whether these politicians already have a correct idea of what the continuation of this struggle will be like. They do, it is true, declare that they will carry on the war, and even if Great Britain should perish they would carry on from Canada. I can hardly believe that they mean by this that the people of Britain are to go to Canada. Presumably only those gentlemen interested in the continuation of their war will go there. The people, I am afraid, will have to remain in Britain and the people in London will certainly regard the war with other eyes than their so-called leaders in Canada. [Berlin address, July 19, 1940]

*Hitler's Words: Two Decades of National Socialism, 1923-1943* (1944), edited by Gordon W. Prange.

## Hoagland, Edward
In the confusion of helicopters and mineral promotions, the question in British Columbia has become the same as everywhere else: How shall we live?

\*

Of course the future takes care of itself. All we know is what is lost, not what will be invented.

*Notes from the Century Before: A Journal from British Columbia* (1969).

## Hodgetts, A.B.
"I think Confederation is a good thing."

"I think it is a bad thing. I'm against it."

"I'm for it."

"What good will it do you?"

"What harm will it do you?"

"No harm, I just don't like it."

"Well, I do."

"Let's have a vote."

Secondary school students in Ontario discussing 1867 in 1967, quoted by A.B. Hodgetts in *What Culture? What Heritage? A Study of Civic Education in Canada* (1968).

## Hoffer, Abram    See Humphry Osmond.

## Hofsess, John
Nationalism needs more than a big mouth.

"How to Survive Middle Age," *Maclean's Magazine*, October, 1973.

## Hogan, J. Sheridan
Jack Frost effectually and gratuitously guards us on three thousand miles of our northern coast, and in this he does us a distinct service, greatly relieving national expenditure and contributing much to our sense of security.

*Canada, An Essay: To Which Was Awarded the First Prize by the Paris Exhibition Committee of Canada* (1955). Quoted by Carl Berger in "The True North Strong and Free" in *Nationalism*

*in Canada* (1966), edited by Peter Russell.

## Hogg, Corporal C.
On the 17th inst., I, Corporal Hogg, was called to the hotel to quiet a disturbance. I found the room full of cowboys, and one Monaghan, or "Cowboy Jack," was carrying a gun and pointed it at me, against sections 105 and 109 of the Criminal Code. We struggled. Finally I got him handcuffed behind and put him inside. His head being in bad shape I had to engage the services of a doctor, who dressed his wound and pronounced it as nothing serious. To the doctor Monaghan said that if I hadn't grabbed his gun there'd be another death in Canadian history. All of which I have the honour to report.

(Signed) C. Hogg, Corporal.

Quoted by A.L. Haydon in *The Riders of the Plains: A Record of the Royal North-West Mounted Police of Canada: 1873-1910* (1910). "Thus when young Corporal Hogg of the Wood Mountain detachment was called upon to quell a disturbance instigated by an armed badman in a North Portal hotel, he reported the subsequent action in words which in their power to say much in little are not unworthy to stand beside Caesar's famous *veni, vidi, vici* message to the Roman senate." Edward McCourt in *Saskatchewan* (1968).

## Hollander, Xaviera
I am sorry the exciting moments of making people happy may be over, thanks to outmoded laws and dishonest manoeuvers, but I guess there will always be new opportunities for an ambitious, active Dutch girl to be happy and give pleasure to others.

*The Happy Hooker* (1972), with Robin Moore and Yvonne Dunleavy.

I now make more money vertically than I ever did horizontally.

The bestselling author moved to Toronto in 1972.

You know what I think Oshawa needs? A good brothel.

Quoted by David Cobb in *Toronto Life*, July, 1973.

## Holman, Eugene
My trip to Toronto to be with you today has reminded me of the farmer visiting New York who was approached during one of those "man-on-the-street" radio broadcasts. They asked him what part of America he called home. "The top part," he replied. "America's all Grade A, but the cream lies in Canada."

"Freedom and Energy Go Together" (1951), *Empire Club of Canada: Addresses 1950-51* (1951). Holman was president of Standard Oil of New Jersey.

## Holmes, John Clellon
. . . the harsh, gray sky darkening with that hint of arctic north that always murmurs the mysterious word "Saskatchewan" to me—with its images of fir forests awesome in winter snow at twilight, and prairie immensities north of Dakota over the line, and finally the terrible majesties of the Canadian Rockies that make the mind ache with awareness of its own significance.

"Gone in October," *Playboy*, February, 1973. The American novelist wrote the earliest beat novel, *Go* (1952).

## Holmes, John W.
Canadians feel that Americans forget about Canada in their foreign relations because they think of it—benevolently, but inaccurately—as some kind of extension of their own country. The Canadian attitude is, however, ambivalent. Canadians are not flattered by being told they are "just like Americans," but on the other hand they would be unhappy if they thought they were being placed in the same category as countries that Americans and Canadians would both call "foreigners."

"The Relationship in Alliance and in World Affairs," *The United States and Canada: The American Assembly* (1964), edited by John Sloan Dickey.

Our problem as Canadians is that we cannot pursue logical conclusions too far. Logic often seems to point in the direction of integration; but integration is what we want to avoid.

*U.S. News & World Report*, July 19, 1971. John W. Holmes is director of the Canadian Institute of International Affairs.

## Holt, Sir Herbert
"We get up in the morning and switch on one of Holt's lights, cook breakfast on Holt's gas, smoke one of Holt's cigarettes, read the morning news printed on Holt's paper, ride to work on one of Holt's streetcars, sit in an office heated by Holt's coal, then at night go to a film in one of Holt's theatres."

Complaint of Montrealers in the late 1920s, quoted by Peter C. Newman in *Flame of Power: Intimate Profiles of Canada's Greatest Businessmen* (1959).

## Holton, Luther H.
Well! John A. beats the devil.

The former Liberal M.P. was amazed when Sir John A. Macdonald's Conservatives were returned to power following the Pacific Scandal in the general election of 1878.

## Hood, Hugh
Everybody in this country has the psychology of a member of a minority group, and not a very important minority group either.

\*

Imagine a Canadian Dream, which implied that everybody in the world ought to share it! Imagine a Committee on Un-Canadian Activities! You can't. Un-Canadianism is almost the very definition of *Canadianism*. ["Moral Imagination: Canadian Thing" (1968)]

\*

Quebec is our conscience. ["Indépendance Blague!" (1968)]

*The Governor's Bridge is Closed* (1973).

## Hoodless, Adelaide
For Home and Country.

Motto of the Federated Women's Institutes of Canada, founded by Mrs. Adelaide Hoodless at Stoney Creek, Ontario, February 19, 1897.

You purify society when you purify the home.

*

A nation cannot rise above the level of its homes, therefore, women must work and study together to raise our homes to the highest possible level.

> Quoted by Ruth Howes in *The Clear Spirit: Twenty Canadian Women and Their Times* (1966), edited by Mary Quayle Innis.

## Hope, Bob

I've never been any place before where they have four seasons in one day. I'm wearing out my body changing clothes.

> American comedian on a Spring visit to Toronto in the 1960s.

## Hopkins, J. Castell

Some years ago I had occasion to state that "Canada only needs to be known in order to be great." Events have since greatly strengthened my belief in the truth of these words and have impressed upon my mind the further fact that to be properly appreciated abroad a people should be familiar with its own past, proud of its own history, filled with confidence in its own resources and strength and conscious of its own national and material development.

> Preface, *The Story of the Dominion: Four Hundred Years in the Annals of Half a Continent* (1901).

After all, History is to the life of a nation what Biography is to the life of an individual.

> *The Story of Canada: A History of Four Centuries of Progress from the Earliest Settlement to the Present Time* (1922).

## Horn, Kahn-Tineta

We're not equal, and we don't want to be. We're different.

*

Whether Indians like it or not, Kahn-Tineta's going to protect them.

> Mohawk model and Indian advocate quoted by Marci McDonald in *Homemaker's Digest*, November-December, 1972.

## Hornby, Sir Edmund

Amongst the Ministers I made many friends—John (usually called Jack) Macdonald, Sir Francis Hincks, Sir William M'Nab, Cartier, Brown, a journalist, and several others. All able men with unlimited powers of consuming champagne. [Quebec, 1855]

*

As usual it was a Psalm-singing Protestant dissenter who, holding seven or eight votes in the palm of his hand, volunteered to do the greasing process for a consideration. Upon my word I do not think there was much to be said in favour of the Canadians over the Turks when contracts, places, free tickets on railways, or even cash was in question. [Quebec, 1858]

> Sir Edmund, a leading British barrister, visited Turkey and Canada on business. *An Autobiography* (1928).

## Hornby, John

The land of feast and famine.

> "John Hornby, a bizarre and mystic little Englishman who roamed the Barrens for a generation, called that stark country 'the land of feast and famine.' He wanted to write a book with that title, but he starved to death before he began it. The phrase remains an apt one and it could well apply to the north as a whole." Pierre Berton in *The Mysterious North* (1959).

## Horning, L.E.  See Wilfrid Eggleston.

## Horowitz, Gad

For consolation, the socialist need only look southward.

> Concluding sentence of *Canadian Labour in Politics* (1968).

The purpose of Canadian nationalism is not to close Canada to the world, but to open Canada to the world by keeping out of the United States.

> "On the Fear of Nationalism," *Nationalism, Socialism and Canadian Independence* (1972), edited by Gad Horowitz.

## Horqarnaq

It is a hard thing to speak the truth. It is

difficult to make hidden forces appear.

Observation of the Eskimo shaman Hor-qarnaq. Knud Rasmussen, *Intellectual Culture of the Copper Eskimos: Report of the Fifth Thule Expedition, 1921-24* (1932).

## Horwood, Harold

There's a distinct ethos in Newfoundland, and it's still there, and will be for a long time to come, I'd say. You don't even have to talk about it; it just *is* a little nation of its own.

Interviewed by Donald Cameron in *Conversations with Canadian Novelists* (1973).

In Newfoundland, a gulch is what mainlanders call a gully. A gully is what mainlanders call a pond. A pond is what mainlanders call a lake.

Fun, isn't it? These verbal musical chairs could go on almost all day.

*Newfoundland* (1969).

## Houde, Camillien

When the time comes, they'll all want me. The Church will want me, St. James's Street will want me, and the people will want me. When the time comes, when the time comes, just you watch Camillien Houde!

Quoted by Sir Anthony Jenkinson in *Where Seldom a Gun Is Heard* (1937).

I did not argue with the people. I joked with them. I said, "If you are for me, work hard for me; but if you are against me, do not work so hard, because we are friends, anyway, whether you are for me or against me. Let us continue to be friends. It is more important that we should be friends than that I should win this election. But I want to win the election.

Quoted by Frederick Edwards in "Who's Houde?" *Maclean's Magazine*, September 15, 1929.

The Province of Quebec is not sufficiently large to contain Maurice Duplessis and Camillien Houde. [After Houde lost the Conservative party leadership to Duplessis, October, 1933]

You know, Your Majesty, some of this is for you.

The long-time mayor of Montreal is said to have made this remark to King George VI and Queen Elizabeth when they heard the cheers of the crowds while driving through Montreal, May 18, 1939.

Your armaments, cannons, rifles, bombs, and battleships, what kind of Christmas tree decorations are those? [Anti-conscription address, Saint-Henri, Winter, 1938]

\*

But now that we're at war, Camillien can't do anything about it. Duplessis can't do anything about it. So what's left for us to do? At least see that we get our fair share of wartime contracts. . . . [Montreal anti-conscription address, October 22, 1939]

Quoted by André Laurendeau in "The Conscription Crisis, 1942," *André Laurendeau: Witness for Quebec* (1973), translated by Philip Stratford.

Montreal is wide-open—but honest.

\*

I would rather pass into legend than into history.

Remarks attributed to the colourful figure who was many times mayor of Montreal between 1928 and 1954.

## Houdini, Harry

Not that way . . . got to get . . . set for it. All right—now hit me. Go on—hit me.

To a startled McGill student (a college boxing champ) who punched Houdini in the stomach before the escape artist could tighten his abdominal muscles to receive the blow. This occurred backstage at the Princess Theatre, Montreal, October 21, 1926. The blow resulted in acute appendicitis, followed by peritonitis, and Houdini's death ten days later in a Detroit hospital. Quoted by William Lindsay Gresham in *Houdini: The Man Who Walked Through Walls* (1959).

## Houocomen, Paulus Jouius von

Truthful witnesses have related that in

a land to the northwest of the Lapps are to be found Pygmaei, who dwell in eternal darkness, so that when they are full grown, they are only as big as our children are when ten years of age. They are a fear-filled people.

> Von der Moscouiten Bottschaft (1534). Quoted by Tryggvi J. Oleson in Early Voyages and Northern Approaches 1000-1632 (1963). For more on pygmies, see Gerhardus Mercator.

### House, Eric
I used to think that one thing led to another. You know, that you *build* a career. But Broadway, parts in Hollywood movies, things like that, they don't necessarily *lead* to anything any more.

> Quoted by Harry Bruce in Saturday Night, November, 1972.

### Houston, James
Must we advise them about our way of life in a voice so strong and sure that we fail to hear the words of wisdom they may have for us?

> "The Eskimos" in Canada (1967), edited by Earle Toppings.

Some people say the animals see the straight path and flee from it in fear, for they know that it was built by men.

> The White Dawn (1971).

It was for me like discovering a fabulous buried treasure. The Eskimo carving tradition had, after all, survived. I felt certain many people in the South would be as excited as I was about the quality of these carvings.

\*

Eskimos, who have more than thirty words for the various types and conditions of snow, do not have a satisfactory word for art. I believe this is because they have never felt the need for it. Like most other hunting societies, they have considered living in harmony with nature as their art. The objects they carve or decorate are to them merely reflections of their total art of living.

> James Houston almost single-handedly created the Eskimo art cooperative system in 1948. "Living Art of the Eski-

mos," The London Observer, October 8, 1972.

### Houston, John
We know that China has a population of around eight hundred million, and we're just hoping that they don't all intend to come here.

> The birthplace of Dr. Norman Bethune, a manse in Gravenhurst, Ontario, was occupied by the Rev. John Houston of Trinity United Church. On April 5, 1972, twenty-eight championship ping-pong players from China were led on a conducted tour through the frame house.

### Howe, C.D.
Mr. Green: I am complaining of what appears to be a constant whittling down of these preferences by the present Canadian government. I am not too sure that this government would not do away with the preferences entirely if they felt they could get away with it as far as the public were concerned.

Mr. Howe: Who would stop us? Don't take yourself too seriously. If we wanted to get away with it who would stop us.

Mr. Green: That is just typical of the minister; if he wanted to get away with anything who would stop him? I tell him he is not yet the dictator of this country, and he is not going to be. He grows more and more dictatorial every session. Some day the Canadian people are going to wake up and realize what a dictator they have running this country.

> House of Commons, May 21, 1951. "Who would stop us?" became a household phrase. The exchange was with Conservative Howard Green.

What's a million?

> What Howe actually said in the House of Commons, June 14, 1951, was: "So I hope the hon. member will agree that to operate a department with 1,100 people for a year, $3 million is not exorbitant. Will he go that far with me?" Out of this grew the famous quip ascribed to Howe: "What's a million?" As Dale C. Thomson in Louis St. Laurent: Canadian (1967) explained: "He had not used the words, but they too became permanently associated with his name."

If we have overstepped our powers I make no apology for having done so. [House of Commons, April 21, 1953, concerning an Order-in-Council banning exports to North Korea]

Her Majesty pays me for doing something useful and I don't think I'm doing anything useful when I sit in the House and listen to the kind of blather that's being talked here.

*

Are we having a debate? . . . I do not think this should be allowed to degenerate into a debate.

*

Mr. Speaker, the answer is that the minister spends nights and days considering the welfare of the people of Canada. [In answer to the rhetorical question, "When is the minister going to consider the welfare of the Canadian people?"]

*

Who wants to hear you? [When George Drew rose to speak on a question of privilege]

*

The prime minister has other things to do than listen to the hon. gentleman. [When an Opposition member rose to speak on a resolution moved by the Liberal leader]

*

Nuts. [Terse response to George Drew when Drew noted that the Conservative party had also contributed to the development of Trans-Canada Air Lines]

*

That's not public enterprise; that's *my* enterprise. [To an Opposition M.P. who reminded him that TCA was a socialist organization]

*

Weasel words. [Rebuttal to an Opposition member's argument]

*

Once a louse, always a louse. [And Donald Fleming's reply: "You should know."]

*

Fulton: May I ask when I will get an answer?
Howe: When we get around to it.

*

If there is some uneasiness in this country about the extent and nature of United States investment in Canada, this is the wrong place to focus it. [The "wrong place" being a debate in the Commons]

*

That would mean coming back to Parliament in three years, and I've more to do than spend my time amusing Parliament. [When Howe's emergency powers were extended for a mere three years in July of 1955, he made this remark]

*

I don't trust this new bunch.

> To his broker, whom he ordered to sell most of his equity stocks, after his defeat and the victory of the Conservative party under John Diefenbaker in June of 1957.

Oh, you and all the other damn Rhodes scholars! Get the hell out of here! [Dismissing a committee of academics from his ministerial office]

Orderly decontrol.

> "The watchword of the day . . . and in Canada, 'orderly' meant 'controlled by C.D. Howe,'" explained Blair Fraser in *The Search for Identity: Canada, 1945-1967* (1967), referring to demobilization at the end of World War II.

Nothing is administratively impossible. [Frequent remark to his assistants]

> Clarence Decatur Howe was sometimes referred to as the "minister of Everything." He represented Port Arthur in the House of Commons from 1935 to 1957 when he lost his own seat. Winston Churchill is reported to have said, "The British Empire has been sold down the river by C.D. Howe," when the British prime minister learned that Howe had ordered Eldorado Mining to fill American uranium requirements before Britain's. Franklin Delano Roosevelt once observed: "What a quarterback C.D. Howe would have made. If one play fails, he always has another up his sleeve." See also J.M. Macdonnell.

**Howe, Gordie**

I don't worry about giving autographs. I'll start to worry when the kids stop asking for them.

Quoted by Foster Hewitt in *Foster Hewitt: His Own Story* (1967).

TO: GORDIE HOWE
(THE GREAT HOCKEY PLAYER)
WHEREVER HE MAY BE
EITHER U.S. OR CANADA

"Gordie is thinking of framing an envelope that arrived at his home last spring" addressed in a childish scrawl. Quoted by Jim Vipond in *Gordie Howe: Number 9* (1968).

## Howe, Joseph
Let the creature live.

Attributed to the young editor and future statesman during a duel in the 1820s. His opponent, John C. Haliburton, standing sixteen paces away, took aim and missed; Howe, making the above declaration, fired into the air.

A live editor is more useful than a dead hero.

Attributed to Howe on his refusal to fight a second duel in Halifax in the 1820s.

My books are very few, but then the world is before me—a library open to all —from which poverty of purse cannot exclude me—and in which the meanest and most paltry volume is sure to furnish something to amuse, if not to instruct and improve.

Letter to George Johnson, January, 1824. [Beck]

But these things are not for us—our wild and beautiful scenes cannot draw for enchantment on legendary lore, and like penniless maidens, must be loved for themselves alone.

"Kentville Falls," September 11, 1828, *Western and Eastern Rambles: Travel Sketches of Nova Scotia* (1973), edited by M.G. Parks.

Genius may require to be breathed into the soul, but it must be fanned by the domestic hearth; and therefore, boys, let not your hours be wasted—let every house be a school house.

"Winter Evenings," *Novascotian*, November 27, 1828. [Beck]

Truly we have tarried long enough with the Senators—let us look abroad and see what other classes are achieving. We have beside us a mountain of Books, Magazines, Pamphlets and Newspapers, that have been accumulating for the last two months, unopened and unread. Like a Turk, in the dim twilight of his Harem, we scarcely know which to choose, but, we shall commence at the apex of the pyramid, and dig downwards.

Editorial, *Novascotian*, May 2, 1833.

The policy of this party has always been to ask for nothing but what was right— and to submit to nothing wrong.

*Novascotian*, July 17, 1834. [Beck]

Nova Scotia is an excellent poor man's country, because almost any man, in any walk of industry, by perseverance and economy, can secure the comforts of life.

*Novascotian*, July 31, 1834.

If this trial tortures them much more than it tortures me, they have themselves to blame. While they wince under the lash, let them remember they knotted the cords for me—that they, a numerous and powerful body, leagued themselves against an humble individual, because he merely performed a duty which they knew he could not honourably avoid.

\*

Could we join heart and hand with a republic which fell upon the rear of Britain, when her front was presented to hostile Europe, in a struggle for the liberties of the world? Were we to permit the American banner to float upon our soil—if the bodies of our fathers did not leap from their honoured graves, their spirits would walk abroad over the land, and blast us for such an unnatural violation.

\*

The nation of which we make a part, and of which we are neither serfs nor bondmen, but free, equal, and unfettered members, has no parallel either in ancient or modern times. It extends to every quarter of the globe; the sun never sets upon its surface; and by whom shall its boundaries be defended?

*

Let not the sons of the Rebels look across the border to the sons of the Loyalists, and reproach them that their press is not free.

*

Your verdict will be the most important in its consequences, ever delivered before this tribunal; and I conjure you to judge me by the principles of English law, and to leave an unshackled press as a legacy to your children. You remember the press in your hours of conviviality and mirth—oh! do not desert it in this its day of trial.

*

Yes, gentlemen, come what will, while I live, Nova Scotia shall have the blessing of an open and unshackled press.

*

Now, gentlemen, upon a calm survey of this case, as I have put it before you, can you, under that indictment, find me guilty of a malicious libel?

Excerpts from the two-day "Address to the Jury," May, 1835. Howe, charged and tried for publishing a libellous letter in the *Novascotian*, was acquitted in ten minutes. [Annand]

Gentlemen, in England the people can breathe the breath of life into their government whenever they please; in this country, the government is like an ancient Egyptian mummy, wrapped up in narrow and antique prejudices—dead and inanimate, but yet likely to last for ever. We are desirous of a change, not such as shall divide us from our brethren across the water, but which will ensure to us what they enjoy.

Election speech, 1836. *The Heart of Howe: Selections from the Letters and Speeches* (1939), edited by D.C. Harvey.

. . . and my pride and hope is, that we shall make Nova Scotia, by her loyalty, intelligence, and spirit, as it were, a Normal school for British North America, to show how far British liberty may be assumed in a Colony, and at what point it should stop, and the people be content.

Speech at Reform dinner, November 23,

1840. *Novascotian*, November 26, 1840. [Beck]

If I can be proscribed today, for defending myself and my friends in the newspapers, another Nova Scotian may be rejected tomorrow because the Governor likes not the colour of his hair.

Address at a public dinner, Cumberland County, fall, 1844. [Annand]

It will be our pride to make Nova Scotia a "Normal School" for the rest of the Colonies, showing them how representative Institutions may be worked, so as to insure internal tranquility, and advancement, in subordination to the paramount interest of and authority of the Empire.

Letter to Charles Buller, February 12, 1848. [Beck]

I am neither a prophet, nor a son of a prophet, yet I will venture to predict that in five years we shall make the journey hence to Quebec and Montreal, and home through Portland and St. John, by rail; and I believe that many in this room will live to hear the whistle of the steam engine in the passes of the Rocky Mountains, and to make the journey from Halifax to the Pacific in five or six days.

Address, Masons' Hall, Halifax, May 15, 1851. [Annand]

Well, sir, we have been told by the poet, that the mind is the standard of the man; and the size of a country is generally measured by the men who are in it.

New Brunswick address, November 8, 1851. [Annand]

Look at the organization of the Colonial office; that department which is especially charged with the government of forty Colonies, and yet has not one Colonist in it! How long are we to have this play of Hamlet with Hamlet himself omitted? . . . Talk of annexation, sir! what we want is annexation to the mother country.

Speech in the Legislative Assembly, February 23, 1854. [Beck]

Our columns of gold and our pyramids

of timber may rise in your Crystal Palaces, but our statesmen in the great councils of the empire, never.

> Letter to the Right Hon. C.B. Adderley, M.P., December 24, 1862. Included by A.J.M. Smith in *The Book of Canadian Prose: Volume I, Early Beginnings to Confederation* (1965).

. . . the Botheration Scheme was ventilated in every part of the Province, and, so far as Nova Scotia is concerned, may now be considered as dead as Julius Caesar.

> "Botheration Letter, No. 12," *Halifax Morning Chronicle*, March 2, 1865. See also William Garvie.

A wise nation preserves its records, gathers up its muniments, decorates the tombs of its illustrious dead, repairs its great public structures, and fosters national pride and love of country, by perpetual references to the sacrifices and glories of the past.

> Address at the Howe Festival, Framingham, Massachusetts, August 31, 1871, *Poems and Essays* (1874).

Boys, brag of your country. When I'm abroad, I brag of everything that Nova Scotia is, has, or can produce; and when they beat me at everything else, I turn round on them and say, "How high does your tide rise?"

\*

Poetry was my first love, but politics was the harridan I married. [Remark made in his later years, frequently reproduced as "Poetry was the maiden I loved, but politics was the harridan I married."]

\*

You don't need a big field to raise a big turnip. [On Nova Scotia]

\*

What's the use of keeping up a cry? We shall be like a goose hissing at a stage coach. We may hiss, but the coach will run us over. [On the futility of persisting in anti-Confederation sentiments, 1868]

> Quoted by George Monro Grant in *Joseph Howe* (1904).

We are sold for the price of a sheepskin.

> *The Novascotian*, August 13, 1866. Bitter remark when it was apparent Nova Scotia would enter Confederation the following year. See also Thomas Chandler Haliburton and Sir Clifford Sifton for other uses of the word "sheepskin."

I often think of that passage, the sense of which is, "We know not what we shall be, but this we know: we shall see Him, and shall therefore be like Him." That is enough for me.

> The great journalist and statesman was sworn in as the first lieutenant-governor of Nova Scotia and died three weeks later. These words come from the last interview he gave and were published in *The Halifax Daily Reporter and Times*, June 2, 1873, the day after his death. [Beck]
> [Beck]: *Joseph Howe: Voice of Nova Scotia* (1964), edited by J. Murray Beck. [Annand]: *The Speeches and Public Letters of The Hon. Joseph Howe* (1858), edited by William Annand.

## Howells, William Dean
I stopped in Toronto, and realized myself abroad without any signal adventures; but at Montreal something very pretty happened to me.

> No one recognized Howells in Toronto, but someone did in Montreal, 1860. *Literary Friends and Acquaintances: A Personal Retrospect of American Authorship* (1900).

## Howison, John
A lawless and unprincipled rabble, consisting of the refuse of mankind, recently emancipated from the subordination that exists in an advanced state of society, and all equal in point of right and possession, compose, of course, a democracy of the most revolting kind. No individual possesses more influence than another; and were any one, whose qualifications and pretensions entitled him to take the lead, to assume a superiority, or make any attempt at improvement, he would be strenuously opposed by all the others. Thus, the whole inhabitants of a new settlement march sluggishly

forward at the same pace, and if one advances in the least degree before the others, he is immediately pulled back to the ranks.

*Sketches of Upper Canada: Domestic, Local, and Characteristic* (1821).

## Hubbard, Elbert

Do you know, when the Millerites over in Buffalo prophesied that the world was going to come to an end on a certain day, do you know what they did? They hiked over to Canada! Now, I sympathize with the move and with the proceeding. My heart is in Canada, part of it, and I have bought a little farm not long ago—out there in Saskatchewan, I like them so much, I like to have a little Canadian real estate.

"The Brotherhood of Man," December 19, 1911, *Addresses Delivered before the Canadian Club of Toronto: Season of 1911-12* (1912).

## Hudon, Gabrielle

Goodbye till 1967!

The twenty-one-year-old draftsman constructed the bomb that killed Wilfred O'Neil, the night watchman who became the first victim of FLQ terrorism. The above remark was made to his mother as police dragged him from the family home at 5:30 A.M., June 2, 1963. Police found fifty sticks of dynamite, and Hudon was sentenced to twelve years—not four, as he had expected. Quoted by Peter Desbarats in "The FLQ Reign of Terror," *Historic Headlines* (1967), edited by Pierre Berton.

## Hudson, Henry

Anno 1607. Aprill the nineteenth, at Saint Ethelburge in Bishops Gate street, did communicate with the rest of the Parishioners these persons Seamen, purposing to goe to sea four days after, for to discover a Passage by the North Pole to Japan and China.

"Divers Voyages and Northerne Discoveries of that Worthy Irrecoverable Discoverer Master Henry Hudson," included by Samuel Purchas in *Hakluytus Posthumus: or Purchas His Pilgrimes:*

*Contayning a History of the World in Sea Voyages and Lande Travells by Englishmen and Others* (1625). See also Llewelyn Powys.

## Hughes, Campbell

A Canadian is someone who drinks Brazilian coffee from an English teacup, and munches a French pastry while sitting on his Danish furniture, having just come home from an Italian movie in his German car. He picks up his Japanese pen and writes to his member of Parliament to complain about the American takeover of the Canadian publishing business.

Quoted by *Time*, March 1, 1971. Hughes, who is the Toronto head of an American multinational publishing firm, adapted but did not originate this definition.

## Hughes, Everett C.

Who shall call whom what and in what situations? An American must be careful, in some circumstances, of calling himself so, since he may be thought to be arrogating to himself as a citizen of the United States, the name of a whole continent. Canadians are North Americans as much as he. But if he doesn't call himself American, the Canadian will; no one will call him a United States-er. . . . Of course we know about "Yankees" and "Canucks" and of qualifying adjectives.

"A Note on Nomenclature," *The United States and Canada: The American Assembly* (1964), edited by John Sloan Dickey.

## Hughes, Helen

I had no idea who he was. They don't tell us, you know. All I knew was, a gentleman would be coming for a sitting at 10:30 in the morning. He just came in and sat down without saying anything.

The Glasgow housewife and psychic medium was consulted by W.L. Mackenzie King. Quoted by Blair Fraser in "The Secret Life of Mackenzie King, Spiritualist," *A Century of Canadian Literature / Un siécle de littérature canadienne* (1967), edited by H. Gordon Green and Guy Sylvestre.

**Hughes, Sir Sam**
"Sir Sam marched up to Kitchener's desk. When he arrived at the desk Kitchener spoke up quickly and in a very stern voice said: 'Hughes, I see you have brought over a number of men from Canada; they are of course without training and this should apply to their officers; I have decided to divide them up among the British regiments; they will be of very little use to us as they are.' Sir Sam replied: 'Sir, do I understand you to say that you are going to break up these Canadian regiments that came over? Why, it will kill recruiting in Canada.' Kitchener answered: 'You have your orders, carry them out.' Sir Sam replied: 'I'll be damned if I will,' turned on his heel and marched out."

> Lord Kitchener was the British secretary of State for War and Sir Sam Hughes the controversial minister of Militia and Defence. The account was written by a Canadian officer present at the meeting, August 26, 1914. Reproduced by Colonel A. Fortescue Duguid in *Official History of the Canadian Forces in the Great War 1914-1919, Volume I: From the Outbreak of the War to the Formation of the Canadian Corps* (1938). The First Canadian Division was never divided. See also Lord Kitchener.

The aeroplane is an invention of the devil and will never play any part in such a serious business as the defence of a nation, my boy!

> To J.A.D. McCurdy who approached the minister of Militia and Defence at the end of August, 1914, to start an air service. Quoted by J.R.K. Main in *Voyageurs of the Air: A History of Civil Aviation in Canada, 1858-1967* (1967).

Give me one million men who can hit a target at five hundred yards and we would not have a foe who could invade our country.

> World War I boast, quoted by Ralph Allen in *Ordeal by Fire: Canada, 1910-1945* (1961).

The soldier going down in the cause of freedom never dies—immortality is his.

> Address to the first contingent of Canadian troops at their departure from Valcartier, Quebec, September 22, 1914. Reproduced by R.C. Brown and M.E. Prang in *Confederation to 1949* (1966).

**Hugo, Dédé**
I am the daughter of Victor Hugo.

> The beautiful daughter of the great French novelist lived in Halifax from 1861 to 1864 as "Miss Lewly." Madly in love with a British officer named Albert Pinsen, Dédé Hugo followed him to his Halifax posting. When Pinsen was sent to Barbados, she followed him there too. But when Pinsen married an English lady in the West Indies, she suffered a collapse and was found wandering the streets of New York saying, "I am the daughter of Victor Hugo." She returned to her father's home in Paris and died there in 1915 at the age of eighty-five. "Victor Hugo's Daughter," *Tales Retold Under the Old Town Clock* (1957), by William Coates Borrett.

**Hull, Bobby**
Hockey is my game—and it sure has been good to me.

> *Hockey Is My Game* (1967).

**Hull, Raymond**
See Dr. Laurence J. Peter.

**Hull, General William**
Inhabitants of Canada. . . . The army under my command, has invaded your country, and the standard of UNION now waves over the territory of Canada. To the peaceable unoffending inhabitant, it brings neither danger nor difficulty. I come to *find* enemies, not to *make* them, I come to protect, not to injure you.

> "A Proclamation" issued by the brigadier-general and commander of the Northwestern Army of the United States, Sandwich, Lower Canada, July 12, 1812. Reproduced by Robert Christie in *A History of the Late Province of Lower Canada, Parliamentary and Political* (1854). For the British reply, see Sir Isaac Brock.

## Hulme, T.E.

Speaking of personal matters, the first time I ever felt the necessity or inevitableness of verse, was in the desire to reproduce the peculiar quality of feeling which is induced by the flat spaces and wide horizons of the virgin prairie of western Canada.

Quoted by Michael Roberts in *T.E. Hulme* (1938). The British philosopher and founder of Imagism expressed these ideas in "Lectures on Modern Poetry" written about 1914. His biographer writes: "In July 1906 he went to Canada, working his way out and back, and doing labouring work on farms and in lumber-camps for eight months. Little seems to be known about this period, except that while in Toronto he used to go to St. Thomas's, a church of Anglo-Catholic tendencies."

## Hume, Joseph

The baneful domination of the mother country.

In a letter to William Lyon Mackenzie of March 29, 1834, the British politician and "philosophical radical" used the above phrase. Mackenzie published the letter in *The Colonial Advocate* on May 22 and found himself accused of treason. Here is the sentence the phrase comes from: "Your triumphant election of the 16th and ejection from the Assembly on the 17th must hasten the crisis which is fast approaching in the affairs of the Canadas, and which will terminate in independence and freedom from the baneful domination of the mother country, and the tyrannical conduct of a small and despicable faction in the colony." Hume denied, in a later letter published by Mackenzie, that he had meant separation from the British connection, but few accepted the denial or clarification.

## Hunter, A.T.

But every loose-waisted, paddle-footed, undrilled man in Canada has come to think that by virtue of being a Canadian he is a natural-born rifle-shot, warrior and strategist. He could rip up and reorganize the War Office in about twenty minutes. This spirit would do no harm if we were sure of not fighting.

"The Fatuous Insolence of the Canadians" (1904), *Empire Club Speeches: Being Addresses Delivered before the Empire Club of Canada during Its Session of 1903-04* (1904). Hunter was secretary of the Ontario Historical Society.

## Hurst, William

They say that Winnipeg was saved from complete disaster by a miracle. It was—a miracle of guts and hard work. The miracle of one hundred thousand multiplied by ten. A million fingers in the dikes.

With this imaginative phrase the Winnipeg city engineer described the efforts of the volunteer dike-builders who stopped the flooding waters when the Red River overflowed its banks on May 5, 1950. Quoted by Frank Rasky in *Great Canadian Disasters* (1961).

## Hurtig, Mel

First let me get something out of the way. While the distinction seems terribly difficult for some to make, and while it has had to be repeated in Canada at least a thousand times too often, it nevertheless appears mandatory to repeat again and again: "It's not necessary to be anti-American to be pro-Canadian."

Address to the World Federalists, Kingston, June 8, 1973. *The Independencer: Magazine of the Committee for an Independent Canada*, September, 1973.

## Huston, Walter

My father who was a contractor then, had a shop on the corner of Bay and Richmond streets in Toronto and he thought perhaps it would be a good idea if his son followed in his footsteps. So, I started at the bottom of the ladder, carrying shingles. I got to the roof the second day and I was carrying scantlings and lumber. It was hot and I decided after two days of that that the stage was a better occupation.

"An Address" (1935), *Empire Club of Canada: Addresses Delivered to the*

*Members During the Year 1934-1935* (1935). The actor, who was born Walter Houghston in Toronto in 1884, is referring to his youthful years at the turn of the century.

Son, always give 'em a good show and travel first class.

> Reply to Gregory Peck who asked the character actor why he was so good. The stage and screen personality will long be remembered for his part in *The Treasure of the Sierra Madre*, directed by his son John Huston in 1947, and for his recording of Kurt Weill's "September Song," released after his death in Hollywood in 1950. Quoted by David Shipman in *The Great Movie Stars: The Golden Years* (1970).

## Hutchison, Bruce

The mystery of William Lyon Mackenzie King is not the mystery of a man. It is the mystery of a people. We do not understand King because we do not understand ourselves.

> *The Incredible Canadian* (1952).

Something strange, nameless, and profound moves in Canada today. It cannot be seen or labeled, but it can be heard and felt—a kind of whisper from far away, a rustle as of wind in prairie poplars, a distant river's voice, or the shuffle of footsteps in a midnight street. It is less a sound than a sense of motion.

Something moves as it has never moved before in this land, moves dumbly in the deepest runnels of a collective mind, yet by sure direction toward a known goal. Sometimes by thought, more often by intuition, the Canadian people make the final discovery. They are discovering themselves.

> *Canada: Tomorrow's Giant* (1957).

The border between the United States and Canada—3,986.8 miles without a single fort or gun to protect it—is the most friendly and least visible line of international power in the world. It is crossed daily by thousands of travellers who hardly notice it in their passage. It is washed by a Niagara of genial oratory and illuminated, or sometimes obscured, by a perpetual diplomatic dialogue. On both sides the border is taken as a fact of nature, almost as an act of God, which no man thinks of changing.

> "The Long Border," *Neighbours Taken for Granted: Canada and the United States* (1966), edited by Livingston T. Merchant.

The Canadian breed sometimes has missed its way. It has never failed a single decisive test when the alternatives were clear. If you can clarify the present alternatives, the right choice will be made again. *Whatever else it may lack, the nation is rich in sanity.*

> "An Open Letter to Pierre Trudeau," *Maclean's Magazine*, July, 1971.

## Hutt, William

We have never considered playing at Stratford-on-Avon any more than we would think of bringing vodka to Poland.

> Actor and associate director of the Stratford Festival, touring Eastern Europe, speaking at a press conference in Warsaw, Poland, February 6, 1973.

## Hutton, Maurice

One ending would be about as good as another for the fiasco of this world.

> "The Folly of the Wise," February 26, 1923. *Addresses Delivered before the Canadian Club of Toronto: Season of 1922-23* (1923).

Herodotus is called "the Father of History." Dubitative persons, full of scruples and misgivings, prefer to call him the "Father of Lies."

> "The Mind of Herodotus," *Many Minds* (1927).

Canada's history is as dull as ditchwater and her politics is full of it.

> Quoted by F.H. Underhill in *Canadian Historical Review*, September, 1935.

## Huxley, Thomas Henry

Last year I became a candidate for a Professorship at Toronto. I took an infinity of trouble over the thing, and got together a mass of testimonials and recommendations, much better than I had any right to expect. From that time to this I have heard nothing of the business—a result for which I care the less, as I believe the chair will be given to a brother of one of the members of the Canadian ministry, who is, I hear, a candidate. Such a qualification as that is, of course, better than all the testimonials in the world.

> Letter of May 3, 1852, quoted by Leonard Huxley in *Life and Letters of Thomas Henry Huxley* (1900), who added: "Nevertheless, after many postponements, a near relative of an influential Canadian politician was at length appointed late in 1853." The professorship of natural history at the University of Toronto paid £350 "with chances of extra fees."

## Huysmans, J.K.
Alas! the days were long past when Des Esseintes, still in the enjoyment of robust health, would, in the middle of the dog-days, mount a sledge he had at home, and then, closely wrapped in furs which he would pull up to his chin, force himself to shiver as he told himself through teeth that chattered of set purpose: "Ah! but the cold is Arctic; it's freezing, freezing hard!" till he actually persuaded himself it *was* cold weather.

> Duc Jean des Esseintes, the decadent sophisticate, appears in the French symbolist novel *A rebours* (1884), best known in English as *Against the Grain*.

# I

## Ikinilik
And of course it may be that all I have been telling you is wrong. For you cannot be certain about a thing you cannot see. And people say so much!

> Elder of the Central Eskimos quoted by Knud Rasmussen in *The Netsilik Eskimos: Social Life and Spiritual Culture: Report of the Fifth Thule Expedition 1921-24* (1931).

## Iles, George
Mere precedence is much. No man will ever have as many descendants as Adam. The eyes of Columbus pointed to every mountain and stream mapped in America.

*

If the leader strides forward too fast, he may be hidden from his followers by the curvature of the earth.

*

Ignorance may find a truth on its doorstep that erudition vainly seeks in the stars.

*

Discovery begins by finding the discoverer.

*

Whoever ceases to be a student has never been a student.

*

If there were no cowards there would be no bullies.

*

Memory is cultivated and praised, but who will teach us to forget?

*

We despair of changing the habits of men, still we would alter institutions, the habits of millions of men.

*

Educated folk keep to one another's company too much, leaving other people much like milk skimmed of its cream.

*

Whatever a man has been he continues to be.

*

Error held in truth has much the effect of truth.

*

A great book is a mine as well as a mint: it suggests and excites as much thought as it presents in finished form.

> *Canadian Stories: Together with . . . Jottings from a Note-Book* (1918).

**Imlach, Punch**
Well, hell, the Lord hates a coward.

> Characteristic expression of hockey coach George Imlach, quoted by Trent Frayne in *Maclean's Magazine*, November 7, 1959.

My job is to win hockey games. If I have to bruise a few guys to do it, that's just too bad. I do what I think is necessary to win.

> Quoted by Jack Batten in *The Inside Story of Conn Symthe's Hockey Dynasty* (1969).

I'm the type of guy who thinks hockey is a war. A war against the other clubs.

> Quoted by Rod McKuen in *The Will to Win* (1971).

**Incarnation, Marie de l'**
See Marie de l'Incarnation.

**Infeld, Leopold**
I remember how I myself gave a talk at that time before a certain club in Canada and said that the secret of the atomic bomb does not exist; that this secret is a myth, and that we are confronted with only two roads to choose from: one is the road to war, the road of such hardship and suffering as humanity has not hitherto known; the other road is the road to international collaboration, of cultural exchange, the road leading to the use of the fruits of science and culture for the benefit of all the people. But my lecture must have been rather weak, for in the question period which followed, a very rich man asked me: "What shall we do to keep the secret of the atomic bomb from getting into Russian hands?"

> Professor Infeld, the mathematical physicist who worked with Einstein, taught at the University of Toronto during the Second World War. He returned to his native Poland in the 1950s. Speech be-

fore the World Peace Council, Vienna, November 4, 1951. "Scientists for Peace," *New Frontiers*, Spring, 1952.

In Toronto I felt cut adrift. . . . It must be good to die in Toronto. The transition between life and death would be continuous, painless and scarcely noticeable in this silent town. I dreaded the Sundays and prayed to God that if he chose for me to die in Toronto he would let it be on a Saturday afternoon to save me from one more Toronto Sunday.

> *Quest: The Evolution of a Scientist* (1941).

**Innes, Hammond**
*There's oil in the Rocky Mountains.* The phrase rang in my head.

> *Campbell's Kingdom* (1952).

It is difficult to convey my feeling, because nobody who hasn't been there can fully appreciate the latent menace of Labrador.

> *The Land God Gave to Cain: A Novel of the Labrador* (1958).

**Innis, Harold Adams**
Democracy will defeat the economist at every turn at its own game.

*

Nationalism provides the only sure basis for internationalism.

> "Government Ownership and the Canadian Scene" (1933), *Essays in Canadian Economic History* (1956), edited by Mary Quayle Innis.

Mechanization moreover implies more effective utilization of physical force. Machine guns are effective keys to the city.

> "Economic Nationalism," *Papers and Proceedings of the Sixth Annual Meeting of the Canadian Political Science Association, 1934* (1934).

Intellectuals in large numbers will sink the raft of any party, and if allowed to write a program will kill it.

> "Discussion in the Social Sciences," *The Dalhousie Review*, Autumn, 1935.

"Minerva's owl begins its flight only in

the gathering dusk . . ." Hegel wrote in reference to the crystallization of culture achieved in major classical writings in the period that saw the decline and fall of Grecian civilization.

"Minerva's Owl," Presidential Address to the Royal Society of Canada, 1947, *The Bias of Communication* (1951).

Canadian nationalism was systematically encouraged and exploited by American capital. Canada moved from colony to nation to colony.

"Great Britain, the United States and Canada" (1948), *Essays in Canadian Economic History* (1956), edited by Mary Quayle Innis.

"It is written but I say unto you" is a powerful directive to Western civilization. [Preface]

*

The ability to develop a system of government in which the bias of communication can be checked and an appraisal of the significance of space and time can be reached remains a problem of empire and of the Western world. ["Paper and the Printing Press"]

*

Culture is not concerned with these questions. It is designed to train the individual to decide how much information he needs and how little he needs, to give him a sense of balance and proportion, and to protect him from the fanatic who tells him that Canada will be lost to the Russians unless he knows more geography or more history or more economics or more science. Culture is concerned with the capacity of the individual to appraise problems in terms of space and time and with enabling him to take the proper steps at the right time. ["A Plea for Time"]

*

It is perhaps a unique characteristic of civilization that each civilization believes in its uniqueness and its superiority to other civilizations. Indeed this may be the meaning of culture—i.e., something which we have that others have not. It is probably for this reason that writings on culture can be divided into those attempting to weaken other cultures and

those attempting to strengthen their own. ["Industrialism and Cultural Values"]

*The Bias of Communication* (1951).

The present Dominion emerged not in spite of geography but because of it.

Quoted by Donald Creighton in *Harold Adams Innis: Portrait of a Scholar* (1957).

### Inugpasugjuk

Two men came to a hole in the sky. One asked the other to lift him up. If only he would do so, then he in turn would lend him a hand.

His comrade lifted him up, but hardly was he up when he shouted aloud for joy, forgot his comrade and ran into heaven.

The other could just manage to peep in over the edge of the hole; it was full of feathers inside. But so beautiful was it in heaven that the man who looked in over the edge forgot everything, forgot his comrade whom he had promised to help and simply ran off in to all the splendour of heaven.

Eskimo legend told by Inugpasugjuk. Knud Rasmussen's *Intellectual Culture of the Iglulik Eskimos: Report of the Fifth Thule Expedition, 1921-24* (1929).

### Irvine, Colonel A.G.

Old Tomorrow would be just the name for Sir John.

Colonel Irvine's nickname for Sir John A. Macdonald stuck. The commissioner of the North-West Mounted Police, meeting with the prime minister late in 1881, found him to be a procrastinator and dubbed him "Old Tomorrow." E.B. Biggar's *Anecdotal Life of Sir John Macdonald* (1891).

### Irvine, William

The member for Winnipeg North Centre is the leader of the party and I am the party.

Because they participated in the Winnipeg general strike of 1919, the two members of the House of Commons—J. S. Woodsworth and William Irvine—were identified as "the labour party." Quoted by F. H. Underhill in *In Search of Canadian Liberalism* (1960).

The man who dares to offend the Montreal interests is the sort of man that the people are going to vote for.

> The Calgary Labour M.P.'s letter to Arthur Meighen, September 25, 1924. Quoted by Roger Graham in *Arthur Meighen: A Biography—II: And Fortune Fled* (1963).

## Irving, Sir Henry
In the Indian language, I am told, Toronto means "The place of meeting." To you and me, ladies and gentlemen, brother and sister subjects of the English throne—[A burst of applause compelled the speaker to pause for some seconds] to us, ladies and gentlemen, to you before the curtain, to us behind it, I hope Toronto may mean "The place of meeting again and again."

> The last words of thanks were drowned in applause. Toronto curtain call, February 24, 1884, quoted by Joseph Hatton in *Henry Irving's Impressions of America: Narrated in a Series of Sketches, Chronicles, and Conversations* (1884).

## Irving, K.C.
We're just a couple of Kent County boys trying to do the best for our province. [To Premier Louis J. Robichaud, 1960]

\*

I am no longer residing in New Brunswick. My sons J. K. Irving, A. L. Irving and J. E. Irving, are carrying on the various businesses. As far as anything else goes, I do not choose to discuss the matter further. [Nassau, January 18, 1972]

> Reclusive New Brunswick capitalist, who retired in 1971, quoted by J. E. Belliveau in *Maclean's Magazine*, May, 1972. See also Louis J. Robichaud.

## Irving, Washington
I was at an age when imagination lends its colouring to everything, and the stories of these Sindbads of the wilderness made the life of a trapper and fur-trader perfect romance to me.

\*

Such was the Northwest Company in its powerful and prosperous days, when it held a kind of feudal sway over a vast domain of lake and forest. We are dwelling too long, perhaps, upon these individual pictures, endeared to us by the associations of early life, when, as yet a stripling youth, we have sat at the hospitable boards of the "mighty Northwesters," the lords of the ascendant at Montreal, and gazed with wondering and inexperienced eye at the baronial wassailing, and listened with astonished ear to their tales of hardships and adventures. It is one object of our task, however, to present scenes of the rough life of the wilderness, and we are tempted to fix these few memorials of a transient state of things fast passing into oblivion; for the feudal state of Fort William is at an end; its council chamber is silent and deserted; its banquet-hall no longer echoes to the burst of loyalty, or the "auld world" ditty; the lords of the lakes and forests have passed away; and the hospitable magnates of Montreal— where are they?

> *Astoria; or Anecdotes of an Enterprise Beyond the Rocky Mountains* (1836).

## Irwin, May
If there was more plumbing there'd be fewer divorces.

> Remark made by the Whitby-born singer-comedienne who ruled Broadway at the turn of the century. Quoted by Stephen Franklin in *The Heroes: A Saga of Canadian Inspiration.*

## Irwin, Thomas J.
Show me the verbal agreement! Show me the verbal agreement!

> Mayor of Sault Ste. Marie to Alderman Harry Lyons, a long-time resident of Steelton, when the two towns amalgamated in 1918. Lyons maintained that there were verbal as well as written agreements. (The remark recalls — and predates — Sam Goldwyn's quip: "A verbal agreement isn't worth the paper it's printed on.")

## Irwin, W. Arthur
Somewhere in the English language there ought to be a word that adequately describes the colossus of the prairies known to the world as the Canadian Wheat Pool. To date, I haven't been able to find one.

"The Wheat Pool," *Maclean's Magazine,* June 1, 1929.

Only journalists can make journalism work.

Quoted by Keith Davey in *Report of the Special Senate Committee on Mass Media, Volume I: The Uncertain Mirror* (1971).

**Isaacs, Avrom**
The opening exhibition conveys some of the excitement and optimism I and the painters involved feel towards these prospects. I also make the best frames in town.

Statement issued by the owner of the Greenwich (later Isaacs) Gallery, announcing the opening of his first group show, 1955. Quoted by Barry Lord in *Toronto Paintings: 1953-1965* (1972).

**Ismay, Lord**
On arrival at Quebec, we found that the Canadian Government had made admirable arrangements. The whole of the Château Frontenac was reserved for the exclusive use of the American and British delegations. All the residents had been moved elsewhere, except for one old lady who was not expected to live a fortnight. It is pleasant to record that she was reported to be still alive, and in occupation of the same room, when we returned for the second Quebec conference a year later.

*The Memoirs of General the Lord Ismay* (1960).

**Ivaluardjuk**
The greatest peril of life lies in the fact that human food consists entirely of souls.

Eskimo belief. Knud Rasmussen's *Intellectual Culture of the Iglulik Eskimos: Report of the Fifth Thule Expedition, 1921-24* (1929).

**Izumi, Kiyo**
I am firmly convinced that architecture, as a form of expression, can be considered an art only when it reflects an understanding of the perceptions of the consumers of the design environment, rather than the perceptions of the architect.

"LSD and Architectural Design," *Psychedelics: The Use and Implications of Hallucinogenic Drugs* (1970), edited by Bernard Aaronson and Humphry Osmund. In 1954, the architect took LSD to help with the design of the Yorkton Psychiatric Centre, Saskatchewan. This was under the direction of Dr. Humphry Osmund.

# J

**Jackson, A.Y.**
In summer it was green, raw greens all in a tangle; in autumn it flamed with red and gold; in winter it was wrapped in a blanket of dazzling snow, and in the springtime it roared with running waters and surged with new life, and our artists were advised to go to Europe and paint *smelly canals.*

"Canadian Art," *Empire Club of Canada: Addresses Delivered to the Members During the Year 1925* (1926).

Nowadays this country has become as remote as Wall Street. If a Canadian wishes to visit the Canadian Arctic, he has to get permission from Washington.

\*

For many years we had a country with

little or no art, now it seems we are to have art without a country.

> *A Painter's Country: The Autobiography of A.Y. Jackson* (1958).

I remember an old lady who had a house full of second-rate European paintings saying, "It's bad enough to have to live in this country without having pictures of it in your home."

> Preface to *James Wilson Morrice* (1966), by Kathleen Daly Pepper.

If we go far enough down this road we'll find Nineveh.

> About a country road in the Kleinburg, Ontario, area. Quoted by Neil Loutit in *The Globe and Mail*, July 17, 1971.

**Jackson, Barry**
One day I hope to see Canadian cities take as much pride in their theatres as they do in their grain elevators.

> Founder and director of the Birmingham Repertory Theatre to an Edmonton theatre audience, November, 1929. Quoted by Betty Lee in *Love and Whisky: The Story of the Dominion Drama Festival* (1973).

**Jackson, William Henry**
See Honoré J. Jaxon.

**Jacob, Fred**
"Oh, he may be a very decent fellow for all I know!" he explained. "But his plays are far too disturbing for Canadians."

> *Peevee* (1928). The playwright referred to is Henrik Ibsen.

**Jacobi, Lou**
Each time you go out on the stage you have to do it as if it's the first time.

> The Jewish comic and character actor was born in Toronto in 1913. Quoted by Frank Morriss in *The Globe and Mail*, April 10, 1967.

**Jacobs, Jane**
We're lucky here, you know. The States serves as a sort of early warning system for Canada. We can look down and see what's going wrong in New York and Cleveland and then try to avoid the same

thing happening here. But it's not easy, because the same destructive forces are at work in Canada.

> American urbanologist resident in Toronto, quoted by Clark Whelton in *The Village Voice*, July 6, 1972.

**Jacobson, Henry**
"The Dirty Thirties! Just put in your book that you met Henry Jacobson and he's seventy-eight years old. Might I say I never took a backward step in my life until that Depression whipped me, took away my wife, my home, a section of good land back in Saskatchewan. Left me with nothing. Write that down."

> Recorded by Barry Broadfoot in "Home, Wife, Land Gone," *Ten Lost Years 1929-1939: Memoirs of Canadians Who Survived the Depression* (1973).

**Jagger, Mick**
"What do you remember of Toronto?" "Not much," said Jagger. "Fatigue. Heat. Not just the heat, but the lack of oxygen. Why isn't there any air conditioning in Canada?"

> Quoted by Robert Stall in *Weekend Magazine*, September 2, 1972, after Jagger played Maple Leaf Gardens in Toronto.

**James, Henry**
Something assures one that Quebec must be a city of gossip; for evidently it is not a city of culture. A glance at the few booksellers' windows gives evidence of this. A few Catholic statuettes and prints, two or three Catholic publications, a festoon or so of rosaries, a volume of Lamartine, a supply of ink and matches, form the principal stock. ["Quebec"]

\*

You purchase release at last by the fury of your indifference, and stand there gazing your fill at the most beautiful object in the world. ["Niagara"]

> *Portraits of Places* (1883).

**James, Captain Thomas**
We had Ice not farre off about us, and some pieces, as high as our Top-masthead.

"That stubborn and pious old Bristol seaman, Captain Thomas James, had provided in his *Strange and Dangerous Voyage*, with a certain grim satisfaction in his hardships, the raw materials for a new *Inferno*, all ice; and Coleridge could no more have escaped in Bristol the shade of his ancient fellow-townsman than the Wedding-Guest could have given the ancient Mariner the slip." John Livingston Lowes in *The Road to Xanadu: A Study in the Ways of the Imagination* (1927).

James's popular account of his Arctic voyage was published in 1633, and it supplied Samuel Taylor Coleridge with some imagery for his great poem *The Rime of the Ancient Mariner* (1798). At least one study of the poem assumed James's account to be the sole source used by Coleridge. The captain left his name behind: James Bay. See also Samuel Taylor Coleridge and Captain Luke Foxe.

## Jameson, Anna

Toronto,—such is now the sonorous name of this our sublime capital,—was, thirty years ago, a wilderness, the haunt of the bear and deer, with a little, ugly, inefficient fort, which, however, could not be more ugly or inefficient than the present one....At present its appearance to me, a stranger, is mostly strangely mean and melancholy. A little ill-built town on low land, at the bottom of a frozen bay, with one very ugly church, without tower or steeple; some government offices, built of staring red brick, in the most tasteless, vulgar style imaginable; three feet of snow all around; and the grey, sullen, wintry lake, and the dark gloom of the pine forest bounding the prospect; such seems Toronto to me now. I did not expect much; but for this I was not prepared. Perhaps no preparation could have *prepared* me, or softened my present feelings. I will not be unjust if I can help it, nor querulous. If I look into my own heart, I find that it is regret for what I have left and lost—the absent, not the present—which throws over all around me a chill, colder than that of the wintry day—a gloom, deeper than that of the wintry night.

\*

"There is no *society* in Toronto," is what I hear repeated all around me—even by those who compose the only society we have. "But," you will say, "what could be expected in a remote town, which forty years ago was an uninhabited swamp, and twenty years ago only began to exist?" I really do not know what I expected, but I will tell you what I did *not* expect. I did not expect to find here in this new capital of a new country, with the boundless forest within half a mile of us on almost every side,—concentrated as it were the worst evils of our old and most artificial social system at home, with none of its *agrémens,* and none of its advantages. Toronto is like a fourth or fifth rate provincial town, with the pretensions of a capital city. We have here a petty colonial oligarchy, a self-constituted aristocracy, based upon nothing real, nor even upon anything imaginary; and we have all the mutual jealousy and fear, and petty gossip, and mutual meddling and mean rivalship, which are common in a small society of which the members are well known to each other, a society composed, like all societies, of many heterogeneous particles; but as these circulate within very confined limits, there is no getting out of the way of what one most dislikes: we must necessarily hear, see, and passively endure much that annoys and disgusts any one accustomed to the independence of a large and liberal society or the ease of continental life.

\*

It is seldom that in this country the mind is ever carried backward by associations or recollections of any kind Horace Walpole said of Italy, that it was "a land in which the memory saw more than the eye," and in Canada hope must play the part of memory. It is all the difference between seed-time and harvest. We are rich in anticipation, but poor in possession—more poor in memorials. Some vague and general traditions, of no interest whatever to the ignorant settlers, do indeed exist, of horrid conflicts between the Hurons and the Iroquois, all along these shores, in the time and before the time of the French dominion; of the enterprise and daring of the early fur traders; above all, of the unrequited labours and sacrifices of the missionaries, whether Jesuits or Moravians, or Methodists, some of whom perished in tortures; others devoted themselves to the most horrible privations—each for what he believed to be the cause of truth, and for the diffusion of the light of salvation; none near to applaud the fortitude with which they died, or to gain hope and courage from their example.

*

I have not often in my life met with contented and cheerful-minded women, but I never met with so many repining and discontented women as in Canada. I never met with *one* woman recently settled here, who considered herself happy in her new home and country: I *heard* of one, and doubtless there are others, but they are exceptions to the general rule.

*

As for the style of architecture, I may not attempt to name or describe it; but a gentleman informed me, in rather equivocal phrase, that it was *"somewhat gothic."*

*

Toronto is, as a residence, worse and better than other small communities—*worse* in so much as it is remote from all the best advantages of a high state of civilisation, while it is infested by all its evils, all its follies; and *better*, because, beside being a small place, it is a *young* place; and in spite of this affectation of looking back, instead of looking up, it must advance—it may become the thinking head and beating heart of a nation, great, and wise, and happy;—who knows?

*

The pity I have for the trees in Canada, shows how far I am being a true Canadian. How do we know that trees do not feel their downfall? We know nothing about it.

*

A man may be as much a fool from the want of sensibility as the want of sense.

*

As the rolling stone gathers no moss, so the roving hearth gathers no affections.

*

O I could beat myself! and now there is no help!—the first moment, the first impression is over—is lost; though I should live a thousand years, long as Niagara itself shall roll, I can never see it again for the first time. Something is gone that cannot be restored. What has come over my soul and senses?—I am no longer Anna—I am metamorphosed—I am translated—I am an ass's head, a clod, a wooden spoon, a fat weed growing on Lethe's bank, a stock, a stone, a petrifaction,—for have I not seen Niagara, the wonder of wonders; and felt—no words can tell *what* disappointment!

*

One of the most gifted and accomplished, as well as most rational and most practical characters I ever met with, once said to me seriously, "I thank God I do not believe in the *impossibility* of anything."

*

A Canadian settler *hates* a tree, regards it as his natural enemy, as something to be destroyed, eradicated, annihilated by all and any means. The idea of useful or ornamental is seldom associated here even with the most magnificent timber trees, such as among the Druids had been consecrated, and among the Greeks would have sheltered oracles and votive temples. The beautiful faith which assigned to every tree of the forest its guardian nymph, to every leafy grove its tutelary divinity, would find no votaries here. Alas! for the Dryads and Hamadryads of Canada!

*Winter Studies and Summer Rambles in Canada* (1838).

**Janes, John**   See John Davis.

**Jarvis, Alan**
Our responsibilities in a once beautiful and unspoiled country, it seems to me, are double now that we are such a privileged and prosperous country.

"A World Without Frontiers" (1956), *Empire Club of Canada: Addresses 1956-57* (1957).

Visitors to Canada who view Canadian painting and graphic art for the first time constantly remark two things: stylistic generalizations are quite impossible to make, but one thing emerges quite clearly —an immense vitality.

> "Art in Canada," *The Atlantic Monthly*, November, 1964.

I attended three universities—Toronto, Oxford, and Cripps.

\*

I'm not very good but I'm very fast and I'm very, very expensive.

> The Brantford-born director of the National Gallery studied at Oxford and served as secretary to Sir Stafford Cripps, minister of Aircraft Production in the British government. Jarvis was a sculptor of some standing. Quoted by Robert Fulford in *The Toronto Star*, December 5, 1972.

### Jasmin, Claude
A man grows out of childhood as he grows into his native land.

> *La petite patrie* (1973).

### Jaxon, Honoré J.
*Fair Play and Free Play* . . . published, when he feels like it, by Honoré Joseph Jaxon, Agitator, Disturber, producer of plans to make men think, and Chronic Objector to those methods of organization which tend to produce "Bossism" and "Machine Rule."

> From a pamphlet published in 1908 by Jaxon who was born William Henry Jackson but changed his name when he was appointed Riel's secretary. After the Rebellion of 1885 he was found insane, but he escaped to the United States where he was involved in labour agitation. Quoted by W.J.C. Cherwinski, *Canadian Historical Review*, June, 1965.

### Jefferis, B.G.
An infallible sign that a young man's intentions are improper, is his trying to excite your passions. If he loves you, he will never appeal to that feeling, because he respects you too much for that. And the woman who allows a man to take advantage of her just to compel him to marry her, is lost and heartless in the last degree, and utterly destitute of moral principle as well as virtue. A woman's

riches is her virtue, that gone she has lost all.

\*

The best writers lay down the rule for the government of the marriage-bed, that sexual indulgence should only occur about once in a week or ten days, and this of course applies only to those who enjoy a fair degree of health. But it is a hygienic and physiological fact that those who indulge only once a month receive a far greater degree of the intensity of enjoyment than those who indulge their passions more frequently. Much pleasure is lost by excesses where much might be gained by temperance, giving rest to the organs for the accumulation of nervous force.

> *Light on Dark Corners: Search Lights on Health: A Complete Sexual Science and a Guide to Purity and Physical Manhood* (25th edition, 1894), by Professor B.G. Jefferis of Chicago and J.L. Nichols of Toronto.

### Jefferson, Thomas
The acquisition of Canada this year, as far as the neighbourhood of Quebec, will be a mere matter of marching, and will give us experience for the attack of Halifax the next, and the final expulsion of England from the American continent.

> Letter to Colonel William Duane, Monticello, August 4, 1812. *The Writings of Thomas Jefferson: Library Edition* (1903), edited by Andrew A. Lipscomb.

### Jefferys, C.W.
Every period has its artistic conventions; even the most original artist can speak only in the idiom of his time.

\*

The pictorial mouse may help the scholastic lion.

> "The Visual Reconstruction of History," *Canadian Historical Review*, September, 1936.

Truth is not only stranger than fiction; it is frequently more artistic.

> "History in Motion Pictures," *Canadian Historical Review*, December, 1941.

A tangible object cannot lie or equivocate so successfully as a word. A building or a four-poster bed expresses the personality of its maker, and unintentionally reveals some secrets that may cast a light upon his character or that of his time.

> The Picture Gallery of Canadian History (1942), Volume I: Discovery to 1763, illustrations drawn and collected by C.W. Jefferys.

## Jelinek, Maria
Hot? Everything's hot when you're skating. No matter what you wear, and no matter how icy the arena is, after five minutes of competition, you're dripping.

> The Czech-born skater and her brother Otto won the world figure skating pairs championship in Prague in 1962. The Globe and Mail, May 18, 1972.

## Jelinek, Otto
If we had to do what we did to win that title every night we'd be dead within a month. In amateur contests you build to one specific performance. Here we do the same act every night; nothing changes.

> Otto Jelinek and his sister Maria joined the Ice Capades after winning the world figure skating pairs championship in Prague in 1962. The Toronto Telegram, November 9, 1963.

## Jellicoe, Admiral John
It is a real pleasure to make the acquaintance of the Toronto people; but it is not a bit of a pleasure to talk to them, as I have had to do for the remaining hours of my stay. I have earned my lunch; or rather, perhaps, I have got to try to earn it.

> "Address," December 8, 1919, Addresses Delivered before the Canadian Club of Toronto: Season of 1919-20 (1920).

## Jenkins, Herbert
In Toronto we size up a man before he's had time to say he's pleased to meet us, and we'd buy a mountain quicker than you'd ask your neighbour to pass the marmalade at breakfast.

\*

John Dene looked about him with interest. He was frankly disappointed. He had

conceived the administrative buildings of the greatest navy in the world as something grand and impressive; yet here was the British Admiralty with an entrance that would compare unfavourably with a second-rate hotel in Toronto.

> The author of John Dene of Toronto: A Comedy of Whitehall (1920) made a name for himself as an English publisher, not as the author of crime and espionage thrillers.

## Jenkinson, Sir Anthony
Toronto is a city of reputations. It has the reputation for being smug, for being religious (they call it Holy Toronto), and for being conservative; and it is reputed to be Canada's most Americanised, most up-and-coming city. All these reputations are, I suppose, justified.

> Where Seldom a Gun Is Heard (1937).

## Jenness, Diamond
They are adapting themselves, too, to our money economy, and learning to work for a daily wage. But when we who created this money economy ignorantly distort and misapply it, how can we teach Eskimos but one step removed from the stone age to use it for their own and others' welfare, and not for increasing human unhappiness?

> Epilogue (1959), The People of the Twilight (1928, 1959).

## Jennings, Charles
"The Voice of CBC Radio"

> Jennings's deep voice was familiar to millions of radio listeners. He earned the sobriquet when he became chief announcer of the CBC upon its formation in 1936. Obituary, Time, July 30, 1973.

## Jerome, Jerome K.
It is one of the joys of England that her people may go to almost any quarter of the globe and find Englishmen all around. It seems as if one could belt the globe and always find friends, Englishmen, and it is one thing that ought to make us proud of being Englishmen that we can always find our friends. I have certainly found a great many here today.

"The Colonial Conference," November 2, 1905, *Addresses Delivered before the Canadian Club of Toronto: Session 1905-1906* (1906).

## Jeune, Father Paul Le
See Le Jeune, Father Paul.

## Jewison, Norman
When you're hungry you take what you can get, and you learn. Now? Now I can afford to say no. That's the real power you get from success.

Toronto-born director of *Fiddler on the Roof*, quoted by Susan Kastner in *The Toronto Star*, March 26, 1968.

## Jewkes, Douglas
I think this calls for a bottle of 7-Up!

First words of the imprisoned Nova Scotian miner to his exhausted rescuers. Jewkes was rescued nine days after the Springhill coal mine caved in, November, 1958, and he later explained the vision that had sustained him: "I dreamed of drinking 7-Up. I could imagine myself falling into a whole well of 7-Up. I thought, if I ever get out of here alive, I'll buy ten cases of 7-Up, and lap it up." He was hired by the elated soft-drink company as a warehouseman. Quoted by Frank Rasky in *Great Canadian Disasters* (1961). See also Byron (Barney) Martin.

## Jodoin, Claude
Nobody loses any status by getting together—whether they call themselves unions or associations. If it's good for the professional associations, and the medical colleges, it certainly should be good for any individual or person as far as Canada is concerned. I'm not criticizing the professional associations or the medical colleges—sometimes I'm jealous, because they have very good union shops.

President of the Canadian Labour Congress. *The Face of Labour: Four Programs from CBC Television*, January-February, 1961.

## John XXIII, Pope
Ah, Toronto.

"His Holiness walked in, a short, rotund person with a very happy smiling face. Just before he reached me, he raised his hands and said, 'Ah, Toronto,' with the emphasis on the last syllable. We conducted as much of a conversation as is usually possible through an interpreter," reminisced Toronto Mayor Nathan Phillips in *Mayor of All the People* (1967). "As we left Pope John, he said something with a smile. He was a jolly person. Monseignor [the interpreter] told us he had said: 'Come back and see me when I can speak English.'" See also Nathan Phillips.

## Johnny Canuck   See Leo Bachle.

## Johnson, Daniel
What is good for the other provinces is not necessarily good for Quebec. The converse is also true: *what is good for Quebec is not necessarily good for the other provinces.*

Leader of the Union Nationale, Legislative Assembly, Quebec, April 23, 1963. Quoted by Frank Scott and Michael Oliver in *Quebec States Her Case: Speeches and Articles from Quebec in the Years of Unrest* (1964).

Some Quebec politicians in the past have been ready to save Confederation even at the expense of Quebec. We want not only to save but develop Quebec, even at the expense of Confederation. But we're not fanatics. There can be no compromise on the essentials, but there's lots of room for negotiation. I guess I'm really paraphrasing Mackenzie King's stand on conscription: separatism if necessary, but not necessarily separatism.

Union Nationale leader quoted by Peter C. Newman in "Daniel Johnson" (1966), *Home Country: People, Places, and Power Politics* (1973).

Egalité ou Indépendance.

Slogan of the victorious Union Nationale party under Daniel Johnson in the Quebec election of 1966.

Canada or Quebec? Wherever the French-Canadian nation finds its freedom, there will its homeland be.

"Canada and Quebec: Can This Marriage Be Saved?" *The Nation Keepers: Canadian Business Perspectives* (1967), edited by Isaiah A. Litvak.

It might be better to amend the marriage contract than to go through all the hardships and explosive damages of divorce.

\*

Divorce after a century together, then a remarriage that is a growing success.

Both remarks are attributed to Daniel Johnson, premier of Quebec from 1966 to 1969, the marriage ceremony being Confederation, the divorce a separation of Quebec from the rest of Canada.

## Johnson, Dick

Ripsi, rantsi,
Humpsy, dumpsy;
I, Dick Johnson,
Killed Tecumseh!

Chorus of "The Dick Johnson Reel" by Jake Falstaff, American poet who died in 1935. The "reel" appeared in Falstaff's *The Bulls of Spring* along with this note: "The old men say their grandfathers heard Dick Johnson sing the chorus of this song in the timberlands of northern Summit County, Ohio."

## Johnson, Edward

It was pretty hard to make the public believe that an artist could have a name like Johnson. Perhaps they were right.

"On Teaching Children Music," December 3, 1928, *Addresses Delivered before the Canadian Club of Toronto: Session of 1928-29* (1929). The singer and later general manager of the Metropolitan Opera in New York adopted a name more in keeping with his profession—Eduardo di Giovanni.

Music is no more the exclusive property of musicians than law is the property of lawyers. Music belongs to the masses.

It would be wonderful if I could live to see Canada made a singing nation.

## Johnson, Eli

I felt so thankful on reaching a land of freedom, that I couldn't express myself. When I look back at what I endured, it seems as if I had entered a Paradise. I can here sing and pray with none to molest me. I am a member of the Baptist Church, and endeavour to live a Christian life.

Johnson settled in Gosfield, Ont., leaving a life of slavery in Virginia. Quoted by Benjamin Drew in *The Refugee: or the Narratives of Fugitive Slaves in Canada* (1856).

## Johnson, George Washington

I wandered today to the hill, Maggie,
    To watch the scene below,
The creek and the creaking old mill,
    Maggie,
    As we used to long ago.
The green grove is gone from the hill,
    Maggie,
    Where first the daisies sprung,
The creeking old mill is still, Maggie,
    Since you and I were young.

First of three verses of "When You and I Were Young" from *Maple Leaves* (1864). This song was once on everyone's lips. The author of the love ballad was born in Wentworth County, Ontario, where he taught school and fell in love with a student, Maggie Clark. They were married the year the poem appeared in Johnson's only book, *Maple Leaves*. The "old mill" stood on the bank of Twenty Mile Creek. Sad to relate, the young bride died two years later, the same year an English composer living in Chicago, J.A. Butterfield, set the poem to music. Johnson taught Latin at Cornell University but eventually returned to Binbrook Township, where he again taught at Glanford School, near Hamilton.

## Johnson, Harry G.

If the public is to be taxed for the privilege of having a national identity—which is what the protectionists are really arguing for—there are far more worthy monuments to national independence than a second-rate manufacturing sector that could be constructed with the money—a decent social security system, a comprehensive public health programme, beautiful cities free of slums, a truly free and high quality educational system, a truly bilingual culture.

Quoted by James Eayrs in "Sharing a Continent: The Hard Issues," in *The United States and Canada: The American Assembly* (1964), edited by John Sloan Dickey.

This kind of attitude, which I find in a lot of Canadian thinking in relation to the United States ("Well, they're very nice guys and they haven't hurt us yet, but who knows, some day they might. . . ."), reminds me of the story of the hermit who lived on a mountain top and wore no clothes but a top hat. He was asked why he wore no clothes and he replied that it was because nobody ever came to visit him anyway. And then he was asked, well, why did he wear the top hat? And he said, "Somebody might come." It seems to me that Canada is being asked to pay a pretty high price for that top hat.

The Toronto-born economist at the University of Chicago answering Walter L. Gordon's criticisms of the integration of the Canadian economy with the American. "External Economic Policy (11)" (1960), *The Canadian Quandary: Economic Problems and Policies* (1963).

So far as national identity is concerned, I have no doubts at all that a Canadian is an animal recognizably distinct from an American, not just in the way he pronounces "out" or "about" or "twenty" but also in his attitudes and general character. My confidence on this score is the result of having observed Canadians in different international contexts, and listening to people of other nationalities discussing Canadian character and behaviour. I won't say that the qualities I think of as typically Canadian are altogether admirable—in addition to seriousness and a fairly high level of competence, they include a certain provinciality of outlook, signs of inferiority feeling, and a tendency at meetings either to orate at a high moral level or to keep quiet and then grumble afterwards about not being listened to—but they are recognizable as a distinct national mixture.

*

Thus, far from contributing to the growth of a stronger, more independent, and

identity-conscious nation, Canadian nationalism as it has developed in recent years has been diverting Canada into a narrow and garbage-cluttered cul-de-sac.

"Problems of Canadian Nationalism" (1961), *The Canadian Quandary: Economic Problems and Policies* (1963).

Instead of welcoming the democratizing influence and attempting to remove or mitigate the socially undesirable side-effects, they resist the forces of modernization and democratization by cultivating hatred of Americans, by seeking to "close the 49th parallel," and by seeking to establish in Canada monopoly privileges for the Canadian-born over everyone else. They have been remarkably successful in disguising petit-bourgeois capitalism as idealistic socialism, and white Canadian Anglo-Saxon supremacy as national independence.

"Canada and Contemporary Society," Convocation Address, Carleton University, May 22, 1970.

## Johnson, Hewlett
Magnificent. Congratulations. Given best Social Credit skill to produce watertight scheme and pressing it forward courageously, Alberta will kindle a world-wide torch.

Cable from the Very Rev. Dr. H.C. Hewlett Johnson, the so-called Red Dean of Canterbury, to William Aberhart when his Social Credit Party was swept into power in Alberta, August 22, 1935. Quoted by John A. Irving in *The Social Credit Movement in Alberta* (1959).

## Johnson, Lyndon B.
Canada is such a close neighbour and such a good neighbour that we always have plenty of problems here. They are kind of like the problems in the home town.

Quoted by Gerald Clark in *Canada: The Uneasy Neighbour* (1965).

## Johnson, Pauline
Go forth, and win the glories of the war.
Go forth, nor bend to greed of white men's hands,

By right, by birth we Indians own these
   lands,
Though starved, crushed, plundered, lies
   our nation low . . .
Perhaps the white man's God has willed
   it so.

> Concluding lines of "A Cry from an
> Indian Wife," *The White Wampum*
> (1895).

\*

And up on the hills against the sky,
A fir tree rocking its lullaby,
Swings, swings,
Its emerald wings,
Swelling the song that my paddle sings.

> Last lines of "The Song My Paddle
> Sings," *The White Wampum* (1895).

\*

The Dutch may have their Holland, the
   Spaniard have his Spain,
The Yankee to the south of us must
   south of us remain;
For not a man dare lift a hand against the
   men who brag
That they were born in Canada beneath
   the British flag.

> Final stanza of "Canadian Born," *Cana-
> dian Born* (1903).

\*

They've shot my flag to ribbons, but in
   rents
   It floats above the height;
Their ensign shall not crown my battle-
   ments
   While I can stand and fight.
I fling defiance at them as I cry,
   "Capitulate? Not I."

> Final stanza of " 'And He Said, Fight
> On,' " the last poem written by E. Paul-
> ine Johnson (whose Indian name was
> "Tekahionwake") shortly before her
> death, March 7, 1913. Texts of all the
> poems are taken from *Flint and Feather:
> The Complete Poems of E. Pauline
> Johnson* (1912), with an introduction by
> Theodore Watts-Dunton.

There are those who think they pay me
a compliment in saying I am just like a
white woman. I am an Indian, and my
aim, my joy, my pride, is to sing the
glories of my people.

> *Legends of Vancouver* (1911).

I desire . . . that no tombstone or monument be raised in my memory. I prefer to
be remembered in the hearts of my
people and my public.

> Will dated nine days before the Indian
> poet's death, quoted by Marjorie Free-
> man Campbell in *The Globe and Mail*,
> February 25, 1961.

### Johnson, Dr. Samuel

About this time it was, that the French
first began to turn their thoughts to
traffick and navigation, and to desire, like
other nations, an American territory. All
the fruitful and valuable parts of the
western world were, already, either occupied, or claimed; and nothing remained
for France, but the leavings of other
navigators, for she was not yet haughty
enough to seize what the neighbouring
powers had already appropriated.

The French, therefore, contented
themselves with sending a colony to Canada, a cold, uncomfortable, uninviting
region, from which nothing but furs and
fish were to be had, and where the new
inhabitants could only pass a laborious
and necessitous life, in perpetual regret
of the deliciousness and plenty of their
native land.

Notwithstanding the opinion which
our countrymen have been taught to entertain of the comprehension and foresight of French politicians, I am not able
to persuade myself, that when this colony
was first planted, it was thought of much
value, even by those that encouraged it
. . . in this region of desolate sterility they
settled themselves, upon whatever principle. . . .

> "The Political State of Great Britain:
> An Introduction" (1756), *The Works of
> Samuel Johnson* (1903), *Volume XIII:
> Reviews and Political Tracts*.

### Johnston, Gordon

Canadian cuckoos never cuckoo—they
only utter gutteral clucks.

> "It Happened in Canada," *The Toronto
> Star*, March 24, 1972.

### Johnston, James

The Chief's Prince Albert friends had
brought him up to date on all the new

Gerda Munsinger jokes. Many of them had been floating across the country for weeks, but it took the Prince Albert people to have enough courage to tell them to Diefenbaker, complete with all the lines, including, "I want my bedtime Tory."

*The Party's Over* (1971).

## Johnstone, Chevalier de
A Canadian in the woods is worth three disciplined soldiers, as a soldier in the plain is worth three Canadians.

> James Johnstone, called Chevalier de Johnstone, was aide-de-camp to Montcalm at the fall of Quebec. Quoted by Francis Parkman in *Montcalm and Wolfe* (1884).

## Joly de Lotbinière, Sir Henri-Gustave
Since we cannot find a comparison on this poor earth emblematic of our future greatness, let us borrow one from the heavens at the risk of losing ourselves in the clouds with the advocates of Confederation; I propose the adoption of the rainbow as our emblem. By the endless variety of its tints the rainbow will give an excellent idea of the diversity of races, religions, sentiments and interests of the different parts of the Confederation. By its slender and elongated form, the rainbow would afford a perfect representation of the geographical configuration of the Confederation. By its lack of consistence—an image without substance—the rainbow would represent aptly the solidity of our Confederation. An emblem we must have, for every great empire has one; let us adopt the rainbow.

> Speech, Legislative Assembly, Quebec, February 20, 1865. *Parliamentary Debates on the Subject of Confederation of the British North American Provinces, 3rd Session, 8th Provincial Parliament of Canada* (1865).

## Jonas, George
And I have slowly come to the conclusion
That I am not a very personal thing,
My food has also known the pleasure of eating,
And some say my own soul could go on living without me.

> "Conclusion," *The Absolute Smile* (1967).

But being a Canadian
By conscious and considered choice
I have to remember no one & nothing
Which in this 1969th year of grace
Suits me just fine ["On the Virtues of Being a Canadian"]

> *

And by midnight or so
While the fires of her manifest destiny smoulder
You'll be all ready to slip across
The world's longest undefended border.

> "American Girl: A Canadian View," *The Happy Hungry Man* (1970).

## Jones, D.G.
Having reached the Pacific, Canadians have begun to turn back on themselves, to create that added dimension Teilhard de Chardin calls the noosphere or, to put it more simply, Canadian culture. Of course, we have been at this for some time, but to use the words of Robert Frost . . . more than ever before we have arrived at a point where we recognize, not only that the land is ours, but that we are the land's.

> Introduction, *Butterfly on Rock: A Study of Themes and Images in Canadian Literature* (1970).

## Jones, Ernest
Life in Toronto was in many ways very pleasant. Curiously enough, one partook of cultural activities more than in London. There, where so many were always available, one had to make an effort to find the necessary free time. In Toronto there was only one serious centre, the Massey Hall, and everything that came there did so only for a week. So it became always a weekly habit to attend, and it was very rewarding, since the most celebrated artists of the musical and theatrical world always included Toronto in their American tours. Any gap would be filled by the Montreal Opera Company, which was very good indeed. Then there were regular visits from the magnificent American orchestras, with their famous conductors, all on a level which London has never reached.

It was not merely that I found myself back in the Biblical and Victorian atmosphere of my boyhood—that would have been bad enough to someone bent on emancipation—but it was the dead uniformity that I found so tedious: one knew beforehand everyone's opinion on every subject, so there was a complete absence of mental stimulation or exchange of thought. I should much like to revisit Toronto now and observe the great change which, I understand, has taken place in this as well as in other respects.

> The psychoanalyst lived in Toronto in 1908 and 1909, before joining Sigmund Freud in Vienna and writing Freud's biography. *Free Associations: Memoirs of a Psycho-Analyst* (1959).

### Jones, Robert M.
Can you sell an icebox to an Eskimo?

The Eskimos often buy refrigerators which they use to keep food from freezing.

*

What is the world's second largest nation?

Most strangers are unaware of Canada's sheer physical size. It is exceeded in area only by the Soviet Union. It has more lakes than the rest of the world combined. And while it contains one of the world's last great undeveloped areas, it is, paradoxically, the fifth largest trading nation on earth and has the third highest standard of living.

> *Can Elephants Swim? Unlikely Answers to Improbable Questions* (1969).

### Jones, Samantha
I don't care if my underwear *does* show, do you?

> The stunning model was born in Buffalo, New York, but was raised in Ottawa. She changed her name from Linda Manhart to Samantha Jones in Paris in 1964. Quoted by Bill Trent in *Weekend Magazine*, March 11, 1967.

### Jordan, Pat
As a politician, I think it is acknowledged he was supreme in his ability to walk a straight fence to the future and keep both ears to the ground.

> Attributed to the Social Credit member from North Okanagan in the British Columbia Legislature, 1973; a tribute to W.A.C. Bennett.

### Jory, Victor
The law keeps the police in handcuffs.

> "Jory is an example of how an actor's face isn't always his fortune," wrote one critic of the American stage and screen star who was born in Dawson City, Alaska, in 1902. Jory was raised in Vancouver and educated (according to *Who's Who in the Theatre* [1970]) at the "University of Canada." Quoted by Jack Edmund Nowlan in *Films in Review*, June-July, 1968.

### Joseph, Dov
The world has accepted us. Jerusalem has become in fact what it has always been in our hearts: the capital of Israel.

*

The last governor of Jerusalem we had known as a people was Pontius Pilate. For the first time in over two thousand years, Jerusalem once again had a Jewish governor.

> Born in Montreal in 1899 and educated in law at McGill and Laval, Dov Joseph was appointed military governor of Jerusalem in 1948. *The Faithful City: The Siege of Jerusalem, 1948* (1960).

### Joseph, Michael
Before the war British publishers were often told by friends in the Canadian book trade that their public preferred the bigger, handsomer American book. They wanted value for money, and had been accustomed to measure value by size and weight. The story has often been told of the Canadian agent who handed one of his travellers an advance copy of a new book from a British publisher and asked, "How many can you sell of that?" The traveller, without opening the book, handed it back and said, "None." The agent, somewhat nettled, said, "None? But you haven't even looked at it." The traveller replied, "I don't need to. It doesn't weigh enough."

> *The Adventure of Publishing* (1949). ·

**Josie, Edith**
Here are the news.

\*

Everything good now.

\*

This is end the news.

\*

I'll bet if they start to make Old Crow big town, they won't do it.

> Indian correspondent for *The White-horse Star* in Old Crow, six hundred miles north of Whitehorse, and author of a collection of her spontaneous and unedited reports, *Here Are the News* (1966). "One of her expressions, 'everything good now,' has become a campus catchphrase at the University of British Columbia. Edith Josie first used it when she described how an Indian died and left his widow with the carcasses of six caribou." Gerald Clark in *Canada: The Uneasy Neighbour* (1965).

**Josselin, John**
New England is by some affirmed to be an island, bounded on the north with the River Canada (so called from Monsieur Cane).

> *New England's Rarities* (1672).

**Joubin, Franc**
This little baby has found me two and a half million dollars worth of uranium ore.

> The first portable radiation counter (the Geiger counter) was developed in Toronto in the 1950s. Joubin prospected the Algoma area with one "little baby." Quoted by J.J. Brown in *Ideas in Exile: A History of Canadian Invention* (1967).

**Joudry, Patricia**
Success or failure is a state of mind.

> The playwright achieved success in Toronto in 1955 with her play *Teach Me How to Cry* and failure with it on Broadway and the West End. *The Toronto Star*, April 2, 1960.

**Joyce, James**
She had interrogated constantly at varying intervals as to the correct method of writing the capital initial of a city in Canada—Quebec.

> The reference is to Molly Bloom in *Ulysses* (1922).

**Judge, Jack**   See Harry Williams.

**Julien, Claude**
True, a united Canada can still fall further and further under the stifling influence of American capital. This is where Europe has a role to play, not for the academic satisfaction of sustaining far-off Canadian independence, but for the very practical reason that Canadian independence is essential to European independence.

> *Canada: Europe's Last Chance* (1968), translated by Penny Williams.

When Lester B. Pearson, the Liberal Prime Minister, came to power in 1963 he inherited from his Conservative predecessor, John Diefenbaker, an issue which was to provoke a serious crisis: American periodicals distributed in Canada were offering English-Canadian business advertising space at rock-bottom prices, which deprived Canadian periodicals of an important part of their income. As a safeguard, a commission proposed a special forty per cent tax on those contracts, and the project was approved by Pearson as it had been by Diefenbaker. Immediately, John F. Kennedy telephoned Pearson from the White House and laid it on the line: either the publications of the *Time-Life* group and the *Reader's Digest* would be exempt from the forty per cent tax, or the United States would slash a $420 million contract intended for the Canadair firm in Montreal; that, added Kennedy, would throw 16,000 men out of work.

> *America's Empire* (1971), translated by Bruce Renaud.

**Julien, Pauline**
We want friendship with Canada. Freedom with friendship.

> Quoted by Blaik Kirby in *The Globe and Mail*, June 19, 1968.

Vive le Québec libre!

> "The federal minister was speaking on the problem of *francophone*. I was in-

*dignée*. These people want to assimilate us. I shouted, *'Vive le Québec libre,'* and that's all.

"I've known Pelletier for a long time. He said: 'You sing better than you shout.' And I said: 'I sing and I can shout too.'

"I heard nothing officially. It was a *cri de coeur*, that's all."

At a conference of francophone nations at Niamey, Niger, in February of 1969, the separatist-minded *chanteuse* Pauline Julien interrupted the speech-making of the secretary of State, Gérard Pelletier, by shouting aloud Charles de Gaulle's ringing declaration. *The Globe and Mail*, March 24, 1969. See also Charles de Gaulle.

## Juliette
I'm no pioneer. Let Sinatra and Peggy Lee do that. I'll do songs the public knows.

Popular singer Juliette Sysak, quoted by Alex Barris in *The Pierce-Arrow Showroom Is Leaking: An Insider's View of the CBC* (1969).

## Jumbo, King of the Elephants
Hath borne his faculties so meek, hath been
So mild in his great office, that his virtues
Will plead like angels, trumpet-tongued, against
The deep damnation of his taking-off.

Jumbo, whose name is a synonym for size, was the best-loved circus elephant of all time. The mammoth pachyderm, born in Africa in 1861 and acquired by P.T. Barnum, was a featured performer in the Barnum and Bailey Circus. Jumbo was struck down and killed by a Grand Trunk Railroad engine at St. Thomas, Ontario, September 15, 1885. Barnum promptly sued the Grand Trunk for $100,000, but a settlement was reached. The above quotation appeared in the *St. Thomas Daily Times*'s obituary notice and comes from Shakespeare's *Macbeth*. Reproduced by V.F.L. Edwards in *The Story of Jumbo* (1935).

## Juneau, Pierre
There are songs yet to be found in Sioux Lookout, Kamloops, Oromocto, Lévis, Corner Brook — wherever there are people.

Introduction to Ritchie York's *Axes, Chops & Hot Licks: The Canadian Rock Music Scene* (1971).

We're just getting a whisper of our own material into the picture. We're just trying to breathe, for God's sake, in an atmosphere completely dominated by U.S. material.

Chairman of the Canadian Radio-Television Commission, quoted in *Quest*, November, 1972.

## Jung, Carl Gustav
There are indeed people who lack a developed persona—"Canadians who know not Europe's sham politeness"—blundering from one social solecism to the next, perfectly harmless and innocent, soulful bores or appealing children, or, if they are women, spectral Cassandras dreaded for their tactlessness, eternally misunderstood, never knowing what they are about, always taking forgiveness for granted, blind to the world, hopeless dreamers. From them we can see how a neglected persona works, and what one must do to remedy the evil.

"The Relations between the Ego and the Unconscious" (1916), *Two Essays on Analytic Psychology* (1966), translated by R.F.C. Hull. For the quoted phrase, see Johann Gottfried Seume.

## Junius
The subject who is truly loyal to the Chief Magistrate will neither advise nor submit to arbitrary measures.—JUNIUS.

No issue of *The Globe and Mail* (or of *The Globe*, before it merged with *The Mail* in 1937) has appeared without these words. The motto of the Toronto newspaper was chosen by its publisher, George Brown, and appeared on the first issue of March 5, 1844. The sentence comes from one of the "Junius Letters," published anonymously in *The London Public Advertiser* between 1769 and 1772. "Junius" has been identified as Laughlin Maclearne, who was a surgeon in the British army and secretary to the Earl of Shelburne, who distinguished between loyalty to the "Chief

Magistrate" (George III) and criticism of the government in power. By implication, *The Globe and Mail* distinguishes between the Crown and the government of the day.

**Jury, Alfred**
The labouring classes have only one man in Parliament, and we have only half of him!

> Alfred Jury was denouncing Daniel J. O'Donoghue as an effective labour

spokesman, at the Canadian Labour Union Convention of 1877, *Proceedings*, August, 1877. See also Daniel J. O'Donoghue.

**Jutra, Claude**
Not making the films you should be making is awful, but making them and not having them shown is worse.

> Director of *Mon Oncle Antoine*, quoted by Alexander Ross in *The Toronto Star*, June 14, 1972.

# K

**Kahn, Herman**
You are a big country now, but you still tend to feel small and fragile. If the U.S. gets a cold, you get pneumonia.

> *The Toronto Star*, August 23, 1972.

**Kallmann, Helmut**
Look for the word *music* in the index of almost any book of Canadian history and you will find that the M's stop at "Murray, James, governor of Quebec!"

> *A History of Music in Canada: 1534-1914* (1960).

**Kalm, Peter**
We can enjoy none of these pleasures in *America*. The history of the country can be traced no further, than from the arrival of the Europeans; for every thing that happened before that period, is more like a fiction or a dream, than any thing that really happened.

*

In *Canada* nobody ever hears the *French* language spoken by any but *Frenchmen*; for strangers seldom come thither; and the *Indians* are naturally too proud to

learn *French*, but obliged the *French* to learn their language.

*

The girls at *Montreal* are very much displeased that those at *Quebec* get husbands sooner than they. The reason for this is, that many young gentlemen who come over from *France* with the ships, are captivated by the ladies at *Quebec*, and marry them; but as these gentlemen seldom go up to *Montreal*, the girls there are not often so happy as those of the former place.

> *Travels into North America* (1770-71), translated from the Swedish by J.R. Forster.

**Kane, Paul**
But the face of the red man is now no longer seen. All traces of his footsteps are fast being obliterated from his once favourite haunts, and those who would see the aborigines of this country in their original state, or seek to study their native manners and customs, must travel far through the pathless forest to find them.

*

Here I consider that my Indian travels finish, as the rest of my journey home to Toronto was performed on board steamboats; and the greatest hardship I had to endure, was the difficulty in trying to sleep in a civilized bed. [October 1, 1848]

> *Wanderings of an Artist among the Indians of North America from Canada to Vancouver's Island and Oregon through the Hudson's Bay Company's Territory and Back Again* (1859).

Better break stones by the wayside; your work will then be appreciated.

> "My memory of the veteran artist is of a gruff and moody man, embittered by the sparing gratitude of a people to whose information and pleasure he had sacrificed his life. 'Better break stones by the wayside; your work will then be appreciated' was the encouraging comment he gave to young artists." Sir Daniel Wilson, quoted by Hector Charlesworth in *The Canadian Scene: Sketches: Political and Historical* (1927). See also Sir George Simpson.

### Karkakonias

If Karkakonias told his children of the medicines of the white man—of his warcanoes moving by fire and making thunder as they move, of his warriors more numerous than the buffalo in the days of our fathers, of all the wonderful things he has looked upon—his children would point and say, "Behold! Karkakonias has become in his old age a maker of lies!" No, my children, Karkakonias has seen many wonderful things, and his tongue is still able to speak; but, until your eyes have travelled as far as has his tongue, he will sit silent and smoke the calumet, thinking only of what he has looked upon.

> The Chipewyan chief travelled to Washington during the Civil War but lapsed into silence when he returned to Pembina. He gave this reason for refusing to tell his people what he had seen. Quoted by William Francis Butler in *The Great Lone Land: A Narrative of Travel and Adventure in the North-West of America* (1872).

### Karloff, Boris

I was fast becoming a disgrace to the family name. In those days black sheep were exported to Canada or Australia. When I blithely flipped a sixpence in the family solicitor's office, the unfortunate losers were the Canadians. . . . I had no idea what Canada was like. It was all a fantastic and frightfully exciting adventure. [Reminiscing in Hollywood in 1936, the actor recalled his departure from Liverpool for Canada, May 7, 1909]

*

I cast around for a name because I felt the name Pratt was not the best stage name one could choose. I remembered the name Karloff, which was on my mother's side, though so far back it didn't make any sense. I took the Boris out of the air, put them together, and I must say the combination has been extraordinarily lucky for me. [This occurred in 1911 on a train between Kamloops and Nelson when the twenty-four-year-old Englishman was a member of a touring company. He made his theatrical début as a sixty-year-old man in Molnar's *The Devil*.]

> "It is not true that I was born a Monster. Hollywood made me one. The Monster was the best friend I ever had," the British-born actor once said. The creator of the original Frankenstein monster looked back on his early theatrical training in western Canada characteristically: "Good experience, but no money!" Quoted by Denis Gifford in *Karloff: The Man, the Monster, the Movies* (1973).

### Karpis, Alvin

My profession was robbing banks, knocking off payrolls, and kidnapping rich men. I was good at it.

> J. Edgar Hoover personally arrested the Montreal criminal in 1936, and was still FBI chief when Karpis was paroled in 1969. "I made that son of a bitch," was Karpis's opinion. *Public Enemy Number One: The Alvin Karpis Story* (1971), as told to Bill Trent.

### Karras, A.L.

The French Canadian fur traders of old

had a name for the moose that was aptly descriptive. They called him *l'orignal*, which embodies in its meaning grotesque, awkward, fantastic, and freak. So the name is fitting for the appearance of the moose, which under certain adverse conditions is anything but beautiful, while at his best he is nothing less than magnificent.

*North to Cree Lake* (1970).

## Karsh, Yousuf
All I know is that within every man and woman a secret is hidden, and as a photographer it is my task to reveal it if I can.

\*

He marched in scowling, and regarded my camera as he might regard the German enemy. His expression suited me perfectly, if I could capture it, but the cigar thrust between his teeth seemed somehow incompatible with such a solemn and formal occasion. Instinctively I removed the cigar. At this the Churchillian scowl deepened, the head was thrust forward belligerently, and the hand placed on the hip in an attitude of anger. So he stands in my portrait in what has always seemed to me the image of England in those years, defiant and unconquerable.

With a swift change of mood, he came towards me when I was finished, extending his hand and saying, "Well, you can certainly make a roaring lion stand still to be photographed."

The Armenian-born Ottawa photographer's account of his famous session with Sir Winston Churchill on December 30, 1941, when the British prime minister was in Ottawa to address Parliament. *Faces of Our Time* (1971). See also Hugh Kenner and George Bernard Shaw.

## Kasemets, Udo
Distinctive Canadian music died its death when the white man took the land from Eskimos and Indians and imported his own brand of music based on Greek theories, written down in Italian notation and duplicated on German-invented printing presses.

*Musicanada*, September, 1969.

## Kash, Eugene
There *may* be more complicated households than ours, but not many.

The musician is married to Maureen Forrester and they have five children. Quoted by Mollie Gillen in *Chatelaine*, September, 1972. See also Maureen Forrester.

## Kattan, Naim
The day of global truth and unities is over, unless one chooses totalitarianism and death.

Baghdad-born Quebec thinker, *Reality and Theatre* (1972), translated by Alan Brown.

## Keate, Stuart
In any world menu, Canada must be considered the vichyssoise of nations—it's cold, half-French, and difficult to stir. [1966]

\*

The national bird of Canada is the grouse. [1971]

From addresses delivered by the publisher of *The Vancouver Sun*.

## Keeler, Ruby
It's amazing. I couldn't act. I had that terrible singing voice, and now I can see I wasn't the greatest tap dancer in the world either.

Ruby Keeler was born in Halifax in 1909 and taken to New York when she was three. A Ziegfeld dancer, she starred with Dick Powell in such films as Busby Berkeley's *Gold Diggers of 1933* and was married to Al Jolson. Quoted by David Shipman in *The Great Movie Stars: The Golden Years* (1970).

## Keeler, Willie
I hit 'em where they ain't.

Remark made by the Canadian-born Baltimore Oriole—renowned for his ability to spray his hits just beyond the reach of opposing fielders—to W. A. Hewitt, sports editor of *The Toronto Star* in 1907. Quoted by Hewitt in *Down the Stretch* (1958).

## Keenleyside, Hugh L.

The boundary between Canada and the U.S. is a typically human creation; it is physically invisible, geographically illogical, militarily indefensible, and emotionally inescapable.

> Adapted by the author from the introduction to his study *Canada and the United States* (1929).

The whole history of the Canadian North can be divided into two periods—before and after the aeroplane.

> *Canadian Geographical Journal*, October, 1949.

Only a strong and wealthy country can really afford a corrupt or inefficient government—and many of them do. [Haldane Prize Essay, Royal Institute on Public Administration, London, England, July, 1954]

One good thing about the little red schoolhouse was that it was generally a long way from home—and the kids had to walk. [Address, Queen's University, 1958]

Too much of our business establishment is top heavy with brass, and too often that brass is paid as though it were gold. [Address, American Society for Public Administration, New York, February 6, 1959]

New York spends more on garbage collection—though with very little effect—than the whole world spends on the United Nations. [Address, Board of Evangelism and Social Service, United Church of Canada, Toronto, February 26, 1959]

Many of our children are developing middle-age spread when they are still in high school. Even their ice cream has to be soft. [Address to a teachers' convention, Calgary, 1965]

Only meagre progress can be expected unless the poorer countries themselves are prepared to do far more than ever before to assist themselves. The austere road of social progress cannot be travelled in a Rolls-Royce.

> *International Aid: A Summary* (1966).

In some of the poorer areas of the world it is sadly true that sex is the only luxury available to the ordinary man. Whether the ordinary woman also considers it a luxury is perhaps open to question. [Address, Third World Conference on Medical Education, New Delhi, November 21, 1966]

It is sometimes said that "when Washington sneezes, London, Tokyo, Bonn and Paris catch cold, and Ottawa—especially if a Liberal Government is in office—comes down with the flu."

> "Letter to an American Friend," *The Star-Spangled Beaver* (1971), edited by John H. Redekop.

Paper has a genius for multiplication that cannot be equalled anywhere else in nature. [To the board of Oxfam-Canada, Toronto, September 24, 1972]

If nothing else, Rideau Hall has saved us from having a White House. [Conference, Canadian Broadcasting League, Ottawa, March 23, 1973]

## Kelland, Otto P.

Take me back to my Western boat,
Let me fish off Cape St. Mary's,
Where the hog-downs sail and the fog-
   horns wail
With my friends the Browns and the
   Clearys.
Let me fish off Cape St. Mary's.

> Last verse of the popular Newfoundland song "Let Me Fish Off Cape St. Mary's."

## Kelley Jr., Thomas P.

"Now I have been in show-biz since 1880, over fifty years; know just about all its angles from Shakespeare to burlesque, and while I realize there will never be a mutual agreement as to who first thought up the pie-in-the-kisser bit, probably the biggest laugh-getter and brightest gem in the crown of comedy, I want to say this:

"For my money there is no doubt as to the identity of its originator. The first time a pie was ever thrown into someone's face in view of an audience and for the sole purpose of entertainment, was just before the turn of the century, behind the hotel of a Newfoundland town with fourteen spectators looking on when its creator, Doc Kelley, the King of the

Medicine Men, threw the freshly baked pumpkin pie into the face of Banjo Gay. I was there, I saw it and I know."

> Sal Salval, a member of Thomas P. (Doc) Kelley's Shamrock Concert Company, quoted by Thomas P. Kelley, Jr., in *The Fabulous Kelley: He Was King of the Medicine Men* (1968). Kelley was born in 1865 and died in 1931. See also Mack Sennett.

## Kelsey, Henry
Thus it continues till you leave ye. woods behind
And then you have beast of severall kind
The one is a black a Buffillo great
Another is an outgrown Bear wch. is good meat
His skin to gett I have used all ye. means I can
He is mans food & he makes food of man
His hid they would not let me it preserve
But said it was a god & they should Starve

> Kelsey, an agent for the Hudson's Bay Company, was the first white man to see the prairies and the first to describe the buffalo, which he spotted on August 20, 1690. His curious description comes from the rhymed introduction he wrote to his *Journal* of 1691, discovered in Northern Ireland in 1926 and first published in *The Kelsey Papers* (1929), introduced by A.G. Doughty and Chester Martin.

## Kelso, John J.
We rush in the keen pursuit of our various ambitions while want pleads at our elbow. It is not that we are hard or indifferent. We are busy. Always busy.

> Kelso founded the Children's Aid Society of Toronto in 1891, the first of its kind in Canada. Quoted by June Callwood in *The Globe and Mail*, December 29, 1973.

## Kemble, Fanny
You would not have to complain of want of hospitality . . . but the unspeakable dirt and discomfort of inns in Montreal and Quebec, the scarcity of eatables and the abundance of fleas and bugs, together with the wicked road from Saint John to Laprairie would make up a sum of suffering for which it would be difficult to find adequate compensation. People intolerable . . . the jargon they speak is intolerable.

> Letter from the actress to Charles Matthews in London, England, concerning theatrical touring conditions in the 1840s, quoted by Betty Lee in *Love and Whisky: The Story of the Dominion Drama Festival* (1973).

## Kemp, The Rev. Mr.
About the year 1790 the Presbyterians of Montreal of all denominations, both British and American, organized themselves into a Church, and in the following year secured the services of the Rev. John Young. At this time they met in the Recollet Roman Catholic Church, but in the year following they erected the edifice which is now known as St. Gabriel Street Church—the oldest Protestant Church in the province. In their early Minutes we find them, in acknowledgment of the kindness of the Recollet Fathers, presenting them with "One box of candles, 56 lbs., at 8d., and one hogshead of Spanish wine at £6.5s."

> "Digest of the *Synod Minutes of the Presbyterian Church of Canada*, by my worthy friend, the Rev. Mr. Kemp, of the Free Church, of Montreal," explains Thomas D'Arcy McGee, who quotes this as "a very striking illustration of the tolerance of French Canadian character." Address, Legislative Assembly, Quebec, February 9, 1865. *Parliamentary Debates on the Subject of the Confederation of the British North American Provinces, 3rd Session, 8th Provincial Parliament of Canada* (1865).

## Kennedy, Betty
My idea of good fashion is that you wear it—it doesn't wear you.

> Popular broadcaster quoted by Sybil Young in *The Canadian Magazine*, November 11, 1972.

## Kennedy, Dan
Believe it or not, the Indian had to learn the whiteman's language to break the first commandment.

*Recollections of an Assiniboine Chief* (1972), by Dan Kennedy (Ochankugahe), edited by James R. Stevens.

## Kennedy, Howard Angus
New Canadians.

The term "New Canadians" for immigrants came into favour around the turn of the century and passed out of favour during the Centennial year when it was replaced by the curious word "ethnic." H.A. Kennedy gave the earlier term currency in his study of Western immigration, *New Canada and the New Canadians* (1907), prefaced by Lord Strathcona. "New Canada, the country I am now to describe, is commonly known as the North-West. It is really the South-West of Canada; and it is coming to be known simply as the West."

## Kennedy, John E.
Advertising is salesmanship in print.

In 1904, Kennedy, a one-time Brockville clothing salesman and former Mounted Policeman, sent the following note to Albert Lasker, then a young Chicago advertising executive: "I am in the saloon downstairs, and I can tell you what advertising is. I know what you don't know. It will mean much to me to have you know what it is and it will mean much to you. If you wish to know what advertising is, send the word 'Yes' down by messenger."

"Word went down to Kennedy, who then appeared in Lasker's office. After an hour they went down to the saloon together, and emerged at midnight," explained John Gunther in his biography of Lasker. "From that time on, Lasker knew what advertising was. First Kennedy asked him what his own ideas were, and Lasker mentioned news. Kennedy said, 'No. News is a technique of presentation, but advertising is a very different thing. I can give it to you in three words.' Lasker said, 'I am hungry. What are those three words?'

"Kennedy said, *'Salesmanship in print.'* "

This famous three-word definition of advertising got Kennedy a job with Las-

ker who hired him for $28,000 a year (increased within two years to $75,000). Kennedy, in his late forties, spearheaded the "reason why" concept of copy and, with Lasker, the concept of modern copywriting. Quoted by John Gunther in *Taken at the Flood: The Story of Albert D. Lasker* (1960).

Conviction is not produced by bare affirmation, but by proof, by inference, by argument—in short, by reason-why talk.

Quoted by H.E. Stephenson and Carlton McNaught in *The Story of Advertising in Canada: A Chronicle of Fifty Years* (1940).

## Kennedy, John F.
We share common values from the past, a common defence line at present, and common aspirations for the future, and indeed the future of all mankind.

Geography has made us neighbours. History has made us friends. Economics has made us partners. And necessity has made us allies. Those whom nature hath so joined together, let no man put asunder.

What unites us is far greater than what divides us.

Address at a joint sitting of the Senate and the House of Commons, May 17, 1961.

I couldn't have called him an s.o.b., I didn't know he was one—at that time.

The American president and Prime Minister John Diefenbaker met in Ottawa in May of 1961 and parted on cordial terms. Theodore G. Sorenson continues the story in *Kennedy* (1965): "Kennedy had inadvertently left behind one of the staff papers he had been using. Diefenbaker not only expropriated the paper but threatened to expose it publicly, claiming that it referred to him as an s.o.b. (Apparently this was a typically illegible reference to the OAS, which the president was urging Canada to join.) Kennedy denied the charge, and dismissed the scribbled letters: 'I couldn't have called him an s.o.b., I didn't know he was one—at that time.' "

Arthur M. Schlesinger in *A Thousand Days* (1965) added: "Kennedy thought the Canadian insincere and did not like or trust him." Kennedy is said to have winced when he heard Diefenbaker speak French and later declared, "It was so bad, I was tempted to try myself."

The working paper, mislaid by Kennedy on his visit of May 16-18, 1961, was written by Walt Whitman Rostow, policy planning director of the U.S. State Department, and according to Peter C. Newman was headed: "What We Want from the Ottawa Trip." Kennedy is said to have scribbled on the paper: "What do we do with the s.o.b. now?" Newman regards this as hardly plausible in *Renegade in Power: The Diefenbaker Years* (1963).

He'll do.

"[Pearson's] visit to London in the first days of May 1963 was little more than a social duty call; but the meeting with President Kennedy, at the presidential house at Hyannis Port a week later, was full of meaning. The talks took place in the easy, cosy atmosphere of an opulent North American home; and Pearson's encyclopaedic knowledge of American baseball statistics quickly established him as a very solid North American citizen. 'He'll do!' Kennedy remarked approvingly, and Pearson proceeded to 'do' all the vital things for which the American government had been waiting so impatiently and so long." Donald Creighton in *Canada's First Century: 1867-1967* (1970).

### Kenner, Hugh
The primary critical question in Canada today is whether it is yet safe to cut the umbilical cord to the wilderness: whether it is time to conduct a new raid on the inarticulate.

\*

Karsh is no Picasso. His tradition is that of the Court Painter: the glamorizer of existing legends and images.

"The Case of the Missing Face" (1948), in *Our Sense of Identity* (1954), edited by Malcolm Ross.

### Kent, Duke of
See Edward Augustus, Duke of Kent.

### Kernighan, Robert Kirkland
This is the land of the true and the leal,
　Where freedom is bred in the bone—
The Southerner never shall place his heel
　On the men of the Northern Zone.

Final version of "The Men of the Northern Zone," *The Khan's Book of Verse* (1925). Kernighan called himself "The Khan" and wrote from "The Wigwam," Rockton, Ontario.

### Kerouac, Jack
You say I'm a snob?—I only wanted to find out why my family never changed their name and perchance find a tale there, and trace it back to Cornwall, Wales and Ireland and maybe Scotland afore that I'm sure, then down over to the St. Lawrence River city in Canada where I'm told there was a Seigneurie (a Lordship) and therefore I can go live there (along with my thousands of bow-legged French Canadian cousins bearing the same name) and *never pay taxes!*

*Satori in Paris* (1966). The novelist was born in Lowell, Massachusetts, of French-Canadian parents.

### Kerr, Graham
It's shiny, it's hard, it's black . . . and one of my favourite pieces of culinary equipment. It's a lump of coal!

Surprisingly, a block of coal can be extremely useful in the kitchen. Provided you wash it first, it especially comes in handy when you want to prepare your potatoes in advance. . . .

Ottawa-based cooking enthusiast, "Graham Kerr—The Galloping Gourmet," *The Trinidad Guardian*, June 22, 1972.

### Kerr, John Chipman
War is Hell, but what is homesteading?

"John Kerr and his brother Roland were homesteading at Spirit River, Alberta, when war was declared. They immediately set out for Edmonton leaving behind a note tacked to the door of their shack which read: 'War is Hell, but what is homesteading?' On the 16th of September 1916, John 'Chip' Kerr won the Victoria Cross while serving with the 49th Battalion during the Battle of the Somme. Roland Kerr was killed in France in 1917." George C. Machum, *Canada's V.C.'s: The Story of Canadians Who Have Been Awarded the Victoria Cross* (1956).

## Kibkârjuk

Heaven is a great land. In that land there are many holes. These holes we call stars. In the land of heaven lives pana (the woman of there) or tapazuma inua (the one that rules over, or owns, what is up there). There is a mighty spirit, and the anatkut hold that it is a woman. To her pass the souls of the dead. And sometimes, when many die, there are many people up there. When anything is spilt up there, it pours out through the stars and becomes rain or snow. The souls of the dead are reborn in the dwellings of pana, and brought down to earth again by the moon. When the moon is absent, and cannot be seen in the sky, it is because it is busy helping pana by bringing souls to earth. Some become human beings once more, others become animals, all manner of beasts. And so life goes on without end.

> The Eskimo legend of "The Land of Heaven" told by Kibkârjuk. Knud Rasmussen, *Intellectual Culture of the Caribou Eskimos: Iglulik and Caribou Eskimo Texts: Report of the Fifth Thule Expedition, 1921-24* (1930).

## Kidd, Bruce

The profit motive simply should have no place in spectator sport. Since a sport like hockey is so much a part of the national culture and since the community contributes so much to the development of its athletes, the staging of hockey games should properly be a community enterprise.

> "Canada's 'National' Sport," *Close the 49th Parallel, Etc.: The Americanization of Canada* (1970), edited by Ian Lumsden.

Hockey is the Canadian metaphor, the rink a symbol of this country's vast stretches of water and wilderness, its extremes of climate, the player a symbol of our national struggle to civilize such a land.

*

Hockey captures the essence of the Canadian experience in the New World. In a land so inescapably and inhospitably cold, hockey is the dance of life, an affirmation that despite the deathly chill of winter we are alive.

> *The Death of Hockey* (1972), by Bruce Kidd and John MacFarlane. See also W.H. Auden.

## Kidd, J. Roby

The pursuit of learning is really the pursuit of fine living.

> "Pursuit of Learning" (1959), *Education for Perspective* (1969).

Good intentions and sentimentalism are not enough. At the first meeting of the Canadian Association for Adult Education in 1935 there was coined a slogan that, while somewhat vulgar, is worth some consideration, "Now and then forget your bleeding heart and use your bloody head!"

> "Education for Perspective" (1967), *Education for Perspective* (1969).

. . . even more important than a guardian and champion of the private citizen is the existence of many persons who will encourage and sustain people to build and renew communities where all human beings can live in dignity and fulfilment. That's what adult education is all about.

> "Adult Education, the Community, and the Animateur," *Citizen Participation: Canada—A Book of Readings* (1971), edited by James A. Draper.

Education can and should make one more sensitive and compassionate—and also tough-minded. These are not warring opposites; these are attributes to be achieved in some large harmony.

> "Education for Perspective," *Probings: A Collection of Essays Contributed to the Canadian Mental Health Association for its Golden Jubilee 1918-1968* (1968).

## Kidd, Captain William

10 FEET BELOW ME LIES £2,000,000.

> William Coates Borrett in "The Oak Island Mystery" in *Tales Retold Under*

*the Old Town Clock* (1957) claims that a flat stone was found buried under ninety feet of earth on Oak Island with these words inscribed on it.

\*

. . . in my late proceedings in the Indies, I have lodged goods and Treasures to the value of one hundred thousand pounds, which I desire the Gouvernment may have the benefitt of, in order thereto I shall desire no manner of liberty, but to be kept prisoner on board such shipp as may be appointed for that purpose.

> Plea to the Speaker of the British House of Commons while awaiting execution for piracy, May 12, 1701. Many believe the notorious buccaneer buried his hoard on Oak Island, Mahone Bay, off the western coast of Nova Scotia. Quoted by R.V. Harris in *The Oak Island Mystery* (1958).

## Kierans, Eric W.

Our problem may be that the challenges we face are of such magnitude that we will have to change not only our situation but, to some degree, our natures.

> Quoted by Peter C. Newman in "Eric Kierans" (1968), *Home Country: People, Places, and Power Politics* (1973).

A nation cannot leap into one another's technology without causing grave structural disturbances in its own economy. Nor can a corporation become a "Cosmocorp" overnight. It must grow into that status steadily or risk collapse.

> Speech at Memorial University, June 3, 1971.

## Kilbourn, Elizabeth

Possibly, the woman artist's talent lies mostly in her ability to make a more human and organic and total use of innovations and discoveries pioneered by men.

> *Women in the Arts in Canada: A Study Prepared for the Royal Commission on the Status of Women in Canada* (1971), by Sandra Gwyn.

## Kilbourn, William

In the end, of course, the general character of the book cannot help reflecting the editor's own prejudices about what matters most. To that extent this book represents the bias of someone who is Methodist in background and enthusiasm, Anglican by adoption, Catholic in doctrine of Church and Sacraments; who believes most things and doubts everything; sees the biblical faith as the best antidote for idolatry; regards the Church as a place for being vulnerable rather than safe, for celebration rather than constriction, for moral disarmament rather than judgement, for acceptance and reconciliation and openness to improbable connections rather than fine distinctions and precise definitions and ringing pronouncements; and who believes that Christianity, for the time being, is better understood as the main question put rather than a set of answers given—though answers there are, for those who will listen, in the holding to that hope that exists beyond hopelessness on the far side of longing and despair.

> *The Restless Church: A Response to the Comfortable Pew* (1966), edited by William Kilbourn.

Even the Canada Council's funds were directed primarily to universities and scholars rather than to artists. Although it spent its budget of one million dollars a year for the arts with superb discrimination and noticeable effect, this amount was only a third of what one single European company, the Vienna State Opera, was receiving annually from its government, and one-fifth the amount that Canada's Department of National Defence was spending annually on military bands. (The latter, curiously enough, did help to subsidize art in a roundabout Canadian way, by supplying several local orchestras with good brass players they could not otherwise have afforded.) Few serious Canadian performers acquired an income-tax problem during the 1950s.

\*

"Returning to Toronto was like finding a Jaguar parked in front of the Vicarage and the padre inside with a pitcher of vodka martinis reading *Lolita*." [Quoting a British visitor, 1959]

> "The 1950s," *The Canadians 1867-1967*

(1967), edited by J.M.S. Careless and R. Craig Brown.

I admire and covet not only American styles and achievements but also the American's generosity of spirit and willingness to take total responsibility for himself and his actions. A Canadian, by contrast, has been called someone who doesn't play for keeps.

> "Some Feelings about the United States," in *The New Romans: Candid Canadian Opinions of the U.S.* (1968), edited by Al Purdy.

If I were asked by some stranger to North American culture to show him the most important religious building in Canada, I would take him to Toronto's Maple Leaf Gardens.

> *Religion in Canada: The Spiritual Development of a Nation* (1968).

The finest business history written in Canada, as well as one of the few great narrative poems of the twentieth century, is E.J. Pratt's epic about the CPR, *Towards the Last Spike.*

\*

Let us begin with a skill-testing question. What Canadian born in humble circumstances, a teacher by profession who rose to be a Bishop, became head of one of the most important organizations in the country then retired from his position to become a foreign missionary, and finally was chosen to be operating head of a world-wide church? Conceivably, one answer to this question might be Paul-Emile Cardinal Léger. He left his teaching post in Rome to run the great archdiocese of Montreal, which he in turn gave up for an African leper colony. He could become the first Canadian Pope. But if he does, he will not be the first but rather the second man to answer the description. The correct reply to the question is in fact Nathan Eldon Tanner of the Church of Jesus Christ of Latter Day Saints, an Alberta schoolteacher and Mormon bishop who became first chief executive of Trans-Canada Pipe Lines, left it in his prime to become a Mormon missionary full time, and in 1965 became Counsellor to the ninety-five-year-old

formal head of the Mormon Church, President David O. McKay, Prophet, Seer, Revelator and Trustee-in-Trust, lineal successor to Brigham Young, and in Mormon belief capable of receiving direct revelations from God.

> *PipeLine: Trans-Canada and the Great Debate—A History of Business and Politics* (1970).

Canada is a land of no one ideology, no single vision; it is a cultural freeport, a way station for travellers (who often move on soon to the other America), a no-man's-land even, or at least no abiding city, a place not easily confused with paradise or the promised land. This "indigestible Canada," this Marx Brothers' Freedonia, this Austro-Hungary of the new world, with its two official peoples and its multitudes of permitted ones, its ethnic islands and cultural archipelagos, its ghettos of the unpasteurized and unhomogenized, this harbour of old Adams unable or unwilling to be reborn or to burn just yet their old European clothes, but growing attached, many of them, as deeply as the Indian or the pioneer to the landscape of farm and city—this Canada has, alas, not even carried diversity and toleration nearly as far as it might (perhaps lest they become principles), since in practice it has been extremely difficult for Asians and West Indians to immigrate to Canada.

> Introduction, *Canada: A Guide to the Peaceable Kingdom* (1970), edited by William Kilbourn. See also Phillip A. Gaglardi.

**Kimball, Elizabeth**
Uncle George was (no matter what Mother may have felt about Uncle Teddy, or the world thinks about Uncle Stephen) the very wittiest man in creation. And if you wonder why, being so witty, he did not become famous like Uncle Stephen, I think the whole thing really depended upon the fact that he couldn't spell, and Uncle Stephen could.

> *The Man in the Panama Hat: Reminiscences of My Uncle, Stephen Leacock* (1970). Uncle George Leacock is the fabulous character described in "My Remarkable Uncle."

## King, Basil

I imagine if I sold three copies of a book in Charlottetown in the course of three years, I am doing well.

*

"When the Canadian author produces a masterpiece we shall sell it."

> King was an ordained minister and novelist popular during the tens and twenties who lived and wrote in Boston. Here he is quoting a Montreal bookseller who made this remark in 1921. "And I looked around the counters," King continued, "and they were piled high with the latest English and American productions which were anything but masterpieces, and he was willing to sell them." "Canadian Culture and the Book-Week," November 22, 1923, *Addresses Delivered before the Canadian Club of Toronto: Season of 1923-24* (1924). The once-popular novelist was born in Charlottetown.

## King, John Mark

God has many bests.

> Moderator of the General Assembly of the Presbyterian Church in 1883 and, until his death in 1899, principal of Manitoba College. The aphorism was often quoted by J.S. Woodsworth.

## King, Paul    See Raymond de Coccola.

## King, W.L. Mackenzie

Were man never to fall, he would be a God; were he never to aspire, he would be a brute.

*

Whenever in social or industrial relations the claims of industry and humanity are opposed, those of industry must make way.

> *Industry and Humanity: A Study in the Principles Underlying Industrial Reconstruction* (1918). The book's motto is "Over all nations is humanity." See also Goldwin Smith.

Hark the herald angels sing
William Lyon Mackenzie King.

> Opening lines of the campaign song in the North York constituency in the election of 1921. Recalled by Alan O. Gib-

bons in *The Canadian Forum*, April, 1974.

It is for parliament to decide whether or not we should participate in wars in different parts of the world, and it is neither right nor proper for any individual or for any groups of individuals to take any step in which in any way might limit the rights of parliament in a manner which is of such great concern to all the people of our country.

> House of Commons, February 1, 1923. "It is for Parliament to decide" or "Parliament will decide" or "Let Parliament decide" was King's way of dealing with difficult situations. "The famous formula," James Eayrs explained in *The Art of the Possible: Government and Foreign Policy in Canada* (1961), "was first pressed into service during the Chanak crisis of 1922." Larry Zolf called it "the greatest magic elixir for any leader to swallow and survive."

There comes to my mind an Italian epitaph to which Sir John A. Macdonald in his day was fond of referring. Over the grave of one who had unnecessarily sought change, there is written, "I was well, I wanted to be better, and here I am."

> "Citizenship" (1925), *The Message of the Carillon and Other Addresses* (1928).

Equal Status!

> Throwing a British halfpenny and a Canadian one-cent piece into the molten metal of the bells for the Peace Tower carillon, Croydon, England, while attending the Imperial Conference in 1926. Quoted by Robert M. Hamilton in *Canadian Quotations and Phrases: Literary and Historical* (1952).

Mr. Esling: My references were to the religious fanatics who today are offending the public by exhibitions of absolute nakedness. In order to bring this right home I would like to know what the Prime Minister would think if he went into his garden in the morning to pick pansies or violets and was confronted by six naked Doukhobors.

Mr. King: I would send for my honourable friend the Leader of the Opposition and the leader of the Progressive Party.

Mr. Bennett: There would be a riot if you overlooked your own supporters.

This celebrated quip was heard in the House of Commons in 1928.

Mr. Mackenzie King: May I conclude what I have to say? So far as giving money from this federal treasury to provincial governments is concerned, in relation to this question of unemployment as it exists today, I might be prepared to go a certain length possibly in meeting one or two of the western provinces that have Progressive premiers at the head of their governments—

Some hon. Members: Oh!

Mr. Mackenzie King:—but I would not give a single cent to any Tory government.

Mr. Bennett: Shame!

Mr. Stevens: Shame!

Mr. Mackenzie King: Do my hon. friends say "shame"?

Mr. Bennett: Yes, shame!

Mr. Mackenzie King: What is there to be ashamed of?

Mr. Stevens: You ought to be ashamed of that.

Mr. Mackenzie King: My hon. friend is getting very indignant. Something evidently has got under his skin. May I repeat what I have said? With respect to giving moneys out of the federal treasury to any Tory government in this country for these alleged unemployment purposes, with these governments situated as they are today, with policies diametrically opposed to those of this government, I would not give them a five-cent piece.

Mr. Cahan: Why give it to a Progressive government?

Mr. Speaker: Order.

House of Commons, April 3, 1930. This is the famous "five-cent piece" speech made by the prime minister in the Commons during the Depression.

The promises of yesterday are the taxes of today.

House of Commons, June 16, 1931. King, leader of the Opposition, replying to the Conservative budget.

Having asked for $20,000,000 at the special session my right hon. friend, finding conditions worse than ever, began to experience difficulty in fixing the amount for the last year. Facing this situation he found it necessary, in order to do what he thought would satisfy the unemployed, to ask not for $20,000,000, $40,000,000, $60,000,000, $80,000,000 or $100,000,000, but to ask this parliament to give a blank cheque which he might fill in for as much as he wished to draw.

House of Commons, February 8, 1932. King, leader of the Opposition, accusing Prime Minister R.B. Bennett of demanding a "blank cheque" from Parliament during the Depression.

You ask what Liberalism is? I believe that Liberalism is the leaven which will make prevail, or the means of making prevail, the law of peace, work and health over the law of blood and of death, no matter where this conflict of laws may be found. This is the very work that we, as Liberals, are engaged upon today.

"The Practice of Liberalism," *The Liberal Way: A Record of Opinion on Canadian Problems as Expressed and Discussed at the First Liberal Summer Conference, Port Hope, September, 1933* (1933).

KING OR CHAOS

This succinct slogan of the Liberal party for the general election of 1935 was devised by the editors of *Maclean's Magazine* and appeared as a double-page spread in the issue of October 15. Floyd S. Chalmers in *A Gentleman of the Press* (1969). W.L. Mackenzie King defeated R.B. Bennett by a substantial majority.

We are fortunate both in our neighbours and in our lack of neighbours. It may be that this fortunate position is not due to any special virtue on our part, that it is an accident of geography and of history, but one has only to be in any European country a day to realize how relatively fortunate a position it is, and what folly it would be to throw it away. It is equally true, I should add, that if some countries have too much history, we have too much geography. . . .

House of Commons, June 18, 1936.

We will be with you to the end.

The conclusion of a stirring wartime address to the battle-weary Britons, Mansion House, London, 1941. Quoted by Ralph Allen in *Ordeal by Fire: Canada, 1910-1945* (1961).

Not necessarily conscription but conscription if necessary.

"There is, fortunately, a third view—a view which I believe accords with the opinion most generally held throughout the Dominion. It is that conscription for service overseas should be inaugurated only if and when, in the opinion of the government, it becomes necessary for the security of our country and for the maintenance of its war effort. That view is the one which is held by the government. It represents the government's policy with respect to conscription for overseas service. In a word, that policy may be described as not necessarily conscription but conscription if necessary." House of Commons, June 10, 1942.

"If, in reference to the very difficult question of service overseas, anyone can conceive of a policy which is better calculated to service the national interest than the one the government has formulated, and which is clearly and concisely expressed in the words: Not necessarily conscription, but conscription if necessary, I shall be the first to advocate its acceptance. I can only say that nothing of the kind has been proposed by any hon. member in the course of the debate." House of Commons, July 7, 1942.

I am proud to believe there is no separation between those who are nearest to us, and I believe in the survival of the human personality. Thus I know that if I have had any success in life it has been due to my father and mother.

Address on the occasion of his twenty-fifth anniversary as leader of the Liberal party, Ottawa, August 7, 1944.

Over and over again, I have thought . . . that some day the world will know some of the things that I have prevented . . . I

must make increasingly clear to the world that prevention of wrong courses of evil and the like means more than all else that man can accomplish. [December 8, 1944]

The Mackenzie King Record: Volume 2: 1944-45 (1968), edited by J.W. Pickersgill and D.F. Forster. In September of 1940, King wrote in his diary, "I really believe my greatest service is in the many unwise steps I prevent."

It is for all to remember that justice is the common concern of mankind. The years of war have surely taught the supreme lesson that men and nations should not be made to serve selfish national ends, whether those ends be isolated self-defence or world domination. Nations everywhere must unite to save and to serve humanity.

Address of the prime minister and leader of the Canadian delegation to the United Nations Conference, Second Plenary Meeting, April 27, 1945. *Basic Documents in Canadian History* (1959), edited by James J. Talman.

My boy, you may one day have some responsibility. I would just give you one bit of advice, to remember that in the course of human history far more has been accomplished for the welfare and the progress of mankind in preventing bad actions than in doing good ones.

Lester Pearson "often recalled a conversation he'd had with King (who acted through most of his tenure as his own secretary of State for External Affairs) on a train going to New York City in the thirties." Quoted by Peter C. Newman in *The Distemper of Our Times: Canadian Politics in Transition: 1963-1968* (1968).

The great thing in politics . . . is to avoid mistakes.

Quoted by Lord Moran in *Churchill: Taken from The Diaries of Lord Moran: The Struggle for Survival: 1940-1965* (1966).

Our best defence in the Arctic is the Arctic itself.

Quoted by James Eayrs in *In Defence*

of Canada: Peacemaking and Deterrence (1972).

I've always found you can control people better if you don't see too much of them.

*

"His actual methods of government are clear enough at a glance. Once, in a revealing moment, he described them to a friend as they strolled on the bank of the Ottawa.

" 'If,' said King, pointing to a distant church spire beyond a bend in the river, 'I try to reach that point directly I shall drown. I must follow the curves of the bank and ultimately I shall get there, though at times I may seem to be going somewhere else.' "

> Quoted by Bruce Hutchison in *The Incredible Canadian* (1952).

If only there had been one more day.

> Characteristic expression, quoted by J. W. Pickersgill in *The Mackenzie King Record, Volume 1: 1939-1944* (1960).

Thank you.

> Dying words, Kingsmere, Quebec, July 22, 1950. See also Helen Hughes, Bruce Hutchison, J.W. Pickersgill, Mercy Phillimore, F.R. Scott.

### King, William
The prejudice which exists against the Coloured Man in the Northern States has followed him even into this free country and operates against his moral improvement.

> Letter to a fellow minister, July 15, 1849, written by the abolitionist who established the Buxton Settlement in southern Ontario. Quoted by Victor Ullman in *Look to the North Star: A Life of William King* (1969) who writes: "No single community in either the United States or Canada contributed so much to the emancipated Negroes as the sons and daughters of Buxton."

### Kinnear, Bill
For Sale—One Home-Made Coffin. Never Been Used. Fit 6′ 2″. Reason for Selling: Improved Health. Phone 97937. Bill Kinnear.

> Classified advertisement, *Saskatoon Star-Phoenix*, June 30, 1945. Reproduced in *Ripley's Believe It or Not! Tombstones and Graveyards* (1966).

### Kinnear, David
Together we make a market. It's an axiom of retailing that two big stores near each other attract more than twice as many customers as they would singly.

> Observation made by the chief executive officer of the T. Eaton Company when both Eaton's and Simpsons located in Yorkdale shopping centre, Toronto, February, 1964. Quoted by William Stephenson in *The Store that Timothy Built* (1969).

### Kipling, Rudyard
Into the mist my guardian prows put forth,
  Behind the mist my virgin ramparts lie,
The Warden of the Honour of the North,
  Sleepless and veiled am I. ["Halifax"]
*
Peace is our portion. Yet a whisper rose,
  Foolish and causeless, half in jest, half hate.
Now wake we and remember mighty blows,
  And, fearing no man, wait! ["Quebec and Montreal"]
*
From East to West the circling word has passed,
  Till West and East is beside our landlocked blue;
From East to West the tested chain holds fast,
  The well-forged link rings true! ["Victoria"]

> These verses from "The Song of the Cities" appeared in Kipling's collection *The Seven Seas* (1896), where the cycle was called "A Song of the English." Fifteen cities are rhapsodized, but only three are Canadian.

A Nation spoke to a Nation,
  A Throne sent word to a Throne:
"Daughter am I in my mother's house,
  But mistress in my own.
The gates are mine to open,
  As the gates are mine to close.

And I abide by my Mother's House,"
Said our Lady of the Snows.

Final verse of "Our Lady of the Snows,"
subtitled "Canadian Preferential Tariff,
1897." Until World War I, the third
and fourth lines were widely quoted to
symbolize Canada's relation to Great
Britain. The poem first appeared in
*The London Times*, April 27, 1897, and
was immediately denounced as an im-
pediment to tourism and immigration.
It was even set to music by Walford
Davies.

The phrase "Our Lady of the Snow"
—in the singular—was used by William
Wordsworth in Poem XIX of *Memorials of a Tour on the Continent* (1820)
to describe the "aërial cleft" of Mount
Righi in Switzerland. Thomas D'Arcy
McGee wrote a poem " 'Our Ladye of
the Snow' "—in the singular, in quotes,
and archaically spelled—about the original church of Notre Dame des Neige on
the southern slope of Mount Royal.
*The Poems of Thomas D'Arcy McGee:
With Copious Notes* (1869), edited by
Mrs. J. Sadlier.

When the early Jesuit fathers preached to
Hurons and Choctaws,
They prayed to be delivered from the
vengeance of the squaws.
'Twas the women, not the warriors,
turned those stark enthusiasts pale.
For the female of the species is more
deadly than the male.

From "The Female of the Species"
(1911).

We giving all gained all.
Neither lament us nor praise.
Only in all things recall,
It is Fear, not Death that slays.

*

From little towns in a far land we came,
To save our honour and a world
aflame.
By little towns in a far land we sleep;
And trust that world we won for you
to keep!

"Epitaphs of the War: 1914-18." These
are called "Two Canadian Memorials."
The first was commissioned for use in
Sudbury but never used. The second
was commissioned by James W. Curran

and used on the Sault Ste. Marie war
memorial. The text of these poems—
and of all the others, unless specified—
has been taken from *Rudyard Kipling's
Verse: Definitive Edition* (1940). Other
poems of Canadian interest include:
"The Prairie," "The Stranger," "Jubal
and Tubal Cain," "A Song of Travel,"
"Romulus and Remus."

There was a young man of Quebec
Who was frozen in snow to his neck,
When asked, "Are you Friz?"
He replied, "Yes I is,
But we don't call this cold in Quebec."

Quoted by Stephen Leacock in "Comic
Verse: The Lighter Notes," *Humour
and Humanity: An Introduction to the
Study of Humour* (1937). There are
numerous versions of this well-known
limerick. Kipling never claimed authorship.

If blood be the price of the Arctic, Lord
God we have paid in full.

"An adaptation of two lines from 'The
Song of the Dead' by Rudyard Kipling:
'If blood be the price of admiralty, Lord
God, we ha' paid in full.' This poem
was written in 1893 to commemorate
British sailors who died in all quarters
of the world. The origin of the adaptation is obscure." Norah Story, *The Oxford Companion to Canadian History
and Literature* (1967).

Is this quite fair? It seems to me very unjust, most wrong, that the thousands of
men who have fought and toiled and
died for the Empire have passed for the
most part without human acknowledge-
ment, while the man who can catch the
popular ear by trying to describe some
of their thoughts and ideas should receive such a welcome as this. Well, the
reward is not to the man himself. You
have done him a great—a very great—
honour, and one I would make bold to
hope is not so much to the author whose
name I bear, as to the ideas that I have
been fortunate enough to reflect.

A thunderous ovation greeted Kipling
when he rose to speak. "The Recessional" had just been sung and the audience was deeply moved. "The Problems

of Empire," October 18, 1907, *Addresses Delivered before the Canadian Club of Toronto: Season of 1906-1907* (1907).

There were days in your progress, anxious days shall I say, but I do not think you realize perhaps how largely Canada bulks, has always bulked in the imagination of the other members of the imperial family. I do not think perhaps you imagine how keenly all over the world men watched in those years to see what part Canada would take among the quicksands and pitfalls prepared and awaiting her, before she set her feet on firm ground. On the other side, as you will remember, there was apathy, not in Canada only; ignorance, not in Canada only; there was poverty, doubt, dissension and ridicule. On the other hand, there was the awakening instinct of a nation in search of its soul, a nation perhaps a little wiser than some of its leaders. Between these two forces was born, I believe, we all believe, the spirit of the land.

"Canada's Path to Nationhood," October 21, 1907, *Addresses Delivered before the Canadian Club of Ottawa: 1903-1909* (1910).

Take everything you like seriously, except yourselves.

Advice to the faculty and students of McGill University where Kipling was awarded his first honorary degree, 1907.

Which reminds me that the other day I saw the Lady herself in the shape of a tall woman of twenty-five or six, waiting for her tram on a street corner. She wore her almost flaxen-gold hair waved, and parted low on the forehead, beneath a black astrachan toque, with a red enamel maple-leaf hatpin in one side of it. This was the one touch of colour except the flicker of a buckle on the shoe. The dark, tailor-made dress had no trinkets or attachments, but fitted perfectly. She stood for perhaps a minute without any movement, both hands—right bare, left gloved—hanging naturally at her sides, the very fingers still, the weight of the superb body carried evenly on both feet, and the profile, which was that of Gudrun or Aslauga, thrown out against a dark stone column. What struck me most,

next to the grave, tranquil eyes, was her slow, unhurried breathing in the hurry about her. She was evidently a regular fare, for when her tram stopped she smiled at the lucky conductor; and the last I saw of her was a flash of the sun on the red maple-leaf, the full face still lighted by that smile, and her hair very pale gold against the dead black fur. But the power of the mouth, the wisdom of the brow, the human comprehension of the eyes, and the outstriking vitality of the creature remained. That is how *I* would have my country drawn, were I a Canadian—and hung in Ottawa Parliament House, for the discouragement of prevaricators.

\*

Canada has given and taken all along the line for nigh on three hundred years, and in some respects is the wisest, as she should be the happiest, of us all.

\*

Again, as always, it was the dignity of the cities that impressed—an austere Northern dignity of outline, grouping, and perspective, aloof from the rush of traffic in the streets. Montreal, of the black-frocked priests and the French novices, had it; and Ottawa, of the gray stone palaces and the St. Petersburg-like shining water frontages; and Toronto, consumingly commercial, carried the same power in the same repose. Men are always building better than they know. . . .

\*

Once, while we halted a woman drove straight down at us from the sky-line, along a golden path between black ploughed lands. When the horse, who managed affairs, stopped at the cars, she nodded mysteriously, and showed us a very small baby in the hollow of her arm. Doubtless she was some exiled Queen flying North to found a dynasty and establish a country. The Prairie makes everything wonderful.

\*

Were I an intending immigrant I would risk a good deal of discomfort to get on to the land in British Columbia; and were I rich, with no attachments outside England, I would swiftly buy me a farm or a house in that country for the mere joy of it.

*

Canada possesses two pillars of Strength and Beauty in Quebec and Victoria. The former ranks by herself among those Mother-cities of whom none can say "This reminds me." To realize Victoria you must take all that the eye admires most in Bournemouth, Torquay, the Isle of Wight, the Happy Valley of Hong Kong, the Doon, Sorrento, and Camps Bay; add reminiscences of the Thousand Islands, and arrange the whole round the Bay of Naples, with some Himalayas for the background.

Real estate agents recommend it as a little piece of England—the island on which it stands is about the size of Great Britain—but no England is set in any such seas or so fully charged with the mystery of the larger ocean beyond.

*

Winnipeg has Things in abundance, but has learned to put them beneath her feet, not on top of her mind, and so is older than many cities. . . . She is a little too modest.

*

One advantage of a new land is that it makes you feel older than Time. I met cities where there had been nothing— literally, absolutely nothing, except, as the fairy tales say, "the birds crying, and the grass waving in the wind."

*Letters to the Family: Notes on a Recent Trip to Canada* (1908). Reprinted in *Letters of Travel 1892-1913* (1920).

To my mind the name of Medicine Hat . . . echoes as you so justly put it in the old Cree and Blackfoot tradition of red mystery and romance that once filled the prairie. Also it hints, I venture to think, at the magic that underlies the city in the shape of your natural gas. Believe me, the very name is an asset, and as years go on will become more and more of an asset. It has no duplicate in the world; it makes men ask questions . . . it has the qualities of uniqueness, individuality, assertion and power. Above all, it is the lawful, original, sweat-and-dust-won name of the city, and to change it would be to risk the luck of the city, to disgust and dishearten old-timers, not in the city alone, but the world over, and to advertise abroad the

city's lack of faith in itself. Men do not think much of a family which has risen in the world, changing its name for social reasons. . . . What, then, should a city be rechristened that has sold its name? Judasville.

> There was agitation in Medicine Hat to change the town's name in 1910. The retentionists were led by the postmaster, Francis F. Fatt, who on November 22, 1910, wrote to Rudyard Kipling "as the Father Confessor of the Empire," imploring his help. On December 9, 1910, Kipling replied from Sussex with a long letter "as a citizen of the Empire and as a lover of Medicine Hat" (which he had visited three years earlier). The full letter appears in a brochure published by *The Medicine Hat News*. For the initial request, see Francis F. Fatt.
>
> "The only commonplace thing about the spot was its name—Medicine Hat, which struck me instantly as the only name such a town could carry," Kipling wrote in 1892. "You people in this district seem to have all Hell for a basement," he told the townsfolk, alluding to the natural gas in the area.

It is her own soul that Canada risks today.

> Message cabled on the eve of the general election, September 21, 1911. The country saved "her own soul," on that occasion at least, by overturning the government. The electorate rejected the reciprocity agreement reached by Prime Minister Sir Wilfrid Laurier and American President William Howard Taft. Laurier was replaced by Sir Robert Borden who favoured imperial preference in matters of trade. One passage of the telegram runs: "It is her own soul that Canada risks today. Once that soul is pawned for any consideration, Canada must inevitably conform to the commercial, legal, financial, social and ethical standards which will be imposed upon her by the sheer, admitted weight of the United States."

Before she realized the grossness of this evil that threatens the world, Canada had sent a division against it. Her answer to the shattering of that division was the despatch of an army corps. How could she do less, they implied, if she wished to live with mankind, or what is more important, with herself? It was as simple as life or death, or the pride that sits rightly on the men and nations that are acquitting themselves honourably at the Armageddon.

> "The Memorial to Canadians Fallen in War," *The Ottawa Citizen*, May 14, 1919. This is Kipling's account of the Canadian soldiers' memorial service at St. Paul's Cathedral, London, England, May 13, 1915.

And always the marvel—to which Canadians seemed insensible—was that on one side of an imaginary line should be Safety, Law, Honour, and Obedience, and on the other frank, brutal decivilisation; and that, despite this, Canada should be impressed by any aspect whatever of the United States.

> "The Very-Own House," *Something of Myself: For My Friends Known and Unknown* (1937). Kipling travelled across Canada in 1906; the next year he was awarded the Nobel Prize for Literature. See also William Wilfred Campbell.

### Kirby, William
The Noblest Motive Is the Public Good.
*
We Observe; We Think; We Reason.
*
Old Niagara For Ever!

> Two mottoes from *The Niagara Mail*, published by Kirby in 1863, followed by one of the publisher's favourite phrases.
>
> *

Poetry in our rude Canada is a field which bears ordinarily more flowers than fruit.

> Letter to Benjamin Sulte, July 25, 1865, quoted by Lorne Pierce in *William Kirby: The Portrait of a Tory Loyalist* (1929).

Je suis un chien qui ronge lo
En le rongeant je prends mon repos
Un temps viendra qui n'est pas venu
Que je morderay qui maura mordu

I am a dog that gnaws his bone

I crouch and gnaw it all alone
The time will come which is not yet
When I'll bite him by whom I'm bit

> This is the famous and mysterious "Golden Dog" inscription which William Kirby saw in 1839 over the lintel of a house on the Rue Baude, Quebec City. His translation appeared in *The Golden Dog (Le chien d'or): A Romance of the Days of Louis Quinze in Quebec* (1877, 1896), The carved stone, with a gilded figure of a dog gnawing a bone and the French rhyme, now adorns the entranceway to the Quebec post office and recalls a tale of vengeance dating back to 1737.

" 'See Naples and die!' That was a proud saying, Count, which we used to hear as we cruised under lateen sails about the glorious bay that reflects from its waters the fires of Vesuvius. We believed the boast then, Count. But I say now, 'See Quebec and live for ever!' Eternity would be too short to weary me of this lovely scene."

> *The Golden Dog (Le chien d'or): A Romance of the Days of Louis Quinze in Quebec* (1877, 1896).

We live in a damned wicked world, and the fewer we praise the better.

> Quoted by Martin Burrell in *Betwixt Heaven and Charing Cross* (1928). See also Henry Clay.

### Kirkconnell, Watson
It is the people that make any country truly great. Merely to be "spacious in the possession of dirt" is no sure title to fame.

> *Canadians All: A Primer of Canadian National Unity* (1941).

### Kishon, Ephraim
Canadian Jewry again demonstrated its love and affection at the second game of the Israelis against a third-league Canadian team when, Shulteiss II falling flat on his face, the stick flew out of his hand and flashed the puck into the Canadians' goal cage. The referee had to stop the game for twenty minutes until the frenetic shouting of the 1,300-strong community had died down. Incidentally, the

game ended with a 498-1 score in the Canadian team's favour, but it must be said that the Lions were greatly hampered by the slippery ground, the irritating sound of the referee's whistle, and the Canadian players.

> "Onward, Lions of Judah!" *Look Back, Mrs. Lot!* (1960), translated from the Hebrew by Yohanan Goldman. Kishon is the Israeli Art Buchwald.

## Kitchener, Lord
You have your orders, carry them out.

> The British secretary of State for War, in 1914, ordering Sir Sam Hughes, minister of Militia and Defence, to break up the First Canadian Division among British formations. Sir Sam's reply was: "I'll be damned if I will." For the full story, see Sir Sam Hughes.

## Kiyooka, Roy
Did you know that Marcel Duchamp was a contemporary of A.Y. Jackson's?

> Art workshop, Simon Fraser University, March, 1973.

## Klein, A.M.
For easier is the yoke than the weight of thought,
Lighter the harness than the harnessed heart!

> Last lines of "Psalm III," *Poems* (1944).

They are upon us, the prophets, minor and major!
Madame Yolanda rubs the foggy crystal.
She peers, she ponders, the future does engage her;
She sees the *Fuehrer* purged by Nazi pistol.

> Opening lines of "Psalm XXV," *Poems* (1944). The poem ends with a call for "that inspiring peasant . . . that prophet . . . who will explicate the folded present." Klein himself answered the call, for these lines constitute a prophecy, and were published a year before Hitler shot himself with a "Nazi pistol."

Where was he born? (Born is the word that I
Use, seeing *littered* is not poesy).

Where was he born? In Braunau at the Inn—
And Austria paid for that original sin!—
Born to a father, old and over-wined
Who had he slept one night, had saved mankind!
At first hight Schicklgruber—'what a name
To herald through the mighty trump of fame'—
*Heil Schicklgruber! Schicklgruber, heil!*
Methinks this lacks the true imperial style,
And certainly no poet's nor mob's tongue
Could shake the shekel-shackle-gruber—song!

> From *The Hitleriad* (1944).

O biblic birds,
who fluttered to me in my childhood illness
—me little, afraid, ill, not of your race—
the cool wing for my fever, the hovering solace,
the sense of angels—
be thanked, O plumage of paradise, be praised.

> From "For the Sisters of the Hotel Dieu," *The Rocking Chair and Other Poems* (1948).

O, like some Anjou ballad, all refrain,
which turns about its longing, and seems to move
to make a pleasure out of repeated pain,
its music moves, as if always back to a first love.

> From "The Rocking Chair," *The Rocking Chair and Other Poems* (1948).

Just say I was born and that I am not dead yet.

> Reply to James Laughlin of New Directions, when the publishers asked the Montreal Jewish poet for a blurb for *The Hitleriad* (1944). Quoted by Miriam Waddington in *The Canadian Forum*, October-November, 1972.

## Klein, Ernest
To know the origin of words is to know the cultural history of mankind.

\*

What the elements are to chemistry,

what the sounds are to music, are words to language. However, words are not only the elements of a language but also of the history of the people speaking it. They are important milestones along the way leading to the majestic Palace of Human Knowledge.

*A Comprehensive Etymological Dictionary of the English Language* (1966).

**Klondike Mike**   See Michael Mahoney.

**Knight, Eric**
Germany and Japan don't want swamps and jungles. They want you—great, rich, sprawling Canada, rich with her endless wheat-bearing acres where a *Herrenvolk* could lord it over a slave population; Canada with its great and untold wealth of unexploited raw material. Those are the goals of Nazi war—Canada, Brazil, Russia, the United States—the vast lands that lie amid untold resources, the lands with living-room for the "super-race" that will allow *you* to become a new sort of white native to carry out their orders.

CBC Radio, March 1, 1942. Quoted by Margaret Fairley in *Spirit of Canadian Democracy: A Collection of Canadian Writing from the Beginnings to the Present* (1945). Knight, the Anglo-American writer, enlisted with the Princess Pats in 1941. He was the author of *The Flying Yorkshiremen* (1937) and *Lassie Come Home* (1940). He died in an airplane crash a year after making this broadcast.

**Knister, Raymond**
There has been no national Burbank to create a Canadian subspecies of the short story as there was to breed Marquis wheat.

\*

We had a new country but old peoples; wealth collectively and in the future, but individual poverty; a store of tradition and a prevalent illiteracy—and so much to be done that we had little time to study how we should do it.

Introduction to *Canadian Short Stories* (1928), edited by Raymond Knister.

I shall not wonder more, then,
But I shall know.

Leaves change, and birds, flowers,
And after years are still the same.

Opening lines of "Change," *Collected Poems* (1949).

**Knopf, Alfred A.**
What this country needs is a Sinclair Lewis.

Remark made by the New York publisher in the early 1960s, quoted by Brian Moore in *Great Canadians: A Century of Achievement* (1965).

**Knowles, R.E.**
There is no such discerning auditor as death.

*The Toronto Star*, April 20, 1929, on the death of Sir Clifford Sifton.

The first essential of an interviewer is to have a fine opinion of oneself. It is necessary to so vary oneself, so to control and direct one's speech, that great men realize that you are no particular fool yourself. There is no such joy to the interviewee as to find a man of magnitude interviewing him. It is fatal to exhibit or cherish an inferiority complex.

Columnist for *The Toronto Star*, quoted by J.H. Cranston in *Ink on My Fingers* (1953).

**Knowles, Stanley**
What shall it profit Canada if we gain a pipeline, and lose a nation's soul? What shall it profit the people of Canada, if we gain a thousand pipelines, and lose Parliament!

"He was aroused by the arrogance of the Liberal tactics to a passionate rage, and at one point during the [1956 pipeline] debate, yelled across to the Treasury Benches. . . ." Quoted by Christina and Peter Newman in "The Great Pipeline Debate," *Historic Headlines* (1967), edited by Pierre Berton.

**Knox, Captain John**   See James Wolfe.

**Kolber, Leo**
The most unethical thing you can do in the business world is to design something that has no profit.

Quoted by Harvey Sheppard in *The Globe and Mail*, January 5, 1972.

### Kootook, David
I will see you again in Spence Bay, or in Heaven.

Letter written to his family by the fourteen-year-old Eskimo lad, November 12, 1972, four days after the crash of the mercy flight taking him from Cambridge Bay to Yellowknife.

Shut up, I am going to die now.

To Marten Hartwell when the pilot sounded out the exhausted Kootook on the subject of cannibalism, November 29, 1972. Kootook refused to eat human flesh and died the following day. Quoted by Colin Smith in *The London Observer*, May 6, 1973. See also Marten Hartwell.

### Koshevoy, Himie
Old garagemen never die, they just retire. / Old actors never die, they just drop apart. / Old beekeepers never die, they just buzz off. / Old hippies never die, they just smell that way. / Old printers never die, they're just not the type. / Old archers never die, they just bow and quiver. / Old wrestlers never die, they just lose their grip. / Old butchers never die, they only meat their fate. / Old lawyers never die, they just lose their appeal. / Old pun books never die, they just get de-pressed. / Old steelmakers never die, they just lose their temper. / Old cheesemakers never die, they just lose their whey.

*Himie Koshevoy's Treasure Jest of Best Puns* (1969). "Some day this book may be considered a turning point of publishing," explains the author on the copyright page. "There are no rights reserved."

### Kosygin, Alexei
Flying over Canada, I saw small fields. Flying over the Soviet Union, you will see enormous fields.

Quoted by Bruce West in *The Globe and Mail*, October 26, 1971.

I personally like Canadians. Very business-like people. They know what they want, which is no mean achievement. And they are proceeding towards their goal boldly, courageously and that, too, is not just a simple thing to do.

CBC-TV interview, October 26, 1971. See also Geza Matrai.

### Kravchenko, Victor
Vancouver. My head was in a whirl. My thoughts were playing leapfrog. I was free! Who was it once said that only those who have been slaves can understand freedom? It seemed to me, walking through the main streets with a group of my shipmates, that I had never before seen so many relaxed, unafraid, happy people in one place at one time.

Soviet engineer Kravchenko's first taste of the Western world, en route from Moscow to Washington, August, 1943. Eight months later he defected and explained his actions in *I Chose Freedom: The Personal and Political Life of a Soviet Official* (1946).

### Kreisel, Henry
The refugee is the everyman of our time.

*The Betrayal* (1964).

### Kreps, Bonnie
One is not born, but rather becomes, a woman or a man.

"Radical Feminism," *Women Unite! An Anthology of the Canadian Women's Movement* (1972).

### Kribs, Louis P.
The Old Man, the Old Flag, and the Old Policy.

Slogan of the Conservative party in the election of 1891, coined by the news editor of *The Toronto Empire*. This marked the first time political slogans were used in Canadian campaigns, and the Conservatives won, returning the "old man," Sir John A. Macdonald, to power. He died a few months later. The "old flag" was the Union Jack, and the "old policy" the National Policy of protective tariffs vs. Liberal reciprocity.

### Kripps, Agnes
When you educate a man, you educate

an individual; but when you educate a woman, you educate a family. And that's what I'm going to do.

> Former Social Credit M.L.A., quoted by Pat Moan in *The Vancouver Sun*, March 17, 1973.

## Kroetsch, Robert
. . . the contradiction that is man; the mind that wrestles with black despair, the spirit that soars.

> *The Words of My Roaring* (1966).

Mile Zero, like mukluks or weak coffee, is a Canadian institution. Mile Zero of the Mackenzie Highway is a stone marker in the farming town of Grimshaw, Alberta; the road, most of it gravel, runs 626 miles to the north. It ends on the far side of Great Slave Lake in Yellowknife, the new capital of the Northwest Territories.

✱

Albertans bow to no one; the multitudes of their own number who flee over the Continental Divide and down to Van-

couver and the Okanagan Valley are so many sheep who deserve the misery of endless rain and a too long summer.

> *Alberta* (1968).

The hope-despair balance is fascinating to me, because that's the razor's edge; that's where we live. We become fascinated with problems of equilibrium. Americans are interested in expansion. This difference has to have an effect on our literature, on our language.

> Interviewed by Donald Cameron in *Conversations with Canadian Novelists* (1973).

## Kunstler, William
I would hope, myself, that every American of draft age came across the border here, or went to Sweden; then, they wouldn't have anybody to fight their wars.

> Address by the radical American lawyer in Toronto about 1969, quoted by Roger Neville Williams in *The New Exiles: American War Resisters in Canada* (1971).

# L

## Labelle, Abbé Antoine
Keep our people together in a land where they can maintain their own individuality.

> Appointed deputy minister of colonization for Quebec in 1888, Abbé Labelle sought to stem French-Canadian emigration to the United States. Quoted by André Siegfried in *Canada* (1973).

## Laberge, Louis
The State Is Our Exploiter.

> Title of working papers distributed by

the Quebec Federation of Labour at its convention in November of 1971.

When one is a victim of aggression one does not waste time preparing the menu for the victory banquet.

> Militant president of the Quebec Federation of Labour, replying to charges that the FLQ lacked specific long-term goals. *The Toronto Star*, February 7, 1972.

## LaBine, Gilbert
On the morning of the 16th of May, about half a mile from where we were

camped, I was following around the shore of an island and I discovered what I considered a beautiful looking vein. I started out and followed it up, and felt sure investigation would prove it to be silver. As I looked over to the shore, a distance of about 300 or possibly 400 feet, I noticed a great wall there that was stained with cobalt-bloom and copper-green. I walked over to this place and investigated it carefully, and found all the associated ores of cobalt, including some silver. Following along, I found a tiny piece of dark ore, probably the size of a large plum. I chipped it off with my hammer, and there it was—pitchblende!

> The prospector who discovered pitchblende, the source of uranium, at Echo Bay, Great Bear Lake, in 1930, recalled the strike six years later at an Ottawa dinner held in his honour. Quoted by Wilfrid Eggleston in *Canada's Nuclear Story* (1965).

People said the North could wait. We went ahead.

> Quoted by Peter C. Newman in *Flame of Power: Intimate Profiles of Canada's Greatest Businessmen* (1959). See also Dr. J. McIntosh Bell.

**Labitzky, Wilhelm**   See Franz Gehring.

**Labonté, Yves**
I did it for kicks.

> For this reason the eighteen-year-old messenger boy planted a bomb in a garbage container on Sherbrooke Street West in Montreal that exploded and killed the nightwatchman, Wilfrid O'Neil, on April 20, 1963. Quoted by Peter Desbarats in "The FLQ Reign of Terror," *Historical Headlines* (1967), edited by Pierre Berton.

**Labouchère, Henry**
British Columbia is a barren, cold mountain country that is not worth keeping. It would never have been inhabited at all, unless by trappers of the Hudson's Bay Company, had the "gold fever" not taken a party of mining adventurers there, and ever since that fever died down the place has been going from bad to

worse. Fifty railroads would not galvanise it into prosperity.

> "The Canadian Dominion Bubble," *Truth*, September 1, 1881. Labouchère was the editor of this British scandal sheet. See also Queen Victoria.

**Lacombe, Father Albert**
Men, women and children, mourn over your great parent; you will no more hear his voice and its eloquent harangues. In your distress and misery you will no more rush to his tent for comfort and charities. He is gone. There is no one like him to fill his place.

> Funeral oration for Crowfoot who died in 1890. Quoted by Pierre Berton in *The Last Spike: The Great Railway, 1881-1885* (1971).

**Ladd, H. Landon**
We are only loggers.

> Slogan of District Two of the International Wood Workers of America, coined by its president, H. Landon Ladd, "after a retired logger heard him speak, and then told him: 'What you say is right, and what you are trying to do is right. But you'll never get it. We are only loggers.' " This is the Newfoundland local. Richard Gwyn's *Smallwood: The Unlikely Revolutionary* (1968).

**Laflèche, Louis-François-Richer**
One will be convinced that the Conquest has not been a misfortune for us, but that it has been the providential means which God used to save us as a people.

> *Quelques considérations sur les rapports de la société civile avec la religion et la famille* (1866). Quoted by Ramsay Cook in *Canada and the French-Canadian Question* (1966).

Speak English, but speak it badly.

> Bishop of Three Rivers from 1870 to 1898, quoted by Télésphore-Damien Bouchard in the House of Commons, June 21, 1944.

**Lafontaine, Sir Louis-Hippolyte**
The very race that has been trodden

underfoot now finds itself, in some sort by this union, in a position of command today. Such is the position in which I leave the people of my race.

> Address at the Montreal banquet to mark his retirement from public life, October, 1851. *Builders of the Canadian Commonwealth* (1923), edited by George H. Locke.

J'aime mon Dieu, et j'aime mon Pays.

> Dying words of the French-Canadian reform leader, 1864. Quoted by G. Mercer Adam in *Canada's Patriot Statesman: The Life and Career of the Right Honourable Sir John A. Macdonald* (1891).

## La Galissonière, Comte de
One might argue that only colonies like St. Domingue and Martinique, which are a source of great wealth and revenues, should be preserved, while others like Canada and Louisiana, which are a burden to France, should be abandoned.

> "Mémoire" (*c.* 1750), quoted by K.A. MacKirdy, J.S. Moir and Y.F. Zoltvany in *Changing Perspectives in Canadian History: Selected Problems* (1967).

## La Hontan, Baron de
I am told, that the fattest went off best, upon the apprehension that these being less active, would keep truer to their Ingagements, and hold out better against the nipping cold of the Winter. [On the "King's Girls," wards of the French king sent to New France as wives for the settlers from 1665 to 1671]

*

For Instance, when the Jesuits Preach up the Incarnation of *Jesus Christ*, they'l answer, *That's Wonderful:* When the Question is put to them, whether they'l turn Christians, they reply, that *they'l consider of it.* . . . Such, Sir, is the Obstinacy and prepossession of this People. [On the Hurons]

> Baron de La Hontan spent ten years in North America. The unorthodox French officer fled to Portugal in 1693 and published his memoirs in The Hague in 1703. *New Voyages to North-America* (1905), translated by Reuben Gold

Thwaites. For his semi-fictional Huron spokesman, see Adario.

I will not say that Justice is more chaste and disinterested here than in France; but, at least, if she is sold, she is sold cheaper. We do not pass through the clutches of advocates, the talons of attorneys, and the claws of clerks. These vermin do not infest Canada yet. Everybody pleads his own case.

> Observation made about 1685 in New France. Quoted by Francis Parkman in *The Old Régime in Canada* (1874).

## Lahr, Bert
Some of the cast cried when they first saw Dawson City, and we *all* cried when we left. The townspeople cried and the cast cried. It was sad.

> The American comedian starred in a musical comedy sponsored by the Dawson City Festival of the Arts, Summer, 1964. Quoted by Edward McCourt in *The Yukon and Northwest Territories* (1969).

## Laidlaw, A.F.
For co-operatives, as for all organizations involved in community education and development, the task is unending. Having once begun it, we can never be done with it.

> "Co-operatives as Agents of Community Education and Development," *Citizen Participation: Canada—A Book of Readings* (1971), edited by James A. Draper.

## Laing, Arthur
The Indian Act is an act which gives the Indian the right to do nothing at all.

> Minister of Indian Affairs in the Trudeau administration, quoted by Ben Swankey in his booklet *National Identity or Cultural Genocide?* (1971).

## Lait, Jack
The most popular beer in Chicago is Canadian Ace.

*

Canadian: A euphemism for "Jew."

> "Loop Lexicon," *Chicago: Confidential* (1950), by Jack Lait and Lee Mortimer.

**Lajeunesse, Marie Louise Emma Cécile**
See Madame Emma Albani.

**La Jonquière, Marquis de**
I have reached the age of sixty-six years, and there is not a drop of blood in my veins that does not thrill for the service of my King.

> Letter from the governor of New France, October 19, 1751, quoted by Francis Parkman in *Montcalm and Wolfe* (1884).

**Lake, John N.**
Arise, Saskatoon, Queen of the North!

> The Temperance commissioner named Saskatoon in 1882, after the Indian word for a purplish berry. "By itself the name is perhaps acceptable, but the combination of Saskatoon Saskatchewan outsiders find difficult to take seriously." Edward McCourt in *Saskatchewan* (1968).

**Lake, Veronica**
The first one was the Canadian epic. It was entitled *Footsteps in the Snow* and deals with dope traffic and ski bums and other goodies. They paid me $10,000 for this, plus expenses. I left immediately after shooting was concluded and still have not seen an edited version. All I know is that it was cold in Canada and I was happy to return to Florida.

> *Veronica* (1971), with Donald Bain.

**Lalemant, Charles**
The harvest is great, the labourers are few; but they have, by God's grace, a courage undaunted by any obstacles, although the promise of success is not yet very great, so rude and almost brutish are the natives.

> "Letter from Father Charles L'Alemant, Superior of the Missions of Canada, to the Very Reverend Father Mutio Vitelleschi, General of the Society of Jesus, at Rome" (1626), *The Jesuit Relations and Allied Documents* (1954), edited by Edna Kenton.

**Lalemant, Jérôme**
The Ocean which separates us from France sees on its eastern side, only rejoicing, splendour, and bonfires; but on its western, nothing but war, slaughter, and conflagrations.

> *

They come like foxes through the woods. They attack like lions. They take flight like birds, disappearing before they have really appeared. [About the Iroquois]

> *

We cannot go back very far in our researches in their past history, as they have no libraries other than the memory of their old men; and perhaps we should find nothing worthy of publication. [About the Algonquins]

> "Relation of What Occurred in the Mission of the Fathers of the Society of Jesus, in the Countries of New France, From the Summer of the Year 1659 to the Summer of the Year 1660," *The Jesuit Relations and Allied Documents* (1954), edited by Edna Kenton.

We are made a spectacle to the world, to angels, and to men.

> The Jesuit threw himself at the feet of Father Brébeuf, quoting I Corinthians 3:9, before he was burned to death by the Iroquois in 1649. Quoted by Francis Parkman in *The Jesuits in North America in the Seventeenth Century* (1867).

**LaMarsh, Judy**
Centennial year was important to Canada, and it will have a lasting effect . . . it was a great year, a watershed in our history. Since 1967, no one has asked what it is to be a Canadian . . . the year 1967 changed us all profoundly, and we will never look back.

> The Honourable Judy LaMarsh was secretary of State during the centennial year. *Memoirs of a Bird in a Gilded Cage* (1968).

You can't fight, fight, fight all the time without becoming less feminine. In politics you have to.

> Address, Women's Canadian Club of Toronto, *The Toronto Star*, January 16, 1969. "Judy LaMarsh is better than genteel, she is alive," according to Robert Fulford, *The Canadian Magazine*, June 4, 1968. See also Bobby Gimby.

## Lambert, John

It may be easily conceived how despicably low the Canadian theatricals must be, when boys are obliged to perform the female characters: the only actresses being an old superannuated demirep, whose drunken Belvideras, Desdemonas, and Isabellas, have often *enraptured* a Canadian audience.

> *Travels through Lower Canada and the United States of North America* (1810).

## Lambert, R.S.

But I imagine quite a few people would be satisfied only if they too met a real poltergeist. To these—in lighter but not disrespectful vein—I offer the following recipe, of which the ingredients are all Canadian:

You must wait until you and your wife are well on in years. Then acquire a more or less tumbledown farmhouse in a remote part of Ontario or the Maritimes. Live there for several years in lonely frugality, and in due course adopt a female adolescent orphan, selecting one with either a poor health record or a neurotic disposition. Then wait and see what happens to your furniture, walls, windows, linen, barns and cattle!

> *Exploring the Supernatural: Ghosts in Canadian Folklore* (1955).

## Lamontagne, Maurice

Should you want to buy furniture, pay cash. Should you buy on terms, and your supplier go bankrupt later, you and your family would go through very unpleasant moments.

> "There never was any question of a gift," the Liberal cabinet minister maintained in the House of Commons, December 18, 1964, alluding to furniture acquired on easy terms. Quoted by Richard Gwyn in *The Shape of Scandal: A Study of a Government in Crisis* (1965).

## Lampman, Archibald

If our country becomes an independent, compacted, self-supporting nation, which is, or ought to be, the dream of all of us, its social and climatic conditions will in the course of time evolve a race of people having a peculiar national temperament and bent of mind, and when that is done, we shall have a *Canadian* literature.

\*

One May evening somebody lent me *Orion and Other Poems,* then recently published. Like most of the young fellows about me I had been under the depressing conviction that we were situated hopelessly on the outskirts of civilization, where no art and no literature could be, and that it was useless to expect that anything great could be done by any of our companions, still more useless to expect that we could do it ourselves. I sat up all night reading and re-reading *Orion* in a state of the wildest excitement and when I went to bed I could not sleep. It seemed to me a wonderful thing that such work could be done by a Canadian, by a young man, one of ourselves. It was like a voice from some new paradise of art, calling to us to be up and doing.

> "Two Canadian Poets: A Lecture by Archibald Lampman," *University of Toronto Quarterly,* July, 1944. The lecture, edited for publication by E.K. Brown, was delivered in Ottawa on February 19, 1891. Lampman was nineteen and a student at Trinity College, Toronto, when he read Roberts's *Orion* which was published in 1880 when Roberts was only a year older than Lampman.

Winter for reading and study; summer for loafing and dreaming and getting near to nature; spring and autumn for joyous and active production. The mind does not mount readily to the higher exertions during the severity of our winter season. [February 6, 1892]

\*

How utterly destitute of all light and charm are the intellectual conditions of our people and the institutions of our public life! How barren! How barbarous! It is true that this is a new and struggling country, but one would think that the simplest impulse of patriotism, if it existed at all in our governing bodies, would suffice to provoke some attempt at remedy. [February 27, 1892]

\*

A country only reaches full national con-

sciousness when it has developed a literature. Our literature is yet to make, and
the literary impulse in the present age,
especially in America, appears to seek its
first outlet in the magazine. [May 28,
1892]

> At the Mermaid Inn: Being Selections
> from Essays on Life and Literature
> which Appeared in The Toronto Globe
> 1892-1893 (1958), edited by Arthur S.
> Bourinot.

I am not a great poet and I never was.
Greatness in poetry must proceed from
greatness of character, from force, fear-
lessness, brightness. I have none of these
qualities. I am, if anything, the very opposite. I am weak; I am a coward. I am
a hypochondriac. I am a minor poet of a
superior order and that is all. [Letter of
August 29, 1895]

\*

I must say, however, that Sunday is a day
that drives me almost to madness. The
prim black and collars, the artificial dress
of the women, the slow trooping to
church, the bells, the silence, the dreariness, the occasional knots of sallow and
unhealthy zealots, whom one may meet at
street corners whining over some awful
point in theology—all that gradually
presses me down till by Sunday night I
am in despair and would fain issue forth
with pot and brush and colour the town
crimson. [Letter of November 2, 1897]

> The distinguished poet was a second-
> class clerk in the Department of Indian
> Affairs in Ottawa. Archibald Lamp-
> man's Letters to E.W. Thomson (1956),
> edited by Arthur S. Bourinot.

And yet to me not this or that
    Is always sharp or always sweet;
In the sloped shadow of my hat
    I lean at rest, and drain the heat;
Nay more, I think some blessèd power
    Hath brought me wandering idly here:
In the full furnace of this hour
    My thoughts grow keen and clear.

> Final stanza of "Heat."

\*

Morning and noon and midnight ex-
    quisitely,

Rapt with your voices, this alone we
    knew,
Cities might change and fall, and men
    might die,
Secure were we, content to dream with
    you
    That change and pain are shadows
        faint and fleet,
    And dreams are real, and life is only
        sweet.

> Final stanza of "The Frogs."

\*

To have done this is to have lived,
    though fame
Remember us with no familiar name.

> From "The Largest Life." The Poems of
> Archibald Lampman (1900), edited by
> Duncan Campbell Scott.

Where the streets are most astir
Sits a bright-eyed usurer,
Like a crinkled spider set
In the centre of his net.

> "The Usurer," written in 1884.

\*

But some day he shall not be called to
    mind
Save as the curse and pestilence of his
    kind.

> "Epitaph on a Rich Man," written in
> 1893. At the Long Sault and Other New
> Poems (1943), foreword by D.C. Scott,
> introduction by E.K. Brown.

## Lamport, Allan

It's like pushing a car uphill with a rope.

\*

If somebody's gonna stab me in the back,
I wanna be there.

\*

That's what I thought you didn't say.

\*

You can lead a dead horse to water, but
you can't make him drink.

\*

Nobody should visit Toronto for the first
time.

\*

Why, I even went so far as to be fair.

\*

Let's not just discontinue it, let's stop it.

> The irrepressible Allan Lamport served
> as mayor of Toronto from 1952 to 1954.
> When he retired as alderman in 1972,

he left behind a whole string of "Lamports" or "Lampys," some authentic, some apocryphal, worthy of Mrs. Malaprop and Sam Goldwyn. See also Slaw Rebchuck.

**Lanctot, Gustave**
This peculiar situation has thrust upon the historians of the country a double task. The first, which is essential, is to inject into history documentary truth and the complex of sociological facts. The second is to infuse into that history a spirit, a faith, and a colour befitting the great achievements narrated and the greater future looming ahead.

> "Past Historians and Present History in Canada," *Canadian Historical Review*, September, 1941.

**Lanctôt, Jacques**
We have a gift for Mr. Cross. You'll have to sign for it.

> Thus began the October Crisis with the kidnapping of James Cross, October 5, 1970. Ron Haggart and Aubrey E. Golden in *Rumours of War* (1971) report that Lanctôt's first words were: "Birthday present for Mr. Cross."

**Landor, Walter Savage**
Once I would bid the man go hang,
From whom there came a word of slang;
Now pray I, tho' the slang rains thick
Across the Atlantic from *Sam Slick*,
Never may fall the slightest hurt on
The witty head of Haliburton,
Wherein methinks more wisdom lies
Than in the wisest of our wise.

> "To Judge Haliburton" first appeared in 1858 and is reprinted from *Poems* (1935), edited by Stephen Wheeler.

**Landy, Eugene E.**
*Canadian black,* noun (among drug users). Marijuana grown in Canada.
*Canadian bouncer,* noun (among drug users). Form of inferior-quality Seconal from Canada.

> *The Underground Dictionary* (1971).

**Langevin, Sir Hector-Louis**
Macdonald is a sharp fox. He is a very well informed man, ingratiating, clever and very popular. He is *the man* of the conference.

> Letter to Jean Langevin, December 4, 1866. Quoted by W.L. Morton in *The Critical Years: The Union of British North America 1857-1873* (1964). Langevin assessed the delegates to the London Conference, December 4, 1866.

For thirty-three years I have been his follower. For thirty-three years I have been his follower.

> Prominent Quebec Conservative and Father of Confederation, on learning that Sir John A. Macdonald was near death. *The Empire*, May 30, 1891. Quoted by Donald Creighton in *John A. Macdonald: The Old Chieftain* (1955).

**Langham, Michael**
In 1954, when I was working as a free-lance director in the British theatre, Tyrone Guthrie invited me to come to the Stratford Festival to direct a play. At the time, like too many Englishmen, I knew next to nothing about Canada—I had never even heard of Stratford, Ontario—and the idea of putting a Shakespearean work into an un-airconditioned tent in an agricultural area during Ontario's reputed hot-house summer seemed rather bizarre. But Guthrie not only gave the proposal of an air of sanity; he made it seem like the only thing worth doing.

> Michael Langham succeeded Guthrie as artistic director in 1955. "Twelve Years at Stratford," *The Stratford Scene 1958-1968* (1968), edited by Peter Raby.

**Langhorne, John**
Cold on Canadian hills, or Minden's plain,
Perhaps that parent mourn'd her soldier slain. . . .

> "The Country Justice," Part I: "Apology for Vagrants," *Poems of Great Britain* (1794), edited by R. Anderson. The English poet, who died in 1779, is remembered today for his translation of Plutarch's *Lives* (1770).

**Langstaff, T.A.**
A real genius at Ottawa has discovered

that you cannot grow wheat on a glacier.

"The Canadian Mountain Regions as a National Asset," *Addresses Delivered before the Canadian Club of Toronto: Season of 1910-1911* (1911).

## Langton, Anne

We have had a thunderstorm today. My mother amused herself during the storm with repeating poetry, one thing I have not done for a very long time. The old world is the world of romance and poetry. I daresay our lakes, waterfalls, rapids, canoes, forests, Indian encampments, sound very well to you dwellers in the suburbs of a manufacturing town; nevertheless I assure you there cannot well be a more unpoetical and anti-romantic existence than ours.

July 2, 1839, *A Gentlewoman in Upper Canada: The Journals of Anne Langton* (1950), edited by H.H. Langton.

## Langton, John

In a former letter I remember saying I was growing a Tory—I feel myself fast approaching to Radicalism again, but not of that sort of which that little factious wretch Mackenzie is leader. I don't know whether you ever heard of him . . . he is a little red-haired man about five feet nothing and extremely like a baboon but he is the O'Connell of Canada.

Letter written from Cobourg by the settler and future auditor general, April 25, 1834. *Early Days in Upper Canada: Letters of John Langton from the Backwoods of Upper Canada* (1926), edited by W.A. Langton.

## Languirand, Jacques

Boomerang: An election promise not kept.

\*

An astronaut is an easily pleased traveller: he agrees to move in a medium that lacks any atmosphere.

\*

According to recent studies, those men who don't understand women fall into two groups: bachelors and husbands.

\*

The bikini was invented by a girl who didn't want men to notice the little red spots around her nose.

*Le dictionnaire insolite* (1962), by the well-known Montreal wit, broadcaster, playwright, and artistic director.

Do you know what it means to be an artistic director? To look after the toilets, the phone, the garbage . . . ?

Quoted by Lawrence Sabbath in *The Montreal Star*, November 25, 1967.

## Lanigan, George Thomas

What, what, what;
What's the news from Swat?
    Sad news,
    Bad news,
Comes by the cable led
Through the Indian Ocean's bed,
Through the Persian Gulf, the Red
Sea and the Med-
Iterranean—he's dead;
The Ahkoond is dead!

"The Ahkoond of Swat" was a once-popular piece of light verse by the Montreal journalist who died in Philadelphia in 1886. The first stanza, reproduced above, follows the inscription: "The Ahkoond of Swat is dead"—Press Dispatch. Edward Lear's "The Akond of Swat" in *Nonsense Songs, Stories, and Botany* (1870) is better known. *Canadian Poetry in English* (Revised and Enlarged, 1954), edited by Bliss Carman, Lorne Pierce, and V.B. Rhodenizer.

## Lanigan, W.B.

The press, more than the pulpit, more even than parliament and the people, is really [the] guide to the destinies of Canada.

Canadian Press, Calgary, 1917. Quoted by M.E. Nichols in *(CP) The Story of The Canadian Press* (1948). Lanigan, freight traffic manager of the CPR, was the brother of George T. Lanigan, the versifier.

## Lansdowne, Lord

I shall expect to hear on arrival that I am in the habit of enforcing seignorial rights after the manner of the old French nobles. [To a friend in the Colonial Office just prior to his appointment as governor general, October 23, 1883]

\*

I made a short reply, first in English and then in French; the audience—almost all French Canadians—listened respectfully to the first and cheered some of the passages, but before I had got out half a dozen words of the French reply, the whole audience burst into rapturous applause, which continued more or less until I had finished. I suppose my French was less bad than some to which they had been used; at any rate it pleased the good folk of Quebec. [Letter to his mother, October 23, 1883, concerning his reception at Quebec City]

> *Lord Lansdowne: A Biography* (1929), by Lord Newton.

I sent for the Mayor of Victoria, and told him that I must have a small—a very small—alteration made in the inscription, before I could consent to drive under it; an alteration of one letter only. The initial "S" must be replaced with an "R," and then I would pledge my word that I would do my best to see that "Reparation" was made to the Province.

> The governor general refused to pass under an arch inscribed "Separation" when he visited Victoria in 1885. Quoted by his private secretary Lord Frederic Hamilton in *The Days before Yesterday* (1920).

### Lapalme, Georges
Our Duplessis has a portable government. He carries it in his brief case wherever he goes.

> Quoted by Pierre Laporte in *The True Face of Duplessis* (1961).

### La Peltrie, Marie-Madeleine de
Visitor: Why don't you give these things you wear to the poor?
La Peltrie: I prefer to see the poor in new clothes.

> The founder of the Ursuline Convent in Quebec, who died November 19, 1671, always wore tattered garments. Adapted from Thomas B. Costain's *The White and the Gold: The French Regime in Canada* (1954).

### Lapointe, Ernest
No interest in Ethiopia, of any nature whatever, is worth the life of a single Canadian citizen.

> Speech by the liberal minister of Justice, Quebec City, 1939, quoted by James Eayrs in *Diplomacy and its Discontents* (1971), who continues: "The next day, from the rostrum of the Palais de Nations at Geneva, the delegate of Haiti uttered another: 'Great or small, strong or weak, near or far, white or coloured, let us never forget that one day we may be somebody's Ethiopia'."

### Lapointe, Joseph-Arthur
They take the vilest burdens and the heaviest loads. / We say: Work's the perpetual privilege of the poor. / And they believe us, being simple and good.

> Second stanza of "The Poor," translated by A.J.M. Smith in *The Poetry of French Canada in Translation* (1970), edited by John Glassco.

### Laporte, Pierre
In the ten years since the Quiet Revolution began, French Canada has experienced an existential phenomenon. French Canadians have become acutely aware of themselves as a people, of the beauty and richness of their culture and of the importance of preserving it. They have also become aware that their language is the cornerstone of their culture and that if their language disappears, their culture will disappear as well. We are, therefore, witnessing a dramatic effort on the part of a numerically small people to protect and strengthen its most fundamental tie, its language. . . . Inevitably, this struggle creates certain frictions, which anarchists, radicals and other extremists are quick to exploit for their own advantage. The result is the present social turmoil.

> Address made by the Quebec minister of Labour and Immigration in Montreal one year before his murder and the discovery of his body at Saint-Hubert, Quebec, October 18, 1970.

My dear Robert. . . . You have the power to dispose of my life. . . . I am convinced that I am writing the most important letter of my life. . . .

> Lines from a note written by Laporte on October 12, 1970, while in the hands of FLQ kidnappers, addressed to Quebec Premier Robert Bourassa. Quoted by Ron Haggart and Aubrey E. Golden in *Rumours of War* (1971).

**La Potherie, Sieur de Bacqueville et de**
Your Highness will find in it nothing but storms, battles, and shipwrecks.

> Claude Charles Le Roy, Sieur de Bacqueville et de La Potherie, warned the Duke of Orléans that his account of d'Iberville's capture of York Factory in 1687 was not a record of glorious deeds. *Documents Relating to the Early History of Hudson Bay* (1931), edited by J.B. Tyrrell.

**Lapp, Dr. Ralph E.**
An attack on missile bases in North Dakota and Montana would inevitably create waves of fallout over Western Canada . . . Canada would be, in a sense, the anteroom of hell. The real hell would be in the United States.

> American nuclear physicist and pacifist speaking in Toronto, January 17, 1972.

**La Rochefoucauld-Liancourt, Duc de**
The inhabitants do not possess the fairest character.

> The French nobleman's assessment of the inhabitants of York (later Toronto) in 1795. *Voyages dans les Etats-Unis d'Amérique, fait en 1795, 1796, et 1797* (1799).

**Larsen, Henry A.**
The weather was bad, with even poorer visibility all the way down the coast of Baffin Island and Labrador. The first vessel we sighted was a Newfoundland fishing schooner, off Bateau Harbour in Labrador where she was heading for the harbour itself. I followed her in to the small fishing village and there we had a few days' well-earned rest. Because of the gale the fishermen were in port and they were surprised to learn who we were and the length of time we had been away from home, although I somehow had a

feeling that they didn't completely grasp the fact that we had come all the way around the Arctic.

> Sergeant Larsen of the RCMP completed his first voyage through the Northwest Passage in his motor schooner *St. Roch* with little fanfare, September, 1942.

\*

On September 27 we passed through the Bering Strait and docked in Vancouver on October 16, at 6:00 P.M. Behind us were 7,295 nautical miles, which we had covered in eighty-six days!

There was nobody to meet us at the wharf. Canada was still at war and had no time for frivolous things.

> Sergeant Larsen completed his return voyage on the *St. Roch* in October of 1944, again without fanfare. *The Big Ship: An Autobiography by Henry A. Larsen* (1967), with Frank R. Sheer and Edvard Omholt-Jensen.

**La Salle, Sieur de**
"Nous sommes tous sauvages: ce 15, 1680."

> La Salle founded Fort Crèvecoeur near the site of Peoria, Illinois, in 1680. Returning, he found it abandoned and in ruins, with the above words written on a plank of wood. Quoted by Francis Parkman in *La Salle and the Discovery of the Great West* (1869).

Here a column was made ready, bearing the arms of France, and inscribed with the words, "LOUIS LE GRAND, ROY DE FRANCE ET DE NAVARRE, REGNE; LE NEUVIEME AVRIL, 1682."

> La Salle raised this column at the mouth of the Mississippi River on April 9, 1682, claiming all of Louisiana (everything from the Alleghanies to the Rockies; from the Rio Grande and the Gulf to the springs of the Mississippi) for Louis XIV. Quoted by Francis Parkman in *La Salle and the Discovery of the Great West* (1869).

**Laski, Harold J.**
You remember what Richard Baxter said when he saw a beggar on the street? "There, but for the grace of God, goes

Richard Baxter." Surely it is well to bear in mind when you examine the careers of our Canadian millionaires, for instance, and study their lives, that it might well be said of the workers, "There, but for the grace of God and possibly a little influence at Ottawa, goes one of our Canadian millionaires." Take the working man into your confidence. While we have a political democracy in England and Canada we must have an industrial democracy as well.

> "Labour and the War," November 15, 1915, *Addresses Delivered before the Canadian Club of Montreal: Season of 1915-16* (1916).

**Laub, Gabriel**
Civilization: Provide Eskimos with central heating so they have to work in order to make money with which to buy refrigerators.

> Laub, a Czech aphorist, writes in German.

**Lauder, Harry**
You were becoming a wee bit Germanized and you did not know it. It was in your talk; in your dialect. I remember the first time I came to Canada, somebody came over to me and said: How do you do Harry "Louder"? That's right. That is the German pronunciation of my name, and he did not know it. You get it right now, though.

> "The War," November 22, 1917, *Addresses Delivered before the Canadian Club of Montreal: Season 1917-18* (1918).

Canada is the mighty tentacle of the British Empire and I have a right to be here.

> "Service and Sacrifice," November 26, 1917, *Addresses Delivered before the Canadian Club of Ottawa: 1917-18* (1918).

Well, I was up in the great West, your Northwest here, last year at a place called Saskatoon; and it came on what they called a blizzard. I had another name for it. I tell you it blew and it blasted and it snowed. Oh, it can snow yonder! Oh! There is nothing to stop it from snowing! It just starts to snow yonder and it snows

on. Well, I was snowed in that day,—I had nothing to do. Mrs. Lauder was away seeing her brothers in Saskatoon, and I was all alone. It was Sunday, and I buried my head under the blankets and I was soon on the Western front. I just closed my eyes and I went away to the Western front,—I went away to where my heart is, and ever shall be yonder;— and I was wandering along when I met Granny's laddie again.

> Sir Harry's audience would catch the reference to "Granny's Laddie," the immensely popular song of the First World War which the Scottish entertainer composed in Saskatoon. Sir Harry would then sing the song that recalls his meeting with a lad from Falkirk who, only seventeen-and-a-half years old, had fought on the front for two years. He had been raised by his grandmother and wanted nothing more than to see her again. "His hair was fair and his eyes were blue," runs the lyric. "The Returned Soldier and Reconstruction," January 20, 1919, *Addresses Delivered before the Canadian Club of Toronto: Season of 1918-19* (1919). A slightly different version of the above, which includes the song lyrics as well, may be found in "The Old Order and the New," January 8, 1919, *Addresses Delivered before the Canadian Club of Montreal: Season of 1918-19* (1919). See also Sir John Willison.

**Laurence, Margaret**
If I had the wings of an angel,
  Or even the wings of a crow,
I would fly to the top of T. Eaton's
  And spit on the people below.

> In *The Stone Angel* (1964), Margaret Laurence explains this is "a verse the children used to chant to the tune of 'The Prisoner's Song.'" For another version of the lyrics, see John Herbert.

What I care about is trying to express something that in fact everybody knows, but doesn't say or can't express.

> Quoted by Donnalu Wigmore in *Chatelaine*, February, 1971.

But you see I write, and most of my generation, I think, write, what I would call a Method novel. Like a Method actor, you get right inside the role.

\*

So when I say "work" I only mean writing. Everything else is just odd jobs.

> Interviewed by Donald Cameron in *Conversations with Canadian Novelists* (1973).

### Laurendeau, André

Am I cherishing an illusion? It seems to me we used to speak better, not so slurred, not so coarse, not so screechy, not so *joual*. But who will settle that? When the universities get their millions, they will be able to commission linguists to conduct an inquiry into the state of our language. Maybe then we shall learn how many good intentions can bring about such pitiful results.

\*

The word *joual* is a summary description of what it is like to talk *joual,* to say *joual* instead of *cheval,* horse.

\*

For one is sure not to mangle French when one learns only English. So the language will die, but it will die virgin and martyr.

> "The Language We Speak," *Le Devoir,* October 21, 1959.

The English papers in Quebec act like British administrators in an African colony. Wise in the arts of political science, the British rarely destroy the political institutions of a conquered country. They keep a close check on the nigger-king but they wink at his whims. On occasion they permit him to chop off a few heads; it's just part of the local folklore. But one thing would never occur to them: to expect the nigger-king to conform to the high moral and political standards of the British.

The main thing is to get the nigger-king to support and protect British interests. Once this collaboration is assured, the rest is less important. Does the princeling violate democratic principles? What else can you expect of the natives? . . . . ["The Nigger-King Hypothesis," *Le Devoir,* July 4, 1958; this celebrated *roi nègre* editorial appeared when no English-language paper in Quebec re-

ported Maurice Duplessis's expulsion of a *Le Devoir* reporter from a press conference]

\*

It has been said that French Canadians have no political ideas, only feelings. Maybe that's true. It should be carefully noted, however, that in general their feelings have been reasonable and moderate. They possess a singular faculty for resistance. They bend in the storm without snapping. They have never shown any inclination to force the hands of destiny. ["A Rebirth of Separatism," August, 1961]

\*

Paris, history reminds us, was worth a mass. Perhaps Canada is worth a royal commission. ["A Proposal for an Inquiry into Bilingualism," *Le Devoir,* January 20, 1962; the following year the Royal Commission on Bilingualism and Biculturalism was established with Laurendeau and Davidson Dunton as co-chairmen]

\*

To give back to human speech its primal fullness one would have to institute a reign of silence.

\*

I doubt that death is real. One always runs the risk of a resurrection. ["You must Drink Your Own Prose to the Dregs," November, 1963]

> *André Laurendeau: Witness for Quebec* (1973), translated by Philip Stratford.

Is it possible to love the State, "that frigid monster"?

> Editorial, *Le Devoir,* March 7, 1963. Quoted by Frank Scott and Michael Oliver in *Quebec States Her Case: Speeches and Articles from Quebec in the Years of Unrest* (1964).

### Laurier, Sir Wilfrid

The proper basis of the British Empire was that it was to be composed of a galaxy of nations under the British Crown.

> House of Commons, December 2, 1907. According to Robert M. Hamilton in *Canadian Quotations and Phrases: Literary and Historical* (1952), Sir Wilfrid first used the felicitous phrase "a gal-

axy of free nations" in a speech in the Guildhall, London, England, July 11, 1902.

Our souls are immortal, but our means are limited. We constantly strive toward an ideal which we never attain. We dream of good, but we never realize the best.

*

Our means are limited, but our nature is perfectible and we have the infinite for our arena.

*

More revolutions have been caused by Conservative obstinacy than by Liberal exaggeration. [Speech before the Club Canadien, Quebec City, June 26, 1877; Skelton]

The eternal principles of justice are far more important than thousands of millions of acres of land. Let us adhere to those principles of justice, and in so doing we will have the surest foundation for securing justice on every occasion. [House of Commons, 1882, concerning a boundary dispute between Manitoba and Ontario; Skelton]

And I will say this, that we are all Canadians. Below the island of Montreal the water that comes from the north from Ottawa unites with the waters that come from the western lakes, but uniting they do not mix. There they run parallel, separate, distinguishable, and yet are one stream, flowing within the same banks, the mighty St. Lawrence, and rolling on toward the sea bearing the commerce of a nation upon its bosom—a perfect image of our nation. We may not assimilate, we may not blend, but for all that we are still the component parts of the same country.

> Toronto address, December 10, 1886. *The Globe*, December 11, 1886.

The subject is a delicate one. I would not wish to say anything disparaging of the capital, but it is hard to say anything good of it. Ottawa is not a handsome city and does not appear destined to become one either.

*

For us, sons of France, political sentiment is a passion; while, for the Englishman, politics are a question of business.

*

While the Frenchman wants you to have his opinion, the Englishman wants you to have opinions of your own.

*

The Englishman respects your opinions; but he never thinks of your feelings.

> Montreal address, May 14, 1884. *Wilfrid Laurier on the Platform* (1890).

" 'Had I been born on the banks of the Saskatchewan,' he was reported as declaring in a sentence that for ten years every Tory editor in Canada kept standing in type, 'I would myself have shouldered a musket to fight against the neglect of governments and the shameless greed of speculators.' " [At a demonstration in the Champ de Mars, Montreal, November 22, 1885, the Sunday following the hanging of Riel; Skelton]

You cannot legislate against geography. [Speech at Somerset, Quebec, August 2, 1887]

Sir, death is the law, the supreme law.

> On Sir John A. Macdonald's death, Ottawa, February 4, 1891, quoted by Lawrence J. Burpee in *Canadian Eloquence* (1910).

It is not enough to have good principles; we must have organization also. Principles without organization may lose, but organization without principles may often win. [Address to the Reform Club, Ottawa, June 19, 1893]

It is true, England was—as the Minister of Finance said on a former occasion, and is yet, isolated—whether splendidly isolated or dangerously isolated, I will not now debate; but for my part, I think splendidly isolated, because this isolation of England comes from her superiority, and her superiority today seems to be manifest.

> House of Commons, February 5, 1896. For the earlier use of the phrase "splendid isolation," see Sir George E. Foster.

I am British to the core.

> Address, Lord Mayor's Banquet, Mansion House, London, England, July 1,

1897, quoted by André Siegfried in *The Race Question in Canada* (1907).

A colony, yet a nation—words never before in the history of the world associated together. [Address at the Queen's Jubilee, London, England, 1897]

If there is anything to which I have devoted my political life, it is to try to promote unity, harmony and amity between the diverse elements of this country. My friends can desert me, they can remove their confidence from me, they can withdraw the trust they have placed in my hands; but never shall I deviate from that line of policy. Whatever may be the consequences, whether loss of prestige, loss of popularity or loss of power, I feel that I am in the right, and I know that a time will come when every man will render me full justice on that score.

House of Commons, March 13, 1900. These remarks were quoted by W.L. Mackenzie King in Parliament on the conscription debate, November 27, 1944.

If we were to be compelled to take part in all the wars of Great Britain, I have no hesitation in saying that I agree with my hon. friend that, sharing the burden, we should also share the responsibility. Under that condition of things, which does not exist, we should have the right to say to Great Britain: If you want us to help you, call us to your councils; if you want us to take part in wars let us share not only the burdens but the responsibilities and duties as well.

House of Commons, March 13, 1900. "My hon. friend" was Henri Bourassa. "If you want us to help you, call us to your councils" became a catchphrase of the period.

For my part—I never made any secret of it—I have the greatest possible admiration for the American people. I have always admired their many strong qualities. But I have found in the short experience during which it has been my privilege and my fortune to be placed at the head of affairs, by the will of the Canadian people, that the best and most effective way to maintain friendship with our American neighbours is to be abso-

lutely independent of them. [House of Commons, July 30, 1903]

We have found that our Canadian independence is quite compatible with our dependency as a colony.

"Address," January 18, 1904, *Addresses Delivered before the Canadian Club of Ottawa: 1903-1909* (1910). It is this address that included the line "the twentieth century belongs to Canada" or its facsimile. For further details about the parentage and progeny of this most famous of all Canadian quotations, see "Who Owns the Twentieth Century?" at the end of the Laurier entries.

"Laurier and the Larger Canada"

Banner at an election rally where Laurier was the principal speaker, Massey Hall, Toronto, *The Globe*, October 15, 1904. "Sir Wilfrid Laurier is easily the first statesman of Great Britain"—*The Daily News*, London, England, September 14, 1904.

Scarcely had I landed in Great Britain when I made a speech. In that very first speech I stated the question fairly to the British people. I told them that we had a preference which we intended to give them, I stated the obstacles, and I asked them to help us to have those treaties removed. I did it in these words: "Either England must advance or Canada must recede." These words were quoted the following day in all the press of Great Britain. They were repeated day after day and week after week, and the consequence was that some two months afterwards the treaties, the obnoxious treaties, were denounced by the British Government. [Sir Wilfrid, in London for the Diamond Jubilee of Queen Victoria in 1897, spoke against the trade treaties Britain had concluded with Germany and Belgium]

\*

We are in the year 1904. We are a nation of six million people already; we expect soon to be twenty-five, yes, forty millions. There are men living in this audience, men over there (pointing to the top gallery), the hope of the country, who before they die, if they live to old age, will see this country with at least sixty millions of people.

*

Sir, I tell you nothing but what you know when I tell you that the nineteenth century has been the century of United States development. The past hundred years has been filled with the pages of their history. Let me tell you, my fellow countrymen, that all the signs point this way, that the twentieth century shall be the century of Canada and of Canadian development. [Cheers] For the next seventy-five years, nay for the next hundred years, Canada shall be the star towards which all men who love progress and freedom shall come.

*

To those, sir, who have life before them, let my prayer be this: Remember from this day forth never to look simply at the horizon as it may be limited by the limits of the Province, but look abroad over all the continent, wherever the British flag floats, and let your motto be, "Canada first, Canada last, and Canada always."

Campaign address, Massey Hall, Toronto, October 14, 1904. Published in *The Globe*, October 15, 1904.

Remember this, that in politics the question seldom arises to do the ideal right. The best that is generally to be expected, is to attain a certain object, and for the accomplishment of this object, many things have to be done which are questionable, and many things have to be submitted to, which, if vigorously investigated, could not be approved of. . . . My object is to consolidate Confederation, and to bring our people, long estranged from each other, gradually to become a nation. This is the supreme issue. Everything else is subordinate to that idea. [Letter to W.D. Gregory, November 11, 1904; Skelton]

This is a difficult country to govern.

Letter to Sir John Willison, March 7, 1905. This is an echo of Sir John A. Macdonald's remark, "Canada is a hard country to govern," and an anticipation of Lester B. Pearson's observation, March 26, 1965: "It has been said that Canada is the most difficult country in

the world to govern. I am perhaps more aware of that than I used to be."

War is everywhere. When Britain is at war, Canada is at war; there is no distinction. If Great Britain, to which we are subject, is at war with any nation, Canada becomes liable to invasion, and so Canada is at war. [House of Commons, January 12, 1910]

I do not pretend to be an imperialist. Neither do I pretend to be an anti-imperialist. I am a Canadian first, last and all the time. I am a British subject by birth, by tradition, by conviction—by the conviction that under British institutions my native land has found a measure of security and freedom it could not have found under any other régime. I want to speak from that double standpoint, for our policy is an expression of that double opinion. [House of Commons, February 3, 1910; Skelton]

I am branded in Quebec as a traitor to the French, and in Ontario as a traitor to the English. In Quebec I am branded as a Jingoist, and in Ontario as a Separatist. In Quebec I am attacked as an Imperialist, and in Ontario as an anti-Imperialist. I am neither. I am a Canadian. Canada has been the inspiration of my life. I have had before me as a pillar of fire by night and a pillar of cloud by day a policy of true Canadianism, of moderation, of conciliation. I have followed it consistently since 1896, and I now appeal with confidence to the whole Canadian people to uphold me in this policy of sound Canadianism which makes for the greatness of our country and the Empire. [Campaign speech, St. John, Quebec, 1911; Skelton]

Follow my White Plume.

On July 11, 1911, Laurier stated: "Henry of Navarre at the battle of Ivry said, 'Follow my white plume, and you will find it always in the forefront of honour.' Like Henry IV, I say to you young men, 'Follow my white plume'—the white hairs of sixty-nine years—and you will, I believe I can say it without boasting, find it always in the forefront of honour." "Sir Wilfrid called not in vain to young Quebec, as age silvered his black locks," explained O.D. Skelton. Quebec backed him but his government was defeated in 1911.

We have long said that when Great Britain is at war we are at war; today we realize that Great Britain is at war and that Canada is at war also.

\*

It would be seen by the world that Canada, a daughter of Old England, intends to stand by her in this great conflict. When the call comes our answer goes at once, and it goes in the classical language of the British answer to the call of duty: "Ready, aye, ready."

> House of Commons, August 19, 1914. Laurier was Opposition leader at the time the special war session was held. For "Ready, aye, ready," see also Arthur Meighen.

What great and enduring achievement has the world ever accomplished that was not based on idealism?

> Address in New York, 1916. Quoted by O.D. Skelton in *The Canadian Dominion: A Chronicle of Our Northern Neighbour* (1919).

For my part I want to fight for England and also for France. To those who do not want to fight either for England or for France I say: *Will you fight for yourselves?* [Montreal address, September, 1916; Skelton]

I have lived too long, I have outlived Liberalism. [To the Liberal caucus in a despairing mood, 1916; Skelton]

Yes, they cheered for me, but they didn't vote for me. [After a triumphal trip across the West, as leader of the Opposition, 1917; Skelton]

Quebec does not have opinions, only sentiments.

> Quoted by Mason Wade in *The French Canadians: 1760-1967* (1968).

In 1896 I was excommunicated by the Roman priests and in 1917 by Protestant parsons.

> Quoted by F.A. McGregor in *The Fall and Rise of Mackenzie King: 1911-1919*

(1962). Laurier faced the Manitoba schools question in 1896 and the conscription issue in 1917.

We French-Canadians belong to one country, Canada; Canada is for us the whole world; but the English-Canadians have two countries, one here and one across the sea. [Skelton]

"An old French Canadian, on his annual visit to Montreal, was told that Queen Victoria had died. Who, then, ruled England, he wanted to know, and was told that the Prince of Wales had succeeded to the throne.

"The inhabitant's eyes lighted up. 'Mon Dieu! but he must have a great pull with Laurier!'" [*The New Orleans Picayune,* September 27, 1908]

If you please, paint me as a ruler of men.

> To Charles Huot who, a few months before Sir Wilfrid's death in 1919, painted the former prime minister's portrait for the Quebec Assembly Chamber. Attributed by Robert M. Hamilton in *Canadian Quotations and Phrases: Literary and Historical* (1952).

C'est fini.

> "A pressure from his hand to the hand of the companion of his life beside him and the whispered words, 'C'est fini,' were the only signs of consciousness in his last hours." Laurier died on February 17, 1919. These dying words, and all quotations above marked "[Skelton]" appear in *Life and Letters of Sir Wilfrid Laurier* (1921), by Oscar Douglas Skelton. See also: John G. Diefenbaker, Joseph Pope, Graham Spry.

### Laurier:
### Who Owns the Twentieth Century?

The Twentieth Century Belongs to Canada.

> Certainly the most celebrated of Canadian aphorisms remains Sir Wilfrid Laurier's simple but strong assertion, "The twentieth century belongs to Canada." The remark has increased in popularity over the last seventy years and shows signs of continuing to please well into the twenty-first century, for the assertion is less a prophecy than it is a

touchstone of national aspiration measured against national achievement. The fine phrase expresses both desire and despair. Here is what Prime Minister Laurier actually said in 1904:

The more I advance in life—and I am no longer a young man—the more I thank Providence that my birth took place in this fair land of Canada. [Cheers] Canada has been modest in its history, although its history is heroic in many ways. But its history, in my estimation, is only commencing. It is commencing in this century. The nineteenth century was the century of the United States. I think we can claim that it is Canada that shall fill the twentieth century. [Cheers] I cannot hope that I shall see much of the development which the future has in store for my country, but whenever my eyes shall close to the light it is my wish—nay it is my hope—that they close upon a Canada united in all its elements, united in every particular, every element cherishing the tradition of its past, and all uniting in cherishing still more hope for the future.

"First Annual Banquet," January 18, 1904, *Addresses Delivered before the Canadian Club of Ottawa: 1903-1909* (1910). The editor of the volume, compiling the addresses five years after Laurier's was delivered, noted in his preface that this was the occasion on which Laurier made his famous declaration. The text does not bear the editor out, but whatever the precise wordage, Laurier's claim to the aphorism can be registered by citing two other early usages. In a campaign address at Massey Hall, Toronto, October 14, 1904, Sir Wilfrid said:

Let me tell you, my fellow countrymen, that all the signs point this way, that the twentieth century shall be the century of Canada and of Canadian development.

The following year he used the expression again, this time in the House of Commons, February 21, 1905:

It has been observed on the floor of the House, as well as outside of this House, that as the nineteenth century had been the century of the United States, so the twentieth century would be the century of Canada.

The assertion was established in the popular mind by 1906. An advertisement for homestead lands in Ernest J. Chambers's *The 'Royal North-West Mounted Police: A Corps History* (1906) includes the assertion in its present form.

Who associates the declaration with James W. Longley? The attorney general of Nova Scotia addressed the Canadian Club of Boston on April 8, 1902, and (as reported by *The Globe*, April 12, 1902) came closest to making the famous statement:

Let me utter one concluding word. Canada is here to stay. The beginning of this century marks an epoch of phenomenal progress in British North America. The nineteenth century was the century of the United States. The twentieth century is Canada's century.

Thus Longley, among the pretenders, has the strongest claim. Other claimants include: Joseph T. Clark, the father of Gregory Clark; the Rev. Dr. James Robertson; J.B. Tyrrell; George Johnson. No matter who can prove precedence, the statement remains identified with Sir Wilfrid. Coming to power in 1896, with his "Ministry of All the Talents," Laurier personified the turn-of-the-century hopes of Canadians for a boundless future.

What follow are other usages of the phrase, some directly relevant, others delightfully irrelevant.

I represent a party which does not yet exist: the party of revolution, civilization.

This party will make the twentieth century.

There will issue from it first the United States of Europe, then the United States of the World.

Written on the wall of Victor Hugo's residence, Place des Vosges, Paris, 1885.

Amidst the happy optimism which pervades Canada at the moment we often hear the speaker say that the twentieth century belongs to Canada. What is true, however, is that Canada belongs to the twentieth century. There is little doubt that for good or ill we shall be shaped in our destiny by the present century.

> Sir Edmund Walker in an address to the Canadian Club of Montreal, January 29, 1912.

Paris was where the twentieth century was.

> Gertrude Stein in the 1920s, quoted by John Bainbridge in *Another Way of Living: A Gallery of Americans Who Choose to Live in Europe* (1968).

I remember a Toronto in which the admirably true phrase—the twentieth century was to be Canada's—was accepted as the general watchword; only nobody had begun to realize what a rotten century the twentieth was going to be.

> B.K. Sandwell in "On Being Sorry for Ourselves," *The Empire Club of Canada: Addresses Delivered to the Members During the Year 1924* (1924).

Let us say, then, that the twentieth century is the century of Canada and of the bathroom.

> B.K. Sandwell in "I Sing the Bathroom," *The Privacy Agent and Other Modest Proposals* (1928).

I've got those weary Twentieth-Century Blues.

> Noël Coward's *Cavalcade* (1931).

Sir Wilfrid Laurier said that the 18th century was England's, the 19th belonged to the United States, and that the 20th would be Canada's. Perhaps I am the only being alive who really believes that. For I do—implicitly. I believe that before the year 2000 Canada's world dominance will be as undisputed a fact as any commonplace of history.

> William Arthur Deacon in *My Vision of Canada* (1933).

Today we think in more modest terms.

> Eugene Forsey in "The Nature of the Canadian Economy," *Social Planning for Canada* (1935), by the Research Committee of the League for Social Reconstruction.

The twentieth century was once supposed to belong to Canada, but it seems more and more likely that only the first quarter of the century was really ours.

> F.W. Burton of St. John's College, Winnipeg, in *The Canadian Journal of Economics and Political Science*, November, 1936.

. . . the hope that in due course it may truly be said that the twentieth century was indeed Canada's.

> D.M. LeBourdais in *Canada's Century* (1951).

The ambition to surpass the United States is not only hopeless but pointless. It is quite clear that, if the twentieth century does not belong to Canada, it does not belong to the United States either: it belongs to all the nations of the world, according to their capacity to make the best of the resources they have.

> Harry G. Johnson in *Canada in a Changing World Economy* (1962).

The twentieth century *did* belong to Canada.

> Brian Moore in *Canada* (1963, 1968).

The future really belongs to those who will build it. The future can be promised to no one.

> Pierre Elliott Trudeau at Yarmouth, Nova Scotia, May 30, 1968.

Some sixty years ago Sir Wilfrid Laurier declared that the twentieth century belongs to Canada. By the middle of the century it had become clear that Canada belongs to the United States.

> Kari Levitt in *Silent Surrender: The Multinational Corporation in Canada* (1970).

The twenty-first century is now just one generation away.

> Ernest Marshall Howse in *People and Provocations* (1965).

The twenty-first century belongs to Japan.

> Herman Kahn, about 1970.

I think if you'll check the books, 'speshully the bankbooks, you'll find out yer

Twentieth-Century still belongs to Fox (whoever he is).

> Don Harron in *Charlie Farquharson's Histry of Canada* (1972).

The 20th Century belongs to the Moon.

> Earle Birney in *What's So Big About Green* (1973).

**Laut, Agnes**
The most brilliant description the writer ever heard of the hereafter was from an old Cree squaw, toothless, wrinkled like leather, belted at the waist like a sack of wool, with hands of dried parchment, and moccasins some five months too odiferous. Her version ran *that heaven would be full of the music of running waters and south winds; that there would always be warm gold sunlight like a mid-summer afternoon, with purple shadows, where tired women could rest; that the trees would be covered with blossoms, and all the pebbles on the shore like dew-drops.*

> From "Story of the Trapper," as quoted by L.J. Burpee and H.J. Morgan in *Canadian Life in Town and Country* (1905). As the authors ask: "If that is not poetry, where shall one find it?"

The chance is always hiding round a corner for the man who goes ahead.

> *Heralds of Empire* (1902).

I don't suppose anything was ever accomplished without somebody being willing to fight a losing battle.

\*

Split the air and you'll get somewhere.

> *Freebooters of the Wilderness* (1910).

What is conservation? About a year and a half ago practical people said: The thing is pure conversation. . . . It is like the heading in the copybook, "Be Good and You will be Happy."

\*

You will see the mighty argosies of the world coming to Canada . . . there is something for you to do. Rise and follow your star.

> "Conservation," February 11, 1910, *Addresses Delivered before the Canadian Club of Ottawa: 1910* (1911).

**Lautens, Gary**
After years of observation, I've come to the conclusion that I'd rather have a friend with warm feelings than a friend with cold facts. Unfortunately, there are a lot of people walking around today with million-dollar brains and ten-cent hearts.

> Quoted by Kay MacKenzie Gold in *How to Build a Life: A Collection of Creeds, Poems and Quotations* (1972).

**Lavallée, Augustin**
> Augustin Lavallée
> teaches music and repairs musical
> instruments and fire-arms

> Circular put out in 1853 by the father of Calixa Lavallée. Quoted by Ernest MacMillan (who called the father "the Harmonious Blacksmith") in *Canadian Portraits: CBC Broadcasts* (1940), edited by R.G. Riddell.

**Lavallée, Calixa**  See Sir Adolphe-Basile Routhier and R. Stanley Weir.

**La Vérendrye, Chevalier de**
Here in Canada more than anywhere else envy is the passion *à la mode*, and there is no escaping it.

> Letter of September 30, 1750. Quoted by Francis Parkman in *A Half-Century of Conflict* (1892).

**Lavergne, Armand-Renaud**
In Canada there are two languages and no patois.

> "The Position of the French Canadian in Canada," December 18, 1911, *Addresses Delivered before the Canadian Club of Montreal: Season of 1911-12* (1912).

If we must conquer our liberties, it is here we should stay. It is not in the trenches of Flanders that we shall win the right to speak French in Ontario. . . . If the Germans are persecutors, there are worse than Germans at our very gates. I'll go further . . . I am not afraid to become a German subject. I ask myself whether the German regime might not be favourably compared with that of the Boches of Ontario.

Address, Legislative Assembly of Quebec, January 13, 1916. Quoted by Mason Wade in *The French Canadians: 1760-1967* (1968).

If the Conscription law is enforced, Canadians have only one choice—to die in Europe or to die in Canada. As far as I am concerned, if my body is to fall in any land, I want it to be on Canadian soil.

Address in Quebec City, July 15, 1917. Quoted by Mason Wade in *The French Canadians: 1760-1967* (1968).

**Law, Andrew Bonar**
I must follow them; I am their leader.

\*

There is no such thing as an inevitable war. If war comes it will be from failure of human wisdom.

\*

If I am a great man, then a good many of the great men of history are frauds.

Remarks attributed to the Canadian-born prime minister of Great Britain; the last remark was made to Lord Beaverbrook during the Ulster crisis, 1913.

You are a curious fellow.

Bonar Law died on October 30, 1923, murmuring these words to his attendant Lord Beaverbrook. Both Law and the Beaver were natives of New Brunswick, and the latter's newspapers helped Law become Britain's first and so far only foreign-born prime minister, a position he held for only 209 days because of ill health. Quoted by Alan Wood in *The True History of Lord Beaverbrook* (1960). See also Lord Beaverbrook.

**Lawrence, Carol**
This is the second time I've performed in Toronto, not counting my honeymoon.

The nightclub singer married Robert Goulet in Toronto. Quoted by Blaik Kirby in *The Globe and Mail*, February 2, 1972. See also Robert Goulet.

**Lawrence, Governor Charles**
That the inhabitants may not have it in their power to return to this Province, nor to join in strengthening the French of Canada or Louisbourg; it is resolved that they shall be dispers'd among his Majesty's Colonies upon the Continent of America. . . .

Decision of the governor and council of Nova Scotia to expel the Acadian population of the province, July 25, 1755. See also Henry Wadsworth Longfellow and Colonel John Winslow.

**Lawrence, D.H.**
I feel a bit like you: nothing nice ever happens, or ever will happen. I dreamed I was made head of a school somewhere, I think, in Canada. I felt so queer about it: such a vivid dream—that I half wonder if it is *my* destiny! A job!—But I manage to make a living still.

Letter written from Florence, June 13, 1927. *The Quest for Rananim: D.H. Lawrence's Letters to S.S. Koteliansky: 1914-1930* (1970), edited by George J. Zytaruk.

**Lawrence, James**
Tell the men to fire faster and not to give up the ship; fight her till she sinks.

Last command of Captain Lawrence of the U.S. *Chesapeake* which was captured by "Brave Broke" of the H.M.S. *Shannon* after a fifteen-minute sea battle outside Boston Harbour, June 1, 1813. Both captains were wounded, Lawrence mortally. Lawrence's dying order, "Don't give up the ship," became the motto of the U.S. Navy, although he did give up the ship. See also Sir Philip Bowes Vere Broke.

**Lawrence, Margaret**
See Margaret Lawrence Greene.

**Layton, Irving**
And me happiest when I compose poems.
  Love, power, the huzza of battle
  are something, are much;
yet a poem includes them like a pool
  water and reflection.

\*

I am their mouth; as a mouth I serve.
  [From "The Birth of Tragedy"]

*

Death is a name for beauty not in use.
  [From "Composition in Late Spring"]

*

A dull people,
but the rivers of this country
are wide and beautiful.
            ["From Colony to Nation"]

*

By the way
she moved
away
I could see
her devotion
to literature
was not
perfect.

      [From "Misunderstanding"] *The Collected Poems of Irving Layton* (1971).

A poem is an Alka-Seltzer tablet: orthodoxies begin to fizz when one is dropped into their midst. Distrustful of abstractions, poetry is in love with the concrete and the particular. ["Poets: The Conscience of Mankind" (1963)]

*

I was once asked: "Whom does the poet write for?" "For God," I answered.
    But you're very welcome to eavesdrop. [Foreword to *Collected Poems* (1965)]

*

My country has been an immense tree on the summit of a sunswept hill from which I plucked hundreds of poems or waited confidently under its boughs for them to fall like heavy fruit into my open lap. When I think of my life under that tree I am filled with an immeasurable thankfulness that extends beyond the coasts of this land to encircle the entire globe.

*

The poet is someone whom life knocks on the head and makes ring like a tuning fork. The knocking begins very early. [Foreword to *The Collected Poems* (1971)]

*

Poems are here to reveal not to argue, and to give pleasure not to pontificate. [Preface (1972)]

      *Engagements: The Prose of Irving Layton* (1972), edited by Seymour Mayne.

What makes us different from Americans is that we are Europeans whose sensibility has been modified by living on this continent. While Americans erased the different qualities the immigrants brought with them, we have carried over some of the European traits, giving us a kind of serenity. We have defied geography to produce this strange country of ours, and now we have to be realistic and stop beating ourselves. We have to realize that despite a small number of people scattered across a big country, despite that many do not read English, despite the presence of the United States, we have produced many good writers. Maybe they're second-string writers, but how many Goethes or Schillers have other countries produced?

      Quoted by Gerald Clark in *Canada: The Uneasy Neighbour* (1965).

Perhaps . . . the answer to the much-asked question "What is a Canadian?" will be found. I hope so though my own instinctive reply is "A Canadian is someone who keeps asking the question 'What is a Canadian?'" But doubtless a graver, more substantial definition is sought by the historian and sociologist.

      Introduction to *Anvil Blood* (1973), a collection of verse by students of York University.

**Leach, Bobby**
I am satisfied. I always keep my word.

      To reporters at his bedside, the Cockney pointed out he had done what he had promised to do—go over Niagara Falls in a steel drum, July 25, 1911. It took Leach twenty-three weeks to recover sufficiently to leave hospital. He died, ironically, after slipping on an orange peel, in Christchurch, New Zealand, in 1926, at the age of seventy. Quoted by Andy O'Brien in *Daredevils of Niagara* (1964).

**Leacock, Stephen**
I, that write these lines, am an Independent, because I will not be a Colonial. This Colonial status is a worn-out, by-gone thing.

      *Great Canada: An Appeal* (1907).

When I go into a bank I get rattled. ["My Financial Career"]

*

The landlady of a boarding house is a parallelogram—that is, an oblong angular figure, which cannot be described, but which is equal to anything. ["Boarding House Geometry"]

*

A man called on me the other day with the idea of insuring my life. Now, I detest life-insurance agents; they always argue that I shall some day die, which is not so. ["Insurance Up to Date"]

*

I mix a good deal with Millionaires. I like them. I like their faces. I like the way they live. I like the things they eat. The more we mix together the better I like the things we mix. ["How to Make a Million Dollars"]

*Literary Lapses* (1910).

Lord Ronald said nothing; he flung himself from the room, flung himself upon his horse and rode madly off in all directions.

"Gertrude the Governess: or, Simple Seventeen," *Nonsense Novels* (1911). "The statement has become part of the English language," noted David M. Legate in *Stephen Leacock: A Biography* (1970). The reason? Theodore Roosevelt made use of the sentence in a political address and credited the literary conceit to Leacock. "All my family, including myself, owe you much for both amusement and instruction," Roosevelt wrote the humourist in 1917. Quoted by Ralph L. Curry in *Stephen Leacock: Humorist and Humanist* (1959). This is one of the few internationally known quotations of Canadian origin.

I was born at Swanmoor, Hants, England, on December 30, 1869. I am not aware that there was any particular conjunction of the planets at the time, but should think it extremely likely.

*

. . . I survived until I took the degree of Doctor of Philosophy in 1903. The meaning of this degree is that the recipient of instruction is examined for the last time in his life, and is pronounced completely full. After this, no new ideas can be imparted to him.

*

Personally, I would sooner have written *Alice in Wonderland* than the whole *Encyclopedia Britannica*.

*

Mariposa is not a real town. On the contrary, it is about seventy or eighty of them. You may find them all the way from Lake Superior to the sea, with the same square streets and the same maple trees and the same churches and hotels, and everywhere the sunshine of the land of hope. [Preface]

*

I think that it was just as they were singing like this: "O—Can-a-da," that word went round that the boat was sinking.

*Sunshine Sketches of a Little Town* (1912).

An English reviewer writing in a literary journal, the very name of which is enough to put contradiction to sleep, has said of my writing, "What is there, after all, in Professor Leacock's humour but a rather ingenious mixture of hyperbole and myosis?"

The man was right. How he stumbled upon this trade secret, I do not know. But I am willing to admit, since the truth is out, that it has long been my custom in preparing an article of a humorous nature to go down to the cellar and mix up half a gallon of myosis with a pint of hyperbole. If I want to give the article a decidedly literary character, I find it well to put in about half a pint of paresis. The whole thing is amazingly simple.

*

No doubt the story-telling habit owes much to the fact that ordinary people, quite unconsciously, rate humour very low: I mean, they underestimate the difficulty of "making humour." It would never occur to them that the thing is hard, meritorious and dignified. Because the result is gay and light, they think the process must be. Few people would realize that it is much harder to write one of Owen Seaman's "funny" poems in *Punch* than to write one of the Archbishop of Canterbury's sermons. Mark Twain's *Huckleberry Finn* is a greater work than *Kant's Critique of Pure Reason,* and Charles Dickens' creation of Mr. Pickwick did more for the elevation of the human race—I say it in all seriousness —than Cardinal Newman's *Lead, Kindly Light, Amid the Encircling Gloom.* Newman only cried out for light in the gloom of a sad world. Dickens gave it. ["Humour As I See It"]

*Further Foolishness* (1916).

The parent who could see his boy as he really is, would shake his head and say: "Willie is no good; I'll sell him." ["The Lot of the Schoolmaster"]

*Essays and Literary Studies* (1916).

There is an old motto that runs, *"If at first you don't succeed, try, try again."* This is nonsense. It ought to read—"If at first you don't succeed, quit, quit, at once." ["Simple Stories of Success, or How to Succeed in Life"]

＊

I wish somehow that we could prohibit the use of alcohol and merely drink beer and whisky and gin as we used to. ["This Strenuous Age"]

*Frenzied Fiction* (1917).

To avoid all error as to the point of view, let me say in commencing that I am a Liberal Conservative, or, if you will, a Conservative Liberal with a strong dash of sympathy with the Socialist idea, a friend of Labour, and a believer in Progressive Radicalism. I do not desire office but would take a seat in the Canadian Senate at five minutes notice.

I believe there are ever so many people of exactly the same way of thinking. ["Politics from Within"]

*The Hohenzollerns in America* (1919).

A man will freely confess that he has no ear for music, or no taste for fiction, or no interest in religion. But I have yet to see the man who announces that he has no sense of humour. ["Have the English Any Sense of Humour?"]

＊

After about ten minutes of his talk they are tired of him. Most people tire of a lecture in ten minutes; clever people can do it in five. Sensible people never go to lectures at all. ["We Have With Us To-night"]

＊

If I were founding a university—and I say it with all the seriousness of which I am capable—I would found first a smoking room; then when I had a little more money in hand I would found a dormitory; then after that, or more probably with it, a decent reading room and a library. After that, if I still had money over that I couldn't use, I would hire a professor and get some text books. ["Oxford as I See It"]

*My Discovery of England* (1922).

There is no way out. Socialism is but a dream, a bubble floating in the air. In the light of its opalescent colours we may see many visions of what we might be if we were better than we are, we may learn much that is useful as to what we can be even as we are; but if we mistake the floating bubble for the marble palaces of the city of desire, it will lead us forward in our pursuit till we fall over the edge of the abyss beyond which is chaos.

*The Unsolved Riddle of Social Justice* (1922).

Do you know, Helga, it rather occurs to me that it's the commonplace people who do things. ["The Soul Call"]

＊

A decision of the courts decided that the game of golf may be played on Sunday, not being a game within the view of the law, but being a form of moral effort. ["Why I Refuse to Play Golf"]

*Over the Footlights* (1923).

The only kind of examination in the subject I can think of would be to say to the pupil, for example, "Have you read Charles Dickens and do you like it?" and when he answered that he didn't care for him but that his uncle read him all the time, to send a B.A. degree to his uncle. ["English as She Is Taught at College"]

*College Days* (1923).

Now education is a peculiar process. You aim at one thing and you hit another. You set out to look for ultimate truth and you don't find it; but incidentally you have acquired a cultivated mind. You pursue studies that you think will be of use in your business. They are not. But by the time you are done with them you yourself are a better man for your business or for any other business.

"Teaching the Unteachable," *The Teachers' Magazine*, June, 1924.

This much however, I will admit, that if a man has a genuine sense of humour, he is apt to take a somewhat melancholy, or at least disillusioned view of life. Humour and disillusionment are twin sisters. Humour cannot exist alongside of eager ambition, brisk success, and absorption in the game of life. Humour comes best to those who are down and out, or who have at least discovered their limitations and their failures. Humour is essentially a comforter, reconciling us to things as they are in contrast to things as they might be.

*

But I have always found that the only kind of statement worth making is an overstatement. A half truth, like half a brick, is always more forcible as an argument than a whole one. It carries further. [Preface]

*

Advertising may be described as the science of arresting the human intelligence long enough to get money from it. ["The Perfect Salesman"]

*The Garden of Folly* (1924).

The general idea, of course, in any first-class laundry, is to see that no shirt or collar ever comes back twice. ["The Laundry Problem"]

*

But anyone can start a movement by beginning with himself. ["Are We Fascinated with Crime?"]

*Winnowed Wisdom* (1926).

I never realized that there was history too, close at hand, beside my very own home. I did not realize that the old grave that stood among the brambles at the foot of our farm was *history*.

"The Place of History in Canadian Edu-

cation," *Report of the Canadian Historical Association 1925* (1926).

To my mind a good woman is one of the greatest things on earth, second only perhaps to a good child or a good man. ["Confessions of a Soda Fiend"]

*The Dry Pickwick and Other Incongruities* (1932).

But how silly it would be if "Old Mother Hubbard went to the cupboard to get her poor dog a bone but when she got there she found only the statutory number of bones left as a legal reserve against the dog, and so he got none."

*

Socialism is only a bright soap bubble, light as ignorance and floating with its own gas. It would only work in a community of impossible people, guided by impossible leaders, and inspired by an inconceivable good-will. The angels, no doubt, are Socialists.

*Stephen Leacock's Plan to Relieve the Depression in Six Days, to Remove It in Six Months, to Eradicate It in Six Years* (1933).

It is difficult to be funny and great at the same time. Aristophanes and Molière and Mark Twain must sit below Aristotle and Bossuet and Emerson.

*

Transitory popularity is not proof of genius. But permanent popularity is.

*Charles Dickens: His Life and Work* (1934).

All ends with a cancellation of forces and comes to nothing; and our universe ends thus with one vast, silent, unappreciated joke. ["Epilogue: From the Ridiculous to the Sublime"]

*Humour: Its Theory and Technique* (1935).

Thank you, Mother England, I don't think I'll "come home." I'm "home" now. ["I'll Stay in Canada"]

*Funny Pieces: A Book of Random Sketches* (1936).

The essence of humour is human kindliness. [Preface]

And for humour, they just don't fit: women are not humorous except by exception. There is no such person as Mrs. Pickwick. ["The humour of Character"]

*

Humour may be defined as the kindly contemplation of the incongruities of life, and the artistic expression thereof. ["On the Nature of Humour"]

*

The mediaeval poet Hans Sachs said that he sang as the birds did, without pay. But most of us are not birds. ["Comic Verse: The Lighter Notes"]

> *Humour and Humanity: An Introduction to the Study of Humour* (1937).

Speaking in a general way one may say that in the West McGill predominates in medicine, Queen's in the Church and Toronto at (not behind) the Bar. Thus McGill attends the sick and when McGill has done its work, Queen's buries them and when they're buried Toronto divides up their estates among the three. It is what Adam Smith so happily called the Division of Labour. ["No Vote of Thanks"]

*

I spoke, I remember, on *The Value of Imbecility in Education*. It was more or less the same kind of talk that I had given at Port Arthur under the title *Our National Heritage*. ["No Vote of Thanks"]

*

The Lord said "let there be wheat" and Saskatchewan was born. ["Saskatchewan and Wheat"]

*

The typical Torontonian is about five feet, nine inches high, with fairly wide shoulders and a dolichocephalic head with an ear on each side of it.

*

French vanishes as one goes west.

*

Leave them alone and pretty soon the Ukrainians will think they won the battle of Trafalgar. . . . ["Monarchy in the West"]

*

Indeed I have always found that the only thing in regard to Toronto which faraway people know for certain is that McGill University is in it. ["So This is Winnipeg"]

*

"If I had known what it was like," I said, "I wouldn't have been content with a mere visit. I'd have been born here." ["British Columbia: Empire Province"]

> *My Discovery of the West* (1937).

There are only two subjects that appeal nowadays to the general public, murder and sex; and, for people of culture, sex-murder. ["Frenzied Fiction"]

*

In other words I am what is called a *professor emeritus*—from the Latin *e*, "out," and *meritus,* "so he ought to be." ["Looking Back from Retirement"]

> *Here Are My Lectures* (1938).

If somebody would give me about two dozen very old elm trees and about fifty acres of wooded ground and lawn—not too near anywhere and not too far from anywhere—I think I could set up a college that would put all the big universities of today in the shade. ["On the Need for a Quiet College"]

*

We may define business in a broad, general way as the art of losing money. ["How to Lose Money (for Amateurs)"]

*

Never mind the difference between the two; it's only that a socialist shares the workroom and a communist shares the bathroom.

*

Call it capitalism if you like and kick it. But it is all we've got. ["How Far Can We Plan"]

> *Model Memoirs and Other Sketches from Simple to Serious* (1938).

But, in the wider sense, what I want to advocate is not to make education shorter, but to make it much longer—indeed to make it last as long as life itself. [Preface]

*

A person who writes for a newspaper very soon learns certain tricks of the trade, arising out of sheer necessity. Thus he must learn to call a murderer an alleged murderer, and the King of England the alleged King of England. This forestalls libel suits. ["Teaching the Unteachable"]

＊

But as to this retirement business, let me give a word of advice to all of you young fellows around fifty. Some of you have been talking of it and even looking forward to it. Have nothing to do with it. Listen; it's like this. Have you ever been out for a late autumn walk in the closing part of the afternoon, and suddenly looked up to realize that the leaves have practically all gone? You hadn't realized it. And you notice that the sun has set already, the day gone before you knew it—and with that a cold wind blows across the landscape. That's retirement. ["When Men Retire"]

*Too Much College: or Education Eating Up Life* (1939).

About the only good thing you can say about old age is, it's better than being dead!

"This Business of Growing Old," *Reader's Digest*, March, 1940.

This is perhaps the oldest country in the world. Till yesterday it seemed destined to eternal solitude.

＊

The palaces of Nineveh are buried under the Mesopotamian sand, and the Assyrian, who once came down like a wolf on the fold and whose banners were gleaming in purple and gold, now sells rugs in a palatial hotel in what was once the "desert of Saskatchewan."

"The Empty Continent," *Canada: The Foundations of Its Future* (1941).

Acknowledging all these debts, I feel also that I owe a good deal of this book to my own industry and effort. [Preface]

*Montreal: Seaport and City* (1942).

I once asked a Christmas Eve group of children if they believed in Santa Claus. The very smallest ones answered without hesitation, "Why, of course!" The older ones shook their heads. The little girls smiled sadly but said nothing. One future scientist asserted boldly, "I know who it is"; and a little make-strong with his eye on gain said: "I believe in it all; I can believe in anything." That boy, I realized, would one day be a bishop. ["Wartime Santa Claus"]

＊

Everybody knows what he is. A sportsman is a man who, every now and then, simply has to get out and kill something. Not that he's cruel. He wouldn't hurt a fly. It's not big enough. ["What Is a Sport?"]

＊

Gentlemen embezzle but don't steal. ["The Struggle to Make Us Gentlemen"]

＊

Old age is the "Front Line" of life, moving into No Man's Land. No Man's Land is covered with mist. Beyond it is Eternity. ["Three Score and Ten"]

＊

Index: There Is No Index.

*My Remarkable Uncle and Other Sketches* (1942).

I can write on this controversy with the friendly neutrality of a Canadian. In Canada we have enough to do keeping up with the two spoken languages without trying to invent slang, so we just go right ahead and use English for literature, Scotch for sermons and American for conversation.

＊

I myself talk Ontario English; I don't admire it, but it's all I can do; anything is better than affectation. ["Good and Bad Language"]

＊

The best definition of humour that I know is: *Humour may be defined as the kindly contemplation of the incongruities of life and the artistic expression thereof.* I think this the best I know because I wrote it myself. I don't like any others nearly as well. Students of writing will do well to pause at the word *kindly* and ponder it well. The very essence of humour is that it must be kindly. "Good jests," said King Charles the Second, that most humorous and kindly king who saved monarchy in England, "ought to bite like lambs, not dogs; they should cut, not wound." The minute they begin to bite and wound that is not humour. That is satire and as it gets more and more satirical the humour dries out of it leaving only the snarl and rasp of sarcasm. ["How to Write Humour"]

It may be those who do most, dream most. ["How Not to Write More Poetry"]

*How to Write* (1943).

With perfect citizens any government is good. In a population of angels a socialistic commonwealth would work to perfection. But until we have the angels we must keep the commonwealth waiting.

"The Utopia of Socialism," *While There Is Time: The Case Against Social Catastrophe* (1945).

I have known that name, the old Brewery Bay, to make people feel thirsty by correspondence as far away as Nevada.

I have a large country house—a sort of farm which I carry on as a hobby.... Ten years ago the deficit on my farm was about a hundred dollars; but by well-designed capital expenditure, by drainage and by greater attention to details, I have got it into the thousands.

To get a new audience I would have had to learn Chinese. So I stopped lecturing.

Quoted by Barbara Nimmo in her preface to *Last Leaves* (1945).

To dig out gold in North Ontario and dig it in, in Tennessee, is on the face of it idiocy.

"Gold," *Last Leaves* (1945).

To go into teaching was a matter of sheer necessity. My education had fitted me for nothing except to pass it on to the other people.

"Teaching School," *The Boy I Left Behind Me* (1946).

You just jot down ideas as they occur to you. The jotting is simplicity itself— it is the occurring which is difficult.

Women have taken over half a man's world, and kept the whole of their own.

I am a great believer in luck, and I find the harder I work the more I have of it.

Many a man in love with a dimple makes the mistake of marrying the whole girl.

There were warnings of apprehension from economists. There always are; apprehension is their business.

The distinction about old McGill is the men who are not there.

I owe a lot to my teachers and mean to pay them back some day.

Socialism won't work except in Heaven where they don't need it and in Hell where they already have it.

The last remark is quoted by Ralph L. Curry in *Stephen Leacock: Humorist and Humanist* (1959). The others are attributed to the most widely known of Canadian writers.

Did I behave pretty well? Was I a good boy?

To a radiologist after an examination for cancer, two hours before his death on March 28, 1944. Quoted by Ralph L. Curry in *Stephen Leacock: Humorist and Humanist* (1959). See also Elizabeth Kimball.

**Lear, Edward**
There was an Old Man of Quebec,—
A beetle ran over his neck;
But he cried, "With a needle
I'll slay you, O beadle!"
That angry Old Man of Quebec.

*The Book of Nonsense* (1846).

**Leather, Sir Edwin**
I suppose I'd been interested in politics ever since I saw George Arliss play Disraeli.

The Toronto-born governor of Bermuda saw the British actor in *Disraeli*, released in 1930. Quoted by Tom Alderman in *The Canadian Magazine*, November 17, 1973.

**Lec, Stanislaw**
You will always find some Eskimos ready to instruct the Congolese on how to cope with heat waves.

*Unkempt Thoughts* (1962), translated from the Polish by Jack Galazka.

## Le Carré, John   See Carré, John le.

## Leclerc, Félix
Many who are only useful believe they are indispensable.

*

I would like to read the book that the hobo and the priest are fighting over.

*

A country is like a woman, one must not always be stuck on it.

*Calepin d'un flâneur* (1961).

## LeClercq, Chrestien
The Gaspesians say that the Beaver is the beloved of the French and other Europeans, who seek it greedily; and I have been unable to keep from laughing on overhearing an Indian, who said to me in banter, "In truth, my brother, the Beaver does everything to perfection. He makes for us knives, kettles, axes, swords, and gives us drink and food without the trouble of cultivating the ground."

*New Relation of Gaspesia with the Customs and Religion of the Gaspesian Indians* (1910), translated by William F. Ganong from the Recollect missionary's *Nouvelle Relation* of 1691.

## Leddy, J.F.
You cannot ignore or escape the fact that you are a part of humanity in close link with the fortunes of men and women all over the globe . . . you are representing others, by default, as well as yourself. You will be casting more votes than your own. And so the key question is: "Whose proxy are you?"

Convocation address, Waterloo Lutheran University, November 5, 1972, delivered by the president of the University of Windsor.

## Lee, Canada   See Anaïs Nin.

## Lee, Dennis
It is not that a permanently unstructured education strikes anyone as a good thing. It is that finding structure yourself to embody your own living necessities, alone or with the advice of people you

respect, is the concealed nine-tenths of the educational process.

*

By "liberal education" I mean any study which liberated a person from unreflecting reliance on the assumptions, structures, models, categories that he had soaked up from his family, school, church and society.

"Getting to Rochdale," *The University Game* (1968), edited by Howard Adelman and Dennis Lee.

Mackenzie was a crazy man,
He wore his wig askew.
He donned three bulky overcoats
In case the bullets flew.
Mackenzie talked of fighting
While the fight went down the drain.
But who will speak for Canada?
Mackenzie, come again.

One stanza from "1838, 1970, 2020," a poem about W.L. Mackenzie, from *Visions 2020: Fifty Canadians in Search of a Future* (1970), edited by Stephen Clarkson.

Among the things which
hesitate to be, is void our
vocation?

"Fourth Elegy," *Civil Elegies and Other Poems* (1972).

## Lee, Ronald
We are the world's oldest living nonconformists. Are we also the world's last?

*Goddam Gypsy: An Autobiographical Novel* (1971).

The aim of the average North American businessman is to go to Florida, bask on the beach and eat bananas. Thousands of Africans do that every day.

Quoted by Don Bell in "Think Not as a Gypsy" in *Saturday Night at the Bagel Factory and Other Montreal Stories* (1972).

## Lefèbvre, Jean-Pierre
I want to demystify the mystique of revolution.

Quebec film director quoted by Roger Manvell in *The International Encyclopedia of Film* (1972).

## Lefolii, Ken

Canada's war on the Indians was not a shooting war, like the Americans'; it was a long war of attrition that is still being waged, and that inflicts new defeats on every generation. The weapon we use is indifference. It leaves an ugly look.

\*

If there is a word for the motifs of Canadianism, the word is Gothic.

*The Canadian Look: A Century of Sights and Styles* (1965).

## Lefroy, John Henry

I do not think this country will ever differ much from this condition in which it now is. The difficulties of the internal navigation will always prevent extensive commerce, even if any valuable production, such as minerals,—not bulky,—should be discovered. It can never support a large population, for the greater part of it is a surface of rock without three inches of soil. I look upon it as an argument against civilization ever being universal, or being of itself a feature of such transcendant importance, that such immense regions are unfitted by nature for the support of a civilized race. [Letter from Athabaska, January 1, 1844]

\*

The great defect in the lady society of Toronto, especially the young lady branch of it, is the want of character. There are very few who possess any one distinguishing taste, acquirement, or characteristic. One cannot be surprised at this considering the deficiencies of the colony in subjects and schools of taste, but it reduces conversation to trifles and matters of the moment. [Letter from Toronto, January 18, 1845]

*In Search of the Magnetic North: A Soldier-Surveyor's Letters from the North-West 1843-1844* (1955), edited by George F.G. Stanley.

## Le Gallienne, Richard

I was once in Canada—years and years ago. Lecturing. In a desolate city called To-ron-to. Heavens! You're not from To-ron-to, are you?

The aging playwright made this remark

in the 1920s to John Glassco in the latter's *Memoirs of Montparnasse* (1971).

## Léger, Jules

From now on you'll be walking behind me.

To his wife Gabrielle, on learning he would succeed Roland Michener as governor general. *Time*, October 15, 1973.

## Léger, Paul-Emile Cardinal

You cannot stand still when billions of people cry out for help. What should you do? Should you give them a sermon or a piece of bread?

Former archbishop of Montreal, now a medical missionary in Cameroon, quoted by Ronald Lebel in *The Toronto Star*, December 24, 1973.

## Leif the Lucky

This country was level and wooded, with broad white beaches wherever they went and a gently sloping shoreline. I shall give this country a name that fits with its natural character and call it Markland.

The site of Markland (Land of Forests) is located by Samuel Eliot Morison, in *The European Discovery of America: The Northern Voyages A.D. 500-1600* (1971), on the east coast of Labrador, near Cape Porcupine. The Viking landfall was made in 1001, and Leif Ericsson's discoveries in the New World are recorded in Icelandic saga.

Nature was so generous here that it seemed to them no cattle would need any winter fodder, but could graze outdoors. There was no frost in winter, and the grass hardly withered. The days and nights were more nearly equal than in Greenland or Iceland. On the shortest day of winter the sun was up between breakfast time and late afternoon.

The site of Vinland, described by Leif the Lucky (Leif Ericsson), is located by Morison at L'Anse aux Meadows, Newfoundland. Here, in 1960, Dr. Helge Ingstad found incontrovertible proof of a Norse colony, including ruins of a forge and steambath, dating from 1001.

## Le Jeune, Paul

Let no one be astonished at these acts of barbarism. Before the faith was received in Germany, Spain, or England, those nations were not more civilized. Mind is not lacking among the Savages of Canada, but education and instruction. They are already tired of their miseries and stretch out their hands to us for help. . . . ["Brief Relation of the Journey to New France, Made in the Month of April Last by Father Paul Le Jeune, of the Society of Jesus" (1632)]

*

Their natural colour is like that of those French beggars who are half-roasted in the Sun, and I have no doubt that the Savages would be very white if they were well covered.

*

They are like the Grecian Philosopher who would wear nothing that he had not made. It would not take many years to learn all their crafts. ["Brief Relation," Tadoussac, 1632]

*

It is very easy to describe a good workman, but quite different to find one. ["Letter from Father Paul Le Jeune, to the Reverend Father Provincial of France, at Paris," Quebec, 1634]

A soul very thirsty for the Son of God, I mean for suffering, would find enough here to satisfy it.

*

The Castor or Beaver is taken in several ways. The Savages say that it is the animal well-beloved of the French, English and Basques,—in a word, by the Europeans. I heard my host say one day, jokingly, Missi picoutau amiscou, "The Beaver does everything perfectly well, it makes Kettles, hatchets, swords, knives, bread; and in short, it makes everything." He was making sport of us Europeans, who have such a fondness for the skin of this animal and who fight to see who will give the most to these Barbarians, to get it; they carry this to such an extent that my host said to me one day, showing me a very beautiful knife, "The English have no sense; they give us twenty knives like this for one Beaver skin."

*

They are so occupied in seeking their livelihood in these woods, that they have not the time, so to speak, to save themselves. ["Relation of What Occurred in New France on the Great River St. Lawrence, in the Year One Thousand Six Hundred Thirty-Four"]

*

Now, as New France is so immense, so many inhabitants can be sent here that those who remain in the Mother Country will have enough honest work left them to do, without launching into those vices which ruin Republics; this does not mean that ruined people, or those of evil lives, should be sent here, for that would be to build Babylons.

*

Behold these tender and delicate Virgins all ready to hazard their lives upon the waves of the Ocean, to come seeking little souls in the rigours of an air much colder than that of France, to endure hardship at which even men would be appalled; and will not some brave Lady be found who will give a Passport to these Amazons of the great God, endowing them with a house in which to praise and serve his divine Majesty in this other world? ["Relation of What Occurred in New France, in the Year 1635"]

> *The Jesuit Relations and Allied Documents* (1954), edited by Edna Kenton.

## Lemaître, François

People say—that someone asked why the prison was placed so far away rather than in the town. The reason is very simple: they wanted to put the prison outside the town rather than the town inside the prison.

> *La quotidienne* (1837). Translated by Margaret Fairley in *Spirit of Canadian Democracy: A Collection of Canadian Writings from the Beginnings to the Present Day* (1945).

## Lemay, Harding

There is nothing more destructive in childhood than a boy's sense that his father doesn't like him.

> *Inside, Looking Out: A Personal Memoir* (1971), by the Quebec-born New York actor-publisher-playwright.

## Lemelin, Roger
I give you the right to insolence, within the guidelines.

> Directive to his editorial writers, from the novelist-turned-publisher of *La Presse*, quoted in *Time*, April 23, 1973.

## Le Messurier, H.W.
We'll rant and we'll roar like true Newfoundlanders,
We'll rant and we'll roar on deck and below;
Until we see bottom inside the two sunkers,
When straight through the Channel to Toslow we'll go.

\*

Farewell and adieu to ye, fair ones of Valen,
Farewell and adieu to ye, girls in the cove;
I'm bound to the westward, to the wall with the hole in,
I'll take her from Toslow the wild world to rove.

> Verses from "The Girls from Toslow," a popular Newfoundland song. "The great majority of the singers had never seen Toslow, nor had they any idea of where it was, but that did not matter, for Toslow existed in the land of imagination; like the Islands of the Blessed, it was everyone's ancestral village, where his fathers had laboured and hoped and loved and passed in the end under its sod or its waves." Harold Horwood in *Newfoundland* (1969). The verses are reproduced from *The Book of Newfoundland* (1937), edited by J.R. Smallwood, where the contemporary folksong is entitled "The Ryans and the Pittmans."

## Lemieux, Jean-Paul
I try to convey a remembrance, a feeling of generations. I sometimes see myself as the central figure, but as a child in the community of generations. I like the feeling of summer in the old days, the feeling of old newsreels or photographs. You get the feeling of fading away.

> Quebec painter, *Weekend Magazine*, August 3, 1963.

## Lemieux, Robert
I have no advice to give to Francis Simard. I have no advice to give to Paul Rose. I have no advice to give to any of the political prisoners. The political prisoners probably have more advice to give me. Political prisoners have more advice to give us all. Political prisoners are the heart of our infested federal prisons.

> Separatist lawyer Robert Lemieux was sentenced to thirty months' imprisonment for contempt of court, July 17, 1973. His client, Jacques Rose, was found guilty of participating in the kidnapping of James Cross. Lemieux made the above reply in the Montreal courtroom and was led away shouting, "Vive le Québec libre!"

## Lemieux, Rodolphe
Talk not of annexation of French Canada! — [Applause] — outside of election time, of course. [Laughter]

> "The Quebec Act," January 12, 1914, *Addresses Delivered before the Canadian Club of Toronto: Season 1913-14* (1914).

You are all immigrants, you gentlemen, but we *Canadians* are the sons of the soil.

> "The Habitant and the War," April 8, 1916, *Addresses Delivered before the Canadian Club of Ottawa: 1915-16* (1916).

## Le Moyne, Jean
Of course there *are* certain balanced attitudes here—on all fours.["The Religious Atmosphere in French Canada" (1951)]

\*

To ask if our novel has added anything new to our knowledge of western woman seems to me to be sheer lunacy. ["Woman and French-Canadian Literature" (1960)]

\*

I want to keep my French heritage, but it is just as important for me to keep my English chattels and to go to the limit of my American gift of invention. I need all that to make the total man.

\*

When I say love, I mean, first of all, the most difficult kind, the love of self, and after that the love of others and the love of things. For the first principle of all love, of all possession, of all gift of self, is this difficult love of oneself. In fact these distinctions describe only different moments of the same love, for love moves within us and around us in a single and uninterrupted motion. ["Saint-Denys-Garneau's Testimony for His Times" (1960)]

\*

All things considered, it is mainly as a North American that I understand myself. For the time being the field of my liberty and unity has at least the scope of a continent. But I intensely envy those who in the far future shall simply and immensely understand themselves as men of the planet Earth. ["Foreword" (1966)]

> *Convergence: Essays from Quebec* (1966), translated by Philip Stratford.

## Lenin, Nikolai

"Skelton wrote with some authority on the subject, for his book, *Socialism: A Critical Analysis,* written in 1910, is said to have prompted Lenin himself to send a note of congratulation to its author for having produced the most damaging case against socialism that he (Lenin) had ever read. Skelton's papers have been lost or destroyed, and my authority for the story is a speech made by the Hon. Stuart Garson, when premier of Manitoba, to the annual meeting of the Regina Liberal Association, November 19, 1947. Mr. Garson's account adds the refinement that when Lenin died, he directed that a copy of Skelton's *Socialism* be interred with him—a fact not easily proved at the present time."

> So writes James Eayrs in *Northern Approaches: Canada and the Search for Peace* (1961). Although an inveterate correspondent, it appears Lenin wrote nothing specifically about Canada or especially for Canadians. (This did not deter Tim Buck from publishing a book called *Lenin and Canada* [1970].) Both Friedrich Engels and Leon Trotsky visited the country and wrote about it. O.D. Skelton was a professor of political economy at Queen's University and under-secretary of State for External Affairs from 1925 to 1941.

## Leonowens, Anna

I was thankful to find, even in this citadel of Buddhism, men, and above all women, who were "lovely in their lives," who, amid infinite difficulties, in the bosom of a most corrupt society, and enslaved to a capricious and often cruel will, yet devoted themselves to an earnest search after truth.

> *The English Governess at the Siamese Court: Being Recollections of Six Years in the Royal Palace at Bangkok* (1870). Anna Leonowens's experiences as a tutor in the royal household in Siam (now Thailand) in 1862-68 were filmed in 1946 as *Anna and the King of Siam.* Rodgers and Hammerstein turned the story into the musical *The King and I* (1951) which, in turn, was filmed in 1956.

> Somewhat less cinematic are Anna Leonowens's post-Siamese experiences. The Welsh-born widow settled in Halifax in 1878 where she lived with her daughter. Mrs. Leonowens among others founded the Nova Scotia College of Art which has since named a gallery in her honour. Then she taught Sanskrit at McGill and died in Montreal in 1914 at the age of seventy-eight. She is buried in Mount Royal Cemetery.

## Le Pan, Douglas

No monuments or landmarks guide the stranger
Going among this savage people, masks
Taciturn or babbling out an alien jargon
And moody as barbaric skies are moody.

> Opening stanza of "A Country Without a Mythology."

\*

You hesitate. The trees are entangled with menace.
The voyage is perilous into the dark interior.
But then your hands go to the thwarts. You smile. And so
I watch you vanish in a wood of heroes,
Wild Hamlet with the features of Horatio.

> Last lines of "Coureurs de Bois," *The Wounded Prince and Other Poems* (1948).

Canadians cannot help sometimes hankering for a world where things would be different. It would be pleasant if there could be more scope for an independent foreign policy, if we could settle our own defence policy more freely, if we could have a more self-sufficient economy without sacrificing the economic advantages that flow from our close association with the United States. If . . . if . . . if . . . if. If wishes were horses, Canadians would certainly ride off in all directions. To outsiders, this may all seem unreasonable and utopian and childish. So it is, if the mood comes too often or is indulged too generously. But it is also natural and human. For has not nationalism often been associated with utopian dreaming, and dreaming not always rigorously grounded in what might be feasible?

\*

These are some of the things I see, or seem to see, when I look at the clouded relationship between Canada and the United States. It is unique. It is full of difficulty. It will take much patient thought and work on both sides to handle the difficulties constructively. But it may prove easier to summon the necessary intelligence and good will if it is realized that the questions at issue are by no means all parochial. In truth, the relationship contains within itself most of the problems of the whole planet, on which we are all adrift together.

> "The Outlook for the Relationship: A Canadian View," *The United States and Canada: The American Assembly* (1964), edited by John Sloan Dickey.

Nor is it very difficult to understand why a Canadian passport should be so popular. Part of the explanation is that with it one can travel easily almost anywhere. Another reason for the popularity of the little blue booklet stamped in gold is that one can speak English or French or Ukrainian or Polish or Chinese and still be a Canadian. One can, in fact, be almost anyone and still be a Canadian; and to be a Canadian is to have a passport to the whole world.

\*

But perhaps there is something that can be plucked and rescued from the en-compassing dimness. An image, a conjoined image of bourgeois and voyageur: the Nor'wester who in youth travels the canoe routes westward and lives on Lake Athabasca or Great Slave Lake as a wintering partner, and who only when he is middle-aged returns to settle permanently in Montreal and to build himself a big house on the side of the mountain where he can look out and see the River of Canada flowing by and remember when he was young and lived hard and was ready for anything that might come at the next portage or the next turn of the river. Bourgeois and voyageur; it is a phrase that can be coaxed into summing up much in Canadian history, making long stretches of it seem more evocative and attractive than they would be otherwise; and sometimes the two qualities can be miraculously combined in the one person. So it must have been with many of the fur traders. And even with Louis Riel, that baffling, rebellious spirit, of whom it is related that when he would receive official visitors at Fort Garry as the leader of the provisional government of the Northwest in 1869, he would be wearing leather moccasins and a frock coat. It will be a long time before either of those trappings will have altogether ceased to indicate something about the Canadian scene and the Canadian consciousness.

> "In Frock Coat and Moccasins" (1964), *Canada: A Guide to the Peaceable Kingdom* (1970), edited by William Kilbourn.

It may be that our persistent unilingualism is to be related to the narrowness of our view of human nature. More generally, it may be that our failure to understand Quebec is the result of almost metaphysical inadequacy.

> Remark made in 1968, quoted in *Saturday Night*, January, 1972.

As I sit writing in the old building of University College here in Toronto, which was built some ten years before Confederation, there is bright sun and a light breeze is rippling the fresh leaves of the maples in the quadrangle outside and holding them in flickering conversation with the green copper roof of the Cloisters. My mind moves first there, where the light sometimes seems Athenian and yet always perfectly autochthonous, and then to East Hall, with its memorial to the three young students of the College who lost their lives in the battle of Ridgeway against the Fenian invaders on the 2nd of June, 1866, while the whole design of Confederation was wavering in the balance. In the eyes of history, the battle was a "meaningless little encounter." But ultimately, who can say? At any rate, that is the spirit I would invoke for this Confederation Day a hundred years later—the spirit of courage in the face of meaninglessness.

"The Canadian Dialectic," *The Montreal Star*, July 1, 1967; reprinted in Andy Wainwright's *Notes for a Native Land: A New Encounter with Canada* (1969).

**Lerner, Sammy**   See Irving Caesar.

**LeRoy, Neil**
Now I want to congratulate our panelist on having been chosen one of Canada's ten best-breasted women!

Freudian slip made by the moderator of "Court of Opinion," a long-running program on CBC Radio, 1950s.

**Lesage, Jean**
Maîtres chez nous. C'est l'temps qu'ça change!

These political slogans—"Masters in our own house," "It's time for a change!" —are associated with the Liberal government of Jean Lesage, premier of Quebec from 1960 to 1966, and his "Quiet Revolution." See also René Lévesque.

The mere presence of the French-Canadian group within the Canadian population as a whole is a guarantee against the invasion of American culture.

Premier of Quebec, Charlottetown, February 2, 1963. Quoted by Frank Scott and Michael Oliver in *Quebec States Her Case: Speeches and Articles from Quebec in the Years of Unrest* (1964).

It was a battle between two regiments of regular soldiers from overseas. The French regiment lost the battle, and went back to France. The British won, and stayed, and were assimilated by the French Canadians. I know lots of their descendants living in Quebec today who can't speak a word of English.

The Quebec premier's view of the conquest in 1759, quoted by Blair Fraser in "League in the West" (1965), *"Blair Fraser Reports": Selections 1944-1968* (1969).

If ever Confederation fails, it will not be because Quebec—the political voice of French Canada—has separated from it. It will be because the way to keep Quebec in it has not been found.

Quoted by Gerald Clark in *Canada: The Uneasy Neighbour* (1965).

**Lescarbot, Marc**
Moreover, the sailors who go from all parts of Europe to fish off Newfoundland, and beyond, a thousand leagues distant from home, find there excellent mines without breaking down cliffs, opening up the earth, living in the darkness of hell (for so must we call the mines, to which in olden times those were condemned who had deserved death). . . .

*

But I shall relate how, in order to keep our table joyous and well provided, an Order was established at the board of the said M. de Poutrincourt, which was called the Order of Good Cheer, originally proposed by Champlain.

*

Moreover, who is there, save a great fool, who would not rather see a forest belonging to himself, than a palace wherein he hath nothing?

The lawyer and writer spent the Winter of 1906-7 at Port-Royal, now Annapolis Royal, Nova Scotia, under Jean de Biencourt de Poutrincourt. *Histoire de la Nouvelle-France* (1609). *The History of New France* (1907), translated by W. L. Grant.

Vrai Neptune, donne nous
Contre tes flots assurance,

Et fais que nous puissions tous
Un jour nous revoir en France,
*Et fais que nous puissions tous*
*Un jour nous revoir en France.*

Pledge to us, great god Neptune,
Against thy ocean arrogance;
Grant us all, as highest boon
That we may meet again in France,
*Grant us all, as highest boon*
*That we may meet again in France.*

> To celebrate Samuel de Champlain's
> return to the little French colony at
> Port Royal, the lawyer Marc Lescarbot
> staged a freshly written masque, Novem-
> ber 14, 1606. *"Le Théâtre de Neptune"*
> was first published in Lescarbot's *Les*
> *muses de la Nouvelle France* (1618), and
> the masque has been translated by Har-
> riette T. Richardson in *The Theatre of*
> *Neptune in New France* (1928). The
> stanza above, from the concluding lines
> of "Hymn to Neptune," inspired Samuel
> Eliot Morison to write, in *Samuel de*
> *Champlain: Father of New France*
> (1972): "This undoubtedly expressed
> the unanimous wish of a homesick
> company."

## Leslie, H.T.

The game of life is not so much in holding a good hand as playing a poor hand
well.

> Lieutenant H.T. Leslie, quoted by Hon.
> Captain Alex. Ketterson in *On Active*
> *Service: Ideals of Canada's Fighting*
> *Men* (1918).

## Levant, Oscar

When I had completed my string
quartet, Schoenberg turned grimly to
me. "At the first playing," he said, "you
will feel desperate."

I wasn't in Toronto when it was
performed by the Kolisch Quartet, but
they sent me the review, which went,
"The Kolisch Quartet played last night
at——Hall. Present at the concert were
——" It went on to describe the guest list.
That was the review.

> *The Memoirs of an Amnesiac* (1966). See
> also Glenn Gould.

## Leverhulme, Lord

One of the Londoners remarked, "You
can always tell a Canadian, can't you?"
"Yes," said another, "but you can't tell
him much."

> "Education and Commerce," *Empire*
> *Club of Canada: Addresses Delivered to*
> *the Members During the Year 1919*
> (1920). Lord Leverhulme, William Hes-
> keth Lever, was the English soap manu-
> facturer.

## Lévesque, René

Too little, too late.

> Lévesque reiterated this phrase through-
> out the late 1950s and early 1960s to
> dramatize English-Canadian concessions
> to Quebec's demands. "Too little and
> too late" goes back to the 1930s, for
> Allan Nevins used it in *Current His-*
> *tory* (1935). The rejoinder is: "Too
> much, too soon."

I am a forty-year-old moderate—believe
it or not—there are young people behind
me who make me feel nervous.

> Quoted in *The Canadian Forum*, July,
> 1963.

That [increased education] is Quebec's
real revolution. That is what brought
about the reawakening of the dream.

Looking back, I personally believe I
felt it (a long time before I recognized
it, naturally) in the fall of 1962. We, the
Liberal government, had just called an
election on the nationalization of private power companies. A couple of
nights later, a small group of us came
up with a campaign slogan: *"Maîtres*
*chez nous"* (Masters in our own home).
The moment those three words rang
out, the search was over. Even though
instinct and common sense cried out
that here, potentially, was much more
than a call for the takeover of a handful
of private utilities.

> "To Be Masters in Our Own House"
> (1968), *Canada: A Guide to the Peace-*
> *able Kingdom* (1970), edited by William
> Kilbourn. The election on November
> 14, 1962, confirmed the Liberal man-
> date. See also Jean Lesage.

We are *Québécois.*

What that means first and foremost—
and if need be, all that it means—is that

we are attached to this one corner of the earth where we can be completely ourselves: this Quebec, the only place where we have the unmistakable feeling that "here we can be really at home."

An Option for Quebec (1968).

Quebec no longer has a government.

Statement made by the separatist leader the evening the War Measures act was imposed, October 16, 1970, when it was believed Ottawa was usurping Quebec's power. Quoted by John Saywell in Quebec 70: A Documentary Narrative (1971).

J'ai le goût du Québec.

"I have a taste for Quebec." Low-key slogan of the Parti Québécois in the provincial election of October, 1973.

### Levine, Les
Man has entered a state of post-consciousness; we are all extensions of a main circuit. Real systems, body technology and ecological conditions control our cultural thrust rather than any previous idea of consciousness we may have had.

Environmental artist, quoted by Douglas Pringle in "Les Levine" in Artscanada, June, 1970.

### Levine, Norman
I remember a night in 1944 in the blackout. Walking down Shaftesbury Avenue towards Piccadilly. Stopped by a voice in the doorway of a shop: "Can you give me a light?" The match flares. She sees your face. You see hers. She noticed the Canadian flashes on my shoulders. "Canadians." She laughed good-humouredly. "Nothing but big cocks and dirty underwear."

Canada Made Me (1958).

### Lévi-Strauss, Claude
A revelation. This is something of a phenomenon. I consider that the culture of the Northwest Indians produced an art on a par with that of Greece or Egypt.

The French structural anthropologist made the above comments at the show "Masterpieces of Indian and Eskimo Art from Canada" organized by the Musée de l'Homme in Paris. Le Droit, November 15, 1969.

### Levitt, Kari
Those who view Quebec separatism as the main threat to Canada's survival, might ask themselves why French Canadians should remain within Confederation when the dominant English-Canadian majority appear to put such a low value on Canada's national independence.

Silent Surrender: The Multinational Corporation in Canada (1970). The Montreal economist is the daughter of Karl Polanyi, the author of The Great Transformation (1944). See also Sir Wilfrid Laurier: Who Owns the Twentieth Century?

### Lewis, David
Beatty: What would be your first act if you became prime minister of Canada? Lewis: Nationalize the CPR, sir.

Exchange between David Lewis, then in his early twenties, and Sir Edward Beatty, president of the CPR and chairman of the selection committee for the Rhodes scholarships, December 1931 or January 1932, CPR board room, Montreal. Lewis was awarded the scholarship, studied at Oxford, and rose to the leadership of the New Democratic Party.

If we can find the resources and methods to produce tanks, bombs and bullets, why can't we find the resources and methods to build homes, schools and playgrounds?
The answer is: we can, if we have the courage to refashion our society to serve the interests of all the people.

Make This Your Canada: A Review of CCF History and Policy (1943), by David Lewis and Frank Scott.

To build the socialist society we must first win; to win we must build the socialist movement; to do that we must work and give and study tirelessly.

Statement in 1935, quoted by Walter D. Young in The Anatomy of a Party: The National CCF 1932-61 (1969).

Corporate welfare bums.

> "The phrase 'corporate welfare bums' was a joint effort; in preparing Lewis's first speech on the issue, Veronica Seale wrote 'the real welfare recipients are the corporations'; in reading this, Lewis changed it to 'the real welfare bums are the corporations,' and Weppler suggested shortening it to 'corporate welfare bums.' Funnily enough, the party didn't realize what a hot property it had in that phrase until it began to appear in headlines, and then they exploited it to the full."
>
> Veronica Seale is an NDP researcher; Murray Weppler, executive assistant to the leader. Lewis's first speech in this issue was made in New Glasgow, Nova Scotia, August 3, 1972. Quoted by Walter Stewart in *Divide and Con: Canadian Politics at Work* (1973).

Welfare is for the needy, not big and wealthy multinational corporations.

> *Louder Voices: The Corporate Welfare Bums* (1972). During the 1972 election year the NDP leader created the catch phrases "corporate rip-offs" and "corporate welfare bums" to describe the practices of those national and multinational businesses that use tax loopholes to pay little or no corporate income tax and apply for incentive subsidies from government.

I'm sure that none of these companies cheats. They are only doing what the law allows them to do. . . . Governments and big business hold hands—in your pockets.

> Election speech, August 3, 1972.

**Lewis, Jerry**
"What do you think of Diefenbaker?" a woman asks, referring to Canada's prime minister of that month.
"What is a Diefenbaker?" asks Lewis.

> Quoted by Richard Gehman in *That Kid: The Story of Jerry Lewis* (1964).

**Lewis, Sinclair**
Do you remember speaking to me, a year and a half ago, about some expedition which goes all through Northern Canada every summer, getting entirely away from civilization, and taking two or three months to make the trip? What is it? Does it occur every year? Would there be any way in which I could go with them—they might be glad to be "written up," and of course I'd stand my share of the expenses. I live far too sedentary a life, and I'd like to do something of that kind.

> Letter to his brother Claude Lewis, December, 1923, about the annual treaty trips undertaken by the Department of Indian Affairs. Both Lewises went on one such trip, and two books resulted: Sinclair Lewis's *Mantrap* (1926), a novel that relies on this excursion for background material; and Claude Lewis's diary, which tells the story of the trip itself: *Treaty Trip: An Abridgment of Dr. Claude Lewis's Journal of an Expedition Made by Himself and His Brother, Sinclair Lewis, to Northern Saskatchewan and Manitoba* in 1924 (1959). Quoted by Mark Schorer in *Sinclair Lewis: An American Life* (1961).

They did not look in the least like lords of the wilderness engaged in watching, under lean shadowing hands, the flight of a distant eagle. They looked like undersized Sicilians who had been engaged in digging a sewer.

> Lewis's view of the Saskatchewan Indians in *Mantrap* (1926).

But it was not till the winter, so carefully did his secret agents have to work in America, that Trowbridge had in full operation the organization called by its operatives the "New Underground," the "N.U.," which had aided thousands of counter revolutionists to escape into Canada.

> *It Can't Happen Here* (1935). In this novel the United States turns fascist and the democrats shift their base of operations north of the border. See also Alfred A. Knopf.

**Lewis, Stephen**
I subscribe to the belief that socialism is not about the public ownership of the means of production, but about the public ownership of power. That means democracy.

Ontario NDP leader and son of David Lewis, in an address to the Canadian Club of Toronto, *The Globe and Mail*, December 8, 1970.

## Lewis, Wyndham

At this juncture it may be as well to tell you that I did not exactly hit it off with the intellectuals of Toronto. Toronto is probably not a good place to be an intellectual in, and I suppose that it is too much to expect that intellectuals from more clement regions (more clement towards the Intelligence) should be welcomed. . . . [Letter to Lorne Pierce, June 17, 1941]

\*

. . . Canada is a small and backward country: the tongue of half of it is French. The English half is probably the dumbest English-speaking population anywhere. It reads less per capita than any other known civilised population. [Letter to Robert Hale, November 9, 1941]

I am reduced to writing articles to fill in the time—and my pocket—on "Will there be a Canadian Renaissance?" The bigger I picture the "renaissance" (whatever they mean by that) the more money I get. So I make it a quite spectacular explosion of intellectual energy. The only intelligent people here—like the painter, Jackson,—regard a marriage with the States as their best bet, and I think the same. Meanwhile I cudgel my brains to imagine Toronto as a sort of Florence or Padua in a great cultural birththroe. By the time I cross that frontier of yours again I shall be a semi-idiot. [Letter to R.D. Jameson, February 14, 1942]

\*

Being here is much the same as if one were in Baffin Land. [Letter to James Johnson Sweeney, December 30, 1942]

\*

Having no human society is no inconvenience to me. Sometimes for six months on end we have seen nobody— we might have been on the sub-arctic continent . . . we are able to make short trips to the States, and it is a blessed relief to breathe that more intelligent air for a while: though oh for a half-hour of Europe!—for relatively agreeable as the States are (after this sanctimonious icebox) the North American continent is not a place I like stopping in for more than a month or two. [Letter to Naomi Mitchison, May 31, 1943]

\*

I made myself his [A.Y. Jackson's] advocate, and was glad to stress the publicity value to Canadians of their zero-land. [Letter to Malcolm MacDonald, August 8, 1943]

\*

Last night I was listening to a Radio celebration of Flaherty, author of *Nanook of the North*. His tremendous advantage was to have lived near Eskimos. Now, Vancouver is not exotic, like Coronation Gulf: but it is worth your while to remember that there are practically no Canadian writers who have familiarized other nations with the Canadian scene. And I continue to feel that the enormous mountains, the Indians and yes the Doukhobors, and other things known to you but not to me, are something definite, an identity not without interest. [Letter to David Kahma, October 26, 1952]

*The Letters of Wyndham Lewis* (1963), edited by W.K. Rose.

Short of a job I shall simply die in a flophouse if I stop here. There is not a minute to be lost if I am to save myself from this last degradation. [Draft of a letter to Frank Morley, October 17, 1941]

Quoted by Walter Michel, *Wyndham Lewis: Paintings and Drawings* (1971).

Lastly in speculating about "Canada," and its future culture, we may be dealing with something that is destined to disappear. But although nations may dissolve, *regions* do not. If at some future time all Americans were politically one, from Coronation Gulf to Magellanes, people who live north of the 49th parallel and the Great Lakes would still be referred to as "Canadians."

\*

Canada will always be so infinitely bigger physically than the small nation who live in it—even if its population is doubled— that this monstrous, empty, habitat must continue to dominate it psychologically and so culturally. ["Nature's Place in Canadian Culture" (1940-44)]

> *Wyndham Lewis in Canada* (1971), edited by George Woodcock.

## Leyrac, Monique

In New York, they understood when I said that my country was not a country—but winter. And that my road was not really a road—but snow.

> The Quebec *chanteuse* made this remark in 1966. For words to the song in question, see Gilles Vigneault.

Famine and wars, these are the things that change the world, not the separation of Quebec.

> Quoted by David Cobb in *The Toronto Telegram*, February 18, 1967.

The other day I was saying if I die—and I want to be burned—I will ask my husband to spread my ashes two places, there and here. You know, I said I couldn't live without Canada—and maybe I couldn't live without France.

> Quoted by Marci McDonald in *The Toronto Star*, June 24, 1972.

## Lightfoot, Gordon

In the early mornin' rain
With a dollar in my hand,
With an achin' in my heart
And my pockets full of sand,
I'm a long way from home,
And I miss my loved one so
In the early mornin' rain,
And no place to go.

> Opening verse of "Early Mornin' Rain," 1964.

I simply write the songs about where I am and where I'm from. I take situations and write poems about them. That's about all there is.

> Quoted by Ritchie Yorke in *Axes, Chops & Hot Licks: The Canadian Rock Music Scene* (1971).

I'm just goin' to keep on doin' what I'm doin'—tiltin' at windmills like every other man or woman I know, searchin' for a better time.

> Quoted by Marci McDonald in *The Toronto Star*, March 11, 1972.

## Lighthall, William Douw

The romantic life of each Colony also has a special flavour—Australian rhyme is a poetry of the horse; Canadian, of the canoe.

> \*

In losing the United States, Britain lost the *smaller* half of her American possessions:—the Colony of the Maple Leaf is about as large as Europe.

> Introduction to *Songs of the Great Dominion: Voices from the Forests and Waters, the Settlement and Cities of Canada* (1889).

Canada is no State—Canada is a World!

> Introduction to *A Wreath of Canadian Song* (1910), edited by C.M. Whyte-Edgar.

## Lillie, Beatrice

If I were asked to describe my entire career on stage I would do so in five words. Audiences have been my downfall. Every time I have tried to take them by surprise they have beat me to it.

> Beatrice Lillie, Lady Peel, has been called "mistress of sophisticated slapstick." She was born in Toronto. *The Star Weekly*, February 27, 1937.

So, you come all the way to New York to see the Toronto girl who made bad, have you? How sweet!

> \*

I've always been very surprised that people consider me funny at all. Maybe it's because I mix grandeur with complete clumsiness.

> Quoted by Jack Karr in *The Toronto Star*, December 16, 1944.

"Have you ever thought, Lady P., what would have become of you if you'd stayed in Toronto?" . . . "Let's think," she mused. "Well, I suppose I would have married some poor, unfortunate Toronto boy, settled down, raised his children, and made his life quite miserable. I wouldn't have experienced any of the excitement of the theatre, but then I wouldn't have had its worries either.

Have I worries? Are you kidding, Buster?"

＊

And yet, wait a minute—I want you to add a little bit from me. And it's this: tell them that, although all I've said, about the dear happy days of long ago—although that's true—still tell them this: that I believe my favourite motto of all, and for all life, is this: "It's better farther on!"

> Lady Peel's "word of greeting," in an interview with R.E. Knowles in *The Toronto Star*, April, 1936.

See you in Toronto . . . can't wait to see the elephants!

> Quoted by Herbert Whittaker in *The Globe and Mail*, April 7, 1962, in New York prior to a Toronto opening.

Never darken my Dior again!

> Beatrice Lillie was dining with the Queen at Buckingham Palace when the waiter accidentally spilled soup down her evening gown. This was her classic reply; the waiter made no response. Quoted by Lore and Maurice Cowan in *The Wit of Women* (1969). Born in Toronto in 1898, Lady Peel—she married and then divorced Sir Robert Peel, Bart.—made her first stage appearance at the Chatham Music Hall in 1914. In *Who's Who in the Theatre* (1970), she listed her recreations as "oil painting, walking, swimming, riding, shooting, and electric-canoeing." She has been called "the ungilded Lillie."

A little bit of heaven had fallen down from the skies one day onto the shores of Lake Ontario. So they sprinkled it with stardust, and it became Irish Toronto.

> *Every Other Inch a Lady: An Autobiography* (1972), with Joan Philip and James Brough.

## Lincoln, Abraham

If, today, he [the president] should choose to say he thinks it necessary to invade Canada, to prevent the British from invading us, how could you stop him? You may say to him, "I see no probability of the British invading us" but he will say to you "be silent; I see it, if you don't."

> Letter to W.H. Herndon, February 15, 1848, from the young lawyer who thirteen years later would be elected president of the United States.

## Lindsay, Vachel

We must have hands across the sea. All citizens of the British Empire chew gum; but they do it behind closed doors. Americans are more open about it; they chew their gum on the street without shame; they seem all to be citizens of that sacred Indian city called Moose Jaw. We know that we chew gum and we don't even deplore it. I might add that Mr. Wrigley told me, confidentially, that he sells more chewing gum in the British Empire than on American soil, and therefore he has built that wonderful tower, all white, on Michigan Boulevard, Chicago, with British money; nevertheless, the folk of the British Empire prefer to imagine that only Americans chew gum.

> "The Modern Troubadour," *Empire Club of Canada: Addresses Delivered to the Members During the Year 1925* (1926).

## Linkletter, Art

There's a vast gulf between the world of children and our own. And every time we bridge that gulf—even if it's only for a moment—we recapture some of the freshness and spontaneity that makes life worth living.

> The TV master-of-ceremonies was born in Moose Jaw in 1912 and raised in California. His NBC-TV show "People Are Funny" ran from 1954 to 1963. *Kids Say the Darndest Things* (1957), with illustrations by Charles W. Schulz and an introduction by Walt Disney.

## Lipset, Seymour Martin

Saskatchewan is a unique and rewarding place for a social scientist to do research, for the province contains a larger proportion of lay social scientists than any other area I have visited. The farmers are interested in their society and its relations to the rest of the world. . . . In travelling about the province I soon learned not to be surprised when a farmer whom I was interviewing would open a book by

Morris, Henry George, Veblen, Major C.H. Douglas, or some technical social scientist.

*

As long as there are social organizations that produce men who do not accept the *status quo,* who see "the inhumanity of man to man" as a crime, there will be hope in the human race.

> *Agrarian Socialism: The Cooperative Commonwealth Federation in Saskatchewan: A Study in Political Sociology* (1950).

The failure of Canada to have a revolution of its own, the immigration of conservative elements and the emigration of radical elements, and the success of colonial Toryism in erecting a conservative class structure, all contributed to making Canada a more conservative and rigidly stratified society.

*

Horatio Alger has never been a Canadian hero.

> *The First New Nation: The United States in Historical and Comparative Perspective* (1964).

### Lipton, Charles

*But in no important industrial country of the world has it ever happened that the workers should organize in unions based in a foreign country.* That had absolutely nothing to do with internationalism! Indeed, such a development was bound to bear within it the danger of the very antithesis of internationalism—imperialism—the domination of workers in one country by bodies located in another country.

> *The Trade Union Movement of Canada: 1827-1959* (1967).

### Lismer, Arthur

The Canadian painter of today has been given courage to express the belief that in this country there is a vast background of unexplored territory. In the objective sense this may be typified by our north country and the boundless west. In the historical sense this may be typified by our religious, racial and pioneer origins. In the industrial sense this may be typified by our vast natural resources. In the

spiritual sense by our hidden yearnings and national creative desires to know our own country and to seek its beauty. A nation's resources are manifold. . . .

> "Canadian Art," December 13, 1926, *Addresses Delivered before the Canadian Club of Toronto: Season of 1926-27* (1927).

It is not hard to say, then, what art should be. Art should be an *awareness,* a sense of *spiritual alertness,* not put on like poetry. The farmer going out to his milking may be aware of its beauty, even though completely inarticulate. [Journal, 1932]

*

We live in a brittle sophisticated world of commercialized entertainment and industrialized movies and radio. We pass through streets that are often ugly and depressing; we analyse and speculate upon the nature of the physical universe, but we fail to keep alive within us the wonder and awe at our actual passage through life. Novels, spectacles, and incidents thrill us for a moment and then leave behind an empty tasteless void as an unpleasant aftermath. We are rarely deeply moved, we are only furiously agitated, mistaking for pleasure what is really an orgy of disturbance, spiritual and mental. ["On Creative Art and Leisure" (1934)]

*

I never sold a painting till I was fifty.

> Quoted by John A.B. McLeish in *September Gale: A Study of Arthur Lismer of the group of Seven* (1955). McLeish claims the last remark as an understandable exaggeration.

A school-teacher asked her class to name a number of the Group of Seven. One little hand shot up and the boy replied, "Well, I know that one of them was called Jack Pine."

> Lismer, a teacher as well as a painter, entertained his students with this story during the 1940s. "Jack Pine" is a well-known canvas by Tom Thomson.

### Little, John

Yet I have done it myself—I have cut capers in chains.

John Little shook off the fetters of slavery in North Carolina and settled in the Queen's Bush (Peel and Wellesley Townships). Quoted by Benjamin Drew in *The Refugee: or the Narratives of Fugitive Slaves in Canada* (1856).

### Little, Rich
One of the things I like about Hollywood is I am now able to impersonate the people right in front of them. They've got to like it because otherwise they'll be considered square.

The "Toscanini of impersonators" was born in Canada. Quoted by Morris Duff in *The Toronto Star*, October 10, 1964.

You could say I am the most famous and richest Ottawa-born impersonator in the world . . . that's because I'm the only one.

Quoted by Peter Goddard in *The Toronto Star*, September 25, 1973.

### Little Bear
I only want to thank you, Redcoats, and the sheriff for your kindness. I am not afraid to die. I may not be able to in the morning, so now I say again to you all—goodbye! How! Acquisanee!

Little Bear, or A-Pis-Chas-Koos, was one of eight Indian chiefs found guilty of taking part in the Frog Lake massacre. He delivered the above remarks the evening before his execution, which took place at Battleford, November 27, 1885.

### Littleton, E.G.P.
Ladies to wear low-necked dresses, without court trains. Gentlemen in full dress. Ladies, whose health will not admit of their wearing low-necked dresses, may, on forwarding to the A.D.C. in waiting a medical certificate to that effect, wear square-cut dresses.

Littleton was military secretary to the governor general, Lord Lorne, Montreal, 1878.

### Litvinoff, Barnet
Canada is often described by what it is not: unlike the U.S.A., unlike Britain; not a new civilization, nor an established one; a grouping of peoples who love their country but not each other. Its Jewish community attracts a similar series of negatives, for the adage that Jews are just like their neighbours, only more so, applies nowhere more strongly than in Canada.

*A Peculiar People: Inside World Jewry Today* (1969).

### Livesay, Dorothy
Perhaps we are a country more feminine than we like to admit, because the unifying, regenerative principle is a passion with us. We make a synthesis of these two seasons, innocence and experience.

Foreword, *Collected Poems: The Two Seasons* (1972).

### Livingston, John A.
We have always had reluctance to see a tract of land which is empty of men as anything but a void. The "waste howling wilderness" of Deuteronomy is typical. The Oxford Dictionary defines wilderness as wild or uncultivated land which is occupied "only" by wild animals. Places not used by us are "wastes." Areas not occupied by us are "desolate." Could the desolation be in the soul of man?

\*

Canoeists and other primitive-trippers are not delighted to encounter others intent on the same private experience. How many visitors constitute the end of wilderness?

"Man and His World: A Dissent," *Wilderness Canada* (1970), edited by Borden Spears.

### Ljungh, Esse W.
A listener is the most lavish producer there is. He or she can soar on sound much higher than the looker can on pictures.

CBC radio producer, quoted by Toni Williams in *The Toronto Telegram*, May 31, 1968.

### Lloyd, Cecil Francis
But if beauty may not die, men may die to beauty, and therein lies the true province and high calling of the artist, not to keep beauty alive, but to prevent poor

earth-worms from becoming so blind that they cannot or will not see her.

> "Sunset and Evening Star," *Sunlight and Shadow* (1928).

There is nothing more cheerful than a little lake on a fine morning in summer, as there is nothing more tranquil and lovely than such a lake on a clear, windless summer night. Blessed be the country that has many little lakes, for to it belongs no small share of the heaven of beauty.

> "Lonely Lakes," *Malvern Essays* (1930).

## Lloyd, Trevor
Unending pursuit of an abstract ideal makes an impersonal world.

> "The Impersonal University," *The University Game* (1968), edited by Howard Adelman and Dennis Lee.

Elections in Canada sometimes produce M.P.s who are chosen more for the capacity to understand their constituents than for their capacity to understand the problems with which the government is faced.

\*

One of the problems for the Canadian public is that the sort of issues facing government at the present day are only comprehensible through the medium of print, and because print is no longer the dominant medium for the general public "the medium censors the message."

> "Government as Dialogue," *Agenda 1970: Proposals for a Creative Politics* (1968), edited by Trevor Lloyd and Jack McLeod.

## Lloyd George, David
Whenever the Germans found the Canadian Corps coming into the line, they prepared for the worst.

> *War Memoirs: Volume VI* (1933-36).

## Lockhart, Gene
The world is waiting for the sunrise;
Ev'ry rose is heavy with dew.
The thrush on high his sleepy mate is
   calling,
And my heart is calling you.

"One of the best songs of 1919 was 'The World Is Waiting for the Sunrise' by Eugene Lockhart and Ernest J. Seitz," wrote Sigmund Spaeth in *A History of Popular Music in America* (1948). "Both the sentiment and the melody of 'The World Is Waiting for the Sunrise' appealed to the people who were searching desperately for some relief from the black misery of the war years."

Lockhart, who was a pianist, was born in London in 1891, and wrote the words of this popular song while touring the country with a group called The Pierrot Players. Ernest Seitz, another member of the group, set it to music. Lockhart wrote other popular songs and made numerous appearances in Hollywood films until his death in 1957. Leslie Halliwell in *The Filmgoer's Companion* (1970) identifies him as a "Canadian character actor at home in genial and shifty parts."

## Lockhart, James
This is to certify that P. Clement has paid all he owed me from the beginning of the world to the present time. J. Lockhart.

> Receipt of James Lockhart, dry goods merchant, Niagara-on-the-Lake, about 1890. Quoted by Janet Carnochan in *History of Niagara* (1914).

## Lodge, Henry Cabot
The fact is England cares nothing about the boundary but their fear of offending the Canadians is something inconceivable. That collection of bumptious provincials bullies them to an extent and they dare not say a word.

> Letter from the U.S. senator in England to his daughter, July 28, 1903. Quoted by Howard K. Beale in *Theodore Roosevelt and the Rise of America to World Power* (1956).

## Loffmark, Ralph
There are only two ways out of public life. One is death, the other is defeat (and I have been defeated).

> Former minister of Health and Welfare in the British Columbia Social Credit

government, quoted in *The Vancouver Sun*, August 30, 1972.

## Lollobrigida, Gina
Canada is okay, because it's close to America.

In the spring of 1960, the Italian cinema star established residence in Toronto with a view to gaining landed immigrant status for her stateless Yugoslavian-born husband Dr. Milko Skofic. Then the marriage broke up and both returned to Europe. Quoted, on a publicity tour, by Doug Fetherling in *The Toronto Star*, December 3, 1973.

## Lombardo, Guy
Corn is always green—like money.

\*

The Sweetest Music This Side of Heaven.

This is the motto of Guy Lombardo and his Royal Canadians, a popular dance band since the 1930s. The bandleader was born in 1902 in London and at the age of twenty-one left for New York where within seven years his radio broadcasts had made him famous. In 1971, the University of Western Ontario presented him with an honorary doctorate.

We will continue to play for lovers, not for acrobats.

Quoted by George T. Simon in *Simon Says: The Sights and Sounds of the Swing Era 1935-1955* (1971).

## London, George
I am convinced that the only way to become a first-class singer is to become a first-class member of the human race.

Quoted by Clyde Gilmour in *Maclean's Magazine*, May 15, 1953. The bass-baritone was born George Burnstein in Montreal and recorded *Boris Godunof* with the Bolshoi in 1960.

## London, Jack
Let me put it on record right here that Ottawa, with one exception, is the hardest town in the United States and Canada to beg clothes in; the one exception is Washington, D.C. The latter fair city is the limit.

"Holding Her Down," *The Road* (1907).

## Lone Ranger, The
See George W. Trendle.

## Lonergan, Father Bernard J.E.
The church always arrives on the scene a little breathless and a little late.

Attributed to the Jesuit theologian about 1963.

## Long, Barbara
Indeed. Toronto, heavy, gray, silly in its provincial prickiness, snittily affirming that it's a failed New York, half-knowing, and drinking a lot of brandy over that knowledge, that it is instead, a failed Boston. . . . Ignorant, smug, Toronto. . . .

"Nothing Left but Xanadu," *The Village Voice*, November 24, 1966.

## Long, Marcus
The fact is that the average teacher has only limited knowledge and even less intellectual interest. . . . No person can be an effective teacher whose interests do not extend beyond the requirements of his school.

Address to teachers in 1955, quoted by Doris French in *High Button Bootstraps: Federation of Women's Teachers' Associations of Ontario: 1918-1968* (1968).

## Longboat, Tom
Too bad I didn't know the hills, Bill. Might'a gone faster. Do better next time.

Regret expressed by the teenage Onondagan Indian runner to his coach Bill Ashley, April 19, 1907, after winning the famed Boston Marathon and breaking the former record by more than five minutes, finishing a half-mile ahead of his nearest competitor. Quoted by Henry Roxborough in *Great Days in Canadian Sport* (1957).

## Longfellow, Henry Wadsworth
Still stands the forest primeval; but under
   the shade of its branches
Dwells another race, with other customs
   and language.

Only along the shore of the mournful
and misty Atlantic
Linger a few Acadian peasants, whose
fathers from exile
Wandered back to their native land to
die in its bosom.
In the fisherman's cot the wheel and the
loom are still busy;
Maidens still wear their Norman caps
and their kirtles of homespun,
And by the evening fire repeat Evangeline's story,
While from its rocky caverns the deep-
voiced, neighbouring ocean
Speaks, and in accents disconsolate
answers the wail of the forest.

This is the last stanza of the final section of the American poet's *Evangeline:
A Tale of Acadie* (1847), a sentimental
but nonetheless movingly written account of the expulsion of the Acadians
in 1775 from "the little village of Grand-
Pré" on "the shores of the Basin of
Minas" in what is today referred to as
New Brunswick's "Evangeline Country."
The original Evangeline was Emmeline
Labische, who died of shock when she
located her lover in Louisiana and found
him engaged to another woman. Longfellow heard the story of the ill-starred
lovers in 1840 in the presence of Na-
thaniel Hawthorne. When the novelist
expressed no interest in it, Longfellow
declared he would turn the story into
an epic poem. See also Governor Charles
Lawrence and Colonel John Winslow.

Should you ask me, whence these stories?
Whence these legends and traditions,
With the odours of the forest,
With the dew and damp of meadows,
With the curling smoke of wigwams,
With the rushing of great rivers,
With their frequent repetitions,
And their wild reverberations,
As of thunder in the mountains?
I should answer, I should tell you,
"From the forests and the prairies,
From the great lakes of the North-
land. . . ."

These are the familiar opening lines of
*The Song of Hiawatha* (1855), which is
partly set in Canada. *Evangeline* and
*Hiawatha* are reprinted from *The Poet-*

*ical Works of Longfellow: Oxford Com-
plete Copyright Edition* (1908).

**Long Lance, Buffalo Child**
See Sylvestre Clarke.

**Longley, James W.**
Let me utter one concluding word. Canada is here to stay. The beginning of this
century marks an epoch of phenomenal
progress in British North America. The
nineteenth century was the century of the
United States. The twentieth century is
Canada's century.

Attorney general of Nova Scotia, addressing the Canadian Club of Boston,
April 8, 1902. *The Globe*, April 12, 1902.
See also Sir Wilfrid Laurier: Who Owns
the Twentieth Century?

**Longstreth, T. Morris**
*Thou shalt not let the Force down* is the
one commandment; and loyalty to this
commandment is the Mounted Police
religion.

\*

Now, discipline is the method of making
difficult things a habit; it is the way of
exacting in a crisis the performance
planned in sober calm.

*The Silent Force: Scenes from the Life
of the Mounted Police of Canada* (1927).

**Loosley, Elizabeth W.**
See John R. Seeley.

**Lord, Barry**
We must take Canada back, by whatever
means our owner makes necessary, and
then give the resources and industries of
this land to its own people. Let us organize a new Canada in which people,
not American-controlled corporations,
come first.

" 'Mericans," *The New Romans: Candid Canadian Opinions of the U.S.*
(1968), edited by Al Purdy.

**Lorimer, James**
In Britain, you don't find special little
book departments labelled "Britannia."
In Sweden, no set of shelves labelled
"Swedenia." We have a long way to go
yet.

"Publishing in Canada" by James Lorimer and Dave Godfrey, *Read Canadian: A Book about Canadian Books* (1972), edited by Robert Fulford, Dave Godfrey, and Abraham Rotstein.

## Lorimier, Chevalier de
Death is nothing to a Frenchman.

> Words of inspiration shouted to Charles Hindenlang who was being led to the Montreal gallows. Lorimier followed shortly after. Quoted by Selwyn P. Giffin in "A Tragedy of Generous Youth," *Open Secrets: Off the Beaten Track in Canada's History* (1929.) See also Charles Hindenlang.

May my execution and the execution of my gallows companions be of use to you. May they show you what you can expect from the English government. I have only a few hours to live, but I want to divide this precious time between my religious duties and my obligations to my fellow countrymen. It is for their sake that I am dying as an infamous murderer on the scaffold; for their sake I have given up my life and children . . . and for their sake I die crying: "Long live Liberty! Long live Independence!"

> From the "Political Testament" of François-Marie-Thomas, Chevalier de Lorimier, hanged on February 15, 1839, for his part in the Rebellion of 1837. Quoted by Marcel Rioux in *Quebec in Question* (1971).

## Lorne, Marquis of
There is a marvellous amount of bitterness and bad language. Half the artists are ready just now to choke the other half with their paint brushes.

> The governor general's reaction to the founding of the Royal Canadian Academy, 1880. Quoted by Moncrieff Williamson in *Robert Harris 1849-1919: An Unconventional Biography* (1970).

Over and over again in Canada have I been asked if such and such a bay was not wonderful like the Bay of Naples, for the inhabitants had often been told so. I always professed to be unable to see the resemblance, of course entirely out of deference to the susceptibilities of the Italian nation. So one of our party, a Scotsman, whenever in the Rocky Mountains he saw some grand pyramid or gigantic rock, ten or eleven thousand feet in height, would exclaim that the one was the very image of Arthur's Seat and the other of Edinburgh Castle. [Winnipeg address, 1881]

*

Etiquette may perhaps be defined as some rule of social conduct. I have found that no such rule is necessary in Canada, for the self-respect of the people guarantees good manners. [Toronto speech, 1883]

> *Memories of Canada and Scotland: Speeches and Addresses* (1884).

In token of the love which thou hast shown
For this wide land of freedom, I have named
A province vast, and for its beauty famed,
By thy dear name to be hereafter known.
Alberta shall it be! Her fountains thrown
From alps unto three oceans, to all men
Shall vaunt her loveliness e'en now; and when,
Each little hamlet to a city grown,
And numberless as blades of prairie grass,
Or the thick leaves in distant forest bower,
Great peoples hear the giant currents pass,
Still shall the waters, bringing wealth and power,
Speak the loved name—land of silver springs—
Worthy the daughter of our English kings.

> *Yesterday and Today in Canada* (1910), by the Duke of Argyle (Lord Lorne). The governor general dedicated this *verse d'occasion* to his wife Princess Louise Caroline Alberta, fourth daughter of Queen Victoria, after he had renamed Alberta (formerly the District of Assiniboia) in 1882.

. . . and I pray that God who has granted

you this great country, that He may, in His own good time, make you a great people.

> On his departure from Canada in 1883, quoted by Wilfred Campbell in *Canada* (1907).

Unto the hills around do I lift up
My longing eyes,
O whence for me shall my salvation come,
From when arise?
From God the Lord doth come my certain aid,
From God the Lord, who heaven and earth have made.

> The first of four verses of "Unto the Hills," a popular hymn which is generally credited to the Marquis of Lorne, later ninth duke of Argyle. The hymn is based on Psalm 121 and was adapted by Lorne to be sung to C.H. Purdy's stately melody. *Methodist Hymn and Tune Book* (1917).

**Lotz, Jim**
Our northern visions and dreams tell us what we are. The realities of the land and its people tell us what we can do.

\*

The north has a profoundly spiritual effect upon man, somehow assuring him of his importance at one time, and convincing him of his insignificance at another.

> *Northern Realities: The Future of Northern Development in Canada* (1970).

**Loudon, Earl of**
Canada must be demolished,—*Delenda est Carthago*,—or we are undone.

> *Review of Military Operations* (1757), quoted by Francis Parkman in *Montcalm and Wolfe* (1884).

**Lougheed, Sir James**
Adultery is the same the world over; it's only the method of approach that varies.

\*

The Senate is a bulwark against the clamour and caprice of the mob.

\*

I think that learned counsel is abusing the privilege of being stupid.

\*

The basic principle of the State is compulsion. This is fundamental in its entire organization. It runs through every system of law, both civil and criminal, through practically all the conventions of society; without it law, order, system and organization could not exist.

> Sir James, called to the Senate in 1889, served as chairman of its Divorce Committee and was later Conservative leader. Quoted by Robert M. Hamilton in *Canadian Quotations and Phrases: Literary and Historical* (1952).

**Louis XIV**
To people Canada, it would be necessary to depopulate France.

> Observation attributed to Louis XIV, king of France, in 1667.

Concerning these new discoveries, you must on no account encourage them unless there be a great need and some obvious advantage to be derived from them. You must hold to the maxim that it is far more worthwhile to occupy a smaller area and have it well populated than to spread out and have several feeble colonies which could easily be destroyed by all manner of accidents.

> Letter to the Comte de Frontenac, April 16, 1676, quoted by W.J. Eccles in *Canada under Louis XIV: 1603-1701* (1964).

The Colony of Canada is good only inasmuch as it can be useful to the Kingdom.

> The Sun King's view of New France in 1702, quoted by Mason Wade in *The French Canadians: 1760-1967* (1968).

**Louis XV**
Are the streets being paved with gold over there? I fully expect to awake one morning in Versailles to see the walls of the fortress rising above the horizon.

> This was the French monarch's reply to Sébastien de Vauban, when the military architect pressed for further funds with which to complete the Fortress of Louisbourg, Cape Breton Island. "The statement was supposed to have been made by Louis XV," explained John Lunn, park superintendent, Fortress of Louis-

bourg, Nova Scotia, February 28, 1973. "The most exact quote, if there ever was one, is lost, and like many such statements, it has not been proved that it was ever uttered."

By the 1740s, Louisbourg was the most expensive fortress in all North America. It fell in 1758, and Quebec fell the following year, and as there was no longer "an alarming drain on the treasury," the loss of New France was celebrated with a magnificent dinner at Versailles.

## Lount, Elizabeth

Truth it is that my dear husband, whom your laws have torn from me and from his helpless children, epoused sincerely the cause of reform. Had their plans succeeded, that reform would have been obtained—the Governor secured—and the Province freed without shedding of a drop of human blood.

*

Those with whom my husband acted were moved by the impulses of noble and generous sympathies. They panted not for offices, for those they enjoyed—they thirsted not for blood, for Canadians were their brothers—they were determined to drive a Nero from his throne, to rid Canada of a tyrant, and to effect a civil resolution that would give happiness and prosperity to the country. Had they been successful, Canadians to the latest posterity would have blest them.

*

O Canada, my own country, from which I am now exiled by a party whose mercy is worse than death—I love thee still. Destruction has overtaken thy brightest ornaments, and the indigent feelings of thy sons burn their hearts, but they dare not give utterance to their thoughts. How many mothers have suffered, like me, the loss of a home and all that could make that home pleasant.

*

Canada will do justice to his memory. Canadians cannot long remain in bondage. They will be free. The lion will give way, and a bold star will eventually ornament the Canadian standard sheet. Then will the name of Canadian martyrs be sung by poets and extolled by orators,

while those who now give law to the bleeding people of Canada will be loathed or forgotten by the civilized world.

Elizabeth Lount, wife of Samuel Lount who, with Peter Mathews, was hanged on April 12, 1838, for taking part in the Rebellion of 1837, addressed this letter of grievance to the chief justice of Upper Canada, John Beverley Robinson. It was published in a Michigan newspaper, *Pontiac Herald*, June 12, 1838, and reprinted by Margaret Fairley as "Who Are the Traitors?" *New Frontiers*, Summer, 1954. After the death of her husband, Mrs. Lount campaigned for amnesty for the exiled Patriots, then moved with her seven children to the American West where she died in 1883. See also: Sir George Arthur, Matthew Lount, Samuel Lount, Egerton Ryerson, Matthew Sheard.

## Lount, Matthew

I would not care if I was dead if I had Mac along with me.

Matthew Lount was the brother of Samuel who was hanged for treason, and the reference is to William Lyon Mackenzie, the leader of the Rebellion of 1837. Quoted by Edwin C. Guillet in *The Lives and Times of the Patriots: An Account of the Rebellion in Upper Canada, 1837-1839* (1938, 1968). See also Elizabeth Lount.

## Lount, Samuel

Be of good cheer, boys. I am not ashamed of anything I've done. I trust in God, and I'm going to die like a man.

The patriot who forged spear-heads for the Rebellion of 1837 was hanged in Toronto, April 12, 1838. Quoted by John Ross Robertson about 1900 in *Old Toronto: A Selection of Excerpts from Landmarks of Toronto* (1954), edited by E.C. Kyte.

"He lived a Patriot, and died for popular rights."

Inscription on the monument erected to honour the memory of Samuel Lount and Peter Mathews, both hanged for treason, April 12, 1838. The monument was erected in 1893 in St. James Cemetery, Toronto. See also Elizabeth Lount.

## Loveless, George

I believe nothing will ever be done to relieve the distress of the working class, unless they take it into their own hands. With these beliefs I left England, and with these views I have returned. Notwithstanding all I have felt and seen, my sentiments on the subject are unchanged. Nothing but union can obtain the great and important object, namely the salvation of the world. Let the producers of wealth firmly and peacefully unite their energies, and what would withstand them? The power and influence of the non-producer would sink into insignificance. The conquest will be won. Our victory is certain.

> George Loveless and four other English agricultural labourers were arrested at Tolpuddle in 1834 and deported to Australia for "illegal combination." Robert Owen led a successful amnesty march. A few years later, Loveless and his family settled on a farm near London, Ontario, with three other of "the Tolpuddle Martyrs"—James Loveless, John Stanfield and James Byrne. Quoted by Charles Lipton in *The Trade Union Movement of Canada: 1827-1959* (1967).

## Low, Colin

Rediffusion on a broad scale of original and creative solutions coupled with free information accessible to all could alter positively the social and environmental situation.

> "The Question of Television Violence," *Challenge for Change*, Autumn, 1972.

## Lowe, Frank

Full speed ahead and damn the toreadors.

&#42;

A bird in the hand is messy.

> "Remember, You Read It Here First," *Weekend Magazine*, March 17, 1973.

## Lowe, Ruth

I'll never smile again
Until I smile at you,
I'll never laugh again,
What good would it do?

For tears would fill my eyes
My heart would realize
That our romance is through.
I'll never laugh again,
I'm so in love with you.
I'll never thrill again
To somebody new.
Within my heart
I know I will never start
To smile again
Until I smile at you.

> Ruth Lowe of Toronto wrote the words and music of this once-popular song, "I'll Never Smile Again," in 1939. It was sung in *Las Vegas Nights* (1941) and made the hit parade. Sigmund Spaeth in *A History of Popular Music in America* (1948) explained that it caught on "through the macabre publicity created by the death of the composer's husband (which had nothing to do with the creation of the song)."

## Lowell, James Russell

Here at last is a state whose life is not narrowly concentered in a despot or a class, but feels itself in every limb; a government which is not a mere application of force from without, but dwells as a vital principle in the will of every citizen.

> "Observations on Canadian Government" (1865), *The Works of James Russell Lowell* (1890).

## Lowell, Robert

The world atop our heads in Maine is
    north,
zeroes through Newfoundland and
    Hudson Bay:
*entremets chinois et canadiens.* ["The
    Races"]
&#42;
High culture is lying with an American
    girl
on the Canadian border, the longest
    border on earth,
each man there noble as the Queen but
    not so rich. ["The End"]

> *Notebook 1967-68* (1969), by the American poet.

## Lower, A.R.M.

"Who reads a Canadian book," it was

asked some years ago, "except by mistake?"

*

We Canadians are a worthy, thrifty people, perfectly safe and constituting no problem to the countries in control of our destinies: we are therefore uninteresting and what we write about is also, for the most part, uninteresting—except to ourselves.

"The Social Sciences in the Post-War World," *Canadian Historical Review*, March, 1941.

If the Canadian people are to find their soul, they must seek for it not in the English language or the French but in the little ports of the Atlantic provinces, in the flaming autumn maples of the St. Lawrence valley, in the portages and the lakes of the Canadian Shield, in the sunsets and relentless cold of the prairies, in the foothill, mountain, and sea of the West and in the unconquerable vastness of the North. From the land, Canada, must come the soul of Canada.

*

In every generation Canadians have had to rework the miracle of their political existence. Canada has been created because there has existed within the hearts of its people a determination to build for themselves an enduring home. Canada is a supreme act of faith.

*

The incident must have impressed on the Prime Minister what he already no doubt knew, that it is not easy to govern a country, part of whose people are more British than the king and part more Catholic than the pope.

*Colony to Nation: A History of Canada* (1946, 1964). The reference in the last quotation is to Sir Wilfrid Laurier's appeal to the Pope in 1896 to stop the Quebec bishops who were instructing their parishioners how to vote.

Our people would have to learn to tolerate men who were not afraid, for the sake of equality, of being "unequal," for

"When everybody's somebody
Then no one's anybody."

Logic carries the worship of the god Equality into all spheres: age, sex, race,

nation, body, mind. [Couplet from Gilbert and Sullivan's *The Gondoliers*]

*Canadians in the Making* (1958).

Canada is a country whose major problems are never solved.

*

The kindliest thing the historian can say about the King war administration is that it consisted of men most of whom were too saturated in Liberal principles to take advantage of these powers. [This evaluation of the Second World War government of Mackenzie King was quoted in the House of Commons by the minister of Justice, Louis St. Laurent, in defence of Liberal tactics, April 16, 1947]

*

Architecturally Ottawa is not a city of history. If it is anything it is a city of the future, not of the past. But I doubt that there are many people in Ottawa who will have the gumption to see that!

*My First Seventy-Five Years* (1967).

### Lowery, R.T.

*The Ledge* has never been raided by the sheriff, snow-slided by cheap silver, or subdued by the fear of man. It works for the trail blazers as well as the bay-windowed and the champagne-flavoured capitalist. One of the noblest works of creation is the man who always pays the printer, he is sure of a bunk in paradise, with thornless roses for a pillow by night, and nothing but gold to look at by day.

Editor and publisher of *The Ledge*, a newspaper that issued from New Denver, British Columbia, around the turn of the century. Quoted by Robert Thomas Allen in *A Treasury of Canadian Humour* (1967).

### Lowry, Malcolm

. . . you should know that it is considered definitely low-minded to try and buy any kind of a book in Canada, even from a bookseller. . . . [Letter to Maxwell Perkins, September 20, 1946]

*

We only live here by grace of being pioneers, and Canada, alas, is forgetting that it is its pioneers who built this country and made it what it was: now it wants to be like everyone else and have auto-camps instead of trees and Coca-Cola stands instead of human beings. In that way, for it has little culture at all, it could destroy its soul: is its own business, no doubt—what we mind is that it threatens to destroy us in the process, an eventuality that it now becomes my duty to try and avoid. [Letter to Stuart Lowry, fall, 1950]

*

And we have no friends in Canada save three fishermen in like case, a cat, five wild ducks, two seagulls, and, of course, a wolf. [Letter to Stuart Lowry, fall, 1950]

*

It may interest you to know that there is a long broadcast tonight or tomorrow night on the subject of Malcolm Lowry, Canada's greatest most successful writer, which we can't listen to because our radio has run down and we can't afford to replenish the battery. The unkindest cut of all. [Letter to Stuart Lowry, fall, 1950]

*

I have done more for Canadian literature than any living Canadian, and that is beside the point except when I say that despite all this I have made a success of my life and had conditions been equal would have made an assured income for life too. . . . [Letter to Stuart Lowry, fall, 1950]

*

The sales in Canada [of *Under the Volcano*] have been 2 copies and apart from some sold by the flying start you gave it in New York, my sole recognition here an unfavourable squib in the *Vancouver Sun*. [Letter to Albert Erskine, February 13, 1951]

*

. . . there is no outlet for one's work in Canada, no magazines, and the U.S. is not interested, should the *mise en scène* be Canada and that *mise en scène* not contain a mounted policeman. It is difficult to make a living at 4000 miles dis-

tance. . . . [Letter to Clenens ten Holder, Summer, 1951]

*

. . . but Canadians can be tough and intolerant babies when they get going, they have an ominous predilection for the use of informers, the Mounted Police have a power and ubiquity that can be considered in anything but the romantic terms of *Rose Marie*, even if they are no doubt decent guys personally: all in all it seems to me British Columbia is a hell of a paradoxical place to ask any Englishman to give up his English passport in, with all that means, no matter how one might believe in or love Canada per se. It's almost a contradiction in terms; and so hence is my position on this score. . . . [Letter to Albert Erskine, early summer, 1954]

*

. . . nevertheless I've as much right to call myself Canadian as Louis Hémon had and I even wrote a Canadian national anthem, though nobody's sung it except me. I had a childish ambition—maybe not so childish—always to contribute something to Canadian literature though, and I wrote a book called *Under the Volcano*, which has become fairly well known, but which people seem to think is written by an American. [Letter to Ralph Gustafson, April 29, 1957]

*Selected Letters of Malcolm Lowry* (1965), edited by Harvey Breit and Margerie Bonner Lowry.

### Lucas, Charles Peyton

I feel that I am out of the lion's paw, and I feel that THERE IS NO CURSE ON GOD'S GREEN EARTH EQUAL TO SLAVERY.

Lucas escaped from slavery in Virginia and settled in Toronto. Quoted by Benjamin Drew in *The Refugee: or the Narratives of Fugitive Slaves in Canada* (1856).

### Luce, Henry R.

I may be in some disagreement with my colleagues. But you said, Sir, you want me to be very plain. I do *not* consider *Time* a Canadian magazine.

Appearing before the Royal Commission on Publications, January 17, 1961, the publisher of *Time Magazine* disagreed with his Montreal editor's definition of *Time* as a Canadian magazine.

Quoted by Peter C. Newman in *The Distemper of Our Times: Canadian Politics in Transition: 1963-1968* (1968).

## Ludwig, Jack

A country which elected, but survived, McKinley, Harding, Coolidge, Hoover, and Nixon as vice-president can't be all bad.

"Balancing the Books," *The New Romans: Candid Canadian Opinions of the U.S.* (1968), edited by Al Purdy.

If I choose to stand in a tradition why not the one to which Tolstoy and Flaubert and Dickens belong, rather than the one that includes Leacock, de la Roche, and Buchan?

Winnipeg-born novelist, quoted by Mordecai Richler in his introduction to *Canadian Writing Today* (1970).

To me the writer is the guy who pays attention to how you get through the twenty-four-hour day, on a second-to-second, minute-by-minute basis.

Interviewed by Donald Cameron in *Conversations with Canadian Novelists* (1973).

## Lumet, Sidney

If you care about your work, every frame matters.

The director of *The Pawnbroker* (1965) was born in Canada in 1924.

## Lynch, Charles

The better you do your work in getting out the stories, the less popular you're likely to be, particularly with the Government.

Quoted by Walt McDayter and Russell

Elman in *A Media Mosaic: Canadian Communications Through a Critical Eye* (1971).

## Lyon, Peyton V.

To be influential with modest means one needs to be modest in demeanour . . . let us tread softly and carry a bulging briefcase of bright ideas.

"Canada Is Becoming a Mouse that Roars" (1960), *The Policy Question: A Critical Appraisal of Canada's Role in World Affairs* (1963).

## Lysenko, Vera

Assimilation is wheat fields and symphonies.

*Men in Sheepskin Coats: A Study in Assimilation* (1947).

## Lytton, Sir Edward Bulwer

I believe that the day will come, and that many now present will live to see it, when a portion at least of the lands on the other side of the Rocky Mountains, being also brought into colonization and guarded by free institutions, one direct line of railway communication will unite the Pacific and the Atlantic.

\*

I conclude, sir, with a humble trust, that the Divine Disposer of all human events may afford the safeguard of His blessing to an attempt to add another community of Christian freemen to those by which Great Britain confides the records of her empire, not to pyramids and obelisks, but to states and commonwealths, whose history will be written in her language.

Address of the colonial secretary to the British Parliament, quoted by Alexander Morris in "The Hudson's Bay and Pacific Territories" (1858), in *Nova Britannia; or, Our New Canadian Dominion Foreshadowed* (1884).

# M

## McAree, J.V.

Experience has taught us that there are some problems for which there is no answer, and that there are circumstances in which the best of men cannot make a move that he will not regret later. There is no right move to make. Every move will be wrong. The ancient wisdom of mankind sums the thing up in the saying about a choice between evils.

> "Insoluble Problems," *The Fourth Column* (1934).

## McArthur, Peter

Art generalizes while science itemizes.

\*

Art is the only enduring expression of science.

\*

An Englishman's social standing seems to depend on the number of people he can afford to despise. The average Englishman has so deep a reverence for antiquity that he would rather be wrong than recent.

> *To Be Taken with Salt: Being an Essay on Teaching One's Grandmother to Suck Eggs* (1903).

Nowadays anyone can write a book, and most everyone does.

> *The Affable Stranger* (1920).

To be born on a farm is the greatest good that can befall a human being. To live on a farm and enjoy all that it has to offer is the greatest good that can be attained by a poet or a philosopher.

> *Around Home* (1925).

A man would need to be a millionaire to be interested in the city.

> *Friendly Acres* (1927).

Some people have so much respect for their superiors they have none left for themselves.

\*

A satirist is a man who discovers unpleasant things about himself and then says them about other people.

\*

To be a place of complete happiness heaven must be a place where we will be allowed to do the things we think ourselves fitted to do on earth.

\*

There are some men who get more satisfaction out of their ignorance than most learned men get out of their knowledge.

\*

Success invariably makes a man philosophical.

\*

Some people make their virtues more unendurable than vices.

\*

Conscience is that within us that tells us when our neighbours are going wrong.

\*

Set even a realist to write autobiography and he instantly becomes an idealist.

\*

When you find a man about whom people speak no evil, it is evidence, not that the man, but that the people are unusual.

\*

I wonder if the history of Canada will ever be written—I mean the real history.

\*

Above all things I love a great dream.

> *The Best of Peter McArthur* (1967), edited by Alec Lucas.

Disaster precedes reform.

\*

A man has to be as willing to forgive himself as to forgive other people.

\*

Every successful enterprise requires three men—a dreamer, a businessman, and a son-of-a-bitch. [A favourite epigram, coined about 1904, with the failure of the humourist's newspaper]

> Peter McArthur, who died in 1924, was a columnist who wrote about farm life in Western Ontario.

**MacAskill, Angus**   See James P. Gillis.

**Macaulay, John**
It is to be observed that the sentencing of females to the Penitentiary causes some inconvenience.

> Concluding paragraph of the first report of the inspectors of the Provincial Penitentiary, Kingston, November 2, 1835. Quoted by J. Alex. Edmison in "The Problem of the Criminal Female," *Saturday Night*, June 11, 1960.

**Macaulay, Lord Thomas Babington**
In order that he might rob a neighbour whom he had promised to defend, black men fought on the coast of Coromandel, and red men scalped each other by the Great Lakes of North America.

> "Frederic the Great" (1842), *Historical Essays Contributed to the "Edinburgh Review"* (1866).

**McBride, Sir Richard**
No Aliens Need Apply.

> Anti-Oriental plank in the platform of the British Columbia politician, defeated in the federal election of 1896. Sir Richard went on to become the province's first native-born premier.

**MacBrien, Sir James H.**
The correct motto of the Force is not "Get Your Man," it is "Maintain the Right." There is a story about getting your man that I might tell you. It is supposed to be the origin of the expression, "Get Your Man." A patrol was sent out five hundred miles to arrest an Indian. He was arrested and they got back within a day's patrol of the post when unfortunately the prisoner was eaten by wolves and they had to go all the way back to the reservation to get another Indian.

> "The Royal Canadian Mounted Police" (1937), *Empire Club of Canada: Addresses Delivered to the Members During the Year 1937-38* (1938).

**MacCallum, J.M.**
If all you young fellows go off to the States, art in Canada is never going to get anywhere.

> Toronto doctor and first patron of the Group of Seven, during the 1920s. Quoted by A.Y. Jackson in *A Painter's Country* (1958).

**MacCallum, Reid**
Positivism and surrealism seem to be the products of a divorce which both agree to maintain and perpetuate. ["Art and Science" (1946)]

*

No: dreams, reveries, pure imagination are not even the material of art, for art is fundamentally a social, common product, and the incommunicable and the irremediably subjective is forever excluded from it. ["Emotion and Pattern in Aesthetic Experience" (1930)]

*

It might be enough to say that to live in the present is to live in love, but as people understand that word so differently, it would be better to end with an unpretentious pun: the present is a present, a gift. ["First and Second Self" (1949)]

> *Imitation and Design and Other Essays by Reid MacCallum* (1953), edited by William Blissett.

**McClelland, Jack**
I want to stress that I am not anti-American. I'm not even pro-Canadian because that would oblige me to condone that peculiar myopia that has become almost a national symbol here. But I care very much for this country. I care very much about our future. And I don't intend to be bullied, smothered or owned by any other country. There are other people who feel as I do. I call them Canadians.

> *Toronto Calendar Magazine*, March, 1972.

**McClintock, Sir Francis Leopold**
I cannot divest myself of the belief that *some record was left here* by the retreating crews, and perhaps some most valuable documents which their slow progress and fast failing strength would

have assured them could not be carried much further.

> Captain McClintock's belief brought results: he found proof of Franklin's death on King William Island. *The Voyage of the "Fox" in the Arctic Seas: A Narrative of the Discovery of the Fate of Sir John Franklin and His Companions* (1859). See also Lady Jane Franklin.

## McCloskey Jr., Paul N.

I suspect, however, that the young men of deep sensitivity who have gone to Sweden or Canada or sought conscientious objector status or willingly undergone jail sentences, would be the same men who, thirty years ago, memorized eye charts and travelled to Canada to enlist in Canadian forces rather than wait for American involvement in the war against Nazi Germany.

> Republican representative from California, House of Representatives, Washington, April 1, 1971.

## McClung, Nellie L.

I believe we'll get you yet, Sir Rodmond.

> To Sir Rodmond Roblin, premier of Manitoba, January 27, 1914. See also Sir Rodmond P. Roblin.

Another trouble is that if men start to vote, they will vote too much. Politics unsettles men, and unsettled men mean unsettled bills—broken furniture, broken vows and—divorce. . . . It has been charged that politics is corrupt. I do not know how this report got out but I do most emphatically deny it. I have been in politics for a long time and I never knew of any division of public money among the Members of the House, and you may be sure, if anything of that kind had been going on, I should have been in on it. Ladies and gentlemen, what I mean is that I would have known about it.

> Address by the suffragette leader ridiculing the manner of Sir Rodmond Roblin, premier of Manitoba, at the mock parliament, Walker Theatre, January 28, 1914. *The Stream Runs Fast* (1945).

Heckler: The Prime Minister would quit politics if a woman were ever elected.

McClung: This proves what a purifying effect women would have on politics.

> Exchange at a public gathering in Brandon during the Manitoba election campaign of 1915.

When I am giving advice to my sons matrimonially, I will tell them to marry a business girl. If they want a creature of selfishness and peevishness, let them marry a petted child of fortune, who has been given everything that the heart can desire, who can order anything she sees that she likes, to be sent home C.O.D.—which is "Call on Dad!"

> "The New Citizenship," October 18, 1915, *Addresses Delivered before the Canadian Club of Toronto: Season of 1915-16* (1916).

Thank you, gentlemen, for thinking of us, unworthy though we be.

> Speech at Portage la Prairie, August 3, 1915, when the Tories decided to back the women's suffrage movement, although the Tory election manifesto clearly stated: "Wifehood, motherhood and politics cannot be associated together with satisfactory results . . . the vote for women will degenerate true womanhood, emotionalize balloting and be illogical and absurd. . . ."

"No woman, idiot, lunatic, or criminal shall vote."

> From the Election Act of the Dominion of Canada, as cited by Nellie L. McClung in *In Times Like These* (1915). See Anonymous: Some Documents.

The hand that rocks the cradle does not rule the world. If it did, human life would be held dearer and the world would be a sweeter, cleaner, safer place than it is now!

\*

Women who set a low value on themselves make life hard for all women.

\*

The economic dependence of women is perhaps the greatest injustice that has been done to us, and has worked the greatest injury to the race.

*

Why is the careless, easy-going, irresponsible way of the young girl so attractive to men? It does not make for domestic happiness; and why, Oh why, do some of our best men marry such odd little sticks of pin-head women, with a brain similar in calibre to a second-rate butterfly, while the most intelligent, unselfish, and womanly women are left unmated? I am going to ask about this the first morning I am in heaven, if so be we are allowed to ask about the things which troubled us while on our mortal journey. I have never been able to find out about it here.

*In Times Like These* (1915).

He said Canada was like a great sand-pile, each little grain of sand beautiful in its own way, but needing cement to bind it to other grains, and it was for us to say whether we could be content to be only a sand-pile, or would we make ourselves a beautiful temple.

*Purple Springs* (1921).

Children are not a handicap to any woman. They open up a new world to their mothers, the rainbow-hued world of childhood, with its delightful confidences and the unforgettable times when, all the world shut out, mother and child wander together through the world of books.

"Can a Woman Raise a Family and Have a Career?" *Maclean's Magazine*, February 15, 1928.

It came as a distinct shock to many Canadian women who had not known they were not persons until they heard it stated that they were.

Until 1929, women were not "persons," at least in the eyes of the Supreme Court of Canada and of five successive Canadian governments. That year the Privy Council of Great Britain ruled that the word "person" in the BNA Act of 1867 did include members of the female sex. See also Anonymous: Some Documents.

As cold and hard a country as ours has one unalterable law—the survival of the fittest. The incompetent were like little candles in the wind.

*

Literature may be light as a cobweb, but it must be fastened down to life at the four corners.

*Clearing in the West: My Own Story* (1936).

A writer must have all the pores of his heart open.

"Quotable Quotes," *Canadian Author and Bookman*, March, 1943.

By nice women . . . you probably mean selfish women who have no more thought for the underprivileged, overworked women than a pussycat in a sunny window for the starving kitten in the street. Now in that sense I am not a nice woman for I do care.

*The Stream Runs Fast* (1945).

## McClure, S.S.

If I were able to give you advice—which I am not—I would give you advice along the following lines. . . . I should reduce the status of the provinces to about that of city charters and make it a real nation, not an assemblage of more or less semi-sovereign states.

"Some Problems of Government," November 26, 1910, *Addresses Delivered before the Canadian Club of Ottawa: 1910* (1911). McClure was a prominent New York editor-publisher and political pundit.

## MacColl, Ewan

In the town of Springhill, Nova Scotia,
Down in the dark of the Cumberland Mine,
There's blood on the coal and the miners lie,
In roads that never saw sun nor sky,
Roads that never saw sun nor sky.

Opening lines and refrain of "The Springhill Mining Disaster" by Ewan MacColl and Peggy Seeger. The Nova Scotia catastrophe in 1958 inspired the American folk singers to write this moving ballad. See also Kaleb Rushton.

## McConachie, Grant

I can still remember him as he looked then: Hollywood's idea of a bush pilot, straight out of Central Casting.

On C.H. "Punch" Dickens in *Great Canadians: A Century of Achievement* (1965).

**McConkey, Oswald Murray**
I give my pledge as a Canadian to defend from waste, to work for the wise use and good management of my country's natural resources—its soil and minerals, its forests, waters and wild life.

> "Conservation Pledge," *Conservation in Canada* (1952).

**MacCormac, John**
A political convention in the United States bears the same relation to a political convention in Canada as bedlam bears to a cemetery.

> *Canada: America's Problem* (1940).

Canada is now wholly within the strategic orbit of the United States.

> *America and World Mastery: The Future of the United States, Canada, and the British Empire* (1942).

**McCormack, John**
The line of the ruling class everywhere is—Property first, Man afterwards. We say: "Man first, Property afterwards!"

> Militant Toronto unionist, 1872, quoted by Charles Lipton in *The Trade Union Movement of Canada: 1827-1959* (1967).

**McCormick, Colonel Robert**
They are so inbred as to be half-witted.

> Opinion of the isolationist-minded publisher of *The Chicago Tribune* on Newfoundlanders, after a four-hour flight delay at Gander, 1952. Quoted by Richard Gwyn in *Smallwood: The Unlikely Revolutionary* (1968).

**McCourt, Edward**
A mobile population creates few traditions. Not that tradition is essential to the creation of great art, but it is an exciting stimulus to the imagination.

> *The Canadian West in Fiction* (1949).

No doubt we on this continent have always tended to exaggerate the importance of mere size; none the less, it is gratifying to know that the 5,000-mile Trans-Canada Highway is the longest continuous road on earth.

*

The Canadian Shield is fascinating country of enormous wealth but there is too much of it. In Canada there is too much of everything. Too much rock, too much prairie, too much tundra, too much mountain, too much forest. Above all, too much forest. Even the man who passionately believes that he shall never see a poem as lovely as a tree will be disposed to give poetry another try after he has driven the Trans-Canada Highway.

> *The Road Across Canada* (1965).

Troy town rose and fell ten times on the hill Hissarlik above the Hellespont; the Indian village sited a few miles west of Moose Jaw went Troy three better—thirteen distinct cultural levels have been uncovered in the Mortlach "midden," first stumbled upon by a local farmer who observed an unusual number of arrowheads in a pasture cowpath.

*

No cities with the possible exception of Sodom and Gomorrah have ever been founded in less congenial physical surroundings than Regina, the Queen City of Saskatchewan.

*

Silence and solitude—the finest gifts Saskatchewan has to offer bedevilled modern man.

> *Saskatchewan* (1968).

**McCrae, John**
In Flanders fields the poppies blow
Between the crosses, row on row,
　　That mark our place; and in the sky
　　The larks, still bravely singing, fly
Scarce heard amid the guns below.

We are the Dead. Short days ago
We lived, felt dawn, saw sunset glow,
　　Loved and were loved, and now we lie
　　In Flanders fields.

Take up our quarrel with the foe:
To you from failing hands we throw
　　The torch; be yours to hold it high.
　　If ye break faith with us who die
We shall not sleep, though poppies grow
　　In Flanders fields.

With the possible exception of Kipling's "Recessional," the most familiar of all war poems is "In Flanders Fields." The poem was written by John McCrae in twenty minutes in the early morning of May 3, 1915, during the second battle of Ypres, Belgium. Born in Guelph in 1872, McCrae was a major and First Brigade surgeon in the Canadian Field Artillery. He was in deep sorrow, for that night he had buried a young friend, Lieutenant Alexis Helmer, and the poem was written out of this personal sorrow. The composition was witnessed by Cyril L.C. Allinson. Helmer's death marked the loss of McCrae's carefree innocence, and the soldier-physician-poet died of double pneumonia on January 28, 1918; he lies buried at Wimereux Cemetery, Boulogne, France.

McCrae published his poem in *Punch* on December 8, 1915. He noted with surprise that his sentiments were shared by millions. But it was only after his death that the poem was recited as part of the official Armistice Day program on November 11, 1918, and has since become an integral part of all Remembrance Day ceremonies in Canada.

So popular was the poem during his lifetime that McCrae supplied friends with hand-written copies, no two of which are identical. The major textural controversy concerns the use of "blow" and "grow." Both words appear in the poem. It is said that McCrae wrote "the poppies blow" for that is what they were doing that May morning, but McCrae accepted the advice of a *Punch* editor that a superior reading would be "the poppies grow," although after publication in the magazine the poet changed his mind and reverted to "the poppies blow." (The only problem with that explanation is that the *Punch* version, which is reproduced above, has the poppies blowing, not growing. As far as the single line is concerned, there is no superior reading; but in the light of the poem as a whole, "the poppies blow" adds variety and complexity, as long as the second-last line ends "though poppies grow." The textual controversy is revived every Armistice Day, when variant holographs are quoted.) The

text of the poem above, from the *Punch* original, is virtually identical with the one Sir Andrew MacPhail included in the posthumous collection of McCrae's poems *In Flanders Fields and Other Poems* (1919) — virtually, because the MacPhail version has an extra comma in the eighth line, making it: "Loved, and were loved, and now we lie"—a not unrhythmical addition. The only detail to add is that "In Flanders Fields" appeared anonymously in *Punch*, but that the authorship was credited to McCrae in the annual index, where his name appeared, misspelled, as "McCree, Lieut.-Col. John." See also Cyril L.C. Allinson.

## McCullagh, George
I have no politics, I am a Canadian.

> Address, June, 1938, quoted by Brian J. Young, "C. George McCullagh and the Leadership League," *Canadian Historical Review*, September, 1966.

If you'll be a good horse, I'll be a good jockey.

> Attributed to the ebullient publisher of *The Globe and Mail* while launching his Leadership League for unemployed youth in the 1930s.

## McCulloch, Thomas
Amidst the infirmities of age, it is a great comfort to old folks, that, whatever destruction time works in their memory, they never find it affecting their judgment. [Letter 7]

*

Since that time I have had much experience of both beasts and fences; and I have always found that good fences make good friends and safe crops. [Letter 9]

*

Let your readers here pause and marvel. And by and by, when their astonishment is surmounted, I may enlarge upon the works and untimely end of the great Censor, who soared beyond Parnassus, and died in a dung heap. [Letter 18]

> The "Letters of Mephibosheth Stepsure" appeared in *The Acadian Recorder* in 1821 and 1822. *The Stepsure Letters* (1960), edited by Douglas Lochhead.

## McCullough, Colin

Scotch is the stream in which all diplomats swim.

> *Life with the Chinese Dragon* (1973).

## McCutcheon, Wallace

I do not want the word Liberal to mean French, and the word Conservative to mean English.

> Progressive Conservative Association of Manitoba, November 14, 1964. Quoted by Peter C. Newman in *The Distemper of Our Times: Canadian Politics in Transition: 1963-1968* (1968).

## MacDermot, Galt

She asks me why,
I'm just a hairy guy.
I'm hairy noon and night,
Hair that's a fright.
I'm hairy high and low,
Don't ask me why, don't know.
It's not for lack of bread,
Like the Grateful Dead.

> Opening lines of "Hair" from *Hair: The American Tribal Love-Rock Musical* (1967), words by James Rado and Gerome Ragni, music by Montreal-born Galt MacDermot.

Theatre is where you can present music and get an audience.

> Quoted by Blaik Kirby in *The Globe and Mail*, June 24, 1972.

## McDonagh, Edward Charles

The car has become a secular sanctuary for the individual, his shrine to the self, his mobile Walden Pond.

> Canadian-born American sociologist, quoted in *Time*, May 10, 1963.

## Macdonald, Lady Agnes

The description of a cowcatcher is less easy. To begin with, it is misnamed, for it catches no cows at all. . . . I turn to him, peeping around the headlight with my best smile. "This is *lovely*," I triumphantly announce, seeing that a word of comfort is necessary, *"quite lovely*; I shall travel on this cowcatcher from summit to sea."

And that is what Sir John A. Macdonald's wife did — ride the cowcatcher through the Rockies, July, 1886. Quoted by Edwin C. Guillet in *"You'll Never Die, John A!"* (1967).

## Macdonald, Brian

You always find you can do a little more than you think you can. All you lose is a little sleep.

> Montreal-born choreographer, appointed head of the Royal Swedish Ballet, 1965.

## Macdonald, Dwight

Suppose that our Northwest were to secede, culturally, from the union and set up its own special Northwestern division of arts and letters; the result would be not unlike the present situation in Canada.

> "Landscape Through a Peephole: An American Glance at Some Canadian Magazines," *Canadian Literature*, Summer, 1959. The New York cultural critic found the batch of literary magazines sent him "in short, provincial— that is dependent on the capital city (London or New York), and yet insistent on a local autonomy which there aren't the resources to sustain."

## Macdonald, Flora

"Flora Macdonald. A name that will be mentioned in history, and if courage and fidelity be virtues, mentioned with honour (Samuel Johnson). The preserver of Bonnie Prince Charlie spent the winter of 1799 here with her husband Capt. Alan Macdonald of the Royal Highland emigrants, when returning to her old home in Skye, after exile from her old new home in North Carolina. Her loyalty and devotion in the midst of troubled days have long been told in Scottish song and story."

> Inscription on a plaque unveiled at the Blockhouse, Windsor, Nova Scotia. The heroic woman herself wrote: "There we continued all winter and spring, covered with frost and snow and almost starved with cold to death, it being one of the worst winters ever seen there." Will R. Bird in *This Is Nova Scotia* (Third Edition, 1955).

## Macdonald, George Sandfield

The historians of Canada (with the conspicuous exception of Garneau) have been literary balloonists. Ascending to a high altitude, they have observed what was on the surface, whilst the character of the Canadian people and its changes in different stages of growth, from the present settlements of the eighteenth century to the confederate nation of today—all this has not yet been written. The people of Canada have been left out of Canadian histories. . . . No work deserving to be called a history of the Canadian people has yet been written.

> *Transactions of the Celtic Society of Montreal* (1884).

## MacDonald, J.E.H.

Let us support our distinctly Native Art, if only for the sake of experiment.

\*

If you must knock, there are a thousand doors in Toronto to knock at. The Artist does not plead for your backing. If you honestly cannot give it, he'd rather have your opposition, because indifference kills his feeling and ambition quickest. And, anyway, the broad strong type of picture marked "Hot Mush" by H.F.G. is a product of Vitality and not Decay.

> MacDonald, a member of the Group of Seven, is replying to an attack by H.F. Gadsby, the Toronto art critic who coined the term "the Hot Mush school." "The Hot Mush School: In Rebuttal of H.F.G.," *The Toronto Star*, December 20, 1913. For the original attack, see H.F. Gadsby.

The Decorative Element is perhaps not so much a component part, as the element in which art lives and moves and has its being. It is an element more in the sense of the universal ether.

> Address at the Arts and Letters Club, Toronto, about 1918, quoted by Peter Mellen in *The Group of Seven* (1970). See also Tom Thomson.

## Macdonald, J.W.G. ("Jock")

There is no manifesto here for the times. There is no jury but time,

> Statement from the catalogue to the

first exhibition of Painters Eleven, Toronto, February 12, 1954. Quoted by William Withrow in *Contemporary Canadian Painting* (1972).

## Macdonald, Sir John A.

Seriously, you would make a decent Conservative, if you gave your own judgment a fair chance and cut loose from Holton and Dorion and those other beggars. So pray do become true blue at once: it is a good standing colour and bears washing.

> Letter to Alexander Tilloch Galt, November 2, 1857, quoted by O.D. Skelton in *The Life and Times of Sir Alexander Tilloch Galt* (1920).

Whatever you do adhere to the Union—we are a great country, and shall become one of the greatest in the universe if we preserve it; we shall sink into insignificance and adversity if we suffer it to be broken.

> Speech in 1861, quoted by E. B. Biggar in *Anecdotal Life of Sir John A. Macdonald* (1891).

I trust that for ages, for ever, Canada may remain united with the mother country. But we are fast ceasing to be a dependency, and are assuming the position of an ally of Great Britain. England will be the centre, surrounded and sustained by an alliance not only with Canada, but Australia, and all her other possessions; and there will thus be formed an immense confederation of freemen, the greatest confederacy of civilized and intelligent men that has ever had an existence on the face of the globe. [Legislative Assembly, April 19, 1861]

Now, gentlemen, what do you think of D'Arcy McGee? I really think you will say: Not guilty, but he must not do it again.

> At a dinner honouring Thomas D'Arcy McGee, November, 1865.

In the Upper House, the controlling and regulating, but not initiating, branch, we have the sober second thought in legislation.

*

A large qualification should be necessary for membership in the Upper House, in order to represent the principle of property. The rights of the minority must be protected, and the rich are always fewer in number than the poor.

> Discussing the proposed Senate, April 6, 1865, quoted by Sir Joseph Pope in *Confederation: Being a Series of Hitherto Unpublished Documents Bearing on the British North America Act* (1895).

I would be quite willing, personally, to leave that whole country a wilderness for the next half-century, but I fear if Englishmen do not go there, Yankees will. . . .

> Letter concerning the settlement of the North-West to Edward Watkin, March 27, 1865. Quoted by P.B. Waite in *The Life and Times of Confederation: 1864-1867* (1962).

A great future would await our country were it not for those wretched Yankees, who hunger and thirst after Naboth's vineyard. War will come some day between England and the United States, and you in India could do us yeoman service by sending an expeditionary force of Ghurkas, Beluchis, etc., to attack San Francisco, and hold that beautiful and unusual city and the surrounding California as hostages for Montreal and Canada.

> Letter to J.S. Maine, Calcutta, April 9, 1867. Quoted by Blair Fraser in "Canada: Mediator or Busybody?" in *Canada's Role as a Middle Power* (1966), edited by J. King Gordon.

By the exercise of common sense and a limited amount of patriotism which goes by the name of self-interest, I have no doubt that the Union will be for the common weal.

> Letter to Sir Ambrose Shea, June 3, 1867, quoted by Donald Creighton in *John A. Macdonald: The Young Politician* (1952).

The Union was treated as if the British North America Act were a private bill, uniting two or three English parishes.

> Quoted by Sir Joseph Pope in *Memoirs of the Right Honourable Sir John Alexander Macdonald* (1894).

Given a Government with a big surplus, and a big majority and a weak Opposition, and you could debauch a committee of archangels.

> To Sir Richard Cartwright about 1869, quoted by Cartwright in his *Reminiscences* (1912).

The great reason why I have always been able to beat Brown is that I have been able to look a little ahead, while he could on no occasion forego the temptation of a temporary triumph. [Concerning George Brown, the Liberal leader, March 5, 1872]

Confederation is only yet in the gristle, and it will require five years more before it hardens into bone. [Letter to Sir John Rose, March 5, 1872]

I must have another ten thousand; will be the last time of calling; do not fail me; answer today.

> Telegram to Sir John Abbott, legal adviser to the CPR which had been granted lucrative contracts by the Conservative government. A few hours later, August 26, 1872, Abbott sent his reply: "Draw on me for ten thousand dollars." Revelation of such campaign-fund contributions brought about the Pacific Scandal of 1873. See also Sir John Abbott,

These hands are clean!

> Words attributed to Macdonald at the time of the Pacific scandal by J.W. Bengough in a cartoon in *Grip*, August 16, 1873. See J.W. Bengough.

Harry, my boy, never write a letter if you can help it, and never destroy one.

> To Colonel H.R. Smith, sergeant-at-arms of the House of Commons from 1872 to 1892, quoted by Sir Joseph Pope in *The Correspondence of Sir John Macdonald* (1921).

They are to be purely a civil, not a military body, with as little gold lace, fuss, and fine feathers as possible: not a crack cavalry regiment, but an efficient police force for the rough and ready—

particularly ready—enforcement of law and justice. [House of Commons, May 3, 1873, introducing the bill to establish the North-West Mounted Police]

If Canada is never sold in the future by a greater traitor than myself, Canada will be a fortunate country.

*

We were fighting an uneven battle. We were simply subscribing as gentlemen, while they were stealing as burglars.

*

I state distinctly, so far as I know, not one single farthing that passed through my hands was expended improperly or contrary to the law.

*

But, sir, I commit myself, the government commits itself, to the hands of this house; and far beyond the house, it commits itself to the country at large. [Loud cheers] We have fought the battle of confederation. We have fought the battle of union. We have had party strife setting province against province; and more than all, we have had in the greatest province, the preponderating province of the Dominion, every prejudice and sectional feeling that could be arrayed against us. I have been the victim of that conduct to a great extent; but I have fought the battle of confederation, the battle of union, the battle of the Dominion of Canada. I throw myself upon this house; I throw myself upon this country; I throw myself upon posterity; and I believe that I know, that, notwithstanding the many failings in my life, I shall have the voice of this country, and this house, rallying around me. [Cheers] And, sir, if I am mistaken in that, I shall confidently appeal to a higher court—to the court of my own conscience, and to the court of posterity. [Cheers] I leave it with this house with every confidence. I am equal to either fortune. I can see past the decision of this House, either for or against me; but whether it be for or against me, I know—and it is no vain boast for me to say so, for even my enemies will admit that I am no boaster —that there does not exist in Canada a man who has given more of his time,

more of his heart, more of his wealth, or more of his intellect and power, such as they may be, for the good of this Dominion of Canada.

The right hon. gentleman resumed his seat, amid loud and long continued cheering.

> Speech delivered by the prime minister in reply to allegations concerning the Pacific railway charter, House of Commons, November 3, 1873. "The Pacific Scandal," reprinted by G. Mercer Adam in *Canada's Patriot Statesman: The Life and Career of the Right Honourable Sir John A. Macdonald* (1891).

When fortune empties her chamberpot on your head, smile—and say "we are going to have a Summer shower."

> Letter to T.C. Patteson, about 1875. Quoted by J.K. Johnson in his edition of *Affectionately Yours: The Letters of Sir John A. Macdonald and His Family* (1969).

Those who dislike the colonial connection speak of it as a chain, but it is a golden chain, and I for one, am glad to wear the fetters. [Paraphrase of a statement in the House of Commons, March 30, 1875]

By the Party, With the Party, For the Country.

> Conservative party slogan, used by Sir John in a Montreal address in a variety of ways, November 24, 1875.

Until that road is built to British Columbia and the Pacific, this Dominion is a mere geographical expression. . . . Until bound by the iron link, as we have bound Nova Scotia and New Brunswick by the Intercolonial Railway, we are not a Dominion in fact.

> Address at the Thomas White dinner, Montreal, reported in *The Mail*, November 29, 1875. Quoted by Donald Creighton in *John A. Macdonald: The Old Chieftain* (1955). See also Sir John's letter of May 1, 1878.

When I was in the Eastern Townships, I heard the cry echoing from rock to rock, across the bosoms of those beautiful lakes, and over the emerald field,—

"Come to our rescue, John A., or we are lost."

> *The Mail,* July 9, 1877. Five days later J.W. Bengough drew a memorable cartoon of this amusing scene. J.W. Bengough's *A Caricature History of Canadian Politics: Events from the Union of 1841, as Illustrated by Cartoons from "Grip," and Various Other Sources* (1886).

I move: That the Speaker do not now leave the Chair, but that this House is of the opinion that the welfare of Canada requires the adoption of a National Policy, which, by a judicious readjustment of the Tariff, will benefit and foster the agricultural, the mining, the manufacturing and other interests of the Dominion; that such a policy will retain in Canada thousands of our fellow countrymen now obliged to expatriate themselves in search of the employment denied them at home, will restore prosperity to our struggling industries, now so sadly depressed, will prevent Canada from being made a sacrifice market, will encourage and develop an active interprovincial trade, and moving (as it ought to do) in the direction of a reciprocity of tariffs with our neighbours, so far as the varied interests of Canada may demand, will greatly tend to procure for this country, eventually, a reciprocity of trade.

> Macdonald, as leader of the Opposition, moved an amendment to the budget speech, March 7, 1878, and declared the principles of his protectionist National Policy.

Again, Lord D. has made the subject of the construction route and requirements of the Canadian Pacific Railway his especial study. Until this great work is completed, our Dominion is little more than a "geographical expression." We have as much interest in B. Columbia as in Australia, and no more. The railway once finished, we become one great united country with a large interprovincial trade, and a common interest.

> Letter to Sir Stafford Northcote, chancellor of the exchequer in Disraeli's cabinet, concerning the reappointment

of Governor General the Lord Dufferin, May 1, 1878. *The Correspondence of Sir John Macdonald* (1921), edited by Sir Joseph Pope. See also the Montreal address reported on November 29, 1875.

Yes, Protection has done so much for me I must do something for Protection!

> To Goldwin Smith on the eve of the 1878 election, quoted by Smith in his letter to *The Globe,* September 23, 1895. "It's devilish hard for a free trader to make a Protectionist speech," he has been quoted as saying.

"Well! John A. beats the devil."

> Luther H. Holton, a former Liberal M.P., was amazed when Sir John's Conservatives were returned to power in the general election of 1878. See Luther H. Holton.

"Old Tomorrow would be just the name for Sir John."

> The prime minister was given this nickname in late 1881 by the commissioner of the North-West Mounted Police. (Other sobriquets include: Old Reynard, Fox Populi, Lord Tomorrow, The Wizard of the North.) See Colonel A.G. Irvine.

I am told that you can come in on the train in the morning and start ploughing in the afternoon. I am told that some in this new country are not content, but you know, ladies and gentlemen, some of us will not be content in heaven if we hear of a place farther west.

> On his first visit to Brandon, about 1881, quoted by Beecham Trotter in *A Horseman and the West* (1925).

Hiving the Grits.

> The phrase the prime minister used to sum up the effect of the Redistribution Act, April, 1882. "It made inroads into Ontario constituencies where the 'Grit' (Liberal) vote was strong." Norah Story, *The Oxford Companion to Canadian History and Literature* (1967).

Any election is like a horse-race, in that you can tell more about it the next day.

> Quoted by Sir Joseph Pope in *Memoirs*

of the Right Honourable Sir John Alexander Macdonald (1894) concerning the election of 1882.

Pacific in trouble; you should be here.

Cable to Sir Charles Tupper in England, December 1, 1883.

"You'll never die, John A.!"

An unidentified person yelled this out at a Toronto gathering to celebrate Sir John's forty years in Parliament. Under the heading "Hail to the Chief!" *The Mail* published Macdonald's speech the following day, December 18, 1884, an excerpt of which follows:

When I look back through my forty years in public life; when I remember how few remain of those who with me entered full of hope, life, and the earnestness of youth; when I bear in mind that those who do remain are like myself, feeble old men—[cries of "No, no! and a voice, "You'll never die, John A.!"]—when I think of all this, feelings of a most solemn nature awake in my mind. . . . I heard a cry just now from one of my friends saying "You'll never die!" [Laughter] Gentlemen, I really do believe that those who die in political opposition to me think so too— [Renewed laughter]—and I fear, though they pray for me and all other like sinners, that in the supplications there is no pious expression of the desire that my life may be long spared. [Loud laughter]

He shall hang though every dog in Quebec bark in his favour.

Prior to Louis Riel's execution on November 16, 1885. Quoted by Sir George R. Parkin in *Sir John A. Macdonald* (1908). Intemperate as it seems, the prime minister's attitude pales beside the sentiment expressed in *The Toronto News*, May 18, 1885: "Strangle Riel with the French flag! That is the only use that rag can have in this country."

If you had a lit-tle more wood, and a lit-tle more water, and here and there a hill, I think the prospect would be improved.

Said in Regina, 1886, quoted by E.B.

Biggar in *Anecdotal Life of Sir John A. Macdonald* (1891).

We are not to be limited to Halifax, Quebec, Montreal or British Columbia, whether it be Port Moody or Victoria— the termini of the Canadian Pacific Railway are Liverpool and Hong-Kong!

Said in Victoria, on the opening of the CPR, 1886.

On reading the above over I see that it will convey the impression that the change of title from Kingdom to Dominion was caused by the Duke of Buckingham. This is not so. It was made at the instance of Lord Derby, then foreign minister, who feared the first name would wound the sensibilities of the Yankees.

Letter to Lord Knutsford in England, July 18, 1889.

If left to ourselves, I have no doubt of a decision in our favour, but I have serious apprehensions which are shared by all our friends here, that a large amount of Yankee money will be expended to corrupt our people . . . Sir C. Tupper will tell you that every American statesman (and he saw them all in '88), covets Canada. The greed for its acquisition is still on the increase, and God knows where it will all end.

Letter to Sir George Stephen, November 10, 1890, *The Correspondence of Sir John Macdonald* (1921), edited by Sir Joseph Pope.

I have no accord with the desire expressed in some quarters that by any mode whatever there should be an attempt made to oppress the one language or to render it inferior to the other; I believe that would be impossible if it were tried, and it would be foolish and wicked if it were possible. [House of Commons, February 17, 1890]

Under the broad foils of the Union Jack we enjoy the most ample liberty to govern ourselves as we please, and at the same time we participate in the advantages which flow from association with the mightiest empire the world has ever seen. Not only are we free to manage our domestic concerns, but, practically, we possess the privilege of making our own treaties with foreign countries, and in our relations with the outside world we enjoy the prestige inspired by a consciousness of the fact that behind us towers the majesty of England.

＊

With my utmost, with my last breath, will I oppose the "veiled treason" which attempts, by sordid means and mercenary proffers, to lure our people from their allegiance.

> "To the Electors of Canada," February 7, 1891. Reprinted by G. Mercer Adam in *Canada's Patriot Statesman: The Life and Career of the Right Honourable Sir John A. Macdonald* (1891).

As for myself, my course is clear. A British subject I was born—a British subject I will die.

> This most memorable of expressions, this vivid assertion of personal principle, may be found in many forms. A few follow.

The cardinal point in our policy is connection with Great Britain. I am a British subject, and British born, and a British subject I hope to die.

> Address at the Thomas White dinner in Montreal, reported in *The Montreal Gazette*, November 26, 1875. Quoted by Donald Creighton in *John A. Macdonald: The Old Chieftain* (1955).

Disguise it as you will, this means separation and independence. The hon. gentleman is moving on by slow degrees to that point. This is a commercial movement; by-and-by we will have something else; until at last we take a step for political independence. I have said to the House before, that a British subject I was born, and a British subject I hope to die. The best interests of Canada are all involved in the connection between the Mother Country and her loving and loyal colony.

> House of Commons, April 21, 1882.

I commend these issues to your determination, and to the judgment of the whole people of Canada, with an un-

clouded confidence that you will proclaim to the world your resolve to show yourselves not unworthy of the proud distinction you enjoy—of being numbered among the most dutiful and loyal subjects of our beloved Queen. As for myself, my course is clear. A British subject I was born—a British subject I will die.

> House of Commons, February 7, 1891. This was Macdonald's last address.

"As to myself—my course is clear. A British subject I was born—a British subject I will die."

> Edwin C. Guillet reproduces a portion of the last address in holograph in *"You'll Never Die, John A.!"* (1967) in this form. The sentiment became a slogan for the last campaign. Macdonald won the election of 1891 but died a few months after assuming office.
>
> Daniel Webster, the American lawyer and patriot, said, July 17, 1850: "I was born an American; I live an American; I shall die an American."
>
> John G. Diefenbaker added a novel twist at the Progressive Conservative Convention in Toronto, September, 1967: "So to each of you, I say I believe in Canada—a Canada undivided. A Canadian I was born, a Canadian I will die." See also Sir Oliver Mowat.

"The Old Man, the Old Flag, and the Old Policy."

> For the slogan of the last campaign, 1891, see Louis P. Kribs.

Look here, McGee, this Government can't afford two drunkards, and you've got to stop. [To Thomas D'Arcy McGee]

＊

I know enough of the feeling of this meeting to know that you would rather have John A. drunk than George Brown sober.

＊

John A. Macdonald, cabinet-maker. [Entering his name in the visitor's book, Legislative Library, on his last visit to Prince Edward Island, 1890]

＊

Like any cabinet-maker, I do the best I can with the lumber you furnish me. [Sir Richard Cartwright quotes Macdonald's reply to a farmer in his *Reminiscences* (1912): "Send me better men to deal with, and I will be a better man."]

*

Mr. Mackenzie (commenting on a clause in a new bill)—"If that is considered an improvement, it is certainly one of a Tory character."
Sir John—"A satisfac-Tory character."

*

Dickey: No, I am still a Conservative, and I shall support you whenever I think you are right.
Sir John: That is no satisfaction. Anybody may support me when I am right. What I want is a man that will support me when I am wrong.

> Famous exchange with Senator A.R. Dickey of Amherst, quoted by E.B. Biggar in *Anecdotal Life of Sir John A. Macdonald* (1891).

During one of the years of Lord Dufferin's administration, the talented Governor General delivered an address in Greek before the University of McGill College, Sir John Macdonald and Sir Hector Langevin being present with him. One of the reporters wrote in his report: "His Lordship spoke in the purest ancient Greek without mispronouncing a word or making the slightest grammatical solecism."
"Good Heavens," said Sir Hector to Sir John, as they read the report. "How did the reporter know that?"
"I told him," replied Sir John.
"But you don't know Greek."
"True," answered Sir John, "but I know a little about politics."

> E.B. Biggar's *Anecdotal Life of Sir John A. Macdonald* (1891). Although Biggar does not record it, there is a variant last line which runs: "True," answered Sir John, "but I do know men."

Let us be English or let us be French, but above all let us be Canadians.

*

When a man has done me an evil turn once, I don't like to give him the opportunity to do so twice.

*

I carried my musket in '37. [Remark

characteristic of his later years]

*

One strong point I admire about Sir Oliver Mowat is his handwriting.

*

A public man should have no resentments.

*

Would you move away please, your breath smells terrible . . . it smells like water.

*

John, I wonder if God Almighty ever made a man as honest as you look. [To "Honest John" Carling, cabinet minister from 1882 to 1891]

*

The task of the politician is to climb the tree and shake down the acorns to the pigs below.

*

A compliment is a statement of an agreeable truth; flattery is the statement of an agreeable untruth.

*

Myself and time against any two men.

*

As far as I am concerned, I've gone through my life with one principle: Be to our faults a little blind, and to our virtues always kind.

> These remarks have been attributed to Sir John A. Macdonald at various times by various writers.

"I do not know whether he originated the phrase, 'Canada is a hard country to govern,' but it was one that was not infrequently on his lips."

> Hector Charlesworth in *The Canadian Scene: Sketches Political and Historical* (1927). See also Sir Wilfrid Laurier for other expressions of this sentiment.

Bowell: I suppose it is late.
Sir John: Yes, Bowell, I suppose it is. I will go. Good night.

> To Sir Mackenzie Bowell, who would become his successor, on leaving the House of Commons for the last time, May 22, 1891. Adapted from E.B. Biggar's *Anecdotal Life of Sir John Macdonald* (1891).

I will let you know tomorrow.

To Sir John Thompson who had just asked the dying prime minister to accept a sinecure, the day before his final stroke on June 6, 1891. Quoted by E.B. Biggar in *Anecdotal Life of Sir John A. Macdonald* (1891).

See also: J.W. Bengough, Sir Charles W. Dilke, Benjamin Disraeli, Lady Agnes Macdonald.

## Macdonald, John Sandfield

We must support our supporters.

*

I am an outside pillar of the Church.

*

What the hell has Strathroy done for me?

To a delegation from a Liberal stronghold that wanted a registry office, *The Globe*, August 24, 1871. Quoted by Bruce W. Hodgins in *John Sandfield Macdonald: 1812-1872* (1971).

## MacDonald, Malcolm

But you are condemning me to exile. All the lights will be on in Ottawa and I shall yearn for the dark of London.

"Malcolm MacDonald, the leader of National Labour, was minister of Health in Churchill's government. He now became U.K. high commissioner to Canada and remained there till early in 1945." Sir Harold Nicolson's *Diaries and Letters: 1939-1945* (1967). On February 18, 1941, Sir Harold wrote: "I had the dreaded meeting of the National Labour Party. Malcolm was in the chair. He told us exactly what had happened about his being sent off to Canada. He had said to Winston, 'But you are condemning me to exile. All the lights will be on in Ottawa and I shall yearn for the dark of London.' He refused to go. He said that he would much rather join up. Winston was evidently touched by this attitude and asked him not to decide till next day. After sleeping it over, 'I saw,' said Malcolm, 'that if Winston asked me to go to Timbuctoo, I should have to accept.' All this sounds awful bunk when one writes it down afterwards, but if you had been there and heard Malcolm speak so simply and frankly, you would have known that the whole thing was true, and that it re-

flects good credit both on the P.M. and on Malcolm."

## MacDonald, Ramsay

Canada is going to be a wonderful country. There are many reasons why I should like to live for one hundred years. One of the reasons is I would like to see this country one hundred years from now. It will be great. It will be rich . . . it will be powerful.

"Address," August 7, 1928, *Addresses Delivered before the Canadian Club of Toronto: Season of 1928-29* (1929). MacDonald was the Labour prime minister of Great Britain.

## MacDonald, Thoreau

The north woods were in his bones and he brought sketches out of the bush as naturally as a hunter brings out fish or partridges.

Son of J.E.H. MacDonald and artist in his own right commenting on Tom Thomson who died mysteriously in 1917.

## MacDonald, Wilson

Norse am I when the first snow falls;
Norse am I till the ice departs.
The fare for which my spirit calls
Is blood from a hundred viking-hearts.

Opening lines of "The Song of the Ski," a verse familiar to generations of school children, from *Out of the Wilderness* (1926).

If I were English, Canada
Should love me like the deuce.
But I was born in Canada
So what the hell's the use!

Last stanza of "The Song of a Bloody Canuck" from *Open House* (1931), edited by William Arthur Deacon and Wilfred Reeves.

He stole, and boasted of his swag.
And, when his victims would rebel,
He wrapped himself in England's flag
And sang, "God Save the King," like Hell.

Final stanza of "The Member of Parliament," *Comber Cove* (1937).

Canadian literature has suffered less

from foreign unfairness than from those internal fault-finders who abound in Canada and whose stock-in-trade is the inferiority of colonialism. These critics are for the most part university professors who know as much about the soul of Canada as a stoker at sea knows about the beauty of a storm. The analogy is perfect, for when multitudinous lakes and countless rivers are calling upon the interpreters to proclaim their beauty these academy-prisoned gentlemen are wrestling with vellum in the stolid atmosphere of classrooms.

*

The critic who discovers a flaw in Canadian literature is considered very clever; but the critic who discovers genius in our poetry or prose is immediately taunted with nationalistic prejudice.

> "The Stigma of Colonialism," *Open House* (1931), edited by William Arthur Deacon and Wilfred Reeves.

### Macdonnell, James McKerras
A Fascist, but a nice Fascist.

> Conservative financial critic's opinion of C.D. Howe. Quoted by Leslie Roberts in *C.D.: The Life and Times of Clarence Decatur Howe* (1957).

### McDougall, J.E.   See Keith Crombie.

### McDougall, John
We put our trust in Providence but kept our powder dry.

> Methodist missionary and Indian commissioner, in *Saddle, Sled and Snowshoe: Pioneering on the Saskatchewan in the Sixties* (1896).

### McElcheran, William
For the mystic what is how. For the craftsman how is what. For the artist what and how are one.

> Designer and sculptor quoted by Eric Freifeld in *Artscanada*, April-May, 1971.

### MacEwen, Gwendolyn
I write basically to communicate joy, mystery and passion . . . not the joy that naively exists with knowledge of pain but that joy which rises out of and conquers pain. I want to construct myths.

> Quoted by Merle Shain in *Chatelaine*, October, 1972.

### McEwen, Tom
These Royal Commissions we have and you hear so much about: It's like someone sitting on a toilet seat. There's a loud report and then it's dropped.

> Observation made in a Vancouver address in the 1950s by a veteran leader of the Communist party and columnist for *The Pacific Tribune*.

### MacFarlane, John   See Bruce Kidd.

### McFarlane, Leslie
Hell, even a ghost has some pride.

> Under contract and using the pseudonym Franklin W. Dixon, the Toronto writer Leslie McFarlane wrote the first sixteen Hardy Boy books, beginning the famous series with *The Tower Treasure* (1926). The remark above is his reaction to the knowledge that the books were not only being updated but also simplified in the 1960s. Quoted by Robert Stall in *Weekend Magazine*, December 15, 1973.

### McFee, Allan   See Max Ferguson.

### McGeachy, J.B.
What is the price of being Canadian? The simplest answer is $10; that is what it costs an Italian or a German to be nationalized here. For the native-born, Canadian nationality is free of charge—a bargain, surely.

*

I shall now read Mark Twain, Stephen Leacock or someone else who wrote sense and possibly listen to some music by Mozart. I am sick of the merchants of doom and dreariness. I have come to the conclusion that the tragic view of life is for six-year-olds and I am getting past the age.

> *A Touch of McGeachy: A Collection of the Best from the Pen of J.B. McGeachy* (1962). "Hamish" McGeachy, the popular columnist and broadcaster, has been quoted by Robert Catherwood in *The Financial Post*, August 5, 1967, as saying:

We sing about the North but live as far south as possible.

## McGee, Thomas D'Arcy

In the articles of paper, ink and type; and in the whole book trade, the reciprocity is all on one side. The Americans have an advantage in this market, of from fifteen to twenty percent over the resident capitalists who might be disposed to embark or who are embarked, in their production. The consequence is the Montreal and Toronto houses are mere agencies for New York publishers, having no literary wares to exchange with Harper, or Putnam, or the Sadliers, or Appleton. Economically, this is an evil; intellectually, it is treason to ourselves. If the design is to Massachusettize the Canadian mind, this is the very way to effect that end: if, on the other hand, we desire to see a Canadian nationality freely developed, borrowing energy from the American, grace from the Frenchman, and power from the Briton, we cannot too soon begin to construct a Grand Trunk of thought, which will be as a backbone to the system we desire to inaugurate. [*New Era*, July 25, 1857]

We should be liberal with the liberal, firm with the hostile, not to be outdone in courtesy by any, and be just to all. [To the Catholics of Canada, June 12, 1858]

I conclude, Sir, as I began, by entreating the House to believe that I have spoken without respect of persons, and with a sole single desire for the increase, prosperity, freedom, and honour of this incipient Northern nation. I call it a Northern nation—for such it must become if all of us do but do our duty to the last.

*

I look to the future of my adopted country with hope, though not without anxiety; I see in the not remote distance, one great nationality bound, like the shield of Achilles, by the blue rim of ocean—I see it quartered into many communities—each disposing of its internal affairs—but all bound together by free institutions, free intercourse, and free commerce; I see within the ground of that shield, the peaks of the Western mountains and the crests of the Eastern waves—the winding Assiniboine, the five-fold lakes, the St. Lawrence, the Ottawa, the Saguenay, the St. John, and the Basin of Minas—by all these flowing waters, in all the valleys they fertilise, in all the cities they visit in their courses, I see a generation of industrious, contented, moral men, free in name and in fact, men capable of maintaining, in peace and in war, a Constitution worthy of such a country. [The hon. gentleman resumed his seat amidst loud and general applause] ["Constitutional Difficulties between Upper and Lower Canada," House of Assembly, Quebec, May 2, 1860]

*

It is possible, I wish I could say it is probable, that the evil may cure itself through internal purgation; but Canadian vigilance must sleep no more except upon its arms. ["Canadian Defences," House of Assembly, Quebec, March 27, 1862]

*

Whenever there was a hair to split the hon. member [Mr. Dunkin] never failed to have his razor at hand. ["Representation by Population," House of Assembly, Quebec, April 1, 1862; McGee is chiding Christopher Dunkin, a fellow M.L.A., who was the ablest critic of Confederation and the author of the Canada Temperance Act of 1864 (called the "Dunkin Act")]

*

I do not believe that it is our destiny to be engulphed into a Republican union, renovated and inflamed with the wine of victory, of which she now drinks so freely—it seems to me we have theatre enough under our feet to act another and worthier part; we can hardly join the Americans on our own terms, and we never ought to join them on theirs. A Canadian nationality, not French-Canadian, nor British-Canadian, nor Irish-Canadian—patriotism rejects the prefix —is, in my opinion, what we should look forward to,—that is what we ought to labour for, that is what we ought to be prepared to defend to the death . . . [we should] cultivate that true catholicity of spirit which embraces all creeds, all classes, and all races, in order to make our boundless Province, so rich in known and unknown resources, a great new Northern nation. ["American Relations and Canadian Duties," an address before the Irish Protestant Benevolent Society of Quebec, May 10, 1862]

*

Let it be the mad desire of others in Europe and America to lay waste populous places; let it be our better ambition to populate waste places. ["Emigration and Colonisation," House of Assembly, Quebec, April 25, 1862]

*

Rest assured, if we remain long as fragments, we shall be lost; but let us be united, and we shall be as a rock which, unmoved itself, flings back the waves that may be dashed upon it by the storm.

*

Who will oppose—who are now opposed to the union? Only those who have a vested interest in their own insignificance. ["Prospects of the Union," Halifax address, August 14, 1864]

*

If we are to succeed in forming a new Confederation of the North, in establishing a free and united Monarchy upon the basis of these separated Provinces, we shall only do so by being just to all men, of every origin, speech, and creed, who may desire to come amongst us, to aid in that great work. ["The Germans in Canada," Address to the German Society of Montreal, December 7, 1864]

*

"For bright, and fierce, and fickle is the South;
But dark, and true, and tender is the North." [These lines are quoted without attribution in McGee's speech at Cookshire, County of Compton, December 22, 1864]

*Speeches and Addresses Chiefly on the Subject of British-American Union* (1865).

We have here no traditions and ancient venerable institutions; here, there are no aristocratic elements hallowed by time or bright deeds; here, every man is the first settler of the land, or removed from the first settler one or two generations at the furthest; here, we have no architectural monuments calling up old associations; here, we have none of those old popular legends and stories which in other countries have exercised a powerful share in the government; here, every man is the son of his own works.

*

We have no aristocracy but of virtue and talent, which is the only true aristocracy, and is the old and true meaning of the term.

*

I will content myself, Mr. Speaker, with those principle motives to Union; first, that we are in the rapids, and must go on; next that our neighbours will not, on their side, let us rest supinely, even if we could do so from other causes; and thirdly, that by making the united colonies more valuable as an ally to Great Britain, we shall strengthen rather than weaken the Imperial connexion.

*

My hon. friend, the member for Hochelaga, though he did a very clever thing the other evening when he disentombed an old newspaper article of mine, entitled "A New Nationality," and endeavoured to fix on me the paternity of the phrase—destined to become prophetic—which was employed by a very distinguished personage in the Speech from the Throne at the opening of the session. I do not happen to remember the article alluded to as one of my first essays in political writing in Canada; but I am quite sure that the almost forgotten publication in which it appeared was never known, even by name, to the illustrious person who delivered the speech on that occasion.

*

Events stronger than advocacy, events stronger than men, have come in at last like the fire behind the invisible writing to bring out the truth of these writings and to impress them upon the mind of every thoughtful man who has considered the position and probable future of these scattered provinces.

*

The acquisition of Canada was the first

ambition of the American Confederacy, and never ceased to be so, when her troops were a handful and her navy scarce a squadron. Is it likely to be stopped now, when she counts her guns afloat by thousands and her troops by hundreds of thousands?

One individual chooses Tuponia and another Hochelaga, as a suitable name for the new nationality. Now I would ask any hon. member of this House how he would feel if he woke up some fine morning and found himself, instead of a Canadian, a Tuponian or a Hochelagander. I think, sir, we may safely leave for the present the discussion of the name as well as the origin of the new system proposed. . . .

> Address to the Legislative Assembly, Quebec, February 9, 1865. *Parliamentary Debates on the Subject of the Confederation of the British North American Provinces, 3rd Session, 8th Provincial Parliament of Canada* (1865). Apparently McGee coined the expression "a new nationality" in an article he wrote, about 1857, when he arrived in Montreal and founded *New Era*. Lord Monck used the phrase in the Confederation debates in 1865 and, two years later, as governor general, included it in the speech from the throne. See Lord Monck.

Prince Edward Island will have to come in, for if she does not we will have to tow her into the St. Lawrence. [Attributed, in 1865, when P.E.I. was anti-Confederation]

Never yet did the assassin's knife reach the core of a cause or the heart of a principle. [Montreal address on the death of Lincoln, 1865]

To the American citizen who boasts of greater liberty in the States, I say that a man can state his private, social, political and religious opinions with more freedom here than in New York or New England. There is, besides, far more liberty and toleration enjoyed by minorities in Canada than in the United States. I would rather be a serf of a Russian Boyar than of that many-headed mon-

ster, public opinion, that will not permit me to have my own private opinions on subjects social, religious, national and political.

> "The New Nation and the Old Empire," *The Montreal Gazette*, December 9, 1865.

In the seaport of Saint Malo, 'twas a
　　smiling morn, in May,
When the Commodore Jacques Cartier
　　to the westward sail'd away;
In the crowded old cathedral all the
　　town were on their knees,
For the safe return of kinsmen from the
　　undiscovered seas;
And every autumn blast that swept o'er
　　pinnacle and pier,
Fill'd manly hearts with sorrow and
　　gentle hearts with fear.

> This is the first of seven stirring stanzas of "Jacques Cartier," one of a dozen verses McGee wrote on Canadian historical themes. *The Poems of Thomas D'Arcy McGee: With Copious Notes* (1869), edited by Mrs. J. Sadlier.

I'd rather turn one simple verse
　　True to the Gaelic ear,
Than classic odes I might rehearse
　　With Senates list'ning near.

> This little verse appears on the title page of *The Poems of Thomas D'Arcy McGee: With Copious Notes* (1869), edited by Mrs. J. Sadlier.

Good morning. It is morning now.

> "And those words were remembered as his last," according to T.P. Slattery in *The Assassination of D'Arcy McGee* (1968). McGee was correcting someone who had called out, "Good night, Mr. McGee," for it was two-thirty, Tuesday morning, April 7, 1868, and within minutes he was shot dead at 71 Sparks St., Ottawa.
>
> See also the Rev. Mr. Kemp and Rudyard Kipling.

### McGeer, Gerry

You see, we have bullets for you but we haven't bread.

> The mayor of Vancouver to delegates of the striking Relief Camp Workers Un-

ion in an allusion to Ottawa's offer of militia instead of relief. Attributed to the outspoken mayor by Arthur "Slim" Evans in his interview with R.B. Bennett, June 22, 1935. Reproduced by Victor Hoar in his edition of *Recollections of the On to Ottawa Trek: Documents Related to the Vancouver Strike and the On to Ottawa Trek* (1973), by Ronald Liversedge.

Now what in Sam Hill would I do with a mace?

When the lord mayor of London visited Vancouver in 1936, he presented the Vancouver mayor with a replica of the London mace. The exuberant McGeer made the above comment shortly after the ceremony. Quoted by Eric Nicol in *Vancouver* (1970) who comments that McGeer "doubtless recognized a mace as a shillelagh that had been to college." McGeer might not have known the mace's value, but King George VI did. Speaking at the Guildhall in London, England, June 23, 1939, after the royal visit, the king said: "Were you, my Lord Mayor, to find yourself in the city hall of Vancouver, you would see there, on the coast of the Pacific Ocean, some 6,000 miles from this Guildhall, an exact replica of the mace which, in this old city of London, is the symbol of your civic authority. The sight would stir the imagination of any man who holds high and ancient office."

It is a long way to Ottawa, but it is ten times as far from Ottawa to Vancouver.

McGeer was summoned to the Senate in 1945. Quoted by Eric Nicol in *Vancouver* (1970).

## MacGeorge, Robert Jackson
The base banner under which they fight, bears the motto, "Expediency is our GOD! RAILROADS are our politics!"

The Very Reverend Jackson MacGeorge, in an editorial in *The Streetsville Weekly Review*, November 25, 1854, is referring to Canadian newspapers. This is sometimes cited as the origin of Sir Allan MacNab's motto "Railroads are my politics." See also Sir Allan MacNab.

## McGillen, Pete
You can't plough a field by turning it over in your mind.

*

If you're too busy to go fishing, you're too busy.

"Outdoors with Pete McGillen" appeared regularly in *The Toronto Telegram* during the 1950s and 1960s.

## McGillivray, Duncan
It is then our luxuries that attract them to the Fort and make us so necessary to their happiness. The love of Rum is their first inducement to industry; they undergo every hardship and fatigue to procure a Skinfull of this delicious beverage, and when a Nation becomes addicted to drinking, it affords a strong presumption that they will soon become excellent hunters.

*The Journal of Duncan M'Gillivray of the North West Company at Fort George on the Saskatchewan, 1794-5* (1929), edited by A.S. Morton.

## McGoun, Lachlan
Tramp, tramp, tramp our boys are
    marching,
Cheer up, let the Fenians come!
For beneath the Union Jack we'll drive
    the rabble back,
And we'll fight for our belov'd Canadian
    home.

It is possible the familiar marching song, so popular during the American Civil War, "Tramp! Tramp! Tramp!," was composed by a Scottish-born house painter living in Napanee while serving with the artillery during the Fenian raids of 1866. *The Oxford Companion to American Literature* (Fourth Edition, 1965) credits the words and music to George Frederick Scott, an American composer best known for the marching song of the Northern troops "Battle Cry of Freedom," and Albert E. Wier in *Songs the Whole World Sings* (1915) attributes the lyrics sung in the United States to George F. Root.

Lachlan McGoun's authorship is claimed by C.C. James in *A Bibliography of Canadian Poetry* (1899), although James reproduces no Canadian version of the lyrics. Without mentioning Mc-Goun, Edith Fowke writes in "Folk Tales and Folk Songs" in *Literary History of Canada: Canadian Literature in English* (1965), edited by Carl F. Klinck: "The Fenian raids of 1866 produced a Canadian parody of 'Tramp, Tramp, Tramp, the Boys are Marching'—a song which later Canadian soldiers adapted for use in the Saskatchewan Rebellion, the Boer War, and World War I." The "Canadian Militia Song" reproduced above appears in *The Canadian Mosaic: The Making of a Northern Nation* (1938), by John Murray Gibbon. See also Anonymous: Martial Airs.

## McGrath, P.T.

But at the present time our country [Newfoundland] is too prosperous, our people are too contented, the outlook is too promising, for us to consider any proposal for union on the part of the Dominion, even if the Dominion were disposed at this time to make one.

> "Why Newfoundland Has Not Entered Confederation," December 8, 1913, *Addresses Delivered before the Canadian Club of Toronto: Season of 1913-14* (1914).

## Machar, Agnes Maule

From Nova Scotia's misty coast to far
    Columbia's shore,
She wakes,—a band of scattered homes
    and colonies no more,
But a young nation, with her life full
    beating in her breast,
A noble future in her eyes—the Britain
    of the West.

      \*

A light among the nations, till nations
are no more.

> "Dominion Day," *Canadian Poems and Lays: Selections of Native Verse, Reflecting the Seasons, Legends, and Life of the Dominion* (1893), edited by W.D. Lighthall.

## McInnes, Graham

Montreal was exotic and Gallic; Quebec was history; Winnipeg was brash and vigorous; Vancouver had the scenery.

But Toronto, Toronto the Good, Hogtown, Babylon-on-the-Humber, what did it have?

Well, I thought it had quite a lot.

> Graham McInnes, the son of Angela Thirkell, the novelist, settled in Toronto in the mid-1930s. *Finding a Father* (1967).

## MacInnes, Tom

The Sun would gain nothing in beauty by appearing but once a year. ["Somewhat Concerning Ballades"]

      \*

Last night in a land of triangles,
  I lay in a cubicle where
A girl in pyjamas and bangles
  Slept with her hands in my hair.

> Last stanza of "Zalinka," *Complete Poems of Tom MacInnes* (1923).

The Divine that can be divined is not the Eternal Divine!

> *Chinook Days* (1926).

Life is a killing experience.

> *The Teachings of the Old Boy* (1927).

## McInnis, Edgar

This sound sense of the possible.

> The essence of the Canadian spirit which seeks "moderation" and "co-operation" to enable Canada to "surmount each successive crisis," according to the historian in *Canada: A Political and Social History* (1947).

## MacInnis, Joseph B.

Underwater man and spaceman are the closest of kin—two frontiersmen exploring two dimensions.

> The "aquanaut" was quoted in 1973.

## McIntyre, James

We have seen thee, queen of cheese,
Lying quietly at your ease,
Gently fanned by evening breeze,
Thy fair form no flies dare seize.

      \*

Cows numerous as a swarm of bees,
Or as the leaves upon the trees,
It did require to make thee please,
And stand unrivalled, queen of cheese.

*

We'rt thou suspended from balloon,
You'd cast a shade even at noon,
Folks would think it was the moon
About to fall and crush them soon.

These stanzas form part of "Ode on the Mammoth Cheese" written by James McIntyre, an Ingersoll coffin-maker and poetaster, to celebrate a mammoth round of cheese weighing over seven thousand pounds, the largest ever moulded by man. The "Ode" first appeared in McIntyre's *Musings on the Banks of the Canadian Thames* (1884). The full story of "the Cheese Poet" is told by William Arthur Deacon in *The Four Jameses* (1927).

## Mackay, J.
Now, having sung Canadian woods and vales,
Its Summer's heat, and Winter's frigid gales,
Let me remark, as climates I compare,
And manners note, 'tis Britain I prefer.
Dear isle! where temp'rate years their empire hold,
Free from extremes of ardent heat or cold.

*Quebec Hill; or, Canadian Scenery: A Poem in Two Parts* (1797).

## Mackay, L.A.
Ontario's such a respectable place;
Drinking's no crime, but it's still a disgrace,
So hide us away behind curtain and screen
While we stealthily go through the motions obscene
In a manner genteel, correctly genteel,
Secret and stuffy, but always genteel.

"Frankie Went Down to the Corner" (1936), *The Ill-Tempered Lover and Other Poems* (1948).

## McKenna, Siobhan
I was aware of the lace curtains parting as I walked down the street. Finally, I decided to give them something to stare at. One day I climbed the telephone pole back of my house and just sat there so that lots of them could see me all at once.

The Irish actress recalling her first visit to Stratford to perform at the Festival in the 1950s. Quoted by William French in "Stratford on Avon—Canada!" in *In Search of Canada* (1971), by the editors of *Reader's Digest*.

## Mackenzie, Sir Alexander
The discovery of a passage by sea, North-East or North-West from the Atlantic to the Pacific Ocean, has for many years excited the attention of governments, and encouraged the enterprising spirit of individuals. The non-existence, however, of any such practical passage being at length determined, the practicability of a passage through the continents of Asia and America becomes an object of consideration. . . . The non-existence of a practicable passage by sea, and the existence of one through the continent, are clearly proved; and it requires only the countenance and support of the British Government, to increase in a very ample proportion this national advantage, and secure the trade of that country to its subjects.

*

These Indians were of a different tribe from those which I had already seen, as our guide did not understand their language. I now mixed up some vermilion in melted grease, and inscribed, in large characters, on the South-East face of the rock on which we had slept last night, this brief memorial—"Alexander Mackenzie, from Canada, by land, the twenty-second of July, one thousand seven hundred and ninety-three."

*Voyages from Montreal on the River St. Laurence, through the Continent of North America, to the Frozen and Pacific Oceans* (1801). The text is taken from *The Journals and Letters of Sir Alexander Mackenzie* (1970), edited by W. Kaye Lamb, who writes: "In 1926 the Historic Sites and Monuments Board erected a monument and tablet to mark the terminus of Mackenzie's journey and this famous inscription was carved in the rock and filled with red cement." The rock is on the shore of Dean Channel, Bella Coola River, British Columbia. Mackenzie was the first explorer to cross the American continent north of Mexico.

"Perhaps the greatest stylistic achievement of all is Alexander Mackenzie's, and not written with ink or inscribed on paper," explained the poet and literary critic A.J.M. Smith in *The Book of Canadian Prose: Early Beginnings to Confederation* (1965). "It was then that Mackenzie achieved his greatest stylistic success, a success inseparably bound up with his heroic exploit. It is a single sentence of monumental grandeur. . . ."

## Mackenzie, Alexander

Let that be the terminus of the Pacific Railway.

"With him nothing was impossible. He laid his finger on the map of British Columbia one day, and finding that it rested immediately on the spot marked Vancouver Island, he said, let that be the terminus of the Pacific Railway. What were mountain ranges or seas of mountains to him? It was an easy matter to promise. It was easy to send a thousand engineers into the field! It was easy to fill the mountains with theodolites and surveyors' chains! It suited him for the moment to make a promise, and a promise was accordingly made." George Stewart in *Canada under the Administration of the Earl of Dufferin* (1878).

Loyalty to the Queen does not require a man to bow down to her manservant, or her maidservant—or her ass.

Quoted by Gordon Donaldson in "Plain Sandy" in *Fifteen Men: Canada's Prime Ministers from Macdonald to Trudeau* (1969). Mackenzie was prime minister from 1873 to 1878.

## MacKenzie, Gisèle

I don't feel that I'm far from home when I'm in the United States.

*The Toronto Telegram*, August 17, 1957. The once-popular singer was born Gisèle LaFleche in Winnipeg.

## Mackenzie, Dr. Norman

They're hanging crepe at Malton and ringing their bells at Boeing.

At the cancellation of the AVRO "Arrow," February 20, 1959. Quoted by James M. Minifie in *Peacemaker or Powder-Monkey: Canada's Role in a Revolutionary World* (1960).

## McKenzie, R. Tait

Supervised and progressive physical education, largely by athletic sports, is an essential part of an educational system from infancy to maturity. It has an educational value nothing can supplant.

Address to the International Conference on Education and Citizenship, Montreal, 1926. The noted educator and sculptor was quoted in the *Carnegie Foundation Bulletin* (1926).

## Mackenzie, Sir William

Why don't you get one of those newfangled things called a motion picture camera?

Casual remark made to Robert Flaherty, about 1915, which led to the filming of *Nanook of the North* (1920). Quoted by Arthur Calder-Marshall in *The Innocent Eye: The Life of Robert J. Flaherty* (1963). See also Robert Flaherty.

The best way to conserve national resources is to develop them.

Remark made by the railroad builder before his death in 1923, quoted by Augustus Bridle in *Sons of Canada: Short Studies of Characteristic Canadians* (1916).

## Mackenzie, William Lyon

We are afraid that the time has not yet come, in which colonial periodicals strictly literary can command encouragement commensurate to the expense of their publication and to what is due to their compilers.

*

Montreal ought to become at no late date the Boston of the colonies.

*

So let it be with British America—let every national distinction cease from among us—let not the native Canadian look upon his Irish or Scottish neighbour as an intruder, nor the native of the British Isles taunt the other about stupidity and incapacity. Rather let them become as one race, and may the only strife among us be a praiseworthy emulation as to who shall attain the honour of conferring the greatest benefits on the country of our birth—or the land of our choice. [*The Colonial Advocate*, March 30, 1826]

\*

There are those doubtless who fear the ignorance of the people of Upper Canada; I, on the other hand, stand more in dread of rulers like ours who are virtually independent of them. The people have an interest in good government, but the rulers have a gain by misrule. ["To the People of York County," *The Colonial Advocate*, July 14, 1831]

\*

Be that as it may, I have no intention of again changing my lodgings. I am here on what I believe to be a good, honourable, and proper errand; and if it pleases the Creator to cut me or mine off, while in what we consider the way of duty, we can bear in mind that he is able to raise up other fit and proper persons to fulfil his wise purposes. Here then we are, *in the House with the Cholera*, and not dismayed. ["Cholera in London," *The Colonial Advocate*, September 13, 1832]

\*

I have probably talked too much politics in my letters, but it should be remembered by the reader that politics is the science which teaches the people of a country to care for each other. If a mischievous individual were to attempt to cut off his neighbour's hand, would that neighbour's other hand and feet do well quietly to permit the amputation of the limb if they could hinder it? All will say, No. This then is politics. That part of our duty which teaches us to study the welfare of our whole country, and not to rest satisfied altho' our own household is well off when our neighbours are in difficulty and danger. The honest politician is he who gives all he can of his time and means to promote the public good, whose charity begins at home *but does not end there*. The man who says he is no politician, is either

ignorant of what he is saying, or a contemptible selfish creature, unworthy of the country or community of which he is a part. ["Dundee and Aberdeen," *The Colonial Advocate*, June 27, 1833]

These are from Mackenzie's newspaper *The Colonial Advocate*, reproduced by Margaret Fairley in her edition of *The Selected Writings of William Lyon Mackenzie: 1824-1837* (1960). See also: Joseph Hume, John Langton, Dennis Lee, Matthew Lount.

### Mackey, Joseph
JOE—THREE DEAD.

Captain Joseph Mackey's plane crashed in the wastes of Newfoundland, taking the lives of his three passengers. One of these was the Nobel Prize winner Dr. Frederick Banting, who died of injuries on February 21, 1941. Wounded and dazed, the pilot tramped this three-word message in the snow to alert the search planes. "Despite my almost hysterical condition," he later explained, "I realized they didn't know the truth. So I tramped out my name in big fifty-foot letters in the snow. 'Joe,' I wrote. Then 'three dead.' " Quoted by Lloyd Stevenson in *Sir Frederick Banting* (1946). See also Sir Frederick Banting.

### McKiernan, Charles    See Joe Beef.

### McKinney, Louise
See Anonymous: Some Documents.

### McKinnon, Catherine
I'm a singer, not a star. I'm a person.

Quoted by Melinda McCracken in *The Globe and Mail*, October 25, 1969.

### MacKinnon, Frank
I've always felt the reason we are so unemotional about our beginning is that Confederation was a constitutional development, and not the result of a popular revolution. If we had only hated George III it might have been different.

Former president of the University of Prince Edward Island quoted by Gerald Clark in *Canada: The Uneasy Neighbour* (1965).

## Mackintosh, Alexander

Dec. 27th—Gave the men 3½ gallons Rum for a Dance.

Dec. 28th—No Duty perform'd by the men this Day.

Alexander Mackintosh, sailing master of *The Nancy of Moy*, a fur-trade vessel on the Great Lakes turned into a man-of-war during the War of 1812, made these entries in his log for 1813. C.H.J. Snider, *Leaves from the War Log of The Nancy* (1936).

## Macklem, Michael

In the East one travels in time. One measures distances not in miles but in years. . . . In the West all dimensions are spatial. There is no past. Everything happens now. Distance is of the essence of one's experience.

"A Book a Mile," *The Tamarack Review*, No. 55, 1970.

## McKnight, West

This is Canada calling!

Characteristic greeting in World War II broadcasts to Europe. "An Overseas Hockey Broadcast," February 17, 1945, *A Pocketful of Canada* (1946), edited by John D. Robins.

## MacLachlan, Alexander

We live in a rickety house,
In a dirty dismal street,
Where the naked hide from day,
And the thieves and drunkards meet.

First stanza of "We Live in a Rickety House."

\*

The Anglo-Saxon leads the van,
And never lags behind,
For was not he ordained to be
The leader of mankind?
He carries very little sail,
Makes very little show,
But gains the havens without fail,
Whatever winds may blow.

First stanza of "The Anglo-Saxon," *Poems and Songs* (1888).

\*

I love my own country and race,
Nor lightly I fled them both,

Yet who would remain in a place
Where there's too many spoons for
the broth?

From "Song."

\*

Here's to the land of forests grand,
The land where labour's free;
Let others roam away from home,
Be this the land for me!
For here 'tis plain the heart and brain,
The very soul, grow vaster,
Where men are free as they should be,
And Jack's as good's his master.

Final stanza of "Young Canada, or Jack's as Good's His Master," *The Emigrant, and Other Poems* (1861).

## McLachlan, J.B.

The ministers when we die tell us that we are dust, and the doctors when we are alive tell us that we are nine-tenths water. These two statements can be proved true of those who vote the Grit or Tory tickets, for their name is MUD. [*The Maritime Labour Herald*, October 21, 1921]

\*

New ideas are born in stables and brought up in jails. Whenever a new cause is struggling its way to recognition its adherents frequently have to die for it. [*The Maritime Labour Herald*, November 17, 1923]

\*

The only difference between jail and a job is that here I am separated from my wife and family. Under capitalism all the workers are in jail all the time. And lots of them haven't got the security of shelter and food that is offered in a penitentiary. [*The Maritime Labour Herald*, November 17, 1923]

\*

These years should have hammered home to your inmost soul that under capitalism the working class has but two courses to follow: crawl or fight.

Quoted by Paul MacEwan in "Labour and Politics in Cape Breton" in *The Cape Breton Highlander*, April 17, 1968.

Sorry I can't attend the funeral but I heartily approve of the event.

Telegram declining an invitation to attend the funeral of Samuel Gompers, middle-of-the-road leader of the American Federation of Labor, in 1924.

Quoted by Tom McEwen in *He Wrote for Us: The Story of Bill Bennett, Pioneer Socialist Journalist* (1951).

James Bryson McLachlan settled in Glace Bay, Cape Breton, in 1902, when he was thirty-three. The Scot exercised considerable influence as secretary of District 26, United Mine Workers of America, and as editor of *The Maritime Labour Herald*. He died in 1936 and is generally referred to today as "Big Jim" McLachlan. David A. Frank, et al., *The People's History of Cape Breton* (1971).

## McLaren, Jack
Sic transit gloria Tuesday!

*Let's All Hate Toronto* (1956).

## McLaren, Norman
Animation is not the art of drawings-that-move, but the art of movements-that-are-drawn.

Quoted by Guy L. Coté in "Animation Films in Canada," *The Journal of the British Film Academy*, Winter, 1956-57.

The purpose of my films is to give the intellect a rest.

"Eye Hears, Ear Sees," CBC-TV, Winter, 1971.

## McLarnin, Jimmy
I never had to be told that wine, women and song would ruin a boxer. I earlier had it drummed into me that they could ruin anybody.

Quoted by Trent Frayne in *Great Canadian Sports Stories* (1967).

You know the secret of fighting? Don't get hit. I fought twenty years and I never would have lasted otherwise.

World welterweight boxing champion who at the age of twenty-nine retired to Vancouver with fame and fortune. Quoted by Jim Kernaghan in *The Toronto Star*, November 6, 1973.

## McLaughlin, John J.
Canada Dry: The Champagne of Ginger Ales.

\*

DOWN FROM CANADA CAME TALES OF A WONDERFUL BEVERAGE

The world's best-selling ginger ale was first prepared in 1890 by John J. McLaughlin, an Oshawa pharmacist whose brother was Sam McLaughlin. The soft drink was originally called "McLaughlin's Pale Dry Ginger Ale" and was popular across Canada because, unlike most carbonated drinks, this one was dry instead of sweet. In 1904, the name was changed to "Canada Dry," and its present popularity dates from 1923 when "The Champagne of Ginger Ales" was introduced to prohibition-dry American drinkers with a full-page advertisement announcing its arrival in *The New York Times*.

## McLaughlin, Robert
An automobile of the latest design
Its use I will never disparage.
But for comfort and pleasure pray give me for mine
A McLaughlin reliable carriage.

From an advertisement for the McLaughlin Carriage Co., Oshawa, 1905.

\*

One Grade Only and that the Best.

Motto of the McLaughlin Carriage Co. "Robert McLaughlin and his sons built a quarter of a million carriages," explained Ken Lefolii in *The Canadian Look: A Century of Sights and Styles* (1965). The slogan was first used about 1895.

## McLaughlin, Colonel Robert Samuel
I have often wondered why some cars succeeded and some failed. One of the strangest facts about the automobile business in North America is that in its fifty-odd years no fewer than 2,400 different makers have manufactured and offered cars for sale; in each case the designers and engineers put the best they knew into the car; each was launched with high hopes—and today you can count on the fingers of two hands the car manufacturers who have survived.

"How the Auto Beat the Horse" by Sam

McLaughlin as told to Eric Hutton in *Maclean's Canada: Portrait of a Country* (1960), edited by Leslie F. Hannon.

The McLaughlins used to joke that, "Sam has wheels in his head." It turned out to be more than a joke, for I was five years old at the time and now at one hundred years old, I am still alive in the making of things that run on wheels, as chairman of the board of General Motors of Canada, which is the direct descendant of the two-vehicle shop my father founded in the year of Canada's Confederation.

"My First Century on Wheels," *Weekend Magazine*, November 13, 1971.

**McLean, George**   See Walking Buffalo.

**McLean, J.S.**
The ordinary man strives to get here and when he falls short of it says, "Gee! I nearly made it." The outstanding man, when he falls just short of it, says, "Hell! Missed it again!"

\*

It is much easier to make money than it is to use it wisely.

James Stanley McLean founded Canada Packers in 1927. Quoted by Douglas Dacre in "The Butcher with a Poet's Soul," *Maclean's Magazine*, October 1, 1951.

**McLean, John**
The name Canada has been variously interpreted. It has been derived from the Cree word Kanâta or Kanâtan, "something which is very neat or clean."

*Canadian Savage Folk: The Native Tribes of Canada* (1896).

**MacLean, Colonel John Bayne**
The reward of work well done is more work.

A favourite maxim of the founder of the Maclean-Hunter Publishing Company. Quoted by Floyd S. Chalmers in *A Gentleman of the Press* (1969). See also Baroness Orczy and Francis Yeats-Brown.

**Maclean, John Philip**
Politics is man's best game, next to war.

*Backroom Boys and Girls* (1973).

**McLean, Ross**
It is the sort of musical that sends the audience home humming the National Anthem.

TV producer on a poor musical comedy, quoted by Clyde Gilmour in *The Toronto Star*, March 17, 1973.

**MacLellan, Gene**
I want to be a person, not a conglomerate.

Prince Edward Island-born songwriter, *The Toronto Star*, June 13, 1972.

**MacLennan, Hugh**
Then, even as the two race-legends woke again remembering ancient enmities, there woke with them also the felt knowledge that together they had fought and survived one great war they had never made, and that now they had entered another; that for nearly a hundred years the nation had been spread out on the top half of the continent over the powerhouse of the United States and still was there; that even if the legends were like oil and alcohol in the same bottle, the bottle had not broken yet. And, almost grudgingly, out of the instinct to do what was necessary, the country took the first irrevocable steps towards becoming herself, knowing against her will that she was not unique but like all the others, alone with history, with science, and the future.

*Two Solitudes* (1945).

Montreal and Canada of only yesterday. And it was out of this cold situation, which became suddenly hot during the Hitler war, that my conception of *Two Solitudes* emerged. Its genesis came in a dream in which I saw a tall, angular blond man arguing noisily with a stocky, darker man. They were shouting at each other in fury and a voice in the dream said to me, "Don't you see it? They're both deaf."

I did not, of course, "invent" the phrase "two solitudes." It comes from a sentence of Rainer Maria Rilke and I still think it is one of the supreme poetic utterances of our century, though actually it was a line of prose in a letter to a friend. . . . "Love consists in this, that two solitudes protect and touch and greet each other." Surely the best practical definition of love ever uttered, whether applied to individuals or to two nations sharing a single state.

> "Two Solitudes that Meet and Greet in Hope and Hate," *Maclean's Magazine*, August, 1971. See also Rainer Maria Rilke.

I'd like to see this country get stirred up about something to find out what goes on underneath.

> *The Precipice* (1948).

Were it not for the United States, Canada would never have been a nation at all, much less the kind she is. ["The Canadian Character"]

*

One good native playwright, working on our radio, would be worth more to this country than a hundred tons of government pamphlets, or a hundred miles of useless road built into the bush before a general election. ["The Tyranny of the Sunday Suit"]

> *Cross-Country* (1949).

If cities have gender, then Montreal, the second-largest French speaking city in the world, is masculine in every one of the innumerable ways in which a self-confident and self-satisfied man can display his maleness. ["City of Two Souls"]

*

The winds of Nova Scotia are still austere and the glacier-scraped headlands of Halifax harbour are stained with red when the tide is out and the sun is low. But I no longer fear that the Homeric beauty of that lovely province will frame the graveyard of a vanished race. ["Husband and Wife"]

> *Thirty and Three* (1954), edited by Dorothy Duncan.

Boy Meets Girl in Winnipeg and Who Cares? [Essay title]

*

Our technology is more lovable than the Russian technology, and in the end it is bound to prevail. We are only beginning. We have just reached the outer fringes of the Solar System. Can any sane man possibly argue that we should stop there? ["Remembrance Day, 2010 A.D."]

> *Scotchman's Return and Other Essays* (1960).

Modern Canadian life has not grown out of us; it has been imposed on us by technology. That may be why the nation seems almost to have out-travelled its own soul. That may be why, for most of us, Canadian history has not so much become a dead thing as an unknown thing.

*

Is it possible for so few people to meet the challenge of this vastness and mystery, of this variety of the land where we live because the network of its rivers enabled a handful of explorers to claim it for us? . . . For surely it is true that so long as the fate of a person or a nation is still in doubt, that person or nation is alive and real. It is only of the dead that no questions are asked.

> *Seven Rivers of Canada* (1961).

This land is far more important than we are. To know it is to be young and ancient all at once.

> *The Colour of Canada* (1967).

In the early October of that year, in the cathedral hush of a Quebec Indian summer with the lake drawing into its mirror the fire of the maples, it came to me that to be able to love the mystery surrounding us is the final and only sanction of human existence.

> *The Watch That Ends the Night* (1961).

The essence of being in your twenties in the Thirties was that no matter how well tuned up you were, you stayed on the ground, or just above it, for ten years.

> "What It Was Like to Be in Your Twenties in the Thirties," *The Great Depres-*

sion: *Essays and Memoirs from Canada and the United States* (1969), edited by Victor Hoar.

**Macleod, James**  See Jerry Potts.

**McLuhan, Marshall**
The new electronic independence recreates the world in the image of a global village.

\*

Schizophrenia may be a necessary consequence of literacy.

\*

Nobody ever made a grammatical error in a non-literate society.

*The Gutenberg Galaxy: The Making of Typographical Man* (1962).

The medium is the message.

"Two independent sources confirm that McLuhan first made this remark at Dr. Alan Thomas's home in Vancouver, July 30, 1959. The occasion was a small reception which he gave following a symposium at U.B.C. on the subject of music and the mass media." E.S. Hallman, CBC, March 16, 1973. This seminal remark first appeared in book form in *Understanding Media* (1964). McLuhan toyed with the observation in the title of *The Medium Is the Massage* (1967), and tinkered with it in *Counterblast* (1969), where he wrote: "The medium is the mess-age."

In a culture like ours, long accustomed to splitting and dividing all things as a means of control, it is sometimes a bit of a shock to be reminded that, in operational and practical fact, the medium is the message. This is merely to say that the personal and social consequences of any medium—that is, of any extension of ourselves—result from the new scale that is introduced into our affairs from each extension of ourselves, or by any new technology.

\*

"The Medium is the Message" because it is the medium that shapes and controls the scale and form of human association and action.

\*

Cubism, by seizing on instant total awareness, suddenly announced that *the medium is the message*. Is it not evident that the moment that sequence yields to the simultaneous, one is in the world of the structure and of configuration?

\*

Money: The Poor Man's Credit Card.

*Understanding Media: The Extensions of Man* (1964).

The young today live mythically and in depth.

\*

Art is anything you can get away with.

\*

Environments are not passive wrappings, but are, rather, active processes which are invisible.

*The Medium Is the Massage: An Inventory of Effects* (1967), with Quentin Fiore.

Canada has no identity and never has had an identity. Any sense of identity we have is our sense of density. So far we have had the advantage of dabbling in identities.

\*

Canada is a Distant Early Warning System for the American experience.

\*

Canada is the only country in the world that knows how to live without an identity.

\*

You can be a French Canadian or an English Canadian but not a "Canadian." We know how to live without an identity, and this is one of our marvellous resources.

"Canada: A Borderline Case," CBC Radio, May 29, 1967.

Life. Consider the alternative.

\*

One of the peculiarities of an electric technology is that it speeds up this process of transformation. Instant and total rehearsal of all pasts and all processes enables us to perceive the function of such perpetual returns as one of purgation and purification, translating the entire world into a work of art.

\*

Help Beautify Junkyards
Throw Something Lovely Away To-Day!

Help Satisfy Our Scrap-e-tiet [Sign at a Toronto junkyard]

*War and Peace in the Global Village* (1968), with Quentin Fiore.

It is important, however, to consider the role of the arts and sciences as Early Warning Systems in the social environment. The models of perception they provide can give indispensable orientation to future problems well before they become troublesome.

\*

Since Sputnik, the planet has become a corporate art form accessible only through the involvement of all our senses at once.

\*

Sophistication is perception.

\*

Good taste is the first refuge of the noncreative. It is the last-ditch stand of the artist.

\*

A man's reach must exceed his grasp or what's a metaphor?

*Through the Vanishing Point: Space in Poetry and Painting* (1968), with Harley Parker.

What we call art would seem to be specialist artefacts for enhancing human perception.

\*

The white man creates the negro. He creates a world into which natives cannot fit.

\*

Publication is a self-invasion of privacy.

\*

The ivory tower becomes the control tower of human navigation.

*Counterblast* (1969).

My work is designed for the pragmatic purpose of trying to understand our technological environment and its psychic and social consequences. But my books constitute the *process* rather than the completed product of the discovery; my purpose is to employ facts as tentative probes, as means of insight, of pattern recognition. . . . I want to map new terrain rather than chart old landmarks.

\*

I don't like to tell people what I think is good or bad about the social and psychic changes caused by new media, but if you insist on pinning me down about my own subjective reactions as I observe the reprimitivization of our culture, I would have to say that I view such upheavals with total personal dislike and dissatisfaction. . . . As a man moulded within the literate Western tradition, I do not personally cheer the dissolution of that tradition through the electric involvement of all the senses. . . . I am not by temperament or conviction, a revolutionary; I would prefer a stable, changeless environment of modest services and human scale.

Interview, *Playboy*, March, 1969.

A cliché is an act of consciousness: total consciousness is the sum of all the clichés of all the media or technologies we probe with.

\*

The Balinese say, "We have no art, we do everything as well as possible."

\*

The more the data banks record about each one of us, the less we exist.

\*

New means create new ends as new services create new discomforts.

*From Cliché to Archetype* (1970), with Wilfred Watson.

Violence is the quest for identity. When identity disappears with technological innovation, violence is the natural recourse.

\*

At the beginning of his very flattering essay on myself in *The Pump House Gang* . . . Tom Wolfe has a drawing of me which at once suggests another title for his essays ("What if he's right?"), namely, "I'd Rather Be Wrong."

*Culture Is Our Business* (1970).

In the vortex of process there are no fixed points of view. Understanding is never a point of view.

Letter, *The Toronto Star*, March 16, 1971.

But Canada as an entity still has value as the DEW Line for the rest of the world, we have the situation of relatively small involvement in the big headaches. The Canadian has freedom of comment, a kind of playful awareness of issues, that is unknown in, say, Paris or London or New York. They take themselves too damn seriously; they have no choice. Here you have a little time to breathe, to think and to feel. It's because Canadians are protected from encountering themselves by layers of colonialism. I'm trying to alert them to the dangers of the 20th century, so they can duck out.

> "The Table Talk of Marshall McLuhan," arranged by Peter C. Newman, *Maclean's Magazine*, June, 1971.

The winner is one who knows when to *drop out* in order to get in *touch*.

*

Twenty-five hundred years of rational culture are in the process of dissolution.

*

Now we can *take today*, since at electric speed *the future of the future is the present*.

> *Take Today: The Executive as Drop-out* (1972), with Barrington Nevitt.

"MCLUHAN READS BOOKS" [Toronto graffiti, 1966]

> See also: Anthony Burgess, Barrows Mussey, A.J.M. Smith, Tom Wolfe.

**McMaster, Andrew Ross**
I say to the minister, and I say to this Government: Trust the people; the heart of the Canadian people is as sound as our No. 1 Hard Manitoba wheat.

> House of Commons, June 24, 1919.

**MacMechan, Archibald**
As soon as our cousins south of the line decide to celebrate Great-grandmothers' Day we will uncritically adopt it too.

> "Canada as a Vassal State," *Canadian Historical Review*, December, 1920. MacMechan's conclusion was: "We invent nothing."

**MacMillan, Sir Ernest**
We must listen to music, not solemnly but thoughtfully, as a language in which are embodied ideas equal to those of painting and literature, and treat the art with the respect due to one of the great revelations made to and through the human mind.

> "Problems of Music in Canada," December 20, 1937, *Addresses Delivered before the Canadian Club of Toronto: Season of 1937-38* (1938).

I am very flattered to be described as a "world figure." I am conscious of becoming a little more rotund as the years go on, but I don't know whether that has anything to do with it.

> "The Enjoyment of Music" (1951), *Empire Club of Canada: Addresses 1951-52* (1952).

**MacMillan, H.R.**
If Canada is underdeveloped, so is Brigitte Bardot. [Objecting to the inclusion of Canada on a list of underdeveloped countries at an industrial conference at Versailles, 1950s]

*

I was born in 1885, the same year as the CPR began. It has managed to do somewhat better than I. [Reflection of the wealthy British Columbia lumber magnate on his eightieth birthday in 1965]

**MacMurchy, Helen**
The mentally defective are those who cannot make, or help to make, a home.

We must make a happy and permanent home for them during their lives. The only Permanent Parent is the State.

> *The Almosts: A Study of the Feeble-Minded* (1920).

**MacMurchy, Marjory**
There are people who believe that no Christmas candle has been set to shine for them. If they can find no other coloured light for Christmas, why should they not look up and see the heaven full of stars. The winter woods are full of Christmas trees, and all December stars are Christmas stars. People who have wearied of every other kind of Christmas will find it difficult to outgrow a star.

Quoted in *Canadian Days: Selections for Every Day in the Year from the Works of Canadian Authors* (1911).

## McMurtry, John

There seems to be a strong correlation between people who relish tough football and people who relish intimidating and beating the hell out of Commies, hippies, protest marchers and other opposition groups. Watching well-advertised strong men knock other people around, make them hurt, is in the end like other tastes. It does not weaken with feeding. It grows.

"Smash Thy Neighbour," *The Atlantic Monthly*, January, 1972.

## MacNab, Sir Allan

Railroads are my politics.

This maxim, or quip, is said to date from 1853, when Sir Allan, president of the Great Western Railway, was leader of the Tory Opposition in the Legislative Assembly of Upper Canada. "Railroads are my politics" appears in an editorial in *The Streetsville Weekly Review*, November 25, 1854, where it refers to the interests of newspaper publishers. See Robert Jackson MacGeorge.

If I am supported by their voice, I shall feel that I am right. If condemned, I am ready to retire into private life,—and perhaps I am now fit for little else.

Resigning under pressure from the joint premiership of the Province of Canada, May 26, 1856. Quoted by G. Mercer Adam in *Canada's Patriot Statesman: The Life and Career of the Right Honourable Sir John A. Macdonald* (1891).

"The chieftain of the Clan MacNab emigrated to Canada with a hundred followers, and, on reaching Toronto, called on his namesake Sir Allan MacNab. He left his card, which bore the words: 'The MacNab.' Sir Allan next day returned the visit, and left *his* card. It said, simply: 'The Other MacNab.' "

*The Wit of the Scots* (1968), by Gordon Irving.

## McNamara, Robert

There is not the remotest set of circumstances, in an imaginable time-frame of the future, in which our two nations could wage war on one another. It is so unthinkable an idea as to be totally absurd.

Attributed to the U.S. secretary of Defense in 1966.

## McNaught, Carlton

Until news and news policies are removed from commercial considerations, and placed in the hands of men and women who are first of all trained reporters and editors, with a degree of economic security suitable to the dignity of their profession, the standards of news itself cannot be raised, no matter how lofty the "codes of ethics" set up by publishers or by newspaper workers themselves.

*Canada Gets the News: A Report in the International Research Series of the Institute of Pacific Relations* (1940).

## McNaught, Kenneth

If politics is the art of the possible, it should be recognized that statesmanship is the art of making things possible. . . .

*A Prophet in Politics* (1959).

## McNaughton, General A.G.L.

The Canadian Army is a dagger pointed at the heart of Berlin.

Press conference, Washington, October, 1942. McNaughton, the "Father of the Canadian Army," was then General Officer Commanding-in-Chief. Quoted by John Swettenham in *McNaughton* (1968-69), who explains that, by October 1943, when the Canadian Army was sent to Italy instead of to Germany, the "famous dagger had become more handle than blade."

The responsibility was mine and nobody else's. The final decision was mine. I said yes. And I say quite frankly that if I were in exactly the same position I would do exactly the same thing tomorrow. [The controversial and costly-in-lives Dieppe raid occurred on August 19, 1942]

The world's memory of Canadians in battle is a bright memory. The Canadians in World War I seemed to shine out of the blood and muck, the dreary panorama of trench warfare. They seemed to kill and die with a special dash of lavishness. [Observation made in 1943]

So be my passing,
My task accomplished and the long day done,
My wages taken. And in my heart
Some late lark singing.
Let me be gathered to the quiet West,
The sundown splendid and serene.

> Lines written by McNaughton at the funeral of a military friend and found among McNaughton's papers following his own death, July 11, 1966. Quoted by John Swettenham in *McNaughton* (1968-69).

## Macnaughton, S.
We doubt if any boy or girl could fail to be enthralled by tales of Braves called "Owl-Child," "Many-tailed-Feathers-round-his-neck," "Black-Evil," "All-and-a-half," "Medicine-pipe-stem," "Good-Young-Men," or even "Big-Belly."

> *My Canadian Memories* (1920).

## Macnee, Patrick
I didn't become an actor at all until Canada. I learned to act from Andrew on all those radio shows. . . .

> The British TV and film actor gained experience working under Andrew Allan of the CBC in Toronto during the 1950s. Quoted by Herbert Whittaker in *The Globe and Mail*, April 21, 1973.

## Macphail, Agnes
Do not rely completely on any other human being, however dear. We meet all life's greatest tests alone. [Address to graduates, Ottawa Ladies' College, 1924]

＊

When I hear men talk about women being the angel of the home I always, mentally at least, shrug my shoulders in doubt. I do not want to be the angel of any home; I want for myself what I want for other women, absolute equality. After that is secured then men and women can take turns at being angels. I stress that angel part, because I remem-

ber that last year an hon. member who spoke from the opposite benches called a woman an angel and in the next breath said that men were superior. They must therefore be gods. [House of Commons, February 26, 1925]

＊

Heckler: Don't you wish you were a man?
Macphail: Yes. Don't you?

> One of the best-known repostes attributed to the first woman elected to the House of Commons (1921-1940). Quoted by Margaret Stewart and Doris French in *Ask No Quarter: A Biography of Agnes Macphail* (1959).

The way to get things out of a government is to back them to the wall, put your hands to their throats, and you will get all they have.

> Address, Southern Progressive Association, Regina, 1927.

I think you and I will live to see other great changes such as social services and an enlargement of the idea of public utilities. If we can sell liquor under government supervision, why not milk? If we can have Hydro as a public utility, then we can have many other things equally necessary.

> "Out of My Experiences," March 4, 1935, *Addresses Delivered before the Canadian Club of Toronto: Season of 1934-35* (1935).

Well, I told them the truth. They say the truth shall set you free. It's certainly set me free.

> In 1940, Agnes Macphail was defeated at the polls. Quoted by Miriam Chapin in *Contemporary Canada* (1959).

## McPhail, Alexander James
Farmers are the only men who will remedy farm conditions.

> Remark made shortly before his death in 1931. Quoted by Grant MacEwan in "Wheat Pool Pilot: Alexander James McPhail," *Fifty Mighty Men* (1958).

## MacPhail, Sir Andrew
Everything a farmer does is done in his spare time.

"The Farmer," *Empire Club of Canada: Addresses Delivered to the Members During the Year 1920* (1921).

The summer fades; life is short; a settled melancholy falls upon the world.

\*

Democracy is fatal to the artist because it measures all human effort by the same human standard, and offers only the same reward.

\*

As democracy grows, liberty disappears.

"Art in Democracy," *The Dalhousie Review*, Volume IV, 1924.

Ideas are born; they develop; they are transformed; but they never die. The history of ideas is the history of the race. They are the real events.

"A History of the Idea of Evolution," *The Dalhousie Review*, Volume V, 1925.

Life is never mean when it is lived at the proper level; and there is no poverty where there is no pretence.

*The Master's Wife* (1939).

## McPherson, Aimee Semple
In the vocabulary of a Canadian, the word "can't" does not exist!

"Her whole career," wrote Lately Thomas in *The Vanishing Evangelist: The Kidnapping of Aimee McPherson* (1959), "was an exemplification of her oft-repeated slogan." The evangelist was born Aimee Elizabeth Kennedy in Ingersoll, Ontario, in 1890, and died in Oakland, California, in 1944. Her disappearance in May of 1926 caused an international scandal. Occasionally the following conundrum is encountered in southwestern Ontario, where she was born. Question: What's the difference between the Welland Canal and Aimee Semple McPherson? Answer: The Welland Canal is a busy ditch.

## Macpherson, C.B.
Possessive individualism.

*The Political Theory of Possessive Individualism: From Hobbes to Locke* (1962). "Its possessive quality is found in its conception of the individual as essentially the proprietor of his own person or capacities, owing nothing to society for them. The individual was seen neither as a moral whole, nor as part of a larger social whole, but as an owner of himself."

## Macpherson, Duncan
My first impression of the prairies is that it is one part horizon, nine parts sky.

\*

Canada, as clumsy as she is, means well.

*Macpherson's Canada* (1969).

## McPherson, Hugo
*Discretion* is surely one of the strongest and most negative virtues of the Canadian character . . . it plays a major part in robbing the scene of colour and vitality.

"Gilding the Muses: The Canada Council," *The Prospect of Change: Proposals for Canada's Future* (1965), edited by Abraham Rotstein.

An art of the people? A folk art? A high art? Film is becoming all of these. In terms of social health and mental anguish, film must help us to reconcile the disparities of the apparently pastoral long-view and the violent blow-up of modern urban life.

"Mental Health and Social Health," *Probings: A Collection of Essays Contributed to the Canadian Mental Health Association for its Golden Jubilee 1918-1968* (1968).

## Macpherson, Jay
Come all old maids that are squeamish
And afraid to make mistakes,
Don't clutter your lives up with boy-
friends,
The nicest girls marry snakes.

Last stanza of "Eurynome."

\*

Say: Wisdom is a silver fish
And love a golden hook.

Last lines of "Go Take the World," *The Boatman* (1957).

## McPhillips, A.D.
Where is the old mailed fist? Has it gone down the drain?

*

I am in sympathy with the resolution but what I say is this. Why go to work and foul our nest with a mess of pottage? We do not need it. We have got it now. Let us not take a chance.

> House of Commons, January 6, 1958. The Conservative M.P. from Victoria was speaking against Diefenbaker's proposed Bill of Rights.

## Macqueen, Thomas

If you wish to wean men from their errors, to make them better or happier, you must first try to make them rational.

> *The Bathurst Courier*, 1847.

Will *nobody* write a few songs for Canada?

> From an editorial in *The Huron Signal*, which Macqueen founded in 1848. Quoted by Henry J. Morgan in *Bibliotheca Canadensis: or A Manual of Canadian Literature* (1867).

Toryism has been the curse of the civilized world—the liberal meaning of it is to exalt and pamper a few individuals in luxuriant indolence at the expense of the sweat and toil and degradation of the great mass of industrous mankind.

> From *The Huron Signal* in 1849, quoted by Margaret Fairley in "Socialist Poet in Upper Canada," *New Frontiers*, Spring, 1955.

## McRuer, J.C.

What is termed "disrespect for law" in fact may only be the manifestation of a burning desire for justice. Order, like law, to be respected, must deserve respect. Disrespect for an order that does not deserve respect ought not to be condemned as degeneration, but commended as a healthy regeneration. What I am concerned about is that lawyers and judges too often regard "order" as a shield for the protection of privilege.

> Former chief justice of Ontario before the American Bar Association meeting, Montreal, September 5, 1966.

## MacTavish, Newton

Upon his tombstone we should engrave these words: "He saved others; himself he did not save."

> This is the essayist's tribute to "The Doctor," *Newton MacTavish's Canada: Selected Essays of Newton MacTavish* (1963).

## McWhirter, Norris and Ross

*Oldest.* The greatest authenticated age to which a human has ever lived is 113 years 124 days in the case of Pierre Joubert, a French-Canadian bootmaker. He was born in Charlesbourg, Quebec Province, Canada, on July 15, 1701, and died in Quebec on November 16, 1814. His longevity was the subject of an investigation in 1870 by Dr. Tache, Official Statistician to the Canadian Government, and the proofs published are irrefutable.

*

*Smallest.* The smallest book printed in movable type is *Short Works* by Robert G. Oliphant of Victoria, B.C., Canada, with 28 pages 11/16 x ⅜ of an inch (area 0.258 of a square inch) and printed in 5½-point type.

*

*Longest.* The longest continuous frontier in the world is that between Canada and the U.S., which (including the Great Lakes boundaries) extends for 3,987 miles (excluding 1,538 miles with Alaska).

> A few "extremes" from the *Guinness Book of World Records* (Tenth Edition, 1971).

## McWilliams, Margaret

God give me work
Till my life shall end
And life
Till my work is done.

> Lines from Mrs. McWilliams's notebook, inscribed on her tombstone when she died in Winnipeg in 1952. She was the founder and first president of the Canadian Federation of University Women. Quoted by Betty Jane Wylie in *The Clear Spirit: Twenty Canadian Women and Their Times* (1966), edited by Mary Quayle Innis.

**Madaule, Jacques**
You are not quite a social being worthy of the term unless you have a fatherland which is your own and incontestably so. In most cases we are born into the fatherland; but alas! it also often happens that we have to reconquer it.

Quoted by René Lévesque in *An Option for Quebec* (1968).

**Madison, James**
I have another idea by which you can make sure of the safety of Canada and it will be less costly. Eliminate all fortifications on the border. It will be cheaper, and without guns neither of us will be able to attack one another, except maybe throw rocks.

Attributed to the American president after the War of 1812.

**Magee, John Gillespie**
Oh, I have slipped the surly bonds of earth,
And danced the skies on laughter-silvered wings. . . .

The American pilot was only nineteen when he was killed in action with the RCAF, December 11, 1941. Archibald MacLeish has ranked his poem "In High Flight" (from which the two lines above have been taken) with Rupert Brooke's "The Soldier" and John McCrae's "In Flanders Fields."

**Magee, Mike**
Fred C. Dobbs is a device. He's an exaggerated character.

Dobbs, the Beamsville farmer, is the creation of broadcaster Mike Magee and no kin of the mad prospector played by Humphrey Bogart in *The Treasure of the Sierra Madre*. Quoted by Bruce Kirkland in *Star Week*, December 16, 1972.

**Magnussen, Karen**
I fall once a day like clockwork. I only hope I've had my fall for the day before I go into the competitions.

The twenty-year-old Vancouverite won the 1973 world figure-skating champi-

onship in Czechoslovakia. Quoted in *Time*, March 12, 1973.

**Maheux, Abbé Arthur**
If one knows his neighbour's tongue, he possesses the key of his house.

*What Keeps Us Apart?* (1944).

**Mahoney, Michael**
Listen, son, it ain't the trail itself that means so much. It's the feller who's going to cross it. Now take White Pass; it's as awkward a goddamn piece of walkin' as you're ever likely to come across. For them that's never been off city pavements, chances are it'll seem a killer. But for a man that knows the bush and is in A number 1 shape—why, hell, there ain't one damn thing to be scared of.

Klondike Mike was the most colourful of the gold-rush characters, and his story is told by Merrill Denison in *Klondike Mike: An Alaskan Odyssey* (1943), who maintains his exploits inspired Jack London's story "Burning Daylight." Mike sometimes claimed he witnessed "The Shooting of Dan McGrew." (It is possible Klondike Mike was the original of the good prospector Jimmy Mahoney in *Rise and Fall of the City of Mahagony* [1927], the musical by Kurt Weill and Bertolt Brecht.)

**Mair, Charles**
In general the Frenchman married the Indian and sank to the level of her tastes and inclination. In general the Englishman married the Indian and raised her to the level of his own.

＊

I am done with the "Canadian Public" which consists of mere cattle. . . . [Letter to Colonel George Taylor Denison, July 17, 1891]

Quoted by Carl Berger in *The Sense of Power: Studies in the Ideas of Canadian Imperialism: 1867-1914* (1970).

Literature is a good stick but a very bad crutch.

A favourite aphorism of the Canada Firster, noted by Norman Shrive in *Charles Mair: Literary Nationalist* (1965).

## Maisonneuve, Sieur de

I have not come here to deliberate, but to act. It is my duty and my honour to found a colony at Montreal; and I would go, if every tree were an Iroquois!

> Maisonneuve founded the colony of Ville-Marie (Montreal) on May 18, 1642. Quoted by Francis Parkman in *The Jesuits in North America in the Seventeenth Century* (1867).

## Maitland, Sir Peregrine

Why do they talk of responsible government when we have responsible government? As Governor of this country I am responsible to the King.

> Attributed to the autocratic lieutenant-governor of Upper Canada (1818-28). Quoted by E.J. Hathaway in *Jesse Ketchum and His Times* (1929).

## Major, André

Clear-mindedness and love cannot exist without revolt, without hatred of all that is an obstacle to such clear-mindedness and love.

*

Fate does not create men's misery; it is, rather, a product of the social structure.

> *Liberté*, March-April, 1963. Quoted by Frank Scott and Michael Oliver in *Quebec States Her Case: Speeches and Articles from Quebec in the Years of Unrest* (1964).

## Malcolm, Andrew I.

The chemophilic society.

> Phrase popularized by the Toronto psychiatrist to describe the drug-oriented Western world today. *The Pursuit of Intoxication* (1971).

## Malraux, André

France needs you. We will build the next civilization together.

*

You are not aware of the meaning you have for France. There is nowhere in the world where the spirit of France works so movingly as it does in the Province of Quebec.

*

I now know that you do not create universal brotherhood at the expense of patriotism, but rather with the help of patriotism, by building on it and with it.

> Montreal address by the novelist and French minister of Culture, October 15, 1963.

## Malthus, T.R.

The Abbé Raynal, who is continually reasoning most inconsistently in his comparisons of savage and civilized life, though in one place he speaks of the savage as morally sure of a competent subsistence, yet, in his account of the nations of Canada, says, that though they lived in a country abounding in game and fish, yet in some seasons and sometimes for whole years, this resource failed them; and famine then occasioned a great destruction among a people who were at too great a distance to assist each other.

> The famous English economist is making reference to Abbé Guillaume Raynal, the influential French *philosophe*. *An Essay on the Principle of Population, or a View of its Past and Present Effects on Human Happiness* (1798).

## Mandel, Eli

Perhaps the ultimate temptation of the contemporary imagination is primitivism.

> Introduction to *Poets of Contemporary Canada 1960-1970* (1972), edited by Eli Mandel.

## Manêlaq

An old woman was once found among corpses. All her neighbours were dead. And she was the only one alive among the dead.
"Have you eaten of human flesh?"
"No."
"Then what have you lived on?"
"Lice."
No one believed her. So they killed her and opened her stomach. It was full of lice. But when her stomach was opened all the lice became alive, put on wings, and flew out over the country and turned into mosquitoes. In that way the old woman took vengeance on the people who would not believe her word.

And she gave them the worst plague of hot summers.

"How the First Mosquitoes Came," an Eskimo legend told by Manêlaq. Knud Rasmussen, *The Netsilik Eskimos: Social Life and Spiritual Culture: Report of the Fifth Thule Expedition, 1921-24* (1931).

**Manion, Robert James**
That life is an adventure is obvious to any man who has attained the age of fifty, and who has had opportunity of touching life at a few diverse points. Whether the adventure be glorious or tragic depends not only on the events themselves, but on the character and mental outlook of the individual.

*Life Is an Adventure* (1936).

No man should enter politics unless he is either independently rich or independently poor.

Quoted by Dalton Camp in *Gentlemen, Players and Politicians* (1970).

**Mann, Larry**
"In show business, at least, the Canadian public's attitude suggests that you don't arrive until you've left. Larry Mann, the actor who finally reluctantly moved to Hollywood in 1965, put it this way to me in an interview in 1964: 'You can be a full-time garbage collector in Toronto and you'll be accepted as such. Nobody says, "If he were any good he'd be collecting garbage in New York!" Or you can be a successful doctor or lawyer or accountant. You're not expected to prove how good you are by moving away to practise medicine or law or accounting in Hollywood or London.' "

Quoted by Alex Barris in *The Pierce-Arrow Showroom Is Leaking: An Insider's View of the CBC* (1969).

I think it interesting to note that no major American network has ever landed a top CBC executive—just CBC writers, directors, actors, singers and musicians. I don't believe this speaks too highly for CBC brass (especially the ones who have come here job hunting at the taxpayers' expense).

*Weekend Magazine*, August 14, 1971. The Toronto character actor now lives in Hollywood.

**Mao Tse-tung**   See Tse-tung, Mao.

**March, Mary**
"She, for it proved to be a woman, tore open her deer-skin cossack exposing her bosoms in an appeal to his manhood. In order to reassure her and allay her fears, he cast his gun aside into a bank of soft snow and then leisurely approached her with signs of amity, he laid hold of her and endeavoured to lead her back."

The Beothuck woman named Demasduit or Waunathoake, renamed Mary March after the month of her capture, at Red Indian Lake, Newfoundland, March 5, 1819. She died soon after. Described by John Peyton, a missionary, and quoted by James P. Howley in *The Beothucks or Red Indians: The Aboriginal Inhabitants of Newfoundland* (1915). See also Nancy Shanawdithit.

**Marchand, Jean**
Things in French Canada were becoming worse and worse, and we thought it essential for the new generation of French Canadians to become involved in federal politics. I made it a condition that Trudeau and Pelletier join me. . . . I was convinced that one French Canadian in Ottawa alone would be destroyed —that there needed to be several of us. And I think it's still true.

Before accepting an invitation to run for Parliament, Marchand insisted on similar invitations for two other of the "Three Wise Men" from Quebec. Quoted by Edith Iglauer in *The New Yorker*, July 5, 1969.

There is no more freedom.

Attributed to the cabinet minister when the Trudeau administration imposed the War Measures Act, October 6, 1970.

**Marconi, Guglielmo**

• • •

Three dots—and no dashes—were the first signal ever carried across the Atlantic Ocean by wireless transmission.

The date was December 11-12, 1901; the signal was a message (three dots mean "s" in Morse Code). Transmission originated at the Marconi installation at Poldhu, on the western coast of Cornwall, and was received at Signal Hill, St. John's, Newfoundland, by Marconi himself, who had raised his four-hundred-foot aerial high above the Newfoundland capital using a box kite—an incongruous seventeenth-century setting, surely, for a significant twentieth-century scientific experiment. Reception of the signal created an immense sensation around the world, and eight years later Marconi received the Nobel Prize in Physics for the "development of wireless telegraphy."

**Maria Monk**   See Monk, Maria.

**Marie de l'Incarnation**
You ask me for seeds and bulbs of the flowers of this country. We have those for our garden brought from France, there being none here that are very rare or very beautiful. Everything is savage here, the flowers as well as the men. [Letter to a French sister, Quebec, August 12, 1653]

*

Farewell, my very dear Mother. I am not as far from you in spirit as in body. We love an immense purpose in which we live and in which also I see you and embrace you, by the union that binds us in it and will bind us there, as I hope, throughout eternity. [Letter to the superior of the Ursulines of Tours, Mother Ursule de Sainte-Catherine, Quebec, September 13, 1640]

*Word from New France: The Selected Letters of Marie de l'Incarnation* (1967), translated by Joyce Marshall.

**Marie Louise, Princess of Bulgaria**
See Marie Louise Chrobok.

**Marie of Rumania, Queen**
See Joseph Boyle.

**Marie-Victorin, Brother**
Like us the tree has a homeland, and it does not thrive in exile. Like us the tree in the forest helps his brother; but trees, too, sometimes fight among themselves and the forest is full of harsh dealings and of silent victories of the strong over the weak. And in the end, like us, the tree, having lived its allotted days, disappears and returns to the earth, while the new vigorous generation grows up towards the sun.

"The Tree," radio address, October, 1943, by the professor of Botany at the University of Montreal. Quoted by Margaret Fairley in "Brother Marie-Victorin," *New Frontiers*, September, 1956.

**Marigny, Alfred de**
Man is an apprentice. Pain is his master, and no one understands who has not suffered.

Although a court of law did not find Alfred de Marigny guilty of the murder of his father-in-law Sir Harry Oakes in Nassau in 1943, Bahamian society did. The playboy worked briefly in Montreal, then settled in South America. Quoted by Geoffrey Bocca in *The Life and Death of Sir Harry Oakes* (1959).

**Markle, Fletcher**
Have Gun Will Travel.

The clever adaptation of the theatrical line "Have Tux Will Travel" was suggested for the TV series *Paladin*, starring Richard Boone (1957-61), by CBC-TV producer Fletcher Markle.

**Marks, Gerald**   See Irving Caesar.

**Marryat, Frederick**
You are at once struck with the difference between the English and the American population, system and ideas. On the other side of the lake, you have much more apparent property, but much less real solidarity and security. The houses and stores of Toronto are not to be compared with those of the American towns opposite. But the Englishman has built according to his means—the American according to his expectations.

*Diary in America, with Remarks on Its Institutions* (1839).

"Oh, dear! what a pity!" cried Percival,

"I shall dream of beavers all night, I'm sure I shall."

\*

"Now, I think that it much better that, as we all go along together, that every man paddle his own canoe. That my thought." [The Indian's remark is frequently cited as the earliest appearance in print of the idiom "every man must paddle his own canoe"]

> The Settlers in Canada: Written for Young People (1844), by Captain Marryat, the popular novelist and sea captain.

## Marsden, Joshua
There is, sir, a solitary loneliness in the woods of America to which no language can do adequate justice. It seems a shutting out of the whole moral creation. . . .

> The Narrative of a Mission, to Nova Scotia, New Brunswick, and the Somers Islands, with a Tour to Lake Ontario (1816).

## Marsh, Lou
What a vast difference between the free and easy contests of the 1880s and the highly commercialized sport of today, wherein the outstanding performers in smaller communities are enticed to larger centres where they give glory to wealthy patrons and drag cash to the pockets of sports-parasites.

> Quoted by William Perkins Bull in From Rattlesnake Hunt to Hockey (1934).

## Marsil, Tancrède
Automatisme

> Aesthetic term first applied to the surreal paintings of Paul-Emile Borduas and others at a group show in Montreal which opened on February 15, 1947. The art critic, writing in Le Quartier Latin, took the word "automatism" from the title of a Borduas canvas. It identifies a Quebec school of painting, as tachisme does in France and as Abstract Expressionism does in the United States. Dennis Reid in A Concise History of Canadian Painting (1973).

## Martin, Byron (Barney)
God must have saved that little hole for me.

> Seventy-four Nova Scotian miners died in the Springhill mining disaster of 1958, but Byron (Barney) Martin survived nine days and eight nights without food or drink. Quoted by Ray Timson in The Toronto Star, November 3, 1958.

## Martin, Chester
More enduring history has been made than written in Canada.

\*

History will continue to be made in Canada whether it is written or not. "Events stronger than advocacy, events stronger than men" will continue to challenge the Canadian character.

> Foundations of Canadian Nationhood (1955).

## Martin, Claire
When you have truly forgiven someone, when you have done it after long thought and not simply because you have forgotten—and blessed with a pitiless memory, I have forgotten nothing—when you have brought yourself to it without watering down your pardon with moral considerations, by which I mean that you pardon your father not as your father but as any human being who has offended you, when you have done all that, which is what I mean by truly forgiving someone, then you feel an inner peace that nothing can match.

> In an Iron Glove (1968), translated by Philip Stratford.

## Martin, Paul
So far as my Delegation is concerned, we do not so much care whether you call it a round table or a cross table conference or a polygonal conference; the important thing is to get those who must be there around a table.

> Acting chairman of the Canadian Delegation to the General Assembly of the United Nations, in a political committee meeting concerning Korean armistice talks, August 19, 1953. Reproduced

by R.A. Mackay in *Canadian Foreign Policy 1945-1954: Selected Speeches and Documents* (1971).

I hope I have not hurt anyone. I have hit hard—I can hit hard, as hard as anyone. But I cannot remember ever having deliberately tried to hurt an honourable member. I have disagreed violently, but I have always made a distinction between ideas and persons.

Quoted by J.P. Whealen in *Meet Paul Martin: A Personal Sketch* (1968).

## Martin, Peter

If Canadians spoke Swahili and dealt in razbuckniks, Canada would have a healthy and vigorous Canadian-owned book publishing industry. But, because we have the misfortune of speaking English and dealing in dollars, our publishing industry is fighting for its survival.

"Brief to the [Ontario] Royal Commission on Book Publishing, March, 1971," *Independence: The Canadian Challenge* (1972), edited by Abraham Rotstein and Gary Lax.

## Martyn, Howe

The multinational firm.

"There was a considerable time-lag between the appearance of what are now called multinational firms and their identification by this term. They were not noticed in part because they did not have a name. . . . The first occurrence the writer has discovered was in a speech by David Lilienthal in Philadelphia in 1958. . . . Prior to finding this precedent, the writer had coined the term independently for the title of a pioneering course of study introduced at the American University, Washington, D.C., in 1961. This was accepted with some reluctance, the dean concerned questioning the title on the grounds that 'multinational' was unfamiliar and not easy to pronounce. The work in this course and the title were described to Dr. Howard Whidden, then foreign editor of *Business Week*, and incidental to his participation in a panel of which the writer was chairman at a conference in Washington on March 21, 1963. On April 20, 1963, a feature article appeared in this magazine with the title 'Multinational Companies.' In 1964, the writer's book, *International Business*, was published with the description on the dust-cover—'Organization, management, and social impact of the multinational corporation.' Quotations from the London edition provided much of the substance of a feature article on October 17, 1964, in the influential *Economist*. . . . The acceptance of the term was so rapid and so general that by 1972, Christopher Tugendhat, a journalist and member of the British Parliament, was able to publish a book on the subject entitled simply *The Multinationals*." Howe Martyn in "Origins of the Multinational Firm," *The Multinational Corporation in World Politics* (1973), edited by Abdul Said.

It is perhaps appropriate that the concept of business "multinationality" was given world currency by a Canadian citizen, Howe Martyn, teaching in the United States. In a letter, May 8, 1973: "I coined the term for a course, finding subsequently, however, a similar earlier use. I prefer my original term 'multinational *firm*' because it avoids the suggestion of an American monopoly of this development conveyed by 'corporation' which is the American term for what others call limited company or *société anonyme*."

## Martyr, Petrus

He found also the men of those lands clothed in skins and not anywhere devoid of intelligence. He says there are great numbers of bears there, which eat fish. For the bears plunge into the midst of a shoal of those fish, and falling upon them with their claws grasping the scales draw them to shore and eat them; on which account, he says, the bears are less dangerous to men.

Reporting on the northern voyages of Sebastian Cabot, in 1515. *The Cabot Voyages and Bristol Discovery Under Henry VIII* (1962), by J.A. Williamson.

## Marx, Groucho

It's better to run to Toronto than to stay in a place you don't wanta.

Groucho Marx played vaudeville in Toronto during World War I. From the record album *An Evening with Groucho* (1967).

## Marx, Karl
Think of the horror! The excellent capitalist has imported bodily from Europe, with his own good money, his own competitors! The end of the world has come!

> *Capital: A Critical Analysis of Capitalist Production* (1912), translated from the third German edition by Samuel Moore and Edward Aveling, edited by Frederick Engels. The original German edition was published in 1886. Marx was commenting on the observation, made by E.G. Wakefield in *England and America* (1833), that capitalists "of Canada and the state of New York," forced to import their labourers, created independent landowners and their future competitors. Noted by Stanley B. Ryerson in *Unequal Union: Confederation and the Roots of Conflict in the Canadas, 1815-1873* (1968).

## Mary, The Blessed Virgin
See Lucia dos Santos.

## Masefield, John
You will therefore understand how greatly I shall appreciate your kindness if you will allow me to include your poem in my anthology, as the most beautiful sea poem of modern times, and the poem which has moved me more than any I have ever read. Perhaps we may some day meet; for life, like the sea, is full of mystery and hidden currents, and one can say with the ancient shipmen, "If we sail west we shall meet with land —it may be the Golden Islands, it may be some other islands—but there will be Queens and Kings there."

> Letter to Duncan Campbell Scott in Ottawa, 1905, concerning Scott's long poem "The Piper of Arll," the reading of which in a New York magazine, December 14, 1895, so profoundly changed the life of the future poet laureate.

In the usual way, I bought the Christmas Number of this American *Truth*, and read it through. It had in it, with some illustrations of phantasy, a longish narrative poem by Duncan Campbell Scott, called *The Piper of Arll*. This was the first poem by a living writer to touch me to the quick. It was narrative; it was delicate phantasy; it was about the sea and singing and a romantic end. . . . I read it till I knew it by heart; even now, I often repeat it to myself.

> *In the Mill* (1941). See also Duncan Campbell Scott.

## Mason, Don
Sighted sub, sank same.

> The American flier spotted a German submarine off the Newfoundland coast, January 28, 1942, and radioed this famous World War II message to the U.S. navy base. It was later learned that the sub had got away; some months later Mason destroyed another Nazi submarine.

## Mason, Michael H.
They are hostile to strangers, and many white pioneers have been done to death by them. This tribe was for many years under the complete domination of one woman, supposed to be partly of European descent.

> The myth of the "white queen" of the Nahanni. *The Arctic Forests* (1924).

## Mason, Walt
Hold me up, mighty waters,
Keep my eye on things above.

> The band played the Episcopal hymn "Autumn" as the *Titanic* sank, south of Newfoundland, April, 1912. The hymn is based on the poem "Little Things" by Walt Mason, a Canadian-born American versifier. Quoted by Walter Lord in *A Night to Remember* (1956).

## Massey, Denton
It is an inconsistency, but why worry about it?

> "Conservatism had to make universal the 'why worry' technique. It had not to encourage the people to think, but to prevent them from thinking; to crush the intellect under the weight of emo-

tions, impulses, and prejudices." Sir
Anthony Jenkinson's *Where Seldom a
Gun Is Heard* (1937). Denton Massey
was an evangelist and cousin of Raymond and Vincent.

### Massey, Raymond

When you have to please Kansas City
and Kensington and try to do both at
once the ultimate product cannot help
but be mediocre.

*

Canada is an example of the little theatre movement reviving the latent theatrical interest of the community.

*

There is no stronger Imperial link than
a continuous and effective interchange
of theatrical endeavour between England
and Canada. I hope to see the day before long when a leading English actor
cannot afford to neglect his Canadian
public but looks forward to his Canadian tour as a logical step in his career
and not as a reason to apply to the
Royal Geographical Society for an explorer's medal.

> "The Future of the Theatre" (1934),
> *Empire Club of Canada: Addresses De-
> livered to the Members During the Year
> 1933-34* (1934).

There are no comedies of manners, because there are no more manners.

*

I believe in censorship because I don't
believe in freedom when it's abused.

*

The two great contributions of the
screen to date are Mickey Mouse and
Charlie Chaplin, one synthetic, the
other select.

*

No actor or actress can pretend to act
on the screen without considerable previous stage experience.

> Remarks made at various times by Ray-
> mond Massey, the Toronto-born actor
> who made his theatrical debut in Sibe-
> ria, entertaining the Canadian Expedi-
> tionary Force in Russia in 1919. He
> created the title role on Broadway of
> *Abraham Lincoln in Illinois* (1938) and
> (as someone said) "took the face off the
> penny and put it into the hearts of mil-

lions of Americans," becoming an American citizen a decade later. On television
he played Dr. Gillespie, mentor of *Dr.
Kildare* (1961-65).

### Massey, Vincent

What name are you going to use?

> To his younger brother Raymond who
> at the age of twenty-five announced that
> he would try his luck on the English
> stage, 1921.

We are the victims of our own intelligence.

> To Colonel Henry E. Osborne, honor-
> ary director, Dominion Drama Festival,
> late 1930s. Quoted by Betty Lee in *Love
> and Whisky: The Story of the Dominion
> Drama Festival* (1973).

There are, however, natural differences
of outlook between Canadians of French
and Anglo-Saxon origin, and we should
understand them. Over the years there
have been many efforts to this end. But
have we, perhaps, been lacking in can-
dour and frankness in our talks with
each other? It is no good to gloss over
the real things on which we may have
different ideas. There are expressions of
*bonne entente* on both sides, but one
can not build national unity simply on
the exchange of compliments. The real
compliment between friends is an honest expression of views in the light of
mutual understanding.

*

There is therefore little need for eulogy
of the "undefended frontier." (Orators
differ as to its length; it extends, apart
from the Canada-Alaska boundary, for
3,986 miles.) Our frontier has long been
immune from conflict, it is true, but it
has suffered grievously from the effects
of rhetoric. As a matter of fact, some of
the realities have been obscured by the
clouds of oratory which hang above this
famous border. It has long been undefended, but realists have observed that
the disparity of population has made
armaments for one country futile and
for the other superfluous.

> *On Being Canadian* (1948).

American influences on Canadian life to

say the least are impressive. There should be no thought of interfering with the liberty of all Canadians to enjoy them. Cultural exchanges are excellent in themselves. They widen the choice of the consumer and provide stimulating competition for the producer. It cannot be denied, however, that a vast and disproportionate amount of material coming from a single alien source may stifle rather than stimulate our own creative effort; and, passively accepted without any standard of comparison, this may weaken critical faculties. We are now spending millions to maintain a national independence which would be nothing but an empty shell without a vigorous and distinctive cultural life. We have seen that we have its elements in our traditions and in our history; we have made important progress, often aided by American generosity. We must not be blind, however, to the very present danger of permanent dependence.

＊

If we as a nation are concerned with the problem of defence, what, may we ask ourselves, are we defending? We are defending civilization, our share of it, our contribution to it. The things with which our inquiry deals are the elements which give civilization its character and meaning. It would be paradoxical to defend something which we are unwilling to strengthen and enrich, and which we even allow to decline.

＊

Canadian achievement in every field depends mainly on the quality of the Canadian mind and spirit. This quality is determined by what Canadians think, and think about; by the books they read, the pictures they see and the programmes they hear. These things, whether we call them arts and letters or use other words to describe them, we believe to lie at the roots of our life as a nation.

*Royal Commission on National Development in the Arts, Letters and Sciences, 1949-51* (1951), commonly called "The Massey Report."

There were four buildings on this corner [at the intersection of King and Simcoe Streets, Toronto]—Government House itself, Upper Canada College, a church, and a saloon (to use the venerable term); a pale little joke of the time was that the four buildings represented legislation, education, salvation, and damnation.

＊

Into our country there flows a perpetual stream of cultural Americana, dubious in quality and alien to the best in our own inheritance. But one must bear in mind that this is equally distasteful to thoughtful Americans. We should know more of what reveals the highest quality of American life and learn from it. The best of what we receive from beyond our borders must be woven into our own fabric.

＊

I published a collection of my speeches —ignoring the warning made in an observation by someone that "speeches don't keep any better than fish."

＊

Nothing touched me quite so much as this comment in a Canadian newspaper: "He made the Crown Canadian." It was too generous a tribute; but that was what I had tried to do.

*What's Past Is Prologue: The Memoirs of the Right Honourable Vincent Massey, C.H.* (1963). The first native-born governor general never did specify which "Canadian newspaper" made this generous tribute.

## Mather, Barry

Once upon a time a little boy asked his Old Man: "Daddy, what is a British Columbian?" The Old Man paused, thought, and then he spoke as follows: "A British Columbian," he said, "is a man who has a California-type house, a Montreal mortgage, an English car, and a Scottish dog. His wife, who comes from Regina or maybe it is Calgary, either has a cat whose forbears came from Persia, or she has a small bird from the tropics which she keeps in a cage allegedly imported from Eastern Canada, but more likely made in Japan. . . . A British Columbian is a man who smokes Virginia cigarettes, drinks South American coffee, eats Ontario cheese,

California oranges, Norwegian sardines, and Alberta butter. . . . I could say more," the Old Man sighed, "but, my boy, that may give you a rough idea. . . ."

However, the little lad had long ceased to listen to his Old Man and was reading a comic book manufactured by some French Canadians in Montreal, about a Texas cowboy saving a Spanish girl from a Mexican.

> Quoted by R.E. Watters, editor, *British Columbia: A Centennial Anthology* (1958).

## Mather, Bruce

I try to write music that I would like to hear. As I, too, am part of the listening public with the same ear structure as everyone else, a portion of the public will react as I do.

> Composer interviewed by *Musicanada*, May, 1968.

## Mathews, Peter

"He was known and respected as an honest and prosperous farmer, always ready to do his duty to his adopted country, and died as he lived—a Patriot."

> Inscription on the monument erected to honour Peter Mathews and Samuel Lount, both hanged for treason, April 12, 1838. The monument was erected in 1893 in St. James Cemetery, Toronto. See also Samuel Lount and Egerton Ryerson.

## Mathews, Robin

We observe that Canadians are pushed aside and considered parochial, or are sometimes examined confidently with instrumentalities forged in other nations to meet non-Canadian needs. Indeed, the Canadian university will become a force to divide Canadians one from the other, to suppress the Canadian past and to prevent the development of a uniquely excellent Canadian future.

> *The Struggle for Canadian Universities: A Dossier* (1969), edited by Robin Mathews and James Steele.

We teach our own literature because it is ours. And when we know ourselves, and respect ourselves, we love our literature, just as we love our grandparents and our children when we know who we are and respect ourselves.

> "Canadian Literature: The Necessary Revolution," *This Magazine Is About Schools*, Fall, 1972.

Canadians are colonized even in their liberation movements.

> *The Toronto Star*, April 2, 1973.

France has culture but no civilization. England has civilization but no culture. The United States has neither. Canada has both.

> Women Teachers' Association of Ontario, Toronto, Spring, 1973.

## Matisse, Henri

About fifteen years ago, I spent two winters in Tangiers in the company of Morrice. You know the artist with the delicate vision, taking delight with a touching tenderness in the rendering of landscapes in closely allied values. He was a man, a true gentleman, a good comrade of great spirit and humour. He never displayed riches. He had as everyone knew a sad weakness for whisky. Despite that we were, outside of working hours, always together. I used to accompany him to the café where I took as many glasses of mineral water as he took glasses of alcohol. (I do not know what more to tell you.) He was a Canadian of Scottish origin belonging to a rich family, himself very well-off, but he never showed it. He was always over hill and dale somewhat like a migrating bird but without any fixed landing place.

> A description of James Wilson Morrice in a letter from the great French painter to Armand Dayot, 1926; quoted by Kathleen Daly Pepper in *James Wilson Morrice* (1966). See also Arnold Bennett.

## Matrai, Geza

Freedom for Hungary!

> Cry of the Hungarian-born Canadian who assaulted Alexei Kosygin while the Soviet premier was strolling with Prime Minister Trudeau across Parliament Hill, Ottawa, October 19, 1971. Trudeau apologized later that day on television:

"I was present at the incident. I can only say that it was a most regrettable one, certainly a very humiliating event for Canadians to have suffered. It makes one ashamed at the way some people in Canada seem to be more interested in problems elsewhere than in exercising Canadian democratic rights and respecting the basic laws in our country."

## Maude, Aylmer

I do not think Canada suffers from the presence of a frugal, laborious, sober, honest and serious people; even if they have their own superstitions and clannish patriotism.

*A Peculiar People: The Doukhobors* (1904). "The money Tolstoy received for his work [*Resurrection*] he gave to assist the migration of the Doukhobors from the Caucasus to Canada," Maude wrote in the introduction to his translation of *Resurrection* (1916), by Leo Tolstoy. See also James Mavor and Leo Tolstoy.

## Maugham, William Somerset

He has the most fascinating sense of colour in the world . . . he's the most delightful interpreter of Paris I know, and when you've seen his sketches—he's done hundreds, of unimaginable grace and feeling and distinction—you can never see Paris in the same way again.

A character in Maugham's novel, *The Magician* (1908), is discussing the painting of Warren (modelled on Morrice). "It is thirty years since I knew Morrice in France, and as you may well imagine my recollections of him are dim. Soon after I met him, however, I wrote what I think was then an accurate portrait of him under the name of Warren in a book called *The Magician*." Maugham's letter to Donald W. Buchanan, March 31, 1935, quoted by Buchanan in *James Wilson Morrice: A Biography* (1936). The character of Philip Carey, the hero of Maugham's *Of Human Bondage* (1915), also owes something to the Montreal-based artist whom Buchanan has called "the nation's first great painter." See also James Wilson Morrice.

Marsh: This was the dumping ground for all the idlers, drunkards and scallywags in England. They had the delusion over there that if a man was too big a rotter to do anything at all in England he'd only got to be sent out here and he'd make a fortune.

Taylor: I guess things ain't as bad as that now. They send us a different class. It takes an Englishman two years longer than anyone else to get the hang of things, but when once he tumbles to it he's better than any of them.

\*

Norah: I thought I hated the prairie through the long winter months, and yet somehow it has caught hold of me. It was dreary and monotonous, and yet I can't get it out of my heart. There's a beauty and a romance in it which fill my soul with longing.

Taylor: I guess we all hate the prairie sometimes, but when you've once lived in it, it ain't easy to live anywhere else.

Speeches from *The Land of Promise*, a three-act comedy Maugham wrote and set in Tunbridge Wells in England, and in Dyer and Prentice in Manitoba, 1912. In the preface to his *Collected Plays* (1931), Maugham explains that he was commissioned to write a part for Irene Vanbrugh and that "perhaps *The Land of Promise* might still hold an audience." It was so popular as a film, a novel based on the screenplay was published in 1914.

## Maurepas, Jean-Frédéric-Phélypeaux

The officials of Canada are looking not for the Western Sea, but for the sea of beaver.

Louis XVI's minister of state, quoted by Joseph Lister Rutledge in *Century of Conflict: The Struggle Between the French and British in Colonial America* (1956).

## Maurois, André

On July 12 I arrived in Halifax and the following day travelled to Montreal by rail. On the station platform I was surrounded by reporters who greeted me in French, with that slight Norman accent which always gives me pleasure when I talk to French Canadians. . . .

We could not remain in Canada. I had no more money; my wife had only a few dollars, just enough to buy two tickets to New York. It was only there that I could earn a living for us.

> About 1940, *Memoirs 1885-1967* (1970), translated by Denver Lindley.

## Mavor, James

One fact, however, must be insisted upon, viz., the Department of the Interior was fully aware that the Doukhobors were reputed to be no individualist farmers, that, on the contrary, they practised a form of communism, the precise form of it as carried out in practice not being known. The department knew also that an explicit condition of the immigration was that the people should be allowed to settle in villages.

> James Mavor, professor of political economy at the University of Toronto, arranged for seven thousand Doukhobors to leave Russia and settle on the prairies in 1898. *My Windows on the Street of the World* (1923). See also Keir Hardie, Aylmer Maude and Leo Tolstoy.

## Mawedopenais

Let the medals you give us be of silver— medals that shall be worthy of the high position our Mother the Queen occupies.

> To the Indian commissioner, Alexander Morris, complaining that his medal was not of the promised silver. Morris replied: "I will tell them at Ottawa *what* you have said, and *how* you have said it."

*

Now you see me stand before you all: what has been done here today has been done openly before the Great Spirit and before the nation, and I hope I may never hear any one say that this treaty has been done secretly: and now in closing this council, I take off my glove, and in giving you my hand I deliver over my birthright and lands: and in taking your hand I hold fast all the promises you have made, and I hope they will last as long as the sun rises and the water flows, as you have said.

Mawedopenais was the chief spokesman of the Ojibway tribes at Fort Francis when Treaty Number 3, or the North-West Angle Treaty, was signed, October, 1873. Quoted by Alexander Morris in *The Treaties of Canada with the Indians of Manitoba and the North-West Territories* (1880).

## May, Dr. Alan Nunn

I still think I did rightly. Many others think so, too.

> On his release from a British prison in 1952, for espionage activities that culminated in the theft of uranium samples, exposed by Igor Gouzenko. Quoted by Frank Rasky in *Gay Canadian Rogues: Swindlers, Gold-diggers and Spies* (1958).

## Mayer, Louis B.

When you come to the end of your rope, tie a knot in it and hang on.

> Advice given to Louis B. Mayer by John E. Wilson, a New Brunswick businessman, while the young Mayer lived with his parents in Saint John; quoted on many occasions in later life by the "big boss" of MGM. Quoted by Bosley Crowther in *Hollywood Rajah: The Life and Times of Louis B. Mayer* (1960).

America like Canada is a land of opportunity.

*

The public are my judges and jury. They really are my masters.

*

I truly had a great mother. Every boy thinks so. I believe she is happy and smiling because I am truly back home.

> Remarks made by Mayer at a luncheon held in his honour, Queen Hotel, Fredericton, published in *The Daily Gleaner*, May 18, 1939.

Each and every year, health permitting, I will visit the university and take part in the Encaenia exercises. At the same time I will take advantage of the opportunity to fish in New Brunswick streams and will go back and tell the world what a grand and glorious land this is.

> Convocation address at the University

of New Brunswick, accepting an honorary LL.D., May 18, 1939.

Louis B. Mayer was at his professional apogee in 1939: his personal income was the highest reported anywhere in the world. Born in 1885 near Minsk, at the age of three he was brought to Saint John. At seventeen, he emigrated to the United States, and in Hollywood he founded Metro-Goldwyn-Mayer in 1924.

Like Roy Thomson, L.B. Mayer is sometimes credited with the crack: "If I can't take it with me, I won't go." He died in Hollywood in October of 1957, murmuring, "Nothing matters, nothing matters." His funeral was attended by many, not all of them mourners. "The reason so many people showed up was because they wanted to make sure he was dead"—this remark is variously credited to Red Skelton and Sam Goldwyn. The funeral oration was a sensitive tribute, read by Spencer Tracy: "The story he wanted to tell was the story of America—the land for which he had an almost furious love, born of gratitude — and of contrast with the hatreds in the dark land of his boyhood across the seas. Though he never lost his love for Canada, which had given him refuge, and an opportunity that found fulfillment in the United States, it was this love for America that made him an authority on America, and his counsel was sought by men in high places."

## Maynard, Fredelle Bruser

I remember, when I was five or six, falling in love with Edward, Prince of Wales. Of the many arguments with which my Mother might have dampened my ardour, she chose surely the most extraordinary. "You can't marry him. He isn't Jewish."

\*

All around me, when I was a child, men broke the land under the fierce promise of the Homestead Act—a quarter section free if within three years you could plough the prairie, raise house and barn, and survive. It can never come again, that free wild perilous world. No one who has known it would willingly return. No one who has left it can forget.

*Raisins and Almonds* (1972).

## Mead, Margaret

When I stand on a street in a Canadian city and look across the street, it couldn't be anywhere but Canada, but how can I prove it?

"How Fast Can Men Change?" (1957), *Empire Club of Canada: Addresses 1956-57* (1957).

## Meighen, Arthur

Above them are being planted the maples of Canada, in the thought that her sons will rest the better in the shade of the trees they knew so well in life. [At Vimy Ridge, July 3, 1921]

Guess-work government.

Description of Mackenzie King's administration by the leader of the Opposition, spring, 1922, when King was unable to decide whether the militia should train that summer. Quoted by Roger Graham in *Arthur Meighen: A Biography — Volume II: And Fortune Fled* (1963).

Let there be no dispute as to where I stand. When Britain's message came then Canada should have said: "Ready, aye ready; we stand by you." [Loud cheers] I hope the time has not gone by when that declaration can yet be made. If that declaration is made then I will be at the back of the Government.

Address of the Conservative leader to the Liberal-Conservative Business Men's Club, Toronto, September 22, 1922, published the following day in *The Mail and Empire*. Meighen was referring to the British government's "invitation" to Canada to send troops to defend the neutrality of Chanak which was threatened by Turkey. Prime Minister Mackenzie King withheld "a declaration of solidarity on the part of the Dominions."

In his jingoistic speech, Meighen deliberately echoed Sir Wilfrid Laurier's declaration in the House of Commons, August 19, 1914, in which Laurier used the British phrase "Ready, aye, ready." See also Sir George E. Foster and Sir Wilfrid Laurier.

A Senate seat is a legitimate aspiration of any Canadian.

> Reply of the prime minister to an ambitious mother who wrote him, "My daughters are both married. May I dream of reaching to the Upper House, Ottawa?" Quoted by F.A. Kunz in *The Modern Senate of Canada, 1925-1963: A Re-appraisal* (1965).

We are not in the same boat, but we are pretty much in the same waters. [Address on Canadian-American relations, 1937]

Difficulties do not crush men, they make them. [Address in 1942]

They [our forefathers] would urge us to be conscious of our mighty heritage, proud of the Imperial Fountain of our freedom and the flag that floats above us, worthy of those ideals of British liberty and justice which have sent their light forth and their truth among all races of men. To our history, our principles, our traditions let us be faithful to the end. ["Responsible Government" (1927)]

*

But, seriously, that is not the duty of the Senate of Canada! Surely if we have one function it is to point the way and try to advance public thinking toward settlement of business problems on business lines. ["Unified Management of Railways," Speech to the Senate, May 25, 1939]

*

Hope springs eternal—but somehow or other troubles never stay long away. ["The Last Hundred Years," Address at St. Mary's, September 13, 1942]

*

Whether now judged right or wrong, whatever I have said, whatever I have done, is going to remain unrevised and unrepented. As it is, it will await whatever verdict may come. ["The CBC—A Party Instrument," Speech to the Conservative Convention, Winnipeg, December 9, 1942]

*

Inflation makes misery unanimous; it is universal poverty. ["Socialism," Speech to the Kiwanis Club of Vancouver, October 21, 1943]

> *Unrevised and Unrepented: Debating Speeches and Others* (1949).

## Melbourne, Lord

"How could one be expected to show an interest in a country like Canada, demanded Lord Melbourne the Prime Minister, where a salmon would not rise to a fly?"

> Prime Minister of Great Britain between 1834 and 1841. James Morris in *Heaven's Command: An Imperial Progress* (1973). Melbourne's favourite political dictum was "Why not leave it alone?"

## Melville, Mother

"There was this old lady in Calgary, they called her Mother Melville, and she used to go down to the jungle on the Bow River and she'd have a purse full of envelopes. Envelopes with stamps on them and a sheet of paper inside each one and she'd go among the boys, all these guys riding the rods and she'd hand out these envelopes and say, 'Write your mother, son, please write her just a line or two. She's worried, I know.' After Mother Melville had gone through, you'd see fifteen or twenty guys sitting around, passing a pencil around, writing notes home."

> Recorded by Barry Broadfoot in "Meet Mother Melville," *Ten Lost Years 1929-1939: Memoirs of Canadians who Survived the Depression* (1973).

## Melzack, Louis

I feel a bookstore should be something like a private library, not a supermarket.

> Founder of the Classic Book Shops chain, *The Canadian Magazine*, August 5, 1972.

## Mencken, H.L.

Jesus, what a swell hotel! *Two* Gideon Bibles—and *one* towel.

> The Baltimore journalist married on September 27, 1930, and spent his honeymoon at the Château Frontenac, Quebec City. Quoted by William Manchester in *Disturber of the Peace: The Life of H.L. Mencken* (1951).

## Mercator, Gerhardus
Here lived pygmies, at the most four feet in height, like those who in Greenland are called Skraelings.

> Legends attest most lands before the dawn of history were populated by giants; Canada was found to be populated by dwarfs. The Flemish geographer Gerhardus Mercator composed the inscription above for his map of northern lands in 1569. "The word Skraeling has as its root *skral*, which means small, wizened, or shrivelled," explains Tryggvi J. Oleson in *Early Voyages and Northern Approaches 1000-1632* (1963). For more about pygmies, see Paulus Jouius von Houocomen.

## Merchant, Livingston T.
We in the United States, friendly and well disposed toward Canada, confident of our power yet conscious of our unsought burdens in the confusing, dangerous world in which we live, all too often tend to assume that Canadians are really just like Americans and should be counted on to react to nearly everything in the same fashion. Nor is it surprising that the general run of Canadians and Americans get on well together as individuals and that each complacently assumes that he "understands" his friend's country.

> Introduction, *Neighbours Taken for Granted: Canada and the United States* (1966), edited by Livingston T. Merchant. Merchant served twice as U.S. ambassador to Canada (1956-58, 1961-62). See also A.D.P. Heeney.

## Mercier, Honoré
We have a right to our national existence as a race apart, and woe to any man who will try to deprive us of it. [1880]

*

In killing Riel, Sir John not only struck our race at the heart but also struck the cause of justice and humanity which, represented by all languages and sanctified by all religious beliefs, demanded mercy for the prisoner of Regina, our poor brother of the Northwest. [Speech, mass rally, Champ de Mars, Montreal, to protest the execution of Louis Riel, November 22, 1885]

> Quoted by J.O. Pelland in *Biographie, discours, conférences, etc., de l'Hon. Honoré Mercier* (1890).

The situation is serious; we are facing the greatest danger ever faced by our political structure; we are asked to participate in a regime which cannot but bear the most disastrous consequences for us. So far, we have lived a colonial life; today, we are forced against our will to assume the responsibilities and dangers of a sovereign state which will not be ours, to expose ourselves to the vicissitudes of peace and war between the world's great powers and to the demanding necessities of military service as it exists in Europe; a political regime is imposed upon us which, through conscription, could scatter our sons from the Polar icelands to the burning sands of the Sahara,—a regime which would condemn us to the compulsory tribute of blood and money and would tear from us our sons, the hope of our country and the consolation of our old days, to precipitate them into far-away and bloody wars which we could neither prevent nor stop. . . .

> Address, Windsor Hotel, Montreal, April 10, 1888, quoted by Ramsay Cook in *French-Canadian Nationalism: An Anthology* (1969).

Men, women, and children, it is for you to choose; you can remain slaves under colonial status, or become independent and free, among other peoples who invite you to the banquet of nations.

> "The Future of Canada," Montreal address, April 4, 1893. Quoted by Mason Wade in *The French Canadians: 1760-1967* (1968).

## Meredith, John
Art should always be a mystery. It isn't possible to totally explain any work of art, anyways, since it is this mysterious quality which makes art so beautiful.

> Quoted by William Withrow in *Contemporary Canadian Painting* (1972).

## Merrick, James G.
So long as the tendency of man is to lapse into savagery, so long will the student prefer to engage in the soul-stirring and back-breaking game of football rather than in the dignified but less inspiring game of cricket.

> Merrick was a champion athlete at the University of Toronto and later Canada's representative on the International Olympic Committee. Observation made in 1893, and quoted by T.A. Reed in *The Blue and White* (1945).

## Merril, Judith
The only estate a writer can own is his name.

*

The fact that Rochdale happened, was permitted to happen, is probably more important than what has happened to Rochdale.

> Ad hoc observations of the science-fiction writer who established the Spaced Out Library in Toronto in 1970. (Rochdale was a student-run "free university" which flourished in the 1960s.)

## Merritt, Charles Cecil Ingersoll
Come on over! There's nothing to worry about here.

> Lieutenant-Colonel Merritt was awarded the Victoria Cross for "matchless gallantry and inspiring leadership whilst commanding his battalion [of the South Saskatchewan Regiment] during the Dieppe raid on the 19th August, 1942. From the point of landing, his unit's advance had to be made across a bridge in Pourville which was swept by very heavy machine-gun, mortar and artillery fire: the first parties were mostly destroyed and the bridge thickly covered by their bodies. A daring lead was required; waving his helmet, Lieutenant-Colonel Merritt rushed forward shouting, 'Come on over! There's nothing to worry about here.'" *The London Gazette*, October 2, 1942. George C. Machum, *Canada's V.C.'s; The Story of Canadians Who Have Been Awarded the Victoria Cross* (1956).

## Metcalfe, Sir Charles
Place the capital in Upper Canada, and the Lower Canadians will be dissatisfied. Place it in Lower Canada, and the Upper Canadians will be so. In proposing Montreal, therefore, I do not mean to promise that such a decision will not produce great dissatisfaction in Upper Canada, for I am inclined to believe that it will, and I have been told that it will lead to a motion for the repeal of the Union.

> Letter to the colonial secretary concerning the location of the capital of the Province of Canada created by the Act of Union. Quoted by John Charles Dent in *The Last Forty Years: Canada Since the Union of 1841* (1881).

## Mezei, Stephen
One can live very well on very little, providing one doesn't have to work too much for it.

*

The difference between the amateur and the professional is that the amateur fights to hurt and the professional fights to win.

> Bon mots from an editor of *The Canadian Theatre Review*.

## Michener, Roland
We stand on the threshold of greatness.

> Speech from the throne delivered by Governor General Michener, House of Commons, October 8, 1970.

## Middleton, Mr. Justice
I cannot find that reproduction of the human race is contrary to morals.

> Decision of the court concerning the "Stork Derby" will of the eccentric lawyer Charles Millar in 1926. See Charles Millar.

## Middleton, General Sir Fred
POUNDMAKER.—I have utterly defeated the half-breeds and Indians at Batoche, and have made prisoners of Riel and most of his council. I have made no terms with them, neither will I make terms with you. I have men enough to

destroy you and your people, or, at least to drive you away to starve, and will do so unless you bring in the teams you took and yourself and councillors, with your arms, to meet me at Battleford on Monday, the 26th. I am glad to hear you have treated the prisoners well and have released them.

(Signed) FRED MIDDLETON,
Major-General.

"I sent back the following not quite grammatical answer" to Poundmaker's request for peace terms, May 23, 1885. Reproduced by General Sir Fred Middleton in *Suppression of the Rebellion in North West Territories of Canada: 1885* (1948), edited by G.H. Needler. See also Poundmaker.

## Middleton, Jesse Edgar
See Jean de Brébeuf.

## Mikita, Stan
If you play to win, as I do, the game never ends.

High-scoring Czech-born hockey star in *I Play to Win* (1969).

## Mill, John Stuart
Canada has been the death of him.

On the death of Lord Durham in 1840. Quoted by John Charles Dent in *The Last Forty Years: Canada Since the Union of 1841* (1881).

## Millar, Charles
Always let the other fellow write the contract. Then you can see where he leaves you an opening, and when you act he hasn't a leg to stand on because he wrote it.

Millar's advice to another Toronto lawyer. When the millionaire lawyer died on October 31, 1926, he left behind the famous "Millar Will," an eccentric document that bequeathed O'Keefe Brewery stock to Baptist ministers and Ontario Jockey Club shares to opponents of horseracing. Clause 5 left the balance of the estate—two thirds of a million dollars—to "the mother who has since my death given birth in Toronto to the greatest number of children as

shown under the Vital Statistics Act." The will was contested for ten years; until the legacy was divided among four sets of parents, each with nine children, some born out of wedlock, to a total of thirty-six Stork Derby babies. "I cannot find that reproduction of the human race is contrary to morals," Mr. Justice Middleton concluded. Quoted by Eric Hutton in "He Started the Stork Derby" in *Maclean's Canada: Portrait of a Country* (1960), edited by Leslie F. Hannon.

## Miller, Henry
"Henry Miller will attempt to play *Hamlet* tonight. The crime will occur in Albany."

When the Broadway actor and manager reminisced, he always recalled this remark made by an anonymous New York critic. Miller, born in England as John Pegge, was brought to Toronto at the age of eleven, where he made his début eight years later in *Macbeth*. Quoted by Daniel Blum in *Great Stars of the American Stage: A Pictorial Record* (1954).

## Miller, Henry
I awoke the other morning, my mind still in a whirl from the continuous effort to recall titles, authors, names of places, events and the most seemingly insignificant data, and what do you suppose I found myself dwelling on? The Plains of Abraham! Yes, my mind was full of Montcalm and Wolfe fighting it out up there towards the roof of the world. The French and Indian War, I believe we call it. Seven long years of fighting. It was probably this battle on the Plains of Abraham, which my weak memory places somewhere in the vicinity of Quebec, that decided the fate of the French in North America. I must have studied this bloody war in detail, in school. In fact, I'm sure I did. And what remains? *The Plains of Abraham*. To be more accurate, more precise, it boils down to a clump of images which could be put in the hollow of a shell. I see Montcalm dying—or was it Wolfe?—in the open air, surrounded by his body-

guard and a cluster of Indians with bald knobs from which a few features protrude, long feathers, buried deep in the scalp. Eagles' feathers probably. Montcalm is making a dying speech, one of those historic "last words," such as—"I regret that I have but one life to give for my country." I no longer remember his words but it seems to me he was saying—"The tide is going against us." What matter, anyway? In a few moments he will be dead, a thing of history. And Canada, except for the Eastern sliver, will be English—worse luck for us! But how is it that I visualize a huge bird perched on his shoulder? Whence that bird of ill omen? Perhaps it is the same bird which got caught in the netting over the cradle in which lay the infant James Ensor, the bird which haunted him all his life. There it is, at any rate, large as life and dominating the infinitude of background in my imaginary piece. For some obscure reason the site of this famous battleground makes a woeful impression upon me: the sky seems to press down on it with all its impalpable weight. Not much space there between land and sky. The heads of the brave warriors seem to brush the cloudless vault of heaven. The battle over, the French will descend the steep face of the promontory by rope ladder. They will take to the rapids in canoes, a handful at a time, the English above raking them mercilessly with grapeshot. As for Montcalm, being a nobleman by birth, and a general, his remains will be removed from the scene with all the honours of war. Night falls rapidly, leaving the helpless Indians to look out for themselves. The British, now having a clear field, romp all over Canada. With stakes and cord the border is marked out. "We" have nothing to fear any more; our neighbours are our own kith and kin. . . .

If this battle isn't included in the fifteen decisive battles of the world it should be. Anyway, I could think of nothing this morning I speak of but battles and battlefields.

"The Plains of Abraham," *The Books of My Life* (1956), by the well-known American novelist.

## Miller, Joaquin

He died at dawn in the land of snows;
A priest at the left, a priest at the right;
The doomed man praying for his pitiless foes,
And each priest holding a low dim light,
To pray for the soul of the dying.
But Windsor Castle was far away;
And Windsor Castle was never so gay
With her gorgeous banners flying!

First of three stanzas of "Riel, the Rebel," *The Complete Poetical Works of Joaquin Miller* (1897). "The prince of all wild-life poets is the Poet of the Sierras, Joaquin Miller, an American of the Americas, to whom the Old World hearkens with delight, but whom the New World eyes askance." Introduction by Charles G.D. Roberts to Miller's *Poems of Wild Life: An Anthology* (1888).

## Miller, Pearl

To hell with Pearl Harbor
Remember Pearl Miller!

The Calgary Highlanders tell the story that the Princess Pats erected this sign in their sergeants' mess shortly before D-Day, after seeing the American slogan "Remember Pearl Harbor."

"Pearl Miller died full of years in 1957 in the sure knowledge that she had become a Calgary legend about whom the natives wove their favourite fantasies, and told their biggest lies . . . the story really ought to be true of a city where the most famous woman in its entire history was the keeper of a common bawdy-house." James H. Gray in *Red Lights on the Prairies* (1971).

## Milne, David

I suppose each painter has his own way of launching into the adventures in shape, colour, texture and space that we call painting. I mostly fall into them. ["Notes for an Exhibition of Little Pictures," October 24, 1936]

The thing that "makes" a picture is the thing that "makes" dynamite—compression. It isn't a fire in the grass; it is an explosion. Everything must hit at once.

＊

All that is needed to appreciate any art

is a capacity for aesthetic feeling; most people lack this entirely and are driven to try to get into contact with painters through their understanding. Even artists fall into the way of trying to make their pictures understandable instead of felt.

Feeling is the power that drives art. There doesn't seem to be a more understandable word for it, though there are others that give something of the idea; aesthetic emotion, quickening, bringing to life. Or call it love: not love of man or woman or home or country or any material thing, but love without an object—intransitive love.

*David Milne 1882-1953* (1967), edited by Ralph Allen.

**Milner, Viscount**
Take British Columbia alone. It would take months to go through it, and years to know it.

"Imperial Unity," Canadian Club Address, Vancouver, October 9, 1908. *Speeches Delivered in Canada in the Autumn of 1908* (1909).

**Milton, John**
Now from the North
Of *Norumbega*, and the *Samoed* shoar
Bursting thir brazen Dungeon, armed with ice
And snow and haile and stormie gust and flaw,
*Boreas* and *Caecias* and *Argestes* loud
And Thrascias rend the Woods, and Seas upturn. . . .

*Paradise Lost*, Book X, *The Poetical Works of John Milton* (1938), edited by H.C. Beeching. The mythical city and kingdom of Norumbega appeared on New World maps in the late 1500s in the region of present-day Nova Scotia. See also Anonymous: Lore: Ontario.

**Milton, Viscount**     See W.B. Cheadle.

**Miner, Jack**
Only humans are wild.

*

A man's reputation is the opinion people have of him; his character is what he really is.

*

Any man who isn't big enough to change his mind has nothing to change.

*

You may do all you can for the other fellow, but it is a failure unless he, himself, is willing to get up in the morning.

For permanent peace by the help of God, let us build more Friendships instead of Warships.

*Wild Goose Jack* (1969).

Understanding birds is easy. They're true to nature. But how do you understand people?

*

Get all the education you can; then add the learning.

*

Today is the tomorrow you worried about yesterday.

*

Canada Geese conduct themselves with dignity, never fight unless it's absolutely necessary to protect their families—and then their wrath is terrible. The gander takes only one mate in a lifetime, and I've never known one to make application for divorce.

*

Anyone who says "silly as a goose" is talking through his hat.

*

Don't put your tongue in high until you get your brain started.

*

I know of no bird or animal that can equal the Canada Goose for getting well after being wounded. It is said that a cat has nine lives; if that is true, the Canada Goose has at least eighteen, nine on each side of the border.

"Minerisms" from the pioneer naturalist who, until his death in 1944, banded wildlife at his famous bird sanctuary at Kingsville, Ontario. As Paul Martin noted, "Jack Miner wrote Kingsville, Canada, across the skies of North America." See also Henry Ford and Edgar A. Guest.

**Minifie, James M.**
Unless Americans can return to the early virtues, principles, and under-

standing which made them great, Canadians may find to their surprise that their own more elastic union has survived that of the dis-United States.

"Eagle's Feather" in *The New Romans: Candid Canadian Opinions of the U.S.* (1968), edited by Al Purdy.

**Minto, Earl of**
Gentlemen, those who have gone before you have bequeathed to you a splendid inheritance. I always remember that apt saying—I forget just now to what distinguished statesman it is due—he said there were three classes of men in the world: "Those who write history, those who read it and those who make it." Canadian men and women have made history and are making it still every day, but the present generation have more time than of old to write and to read it.

"Address," January 18, 1904, *Addresses Delivered before the Canadian Club of Ottawa: 1903-1909* (1910). The Earl of Minto was the governor general from 1898 to 1904.

**Mintzberg, Henry**
Advocates of strategic planning suggest that we must build throughways, not find our way through the forest as Champlain once did.

"A Framework for Strategic Planning," *An Industrial Strategy for Canada* (1972), edited by Abraham Rotstein.

**Miron, Gaston**
we will make you, Land of Quebec
a bed of resurrections

Lines from "October," translated by Fred Cogswell in *One Hundred Poems of Modern Quebec* (1970).

We have to mine the national past for the themes, the traits that have marked us. These can be negative, destructive; we have to face them. French Canadians have always, for example, been given to nostalgia, to living in a dream world woven from the past.

Leading Quebec poet quoted by Malcolm Reid in *The Shouting Signpainters: A Literary and Political Account of Quebec Revolutionary Nationalism* (1972).

**Mirvish, Ed**
Don't Just Stand There, Buy Something!

This Way You Lucky People—Come in and Get Lost!

There's No Place Like This Place Any Place!

Honest Ed's Not a Baker . . . But He Saves You "Dough"!

It's Fun to Shop at . . . HONEST ED'S!

Slogans from "Honest Ed's," the well-known discount department store in Toronto operated by Edwin Mirvish since 1948. "Ed had invented a discount house. It was the first in North America, a store that sold goods for less than you paid in other, more fancy, more serious stores." Quoted by Jack Batten in *Honest Ed's Story: The Crazy Rags to Riches Story of Ed Mirvish* (1972).

**Mitchell, John**    See Patrick Slater.

**Mitchell, Joni**
We are stardust
We are golden
And we've got to get ourselves
Back to the garden.

Refrain from "Woodstock," from the album *Ladies of the Canyon* (1969).

It's life's illusions I recall;
I really don't know life at all.

From "Both Sides, Now," a popular ballad by Joni Mitchell, born Roberta Joan Anderson in Fort Macleod, Alberta.

**Mitchell, Roy**
An audience is something which requires to be made and there can be no great communication until it has been made, until it has been compacted into one emotional content and one mind by the creation of an atmosphere, the introduction of the characters, the delivery of the theme, by suggestions of time and place and by the arousing of an interest in the march of the story.

"Motion and the Actor," *Yearbook of*

*the Arts in Canada: 1928-29* (1929), edited by Bertram Brooker.

The man who is ever on the watch for a far-off glitter delivers us always into bondage.

*

A hundred times a day artists of the theatre have to decide between the living art of motion and the sayings, pictures and music that obsess it.

*

If we are to be an art we must do as the other arts do, retain control of our superb moments.

Creative Theatre (1929), by the progressive and imaginative director of Hart House Theatre at the University of Toronto during the 1920s.

## Mitchell, W.O.
"Jake and the Kid."

A series of humorous stories, first published in *Maclean's Magazine* during World War II, then serialized on CBC radio and television, finally collected as *Jake and the Kid* (1961). The stories were about Jake, a cranky hired hand, and a lively youngster called the Kid, who lived in Crocus, Saskatchewan.

He looked up to find that the street had stopped. Ahead lay the sudden emptiness of the prairie. For the first time in his four years of life he was alone on the prairie.

*

Why did people die? Why did they finish up? What was the good in being a human? It was awful to be a human. It wasn't any good.

The musings of the young boy in the novel *Who Has Seen the Wind* (1947).

If it isn't alive, it isn't ever going to be art.

Interviewed by Donald Cameron in *Conversations with Canadian Novelists* (1973).

## Mitford, Nancy
Just the right age, but what of Nova Scotia? An atlas, hastily consulted, showed it to be horribly marine. "A transatlantic Isle of Wight" as Linda put

it. "No thanks." Sea breezes, in so far as they are good for the complexion, were regarded by us as a means and not an end, for at that time it was our idea to live in capital cities and go to the Opera alight with diamonds. "Who is that lovely woman?" and Nova Scotia was clearly not a suitable venue for such things.

*

She had never felt interest or curiosity towards those unsuitable people in Canada, they were one of the unpleasant things of life and she preferred to ignore them.

*

Now fancy moving, in Canada. You'd think one place there would be exactly the same as another, wouldn't you? Sheer waste of money, you'd think.

Love in a Cold Climate (1949). See also Dénis Diderot.

## Moir, David Macbeth
Listen to me, as when ye heard our
    father
Sing long ago the song of our shores—
Listen to me, and then in chorus gather
    All your deep voices, as ye pull your
      oars:
      *Fair these broad meads—these*
        *hoary woods are grand;*
      *But we are exiles from our fathers'*
        *land.*

From the lone shieling of the mistry
    island
Mountains divide us, and the waste
    of seas—
Yet still the blood is strong, the heart is
    Highland,
And we in dreams behold the
    Hebrides:
      *Fair these broad meads—these*
        *hoary woods are grand;*
      *But we are exiles from our fathers'*
        *land.*

Two of five stanzas of "Canadian Boat-Song (from the Gaelic)," reproduced from G.H. Needler's *The Lone Shieling: Origin and Authorship of the Blackwood "Canadian Boat-Song"* (1941). Once widely quoted and thought to be by the novelist John Galt, this poem appeared anonymously in *Blackwood's,*

September, 1829. Professor Needler demonstrates textually that it was not by Galt but by David Macbeth Moir, a Scottish versifier and contributor to the periodical, who had never visited North America but had been in correspondence with Galt at the time of the composition of the poem. A "shieling" or "shealing" is a rough hut on a small pasture. The poem is not "in any real sense a boat-song, but the lament of Highlanders from the Hebrides exiled in Upper Canada" or on Cape Breton Island, according to Professor Needler. Hugh MacLennan said it has "possibly the most haunting verses ever composed in Canada." "Canadian Boat-Song (from the Gaelic)" should not be confused with Moore's "A Canadian Boat Song: Written on the River St. Lawrence." See also Thomas Moore.

## Moiseiwitsch, Tanya
I'm happy to see everything I design on the stage—that means it isn't taking up storage space.

Quoted by Roy Newquist in *Showcase* (1966).

## Molson, Senator Hartland
We don't really own the Canadiens. The public of Montreal, in fact the entire Province of Quebec, owns the Canadiens. This club is more than a professional sports organization. It is an institution—a way of life.

Remark made by the president of the Montreal Canadiens Hockey Club in 1957. Quoted by Stan Fischler in *Rocket Richard: The Flying Frenchman* (1971).

## Molson, John
This day bought 8 bu. of barley
MY COMMENCEMENT ON THE GRAND STAGE OF THE WORLD.

Entry for July 28, 1786, in the diary of John Molson, the Montreal brewer.

## Molson, John Henry
Wealth will not take care of itself if it is not vigilantly cared for.

Son of the founder of Molson's Brewery.

## Moltke, Helmuth von
The feeling in America is friendly to Germany . . . perhaps the United States can be persuaded to mount a naval demonstration against England, for which, as a reward of victory, Canada beckons.

Memorandum from Field Marshal von Moltke, the German chief of general staff, to the German minister of Foreign Affairs, August 5, 1914. Adapted from Charles F. Winter's *Lieutenant-General the Hon. Sam Hughes, K.C.B., M.P., Canada's War Minister, 1911-1916* (1931).

## Monck, Lady Elizabeth
In a fog, near that stupid Newfoundland, June 21, 1867.

Entry in the journal of Lady Monck, corrected afterward to "not at all near it." *Monck Letters and Journals 1863-1868: Canada from Government House at Confederation* (1970), edited by W.L. Morton.

## Monck, Lord
A careful consideration of the general position of British North America induced the conviction that the circumstances of the times afforded the opportunity, not merely for the settlement of a question of personal politics, but also for the simultaneous creation of a new nationality.

Speech from the throne, Parliament of Canada, Quebec, January 19, 1865. Reported in *The Globe*, January 20, 1865.

I am obliged to go to Ottawa tomorrow for a few days for some business, but I expect that you will find us still here when you come out.

Letter from Sir Charles Stanley, Fourth Lord Monck, at Spencer Wood, Quebec City, June 26, 1867, to his son Henry. *Monck Letters and Journals 1863-1868: Canada from Government House at Confederation* (1970), edited by W.L. Morton, who supplied the following footnote: "The 'business' was of course the proclamation of the Dominion of Canada. Nothing could better illustrate Monck's matter-of-factness on this occasion, mistaken and exasperating—in his treating so great an occasion as another item of business."

In addressing for the first time the Parliamentary Representatives of the Dominion of *Canada*, I desire to give expression to my own deep feeling of gratification that it has been my privilege to occupy an official position which has made it my duty to assist at every step taken in the creation of this Great Confederation.

I congratulate you on the Legislative sanction which has been given by the Imperial Parliament, to the Act of Union, under the provisions of which we are now assembled, and which has laid the foundation of a new Nationality that I trust and believe will, ere long, extend its bounds from the *Atlantic* to the *Pacific* Ocean.

＊

Your new nationality enters on its course backed by the moral support, the material aid, and the most ardent good wishes of the Mother Country. Within your own borders peace, security and prosperity prevail, and I fervently pray that your aspirations may be directed to such high and patriotic objects, and that you may be endowed with such a spirit of moderation and wisdom as will cause you to render the great work of Union which has been achieved, a blessing to yourselves and your prosperity, and a fresh starting point in the moral, political and material advancement of the people of *Canada*.

> Speech from the throne, November 7, 1867. *Journals of the House of Commons of the Dominion of Canada . . . being the 1st Session of the 1st Parliament of the Dominion of Canada* (1868).

My knowledge of public opinion in Canada has now become ancient history —but when I knew it I always thought that the exuberant loyalty which appeared so strong on the surface would not continue to exist if it were subjected to the strain of any national sacrifice. There was then, however, no indication of any desire to identify their future with that of the United States.

> Letter written to Goldwin Smith from

London, England, February 14, 1887. Quoted by Arnold Haultain in *A Selection from Goldwin Smith's Correspondence* (1913).

## Monck, Henry Wentworth

Invite all the Great Powers to Europe to a grand convention, in the hope that they may find it possible to agree to reduce simultaneously their enormous armies . . . until the great nations shall begin to realize that they can be quite as secure with one thousand soldiers each, as they are at present with half a million or more.

> Petition to Queen Victoria in 1887 from the visionary who was born at March, near Ottawa, and sat for the figure of Christ in Holman Hunt's canvas "Christ in the Temple." Quoted by Thérèse C. Thompson in "The Prophet of March," *Flamboyant Canadians* (1964), edited by Ellen Stafford.

## Monk, Maria

The Superior now informed me, that having taken the black veil, it only remained that I should swear the three oaths customary on becoming a nun: and that some explanation would be necessary from her. I was now, she told me, to have access to every part of the edifice, even to the cellar, where two of the sisters were imprisoned for causes which she did not mention. I must be informed that one of my great duties was to obey the priests in all things; and this I soon learnt, to my utter astonishment and horror, was to live in the practice of criminal intercourse with them.

> Maria Monk was (in the words of Norah Story in *The Oxford Companion to Canadian History and Literature* [1967]) "a notorious imposter, who arrived in New York from Montreal in a state of advanced pregnancy [who] claimed to be a nun who had 'escaped' from the Hotel-Dieu convent." *The Awful Disclosures of Maria Monk, as exhibited in a Narrative of Her Sufferings during a Residence of Five Years as a Novice, and Two Years as a Black Nun, in the Hôtel-Dieu Nunnery at Montreal* (1836), written with the assistance of the Rev.

George Bourne. See also Maria Monk's "daughter," Mrs. Lizzie St. John Eckel.

## Monroe, James

In the mean time the acquisition *of Canada is not an object with us,* we must make valuable what we have already *acquired* and at the same time take such measures as *to weaken it as a British province.*

Letter written to Thomas Jefferson from Trenton, New Jersey, November 1, 1784, *The Papers of Thomas Jefferson: Volume 7* (1953), edited by Julian P. Boyd.

. . . that the American continents, by the free and independent condition which they have assumed and maintained, are henceforth not to be considered as subjects for future colonization by any European powers.

Annual message of the American president to Congress, December 2, 1823, "The Monroe Doctrine."

## Monroe, Marilyn

When they said Canada, I thought it would be up in the mountains somewhere.

The movie star was interviewed on the set of *Niagara* by Jock Carroll in 1952, *The Death of the Toronto Telegram and Other Newspaper Stories* (1971).

## Monsarrat, Nicholas

Next time you say: "Toronto the Good," and a man from Montreal chips in with: "Good for what?" you can at least answer: "Good for Stratford, Ontario."

*Canada Coast to Coast* (1955).

To go to Stratford today is more than a duty—it is a pleasure.

Remark made in 1953, from *To Stratford with Love* (1963).

Canada isn't exactly underdeveloped, but living here is like living in a civilized Congo: there's just as much search for identity.

Quoted by Gerald Clark in *Canada: The Uneasy Neighbour* (1965).

Between the frowning Scottish elder and the peeping priest, Canada had apparently broken its frontiers and peopled its land, all without a single twinkle in the eye.

*Life Is a Four-Letter Word: Volume II—Breaking Out* (1970).

## Montcalm, Marquis de

As for Quebec, it is as good as the best cities of France, except ten or so. [Letter to his wife, 1756]

*

Kill me, but spare the English who are under my protection. [To the Indian allies who helped him take Fort William Henry, August 9, 1756]

*

What a country! Here all the knaves grow rich, and the honest men are ruined. [1759]

*

A little is precious to those who have nothing. [When the cargo from France in the Spring of 1759 was smaller than expected]

*

We will save this unhappy colony, or perish. [February, 1759]

*

Oh, when shall we get out of this country! I think I would give half that I have to go home. . . . [Letter to his wife, March 18, 1759]

*

I shall always say, Happy he who is free from the proud yoke to which I am bound. When shall I see my château of Candiac, my plantations, my chestnut grove, my oil-mill, my mulberry trees? *O bon dieu! Bon soir; brûlez ma lettre.* [Letter to his wife, March 23, 1759]

*

Can we hope for another miracle to save us? I trust in God; he fought for us on the eighth of July. Come what may, his will be done! [April, 1759]

*

It seems as if they were all hastening to make their fortunes before the loss of the colony; which many of them perhaps desire as a veil to their conduct. [Letter in cipher to Maréchal de Belleisle, minister of War, shortly before the Conquest]

*

We need not suppose that the enemy

have wings. [Letter to the Marquis de Vaudreuil-Cavagnal, July 27, 1759; the image is usually associated with the last governor of New France, and not with Montcalm; see also the Marquis de Vaudreuil-Cavagnal]

*

I swear to you that a hundred men posted there would stop their whole army. [Letter to the Marquis de Vaudreuil-Cavagnal, July 29, 1759; Montcalm is referring to the path from the water's edge to the Plains of Abraham, then called Anse au Foulon, now called Wolfe's Cove]

*

I am overwhelmed with work, and should often lose temper, like you, if I did not remember that I am paid by Europe for not losing it. Nothing new since my last, I give the enemy another month, or something less, to stay here. [Last letter written by Montcalm, to Brigadier-General François-Charles de Boulamaque, September 11, 1759]

> Quoted by Francis Parkman in *Montcalm and Wolfe* (1884).

Oh that I had served my God as faithfully as I have served my King.

*

There they are, where they have no right to be.

> Two remarks attributed to Montcalm, on learning the English had taken battle formation on the Plains of Abraham, September 13, 1759. "War is the grave of the Montcalms"—old French saying. "In truth, the funeral of Montcalm was the funeral of New France," Francis Parkman in *Montcalm and Wolfe* (1884). For Montcalm's dying words and a description of his death, see Francis Parkman. See also Lord Aylmer and Walter Carruthers Sellar.

### Montesquieu, Charles de

Generally, the effect of colonizing a country is to weaken the one from which people are drawn without populating the one to which they are sent.

> Letter CXXI, *The Persian Letters* (1721).

When the savages of Louisiana want

fruit, they chop down the tree at its roots and pick the fruit. That is despotic government.

> *L'esprit des lois* (1748), by Charles Louis de Secondat, Baron de la Brède et de Montesquieu.

### Montgomery, John

"John Montgomery, you have been found guilty of high treason," said Chief Justice John Beverley Robinson. "Have you anything to say before the judgment of the court is passed upon you?"

"I have," replied Montgomery bitterly. "I have not had a fair trial. There are witnesses here who have sworn my life away. The perjured evidence of William Gymer, William Crew, and David Bridgeford will haunt them in after years. These perjurers will never die a natural death; and when you, sir, and the jury shall have died and perished in hell's flames, John Montgomery will yet be living on Yonge Street."

> Prophecy allegedly made in the dock of the Toronto court house in the presence of Chief Justice John Beverley Robinson, April 2, 1838. Eight days later the proprietor of Montgomery's Tavern, which acted as a meeting place for the rebels of 1837, was convicted of high treason. He was sentenced to death but the sentence was commuted to imprisonment. Montgomery escaped to the United States and was eventually pardoned. He died in 1879, in his ninety-sixth year.
>
> Edwin C. Guillet in *The Lives and Times of the Patriots: An Account of the Rebellion in Upper Canada, 1837-1838* (1938, 1969) wrote: "An obituary notice in the Picton *Times* of January 29, 1880, is the basis of the alleged address to the court, which had been one of his favourite stories as an old man. The prophecy was partially fulfilled, for one man shot himself and another cut his throat, and Montgomery outlived judge, jurors, witnesses, and prosecutors."

### Montgomery, L.M.

Isn't it strange—the horror with which we shrink from the thought of losing our individuality? Total annihilation would be preferable to becoming anybody else, even though that anybody else might be a hundred-fold better and nobler than ourselves. [Cavendish, December 16, 1906]

It is merely a juvenile story, ostensibly for girls; [but] as I found the MS. rather interesting while reading it over lately I am not without hope that grown-ups may like it a little. Its title is *Anne of Green Gables* and the publishers seem to think it will succeed as they want me to go right to work on a sequel to it. [Cavendish, May 2, 1907]

I beg leave to call your attention to a new and original thought which you have not probably heard before. It is this —"every rose has its thorns." [Cavendish, December 22, 1908]

> The Green Gables Letters from L.M. Montgomery to Ephraim Weber 1905-1909 (1960), edited by Wilfrid Eggleston.

Elderly couple apply to orphan asylum for a boy; a girl is sent them.

> Notebook entry, about 1907, that led to the writing of *Anne of Green Gables* (1908). Quoted by Hilda M. Ridley in *The Story of L.M. Montgomery* (1956).

I've done my best, and I begin to see what is meant by the "joy of strife." Next to trying and winning, the best thing is trying and failing.

A little "appreciation" sometimes does quite as much good as all the conscientious "bringing-up" in the world.

> Anne of Green Gables (1908).

"Have you ever noticed," asked Anne reflectively, "that when people say it is their duty to tell you a certain thing you may prepare for something disagreeable? Why is it that they never seem to think it a duty to tell you the pleasant things they hear about you?"

"Having adventures comes natural to some people," said Anne serenely. "You just have a gift for them or you haven't."

> Anne of Avonlea (1909).

"Canada is the finest country in the world, Miss Cornelia."
"Nobody ever doubted that," said Miss Cornelia complacently.

> Rainbow Valley (1919).

"Snow in April is abominable," said Anne. "Like a slap in the face when you expected a kiss."

> Anne of Ingleside (1939).

The critics condemn my books because of what they call my lack of realism. My reply to them is that sunsets are just as real as pigstyes and I prefer writing about sunsets.

> Address to the Toronto Women's Press Club about 1936.

Peace! You never know what peace is until you walk on the shores or in the fields or along the winding red roads of Prince Edward Island in a summer twilight when the dew is falling and the old old stars are peeping out and the sea keeps its mighty tryst with the little land it loves. You find your soul then. You realize that youth is not a vanished thing but something that dwells forever in the heart.

> Quoted by Ian Sclanders in "Lucy of Green Gables," *Maclean's Canada: Portrait of a Country* (1960), edited by Leslie F. Hannon.

## Montgomery, Richard
I will dine in Quebec on Christmas day or in Hell.

> Adapted from a remark made in December, 1775, as quoted by George F.G. Stanley in *Canada Invaded: 1775-1776* (1973).

Push on, brave boys, Quebec is ours!

> The last command of the popular American hero, Brigadier-General Richard Montgomery, who was shot through the head and both thighs, Près-de-Ville, outside the Quebec ramparts, New Year's Eve, 1775. Montgomery commanded the American Revolutionary Army which had taken Montreal in November and, joined by the forces under

Benedict Arnold, the army intended to storm the capital of New France. Quoted by John Codman II in *Arnold's Expedition to Quebec* (1901).

## Montgomery of Alamein, Field-Marshal
In the distance I seem to catch a glimpse of a great nation of fifty million people, and more; a virile people, ideally located, who through its strength enjoy peace and security. This great Nation, joined by close ties of blood and battle to the Old World and the New World, seems to me to form a hinge between the two.

> The chief of the Imperial general staff also referred to Canada as "a priceless hinge of pure gold" in a radio broadcast "to the people of Canada" in September of 1946. *The Memoirs of Field-Marshal The Viscount Montgomery of Alamein, K.G.* (1958).

## Montrueil
In this country a thousand men could stop three thousand.

> Letter to a French minister, June 12, 1756, quoted by Francis Parkman in *Montcalm and Wolfe* (1884).

## Moodie, Colonel Robert
I am shot—I am a dead man.

> Dying words of the officer shot by the rebels before he could inform the authorities of the uprising, near Montgomery's Tavern, December 4, 1837. Quoted by John Charles Dent in *The Story of the Upper Canadian Rebellion* (1885).

## Moodie, Susanna
The aristocracy of wealth is bad enough; but the aristocracy of dress is perfectly contemptible. Could Raphael visit Canada in rags, he would be nothing in their eyes beyond a common sign-painter.

\*

My love for Canada was a feeling very nearly allied to that which the condemned criminal entertains for his cell.
. . .

\*

"I've never know'd an English gentleman to get on in the bush." [Neighbour's remark]

\*

Reader! it is not my intention to trouble you with the sequel of our history. I have given you a faithful picture of a life in the backwoods of Canada, and I leave you to draw from it your own conclusions. To the poor, industrious working man it presents many advantages; to the poor gentleman, *none!*

\*

If these sketches should prove the means of deterring one family from sinking their property, and shipwrecking all their hopes, by going to reside in the backwoods of Canada, I shall consider myself amply repaid for revealing the secrets of the prison-house, and feel that I have not toiled and suffered in the wilderness in vain.

\*

We found that manual toil, however distasteful to those unaccustomed to it, was not after all such a dreadful hardship; that the wilderness was not without its rose, the hard face of poverty without its smile. If we occasionally suffered severe pain, we as often experienced great pleasure, and I have contemplated a well-hoed ridge of potatoes on that bush farm with as much delight as in years long past I had experienced in examining a fine painting in some well-appointed drawing room.

> *Roughing It in the Bush; or, Forest Life in Canada* (1852).

To the honest sons of labour Canada is, indeed, an El Dorado—a land flowing with milk and honey; for they soon obtain that independence which the poor gentleman struggles in vain to realize by his own labour in the woods.

> *Life in the Clearings versus the Bush* (1853).

Beautiful—most beautiful in her rugged grandeur is this vast country. How awful is the sublime solitude of her pathless woods! what eloquent thoughts flow out of the deep silence that broods over them! We feel as if we stood alone in the presence of God, and nature lay at his feet in speechless adoration.

Has Canada no poet to describe the glories of his parent land—no painter that can delineate her matchless scenery of land and wave? Are her children dumb and blind, that they leave to strangers the task of singing her praise?

The standard literature of Canada must be looked for in her newspapers.

"Introduction," *Mark Hurdlestone, The Gold Worshipper* (1853). *Life in the Clearings by Susanna Moodie, to which is added this author's Introduction to Mark Hurdlestone* (1959), edited by Robert L. McDougall.

## Moody, Dr. T. Glendon
If it hurts, don't pay me.

How many dentists would make such an offer? Dr. Moody, Vancouver's "painless dentist," did, in 1915, because he had invented "Oralthesia — the most wonderful discovery of the age—the one and only sure, safe antidote to pain in the dental chair." Quoted by David Parry in *The Canadian Magazine*, December 2, 1972.

## Moore, Brian
He doesn't want to talk about Canada. . . . There you have the Canadian dilemma in a sentence. Nobody wants to talk about Canada, not even us Canadians. You're right, Paddy. Canada is a bore.

*The Luck of Ginger Coffey* (1960).

Have I left it? It reminds me of the story of James Joyce when he was asked why he had left the Church. "That's for them to say," he said. I feel the same way.

Reply to Gerald Clark's question why he left Canada for the United States, quoted in *Canada: The Uneasy Neighbour* (1965).

Cynics have said that it would be cheaper for the government to house Canada's total Eskimo population in the swank Château Laurier Hotel in Ottawa than it is to maintain the present Eskimo welfare services in the Arctic.

\*

The story of Canada's development of its North, then, can be summed up fairly accurately in one sentence: where there are profits, there are people.

\*

Possibly the only definition of Canadianism that some citizens might agree on is the wry observation that "a Canadian is someone who has turned down a chance to go and live in the United States."

\*

Developed or not, the North remains all important to the Canadians' self-image. It makes their country the second largest on earth. . . . Above all, its brooding physical presence over the land is a warning that Canadians have not yet conquered their universe.

*Canada* (1963, 1968).

It was, perhaps, the final irony in this Canadian drama. Two men had been kidnapped. The French Canadian lay dead. The Englishman went free.

*The Revolution Script* (1971).

Fiction is a great release from the dreadful facts we live with.

Interviewed by Donald Cameron in *Conversations with Canadian Novelists* (1973).

## Moore, Dora Mavor
Around here the managing director scrubs floors if necessary!

Mrs. Moore was managing director of the New Play Society in Toronto in the 1950s.

## Moore, H. Napier
I have made the assertion repeatedly, amidst tremendous laughter, that we haven't had a depression at all in this country, that really we have been getting over a very bad boom.

"The Melancholy of Laughter" (1935), *Empire Club of Canada: Addresses Delivered to the Members During the Year 1934-35* (1935).

## Moore, Mavor
No wonder our face looks blank to others. Even in films a Canadian to date has been either a half-breed trapper or a Mountie, or a contrivance for casting an Englishman in a Hollywood picture or an American in an English one.

\*

If we are not ourselves, we shall be less than others.

"Theatre in English-Speaking Canada," *The Arts in Canada: A Stock-Taking at Mid-Century* (1958), edited by Malcolm Ross.

If we fail this generation, we shall deserve the Maple Leaf as a symbol: a red face with a blank expression, and a pointed head.

*Maclean's Magazine*, June 4, 1966.

## Moore, Thomas
Faintly as tolls the evening chime
Our voices keep tune and our oars keep
time.
Soon as the woods on shore look dim,
We'll sing at St. Ann's our parting hymn.
Row, brothers, row, the stream runs fast,
The Rapids are near and the daylight's
past.

Why should we yet our sail unfurl?
Why is not a breath the blue wave to
curl;
But when the wind blows off the shore,
Oh! sweetly we'll rest our weary oar.
Blow, breezes, blow, the stream runs fast,
The Rapids are near and the daylight's
past.

Utawas' tide! this trembling moon
Shall see us float over thy surges soon.
Saint of this green isle! hear our prayers,
Oh, grant us cool heaven and favouring
airs.
Blow, breezes, blow, the stream runs fast,
The Rapids are near and the daylight's
past.

"I wrote these words to an air which our boatmen sung to us frequently. The wind was so unfavourable that they were obliged to row all the way, and we were five days in descending the river from Kingston to Montreal, exposed to an intense sun during the day, and at night forced to take shelter from the dews in any miserable hut upon the banks that would receive us. But the magnificent scenery of the St. Lawrence repays all such difficulties." From the notes to "A Canadian Boat Song: Written on the River St. Lawrence" by Thomas Moore

in 1804, and first published in *Epistles, Odes and Other Poems* (1806).

Moore's poem is frequently confused with "Canadian Boat-Song (from the Gaelic)," which first appeared in *Blackwood's*, September, 1829; see David Macbeth Moir. Curiously, although both were popular in the Canadas during the nineteenth century, neither poem was written by a Canadian about a boat or as a song. Of the two, Moore's was the better known, Moir's the more moving. The Scotsman never set foot on North American soil; the Irishman wrote his lyric at Ste. Anne de Bellevue while visiting with the explorer Simon Fraser.

\*

I dreamt not then that, ere the rolling
year
Had fill'd its circle, I should wander
here
In musing awe; should tread this wondrous world,
See all its store of inland waters
hurl'd
In one vast volume down Niagara's
steep,
Or calm behold them, in transparent
sleep,
Where the blue hills of old Toronto
shed
Their evening shadows o'er Ontario's
bed;
Should trace the grand Cataraqui, and
glide
Down the white rapids of his lordly
tide....

Lines from "To the Lady Charlotte Rawdon, from the Banks of the St. Lawrence," 1804. *The Poetical Works of Thomas Moore: Reprinted from Early Editions, with Explanatory Notes, Etc.* (1910). See also Thomas D'Arcy McGee.

## Moran, Lord
The atmosphere of Ottawa after Washington is like Belfast after Dublin.

*Churchill: Taken from The Diaries of Lord Moran: The Struggle for Survival (1940-1965)* (1966).

## Morgan, Henry
Those were the days when we made history and took our whiskey straight.

Letter to Charles Mair, December 4, 1899, concerning the Canada First movement of the 1860s and 1870s, quoted by Carl Berger in *The Sense of Power: Studies in the Ideas of Canadian Imperialism: 1867-1914* (1970).

## Morgan, Henry
I think Canada's a wonderful country and we're going to keep it that way.

New York television personality living in Toronto, 1971.

A kleptomaniac can't help helping himself.

Credited by Leo Rosten in *Rome Wasn't Burned in a Day: The Mischief of Language* (1972) to "Henry Morgan—the comedian, not the pirate; the two categories are not always resolutely separated."

## Morin, Nicole
I'm fully aware my body opens many doors for me professionally. But it is what happens once I'm inside these doors that is really important.

Bosomy film actress, quoted by Peter Goddard in *Star Week*, May 6, 1972.

## Morison, Dr. R.S.
A thousand years from now people will know Montreal as the place where Wilder Penfield made his classic maps of the cerebral cortex, Hans Selye made "stress" a household word, and Jacques Genest helped to blaze a trail through the Laurentian mountains to an understanding of hypertension.

Address of the director of Medical and Natural Sciences, Rockefeller Foundation, at a meeting of the Canadian Medical Association at Ste. Adèle, 1964. Quoted by H.E. MacDermot in *One Hundred Years of Medicine in Canada 1867-1967* (1967).

## Morison, Samuel Eliot
No other European colony in America is so much the lengthened shadow of one man as Canada is of the valiant, wise, and virtuous Samuel de Champlain, Xaintongeois (of Saintonge).

*

Even the humble and inconspicuous Pilgrim Fathers enjoyed more publicity in England than all Canada and L'Acadie obtained in France. This helps to explain the bitterness of French-Canadian nationalists toward Mother France, who neglected their ancestors when they were few, poor and needy, and "abandoned" them to the English after they had formed a viable society. The third Republic honoured (?) Champlain by naming a second-class cruiser after him in 1874, and a store ship in 1919.

*Samuel de Champlain: Father of New France* (1972).

I remember how the marketwomen of Paris, wheeling barrows of apples of doubtful origin, used to cry them as "Canada! des vraies Canada!"

*The European Discovery of America: The Northern Voyages A.D. 500-1600* (1971). See also: Biarni, Brendan the Apostle, Hélène Champlain.

## Moriyama, Raymond
I'm constantly reminded of what my grandfather told me: the moon shines just as much on a handful of water as on a lake. We may find truth under a pebble. Truth is probably very small.

Quoted by Marjorie Harris in *Maclean's Magazine*, March, 1970.

Architecture is a backdrop for worthwhile human activity.

Vancouver - born Toronto architect, quoted in *Time*, July 9, 1973.

## Morley, Christopher
The scene of the tale is said to be England. And yet, to the zealous observer, there will seem to be some flavours that are hardly English. . . . I am wondering about this, and I conclude that perhaps it is due to the fact that Miss de la Roche lives in Toronto, that delightful city where the virtues of both England and America are said to be subtly and consummately blended. Her story, as simple and refreshing as the tune of an old song, and yet so richly spiced with humour, perhaps presents a blend of qualities and imaginations that we would

only find in Canada; for the Canadians, after all, are the true Anglo-Americans.

Foreword to Mazo de la Roche's *Explorers of the Dawn* (1922).

## Morley, Robert
Have I a message for Toronto? I'm hoping Toronto has a message for me.

Quoted by Herbert Whittaker in *The Globe and Mail*, August 30, 1972.

I don't suppose we found out much about Canada or the Canadians, but we learnt a little about a country of which the English know nothing, which is not surprising when you think how little Canadians seem to know about their land either.

*The London Observer*, December 24, 1972.

## Morrice, James Wilson
Fine work, almost criminally fine. I once disliked some of his pictures, but now I like them all. His is the savage work that one would expect to come from America—but it is always France that produces anything emphatic in art. [Letter to Edmund Morris, January 30, 1911, about a Cézanne exhibition]

I have not the slightest desire to improve the taste of the Canadian public. [Letter to Edmund Morris, February 12, 1911]

Quoted by J. Russell Harper in *Painting in Canada: A History* (1966).

My name is written all over it. [Refusing to sign a painting]

Quoted by Donald W. Buchanan in *James Wilson Morrice: A Biography* (1936). The Franco-Canadian painter is described in Bennett's *Buried Alive* (1908) and in Maugham's two novels *The Magician* (1908) and *Of Human Bondage* (1915). See also: Arnold Bennett, Henri Matisse, William Somerset Maugham.

## Morris, Alexander
A new nationality.

The concept of a new nationality of the North has been credited to Thomas

D'Arcy McGee, Lord Monck and Alexander Morris. Morris is best-remembered as the author and negotiator of *The Treaties of Canada with the Indians of Manitoba and the North-West Territories* (1880). As a young lawyer he delivered a lecture in Montreal in 1858 which included the phrase "a new nationality." This was published as *The Hudson's Bay and Pacific Territories* (1859). See also Thomas D'Arcy McGee and Lord Monck.

Canada was bound to the North-West by the ties of discovery, possession, and interest. ["Speech on the Resolutions for the Acquisitions of the North-West Territory," House of Commons, December 5, 1867]

*

. . . who can doubt of the reality and the accuracy of the vision which rises distinctly and clearly-defined before us, as the Great Britannic Empire of the North stands out in all its grandeur, and in all the brilliance of its magnificent future! . . . who can doubt of the future of these British Provinces, or of the entire and palpable reality of that vision which rises so grandly before us of the Great British Empire of the North—of that new English-speaking nation which will at one and no distant day people all this Northern continent—a Russia, as has been well said, it may be, but yet an English Russia, with free institutions, with high civilization, and entire freedom of speech and thought—with its face to the south and its back to the pole, with its right and left resting on the Atlantic and the Pacific, and with the telegraph and the iron road connecting the two oceans! ["The Hudson's Bay and Pacific Territories," Mercantile Library Association of Montreal, winter, 1858]

*

I was told at one meeting in Montreal that I had Canada on the brain. Well, gentlemen, a great many others have Canada on the brain now. [Speech at the Annual Dinner, St. Andrew's Day, Selkirk St. Andrew's Society, as lieutenant-governor of Manitoba (1872-78)]

*Nova Britannia; or, Our New Canadian Dominion Foreshadowed* (1884).

And why is all this done? I will tell you; it is because you are the subjects of the Queen as I am. She cares as much for one of you as she does for one of her white subjects. The other day a party of Iroquois Indians were taken to England across the ocean; the Queen heard of it and sent to them, saying, "I want to see my red children," took their hands and gave each of them her picture, and sent them away happy with her goodness. [Address preparatory to the signing of the Treaties of Forts Carlton and Pitt, August 18, 1876]

*

I said to myself, we must teach the children to prepare for the future; if we do not, but a few suns will pass and they will melt away like snow before the sun in spring-time. . . . My words, when they are accepted, are written down, and they last, as I have said to the others, as long as the sun shines and the river runs. [Address preparatory to the signing of the Treaties of Forts Carlton and Pitt, September 7, 1876]

> Alexander Morris was lieutenant-governor of Manitoba and the negotiator of a succession of important treaties. *The Treaties of Canada with the Indians of Manitoba and the North-West Territories, including the Negotiations on which They Were Based, and Other Information Relating Thereto* (1880). See also Mawedopenais.

### Morris, Clara
There is no habit more tenacious than the habit of work.

> *The Life of a Star* (1906), by the Canadian-born Broadway leading lady.

### Morris, James
It was the proud boast of the grandest Anglo-Canadian mansions that not a stick of furniture in the house, not a knife, not a single painting of Highland cattle in a gloomy brownish glen, was home-produced—all came, as they liked to say, from the Old Country.

*

In the emancipation of Queen Victoria's Canada we may detect some prophetic glimpses of the anxieties that occur, when great Empires disintegrate at last, and leave their distant children to evolve identities of their own.

*

Canada was the idealist's end of Empire —a people united in reconciliation, a colony emancipated, a wilderness civilized, the principles of parliamentary democracy transferred in triumphant vindication from an ancient capital to a new.

> *Pax Britannica: The Climax of an Empire* (1968).

In theory the whole country was British. Since the end of the French wars Canada had formed one of the weirder of the Crown's dependencies, peopled, where it was peopled at all, mostly by Frenchmen, American loyalists and dispossessed Highlanders.

*

The insects were terrible, too: blackflies, buffalo gnats, deerflies, mooseflies, legs, no see-ums, creepin' fire and ubiquitous, unspeakable mosquitoes . . . who are said to inhabit the Canadian north in an incidence of five million to the acre: a naked man would be sucked dry of all his blood in three and one-half hours, and even the caribou, some theorists believe, are driven to their migrations by the insect bites.

> *Heaven's Command: An Imperial Progress* (1973).

### Morris, Jan    See James Morris.

### Morris, Jerrold
Few Canadian nudes are energetic, pathetic or ecstatic.

> *The Nude in Canadian Painting* (1972).

### Morris, Leslie
"Write as you fight" is a fine old motto.

> Introduction by Morris to *Our Fight for Canada: Selected Writings (1923-1959)* (1959), by Tim Buck.

Social change, ripening to the point of radical social transformation, is the law of development of human society.

> "The 'Great Divides' in Human History," *The Canadian Tribune*, Novem-

ber 9, 1964. This was the veteran Communist's last article, and it has been reprinted in *Look On Canada, Now: Selected Writings of Leslie Morris 1923-1964* (1970).

**Morris, Sir Lewis**
We hold a vaster empire than has been!

This line first appeared in "Song of Empire," a poem by Sir Lewis Morris to celebrate Queen Victoria's Jubilee, June 20, 1887. Of the author, Sir Paul Harvey wrote in *The Oxford Companion to English Literature* (Third Edition, 1946): "His simplicity of expression, melodious verse, cheerful optimism, and occasional exaltation made his work extremely popular, in spite of its poetic mediocrity." Nevertheless, his sentiments found sympathetic hearts in the Dominions, especially Canada. William Wilfred Campbell conceived of Canada as a "Vaster Britain." For the phrase, as it appeared on the two-cent stamp in 1898, see Sir William Mulock.

**Morris, Richard**
Give us a place to stand
And a place to grow
And call this land
Ontario.

\*

Give us a land of lakes
And a land of snow
And we will build
Ontario.

\*

A place to stand,
A place to grow,
Ontar-i-ar-i-ar-io.

A few lines from the rousing "Ontar-i-ar-i-ar-io," the theme song from *A Place to Stand*, a documentary film directed by Christopher Chapman for the Ontario government which won an Academy Award for short subjects (live action) in 1967. The song proved so popular it was eventually released as a disc. The lyrics are by Richard Morris, the music by Dolores Claman.

**Morriseau, Norval**
People say that heaven is up in the great skies beyond the stars. If a rocket ship left the earth today, I understand it would travel for a long time and still not reach anywhere, for space is vast. As for those of my people who claimed to have gone some place after they were dead and then come back in a matter of two to three days, my idea is, where could they have gone? If the rocket ship could travel for ever without finding heaven, then there must be a heaven right here on earth that we pass every day without being able to penetrate its invisible wall. When a human body dies, and the soul leaves the body, then the soul itself can pass through this wall that we cannot pass in our human bodies.

*Legends of My People, The Great Ojibway* (1965), edited by Selwyn Dewdney.

My teacher? Who could teach me this? Only legends.

At the Toronto opening of the young Ojibway artist's first show in the early 1960s.

**Morse, Eric W.**
The challenge of wilderness travel in Canada is two-edged: the personal challenge to *explore*, and the public challenge to *preserve*—while yet we are able.

"Challenge and Response: The Modern Voyageur," *Wilderness Canada* (1970), edited by Borden Spears.

**Mortimer, Lee**   See Jack Lait.

**Morton, Desmond**
It doesn't matter whether the North Bay *Nugget* belongs to Roy Thomson, Max Bell, or a local drygoods merchant. They are all, without a single exception, in the same kind of hands. They all belong to the Canadian business community and they do what that community wants. And if Canadian businessmen assume an automatic, infallible identity between their views and those of every right-thinking Canadian, they are hardly unique among the oligarchs of history.

Professor of law, quoted by Keith Davey in *Report of the Special Senate Committee on Mass Media, Volume I: The Uncertain Mirror* (1971).

## Morton, Lindsay

The whole thing resolved itself into a question of dying decently.

Pathetic comment of an English mining agent who crouched with his family on the shore of the lake while the South Porcupine gold camp burned to the ground in 1911. Quoted by Frank Rasky in *Great Canadian Disasters* (1961).

## Morton, W.L.

The line which marks off the frontier and the farmstead, the wilderness from the baseline, the hinterland from the metropolis, runs through every Canadian psyche.

*

If then Canada's destiny is in its own hands, why is it disturbed by fear and resentment of America? The answer is plain. What Canada really fears is not the old America, but America in its new role of world power. It fears that America in seeking to maintain its world power will make demand after demand on Canada, each reasonable in itself, until the substance of independence is modified out of existence.

*

As America is united at bottom by the covenant, Canada is united at the top by allegiance. Because Canada is a nation founded on allegiance and not on compact, there is no process in becoming Canadian akin to conversation, there is no pressure for uniformity, there is no Canadian way of life. Any one, French, Irish, Ukrainian or Eskimo, can be a subject of the Queen and a citizen of Canada without in any way changing or ceasing to be himself. This is a truth so fundamental that it is little realized and many, if not most, Canadians would deny its truth, but it is central to any explanation or understanding of Canadian nationhood.

*

Not life, liberty, and the pursuit of happiness, but peace, order, and good government are what the national government of Canada guarantees. Under these, it is assumed, life, liberty, and happiness may be achieved, but by each according to his taste. For the society of allegiance admits of a diversity the so-ciety of compact does not, and one of the blessings of Canadian life is that there is no Canadian way of life, much less two, but a unity under the Crown admitting of a thousand diversities.

*The Canadian Identity* (1961).

A Canadian is someone who knows he is going somewhere, but isn't sure where.

Quoted by Gerald Clark in *Canada: The Uneasy Neighbour* (1965).

If one must travel to Nowhere, there is no more comfortable way than on a tide of oil.

"The Bias of Prairie Politics," *Historical Essays on the Prairie Provinces* (1970), edited by Donald Swainson.

Nationalism may be a bad thing, but nihilism is worse. [Attributed]

## Mosher, Aaron R.

These are Mosher's Rules of Order!

Characteristic retort at union conventions to any delegate who invoked Robert's Rules of Order. Mosher was president of the Canadian Brotherhood of Railway Employees from its inception in 1908 until 1952.

## Mosley, Sir Oswald

When Britain at last decided on great policies, it should ask the Queen of England to go, together with the President of France, to invite Canada to enter the European community. I reiterate that Europe can only be made, and great things can only be done, in a great way.

*My Life* (1968), by the British fascist.

## Mother Damnable

All the land to the west of this shall remain wild and unpeopled for two hundred years. Then it shall give food to the eastern tribes of men. ["West of this" has been interpreted as west of Winnipeg; "two hundred years" would bring the year to 1900, when the West began producing wheat for the East]

*

All the world shall one day be divided into two great countries; one of these shall almost destroy itself, but shall afterwards become greater than before. [It is assumed Mother Damnable meant North America when she said "all the world," and that this was a reference to the American Civil War]

*

A country shall rise up that shall take its name from the great Master of Life, and shall be blessed by him and shall prosper, and shall spread to the west and fill the western country with white men; and the face of the country shall be divided like crystal. ["Master of Life" would be Manitou, so this might be a prophecy of the birth of Manitoba; "divided like crystal" might be an imaginative image for surveyors' sections]

> Mother Damnable was the name the English gave Wampohama, a Huron woman who lived among the Crees on the shore of Lake Winnipeg. There is no record of her birth but in 1648 she is said to have married a Huron chief. Mother Damnable lived like a recluse and was respected as a shaman. She died about 1700, leaving the world richer (if not wiser) for her prophecies, made on her deathbed. *A Short Account of the Old Indian Witch, Wampohama, better known to the early settlers as Mother Damnable, Together with her Extraordinary Prophecies, already partially fulfilled, concerning the Future Destinies of What are Now Winnipeg, Manitoba, and the Great North-West* (1882).

### Motherwell, W.R.

Our CCF friends over there are all full of an abundance of hot air and heifer dust. [Remark made in the House of Commons in 1934]

*

I may still have a seat but no place to put it. [Complaining to R.B. Bennett in 1925 that redistribution would deprive him of his seat]

*

When a man drops out at the age of eighty, people can't say he's a quitter.

> The "Honourable W.R." retired from federal politics in 1938, two years short of eighty. The last two remarks are quoted by Grant MacEwan in "Fighting Farmer from Sintaluta," *Fifty Mighty Men* (1958).

### Mountain, Bishop Jacob

If ye have faith as a grain of mustard seed, ye shall say unto this mountain, Be ye removed and planted in the Sea.

> "A charming story is told as to the appointment of Rev. Jacob Mountain, in 1793, to the See of Quebec, which then included all the Canadian Provinces. It is said that when consulting with William Pitt as to the appointment of a Bishop to Canada, he took the liberty of conveying a hint to the Prime Minister by combining Matt. xvii, 20 and Luke xvii, 6. . . ." E.J. Hathaway in *Jesse Ketchum and His Times* (1929).

The good people of England are so fond of their Constitution that they will force it upon those who are totally unfit to receive it: as if, because Roast Beef is wholesome and nourishing for strong men, we should cram it down the throats of infants, who are totally incapable of digesting it.

> Letter of the Protestant bishop, March 6, 1810. Quoted by Peter Burroughs in *The Canadian Crisis and British Colonial Policy, 1828-1841* (1972).

### Mountbatten, Philip

"On the Canadian prairies a woman calls out: 'I've got a life-size picture of you!' Philip calls back: 'How ghastly!' "

> Pierre Berton in *The Royal Family: The Story of the British Monarchy from Victoria to Elizabeth* (1954).

Tell me, are our people in Quebec still loyal?

> To a startled James Eayrs during the visit in 1964 of H.R.H. The Prince Philip, Duke of Edinburgh. Quoted by Eayrs in *The Toronto Star*, February 14, 1972.

Not another one?

> On being presented with yet another ceremonial cowboy hat at the Calgary Stampede in 1969. (Later, in Vancouver, the Prince apologized, and explained: "Once given the key to the city, you don't go on getting keys to the city.")

*

I declare this thing open—whatever it is.

Shortly after apologizing for the Calgary cowboy hat incident, Prince Philip opened the new annex to the Vancouver City Hall, but forgot its name. "It was raining, and I wanted to get on with it: especially as the total audience was about fifteen passing shoppers under umbrellas," explained the Prince later. (The annex is now known in Vancouver as The East Thing.) Quoted by Basil Boothroyd in *Philip: An Informal Biography* (1971).

The monarchy exists in Canada for historical reasons and it exists in the sense that it's a benefit or it was considered to be a benefit to the country or to the nation.

*

I think it is a complete misconception to imagine that the monarchy exists in the interest of the monarchy. It does not. It exists in the interest of the people in the sense that we do not come here for our health . . . we can think of other ways of enjoying ourselves.

*

If at any stage people feel that it has no further part to play then for goodness sake let's end the thing on amicable terms without having a row about it. [Ottawa press conference, October, 1969]

See also Harold Brine.

**Mowat, Farley**
For those with eyes to see, the North is vitally and vividly alive. Long, long ago, men of other races out of another time recognized this truth and learned to call the northern regions "home."

*Canada North* (1967).

You must rid yourself of this delusion because, as I see things, there is no guarantee that the privileged position presently enjoyed by Canadians as "most-favoured serfs" will last. The day is near when the Yankees will see no further need to pamper us—they'll own us outright . . . and remember—a man who sells *himself* into slavery does not earn the gratitude of his master; instead he earns a deep contempt. We Canadians have well earned such contempt—and a wise slave knows that a contemptuous master is more to be feared, in the long run, than an angry one.

"Letter to My Son" in *The New Romans: Candid Canadian Opinions of the U.S.* (1968), edited by Al Purdy.

I have my own vision of the high North. I envision it being transformed—restored—into a symbol of sanity in a world where madness is becoming the accepted mode of action.

*Tundra: Selections from the Great Accounts of Arctic Land Voyages* (1973).

**Mowat, Sir Oliver**
For myself I am a true Briton. I love the old land dearly. I am glad that I was born a British subject; a British subject I have lived for three score years and something more. I hope to live and die a British subject. I trust and hope that my children and my grand-children who have also been born British subjects will live their lives as British subjects, and as British subjects die.

Address in Toronto, February 18, 1891, while prime minister of Ontario. Quoted by C.R.W. Biggar in *Sir Oliver Mowat: A Biographical Sketch* (1905).

**Moynihan, Daniel**
You have a conservative tradition as well as a liberal tradition, and these supplement and complete and sustain each other. The United States lacks and has suffered for the absence of what could be called a conservative tradition. The people we call conservatives are really nothing more than rich anarchists.

Toronto address, *The Toronto Star*, April 14, 1972.

**Mozart, Wolfgang Amadeus**
But as to merit, I know
For sure, yes, yes, I swear . . .
The likes of us you will not find
From Paris to Canada,
From Paris to Canada,
From Paris to Canada.

From "Guglielmo's Aria" which Lorenzo da Ponte wrote for *Così Fan Tutti*. Mozart set the words to music in Vienna, December of 1789, but the aria is seldom performed, except in Canada. K. 384, Appendix, *Sämtliche Werke*.

## Mrozek, Slawomir
This place is nice and empty. What you should do is organize reverse immigration, and make it even emptier while you still have a chance.

> Polish playwright's reaction to Canada, 1969.

## Muggeridge, Malcolm
It would be preposterous to suggest that Lord Beaverbrook's Personality Cult in New Brunswick is seriously comparable with Stalin's in Russia. One might as well compare a pair of old-fashioned bellows with a hurricane. Yet the principle is the same, the passion of a human ego to occupy the wide open spaces of history, to ensure that the notice achieved or enforced in life shall endure after death.

> "The Cult The Beaver Built," *Maclean's Magazine*, November 2, 1963.

## Muir, Alexander
In days of yore, from Britain's shore,
Wolfe, the dauntless hero, came,
And planted firm Britannia's flag
On Canada's fair domain.

Here may it wave, our boast and pride,
And, joined in love together,
The Thistle, Shamrock, Rose entwine
The Maple Leaf forever!

The Maple Leaf, our emblem dear,
The Maple Leaf for ever;
God save our Queen, and Heaven bless
The Maple Leaf for ever.

> First verse and chorus of "The Maple Leaf Forever," *Selections from Scottish Canadian Poets: Being a Collection of the Best Poetry Written by Scotsmen and their Descendants in the Dominion of Canada* (1900), edited by Dr. Daniel Clark. "The Maple Leaf Forever" was written in the year of Confederation by Alexander Muir, a Toronto school teacher and later principal. One day in the fall, Muir was walking when a maple leaf floated down and clung persistently to his sleeve. He tried to brush it off, then jokingly remarked "the maple leaf for ever." He then wrote the poem

which he fitted to his own music. He had a thousand copies printed for thirty dollars but the work was pirated by a music publisher who copyrighted it, promoted it and sold it widely without payment to Muir.

The pro-British words have never been acceptable to French Canadians. The first two lines are sometimes toned down: "In days of yore the hero, Wolfe, / Britain's glory did maintain. . . ." The last two lines of the first verse are similarly altered: "With lily, thistle, shamrock, rose, / The Maple Leaf forever."

## Müller, Max
To my mind the structure of such a language as the Mohawk is quite sufficient evidence that those who worked out such a work of art were powerful reasoners and accurate classifiers.

\*

It has long been a puzzle to me why this most tempting and promising field of philological research has been allowed to lie almost fallow in America,—as if these languages could not tell us quite as much of the growth of the human mind as Chinese, or Hebrew, or Sanscrit.

> "Professor Max Müller, who took the opportunity afforded by the presence of a Mohawk undergraduate at Oxford to study his language, writes of it in emphatic terms"—letters written in 1882 to Horatio Hale, quoted in Hale's *The Iroquois Book of Rites* (1883).

## Mulock, Sir William
"WE HOLD A VASTER EMPIRE THAN HAS BEEN"

> Sir William Mulock, postmaster-general under Laurier, arranged the issue of Canada's first commemorative stamp in 1898 to honour the "Imperial penny postage." The two-cent stamp, the first printed in multiple colours, bore the legend "We Hold A Vaster Empire Than Has Been," in English only. "On an engraved outline map of the world in black, the seven seas were printed by offset in blue and the British Empire in red. The stamp was the object of public criticism because of the difficulty of registering the colours accurately; the red

showed on areas that were not under British control." J.R. Carpenter, "Postage Stamps," *Encyclopedia Canadiana* (1963). See also: William Wilfred Campbell, Sir Lewis Morris, F.H. Underhill.

## Mulvaney, Charles Pelham
He heard the sentence with a smile on his lips.

Description of Louis Riel receiving the death sentence in court, September 18, 1885. *The History of the North-West Rebellion of 1885* (1885).

## Münchausen, Baron
"Pray, my dear Baron, were you ever at the Falls of Niagara?"

"Yes, my lady," replied I, surprised at such a strange association of ideas; "I have been, many years ago, at the Falls of Niagara, and found no more difficulty in swimming up and down the cataracts than I should to move a minuet."

At that moment she dropped her nosegay.

*

In these cold climates I observed that the eagles flew with greater rapidity, in order, I suppose, to keep their blood in circulation. In passing Baffin's Bay I saw several large Greenlandmen to the eastward, and many surprising mountains of ice in those seas.

While I was surveying these wonders of nature it occurred to me that this was a good opportunity to discover the north-west passage, if any such existed, and not only obtain the reward offered by the government, but the honour of a discovery pregnant with so many advantages to every European nation. But while my thoughts were absorbed in this pleasing reverie I was alarmed by the first eagle striking its head against a solid transparent substance, and in a moment that which I rode experienced the same fate, and both fell down seemingly dead.

*The Travels and Surprising Adventures of Baron Münchausen* (1785), by Rudolf Erich Raspe.

## Munger, William
England's Star has passed its zenith. Russia will one day, and that at no distant period, control England's Asiatic possessions. When that happens, as a natural consequence the United States will take possession of the Bahamas and all the British West Indies islands; and Canada will fall into our lap like a ripe apple.

Congressman from Ohio, quoted by Paul F. Sharp in *Whoop-Up Country: The Canadian-American West: 1865-85* (1955).

## Munk, Jens
Herewith goodnight to the whole world and my soul into the hand of God.

Concluding words of the will drawn up by Jens Munk, June 4, 1620. The Danish sea captain was searching for the Northwest Passage. Wintering on the west coast of Hudson Bay near Churchill River, he watched sixty-one of his men die of scurvy, so he drew up his will. Munk and two others survived the winter and managed to sail the smaller of their two ships back to Europe.

## Munro, Alice
So a house is not the same for a woman. She is not someone who walks into the house, to make use of it, and will walk out again. She *is* the house; there is no separation possible.

Quoted by Richard Needham in *The Globe and Mail*, August 15, 1972.

## Munro, William Bennett
If MacDonald is entitled to be called the Father of Confederation it would appear that Alexander Hamilton has some claim to be designed as its grandfather.

*American Influences on Canadian Government* (1929).

## Munsinger, Gerda
Perhaps it's about Sévigny?

First words to Robert Reguly who traced Mrs. Gerda Munsinger, intimate of at least one cabinet minister, to Munich.

*

If I were a spy, would I be working for a living?

Mrs. Munsinger was a hostess in a Munich nightclub. "Star Man Finds

Gerda Munsinger," *The Toronto Star*, March 11, 1966.

I knew Pierre as a man. He knew me as a woman. That's all there was to it.

The reference is to Pierre Sévigny, then associate minister of National Defence in the Diefenbaker government. Quoted by Peter C. Newman in *The Distemper of Our Times: Canadian Politics in Transition: 1963-1968* (1968) who called this "the most fitting epitaph to the affair."

I want my bedtime Tory.

Attributed by James Johnston in *The Party's Over* (1971). See also: Lucien Cardin, Gillis Purcell, Robert Reguly, Pierre Sévigny.

## Murphy, Emily Ferguson
It was as pleasant an experience as running a rapids without a guide. Besides, the lawyers and police officials looked so accustomed and so terribly sophisticated. Indeed, I have never seen brass buttons so bright and menacing as on this particular day. All the men became embarrassed and started to stammer over their manner of addressing me. One said "Your Worship" and others "Your Honour." A negro said "Your Majesty" and the rest said "Sir."

In 1916, at the age of forty-eight, Mrs. Emily Gowan Ferguson Murphy became the first lady magistrate in the British Empire. The Edmonton feminist also led the battle to admit women to the Senate. Quoted by Byrne Hope Sanders in *Canadian Portraits: Famous Women* (1958). See also Anonymous: Some Documents.

## Murphy, Harvey
You don't know the difference between communism and rheumatism!

Reply of the sometime vice-president of the Union of Mine, Mill and Smelter Workers to charges that the union was communist-dominated, at the Mine-Mill Convention, Royal York Hotel, Toronto, 1959. (It was alleged that Murphy was Canada's only graduate of the LSE—the Lenin School of Espionage, in Moscow.)

## Murray, Anne
Thanks. The Maritime mafia has just scratched the surface.

Accepting the 1970 Juno Award of the Canadian music industry's weekly magazine *RPM* as the top female vocalist of the year.

## Murray, Gladstone
As I said, when broadcasting from New York, I think the declared intention of Canada to establish public service broadcasting is a normal sign—a symbol of a developing national consciousness.

"Should Broadcasting Be Controlled?" (1933), *Empire Club of Canada: Addresses Delivered to the Members During the Year 1933-34* (1934).

## Murray, Ma
Only flush for No. 2, curtail bathing to the Saturday-night tub, go back to the old washrag, which could always move a lot of B.O. if applied often enough.

Gratuitous advice to readers of *The Alaska Highway News* during the water shortage at Fort St. John, B.C., in 1946.

*

Printed in the sage brush country of the Lillooet every Thursday, God Willing. Guarantees a chuckle every week and a belly laugh once a month, or your money back. Subscription: $5 in Canada. Furriners: $6. This week's circulation 1769, and every bloody one of them paid for.

Editorial page, *Bridge River-Lillooet News*, published during the 1950s by the peppery veteran journalist Ma (for Margaret) Murray. Quoted by Georgina Keddell in *The Newspapering Murrays* (1967).

## Murray, Margaret
One Flag, One Throne, One Empire

Dr. Murray founded the Imperial Order Daughters of the Empire in Montreal on February 13, 1900, and chose the I.O.D.E. motto above.

## Mussey, Barrows
The difference between McLuhan and me is that, by temperament—and by experience too—I am the sort who says the

Wright Brothers will never get it off the ground. He is the one who says that every family in America will have a private plane by 1950.

> American writer, quoted in *McLuhan: Hot & Cool* (1967), edited by Gerald Emanuel Stearn.

## Mutchmore, James Ralph
If you think it, say it. Get it out. Then people can argue about it, and, if you are wrong, you will at least know.

*

It has been said that the Church is an anvil which has worn out many hammers.

> Credo of the outspoken moderator of the General Council of the United Church from 1962 to 1964.

I believe the United Church should be a uniting church.

> *Mutchmore: The Memoirs of James Ralph Mutchmore* (1965). The former moderator favoured church union as fervently as he denounced "the three b's"—betting, beer and bingo.

## Myers, Gustavus
The rapid concentration of wealth in Canada is no mere fancy. Already, it is estimated, less than fifty men control $4,000,000,000, or more than one-third of Canada's material wealth as expressed in railways, banks, factories, mines, land and other properties and resources.

> *A History of Canadian Wealth* (1914).

## Myers, Martin
First you're an unknown, then you write one book and you move up to obscurity.

> *The Canadian Magazine*, March 24, 1973.

"Why, my business. What business would it be? I am only in one business. Lost civilizations. I am a seeker, collector, and student of things past. I collect junk."

> *The Assignment* (1971).

## Myleykovskiy, A.G.
In order to mobilize the masses to struggle against American imperialism, one should use the slogan "Fight the Sale," the sale of the natural wealth of Canada, in order to protect her natural development.

*

The Workers' Progressive Party of Canada is the party that first in history acknowledged the right of French Canada to national self-definition (including the right to separation) as an independent, equal nation.

*

... the tactic of the Canadian bourgeois of playing on the Anglo-American rivalry ... thanks chiefly to the possibility of benefitting simultaneously from American capital and the colonial monopoly of British imperialism.

> Three excerpts from *Canada and the Anglo-American Controversies* (1958), a study published in Moscow in the Russian language.

## Myrdal, Gunnar
The first thing I'd do is nationalize all the American trade unions. Canadian unions must be independent. Let them cry how much they want.

*

I was in Quebec City recently, a marvellous, wonderful place. I saw some models of French sculpture, but my motel was as American as you can imagine; the food was completely American. The only difference was the language, for Lord's sake, plus a few intellectuals who make poetry and stuff. Hell, that's not French culture. They're as far away from France as the rest of the Canadians are from England. I mean, how in hell can they be independent? It's all nonsense.

> Swedish social scientist quoted by Peter C. Newman in "Sweden" (1971), *Home Country: People, Places, and Power Politics* (1973).

# N

## Nader, Ralph
My guess is that Canada will remain like the Japanese wife—one step behind. The cue will come from Washington.

> Toronto address, May 27, 1971, reported the following day in *The Toronto Star*.

Canada is to the U.S. as Chrysler is to G.M.

> *The Toronto Star*, May 1, 1972.

## Naismith, Dr. James A.
Permit me to add my hearty congratulations to the many that must have poured in from your host of friends and admirers on this your twenty-first birthday. Your record is without parallel in the history of basketball. There is no team I mention more frequently in talking about the game. My admiration is not only for your remarkable record of games won but for your record of clean play, versatility of meeting teams at their own style and more especially for your unbroken record of good sportsmanship. My admiration and respect go to you because you have remained unspoiled by your success and have maintained the womanly graces notwithstanding your participation in a strenuous game. You are not only an inspiration to all basketball players throughout the world, but a model for all girls' teams. The Grads have the greatest basketball team that ever stepped out on a floor.

> Letter to J. Percy Page in 1940, the year the coach disbanded the Edmonton Grads basketball team after the all-girl team had played for twenty-four years. The tribute was a great one, for it came from the Almonte medical doctor who in 1891 had invented basketball and codified its thirteen basic rules. Quoted by Henry Roxborough in *Great Days in Canadian Sport* (1957).

## Nakano, Takeo
My hands tremble
As I sign my naturalization papers
Making me a Canadian citizen
And Canada my final resting place.

> A *waka* translated from the Japanese by Robert Y. Kadoguchi. *Volvox: Poetry from the Unofficial Languages of Canada* (1971), edited by J. Michael Yates.

## Nakasuk
In the old days the shamans could do everything.

> Belief of the Eskimo Nakasuk. Knud Rasmussen's *The Netsilik Eskimos: Social Life and Spiritual Culture: Report of the Fifth Thule Expedition, 1921-24* (1931).

## Nâlungiaq
It is said that it is so, and therefore it is so.

＊

That is all I can tell you about the world, both the one I know and the one I do not know. If only I could dream I would know more; for people who can dream hear and see many things. *We believe in dreams, and we believe that people can live a life apart from real life, a life they can go through in their sleep.*

> Eskimo belief related by Nâlungiaq. Knud Rasmussen's *The Netsilik Eskimos: Social Life and Spiritual Culture: Report of the Fifth Thule Expedition, 1921-24* (1931).

## Nanook of the North
Yes, yes, the aggie will come first. Not a man will stir, not a harpoon will be thrown until you give the sign. It is my word.

> Nanook, the most famous Eskimo of all time, agreed to abide by the new rules laid down by Robert Flaherty for the "shooting" of the *agee* or walrus. The Eskimo hunter was the star of Flaherty's documentary feature film *Nanook of the North* (1920) filmed in the Canadian Arctic. The name Nanook means "The Bear." Quoted by Richard Griffith in *The World of Robert Flaherty* (1953). See also Robert Flaherty.

## Nansen, Fridtjof

The land of the great white silence will never more ring with the happy mirth of these lovable children of the twilight.

> Preface by the Norwegian Arctic explorer to *The People of the Twilight* (1928), by Diamond Jenness.

## Napoleon   See Napoleon Bonaparte.

## Naukatjik

Women become dangerous when they have no husbands to lie with them.

> Observation of the Eskimo Naukatjik. Knud Rasmussen's *Intellectual Culture of the Iglulik Eskimos: Report of the Fifth Thule Expedition, 1921-24* (1929).

## Neagle, Anna

We took tremendous pains with Victoria, to get things just right, and we had to come to Canada to get them so. In England we had nowhere an authentic picture of her as a young girl. We had to come to Montreal to see a statue of Victoria as a young queen.

> The British leading lady played the monarch in *Victoria the Great* (1937). "The British Motion Picture Industry," October 18, 1937, *Addresses Delivered before the Canadian Club of Toronto: Season of 1937-38* (1938).

## Neatby, Hilda

Like many other Canadians, however, I am disturbed at the apparent indifference of the experts to the disappearance of the old-fashioned concept of the "educated person" who chose to rest his reputation on his bearing and conversation, rather than on degrees and "research."

> So Little for the Mind (1953). The title of this influential book comes from Cardinal Newman: "Any self-education in any shape, in the most restricted sense, is preferable to a system of teaching which, professing so much, really does so little for the mind."

## Needham, Richard J.

Ruined by a book! Such was my awful fate. Henry Miller had no effect on me;

D.H. Lawrence left me cold; I yawned my way through Frank Harris's memoirs. But then I came across a copy of Eaton's catalogue; and, leafing idly through it, discovered photographs of men wearing full-length winter undergarments.

> Needham's Inferno (1966).

If Canada's young people were educated, they would be a troublesome lot, always rocking the boat, and wanting to change things, and questioning the infinite mercy and wisdom of the authorities. Accordingly, the authorities prevent Canada's young people from getting an education by keeping them locked up in institutions called schools, where they are bored, bullied, and brainwashed into total apathy.

> The Garden of Needham (1968).

Every woman needs one man in her life who is strong and responsible. Given this security, she can proceed to do what she really wants to do—fall in love with men who are weak and irresponsible.

\*

One of Canada's greatest tragedies is that sober second thoughts so often prevail.

\*

The first half of our lives is ruined by our parents, and the second half by our children.

\*

There's a happiness that comes only to those who have given up the idea of happiness.

\*

It's marvellous being a woman in Toronto; you get to meet so many interesting women.

\*

I used to look down on the world for being corrupt, but now I adore it for the utter magnificence of that corruption.

\*

A truly immoral man, I suppose, is the one who advises people to behave as in fact they are behaving.

\*

The only journalism course I feel qualified to give consists of five words, "Travel, suffer, love, read, write."

> A Friend in Needham, or a Writer's Notebook (1969).

A husband suspects one other man; a wife, all other women. [April 30, 1971]

*

We spend our lives preparing for delights which don't come, and recovering from disasters which do. [May 25, 1971]

*

Some women are buried in coffins, but the majority are buried in bungalows. [April 28, 1972]

> From "A Writer's Notebook," Needham's column in *The Globe and Mail.*

Nobody should be married, but everybody should have been.

*

Canada is a country where mothers take their daughters to the ballet, and fathers take their sons to the hockey game.

> *Homemaker's Digest,* January-February, 1972.

## Neel, Boyd
Opera is a convention with a tradition always attached to it. Part of the tradition is the acceptance of the convention.

> "Opera," *The Arts in Canada: A Stock-Taking at Mid-Century* (1958), edited by Malcolm Ross.

## Nélligan, Emile
She was a Golden Ship: but there showed through
Translucent sides treasures the blasphemous crew,
Hatred, Disgust and Madness, fought to share.

> From "The Golden Ship," *Selected Poems* (1960), translated by P.F. Widdows.

## Nelson, Robert
We have been oppressed by the hand of a Transatlantic power, and unjustly and cruelly castigated with the rod of unrelenting misrule for a long series of years —so long, that the measure of Tyranny has filled to overflowing.

> "Proclamation," March, 1838, issued by the *soi-disant* president of the Provisional Government of the State of Lower Canada. Reproduced by Robert Christie in *A History of the Late Province of Lower Canada, Parliamentary and Political* (1854).

## Nelson, Wolfred
As for me, I am of a different opinion from that of M. Papineau. I claim the time has come to melt down our pewter plates and spoons into bullets.

> Dr. Nelson, a leader of the rebellion in Lower Canada, cried this out at a political meeting, St. Charles, October 23, 1837. Quoted by Alfred D. DeCelles in *The "Patriotes" of '37: A Chronicle of the Lower Canadian Rebellion* (1920).

We rebelled, my Lord—but start not at the avowal. We rebelled neither against Her Majesty's person or her government, but against colonial misgovernment, and we abide the issue—the penalty is ours.

> Letter addressed to Lord Durham from Montreal's New Jail, June 18, 1839, and signed by Nelson and other insurrectionists. Reproduced by Robert Christie in *A History of the Late Province of Lower Canada, Parliamentary and Political* (1854).

## Nelsova, Zara
Look at a man. He always has to wear black evening clothes when he plays a concert. I am never happy wearing black on the platform. I feel it sometimes has a bad effect on the audience. I never wear red if I'm going to play the classics —Bach or Haydn. I do wear striking colours if I'm to play Dvorak or Bloch. I would never wear a pastel colour to play Strauss' "Don Quixote": I always wear pastels to perform Debussy and Fauré.

> The Winnipeg-born cellist was quoted by Suzanne Morrison in *The Toronto Star,* March 23, 1966.

## Netsit
A tiny little gnat once flew out into the world. It was so small that it thought people took no notice of it at all. But, being hungry, it settled on a baby's hand, and, as it sat there, it heard someone say:

"Ooh, that horrible gnat! Smash it, quick!"

But suddenly the gnat was able to speak, and it answered in such a fashion that the boy heard it: "Ah, spare my life, spare my life! I have a little grandson who will cry if I don't come home."

Fancy—so little, and yet a grand-father!

> Eskimo fable told by Netsit. Knud Rasmussen's *Intellectual Culture of the Copper Eskimos: Report of the Fifth Thule Expedition, 1921-24* (1932).

### Nevers, Edmond de

Certainly it cannot be too often repeated, that the most solid basis for a nation is the possession of the land; that the question of "repatriation," that is of the return to the agricultural districts of the province of Quebec, remains the order of the day. Lay hold of the land, as far as circumstances will permit.

> *L'avenir du peuple canadien-français* (1896). Quoted by Ramsay Cook in "Quebec: The Ideology of Survival" in *The Prospect of Change: Proposals for Canada's Future* (1965), edited by Abraham Rotstein.

The young French Canadian is perhaps the only child in America who has what could be called an ideal, and whose dream is not merely to become an Astor or a Vanderbilt!

> Attributed to the writer, who died in 1906, by Abbé Groulx. Quoted by Susan Mann Trofimenkoff in *Abbé Groulx: Variations on a Nationalist Theme* (1973).

### Nevitt, Barrington

See Marshall McLuhan.

### Newbolt, Sir Henry

Whatever you are, it would be a very strange thing, if you do not produce a great literature when you feel the need of it. I am not sure that the way in which you feel the need of it at this moment is exactly the way I mean. You seem sometimes—at least the gentleman who asked me that question—seemed to me to be demanding a great literature and a great art much as he might demand a big Government building or a fine university. That is the sort of thing that you can go out and get, or, if it is not got, demand to know whose fault it is. Now, that is not the way with literature and art. You do not build a literature or an art out of stones and mortar, and you do not get it by paying dollars for it. You get it only because the nation which already has a national spirit and a national landscape and a national atmosphere and a set of national ideals cannot rest satisfied till it has expressed them for itself. And I hazard the conjecture, very humbly, that possibly at this moment you are still contented with ideals so very nearly like the English ones that you have not felt a very strong impulse to put things differently for yourselves. But you will.

> "Literature and Life," February 27, 1923, *The Canadian Club of Ottawa Year Book: 1922-23; 1923-24* (1925).

### Newcastle, Duke of

Annapolis, Annapolis! Oh, yes, Annapolis must be defended; to be sure, Annapolis should be defended—where is Annapolis?

> The Duke of Newcastle was an ineffectual prime minister of Great Britain; in 1754 he uttered this absurdity as recorded by Horace Walpole in *Memoirs of the Last Ten Years of the Reign of George II* (1846). Quoted by Francis Parkman in *Montcalm and Wolfe* (1884). See also George II and Tobias Smollett.

### Newlove, John

Beauty's whatever
makes the adrenalin run. . . .

> "The Double - Headed Snake," *Black Night Window* (1968).

### Newman, Peter C.

Many of tomorrow's Canadian business princes will build their domains under the wide sub-Arctic horizon, where birch trees take a century to grow twelve inches and indigo delphiniums sprout six feet in one nightless summer.

> *Flame of Power: Intimate Profiles of Canada's Greatest Businessmen* (1959).

The right instincts were in him, but throughout his stormy stewardship, they languished in the cupboard of his soul.

He gave the people a leadership cult, without leadership.

Assessment of John Diefenbaker by the political journalist. *Renegade in Power: The Diefenbaker Years* (1963).

We had spent a hundred years trying to become a nation; now we *were* a nation and it was hell.

\*

Politicians measure out their lives in terms of conventions and elections—and of the two, conventions are the more intensely exciting.

\*

Jean Lesage could never make up his mind whether he wanted to be the next prime minister of Canada or the first president of Quebec.

\*

Pierre Elliott Trudeau's face, which might have been carved in alabaster to commemorate some distant war of the Crusades, closes in mask-like as he walks into the future, burdened with hope.

*The Distemper of Our Times: Canadian Politics in Transition: 1963-1968* (1968).

It is far too much to claim for *Home Country* that it's the chronicle of a time. But it is the chronicle of a political education, my own. And what I've learned is not to believe in magical leaders any more; that character and compassion are more important than ideology; and that even if it's absurd to think you can change things, it's even more absurd to think that it's foolish and unimportant to try.

*Home Country: People, Places, and Power Politics* (1973).

**Newman, Sydney**
I do like art that has something to say and art that is of use, whether that use is merely to give pleasure or whether it is a practical use. This roughly is me.

Quoted by Philip Purser in "Head of Drama," *Contrast: The Television Quarterly*, Autumn, 1962. Newman is commissioner of the National Film Board.

**Nichols, J.L.**   See B.G. Jefferis.

**Nichols, Mike**
Drink Canada Dry? If you complain about American ownership of your re-

sources I'll tell the Americans to buy their ginger ale elsewhere.

Attributed to the American satirist in Vancouver while filming *Carnal Knowledge* (1971).

**Nicholson, L.H.**
What is more indicative of the health and progress of a country than the style of its laws, the manner in which they are observed and—this is where we come in—the manner in which they are enforced?

Commissioner of the RCMP addressing the Conference of the International Associations of Chiefs of Police, Detroit, 1953. Quoted by Alan Phillips in *The Living Legend: The Story of the Royal Canadian Mounted Police* (1954).

**Nicol, Eric**
In the ensuing battle both the British and French generals were mortally wounded, but the British refused to admit that it was a draw. The French therefore went back to their farms swearing that they would have "la revanche du berceau," a French expression meaning the family allowance.

*An Uninhibited History of Canada* (1959), by Eric Nicol, illustrated by Peter Whalley.

Very little is known about the War of 1812 because the Americans lost it.

*Say Uncle: A Completely Uncalled-for History of the United States* (1961), illustrated by Peter Whalley.

Was Lenin pro-Communist?

*Russia, Anyone? A Completely Uncalled-for History of the U.S.S.R.* (1963), illustrated by Peter Whalley.

To paraphrase Henry Ford slightly, of early Vancouver it may be said that history is bunkhouse.

*Vancouver* (1970).

Confederation has been like a mail-order bra: intended to contain and uplift, it has instead drawn attention to the cleavage.

\*

The provinces were literally railroaded into Confederation.

*

Is Confederation a myth?

*100 Years of What?* (1966), illustrated by Peter Whalley.

Failure, after all, is the sugar of life: the more lumps you take, the sweeter you are.

*A Scar Is Born* (1968).

. . . the tested formula for becoming rich as an author is to write regularly to an uncle who is dying from a surfeit of oil wells.

*One Man's Media—and How to Write for Them* (1973).

**Nicolson, Sir Harold**
On to Niagara Falls. We cross the Peace Bridge between America and Canada. A tiny little bridge. Above the Canadian end of it is a Union Jack. I take off my hat. I show my passport to an official. "From the Old Country?" he asks. I get a lump in my throat. I am no longer on foreign soil. We then motor along the Canadian side till we get to the falls. They are small and disappointing. A fine flow of water and much steam and spray. But a fraud really. Then motor back to the United States. At the frontier-post the man asks me how long I have been resident in Canada. "Between twenty and twenty-five minutes," I answer.

March 3, 1933, *Diaries and Letters 1930-1939* (1966), edited by Nigel Nicolson. For the complementary reaction of his wife, see Vita Sackville-West. See also Malcolm MacDonald.

**Nielsen, Leslie**
Playing one character over and over again is not my notion of being an actor. It's like a painter having a five-year contract with the Hilton Hotel chain. He paints the same picture in every room of every hotel for five years. He will make a lot of money. But what kind of satisfaction would that be for a genuine painter?

Regina-born American TV actor (brother of Eric Nielsen, Tory M.P.), quoted by David Steele Turner in *Act-*

ors about *Acting, Loving, Living, Life* (1972).

**"Nigger Dan"**   See Daniel Williams.

**Nihon, Alexis**
I only buy, and then rent; I never sell.

Belgian-born Montreal industrialist and inventor of the tubeless tire, quoted by Paul King in *The Canadian Magazine,* July 29, 1972.

**Nin, Anaïs**
Canada was a generous, warmhearted host.

The reference is to the American Negro actor, Canada Lee, who died in 1952. *The Diary of Anaïs Nin: 1939-1944* (1969), edited by Gunther Stuhlmann.

**Niven, David**
The fog lifted and everyone was pointing. A mile or so away was a gigantic fortress sailing majestically along. Pale pink in the setting sun on one side and blue-green on the other. It towered out of the water and with nine-tenths out of sight below the surface, imagination boggled at the size of the whole. [On first sighting Quebec City]

*

I hope that the statute of limitations applies in this case and that the Mounties will not be sent to pull me in, and if it will help at all, I offer my belated apologies to the author, Tyrwhitt-Drake, who long before had written a book called *Fox Hunting in Canada.* I found it in the hospital library, copied some of it assiduously and sold four articles to the local newspaper under the title "Hunting of the Canadian Fox." It paid the doctor's bill.

The future film actor was confined to the Ottawa General Hospital for a tonsillectomy during the 1930s. *The Moon's a Balloon* (1971).

**Niviaksiak**
To hunt the great bear, you must *feel* like a bear.

*

Ah, it is dark! I am falling.

The last cry of the Cape Dorset printmaker whose art was obsessed with the image of the bear. Niviaksiak died on a hunting expedition face to face with a giant polar bear. He did not fire on the bear, nor did the animal harm his prostrate body, yet he died. The artist's death in 1959 has always puzzled the Eskimos. Quoted by Lawrence Elliott in "The Remarkable Eskimo Artists of Baffin Island" in *Canada—This Land, These People: A Reader's Digest Collecion* (1968). George Swinton in *Eskimo Sculpture/Sculpture Esquimaude* (1965).

## Nixon, Richard M.
With regard to the Japanese, I think I can best summarize our dilemma in this way: After the Japanese were here I found that, both from the information they gave and the information we had ourselves, Japan is our biggest customer in the world.

> Press conference, White House, Washington, September 16, 1971. Peter C. Newman noted: "The fact is that in 1970 United States–Canadian trade exceeded the value of United States–Japanese trade by some $10 billion. Our purchases from the United States (and if this sounds like north country boasting, forgive me, for it is the absolute truth) have for many years approached in value the total of the combined purchases of America's four next largest trading partners—Japan, West Germany, Britain and France." ("I Love Canada," *The New York Times*, January 28, 1972)

What we are really saying is simply this: That while we do not have a wall between us, while we do have this great unguarded boundary, this does not mean that we are the same, it does not mean that we do not have differences, but it does mean that we have found a way to discuss our differences in a friendly way, without war, and this is the great lesson for all the world to see.

> Speech at Uplands Airport, Ottawa, April 13, 1972.

To all of you who have welcomed Mrs. Nixon and me so warmly on this occasion, I trust you will make allowance for my attempt to speak in the language I studied thirty-seven years ago. When I

tried it today, before I came, on our top linguist in the American government, General Walters, he said, "Go ahead, you speak French with a Canadian accent."

Hon. Members: Hear, hear!

Mr. Nixon: I will have to admit that I am not very much at home in the French language but, as a former parliamentarian in my own country, I feel very much at home in this Chamber.

\*

Canada is the largest trading partner of the United States.

Hon. Members: Hear, hear!

Mr. Nixon: It is very important that that be noted in Japan, too.

Hon. Members: Hear, hear!

\*

We must also build a new spirit of partnership within the Western hemisphere that we share together. It has been said that Canada is bounded "on the north by gold, on the west by the East, on the east by history, and on the south by friends."

Hon. Members: Hear, hear!

Mr. Nixon: We hope that this will always be the case.

> Address before a joint sitting of the Senate and the House of Commons, April 14, 1972. For the quoted remark, see Dorothy Duncan and Frances Shelley Wees.

## Noah, Mordecai Manuel
Hear, O Israel, the Lord is our God—the Lord is one. Ararat, a City of Refuge for the Jews, founded by Mordecai Manuel Noah, in the Month of Tisri 5586—Sept. 1825 in the Fiftieth Year of American Independence.

> The New York journalist and politician of Portuguese-Jewish descent attempted to found on Grand Island in the Niagara River the city of Ararat, a temporary refuge for those Jews who planned to settle in the Holy Land. The above inscription comes from the cornerstone Noah laid in 1825.

## Noël, Jacques
Here in this Countrey are Cinamon and Cloves, which they call in their language Canodeta.

"Letter Sent to M. John Growte student in Paris from Jaques Noel of S. Malo, the grand nephew of Jaques Cartier" (1587), *The Principal Navigations, Voyages, Traffiques, and Discoveries of the English Nation* (1589), by Richard Hakluyt.

**Nolan, Patrick James**
R.B. Bennett, Q.C.: Mr. Clerk, send to the library for Anson on *Contracts*.
Paddy Nolan, Q.C.: Mr. Clerk, send to the library for Bennett on *Bluff*.

Exchange in the Alberta Court of Appeals, about 1920, recalled by Senator Paul Martin. Calgary Bob Edwards once said of the Calgary lawyer: "All the best criminals go to Paddy Nolan."

**Noorduyn, Robert**
The Norseman.

This is the name given the world's first bush aircraft, designed and built in Montreal by the founder of Noorduyn Aviation Ltd. in 1935.

**Norman, Herbert**
Will this never end?

*

I've become an embarrassment to my country.

*

I have lived under illusions too long.

The Canadian ambassador to Egypt took his own life by leaping from the roof of a Cairo apartment building, April 4, 1957. He had endured six years of having his loyalty questioned by the witch-hunting U.S. Senate Subcommittee on Internal Security. Quoted by Sidney Katz in "What Kind of Man *Was* Herbert Norman?" *Maclean's Magazine*, September 28, 1957. See also Ralph Allen.

**Normand, Jacques**
You have to go after money where it is found, and that is among the poor. The poor have so little money, but they are so numerous.

*Parlez-moi d'humour* (1965), edited by Jacques de Roussan.

**Norstad, General Lauris**
Having been born and raised in the State of Minnesota, I might claim that geographical proximity has given me a particularly close relationship with you and your country. My own part of the United States is literally only a stone's throw away from Canada and, if stones are sometimes thrown across this friendly border, and they are, perhaps it is a good thing. It keeps us aware of one another, compels us from time to time to reassess the importance of our relationship, to appreciate how much we mean to one another.

"NATO Strategy" (1959), *Empire Club of Canada: Addresses 1959-60* (1960).

Reporter: Does it mean, Sir, that if Canada does not accept nuclear weapons for these airplanes that she is not actually fulfilling her NATO commitments?
Norstad: I believe that's right. She would be meeting it in force but not under the terms of the requirements that have been established by NATO.

Two days after his retirement as supreme commander of NATO, General Norstad visited Ottawa, the last call in his round of farewells. He made this reply at a press conference, January 3, 1963, which helped topple the Conservative government of John Diefenbaker. Quoted by Peyton Lyon in *Canada in World Affairs: 1961-1963* (1968).

**Northcliffe, Lord**
There is no ignorance of Canada now in the United Kingdom.
I wish there were a little knowledge of the British Empire in Canada.

"Our Business Partner, John Bull," October 23, 1908, *Addresses Delivered before the Canadian Club of Toronto: Season of 1908-1909* (1909).

**Norwood, Gilbert**
Culture is suspiciously examined at every Customs office; barbarism laughs at frontiers. ["A Strange Duel"]

*

Each of us has achieved, or possesses, what is in the eyes of someone else the unattained crown of his life. ["Those Magic Isles"]

*Spoken in Jest* (1938).

## Nostradamus, Michel
Du Mont Royal naistra d'une casane,
Qui duc, & compte viendra tyranniser,
Dresser copie de la marche Millane,
Favence, Florence d'or & gens espuiser.

Out of Montreal shall be born in a
cottage,
One that shall tyrannize over duke and
earl,
He shall raise an army in the land of the
rebellion,
He shall empty Favence and Florence of
their gold.

> *Centuries* (1555), Century VII, 32. *The*
> *Complete Prophecies of Nostradamus*
> (1947), translated by Henry C. Roberts,
> whose interpretation of this "dark
> prophetic verse" is: "A Canadian leader,
> of lowly birth, shall be raised to great
> power and eventually assume command
> over men of the nobility."

## Novick, Julius
"Canadian playwright." The words seem
a little incongruous together, like "Panamanian hockey-player," or "Lebanese
fur-trapper."

\*

Quick! Can you name three Canadians?
Any three Canadians at all?

> The American drama critic reviewed
> George Ryga's *The Ecstasy of Rita Joe*
> at the Washington Theatre Club in *The*
> *New York Times*, May 13, 1973.

## Nowlan, Alden
Perhaps the ultimate indignity is loneliness without privacy.

\*

Men and women are not equal; each is
superior to the other.

\*

The day the child realizes that all adults
are imperfect he becomes an adolescent;
the day he forgives them, he becomes an
adult; the day he forgives himself he
becomes wise.

\*

Without God we have no rights, only
such privileges as may be granted us by
the state.

> "Scratchings," *Between Tears and*
> *Laughter* (1971).

No, Canada has never been staid and
grey, but a great many Canadian intellectuals have been colour blind.

\*

I had never heard of Ulysses, but before
I was ten years old I knew that I was
descended from classic heroes. [About
his Maritime background]

\*

Perhaps, then, Canada is not so much a
country as magnificent raw material for
a country; and perhaps the question is
not "Who are we?" but "What are we
going to make of ourselves?"

> "Alden Nowlan's Canada," *Maclean's*
> *Magazine*, June, 1971. The New Bruns-
> wick author once said: "I write for the
> same reason I'm 6'3" tall. I can't do
> anything about it."

## Nuliajuk
And of course it may be that all I have
been telling you is wrong. For you cannot be certain about a thing you cannot
see. And people say so much!

> Remark made ironically by the Eskimo
> Nuliajuk. Knud Rasmussen, *The Netsi-*
> *lik Eskimos: Social Life and Spiritual*
> *Culture: Report of the Fifth Thule Ex-*
> *pedition, 1921-24* (1931).

## Nuligak
I, Nuligak, will tell you a story.

> Opening sentence of the first autobiog-
> raphy dictated by an Eskimo. *I, Nuligak*
> (1971), edited and translated by Maurice
> Metayer.

## Nye, Bill
Are you related to the Bowells of Compassion, Ohio?

> The American humourist asked this of
> Sir Mackenzie Bowell, prime minister
> from 1894 to 1896; quoted by Stephen
> Leacock in "The Expression of Hum-
> our: Words," *Humour and Humanity:*
> *An Introduction to the Study of*
> *Humour* (1937).

## Nynych, Stephanie
There is nothing wrong with one thinking oneself beautiful as long as one
doesn't think that others aren't.

> . . . *Like I See It* (1972).

# O

## Oakes, Sir Harry
Bennett! Listen, when a man makes money he has to keep two jumps ahead of the people trying to take it from him. The "have-nots" today are completely in command. Stalin takes it all. Bennett takes all but fifteen per cent. The difference between them is fifteen per cent. Bennett wouldn't like to hear it put that way, would he? . . . No, sir. Pride of ownership used to belong to all men, but it's getting narrower. Pride of possession today belongs to the politicians. You find it. They take it.

> To Gregory Clark after Sir Harry moved to the Bahamas in 1935 to escape the discriminatory taxation of R.B. Bennett's Conservative government. The mining executive was mysteriously murdered in Nassau in 1943. Quoted by Geoffrey Bocca in *The Life and Death of Sir Harry Oakes* (1959). See also Roza Brown, Alfred de Marigny, and William H. Wright.

## Obodiac, Stan
I shudder to think what would have happened to the Canadian World War II effort if we had depended on track and swimming participants instead of mannish hockey players.

> Publicity director of Maple Leaf Gardens, quoted in *The Toronto Telegram*, June 7, 1970.

## Obolensky, Serge
When we had recovered, and were back at Calgary, we went into the Ritz Hotel dining room for dinner, and to my astonishment the orchestra began playing the Imperial Russian anthem. It startled me to hear it. The orchestra leader was a Russian émigré. And there was also present a Russian officer who had successfully arranged to locate, on Calgary farms, a large group of White Russians from China.

> The émigré Russian prince and his new wife explored Alberta in 1924, where

they thought of acquiring a farm, but decided otherwise. *One Man in His Time: The Memoirs of Serge Obolensky* (1958).

## O'Brien, Andy
Championship is a state of mind.

> "Ring Champ's Fight with Fear," *My Friend the Hangman: Dramatic Encounters in Sport, Crime and War* (1970). See also Nicolai Zabotin.

## O'Byrne, Henry
Look, George! Look! It's land. See that beacon on the shore? Get digging. We're going to make it!

> Encouragement shouted by coach Henry O'Byrne to George Young, January 15, 1927, when the sixteen-year-old marathon swimmer had covered most of the twenty miles of Catalina Strait. After sixteen hours he was ready to quit when O'Byrne spied the light on the mainland shore. Young won $25,000. Quoted by Henry Roxborough in *Great Days in Canadian Sport* (1957).

## O'Callaghan, Edmund Bailey
*Henceforth, there must be no peace in the Province—no quarter for the plunderers.* Agitate! Agitate! AGITATE! Destroy the Revenue; denounce the oppressors. Everything is lawful when the fundamental liberties are in danger. "The guards die—they never surrender."

> O'Callaghan was a supporter of Louis-Joseph Papineau. "Resolutions on Canada Affairs," March 6, 1836, reproduced by Robert Christie in *A History of the Late Province of Lower Canada, Parliamentary and Political* (1854).

## O'Donoghue, Daniel J.
Your Excellency, I represent the rag, tag and bobtail!

> The words "that Daniel O'Donoghue flung at Lord Dufferin, governor general of Canada, on being somewhat

haughtily asked for his credentials," in the mid-1870s, are quoted by Doris French in *Faith, Sweat and Politics: The Early Trade Union Years in Canada* (1962). Mackenzie King called "Irish Dan" the Father "of the Trade Union Movement in Canada." Charles Lipton in *The Trade Union Movement in Canada: 1827-1959* (1966) disagreed: "During the 1950s the leadership of the Trades and Labour Congress of Canada fostered the idea that O'Donoghue was the 'father of the Canadian labour movement.' We have discovered no evidence that the pioneers considered O'Donoghue their father, and sometimes they wondered if he was their brother. The truth is that O'Donoghue was a bit of an opportunist." See also Alfred Jury.

**O'Gorman, P.T.**
Witness the French-Canadian politician, who, in the course of a Parliamentary debate, remarked that he had "spent a week in Toronto, one Sunday."

*Magnificent Ontario* (1950).

**O'Grady, Standish**
Thou barren waste; unprofitable strand,
Where hemlocks brood on unproductive land,
Whose frozen air on one bleak winter's night
Can metamorphose *dark brown hares to white*!

"Winter in Lower Canada," *The Emigrant: A Poem in Four Cantos* (1841).

**O'Hagan, Thomas**
As regards Canadian literary criticism, it is woefully lacking in scholarship, poise and judicial discrimination. All our goslings are swans.

"What is Criticism," *Canadian Bookman*, June, 1927.

**O'Hara, Geoffrey**
K-K-K-Katy, beautiful Katy,
You're the only g-g-g-girl that I adore,
When the m-m-m-moon shines over the cow-shed,
I'll be waiting at the k-k-k-kitchen door.

This "stammering song" was the hit of 1918 and has remained popular ever since as a novelty number. The words and music were written by Geoffrey O'Hara, a successful Tin Pan Alley composer born in Chatham, Ontario, in 1882. "Does anybody who reads this not know who wrote 'K-K-K-Katy?' " Augustus Bridle asked in "Who Writes Our Music?" in *Maclean's Magazine*, December 15, 1929. The silly song is associated with the ending of World War One and the relief that this event occasioned. There are many parodies along the lines of:

K-K-K-K-P,
Dirty old K.P.,
That's the only army job that I abhor,
When the m-moon shines over the guardhouse,
I'll be mopping up the k-k-k-kitchen floor.

*"Sound Off!" Soldier Songs from the Revolution to World War II* (1942), edited by Arthur Dolph.

**O'Hara, John**
"A bunch of Americans . . . are trying to do something about Canada."
"To do what about Canada?"
"Oh—to try to straighten things out between them and us."
"We having trouble with *them*, too? I thought they were our friends," she said.
"That's just what they don't like. Americans taking them for granted. . . . Oh, it isn't a crisis. It's a long, drawn-out affair. Been going on since the war."

"The Clear Track," *The Horse Knows the Way* (1964).

**Olcott, Sidney**
My first great historical picture was entitled *Henry Hudson's Discovery of the North River*. We made this masterpiece with a cast of six people, three of whom were Indians who attacked Hudson's ship. It was another of those famous one-day pictures.

The Irish-Canadian producer-director, born John S. Alcott, was a big name in silent pictures. He died in Hollywood in 1949, at the age of seventy-six.

## O'Leary, Grattan

One of the great problems before Canada today is not to save capitalism from socialism or communism, but to save capitalism from certain capitalists.

> "The Public and the Politician" (1933), *Empire Club of Canada: Addresses Delivered to the Members During the Year 1933-34* (1934).

A senatorship isn't a job, it's a title. Also it's a blessing, a stroke of good fate; something like drawing a royal strait flush in the biggest pot of the evening, or winning the Calcutta Sweep. That's why we think it wrong to think of a senatorship as a job; and wrong to think of the Senate as a place where people are supposed to work. Pensions aren't given for work.

> Remark made in 1942, twenty years before the speaker was summoned to the Senate. Quoted by R. MacGregor Dawson in *The Government of Canada* (1952).

We have forgotten the truth that there is no sense in pasting wings on a man unless you can give him a winged nature.

> "Address" (1950), *Empire Club of Canada: Addresses Delivered to the Members During the Year 1949-50* (1950).

In Canada's capital, the city of Ottawa, there is an old canal which winds through the town. Weeping willows grow beside it and arch over it and not one Canadian in ten thousand knows when or why it was built. It was built more than a century ago by a British engineer to help defend Canada against the United States; and the fact that today this old canal is but a museum piece, its origin unknown or unremembered, tells the blessed thing that has come between these two countries and which today has roots deeper than before.

> "Canada's Political Philosophy," *Canada: Nation on the March* (1953), introduction by H. L. Enman.

I vote with the Tories but dine with the Grits.

\*

George, you know the trouble with you is you don't read any poetry. [To Conservative leader George Drew, early 1950s]

> Quoted by Alan Phillips in "The Last Angry Tory" in *Maclean's Magazine*, June 7, 1958.

So far, we've had nothing but props and music. The curtain goes up and the play never begins.

> The Conservative senator's view of the first nine months of the Trudeau administration, quoted by Frances Russell in *The Globe and Mail*, March 11, 1968.

## Oliphant, Betty

Quality, quality is what really counts.

> A director of the National Ballet, quoted by Nathan Cohen in *The Toronto Star*, March 22, 1969.

## Oliver, John

There are times when it requires more courage to stand still than to go forward.

\*

If you would meet your debts you must doff the broadcloth and don the overalls.

\*

It is not the business of the Government to maintain the people—it is the business of the people to maintain the Government.

\*

It's a fine thing to have your head in the air, but it's always best to have your feet on the ground.

> The incorruptible, self-educated premier of British Columbia, quoted by James Morton in *Honest John Oliver: The Life Story of the Honourable John Oliver, Premier of British Columbia, 1918-1927* (1933).

## Oliver, Michael

Canada is a self-made country, and, as Talleyrand once remarked about a self-made man, "I am sure God is pleased that He need not accept the responsibility."

> Introduction, *Quebec States Her Case: Speeches and Articles from Quebec in the Years of Unrest* (1964), edited by Frank Scott and Michael Oliver.

## Olivier, Sir Laurence
How nice.

> Said to be the British actor's reply when approached in New York by Tom Patterson to help found the Stratford Festival, 1952. Luckily Tyrone Guthrie was more enthusiastic.

## Ollivier, Maurice
Responsible government exists when the Executive is responsible to a legislature and is kept in power by the vote of the majority of that assembly, elected by the people. Therefore, there is responsible government when the Ministry is made up of chiefs of administrative departments who remain at the head of their respective departments only as long as they are supported by the majority of the assembly.

> *British North America Acts and Selected Statutes: 1867-1962* (1962).

## Olson, Sigurd F.
There are few places left on the North American continent where men can still see the country as it was before Europeans came and know some of the challenges and freedoms of those who saw it first, but in the Canadian Northwest it can still be done.

> *The Lonely Land* (1961).

It may well be that with their help the Canadian north, with its vast expanses of primeval country, can restore to modern man a semblance of balance and completeness. In the long run, these last wild regions of the continent might be worth far more to North Americans from a recreational and spiritual standpoint than through industrial exploitation. If this vision could be realized, even in part, these people might once more be proud of their heritage.

> *Runes of the North* (1963), by the Minnesota naturalist.

## O'Neill, "General" John
Whatever I have done in connection with the Fenian Brotherhood, was done for Ireland, from conviction and not to please any particular class of persons.

\*

As to the propriety of invading Canada, I have always had but one opinion: Canada is a province of Great Britain; the British flag floats over it and English soldiers protect it, and, I think, Wherever the English flag and English soldiers are found, Irishmen have a right to attack. In striking at England through Canada we attempted no more than was done by the American Republic in the war of the Revolution.

> *Official Report of Gen. John O'Neill, President of the Fenian Brotherhood; on the Attempt to Invade Canada, May 25, 1870* (1870).

## O'Neill, John
I am a sociologist, God help me.

> *Sociology as a Skin Trade: Essays Towards a Reflexive Sociology* (1972), by the York University social scientist.

## Onions, C.T.
*Canada.* 1850. (Adapted from the Spanish, form of *caño*, gutter.) In Western U.S.: A narrow valley or glen; a small cañon.

> *The Shorter Oxford English Dictionary on Historical Principles* (Third Edition, 1964).

## Opekokew, Delia
A real conflict is going to erupt one of these days. We are going to do more than stay in our teepees saying "Ugh!"

> Conference on Educational Reform for Minorities, University of Windsor, May, 1971.

## Orban, William
*5BX Plan for Physical Fitness.*

> Little did the Queen's Printer know that the slim booklet of Air Force exercises it issued in 1958 at fifty cents a copy would become a world-wide bestseller. The publication was the work of Dr. William Orban, physical fitness consultant to the Royal Canadian Air Force, and Dr. Orban's title refers to the "five basic exercises" he evolved for the use of the fliers.
>
> In 1962, Simon and Schuster reprinted *5BX* as a paperback in the

United States, and within a decade three million copies were sold in English, and another four million in other languages.

Credit for conceiving the 5BX plan is sometimes accorded to John Kearns Kett, RCAF physical-education instructor.

## Orczy, Baroness Emmuska

To the President, Directors and all connected with that marvellous organization the Canadian Pacific Railway . . . I could not have written the book had it not been for the happy time you gave me in Canada. In all gratitude and friendship, therefore, I dedicate *Blue Eyes and Grey* to you.

> This must be the only novel ever dedicated to a railroad. The Hungarian-born popular novelist who created the Scarlet Pimpernel visited Canada in 1925, rode on the CPR, and in 1928 wrote *Blue Eyes and Grey*, a romance set in the West. "The whole trip now seems like a beautiful dream," she said in a letter to Colonel John Bayne MacLean, as quoted by Floyd S. Chalmers in *A Gentleman of the Press* (1969).

## O'Reilly, Judge Peter

Boys, I am here to keep order and administer the law. Those who don't want law and order can "git." But those who stay with the camp, remember on what side of the British Columbia line the camp is. For, boys, if there is shooting in Kootenay, there will be hanging in Kootenay.

> To American miners at Wilde Horse Creek, British Columbia, 1864. Quoted by Frank Rasky in *Great Canadian Disasters* (1961).

## Orekoff, Michael   See Michael Verigin.

## Orkin, Mark M.

Canajan.

> "The nash null language of Anglos." Canajun is to English what joual is to French, according to the lawyer and philologist.

\*

Eh?

> "Rhymes with hay. The great Canadian monosyllable and shibboleth, 'eh?', is

all things to all men." As in the expression "Sir John, Eh?" *Canajan, Eh?* (1973).

## Orpingalik

This is what I call this song, for it is just as necessary to me to sing it as it is to breathe.

> "My Breath" is the title of a poem by the Eskimo singer Orpingalik. Knud Rasmussen, *The Netsilik Eskimos: Social Life and Spiritual Culture: Report of the Fifth Thule Expedition, 1921-24* (1931).

## Orr, Bobby

Hockey is all action.

> *Orr on Ice* (1970), with Dick Grace.

I don't even like to think about money *and* hockey. I played just as hard when I only got a ten-dollar bill once a week.

> Defenceman for the Boston Bruins not commenting on his salary, bonuses, prizes and commercial endorsements. Quoted by Bill Surface in *In Search of Canada* (1971), by the editors of *Reader's Digest*.

## Osborne, Colonel Henry E.

If this organization becomes a success, it will have been founded on love and whisky.

> Honorary director of the Dominion Drama Festival from 1933 to 1939, quoted by Betty Lee in *Love and Whisky: The Story of the Dominion Drama Festival* (1973). This was a self-fulfilling prophecy, for during the 1950s the festival would be sponsored by Calvert Distillers.

## Osborne, John

You don't have to look interested, dear. She's not interested in all that horse manure about Canada.

> Archie Rice's line in *The Entertainer: A Play* (1957).

## Oshaweetuk

It must be tiresome for someone to paint this same picture on every package.

> The Cape Dorset carver, having no

knowledge of the process of printing, assumed the images on James Houston's cigarette package were hand-drawn. It occurred to Houston that the Eskimos could be print-makers as well as carvers. This took place in 1957. Quoted by Lawrence Elliott in *Canada—This Land, These People: A Reader's Digest Collection* (1968).

## Osler, Sir William

Speck in cornea . . . 50¢

First fee recorded in the young physician's account-book, Dundas, Ontario, 1874. Quoted by Harvey Cushing in *The Life of Sir William Osler* (1925) who notes that this was "an entry he was later to point out to aspiring young M.D.'s in later years with a twinkle in his eye."

A patient with a written list of symptoms—neurasthenia.
*

An excellent recipe for longevity is this: cultivate a minor ailment, and take very good care of it.
*

A physician who treats himself has a fool for a patient.
*

Care more particularly for the individual patient than for the special features of the disease.
*

Divide your attention equally between men and books.
*

Gall-bladders are superfluous organs—like the appendix—one of those afterthoughts of the Almighty.
*

Half of us are blind, few of us feel, and we are all deaf.
*

Happiness lies in the absorption in some vocation which satisfies the soul.
*

Humanity has but three great enemies: fever, famine and war; of these by far the greatest, by far the most terrible, is fever.
*

I have careful records of about five hundred deathbeds, studied particularly with reference to the modes of death and the sensations of the dying. . . . Ninety suffered bodily pain or distress of one sort or another, eleven showed mental apprehension, two positive terror, one expressed spiritual exaltation, one bitter remorse. The great majority gave no sign one way or the other; like birth, their death was a sleep and a forgetting.
*

I have two fixed ideas . . . the first is the comparative uselessness of men above forty years of age. This may seem shocking, and yet read aright the world's history bears out the statement. . . . My second fixed idea is the uselessness of men above sixty years of age, and the incalculable benefit it would be in commercial, political, and in professional life if, as a matter of course, men stopped work at this age. . . . In that charming novel, *The Fixed Period*, Anthony Trollope discusses the practical advantages in modern life of a return to this ancient usage [of retiring sexagenarians from public life], and the plot hinges upon the admirable scheme of a college into which at sixty men retired for a year of contemplation before a peaceful departure by chloroform. That incalculable benefits might follow such a scheme is apparent to anyone who, like myself, is nearing the limit, and who has made a careful study of the calamities which may befall men during the seventh and eighth decades. Still more when he contemplates the many evils which they perpetuate unconsciously, and with impunity. As it can be maintained that all the great advances have come from men under forty, so the history of the world shows that a very large proportion of the evils may be traced to the sexagenarians—nearly all the great mistakes politically and socially, all the worst poems, most of the bad pictures, a majority of bad novels, not a few of the bad sermons and speeches. . . . The teacher's life should have three periods, study until twenty-five, investigation until forty, profession until sixty, at which age I would have him retired on a double allowance. Whether Anthony Trollope's suggestion of a college and chloroform should be carried out or not I have become a little dubious, as my own time is getting so short.

"OSLER RECOMMENDS CHLOROFORM AT SIXTY" was the response of the world press to Dr. Osler's tongue-in-cheek suggestion in "The Fixed Period," his valedictory address, Johns Hopkins University, Baltimore, February 22, 1905. The world-famous medical teacher was fifty-five at the time and refused to retract a word of it, although when the address was published in book form he added this note: "To every man over sixty whose spirit I may have thus unwittingly bruised, I tender my heartfelt regrets." Quoted by Harvey Cushing in *The Life of Sir William Osler* (1925).

In neurasthenia or insanity, *"cherchez la femme"*—woman is at the bottom of most troubles.

*

In science the credit goes to the man who convinces the world, not to the man to whom the idea first occurs.

*

It cannot be denied that in dealings with the public just a little touch of humbug is immensely effective, but it is not necessary.

*

It is easier to buy books than to read them and easier to read them than to absorb them.

*

It is one of the greatest blessings that so many women are so full of tact. The calamity happens when a woman who has all the other riches of life just lacks that one thing.

*

Know syphilis in all its manifestations and relations, and all other things clinical will be added unto you.

*

Lift up one hand to heaven and thank your stars if they have given you the proper sense to enable you to appreciate the inconceivably droll situations in which we catch our fellow creatures.

*

Live in the ward. [Advice to interns and doctors generally]

*

Look wise, say nothing, and grunt.

Speech was given to conceal thought.

*

One of the first duties of the physician is to educate the masses not to take medicine.

*

Outside of the asylum there are also the two great types, the student-lark who loves to see the sun rise, who comes to breakfast with a cheerful morning face and in hilarious spirits . . . the student-owl with his saturnine morning face, thoroughly unhappy, cheated by the wretched breakfast-bell of the two best hours of the day for sleep. . . .

*

Patients should have rest, food, fresh air, and exercise—the quadrangle of health.

*

Save the fleeting minute; learn gracefully to dodge the bore.

*

The best thing nature can do with gall stones is to close the stone quarry and shut down the business.

*

The desire to take medicine is perhaps the greatest feature which distinguishes man from animals.

*

The natural man has only two primal passions, to get and to beget.

*

The philosophies of one age have become the absurdities of the next, and the foolishness of yesterday has become the wisdom of tomorrow.

*

The practice of medicine is an art, based on science.

*

The quest for righteousness is Oriental, the quest for knowledge Occidental.

*

The Scots are the backbone of Canada. They are all right in their three vital parts—heads, hearts and haggis.

*

The value of experience is not in seeing much, but in seeing wisely.

*

The young physician starts life with twenty drugs for each disease, and the old physician ends life with one drug for twenty diseases.

*

There are no straight backs, no symmetrical faces, many wry noses, and no even legs. We are a crooked and perverse generation.

*

Throw away, in the first place, all ambition beyond that of doing the day's work well.

*

To have striven, to have made an effort, to have been true to certain ideals—this alone is worth the struggle. Now and again in a generation one or two snatch something from dull oblivion.

*

To know just what has to be done, then to do it, comprises the whole philosophy of practical life.

*

To study the phenomena of disease without books is to sail an uncharted sea, while to study books without patients is not to go to sea at all.

*

To talk of diseases is a sort of Arabian Nights' entertainment.

*

Varicose veins are the result of an improper selection of grandparents.

*

We are here to add what we can to, not to get what we can from, life.

*

When schemes are laid in advance, it is surprising how often the circumstances fit in with them.

*

With half an hour's reading in bed every night as a steady practice, the busiest man can get a fair education before the plasma sets in the periganglionic spaces of his grey cortex.

*

You can grow corns or potatoes, but you cannot grow brains. Brains come hard and they come high.

*

The most vivid recollections of my boyhood in Canada cluster about the happy spring days when we went off to the bush to make maple sugar—the bright sunny days, the delicious cold nights, the camp-fires, the log cabins, and the fascinating work tapping the trees, putting in the birch-bark spouts, arranging the troughs, and then going from tree to tree, collecting in pails the clear sweet sap. One memory stands out above all others, the astonishment that so little sugar was left after boiling down so great a cauldron of liquid. And yet the sap was so abundant and so sweet. The workers of my generation in the bush of science have collected a vaster quantity of sap than ever before known; much has already been boiled down, and it is for you of the younger generation while completing the job to tap your own trees. [1911]

*The Life of Sir William Osler* (1925), by Harvey Cushing. *Sir William Osler: Aphorisms from His Bedside Teachings and Writings* (1950), collected by Robert Bennett Bean and edited by William Bennett Bean.

### Osmond, Humphry
Psychedelic.

This neologism, which means "mind-expanding," was coined by Dr. Humphry Osmond to describe the effects of hallucinogenic drugs. It first appeared in print in "A Review of the Clinical Effects of Psychotomimetic Agents," *Annals of the New York Academy of Science*, 66, 1957. Dr. Osmond, who was director of psychiatric research in the department of public health in Saskatoon, was engaged in experiments with mescaline with Dr. Abram Hoffer, then professor of psychiatry, University of Saskatchewan. One "smogless May morning in Hollywood," Dr. Osmond administered mescaline to Aldous Huxley; the novelist described his experience in *The Doors of Perception* (1954), and the LSD craze began. *Psychedelics: The Use and Implications of Hallucinogenic Drugs* (1970), edited by Bernard Aaronson and Humphry Osmond.

### O'Sullivan, John L.
Texas, we repeat, is secure; and so now, as the Razor Strop Man says, "Who's the next customer?" Shall it be California or Canada?

*The New York Morning News*, July 7, 1845. Quoted by F. Merk in *Manifest Destiny and Mission in American His-*

*tory* (1963). O'Sullivan, a U.S. congressman, coined the phrase "manifest destiny," and used it for the first time in the same publication on December 27 of the same year.

## Ouellette, Fernand

It seems essential that all available energy be mobilized. Will a dynamic, progressive society place Quebec on the same footing as the rest of Canada? Then, and only then, shall we find out whether Confederation was really a hoax.

> "The Historical Background of Separatism in Quebec," *Canadian Historical Review*, September, 1962.

My native tongue is not French, it is *Franglais*. Learning French was almost like learning a foreign language.

> *Franglais*: term used in France for the anglicized French language. *Liberté*, March-April, 1964.

## Owen, Don

I feel you have to be able to make a movie the way a writer writes a novel, changing, adapting, erasing a paragraph, putting in something that comes along.

> Quoted by Herman Voaden in his edition of *Don Owen's Nobody Waved Good-Bye* (1971).

# P

## Paassen, Pierre van

The test of the civilization of any people is the way they treat a foreigner; as a foreigner myself, coming as a young man to Canada, I have nothing but praise for the way I was received in Canada.

> "Frontiers of Hope and Despair" (1934), *Empire Club of Canada: Addresses Delivered to the Members During the Year 1933-34* (1934).

Before attempting to write a story, I strolled into the office of *The Toronto Daily Star*, another afternoon paper, and was ushered into the presence of the managing editor, a Mr. John R. Bohn. "What exactly could you do?" he asked kindly enough. "Well, perhaps you could use someone," I said, "to watch the foreign press. I have a working knowledge of several languages," and I named a whole string, adding one each time he raised his left eyebrow in feigned astonishment. "That's fine, that's extraordinary," said Mr. Bohn, "but what we

really need here in this office is someone who understands Bulgarian." That was the one European language, I think, I had failed to mention.

> *Days of Our Years* (1940). Van Paassen was hired and went on to become an internationally respected war correspondent.

## Pacey, Desmond

The decisive point is that Canada's youth is in reality an advantage rather than a handicap. Her future is almost certain to be greater than her past, and this is the basis for the perpetual hopefulness which pervades her literature and her literary criticism. [General Introduction]

\*

Our literary history may not be glorious, but it is ours and we should be aware of it—even if only to learn from our own mistakes. [Conclusion]

*Creative Writing in Canada: A Short History of English-Canadian Literature* (Revised Edition, 1961).

**Page, P.K.**
The important thing is to evolve. To become fully awake is the major task.

Quoted by Merle Shain in *Chatelaine*, October, 1972.

**Pakan**
Tell the people of Edmonton that we choose to live in peace. They have nothing to fear from us. We have peaceful purposes and will be fully occupied in carrying them out. We will work to extend our farms and schools and build better homes. We are still Indians but we will prove that Indians can farm and adjust to the new way of living.

Pakan refused to support Riel in the Rebellion of 1885 and so gained his name which means "a tough nut, hard to crack." He was chief of the Wood Crees who settled at Whitefish Lake, Saskatchewan.

**Palardy, Jean**
If the French want to see an authentic eighteenth-century French fortress, then, you know, they will just have to come to Louisbourg.

Quoted by Kenneth Koyen in *Holiday*, Summer, 1972.

**Palmer, Daniel David**
Chiropractic art consists in the aptitude of adjusting vertebrae, of which art I am the originator.

❋

Chiropractic deals with biology. It is the only comprehensive system which answers the timeworn question, "What is life?"

"The Moral and Religious Duty of a Chiropractor," *The Chiropractic Adjustor: A Compilation of the Writings of D.D. Palmer* (1921), edited by B.J. Palmer. The word "chiropractic" was coined by D.D. Palmer, a native of Port Perry, Ontario, who founded the Palmer School of Chiropractic in Davenport, Iowa, in 1903. The word is Greek for

"doing by hand" and stems from Palmer's experience in September of 1895 when he treated a deaf patient with spinal manipulation. A familiar saying of his runs: "Chiropractic is founded upon the relationship of bones, nerves and muscles."

**Palmer, Howard**
Land of the Second Chance.

Title of a comprehensive study of ethnic groups in southern Alberta, written by Howard Palmer and published in 1972.

**Palmerston, Lord**
I cannot admit that it is a question for consideration and decision whether our North American Provinces are to be fought for or abandoned. There may be much to be said for the theory put forward by some, that our Colonies are an encumbrance and an expense, and that we should be better without them, but that is not the opinion of England, and it is not mine.

Confidential despatch from the British prime minister to Lord Monck, July, 1864. Quoted by W.L. Morton in *The Critical Years: The Union of British North America 1857-1873* (1964), who calls the remark "this last roll of Palmerstonian thunder."

"Palmerston said of the Hudson's Bay Company that its functions should be to strip the local quadrupeds of their furs, and keep the local bipeds off their liquor."

James Morris in *Heaven's Command: An Imperial Progress* (1973).

**Papandreou, Andreas G.**
For my generation that following the defeat of Fascism and Naziism hoped for a democratic, peaceful, progressive world, it is not easy to contemplate a new totalitarian era. Yet, we have to retain our optimism. For optimism is the prerequisite to action. And action by now is not our right, but our duty.

*Man's Freedom* (1970). The once-exiled Greek leader and head of the Panhellenic Liberation Movement is professor of Economics at York University. A phrase associated with him is *Paternalistic Capitalism*, the title of a study of the capitalistic ethos published in 1972.

## Papen, Franz von

During the first few weeks of the conflict I was plagued by all sorts of people with plans for the conduct of the war, new inventions, and all manner of unlikely projects. One of them was a young man who had the idea of hindering the transport of troops and war material from Canada in order to delay as far as possible the arrival of British aid in France. The idea seemed attractive to me and the attempt to delay the arrival of British and Canadian divisions in France a worthwhile project. The young man in question suggested that the railway bridge over the Welland Canal in Canada should be blown up. Canada was a belligerent, and this sort of activity seemed perfectly justified.

> Von Papen was vice-chancellor of Germany from 1933 to 1934. *Memoirs* (1953), translated by Brian Connell.

## Papineau, Louis-Joseph

I love my country—I have loved her wisely!—I have loved her madly! "My country first!" I learned to lisp at my father's knee.

> Montreal election address, August 11, 1827, quoted by George H. Locke in *Builders of the Canadian Commonwealth* (1923).

Be neither clericals nor anti-clericals: be true.

> Quoted by Lionel-Adolphe Groulx in *Notre maître, le passé* (1924-44).

You will believe me, I trust, when I say to you, I love my country. . . . Opinions outside may differ; but looking into my heart and my mind in all sincerity, I feel I can say that I have loved her as she should be loved.

> Quoted by Alfred D. DeCelles in *The "Patriotes" of '37: A Chronicle of the Lower Canadian Rebellion* (1920).

The time has gone by when Europe could give Monarchies to America; on the contrary, a new epoch is now approaching when America will give Republics to Europe.

> Address in the House, 1835, quoted by John Mercier McMullen in *The History of Canada from Its First Discovery to the Present Time* (1892).

Our people don't want english capital nor english people here,—they have no ambition beyond their present possessions, & never want to go beyond the sound of their own Church Bells.

> Quoted by Stewart Derbishire in "Report to Lord Durham on Lower Canada, 1838," edited by Norah Story, *Canadian Historical Review*, March, 1937.

It is within ourselves, by studies, occupations, amusements within our reach, whether rich or poor, that we can find life as it is for everyone, good and bad, and quite bearable if we are moderate.

*

With money, one lives in Canada if one hopes to do good . . . one lives in orange-groves if one has the sad conviction of not being able to do good to the country where he is born.

> Letter to his wife Julie, written in exile in Paris, June 20, 1845. Quoted by Jean Bruchési in *Our Living Tradition: Second and Third Series* (1959), edited by Robert L. McDougall. See also Wolfred Nelson.

## Pâquet, Monseignor Louis-Adolphe

We are not only a civilized race, we are the pioneers of civilization; we are not only a religious people, we are the messengers of the religious idea; we are not only submissive sons of the Church, we are, we ought to be, numbered among its zealots, its defenders, and its apostles. Our mission is less to manipulate capital than to change ideas; it consists less in lighting the fires of factories than in maintaining and radiating afar the hearthlight of religion and thought.

> Quebec City Address, St. Jean-Baptiste Day, 1902. Quoted in another version by Mason Wade in *The French Canadians: 1760-1967* (1968).

**Paré, Lorenzo**
Our nationalism is a defence mechanism. It is not a way of life.

Quoted by Guy Sylvestre in "Tradition and Change in French Canada" and translated by Glenn Shortliffe in *The Arts in Canada: A Stock-Taking at Mid-Century* (1958), edited by Malcolm Ross.

**Parent, Etienne**
Nos institutions, notre langue, nos lois.

Motto of the Quebec City newspaper *Le Canadien* when it was revived on May 7, 1831, under the editorship of Etienne Parent.

**Parizeau, Jacques**
The main opponent of Coca-Cola is Pepsi-Cola, not the Parti Québécois.

Reply to criticism that the mock budget prepared by the separatist party for the election of October 29, 1973, would alarm big business and depress the Quebec economy. Quoted by William Borders in *The New York Times*, October 21, 1973.

**Parker, Dorothy**
It is also, I am afraid, true that, deep in New York, there are certain spells during certain evenings—cognac is best for a starter—when my English slips from me like the shucked skin of a snake, and I converse only in the elegant French tongue. But what French! O God, O Montreal, what French!

"The Grandmother of the Aunt of the Gardener" (1931), *Constant Reader* (1970). See also Samuel Butler.

**Parker, Edgar Randolph ("Painless")**
All my life I've tried to be dignified. But, you know, I'm not dignified. You can't turn a showman into an ethical dentist.

Quoted by Ian Sclanders in "Painless Parker: The Outlaw Dentist," *Maclean's Magazine*, December 15, 1949. The New Brunswick-born dentist with a sense of showmanship legally changed his name to Painless Parker to advertise his practice without contravening the dental code. Bob Hope played the role of Pain-

less in *The Paleface* (1947), a film about the zany dentist who died in 1952.

**Parker, Sir Gilbert**
You are playing on the shores of life, and so am I. You are beginning to think and dream, and so am I. We are only children till we begin to make our dreams our life. So I am one with you, for only now do I step from dreams to action.

*When Valmond Came to Pontiac: The Story of the Lost Napoleon* (1895).

**Parker, Harley**
Good taste is the first refuge of the witless.

Quoted by Marshall McLuhan in *Counterblast* (1969).

Someone has said: "We don't know who discovered water but we're sure it wasn't a fish." Unfortunately, man in relation to his environment is in the same state of unawareness.

"Art and Pollution: A Proposal," *Artscanada*, April, 1970. See also Marshall McLuhan.

**Parkin, John C.**
As I see it, the environment is a total system which should be so carefully designed as to ensure the appropriate ecological relationship between man and his physical surroundings. Our species is extraordinarily adaptable, but not so adaptable that we can much longer maintain so reckless a disregard for our surroundings.

"Interface and Interplay," *Probings: A Collection of Essays Contributed to the Canadian Mental Health Association for its Golden Jubilee 1918-1968* (1968).

Ethics are merely a form of collective bargaining at the professional level.

Address, Saskatchewan Symposium on Architecture, Regina, October 21, 1961.

A tree trunk takes up no more space than a service pole.

"Toronto 1980," *The Globe and Mail*, November 4, 1961.

## Parkinson, C. Northcote

Canada, with one policeman to 662, has a crime index of 4,183.4—nearly double that of Britain and more than three times that of the Netherlands where the police force numbers only 1 in 836. The Royal Canadian Mounted Police have a well-deserved reputation for getting their man but the fact remains that they have to do this too often.

> The Law of Delay: Interviews and Out-erviews (1970), by the British humourist and originator of "Parkinson's Law."

## Parkman, Francis

In these ancient wilds, to whose ever verdant antiquity the pyramids are young and Nineveh a mushroom of yesterday; where the sage wanderer of the Odyssey, could he have urged his pilgrimage so far, would have surveyed the same grand and stern monotony, the same dark sweep of melancholy woods,— here, while New England was a solitude, and the settlers of Virginia scarcely dared venture inland beyond the sound of a cannon-shot, Champlain was planting on shores and islands the emblems of his faith.

*

Spanish civilization crushed the Indian; English civilization scorned and neg-lected him; French civilization embraced and cherished him.

> Pioneers of France in the New World (1865).

A happier calamity never befell a people than the conquest of Canada by the British arms.

> The Old Régime in Canada (1874).

The most momentous and far-reaching question ever brought to issue on this continent was: Shall France remain here or shall she not?

*

America owes much to the imbecility of Louis XV and the ambitious vanity and personal dislikes of his mistress.

*

In truth, the funeral of Montcalm was the funeral of New France.

*

Here Wolfe himself led the charge, at the head of the Louisbourg grenadiers. A shot shattered his wrist. He wrapped his handkerchief about it and kept on. Another shot struck him, and he still advanced, when a third lodged in his breast. He staggered, and sat on the ground. Lieutenant Brown, of the gren-adiers, one Henderson, a volunteer in the same company, and a private soldier, aided by an officer of artillery who ran to join them, carried him in their arms to the rear. He begged them to lay him down. They did so, and asked if he would have a surgeon. "There's no need," he answered; "it's all over with me." A moment after, one of them cried out: "They run; see how they run!" "Who run?" Wolfe demanded, like a man roused from sleep. "The enemy, sir. Egad, they give way everywhere!" "Go, one of you, to Colonel Burton," returned the dying man; "tell him to march Webb's regiment down to Charles River, to cut off their retreat from the bridge." Then, turning on his side, he murmured, "Now, God be praised, I will die in peace!" and in a few moments his gallant soul had fled.

Montcalm, still on horseback, was borne with the tide of fugitives towards the town. As he approached the walls a shot passed through his body. He kept his seat; two soldiers supported him, one on each side, and led his horse through the St. Louis Gate. On the open space within, among the excited crowd, were several women, drawn, no doubt, by eagerness to know the result of the fight. One of them recognized him, saw the streaming blood, and shrieked, *"O mon Dieu! mon Dieu! le Marquis est tué!"* "It's nothing, it's nothing," replied the death-stricken man; "don't be troubled for me, my good friends." (*"Ce n'est rien, ce n'est rien; ne vous affligez pas pour mois, mes bonnes amies."*)

In the night of humiliation when Vaudreuil abandoned Quebec, Mont-calm was breathing his last within its walls. When he was brought wounded from the field, he was placed in the house of the Surgeon Arnoux, who was then with Bourlamaque at Isle-aux-Noix, but whose younger brother, also a surgeon, examined the wound and pronounced it mortal. "I am glad of it," Montcalm said quietly; and then asked how long he had to live. "Twelve hours, more or less," was the reply. "So much the better," he returned. "I am happy that I shall not live to see the surrender of Quebec." He is reported to have said that since he had lost the battle it consoled him to have been defeated by so brave an enemy; and some of his last words were in praise of his successor, Lévis, for whose talents and fitness for command he expressed high esteem. When Vaudreuil sent to ask his opinion, he gave it; but when Ramesay, commandant of the garrison, came to receive his orders, he replied: "I will neither give orders nor interfere any further. I have much business that must be attended to, of greater moment than your ruined garrison and this wretched country. My time is very short; therefore pray leave me. I wish you all comfort, and to be happily extricated from your present perplexities." Nevertheless he thought to the last of those who had been under his command, and sent the following note to Brigadier Townshend: "Monsieur, the humility of the English sets my mind at peace concerning the fate of the French prisoners and the Canadians. Feel towards them as they have caused me to feel. Do not let them perceive that they have changed masters. Be their protector as I have been their father."

Bishop Pontbriand, himself fast sinking with mortal disease, attended his death-bed and administered the last sacraments. He died peacefully at four o'clock on the morning of the fourteenth. He was in his forty-eighth year.

*Montcalm and Wolfe* (1884). New France fell to the British forces on the Plains of Abraham, outside the walls of Quebec. General James Wolfe died September 13, 1759, and was buried in Greenwich, England. Louis-Joseph de Montcalm-Gazon, Marquis de Montcalm de Saint-Servan, who was mortally wounded, died the following day and was buried in the Ursuline Chapel in Quebec. See the Index for further references to Wolfe and Montcalm.

**Parlby, Irene**
If the mills of God grind slowly, the mills of Parliament sometimes seem to stop altogether—that is, of course, so far as great fundamentals are concerned.

Speech in 1928 by Dr. Parlby of Alberta, the second woman cabinet minister in the British Empire. See also Anonymous: Some Documents.

**Parlow, Kathleen**
With all the things that have been said about me, nobody has mentioned the greatest asset I have. Here is a woman who doesn't want to talk in public and I should think that a female who doesn't want to talk should be cherished.

The famous Calgary-born violinist died in Toronto in 1963. *The Globe and Mail*, January 30, 1941.

**Parmenius, Stephen**
Now I ought to tell you about the customs, territories and inhabitants: and yet what am I to say, my dear Hakluyt, when I see nothing but desolation? There are inexhaustible supplies of fish, so that those who travel here do good business.

Letter written in Latin to Richard Hakluyt from St. John's, Newfoundland, August 6, 1583, by the young scholar and poet on Humphrey Gilbert's expedition, who perished twenty-three days later in a shipwreck off Sable Island. Parmenius, the first known Hungarian to set foot on the North American continent, was the first known poet to do so as well. Quoted by David B. Quinn and Neil Cheshire in *The New Found Land of Stephen Parmenius: The Life and Writings of a Hungarian Poet Drowned on a Voyage from Newfoundland, 1583* (1972).

**Parmenter, Ross**
The need for devotion to something outside ourselves is even more profound than the need for companionship. If we are not to go to pieces or wither away, we must have some purpose in life; for no man can live for himself alone.

American music critic born in Canada. "The Doctor and the Cleaning Woman," *The Plant in My Window* (1949).

## Partridge, Eric

Canadians have a very distinctive variety of English, far more different from that spoken in Britain than is the English spoken by Australians; yet Canadians— so imperceptibly, so constantly has the process operated—"just get on with the job"; having this very different English, they therefore do not feel the need to have it at all.

> *British and American English Since 1900* (1951).

## Patch, Sam

To show people that some things can be done as well as others.

> This is Sam Patch's answer to the question of why he "lept." On October 22, 1829, the Nantucket millhand, twenty-three, became the first of the Niagara "daredevils." From a specially constructed platform on Goat Island, he leapt the 118 feet into the boiling cauldron at the foot of the Horseshoe and American Falls. He died later that year on November 13—a Friday—attempting the same feat at Genesee Falls near Rochester, New York. The man who asked him why he risked his life was the Hartford divine Horace Bushnell. Mrs. M.B. Cheney's *Life and Letters of Horace Bushnell* (1880). William Lyon Mackenzie describes the Niagara leap in *Sketches of Canada and the United States* (1883).

## Patmore, Derek

A writer of our acquaintance, sitting on the train going west across the repetitive prairies, finally burst out savagely, "This country could do with a great deal of editing!"

\*

Someone quoted us a typical example of the Canadian attitude of Americans: "We like the Americans we know," said the speaker, "we just don't like the United States."

> *Canada* (1967), by Derek Patmore and Marjory Whitelaw.

## Patrick, Lester

All right! If there's no one else in sight, I'll go in myself.

> Patrick was manager of the New York Rangers during the 1928 Stanley Cup final round when the goalkeeper was injured. Patrick, then forty-four, although he had never played goal, donned the pads and the Rangers won. Quoted by Henry Roxborough in *Great Days in Canadian Sport* (1957).

## Patterson, Edward

When the coloured people here are insulted it is by the *ruffians* in Canada.

> Patterson escaped from slavery in Maryland and settled in Hamilton. Quoted by Benjamin Drew in *The Refugee: or the Narratives of Fugitive Slaves in Canada* (1856).

## Patterson, Tom

This is Tom Patterson. Will you come to Canada and give advice? We want to start a Shakespeare festival in Stratford, Ontario. We will pay your expenses and a small fee.

> This long-distance telephone call from Tom Patterson in Stratford to Tyrone Guthrie in Northern Ireland during the summer of 1952 resulted in the founding of the Stratford Festival. Quoted by Tyrone Guthrie in *A Life in the Theatre* (1959).

I guess those five words will never fade from my mind.

> The five words are "When do you want me?" This was Tyrone Guthrie's response to Tom Patterson's invitation to visit Stratford in 1952 to give advice on the plans for an annual Shakespearian festival. Quoted by Rosemary Pitcher in "All the Town's a Stage," *Weekend Magazine*, July 14, 1973.

DECIDED PROCEED STOP ASSURE YOU FULL STEAM AHEAD.

> Cable from Patterson of the Festival Committee in Stratford assuring Alec Guinness and Tyrone Guthrie, both in London, England, that there would indeed be a Stratford Festival, 1952. Quoted by Guthrie in "First Shakespeare Festival at Stratford, Ontario," *Renown at Stratford: A Record of the Shakespeare Festival in Canada* (1953), by

Tyrone Guthrie, Robertson Davies, and Grant Macdonald.

We had to go to New York or London to see the best in the arts. Now, we can see the best right here.

> "Canada's Big League Theatre" (1956), *Empire Club of Canada 1956-57* (1957). For the "Stratford adventure," see also: Alec Guinness, Tyrone Guthrie, Siobhan McKenna, Nicholas Monsarrat, Sir Laurence Olivier, Frederick Valk, Herbert Whittaker.

**Pattullo, T.D.**
I remember some years ago a friend of mine was teaching his little boy the Lord's Prayer, and the little fellow said: "Our Father which art in Heaven, halibut be Thy name."

> "British Columbia," January 12, 1922, *The Canadian Club of Ottawa Year Book: 1922-23; 1923-24* (1925). Pattullo was premier from 1933 to 1941.

**Paul, Charles F.**
Militant suffragettes have threatened to break the windows of the Canadian Pacific Railway offices in Trafalgar Square [where settlers are recruited for western Canada], and as a precaution they have been temporarily boarded up. The railway company, however, have replied to the militant vote-seekers by displaying a large sign, sixteen feet long, bearing the words, "We are looking for settlers, not for suffragettes."

> *Saturday Night*, March, 1913.

If you drive modesty out of the world, you will go a long way toward driving out sexual morality also.

> *Saturday Night*, July, 1914. Paul was the editor of this monthly from 1909 to 1926.

Now it would be foolish and impossible to try and prevent the manufacture of films containing Canadian snow scenes; but there is no vestige of a doubt that when exhibited overseas they have a detrimental effect on immigration, particularly in those countries from which we are most anxious to attract population. . . . Everything that can be done should be done, to encourage the circulation of screen pictures that demonstrate that snow scenes and dog-trains are but a minor phase in Canadian life.

> *Saturday Night*, October, 1922.

If the walls of the Canadian section of the British Empire Exhibition are to be covered with crude cartoons of the Canadian Wilds, devoid of perspective, atmospheric feeling and sense of texture, it is going to be a bad advertisement for this country. We should advise the Department of Immigration and Colonization to intervene to prevent such a catastrophe.

> *Saturday Night*, September 15, 1923. A reaction to paintings by the Group of Seven.

**Payne, John**
If drinking to your success would Take Cape Briton [*sic*], you must be in Possession of it now, for it's a standing Toast.

> Letter of John Payne of Boston to Colonel Robert Hale, April 24, 1745, when Hale set out to take Louisbourg. Quoted by Francis Parkman in *A Half-Century of Conflict* (1892).

**Pearl, Bert**
It's . . . the Happy Gang!

> "The Happy Gang" came on the air June 14, 1937, and over the years employed the talents of Cliff McKay, Bobby Gimby, Lloyd Edwards, Joe and Bert Niosi, Jimmy Namaro, Lou Snider, and a host of others. The CBC Radio program was a vehicle for Bert Pearl and was sponsored by Colgate-Palmolive-Peet. E. Austin Weir in *The Struggle for National Broadcasting in Canada* (1965) writes that the five-days-a-week program "ran for twenty-two years and was the most popular of all Canadian daytime programs." Pearl, who was born in Winnipeg in 1913 and retired to Hollywood in the 1960s, was known as "that five foot two and a half of sunshine."

**Pearson, Arthur M.**
Buy land. They've stopped making it.

Saskatchewan senator, chairman of the Special Senate Committee on Land Use, to Senator David Croll. Quoted by George Bain in *The Globe and Mail*, March 17, 1973.

## Pearson, Hesketh

A visit to Niagara Falls made me homesick, and I went on to Quebec for a few days at the Château Frontenac, where I read Gilbert Parker's *The Seats of the Mighty* and succumbed to another hard-up story from a man who lived at Levis on the opposite shore and had invented something that would make a fortune if he could exploit it in England. Like an idiot I parted with a portion of my rapidly diminishing capital, and soon lost sight of him. I have a dim idea that his invention had something to do with harness for horses; but as I can never take the smallest interest in any sort of invention, my enquiries into this were perfunctory.

*Hesketh Pearson by Himself* (1965). The noted biographer's visit to America was made in 1908.

## Pearson, Lester B.

. . . it is perhaps fitting that this fastest of all games has become almost as much of a national symbol as the maple leaf or the beaver. Most young Canadians, in fact, are born with skates on their feet rather than with silver spoons in their mouths.

The future prime minister paying tribute to hockey. "Love of Sport," *Canada: Reprinted from the Canadian Number of "The Times," May 15, 1939* (1939).

If Lester is my name, Mike is what I am usually called. This change goes back to World War I when I was training with the RFC. My Squadron Commander felt that Lester was no name for an aspiring fighter pilot and decided to call me Mike. It stuck, and I was glad to lose Lester.

Preface, *Mike: The Memoirs of the Right Honourable Lester B. Pearson: Volume I, 1897-1948* (1972).

"One day in 1963, after he became prime minister, he was driving past the Victoria College library in Toronto on his way to a civic reception in his honour, and the sight of the building prompted him to tell this anecdote about his enlistment:

" 'I was in the library in 1915, studying a Latin poet, and all of a sudden I thought: "War can't be this bad." So I walked out and enlisted.' "

John Robinson Beal in *The Pearson Phenomenon* (1964).

I accept now with equanimity the question so constantly addressed to me, "Are you an American?" and merely return the accurate answer, "Yes, I am a Canadian." ["Canada and the United States," January 31, 1941; *Words*]

"How long, Mr. Pearson, have you been a member of the Liberal party?"

"Since I was sworn in as a Minister a couple of hours ago."

The new member for Algoma East was sworn in as secretary of State for External Affairs on September 10, 1948. "I should have learned by now that, while quips can get a politician headlines, they can also get him more easily into trouble than more serious observations." *Mike: The Memoirs of the Right Honourable Lester B. Pearson: Volume I, 1897-1948* (1972).

In this position I am doing my best, I am sure without complete success, to live up to a motto which I am told President Truman keeps on his desk in Washington and which reads: "Always do right—this will please some people and astonish the rest." ["To the United Nations Correspondents' Association," November 11, 1952, as president of the U.N. General Assembly; *Words*]

The Canadian-American situation is one something like that of living with your wife. Sometimes it is difficult and even irritating to live with her but it is always impossible to live without her. [As secretary of State, March 15, 1955]

The grim fact is that we prepare for war like precocious giants and for peace like retarded pygmies. [Acceptance speech, Nobel Prize for Peace, Oslo, December 10, 1957]

In such an agreement, a U.S. finger would be on the trigger; but a Canadian finger would be on the safety catch. ["On Canadian Defence Policy," January 12, 1963, concerning joint control of nuclear weapons on Canadian soil; *Words*]

It will not be an easy time, but it will, I pledge you, be a time to excite the daring, to test the strong, and to give new promise to the timid. [On being sworn in as head of a minority government, April 22, 1963]

Independent, they would be even more dependent. [Attributed to the prime minister after the first FLQ bombings in Quebec]

We worry when you look hard at us, but we are also touchy about being overlooked. [Commemoration address, Notre Dame University; *The New York Times*, June 10, 1963]

The strongest pressure in the world can be friendly pressure. [About 1963]

The chairman, a taciturn and weather-beaten farmer, spoke: "I have been asked to introduce Mr. Pearson, who has been asked to speak to us. I have. He will." [At a constituency meeting]

\*

Welcome Liberace and Our Prime Minister [Sign, Holiday Inn, in an Ontario city, 1963]

\*

I Like Milk [Chant of a child sporting an "I Like Mike" button, 1963]

> *Mike: The Memoirs of the Right Honourable Lester B. Pearson: Volume II, 1948-1957* (1973), edited by John A. Munro and Alex. I. Inglis.

They can't start a war if we don't answer the phone. [The "hot line" rang in the prime minister's office, but the new P.M. and Paul Martin could not find it; Winter, 1964]

This is the flag of the future, but it does not dishonour the past.

> House of Commons, December 15, 1964. Canada acquired its own flag at 2:30 A.M., December 16, 1964. The "Maple

Leaf" was officially raised and flown for the first time on February 15, 1965.

It has been said that Canada is the most difficult country in the world to govern. I am perhaps a little more aware of that than I used to be. [Campbellford, Ontario, March 26, 1965; for similar remarks by other prime ministers, see Sir Wilfrid Laurier]

A liberal is a man of the centre, moving forward. . . . Liberalism is the middle way between extremes. But while we are in the middle of the road, we don't stand still. [TV interview, October 20, 1966]

The words of General de Gaulle's speech that shocked and distressed me most, however, as I listened to them almost in disbelief on television, were those which referred to his motor journey that afternoon from Quebec City to Montreal: "Je vous salue de tout mon coeur. Je vais vous confier un secret que vous ne répéterez pas. Ce soir, ici, et toute le long de ma route, je me trouvais dans une atmosphère du même genre que celle de la libération." [I salute you with all my heart. I am going to trust you with a secret that you will not repeat. This evening, here, and all along my route, I found myself in an atmosphere of the same kind as that of the liberation.] The "liberation" to which General de Gaulle referred in describing this entry into Montreal was the freeing of Paris from the Nazis, for which so many Canadians, with other allied soldiers, gave their lives. [Reply to Charles de Gaulle's Montreal address, July 24, 1967]

We moved from British influence to American influence without much feeling of purely national identity in between. [Interview upon retirement, 1967]

Then I think of the time I went to Camp David to order LBJ to stop bombing North Vietnam or else; and got away alive and happy to tell the tale, which no one believed. ["Adieu to the Parliamentary Press Gallery," March 30, 1968; *Words*]

One might as well say that the football squad is no place for the honour student in English because "the environment is alien."

The former prime minister thus took James Eayrs to task "for asserting that public service is uncongenial for the inquiring mind." In *Diplomacy and Its Discontents* (1971), Eayrs replied: "It was not for literature that Lester Pearson received his Nobel Prize—nor for logic either."

We'll jump off that bridge when we get to it. [Characteristic expression, also attributed to Pearson's contemporary, the American president, L.B. Johnson]

Politics is the skilled use of blunt objects. ["The Tenth Decade," CBC-TV, 1972]

Not to seek success but to deserve it.

This was said to be Pearson's personal motto. (Often identified as a line from Shakespeare's *Timon of Athens* (1623), it more likely derives from this once-famous couplet from Joseph Addison's play *Cato* (1712): " 'Tis not in mortals to command success, / But we'll do more, Sempronius; we'll deserve it."
*Words and Occasions: An Anthology of Speeches and Articles Selected from His Papers by the Right Honourable L.B. Pearson* (1970). See also Charles de Gaulle and W.L. Mackenzie King.

### Pearson, Maryon
I married him for better or for worse, not just for lunch. [Attributed to Mrs. Lester B. Pearson, about 1967]

Behind every successful man there is a surprised woman.

Quoted by Lester B. Pearson in *Mike: The Memoirs of the Right Honourable Lester B. Pearson: Volume I, 1897-1948* (1972).

### Pearson, Peter
There's something about this country that allows exceptional films to be made only by accident. The talent and resources of this country are unlimited, and it's rather sad that these talents, over and over again, are wasted and wither up.

Accepting an Etrog Award as best direc-

tor for *Best Damn Fiddler from Calabogie to Kaladar* at the 1971 Canadian Film Awards. Quoted by Daniel Stoffman in *The Toronto Star*, October 21, 1971.

### Peary, Robert
I have the Pole, April 6, 1909.

The American naval officer sent this telegram from Smokey Tickle, Labrador, on September 6, 1909, claiming to be the first person to reach the North Pole. Farley Mowat in *The Polar Passion: The Quest for the North Pole* (1967) credits Dr. Frederick Cook with attaining the Pole a year earlier. See also Dr. Frederick Cook.

### Peden, W.J.
During off-hours in early morning when Madison Square Garden spectators were few, the six-day bicycle race could become monotonous. So, when in slow pursuit, I would occasionally hold *Reader's Digest* in one hand and read a page while steering with the other.

Torchy Peden, the youngster from Victoria, became one of the most colourful and successful six-day bicycle riders in the world. Quoted by Henry Roxborough in *Great Days in Canadian Sport* (1957).

### Pedley, Constable A.
Fresh troubles were at hand, however.

Constable Pedley of the RCMP escorted an insane and violent evangelist from Fort Chipewyan to Fort Saskatchewan, some four hundred miles, December, 1904. The missionary's life was saved and within six weeks he was completely recovered. But on the return journey, Constable Pedley broke down and had to be institutionalized at Brandon for six months before being released. The understatement from Pedley's report was quoted by A.L. Haydon in *The Riders of the Plains: A Record of the Royal North-West Mounted Police of Canada: 1873-1910* (1910).

### Peel, Lady   See Beatrice Lillie.

### Peel, Paul
Rest? How can I rest if I do not paint? It is no rest to be idle.

Quoted by Adrian Macdonald in *Canadian Portraits* (1925). The artist painted "After the Bath" which so moved Sarah Bernhardt she tried to buy it. See Sarah Bernhardt.

## Peers, Frank W.

Broadcasting which operates as an auxiliary to advertising must treat man as essentially a consumer, a buyer of goods; and the programs are subservient to that end. A full broadcasting service operates on quite another principle, appealing to man as an active and creative person, Aristotle's "political being," with a potential for growth. National control, then, is not an end in itself, and never has been in Canada. It is the necessary condition for a system designed, in the North American context, to assist Canadians to know the changing society around them, and to adapt successfully to it. The framework of such broadcasting was established in Canada forty years ago. The struggle to improve, even to maintain it, is greater today than ever before, and more crucial still to our survival as a nation.

*The Politics of Canadian Broadcasting: 1920-1951* (1969).

## Peguis

Before you whites came to trouble the ground, our rivers were full of fish and woods of deer. Our creeks abounded with beavers and our plains were covered with buffaloes. But now we are brought to poverty. Our beavers are gone forever; our buffaloes are fled to the lands of our enemies. The number of our fish is diminishing. Our cats and our rats are few in number. The geese are afraid to pass over the smoke of our chimneys and we are left to starve while you whites are growing rich on the very dust of our fathers, troubling the plains with the plough, covering them with cows in the summer and in the winter feeding your cattle with hay from the very swamps whence our beavers have been driven.

All right. I am the highest ruler in these parts. I will take the name of King. I will be William King.

Peguis was a Saulteaux chief whose name means "Destroyer." Baptized by a Red River missionary, he adopted an English name in 1838.

## Pellan, Alfred

A painter should be like a fisherman. He should keep the fish he wants and throw the rest back. Then, of course, he should carefully mount the fish he keeps.

Attributed to the Quebec painter, 1949.

## Pelletier, Gérard

Our Government has been accused of suppressing the Canadian coat of arms, but it really doesn't matter. We could put Schenley's coat of arms on government buildings and no one would know the difference. These symbols do not mean a thing in the twentieth century.

Schenley's refers to the well-known distillers. "Encounter," CBC-TV, July 20, 1970. Quoted by John G. Diefenbaker in *Those Things We Treasure: A Selection of Speeches on Freedom and in Defence of Our Parliamentary Heritage* (1972).

We were the first generation to say, "God damn it, we'll stay home and change the place."

Pelletier is referring to the "Three Wise Men" from Quebec (Marchand, Trudeau and himself) who opposed Duplessis in Quebec in the 1950s and separatism from Ottawa in the 1960s. Quoted by Edith Iglauer in *The New Yorker*, July 5, 1969.

Authoritarianism is the temptation of power; alarmism that of opposition.

*The October Crisis* (1971), translated by Joyce Marshall.

What language do you listen to music in?

Reply to criticism that the secretary of State had authorized all-French narration for an outdoor concert on Parliament Hill, July 1, 1972. Quoted by *Time*, July 17, 1972. See also Pauline Julien.

## Pelletier, Wilfred

For every north american indian who

begins to disappear i also begin to disappear.

Title of a collection of essays on Indian relations, edited by Pelletier and published in 1971.

**Penfield, Wilder**
"Work today and be happy tomorrow"—that's the physician's rule of life.

*The Torch* (1960).

There are times when compassion should prompt us to forego prolonged and costly treatment. If a man must die, he has the right to die in peace, as he would prefer to do if asked. Positive action to take a life is not permitted. But the negative decisions that ease and shorten suffering have always been ours to make.

*

The span of life, for those who escape its early perils, is about the same today as when David played on his harp before King Saul.

*

Rest, with nothing else, results in rust. It corrodes the mechanisms of the brain. The rhubarb that no one picks goes to seed.

*The Second Career* (1963).

The second career of every man or woman should begin early. It may well outlast the bread-winning jobs.

*

The brain of a man or woman that is made bilingual or multilingual early in life becomes a superior instrument.

*

In all our studies of the brain, no mechanism has been discovered that can force the mind to think, or the individual to believe, anything. The mind continues free. This is a statement I have long considered. I have made every effort to disprove it, without success. The mind, I must conclude, is something more than a mechanism. It is, in a certain sense, above and beyond the brain, although it seems to depend upon brain action for its very existence. Yet it is free.

*Second Thoughts: Science, the Arts and the Spirit* (1970).

**Penlington, Norman**
The federation of the British North American colonies in 1867 was essentially the product of American pressure, British support, and Canadian need. Without American pressure, British North Americans would not have willed to solve their problems together; without British support they would have despaired of doing so.

*Canada and Imperialism: 1896-1899* (1965).

**Penn, William**
To the Emperor of Canada.

William Penn addressed his letter concerning peace and trade to "The Emperor of Canada," June 21, 1682, shortly before the Quaker leader sailed from England to settle in the area now called Pennsylvania. Quoted by George Johnson in *Alphabet of First Things in Canada: A Ready Reference Book of Canadian Events* (Third Edition, 1897).

**Pentland, Barbara**
We are actually the first generation of Canadian composers. Before our time music development was largely in the hands of imported English organists, who however sound academically, had no creative contribution to make of any general value.

*Northern Review*, April, 1950.

Question: What should be the place and pattern of music in general education?
Answer: Capture the ears of the young before Muzak and the school system get them!

Composer interviewed by *Musicanada*, July-August, 1969.

**Penz, Peter**   See Ian Adams.

**Pepin, Jean-Luc**
Mr. Speaker, before requesting permission to table a return, may I rise on a question of privilege?
Mr. Speaker, yesterday my name was pronounced in this chamber.
I do not mind being called "Jeen," "John" or "Jake," although I prefer to

be called "Jean." I do not mind being called "Lac," "Luke" or "Luck," although I prefer being called "Luc." I do not mind being called "Piep-in," "Papin" or "Peppin" although I prefer being called "Pepin." The only name I resent is "Peep-in."

Mr. Speaker: The minister has not established the basis of his point of order or question of privilege. This is hardly a "pépin" [problem].

> House of Commons, February 16, 1971.

It's all right to lose once, but to lose twice in the same week is a bit of a shock.

> The federal minister of Trade and Commerce was defeated by a handful of votes in the election of October 30, 1972. The first recount reversed the standings; the second reversed the revised standings. Quoted in *The New York Times*, November 12, 1972.

## Percival, Lloyd
The average Canadian male is weakest in his arms. He just doesn't use 'em enough. We may soon reach the stage where the Canadian bride carries the Canadian groom over the threshold.

> Former athlete and founder of the Fitness Institute, quoted by Bob Pennington in *The Toronto Star*, April 15, 1972.

## Perram, Walter H.
If we adopt this American formation I am afraid we shall never again see a real football match in Canada, for it is not football to toss the ball about the field from hand to hand.

> Perram was captain of the All-Canadian rugby football team when it played Harvard University in 1876. Quoted by *The Mail* in 1876.

## Perrault, Pierre
A country is nothing but an experiment in pride. We shall not escape unscathed . . . for we have committed the indiscretion of loving the land as a country.

> Quoted by René Lévesque in *An Option for Quebec* (1968).

## Perry, Oliver Hazard
We have met the enemy and they are ours; two ships, two brigs, one schooner and one sloop.

> Despatch of the American commodore to William Henry Harrison at Sandusky, September 12, 1813, two days before the Battle of Lake Erie, in which Commodore Perry defeated British Captain R.H. Barclay. Quoted by Thomas H. Raddall in *The Path of Destiny: Canada from the British Conquest to Home Rule: 1763-1850* (1957).

## Perry, Robert L.
To agree, to disagree, to harness diversity, to respect dissent; perhaps this is the real essence of Canada.

> *Galt, U.S.A.* (1971).

## Peter, Dr. Laurence J.
The Peter Principle – In a hierarchy, every employee tends to rise to his level of incompetence.

> *The Peter Principle* (1969), by Dr. Laurence J. Peter, a Canadian-born psychologist teaching in California, and Raymond Hull, a freelance author living in British Columbia.

## Peterson, Oscar
Like, I'm invited to do a command performance for the Queen in England. President Nixon has asked that I do a concert at the White House. But I don't get any requests from Trudeau. It sometimes seems pretty hopeless getting through to Canadians that yes, we Canadian artists do exist.

> Montreal-born jazz pianist, quoted by Shari Steiner in *The Toronto Star*, December 6, 1969.

## Petrovich, Mike
Are we old enough to die but not to live?

> Quoted by Don Bell in *Saturday Night at the Bagel Factory and Other Montreal Stories* (1972).

## Phelps, Arthur L.
If I were to offer, not a definition, but a working description of an alert Canadian citizen just now, I could say he is

one (man or woman) increasingly aware of being North American in the continental sense without being American in the national sense.

> Address, University of New Brunswick, February 18, 1947. This is usually quoted in a more succinct form: "A Canadian is a fellow who has become a North American without becoming an American."

**Philip, Prince**   See Philip Mountbatten.

**Phillimore, Mercy**
Mr. King was an investigator. He did not accept the spirit hypothesis and he had the courage to say so, but he never ceased to be critical in appraising evidence. He was a highly intelligent man with shrewd judgment, and to say he consulted mediums for advice in statecraft is preposterous. It is also outrageous, an insult to his memory.

> Secretary of the London Spiritualist Alliance, in England, speaking to Blair Fraser about W.L. Mackenzie King's spiritualist interests. Reprinted by H. Gordon Green and Guy Sylvestre in *A Century of Canadian Literature / Un siécle de littérature canadienne* (1967).

**Phillips, Alan**
The Mounties inspire such widespread faith that a lad from Dunmanway, Cork, once sent off a letter addressed to: Santa Claus, c/o The Mounties, Canada. The Commissioner's office obligingly sent the boy a reply signed "Santa."

> *The Living Legend: The Story of the Royal Canadian Mounted Police* (1954).

**Phillips, Colonel Eric**
One of the secrets of being an executive is never do anything that you can get someone to do for you.

> Quoted in the industrialist's obituary notice, *The Globe and Mail*, December 28, 1964.

You can't drink yourself sober, you can't spend yourself rich, and the power to tax is the power to destroy. [Last address to the board of the Argus Corporation, 1964]

**Phillips, Nathan**
No one ever tried harder than I to live up to the name, and I believe that I *was* Mayor of All the People, regardless of race, colour, creed, national origin or political affiliation.

> *

The Royal Couple spent a busy day in Toronto. Everywhere they went, the good humour of Prince Philip was evident, even in the ninety-two-degree heat on the way to the Grenadier Restaurant where the Royal Couple had tea with Parks Commissioner George Bell and Mrs. Bell and my wife and me. The Prince looked at Grenadier Pond and said to a fourteen-year-old Boy Scout: "The water looks good. I think I'll go in for a swim." The youth replied: "But it is polluted, sir." "If we both went in," replied the Prince, "it would be more polluted."

> *Mayor of All the People* (1967). See also Pope John XXIII.

**Phillips, R.A.J.**
Today only a few people are caught by the magnetism of the North.

> *

When Columbus made his well-remembered voyage to the Caribbean, Canada had been known to Europeans for more than five hundred years.

> *Canada's North* (1967).

**Phipps, R.W.**   See Nicholas Flood Davin.

**Phips, Sir William**
Your answer positive in an hour returned by your own trumpet, with the return of mine, is required upon the peril that will ensue.

> Phips, leader of the British forces, sent his courier to Comte de Frontenac with this order to surrender Quebec immediately, October 15, 1690. Quoted by Francis Parkman in *Count Frontenac and New France under Louis XIV* (1877). For the famous reply, see Comte de Frontenac.

**Piapot**
You can kill me and scalp me but you can't scare me. . . . You talk like a child

but you cannot scare me. . . . Nobody will find the Great Spirit through fear. That is not His plan. His voice can be heard by Indians as well as Whites but Indians are the best listeners. I have more faith in what I have heard from the Great Spirit than what I have heard from you.

The Cree chief, whose name translates as "one who knew the secrets of the Sioux," died in the Cypress Hills in 1908.

## Picard, Laurent
I don't think it should be an objective to be gray.

CBC executive, quoted by Jack Miller in *The Toronto Star*, May 13, 1972.

## Pickersgill, J.W.
"Clear it with Jack."

"Between 1937 and 1948 he had functioned as Mackenzie King's chief adviser and it was during this epoch that the phrase 'clear it with Jack' first became a password to power in Ottawa." Peter C. Newman in *The Distemper of Our Times: Canadian Politics in Transition: 1963-1968* (1968). According to Dale C. Thomson in *Louis St. Laurent: Canadian* (1967) the phrase that "became a watchword on Parliament Hill" was "Check it with Jack."

Mr. King, it is wonderful. Do you realize that this is a larger majority than you received in any election except 1940?

To Prime Minister Mackenzie King, July 23, 1948, when Newfoundland was only 52% in favour of Confederation with Canada. King's reply was, "I hadn't realized that at all, Pickersgill. That puts a different light on the whole situation." Quoted by Richard Gwyn in *Smallwood: The Unlikely Revolutionary* (1968).

We all want to increase the population of this country and for that purpose if they are equally good people I don't believe that any immigrant, no matter where he comes from or how good he is, is as good as another Canadian baby, because the immigrant has to learn to be a Canadian and the baby is a Canadian to start with.

From a speech made by the minister of Citizenship and Immigration in Victoria, April 15, 1955, repeated April 18 in the House of Commons. George Drew replied: "I would hope that he would remember that Sir John A. Macdonald was an immigrant to this country." Roland Michener added: "Would the minister consider the desirability of changing the name of this portfolio to that of minister of citizenship and propagation?"

I enjoy a reasonable sense of irresponsibility. [Adapted]

*

It is not merely for the well-being of Canadians but for the good of mankind in general that the present Liberal government should remain in office. [Prior to the 1957 election]

*

The real trouble with the Conservative party is that basically it has been a party of Anglo-Saxon racists. They really don't believe in the equality of all Canadians. They really don't believe the French have any right in this country, unless they act like a conquered people.

Quoted by Peter C. Newman in "Jack Pickersgill" (1973), *Home Country: People, Places, and Power Politics* (1973).

I am sure that this country will survive this government, as it survived the last Tory regime. But why, sir, why do we have to suffer these things once in every generation?

Characteristic remark in the House of Commons when the Tories under John Diefenbaker swept the country in the general election on March 31, 1958.

Mackenzie King genuinely believed and frequently said that the real secret of political leadership was more in what was prevented than in what was accomplished.

*The Mackenzie King Record* (1960), Volume I.

## Pickford, Mary
It brought me into the world without a silver spoon in my mouth, but it taught me the lesson which the sterner laws of the North always seem to teach its sons

and daughters, that you must look ahead, and not think only of the passing moment; that bigness should belong to your own life as well as to the map of your own country, and that if you come from the land of the beaver you should always be happy in working like a beaver.

> Mary Pickford was born Gladys Mary Smith in Toronto in 1893 and achieved international fame in films as "America's Sweetheart."

"What's your name?" he [David Belasco] asked right off.
"At home in Toronto, I'm Gladys Smith; but on the road I'm Gladys Milbourne Smith."
This struck him very funny, though he tried to conceal his amusement.
"We'll have to find another name for you. What are some of the other names in your family?"
I told him. . . .
"Well, my little friend, from now on your name will be Mary Pickford, and will you come back, please, with your aunt, tomorrow night and see our play?" [Conversation with the New York theatrical producer when Miss Pickford was nineteen]

*

Up to that time the family had always called me Gladys. They had never taken the "Mary" business very seriously. But on the March day of 1909, on East Fourteenth Street in New York, Gladys was sent back to Canada and Mary Pickford was to embark on a great and thrilling career.

*

Opening night in New York was one of unprecedented terror for me. I was concerned for one thing about my diction. The dialogue director had cautioned me so much about my Canadian "*r*'s" that I was terrified every time I said the word "garden."

> *Sunshine and Shadow* (1955), foreword by Cecil B. De Mille.

Last night I had a dream about Toronto. I was on my bicycle, cruising about in front of the old house. And, as usual in my dreams, I was a little girl again. A little girl in Toronto, with long golden curls.

> Telephone interview from Hollywood conducted by Clyde Gilmour in *The Toronto Telegram*, June 22, 1968. From this interview Gilmour learned that Miss Pickford retained her Canadian citizenship all through her Hollywood career.

My strongest ties and memories have always remained rooted in my Canadian childhood.

> Statement delivered by Buddy Rogers, Mary Pickford's husband, at the unveiling of a plaque marking the site of her childhood home, now occupied by the Hospital for Sick Children, Toronto, May 27, 1973.

## Pickthall, Marjorie
Do the French lilies reign
Over Mont Royal and Stadacona still?

*

Whither I go I know not, nor the way,
Dark with strange passions, vexed with
    heathen charms,
Holding I know not what of life or
    death;
Only be Thou beside me day by day,
Thy rod my guide and comfort, under-
    neath
Thy everlasting arms.

> Lines from "Père Lalement," *The Select-ed Poems of Marjorie Pickthall* (1957), edited by Lorne Pierce.

To me the trying part is being a woman at all. I've come to the ultimate conclusion that I'm a misfit of the worst kind, in spite of a superficial femininity—emotion with a foreknowledge of impermanence, a daring mind with only the tongue as an outlet, a greed for experience plus a slavery to convention—what the deuce are you to make of that?—as a woman? As a man, you could go ahead and stir things up *fine*.

> Letter, December 27, 1919, quoted by Lorne Pierce in *Marjorie Pickthall: A Book of Remembrance* (1925).

## Pidgeon, Walter
My Metro years were the best. I'd like to have them all back again. Favourite

pictures? Any of the ones with Greer Garson.

> The MGM actor, called "that handsome piece of screen furniture" by James Agate, was born in East Saint John, New Brunswick, in 1897. Quoted by David Shipman in *The Great Movie Stars: The Golden Years* (1970).

### Pierce, Lorne
Landmarks soon become hitching posts.

＊

Never again can the whim of a foreign publisher numb us. Never again will a publisher tell us what we must or must not do, and when we must or must not do it. We have grown up.

> *The House of Ryerson: 1829-1954* (1954).

Nothing survives by right but only by reason. Besides, nothing is static that lives. A divine yeast works in all created things that live and breathe and need the light.

＊

Canada has had no Jonathan Edwards, Jefferson, Franklin, or Tom Paine, no recognized spokesmen accepted as symbols of enlightenment, government, common sense, or the dignity of the common man. Canadian soil has not been friendly to the cult of the Great Man, the Tycoon perhaps, but not the Prophet.

> *A Canadian Nation* (1960), by the long-time editor of The Ryerson Press.

No great literature or art is possible without a great people, a people ripened by experience, stirred by curiosity, and alive to wonder—a people with the daring capacity to expect the wonderful and then attempt to realize it.

＊

I once defined a publisher as: Somebody looking for someone who has something to say.

> *An Editor's Creed* (1960).

### Pierre le Canadien   See Peter Dmytruk.

### Pike, Warburton   See Saltatha.

### Pike, Zebulon
Pike's Peak or Bust!

Zebulon Pike, the American military explorer, claimed the territory of Minnesota for President Thomas Jefferson, and in 1806 discovered the famous peak that bears his name. Pike mistakenly believed the granite-yielding mountain near Cripple Creek, Colorado, was unscalable.

As a brigadier-general he led the invasion of York in an attempt to claim the town that would later become Toronto for President James Madison. But he was killed at Fort York, April 27, 1813, when hit by a boulder from an exploding magazine. The rallying cry "Pike's Peak or Bust" has nothing to do with the War of 1812, for it was first heard in 1858 when American prospectors discovered gold in the Rockies in the vicinity of Pike's Peak.

### Pilon, Jean-Guy
When the day comes that this cultural minority, hitherto only tolerated in this country, becomes a nation unto itself within its own borders, our literature will take a tremendous leap ahead. Because the writer, like everyone else in this society, will feel free. And a free man can do great things.

> *Le Quartier Latin*, February 27, 1962, quoted by Pierre Elliott Trudeau in "New Treason of the Intellectuals" (1962), *Federalism and the French Canadians* (1968), who comments: "It would seem, too, that Pilon is a good poet. I would like him to tell me—in prose, if he likes—how national sovereignty is going to make him 'a free man' and 'capable of doing great things.' If he fails to find within himself, in the world about him and in the stars above, the dignity, pride and other well-springs of poetry, I wonder why and how he will find them in a 'free' Quebec."

Before we can learn the words necessary to live, it is already time to learn to die.

> Last line of the prose poem "The Needs of the Land! . . . ," translated by Louis Dudek in his anthology *Poetry of Our Time: An Introduction to Twentieth-Century Poetry* (1965).

I grew too rich
I set my house afire, without even
looking at the blaze

> Lines from "The Burning," translated by G. V. Downes in *The Poetry of French Canada in Translation* (1970), edited by John Glassco.

Everything is still to be said.

> Title of a poem translated by Fred Cogswell in his *One Hundred Poems of Modern Quebec* (1970).

## Pinsent, Gordon
I think everyone needs to bend over a little and help things along . . . if the talent in this country can just go to bed with the money in this country, maybe it can all come together. Otherwise we're just going to be left on the sidelines with our dreams.

> Writer-star of *The Rowdy Man,* quoted in *The Globe and Mail,* July 7, 1973.

## Pitseolak
I have lost the time when I was born but I am old now—my sons say maybe I am seventy.

\*

I have heard there is someone—not a human being but a spirit—in the moon. When I heard that the two men had landed on the moon I wondered what the spirit thought of these two men landing on his land.

> *Pitseolak: Pictures Out of My Life* (1971), edited by Dorothy Eber.

## Pitt, William
Some are for keeping Canada, some Guadaloupe. Who will tell me what I shall be hanged for not keeping.

> William Pitt the Elder was prime minister of Great Britain when Quebec was taken in 1759. Quoted by Hilda Neatby in *Quebec: The Revolutionary Age 1760-1791* (1966). The rhetorical question was supposedly asked in the British House of Commons.

Join, my love, with me, in most humble and grateful thanks to the Almighty. The siege of Quebec was decided on May 17, with every happy circumstance. . . . Happy, happy day! My joy and hurry are inexpressable.

> Letter to his wife Hester, quoted by Oliver Warner in *With Wolfe to Quebec: The Path to Glory* (1972).

## Pitt, William
It will be experience which will teach them that English laws are the best. But it must be admitted that they ought to be governed to their satisfaction.

> William Pitt the Younger was prime minister of Great Britain from 1783 to 1801, and is said to have had this reaction to the passage of the Quebec Act in 1774. Quoted by Mason Wade in *The French Canadians: 1760-1967* (1968).

## Piuvkaq
A wonderful fate
Getting wishes fulfilled!
But all too often they
Slip apart.

> From an Eskimo poem "The Joy of a Singer" by Piuvkaq. Knud Rasmussen, *The Netsilik Eskimos: Social Life and Spiritual Culture: Report of the Fifth Thule Expedition, 1921-24* (1931).

## Plamondon, Huguette
You must realize one thing: organized labour is composed of human beings, and we're allowed to make mistakes like any other group in society. But one thing that you must remember: if we exist today, it's on account of the capitalists. They gave us birth; had they treated their workers on a decent basis, not exploited them, not abused them, we wouldn't be organized today. Their abuse of us has given birth to unions, and that's why I say that we're a "must" in this society.

> Field representative, United Packinghouse, Food, and Allied Workers. *The Face of Labour: Four Programs from CBC Television, January-February,* 1961.

## Plante, Jacques
My business is getting shot at. When I stop pucks, business is good. When I don't, business is bad.

*

Question: Do you find hockey is fun anymore?
Answer: Hockey is fun when you're winning.

> Controversial goaltender of the National Hockey League who, by the end of the 1970-71 season, had stopped 28,545 pucks. Quoted by Andy O'Brien in *The Jacques Plante Story* (1972).

### Plante, Pax
Against the Montreal underworld, even the King of England is powerless!

> Quoted by Alain Stanké in *Pax, lutte à finir avec la pègre* (1972), the biography of Quebec's leading crime-fighter.

### Plaskett, Joseph
Many of us might still be hankering to paint the Canadian Shield if the war had not helped to put us more closely in touch with the contemporary thought of Europe.

> Quoted by Robert Ayre in "Painting" in *The Arts in Canada: A Stock-Taking at Mid-Century* (1958), edited by Malcolm Ross.

### Plaut, W. Gunther
The mental highways are far more important than those built of asphalt and cement.

> "To Change the Patterns," *Probings: A Collection of Essays Contributed to the Canadian Mental Health Association for its Golden Jubilee 1918-1968* (1968).

### Pleshette, Suzanne
I'm not afraid of failure. I've had it.

> Canadian-born Hollywood actress, quoted by Jack Hirschenberg in *The Toronto Star*, March 24, 1963.

### Plessis, Monseigneur Joseph-Octave
Jesus Christ, in giving you a religion designed to lead you to heaven, has not asked you to control and supervise the sovereigns under whom you live.

> Remark made in 1810 by the bishop of Quebec, quoted by Pierre Elliott Trudeau in "Some Obstacles to Democracy"

(1958), *Federalism and the French Canadians* (1968).

### Plummer, Christopher
An actor is never established.

> Toronto-born, Montreal-raised stage actor, quoted by Carol Kennedy in *The Montreal Star*, May 20, 1967. "Christopher Plummer is like aluminum: light but metallic." (David Shipman)

### Plunkett, Al
Make 'em cry one minute and laugh the next and you've got 'em.

*

Some of the men we entertained at five o'clock were dead at seven-thirty.

> Al Plunkett was the star and the brother of Merton W. Plunkett who formed "The Dumbells Review" in 1917 to entertain overseas troops. The group played across Europe, Britain, the United States and Canada until disbanding in 1929. Quoted by Max Braithwaite in "The Rise and Fall of the Dumbells," *Maclean's Magazine*, January 1, 1952.

### Polanyi, Karl
The discovery of society is, indeed, the anchor of freedom.

> *The Great Transformation* (1944). The distinguished political economist spent the last years of his life in Canada.

### Pollock, Harry J.
The paths of glory lead to the U.S.A.

> Remark made by the founder of the James Joyce Society of Canada, 1970.

### Polo, Marco
It is also on islands in that sea (north of Bargu at Lake Baikal) that the Gerfalcons are bred. You must know that the place is so far to the north that you leave the North Star somewhat behind you towards the south! The Gerfalcons are so abundant there that the Emperor of China can have as many as he likes to send for. And you must not suppose that those Gerfalcons which the Christians carry into the Tartar dominions go to the Great Khan; they are carried only to the Prince of the Levant.

"Only the Canadian archipelago can be meant, and this identification is greatly strengthened if Bargu is rightly believed to lie south of Lake Baikal, for the meridian through the lake would strike Ellesmere Island in the Canadian Arctic," according to Tryggvi J. Oleson in *Early Voyages and Northern Approaches 1000-1632* (1963). The Venetian traveller dictated his memoirs in 1298; the quotation comes from *The Book of Marco Polo* (1903), edited by Sir Henry Yule. See also Martin Behaim.

**Pompadour, Madame de**
Now that Montcalm is dead, the King will have some peace!

*

It makes little difference; Canada is useful only to provide me with furs.

*

Now the King can sleep.

*

We can be happy without Canada.

Said to be the sentiments of Jeanne Antoinette Poisson, Marquise de Pompadour, mistress of Louis XV, on learning of the fall of Quebec in 1759. See also Dénis Diderot and Louis XV.

**Ponte, Lorenzo da**
See Wolfgang Amadeus Mozart.

**Pontiac**
Father, when our great father of France was in this country, I held him fast by the hand. Now that he is gone, I take you, my English father, by the hand, in the name of all nations, and promise to keep this covenant as long as I shall live.

At a meeting of Indians at Oswego, July 23, 1766. Quoted by Francis Parkman in *The Conspiracy of Pontiac and the Indian War after the Conquest of Canada* (1870).

**Pooley, Sophia**
I guess I was the first coloured girl brought into Canada. The white men sold us at Niagara to old Indian Brant, the king. I lived with old Brant about twelve or thirteen years as nigh as I can tell.

Sophia Pooley, born in New York State but spirited across the border before the American Revolution, was sold to the Mohawk chief, Joseph Brant. When Benjamin Drew interviewed her for *The Refugee: or the Narratives of Fugitive Slaves in Canada* (1856), she was in her nineties and living in the "Queen's Bush" (Peel and Wellesley Townships).

**Pootagok**
Joyfully I See Ten Caribou.

Lovely title of an Eskimo print, a self-portrait of the artist. Reproduced by Ken Lefolii in *The Canadian Look: A Century of Sights and Styles* (1965).

**Pope, Alexander**
But where the extreme of vice, was ne'er agreed:
Ask where's the North? At York, 'tis on the Tweed;
In Scotland, at the Orcades; and there,
At Greenland, Zembla, or the Lord knows where.

Epistle II, *An Essay on Man* (1733). *The Poetical Works of Alexander Pope* (1860), edited by H.F. Cary. The mythical kingdom of Zembla was sometimes located in the Canadian Arctic.

**Pope, Joseph**
We have all the liberty that is good for us, and some people think a good deal more.

Last letter to his son, September 16, 1925. *Public Servant: The Memoirs of Sir Joseph Pope* (1960), edited by Maurice Pope.

**Porter, John**
The Vertical Mosaic.

"One of the most persistent images that Canadians have of their society is that it has no classes," wrote John Porter in his major opus *The Vertical Mosaic: An Analysis of Social Class and Power in Canada* (1965). The social scientist from Carleton University examined the mosaic structure of Canadian society from two angles: horizontally, to study ethnicity; vertically, to study class. He came to the conclusion that Canadians are more class-ridden than Americans but less aware of it. Canadians see their society as a national mosaic; Americans have traditionally pictured theirs as a melting-pot.

"Here individuals of all nations are melted in a new race of men. The American is a new man who acts upon new principles," observed Jean de Crèvecoeur in *Letters from an American Farmer* (1782). The American is a member of "a new race of men," the Canadian a citizen of a new "northern nationality," to use Alexander Morris's expression which dates from 1858. See Alexander Morris for his use of this phrase. See also Thomas D'Arcy McGee and Lord Monck for their uses of the phrase in the 1860s.

The image of the American melting-pot was supplied by Israel Zangwill who, in 1908, wrote: "America is God's Crucible, the great old merging into the Melting-Pot where all the races of Europe are melting and reforming!" An early, if not the earliest, use of the word "mosaic" in its Canadian sociological context appears in *Romantic Canada* (1922); see Victoria Hayward. Four years later a study of the foreign-born was published, *Our Canadian Mosaic* (1926); see Kate A. Foster. "A mosaic of cultures, with a Canadian pattern, or the melting pot?" is the title of an editorial in *The Canadian Nation*, December, 1928. See also John Murray Gibbon, who received the Governor General's Award for *Canadian Mosaic: The Making of a Northern Nation* (1938).

The word "mosaic" has a metaphoric interest all its own. *The Shorter Oxford English Dictionary* (Third Edition, 1963) defines it in artistic terms as "the process of producing pictures or patterns by cementing together small pieces of stone, glass, etc., of various colours." The term "mosaic vision" is defined as "the manner of vision of the compound eye of an anthropod" or insect. *The Random House Dictionary* (1967) defines "mosaic disease" as any of several diseases of plants, characterized by mottled green or green and yellow areas on the leaves." *Van Nostrand's Scientific Encyclopedia* (Fourth Edition, 1968) has the following entry for "Mosaic Structure": "A sub-

structure inside a crystal in which small regions of the crystals, separated by subboundaries, have slightly different orientations." The word "mosaic" is not related to the Biblical "Mosaic" for it derives from the Greek for "muse." A mosaic is, literally, "a work pertaining to the Muses"—an inspired way to look at Canada!

Ideology did not end in Canada. It simply did not begin.

"Canadian Character in the Twentieth Century" (1967), *Canada: A Sociological Profile* (1971), edited by W.E. Mann.

### Porter, McKenzie
A republic can swallow a top hat but not a crown.

*The Toronto Telegram*, May 3, 1971.

### Potts, Jerry
Macleod: What do you think we'll find on the other side of this hill, Jerry?
Potts: Nudder hill.

\*

Macleod: What is he saying, Potts?
Potts: He wants grub! [Or: Dey damn glad you're here; after a long Indian harangue]

\*

Macleod: What's the matter, Jerry, are you lost?
Potts: No. Stones lost.

Exchanges between the halfbreed scout and interpreter for the North-West Mounted Police and assistant commissioner James Macleod, near Fort Whoop-Up, Fall, 1874. Stories about Potts are told by T. Morris Longstreth in *The Silent Force: Scenes from the Life of the Mounted Police of Canada* (1927) and by Hugh A. Dempsey in *Jerry Potts, Plainsman* (1966).

### Pound, Ezra
I trust the Alberta Elections have renewed your faith in humanity. [Letter of September 1, 1935, to John Buchan, before his Canadian appointment; a reference to the Social Credit victory]

\*

Thank God for one Brit. peer who didn't BUY it or get it by DIRT. [Buchan was appointed governor general on November 2, 1935, and the poet congratulated him a few months later]

Quoted by Janet Adam Smith in *John Buchan: A Biography* (1965).

## Poundmaker

Eagle Hills, May 19th, 1885. Sir.—I am camped with my people at the east-end of the Eagle Hills, where I am met by the news of the surrender of Riel. No letter came with the news, so that I cannot tell how far it may be true. I send some of my men to you to learn the truth and the terms of peace, and hope you will deal kindly with them. I and my people wish you to send us the terms of peace in writing, so that we may be under no misunderstanding, from which so much trouble arises. We have twenty-one prisoners, whom we have tried to treat well in every respect. With greetings,

His
(Signed) POUNDMAKER    X
Mark.

Poundmaker's letter to Sir Fred Middleton at Duck Lake. Reproduced by Middleton in *Suppression of the Rebellion in the North West Territories of Canada: 1885* (1948), edited by G.H. Needler. For the reply, see Sir Fred Middleton.

The law is a hard, queer thing. I do not understand it.

*

I am not guilty. What I did was for the Great Mother. When my people and the whites met in battle, I saved the Queen's men. I took the firearms from my following and gave them up at Battleford. Had I wanted war, I would not be here but on the prairie. You did not catch me. I gave myself up. You have me because I wanted peace.

Speech in his own defence at his trial for "levying war against Her Majesty," 1885, for which he was sentenced to three years in Stony Mountain Penitentiary, Alberta.

Hang me now. I would rather die than be locked up.

Poundmaker's reply to the judge when he heard his sentence. *Daily Intelligencer* (Belleville), August 19, 1885. Reprinted in *The Riel Rebellion 1885* (1972), compiled by Nick and Helma Mika. The great Cree chief died in 1886, shortly after his release from penitentiary.

## Power, Charles G.

A politician is anyone who manages to get elected: more to the point, he is someone who is elected again.

*

The political game is a great one to play. It is exciting even to watch; it brings with it disappointments and frustrations, but there are compensations in the acquaintances it brings, in the friendships formed, and in the knowledge acquired of humanity, sometimes at its worst, more often at its best.

*A Party Politician: The Memoirs of Chubby Power* (1966), edited by Norman Ward.

## Powys, Llewelyn

There he sat in the tiny boat, dressed "in a motley gown," the possessed sea-captain who had sailed to the North, and sailed to the East, and sailed to the West in his endeavour to find a passage through the ice-bound ramparts of the planet itself. There he sat, this dreamer, in his coat of many colours, until to the eyes of the mutineers, who watched the shallop grow smaller and smaller in the wake of their stolen vessel, he became a mote, a speck, a nothing, lost to sight on the unresting waves of the wharfless wilderness that had been by him, so resolutely, so desperately discovered.

*Henry Hudson* (1928). The English navigator was cast adrift in James Bay in 1611. See also Henry Hudson.

## Pratley, Gerald

What we need is not an "industry" but a firm financial foundation on which, hopefully, dozens of independent artists in film can find the means to regular employment, to travel the entire country if they wish, or work in the cities of their choice. There is hardly a film maker today who requires studios to work in; all he needs are laboratories for editing, recording and processing. These we have in abundance. If only film makers could raise the money to make films as easily as some people seem to find it to go into processing!

*Impact,* February, 1972.

### Pratt, E.J.

It took the sea a thousand years,
A thousand years to trace
The granite features of this cliff,
In crag and scarp and base.

It took the sea an hour one night,
An hour of storm to place
The sculpture of these granite seams
Upon a woman's face.
["Erosion" (1932)]

*

There is no silence upon the earth or
    under the earth like the silence under
    the sea;
No cries announcing birth,
No sounds declaring death.
[Opening lines of "Silences" (1937)]

*

                Where was the source
Of his strength . . . not in these the
    source—
But in the sound of invisible trumpets
    blowing
Around two slabs of board, right-angled,
    hammered
By Roman nails and hung on a Jewish
    hill.

From "Brébeuf and His Brethren" (1940), *The Collected Poems of E.J. Pratt* (Second Edition, 1958), edited by Northrop Frye.

Lord grant us capacity,
Longevity, elasticity,
Avoiding obesity.

A humorous grace, quoted by Earle Birney in "E.J. Pratt and His Critics," *Our Living Tradition: Second and Third Series* (1959), edited by Robert L. McDougall. See also F.R. Scott.

### Préfontaine, Yves

I live in a land where cold has conquered green things, reigns grey and heavy over phantom trees.

Lines from the prose poem "Country to Let" translated by G.V. Downes in *The Poetry of French Canada in Translation* (1970), edited by John Glassco.

### Preston, Sergeant

See George W. Trendle

### Preston-Muddock, J.E.

Flin Flon.

This Manitoba town may well be the only one in the world named after the hero of a dime novel. In 1913, near the site of Flin Flon, a prospector found a dog-eared copy of J.E. Preston-Muddock's *The Sunless City* (1905). The hero of the dime novel is Professor Josiah Flintabbatey Flontin, nicknamed Flin Flon. He finds a "sunless city" rich in gold and ruled by women located at the centre of the earth. The settlement in the area was named after him. John Fisher agitated for a suitable memorial to the fictitious inventor, and in 1962 a twenty-four-foot fiberglass figure, designed by the cartoonist Al Capp, was erected at Flin Flon.

### Priestley, J.B.

What an entrance these three could make!

The striking appearance of the theatrical trio—Murray Davis, Donald Davis, and their sister Barbara Chilcott—inspired J.B. Priestley to write an original play. *The Glass Cage* received its world premier at the Davis's Crest Theatre in Toronto, March 5, 1957. It did less well on the West End.

It has a rather sad tone, as if someone once dear and now lost and forgotten is still being endlessly regretted. Many of the men hardly move their lips, conversing in a melancholy mumble. Even the gay and pretty girls, for all their sparkling glances, sound as if they were inwardly fixed in some sad enchantment. You look up in the aeroplane to see the handsome stewardess smiling at you, like a favourite niece; and then she murmurs, "Would you care for some carfee?"

The British playwright discussing Canadian speech patterns, 1953. Quoted by Joseph Barber in *Good Fences Make*

Good Neighbours: Why the United States Provokes Canadians (1958).

The best of Leacock lies somewhere between—though at a slight angle from—the amiable nonsense of characteristic English humour (e.g., Wodehouse) and the hard-hitting wit and almost vindictive satire of much American humour.

*

The Canadian is often a baffled man because he feels different from his British kindred and his American neighbours, sharply refuses to be lumped together with either of them, yet cannot make plain his difference.

Introduction to The Bodley Head Leacock (1957), edited by J.B. Priestley.

## Pringle, Gertrude
### Things That Are Not Done
Among the unspeakable things that put a man completely beyond the social pale are the following:

Having the razor used on his head and neck, giving a convict-like appearance, instead of having the hair cut with the scissors and tapered gradually off.

Using a tooth-pick at table or anywhere in public.

Manicuring his nails in public.

Being photographed in evening clothes.

Wearing a white tie with a dinner jacket.

Stretching himself full length on a sofa when making an evening call.

Borrowing money from a woman.

Etiquette in Canada: The Blue Book of Canadian Social Usage (1932).

## Pritchard, William
A statesman is a man who honestly desires to do something for his country, and a politician is a man who wants, in any way at all, his country to do something for him.

Address to the jury, March 23-24, 1920. Winnipeg 1919: The Strikers' Own History of the Winnipeg General Strike (1973), edited by Norman Penner.

## Pritchett, V.S.
All across Canada we were struck by the smallness of the flowers.

*

They [the Rockies] are less friendly than the Andes—they are grayer; they lack the urbanity and—I may as well say it—the intelligence of the Alpes. This is absurd anthropomorphism, I know, but I am thinking of the poverty of human association in the scene. . . .

*

Montreal has something of American luxury, the sagacity of London, the briskness of New York, the gaiety of Europe.

*

[Canada gives one] an impression of restraint rather than exuberance; of tidiness. . . .

*

The real nightmare of the Canadian is not fear of economic swamping by the rich neighbour with whom he has so much in common, but the old fear of disintegration.

*

The Canadian spirit is cautious, observant and critical where the American is assertive; the foreign policies of the two nations are never likely to fit very conveniently, and this, again, is just as well, for the peace of the world depends on a respect for differences.

"Across the Vast Land," Holiday, April, 1964.

An investor arrived who belonged to a sect called the Church of the Last Purification, of Toronto, Canada.

*

And here in Mr. [Hubert] Timberlake was a man who had not merely performed many miracles—even, it was said with proper reserve, having twice raised the dead—but had actually been to Toronto, our headquarters, where this great and revolutionary revelation had first been given.

"The Saint," The Sailor, Sense of Humour, and Other Stories (1956).

## Prowse, D.W.
Dear, delightful day of Arcadian simplicity! when we had no debt and port wine was a shilling a bottle.

*

The history of St. Pierre and Miquelon

is a small fragment of the history of France, a Liliputian reproduction of that ancient and tragic story. The little island has had, like the mother country, its Revolution, its Reign of Terror, its Tree of Liberty, its Jacobin Club, and under the Empire a miniature *coup d'état*; all, however, was on a very small scale, a veritable tempest in a teapot.

> *A History of Newfoundland from English, Colonial, and Foreign Records* (1895).

### Pruszynski, Stash
AFTER THE RIOT, EAT AT JOE'S.

> Sign carried during a McGill riot by the Polish-born journalist. Quoted by Don Bell in *Saturday Night at the Bagel Factory and Other Montreal Stories* (1972).

### Pryce-Jones, Alan
I appear respectable again, riding the waves of sloth towards some climax as dramatic as the twenty-foot tidal drop at Saint John, in the Bay of Fundy. For forty-five minutes, in that New Brunswick harbour, between the ebb and flow of the tide, a ship can traverse the gorge between river and harbour. Forty-five minutes and no more. Just about the time taken by a bout of activity between spells of *accidie*.

> "Viewpoint," *Times Literary Supplement*, October 27, 1972. The British critic wrote, in a review of Edmund Wilson's *O Canada:* ". . . Toronto, a city of penetrating gloom in which Scottish dourness is pierced, from time to time, by unexpected flashes of gaiety."

### Pryde, Duncan
Where are the Eskimo managers of Hudson's Bay posts? Where are the Eskimo police, the radio operators, the nurses? I'll tell you where they are. They are down at the welfare office drawing relief.

> *Time*, May 2, 1969.

### Purcell, Gillis
There was a young lady from Munich
Whose bosom distended her tunic.
   Her main undertaking
   Was cabinet making
In fashions *bilingue et unique*.

> This limerick, which celebrates the achievements of Gerda Munsinger, won first prize in a limerick contest sponsored by *Maclean's Magazine* in 1967.

The standard description of The Canadian Press is "the co-operative news association of the daily newspapers of Canada." It is familiarly called CP, although it shares this label with, among others, a country-wide railway and a meat-packing firm. But I heard the most memorable definition of the outfit thirty years ago from the lips of J.R. Burnett, then editor and publisher of *The Charlottetown Guardian*. It was at an annual meeting of CP members and Mr. Burnett was furious about something. He said: "That's the trouble with The Canadian Press. It's one of those faceless corporations with no soul to save and no ass to kick."

> Excerpt from an address by the general manager at CP's Fiftieth Anniversary Dinner, Toronto, April, 1967. See also Victor Sifton.

### Purchas, Samuel
Merchants might get the World, and give us the World better, if Charitie were their Needle; Grace, their Compas; Heaven their Haven, and if they would take their height by observing the Sunne of Righteousness in the Scripture-astrolabe, and sounding their depth by a Leading Faith, and not by a Leadden bottomlesse Covetousness: that is, if they would seeke the Kingdome of Heaven first, all things should bee added; they should finde Worlde enough in the Indian, and Polare Worlds, and wee and they should arrive at better knowledge of the Creator and Creatures.

\*

We have now compassed the World in the Courses of so many Planets, every of which had a peculiar wandering, and yet none erring from the publike benefit of the Universe.

> *Hakluytus Posthumus, or Purchas His Pilgrimes: Contayning a History of the World in Sea Voyages and Lande Travells by Englishmen and Others* (1625); reproduced from the edition of 1905.

**Purdy, Alfred**
And this is a country where the young
leave quickly
unwilling to know what their fathers
know
or think the words their mothers do not
say—

"The Country North of Belleville,"
*Selected Poems* (1972).

I write poems like spiders spin webs, and
perhaps for much the same reason: to
support my existence.

Interviewed by Gary Geddes in *Canadian
Literature*, Summer, 1969.

**Pytheas**
"Pytheas . . . describes Thule and other
neighbouring places, where, according to
him, neither earth, water, nor air exist,
separately, but a sort of concretion of
all these, resembling marine sponge, in
which the earth, the sea, and all things
were suspended, thus forming, as it
were, a link to unite the whole together.
It can neither be travelled over nor
sailed through. As for the substance, he
affirms that he has beheld it with his own
eyes; the rest, he reports on the authority of others."

The Greek geographer and historian
Strabo, who wrote *The Geography* about
A.D. 20, gave this account of the Arctic
regions as reported by the Greek geographer Pytheas of Marseilles who lived
about 300 B.C. The original account has
not survived. *The Geography* (1854),
translated by H. Hamilton and W. Fal-
coner.

# Q

**Qaqortingneq**
This is all that our forefathers have told
us . . . I myself know nothing for my
own part, I only repeat what I have
heard.

The conclusion of a story by Qaqortingneq. Knud Rasmussen's *The Netsilik
Eskimos: Social Life and Spiritual Culture: Report of the Fifth Thule Expedition, 1921-24* (1931).

**Quaife, Richard T.**
I mean, there comes a time when a man
has to stand up and make a decision.

Quaife made his decision in the middle
of a rush-hour traffic jam when he pulled
the bus he was driving over to the curb,
announced to his forty-odd passengers he
was quitting, and telephoned his resignation to the Calgary Transit System. The
forty-one-year-old father of four children
and three foster children later explained
that he had had enough and thought it
was time for a change. Quoted by Chris
Dennett in *The Toronto Star*, July 20,
1973.

**Queen Elizabeth**    See Elizabeth II.

**Queen Mother, The**
See Elizabeth the Queen Mother.

**Quen, Jean de**
As the weeks are composed of both days
and nights; the Seasons of heat and cold,
of rain and shine; so also we may say our
year has been but a mingling of joys and
sorrows, of successes and failures.

Relation of 1655-56, *The Jesuit Relations
and Allied Documents* (1954), edited by
Edna Kenton.

## Quesnel, Joseph
Parcours tout l'univers, de l'Inde en
  Laponie,
Tu verras que partout ou fête la génie,
Hormis en ce pays; car l'ingrat Canadien
Aux talents de l'esprit, n'accorde jamais
  rien.

> "Epitre à M. Généraux Labadie" (1804),
> *Le répertoire national* (1848), by the
> playwright and opera composer who
> settled in Montreal. The stanza trans-
> lates: "Travel the universe, from India
> to Lapland, / And everywhere you will
> find the celebration of genius; / Except
> in this country: for the Canadian ingrate
> / Never sets any store by the talents of
> the spirit."

## Quilico, Louis
Dear God, you gave me a voice, I didn't
ask for it. So help me.

> Quilico's mock prayer, quoted by Blaik
> Kirby, *The Globe and Mail*, February
> 12, 1972.

The way I look at it, it's a feather in my
hat—but not the feather-holder. I've had
the hat before.

> The Canadian baritone made his début
> at the Metropolitan Opera in New York
> rather late in his career, replacing a
> principal in *Pelléas and Mélisande* on
> two days' notice. Quoted by Stan Fischer
> in *The Toronto Star*, February 11, 1972.

## Quinn, Eddie
The only thing on the level is mountain-
climbing.

> Remark associated with the Montreal
> wrestling promoter during the 1920s and
> 1930s, quoted by Tim Burke in *The
> Montreal Gazette*, March 17, 1973.

## Quinn, T. Emmett
To increase scoring, the puck should be
painted green and reduced to half size,
thus making it more difficult for the goalkeeper to see and stop it. Players should
be compelled to carry rolls of bills in
hip pockets, so that major fines could be
paid on the spot. Instead of giving a
minor penalty, the referee should stop
play, take the offender aside, talk to him
and try to reform him.

> Tongue-in-cheek suggestions to improve
> the game of hockey made by the presi-
> dent of the National Hockey Association
> in 1914. Quoted by Henry Roxborough
> in *The Stanley Cup Story* (1964).

## Qúpaq
Luck nearly always follows after misfortune. If this were not so, people would
soon die out.

> Eskimo saying related by Qúpaq. Knud
> Rasmussen's *The Netsilik Eskimos: So-
> cial Life and Spiritual Culture: Report
> of the Fifth Thule Expedition, 1921-24*
> (1931).

# R

## Rabelais, François
But on the fourth day they reached an
island called Medamothy, with a fine
and delightful prospect, by reason of the
vast number of lighthouses and high
marble towers in its circuit, which is not
less grand than Canada. Pantagruel en-
quiring who governed there, heard that
it was . . . .

  *

Antiphanes said that Plato's philosophy
was like words which being spoken in
some country during a hard winter are
immediately congealed, frozen and not

heard; for what Plato taught young lads could hardly be understood by them when they were grown old. Now, he continued, we should philosophize and search whether this be not the place where those words are thawed. . . .

> Both excerpts come from Book IV of *Gargantua and Pantagruel* which was published in 1552, one year before the death of the great French stylist and humourist. The explicit reference to this country, "no less large than Canada" (*n'estoit moins grand que de Canada*), occurs in chapter two. A long passage about the "frozen words" may be found in chapter fifty-six, and as Rabelais based Books III and IV on the narratives of Jacques Cartier, the country of the "frozen words" appears to be New France. (Marius Barbeau went so far as to maintain that Rabelais was the author of Cartier's *Voyages*.) It was a gracious gesture of Rabelais to bequeath to us such an imaginative metaphor: an island in the St. Lawrence where "frozen words" might be thawed, and heard, if not understood.

### Raby, Peter

Romantic dreams become nightmares because, for the most part, they are the dreams of men who have seen reality face to face. People who dismiss Shelley as a pale dreamer forget "I met Murder on the way. He had a mask like Castlereagh." Schumann called Chopin "A cannon under roses," and Baudelaire said of Delacroix "A volcanic crater hidden by bunches of flowers." In Dumas too there is a hard core.

> "The Three Musketeers," *The Stratford Scene 1958-1968* (1968), edited by the dramaturge Peter Raby.

### Radclive, John Robert

My family deserted me and changed their names, but I kept right on with the job, because I argued with myself that if I was doing wrong, then the government of the country was wrong. I held that I was the Minister of Justice at a hanging and that if I was a murderer then he was also a murderer. . . .

I used to say to condemned persons as I beckoned with my hand, "Come with me." Now at night when I lie down, I start up with a roar as victim after victim comes up before me. I can see them on the trap, waiting a second before they face their Maker. They taunt me and haunt me until I am nearly crazy with an unearthly fear. I am two hundred times a murderer, but I won't kill another man.

> Canada's leading public executioner speaking in 1912; quoted by Frank W. Anderson in *A Concise History of Capital Punishment in Canada* (1973).

### Raddall, Thomas H.

Our sons would never give themselves wholly to anything but this rocky homeland on the sea's edge, where life is a struggle that demands a man's utmost and will take no less, where beauty alone is bountiful and only death comes easily; where courage springs from the eternal rock like the clear singing river, like the deep-rooted forest itself.

> *His Majesty's Yankees* (1942).

When they founded the town in 1749 His Majesty's Board of Trade and Plantations decided to name it in honour of their president George Junk. He happened to be Earl of Halifax and they chose the title rather than the family name. Haligonians are truly grateful.

> "The Canadian Age," *Century 1867-1967*.

### Radisson, Pierre-Esprit

We were Caesars, being nobody to contradict us.

> The French explorer, who wrote his memoirs in imperfect English, spelled the name "Cesar." "Lake Superior Voyage" (1661), *The Explorations of Pierre Esprit Radisson* (1961), edited by Arthur T. Adams. Grace Lee Nute called her study *Caesars of the Wilderness* (1943). See also Sieur des Groseilliers.

They tied me to a post, where I stayed a full hour without the least molestation. A woman came there with her boy, enticed him to cut off one of my fingers with a flint stone. The boy was not four years old. This child takes my finger and begins to work, but in vain because he had not the strength to break my fingers; so my poor finger escaped, having no other hurt done to it but the flesh cut around it. His mother made him suck the very blood that runned from my finger. I had no other torment all that day. At night I could not sleep because of the great pain.

> The adventurer was tortured by Indians in 1684. *The Explorations of Pierre Esprit Radisson* (1961), edited by Arthur T. Adams.

## Ragueneau, Paul
We ourselves set fire to it, and beheld it burn before our eyes, in less than one hour, our work of nine or ten years. . . .

> Father Superior at Sainte-Marie among the Hurons, when the missionary fort was burnt in 1649 prior to the Iroquois attack. "Relations" (1649), *The Jesuit Relations and Allied Documents* (1954), edited by Edna Kenton.

## Raine, Norman Reilly
"I'm fired? Who says I'm fired?" Tugboat Annie Brennan leaned across the desk of the president of the Deep-Sea Towing and Salvage Company, and thrust her formidable jowls into his red, embarrassed face. She repeated, with husky emphasis: "Who says so?"

> "Tugboat Annie," *The Saturday Evening Post*, July 11, 1931. This is the opening paragraph of the first in the popular series of stories published in *Satevepost* during the thirties and forties. In 1933, Mervyn Le Roy directed Cobourg-born Marie Dressler and Wallace Beery in the even more popular film *Tugboat Annie*. Norman Reilly Raine, born in Pennsylvania and educated in England, fought with the Canadian Expeditionary Force during World War One and in 1926 was assistant editor of *Maclean's Magazine*. He received an Academy Award for the best screenplay of 1937 with *The Life of Emile Zola*. The "Tugboat Annie" stories were never collected. According to *Who's Who in America: Third Edition 1972-1973* (1973), Raine,

born in 1895, is "now engaged in scenario and short story writing."

## Ralston, J.L.
In the stand I have taken I have considered that my first thought should be my duty to our fighting men in the overseas army.

> Key sentence in the letter of resignation written by the minister of National Defence to Prime Minister Mackenzie King, November 2, 1944, over the conscription crisis. King's reply was masterful: "In your letter you also say 'In the stand I have taken I have considered that my first thought should be my duty to our fighting men in the overseas army.' I need scarcely say that I have always had the same thought and conception of duty towards all our fighting men."

## Rampa, T. Lobsang
We came to Canada because we thought that this country would offer us peace. We have not been mistaken. It has been satisfactory.

\*

The best thing would be for the people to give up the French language (except as a cultural courtesy) . . . that they also give up English (except as a cultural courtesy), they could then practise telepathy.

> Quoted by Alain Stanké in *Rampa, imposteur ou initié?* (1973). Rampa is the author of numerous books about "the third eye" and for the last twenty years has lived in various cities across Canada.

## Randall, Robert
In memory of Robert Randall, Esq., M.P.P., the victim of Colonial Misrule, who died May 21st, 1831, aged 68 years.

> Inscription on the tombstone of the reformer who tried in vain to redress the many personal injustices done him, Drummond Hill Cemetery, Niagara Falls.

## Randell, Captain John
I'll see you in hell first.

> Captain John Randell's reply to the U.S. Coast Guard's order to surrender the

*I'm Alone,* a ninety-ton schooner registered at Lunenberg, running 2,800 cases of rum, brandy and whisky to a Louisiana port, before the *I'm Alone* was sunk on March 20, 1929, outside territorial waters in the Gulf of Mexico. The loss of the ship and one sailor created an international incident. It took two judges six years to decide in Canada's favour. Quoted by Harry Bruce in "The *I'm Alone* Incident," *Historic Headlines* (1967), edited by Pierre Berton.

## Randolph, John

Ever since the report of the committee on foreign relations came into the House, we have heard but one word—like the whip-poor-will, but one eternal monotonous tone — Canada! Canada! Canada!

\*

The people of Canada are first to be seduced from their allegiance, and converted into traitors, as a preparation for making them good American citizens.

\*

A war not of defence, but of conquest, of aggrandizement, of ambition—a war foreign to the interests of this country; to the interests of humanity itself.

> Addresses in the U.S. House of Representatives prior to and during the War of 1812 by John Randolph, Republican leader from Virginia. The last comes from his speech in the House on December 10, 1811.

## Rasky, Frank

The legend arose that a green correspondent [covering the Winnipeg flood in May 1950] cabled his London editor: GOD LOOKED DOWN FROM THE PEMBINA HILLS NEAR WINNIPEG TODAY ON AN AWESOME SCENE OF DESTRUCTION. . . . The editor wired back: FORGET FLOOD. INTERVIEW GOD.

> *Great Canadian Disasters* (1961). Rasky's chestnut pre-dates the Winnipeg flood and may have originated with press coverage of the Johnstown, Pennsylvania, flood disaster of 1869.

## Rasmussen, Knud

Without doubt the Caribou Eskimos are among the most hardy races in the world. Their land offers them severe living conditions, and yet they think it is the best in the world. To us the great contrasts in the various seasons were the most striking features in their life; for they either live in a state of dire need or in an abundance so wonderful that it makes them forget all their troubles.

> *Intellectual Culture of the Caribou Eskimos: Igulik and Caribou Eskimo Texts: Report of the Fifth Thule Expedition, 1921-24* (1930).

There is scarcely any country on earth that presents conditions more severe and inclement for man than the most easterly parts of the Northwest Passage, for it lies waste and bare of all that is otherwise considered necessary for life; and yet there the Netsilingmiut for generations have known how to wage the struggle for existence, in such a manner that strangers coming among them will involuntarily receive the impression that it is a people who desire no better hunting ground than these, the very ones where their ancestors developed that special culture which they have faithfully handed down from father to son.

\*

Just after midnight, when the air was coolest and the snow had stiffened a little where there was no water underneath, we said goodbye to the village. All the men and women stood round our sledges and wished us luck on our journey. There the parting word is always:

"May you get to the place you are aiming for."

> *The Netsilik Eskimos: Social Life and Spiritual Culture: Report of the Fifth Thule Expedition, 1921-24* (1931).

The whole world is the tomb of brave men.

> From the funeral oration of the Danish anthropologist and Arctic explorer in 1923, over the remains of seamen who seventy-five years earlier had died at Starvation Cove. Quoted by Leslie H. Neatby in *In Quest of the North West Passage* (1958). (The Athenian statesman

Pericles said, "The whole earth is the tomb of illustrious men.")

**Raspe, Rudolf Erich**
See Baron München.

**Rawhide**   See Max Ferguson.

**Rayner, Gordon**
I prefer a reality as close to my dreams as possible; consequently what I have to do outside of my dreams is to make more of my time the way I would like it ideally. Part of the struggle is just the pain and pleasure of creating art.

> Quoted by William Withrow in *Contemporary Canadian Painting* (1972).

**Reade, John Collingwood**
There has never been a time of quietude and security throughout the world. Human society, like the earth on which it lives, is always trying to adjust itself to great stresses.

> "The Approaching Climax" (1945), *Empire Club of Canada: Addresses Delivered to the Members During the Year 1944-45* (1945).

**Reaney, James**
I think also that any sensible person would say that what you do with a tradition, after picking out the part of it that seems to go well with you, is follow it. That is, do it over again. I don't mean turning out facsimiles but related works: let me give a sardonic instance first. When *Brébeuf and His Brethren* first came out, a friend of mine said that the thing to do now was to write the same story from the Iroquois point of view.

*

If you just hole up in Canada and refuse to educate yourself you are going to be provincial. But if you flee the country, cut yourself off from your roots, you may end up not even being that. The solution seems to be that the Canadian poet has to stay in the country and at the same time act as if he weren't in it. It looks as if I'm saying that the Canadian poet has to be some sort of poltergeist. He probably has to be.

> "The Canadian Poet's Predicament,"

*University of Toronto Quarterly*, April, 1957.

. . . we poor idiot Canadians have to have some literary ancestors. Your great-grandmother may have been an extremely second-rate type but she is part of the potentially first-rate you and has to be taken into account.

*

I remember as a child feeling that the Promised Land of our Bible at home lay just on the other side of a hogsback hill to the south of our farm.

*

Evil is a basis for unity, not something to be fled from and rejected.

> "Isabella Valancy Crawford," *Our Living Tradition: Second and Third Series* (1959), edited by Robert L. McDougall.

The world of Canadian poetry is like some lonely farmhouse at the centre of a remarkably large and bleak farm. One enters the farmhouse to find the inhabitants all busy at making wonderfully strange carvings apparently unrelated to the prairie fields and Yonge streets that lie outside. I say "apparently" unrelated because the more we stay with the carvers the more we realize that the carvings *are* related, related in a very freeing way to the whole farm of ten fields and two wastelands.

> "The Third Eye" (1960), *A Choice of Critics: Selections from Canadian Literature* (1966), edited by George Woodcock.

And like dear bad poets
  Who wrote
  Early in Canada
And never were of note.

*

What did the Indians call you?
For you do not flow
With English accents.

> "To the Avon River above Stratford, Canada," *Twelve Letters to a Little Town* (1962).

We need art. Not Canadian art. But just art. When I think of the last twenty years here, the thing that happened that made the most difference to me—was the success of the Stratford Shakespeare Festival. If we can do Shakespeare that well, we must be more awake than we suspected. The more we do Shakespeare, the more imaginatively awake will we be. Literature, the Bible, and Shakespeare tell you more about the potentialities of Canada than Canada does itself.

*

You find Canadian history dull and if you were teaching it, what would you teach in the second term?

Better to be a nation without a history than to have too much of it as, say, Bulgaria has. We have just enough. I can remember once at a party somebody sneering at one of the Riel Rebellions: only seven people killed. What on earth would he be satisfied with? Tamburlaine's pyramid of human skulls?

> "Local Grains of Sand" (1964), *Canada: A Guide to the Peaceable Kingdom* (1970), edited by William Kilbourn.

What did I most enjoy about the whole venture? John Hirsch used to say that Act II [of the Stratford Festival's production of *Colours in the Dark*] was like a crystal which you could turn various ways, various lights, different lights, different meanings. That's the kind of art I'd like to create out of where I was born —something that's never finished.

> "Colours in the Dark," *The Stratford Scene 1958-1968* (1968), edited by Peter Raby.

Shall I tell you a story of the jealous Moor or of the old king and his three daughters? No. I shall tell you a story of myself when fifteen years ago I was sixteen.

> Prologue to the play *The Sun and the Moon*, quoted by Ross Woodman in *James Reaney* (1971).

### Rebchuck, Slaw
This agenda shouldn't take long, there's nothing contagious on it.

*

Just give me the headlights. [To a city clerk presenting a report]

*

If you scrape down to the bottom of the barrel, you'll find a rotten apple.

*

We're in total darkness but I see the light.

*

How come I never get any plums or apples or peaches or pears? [On the subject of aldermen going on junkets]

*

Let's get it in black and writing.

*

That's putting the horse before the cart . . . well, isn't that what you normally do, put the horse before the cart?

*

They're making a mountain out of a molehole.

*

I was caught down with my pants short.

*

You can't have a gain without a loss. [On a surplus city budget]

> "They're planned because I believe that more truth can be said in jest than in seriousness," explained Slaw Rebchuck, Winnipeg insurance agent and alderman since 1949, councillor since 1962. Whether Rebchuck's malapropisms are calculated or not, they are as honoured in the West as those of Allan Lamport (another insurance agent and former alderman) are in the East. Quoted by Don Atkinson in *The Winnipeg Tribune*, August 2, 1969.

### Red Jacket
Brother, the Great Spirit has made us all, but He has made a great difference between His white and His red children. He has given us different complexions and different customs. To you He has given the arts. To these He has not opened our eyes. We know these things to be true. Since He has made so great a difference between us in other things, why may not we conclude that He has given us a different religion according to our understanding? The Great Spirit does right. He knows what is best for His children; we are satisfied.

*

Brother, if you white men murdered the Son of the Great Spirit, we Indians had nothing to do with it, it is none of our affair. If he had come among us, we would not have killed him; we would have treated him well. You must make amends for that crime yourselves.

> Red Jacket delivered a sermon on tolerance to a missionary busy evangelizing in Mohawk country in 1815. The Iroquois war chief was a considerable orator. Quoted by Fraser Symington in *The Canadian Indian: The Illustrated History of the Great Tribes of Canada* (1969).

### Redekop, John H.
The recent (1969) tour of the giant U.S. *Manhattan* through Canadian Arctic waters is relevant at this point. The ship did not fly the Canadian flag in Canadian waters. Not a word appeared in the lengthy account in *Life* about the role of the Canadian ice-breaker, the *John A. Macdonald*, which on at least five occasions had to come to the rescue of the big tanker. By and large, American mass media simply ignored the fact that the *Manhattan* success would have been impossible without the constant aid of Canadian ice-breakers or the ten years of diligent and persistent research conducted by Canada, especially the national government. The story was told as being but another example of the success of American technology!

> "Some of My Best Friends are American," *The Star-Spangled Beaver* (1971), edited by John H. Redekop.

### Redesdale, Lord
"Adolf Hitler hit on the idea of a Swastika for the Nazi party's emblem after his girlfriend, Unity Freeman-Mitford—known as his Nordic Goddess—told him about it.

"Unity was the daughter of the eccentric British peer, Lord Redesdale, who lived in an old log cabin a mile and a half outside Swastika [a mining village near Kirkland Lake in Northern Ontario].

"Lord Redesdale had five other daughters—Diana, who married successively the Hon. Bryan Guinness and Sir Oswald Mosley; Nancy, who wrote novels; Jessica, who married the Communist nephew of Sir Winston Churchill; Pam-

ela, whom some called 'the nice one'; and Deborah who married a duke and became the Duchess of Devonshire."

> Adapted from the "Golden Anniversary (1919-1969) Souvenir Edition" of the *Northern Daily News,* Kirkland Lake, July 10, 1969.

Thus circumstantial evidence exists to suggest that the Nazi Party would not have adopted the swastika as its emblem had there not been a village by that name in northern Ontario. (During the Second World War there was pressure to change the name to Winston, but the villagers met en masse, September 13, 1940, and resisted. They noted that their use of the symbol went back to 1904, predating the Nazis' use and that the "twisted cross" was an honourable Hindu symbol. Roy Thomson, then a fledgling broadcaster in Timmins, said: "At Swastika we have played our part and contributed to the war effort in every way possible.")

### Reeve, Ted
Having played football for various teams until I grew homesick every time I passed a hospital; having bounded gracefully about lacrosse fields until I was decorated with the dandiest hemstitching; having coached football teams until practically immune to the bludgeonings of fate, I have finally become numb enough to produce a book.

> Foreword to *Sporting Extras* (1938) by Ted Reeve, otherwise known as "Old Bones" or "The Moaner." Edward H. Reeve, a great athlete and notable sports columnist, was honoured for both football and lacrosse in the Sports Hall of Fame.

The crowd's as happy as hell. He just lit a cigar.

> To a group of anxious lacrosse players, quoted by Robert Thomas Allen in *A Treasury of Canadian Humour* (1967).

When I joined the paper in 1923, they said it was steady work.

> Remark made by the sports columnist when *The Toronto Telegram* folded in 1971. Quoted by Jock Carroll in *The*

*Death of the Toronto Telegram and Other Newspaper Stories* (1971).

## Regnault, Christophe

This is what these savages told us of the taking of the Village of St. Ignace, and about Fathers Jean de Bréboeuf and Gabriel L'Allemant:

"The Iroquois came, to the number of twelve hundred men; took our village and seized Father Bréboeuf and his companion; and set fire to all the huts. They proceeded to vent their rage on those two Fathers, for they took them both and stripped them entirely naked, and fastened each to a post. They tied both of their hands together. They tore the nails from the fingers. They beat them with a shower of blows from cudgels, on the shoulders, the loins, the belly, the legs and the face—there being no part of their body which did not endure this torment." The savages told us further, that, although Father de Bréboeuf was overwhelmed under the weight of these blows, he did not cease continually to speak of God, and to encourage all the new Christians who were captives like himself to suffer well, that they might die well, in order to go in company with him to Paradise. While the good Father was thus encouraging these good people, a wretched Huron renegade,—who had remained a captive with the Iroquois, and whom Father de Bréboeuf had formerly instructed and baptized,—hearing him speak of Paradise and Holy Baptism, was irritated, and said to him, "Echon" that is Father de Bréboeuf's name in Huron, "thou sayest that Baptism and the sufferings of this life lead straight to Paradise; thou wilt go soon, for I am going to baptize thee, and to make thee suffer well, in order to go the sooner to thy Paradise." The barbarian, having said that, took a kettle full of boiling water, which he poured over his body three different times, in derision of Holy baptism. And, each time that he baptized him in this manner, the barbarian said to him with bitter sarcasm, "Go to Heaven, for thou art well baptized."

\*

Those butchers, seeing that the good Father began to grow weak, made him sit down on the ground; and one of them, taking a knife, cut off the skin covering his skull. Another one of those barbarians, seeing that the good Father would soon die, made an opening in the upper part of his chest, and tore out his heart, which he roasted and ate. Others came to drink his blood, still warm, which they drank with both hands,—saying that Father de Bréboeuf had been very courageous to endure so much pain as they had given him, and that, by drinking his blood, they would become courageous like him.

This is what we learned of the Martyrdom and blessed death of Father Jean de Bréboeuf, by several Christian savages worthy of belief, who had been constantly present from the time the good Father was taken until his death. These good Christians were prisoners to the Iroquois, who were taking them into their country to be put to death. But our good God granted them the favour of enabling them to escape by the way; and they came to us to recount all that I have set down in writing.

> "A Veritable Account of the Martyrdom and Blessed Death of Father Jean de Bréboeuf and of Father Gabriel l'Allement, in New France, in the Country of the Hurons, by the Iroquois, Enemies of the Faith," *The Jesuit Relations and Allied Documents* (1954), edited by Edna Kenton. Bréboeuf's death occurred on March 16, 1649. See also Jean de Brébeuf.

## Reguly, Robert
STAR MAN FINDS GERDA MUNSINGER

Munich—The girl Canada calls Olga Munsinger is alive and well.

Her real name is Gerda Munsinger. She is tall, blonde and shapely.

I found her in a chintzy flat in an affluent district of Munich, wearing a gold September birthstone ring that was the gift of a former Canadian cabinet minister. . . .

> *Star* reporter Robert Reguly made "the scoop of the sixties" when he found Mrs. Munsinger (the former Miss Garmisch-Partenkirchen, who was intimate with

at least one Canadian cabinet minister) alive and well and living in Munich. *The Toronto Star*, March 11, 1966. See also Gerda Munsinger.

**Reid, Kate**
Three-quarters of acting is listening.

Quoted by Herbert Whittaker in *The Globe and Mail*, November 25, 1967.

Acting is not being emotional, but being able to express emotions.

Quoted by Joanne Strong in *The Globe and Mail*, June 4, 1973.

**Reid, Malcolm**
The young people I am speaking of will not stop shouting until the walls come down.

*The Shouting Signpainters: A Literary and Political Account of Quebec Revolutionary Nationalism* (1972).

**Reid, R.G.**
What can one say, the will of the people has spoken.

Response of the premier of Alberta to the election results the evening of August 22, 1935, when the United Farmers of Alberta lost every seat in the legislature to William Aberhart's new Social Credit party. Quoted by John A. Irving in *The Social Credit Movement in Alberta* (1959).

**Reid, Weir**
Fortunately, there are still those among us who have a healthy irreverence toward power, even as they seek it.

Weir Reid led Sudbury's United Mines, Mill and Smelter Workers in its fight against control by American unions. Quoted by *Time*, May 3, 1971.

**Repo, Satu**
Although I have experienced war and refugee camps and even spent a short time in a mental hospital, it was at a School of Social Work that I finally lost my social innocence: the feeling that social institutions are rational and benevolent, working in the best interests of all citizens, and that, broadly speaking, the interests of all individuals are in

harmony with each other and with the goals of society.

*

What is reality and what is fantasy is always determined by those in power.

"Therapy and the Powerless: Memoirs of a Social Work Student," *This Book Is About Schools* (1970), edited by Satu Repo.

**Reston, James B.**
Canadians and Americans communicate with each other more than any other sovereign peoples in the world. They visit one another more, buy more of each other's products, and work together on common problems more than any two nations in the world. And yet there does seem to be a problem.

*

Our general attitude toward this [investment and branch plant operations] in the United States is that the Canadians ought to be grateful to us for producing jobs and raising their standard of living, but what seems to Americans as a perfectly normal and even beneficent form of business is often regarded by other peoples as a form of economic imperialism and maybe even a threat to their independence.

"Can Improved Communication Help?" *Neighbours Taken for Granted: Canada and the United States* (1966), edited by Livingston T. Merchant. Reston — the Pulitzer Prize-winning columnist — is an editor of *The New York Times*.

**Revillon, Victor**
"Everything from a Needle to an Anchor."

Motto of "Revillon Brothers, Pioneer General Wholesaler of Western Canada, Edmonton, Alberta"—from an advertisement in 1906. The Montreal office also advertised in the same publication as "Dealers in and Exporters of Furs," with offices in: Paris, Moscow, London, Nijny, New York, Nicolaiv, Leipzig, Khabarosk, Shanghai, Bokhara, Edmonton, Prince Albert. From Ernest J. Chambers's *The Royal North-West Mounted Police: A Corps History* (1906).

Victor Revillon was the founder of the French fur-trading empire which in Canada operated as Revillon Frères Trading Company until 1936 when it was bought out by the Hudson's Bay Company.

## Rexroth, Kenneth

The systematic conquest of the old Northwest by red-coated soldiers and land speculators has moved few boyish hearts, even in New England. But the story of the boats of Champlain poking their way into the dark, leafy wilderness, the heroic death of Father Jogues, the pathetic death of La Salle, the joyful portages of Marquette and Joliet—even the cognac, riot and abandoned women in besieged Montreal—are as moving as the tribulations and defiance of Milton's Satan.

"Notes on Historians," *Assays* (1961).

## Reynolds, Sir Joshua

He has treated the subject as it ought to be treated. I retract my objections. I foresee that his picture will not only become one of the most popular, but will occasion a revolution in art.

Sir Joshua Reynolds objected to Benjamin West's plan to dress the figures in "The Death of Wolfe" (1770) in contemporary rather than classical garb, but when he saw West's magnificent canvas, he changed his mind and arranged for the American artist to be appointed historical painter to the court. Quoted by Oliver Warner in *With Wolfe to Quebec: The Path to Glory* (1972). See also Benjamin West.

## Reynolds, Quentin

He'd discovered a weapon with which he could fight these men—the weapon of faith.

*

Trust George DuPre? I would have bet my life on him.

*The Man Who Wouldn't Talk* (1953). The problem was DuPre talked too much and had more imagination than faith. For the hoax that took Quentin Reynolds for a ride, see George DuPre.

## Rhind, Pauline Elizabeth

Recipe for living: Equal amounts of work, play, love and philosophy.

*Earth & Sun & High Rise Recipes for Singles* (1972).

## Rhodes, E.N.

A country's worth is not according to the number of square miles it possesses, but according to the square people it contains. Nova Scotia is very happy in this regard.

Premier of Nova Scotia, *The Book of Canada: Published by the Canadian Medical Association* (1930), edited by Chester Martin, W. Stewart Wallace, and T. C. Routley.

## Rhys, Charles Horton

Toronto is the handsomest town we have yet seen. Wide streets, good shops, lovely gardens, handsome public buildings, churches rich in spires and traceried windows, spacious hotels, and elegant equipages. We put up at the Revere House, and during our stay there was a grand Scottish gathering. Such piping and dancing, and throwing the caber! Glorious weather, bands playing, handsome women, wonderful calves (the men, I mean—that is, the men's legs). . . .

*A Theatrical Trip for a Wager! Through Canada and the United States* (1861).

## Rice, Gitz

Oh, Mademoiselle from Armentières,
Parlez-vous,
Oh, Mademoiselle from Armentières,
Parlez-vous,
She hasn't been kissed in forty years,
Hinky-dinky, par-lee-voo.

It was in 1915 that Gitz Rice, a sergeant in the Canadian Army, sat down at a little café in Armentières, a small French town near Lille, and watched a chic barmaid serve drinks. Then and there he composed the words of the world-famous "Mademoiselle from Armentières." He performed his composition a few days later before the Fifth Battery, Montreal, stationed in France.

Gitz Rice, born Ingram Rice in New

Glasgow, Nova Scotia, was a former printing-ink salesman with a gift for tunesmithery. He acquired a following on Tin Pan Alley for his popular songs and arrangements. Among the hits of the twenties and thirties, composed before his death in New York in 1947, were "My Buddy" and "Dear Old Pal of Mine."

"Mademoiselle from Armentières" became what Burton Stevenson called "the folk song of the Great War." It is sometimes known by its refrain, "Hinky Dinky Parlay Voo." The word "Armentières" should be mispronounced in the English fashion as "Armenteers." There are later versions, too numerous to reproduce, with penultimate lines that run: "The French they are a peculiar race," "She wore her dress awfully loose," "She waggled her headlights and caboose," etc. And then there is the barmaid's rival, "Mademoiselle from St. Nazaire" who "never heard of underwear."

Composition of the ditty has been falsely credited to "Red" Rowley (for the words) and Alfred James Walden (whose tunes appeared under the name of Harry Wincott). Sigmund Spaeth, in his authoritative analysis, *A History of Popular Music in America* (1948), credits Gitz Rice with the words, but the music (based on a French song "Mademoiselle de Bar-Le Duc") he ascribes to Alfred James Walden. Spaeth suggests that the ditty was written by Rice in England and first performed there by a music-hall entertainer, Sergeant "Red" Rowland (not Rowley), as late as 1917. It seems clear that at the very least Gitz Rice wrote the words of one of the catchiest and most popular songs of all time. It seems likely that, in addition to writing the words, he composed or adapted the tune and sang the song for the first time in France in 1915.

## Rich, John

If everybody contemplates the infinite instead of fixing the drains many of us will die of cholera.

"The Emotional Revolution," *Agenda 1970: Proposals for a Creative Politics*

(1968), edited by Trevor Lloyd and Jack McLeod.

## Richard, Henri "Pocket"

Once you are alone in front of a goalie, size doesn't matter. A hard low shot fired by a small player can be just as dangerous as one by a big fellow.

The younger brother of Rocket Richard, called "Pocket" because of his height and weight (5′ 7″, 160 lbs.). Quoted by Andy O'Brien in *Young Hockey Champions* (1969).

## Richard, Maurice "Rocket"

I have nothing to regret. What's done is done; I have no excuses. Some days were good days, some days were bad days. But I cannot recall any day that I did not try my best—so how can I regret even the bad days?

Quoted by Andy O'Brien in *Rocket Richard* (1961).

## Richardson, Herbert W.

How a man views the world always expresses his own view of himself—even though he may not be aware of this.

*Nun, Witch, Playmate, The Americanization of Sex* (1971).

## Richardson, Judge Hugh

Louis Riel, You are charged with treason. You let loose the flood gates of rapine and bloodshed, and brought ruin and death to many families, who, if let alone, were in comfort and a fair way of affluence. For what you did you have been given a fair and impartial trial. Your remarks are no excuse for your acts. You committed acts that the law demands an account for at your hands. The jury coupled with their verdict a recommendation to mercy. I can hold out no prospect for you, and I would recommend you to make your peace with God. For me, only one duty and a painful one to perform remains. It is to pass sentence upon you. If your life is spared, no one will feel more gratified than myself, but I can hold out no hope. The sentence of this Court upon you,

Louis Riel, is that you be taken to the guard-room of the Mounted Police of Regina, whence you came, and kept there until September the eighteenth, and from thence to the place of execution, there to be hanged by the neck until dead, and may the Lord have mercy upon your soul!

> Stipendiary Magistrate Hugh Richardson passed the sentence of death on Louis Riel on July 31, 1885. A succession of appeals delayed the execution from September 18 until November 16 of that year. The wording of the sentence, which has been reproduced from an anonymous contemporary book *The Story of Louis Riel the Rebel Chief: Illustrated* (1885), differs slightly from the official transcript, *The Queen* vs. *Louis Riel* (1886). See also Louis Riel.

### Richardson, James Cleland
Will I gie them wund?

> "The Scottish-born piper with the 16th Canadian Infantry Battalion was eighteen years old when he requested permission to play his company over the top at Regina Trench on the Somme, October 8, 1916. As the Company approached the objective, it was held up by very strong wire and came under intense fire, which caused heavy casualties and demoralized the formation for the moment. Realizing the situation, Piper Richardson strode up and down outside the wire, playing his pipes with the greatest coolness. The effect was instantaneous. Inspired by his splendid example, the company rushed the wire with such fury and determination that the obstacle was overcome and the position captured.
>
> "Later, after participating in bombing operations, he was detailed to take back a wounded comrade and prisoners.
>
> "After proceeding about 200 yards Piper Richardson remembered that he had left his pipes behind. Although strongly urged not to do so, he insisted on returning to recover his pipes. He has never been seen since, and death has been presumed accordingly owing to lapse of time." *The London Gazette*, October 22, 1918. He was awarded the

Victoria Cross posthumously. George C. Machum, *Canada's V.C.'s: The Story of Canadians Who Have Been Awarded the Victoria Cross* (1956).

### Richardson, Major John
Canada, alone, in the wide universe, forms the exception. The few men of talent who exist within her bosom, have never met with that attention which it is the pride of the nations to which I have alluded to bestow upon those who undertake to instruct, inform, or amuse their minds; and so far has this apathetic feeling been carried, that in my own case it was left to the people of the United States to inform them that they possessed a writer not less favourably known in Europe than among themselves, of whose existence they (the Canadians) were ignorant, and to whose success they were indifferent.

> The author of *Wacousta; or The Prophecy* (1832) and other romances was more popular in the United States than in the Canadian colonies.

Few of the occurrences that took place were known, except through report, principally oral, and from the solitary traveller passing through the district, for newspapers there were—not earlier than 1812—a luxury almost unknown in that semi-barbarous province, which, even at the present day, when *affecting* a position among the nations of the earth, cannot boast in literature of three native authors, while it compels even those to court a strange soil for the harvest that awaits the man of talent and application in every portion of the civilized world.

> Major Richardson discussing news of the War of 1812 in his novel, first published in 1851, called *Westbrook, the Outlaw; or, The Avenging Wolf, an American Border Tale* (1973).

### Richardson, Thomas
Canada is a large country in North America. A remarkable earthquake happened here in 1663, which overwhelmed a chain of mountains above 3,000 miles long, and changed their immense tract into a plain. It is now in the

possession of the English. York and Quebec are the chief towns.

*A Juvenile Gazetter* (1830).

## Richler, Mordecai

"A man without land is nobody. Remember that, Duddel."

Grandfather's advice to young Duddy and the motif of *The Apprenticeship of Duddy Kravitz* (1959).

"I'm world-famous," Dr. Parks said, "all over Canada."

*The Incomparable Atuk* (1963).

To be a Jew and a Canadian is to emerge from the ghetto twice, for self-conscious Canadians, like some touchy Jews, tend to contemplate the world through a wrong-ended telescope, as witness what is still my most cherished Canadian newspaper headline: 1960 WAS A GOOD YEAR FOR PLAYWRIGHTS FROM OUTSIDE CANADA.

Foreword, *Hunting Tigers Under Glass: Essays and Reports* (1968).

It was nice, very nice, that Walter Pidgeon, *Canadian-born*, was a Hollywood star, but if you wanted Lauren Bacall, you had to be Bogart. An urban American.

\*

When I return to Canada from time to time, what I always find most tiresome is the cultural protectionism, the anti-Americanism. No heritage is worth preserving unless it can survive the sun, the mixed marriage, or the foreign periodical. Culture cannot be legislated or budgeted or protected with tariffs. Like potatoes.

\*

However, if I still feel the longest unmanned frontier is an artificial one, I no longer look forward, as I once did, to the day when it might disappear and we would join fully in the American adventure. Vietnam and Ronald Reagan, among other things, have tempered my enthusiasm. Looked at another way, yes, we *are* nicer. And suddenly that's important.

"The North American Pattern" in *The New Romans: Candid Canadian Opinions of the U.S.* (1968), edited by Al Purdy.

Canadians represent, as it were, the least militant North American minority group. The white, Protestant, heterosexual ghetto of the north.

\*

Then, to repeat a favourite story of mine, there is the editor of a major New York publishing house who told me that one afternoon he and his associates compiled a list of twelve deserving but ineffably dull books with which to start a publishing firm that was bound to fail. Leading the list of unreadables was *Canada: Our Good Neighbour to the North*.

Introduction, *Canadian Writing Today* (1970).

"Listen your Lordship, I'm a respecter of institutions. Even in Paris, I remained a Canadian. I puffed hashish, but I didn't inhale."

*St. Urbain's Horseman* (1971).

Canada is one of the few places left where the small decencies are observed. If, as a young man, I was scornful of the country because we always seemed so far behind style-setting New York, I now thank God for the cultural lag. Ours, after all, is the good neighbourhood. A society well worth preserving.

*Life Magazine*, April 9, 1971.

The Canadian kid who wants to grow up to be Prime Minister isn't thinking big, he is setting a limit to his ambitions rather early.

\*

What I choose to celebrate, they are ashamed of.

\*

Ultimately I think all writers are parochial, they're stuck with the material to hand. I'm a Canadian and a Jew, and I write about being both. I worry about being away so long from—well, the roots of my discontent.

\*

Fundamentally, all writing is about the

same thing: it's about dying, about the brief flicker of time we have here, and the frustrations that it creates.

Quoted in *Time*, May 31, 1971.

The Canadian distributor, bracingly realistic, did not detain me overlong with *recherché* chitchat about style, content or influences. "Have you written a thick book or a thin book?" he demanded.

A thin one, I allowed.

"Thick books sell better than thin ones here." ["Why I Write" (1971); the thin book is *The Acrobats*, Richler's first novel, published in 1954.]

\*

Wherever I travel I'm too late. The orgy has moved elsewhere. ["A Sense of the Ridiculous" (1969)]

*Shovelling Trouble* (1972).

I'm not the kind of writer who can change or expects to change anything. What I do hope to do is set down a sort of honest record of things of our time and our place, to balance . . . I don't know if you've read something I once wrote in a *New American Review*, where I spoke of the writer as a kind of loser's advocate, as a witness to injustices in this world, and said that the writer should speak for those people who are not getting a fair share of the sun. I don't mean social justice really, although of course I want to see more social justice. I mean other things, wider ramifications of injustice.

Interviewed by Graeme Gibson in *Eleven Canadian Novelists* (1972).

## Richmond, Duke of
Indeed, my friend, you bite very hard!

"Charles Gordon Lennox, Fourth Duke of Richmond, was appointed governor-in-chief of Canada in 1818," explains Norah Story in *The Oxford Companion to Canadian History and Literature* (1967). "He died suddenly, near Richmond, Upper Canada, from hydrophobia, after being bitten by a pet fox. . . ." Quoted by Robert M. Hamilton in *Canadian Quotations and Phrases: Literary and Historical* (1952).

## Richthofen, Manfred von
See A. Roy Brown.

## Ridout, Godfrey
Question: Is there a distinctive Canadian music?

Answer: Show me a distinctive Canadian!

Composer interviewed by *Musicanada* June-July, 1968.

## Riel, Louis
You go no farther!

"There was no violence. The métis simply stood on the chain while Riel declared that the territory south of the Assiniboine belonged to the people of Red River and not to Canada, and that the métis would not allow the survey to proceed any farther. This was no unplanned impulsive act." George F.G. Stanley in *Louis Riel* (1963). The British surveyors were stopped on October 11, 1869. The four decisive words have no source other than tradition.

Tell them our great thought is to resist being made Irishmen of.

Quoted by John Malcolm Reid in *The London Free Press*, December 16, 1869. Quoted by W.L. Morton in "The Bias of Prairie Politics," *Historical Essays on the Prairie Provinces* (1970), edited by Donald Swainson.

I am the half-breed question.

About 1884. Quoted by O.D. Skelton in *Life and Letters of Sir Wilfrid Laurier* (1921), who explains: "At the same time he threw out hints, which did not reach those in authority, that if the government would again pay him a sum to leave the country, say $100,000 or $35,000, or perhaps only $10,000 the half-breed question could be settled: 'I am the half-breed question.' "

Your Honours, Gentlemen of the Jury: Oh my God! help me through thy grace and the divine influence of Jesus Christ. Oh my God! bless me, bless this honourable Court, bless this Honourable Jury, bless my good lawyers who have come 700 leagues to try to save my life, bless also the lawyers for the Crown, because they have done, I am sure, what they thought their duty. They have shown me fairness which at first I did not expect from them. Oh my God! bless all those who are around me through the grace and influence of Jesus Christ Our Saviour, change the curiosity of those who are paying attention to me, change that curiosity into sympathy with me.

\*

The day of my birth I was helpless and my mother took care of me although she was not able to do it alone, there was some one to help her to take care of me and I lived. Today, although a man, I am as helpless before this Court, in the Dominion of Canada and in this world as I was helpless on the knees of my mother the day of my birth. The North West is also my mother, it is my mother country, and although my mother country is sick and confined in a certain way, there are some from Lower Canada who came to help her to take care of me during her sickness, and I am sure that my mother country will not kill me more than my mother did. . . .

\*

If it is any satisfaction to the doctor to know what kind of insanity I have, if they are going to call my pretentions insanity, I say humbly, through the grace of God I believe I am the prophet of the New World.

\*

We took up arms against the invaders from the East without knowing them. They were so far apart from us, on the other side of the Lakes, that it cannot be said that we had any hatred against them. We did not know them. They came without notification. They came boldly. We said: Who are they? They said: We are the possessors of the country. Well, knowing that it was not true, we done against those parties coming from the East what we used to do against the Indians from the South and from the West, when they would invade us.

\*

I suppose the Half-breeds in Manitoba, in 1870, did not fight for two hundred and forty acres of land, but it is to be understood that there were two societies who treated together. One was small, but in its smallness it had its rights. The other was great, but in its greatness it had no greater rights than the rights of the small, because the right is the same for every one, and when they began by treating the leaders of that small community as bandits, as outlaws, leaving them without protection, they disorganized that community.

\*

I know that through the grace of God I am the founder of Manitoba.

\*

Do you own the lands? In England, in France, the French and the English have land, the first who were in England, they were the owners of the soil and they transmitted to generations. Now by the soil they have had their start as a nation. Who starts the nations? The very same one who creates them, God. God is the master of the universe, our planet is his land, and the nations, the tribes are members of his family, and as a good Father he gives a portion of his lands to that nation, to that tribe, to everyone, that is his heritage, that is his share of the inheritance, of the people, or nation or tribe.

\*

This is the principle. God cannot create a tribe without locating it, we are not birds, we have to walk on the ground, and that ground is enriched with many things which besides its own value increases its value in another manner, and when we cultivate it, we still increase that value.

\*

If they declare me insane, I have been astray. I have been astray not as an impostor, but according to my conscience. Your Honour that is what I have to say.

Excerpts from "The Prisoner's Address," *The Queen* vs. *Louis Riel, Accused and Convicted of the Crime of High Treason* (1886). The address was delivered in Regina on July 31, 1885. Riel prefaced his eloquent defence speech with these words: "I cannot speak English very well, but I am trying to do so, because most of those here speak English."

I have received my divine notification with uplifted arms and bowed head. Since then I have been working for humanity, and already with what success the world knows. Deeds are not accomplished in a few days, or in a few hours. A century is only a spoke in the wheel of everlasting time. By formulating I have brought about practical results. Much work is still undone. [*Weekly British Whig*, August 27, 1885]

> Reprinted in *The Riel Rebellion 1885* (1972), compiled by Nick and Helma Mika.

Every day in which I have neglected to prepare myself to die, was a day of mental alienation.

> Quoted by Nicholas Flood Davin, "Interview with Riel," *The Regina Leader*, November 16, 1885.

I have nothing but my heart, and I gave it long ago to my country. [To a jail guard who asked for a souvenir]

Our Father which art in heaven, Hallowed be thy name. Thy kingdom come. Thy will be done in earth, as it is in heaven. Give us this day our daily bread. And forgive us our debts, as we forgive our debtors. And lead us not into temptation, but deliver us from evil—

> These were Louis Riel's last words from the scaffold. By pre-arrangement, the public executioner cut short his recital of the Lord's Prayer (Matthew 6:9-13) at the word "evil." From the crowd were clearly heard voices saying: "The God damned son of a bitch is gone at last," "Yes, the son of a bitch is gone for certain now." Riel died about nine o'clock the morning of November 16, 1885, a cold but clear day. The hangman, John Henderson, a former prisoner of Riel's during the first uprising, received fifty dollars from the sheriff for executing him. George F.G. Stanley, *Louis Riel* (1963).

RIEL, 16 NOVEMBRE 1885

"Louis Riel is buried in the grounds of the Basilica in St. Boniface...above the spot where Louis lies stands a brown granite tombstone. On it are inscribed these simple words." George F.G. Stanley, *Louis Riel* (1963).

"In recommending him to the mercy of the court, we did so because we considered that while the prisoner was guilty, and we could not by any means justify him in his acts of rebellion, at the same time we felt that had the Government done their duty and redressed the grievances of the half-breeds of the Saskatchewan, as they had been requested time and again to do, there never would have been a second Riel rebellion, and consequently no prisoner to try and condemn. We could not but condemn in the strongest terms possible the extraordinary dilatoriness of Sir John Macdonald, Sir David McPherson and Lieutenant-Governor Dewdney and I firmly believe that had these three been on trial as accessories, very little mercy, if any, would have been shown them by the jury."

> Letter from "a juryman at Riel's trial," quoted by Edward Blake in an address published as a pamphlet *Ministers on Trial* (1886). See also: John Bruce, Greg Curnoe, Sir John A. Macdonald, Charles Pelham Mulvaney, Judge Hugh Richardson, John Ross Robinson, Thomas Scott.

## Rilke, Rainer Maria
And this more human love (that will fulfill itself, infinitely considerate and gentle, and good and clear in binding and releasing) will resemble that which we are with struggle and endeavour preparing, the love that consists in this, that two solitudes protect and touch and greet each other.

> Letter Seven, Rome, May 14, 1904, *Letters to a Young Poet* (1934), translated from the German by M.D. Herter Norton. Hugh MacLennan found the title and theme of his novel *Two Solitudes* (1945) in this passage by the great German poet.

## Rinfret, Fernand
On lit Proust à Rideau Hall.

> "There is someone reading Proust in

Rideau Hall." A graceful tribute to John Buchan, Governor General Lord Tweedsmuir, by a French-Canadian writer. Quoted by Janet Adam Smith in *John Buchan: A Biography* (1965).

## Riopelle, Jean-Paul

When I feel hesitant I don't paint. When I paint I don't feel hesitant.

> CBC-TV's "Telescope," May 21, 1965.

To progress is to destroy what one thought had been acquired.

\*

I see no difference whatever between the past and the present. The works of the past are neither closer nor farther removed. There has been no evolution: what has occurred should simply allow us to see better.

> Quoted by Pierre Schneider in *Catalogue de l'exposition du Musée du Québec* (1967).

There is no figuration, there is only expression—and expression is just someone in front of things.

> Quoted by Arthur Bardo in *The Montreal Star*, September 19, 1969.

## Rioux, Marcel

Far from becoming "a province like the others," Quebec became more and more a province not like the others. The most astute Quebeckers began to wish that Quebec were not a province at all. Little by little, the Quiet Revolution turned into the "Quebec question." The English-speaking Canadians were soon to ask, "What does Quebec want?" The French Canadians, astonished by their own audacity, did not know what to reply.

\*

That will be the end of a long story—and the beginning of another. [On the coming of independence for Quebec]

> *Quebec in Question* (1971), translated by James Boake.

## Ripley, Robert L.

A. Forrester of Toronto—ran 100 yds. backwards in 14 seconds.

> An item from the first "Believe It or Not!" cartoon, *The New York Globe*, December 19, 1918. Reprinted in *Ripley's Believe It or Not!* (1929).

The best days of my life I spent in Hell and Hell, you may or may not know, is a most delightful city in Norway, and I was there about a year ago and it is a very pleasant little place. Hell reminded me of Toronto—all green trees and public parks. I have not been able to find since I came here whether I am just entering a public park or leaving it. There doesn't seem to be any way for a stranger to tell. . . . But Hell is a delightful place. I am sure I cannot wish any man in Toronto any better luck if he decided to leave Toronto than to go to Hell.

> "Believe It or Not," October 3, 1932, *Addresses Delivered before the Canadian Club of Toronto: Season of 1932-33* (1933).

## Ritchie, J.A.

The wholesome Sea is at her gates,
　　Her gates both East and West,
Then is it strange that we should love
　　This Land, Our Land, the best?

> These strangely haunting (if Kiplingesque) lines are inscribed in stone over the main entrance to the Parliament Buildings in Ottawa: "THE WHOLESOME SEA IS AT HER GATES . . . HER GATES BOTH EAST AND WEST." They date from 1920, when the buildings were rebuilt after the great fire, and first appeared that year in a poem "There Is a Land" written by J.A. Ritchie, K.C., an Ottawa barrister and poetaster.

## Rittinghausen, Eva

In Trudeau's life there are more women than just me . . . yes, he's the No. 1 catch of the international jet set.

> In London to attend the Commonwealth Prime Ministers' Conference, the bachelor prime minister made the mistake of dining in Chelsea with the talkative Mrs. Rittinghausen, a Canadian-born woman of German ancestry. Quoted in *The Globe and Mail*, January 6, 1969. Visibly irritated, Trudeau replied: "My personal friends do not talk about my personal affairs in public. Therefore, if

someone is, they are not personal friends, they may be passing acquaintances." Mrs. Rittinghausen is reported to have explained: "It was love at first sight—I love to give and why shouldn't it be to Canadians." See also Pierre Elliott Trudeau.

## Rivard, Adjutor
O God, do Thou bless the houses where the cradle is held in honour! Bless those hearths where many a birth comes to cheer the ancient cradle and bring it perpetual youth! Bless the families who hold in reverence the virtues of former days, to the glory of our Church and of our Country!

"The Cradle," *Chez Nous: Our Quebec Home* (1924), translated by W.H. Blake.

## Rivard, Antoine
A great criminal lawyer must be an actor. He must use tragedy sparingly and know when and how to use it. And, above all, he must be a good comedian. I think a lawyer, before he studies law, should study under a great actor as did the great lawyers of France a century ago.

Quoted by Frank Hamilton in "The Case Book of Antoine Rivard" in *Maclean's Canada: Portrait of a Country* (1960), edited by Leslie F. Hannon.

## Rivard, Lucien
I'm going out to flood the rink.

With words to this effect, Lucien Rivard gained access to the prison yard and leapt over the wall of Bordeaux Jail. The convicted drug peddlar made good his escape at 6:30 P.M., March 2, 1965, when the weather was balmy and the temperature in the forties. Rivard, nicknamed "The Gallic Pimpernel," was recaptured July 16 and extradited to the United States. M. Justice Dorion is said to have observed: "I suppose he was getting fed up waiting for his bail to be approved." *The Shape of Scandal: A Study of a Government in Crisis* (1965), by Richard Gwyn.

## Roberts, Sir Charles G.D.
Awake, my country, the hour is great with change!

Under this gloom which yet obscures the land,
From ice-blue strait and stern Laurentian range
　　To where giant peaks our western bounds command,
A deep voice stirs, vibrating in men's ears. . . .

*

Awake, my country, the hour of dreams is done!
Doubt not, nor dead the greatness of thy fate.

Lines from "An Ode for the Canadian Confederacy" (1886).

O Child of Nations, giant-limbed,
　　Who stand'st among the nations now
Unheeded, unadorned, unhymned,
　　With unanointed brow,—

How long the ignoble sloth, how long
　　The trust in greatness not thine own?
Surely the lion's brood is strong
　　To front the world alone!

Two of the fourteen stanzas of "Canada" (1886). *Selected Poems of Sir Charles G.D. Roberts* (1936).

A good Canadian Nationalist *must* be a good British Imperialist. [About 1900]
*
I live *for* poetry *by* prose. [Frequent remark]

Quoted by E.M. Pomeroy in *Sir Charles G.D. Roberts: A Biography* (1943). See also Rudyard Kipling.

## Roberts, J.H.
Very heavy casualties in men and ships. Did everything possible to get men off but in order to get any home had to come to sad decision to abandon remainder. This was joint decision by Force Commanders. Obviously operation completely lacked surprise.

Message conveyed by pigeon to the Headquarters First Canadian Corps from Major-General J.H. Roberts, after the raid on Dieppe, August 19, 1942. Reproduced by C.P. Stacey in *Official History of the Canadian Army in the Second World War, Volume I: Six Years of War* (1955).

**Roberts, Kenneth**
On every side of us are men who hunt perpetually for their personal Northwest Passage, too often sacrificing health, strength, and life itself to the search; and who shall say they are not happier in their vain and hopeful quest than wiser, duller folks who sit at home, venturing nothing and, with sour laughs, deriding the seekers for that fabled thoroughfare?

Foreword to *Northwest Passage* (1937).

**Robertson, Heather**
The farmer is the guardian of the western dream; without him, the West is just the East.

*Grass Roots* (1973).

**Robertson, John Ross**
Riel had but little of the Napoleonic look, credited to him by his admirers on the American side of the line, and with a prominent Jewish nose and deep penetrating eyes, he has more of the animal in him than should be allotted to a man of his physique.

The future publisher of *The Toronto Telegram* interviewed Riel at Fort Garry in January of 1870. Quoted by Ron Poulton in *The Paper Tyrant: John Ross Robertson of The Toronto Telegram* (1971).

**Robertson, Norman**
I suppose we have here all the people in Canada interested in having Newfoundland join Canada.

To a group of four others in the office of the under secretary of External Affairs, Ottawa, August, 1946. Quoted by R.A. MacKay in "Smallwood in Ottawa, 1946," *The Political Economy of Newfoundland, 1929-1972* (1973), edited by Peter Neary.

**Roberval, Sieur de**
To declare unto you the state of the Savages, they are people of a goodly stature, and well made, they are very white, but they are all naked: and if they were apparelled as the French are,

they would bee as white and as fayer: but they paynt themselves for feare of heat and sunne burning.

\*

They have a King in every Countrey, and are wonderfull obedient unto him: and they doe him honour according unto their manner and fashion.

"The maners of the Savages," from "The Voyage of John Francis de la Roche, knight, Lord of Roberval, to the Countries of Canada, Saguenai, and Hochelaga . . . April, 1542," quoted by Richard Hakluyt in *The Principal Navigations, Voyages, Traffiques, and Discoveries of the English Nation* (1589).

**Robeson, Paul**
A great joy during the period when I was not even permitted to travel to Canada (for which no passport is required from the United States), were the concerts at the border that were sponsored by the metal miners of Canada. In 1952 I had been invited to attend the Canadian convention of their union, the Mine, Mill and Smelter Workers, and when the State Department barred me from coming to them, the miners arranged for a concert to be held at Peace Arch Park, on the border between the State of Washington and the Province of British Columbia. I shall always remember that concert on May 18, 1952, when 30,000 Canadians came from many miles away to hear me, to demonstrate their friendship and to protest against all barriers to cultural exchange.

For three more years these concerts were held at that border, until finally the State Department was forced to retreat from its arbitrary and illegal ban on my travel to places which require no passport. The hand of brotherhood—yes, I found that hand in Canada, too.

*Here I Stand* (1958).

**Robichaud, Louis J.**
If there is a man who wants to run this province, let him present himself to the people and be elected to office. [An allusion to K.C. Irving, New Brunswick's one-man conglomerate]

*

Where I come from, we measure a man's stature from the shoulders up.

Louis J. Robichaud was called "Little Louie" when he was premier of New Brunswick in the 1960s because of his height—a mere five feet, four inches. See also Hugh John Flemming and K.C. Irving.

## Robins, John D.
A normal animal must be content with four limbs; no such restriction is placed upon the branches of a tree. Possibly, when man has attained the trustworthiness of the tree, he may be allowed its freedom.

*

I can approach a solitary tree with pleasure, a cluster of trees with joy, and a forest with rapture; I must approach a solitary man with caution, a group of men with trepidation, and a nation of men with terror.

*The Incomplete Angler* (1943).

## Robins, Toby
I was always star material in Canada. But that was because there were no other actors.

Quoted by Urjo Kareda in *The Toronto Star*, October 8, 1968.

There is no future for an actress in Canada. The Meccas are elsewhere.

Quoted by Herbert Whittaker in *The Globe and Mail*, September 14, 1968. The Toronto-born West End actress is married to the producer Bill Freedman.

## Robinson, John "Black Jack"
Success is the god of politics and expediency is the supreme law of public life in Canada. Statesmen no longer do right because it is right. The justice or the injustice of every act is established by the answer to the question, Will It Pay?

*

TEARS AND TAXES ARE THE PRICE OF LIBERTY. The pockets that pay are more blessed than the eyes that weep. [An editorial urging the conscription of wealth, June 18, 1917]

John Robinson—called "Black Jack" to distinguish him from his publisher John Ross Robertson—was the fighting editor of *The Toronto Telegram* from 1880 until his death in 1928. Quoted by Ron Poulton in *The Paper Tyrant: John Ross Robertson of The Toronto Telegram* (1971).

## Robinson, Sir John Beverley
The Kingdom of Canada.

The union of the colonies of Upper and Lower Canada under the monarchy was proposed by Robinson in *Letters from Mr. Commissioner Robinson on the Canada Trade and Canada Union Bills* as early as 1882. Sir John A. Macdonald incorporated the phrase "The Kingdom of Canada" in the first draft of the British North America Act, but in later drafts "Kingdom" was discarded in favour of "Dominion" which, it was felt, would sound less monarchical to the republic to the south.

## Robinson, Judith
There is an old Canadian proverb which says a fool and his heritage are soon parted.

*This Is On the House* (1957).

## Robitaille, Gérald
Being alive implies all the possibilities of death. *La vie est belle!*

*

Paris is a décor in which dreams are lived.

*Images* (1970), by the Canadian-born secretary to Henry Miller.

## Roblin, Duff
I know the worth of this unprecedented idea, the idea of unity without uniformity which is the distinctive mark of Canada, the stamp of the Canadian identity. That is why, despite some present-day trends and fashions, I do not—I cannot—imagine a Canada without Quebec, or a Quebec without Canada. . . .

Premier of Manitoba in the 1960s, quoted by James M. Minifie in *Open at the Top: Reflections on U.S.-Canada Relations* (1964).

## Roblin, Sir Rodmond P.
I am opposed by all the short-haired women and the long-haired men in the province.

> The premier of Manitoba criticized the women's suffrage movement in 1912. According to Henry F. Woods in *American Sayings: Famous Phrases, Slogans and Aphorisms* (1945), the phrase "long-haired men and short-haired women" was fairly common in the United States in the 1920s. Roblin may have originated it.

" 'What in the world do women want to vote for? Why do women want to mix in the hurly-burly of politics? My mother was the best woman in the world, and she certainly never wanted to vote! I respect women,' he went on, 'I honour and reverence women, I lift my hat when I meet a woman. . . . Now you forget all this nonsense about women voting,' he went on in his suavest tones. 'You're a fine, smart young woman, I can see that. And take it from me, nice women don't want to vote.' "

> Quoted by Nellie L. McClung in *The Stream Runs Fast* (1945), when she solicited the support of the premier of Manitoba for the Winnipeg Political Equality League, January, 1914. See also Nellie L. McClung.

Look at the States across the line where there is woman suffrage. In Chicago there are women's clubs scattered everywhere, showing how women are deserting the home, yet even then, when they have suffrage, they are not using the privilege. In Colorado, they shrink from the polls as from a pestilence. I believe woman suffrage would be a retrograde movement, that it would break up the home, and that it would throw the children into the arms of the servant girls.

> *The Manitoba Free Press*, January 28, 1914.

## Robson, Joseph
The Company have for eighty years slept at the edge of a frozen sea; they have shown no curiosity to penetrate further themselves, and have exerted all their art and power to crush that spirit in others.

> *An Account of Six Years' Residence in Hudson's-Bay, from 1733 to 1736, and 1744 to 1747* (1752). Critics characterized the Hudson's Bay Company's unwillingness to establish inland posts to compete with the French and English traders as "the sleep by the frozen sea."
>
> "The Company had been accused of falling asleep by the frozen sea.
>
> "They were not asleep. They had heard every word the rude fellows were saying. And, through it all, had gone on making profits." *The Great Fur Opera: Annals of the Hudson's Bay Company 1670-1870* (1970), by Ronald Searle and Kildare Dobbs.

## Roby, Yves   See Jean Hamelin.

## Roche, Mazo De la
See De la Roche, Mazo.

## Rochefoucauld-Liancourt, Duc de La
See La Rochefoucauld-Liancourt, Duc de.

## Rockefeller, James S.
When I came up I was told Mr. Gordon was an accountant.

\*

Yes, I remember saying those words ["If we proceed, we proceed at our own peril"], and he nodded his head and said yes. He did not use those words; I used those words. I remember very well.

> Minutes and Proceedings, House of Commons Standing Committee on Finance, Trade and Economic Affairs, January 24 to February 22, 1967. James S. Rockefeller was chairman of Citibank, the future growth of whose subsidiary, Mercantile Bank, was being limited by the finance minister. See also Walter L. Gordon.

## Rockefeller Jr., John D.
Politically, Canada and the United States are two entirely separate and distinct units, and probably will always so remain. Geographically, they are separated only by a surveyor's line three thousand miles in length, without forts

or guards from one end to the other. For over a hundred years these two peoples have lived in peace and happiness as close neighbours, settling such questions as have naturally arisen in an orderly and friendly manner. This is very significant. Does it not point to the fact that in ideals and aims these two great peoples are alike? Does it not suggest that they are brothers in spirit, whatever the genealogist may say? I like to feel that it does, and I know my fellow-countrymen generally share that view.

"Brotherhood Among Men and Nations," April 12, 1918, *Addresses Delivered before the Canadian Club of Montreal: Season of 1917-18* (1918).

**Rockman, Arnold**
In order to invent the airplane you must have at least a thousand years' experience dreaming of angels.

Characteristic remark of the York University social scientist and typographer, 1960s.

**Roditi, Georges**
They speak the French of a province which does not exist.

Paris publisher referring to the Québécois. Quoted by Nicholas Monsarrat in *Life Is a Four-Letter Word: Volume II: Breaking Out* (1970).

**Rogers, Robert D.**
Went in Boats to cut out the Steam Boat Caroline, found her moored at a wharf & Storehouse at Schosser set fire to her & sent her adrift down the river towards the falls.

Diary entry, December 29, 1837, by Robert D. Rogers, an officer of the Cobourg Rifle Corps. Quoted by F.M. de la Fosse, in "Diary of Lieutenant-Colonel Robert D. Rogers," *Canadian Historical Review*, December, 1932.

**Rogers, Will**
Marie Dressler is the real queen of our movies . . . she was a sensational musical-comedy star when your fathers and mothers had to get a marriage licence to see Niagara Falls.

Foreword to *My Own Story* (1934), by Marie Dressler as told to Mildred Harrington. See also Marie Dressler.

**Rohmer, Richard**
Mid-Canada Development Corridor.

This concept was originated and popularized by Richard Rohmer, a Toronto and Northwest Territories lawyer and influential citizen. "Mid-Canada is largely a habitable region with a cool but acceptable climate and a rugged but accessible terrain." This appears in *Mid-Canada Development Corridor: A Concept* (1967), a pioneering report undertaken for Rohmer by Acres Research and Planning Limited. Two years later Lakehead University hosted the first Mid-Canada Conference "to examine the advantages of establishing a nation-wide policy and plan for the development of Canada's Mid-North." In 1970, Rohmer published *The Green North: Mid-Canada Corridor.*

The great resources giant of the Canadian Arctic sleeps no longer. It is wide awake, growing rapidly. It is undisciplined, uncontrolled, and uncoordinated. It must be taken in hand and moulded by clearly defined national policies and goals designed to benefit all Canadians. This action must be taken *now*, immediately.

It is imperative!

*The Arctic Imperative: An Overview of the Energy Crisis* (1973).

**Rolph, Dr. John**
Lawyers and physicians have no Clergy Reserves. They depend upon the support of the community which benefits by their labours. The professors of law and physic are well represented in this Assembly, and bear ample testimony to the generosity of the people toward them. Will good, pious and evangelical ministers of our holy religion be likely to fare worse than the physicians of the body, or the agents of our temporal affairs?

Address in the Upper Canadian Assembly, 1836, quoted by J.H. Stewart Reid, Kenneth McNaught and Harry S. Crowe in *A Source-book of Canadian History:*

*Selected Documents and Personal Papers* (1959).

## Rolph, Dr. Thomas
It is really melancholy to traverse the province and go into many of the common schools; you will find a herd of children instructed by some anti-British adventurer, instilling into the young and tender minds sentiments hostile to the parent state . . . and American spelling books, dictionaries and grammar, teaching them an anti-British dialect and idiom.

Rolph travelled through Upper Canada in 1832-33. Quoted by J.G. Hodgins in *Documentary History of Education in Upper Canada* (1895).

## Roman, Stephen B.
It is our responsibility to illustrate to the public at large that there is no alternative to private enterprise.

*

There are good days and there are bad days. But there is always a challenge and a romance in mining.

Quoted by George Lonn in *Builders of Fortunes* (1963).

I am a concerned Canadian. I believe in every segment of our society, and I believe that every segment of that society should produce according to its ability, and thus receive the benefits according to its responsibility and obligations.

*The Toronto Star*, May 2, 1972. Roman heads Denison Mines Ltd., the world's largest supplier of uranium, which he tried to sell to an American oil company in 1970.

I resent that they think that because the chairman is an immigrant boy from Slovakia and the president is a Polack, we are third-class citizens.

Statement to the press on learning that the Trudeau administration would block the sale of Denison Mines Ltd. to U.S. interests, 1970.

## Ronald, William
Everybody wants a spotlight—there's a need—a sweet dry cry from all the ranks.

Abstract artist and broadcaster. "He Must Search," *Probings: A Collection of Essays Contributed to the Canadian Mental Health Association for its Golden Jubilee 1918-1968* (1968).

Painting, you are at war. The ones that make it as art are the ones you defeat.

Quoted by William Withrow in *Contemporary Canadian Painting* (1972).

## Ronsard, Pierre de
Go to the regions
Where our religions have never been
heard of,
To Peru, Canada, Callicuth, Canibales,
And there, show by example, your cardinal virtues.

"Continuation du Discours," *Discours des Misères de ce Temps* (1562), by the French court poet.

## Rooke, John K.
Please don't believe
The use of force
Is how we change the social course;
The use of force
You surely know
Is how we keep the status quo.

"The Use of Force," *The Canadian Forum*, February, 1940.

## Roosevelt, Franklin Delano
Why, what would the people of New York City do if the subways were all owned in Canada. There'd be a revolution!

FDR's reply, when advised to take stronger measures against South American politicians resisting U.S. business interests. Quoted by Peter C. Newman in *Maclean's Magazine*, March, 1972.

The Dominion of Canada is part of the sisterhood of the British Empire. I give to you assurance that the people of the United States will not stand idly by if domination of Canadian soil is threatened by any other Empire. We can assure each other that this hemisphere, at least, shall remain a strong citadel wherein civilization can flourish unimpaired.

Upon receiving an honorary degree from Queen's University, Kingston,

August 18, 1938. Earlier that day the American president dedicated the nearby Ivy Lea Bridge which links the two countries. A few years later Stephen Leacock waxed eloquent about the event in "All Right, Mr. Roosevelt," *Last Leaves* (1945): "You remember, Mr. Roosevelt, when you opened up that new Friendship Bridge across the river near Gananoque . . . those people on the two sides of the ribbons you cut had been waiting to come across and hug one another again for a hundred and fifty years."

## Roosevelt, Theodore

Let the fight come if it must; I don't care whether our sea coast cities are bombarded or not; we would take Canada.

> Letter, December 20, 1895, quoted by Howard K. Beale in *Theodore Roosevelt and the Rise of America to World Power* (1956).

I will appoint three commissioners to meet three of their commissioners, if they so desire, but I think I shall instruct our three commissioners when appointed that they are in no case to yield any of our claim.

> The American president to John Hay, July 16, 1902. Quoted by Thomas A. Bailey in "Theodore Roosevelt and the Alaska Boundary Settlement," *Canadian Historical Review*, June, 1937. This is another instance of Teddy Roosevelt's "big-stick" diplomacy.

## Root, Elihu

I ask you, my friends, to join me in a sentiment—to the Canadian settlers in New England and to the American settlers in the Canadian West—may they ever with loyal memory do honour to the lands of their birth, may they ever with loyal citizenship do God's service to the countries of their adoption.

> Elihu Root was the U.S. secretary of State at the time, and in 1912 the recipient of the Nobel Peace Prize. "Relations between the United States and Canada," January 28, 1907, *Addresses Delivered before the Canadian Club of Ottawa: 1903-1909* (1910).

## Rose, Fred

But, honest to God, I'm innocent.

> To a reporter as the RCMP came to arrest the M.P. for espionage activities exposed by Igor Gouzenko, 1948. Quoted by Frank Rasky in *Gay Canadian Rogues: Swindlers, Gold-Diggers and Spies* (1958).

## Rosebery, Lord

Cinderella of the Empire.

> Epithetical description of Newfoundland, quoted by J.R. Smallwood in *I Chose Canada: The Memoirs of the Honourable Joseph R. "Joey" Smallwood* (1973). Lord Rosebery was prime minister of Great Britain (1894-95); according to James Morris, this "most eloquent of imperialists . . . probably invented the phrase 'Commonwealth of Nations,' in its British Imperial sense" in 1884.

## Rosenberg, Stuart E.

Increasingly, in Canada and the United States, the problem of intermarriage has become one of the chief concerns of the Jewish community. Paradoxically, among the freedoms now open to Jews in North America is the freedom to opt out—not to be a Jew.

> *The Jewish Community in Canada: Volume II: In the Midst of Freedom* (1971).

## Rosenthal, Joe

Since our forbears first set foot on this continent, the white man has been taking from the Indian: his food, his source of livelihood, his traditional way of life. The only thing the white man has refused to accept is perhaps the most valuable thing he had to offer: his unique sense of values.

> *Indians: A Sketching Odyssey* (1971).

## Ross, Alexander

There is a time to give, and a time to withhold from giving. Progress is to be secured little by little, and especially by giving at the right time those particular things that can be received with thankfulness.

*The Red River Settlement: Its Rise, Progress and Present State* (1856).

One day while in a jocular mood the old man began to talk over his past life. It was full of adventure, and may appear amusing to others as it did to us. I shall give it as nearly as I can in his own words. "I have now," said he, "been forty-two years in this country. For twenty-four I was a light canoeman. I required but little sleep, but sometimes got less than I required. No portage was too long for me; all portages were alike. My end of the canoe never touched the ground till I saw the end of it. Fifty songs a day were nothing to me. I could carry, paddle, walk and sing with any man I ever saw. During that period I saved the lives of ten *bourgeois,* and was always the favourite because when others stopped to carry at a bad step and lost time, I pushed on—over rapids, over cascades, over chutes; all were the same to me. No water, no weather ever stopped the paddle or the song. I have had twenty wives in the country; and was once possessed of fifty horses and six running dogs trimmed in the first style. I was then like a *bourgeois,* rich and happy. No *bourgeois* had better-dressed wives than I; no Indian chief finer horses; no white man better-harnessed or swifter dogs. I beat all the Indians at the race, and no white man ever passed me in the chase. I wanted for nothing; and I spent all my earnings in the enjoyment of pleasure. Five hundred pounds twice told have passed through my hands, although now I have not a spare shirt to my back nor a penny to buy one. Yet, were I young I should glory in commencing the same career again. I would spend another half-century in the same fields of enjoyment. There is no life so happy as a *voyageur's* life; none so independent; no place where a man enjoys so much variety and freedom as in the Indian country. *Huzza, huzza pour le pays sauvage!"*

After this *cri de joie* he sat down in the boat and we could not help admiring the wild enthusiasm of the old Frenchman. He had boasted and excited himself till he was out of breath and then sighed with regret that he could no longer enjoy the scenes of his past life.

The Hudson's Bay Company historian is quoting an anonymous *coureur-de-bois* in *The Fur Hunters of the Far West: A Narrative of Adventures in the Oregon and Rocky Mountains* (1855).

### Ross, Brigadier-General Alexander

It was Canada from the Atlantic to the Pacific on parade. I thought then, and I think today, that in those few minutes I witnessed the birth of a nation.

Battle of Vimy Ridge, Easter Monday, 1917. Quoted by D.E. Macintyre in *Canada at Vimy* (1967).

### Ross, Alexander

The Americans just bought my father's grave.

Quoted by Walter Stewart in *Shrug: Trudeau in Power* (1971). The Toronto writer and magazine editor explained: "My father's remains are interred in Forest Lawn Cemetery in Burnaby, B.C. This cemetery was recently bought out by an American chain of funeral homes, which prompted my immortal remark. And which, incidentally, made me a life-long nationalist. A venture capitalist has recently bought back my father's grave from the Americans . . . far better that my father's grave should be owned by Canadian rip-off artists than by American ones."

### Ross, George W.

Among the titles suggested were the following:—"Flag Day," "Britannia Day," "Patriotic Day" and "Empire Day." None of these titles, except the last, seems to me to be acceptable. . . . "Empire Day" suggests that larger British sentiment which I think now prevails throughout the Empire, and to which Canada has for many years contributed not a little. . . . As to the time most convenient for the celebration of such a day, from suggestions received, and from a careful consideration of the whole question, I would respectfully advise that the school day immediately preceding the 24th of May be the day selected. . . . For this and the next generation or two, the recollection of her illustrious reign will on reflection quicken the pulse of the many hundreds of thousands of school children as they remember the greatness of the Empire over which she reigned so long. [A reference to Queen Victoria]

＊

There can be no future for Canada worthy of the traditions of the lands from which she has been stocked, or worthy of the opportunities for nationhood which now seem to be thrust upon her, unless we gird up our loins, and with a resolute and studied purpose endeavour to develop a national spirit.

> Memorandum to the Dominion Teachers' Association, July 23, 1898, from the Ontario minister of Education, George W. Ross, who was responding to a series of letters written a year earlier by Mrs. Clementina Fessenden, a school teacher in Hamilton. Empire Day outlasted the empire itself, at least in Toronto where it was being observed a half century later. Quoted by J. Castell Hopkins in *The Origin and History of Empire Day* (1910). See also Mrs. Clementina Fessenden and Earl Grey.

The ink was scarcely dry upon our Constitution when we began to think constitutionally.

> "The Evolution of Canadian Sentiment" (1905), *Builders of the Canadian Commonwealth* (1923), edited by George H. Locke.

Nations are not born in a day. Great movements make their way painfully often, but always slowly, to a climax. "There is first the blade, then the ear, then the full corn in the ear." May we trust that the blade has disappeared, and that the harvest, when it comes, as come I trust it will, will be of the full-ripened corn of a loyal and well-informed public opinion, which will garner for the historian the story of a federation so complete and so comprehensive as to leave the story of Caesar and Alexander but a paltry page in the archives of the universe.

> "Shall Canada Be Always a Dependency of the Empire?" Address before the National Club, Ottawa, October 28, 1908.

## Ross, Sir John

They first pointed to the ships, eagerly asking, "What great creatures those were?" "Do they come from the sun or the moon?" "Do they give us light by night or by day?" Sacheuse told them that he was a man, that he had a father and mother like themselves; and, pointing to the south, said that he came from a distant country in that direction. To this they answered, "That cannot be, there is nothing but ice there."

> *A Voyage of Discovery Made under the Orders of the Admiralty . . .* (1819). John Ross, captain of the *Sabine*, sailed into Melville Bay and was thus greeted by the Polar Eskimos, August 10, 1818.

But let them remember that ice is stone; a floating rock in the stream; a promontory or an island when aground not less solid than if it were a land of granite.

＊

Let no man imagine that he knows what a present is worth till he has found what happiness can be produced by a blue bead, a yellow button, a needle, or a piece of an old iron hoop.

> *Narrative of a Second Voyage in Search of a Northwest Passage* (1835).

## Ross, Malcolm

Surely Canadians have taken to ballet as happily as the Russians have taken to hockey.

> "Editor's Introduction," *The Arts in Canada: A Stock-Taking at Mid-Century* (1958).

## Rotha, Paul

The National Film Board is a unique venture in national publicity and education through visual media; it is indeed a model to other nations. Its future will depend not only on its obviously fine teamwork but on whether it can develop personalities whose creative contribution can rise above the general need for continual output.

> *The Film Till Now: A Survey of World Cinema* (Revised Edition, 1960), with additional material by Richard Griffith.

## Rotstein, Abraham
Much will have to change in Canada if the country is to stay the same.

"The Precarious Society" (1964), *The Precarious Homestead: Essays on Economics, Technology and Nationalism* (1973).

In the course of the Watkins task force in 1967, we realized for the first time that what we had always regarded as a kind of inbred, myopic, bilateral little affair between Canada and the United States was real and it struck us like a thunderclap—the local manifestation of a global explosion of American corporations. The issue of foreign investment wasn't a narrow little thing between Canada and the United States. In relation to the explosion of multi-national corporations, Canada was the Dew line for the rest of the world.

"Foreign Ownership of Industry—a New Canadian Approach," *The Round Table*, July, 1968.

I leave aside the overwhelming cultural dependence, the significant military dependence and the constraints on foreign policy which the American connection has imposed. At this late date we do not need to be persuaded of the facts; we need some way to keep from being mesmerized by them.

Introduction to *Reclaiming the Canadian Economy: A Swedish Approach through Functional Socialism* (1970), by Gunnar Adler-Karlsson.

The nation-state remains, in the end, the central locus of power and authority in our society and, until such time as transcending institutions have been created, we may envisage that it will remain to protect its members by moderating the intrusion of such technological forces as the spreading American corporation. For this reason, I remain conservative in regard to Canadian survival and a radical in regard to the emergent institutions necessary to achieve this task.

"Binding Prometheus," *Close the 49th Parallel, Etc.: The Americanization of Canada* (1970), edited by Ian Lumsden.

Canada now stands as a DEW line for the rest of the world, revealing in high definition what may be expected from the global penetration of the American corporation. ["The Watkins Report" (1968)]

*

To recognize on the moral plane that "technology is ourselves" is to stagger under the burden of an immense responsibility. We can no longer dissociate ourselves from, or contract out of, the vast network of compulsion and anonymous tyranny that the technological society creates. We ourselves are its source when we opt for the reign of the machine.

*The Precarious Homestead: Essays on Economics, Technology and Nationalism* (1973).

I am afraid of the worst, but I am not sure what that is.

*

Radicalism in Canada has to mean nationalism.

Aphorisms that date from 1972, popularized by the influential political economist. See also Stephen Clarkson.

## Rouleau, Judge C.B.
If I really thought you were guilty, I would give you ten years.

Dispensing a two-year sentence to a Chinese, 1900. The Saskatchewan town of Rouleau is named after the Edmonton judge and member of the North-West Territories Council.

## Rousseau, Jean-Jacques
The first European penetrating the communities of uncivilized peoples ought to be hung at the frontier. . . .

Declaration of the French writer in 1753, quoted by George F.G. Stanley in *New France: The Last Phase 1744-1760* (1968).

The savages of northern America have governed themselves in this way to our day, and they are very well governed.

*The Social Contract* (1762), Book III.

## Roussel, Timothée
Maison du Chien d'Or

"In 1688 he had a stone house built in Buade street, later called 'Maison du Chien d'Or' ('House of the Golden Dog') because of an inscription that he caused to be placed on it." Roussel was a surgeon in Quebec. Quoted by Gabriel Nadeau, "Timothée Roussel," *Dictionary of Canadian Biography: Volume I: 1000-1700* (1965). See also William Kirby.

## Roussopoulos, Dimitri
There is no young person in Quebec who considers himself a militant or an activist in any sense who is not an independentist and a socialist. It is like putting on our coat in the morning.

"The Quiet Revolution Now," *This Magazine is about Schools*, Spring, 1970.

## Routhier, Sir Adolphe-Basile
O Canada! terre de nos aïeux,
Ton front est ceint de fleurons glorieux.
　Car ton bras sait porter l'épée,
　　Il sait porter la croix;
　Ton histoire est une épopée
　　Des plus brillants exploits;
　Et ta valeur, de foi trempée,
Protègera nos foyers et nos droits.

First of four verses of "Chant national," better known as "O Canada." The words were written by Sir Adolphe-Basile Routhier and set to music by Calixa Lavallée for the Fète Nationale des Canadiens-française in Quebec City on St. Jean-Baptiste Day, June 24, 1880. The Quebec City lawyer and versifier published the lyrics in a volume called *Les Echos* (1882), from which the verse above is taken. Calixa Lavallée's tune shares a few bars with "The March of the Priests" from Act II of *The Magic Flute*, which has led some listeners to conclude, falsely, that the tune was composed by Mozart.

　Here is a translation by William McLennan from *Songs of Old Canada* (1886): "O Canada! land of our sires, / Whose brow is bound with glorious bays, / The sword thy valorous hand can wield / And bear the Cross that faith inspires, / What mighty deeds hast thou beheld, / An epogee of glorious sights! / The faith, thy shield through all thy days, / Shall still protect our homes and rights, / Shall still protect our homes and rights." (The final line is usually repeated.)

　In 1967, Parliament recognized the melody and the French lyrics of "O Canada" and proclaimed them the national anthem. For the official English lyrics, see R. Stanley Weir. For "The Maple Leaf Forever," see Alexander Muir. For "God Save the King," see Anonymous: Songs.

## Rovere, Richard H.
What would happen in Canada if full sovereignty were invoked and the southern border were sealed tight against American mass culture—if the airwaves were jammed, if all our comic books were embargoed, if only the purest and most uplifting of American cultural commodities were allowed entry? Native industries would take over obviously. Cut off from American junk, Canada would have to produce her own.

*Maclean's Magazine*, November 5, 1960.

## Rowell, N.W.
The last man who spoke to me as I left the Canadian front was the chauffeur, Bouillon, a French Canadian, and when he bade me good-bye he said: "When you go back to Canada will you tell the boys to come out and help us? Tell them not to be afraid. It is just like baseball, only instead of catching the ball you dodge the shells, and you soon get used to that."

"The War and Our Canadians at the Front," November 7, 1916, *Addresses Delivered before the Canadian Club of Montreal: Season of 1916-17* (1917).

Fifty thousand Canadian soldiers under the sod in Europe is the price Canada has paid for the European statesmanship which drenched the continent in blood. [League of Nations, Geneva, December 8, 1920]

National unity must be based on provincial autonomy, and provincial autonomy cannot be assured unless a strong feeling of national unity exists throughout Canada.

*Report of the Royal Commission on*

*Dominion - Provincial Relations* (1940), Book II, Section G. Commonly called The Rowell-Sirois Report.

**Rowse, A.L.**
I made friends with old Sir Robert Borden, the former Prime Minister of Canada, who came to give the Rhodes Lectures and stayed a couple of terms—charming old boy, very grave and deliberate of speech, with beautiful old-fashioned manners, spats and immensely crinkled, curly grey hair parted in the middle. When he went back to Canada he wrote me now and again, and sent me the poems of Archibald Lampman, which I failed to appreciate.

*All Souls, 1930s. A Cornishman at Oxford: The Education of a Cornishman (1965).*

**Roxborough, Henry**
Sport is one area where no participant is worried about another's race, religion or wealth; and where the only concern is "Have you come to play?"

*One Hundred—Not Out: The Story of Nineteenth Century Canadian Sport (1966).*

**Roy, Gabrielle**
Then Manitoba seemed to her to grow bored. So vast, so little bestrewn with names, almost entirely given over to these wise, naked stretches which represented lakes and uninhabited space! Emptier and emptier, bare paper without a printed word, the further you went into the North. It seemed that all the place-names had clustered together on this map as though to warm each other, that they had all crowded together in the same corner of the South.

*Where Nests the Water Hen (1951), translated by Harry Binsse.*

It's futile to say which is the most important, the man of action who fights for the rights of his brother, or the poet, the bird that sings at dusk between the bars of the prison. Who is to say who is the most precious of the two to the prisoner . . . ?

Interviewed by Donald Cameron in *Conversations with Canadian Novelists (1973).*

**Rubinoff, Lionel**
May heaven protect us, then, from intellectuals in search of their Canadian identity and from philosophers of history in search of Canadian destiny.

"National Purpose and Ideology" from Andy Wainwright's *Notes for a Native Land: A New Encounter with Canada* (1968).

It is only . . . through the imaginative transcendence of evil that the future of mankind can be secured.

*The Pornography of Power* (1968).

**Rumilly, Robert**
"Patronage!" The udder of democracy!

*History of Saint-Laurent* (1970), translated by Cameron Nish.

**Rupert, Prince**
Pro Pelle Cutem

"Skin for the Sake of the Fleece," motto on the coat-of-arms of the Hudson's Bay Company, granted by letters patent May 2, 1670. For the official title of the H.B.C., see Charles II.

**Rush, Ian C.**
The rubber business is highly volatile. It bounces around.

President of Polymer, explaining why his firm had just fired three hundred employees. CBC-TV's "Weekend," 1971.

**Rush, Richard**
And it [Canada] agrees, that all other armed vessels on these lakes shall be forthwith dismantled, and that no other vessels of war shall be there built or armed.

Historic "arms-limitation" clause (which reduced the number of naval vessels on Lake Champlain and the Great Lakes to a total of eight). The Rush-Bagot Agreement, 1817, between Great Britain and the United States, Washington, April 28-9, 1817. Richard Rush was acting secretary of State. See also Charles Bagot.

## Rushton, Kaleb

Three days passed and the lamps gave
 out,
And Kaleb Rushton he up and said,
"There's no more water nor light nor
 bread,
So we'll live on songs and hope instead.
We'll live on songs and hope instead."

> From the ballad "The Springhill Min-
> ing Disaster" by Ewan MacColl and
> Peggy Seeger. Kaleb Rushton was a sur-
> vivor of the 1958 Nova Scotia cave-in.
> See also Ewan MacColl.

## Russell, Harold

It is not what you have lost but what you
have left that counts.

> Russell, who was born in Sydney, Nova
> Scotia, lost both hands in the Second
> World War. He played the role of a
> handicapped veteran in Cecil B. De
> Mille's *The Best Years of Our Lives*
> (1945) which earned him two Oscars—for
> best supporting actor and a special
> award for bringing hope and courage to
> his fellow veterans. The only person ever
> to receive two Oscars for the same role,
> he retired from acting and entered
> public relations. In 1949, he published
> his biography, *Victory in My Hands*.

## Russell, Robert B.

We must establish the same form of
government as they have it in Russia
so that we may have a Russian democracy here. The only way to prevent the
coming revolution in Canada is for the
government to establish a form of government such as the Bolsheviks have
established in Russia and are now establishing in Germany.

> Address to workers at the Walker
> Theatre in Winnipeg, December 22,
> 1918. Russell later helped lead the Win-
> nipeg general strike of 1919. *The Winni-
> peg Citizen*, June 11, 1919.

## Rutherford, Ann

I was Polly Benedict, Andy Hardy's girl
friend, the girl next door, and to have
taken a drink in public would have let
down all the girls who wrote to me.

\*

I knew I was a certain type who sold a

certain number of tickets.

\*

And all I wanted was for it not to end
until I was ready to have it end.

> Born in Toronto in 1920 and raised in
> California, Ann Rutherford appeared
> opposite Mickey Rooney in *Love Finds
> Andy Hardy* (1938) and retired from the
> screen ten years later.

## Rutherford, Ernest

There is a saying that "it is the first step
that counts," and it is clear that to
McGill belongs whatever credit is due
for the early ideas and experiments
which opened up the way into the unknown.

> Rutherford was professor of Physics at
> McGill University from 1898 to 1907,
> where he did work in radioactivity that
> led to his receiving the Nobel Prize for
> Chemistry the following year. Quoted by
> Rollo O. Earl in "Science," *The Culture
> of Contemporary Canada* (1957), edited
> by Julian Park.

## Ryan, Claude

Tomorrow, as today, Montreal will be
only 350 miles from Toronto. Thus we
will have French and English existing
side by side, exchanging goods, services
and ideas, depending on each other in
many ways.

> "Claude Ryan's Answer," *Maclean's
> Magazine*, May, 1971.

## Ryan, "Red"

I'm through. Besides. I would rather do
anything than break the trust placed in
me by my kind chaplain, Dr. Kingsley.
My great ambition is to prove to my
relatives and friends that I'm a changed
man.

> Norman "Red" Ryan, the notorious
> bank-robber, explaining why he was
> being a model prisoner, shortly before
> his parole. Once out of prison, he re-
> turned to a life of crime. Quoted by Roy
> Greenaway in *The News Game* (1966).

You've got me, boys. I've had enough.

> Ryan's dying whisper after a gunbattle
> with the Sarnia police, May 23, 1936.

Quoted by Harold Dingman, *The Globe*, May 25, 1936.

**Ryder, Gus**
I would like to repeat the last-minute message I gave to Marilyn Bell at Youngstown before she started her great swim.

"Kneel and ask the Greatest Coach and Instructor for divine guidance and strength to make this voyage, and in our boat waiting for you we will do the same."

*

Come on, Marilyn—that's the girl. Remember the little crippled kids at the Lakeshore. They're all cheering for you!

> Quoted by Ron McAllister in *Swim to Glory: The Story of Marilyn Bell and the Lakeshore Swimming Club* (1954).

IF YOU QUIT, I QUIT / DON'T LET THE CRIPPLED KIDS DOWN

> Two messages chalked on a small blackboard by Gus Ryder, Marilyn Bell's trainer, and held up for the sixteen-year-old swimmer to read during the last stretch of her marathon swim across Lake Ontario, September 9, 1954. Quoted by June Callwood in "How Marilyn Swam the Lake" in *Maclean's Canada: Portrait of a Country* (1960), edited by Leslie F. Hannon. See also Marilyn Bell.

**Ryerson, Egerton**
The diffusion of Christianity is the most important subject that can engage the attentions of men.

> "The first sentence of Ryerson's to appear in print," in 1826, according to Robin S. Harris who quotes it in *Our Living Tradition: Second and Third Series* (1959), edited by Robert L. McDougall.

At eight o'clock today, Thursday, 12th April, Lount and Mathews were executed. The general feeling is in total opposition to the execution of those men. Sheriff Jarvis burst into tears when he entered the room to prepare them for execution. They said to him very calmly, "Mr. Jarvis, do your duty; we are pre-pared to meet death and our Judge." They then, both of them, put their arms around his neck and kissed him. They were then prepared for execution. They walked to the gallows with entire composure and firmness of step. Rev. J. Richardson walked alongside of Lount, and Dr. Beatty alongside of Mathews. They ascended the scaffold and knelt down on the drop. The ropes were adjusted while they were on their knees. Mr. Richardson engaged in prayer; and when he came to that part of the Lord's Prayer, "Forgive us our trespasses, as we forgive those that trespass against us," the drop fell!

> Convicted of treason, Samuel Lount and Peter Mathews were hanged on April 12, 1838, for taking part in the Rebellion of 1837. *The Story of My Life* (1883).

On the importance of education generally we may remark, it is as necessary as the light—it should be as common as water, and as free as air. . . . Education among the people is the best security of a good government and constitutional liberty, it yields a steady, unbending support to the former, and effectually protects the latter. An educated people are always a loyal people to good government; and the first object of a wise government should be the education of the people. . . . Partial knowledge is better than total ignorance; and he who cannot get all he may wish, must take heed to acquire all he can. If total ignorance be a bad and dangerous thing, every degree of knowledge lessens both the evil and the danger.

> An early editorial from the *Christian Guardian*, founded by Egerton Ryerson in 1829, quoted by Peter Sandiford in "Canadian Education: Past and Present," *Handbook of Canada: Issued by the Local Committee on the Occasion of the Meeting of the British Association for the Advancement of Science at Toronto, August, 1924* (1924).

One topic more and I have done. Society contains not the whole of man. Human societies die; man never dies. Man has a higher destiny than that of states.

"A Lecture on the Social Advancement of Canada," *Journal of Education for Upper Canada*, December, 1849.

The political destiny of our country seems to be involved in utter uncertainty and impenetrable obscurity.

Letter to Sophie Ryerson, May 28, 1865,

*My Dearest Sophie* (1955), edited by C.B. Sissons.

How mysterious are the ways of Providence—how dark, crooked, and perverse the ways of man.

*The Story of My Life* (1883), edited by J.G. Hodgins.

# S

**Sabia, Laura**
If men could get pregnant, abortion would be a sacrament.

Remark made in 1971 by the head of the National Action Committee on the Status of Women. (The quip may have originated with the American liberationist, Florynce Kennedy.)

**Sackville-West, Vita**
Niagara is really some waterfall! It falls over like a great noisy beard made of cotton-wool, veiled by spray and spanned by rainbows. The rainbows are the most unexpected part of it. They stand across like bridges between America and Canada, and are reproduced in sections among the boiling foam. The spray rises to the height of a sky-scraper, shot by sudden iridescence high up in the air. There is a strange and impressive alliance between the works of God and the works of man: factory-chimneys line the cliff; great pylons stretch away across the country. It was a sunny day, and only remnants of snow lay about. But there were grand icicles on the cliffs.

I think it is very good for you and me to have come to America. I am glad we did. I am getting a lot out of it. There may be moments when we are tired and nauseated and bored. But on the whole it is infinitely valuable.

Letter written from Niagara Falls, January 31, 1933, to Harold Nicolson in Stockbridge, Massachusetts; Nicolson's *Diaries and Letters 1930-1939* (1966), edited by Nigel Nicolson. For the polar opposite reaction, see Sir Harold Nicolson.

**Safarian, A.E.**
The greatest cost of chauvinism, here as elsewhere, is the inability to see one's own interests.

"Foreign Ownership and Control of the Canadian Economy," *The Prospect of Change: Proposals for Canada's Future* (1965), edited by Abraham Rotstein.

**Safdie, Moshe**
Habitat is in the tradition of spontaneous self-made environments, the beginnings of a contemporary vernacular.

*Beyond Habitat* (1970), edited by John Kettle. The Israeli-born Montreal architect designed Expo 67's Habitat.

**Sagard-Théodat, Gabriel**
I had hoped to promote a peace between the Hurons and the Iroquois so that Christianity could be spread among them and to open the road to trade with many nations who were not accessible, but some members of the Company advised me that it was not expedient since

if the Hurons were at peace with the Iroquois, the same Iroquois would lead the Hurons to trade with the Dutch and divert them from Quebec which is more distant.

> Le grand voyage du pays des Hurons (1632). The Recollet missionary's account was translated by H.H. Langton as *The Long Journey to the Country of the Hurons* (1939).

It is difficult, almost impossible, for all the French still unused to this Indian country to make long trips and *courir les bois et forests*.

> The italicized phrase means "to get about in the woods and forests" and first appeared in the missionary's *Histoire du Canada* (1636). According to R.M. Saunders in "Coureur de Bois: A Definition," *Canadian Historical Review*, June, 1940, this is the first use in print of the phrase that later became *coureur-de-bois*.

### Sahl, Mort
My whole life is a movie. It's just that there are no dissolves. I have to live every agonizing moment of it. My life needs editing.

*

Nationalist: Do you realize that this country hasn't even got a flag?
Comedian: That's a start.

> Exchange in Toronto in 1961. The nightclub satirist was born Morton Lyon Sahl in Montreal in 1927. See also Nicolai Zabotin.

### St. Brendan   See Brendan the Apostle.

### St. Denis, Michel
I don't find it horrible enough.

> Anglo-French theatre director criticizing a student production at the Dominion Drama Festival in 1937. Quoted by Betty Lee in *Love and Whisky: The Story of the Dominion Drama Festival* (1973).

### Saint-Exupéry, Antoine de
Terre des Hommes.

> Although he died in a plane crash in 1945, the French aviator-author pro-

vided Expo 67's theme: "Terre des Hommes/Man and his World."

> Saint-Exupéry published a book of lyrical reflections *Terre des Hommes* in 1939, which included the following passage: "To be a man is to feel that through one's own contribution, one helps to build the world." The book was translated into English and published later that year as *Wind, Sand and Stars*.

### St. Laurent, Jeanne
I am a wife and mother and happy in my career.

> Frequent remark of the wife of Louis St. Laurent who was prime minister from 1948 to 1957.

### St. Laurent, Louis
I didn't know at first that there were two languages in Canada. I just thought that there was one way to speak to my father and another to talk to my mother.

I cannot see him. We are maintaining friendly diplomatic relations with the Russian Embassy. I cannot take any part in a quarrel between an employee in the Embassy and his employers. After all, this might become a rather serious international incident.

> St. Laurent was minister of Justice when Igor Gouzenko waited in his office with proof that a Soviet espionage network was operating in Canada. St. Laurent explained to his secretary he would be unable to meet with Gouzenko, September 6, 1945. Quoted by Frank Rasky in *Gay Canadian Rogues: Swindlers, Gold-diggers and Spies* (1958).

A small power is in a sense by its very smallness relieved from much of the responsibility which participation in decisions involves, and which the implementation of such decisions requires. At the other extreme the great powers can protect their positions with the veto. A "middle power" such as Canada, however, is in a different position. Its economic strength and political influence are of importance, and its prestige is high. The material and moral contribution which Canada can make to collective action, as the last two wars have shown, is significant.

> House of Commons, April 29, 1948. This is an early use of the phrase "middle power" to rank Canada's world influence, made by the secretary of State in connection with Canada's seat on the Security Council of the United Nations.

Without sacrificing the universality of the United Nations, it is possible for the free nations of the world to form their own closer association for collective self-defence under article 51 of the charter of the United Nations . . . the formation of such a defensive group of free states would not be a counsel of despair but a message of hope.

> House of Commons, April 29, 1948. The secretary of State's speech led to the formation of the North Atlantic Treaty Organization (NATO).

Socialists are Liberals in a hurry.

> "In Saskatchewan, where the CCF Party was in power, he commented good-naturedly that most of the supporters of the Socialist government were merely 'Liberals in a hurry.'" Dale C. Thomson in *Louis St. Laurent: Canadian* (1967). Thomson gives as his source for the birth of this delightful adage the coverage of the speech by *The Montreal Gazette*, April 25, 1949. Prime Minister St. Laurent must not be given full credit: the phrase "Liberals in a hurry" was applied to those Progressives and Liberal-Progressives in the House of Commons who joined the Liberal party in 1926.

"Uncle Louis is going to be hard to beat."

> Campaigning in the West in 1949, a conservative paper published a description of the new Liberal leader as "Uncle Louis." "The nickname stuck, and St. Laurent had found his feet," explained Dale C. Thomson in *Louis St. Laurent: Canadian* (1967).

Well, we will do what we consider to be our duty, and the Canadian people can decide if they want to follow us.

> CBC Radio talk, September 4, 1951, quoted by Dale C. Thomson in *Louis St. Laurent: Canadian* (1967).

It has been said that Great Britain acquired her Empire in a state of absence of mind. Apparently we have administered these vast territories of the North in an almost continuing absence of mind.

> House of Commons, December 8, 1953, on second reading of the bill to establish the Department of Northern Affairs and National Resources.

They have just got tired of seeing us around.

> This is how St. Laurent explained the Liberal defeat to Milton Gregg, his defeated Labour minister, June 10, 1957. Quoted by Dale C. Thomson in *Louis St. Laurent: Canadian* (1967).

Get defeated in an election!

> When asked the secret of his good spirits and robust health in his seventy-ninth year, the former prime minister gave the above answer, as noted by *The Montreal Star*, January 31, 1962. Quoted by Dale C. Thomson in *Louis St. Laurent: Canadian* (1967).

### St. Laurent, Madame de
My memory will always recall Quebec and Beauport, and a friendship which has triumphed over twenty years of absence. . . .

> Letter of Julie de Montgenet, Madame de St. Laurent, to Major Louis Ignace de Salaberry, November 3, 1814. For the genesis of this great Canadian romance, see Edward Augustus, Duke of Kent.

### St. Pierre, Paul
Canadian politics in British Columbia is an adventure, on the prairies a cause, in Ontario a business, in Quebec a religion, in the Maritimes a disease.

> St. Pierre, a writer, was the Liberal M.P. for Coast Chilcotin from 1968 to 1972.

### Sainte-Marie, Buffy
I'm just a mouthpiece . . . I'm a visible Indian. People know me and my works,

which lets me draw attention to what's going on.

\*

What kid wants to be told in school that his grandfather was a savage.

\*

It has been the aim of the government from the beginning to annihilate Indians. Instead of the War Department now, we have the Department of Indian Affairs, whose job it is to assimilate Indians.

> Quoted by Melinda McCracken in *The Globe and Mail*, March 16, 1970. The singer was born on the Piapot Reserve, Craven, Saskatchewan, in 1941.

## Sala, George Augustus
"If we may accept the authority of George Augustus Sala, this is the longest street in the world."

> The English journalist was referring to Yonge Street in Toronto. Reported by Charles G.D. Roberts in *The Canadian Guide-Book: Appletons' Guide* (1895).

## Sales, Sammy
I love show business and the theatre. I just wish I could afford it.

> Quoted by Morris Duff in *The Toronto Star*, October 31, 1959.

## Salinger, Pierre
Just you wait and see, they won't fight to protect Canada.

> President Kennedy's press secretary wagged his finger at U.S. draft-dodgers and draft-evaders who sought sanctuary in Canada during the late 1960s. Salinger's childhood was spent in Toronto.

## Salsberg, J.B.
Some of you may have been led to believe that Fifth Avenue, Piccadilly, the Champs Elysées are important. I suppose they have their place; but there is no comparison, none of them can compare with this broad, throbbing, full-of-life thoroughfare known as Spadina Avenue, the heart of my constituency.

> Polish-born Labour Progressive M.P., Ontario Legislature, April 4, 1951, "St.

Andrew: A Portrait," *New Frontiers*, Summer, 1955.

If the only way to socialism is over the mountains of dead including my own comrades then I do not want that kind of socialism.

> Address to the Central Committee of the Communist Party of Canada in 1956, setting forth the reasons for severing his long-term connections with the party.

We just couldn't believe that these men who were building the brave new world could be responsible for the purges, the trials, and executions. . . .

> One-time Communist member of the Ontario Legislature, explaining why he broke with the party over the issue of Jewish repression. Quoted by Philip Sykes in *The Toronto Star*, November 10, 1972.

## Saltatha
To the man who is not a lover of Nature in all her moods the Barren Ground must always be a howling, desolate wilderness; but for my part, I can understand the feeling that prompted Saltatha's answer to the worthy priest, who was explaining to him the beauties of Heaven. "My father, you have spoken well; you have told me that Heaven is very beautiful; tell me now one thing more. Is it more beautiful than the country of the musk-ox in summer, when sometimes the mist blows over the lakes, and sometimes the water is blue, and the loons cry very often? That is beautiful; and if Heaven is still more beautiful, my heart will be glad, and I shall be content to rest there till I am very old."

> Attributed to Saltatha, a brave of the Yellowknife tribe and companion of Warburton Pike who quotes the speech in *The Barren Ground of Northern Canada* (1892). See also the Dogrib Indian quoted by P.G. Downes.

## Saltzman, Harry
We created a form of modern mythology. James Bond is the Supreme legend in modern times. Every man would like to be a superman, and every woman

would like to be possessed by one. Bond is their idea of Superman.

> Quoted by Pearl Sheffy in *The Toronto Star*, October 9, 1965. The London-based film producer, a native of eastern Canada, is talking about the James Bond films, which he produces with Albert Broccoli, the son of the American who named the vegetable.

## Samuel, Sigmund
For more than twenty years, I have not kept a penny from the business for myself. It has all been returned to the community. A man must show his gratitude if he can.

> *In Return: The Autobiography of Sigmund Samuel* (1963), by the metal magnate and philanthropist.

## Sandburg, Carl
If two Canadians understand snow
they are then both Canadians.
If one Canadian understands snow
and another doesn't understand
snow at all, then one is a Canadian
and the other is no Canadian at all.

> From "Canadians and Pottawatomies" (1928), *Complete Poems* (1950).

## Sandiford, Peter
The reform of society will come, not through the indoctrination of the young, but from the intellectual conversion and convictions of the adult.

> Observation made in 1935 and quoted by J.R. Kidd in "Present Developments and Trends" in his *Adult Education in Canada* (1950).

## Sandwell, B.K.
There is no land—I say this is true of any land upon the surface of the earth—there is no land, that will support life, that the race which inhabits it will not in due time come to love.

> *

*The London Times* in a recent review of the latest book of Mr. George Moore remarked that it was perhaps the best example yet extant, not of English writing, but of Irish writing—of the Irish language; that Mr. Moore, while he was

using English words, was undoubtedly writing in an Irish language. And I can see no reason why we in Canada, when we have developed a style of our own, should not describe ourselves as using an English vocabulary, but a Canadian language.

> "Canadian Literature," March 13, 1920, *The Canadian Club Year Book: 1919-20* (1920).

I remember a Toronto in which the admirably true phrase — the twentieth century was to be Canada's—was accepted as the general watchword; only nobody had begun to realize what a rotten century the twentieth was going to be.

> "On Being Sorry for Ourselves," *Empire Club of Canada: Addresses Delivered to the Members During the Year 1924* (1924).

A poem about the drains or the abattoirs in Montreal is in no wise different from a poem about the drains or the abattoirs in Chicago. But the Canadian woods are different from anybody else's woods, and the Canadian woods poetry was different. Back to the woods, ye Muse of Canada—back to the woods! ["The Deforestation of Canadian Poetry"]

> *

Privacy will be, obviously, the opposite of Publicity. ["The Privacy Agent"]

> *

The twentieth century is the bathroom's century. True, the bathroom shares that century with the Dominion of Canada; but now that we have experienced nearly thirty years out of the hundred, I feel that Canada can well afford to let the bathroom have what is left. . . . Let us say, then, that the twentieth century is the century of Canada and of the bathroom. ["I Sing the Bathroom"]

> *The Privacy Agent and Other Modest Proposals* (1928).

If Canada does not often produce great artists, scientists, and professional men, it is not because the material is not amongst us, but because we do not know how to handle it. The characteristics of genius too often arouse our suspicion and distrust, whence it comes that our prophets are so often without honour in their own country. Perhaps if Canada had been a little different, Norman Bethune would not have died in China.

*Saturday Night,* December, 1939.

Let the Old World, where rank's yet
vital,
Part those who have and have not title.
Toronto has no social classes—
Only the Masseys and the masses.

"On the Appointment of Governor-General Vincent Massey, 1952," F.R. Scott and A.J.M. Smith's *The Blasted Pine: An Anthology of Satire, Invective and Disrespectful Verse Chiefly by Canadian Writers* (1957).

Yet the beaver was in its day the most notable, the most respected, of all Canadian fauna. Like the Canada Goose, it has a scientific name which clearly recognizes its association with this northern land. But it is even more Canadian than the Canada Goose, in that it was for many generations accepted as the symbolic animal of the nation. It was to Canada what the bulldog is to England and the eagle is to the United States. It got into heraldry, where it associates with such gorgeous creatures as the unicorn, the phoenix, and the martlet or bird-with-no-feet which roots in the coat-of-arms of McGill University. ["Alas, the Beaver is Obsolete!"]

*The Diversions of Duchesstown and Other Essays* (1955).

I am what librarians have made me with a little assistance from a professor of Greek and a few poets.

Quoted by J.R. Kidd in *Learning and Society* (1963). Sandwell was the influential editor of *Saturday Night* from 1932 to 1951.

## Sangster, Charles

One voice, one people, one in heart
And soul, and feeling, and desire!
Re-light the smouldering martial fire,
Sound the mute trumpet, strike the
lyre,

The hero deed can not expire,
The dead still play their part.

*

Some souls are the Hesperides
Heaven sends to guard the golden
age,
Illuming the historic page
With records of their pilgrimage;
True Martyr, Hero, Poet, Sage:
He was one of these.

Two verses from "Brock," *Hesperus, and Other Poems and Lyrics* (1860). Sangster's ode to the hero of the War of 1812 was widely read in its day.

When they get a man into the Civil Service, their first duty is to crush him flat, and if he is a fool or a poet, or dares to think of any nonsense of that kind, draw him through a knot or a gimlet hole a few times, pile on the agony of toil, toil until his nerves are flattened out, all the rebound knocked out of him, and then—superannuate him on what he can squeeze out of them through friends or enemies, and tell him he should be thankful for small favours of the most microscopic pattern.

Letter to William Douw Lighthall, November 15, 1888, quoted by Desmond Pacey in *Ten Canadian Poets: A Group of Biographical and Critical Essays* (1958).

## Santos, Lucia dos
Poor Canada!

An apparition of the Blessed Virgin Mary appeared to three shepherd children from the town of Fátima in central Portugal. They said they saw the figure of a lady brighter than the sun, standing on a cloud in an evergreen tree, a total of six times, from May 13 to October 13, 1917. The last vision was of the sun which appeared to stop and then to dance. The site of the visitation is now marked by the Basilica of Our Lady of Fátima.

Within two years of the event, two of the girls were dead, but the third, Lucia dos Santos, who became a Carmelite nun, at various times has disclosed further messages that were revealed to her in 1917. Some Catholics in Quebec believe that at least one of the prophecies concerns Canada. As Jacques Godbout wrote in "Five Civilizations" in *The Toronto Star*, December 30, 1972:

> " 'Poor Canada!' said the Virgin Mary in Portuguese to the children of Fátima, who didn't know how to read or write, who didn't even know geography, and had not yet been introduced to television.
>
> " 'Poor Canada!' said the apparition; and the parish priest of Fátima repeated it to the bishop, who mentioned it to the archbishop, who confided the phrase to the papal nuncio, who reported it to the Pope, who much later said a few words about it to Cardinal Léger, then pastor of Montreal, and when, in their turn, the whole French-Canadian population heard about it, they fell on their knees in order to save the country."

**Sapir, Edward**
Thus, it must be conjectured that lipstick is less secure in American culture as an element of fashion than rouge discretely applied to the cheek.

> The German-born anthropologist was associated with the National Museum in Ottawa from 1910 to 1925, and was succeeded by Diamond Jenness. "Fashion" (1931), *Selected Writings of Edward Sapir in Language, Culture and Personality* (1949), edited by David G. Mandelbaum.

**Sarah Binks**   See Paul Hiebert.

**Saroyan, William**
Whatever happened to Morley Callaghan?

> To a Canadian World War Two correspondent, quoted by Barbara Moon in "The Second Coming of Morley Callaghan," *Maclean's Magazine*, December 3, 1960.

**Sarrazin, Michael**
If you've gone through public school and had boring Canadian history shoved at you, you'd realize that nothing really interesting has ever gone on in Canada. When I found out that John A. Macdonald was a juicer I thought that was

terrific. So what else is there? Nelson Eddy, Jeanette MacDonald and Laura Secord running through the woods. Trudeau? Oh God, I'd never want to play Trudeau. I hope I never get that bald.

> Quoted by Betty Lee in *The Globe and Mail*, December 5, 1970.

Although it's a huge environment, there's a community feeling in Canada. I'm always uptight in places like New York and Los Angeles, but I come back to Toronto and there are still people who say please, and thank you, and how are you.

> Quoted by Eve Rockett in *Chatelaine*, June, 1972.

**Sartre, Jean-Paul**
The barman smiled.
"In the reign of Louis-the-Well-Beloved, sir, France had already committed every fault there was to commit."
"Ah," said Gomez: "You're a Canadian."
"I'm from Montreal," said the barman.
Gomez laid the paper down on the counter. After a brief pause he said:
"Don't you ever get any French in here?"

> *Iron in the Soul* (1950), translated by Gerald Hopkins.

And then all round Paris lies France, furrowed with one-way roads, and then the seas dyed blue or black, the Mediterranean blue, the North Sea black, the Channel coffee-coloured, and then the foreign lands, Germany, Italy — Spain white, because I did not go and fight there—and all the round cities, at fixed distances from my room, Timbuctoo, Toronto, Kazan, Nijni-Novgorod, immutable as frontier points.

> *The Age of Reason* (1945).

There's no question of your obtaining socialist independence gradually in Quebec. So it must of course be through violence. I do not say this light-heartedly, it is the same everywhere.

> Videotape interview shown in Montreal, January 16, 1971. Quoted by Gérard

Pelletier in *The October Crisis* (1971), translated by Joyce Marshall.

## Saunders, A.C.
In this province by the sea there is neither great wealth nor poverty, but rather a happy contentment which pervades the homes of the highest and lowest.

Premier of Prince Edward Island. *The Book of Canada: Published by the Canadian Medical Association* (1930), edited by Chester Martin, W. Stewart Wallace, and T.C. Routley.

## Saunders, Sir Charles E.
Marquis is still King, and it looks as if, when the day comes for Marquis to step out, it is likely to be one of his descendants who will be crowned.

Address to the Royal Canadian Institute, Toronto, November, 1929, by the Dominion cerealist who, in 1903, developed Marquis wheat, a famous strain of hard, fast-ripening wheat. Sir Charles developed the strain but always claimed that it was made by "God Almighty." See also his father, William Saunders.

## Saunders, Marshall
My name is Beautiful Joe, and I am a brown dog of medium size. I am not called Beautiful Joe because I am a beauty . . . I know that I am not beautiful, and I know that I am not a thoroughbred. I am only a cur.

*

You may depend upon it, a four-legged creature, unlike a two-legged one, has a reason for everything he does.

*Beautiful Joe: An Autobiography* (1894), a phenomenally successful first-person animal story for children. "Beautiful Joe died at Meaford, Ontario, September 13th, 1899, in the 18th year of his age." Henry James Morgan in *Types of Canadian Women and of Women Who Are or Have Been Connected with Canada* (1903).

## Saunders, Robert
I trust the young lady will run for office against me. She has beauty, brains and is a wonderful speaker. It is a combination I could not beat.

The mayor of Toronto at a civic reception accorded Barbara Ann Scott in 1948 when she returned from Switzerland where she had won the women's figure-skating championship. Quoted by Henry Roxborough in *Great Days in Canadian Sport* (1957). See also Barbara Ann Scott.

## Saunders, William
*Marquis:* This wheat is a selected superior strain of the variety formerly grown at the Farm under the name Markham—Hard Red Calcutta (female) X Red Fife (Male). Kernels rather dark red, hard, and about medium size, rather short. Heads of medium length, beardless, pointed. Chaff, yellowish and smooth. Straw, stiff and of medium or rather below medium length. Ripens a few days before Red Fife. Produces very strong flour of good colour.

William Saunders was the first Dominion cerealist in Ottawa. He arranged for his son Sir Charles E. Saunders to carry on his work, and the father watched the son develop the famous Marquis strain in 1903. "Annual Report for 1906," quoted by Elsie M. Pomeroy in *William Saunders and His Five Sons: The Story of the Marquis Wheat Family* (1956). See also Sir Charles E. Saunders.

## Scammell, A.R.
Oh! this is the place where the fishermen gather,
In oil skins and boots and Cape Anns battened down;
All sizes of figures with squid lines and jiggers,
They congregate here on the squid-jiggin' ground.

First verse of the famous Newfoundland air "The Squid-Jiggin' Ground," written in 1944 and published in *My Newfoundland* (1966).

## Schafer, R. Murray
Someone once said that the two most important things in developing taste were sensitivity and intelligence. I don't think this is so; I'd rather call them

curiosity and courage. Curiosity to look for the new and the hidden; courage to develop your own tastes regardless of what others may say or think.

> The Composer in the Classroom (1965).

Before ear training it should be recognized that we require ear cleaning.

＊

Noise is any sound signal which interferes. Noise is the destroyer of things we want to hear.

＊

Silence is a pocket of possibility. Anything can happen to break it.

＊

Rhythm says: "I am here and I want to go there."

> Ear Cleaning: Notes for an Experimental Music Course (1967).

Question: What is your favourite form of music?

Answer: Music that speaks directly; music that is created perilously; music created by composers who risk everything; dangerous music. "For beauty is nothing but the beginning of terror." (Rilke)

> Composer interviewed by Musicanada, October, 1968.

Today all sounds belong to a continuous field of possibilities lying within the comprehensive dominion of music.

＊

Behold the new orchestra: the sonic universe!

> The New Soundscape: A Handbook for the Modern Music Teacher (1969).

"Poetry is when words sing"—six-year-old boy.

＊

Language is sound as sense. Music is sound as sound.

> ... When Words Sing (1970).

### Schendel, Michael van
Quebec has been the name of a sickness.

> Quoted by Malcolm Reid in The Shouting Signpainters: A Literary and Political Account of Quebec Revolutionary Nationalism (1972).

### Schreyer, Edward
I don't for a moment accept, on general principles, that a free-enterprise press is unalterably opposed to any NDP government, but if you want to get down to certain specifics I suppose I could make a bloody good argument to support the theory.

> Premier of Manitoba quoted by John Fraser in The Globe and Mail, April 24, 1973.

### Schultz, John Christian
I got . . . the Rope which bound poor Scott's hands when he was shot. I send it by express. Use it at Indignation meeting and then present to the Master of Orange Lodge.

> Schultz and Thomas Scott were made prisoners of Louis Riel at Fort Garry in 1869. Schultz made good his escape, but Scott was executed. Letter to Colonel George Taylor Denison, July 20, 1870, quoted by Carl Berger in The Sense of Power: Studies in the Ideas of Canadian Imperialism: 1867-1914 (1970).

### Scott, Barbara Ann
Well! I guess I better start right away to become the hardy, outdoor type.

> The Ottawa skater's reply to an expert who predicted she would lose the Olympic gold medal in 1948 because the tournament was held outdoors, whereas she had won the European women's figure-skating title on indoor ice. Quoted by Henry Roxborough in Great Days in Canadian Sports (1957).

When I was in Europe, my listings read: "Scott, Canada." I had thought of myself less as an individual than as a representative of my country.

＊

48-U-1

> Licence plate number of the cream-coloured Buick roadmaster presented to Miss Scott by the City of Ottawa when she returned from winning an Olympic medal on February 6, 1948. Miss Scott called the rebus "a pun that I think is very sweet." (To protect her amateur status she was forced to return the gift, only to reclaim it a year later when she

turned pro.) *Skate with Me* (1950). In 1955, she married a Chicago publicist and became Mrs. Thomas Van Dyke King. See also Robert Saunders.

## Scott, Duncan Campbell

There was in Arll a little cove
Where the salt wind came cool and free:
A foamy beach that one would love,
If he were longing for the sea.

> First of forty stanzas of "The Piper of Arll," *Selected Poems of Duncan Campbell Scott* (1951), edited by E.K. Brown. The legend-like poem first appeared in the Christmas issue of a New York paper called *Truth*, December 14, 1895. It was read and memorized by a young worker in a carpet factory in Yonkers and the experience changed his life: John Masefield resolved to become a poet. Scott's "The Piper of Arll" first appeared in hard covers in *Labour and the Angel* (1898). See also John Masefield.

He had two girls,
One is Virginie;
What God calls the other,
Is not known to me.

> Final stanza of "At the Cedars," *Selected Poems of Duncan Campbell Scott* (1951), edited by E.K. Brown.

Revolt is essential to progress, not necessarily the revolt of violence, but always the revolt that questions the established past and puts it to the proof, that finds the old forms outworn and invents new forms for new matters.

＊

But let it pass,—modernity is not a fad, it is the feeling for actuality.

> "Poetry and Progress," Presidential address delivered before the Royal Society of Canada, May 17, 1922, *The Circle of Affection and Other Pieces in Prose and Verse* (1947).

I have long been quite satisfied not to be taken seriously as a poet. I don't seem to be able to gain the attention of important papers or reviews, but I am not grieving. Probably I would not be able to live up to popularity.

> Scott's death in Ottawa in 1947 was hardly noted. Quoted by E.K. Brown in

"Memoir," *Selected Poems of Duncan Campbell Scott* (1951), edited by E.K. Brown.

Let your soul grow a thing apart,
    Untroubled by the restless day,
Sublimed by some unconscious art,
    Controlled by some divine delay.

For life is greater than we think,
    Who fret along its shallow bars:
Swing out the boom to float or sink
    And front the ocean and the stars.

> "The Ideal," *Selected Poems of Duncan Campbell Scott* (1951), edited by E.K. Brown.

## Scott, Canon F.G.

Was it in vain that Buddha taught,
    Or that Mohammed lived and died?
    Have they not, working side by side
In differing climes, God's purpose
        wrought?
    ＊
Oh dream not the Almighty's powers
    Must ever work in one known way:
Nor think those planets have no day,
Whose suns are other suns than ours.

> From "Catholicism," *Justin and Other Poems* (1885).

I am getting old, but I am going to dedicate the rest of my life to fighting labour's battles.

> On June 8, 1919, when the Winnipeg general strike was at its height, Canon Scott was summoned back to Ottawa, but he made the strikers this promise. *Winnipeg 1919: The Strikers' Own History of the Winnipeg General Strike* (1973), edited by Norman Penner.

Never again but in dreams will one see the great battalions marching on the battle-ploughed roads of France and Flanders. Never again will one see them pouring single file into the muddy front trenches. All that is over.

> *The Great War as I Saw It* (1922), by the archdeacon of Quebec, senior chaplain during World War One, and father of F.R. Scott.

## Scott, F.R.

Only in times of peace can the wastes of capitalism be tolerated.

"The Efficiency of Socialism," *Queen's Quarterly*, Summer, 1935.

I used to say to my classes in constitutional law, "We have a *rendez-vous* with the BNA Act. It's going to come some day!"

"Address" (1964), *The Future of Canadian Federalism* (1965), edited by P.-A. Crépeau and C.B. Macpherson.

There are two miracles of Canadian history. The first is the survival of French Canada, and the second is the survival of Canada.

Remark made in 1952, quoted by Ramsay Cook in *Canada and the French-Canadian Question* (1966).

Till power is brought to pooling
And outcasts share in ruling
There will not be an ending
Nor any peace for spending.

From "Dedication" (1945). When the poem was first published in 1941 the second word in the second line was originally "masses," not "outcasts."

*

Who shall bend to single plan
The narrow sacrifice of man?
Find the central human urge
To make a thousand roads converge?

Final stanza of "Conflict" (1945).

*

Shall we go round the mulberry bush, or shall
We gather at the river, or shall we
Appoint a Poet Laureate this fall,
Or shall we have another cup of tea?

O Canada, O Canada, Oh can
A day go by without new authors springing
To plant the native maple, and to plan
More ways to set the selfsame welkin ringing?

Last two stanzas of "The Canadian Authors Meet" (1945).

*

The rain of the monsoon falls, an inescapable treasure,
Hundreds of millions live
Only because of the certainty of this season,
The turn of the wind.

*

Today, while Europe tilted, drying the Baltic,
I read of a battle between brothers in anguish,
A flag moved a mile.

*

We grow to one world
Through enlargement of wonder.

Lines from "A Grain of Rice" (1954).

*

The advantages of living with two cultures
Strike one at every turn,
Especially when one finds a notice in an office building:
"This elevator will not run on Ascension Day";
Or reads in the *Montreal Star*:
"Tomorrow being the Feast of the Immaculate Conception,
There will be no collection of garbage in the city";
Or sees on the restaurant menu the bilingual dish:

DEEP APPLE PIE

TARTE AUX POMMES PROFONDES

"Bonne Entente" (1954).

*

If you want to be righteous and rich
And to know you have God on your side
You won't find a cosier niche
Than Toronto can always provide.

From "Ode to Confederation," *The Eye of the Needle* (1957).

*

When Lalemant and de Brébeuf, brave souls,
Were dying by the slow and dreadful coals,
Their brother Jesuits in France and Spain
Were burning heretics with equal pain.
For both the human torture made a feast:
Then is priest savage, or Red Indian priest?

"Brébeuf and His Brethren" (1957). A reference to E.J. Pratt's long poem.

*

Where are the coolies in your poem, Ned?

First line of "All the Spikes but the Last," *The Eye of the Needle* (1957).

The reference is to E.J. Pratt who, in 1952, published the heroic epic *Towards the Last Spike*.

Onward the mighty waters flow,
But where, Oh where, is Charbonneau?

"Old Montreal Ballad," *The Eye of the Needle* (1957).

*

How shall we speak of Canada,
Mackenzie King dead?
The Mother's boy in the lonely room
With his dog, his medium and his ruins?

He blunted us.

We had no shape
Because he never took sides,
And no sides
Because he never allowed them to take
    shape.

He skilfully avoided what was wrong
Without saying what was right,
And never let his on the one hand
Know what his on the other hand was
    doing.

The height of his ambition
Was to pile a Parliamentary
    Commission on a Royal Commission,
To have "conscription if necessary
But not necessarily conscription,"
To let Parliament decide—
Later.

Postpone, postpone, abstain.

Only one thread was certain:
After World War I
Business as usual,
After World War II
Orderly decontrol.
Always he led us back to where we were
    before.

He seemed to be in the centre
Because we had no centre,
No vision
To pierce the smoke-screen of his
    politics.

Truly he will be remembered
Wherever men honour ingenuity,
Ambiguity, inactivity, and political
    longevity.

Let us raise up a temple
To the cult of mediocrity,

Do nothing by halves
Which can be done by quarters.

"W.L.M.K." (1957). "Dedicated to the end (we hope) of an era."—Author's note, *The Eye of the Needle* (1957).

*

I went to bat for the Lady Chatte
Dressed in my bib and gown.
The judges three glared down at me
The priests patrolled the town.

First stanza of "A Lass in Wonderland" (1964). In 1959, the author—a member of the faculty of law of McGill University—successfully defended D.H. Lawrence's novel *Lady Chatterley's Lover* against a charge of obscenity laid in Quebec, after the three judges of the Quebec Court of Appeal had condemned the book.

*

I looked the sun straight in the eye.
He put on dark glasses.

"Eclipse" (1964).

*

Let us give new names
To the stars.
What does Venus mean
Or Mars?

From "New Names" (1964).

*

The world is my country
The human race is my race
The spirit of man is my God
The future of man is my heaven

"Creed" (1964). The texts of all poems, unless otherwise credited, are taken from *F.R. Scott: Selected Poems* (1966).

Put wings
on happenings,

plucking the live moment
from the torrent.

*

Free the old
from its mould

yet be beholden
to the proven.

*

Use sense
with reticence

fusing the notion
with the passion.

\*

Genitalia?
Inter alia

but as part
of a whole heart.

\*

Each verse
a universe.

In all ways
praise.

> From "Poem for Living," *The Dance Is One* (1973).

A flower should not mean, but bee.

\*

Newspapers are born free, and everywhere they are in chains.

\*

Canada won its independence mostly by fighting against Germans.

> Unpublished aphorisms from the Montreal man of letter's commonplace book, 1973. See also David Lewis.

## Scott, Jack

Perhaps it's time for the nations of the world to forget about the whole tenuous idea of a lasting peace and just settle down to making some rules for a nice, safe war.

> "War for Gain," *From Our Town* (1959), by the Vancouver columnist.

## Scott, R.B.Y.

It is surely an inescapable conclusion that a social structure in which the rights of property are paramount, and an economic order in which the motive power is acquisitiveness and the certain result a division of society into rich and poor, are incompatible with the mind of Christ.

> "The Biblical Basis," *Towards the Christian Revolution* (1936), edited by R.B.Y. Scott and Gregory Vlastos.

## Scott, Thomas

I prefer the manners of the native Indians to the insipid conversation of our own officers. The Chief of the Five Nations speaks twelve Indian languages, besides English, French, German and Spanish. He translated your "Lady of the Lake" as well as the Scriptures into Mohawk, and yet with the most polished manner of civilized life, he would not disdain to partake of the blood of his enemy at the banquet of sacrifice; yet I admire and love this man.

> Letter to Sir Walter Scott from his younger brother Thomas who settled in the Brantford area, 1815. Quoted by Frank Yeigh in "Scott, Carlyle, Dickens, and Canada," *Queen's Quarterly*, Spring, 1930. According to the journal of a Captain Langston, 1817, Scott's novels "are supposed to be sketched by Mr. and Mrs. [Thomas] Scott, but finished for the press by their brother Walter. Such is the opinion of the officers of the 70th!!!" Thomas Scott was buried in Quebec City. See also Sir Walter Scott.

## Scott, Thomas

The métis are a pack of cowards. They will not dare to shoot me.

> Letter written shortly before his execution at Fort Garry, March 4, 1870. Quoted by George F.G. Stanley in *Louis Riel* (1963).

For God's sake either finish me, or take me out of this, for I am freezing.

> *The Globe*, March 26, 1885. These are said to be Scott's last words. (It was believed that Scott was not dead when placed in his coffin and could be heard making the above demand eleven hours later.) The above statement is from a news report reprinted by Nick and Helma Mika in their edition of *The Riel Rebellion 1885* (1972).

## Scott, Sir Walter

Of five brothers, all healthy and promising, in a degree far beyond one whose infancy was visited by personal infirmity, and whose health after this period seemed long very precarious, I am, nevertheless, the only survivor. The best loved, and the best deserving to be loved, died before this day in a distant and foreign land.

> The novelist wrote this letter about his younger brother who died in Quebec on February 4, 1823. Quoted by Frank Yeigh in "Scott, Carlyle, Dickens, and

Canada," *Queen's Quarterly*, Spring, 1930. See also Thomas Scott.

## Scriven, Joseph Medlicott
What a Friend we have in Jesus,
All our sins and griefs to bear!
What a privilege to carry
Everything to God in prayer!
Oh, what peace we often forfeit,
Oh, what needless pain we bear—
All because we do not carry
Ev'rything to God in prayer!

> First of three verses of "What a Friend We Have in Jesus," written about 1857 by a resident of the Port Hope area of Ontario who "has been known to divest himself of his clothing, in order to cover the nakedness and relieve the sufferings of destitute ones." Scriven died, August 10, 1886, at the age of sixty-six, his last reported words being: "I wish the Lord would take me home." Quoted by the Rev. Jas. Cleland in *What a Friend We Have in Jesus and Other Hymns by Joseph Scriven with a Sketch of the Author* (1895). The hymn, sometimes called "Pray without Ceasing," was set to music by Charles C. Converse, an Albany lawyer and musician, and soon became an international evangelical favourite.

## Searle, Ronald
See Jane Clapperton and Kildare Dobbs.

## Secord, Laura
It was while the Americans had possession of the frontier, that I learned the plans of the American commander, and determined to put the British troops under Fitzgibbon in possession of them, and, if possible, to save the British troops from capture, or, perhaps, total destruction. In doing so, I found I should have great difficulty in getting through the American guards, which were out ten miles in the country. Determined to persevere, however, I left early in the morning, walked nineteen miles in the month of June, over a rough and difficult part of the country, when I came to a field belonging to a Mr. DeCamp, in the neighbourhood of the Beaver Dam. By this time daylight had left me. Here I found all the Indians encamped; by moonlight the scene was terrifying, and to those accustomed to such scenes, might be considered grand. Upon advancing to the Indians they all rose, and, with some yells, said "Woman," which made me tremble. I cannot express the awful feeling it gave me; but I did not lose my presence of mind. I was determined to persevere. I went up to one of the chiefs, made him understand that I had great news for Capt. Fitzgibbon, and that he must let me pass to his camp, or that he and his party would be all taken. The chief at first objected to let me pass, but finally consented, after some hesitation, to go with me and accompany me to Fitzgibbon's station, which was at the Beaver Dam, where I had an interview with him. I then told him what I had come for, and what I had heard—that the Americans intended to make an attack upon the troops under his command, and would, from their superior numbers, capture them all. Benefitting by this information, Capt. Fitzgibbon formed his plans accordingly, and captured about five hundred American infantry, about fifty mounted dragoons, and a field-piece or two was taken from the enemy. I returned home next day, exhausted and fatigued. I am now advanced in years, and when I look back I wonder how I could have gone through so much fatigue, with the fortitude to accomplish it.

> Quoted by Gilbert Auchinleck in *A History of the War Between Great Britain and the United States of America during the Years 1812, 1813 & 1814* (1855). Mrs. Secord's account of her celebrated trek appeared in "History of the War of 1812," *Anglo-American Magazine*, November, 1853.
>
> The Loyalist lady was thirty-eight when she made her famous walk through the woods in June of 1813. See also James FitzGibbon.
>
> "For forty years her exploit went almost unrecognized. A magazine article of 1853 was the first printed mention of it. In 1860 the then Prince of Wales, later King Edward VII, visited Canada to lay the foundation stone of the

Ottawa Parliament Buildings, spent some days at Niagara Falls, and learning of Laura's story, sent her a cheque for one hundred pounds." (B.K. Sandwell)

**Seeger, Peggy**    See Ewan MacColl.

**Seeley, John R.**
One such community from among the many of its kind has been chosen. It will be called "Crestwood Heights."* It is "somewhere in central Canada"; the time falls in the years immediately following World War II. [*Footnote: The authors and their associates had great difficulty in creating a pseudonym that would suitably denote the psychological and social overtones of the original name. The one selected very nearly catches these subtle nuances. Among the pseudonyms thought of were: Hillgrove, Interwalden, Uppertown, Maple Heights, Montsylvania, Hillbrow Heights, Richview Heights, Hilltop Heights, Woodmount, Newmount and Urban Heights.]

> Text and footnote from *Crestwood Heights* (1956), by John R. Seeley, R. Alexander Sim, and Elizabeth W. Loosley. One wonders how well the classic sociological study of the Toronto borough of Forest Hill would have fared had it been called *Montsylvania*.

If Canada is to be more than a geographical expression, her nationhood will be born in her Universities. And if her Universities are to discover any merit or mission, then students will educate the educators into that discovery—and salvation. May they come to it before it is too late.

> "The 'Berkeley Issue' in Times and Place," *The University Game* (1968), edited by Howard Adelman and Dennis Lee.

Anyone who is not crazy is—plain crazy.

> "Sanity in a Revolutionary Time," *Probings: A Collection of Essays Contributed to the Canadian Mental Health Association for its Golden Jubilee 1918-1968* (1968).

**Seitz, Ernest**    See Gene Lockhart.

**Selke, Frank J.**
I predict that the boys from Old Quebec will always excel at hockey. There is something about their zeal and their temperament which makes hockey their natural game. In 1980, as in 1960, the habitants' rallying cry should still be *"Les Canadiens sont là!"*

> Selke managed the Montreal Canadiens when they won five successive Stanley Cups. *Behind the Cheering* (1962).

**Selkirk, Lord**    See Stanley Baldwin.

**Sellar, Robert**
But no suppression of facts, no titles the crown is misled to confer, no Windsor uniforms, no strutting in swords and cocked hats, no declarations and resolutions of Parliament, no blare of party conventions, no lies graven on marble, no statues of bronze can change the truth, that the true makers of Canada were those who, in obscurity and poverty, made it with axe and spade, with plough and scythe, with sweat of face and strength of arm.

> *A Scotsman in Upper Canada: The Narrative of Gordon Sellar* (1915). This is a fictional account of an immigrant's experiences in Upper Canada in 1825 written by Robert Sellar.

**Sellar, Walter Carruthers**
Would it have been a Good Thing if Wolfe had succeeded in writing Gray's Elegy instead of taking Quebec?

> "Test Paper V," *1066 and All That* (1930), by Walter Carruthers Sellar and Robert Julian Yeatman. See also James Wolfe.

**Selye, Hans**
*Facts must be correct; theories must be fruitful.* A "fact," if incorrect, is useless—it is not a fact—but an incorrect theory may be even more useful than a correct one if it is more fruitful in leading the way to new facts.

> *From Dream to Discovery: on Being a Scientist* (1964).

Life is largely a process of adaptation to the circumstances in which we live.

*

Stress is essentially the rate of all the wear and tear caused by life.

*

Stress is the state manifested by a specific syndrome which consists of all the nonspecifically induced changes within a biologic system.

*The Stress of Life* (1956).

Work is what we have to do; play is what we like to do.

*The Toronto Star*, December 6, 1972.

## Sennett, Mack

I was a Canadian farm boy with no education. I moved to the United States and worked as a boilermaker. A man who was to become President helped me, in an odd sort of way, and I wound up as a motion-picture producer, many times a millionaire when I was on top of the heap. Where else but in America could a thing like this happen?

*

In Canada where I was fetched up life was cold and serious. Canadians are not congenitally comic. To this day they have not caught onto getting funny with cops, the naturalest comedians in the world. Ever hear of them cracking wise at the Royal Canadian Mounted Police?

The man who choreographed the cinematic slapstick of the Keystone Kops was born Michael Sinnott in Richmond, Quebec, in 1880. Gene Fowler called him "the sensitive boiler maker" in his biography, *Father Goose: The Story of Mack Sennett* (1934). The passages above appear in *King of Comedy* (1954), as told to Cameron Shipp.

You know, the art of screen slapstick has been mostly lost. Yet people love slapstick. The lowering of dignity is always funny. There is a great deal of humour in the combination of surprise and violence. I myself like to laugh and I enjoy comedy and that's why I like slapstick. Any little success I have had was because I was one of the mob and catered to the mob.

*

Those were a special kind of pie. They were full of a sort of paste and sticky stuff so that when they hit, they didn't splatter too much, but dripped nice and gooey.

Sennett believes pie-wielding was introduced on the screen in 1913 when on the spur of the moment Mabel Normand threw a custard pie at Ben Turpin. Quoted by Ezra Goodman in *The Fifty Year Decline and Fall of Hollywood* (1961). See also Thomas P. Kelley, Jr.

No "think" gags. When the audience is thinking they can't be laughing.

*

"Nothing was sacred to Mack and his irreverent buffoons. 'All is vanity,' said Ecclesiastes. 'That ain't the half of it,' said Sennett. 'All is ridiculous!' Virtue, authority, sweet love, wealth—all ridiculous."

Quoted by Frank Capra in *The Name Above the Title: An Autobiography* (1971). See also Calvin Coolidge and Marie Dressler.

## Service, Robert

This is the Law of the Yukon, that only
 the Strong shall thrive;
That surely the Weak shall perish, and
 only the Fit survive.
Dissolute, damned and despairful,
 crippled and palsied and slain,
This is the Will of the Yukon,—Lo, how
 she makes it plain!

Final stanza of "The Law of the Yukon," *The Spell of the Yukon and other Verses* (1907).

*

Fate has written a tragedy; its name is
 "The Human Heart."
The Theatre is the House of Life,
 Woman the mummer's part;
The Devil enters the prompter's box
 and the play is ready to start.

Final stanza of "The Harpy" (1907).

*

A bunch of the boys were whooping it
 up in the Malamute saloon;
The kid that handles the music-box was
 hitting a jag-time tune;

Back of the bar, in a solo game, sat
    Dangerous Dan McGrew,
And watching his luck was his light-o'-
    love, the lady that's known as Lou.

> First verse of "The Shooting of Dan
> McGrew" (1907).

\*

There are strange things done in the
    midnight sun
    By the men who moil for gold;
The Arctic trails have their secret tales
    That would make your blood run
    cold;
The Northern Lights have seen queer
    sights,
    But the queerest they ever did see
Was that night on the marge of Lake
    Laberge
    I cremated Sam McGee.

> Refrain of "The Cremation of Sam
> McGee" (1907). This famous poem con-
> tains the oft-quoted line: "A promise
> made is a debt unpaid."

\*

Imagination is the great gift of the gods.
Given it, one does not need to look
afar for subjects. There is romance in
every face.

> *Ballads of a Bohemian* (1921).

\*

Oh Lip-stick Liz was in the biz'
That's the oldest known in history;
She had a lot of fancy rags,
Of her form she made no mystery.
She had a man, a fancy man,
His name was Alexander;
And he used to beat her up because
He couldn't understand her.

> First verse of "Lip-Stick Liz," *Bath-Tub
> Ballads* (1940). All texts are taken from
> *The Complete Poems of Robert Service*
> (1944). "The Poet of the Yukon" died
> on September 11, 1958, and is buried at
> Lancieux, Brittany. It is not widely
> known that he made an appearance in
> the Hollywood movie *The Spoilers*
> (1942), with Marlene Dietrich. See also
> Joseph Boyle and William Briggs.
>     "And although quotability is no
> proof of literary merit, it is worth noting
> that Service occupies more space in
> Bartlett's *Familiar Quotations* than all
> other Canadian poets put together."

Edward McCourt in *The Yukon and
Northwest Territories* (1969).

## Seton, Ernest Thompson

Have the wild things no moral or legal
rights? What right has man to inflict
such long and fearful agony on a fellow-
creature, simply because that creature
does not speak his language?

> "Redruff," *Wild Animals I have Known*
> (1895).

At the time I knew only that "we were
going to Canada." Pictures of log houses
with pointed spruce-trees all around,
and bears and wolves in the background,
gave me thrills of mixed interest and
fear.

\*

There are three enemies to a lost man—
cold, hunger, and, last and most terrible,
fear. Don't get scared, and all will be
well.

> *Trail of an Artist-Naturalist: The Auto-
> biography of Ernest Thompson Seton*
> (1951).

## Seume, Johann Gottfried

A Canadian, still a stranger to Europe's
sham politeness, and still possessing in
his breast a heart as God gave it to him,
still free from "culture," far off in Quebec's icy forests, brought for sale what he
had hunted with his bow. Without any
sly rhetoric he gave up the wild fowl for
the pittance they offered him and hur-
ried contented back with his meagre
reward to his well-concealed tribal home
and into the arms of his dark-skinned
wife.

> This is a prose translation of the open-
> ing lines of "The Wild One," a German
> poem by Johann Gottfried Seume. While
> a student, Seume was seized by Hessian
> recruiting officers, sold into the English
> army, and drafted for service in Canada.
> He bought his freedom and returned to
> Germany in 1783, where he died in 1810.
> "Der Wilde," *Sämmutliche Werke*
> (Leipzig, 1839). For an intriguing use
> of this quotation, see Carl Gustav Jung.

## Sévigny, Pierre

Men go on only to withdraw and cede
their place to younger men.

*This Game of Politics* (1965). See also Gerda Munsinger.

## Seward, William H.
The policy of the United States is to propitiate and secure the alliance of Canada while it is yet young and incurious of its future. But on the other hand, the policy which the United States actually pursues is the infatuated one of rejecting and spurning vigorous and evergrowing Canada, while seeking to establish feeble states out of decaying Spanish provinces on the coast and islands of the Gulf of Mexico. I shall not live to see it, but the man is already born who will see the United States mourn over this stupendous folly.

> *Cruise to Labrador* (1857), by the future U.S. secretary of State.

So I look upon Prince Rupert's Land and Canada, and see how an ingenious people, and a capable, enlightened government, are occupied with bridging rivers and making railroads and telegraphs to develop, organize and create and preserve the great British provinces of the north; by the Great Lakes, the St. Lawrence and around the shores of Hudson's Bay, and I am able to say, "It is very well; you are building excellent states to be hereafter admitted to the American Union."

> Speech at St. Paul, Minnesota, while campaigning on the Republican ticket, reported in *The New York Herald*, January 25, 1861.

I know that Nature designs that this whole continent, not merely these thirty-six States, shall be, sooner or later, within the magic circle of the American Union.

> Boston address after Seward acquired Alaska for the United States, reported in *The Montreal Gazette*, June 27, 1867.

It would be long before either Canada or Mexico can realize its [immigration's] invigorating power. This may seem hard, but it is clear that only one great nation can be built on one continent at one time. The remedy for both of those countries is the same—accession to the United States. Canada has hesitated long, but it will see and feel this truth at last—that it is better to be an equal constituent member of a great, powerful, and free nation, than a small, feeble, and isolated state, even though equally free.

> *Travels Around the World* (1873), edited by Olive Risley Seward.

## Seymour, Lynn
I wear my heart on my shoulder. If something emotional happens in my life I come out in spots or fall over.

> The *prima ballerina* was born Lynn Springbett in Wainwright, Alberta. Quoted by John Gale in *The Montreal Star*, March 22, 1965.

## Shadbolt, Jack
The greatest asset to an improvising artist is his sensitivity to the poetic—both to the physical poetry of his medium and, even more important, to the evocative overtones of his imagery. He must cultivate a disciplined suggestibility: for such a proliferative process as rapid improvisation tosses up all sorts of melodramatic possibilities.

> *In Search of Form* (1968).

## Shafer, Morley
Any peace is honourable.

> The Toronto-born television reporter covered the Vietnam War for CBS and incurred Richard Nixon's wrath when he criticized the American president's "peace with honour" policy. *The Toronto Star*, January 27, 1973.

## Shaffer, Ivan
If you are over thirty-five, if you are in business for yourself, and if your wife has her own car (even if it's leased and you are charging it to the business), you have probably lost money buying and selling Canadian mining stocks.

> *The Stock Promotion Business: The Inside Story of Canadian Mining Deals and the People behind Them* (1967).

## Shain, Merle
Loving can cost a lot but not loving

always costs more, and those who fear to love often find that want of love is an emptiness that robs the joy from life.

\*

Orgasms really have very little to do with making love, and men who require their woman to respond with *petit mal* seizures that can be picked up on the Richter scale are not making love but asking for reassurance.

\*

The world is divided into couples, and so being single can feel like playing musical chairs and every time they stop the music, you're the one who's out.

\*

There are no perfect men of course, but some are more perfect than others, and we can use all of those we can get.

*Some Men Are More Perfect Than Others: A Book about Men, and Hence about Women, and Love and Dreams* (1973).

### Shakespeare, William

Antipholus: Where America, the Indies?

Dromio: O, sir, upon her nose, all o'er embellished with rubies, carbuncles, sapphires, declining their rich aspect to the hot breath of Spain; who sent whole armadoes of caracks to be ballast at her nose.

*The Comedy of Errors*, Act III, Scene 2. Written about 1591, this play includes Shakespeare's single reference to the New World. There is, however, the Dane's remark in *Hamlet*, Act II, Scene 2: "I am mad north-north-west; when the wind is southerly, I know a hawk from a handsaw." A reference to the Northwest Passage, to madness or to both?

Now is the winter of our discontent
Made glorious summer by this sun of
York.

The opening lines of *The Tragedy of King Richard III*, written about 1593, were the first words heard from the open stage of the Stratford Festival, recited by Alec Guinness. According to Nicholas Monsarrat, the words were "absolutely prophetic of all that was to

come." Herbert Whittaker wrote, "July 13, 1953, was the most exciting night in the history of Canadian theatre." For the "Stratford adventure," see also Tom Patterson.

### Shanawdithit, Nancy

"A gentleman put a looking glass before her and her grimaces were most extraordinary, but when a black pencil was put into her hand and a piece of white paper laid upon the table, she was in raptures. She made a few marks on the paper apparently to try the pencil; then in one flourish she drew a deer perfectly, and what is most surprising, she began at the tip of the tail."

Shanawdithit, believed to be the sole survivor of the Beothuck Indians, was captured April 22, 1823, and died in St. John's, June 6, 1829. The Rev. William Wilson in *Newfoundland and Its Missionaries* (1866), quoted by James P. Howley in *The Beothucks or Red Indians: The Aboriginal Inhabitants of Newfoundland* (1915). See also Mary March.

### Shanley, Charles Dawson

For I saw by the sickly moonlight,
    As I followed, bending low,
That the walking of the stranger
    *Left no footmarks on the snow.*

From "The Walker of the Snow," *Canadian Poems and Lays: Selections of Native Verse, reflecting the Seasons, Legends, and Life of the Dominion* (1893), edited by W.D. Lighthall.

### Shatner, William

Actresses never retire. They just raise children.

The American TV actor was born in Toronto and married a former actress. Quoted by Sam Solomon in *The Toronto Star*, December 5, 1967.

### Shaughnessy, Baron

Take good care of the Canadian Pacific Railway.

To Edward Beatty in 1923, the year Baron Shaughnessy died. The Baron succeeded Van Horne as president of the CPR and was himself succeeded by Beatty. Quoted by R.G. MacBeth in *The Romance of the Canadian Pacific Railway* (1924).

### Shaunon, Robert W.
Perhaps the reader may ask, of what consequence is it whether the author's exact language is preserved or not, provided we have his thought? The answer is, that inaccurate quotation is a sin against truth. It may appear in any particular instance to be a trifle, but perfection consists in small things, and perfection is no trifle.

> "Misquotation," *The Canadian Magazine*, October, 1898.

### Shaw, George Bernard
It is quite a mistake to suppose that conventional morality is all of one piece the world over. London cannot live on the morals of the Italian peasant or the Australian sheepfarmer. What is more, high civilization is not compatible with the romance of the pioneer communities of Canada.

> "The Cinema as Moral Leveller," *New Statesman*, June 27, 1914. Quoted by J. Percy Smith in *The Unrepentant Pilgrim: A Study of the Development of Bernard Shaw* (1965).

The French Canadians, who are of the same race with us only in the sense that we all belong to the human race, cling to us just as hard. They all follow us to war so boldly that we begin to have misgivings as to whether someday they may not make us follow them to war.

> *The Intelligent Woman's Guide to Socialism and Capitalism* (1928).

Don't tell Canadians that I was a British spy masquerading as a pro-German during the War. You started a serious heath fire with that.

> Postcard to Maurice Colbourne, a British lecturer touring the Empire. "Bernard Shaw and the Empire," *Empire Club of Canada: Addresses Delivered to the Members During the Year 1930* (1931).

Since when does the Canadian Government know a good picture when it sees one? And in any case why did they not commission Augustus John at a thousand guineas and make sure of the job? If John did it, the job would be good—or at any rate everybody would think so.

> "I explained that the Government of Canada wished to have a good portrait of him in the National Archives at Ottawa," wrote Yousuf Karsh in *Faces of Our Time* (1970) about his photographic session with G.B.S. in 1943. "Plucking up my courage, I suggested that perhaps I had been assigned to make the portrait for that same reason."

So far we have not budged a step, and shall not unless Hitler pushes us out by the scruffs of our necks. In that case we shall certainly come to Canada, as we have a joint annuity there to die on. And Vancouver is the pick of Canada. . . .

> Quoted by Eric Nicol in *Vancouver* (1970) who explains that "a resident, Mrs. Fitz James, received a postcard from" G.B.S. during the Battle of Britain.

"I told him that I had received a cable to the effect that *Heartbreak House* had been a success at Hart House Theatre. He replied, 'It naturally would be, it's a very good play.' Shaw's talk was as brilliant as I expected it would be, but I couldn't overcome a feeling that there was an element of artificiality in it. The epigrams seemed rather to get in the way. I would have liked to hear his sober view about many things, but Shaw without iridescence would not have been Shaw."

> Quoted by Vincent Massey in *What's Past is Prologue: The Memoirs of the Right Honourable Vincent Massey, C.H.* (1963). See also Arthur Stringer.

### Shaw, John
The greatest nations of antiquity and of modern times have been those that cultivated athletic sports. Long may they prosper. If the time comes that Canada needs defenders, she will draw them from the ranks of rowers, boxers, lacrosse and hockey players.

> Address by the mayor of Toronto in 1904 at a reception to honour Lou Scholes

who had just returned from winning the celebrated Diamond Sculls, the highest award in amateur sculling.

**Shawundais**   See John Sunday.

**Sheard, Joseph**

I'll not put a hand to it. Lount and Mathews have done nothing that I might not have done myself, and I'll never help to build a gallows to hang them.

> Refusing to serve as foreman of the work crew ordered to erect the scaffold from which Peter Mathews and Samuel Lount were hanged, April 12, 1838, for taking part in the Rebellion of 1837. Sheard, an architect, later served as mayor of Toronto; his Christian name is sometimes given as Matthew. *Old Toronto: A Selection of Excerpts from Landmarks of Toronto* (1954), edited by E.C. Kyte.

**Shearer, Douglas**

I was now working for MGM, employed for this particular publicity stunt, which was what they called it. For that they paid me very well, seventy-five bucks. And I decided it was time I sold my return ticket for Montreal and stay on. I had become fascinated by the country as well as the industry. I had had enough background in industrial plants and mechanics so that I thought the competition wouldn't be too tough. I visualized the possibilities of a place for myself. And the weather was fine compared to that of Montreal.

> The brother of Norma Shearer, interviewed by Bernard Rosenberg and Harry Silverstein in *The Real Tinsel* (1970). When he left Montreal for Hollywood in the 1920s, Shearer was quoted as saying: "Thirty-dollar-a-week jobs were just as hard to get as those for thirty thousand dollars a week." He worked for MGM as a stuntman and then as a technician.

**Shearer, Norma**

I consider myself one of the world's luckiest persons.

*

In a picture things are *made* to work out.

*

. . . nobody but myself was trying to do me in.

> Norma Shearer was born in Montreal in 1900 and became a popular film actress. When her husband, Irving Thalberg, head of production at MGM, died, she lost her discernment and declined starring roles in *Mrs. Miniver* and *Gone with the Wind* and left films altogether. Quoted by David Shipman in *The Great Movie Stars: The Golden Years* (1970). About her marriage to Thalberg, there is Joan Crawford's remark: "How can I compete with Norma Shearer when she sleeps with the boss?" See also Florenz Ziegfeld.

**Shebib, Don**

I know a whole lot of people here are pushing hard to make Hollywood Establishment films. The trouble is, of course, that they won't be nearly as good as Hollywood Establishment films. So why the hell bother?

> Director of *Goin' Down the Road*, quoted by Betty Lee in *The Globe and Mail*, October 31, 1970.

I'm still not totally dedicated to making features. There's no market, really, for the kind of films I'd like to make. Pieces of film texture—because film drama is inherent in going from texture to texture—can't be sustained for a long time, certainly not for ninety minutes. I look forward to the time when public theatres will be running films that are six, or fifteen, or forty-five minutes.

> Quoted by Kaspars Dzeguze in *The Globe and Mail*, November 18, 1972.

**Shephard, Esther**   See Paul Bunyan.

**Sheppard, Edmund E.**

It would manifestly benefit Ontario if a ship canal connected our lake with the St. Lawrence and the ocean. We have convicts enough in Canada to build it within a few years if all those sentenced to a long term were employed upon it.

*Saturday Night*, December, 1889.

If women keep on demanding a vote, cropping their hair, opposing us in the professions, wearing our coats, hats and shirts, and if men continue nursing babies, promoting female dress reform, and using curling tongs, first thing we know there will be a blurred line denoting a merging of the sexes. That would be a fine development in human anatomy with which to mark the close of the nineteenth century.

> *Saturday Night*, May 13, 1893. Sheppard founded *Saturday Night* in 1887 and edited it until 1906.

## Sherbrooke, Lord
Now you ought to make it your business to get rid of the Dominion.

> To Lord Dufferin after his appointment as governor general in 1872. "To which I replied that I certainly did not intend to be handed down to history as the Governor General who had lost Canada." Quoted by Herbert Paul in *The Life of Froude* (1905). See also Lord Dufferin.

## Sherring, William J.
I have an idea that some of the Americans are in the race for the sole purpose of pacing their best runner; but they won't fool me. If the early pace is too fast I'll drop back. You can bet I'll be right in the fight the last few miles and the fellow that beats me will have to be a dandy.

> Writing to a Hamilton newspaperman prior to winning the marathon in Athens in 1906, handily defeating the world's best distance runners and becoming international champion. Quoted by Henry Roxborough in *One Hundred —Not Out* (1966).

## Sherwood, Robert E.
I never realized how patriotic I was to my own country, until I found myself serving under an alien flag, and doing obeisance to a little shrimp in Buckingham Palace.

> A recent Harvard graduate, Sherwood enlisted in the Black Watch, trained in Montreal and shipped overseas. He wrote a long letter to his tutor Albert Hunt in 1917 which praised the Canadian war effort but included the above sentence. The letter was published in the *Lampoon* which Harvard had to recall in order to censor the "offending sentence." John Mason Brown in *The Worlds of Robert E. Sherwood: Mirror to His Time 1896-1939* (1965) claims it "had been inked out in gold."

In a few days—or maybe, a few hours, how do I know?—I'll be up in that terror. How can any man live through that? Let's face it—I'm going to be killed in this war. And that's the end of me. And what have I done with my life? Who am I? Just another lousy (literally lousy) private in the Canadian Army. And all of these nice, decent guys who are here with me—guys from New Brunswick, Ontario, Alberta, British Columbia and the banks of the Saskatchewan—they're going to be killed, too. Maybe some of them have had lives that mean something—I haven't. But why should they have to die? Why should I have to die before I've realized some part of myself? Why? Why?

> Quoted by John Mason Brown in *The Worlds of Robert E. Sherwood: Mirror to His Time 1896-1939* (1965). Brown implies these were the future playwright's thoughts when his French trench was under German bombardment, as he recalled them in the 1950s when he accepted an honorary doctorate at Bishop's University. Sherwood's experiences with the Black Watch supplied much of the background to *The Road to Rome*, his first play produced in 1927. *There Shall Be No Night*, a great success in 1940, had a portion of its royalties earmarked for the Canadian war effort.

Endless views of Canadian Northwest Mounted Policemen trudging through blizzards, and then entering log cabins with flour sprinkled over their mackinaws.

> Capsule review of the film *Over the Border*, quoted by Max Wilk in *The Wit and Wisdom of Hollywood: From the Squaw Man to the Hatchet Man* (1971).

## Shields, Dr. T.T.
You have observed that the Roman Catholic Church never builds a church on a back street?

"One Sacrifice for Sins Forever," sermon preached at Jarvis Street Baptist Church, Toronto, Sunday evening, October 11, 1931. Quoted by Leslie K. Tarr in *Shields of Canada* (1967).

## Shimkus, Joanna
You don't think I could *invent* a name like that.

The stunning model was born in Halifax in 1944 and modelled in Paris at nineteen. She broke into Hollywood pictures at twenty-five. Quoted by Geoffrey Minish in *The Toronto Star*, March 16, 1968.

I like the way I look. I need my imperfections.

Quoted by Ivor Davis in *The Globe and Mail*, January 16, 1971.

## Shin, Hoei
Fusang

The Chinese Buddhist missionary Hoei Shin wrote an account of his travels in which he claimed to have discovered a new country in A.D. 499 where the trees were thousands of feet high and of vast girth. He named this country Fusang (or Fu Sang or Fon Sang); his description appears in the ancient collection *Lung Wei Pi Shu*.

Fusang has been identified with British Columbia; if so, Hoei Shin was the discoverer of America—and Canada. It was not until 1579 that the first European, Sir Francis Drake, sighted the West Coast of the New World. See also Harold Griffin.

## Ship, Reuben
The Investigator took a deep breath before speaking. "In all humility I dedicate myself to the task of bringing to light the facts of their monstrous conspiracy that threatens our way of life Up Here. I shall pursue this objective, relentlessly, disregarding all attempts at intimidation by persons in high places who may be implicated by these facts;

and I shall not cease until I have fixed the blame for a thousand years of treason!"

CBC Radio broadcast Reuben Ship's political satire on Joseph McCarthy in May of 1954. The unnamed demagogue was played by John Drainie and the program directed by Andrew Allan. A bootleg recording was sold in the United States, and the script was published in Britain as *The Investigator: A Narrative in Dialogue* (1956).

## Shirley, William
*Delenda est Canada!*

Echoing Cato the Elder in the Roman Senate, the governor of Massachusetts addressed the Assembly in 1746 and raised 3,500 men to take Louisbourg from the French. The commander-in-chief of the British forces in North America failed, and nine years later failed at Niagara. Quoted by Francis Parkman in *A Half-Century of Conflict* (1892).

## Shortt, Adam
Oh, a man's got to die of something!

Political economist quoted by Arthur R.M. Lower in *My First Seventy-Five Years* (1967).

## Shtern, Sholem
The fist and sword have always sought to force and rule, but word and pen have always been victorious.

"The Lantern that Shines in Prison," translated from the Yiddish by Ruth Borchiver, *New Frontiers*, Spring, 1955.

## Shulman, Milton
I don't really find it difficult to be a critic. You just had to learn the right mental approach. You simply have to be able to separate your objective reactions from your subjective reactions. And the forms you're writing about don't matter too much. Theatre or film . . . there's really not too much difference between one form and another.

Quoted by Don Rubin in *The Toronto Star*, January 10, 1969. The corrosive critic of the *Evening Standard* was born in Toronto in 1913 and graduated from Osgoode Hall before becoming a British theatrical producer and then critic.

## Shulman, Morton
Anyone can make a million.

Title of a bestselling guide to the stock market published in 1966. Its sequel, *Anyone Can Still Make a Million*, appeared in 1973.

As time goes by there are fewer and fewer novelties.

Quoted by Pat Annesley in *Toronto Life*, July, 1972.

## Shumiatcher, Morris C.
The Buckskin Curtain.

"I think the Indian Canadian wishes to enlarge the world in which he lives beyond the buckskin curtain of his reserve. He may not be interested in becoming a citizen in the abstract sense, but he does wish his children to attend the white man's schools which may be close at hand." The Regina lawyer coined this phrase in "The Buckskin Curtain," *The Beaver*, Autumn, 1959.

Freedom is not a legacy that is bequeathed from father to son or that can be inherited by one generation from another. It is a living organism into which each man in every age must breathe the breath of life. Its growth is in struggle and its strength derives from adversity. Its vitality is nurtured when men rescue it from those who assault it. And when it has been successfully defended, it invigorates and enriches those who have caused it to prevail and rejuvenates the society in which it has survived.

*Assault on Freedom: Reflections on Saskatchewan's Medical Care Crisis* (1962).

## Shuster, Frank
Just remember, baby, there's more to life than happiness.

Quoted by Susan Kastner in *The Toronto Star*, December 30, 1965. See also Johnny Wayne.

## Shuster, Joe
I never met a girl who matched up to Lois Lane.

Superman, the cartoon character, was invented and first drawn by Joe Shuster, the Toronto-born cousin of Frank Shuster, a *Toronto Star* staffer. (It is interesting to note that Clark Kent first worked for the *Daily Star*, then the *Daily Planet*, and now a TV station.)

The story-line was created by Shuster's Cleveland highschool friend Jerry Siegel, and first appeared in *Action Comics* in 1938. World-wide newspaper syndication, radio, film and TV exposure soon followed. Shuster sold his interest in the strip to National Periodicals Publications Inc., but as Alexander Ross wrote in "Return of the Old Invincibles" in *Maclean's Magazine*, March 19, 1966, "He's trying to paint pop art—*serious* strips—and hopes eventually to promote a one-man show in some chic Manhattan gallery." According to Jules Feiffer in *The Great Comic Book Heroes* (1965), "No one drew skyscrapers like Shuster."

"Yes. Superman was conceived by Toronto-born Joe Shuster who originally worked not for the *Daily Planet* but for a newspaper called *The Star*, modelled on the *Toronto Star*. This makes his assumed identity of bland Clark Kent not merely understandable, but artistically inevitable. Kent is the archtypical middle-class Canadian WASP, superficially nice, self-effacing, but within whom there burns a hate-ball, a would-be avenger with superhuman power, a smasher of bridges, a breaker of skyscrapers, a potential ravager of wonder women. And (may those who have scoffed at Canadian culture in the past, please take note) a universal hero." Mordecai Richler in "The Great Comic Book Heroes," *Hunting Tigers under Glass: Essays and Reports* (1968).

Faster than a speeding bullet!
More powerful than a locomotive!
Able to leap tall buildings at a single bound!
Look! Up in the sky!
It's a bird!
It's a plane!
IT'S SUPERMAN!

541

Quoted by E. Nelson Bridwell in *Super-man: From the Thirties to the Seventies* (1971). "This looks like a job . . . for Superman!"

## Sibley, Mrs. R.A.
Fever and Ague.—Four ounces galangal root in a quart of gin, steeped in a warm place; take often.—Mrs. R.A. Sibley.

> Mrs. Sibley was one of many contributors to *The Canadian Home Cook Book* (1877), "compiled by Ladies of Toronto and Chief Cities and Towns in Canada."

## Siegfried, André
The university in Canada, instead of being a centre for new ideas and the evolution of the future, is a potent instrument of conservatism. There is something venerable and poetic about Laval, which is invested with a charm for the French visitor, but it has to be admitted that for signs of progress we must look elsewhere.

*

It is safe now to predict that Canada will become less and less British and more and more American. The best we can wish for—a wish that may well be realized—is that she may become Canadian first and foremost.

*

It is not the American nation that menaces the Canadian nation; rather it is the American form of civilization that threatens to supplant the British.

*

The [Canadian] census of 1901 records only 4,181 cases of persons declaring that they belonged to no religion and only 3,613 professed "agnostics," this word being explained in a note as comprising "atheists, freethinkers, infidels, sceptics and unbelievers." The Englishman is never really at ease until he is duly catalogued.

> *The Race Question in Canada* (1907).

. . . the relationship which exists between the French and English Canadians . . . is a *modus vivendi* without cordiality.

*

I remember having breakfasted with a French Canadian in Montreal and having dined with an English Canadian family in Toronto on the same day. The contrast was quite a shock to my senses. It was like experiencing the different pressures in a diving bell. Involuntarily I thought of the uncompromising formula of Maurice Barrès: "Prayers that do not mingle."

*

At the beginning, in the middle, and at the end of any study of Canada, one must reiterate that Canada is American.

*

In the Montreal telephone directory, the Macs fill six pages. Tear them out, and Montreal is no longer a financial capital, but simply an immense French village with a little English garrison!

*

Many countries—and they are to be envied—possess in one direction or another a window which opens out on to the infinite—on to the potential future. . . . The North is always there like a presence; it is the background of the picture without which Canada would not be Canadian.

> *Canada: An International Power* (1937), translated by H.H. and Doris Hemming.

## Sifton, Sir Clifford
The Last Best West, Beyond Which One Cannot Dream of Anything Better.

*

Come to Alberta and Go into Partnership with the Canadian Pacific.

*

The World's Bread Basket is Western Canada.

> These slogans are usually associated with the vigorous immigration policy of Sir Clifford Sifton, minister of the Interior from 1896 to 1905.

Peasants in sheepskin coats.

> The phrase is associated with Sir Clifford who encouraged the immigration to western Canada of Ukrainian and Doukhobor farmers and labourers. Such settlers were often referred to as "Sifton's Sheepskins."
>
> Sifton is quoted by Vera Lysenko in *Men in Sheepskin Coats: A Study in Assimilation* (1947) as saying: "If one should examine twenty people who turn

up at Hamburg to emigrate, he might find one escaped murderer, three or four wasters and ne'er-do-wells, some very poor shopkeepers, artisans or labourers, and there might be one or two stout, hardy peasants in sheepskin coats. Obviously the peasants are the men who are wanted here."

See Thomas Chandler Haliburton and Joseph Howe for the use of the word "sheepskin" in another context.

So far as Winnipeg is concerned it is a discouraging place and always was, but I would not fret about it. I think it will come around all right. If it does not we can always have the satisfaction of consigning it to a warmer place. [Letter to Sir John Willison, December, 1899]

Canada is not required to be bribed into loyalty.

This is a paraphrase of a remark made in Ottawa in December, 1903. Lord Rosebery added: "Only two days ago Mr. Sifton, one of the Canadian Ministers, declared with indignation that Canada did not require to be bribed into loyalty. That sentence, as I believe, will be re-echoed in every part of our English-speaking Empire."

I shall be content, when the history of this country shall be written, to have the history of the last eight or nine years, so far as western administration is concerned, entered opposite my name. [Remark, 1906]

There is only one policy for Canada and that is to stand on its own legs like any other country.

December 22, 1920, quoted by John W. Dafoe in *Clifford Sifton in Relation to His Times* (1931).

When I speak of quality I have in mind, I think, something that is quite different from what is in the mind of the average writer or speaker upon the question of Immigration. I think a stalwart peasant in a sheep-skin coat, born on the soil, whose forefathers have been farmers for ten generations, with a stout wife and a half-dozen children, is good quality.

"The Immigrants Canada Wants," *Maclean's Magazine*, April 1, 1922. Sir Clifford was regularly criticized for settling "peasants in sheep-skin coats"—Ukrainians mainly—on the prairies.

I have no confidence whatever in any of the schemes propounded for relief. I never accomplished anything myself except by hard work, frugality and self-denial, and I don't believe anybody else ever did. This is the road that Western Canada, in common with the rest of humanity, has to travel.

Letter to John W. Dafoe, January 5, 1923. Quoted by Ramsay Cook in *The Politics of John W. Dafoe and the Free Press* (1963).

It seems to me that most of the things that I was abused about were easily defensible as in the public interest. Some things that I rather expected to be taken to task about passed unnoticed, or earned me commendation.

Quoted by John W. Dafoe in *Clifford Sifton in Relation to His Times* (1931). See also R.E. Knowles.

### Sifton, Victor

I assure you, gentlemen, my presidential address will be as brief as Mr. Purcell has been able to make it.

Chairman of the board of F.P. Publications in the 1950s, paying tribute to Gillis Purcell, general manager of Canadian Press. Quoted by Russell Braddon in *Roy Thomson of Fleet Street* (1965).

### Silverheels, Jay

Kemo Sabe.

Tonto's reply to the Lone Ranger in countless radio, film and TV adaptations of Frank Striker's character, a kind of western Robin Hood. The role of "the faithful Indian scout and companion" to "the mysterious Masked Rider of the Plains" was first played by Chief Thundercloud, but then fell to the lot of a Canadian athlete and actor who called himself Jay Silverheels. He was born Harry Smith at the Six Nations reserve near Brantford in 1920, the son of the most-decorated Canadian Indian in

World War I. The Mohawk actor was discovered by Joe E. Brown and first played Tonto in 1949. According to *Nova Magazine*, January, 1973: "He occasionally appears on television, sometimes reading his own poetry, and has paired up again with the Lone Ranger for television and radio commercials for aftershave." See also George W. Trendle.

**Sim, R. Alexander**   See John R. Seeley.

**Simard, Jean**
When a European writer takes up his pen, it is a tool heavy with years and experience, still slightly warm from the thousands of lettered hands that have manipulated it before him. Whereas ours have held only the axe! We are the first intellectuals in a nation of woodcutters.

> *Répertoire* (1961).

**Simcoe, Elizabeth Posthuma**
I like the parties at the Chateau excessively, for there are forty or fifty people in an evening, and I think it very amusing to walk about the room and have something to say to everybody without a long conversation with any.

> Quebec, December, 1794. *Mrs. Simcoe's Diary* (1965), edited by Mary Quayle Innis.

**Simcoe, John Graves**
I cannot dismiss you without earnestly desiring you to promote by precept and example, among your respective counties, the regular habits of piety and morality, the surest foundations of all private and public felicity; and at this juncture, I particularly recommend to you to explain, that this province is singularly blest, not with a mutilated constitution, but with a constitution which has stood the test of experience, and which is the very image and transcript of that of Great Britain; by which she has long established and secured to her subjects as much freedom and happiness as is possible to be enjoyed under the subordination necessary to civilized society.

> Address at the closing of the first session of the first parliament of Upper Canada, October 15, 1792. *Letter to Sir Joseph Banks . . . To Which Are Added Five Official Speeches* (1890).

There was to be one Church, one university to guard the constitution . . . there at every street corner was to be a sentry, there the very stones were to sing, "God Save the King."

> This is how the governor of Upper Canada envisioned York, later Toronto, as a "palladium of British loyalty." Quoted by E.M. Gundy in "The Romance of Pioneer Life in Ontario," *The New Outlook*, July 8, 1925.

**Simms, James**
I know not with what weapon the Honourable Member will attack me, except it be with the jawbone of an ass.

> Attorney general of Newfoundland to a member of the legislature who had declared: "I will attack Her Majesty's Attorney-General," about 1826. Quoted by W.D. Prowse in *A History of Newfoundland from English, Colonial, and Foreign Records* (1895).

**Simpson, Sir George**
. . . it has occurred to me however that Philanthropy is not the exclusive object of our visits to these Northern Regions, but that to it are coupled interested motives, and that Beaver is the grand bone of contention.

\*

Connubial alliances are the best security we can have of the goodwill of the Natives, I have therefore commended the Gentlemen to form connections with the principle Families immediately on their arrival, which is no difficult matter as to the offer of their Wives & Daughters is the first token of their Friendship & hospitality.

> Letter to the governors of the Hudson's Bay Company from Fort Wedderburn, May 18, 1821. *Journal of Occurrences in the Athabasca Department by George Simpson, 1820 and 1821, and Report* (1938), edited by E.E. Rich.

Russia, though apparently the most unwieldy state on earth, is yet more decidedly one and indivisible than any other dominion in existence.

> Narrative of a Journey Round the World, During the Years 1841 and 1842 (1847).

In taking the sketch of the buffalo hunt you were good enough to send me last year, you must have stood in the rear of the herd; a side view would have given a better idea of the appearance of the animals, as from the hind view, it required a little explanation to make a stranger understand that the mass of dark objects before him, were intended either for buffalo or any other living animal.

> Letter from "the little emperor" (as the governor of the Company was called) to the artist Paul Kane, 1847, quoted by Russell Harper in Paul Kane's Frontier (1971).

### Simpson, Jimmy
If the Communists wouldn't organize demonstrations, it wouldn't be necessary for the police to break them up.

> Mayor of Toronto quoted by Tom McEwen in He Wrote for Us: The Story of Bill Bennett, Pioneer Socialist Journalist (1951).

### Simpson, Robert
The Dream Book.

> This is the name of the semi-annual, mail-order catalogue issued by Robert Simpson Company and Sears-Roebuck, from the 1960s on. The title recalls the phrase Western Canadian Indians used for early mail-order catalogues: the Wish Book.

### Sinclair, George
In total, advertising persuasively states the viewpoint that people should want the best of material life. For those who have not found the means of purchasing that life, for the dispossessed, advertising may well be instigation to revolution. But to want the situation otherwise is to ask men to be adjusted to poverty and ignorance. That, I believe, would be madness.

> "Advertising and Mental Health," Probings: A Collection of Essays Contributed to the Canadian Mental Health Association for its Golden Jubilee 1918-1968 (1968).

### Sinclair, Gordon
I am at least one newspaperman who went to the Orient and came back not knowing who was going to win.

> "Footloose in China," April 17, 1939, Addresses Delivered before the Canadian Club of Toronto: Season of 1938-39 (1939).

People won't accept my style of news. I use slang, cuss words, sex. Some of my acquaintances are garbage men, harlots, newsboys, waitresses. I get drunk. I exaggerate. I don't believe in goodness.

> Original excuse for refusing to move from newspaper work to broadcasting, 1944.

*

The best thing in all the world to be is a rich man in your own country.

> Advice of "a rich and quiet nobleman of Siam," quoted with approval by Gordon Sinclair in Will the Real Gordon Sinclair Please Stand Up (1966).

Nobody has asked me but if I were to choose a national bird for Canada, it would be the starling. He struts self-reliantly, asks no favours of anybody, and never puts out his claw for relief.

> The Globe and Mail, January 10, 1972.

The four elements of news are: love, money, conquest, disaster.

> From a news broadcast on CFRB, Toronto, 1972.

I can name you five thousand times when the Americans raced to the help of other people in trouble. Can you name me even one time when someone else raced to the Americans in trouble?

> From a "Let's Be Personal" broadcast heard over CFRB in Toronto, June 5, 1973, and released as a best-selling recording in the United States, the royalties of which the broadcaster earmarked for the American Red Cross.

## Sinclair, Lister

"But we all hate Toronto."

"That's just it. We *all* hate Toronto! It's the only thing everybody's got in common."

"We All Hate Toronto," *A Play on Words and Other Radio Plays* (1948).

A lot of people have the wrong idea of me. I'm an omnibrow—not a highbrow, not a lowbrow—an omnibrow.

Quoted by Marci McDonald in *The Toronto Star*, July 8, 1972.

## Sinden, Harry

It's easy. All you have to do is win.

＊

It was never in doubt. [Team Canada's victory over the Soviet team, Moscow, September 27, 1972]

＊

Nyet, nyet, Soviet! / Da, da, Canada! [Chanted by three thousand Canadian hockey fans attending the Moscow games, September, 1972; *nyet*, no; *da*, yes]

＊

Our last word has to be something more than: "We won, didn't we?"

＊

"I don't want any of you guys to go out of your way," I told the players, "but if he happens to skate by, and gets in your way, give him a tickle." [Referring to the Russian hockey star Kharlamov]

*Hockey Showdown: The Canada-Russia Hockey Series* (1972). Sinden, general manager of the Boston Bruins, was coach of Team Canada.

## Singh, Khushwant

Though in the intervening long summers and winters I have wandered over many lands in many climes and lived among diverse races—black, brown, yellow, and white—I remain as convinced as I was twenty years ago that there is no country in the world as beautiful as Canada, and there are no people in the world nicer than Canadians.

To me, coming back to Canada is like coming back to my spiritual home. Canada quickened in me the impulse to appreciate the best there is in life; the ability to perceive beauty in things that are beautiful; the ability to love people who are lovable. It was in Canada that the desire to write came upon me. It was in Canada that I first saw my name in print. I owe more to this country and its people than I can put in words.

Many among you will be embarrassed by this kind of soppy sentimentalism. Well, I am a soppy sentimentalist.

"Oriental Pearl in the World Oyster," *Man and His World: The Noranda Lectures, Expo 67* (1968), introduced by Helen S. Hogg.

## Sinnott, Michael    See Mack Sennett.

## Sirois, J.N.    See N.W. Rowell.

## Sirois, Dr. Jean

To summarize in a single sentence let us say: Canadian neurology will possess French individualism and ingenuity, English fair play, and American goodwill.

Quebec neurologist quoted in 1957 by H.E. MacDermot in *One Hundred Years of Medicine in Canada 1867-1967* (1967).

## Sissons, C.B.

I can tell you now that my second-class students did better in the world than my first.

When the professor of history at the University of Toronto retired in 1947, he made this admission to one of his "B" students, Lester B. Pearson.

## Sissons, Jack H.

Justice shall be taken to every man's door.

Maxim of the first justice of the Territorial Court of the Northwest Territories from 1955 to 1965. Judge Sissons, whose bailiwick covered one-third of Canada's land mass, was called Ekoktoegee by the Eskimos—"The One Who Listens to Things." *Judge of the Far North: The Memoirs of Jack Sissons* (1968).

## Sitting Bull

We did not give you our country; you took it from us. Look how I stand with these people. Look at me. You think I am a fool, but you are a greater fool than I am. This house, the home of the English, is a medicine house and you come here to tell us lies. We do not want to hear them. Now I have said enough. You can go back. Say no more. Take your lies with you. I will stay with these people. The country we came from belonged to us; you took it from us; we will live here.

> After the battle of Little Bighorn in 1876, Sitting Bull found sanctuary in the Canadian West. He made this reply to General Alfred Terry who urged him to return with his small band of Sioux to the United States. Quoted by John Peter Turner in *The North West Mounted Police 1873-1893* (1955).

## Skelton, O.D.
A former master dispenser of patronage, Sir Charles Tupper, had devised an ingenious plan. Sir William Van Horne complained to Sir Charles that he was sending a preposterous number of recommendations for passes on the Canadian Pacific. "True," Sir Charles replied, "but it is difficult to decline what people consider costs me nothing. Hereafter, when I send you a letter recommending a pass, and sign it 'Yours truly,' throw it into the waste-basket; when I sign it 'Yours sincerely,' please give it consideration; but when I sign it 'Yours very sincerely,' you simply must not refuse it." "And," added Sir William, "after that, every blessed letter from Tupper asking for a pass was signed, 'Yours very sincerely.' "

> *Life and Letters of Sir Wilfrid Laurier* (1921).

## Skelton, Robin
Canada has given me both a home and a cause. It is a country in which every gesture counts. It is a country of welcomes. It is a country of possibilities. There is more potential greatness in Canada, I am sure, than anywhere else on earth.

> "O Canada!" from Andy Wainwright's *Notes for a Native Land: A New Encounter with Canada* (1969).

## Skvorecky, Josef
I can't force myself to think about nudity in the movies, or about drugs or pollution. Such things are a luxury. Sure it's nice to see a naked girl on the screen, but the issues that really interest me are justice and the right of innocent people to a fair trial.

> Czechoslovakian literary figure living in Toronto, quoted by Peter C. Newman in "Josef Skvorecky" (1970), *Home Country: People, Places, and Power Politics* (1973).

## Slade, Bernard
My theory is that if you can make it in Canada, you can make it anywhere.

> TV script editor of *The Flying Nun* and creator of *The Partridge Family* and *Brigit Loves Bernie*, Slade was born in St. Catharines. Quoted by David Cobb in *The Canadian Magazine*, June 17, 1972.

## Slade, Mark
Films say nothing. People do the saying.

> *Language of Change: Moving Images of Man* (1970).

## Slater, Patrick
What a pity public hangings were ever done away with! Had they continued a few years longer, the horrible practice of hanging men would have passed away under the pressure of public opinion.

\*

"Here's to the worn-out hearts of those who saw a nation built, and to the proud, fun-loving young hearts that have it in their keeping." [Final toast]

> *The Yellow Briar: A Study of the Irish on the Canadian Countryside* (1933), written by John Mitchell under the pseudonym Patrick Slater.

I ask, therefore, that I be taken into custody on the charge of stealing certain moneys from clients and others, particulars of which I shall supply you. I do not wish to give their names publicity without their consent. My defalcations exceed the sum of $20,000.

> Letter of self-accusation sent to the at-

torney general of Ontario by the Toronto lawyer and author John Mitchell who wrote as Patrick Slater. At his own insistence Mitchell was tried, convicted of theft and sentenced to six years in a penitentiary. Quoted by Dorothy Bishop in her preface to the 1970 edition of *The Yellow Briar* (1933).

## Slezak, Leo

"If somebody in Canada wants to give you something free—call the police!"

Advice given the famous Viennese opera tenor in Montreal, after losing money to a real-estate swindler who had offered him free land. *Meine sämtlichen Werke* (1963).

## Slocum, Joshua

I was born in the breezes, and I had studied the sea as perhaps few men have studied it, neglecting all else.

\*

To know the laws that govern the winds, and to know that you know them, will give you an easy mind on your voyage around the world; otherwise you may well tremble at the appearance of every cloud.

\*

There was not a moment to spare. . . . I sprang from the oars to my feet, and lifted the anchor above my head, threw it clear just as she was turning over. I grasped her gunwale and held on as she turned bottom up, for I suddenly remembered that I could not swim.

*Sailing Alone Around the World* (1900). Between April of 1895 and July of 1898, the Nova Scotian seafarer Joshua Slocum sailed alone around the world, the first man to do so. On his derelict oyster sloop *Spray* he sailed 46,000 miles, without being able to swim.

Some far away places.

"B.H. Kidder of Oak Bluffs wrote the *Vineyard Gazette* that he saw Slocum later in Bridgeport, Connecticut, asked him where he was going, and that Slocum replied, 'Some far away places.' It does not seem likely, however, that the year was 1909." Walter Teller's *Joshua Slocum* (1971). That was the year Slocum disappeared and was presumed dead.

## Slonim, Reuben

It's easier to get along with Israelis than with lovers of Israel.

*Both Sides Now: A Twenty-Five-Year Encounter with Arabs and Israelis* (1972).

## Slopen, Beverley

There is no cure for masochism.

Remark of the Toronto writer and publicist, 1973.

## Smallwood, J.R.

It is a fact that for centuries we have lived by *killing* cod and other fish; by *killing* seals in the water and on the ice, and animals on land; by *cutting down* trees. Has all this developed in us a trait of destructiveness, or narcotized what ought naturally to be an instinct for creativeness?

*The Book of Newfoundland* (1937).

The only thing wrong with Confederation is that we didn't join in 1867. [Remark made about 1948]

\*

I never thought I'd see the day. [On April 1, 1949, the day Newfoundland joined Confederation]

\*

We have made other mistakes. I have made more than one mistake. The only man who makes no mistakes is a man who does nothing, and that is a mistake. Therefore he makes one. I have made mistakes. They have been, perhaps, mistakes of the heart. [Address in the Legislature, March, 1951]

\*

I am king of my own little island, and that's all I've ever wanted to be.

After six years of dealing with Jean Lesage, I have learned to deeply respect the humility of Charles de Gaulle. [To Peter C. Newman in 1967]

\*

This is *our* river, this is *our* waterfall, this is *our* land . . . we are developing it mainly, chiefly, principally for the benefit of Newfoundland. Newfoundland first, Quebec second, the rest of the world last. [Unveiling the Churchill

Falls power project, Labrador, July 17, 1967]

*

This poor bald rock. . . .

> Joseph Roberts (Joey) Smallwood became "the only living Father of Confederation" and first premier of Newfoundland when the island joined the mainland in 1949. The quotations appear in Richard Gwyn's *Smallwood: The Unlikely Revolutionary* (1968).

Confederation is good for the children.

> "Mothers, Read This," an editorial in *The St. John's Confederate*, May 31, 1948. Quoted by Peter Neary in *The Political Economy of Newfoundland, 1929-1972* (1973).

I was laid off.

> Reason given for his resignation as premier of Newfoundland after twenty-two years in public life, January 18, 1972.

It's not where you are. It's where you're headed that matters.

> *Time*, February 14, 1972.

God, I wanted success and I wanted Newfoundland to share in that success.

> Reply to charges of conflict of interest made by a provincial royal commission, *The Toronto Star*, July 8, 1972.

The province needs a cultural revolution.

> Ex-premier's address to students of Memorial University, Spring, 1973, after a visit to China. "If I were ten years younger, I would like to settle down for two or three years in China to help them build the society they are building." *The Toronto Star*, April 26, 1973.

My misfortune as a politician was that there was no other Premier with whom Newfoundlanders could compare me. They could compare me with perfection, but that was a comparison in which I could only lose.

> *I Chose Canada: The Memoirs of the Honourable Joseph R. "Joey" Smallwood* (1973), by the "only premier" from 1948 to 1972.

Nehru, my cod to thee.

> Message for Jawaharlal Nehru to accompany a boatload of cod for India's starving millions.

**Smart, Christopher**
Glorious the northern lights astream;
Glorious the song, when God's the theme. . . .

> *Song to David* (1763).

**Smart, James A.**
Granary of the Empire.

> Description of the prairie provinces, first used as the motto for a Canadian exhibition in London, England, 1901. It originated with the federal deputy minister in charge of the display, according to William Thomas Preston in *My Generation of Politics and Politicians* (1927).

**Smet, Pierre-Jean de**
The Indian has the gift of being everywhere without being anywhere.

> Quoted by Fraser Symington in *The Canadian Indian: The Illustrated History of the Great Tribes of Canada* (1969).

**Smith, A.E.**
Communism is Canadian because it shows that there is a way out of the conditions of hatred, crime, disease, poverty, unemployment and war.

> *All My Life: An Autobiography* (1949).

**Smith, A.J.M.**
"Why is *The McGill Daily*?"
Asked the pessimist sourly.
"Thank God," said the optimist gaily,
"That it isn't hourly!"

> "The McGill Daily" (1926), *The Blasted Pine: An Anthology of Satire, Invective and Disrespectful Verse* (1957), edited by F.R. Scott and A.J.M. Smith.

If you write, apparently, of the far north and the wild west and the picturesque east, seasoning well with allusions to the Canada goose, fir trees, maple leaves, snowshoes, northern lights, etc., the public grasp the fact that you are a Canadian poet, whose works are to be bought from the same patriotic motive that prompts the purchases of Eddy's matches or a Massey-Harris farm implement, and read along with Ralph Connor and Eaton's catalogue.

\*

The heart is willing, but the head is weak. Modernity and tradition alike demand that the contemporary artist who survives adolescence shall be an intellectual. Sensibility is no longer enough, intelligence is also required. Even in Canada.

"Wanted: Canadian Criticism," *The Canadian Forum*, April, 1928.

This is a beauty
of dissonance,
this resonance
of stony strand. . . .

\*

This is the beauty
of strength
broken by strength
and still strong.

From "The Lonely Land" (1926).

\*

And I will sing to the barren rock
Your difficult, lonely music, heart,
Like an old proud king in a parable.

Last stanza of "Like an Old Proud King in a Parable" (1943).

\*

McLuhan put his telescope to his ear;
What a lovely smell, he said, we have here.

"The Taste of Space," *Poems: New and Collected* (1967). (McLuhan's response was: "Synaesthesia!")

But the Canadian poet has one advantage—an advantage that derives from his position of separateness and semi-isolation. He can draw upon French, British, and American sources in language and literary convention; at the same time he enjoys a measure of detachment that enables him to select and adapt what is relevant and useful. This gives to contemporary Canadian poetry in either language a distinctive quality—its eclectic detachment. This can be, and has been, a defect of timidity and mediocrity; but it can also be, as it is hoped this book will show, a virtue of intelligence and discrimination.

Introduction to *The Oxford Book of Canadian Verse in English and French* (1960), edited by A.J.M. Smith.

## Smith, Adam

The French colony of Canada was, during the greater part of the last century, and some part of the present, under the government of an exclusive company. Under so unfavourable an administration its progress was necessarily very slow in comparison with that of other new colonies; but it became much more rapid when this company was dissolved after the fall of what is called the Mississippi scheme. When the English got possession of this country, they found in it near double the number of inhabitants which Father Charlevoix had assigned to it between twenty and thirty years before. That Jesuit had travelled over the whole country, and had no inclination to represent it as less considerable than it really was.

*An Inquiry into the Nature and Causes of the Wealth of Nations* (1776).

## Smith, Alexis

To maintain an actress's position in Hollywood one must have an enormous preoccupation with self.

The leading lady of the 1940s was born in Penticton in 1921 and taken the next year to Los Angeles. She is married to Craig Stevens. "It's not Warners that typed me. I typed myself—I played all my roles alike because I didn't know any better." Quoted by Lennard Decarl in *Films in Review*, June-July, 1970.

## Smith, Arnold

We can't go on living on a planet that's two-thirds slum—not with safety.

\*

We need to learn to share a planet. Belonging to the Commonwealth can help.

Arnold Smith is secretary-general of the Commonwealth of Nations.

## Smith, Denis

The range of choices before Quebec was always limited; but Pierre Trudeau, by his rationalism, has radically narrowed and distorted those choices. And the major dialectical opponent that his approach has created is not René Lévesque the pragmatist, but Pierre Vallières the fellow absolutist. The triangle of forces in which Pierre Trudeau is caught as both agent and victim—and Canada along with him—has taken the shape of classical tragedy.

> Bleeding Hearts . . . Bleeding Country: Canada and the Quebec Crisis (1971).

**Smith, Donald**   See Lord Strathcona.

## Smith, Goldwin
Ah! Politics, politics, always politics.

> Quoted by Hector Charlesworth in Candid Chronicles: Leaves from the Note Book of a Canadian Journalist (1925).

Style! I have no style. I merely wait till the mud settles. [May, 1904]

\*

That all the elements for a gigantic revolution exist in Russia is not to be gainsaid. But what would you have? A bloody and weltering anarchy. And the outcome of that would be—What? Well, people forget the army, the gigantic army—a million men probably. The army would be dislocated from the State and would follow a leader of its own—and that leader might, for aught we know, be a truculent Cossack. [January, 1905]

\*

If I were the Tsar, I should order all the Grand Dukes and their families out of Russia—for safety's sake; and then *I should rule without them!* [March, 1905]

\*

I was talking to him about an elaborate *édition de luxe* of the *Lives of Makers of Canada* at (I think) a guinea a volume. At once he fired up. "Where will it sell?" he asked. "These people are all carried away by the erroneous idea that there is a unified 'Canada.' There isn't. It might sell in Ontario; but what does a Doukhobor running naked over the prairie looking for Christ care about the life or politics of George Brown for example?" [Conversing with a Toronto publisher, November, 1905]

\*

ABOVE ALL NATIONS IS HUMANITY.

> "The motto engraved, by his own orders, on that stone seat, his own gift, on the Campus of Cornell. . . ." (W.L. Mackenzie King chose a similar motto for his *Industry and Humanity* [1918]: "Over all nations is humanity.") Quoted by Arnold Haultain in *Goldwin Smith: His Life and Opinions* (1913).

"Graft" was the slang name for corruption among the people, who complained truly but helplessly that everything was full of it. At a farmers' picnic I drew a farmer aside and asked him what was the difference in principle between his party and the other. He was long in answering, but at last he replied, "We say the other fellows are corrupt." The world will not go on in this way for ever.

\*

There are in Canada no social materials for a House of Lords, nor is there anything like that independent gentry which has furnished the conservative element in the House of Commons. The leading men in Canada are commercial, and cannot leave their business offices for Ottawa; or if they do, it is on business of their own.

\*

The union of the Canadian Provinces resembles, as a wit said in the debate, not that of a bundle of rods, gaining strength by their union, to which a confederationist had complacently compared it, but that of seven fishing-rods tied together by the ends.

\*

Canada, or rather be it said Ontario, cooped up as it is and severed from the great literary and publishing centres, is not a field in which literary distinction is to be earned.

\*

If his strong point was having been a stone-mason, his weak point was being a stone-mason still. [On Prime Minister Alexander Mackenzie]

> Reminiscences (1910), edited by Arnold Haultain.

I am no more against Colonies than I am against the solar system. I am against dependencies, when nations are fit to be independent.

The Empire (1863).

Communism as a movement is a mistake. But there is a communism which is deep seated in the heart of every man, which makes him feel that the hardest of all labour is idleness in a world of toil, and the bitterest of all bread that eaten by the sweat of another's brow.

Address, Montreal Mechanics' Institute, *Ontario Workman*, January 2, 1873. Quoted by Charles Lipton in *The Trade Union Movement of Canada: 1827-1959* (1967).

If public life is the noblest of all callings, it is the vilest of all trades.

*Lectures on Modern History* (1861). "Politics, the noblest of all callings, but the meanest of all trades. . . ." *Essays on Questions of the Day, Political and Social* (1893).

But in this country what is there for Conservatives to conserve or for Reformers to reform?

*Canadian Monthly and National Review*, April, 1872.

French Canada is a relic of the historical past preserved by isolation, as Siberian mammoths are preserved in ice.

*

Canadian nationality being a lost cause, the ultimate union of Canada with the United States appears now to be morally certain; so that nothing is left for Canadian patriotism but to provide that it shall be a union indeed, and not an annexation. . . .

*The Political Destiny of Canada* (1878).

Not Party, But the People.

Motto for *The Bystander: A Monthly Review of Current Events, Canadian and General*, February, 1880. In the January issue, Smith explained: "Our point of view is Canadian, but outside the Canadian Parties."

A Gothic pile, with the variety of forms and outlines in which its charm resides, or an Elizabethan manor-house, with its many gables, must in Canada be a mere snow-trap. [The "Gothic pile" is a reference to the newly constructed Parliament Buildings in Ottawa; *The Bystander*, February, 1880]

At present we have for a population of four millions, eight kings, one central and seven provincial, as many parliaments, and sixty-five ministers of the crown; while England is content with a single king, a single parliament—the members of which are not paid—and a single cabinet, seldom containing as many members as the cabinet at Ottawa. We have also judges and chief-justices as the stars of heaven in number. [*The Bystander*, March, 1880]

To make a nation there must be a common life, common sentiments, common aims, and common hopes. Of these, in the case of Quebec and Ontario, there are none.

*

Ontario by herself might be a nation. There is nothing at least in the nature of things, however much there may be in actual circumstances, to prevent her. [*The Bystander*, December, 1889]

It is perfectly true that the works of a journalist are ephemeral; they go into the nether world of old files and are forgotten. But does not the same fate befall a good many books? Look at the back stacks of any great library. What a necropolis of the immortals in there. [Address, Canadian Press Association, June 3, 1881]

The father of confederation was deadlock.

Quoted by G. Mercer Adam in *Canada's Patriot Statesman: The Life and Career of the Right Honourable Sir John A. Macdonald* (1891).

"Rich by nature, poor by policy," might be written over Canada's door. Rich she would be if she were allowed to embrace her destiny and be part of her own continent; poor, comparatively at least, she is in striving to remain a part of Europe.

*Canada and the Canadian Question* (1891). The phrases within quotation marks appeared a few years earlier in

Smith's introduction to *Handbook of Commercial Union* (1888), by G. Mercer Adam.

A romantic age stands in need of science, a scientific and utilitarian age stands in need of the humanities. [*The Week*, April 28, 1893]

Ottawa is a sub-arctic lumber-village converted by royal mandate into a political cockpit.

> Quoted by Edwin C. Guillet in *Pioneer Inns and Taverns* (1956).

When this man is gone who will then take his place? What shepherd is there who knows the sheep, or whose voice the sheep know? Who else could make Orangemen vote for Papists or induce half the members for Ontario to help in levying on their own province the necessary blackmail for Quebec? Yet this is the work which will have to be done if a general break-up is to be averted. Things will not hold together of themselves. [On Sir John A. Macdonald]

> Remark attributed to Goldwin Smith. The British-born journalist settled in Toronto in 1871 where he died in 1910. See also Wilfrid Eggleston.

The ultimate Union of this Northern Continent seems to me as certain as the rising of tomorrow's sun. It may be distant; it is not likely to come in my time; but it will come. Nature has made up her mind, and in the end she will have her way.

*

You must catch me soon or not at all. I am very near my end.

> This passage comes from Smith's letter to Sir Horace Curzon Plunkett, May 31, 1910. Arnold Haultain, in his edition of *A Selection from Goldwin Smith's Correspondence* (1913), explains: "This was the last letter to which Goldwin Smith attached his signature. He died a week after dictating this letter, viz. on June 7, 1910."

**Smith, H. Allen**     See Charles Fort.

**Smith, I. Norman**
Canada's sense of destiny has depended much on whether one sat on a tractor or in an office; whether one lived in 1758, 1867, or 1965; whether one was Indian, Eskimo, French, English, Irish, or Slav; whether one liked Ed Sullivan or Noël Coward, a Queen or a President.

It depends, too, on whether one believes democracy means majority rule or minority rights. . . .

> "The Canadian Sense of Destiny," *Neighbours Taken for Granted: Canada and the United States* (1966), edited by Livingston T. Merchant. I. Norman Smith was editor of *The Ottawa Journal*.

**Smith, Leo**
A German poet once launched the following paradox: "There is no art; there are only artists." A survey of music in Canada offers such difficulties that one is tempted to parody the above as follows: There is no Canadian music; but there are musicians living in Canada, and, to a lesser extent, Canadian musicians.

> "A Survey of Music in Canada," *Handbook of Canada: Issued by the Local Committee on the Occasion of the Meeting of the British Association for the Advancement of Science at Toronto, August, 1924* (1924).

**Smith, Olivia**
There is one thing you have forgotten in your deliberations and that is justice to women. I hope that at your future meetings you will give more attention to the cause of women. That is all I have to say.

> As the lieutenant-governor was about to prorogue the Ontario legislature on March 19, 1910, the House was startled by a militant suffragette rising from the gallery and making the above statement. She made a quick exit and was never heard from again. But it was learned she was an Englishwoman named Olivia Smith and that she had been imprisoned for similarly disrupting the British House of Commons. "Woman's Work and the Public Policy in Canada," *The Canadian Annual Review of Public Af-*

*fairs, 1910* (1911), edited by J. Castell Hopkins.

## Smith, Ray
North America is a large island to the west of the continent of Cape Breton. (Pronounced: Caybrittn)

*Cape Breton is the Thought Control Center of Canada* (1969).

## Smith, Sidney
If physical expansion involves academic deterioration, we ought not to enroll one extra student.

Quoted by Claude T. Bissell in "The University and the City" (1958), *Empire Club of Canada: Addresses 1957-58* (1958). Smith, president of the University of Toronto, made this statement in 1957.

## Smith, William J.
It takes a lot of labour to move a ton of freight one mile.

National president, Canadian Brotherhood of Railway, Transport, and General Workers. *The Face of Labour: Four Programs from CBC Television*, January-February, 1961.

## Smith, William Wye
O, the East is but the West, with the sun a little hotter;
And the pine becomes a palm by the dark Egyptian water;
And the Nile's like many a stream we know that fills its brimming cup;
We'll think it is the Ottawa as we track the batteaux up!
Pull, pull, pull! as we track the batteaux up!
It's easy shooting homeward when we're at the top.

This is the first of four stanzas of "The Canadians on the Nile" by the Rev. W.W. Smith of St. Catharines. The verse commemorates the Canadian Expeditionary Force of *voyageurs* sent to the relief of General "Chinese" Gordon at Khartoum in 1885. *A Treasury of Canadian Verse: With Brief Biographical Notes* (1900), edited by Theodore H. Rand.

## Smohalla
My young men shall never work. Men who work cannot dream; and wisdom comes to us in dreams. . . . You ask me to plough the ground. Shall I take a knife and tear my mother's bosom? You ask me to dig for stone. Shall I dig under her skin for her bones? You ask me to cut grass and make hay and sell it to the rich like white men. But how dare I cut my mother's hair?

Chief Smohalla was leader of the Columbia River band of Indians known as the "Dreamers." Quoted by Fraser Symington in *The Canadian Indian: The Illustrated History of the Great Tribes of Canada* (1969).

## Smollett, Tobias
Captain C. treated the Duke's character without any ceremony. "This wiseacre," said he, "is still abed; and I think the best thing he can do is to sleep on till Christmas; for when he gets up he does nothing but expose his own folly. In the beginning of the war he told me in a great fright that thirty thousand French had marched from Acadia to Cape Breton. Where did they find transports? said I.—Transports! cried he, I tell you they marched by land.—By land to the island of Cape Breton!—What is Cape Breton an island?—Certainly.—Ha! are you sure of that?—When I pointed it out on the map, he examined it earnestly with his spectacles; then, taking me in his arms,—My dear C., cried he, you always bring us good news. Egad! I'll go directly and tell the King that Cape Breton is an island."

*The Expedition of Humphry Clinker* (1771). Francis Parkman, who quotes this passage in *Montcalm and Wolfe* (1884), regards it as an imaginary instance of the very real ignorance of the Duke of Newcastle. See also the Duke of Newcastle.

## Smuts, Jan Christian
You and I have transformed the structure of the British Empire.

To Sir Robert Borden at the Imperial War Conference in London, April 16, 1917, after the prime minister of Canada and the prime minister of the Union of South Africa secured "a full recognition of the Dominions as autonomous nations of an Imperial Commonwealth." The same day Smuts recommended that the term British Empire be replaced by the term British Commonwealth of Nations. *Robert Laird Borden: His Memoirs* (1938), edited by Henry Borden. See also Sir Robert Borden.

Canada proved herself there [on the vast Western Front], and it could never be the same Canada again, as her subsequent history has already shown. Vimy Ridge was followed by Passchendaele and Amiens, to mention only the highlights. Canada had found her consciousness, found herself, and found her secure place in the great world. There her title-deeds to the future were written.

> Foreword to *Arthur Currie: The Biography of a Great Canadian* (1950), by Hugh M. Urquhart.

## Smythe, Conn
Gentlemen and Frenchmen. . . . [Start of a speech to the NHL on the presentation of the Hart Trophy to Bobby Orr, following a speaker who held forth in French]

*

If you can't lick 'em in the alley, you can't beat 'em on the ice.

> "I've tried to explain a hundred times what I meant when I said [that]. I did not mean that you scare the other guy but that you show him there is no fear in you." Quoted by Bob Pennington, *The Toronto Star*, October 1, 1973. This widely quoted aphorism first appeared in print in an interview with Trent Frayne in 1952.

Everybody has an incentive, and if you can bring out that incentive you've got a winner.

> Quoted by Trent Frayne in *Maclean's Magazine*, January 1 and 15, 1952.

## Snookum Jim
Dear Friend
My partner Will Geary got to putting on airs and I shot him and he is dead the potatoes is looking well. Yours truly

> SNOOKUM JIM

"An authentic letter written by a Whoop-Up resident" to the RCMP at Benton, quoted by T. Morris Longstreth in *The Silent Force: Scenes from the Life of the Mounted Police of Canada* (1927).

## Snow, Hank
And this was my one big dream, to have a damn place where I could make as much noise as I damn well wanted to, or leave the lights burning all night, or go to the refrigerator and get something to eat whenever I wanted.

> Nova Scotia-born star of the Grand Ole Opry, quoted by Jo Durden-Smith in *Maclean's Magazine*, April, 1972.

## Snow, Michael
The film is a cosmic strip.

> Quoted by Charlotte Townsend in "Converging on *La Région Centrale*" in *Artscanada*, February-March, 1971.

## Snowball, Jeannie
Ookpik.

> This small sealskin version of the Arctic owl was first sewn by Jeannie Snowball, an Eskimo widow in her sixties living in Fort Chimo. Ookpik means "happy little Arctic owl." Discovered by Frank Hamilton of the Department of Trade and Commerce, the doll was the hit of the Philadelphia Trade Fair, November, 1963. Ookpik has been called Canada's greatest symbol since the beaver. As balladeer Maryellen Greer described him: "He looked like an owl in front, / And just like a duck behind." *The Globe and Mail*, March 7, 1964. See also Frank Hamilton.

## Somers, Harry
I maintain you can create a whole composition out of one note, by applying basic principles.

> "Composer in the School," *Musicanada*. May, 1969.

From about the age of eight, I think, I had the idea I wanted to become a composer—mainly, at that time, in order to become very, very famous.

Quoted by Peter Such in *Soundprints: Contemporary Composers* (1972).

## Souster, Raymond
". . . But only God can make a tree."
(He'll never try it in Sudbury.)

"Very Short Poem."

*

Still grabbing
at that golden ring?

The ride's the thing.

"Merry - Go - Round," *Selected Poems* (1972).

## Southam, Harry Stevenson
Two papers are better than one.

H.S. Southam — the son of William Southam (who founded the newspaper dynasty) and the father of Robert Southam—died in 1954. Quoted by Charles Bruce in *News and the Southams* (1968).

## Sparks, Ned
I reasoned that all persons live somewhat under a shell. Their exteriors do not disclose their real personalities. A highly emotional or sentimental person will often hide his true feelings beneath a gruff exterior. And so I came to a conclusion. My new character would be a grumpy, hard-boiled, growling individual, impervious to any tender sentiment. But at the same time he would convey to his audience that all the bluster was merely a mask.

*The New Yorker* referred to the Guelph-born, St. Thomas-raised film actor as "the acrid Ned Sparks." Interviewed by Harold Feffernan in *The Detroit Times*, May 8, 1936. He was the original dead-pan comic, "the man who never smiled."

## Sparshott, Francis
Only those to whom what we say is not very important can be expected to understand what it is that we are saying.

"Philosophy and the 'Creative Process,'" *West Coast Review*, Spring, 1966.

Most of life and most of art is best enjoyed quietly.

*

One has apparently to choose between

a competent discussion of trivialities and a series of emotional outbursts about what matters.

*Looking for Philosophy* (1972).

## Spector, Maurice (Max)
Many who came chiefly to cheer went away to think.

When the Communist Party of Canada's leading political thinker sided with Trotsky rather than Stalin, after attending the Comintern's Sixth World Congress in Moscow in 1928, he made his views known and was expelled from the party in November of 1928. Letter to the American Trotskyite James P. Cannon, quoted by William Rodney in *Soldiers of the International: A History of the Communist Party of Canada 1919-1929* (1968).

## Spencer, Herbert
How the region [of the Thousand Islands] could have been formed—how the St. Lawrence could have cut these multitudinous channels, dividing tree-covered masses of rock of all sizes,—it is difficult to understand. But it is the romance of the scene which chiefly impresses one. Obviously this trait has prompted inhabitation; for here a small hotel, and there a villa, peeps out amid the trees. It has become the fashion among wealthy Americans to have one of these small water-guarded areas as a summer abode: gratification being doubtless given to a sentiment which is active during boyhood and is not altogether dead in adult life.

Picking us up next day, a steamer for Toronto carried us through another region of "The Thousand Islands," and presently on to Lake Ontario. "In the afternoon we came unto" a town, in which it could not be said that "it seemed always afternoon"; but in which, contrariwise, the vivacity of morning seemed conspicuous. This was Kingston, where the steamer stopped for a time to take in wood.

*An Autobiography* (1904). The British philosopher's visit was made in 1882.

## Spengler, Oswald

In the case of Canada, not merely great regions, but the *whole country* has been picketed out in equal rectangles for future development.

*The Decline of the West* (1918-22), translated from the German by Charles Francis Atkinson.

## Spicer, Keith

Westmount Rhodesians.

Phrase employed by the commissioner of official languages at a luncheon meeting of the Canadian Studies Institute, Johns Hopkins University, Baltimore, April, 1973. Spicer was asked, "Are you preoccupied with safeguarding the linguistic rights of English-speaking Quebecers?" In his reply, Spicer compared the Anglo-Saxons in the wealthy Montreal district of Westmount with the "outlaw regime" of Ian Smith's Rhodesia.

## Spry, Graham

Radio broadcasting is not to be considered or dismissed as a business only. It is no more a business than the public school system, the religious organizations, or the varied literary, musical, and scientific endeavours of the Canadian people. It is a public service. It is a national service. As a public and national service it should be controlled.

April 18, 1932. Quoted by E. Austin Weir in *The Struggle for National Broadcasting in Canada* (1965).

We sought, if J.W. Dafoe's words on a great subject may be used, to have "affinities with Machiavelli as well as Sir Galahad."

"The Origins of Public Broadcasting in Canada: A Comment," *Canadian Historical Review*, June, 1965. Dafoe had described Sir Wilfrid Laurier as "a man who had affinities with Machiavelli as well as with Sir Galahad" in *Laurier: A Study in Canadian Politics* (1922).

But when polling day came, I was defeated by large and enthusiastic majorities. . . .

"The CCF Party in Its Formative Years,"

*The Great Depression* (1969), edited by Victor Hoar.

Without communication, there is no society, whether it be a hive of bees, a troop of Boy Scouts, a bar association, or a nation.

Quoted by Harry J. Boyle in *Content*, March, 1972.

## Srul, Irving Glick

I respect any music that seems to extend itself inevitably.

Composer interviewed by *Musicanada*, October, 1967.

## Stacey, C.P.

Canada is an unmilitary community. Warlike her people have often been forced to be; military they have never been.

Opening words of *Official History of the Canadian Army in the Second World War, Volume I: Six Years of War* (1955). See also George F.G. Stanley.

## Stanfield, Robert L.

My Centennial project is to try to love Toronto.

Nova Scotia premier, quoted in *The Toronto Star*, January 27, 1967.

The way I make a speech, people know I'm not out to impress them, so I must be telling the truth. . . . They will accept me as I am, or not at all.

Leader of the Conservative party, 1968, quoted by Walter Stewart in *Shrug: Trudeau in Power* (1971).

The only minister sticking with Trudeau is Billy Graham.

\*

They say Mitchell Sharp actually resigned six months ago—they just haven't figured out what he said.

\*

Energy Minister J.J. Greene is going to publish his collected speeches—with the help of Masters and Johnson—called How to Really Enjoy Several Different Positions.

\*

Am I going too fast for you fellows?

*

It's a thankless, lonely job. Particularly when you're bad at it. But where else could you find a man so totally dedicated to spreading poverty in this country. [A reference to Finance Minister Edgar Benson]

*

I guess it is only between joining and leaving that there's no freedom at all. [A reference to Trudeau's remark that Paul Hellyer was free to join or leave the Liberal party]

*

I knew he would never marry Barbra Streisand or any American girl. I can recall him saying the States has no place in the bedrooms of the nation.

*

I don't think I'd do too well in the Senate. I speak too fast for them.

> Luncheon speech, Variety Club, Toronto, May 27, 1971.

There's only one me, and I'm stuck with him.

> CBC-TV's "Weekend," March 18, 1973.

## Stanley, Lord
I have been thinking for some time it would be a good thing if there were a challenge cup which could be held from year to year by the leading hockey club in Canada. I am willing to give such a cup.

> Governor General Lord Stanley donated the trophy that bears his name in 1893. The Stanley Cup cost ten guineas but has become the most coveted award in all hockey. Quoted by Henry Roxborough in *The Stanley Cup Story* (1964).

## Stanley, George F.G.
An unmilitary people.

> *Canada's Soldiers: The Military History of an Un-Military People* (1960). See also C.P. Stacey.

New France began as an economic venture on the part of old France. It came to an end because old France never regarded it as anything else; never, certainly, as a possibly distinct national entity. The concept of a colony as a new

national expression, with an ethos of its own and an economy of its own, was completely foreign to eighteenth-century thought.

> *New France: The Last Phase 1744-1760* (1968). See also Louis Riel.

## Starnes, Richard
Canadians are generally indistinguishable from the Americans, and the surest way of telling the two apart is to make the observation to a Canadian.

> Scripps-Howard columnist, quoted by Gerald Clark in *Canada: The Uneasy Neighbour* (1965).

## Starrett, Vincent
I was born in a bookshop or so close to it as to be able to claim the distinction. . . . It was the early morning of Tuesday, October 26, 1886, and the scene was No. 26 Oxford Street in the City of Toronto. In its prime it was a handsome enough middle-class dwelling, I have been told, but I have no memory of it whatever and no particular affection for it. I saw it consciously for the first time about thirty years ago and was not impressed.

*

Victorian Toronto in the last years of the old century was an interesting place to be born, for the old Tory capital was like a bit of old London itself.

> *Born in a Bookshop: Chapters from the Chicago Renascence* (1965).

## Stathakis, George L.
If I die, the turtle will carry the secret of the trip and reveal it at the proper time.

> Stathakis was a Greek-born Buffalo chef and mystic who went over Niagara Falls in a barrel on July 5, 1930. He perished, but his pet turtle crawled out of the barrel and lived for many years without revealing a word of "the secret." Quoted by Andy O'Brien in *Daredevils of Niagara* (1964).

## Stearn, Jess
"Reincarnation could be compared to attending school. Each life is a grade. If one learns his lessons well, he is pro-

moted to a higher grade. But if he doesn't understand, he must repeat his year."

It was a pretty good analogy.

*The Search for the Girl with Blue Eyes* (1968). The American author of books on psychic matters is quoting Joanne MacIver, a young twentieth - century Orillia girl who, under hypnosis, recalled being not Cleopatra in ancient Egypt but Susan Ganier, a nineteenth-century Ontario farm girl.

### Stedman, Raymond William
*Canadian Mounties v. Atomic Invaders* is an example of a title fad [in movie serials] that was perhaps symptomatic of waning creativity.

*The Serials: Suspense and Drama by Installment* (1971). A serial by this name was actually produced in Hollywood in the 1950s. See also Franklin Adreon.

### Steele, James
A loyal ally does not spy; he simply exchanges information.

"Canada's Vietnam Policy," in Stephen Clarkson's *An Independent Foreign Policy for Canada?* (1968). See also Robin Mathews.

### Steele, Sir Samuel Benfield
The changes which had taken place during my absence of seven years made me rub my eyes and wonder if I were dreaming. Hundreds of thousands of settlers had come into the great west. . . . It was the same all over western Canada, and we, who had been the pioneers of this glorious change, were permitted by Providence to see the fruits of our labours and our hardships.

*Forty Years in Canada: Reminiscences of the Great North-West with Some Account of His Service in South Africa* (1915). Sir Sam had a distinguished career with the Mounted Police; from 1901 to 1907, he served with British forces in South Africa.

### Steenman, L.F. See Anonymous: Songs.

### Stefansson, Vilhjalmur
I was brought up to believe that "primi-

tive" people have certain mental qualities called "instinctive," through which they vastly excel us along certain lines; and that, to balance this superiority, they are far our inferiors in certain other ways. My observation has been to the contrary, and inclines me to believe that there are no points in which they are any more inferior to us than might be expected from the environment under which they have grown up from childhood. Neither have they, so far as I have seen, any points of superiority over the white man, except those which are developed directly by the environment.

*My Life with the Eskimos* (1913).

But really what I have more at heart than anything else is that you do something, something intelligent for the Eskimo. That is the thing, really, that I am pleading for now. That is what brought me to Canada, and it is more or less incidental that I am trying to get support for another reason.

"Our Northland, Its People and Resources" (1913), *Empire Club of Canada: Addresses Delivered to the Members During the Sessions of 1912-13 and 1913-14* (1915).

The friendly Arctic.

In his major work *The Friendly Arctic: The Story of Five Years in Polar Regions* (1921), Stefansson's theme is that the North, far from being forbidding, is generally friendly.

If you take my word for this and look into it, you will see that instead of Canada being a grain country with a vast hinterland of no value, it is really a great land with a southern fringe of orchard land and a vast hinterland of valuable grazing country.

The Manitoba-born Arctic explorer felt there was a future in deer-meat, so he referred specifically to the northern deer-grazing country. "The Canadian North," April 28, 1919, *Addresses Delivered before the Canadian Club of Montreal: Season of 1918-19* (1919).

The northward course of empire.

Stefansson adapted the familiar phrase "Westward the course of empire takes its way" for the title and theme of his book *The Northward Course of Empire* (1922) which emphasizes the Arctic explorations of the fur traders. The phrase is associated with Bishop Berkeley, who used it in 1752 in a verse entitled "On the Prospect of Planting Arts and Learning in America," and with John Quincy Adams in 1802. "In spite of our hopes for *The Northward Course of Empire*, it sold less than two hundred copies in Canada," Stefansson wrote in his autobiography. Elsewhere he noted that a Russian translation of the same work sold twenty thousand copies.

It is great good fortune that we still have our frontier land in which pioneers may struggle and build, where they may dream their dreams of empire, and eventually write upon pages now blank the story of those realized dreams.

> *The Northward Course of Empire* (1922).

The philosophers of the Middle Ages demonstrated both that the earth did not exist and also that it was flat. Today they are still arguing about whether the world exists, but they no longer dispute about whether it is flat.

> *The Standardization of Error* (1927).

We should not regard the Eskimos as foreigners but as friends. They are your fellow citizens. Their future is bound up in our future. If Canada is but a thin southern strip across which plies a shuttle railway we shall have no remarkable future.

> Quoted by Margaret Fairley in *Spirit of Canadian Democracy: A Collection of Canadian Writings from the Beginnings to the Present Day* (1945).

Discovery has been my life. First the discovery, as a boy, of the New World. Then the discovery of the new ideas that were sprouting like prairie wheat in that world. Then the discovery of ancient people and unknown lands, and now, at last, the discovery of what discovery itself has done to my life.

\*

Today, rather than pretend to an atheism that can no more be proved than can the existence of God, I prefer to think that agnosticism is the only *modest* faith.

\*

The explorer is the poet of action and exploring is the poetry of deeds.

\*

False modesty is better than none.

\*

A land may be said to be discovered the first time a European, preferably an Englishman, sets foot on it.

\*

I have examined all the arguments in favour of no life in the Arctic Sea, and it seems to me that they are the kind of arguments that would appeal to a philosopher but would *not* appeal to fish.

\*

What is the difference between unethical and ethical advertising? Unethical advertising uses falsehoods to deceive the public; ethical advertising uses truth to deceive the public.

> *Discovery: The Autobiography of Vilhjalmur Stefansson* (1964).

The Russians live North and look North, but the Canadians live North and look South.

\*

The trouble lies in the fact that a Canadian Prime Minister has never been exiled to the Arctic.

\*

On the basis of my years with the Stone Age Eskimos I feel that the chief factor in their happiness was that they were living according to the Golden Rule.

\*

One of the advantages of skin clothing over woollens in Arctic exploration is that you can eat them in an emergency, or feed them to your dogs if the need is not quite so pressing. This puts actual starvation off by a week or so.

> Remarks attributed to the vigorous and outspoken Arctic explorer who died in 1962.

## Stegner, Wallace

In the end, I decide not to fault Whitemud for not being what only centuries of growth and the accidents of wealth and human genius could make it. Let it be, at least for a good long while, a seedbed, as good a place to be a boy and as unsatisfying a place to be a man as one could well imagine. Unless North American tourists discover the beauty of the geometric earth and the enormous sky brimming with weather, and learn the passion of loneliness and the mystery of a prairie wind, Whitemud is going to have too little to work with; it will remain marginal or submarginal in its community and cultural life. . . . Give it a thousand years.

    *

It is a country to breed mystical people, egocentric people, perhaps poetic people. But not humble ones. At noon the total sun pours on your single head; at sunrise or sunset you throw a shadow a hundred yards long. It was not prairie dwellers who invented the indifferent universe or impotent man. Puny you may feel there, and vulnerable, but not unnoticed. This is a land to mark the sparrow's fall.

> *Wolf Willow: A History, a Story, and a Memory of the Last Plains Frontier* (1962). The American author writes warmly of the Cypress Hills and the plains immediately below, where Saskatchewan and Manitoba meet up with the Montana border. From 1914 to 1920, the author's family homesteaded these regions.

### Stein, David Lewis
Well groomed, we stand on broadloomed floors
Inhaling deeply the smell of money,
Well-adjusted children of the new era
Blankly awaiting the next pogrom.

> "Poem," *First Flowering: A Selection of Prose and Poetry by the Youth of Canada* (1956), edited by Anthony Frisch.

The past is gone; the present is full of confusion; and the future scares hell out of me.

> "Brown School," *Toronto Life*, September, 1972.

### Stein, Gertrude
Hemingway seemed very much not to have liked Canada.

> Letter to Sherwood Anderson, 1924. See also Ernest Hemingway.

### Steinbeck, John
Niagara Falls is very nice. It's like a large version of the old Bond sign on Times Square. I'm very glad I saw it, because from now on if I am asked whether I have seen Niagara Falls I can say yes, and be telling the truth.

> *Travels with Charley: In Search of America* (1962).

### Steinberg, David
If I stay in California much longer, I'll melt like butter.

> Winnipeg - born satirist, quoted by Charles Higham in *The New York Times*, July 16, 1972.

### Steinberg, Nathan
If a man goes without food for one day, he will lie. If he goes without food for two days, he will steal. If he goes without food for four days, he will riot and kill. The food business is the most essential in the world, and the largest.

> Supermarket magnate quoted by Peter C. Newman in *Flame of Power: Intimate Profiles of Canada's Greatest Businessmen* (1959).

### Steinberg, Sam
We started with a philosophy, and we have carried it out. The starting point was my mother's principle of keeping customers happy by giving them a little extra, and we haven't changed.

> Supermarket magnate quoted by Peter C. Newman in *Flame of Power: Intimate Profiles of Canada's Greatest Businessmen* (1959).

### Stendhal
Mr. Hall found Canada to be inhabited by Frenchmen who speak the language which was current around the end of Louis XIV's reign. At the moment when he enters the city of Mont-Réal, it is in the throes of an election. On all the walls he reads these words, written with chalk in letters two feet high: *Papineau pour toujours*. Papineau was the popu-

lar candidate. But instead of shouting *Vive Papineau,* as one would do in France, the French of Canada translated the phrase used in England in such circumstances, "Papineau *forever!*"

\*

Canada has often been discontented with the government of England; one can believe that easily. Now Mr. Hall wants to persuade us that Canadians are happier under a government which is jealous and hungry for money than they would be if they were self-governing. I admit I've never read anything so extraordinary. I reread the passage twice to see if it wasn't tongue-in-cheek, as the English often are. Canada sends an enormous amount of contraband English merchandise to the United States. That's what provides employment for those French country folk whom we saw constantly engaged in conversation with their horses. This contraband activity and its attendant monetary advantages may stave off for half a century Canada's union with the United States.

> The great French novelist reviewed *Travels in North America, in the Years 1827 and 1828* (1829), by Basil Hall, a British traveller, in 1830. *Mélanges d'art et de littérature* (1867).

### Stengel, Casey

Well, you see, they have these polar bears up there and a lot of fellows trip over them trying to run the bases and they're never much good anymore except maybe for hockey or hunting deer!

> The irrepressible Casey Stengel on why so few Canadians play major-league baseball in the United States, 1973.

### Stephen, George

Stand fast, Craigellachie!

> The Canadian Pacific Railway was all but bankrupt in November of 1884 when President George Stephen raised last-minute capital in London, England, by selling his own bonds and those of his cousin Donald Smith, Lord Strathcona, an influential Montreal investor in the railway. "It was this small bit of Highland good cheer that prompted the president to send off to Smith one of the

most memorable cablegrams in Canadian history . . . and certainly the shortest," wrote Pierre Berton in *The Great Railway: Illustrated* (1972). "And Donald Smith, when he read it in Montreal, must himself have heard, as in the distance, the clash of warring claymores and the wild skirl of battle."

Craigellachie is Gaelic for "the rock of alarm." According to *The Encyclopaedia Britannica* (Eleventh Edition, 1910-11), "It is situated on the Spey amidst scenery of surpassing loveliness. The slogan of the Grants is 'Stand fast Craigellachie!' The place has become an important junction of the Great North of Scotland railway system." Of local manufacture is "Stand Fast" whisky. Because he stood fast, Lord Strathcona was offered the honour of driving in the "last spike" at Craigellachie, Eagle Pass, British Columbia, November 7, 1885. The Canadian Craigellachie is a point on the CPR route between Sicamous and Revelstoke. A plaque marking the spot includes this inscription: "Here on November 7, 1885, a plain iron spike welded East to West."

See also Lord Strathcona.

### Stephenson, Sir William

As a whole, Intelligence operations consist less of the blood-chilling adventures we read about than of hard work, endless patience, highly developed technical skills, and infinitely careful and competent organizations. War has become a thing of instantaneous combustion, engulfing civilian and soldier alike. Surely it is plain that against enemy attack today, the first defence must be information: to find out when and where an aggressor intends to strike. That is the role of Secret Intelligence, and without it all other means of defence could prove to be of sadly limited avail.

> Quoted by H. Montgomery Hyde in *The Quiet Canadian: The Secret Service Story of Sir William Stephenson* (1962). During World War Two, the task of coordinating British and American intelligence systems was "under the direction of a quiet Canadian, William Stephenson" (the phrase is Robert E. Sherwood's). Sir William, born in Mani-

toba in 1896, invented wireless photo-transmission at the age of twenty-six. Stephenson may have been Ian Fleming's model for "M" in the James Bond books. See also Ian Fleming.

## Stern, Karl

It is no coincidence that in Hebrew the word *Yadoa* is the word for knowing and for the physical consummation of love.

*The Pillar of Fire* (1951).

For phenomenology and existential philosophy have taught us once more something that classical philosophers knew long ago: if one wants to get closer to the ontological mystery behind the facts of nature, there is only one reliable place to go—to the hearts of men.

*The Flight from Woman* (1965).

## Sterne, Laurence

There is a Northwest Passage to the intellectual world.

*Tristram Shandy* (1759-67), Book V, Chapter 42.

## Stevens, Wallace

My eye was particularly taken by three things—or say four—on the trip from start to finish; first, Montreal's Frenchness, second, Lake Superior's austerity, third Winnipeg's cool sunnyness, and fourth the rock character of mountains above the timber-line. [August 2, 1903]

Journal entry of the American poet, dated at Palliser, British Columbia. *Letters of Wallace Stevens* (1966), edited by Holly Stevens.

## Stewart, Alexandra

I'm not an actress. I never studied the theatre. I just wanted to ride horses.

Quoted by Leslie F. Hannon in *The Star Weekly*, October 24, 1964. The beautiful actress was born Sandra Maureen Stewart in Montreal and moved to Paris to model in 1957.

## Stewart, Andrew

Canadian content.

Andrew Stewart was chairman of the Board of Broadcast Governors when it popularized the two-word phrase "Canadian content." The BBG, a forerunner of Pierre Juneau's CRTC, was required by the Broadcasting Act of 1958 to ensure that all radio and TV be "basically Canadian in content and character." The BBG ruled that all TV stations would be required to telecast a minimum of "45% Canadian content" as of April 1, 1961, and "55% Canadian content" as of April 1, 1962. The CBC met this requirement with ease, but the private stations never did, so the regulations were relaxed to require that they maintain these levels during the summer and outside of prime time.

## Stewart, Basil

Once they took anybody, now they scrutinize. It was this scrutiny which prompted the now well-known suffix to an advertisement in a Winnipeg paper asking for road labourers—"No English need apply."

*

Geographically considered Canada is in just the same position to the United States as Scotland is to England, and its final political union is no more improbable today than was that of England and Scotland, say, two hundred and fifty years ago.

*The Land of the Maple Leaf; or, Canada As I Saw It* (1908). For more on "No English Need Apply," see Keir Hardie.

## Stewart, Dr. D.A.

A doctor advocating a commodity generally is putting up for sale along with his commodity something that does not belong to him: the age-old inherited confidence of people in the medical profession. To sell a harmless or useful product in that way is not so bad as to sell nostrums, but the principle is the same. One committee member thought quite appropriate the answer of a wife, when her husband asked if a collar could be worn again—"if it's doubtful it's dirty."

Manitoba doctor, chairman of the Code of Ethics Committee of the Canadian Medical Association, 1937. Quoted by

H.E. MacDermot in *One Hundred Years of Medicine in Canada 1867-1967* (1967).

## Stewart Jr., George

We have had to write our books under our breath, as it may be said, and the marvel is that we have been able to produce, under such depressing circumstances, so many works of even respectable merit.

\*

Every now and then we hear the question: Why does Canada not have a magazine? The Canadians read magazines and pay for them. That is true; but it is also true that they want the best. Their standard is high, and unless the publisher can supply a publication which can compete with the important old world and United States serials, they will not have it, no matter how patriotic they may suppose themselves to be. Of course, the day is coming when Canada will have its great monthly and still greater quarterly, but the time is not yet ripe.

> "Literature in Canada," *Canadian Leaves: History, Art, Science, Literature, Commerce: A Series of New Papers Read before the Canadian Club of New York* (1887), edited by G.M. Fairchild, Jr.

## Stewart, Reginald

There are just as many children beating drums and blowing horns in the jungles of Africa as there are in the drawing-rooms of America.

> "Good Music Made Popular" (1934), *Empire Club of Canada: Addresses Delivered to the Members During the Year 1934-1935* (1935).

## Stewart, Walter

When I read about an American soldier firing a clip of tracer bullets into a group of women and children in some Mekong hamlet, I feel a quiet thrill of pride. The vivid description of a fighter-bomber snarling across the hills near Khe Sanh, spraying napalm, sends a surge of patriotism coursing through my veins. An eyewitness account of bombs wrenching at rice paddies along the Ho Chi Minh Trail stirs me like a cry of

bugles. After all, it's our war, too. The bullets for that soldier's weapon may have ridden in a De Havilland Caribou built at Malton, Ontario; that napalm-spraying fighter-bomber was almost certainly equipped with a Canadian-made Marconi Doppler Navigation System; those bombs along the Ho Chi Minh Trail may have been made from dynamite shipped out of Valleyfield, Quebec, and disgorged by a bombing computer fashioned in Rexdale, Ontario.

Why should the Americans have all the glory? We do our part, too.

> *Shrug: Trudeau in Power* (1971).

Votes are where you can grovel for them, I guess.

\*

If the two most noted words in Trudeau's vocabulary are Anglo-Saxon in origin, those in Stanfield's are French: *noblesse oblige*.

\*

If it's Tuesday, this must be bilingualism. [Quick characterization of the Liberal party's ability "to hold any number of positions on any question up for discussion"]

> *Divide and Con: Canadian Politics at Work* (1973).

## Stobo, Robert

The major's service at Quebec was all obedience to command, and information to his great patron, best and almost only known; he pointed out the place to land, where afterwards they did, and were successful.

> It is an open question whether Stobo, the Scottish-born American espionage agent, told James Wolfe of the path at Anse-aux-Foulons leading to Quebec. *The Memoirs of Major Robert Stobo of the Virginia Regiment* were not published until 1800 and are told in the third person. Quoted by Robert C. Alberts in *The Most Extraordinary Adventures of Major Robert Stobo* (1965).

## Stock, Brian

If one gathers the best natural scenery from Switzerland, France, Scotland, Russia, and Roumania and lumps them together, one does not have a country.

\*

One cannot resist climate, people, and countryside forever. One cannot go on believing in a *patria* which does not exist.

> "Why Young Men Leave," *The Atlantic Monthly*, November, 1964.

### Stolk, Mary Van
There are no lobbyists for children.

> *The Battered Child in Canada* (1972).

### Stopes, Marie
Notwithstanding my marriage, my legal name is Marie C. Stopes . . . privately, for the few friends who cannot escape the bonds of custom, I add the name of my husband by hyphen—Stopes-Gates.

> The author of *Married Love* (1918) was married to an impotent Montreal doctor and was still a virgin when the book appeared.

### Stott, Denis
Intelligence is like witchcraft. It's a convenient, all-embracing mystical term for a commodity that is unseen, unreachable and indefinable, so any use of the term intelligence as a measure of a person's abilities is pre-scientific and meaningless.

> *The Parent as Teacher* (1971).

### Stowe, Harriet Beecher
Montreal is a most religious city . . . Montreal is a mountain of churches. Every shade and form of faith is here well represented in wood or stone and the gospel feast set forth in every form and shape to suit the spiritual appetite of all inquirers.

> The author of *Uncle Tom's Cabin* (1852) visited Montreal in 1869. Quoted by Edgar Andrew Collard in *Montreal Yesterdays* (1962). The author's brother, Henry Ward Beecher, visited the city ten years later.

### Stowe-Gullen, Augusta
Victoria College! With a Queen's name, they can't refuse a woman!

> Augusta Stowe was the first woman doctor to train and practise in Canada. She graduated from Victoria University and the Toronto School of Medicine in 1883, the year she married Dr. B. Gullen. Her mother, Dr. Emily Howard Stowe, had been in practice for three years, having graduated in New York. Quoted by Byrne Hope Sanders in *Canadian Portraits: Famous Women* (1958).

When women have a voice in national and international affairs, *wars will cease forever.*

> Quoted by Jean Bannerman in *Leading Ladies: Canada: 1639-1967* (1967).

### Strabo    See Pytheas.

### Strachan, John
I had almost forgot to tell you that, seeing no prospect of my ever being able to return home, I married last spring and find myself happy in the connexion. My wife has an annuity of three hundred a year during her life. She has a great share of beauty, in her twenty-second year, and as good an education as this country could afford, which by the way is not great. [Letter to Dr. James Brown, Cornwall, October 20, 1807]

\*

Nobody would ask for the vote by ballot but from gross ignorance; it is the most corrupt way of using the franchise.

> The latter quote is Strachan's answer to Question No. 556, "The vote by ballot is prayed for in many petitions both to the Assembly and to His Majesty; what is your opinion of this mode of voting?" *The Seventh Report from the Select Committee of the House of Assembly of Upper Canada on Grievances . . . W.L. Mackenzie, Chairman* (1835). Reproduced by J.L.H. Henderson, editor of *John Strachan: Documents and Opinions* (1969).

Can you tell me, Sir, the reason why the public buildings and library at Washington should be held more sacred than those at York?

> Letter to Thomas Jefferson, written from York (later Toronto), January 30, 1815. Reproduced by William F. Cog-

gin in *1812; the War, and its Moral: A Canadian Chronicle* (1864).

The law! the law! Never mind the law; toorn him oot, toorn him oot!

> When Barnabas Bidwell was elected to the Legislative Council of Upper Canada in November of 1821, the Rev. John Strachan urged the legal or illegal dismissal of the noted reformer. On January 22, 1822, Bidwell was declared ineligible to sit in the House; a "late loyalist," he had emigrated from the United States twelve years earlier but had neglected to apply for British citizenship. Quoted by John Charles Dent in *The Story of the Upper Canadian Rebellion* (1885).

### Strachey, John
I cannot see why America should have such a terrible effect on Canada. I want to see this country develop her special form of culture, her special political forms, deal with the great problems of the world and set a good example to the world. I cannot see why Canada cannot do that perfectly. One doesn't want to make her the richest and most luxurious city in the world but a state of the best citizens and that is what she can do.

> "Stands England Where She Did?" October 9, 1925, *Addresses Delivered before the Canadian Club of Toronto: Season of 1925-26* (1926). Strachey was, at the time, editor of *The Spectator*.

When I was here last I found the official leaders of the Communist party in jail. I am glad to see that this is no longer the case, but the statute under which they were put in jail is still on the statute books and it does seem to me that Canada is to some extent at the turning point.

> "What Is the Cause of War" (1935), *Empire Club of Canada: Addresses Delivered to the Members During the Year 1934-35* (1935). The English Marxist and M.P. was denied admission to the U.S. on his lecture tour.

### Straiton, John
We once tested some advertising ideas for a stereo set in Toronto and in Chi-cago. The phrase "Made in Canada by Canadian Craftsmen" was rated better in Chicago than in Toronto. I know that Canadian whiskey is the biggest selling whiskey in the U.S. They like our spirit, anyhow.

> "Are Canadians Simply Americans on Snowshoes?" October 22, 1970, *The Empire Club of Canada: Addresses 1970-71* (1971).

Without advertising, it's Russia.

> Vice-chairman, Ogilvy and Mather, quoted by Joanne Strong in *The Globe and Mail*, May 28, 1973.

### Strand, Mark
We all have reasons
for moving.
I move
to keep things whole.

> Last stanza of the poem "Keeping Things Whole" (1963), by the poet who was born in Prince Edward Island in 1934 and now lives in the United States. *The Contemporary American Poets: American Poetry Since 1940* (1969), edited by Mark Strand.

### Stratas, Teresa
Don't call me Callas.

> Quoted by George Kidd in *The Toronto Telegram*, January 10, 1958.

Little Callas? Not me!

> Quoted by Leon Kossar in *The Toronto Telegram*, January 28, 1958.

Everybody's given me a big break some time or other, it seems.

> Quoted by Ralph Hicklin in *The Globe and Mail*, August 11, 1962. The operatic diva was born Anastasia Stratakis in Toronto in 1938.

I have only one real, unchanging friend —my music.

> Quoted by Blaik Kirby in *The Toronto Star*, June 18, 1963.

### Strathcona, Lord
I had neither the training nor the talents to accomplish anything without hard work, and fortunately I knew it.

Donald Smith, Lord Strathcona, quoted by Joseph Gilpin Pyle in *The Life of James J. Hill* (1916).

Northern people have always stood for courage and unconquerability. They have the muscle, the wholesomeness of life, the strength of will.

Strathcona risked his fortune on the CPR and was invited to drive in the "last spike," November 7, 1885. "Then came the final day when Donald Smith drove a gold [*sic*] spike into the heart of the Rockies, and ended them." Stephen Leacock, as quoted by Eric Nicol in *Vancouver* (1970). See also George Stephen.

## Stravinsky, Igor
I like Toronto because nobody hates me here—unlike New York or Vienna.

Attributed to the late composer by John Kraglund in *The Globe and Mail*, May 6, 1972.

## Street, A.G.
You and the plough have become one, a common intelligence with but one idea only, to plough—on and on and on. Your mind stands calmly aloof, rejoicing in a thing in which it has no conscious part, noting with a detached satisfaction the perfect furrow, which falls away on your right in an infinite ribbon.

*Farmer's Glory* (1934). Street farmed for a few years in Manitoba until the outbreak of World War I took him back to England.

## Strickland, Major Samuel
The shores were dotted with farmhouses and adorned with fine gardens and orchards, while lovely islands, covered with lofty trees, rose from the river and delighted the eye. I thought Canada then—and I have never changed my opinion since—the most beautiful country in the world. [St. Lawrence above Ile d'Orléans]

\*

Nothing, indeed, but industry and enterprise is needed to change the waste and solitary places of Upper Canada into a garden of Eden, which it is designed by the Supreme Architect to become.

\*

A man of education will always possess an influence, even in bush society: he may be poor, but his value will not be tested by the low standard of money, and notwithstanding his want of the current coin of the realm, he will be appealed to for his judgment in many matters, and will be inducted into several offices, infinitely more honourable than lucrative.

\*

Reader, did you ever see a ghost? A tall spectral-looking figure, with large saucer eyes, glides before you; and ere you summon courage to address it, vanishes from your astonished sight? Well, Canada is no place for ghosts. The country is too new for such gentry. We have no fine, old, ruined castles, crumbling monastic walls, or ivy-clad churches—no shelter here but the wild, wild wood.

*Twenty-Seven Years in Canada West; or, The Experience of an Early Settler* (1853), edited by Agnes Strickland.

## Stringer, Arthur
Society, my dear, is like salt water, good to swim in but hard to swallow.

\*

To wear love's brand you must bear love's burn.

*The Silver Poppy* (1903).

The sad truth is our whole busy bunch of novelists and story-tellers and verse writers today constitute nothing more than an attenuated choir of street sparrows, chirping disconsolately from the rafters of a locomotive round house. Canada's great artists today are Shaughnessy and Mann and Mackenzie and Charlie Hays and those epic-minded workers who are writing a new kind of blank verse in town sites and railway iron and grain routes.

*The Globe*, New Year's edition, 1910.

For as Earl Grey said when he was Governor General of this Dominion: "Canada has been too busy writing her history with the gun and the axe and the plough to bother about writing it with the pen." Or, to quote his exact words when speaking of Canadians: "Their energies are so much absorbed in this task that it would be unreasonable to expect them to be in the van of movements which aim at the realization of the higher and nobler life."

\*

I recall how some cynical Demosthenes of the daily press once put the rhetorical question—I do not know whether it was Hector Charlesworth or not—Where are our Canadian poets? And a new cynical Toronto editor said: "On the train to New York."

"The Interpreters of Canada," *Empire Club of Canada: Addresses Delivered to the Members During the Year 1932* (1932).

As a member of those melancholy expatriates who have been dubbed the League of Fallen Maple Leaves I have learned to tread lightly when I venture back to the land of my birth.

\*

For art is a flower that can't be forced.

\*

You know, I'm at last beginning to understand why the beaver is our national emblem. I thought, once, it was due to the industriousness of what had been designated as merely amplified rat. But I was wrong there. For outside its industry the beaver has one peculiar and distinguishing trait. That peculiarity stems from the conviction that its home isn't inhabitable until it has been well damned.

\*

We Canadians, of course, have had to get used to being told we don't amount to much. The late lamented Kaiser, when he concocted his cultural map of the world, marked Canada off as a blank. Sara Bernhardt, when last in this country on one of her repetitious farewells, complained that we had no poets and no poetry. Robert Barr said we spent more money on our booze than on our books. When a group from the Canadian Authors' Association journeyed to England and visited George Bernard Shaw that Chesterfieldian Irishman announced that he was under the impression Canada *had* no authors. Much of Shaw's emi-

nence, of course, has been achieved through his rudeness and his tendency to stand Truth on her head. For when this same association of authors invited him to Canada his gracious response was that he had no intention of visiting an outlandish country of savages where a man of Shavian alertness would promptly die of intellectual starvation.

"Canada Finds Her Voice" (1949), *Empire Club of Canada: Addresses Delivered to the Members During the Year 1948-49* (1949). Stringer, born in Chatham, achieved popular success in the United States with his novels. He died in New Jersey in 1950.

### Stykolt, Stefan

Economics is an art. But it is an art without aesthetic rewards. The financial rewards, though, can be very great, which is why it's an art more open to corruption than others.

\*

All the evils of publishing can be traced to one source—copyright.

Quoted by Kildare Dobbs in *The Living Name: A Tribute to Stefan Stykolt from Some of His Friends* (1964), edited by W.J. Stankiewicz.

### Styles, W.A.L.

An expletive, highly picturesque and commonly used by the North West voyageurs, was: "Crush my soul on the end of a fence rail!"

*Unusual Facts of Canadian History* (1947), introduced by Stephen Leacock.

### Sullivan, J.A. (Pat)

Life with the Communists is full of surprises—none of them pleasant.

*Red Sails on the Great Lakes* (1955).

### Sullivan, R.B.

The future safety and tranquillity of the Province must depend more upon external circumstances, over which this Government has no control, than upon the management of internal affairs. There are no mountains or seas, or differences of language to separate this Province from the United States, and this Province must be materially affected by the state of Politics and of the popular mind in the neighbouring republic.

*

In many parts of the Province the teachers are Americans, for the sake of obtaining employment they have swallowed the oath of allegiance which agrees so ill with them that the rest of their lives is spent in attempts to disgorge it. These men are utterly ignorant of every thing English and could not if they tried instruct their pupils in any of the duties which the connection of the Province with England casts upon them. The books they use are all American filled with inflated accounts of American independence and the glorious wars with England. The exploits of General Jackson and the heroes of '76 fill the youthful mind to the exclusion of every thing glorious or interesting in English history. The young man grows up without a single prepossession in favour of his country; he looks upon a British soldier as a person whom it would be honourable and glorious to oppose with the rifle. The British Government in his mind is a chimerical monster four thousand miles off, which notwithstanding that it has been beaten to nothing by American prowess, and excelled in every thing by American ingenuity still drags on an antiquated existence, which it holds almost at the will of the United States.

*

. . . it is strange to observe that while in the state of New York, the course of instruction and the books which are used are under the strictest surveillance and direction of the Government, all this in Upper Canada is left to the care of a few illiterate, ignorant and sometimes disloyal local Township trustees.

> Letter of R.B. Sullivan, member of the Executive Council of Upper Canada, to Sir George Arthur, lieutenant-governor of Upper Canada, June 1, 1838, *The Arthur Papers: Being the Canadian Papers Mainly Confidential, Private, and Demi-Official of Sir George Arthur, K.C.H.* (1957), edited by Charles R. Sanderson.

## Sulzberger, Arthur Hays
The Scotch in Ontario may brood a little too darkly on sins material and immaterial, especially after the merriment of Hogmanay, but the habit of introspection is beneficial.

> "Power and Responsibility" (1952), *Empire Club of Canada: Addresses 1951-52* (1952). Sulzberger was publisher of *The New York Times*.

## Sunday, John
Brothers and sisters, I will tell you what the good missionaries are like—they are like sun-glasses, which scatter light and heat wherever they are held; so do the ministers of Christ spread the light of truth amongst the people, which warms their hearts and makes them happy.

> Sunday, a Mississauga Indian named Shawundais ("Sultry Heat"), was converted in 1826 and became a missionary among his people.

*

My family lives at Alderville, but I live everywhere.

> Familiar remark of the far-travelling missionary who died at Alderville, Ontario, December 14, 1875. Quoted by John Maclean in *Canadian Savage Folk: The Native Tribes of Canada* (1896).

## Sutherland, Donald
People say, "What are you going to Toronto for?" Either you're going there for a location or a vacation. Certainly not for a vocation.

> Quoted by Robert McDonald in *The Toronto Star*, August 18, 1967.

Why not? All my intensities are defined by my roots, and my roots are entirely Canadian. I'm as Canadian as you'll ever find. Whatever that means.

> Quoted by Paul King, who asked the film star if he still felt like a Canadian, in *The Canadian Magazine*, March 28, 1970. Sutherland was born in Saint John in 1936 and from 1965 to 1971 was married to Tommy Douglas's daughter. See also Shirley Sutherland.

## Sutherland, John

If God still talks to these poets in private, he carries less weight than Karl Marx or Sigmund Freud. The seven-day fireworks of the world's creation matter less than the creation of the socialist state; the cure of earthly ills is to be achieved by economics or psychology rather than by divine intervention.

Preface to *Other Canadians* (1949).

A horse that talked would be a phenomenon but a horse that talked only of itself would be a horror. But we would not mind a horse that talked only of horses.

\*

A writer is no longer a man but an environment.

"The Great Equestrians," *Northern Review*, Summer, 1956. *John Sutherland: Essays, Controversies and Poems* (1972), edited by Miriam Waddington.

## Sutherland, Ronald

Surely there are more clergymen per book in Canadian literature than in the literature of any other country.

*Second Image: Comparative Studies in Québec/Canadian Literature* (1971).

So what if Canadian cultural activity is experiencing a veritable explosion? The starfish off Australia's coral reef are also increasing spectacularly, and that may be a phenomenon of greater importance because they could end up doing in one of nature's most useful and beautiful masterpieces.

"Canada's Elizabethan Age," *The Times Literary Supplement*, October 26, 1973.

## Sutherland, Shirley

Well, we're rich now—ah, wealthy. I've lived in rich environments and in poor environments, and if there's something that upsets you about living in a rich environment, there's something wrong with you.

Shirley Sutherland, Tommy Douglas's daughter, was married to Donald Sutherland from 1965 to 1971. Quoted by Stewart Warner in *The Star Weekly*, August 24, 1968. See also Donald Sutherland.

## Sutton, Horace

Canada is clean, healthy, young, polite, unspoiled and, as I say, just upstairs.

*Footloose in Canada* (1950), by the New York travel writer.

## Swankey, Ben

An Indian reserve is a big bottle. The bottle is wide at the base and holds a great many people. It has, however, a very narrow neck. In the neck, the Indian Agent is a stopper. Outside the bottle is the world. To the Indians, the world is the Indian Affairs (Branch) and assorted white men. Inside are the Indians, the chief and council are the cream, and they're at the top of the bottle near the stopper. Periodically the bottle is open and some children and a few adult Indians are let out; sometimes money is put in, then the stopper is replaced. No information passes through the glass walls. Indians don't know much of what's happening outside, and the outside knows less about them. Few outside get past the stopper.

Ben Swankey, in his booklet *National Identity or Cultural Genocide?* (1971), is quoting "a former official of the Indian Affairs Branch" of the federal government.

## Sweet Grass

When I hold your hand I feel as if the Great Father were looking on us both as brothers. I am thankful. May this earth here never see the white man's blood spilt on it. I thank God that we stand together, that you all see us; I am thankful that I can raise up my head, and the white man and red man can stand together as long as the sun shines.

The principal Cree chief at the negotiations leading to the signing of the treaties at Forts Carlton and Pitt, September 9, 1876. Alexander Morris's *The Treaties of Canada with the Indians of Manitoba and the North-West Territories* (1880).

**Sweezey, R.O.**
... he thought that a contribution would be in order to the Ontario Conservative Party because we would probably be having a lot more dealings with the Ontario people, and that gratefulness was always regarded as an important factor in dealing with democratic governments.

> Statement regarding large contributions, Special Committee on the Beauharnois Power Project, Ottawa, July 17, 1931. *Appendix to the Sixty-Ninth Volume of the Journals of the House of Commons, Session 1931* (1931).

**Swinburne, Algernon Charles**
You fellows in Canada are doing the best work that is being done by your contemporaries in the English language.

> The British poet made this remark to Charles G.D. Roberts in 1899, at Theodore Watts-Dunton's home, No. 2, "The Pines," England. Swinburne was referring to the writing of Roberts, Carman, Lampman and the two Scotts—D.C. and F.G. On a later visit, shortly before Swinburne's death in 1909, Roberts mentioned the writing of Pauline Johnson. "Now, Algernon, don't forget our dear Pauline!" chided Watts-Dunton. Swinburne replied, "I could never forget her." Both remarks are quoted by E.M. Pomeroy in *Sir Charles G.D. Roberts: A Biography* (1943).

**Swinton, George**
If the *inuit* could not change, they would no longer be.

> *Sculpture/Inuit: Masterworks of the Canadian Arctic* (1971), by George Swinton, William E. Taylor, and James Houston. *Inuit* (or *innuit*, "men") is the name the Eskimos give themselves.

**Sydenham, Lord**
I am ready to hang myself half a dozen times a day. . . . I long for September, beyond which I will not stay if they were to make me Duke of Canada and Prince of Regiopolis as this place is called.

> The autocratic governor general's release was more complete than even he

desired. Thrown by his horse, he died fifteen days later, September 19, 1841. Letter to Lord John Russell, June 5, 1841, quoted by John Charles Dent in *The Last Forty Years: Canada Since the Union of 1841* (1881).

**Sykes, Rod**
That "Eastern Bastard" is My Brother!

> Bumper sticker promoted by the mayor of Calgary to offset the ill effects of an earlier sticker that appeared on Alberta cars during the oil crisis of November, 1973: "Let the Eastern Bastards Freeze in the Dark." Quoted by James H. Gray in *The Toronto Star*, December 15, 1973.

**Sylvestre, Guy**
It is easy to say where French Canada has come from; much less so to see where it is going.

> "Tradition and Change in French Canada," translated by Glen Shortliffe, *The Arts in Canada: A Stock-Taking at Mid-Century* (1958), edited by Malcolm Ross.

It is finally through poetry that French-Canadian literature has reached its maturity, and it is the poets who have created a climate favourable to the progress of letters.

\*

This literature is, after all, American, written in French, in a British country, and not without a certain anguish.

> "Les Lettres," *Esquisses du Canada Français* (1967).

**Symington, Mona**
There's a dusky, husky maiden in the Arctic,
And she waits for me but it is not in vain,
For some day I'll put my mukluks on and ask her
If she'll wed me when the ice worms nest again.

> First verse of "When the Ice Worms Nest Again," words and music by Mona Symington, Marion Williamson and Joyce Kolgan. Although there is a worm found in the Yukon icefields, the "ice

worm" referred to here and in the works of Robert Service is a joke: a bit of spaghetti with eyes painted on, sometimes added to a cocktail. A version of "When the Ice Worms Nest Again" was reproduced by C.E. Gillham in *Raw North* (1947).

## Symons, Scott
Canadians are, after all, simply romantics who lost the courage of their hopes.

*

Everything is a part of everything else. Everything *is* everything else. Everything is not only universal, but its own universe. . . . Everything is either Alleluia or anguish.

> *Heritage: A Romantic Look at Early Canadian Furniture* (1971).

# T

## Taché, Archbishop Alexandre-Antonin
A little axle grease will make the Red River Cart go a long way and so will friendship, if applied wisely.

> First archbishop of St. Boniface, quoted by Dan Kennedy (Ochankugahe) in *Recollections of an Assiniboine Chief* (1972).

## Taché, Sir Etienne-Pascal
Be satisfied we will never forget our allegiance till the last cannon which is shot on this continent in defence of Great Britain is fired by the hand of a French Canadian.

> Address, Quebec Assembly, April 24, 1846. Quoted by Jacques Monet in *The Last Cannon Shot: A Study of French-Canadian Nationalism 1837-1850* (1969).

## Taché, Eugène
Je me souviens.

> The motto of the Province of Quebec was first inscribed beneath its coat of arms on February 9, 1883. The phrase, which translates "I remember" and is an allusion to the glory of the *Ancien Régime*, was suggested by the architect Eugène Taché.

## Taché, Joseph-Charles
Such legends and tales, into which the people have poured their hearts, with which they have sought to satisfy, within certain limits, that craving for the marvellous which is deep in our nature; such traditions, attached to this or that place in every inhabited country, constitutes a notable part, the foundation, one may say, of all national literature.

> *Forestiers et voyageurs* (1884).

## Taft, William Howard
Now is the accepted time. Canada is at the parting of the ways. Shall she be an isolated country, as much separated from us as if she were across the ocean, or shall her people and our people profit by the proximity that our geography furnishes and stimulate the trade across the border that nothing but a useless, illogical and unnecessary tariff wall created?

> Illinois state legislature, Springfield, February 11, 1911. He added: Canada is "attached to the Empire only by a light and imperceptible bond."

I have lived in Canada in the summer time for thirteen years out of twenty-two. I have an intense interest in your development, profound confidence in the great future of your Dominion, and great admiration for the policy of the Mother Country in lightening the bonds that unite you to the Empire, so far as the control of your destiny and your political government is concerned, with the result that as those regions are lightened the bond between mother and daughter grows stronger.

> "The Monroe Doctrine," February 11, 1915, *Addresses Delivered before the Canadian Club of Toronto: Season of 1914-15* (1915).

Something was said about reciprocity—in an indefinite way [Laughter]; but I am content to wait [Laughter and applause]; I don't want to be vindicated all at once. [Laughter]

*

Now, in that very history we find that it was not such an easy thing to maintain that hundred years of peace. . . . When the shibboleth of one of our presidents was "Fifty-four forty or fight," and we didn't get "Fifty-four forty," and we didn't fight.

> "Fraternal Relations," *Empire Club of Canada: Addresses Delivered to the Members During the Year 1919* (1920).

## Tagore, Rabindranath

May I indulge in a generality and say with conviction that Canada being a young country is full of possibilities that are incalculable. She has neither exhausted her material resources nor those of her mind and character. She has not yet produced in her psychology the self-toxin of fatigue that old civilizations suffer from in the shape of cynicism and spiritual insensitiveness. Her creative youth is still before her. . . . Canada is too young to fall a victim to the malady of disillusionment and scepticism, and she must believe in great ideals in the face of contradiction—for she has the gift of youth, she has the direct consciousness of the stir of growth within, which should make her trust her own self, which is the only sure way of trusting the world.

> The great Bengali poet and philosopher, Rabindranath Tagore, visited

Vancouver and Victoria in 1929, where he addressed the Sikh communities. The above remarks were made in Victoria, April 6, 1929.

## Talbot, Edward Allen

The streets of York are regularly laid out, intersecting each other at right angles. Only one of them, however, is yet completely built; and in wet weather the unfinished streets are, if possible, muddier and dirtier than those of Kingston. The situation of the town is very unhealthy, for it stands on a piece of low marshy land, which is better calculated for a frog-pond or beaver-meadow than for the residence of human beings.

*

It is impossible to walk the streets of Montreal on a Sunday or holiday, when the shops are closed, without receiving the most gloomy impressions; the whole city seems one vast prison.

> *Five Years' Residence in the Canadas; Including a Tour through Part of the United States of America in the Year 1823* (1824).

## Talbot, Colonel Thomas

Charlevoix was, I believe, the true cause of my coming to this place. You know he calls this the "Paradise of the Hurons." Now I was resolved to get to paradise by hook or by crook, and so I came here.

> Remark made at Port Talbot, July 10, 1837, to Anna Jameson and quoted in her *Winter Studies and Summer Rambles in Canada* (1838).

## Talese, Gay

It had become one of the corporate jokes within *The Times* that most of the money earned did not come from publishing the greatest newspaper in the world but from the forty-two per cent interest that [Adolph Simon] Ochs had bought in 1926 in a paper-making mill in Canada. *The Times* made more money producing paper without words than paper with words. The Spruce Falls Power & Paper Co. Ltd., of Toronto, which supplied two-thirds of *The Times'* paper, had accounted for fifty-three per cent of The New York Times Company's total profit in recent years.

> *The Kingdom and the Power* (1969).

## Talon, Jean

My chief purpose in this is to populate the environs of Quebec with a goodly number of people capable of contributing to its defence without the king having to pay any of them.

> Intendant of New France to Colbert, October, 1667. Quoted by Sir Thomas Chapais in *Jean Talon: Intendant de la Nouvelle-France* (1904).

The girls destined for this country, besides being strong and healthy, ought to be entirely free from any natural blemish or anything personally repulsive.

> Letter to Jean-Baptiste Colbert, November 10, 1670, quoted by Francis Parkman in *The Old Régime in Canada* (1874).

## Tangay, Eva

As a matter of fact, I'm not beautiful, I can't sing. I do not know how to dance. I am not even graceful.

> The "I Don't Care" girl, born in Marbleton, Quebec, was the highest-paid actress and singer in the United States in 1912. "I Don't Care" was the hit song of *The Chaperons*, the Broadway show that made her queen of vaudeville in 1904. She died in penurious obscurity in Hollywood in 1947. Quoted by Stephen Franklin in *The Heroes: A Saga of Canadian Inspiration* (1967) who wrote: "She heralded the emancipation and excess of the Roaring Twenties in the 1910s; she changed the whole style of singing and dancing; she was the symbol of the awakening, free-thinking female."

## Tanner, Elaine

I did everything I wanted to do in swimming. There was the travel, the world records, and competing in the Olympics. Now I have a new life to look forward to.

> Before the age of twenty, the champion swimmer won numerous medals at the Mexico Olympics, the Commonwealth Games in Kingston, Jamaica, and the Pan-Am Games at Winnipeg. Then she married Ian Nahrgang of Prince George. *Canadian Panorama*, November 4, 1972.

## Tanner, Nathan E.

All the wheels of industry turn on oil.

> "Petroleum Development," *Canada; Nation on the March* (1953), introduction by H.L. Enman.

It was a very difficult time, with so much political opposition, but most people didn't understand what it was all about. I feel justified in what I did. It was an accepted and common thing for the president of a firm to be offered options on stock.

\*

No matter where I've laboured, I feel I've always been in the service of the Lord.

> Nathan E. Tanner advanced from Alberta Social Credit mines minister and Trans-Canada Pipe Line president to second counsellor to the president of the Church of Jesus Christ of Latter-Day Saints. He is commenting on stock options that netted him at least one million dollars. *Canadian Panorama*, May 20, 1972. See also George DuPre and William Kilbourn.

## Tarasov, Anatoly

Canadian professional hockey is proud and touchy. Canada is the birthplace of this tremendous game. You invented it and you always want to be the best. Prove it, then, in honest battle.

> Coach of championship Russian hockey teams quoted in *The Canadian Magazine*, April 19, 1969.

## Tard, Louis-Martin

In all societies there have been individuals who claimed to be able to heal their fellow man with their strange practices; they used to be called sorcerers. Today they are known as doctors and their practices are known as medicine.

\*

An agronomist is a specialist in agricultural questions who happens to be cultivated.

*Si vous saisissez l'astuce* (1968), by the
Montreal humourist.

## Tardivel, Jules-Paul

God planted in the heart of every
French-Canadian patriot a flower of
hope. It is the aspiration to establish, on
the banks of the St. Lawrence, a New
France whose mission will be to continue in this American land the work of
Christian civilization that old France
carried out with such glory during the
long centuries.

> *Pour la patrie* (1895). Quoted by Ram-
> say Cook in *Canada and the French-
> Canadian Question* (1966).

It is not necessary that we possess industry and money. We will no longer be
French Canadians but Americans almost
like the others. Our mission is to possess
the earth and spread ideas. To cling to
the soil, to raise large families, to maintain the hearths of intellectual and spiritual life, that must be our role in America.

> The Kentucky-born Quebec national-
> ist's declaration of faith, made in 1902.
> Quoted by Ramsay Cook in "Quebec:
> The Ideology of Survival" in *The Pros-
> pect of Change: Proposals for Canada's
> Future* (1965), edited by Abraham Rot-
> stein.

## Tarte, Israël

At the moment when the corpse of Riel
falls through the trap and twists in con-
vulsions of agony, at that moment an
abyss will be dug that will separate Quebec from English-speaking Canada, especially Ontario.

> Statement made before Riel was hanged
> on November 16, 1885.

Elections are not won by prayers alone.

> This celebrated remark was made in
> 1896 when Sir Wilfrid Laurier and
> Tarte won re-election. Tarte was Lau-
> rier's Quebec lieutenant and the Liberal
> party's bagman.

You are evidently under the impression
that we are a kind of backward people,
of simple-minded fellows, who cannot
keep pace with their English fellow citi-

zens. On that point you are altogether
astray. The "habitant," as you call him,
is a wide awake "boy." He has, in my
humble opinion, more political sagacity
than many of his fellow-citizens of English origin — not because he has more
intelligence, but because he has been
obliged to conquer his liberty inch by
inch.

*

The French genius is not the same as
the Anglo-Saxon genius. We are French,
you are English. Would you permit me
to add that we are Canadians to the fullest extent of the word while, on many
occasions, you are more British than Canadians. If there is any trouble in future,
the trouble will come out of that difference.

> "A Quebec Politician Regrets English-
> Canadian Ignorance of French Cana-
> dians," Israël Tarte to Sir John Willi-
> son, November 28, 1900. *A Century of
> Canadian Literature / Un Siècle de Lit-
> térature Canadienne* (1967), edited by H.
> Gordon Green and Guy Sylvestre.

## Taschereau, Louis-Alexandre

Watch this young man. He will go far.

> The Quebec Liberal premier crossed the
> floor of the House to greet the new
> Conservative deputy from Trois-Ri-
> vières, Maurice Duplessis, on the open-
> ing of the Quebec Parliament, January
> 10, 1928. In less than ten years Duples-
> sis's new Union Nationale party would
> defeat Taschereau's government.

Here was felt the first beating of the
Canadian heart, and here beat the hearts
of two great races, in the happiest harmony which alone makes for a lasting
prosperity.

> Premier of Quebec, *The Book of Cana-
> da: Published by the Canadian Medical
> Association* (1930), edited by Chester
> Martin, W. Stewart Wallace, and T.C.
> Routley.

## Taschereau, Robert

Over two-thirds of the book, or 250
pages, deal with filthy, obscene descriptions that are offensive to decency and
utterly unnecessary for what we have
been told is the purpose of the book.

Part of the dissenting opinion of the justice of the Supreme Court of Canada on the merits of *Lady Chatterley's Lover* (1928). F.R. Scott successfully defended D.H. Lawrence's novel against charges of obscenity in 1959. See also F.R. Scott.

**Tatanga Mani**   See Walking Buffalo.

**Taylor, A.J.P.**
Max Aitken Lord Beaverbrook was quite a Somebody. Those who loved him have one dream in life: that the telephone will ring again and the familiar voice ask, "What's the news?"

> *Beaverbrook* (1972). See also Lord Beaverbrook.

**Taylor, Annie Edson**
Did I go over the falls yet?

\*

Nobody ought ever to do that again.

\*

It's a terrible nightmare—I don't want to experience it again. I'd sooner be shot from a cannon.

> The forty-three-year-old Michigan school teacher was the first person to go over Niagara Falls and live. These were the first words she spoke after emerging from her home-made barrel, sometime after four o'clock, Sunday, September 24, 1901. Her story is told by Andy O'Brien in *Daredevils of Niagara* (1964). See also Anonymous: Select Epitaphs.

**Taylor, Bayard**
"This is no longer America," said my friends. There was not a feature in all the wide view (except our double-decked steamer), to remind us of the New World; yet, on the other hand, we could not have referred it to any one portion of Europe. The sky, the air, the colors of the landscape, were from Norway; Quebec and the surrounding villages suggested Normandy — except the tin roofs and spires which were Russian, rather; while here and there, though rarely, were marks of English occupancy. The age, the order, the apparent stability and immobility of society, as illustrated by external things, belonged decidedly to Europe. This part of Canada

is but seventy or eighty years older than New England, yet there seems to be a difference of five hundred years. A century of foreign domination has made no material change in the character and habits of the French population. In fact, the change in the peasantry of France has been much greater during the same period. That magic atmosphere of the Past, which makes Europe so attractive to an American, already spreads a thin veil over these Canadian shores.

> "Up the Saguenay," *At Home and Abroad: A Sketch-Book of Life, Scenery and Men: Second Series* (1862).

**Taylor, E.P.**
I only like winners.

> Quoted in *Holiday*, April, 1964.

Canadian nationalism! How old-fashioned can you get?

> Remark made in the Winter of 1963, quoted by George L. Grant in *Lament for a Nation: The Defeat of Canadian Nationalism* (1965).

I'm a Bahamian.

> Quoted by *The Sunday Times*, December 22, 1968.

Me, ruthless? Certainly not. But when I'm right and management's consistently wrong, of course I get rid of management.

\*

I look for companies that will not only grow with the country, but faster than the country. I look for companies where no very large shareholder exists. With my partners, I buy enough stock to give us effective control. Then the company holds our view.

> Quoted by Peter C. Newman in *Flame of Power: Intimate Profiles of Canada's Greatest Businessmen* (1959), who concludes: "Taylor is condemned by socialists as 'the crushing Croesus of big business,' by Communists as 'E(xcess) P(rofits) Taylor—the mad miser of millions,' and by righteous temperance advocates as the beer baron personally responsible for the plight of every Canadian alcoholic."

I think if the old boys don't get out, it gets very discouraging for the younger people underneath.

> After resigning the chairmanship of the Argus Corporation. Quoted by Hugh Windsor in "The New Corporate Princes," *The Globe Magazine*, May 29, 1971.

## Taylor, Harry "Kamoose"

### CODE OF RULES

1. Guests will be provided with breakfast and supper but must rustle their own dinner.

2. Boots and spurs must be removed at night before retiring.

3. Dogs are not allowed in the bunks, but may sleep underneath.

4. Candles, hot water and other luxuries charged extra, also soap.

5. Two or more persons must sleep in one bed when so requested by the proprietor.

6. Baths furnished free down at the river, but bathers must furnish their own soap and water.

7. Jewelry or other valuables will not be locked in the safe. The hotel has no such ornament as a safe.

8. The proprietor will not be responsible for anything. In case of fire, guests are requested to escape without unnecessary delay.

9. Guests without baggage may sleep in the vacant lot.

10. Meals served in bedrooms will not be guaranteed in any way. Our waiters are hungry and not above temptation.

11. All guests are requested to rise at 6 A.M. This is imperative as sheets may be needed for tablecloths.

12. No tips to be given to any waiters or servants. Leave them with the proprietor and he will distribute them if considered necessary.

13. The following tariff subject to change: Board $25 a month. Board and Lodging with wooden bench to sleep on, $50 a month. Board and lodging with bed, $60 a month.

14. When guests find themselves or their baggage thrown over the fence, they may consider that they have received notice to quit.

> "Code of Rules," Hotel Fort Macleod, September 1, 1882. Reproduced by Grant MacEwan in "The Keeper of Hotel Fort Macleod: Harry Taylor" in *Fifty Mighty Men* (1958). Innkeeper Taylor's nickname "Kamoose" is said to be Indian for "wife-stealer."

### NEW TEN COMMANDMENTS

He that loves not Wine, Women, or Song remains a fool his whole life long.

I. When thirsty thou shalt come to my house and drink.

II. Thou shalt always keep my name in memory, and forget all others in the same business.

III. Thou shalt honour me and my bartender, so thou shalt live long in the land, and continue to drink at my home forever.

IV. Thou shalt honour me and mine, that thou mayest live long and see us again.

V. Thou shalt not break or destroy anything on my premises, else thou shalt pay for it double its value.

VI. No singing; thou shalt not raise thy voice in song, or thy feet in gaiety.

VII. Thou shalt not dare to pay thy bills in bad money nor ever "Chalk" or "Slate."

VIII. Thou shalt not steal from me, for I need all I have and more too.

IX. Thou shalt not expect too large glasses, as the landlord must live on the profits.

X. After eating and drinking at my home, thou shalt pay me promptly, for the landlord never likes to "Chalk," especially to poor customers.

> Taylor was a whisky trader who went into the hotel business at Macleod in 1874 when the Mounted Police arrived in the West. "New Ten Commandments" appeared in an advertisement for his Macleod Hotel in *The Lethbridge News*, March 13, 1889.

## Taylor, Nathaniel (Nat)

At an NFB symposium, years ago, I was asked a loaded question: Did I support a quota system (on foreign films) for Canada? I answered right away, "Yes, if the government will legislate that peo-

ple have to go to see Canadian films."
That's the whole answer.

> The motion-picture exhibitor added
> that a requirement of a successful fea-
> ture film was "some kind of schmaltz."
> Quoted by Kaspars Dzeguze in *The
> Globe and Mail*, October 14, 1972.

## Taylor, Sir Thomas W.

I am not here to dispense Justice, I am
here to dispose of this case according to
law. Whether this is or is not justice is a
question for the legislature to determine.

> Sir Thomas served as chief justice of
> Manitoba from 1887 to 1899.

## Teach, Edward

I've buried my money where none but
Satan and myself can find it, and the one
that lives the longest takes all.

> Teach, popularly known as "Black-
> beard the Pirate," was the terror of
> the Atlantic during the eighteenth cen-
> tury. His booty is believed by many to
> be buried in the Money Pit of Oak
> Island in Mahone Bay off the western
> coast of Nova Scotia. Quoted by R.V.
> Harris in *The Oak Island Mystery*
> (1958).

## Tecumseh

"After a pause, Tecumseh, who was evidently struck with the commanding figure and fine countenance of the general,
turning round to his people, stretched
out his hand, and exclaimed with a long
ejaculated—Ho-o-o-e: 'This is the man.'
"The general used to call Tecumseh
'the Wellington of the Indians.'"

> The general was Sir Isaac Brock. *The
> Life and Correspondence of Major-
> General Sir Isaac Brock, K.B.* (1847), by
> Ferdinand Brock Tupper. Reproduced
> by Carl F. Klinck in *Tecumseh: Fact
> and Fiction in Early Records* (1961).

"Being in company with some British
officers, he was asked his opinion of Gen.
Brock, in comparison with the merits of
their present general. He answered—
'Gen. Brock very brave man, great gen-
eral. He say, Tecumseh, come, *we* go.
Gen. Proctor say, Tecumseh, *you* go.
Proctor no Brock.'"

Henry Trumbull's *History of the Indian
Wars: To Which is Prefixed a Short
Account of the Discovery of America by
Columbus* (1846).

The Pale Faces who fought against our
fathers, the British, are our enemies.
They came to us hungry, and they cut
off the hands of our brothers, who gave
them corn. We gave them rivers full of
fish, and they poisoned our fountains.
We gave them mountains and valleys
full of game, and in return they gave
our warriors rum and trinkets and—a
grave. The shades of our slaughtered
fathers can find no rest, their eyes can
see no herds on the hills of the light in
the hunting grounds of the dead. Until
our enemies are no more we must be as
one man, one chief whose name is
DEATH!—I have spoken.

> *Notes on Niagara: 1759-1860*, Niagara
> Historical Society, Number 32.

You have got the arms and ammunition
which our great father, the king, sent for
his red children. If you have any idea of
going away, give them to us, and you
may go, and welcome, for us. Our lives
are in the hands of the Great Spirit. We
are determined to defend our lands, and
if it be His will, we wish to leave our
bones upon them.

> Speech at a council of war, September
> 18, 1813, Malden, Upper Canada.
> Quoted by Major John Richardson in
> *The War of 1812* (1843). Reproduced
> by Carl F. Klinck in *Tecumseh: Fact
> and Fiction in Early Records* (1961). Te-
> cumseh was killed seventeen days later.

"—Tecumseh fell dead and we all ran."

> The great Shawnee chief died during
> the Battle of Moraviantown, on the
> Thames River, October 5, 1813. The
> words of "a Potawatamie chief" quoted
> by Benjamin Drake in *Life of Tecum-
> seh* (1841), reproduced by Carl F. Klinck
> in *Tecumseh: Fact and Fiction in Early
> Records* (1961). The Shawnee chief's
> name means "Shooting Star." See also
> Black Hawk and Dick Johnson.

## Tekahionwake   See Pauline Johnson.

## Tekakwitha, Kateri
I will love thee in Heaven.

> Dying words of the first Indian saint, April 17, 1860. Other sources claim her last words were: "Jesus, I love thee!" Quoted by Ellen H. Walworth in *The Life and Times of Kateri Tekakwitha: The Lily of the Mohawks* (1891).

## Templeton, Charles
I don't want to do one thing all my life.

> This versatile man has been a cartoonist, evangelist, newspaper editor, candidate for the Ontario Liberal leadership, television director, magazine editor, radio broadcaster, inventor, author, and who-knows-what-else. Quoted by Merle Shain in *The Toronto Telegram*, February 22, 1969, who recalled a couplet heard on CBC-TV's "Nightcap": "Where have all the good jobs gone? / They've to Charlie Temp-le-ton."

## Templeton, Gilbert
RAZ-MAH. Templeton's TRCs.

> These are familiar trade names of patent medicines manufactured by Templeton's Ltd., Chemists. James Templeton, a Calgary druggist, began selling Templeton's Pink Powders in 1890 for relief from rheumatic pain. An improved version in capsule form, called Templeton's Rheumatic Capsules, went on sale in 1907. In the 1930s, the Food and Drug Division decided "rheumatic" should not appear on the label, so Templeton's Rheumatic Capsules became Templeton's TRCs. RAZ-MAH was developed in 1920 for the relief of bronchial asthma, chronic bronchitis and hay fever. The name is derived from the "RX" symbol used for medical prescriptions. Gilbert Templeton, the founder's son, is president of the Toronto-based firm. His soothing voice is familiar to generations of radio listeners as he extols the properties of his medicines.

## Templeton, Jean
Just once, though, I'd like to learn something from success.

> *The Toronto Telegram*, August 15, 1964.

You know, dandruff can cause you a lot more trouble.

> A reference to the effect of epilepsy on her career as a comedienne, quoted by Pierre Berton in *The Cool Crazy Committed World of the Sixties: Twenty-One Television Encounters* (1966).

## Tennant, Veronica
I realized that if I didn't dance, a part of me would die; it wouldn't be the same Veronica Tennant.

> *

Short? Sure, I'm short for a dancer, five-foot-three. I'm about the shortest dancer in the company. I'm told I appear taller on stage and that's a compliment to me. If you have presence, you seem taller.

> Quoted by Sid Adilman in *The Toronto Telegram*, April 17, 1971.

It's a special joy, it seems, every time I get on the stage.

> Quoted by John Fraser in *The Globe and Mail*, October 14, 1972.

## Tennyson, Alfred Lord
To England under Indian skies,
    To those dark millions of her realm!
To Canada whom we love and prize,
    Whatever statesman hold the helm.
        Hands all round!

> From "Hands all Round," published February 7, 1852, two years after his appointment as poet laureate.

Not here; the White North has thy bones,
    And thou, heroic sailor soul,
Are passing on thy happier voyage now
    Toward no earthly pole.

> Lines written in 1875 for the monument in Westminster Abbey to Sir John Franklin who perished in the Arctic in 1847 but whose body was never found.

You, the Mighty, the Fortunate,
You, the Lord-territorial,
You, the Lord-manufacturer,
You, the hardy, laborious,
Patient children of Albion,
You, Canadian, Indian,
Australasian, African,
All your hearts be in harmony,
All your voices in unison,

Singing "Hail to the glorious
Golden year of her Jubilee."

Stanza X of "On the Jubilee of Queen
Victoria," published in 1887 and "writ-
ten to celebrate the fiftieth year of the
Queen's reign."

Witness, too, the silent cry,
The prayer of many a race and creed,
and clime—
Thunderless lightnings striking under
sea
From sunset and sunrise of all thy realm,
And that true North, whereof we lately
heard
A strain to shame us, "Keep you to your-
selves;
So loyal is too costly! friends—your love
Is but a bruthen: loose the bond, and go."
Is this the tone of empire? here the faith
That made us rulers? this, indeed, her
voice
And meaning, whom the roar of Hougou-
mont
Left mightiest of all people under heav-
en?
What shock has fool'd her since, that she
should speak
So feebly? wealthier—wealthier—hour by
hour!
The voice of Britain, or a sinking land,
Some third-rate isle half-lost among her
seas?

"To the Queen," epilogue to "O Loyal
to the Royal in Thyself," *Idylls of the
King* (1873). "That true North" is a
direct reference to Canada, composed
immediately upon reading a "villainous"
editorial in *The Times* of October 30,
1872, in which Canada was advised to
seek its independence: "Take up your
freedom; your days of apprenticeship
are over." This passage, like all others,
is reproduced from *Tennyson's Poetical
Works* (1897), edited by Eugene Parsons.

The tribute did not go unnoticed. On
March 3, 1873, Lord Dufferin, governor
general of Canada, wrote the poet:
"Canada may well be proud that her
loyal aspirations should be thus imper-
ishably recorded in the greatest poem
of this generation." Dufferin wrote a
total of three letters to the laureate
(these appear in *Alfred Lord Tennyson:
A Memoir by His son* [1897]); Tennyson
dedicated a poem to Dufferin (it appears in *Demeter, and Other Poems*
[1889]).

"That true North" is a lovely phrase
for a feeling that may well have informed more than the epilogue to *The
Idylls of the King*. To some extent Tennyson thought in geographical terms in
"The Passing of Arthur" when he described the aged king boarding his
"dusky barge" and setting sail into the
western sunset. In those far-off regions
Arthur heard a great cry "from beyond
the limit of the world." In Tennyson's
day the West and the North were frequently linked (as in the phrase "the
Northwest"). Perhaps King Arthur
reigns over the ever-loyal Canadians in
"that true North" where he fights "The
darkness of that battle in the West, /
Where all of high and holy dies away."

For Tennyson's "opposite number,"
see James Gay.

**Tennyson, Bertram**

The world is fair in this new land, and
yet I envy you,
For we have not the primrose pale, and
though 'tis just as blue,
The violet, in exile here, throws out a
scentless bloom;
The rose is fair as England's rose, but
has not its perfume.

One of many stanzas from "Broncho
Days."

\*

Have we not stood together in the van;
Whether at Queenston Heights, or Lun-
dy's Lane?
Or later, on the scorching wide Soudan,
Our loyal aid has not been all in vain;
And should the sun break on a wilder
day,
And Britain cry, "Push on, brave volun-
teer,"
'Tis but the word to point us out the
way
We knew before; and, with no touch of
fear,
Learn thou, where Britons go, Canadians
also dare.

One of many stanzas from "Canada to
Britain." *The Land of Napioa and*

*Other Essays in Prose and Verse* (1896) was written by the poet laureate's nephew and published in Moosomin, then in that part of the Northwest Territories that is now in Alberta. He was the son of Horatio, Tennyson's youngest brother. "Bertram Tennyson was a sailor, a soldier, and a barrister, besides being something of a poet and an artist," explained Agnes Grace Weld in *Glimpses of Tennyson and Some of His Relations and Friends: With an Appendix by the Late Bertram Tennyson* (1903).

**Tennyson, Emily Lady**
He has just written "O loyal to the royal in thyself." A. burnt with indignation and shame at one eminent statesman saying to him, "Would to God Canada would go!"

> Journal entry, Christmas, 1872. Quoted by Lorne Pierce in *Alfred, Lord Tennyson and William Kirby: Unpublished Correspondence to Which Are Added Some Letters from Hallam, Lord Tennyson* (1929).

You Canadians should be proud of the founders of your country. The United Empire Loyalists were a grand type of loyal, law-abiding, God-fearing men. No country ever had such founders, no country in the world. No, not since the days of Abraham!

> These remarks were addressed "a year or two before her death" to George T. Denison who recorded them in *Soldiering in Canada: Recollections and Experiences* (1900). Lady Emily Tennyson, the laureate's widow, died in August of 1896.

**Tennyson, Hallam Lord**
He watched Canada to the last with great interest . . . and may Canada be ever that "True North."

> Letter from the son of the poet laureate, Hallam, Lord Tennyson, Isle of Wight, to William Kirby, November 3, 1892. Quoted by Lorne Pierce in *Alfred, Lord Tennyson and William Kirby: Unpublished Correspondence to Which Are*

> Added Some Letters from Hallam, Lord Tennyson* (1929).

**Terry, Ellen**
Oh it was awful—wonderful—magnificent! I have never experienced anything so surprising,—it is like flying; for a moment you cannot breathe!

\*

Yes, it is a pleasant pastime. The Canadians are quite right,—it beats skating, ice-boating, trotting, everything in the way of locomotion; what matters the cold, with such exercise as toboganning.

> The famous actress learned the joys of tobogganing in Toronto, February 24, 1884. Quoted by Joseph Hatton in *Henry Irving's Impressions of America: Narrated in a Series of Sketches, Chronicles, and Conversations* (1884).

**Thayendanegea**    See Joseph Brant.

**Theall, Donald F.**
It could be argued that the development of Marshall McLuhan and Northrop Frye at the same university was not accidental. Although in some ways they seem superficially quite distinct, there are really many similarities, and over a period of time McLuhan has come more and more to manifest an interest in the theory of archetypes which formed an important part of Frye's literary theories. Frye and McLuhan are both interested in broad historical patterns, in very generalized groups of images and in neutrally oriented ways of approaching the cultural objects that they wish to analyze. Both of them are interested more than might ordinarily be expected in the theoretical influence of James Joyce and the symbolist poets such as Mallarmée and Valéry. Although the early McLuhan did not seem to share Frye's interest in Blake, by the writing of *War and Peace in the Global Village* McLuhan seemed to share a considerable commitment to some of Blake's apocalyptic views. In very different ways, both of them wish to find methods to replace the *history of ideas* approach to culture, Frye by developing a scientific criticism, McLuhan by transforming the

history of ideas into a *history of artistic techniques* and then into a *history of of technologies.*

> "The Influence of the Canadian University Milieu on McLuhan: A Speculative Note," *The Medium Is the Rear View Mirror: Understanding McLuhan,* Donald F. Theall (1971).

**Thomas, Bob**   See Russell Birdwell.

**Thomas, Dylan**
The plane trip was ghastly. It seemed to go on forever, and all my fellow passengers seemed either actively unpleasant or moronic. The plane was stiflingly hot, & there wasn't any of the usual slight plane ventilation because of the height we travelled: in the stratosphere. We couldn't put down at the airport in Newfoundland because of icy weather conditions, so had to land somewhere in Canada. We got out for an hour: the cold was unbelievable, all the airport ground crew dressed up like Hudson Bay trappers and beating their great grizzly - bear - gloved hands together & stamping on the snow. And when we did, after several stifling eternities spent high as the moon, arrive in New York, it was to find it one of the coldest days there for years: when we got off the plane it was four below zero.

> Letter to Mr. and Mrs. D.J. Thomas, February 26, 1950, from New York, *Selected Letters of Dylan Thomas* (1966), edited by Constantine Fitzgibbon.

I enclose a letter from McGill University, Montreal. This letter seems, to me, to mean that McGill is prepared to transport me (I suppose at a good fee) all the way from Wales to Montreal. And (I suppose) back. . . . And as I don't particularly want to go to Montreal, soak McGill for twice (at least) as much as I get in the States—plus, of course, full expenses *by air.*

> Letter to Brinnin, January 6, 1952, in *Dylan Thomas in America: An Intimate Journal* (1955), by John Malcolm Brinnin. Thomas gave readings at McGill and the University of British Columbia.

**Thomas, Lowell**
My head size became distorted, but before I left Canada it was put in its proper place again. I made my last speech . . . in Halifax the night before the Dominion election. I was to speak in Nelson Hall, and the man who was to introduce me was called away to speak at some neighbouring town, and at the last minute the committee had to call in someone else, and the man who was called in to introduce me was an Englishman just out from the British Isles. And he said, "I understand that the speaker tonight is the author of a book." Then he went on, "As I came into the auditorium I met a man who had read the book." And then in the charming British way he put me in my place by adding, "I understand it is readable, in fact you might say quite." And he sat down. So I went back home quite normal I assure you.

> "Strange Tales from the Far East," November 20, 1933, *Addresses Delivered before the Canadian Club of Toronto: Season of 1933-34* (1934).

**Thompson, Andrew**
I'm a quiet person. A civilized person doesn't have to beat his hands and shout to show he's tough.

> Senator Thompson was quoted by David van Praagh in "The Quiet Ulsterman" in *The Globe Magazine,* January 16, 1965.

**Thompson, David**
Previous to the discovery of Canada (about 320 years ago), this Continent from the Latitude of forty degrees north to the Arctic Circle, and from the Atlantic to the Pacific Ocean, may be said to have been in the possession of two distinct races of Beings, Man and the Beaver. Man was naked and had to procure clothing from the skins of animals. . . .

\*

Thus I have fully completed the survey of this part of North America from sea to sea, and by almost innumerable astronomical Observations have determined the positions of the Mountains, Lakes and Rivers, and other remarkable places on the northern part of this Continent; the Maps of all of which have been drawn, and laid down in geographical position, being now the work of twenty-seven years.

*David Thompson's Narrative of His Explorations in Western America 1784-1812* (1916), edited by J.B. Tyrrell, who called David Thompson "one of the greatest geographers of the world."

Hudson's Bay is certainly a country that Sinbad the Sailor never saw, as he makes no mention of mosquitoes. [Prince of Wales's Fort, now Churchill, Manitoba, 1784-85]

\*

Many reflections come on my mind; a new world was in a manner before me, and my object was to be at the Pacific Ocean before the month of August. How were we to find provisions, and how many men would remain with me, for they were dispirited? Amidst various thoughts I fell asleep on my bed of snow. [January 10, 1811; to Victor G. Hopwood this was "the most dramatic moment of Thompson's *Travels*" when the explorer faced the Athabasca Pass in the Rocky Mountains and the completion of his journey to the Pacific]

\*

We continued our journey, amused with the seals playing in the river; on the fifteenth, near noon, we arrived at Tongue Point, which at right angles stretches its steep rocky shores across the river for a full half a mile, and brought us to a full view of the Pacific Ocean, which to me was a great pleasure, but my men seemed disappointed. They had been accustomed to the boundless horizon of the great lakes of Canada, and their high rolling waves; from the ocean they expected a more boundless view, a something beyond the power of their senses which they could not describe, and my informing them that directly opposite to us, at the distance of five thousand miles, was the empire of Japan, added nothing to their ideas, but a map would. The waves being too high for us to double the point, we went close to the river bank where there is a narrow

isthmus, of one hundred yards, and carried across it. [Columbia River, July 14, 1811]

*Travels in Western North America, 1784-1812* (1971), edited by Victor G. Hopwood.

## Thompson, Gordon V.

What is the market for the Canadian song writer? The answer is, almost none whatever.

Toronto music publisher, "The Canadian Song Market," *The Canadian Author and Bookman*, March, 1943.

## Thompson, Sir John

He who serves Canada serves the Empire, and he who serves the Empire serves Canada as well.

Belleville address, September 21, 1893. quoted by J. Castell Hopkins in *Life and Work of the Rt. Hon. Sir John Thompson . . . Prime Minister of Canada* (1895).

## Thompson, Phillips

Labour is just as much interested in the maintenance of capitalism, that is to say, the supremacy of capital, as the slave was in the perpetuation of the slave power.

\*

Land ought not to be a commodity, because like air and water it is necessary to human existence; and all men have by birthright equal rights to its use.

\*

Political economy needs to be re-written from the standpoint of the Sermon on the Mount and the Declaration of Independence.

*The Politics of Labour* (1887).

John Brown
Went down
Thirty days;
Couldn't raise
Three dollars,
Peeler hollers,
You're clear
Out of here;
In that room
Wait your doom.

Labour reporter Phillips Thompson covered the police court for *The Toronto Telegram* under the name Jimuel Briggs, about 1870. Recalled by Sir John Willison in *Reminiscences Political and Personal* (1919), who commented: "What curious fag-ends repose at the back of one's memory."

## Thompson, Robert

The Americans are our best friends, whether we like it or not.

\*

Parliament is being turned into a political arena.

\*

You've buttered your bread, now you have to lie in it.

\*

Social Credit is above politics.

"Thompsonisms" from the former leader of the Social Credit party, quoted by Peter C. Newman in "Robert Thompson" (1967), *Home Country: People, Places, and Power Politics* (1973).

## Thompson, Samuel J.

The march back to Toronto was very leisurely executed, several of the mounted officers carrying dead pigs and geese slung across their saddle-bows as trophies of victory.

After routing William Lyon Mackenzie's rebels, December 7, 1837. *Reminiscences of a Canadian Pioneer for the Last Fifty Years: An Autobiography* (1884).

## Thompson, Tommy

PLEASE WALK ON THE GRASS

This friendly invitation was devised by Thomas W. Thompson, parks commissioner, Metropolitan Toronto. The first sign was erected in Edwards Gardens in 1960. The five words have become the motto of the Parks Department.

## Thompson, William Irwin

To understand history, one must stand outside history, not just to avoid bias, but to be able to perceive distinctness and relations. Any simple stand to the Left or the Right is still a movement on the same political plane. But above the American Left and Right is Canada, a place free of the American Dream and the European Nightmare. No longer a colony, not yet an independent national power, Canada, like Switzerland, is *The Peaceable Kingdom* to which those weary of conflict go to escape the burden of a national destiny. As the Canadian historian John Conway has remarked: "America is Faustian and Dionysian; Canada is not." In the opposition between Apollonian Canada and Dionysian America, one can see that once again the unique excellence of both countries is also their tragic flaw. Los Angeles is one very obvious example of an edge, but Toronto is also a city at the edge of American history. With its draft dodgers, deserters, and émigré academics, it is almost Tolkien's Rivendell, safe from the ragings of the archaic darkness of Sauron and the Ring wraiths. Whether one can live permanently in Rivendell is a question I ask myself daily, but at the moment Toronto seems the perfect retreat in which to look from one end of history to the other.

At *the Edge of History* (1971). "The future is beyond knowing and the present is beyond belief," according to the professor of English, York University, Toronto.

## Thomson, Kenneth

I find myself swept along by circumstances. Dad creates them. I often say it is like being a man carrying two bags, one in either hand. One bag is advantages, one is disadvantages, but they are both heavy.

Quoted by Margaret Penman in *The Toronto Telegram*, February 4, 1967.

## Thomson, Roy

My name's Thomson . . . call me Roy.

\*

Know of any newspapers for sale?

\*

What is editorial content? The stuff you separate the ads with.

If any of our editors were to come out against either God or the Monarchy, I guess we'd have to do something.

\*

You know, it's just like having a licence

to print your own money. [To colleagues after being awarded a licence to operate a TV station in Scotland, Fall of 1957; usually quoted as "A TV franchise is a licence to print money"]

*

Primarily, I'm a money-making man.

*

There is nothing sinful about being rich.

*

Everybody wants to make money—but how many want it enough to work for it?

*

What are orthodox [business] methods? They're rules adopted by old established outfits to prevent young new outfits from making money. Well, I couldn't afford to be orthodox when I was young: I had to make money! Now, of course, it's different, I can afford to follow the rules. Now I've made a lot of money and I'm hell-bent on convention!

*

I believe a newspaper should represent all shades of political opinion and that its readers are entitled to ALL the news, presented in an impartial manner and not coloured to suit the political views of its management. I also believe that those in public office should be given credit when credit is due, and criticized when their actions call for criticism—and this irrespective of party, creed or belief.

On May 7, 1934, Roy Thomson acquired his first newspaper, *The Timmins Press*, for a down payment of two hundred dollars. He published the above "Announcement" of new ownership and editorial policy on the front page. Forty years later, the Thomson chain owned and operated over two hundred newspapers and allied interests.

*

"When asked how many newspapers he wanted altogether, he replied: 'Fifty-two—one for each week of the year.' After he had exceeded that number, he liked to say: 'I want one for each *day* of the year.'"

*

"When Paul Martin, the cabinet minister, formally opened the Guelph *Mer-*

*cury*'s new building, he said in his speech that whenever he entered a strange town he always bought a paper. At this Thomson grinned broadly, and interjected: 'Me too—and its plant!'"

*

Edinburgh's idea of stop-press news is a picture of some mouldy old ruin with a description of what it was like two centuries ago!

*

I'm frank, brutally frank. And even when I'm *not* frank, I *look* frank.

*

I don't like spending money.

*

My only two loves are my family and my business. And if I *had* to choose between the two . . . well, I don't know, I'd probably choose my business, because my family can now look after itself.

*

Anyone who doesn't buy at a discount or at sales needs his head read.

"Deliberately then he posted his United Kingdom citizenship papers, marked 'For attention,' to Harold Macmillan; and a few days later received them back from Admiralty House, marked 'Duly noted.'"

*

John Diefenbaker: Why burden your sons and successors with the incubus of this thing [a hereditary title]?

Lord Thomson of Fleet: It's the best way I can prove to Canadians that I'm a success.

*

Canada intimated that they wouldn't mind Lord Thomson of Mississauga, but that's all—and that's a hell of a name anyway. I can't even spell it myself. [The Thomson estate is in Mississauga, near Toronto]

*

Nikita Khrushchev: You can't take it with you.

Lord Thomson of Fleet: Then I'm not going.

*

How much would it cost me to buy *Pravda*? [To Premier Khrushchev in Moscow, 1963]

*

Lord Thomson: I have a magpie mind. I like anything that glitters.

Reporter: Newspapers don't glitter, sir.

Lord Thomson: No, but their balance sheets do.

*

I'm not an editorial proprietor; I'm a business proprietor.

*

My favourite colour. Gold!

*

I think I've made a very important contribution to British journalism. I hope when I leave that my epitaph would be that my newspapers were better than when I got them and that they have contributed something to the enhancement of life and to the knowledge of the people who read them.

> Roy Thomson is endlessly quotable; even his title seems endless: Lord Thomson of Fleet and of Northbridge in the City of Edinburgh. His quips come from a number of sources, including: Russell Braddon's *Roy Thomson of Fleet Street* (1965); Margaret Penman, *The Toronto Telegram*, February 4, 1967; Irwin Ross, "No Sense at all in Stopping," *In Search of Canada* (1971), by the editors of *Reader's Digest*; Peter C. Newman, "The Table Talk of Roy Thomson," *Maclean's Magazine*, December, 1971. See also Lord Beaverbrook and Kenneth Thomson.

### Thomson, Tom

Some day they will know what I mean.

> The painter, who died mysteriously in 1917, frequently made this reply when his art was criticized. Quoted by Blodwen Davies in *Tom Thomson: The Story of a Man Who Looked for Beauty and for Truth in the Wilderness* (1935, 1967).

Take everything as it comes; the wave passes, deal with the next one.

> Arthur Lismer "would once in a while recall a saying of Tom Thomson in the old Algoma days when he was out with Lismer in a canoe in rough water," explained John A.B. McLeish in *Sep-*

> *tember Gale: A Study of Arthur Lismer of the Group of Seven* (1955).

"To the Memory of Tom Thomson Artist Woodsman and Guide who was drowned in Canoe Lake July 8th 1917. He lived humbly but passionately with the wild. It made him brother to all untamed things of nature. It drew him apart and revealed itself wonderfully to him. It sent him out from the woods only to show these revelations through his art. And it took him to itself at last. His fellow artists and other friends and admirers join gladly in this tribute to his character and genius. His body is buried at Owen Sound, Ontario, near where he was born August 1877."

> Inscription on Thomson's Cairn, Canoe Lake, Algonquin Park. Reproduced by Ottelyn Addison and Elizabeth Harwood in *Tom Thomson: The Algonquin Years* (1969). The inscription was written and the memorial plaque designed by J.E.H. MacDonald and erected September 27, 1917.

### Thoreau, Henry David

I fear that I have not got much to say about Canada, not having seen much; what I got by going to Canada was a cold.

*

Soon the city of Montreal was discovered with its tin roofs shining afar. Their reflections fell on the eye like a clash of cymbals on the ear.

*

The names of the squares reminded you of Paris,—the Champ de Mars, the Place d'Armes, and others, and you felt as if a French revolution might break out any moment.

*

On every prominent ledge you could see England's hands holding the Canadas, and I judged by the redness of her knuckles that she would soon have to let go.

*

Through the words Canada East on the map stretching over many rivers and lakes and unexplored wildernesses, the actual Canada, which might be the colored portion of the map, is but a little clearing on the banks of the river, which one of those syllables would more than cover.

\*

Their very *rivière* meanders more than our *river*.

\*

But in Canada you are reminded of the government every day. It parades itself before you. It is not content to be the servant, but will be the master; and every day it goes out to the Plains of Abraham or to the Champ de Mars and exhibits itself and its tools.

\*

In short, the inhabitants of Canada appeared to be suffering between two fires,—the soldiery and the priesthood.

\*

I have been told that two townsmen of mine, who were interested in horticulture, travelling once in Canada, and being in Quebec, thought it would be a good opportunity to obtain seeds of the real Canada crook-neck squash. So they went into a shop where such things were advertised, and inquired for the same. The shopkeeper had the very thing they wanted. "But are you sure," they asked, "that these are the genuine Canada crook-neck?" "O yes, gentlemen," answered he, "they are a lot which I have received directly from Boston." I resolved that my Canada, crook-neck seeds should be such as had grown in Canada.

*A Yankee in Canada* (1866).

To a great extent the feudal system still prevails there (in Canada), and I saw that I should be a bad citizen, that any man who thought for himself and was only reasonably independent would naturally be a rebel. You could not read or hear of their laws without seeing that it was a legislating for a few and not for all. That certainly is the best government where the inhabitants are least often reminded of the government. (Where a man cannot be a poet even without danger of being made poet-laureate! Where he cannot be healthily neglected, and grow up a man, and not be an Englishman merely!) Where it is the most natural thing in the world for a government that does not understand you, to let you alone. Oh, what a government were there, my countrymen! [August 21, 1851]

\*

Why should Canada, wild and unsettled as it is, impress one as an older country than the States, except that her institutions are old. All things seem to contend there with a certain rust of antiquity, such as forms on old armour and iron guns, the rust of convention and formalities. If the rust was not on the tinned roofs and spires, it was on the inhabitants. [September 11, 1851]

*The Journals of Henry D. Thoreau* (1906), edited by Bradford Torrey and Francis H. Allen.

### Thorgilsson, Ari

Both east and west in the country they found human habitations, fragments of skin boats and stone implements from which it was evident that the same kind of people had been there as inhabited Wineland and whom the Greenlanders called Skrellings.

*The Book of the Icelanders* (1122-23). "This is the earliest mention of Vinland in Icelandic literature," according to Tryggvi J. Oleson in *Early Voyages and Northern Approaches 1000-1632* (1963). The location of Wineland (or Vinland) has been narrowed down to Newfoundland.

### Thorndike, Dame Sybil

That is what you don't get with a cinema. You never get your own performance. The thing we give, that we feel as actors in the performance of "The Distaff Side" in Toronto is different to what we give in Boston. Something that Toronto gives to us we are handing back to Toronto; something that Boston gives us we hand back to Boston. They are different things.

"The Theatre" (1935), *Empire Club of Canada: Addresses Delivered to the Members During the Year 1934-35* (1935).

### Thornton, Sir Henry

We regard the use of radio as a national trust. It is essentially both a national and a local-service institution. As such it adds to the social and economic life of the nation. Service to the listener is the primary consideration. In the final analysis the listener himself makes the program. The future of broadcasting rests with the individual who turns the dial.

\*

There is a new marvel of science which is already playing an important part in the art of indirect advertising and which is destined to become a still larger factor in the future. It is radio broadcasting. There are certain necessary and proper limitations with respect to the employment of this agency and it is essential that broadcasting be surrounded with such safeguards as will prevent the air becoming what might be described as an atmospheric bill board.

> Address to the Advertising Clubs of the World, Philadelphia, June 21, 1926. Quoted by E. Austin Weir in *The Struggle for National Broadcasting in Canada* (1965).

## Thorvald
We have won a fine and fruitful country, but will hardly be allowed to enjoy it.

> The Vikings established a colony at L'Anse au Meadow, Newfoundland, around A.D. 1000. The lament about "a fine and fruitful country" is attributed to Thorvald, brother of Leif the Lucky, and is his dying prophecy, made with a Beothuck arrow in his belly.

## Threlfall, Reg
They lost because they forgot to remember and started to think.

> Threlfall was the Winnipeg Blue Bombers' coach when, after an early lead, they lost the Grey Cup to the Toronto Argonauts.

## Tibbetts, Benjamin Franklin
Oh, how wonderful is the harp of a thousand strings that is still in tune.

> Remark made to a friend around 1845, about the intricate older ships' engines being replaced by the simplicity of his own invention, the double-expansion steam engine. Quoted by J.J. Brown in *Ideas in Exile: A History of Canadian*

*Invention* (1967).

## Tiger, Lionel
The male bond.

> The McGill-educated anthropologist wrote *Men in Groups* (1970) which helped popularize the concept of "the male bond," a term used to characterize the behaviour of men (but not women) in forming groups.

To those who think that the law of gravity interferes with their freedom, there is nothing to say.

> Lionel Tiger and Robin Fox's *The Imperial Animal* (1971).

## Tiktak
I do not think out what I will do. My thought comes out while I work. My work expresses my thought. My work is what I think. My work is my thought.

> Quoted by George Swinton in "The Sculptor Tiktak" in *Artscanada*, June, 1970.

## Tilley, Sir Samuel Leonard
"His Dominion shall be from sea to sea."

> At the London Conference in December of 1866, it was felt that the working title of the new country "The Kingdom of Canada" would "wound the sensibilities of the Yankees" (Sir John A. Macdonald's phrase in his letter to Lord Knutsford, July 18, 1899). The title appeared in early drafts of the British North America Bill, but at the suggestion of the New Brunswick statesman and a Father of Confederation, "Kingdom" was replaced by "Dominion."
>
> Tilley's inspiration, it is said, derived from one of two biblical passages, although the word "dominion" has long been used in the sense of "a territory subject to a sovereign ruler." The arms of the Dominion of Canada bear the Latin inscription *"Ad mari usque ad mare"* ("From sea to sea"). The two biblical passages are: "He shall have dominion also from sea to sea, and from the river unto the ends of the earth." (Psalm 72:8) ". . . and His Dominion shall be from sea even to sea, and from the river even to the ends of the earth." (Zechariah 9:10)

**Timbres, Harry G.**
Speaking out of my own experience thus far, I can say there is no lip-service here. I wonder if our American emphasis upon personal liberty and upon the right to criticize even when we don't know what we are criticizing has caused us to be sceptical of a sincerity which is more interested in making social justice work than in cavilling about who are going to be its agents. If this is true, we are certainly the losers.

Letter written from Russia, August 26, 1936, by Dr. Harry Timbres, the Missouri-born, Alberta-raised medical doctor who with his wife settled on the Volga, where he died in 1937. Harry and Rebecca Timbres, *We Didn't Ask Utopia: A Quaker Family in Soviet Russia* (1939).

**Tisdall, Dr. Frederick**
See Dr. Alan Brown.

**Tocqueville, Alexis de**
The physiognomy of a government can best be judged in its colonies, for there its characteristic traits usually appear larger and more distinct. When I wish to judge of the spirit and faults of the administration of Louis XIV, I must go to Canada. Its deformity is there seen as through a microscope.

Quoted by Francis Parkman in *The Old Régime in Canada* (1874).

The French of Canada, who loyally preserve the tradition of their ancient mores, are already finding it difficult to live on their land, and this small nation which has only just come to birth will soon be a prey to all the afflictions of old nations. The most enlightened, patriotic and humane men in Canada make extraordinary efforts to render people dissatisfied with the simple happiness that still contents them.

*Democracy in America* (1835). A translation by George Lawrence, edited by J.P. Mayer and Max Lerner, was published in 1966.

We arrive at the moment of crisis. If the Canadians do not come out of their apathy within twenty years, it will be too late.

Quoted by George Wilson Pierson in *Tocqueville and Beaumont in America* (1938).

They are as French as you and I. They even resemble us more closely than the Americans of the United States resemble the English. . . . We felt that we were at home, and everywhere we were received like compatriots, children of *old France*, as they say here. To my mind the epithet is badly chosen. Old France is in Canada; the new is with us. . . .

Quoted by George W. Pierson in *Tocqueville in America* (1959). The French author spent ten days in Lower Canada, from August 24 to September 2, 1831.

. . . I will therefore limit myself to generalities (and from me to you only) in saying that the situation in Canada seems to me to be an extremely serious one, and one deserving of the closest attention by your legislators. French Canadians are a separate people in America, a people of a distinct and vivacious national character, a new and healthy people whose origins are entirely warlike, with its language, its religion, its laws, its customs, a nation more densely populated than any other of the new world; which could be conquered but not dissolved by force to be absorbed into the milieu of the Anglo American race. Time alone could bring about that result; neither legislation, nor the sword.

Letter from Alexis de Tocqueville at Compiège, January 3, 1838, to Henry Reeve, clerk of the Privy Council of Great Britain. Reeve was translating *Democracy in America*, and as a result of the Rebellion of 1837 wrote to Tocqueville requesting his views on the French in Canada. "A Letter from Alexis de Tocqueville on the Canadian Rebellion of 1837" was first published by Edgar McInnis in the *Canadian Historical Review*, December, 1838.

**Tolmie, S.F.**
British Columbia is Canada's westernmost province and the geographic centre of the British Empire.

Premier of British Columbia, *The Book of Canada: Published by the Canadian Medical Association* (1930), edited by Chester Martin, W. Stewart Wallace, and T.C. Routley.

## Tolstoy, Leo

My view of this movement among the Canadian Doukhobors is that materially they have injured themselves. But this movement has shown that there lives in them what is most precious and important—a religious feeling, not passive and contemplative, but active, drawing them to the renunciation of material advantages. . . .

> Tolstoy is referring to the nude marches the Doukhobors made about 1902. Quoted by Aylmer Maude in *A Peculiar People: The Doukhobors* (1904). See also Aylmer Maude and James Mavor.

## Tom, Uncle   See Josiah Henson.

## Tompkins, Father James

Give the people ideas and they'll put them to work.

*

The only way a man achieves greatness is by getting it from the people—the people make giants.

*

It is the hardest thing in the world to have faith in man—and to keep it up.

*

There's no such thing as a Catholic co-operative store, a Methodist store, or a pious store . . . two plus two makes four in the accounts no matter what religion you have.

*

God help us, man, can you tell me any Catholic way of canning lobsters? [To the charge that Father Tompkins was "making good Catholics out of all those Nova Scotia fishermen"]

> Quoted by E.A. Corbett in "Dr. James Tompkins," *Pioneers in Adult Education in Canada* (c. 1955), edited by Harriet Rouillard.

Perhaps our problems are our own fault.

*

Practise self-help.

*

You must have faith that uneducated men can learn and can educate themselves. You must have faith that the people will develop their own leaders.

> Characteristic maxims, quoted by J.R. Kidd in his *Adult Education in Canada* (1950).

The little people together is a giant. You've got to give them ideas. Then they'll blow the roof off.

*

Ideas have hands and feet. They'll do work for you.

*

Practical education—co-operative action.

*

Adult education should be designed for the best brains we have, to wrestle with the worst problems we have.

*

When a man gets up on his hind legs, no one can walk on him.

> The Reverend Dr. James J. Tompkins helped found the co-operative Antigonish Movement at St. Francis Xavier University during the 1920s. Quoted by John R. Chafe in "God's Greatest Nuisance" in *In Search of Canada* (1971), by the editors of *Reader's Digest*. See also M.M. Coady.

## Tonnancour, Jacques de

If the modern artist sways on his tightrope and so often falls, have mercy on him for you are on the tightrope too.

> Quoted in *Maclean's Canada: Portrait of a Country* (1960), edited by Leslie F. Hannon.

## Tonto   See Jay Silverheels.

## Tonty, Henri de

As M. de la Salle advanced to remind him of his duty, he received three balls in his head, and fell down dead.

> A gripping, one-sentence account of the murder of La Salle in 1685 in present-day Texas. *An Account of M. de la Salle's last Expedition and Discoveries in North America* (1698), by the French officer nicknamed "Tonty of the Iron Hand."

## Tousignant, Claude
If I still have to "explain" my paintings, then my past work has been as good as useless; for the future, I have decided to let my paintings speak for themselves.

Quoted by William Withrow in *Contemporary Canadian Painting* (1972).

## Towers, Graham
Committee member: Two years ago you said the exact opposite. Can you explain that?
Graham Towers: Certainly. I was wrong.

Attributed to the first governor of the Bank of Canada, before a parliamentary committee in the 1940s by Grattan O'Leary in *Maclean's Magazine*, June 7, 1958.

A Governor of a Central Bank is so limited in what he can say that unless he can talk about something else he may not be found very interesting.

"That remark was made to me by the Governor of a Central Bank in one of the other Dominions," Towers explained in "Central Banking in Canada," January 6, 1936, *Addresses Delivered before the Canadian Club of Toronto: Season of 1935-36* (1936).

## Town, Harold
Collage seems to me the one medium most suited to the age of conspicuous waste, and it's marvellous to think of the garbage of our age becoming the art of our time.

*Collage: Personalities, Concepts, Techniques* (1962), by Harriet Janis and Rudi Blesh.

There was a time, I guess it was in 1952, when I was doing a lot of paintings that had to do with neon signs. And certainly the neon wasn't pretty but it fascinated me for two or three years. I suddenly realized, walking up that hideous bit of Bay Street from Wellesley Street to Bloor which has mostly showrooms for cars and automobile parts—I suddenly realized these signs were beautiful, all those gorgeous blues, and I realized that if an Egyptian from the time of one of the great Pharaohs were to walk down the street he would have found them a mystery, an overwhelming mystery. There's everything there.

*

Every time I look at the hill across the way, I realize that everything I've done is insignificant. Things are so beautiful.

"Harold Town Talks" (1960), interviewed by Elizabeth Kilbourn, *Canada: A Guide to the Peaceable Kingdom* (1970), edited by William Kilbourn.

## Townshend, George
"Oh, General, if Quebec falls, will Your Highness spare the women?"
"That depends. Don't write any more petitions. Send fifty beautiful virgins to me at once—and we shall see."

Brigadier-General Townshend despised General James Wolfe, whom he succeeded when Wolfe died taking Quebec, 1759. The mock dialogue accompanies one of Townshend's caricatures of Wolfe, and is quoted by Christopher Hibbert in *Wolfe at Quebec* (1959). "I never served so disagreeable a campaign as this," Townshend wrote. "It is war of the worst shape."

## Toye, William
With two colonial beginnings, two languages, two main religions, Canada is really two countries, held together by three nation-saving bywords—conservatism, caution and compromise. . . .

Introduction, *A Book of Canada* (1962), edited by William Toye.

## Toynbee, Arnold J.
If the future of mankind in a unified world is going to be on the whole a happy one, then I would prophesy that there is a future in the Old World for the Chinese, and in the island of North America for the *Canadiens*. Whatever the future of mankind in North America, I feel pretty confident that these French-speaking Canadians, at any rate, will be there at the end of the story.

*Civilization on Trial* (1948).

If the great Powers stubbornly insist on clinging to the old concept of nationalism—which is out-dated now—peoples who have not found nationalism a happy experience may be the only ones who can give the world the fresh solution that it needs. I suspect that the coming people in the Americas may be the French-Canadians; and in Asia, the Chinese.

> "History Warns Modern Man," an interview with Gretta Palmer, *World Review*, March, 1949.

**Toynbee, Philip**
The fifty-first State of the Union is a common and bitter Canadian comment of Canadians about their own country. But *why* are Americans so deeply hated by their immediate neighbours, both north and south? Not, certainly, because they are unpleasant people: the great majority of U.S. visitors to Canada and Mexico are civil, modest and friendly. The reason, surely, is that normal human greed in both countries has encouraged U.S. investment to such an extent that both have largely lost their dignity and individuality. Then bitter and anti-U.S. resentment follows, even (particularly?) among all those, of all classes, who have profited most from the squalid transaction.

> "Pockets of Sanity in a Land of Madness," *The London Observer Magazine*, January 27, 1974.

**Tracy, Spencer**   See Louis B. Mayer.

**Traill, Catherine Parr**
As to ghosts or spirits they appear totally banished from Canada. This is too matter-of-fact country for such supernaturals to visit. Here there are no historical associations, no legendary tales of those that came before us. Fancy would starve for lack of marvellous food to keep her alive in the backwoods. We have neither fay nor fairy, ghost nor bogle, satyr nor wood-nymph; our very forests disdain to shelter dryad or hamadryad. No naiad haunts the rushy margin of our lakes, or hallows with her presence our forest-rills. No Druid claims our oaks; and instead of pouring with mysterious awe among our curious limestone rocks, that are often singular-

ly grouped together, we refer them to the geologist to exercise his skill in accounting for their appearance: instead of investing them with the solemn characters of ancient temples or heaven altars, we look upon them with the curious eye of natural philosophy alone. [May 9, 1833]

\*

"I should like to know, then, what Canada is good for?" she said angrily.

"It is a good country for the honest, industrious artisan. It is a fine country for the poor labourer who, after a few years of hard toil, can sit down in his own log-house and look abroad on his own land and see his children well settled in life as independent freeholders. It is a grand country for the rich speculator who can afford to lay out a large sum in purchasing land in eligible situations; for if he have any judgment he will make a hundred per cent as interest for his money after waiting a few years. But it is a hard country for the poor gentleman whose habits have rendered him unfit for manual labour."

> Conversation between "a very fine lady" and "the son of a naval officer of some rank in the service busily employed in making an axe-handle out of a piece of rock-elm." *The Backwoods of Canada: Being Letters from the Wife of an Emigrant Officer* (1836).

. . . Any short-comings that may be noticed by our friends, must be excused on the score of the work being wholly Canadian in its execution.

> *Canadian Wild Flowers* (1869).

**Tremlett, Thomas**
To the first charge Your Excellency I answer that it is a lie, to the second charge I say that it is a d----d lie, and to the third charge that it is a d----d infernal lie, and Your Excellency I have no more to say.

> Reply of the chief justice of Newfoundland to three charges of partiality and corruption, October, 1811. Although exonerated, Tremlett changed posts in 1813 with the chief justice of Prince Edward Island. Quoted by D.W. Prowse in *A History of Newfoundland from*

*English, Colonial, and Foreign Records* (1895). See also Caesar Colclough.

## Trendle, George W.
On, King! On, you huskies!

Frequent cry of Sergeant Preston, the gold rush Mountie, to his lead husky King. Preston starred in "Challenge of the Yukon," a radio serial popular during the 1940s. Trendle, a Detroit broadcaster, is better known as the creator of "The Lone Ranger."

## Trent, John
There's nothing like failure to give you success.

Director of CBC-TV's "Jalna" series. *The Toronto Star*, June 22, 1973.

## Triquet, Paul
Never mind them, they can't shoot. . . . There are enemy in front of us, behind us and on our flanks, there is only one safe place—that is on the objective.

"On 14th December, 1943, Captain Triquet's company of the Royal 22e Régiment with the support of a squadron of a Canadian Armoured Regiment was given the task of crossing the gully and securing Casa Berardi. Difficulties were encountered from the outset. The gully was held in strength and on approaching it the force came under heavy fire from machine guns and mortars. All the company officers and 50 per cent of the men were killed or wounded. Showing superb contempt for the enemy, Captain Triquet went round reorganizing the remainder and encouraging them with the words, 'Never mind them, they can't shoot.' Finally when enemy infiltration was observed on all sides shouting, 'There are enemy in front of us, behind us and on our flanks, there is only one safe place—that is on the objective,' he dashed forward and with his men following him broke through the enemy resistance. In this action four tanks were destroyed and several enemy machine-gun posts silenced." *The London Gazette*, March 6, 1944. George C. Machum, *Canada's V.C.'s: The Story of Canadians Who Have Been Awarded the Victoria Cross* (1956).

## Trollope, Anthony
I must confess that in going from the States into Canada, an Englishman is struck by the feeling that he is going from a richer country into one that is poorer, and from a greater country into one that is less.

*

Toronto as a city is not generally attractive to a traveller . . . the streets in Toronto are framed with wood, or rather planked, as are those of Montreal and Quebec; but they are kept in better order. I should say that the planks are first used at Toronto, then sent down by the lake to Montreal, and when all but rotted out there, are again floated off by the St. Lawrence to be used in the thoroughfares of the old French capital. But if the streets of Toronto are better than those of the other towns, the roads round it are worse.

*North America* (1862), by the British novelist.

## Trollope, Frances
I frequently heard vehement complaints, and constantly met the same in the newspapers, of a practice stated to be very generally adopted in Britain of sending out cargoes of parish paupers to the United States. A Baltimore paper heads some such remarks with the words

"INFAMOUS CONDUCT!"

and tells us of a cargo of aged paupers just arrived from England, adding, "John Bull has squeezed the orange, and now insolently casts the skin in our faces." Such being the feeling, it will be readily believed that these unfortunates are not likely to meet such kindness or sympathy in sickness, or in suffering of any kind. If these American statements be correct, and that different parishes are induced, from an excessive population, to pay the voyage and out-fit of some of their paupers across the Atlantic, why not send them to Canada?

*Domestic Manners of the Americans* (1832), by the mother of the novelist Anthony Trollope.

## Trotsky, Leon
The whole business was so offensive, so

clearly a discrimination against the Russian revolutionaries, in contrast to the treatment accorded other passengers not so unfortunate as to belong to a nation allied to England, that some of the Russians sent a violent protest to the British authorities. I did not join with them because I saw little use in complaining to Beelzebub about Satan. But at the same time we did not foresee the future. . . .

While a group of sailors were holding me fast, my older boy ran to help me and struck an officer with his little fist. "Shall I hit him again, papa?" he shouted. He was eleven then, and it was his first lesson in British democracy.

The police left my wife and children in Halifax; the rest of us were taken by train to Amherst, a camp for German prisoners. And there, in the office, we were put through an examination the like of which I had never before experienced, even in the Peter-Paul fortress. For in the Czar's fortress the police stripped me and searched me in privacy, whereas here our democratic allies subjected us to this shameful humiliation before a dozen men.

> Leon Trotsky's incarceration in Canada occurred on April 3, 1917, when he and his family were forcibly removed from a Norwegian vessel at Halifax. His wife and children were kept under close surveillance in Halifax while Trotsky was incarcerated in a prisoner-of-war camp at Amherst. He was released on April 29 and with his family returned to Russia where he played a prominent role in the October Revolution. The passage above appears in *My Life: An Attempt at an Autobiography* (1931). The possibility that the provisional government in St. Petersburg had requested the British authorities to detain Trotsky is raised by Isaac Deutscher in *The Prophet Armed: Trotsky: 1879-1921* (1954). No doubt the revolutionary was familiar with Dostoyevsky's observation: "The degree of civilization in a society can be judged by entering its prisons."

**Trotter, Beecham**
A good friend says, sometimes, that the difference between Canada and the United States is that the United States are a great country, with a great people, who are not as great as they think they are; and Canada is a great country, inhabited by a great people who are much greater than they believe themselves to be.

> *A Horseman and the West* (1925).

**Trottier, Pierre**
We have used winter to create a beautiful myth with which to apologize for our tardiness in regard to history, progress, civilization, culture, art. . . . Our winter, though, has paid us back in kind. It has readily accepted its double role of judge and justifier. Before its tribunal, our fear of living, our inability to exist, our lack of substance on this earth, all receive their absolution and condemnation: absolution for all our failings of the past, and simultaneous condemnation for those of the future. Peace be with you, my son, and sin again! Our winter whitewashes us, without ever giving us a taste for true colour, but only for that of the colour print.

> "Return to Winter" (1963), translated by Ben Shek, *Canada: A Guide to the Peaceable Kingdom* (1970), edited by William Kilbourn.

**Trudeau, Margaret**
I sort of feel right now that we are in some kind of vacuum—Pierre and I—in a very lovely bubble, except for his job.

> Interviewed by Dan Turner, *The Toronto Star*, June 23, 1973.

**Trudeau, Pierre Elliott**

OBITER DICTA

*Le raison avant la passion.* [Reason over Passion; said to be Trudeau's personal maxim]

The flag is a matter of complete indifference in Quebec.

\*

The glue of nationalism must become as obsolete as the theory of the divine right of kings. [Interview, June 11, 1964]

I am opposed to nationalism in all its forms, whether it be French-Canadian,

Jewish, Irish, or any other. [October, 1965]

Warner Troyer: How badly do you want to be prime minister?

Trudeau: Not very badly. But I can give you another quotation, from Plato—that men who want very badly to head the country shouldn't be trusted. [CBC-TV interview, Toronto, March 26, 1967]

I wouldn't lift a finger to get rid of the monarchy . . . I think the monarchy, by and large, has done more good than harm to Canada. [June, 1967]

There's no place for the state in the bedrooms of the nation.

> The then minister of Justice tossed off this now-celebrated *bon mot* in an Ottawa interview, December 22, 1967. (What he actually said, in reference to changes in the Criminal Code, was, "The state has no place in the nation's bedroom.") Trudeau alluded to his own aphorism at the Commonwealth Prime Ministers' Conference in London, England, January 16, 1969, when he turned against reporters who were plaguing him about his association with Eva Rittinghausen. "I think you once agreed when I said that the state had no place in the bedrooms of the nation. I think we could even say that the nation has no place in the bedrooms of the state, and certainly not the press anyhow." See also Eva Rittinghausen.

We must remain whole, and we must remain complete. National unity is the framework to which everything else is knit. [March 2, 1968]

An exciting party should have both blondes and brunettes. [March 10, 1968]

I would feel embarrassed to have the full support of Quebec at the leadership convention. [March 11, 1968]

Q. Will you give up your Mercedes?
A. Are you talking of the car now, or the girl?
Q. The car.
A. I won't give up either. [April 3, 1968]

A policy of bilingualism does not mean that everyone must speak two languages.

It means that a citizen can use either French or English when dealing with the state, and that, whenever numbers make it practical, he can educate his children in either language. Of course, a bilingual state is more expensive than a unilingual one, but it is a richer state. The alternative is to confine French-speaking Canadians to Quebec, and then we cannot afford the incalculable price of the resulting separation.

\*

Canada will be a strong country when Canadians of all provinces feel at home in all parts of the country, and when they feel that all Canada belongs to them. We wish nothing more, but we will accept nothing less. Masters in our own house we must be, but our house is the whole of Canada. [Address, Liberal Convention, Ottawa, April 5, 1968]

To govern is to choose. [April 24, 1968]

Some commentators have suggested that I do not really exist, that I am the figment of the imagination of certain newspaper columnists and television producers. Personally, I reject this extreme view. [Montreal, May 6, 1968]

Assistant: What shall we do, sir, about the Abortion Bill?
Trudeau: Pay it! [Attributed]

I've done some nasty things in my life but I've tried not to do them twice. [Attributed]

Luck, that's when preparation and opportunity meet. [Attributed]

I can't give you too many kisses. The press is watching. Perhaps later. [To a pretty campaigner, May 18, 1968]

Trudeau: Well, there is some question as to my age. Do not ask me about that.
Interviewer: Well, you're certainly a young man, and if I am correct, sir, and may say so, forty-eight years of age.
Trudeau: Well, some say that. Some say other figures. I will have to ask my sister again. I am not too sure.
Interviewer: Well, it certainly is not old.
Trudeau: Oh, it's not old by any means. Even if I were fifty-eight, I

would not be old. [CKNX Wingham, May 21, 1968]

Voice in the crowd: Canada is owned by the United States.

Trudeau: There is a man with an inferiority complex. [Winnipeg, May 23, 1968]

I seek a clear mandate for a strong federalism. [June 7, 1968]

We have heard from the leaders of the other parties that the country is really going down the drain economically, that we are in a terrible mess, and that things really are in a very, very difficult position for Canadians. When you hear them, when you think of the kind of future they see for Canada, it is a wonder they want the job of prime minister. [June 11, 1968]

Voice in the crowd: Vive la France!

Trudeau: Si vous voulez. Vive la France, et vive les Anglais, aussi. Et vive la république des patates frites. [Chatham, June 11, 1968]

The truth is that I was going to Cuba in a canoe, but this was in 1961 with some friends of mine. This was a sporting event. I should tell you I have canoed down most of the great rivers, not only of Canada but of the world. [June 14, 1968]

It is not of communism that we should be afraid, but rather of the fact that people are starving to death. We should be ashamed of it. [Quebec, June 15, 1968]

Voice in the crowd: Where did you get that tan?

Trudeau: The tan? Riding in an open convertible between rallies which draw more people than your rally is doing, I will tell you that. But you are welcome to ours. [Saskatoon, June 18, 1968]

If we do not develop this country, there are nations, not only who will come through their capital, but they will come through their technology, they will come through their population, and they will say, "By what right does this small Canadian population live in such a wealthy country and not exploit its resources?" [Fort William, June 18, 1968]

I am less worried about what is over the Berlin Wall than about what might happen in Chicago or in New York or in our own great cities in Canada. [Attributed]

The Just Society [Campaign slogan, summer, 1968]

When you spend money abroad it is not inflationary. [To Ottawa reporters after returning from a Mediterranean cruise, September 10, 1968]

There are poor people in the cabinet, and there are certainly people in the cabinet that are getting poor, I can tell you that. [Press conference, Ottawa, September 11, 1968]

The attainment of a just society is the cherished hope of civilized men.

Speech from the throne, House of Commons, September 12, 1968. The throne speech referred to the Liberal party's slogan "The Just Society."

Q. Mr. Prime Minister, I would like to know how and when you are going to sell the western Canadian farmers' wheat?

A. Well, why should I sell the Canadian farmers' wheat? [Liberal party gathering, Manitoba, December 13, 1968]

I'm doing it now in the hopes that I will reach the stage like Mackenzie King, where, perhaps, after many less years, I'll be able to make all the other people do the work and just go home with my diary. [TV interview, January 1, 1969]

Compromise is possible if it looks in the right direction.

*

Canada is the product of understanding, not conflict; we are the trustees of reasonableness, not violence. [Commonwealth Prime Ministers' Conference, London, England, January 10, 1969]

I think that all of us feel a sense of guilt, not so much toward the Indian as toward the fact that we haven't really addressed our minds to this problem.

\*

Would I call myself a socialist or a capitalist? I rarely call myself anything; other people do the calling. I do not believe in labels very much. [To students at Canada House, London, England, January 13, 1969]

Student: Why don't you come in and talk to us?

Trudeau: It's a matter of scheduling, I have a tight schedule. . . .

Student: You wouldn't want to let down all these beautiful girls, would you?

Trudeau: It's a matter of inelasticity. [To students in Washington, March 25, 1969]

Americans should never underestimate the constant pressure on Canada which the mere presence of the United States has produced. We're a different people from you and we're a different people partly because of you. . . . Living next to you is in some ways like sleeping with an elephant. No matter how friendly and even-tempered is the beast, if I can call it that, one is affected by every twitch and grunt. . . . It should not therefore be expected that this kind of a nation, this Canada, should project itself . . . as a mirror image of the United States.

> Address to the National Press Club, Washington, March 26, 1969. Trudeau returned to the elephant image in an interview in Wellington, New Zealand, May 14, 1970, when he told the TV audience: "Now, obviously when you're contending with an elephant you can't hope to be stronger and better and bigger than the elephant. What you can do is select those areas in which perhaps you can perform better. You know, man is smaller than an elephant but perhaps he has certain talents which the elephant doesn't have."

Flying? I think it will last as long as sex. [After a 900 m.p.h. jet ride, May 19, 1969]

My father taught me order and discipline, and my mother freedom and fantasy.

\*

My teachers used to say that for a Catholic I was pretty much of a Protestant.

\*

I am very eclectic . . . I have probably read more of Dostoyevsky, Stendhal, and Tolstoy than the average statesman, and less of Keynes, Mill and Marx.

\*

It takes up too much time, being afraid.

\*

The Just Society is the kind of society freedom would establish.

\*

If we don't solve our own problems, other people will—and the world of tomorrow belongs to the people who will solve them.

> Interviewed by Edith Iglauer in *The New Yorker*, July 5, 1969.

If you want to see me again, don't bring signs saying "Trudeau is a pig" and don't bring signs that he hustles women, because I won't talk to you. I didn't get into politics to be insulted. And don't throw wheat at me either! [Saskatoon, July 17, 1969]

There is the need to explain people to people, and people to themselves, much more than has ever been done. I personally never realized the extent to which the different parts of our country didn't explain themselves to each other. [Ottawa interview, August, 1969]

How many other Riels exist in Canada, beyond the fringe of accepted conduct, driven to believe that this country offers no answer to their needs and no solutions to their problems?

\*

It is all too easy, should disturbances erupt, to crush them in the name of law and order. We must never forget that, in the long run, a democracy is judged by the way the majority treats the minority. Louis Riel's battle is not yet won. [Address at the unveiling of the Louis Riel Monument, Regina, October 2, 1969]

The hon. stinker. [Trudeau once referred to a member of the House of Commons in this way, a variation of "the hon. gentleman," which is how Hansard reports personal references]

Mangez de la merde!

> "Let them eat shit!" A variation on Marie-Antoinette's classic reply, on being told her people had no bread, "Qu'ils mangent de la brioche!" ("Let them eat cake!") The prime minister was heard yelling this at "the Lapalme boys," striking mail-truck drivers who, on the expiry of their contract on April 1, 1970, were not rehired by the federal government when it took over the operations of the Lapalme company.

A very regrettable side effect. [A new definition of unemployment as "a very regrettable side effect of inflation," House of Commons, April 16, 1970]

Biafra? Where's Biafra? [Widely reported when Nigeria forcibly re-established its control over secessionist Biafra, April, 1970; in editorial cartoons the rhetorical question was addressed to Mitchell Sharp, who only shook his head sadly]

You know, it's their own health, but the same people who get high on pot five or three times a week very often are the same people who say, "What's the government going to do about pollution?" and who go around polluting their own lungs. [To youths in Whitehorse, August 4, 1970]

I do not personally share with any acuteness the sense of regret expressed by some commentators that Canadians pay insufficient heed to their past. The past we must understand and respect, but it is not to be worshipped. It is in the future that we shall find our greatness. [House of Commons, October 9, 1970]

It is more important to maintain law and order than to worry about those whose knees tremble at the sight of the army. [Ottawa, October 12, 1970]

Trudeau: Yes, well there are a lot of bleeding hearts around who just don't like to see people with helmets and guns. All I can say is, go on and bleed, but it is more important to keep law

and order in the society than to be worried about weak-kneed people who don't like the looks of. . . .

Rafe: At any cost? How far would you go with that? How far would you extend that?

Trudeau: Well, just watch me.

Rafe: At reducing civil liberties? To what extent?

Trudeau: To what extent?

Rafe: Well, if you extend this and you say, O.K., you're going to do anything to protect them, does this include wiretapping, reducing other civil liberties in some way?

Trudeau: Yes, I think the society must take every means at its disposal to defend itself against the emergence of a parallel power which defies the elected power in this country and I think that goes at any distance. So long as there is a power in here which is challenging the elected representatives of the people, I think that power must be stopped and I think it's only, I repeat, weak-kneed bleeding hearts who are afraid to take these measures.

> This widely quoted interview with CBC-TV reporter Tim Rafe took place during the FLQ crisis, October 13, 1970, and the transcript was published the following day in *The Toronto Star*. The prime minister, under fire for invoking the stiff War Measures Act, was justifying to the nation his show of force. (A phrase from the interview supplied Denis Smith with the title of a study of the use—and misuse—of power: *Bleeding Hearts . . . Bleeding Country: Canada and the Quebec Crisis* [1971].)

Lack of absolute power corrupts absolutely.

> Trudeau is making a veiled reference to the rumour, reported by Peter C. Newman in *The Toronto Star* during the October 1970 crisis, that publisher Claude Ryan and others were about to form an alternate government to replace the recently elected Quebec administration of Robert Bourassa. The prime minister simply varied Lord Acton's dictum of 1887, "Power tends to corrupt and absolute power corrupts absolutely," yet he failed to add, although

Acton did, "Great men are almost always bad men."

Therefore, His Excellency the Governor-General-in-Council, on the recommendation of the prime minister, is pleased to direct that a proclamation be issued proclaiming that apprehended insurrection exists and has existed as and from the fifteenth day of October, one thousand nine hundred and seventy.

Formal statement made by the prime minister within hours of the imposition of the War Measures Act (Public Order Regulations, 1970), 4:00 A.M., October 16, 1970. Reproduced by John Saywell in *Quebec 70: A Documentary Narrative* (1971).

I acted on the information I have been accumulating since I was three years old. [House of Commons, October 27, 1971]

Monsieur le président, qu'on lis in English or in French la position est la même; le communiqué does not talk about ce qu'on disait en réponse to the Leader of the Opposition. [Bilingual answer to Marcel Lambert's bilingual question in the House of Commons]

There is no such thing as a model or ideal Canadian. What could be more absurd than the concept of an "all-Canadian" boy or girl. [Canadian-Ukrainian Congress, November 1, 1971]

I've written often enough that the country is held together only by consent, not by force of arms. If any part of our country wants to leave Canada I don't think force of arms will be used to prevent it. [Interview with Tom Buckley, *The New York Times Magazine*, December 6, 1970]

Unemployment [is the main problem facing Canadians], I guess. The switch is because we have won last year's victory, the one against inflation.

When asked to identify the main problem facing Canadians, and why the nation faces a new one, Trudeau made this reply on December 23, 1970. Quoted by Walter Stewart in *Divide and Con: Canadian Politics at Work* (1973).

But we have by no means attained an age of great wisdom. I wish that we had; a glance about this troubled planet, however, indicates that men have not yet turned their backs upon destruction. Even in my own country, as we recently had the shock of discovering, violence is no stranger. [President's luncheon, Islamabad, Pakistan, January 7, 1971]

Fuddle-duddle.

House of Commons, February 16, 1971. John Lundrigan, member for Gander-Twillingate, addressed a question to the prime minister: "I would ask the hon. gentleman if he would condescend to tell us whether any new programs are to be announced now — let them eat what? I did not get what the prime minister just said." As Hansard observed: "Some hon. Members: Shame!" Lundrigan continued: "On a question of privilege, I want to say two things. First, I hope that the remark of the prime minister has been recorded. Second, he does not have the guts to say to the people of Canada what he has just said across the floor of the House. . . . Mr. Speaker, I am not permitted to use four-letter words in the House so I cannot quote from the record what the prime minister said. But let me say to the Lapalme workers that what they heard from the prime minister was mild compared with what he has just said to the House of Commons today."

"Some hon. members: Hear, hear!"
"Some hon. members: Oh, oh!"

Then the prime minister rose: "Mr. Speaker, the hon. member has accused me of uttering a four-letter word in this House. That is an absolute untruth. . . . I challenge any member opposite to say that they heard me utter a single word, and I challenge the Hansard reporter to say whether or not he has recorded anything of that sort."

Members of the press gallery who observed the unbecoming incident reported that the prime minister mouthed an obscenity without uttering it. Although not usually at a loss for words, this time Trudeau was. Later, outside the House, he explained to George Bain and other reporters that the words he had mouthed —but had not uttered—were "fuddle-duddle."

This was a happy invention, and the ingenious and handy euphemism was an instant hit across the country—but not beyond its borders. "Fuddle-duddle," which recalls nonsense phrases from nursery rhymes like "fiddle-faddle" and "fiddle-diddle," does not appear in Oxford or Webster and is a genuine Canadianism. A member of the Opposition immediately offered a pun: "The prime minister wishes to be obscene and not heard."

Canadians by and large tend to think of Canada as a land of immense potential. Not just as a big land, which it unquestionably is. Or a privileged land as many others enviously regard us. But as a land of limitless promise. A land, perhaps, on the threshold of greatness. [Toronto Liberal Association, March 3, 1971]

I've never been a president and wonder what it would be like. [Toronto dinner, April 15, 1971]

[I can foresee the day when Canada and Russia might] reach agreement on a program of trans-Arctic co-operation of a yet unforeseen nature. That may be a dream, but surely there is an element of reality in it—the reality of two peoples overcoming the rigors of the same climate, subduing the same untamed reaches, taking up the challenge of our common Everest, the Far North. [Leningrad speech, May 27, 1971]

Americans are not only our neighbours and allies, but they are even our friends. [To Leonid Brezhnev, Moscow, May, 1971]

There is no necessary relation between inflation and unemployment. [Port Hope, September 10, 1971]

We're not going to move away from the U.S. We're going to be friends willy-nilly, and probably more willy than nilly. [Interview, December 21, 1971]

And I concede your point too, that it's likely we heard more from the vested interests than we did from the little taxpayer who didn't have . . . the high-paid lawyers to speak for him . . . I suppose in participatory democracy there will always be some whose voice is louder than others.

CTV interview concerning the abortive white paper on taxation, December 28, 1971. This admission supplied David Lewis with the title of his book *Louder Voices: The Corporate Welfare Bums* (1972).

Student: But tell me, what does Pierre Trudeau really think about the problems of the Canadian economy when he's lying in bed at night.
Trudeau: When I'm lying in bed at night, I really don't think about the problems of the Canadian economy. [CBC-TV student interview, Ontario]

The baby is fine. It has changed my own life quite a bit. You want to quote someone, I'll quote Claudel who says that his relations with mankind have changed since he has become father of one of them. And I think that's true. [TV interview, January 9, 1972]

I like to quote myself that "a politician should be slightly ahead of the people but still in contact." [August 16, 1972]

Inflation has been beaten. [August, 1972]

I see a campaign as a bath of fire in which you're purified, and settle all the piddling little questions of whether this little thing was right or wrong. What's your over-all judgment. Is it yes or no?

Campaign speech, September 2, 1972, quoted by Walter Stewart in *Divide and Con: Canadian Politics at Work* (1973).

I'll tell you one thing that's certain. From now on, no more philosopher-king.

To a cabinet minister on election night, October 30, 1972, when it became apparent there would be a minority government. (CBC pundit Larry Zolf later quipped: "Trudeau has moved from philosopher-king to Mackenzie King in only four years.")

I want to say I'm sorry for all those who didn't win. I just wanted to tell them to cheer up . . . I'm sure there are a lot of broken dreams. [Press conference,

October 31, 1972, following the near-defeat at the polls]

WRITINGS

What sets a canoeing expedition apart is that it purifies you more rapidly and inescapably than any other. Travel a thousand miles by train and you are a brute; pedal five hundred on a bicycle and you remain basically a bourgeois; paddle a hundred in a canoe and you are already a child of nature.

*

How does the trip affect your personality? Allow me to make a fine distinction, and I would say that you return not so much a man who reasons more, but a more reasonable man.

*

A good camper knows that it is more important to be ingenious than to be a genius.

*

I know a man whose school could never teach him patriotism, but who acquired that virtue when he felt in his bones the vastness of his land, and the greatness of those who founded it.

> "Exhaustion and Fulfilment: The Ascetic in a Canoe," *Wilderness Canada* (1970), edited by Borden Spears. Trudeau's essay, a moral meditation on physical sensation, first appeared in 1944.

Let us overthrow the totems, break the taboos. Or better, let us consider them cancelled. Coldly, let us be intelligent. ["Politique fonctionnelle" (1950)]

*

In reality, though, the first thing to ask of history is that it should point out to us the paths of liberty. The great lesson to draw from revolutions is not that they devour humanity but rather that tyranny never fails to generate them. ["When the People Are in Power" (1958)]

*

In the last analysis any given political authority exists only because men consent to obey it. In this sense what exists is not so much the authority as the obedience. ["To Prevent Sedition . . ." (1958)]

*Approaches to Politics* (1970), translated by I.M. Owen.

Chinese Marxists are like Quebec collegians. On questions of religion and sex, they lose their sang-froid.

> *Two Innocents in Red China* (1968), by Jacques Hébert and Pierre Elliott Trudeau, translated by I.M. Owen from the original 1961 edition.

The political philosophy of the Liberal Party is simplicity itself: "Say anything, think anything: better still, think nothing, but put us in power, for we are best fitted to govern." ["The Abdication of the Spirit," *Cité Libre*, April, 1963]

Historically, French Canadians have not really believed in democracy for themselves; and English Canadians have not really wanted it for others. Such are the foundations upon which our two ethnic groups have absurdly pretended to be building democratic forms of government. No matter the ensuing structure has turned out to be rather flimsy.

*

And, as everyone knows, the army is a poor training corps for democracy, no matter how inspiring its cause.

*

French Canadians are perhaps the only people in the world who "enjoy" democracy without having had to fight for it. ["Some Obstacles to Democracy in Quebec" (1958)]

*

The true tactical position of the *democratic* socialist is on the left, *but no further.*

*

The basis of a socialist ideology is to work out a certain set of human values, for the fostering of which society is held collectively responsible. ["The Practice and Theory of Federalism" (1961)]

*

This is what I call la nouvelle trahison des clercs: this self-deluding passion of a large segment of our thinking population for throwing themselves headlong —spiritually and mentally—into purely escapist pursuits. ["New Treason of the Intellectuals" (1962)]

*

In other words, the nation first decides

what the state should be; but then the state has to decide what the nation should remain. ["Federalism, Nationalism and Reason" (1964)]

*

The only constant factor to be found in my thinking over the years has been opposition to accepted opinions. Had I applied this principle to the stock market, I might have made a fortune. I chose to apply it to politics, and it led me to power—a result I had not really desired, or even expected.

*

My political action, or my theory—insomuch as I can be said to have one—can be expressed very simply: create counterweights. [Foreword (1967)]

> *Federalism and the French Canadians* (1968).

Man reached out and touched the tranquil moon. Puisse ce haut fait permettre à l'homme de redécouvrir la terre et d'y trouver la paix.

> This brief but eloquent statement was one of seventy-three from world leaders miniaturized and reproduced on a disc the size of a fifty-cent piece. Taken to the moon on the Apollo flight, the disc was deposited on the lunar surface by Neil Armstrong, July 20, 1969. The translation runs: "May that high accomplishment allow man to rediscover the earth and there find peace."
>
> The Trudeau material comes from many contemporary sources, including the following publications: *The Gospel According to Saint Pierre* (1969), edited by Brian Shaw; *The Best of Trudeau* (1972); *Pierre Elliott Trudeau's Conversation with Canadians* (1972), foreword by Ivan L. Head.
>
> See also: John Diefenbaker, Jean-Guy Pilon, Sir Wilfrid Laurier: Who Owns the Twentieth Century?, Margaret Trudeau.

## Trudel, Marcel

If we have a separate state there is a great danger we will fall into a dictatorship. Confederation—with guarantees for civil liberties provided by Ottawa—is a corrective against the tendencies to which we French Canadians respond.

> Quoted by Gerald Clark in *Canada: The Uneasy Neighbour* (1965).

It is persistently maintained in certain circles that it is impossible to write a Canadian history of equal validity for our two main language groups. This amounts to saying that history should serve the particular ends of each of them. But history's prime function is to convey an understanding of society as it was in the past, and, more specifically in this case, to acquaint both French and English Canadians with the adventure they have shared on North American soil. . . . The teaching of history hitherto has been far from this; more often than not it has only tended to set one group against the other. If Canada is more than ever before threatened with schism, we believe we must look for the cause very largely in the manner in which today's citizens have learned the history of their country.

> *Canadian History Textbooks: A Comparative Study* (1970), Studies of the Royal Commission on Bilingualism and Biculturalism.

## Trueman, Albert W.

What more important thing can be done for the future of Canada than to provide the means by which the highest intelligences of the country, both academic and artistic, may develop their highest potentialities?

> "The Canada Council and the Talented Individual," *Third Annual Report of the Canada Council* (1960).

Our golden apple is divisible but it cannot be endlessly divided if it is to provide any sustenance worth having.

*

When the golden apple is divided it is perhaps the part put in young hands that will be in the safest keeping.

> Introduction, *Fourth Annual Report of the Canada Council* (1961).

The Canada Council is only one partner in the enterprise of patronage.

> Introduction, *Sixth Annual Report of the Canada Council* (1963).

## Truman, Harry S.
Canada has achieved internal unity and material strength, and has grown in stature in the world community, by solving problems that might have hopelessly divided and weakened a less gifted people.

\*

Canada and the United States have reached the point where we no longer think of each other as "foreign" countries. We think of each other as friends, as peaceful and co-operative neighbours on a spacious and fruitful continent.

> The American president addressed a joint meeting of the Senate and the House of Commons, June 11, 1947.

## Truscott, Steven
In all the world today, only two people really know for sure that I'm innocent. One of them is me. The other is the killer.

> *The Steven Truscott Story* (1971), as told to Bill Trent.

## Tse-tung, Mao
A mobile operating unit. Functioning close to the front . . . yes, that would be good. It would be good for our fighters to know they would receive immediate treatment for their wounds. . . . Then it is clear. You will organize the mobile operating unit at once.

> The Chinese Communist leader to Dr. Norman Bethune, Yenan, North China, March-April, 1938. Mao's words come from Bethune's diary as quoted by Ted Allan and Sydney Gordon in *The Scalpel, the Sword: The Story of Dr. Norman Bethune* (1952).

What kind of spirit is this that makes a foreigner selflessly adopt the cause of the Chinese people's liberation as his own? It is the spirit of internationalism, the spirit of communism, from which every Chinese Communist must learn . . . this is our internationalism, the internationalism with which we oppose both narrow nationalism and narrow patriotism.

\*

Comrade Bethune's spirit, his utter devotion to others without any thought of self, was shown in his boundless sense of responsibility to his work and his boundless warm-heartedness towards all comrades and the people. Every Communist must learn from him. . . .

> *Quotations from Chairman Mao Tsetung* (1966), edited by Lin Piao. Mao's tribute to the Orillia-born medical doctor who died in northern China on November 12, 1939, was written on December 21, 1939 ("In Memory of Norman Bethune," *Selected Works*). As part of "the little red book," the tribute has received extraordinary distribution — perhaps one hundred million copies have been printed.

The chairman of the People's Republic went on to say: "I saw Comrade Bethune only once. Afterwards he wrote me many letters. But as I was busy, I wrote back only one letter and do not know if he ever received it. I feel deeply grieved over his death. Now all of us commemorate him; thus we can see how profoundly people are moved by his spirit. We must all learn from him the spirit that is so completely free from selfishness. Starting from that point, one can become a person of great use to the people."

To Robert Payne, in *Mao Tse-tung* (1968), the Chinese leader "appears to have written this sermon out of an obscure sense of guilt, remembering that he had failed to answer the doctor's letters and perhaps taken him too much for granted." See also Norman Bethune.

## Tubman, Harriet
I think slavery is the next thing to hell. If a person would send another into bondage, he would, it appears to me, be bad enough to send him into hell, if he could.

> Harriet Tubman fled slavery in the American South and settled in St. Catharines. Quoted by Benjamin Drew in *The Refugee: or the Narratives of Fugitive Slaves in Canada* (1856).

## Tucker, Albert
The contribution of education to a distinctive Canadian consciousness is largely accidental.

> Principal of Glendon College, York Uni-

versity, quoted by Donna Dilschneider in *The Toronto Star*, September 13, 1972.

**Tumpane, Frank**
I often wonder at the restraint of a woman of say, forty-three, who finds her escort gaping at some bunny girl with that simple-minded fatuous look that males acquire on such occasions. How does she keep herself from pouring her martini over the silly ass's head?

*The Toronto Telegram*, March 3, 1966.

**Tupper, Sir Charles**
I say what Canada wants is a national policy—a policy that shall be in the interest of Canada, apart from the principles of free-trade, apart from the principles of protection.

House of Commons, February 25, 1876. Tupper's speech included the phrase "national policy" which two years later Sir John A. Macdonald would appropriate for his protectionist National Policy.

The human mind naturally adapts itself to the position it occupies. The most gigantic intellect may be dwarfed by being cabin'd, cribbed, and confined. It requires a great country and great circumstances to develop great men.

*

The fact is, if we are known at all across the Atlantic, notwithstanding the immense resources of these Maritime Provinces, it is because we happen to be contiguous to Canada. Everything connected with our interests tells us of the insignificance of our position.

Address made in 1865 by the Nova Scotian leader, quoted by George H. Locke in *Builders of the Canadian Commonwealth* (1923). See also O.D. Skelton.

Sir Wilfrid is too English to me.

Sir Charles was prime minister for two months in 1896 after defeating Sir Wilfrid Laurier.

**Turcotte, Father J.G.**
Trois-Rivières is the second-largest French-speaking city in the world.

"The clue to the explanation lies in the phrase beloved by economists and statisticians — *per capita*," explains Leslie Roberts in *The Chief: A Political Biography of Maurice Duplessis* (1963). "Nowhere but in Paris . . . does over ninety-five per cent of the population speak French as their sole language."

**Turner, John**
A crisis has never been avoided by silence. A confrontation is always the only way to bring an issue to a head.

*Politics of Purpose* (1968).

There are two kinds of problems, those that get better . . . and those that get worse.

Quoted by Barbara Frum in *Maclean's Magazine*, August, 1973.

**Turner, Richard E.W.**
Never let it be said the Canadians had let their guns be taken!

Lieutenant Turner of the Royal Canadian Dragoons was awarded the Victoria Cross for valour at Leliefontein, Komati River, Union of South Africa, November 7, 1900. Quoted by John Swettenham in *Valiant Men: Canada's Victoria Cross and George Cross Winners* (1973).

**Tuttle, Charles R.**
The highest latitudes produce the greatest men.

*Our North Land* (1885).

**Twain, Mark**
I have seen the cab which Champlain employed when he arrived overland from Quebec; I have seen the horse which Jacques Cartier rode when he discovered Montreal. I have used them both; I will never do it again.

*

Well, never mind, what you lack in weather you make up in the means of grace. This is the first time I was ever in a city where you couldn't throw a brick without breaking a church window. Yet I was told that you were going to build one more. I said, the scheme is good, but where are you going to find the room? They said, we will build it on top of another church and use an elevator.

This shows that the gift of lying is not yet dead in the land.

\*

The burglar took the diamond studs, but left the shirt; only a reformed Toronto publisher would have left the shirt. [Referring to the loss of cufflinks in a rash of burglaries]

\*

I can speak French but I cannot understand it.

\*

But as I have already intimated, I will close this oration with a few sentiments in the French language. I have not ornamented them with flowers of rhetoric, for, to my mind, that literature is best and most enduring which is characterized by a noble simplicity. J'ai le belle bouton d'or de mon moncle, mais je n'ai pas celui du charpentier. Si vous avec le fromage du brave menuisier, c'est bon; mais, si vous ne l'avez pas, ne te désole pas, prenez le chapeau de drap noir de son beau-frère malade. Tout à l'heure! Qu'est-ce que vous dites? Pâté de foie gras! Revenons à nos moutons! Pardon, Messieurs, pardonnez-moi; essayant à parler la belle langue d'Ollendorff strains me more than you can possibly imagine. But I mean well, and I've done the best I could.

> Mark Twain established legal residence in Montreal for six months in 1881 in order to copyright his books throughout the British Empire, for his works were being pirated by unscrupulous Toronto publishers who were selling unauthorized editions in the United States. The humourist addressed a farewell banquet at the Windsor Hotel, December 7, 1881, where the above remarks were heard. Quoted by Stephen Leacock in "Mark Twain and Canada," *Queen's Quarterly*, Spring, 1935.

I have never seen real mud since I left Missouri until today.

> On visiting Winnipeg, 1895, "More of Mark Twain in Canada," *Queen's Quarterly*, Summer, 1935.

Those sons of up there will steal anything they can get their hands on . . . possible suits for damages and felony would be no more restraint upon them, I think, than would the presence of a young lady be upon a stud horse who had just found a mare unprotected by international copyright.

> The American novelist regarded John Ross Robertson and other Toronto publishers who plagiarized his books as "all born pirates," 1880s. Quoted by Ron Poulton in *The Paper Tyrant: John Ross Robertson of the Toronto Telegram* (1971).

**Tweed, Tommy**
A foretaste of hindsight.

> This intriguing phrase was devised by the popular actor-writer in the late forties for a CBC satire on dominion-provincial relations involving a production of "Little Red Riding Hood."

Red Sails in the Dust Bowl.

> Title of a radio play satirizing a scheme to irrigate the prairies with canals, broadcast by the CBC during the 1940s.

**Tweedsmuir, Baron**
I remember in the war in Italy, we would creep through the darkness of the hills on night advances. The Italian villagers that we encountered would whisper: "Are you English?" "No." "Are you American?" "No." "Then who are you?" "Canadians," we would reply. That seemed to puzzle them.

> "Twenty-five Years in Canada" (1961), *Empire Club of Canada: Addresses 1961-62* (1962). Baron Tweedsmuir is a son of John Buchan, Lord Tweedsmuir, who was governor general from 1935 to 1940. See also John Buchan.

**Tweedsmuir, Lord**   See John Buchan.

**Tyrrell, Joseph B.**
It's a man's duty to live as long as he can.

> The greatest land explorer of his day died in 1957 at the age of ninety-nine. Quoted by Pierre Berton in *Great Canadians: A Century of Achievement* (1965).

**Tyson, George**
"Captain Hall very bad again. He talks

wildly—seems to think someone means to poison him; calls for first one and then another, as if he did not know who to trust. When I was in, he accused —— and —— of wanting to poison him. When he is more rational he will say, 'If I die you must still go on to the Pole,' and such remarks. It is a sad affair; what will become of this expedition if Captain Hall dies, I dread to think."

> Diary entry, November 3, 1871. Quoted by Mrs. Euphemia V. Blake in *Arctic Experiences: containing Capt. George E. Tyson's Wonderful Drift on the Ice-Floe* . . . (1874). Hall died five days later. See also Charles Francis Hall.

**Tyson, Ian**
Four strong winds that blow lonely,
Seven seas that run high,
All those things that don't change come
    what may.

But our good times are all gone
And I'm bound for movin' on,
I'll look for you if I'm ever back this
    way.

> Refrain of "Four Strong Winds" composed in 1963 by Ian Tyson of Ian and Sylvia.

**Tzara, Tristan**
A great Canadian philosopher has said *le pensée* (thought) and *la passé* (the past) are also very charming.

> Obscure comment by the founder of Dada; "Seven Dada Manifestoes" (1916-20)), *The Dada Painters and Poets: An Anthology* (1951), edited by Robert Motherwell, who adds, "The genders of *la pensée* and *le passé* are reversed. This is a standard way of making comic Americans speak French. Perhaps Tzara had in mind an English Canadian, perhaps not."

# U

**Ullmann, Liv**
I like to be regarded as a star. I like to be at the center of things in a press conference, stay at fancy hotels, and swim in luxury. But that's only for a short time. After such a day I also like to go back to my room, close the door and just be myself.

> The radiant Norwegian actress, born in Tokyo in 1940, spent her first five years living in what she remembers as the "Little Norway" district of Toronto. Ingmar Bergman cast her in five films during the 1960s.

**Uncle Tom**   See Josiah Henson.

**Underhill, Frank H.**
An honest attempt to enumerate the points in which our Canadian civilization differs from that of the United States is apt to be almost as brief as the famous essay upon snakes in Ireland.

> "O Canada," *The Canadian Forum*, December, 1929.

. . . in Canada there is little of that personal intercourse between practical statesmen and university dons which is a unique and charming feature of English life, raising the intellectual level of politics and saving the universities from becoming the breeding ground of Ph.D.s. ["Goldwin Smith" (1933)]

Ultimately, the reason why William Lyon Mackenzie King has been our highly respected prime minister for twenty years is that the anything-but-respectable William Lyon Mackenzie was beaten in 1837. ["Twenty-five Years as Prime Minister" (1946)]

The real division in the world today is not between socialism and capitalism, it is between freedom and totalitarianism. ["Random Remarks on Socialism and Freedom" (1947)]

He [W.L. Mackenzie King] has been the representative Canadian, the typical Canadian, the essential Canadian, the ideal Canadian, the Canadian as he exists in the mind of God. ["The End of the King Era" (1948)]

For . . . we cannot escape the fact that we live on the same continent as the Americans, and that the longer we live here the more we are going to be affected by the same continental influences which affect them. It is too late now for a Canadian cultural nationalism to develop in the kind of mediaeval isolation in which English or French nationalism was nurtured. The so-called "alien" American influences are not alien at all; they are just the natural forces that operate on a continental scale in the conditions of our twentieth-century civilization. ["Notes on the Massey Report" (1951)]

If we could get off by ourselves on a continent island, far away from the wicked Americans, all we should achieve would be to become a people like the Australians. (And even then the American goblin would get us in the end, as he is getting the Australians.) Let us be thankful, then, that we live next door to the Americans. But if we allow ourselves to be obsessed by the danger of American cultural annexation, so that the thought preys on us day and night, we shall only become a slightly bigger Ulster. ["Notes on the Massey Report" (1951)]

My guess is that the Canadian voter had

been in a deep slumber for twenty-odd years before 1957, sleeping steadily on his left side, his Liberal side; that early in 1957 he began to stir uneasily in his sleep, to such an extent that the political doctors watching around his bedside gave out almost daily bulletins that he was waking up; but they were wrong; and on March 31, 1958, still sleeping, he turned over on his right side, his Conservative side, and he will probably continue to sleep steadily on this side for another twenty years, dreaming happily all the time of Stanley Cup and Grey Cup finals, of nerve-wracked weekends on crowded highways, and of split-level ranch-houses. [Convocation Address, Queen's University, May 16, 1959]

*In Search of Canadian Liberalism* (1960).

The artistic cult of the North is, as a matter of fact, pure romanticism at its worst, and bears little relation to the real life of Canada. Far from seeking inspiration among the rocks and winds, the normal Canadian dreams of living in a big city where he can make his pile quickly and enjoy such urban luxuries as are familiar to him in the advertising columns of our national magazines.

"False Hair on the Chest," *Saturday Night*, October 3, 1936.

There is more in common between two managers, one of whom is a socialist, than there is between two socialists, one of whom is a manager.

A nation is a body of people who have done great things together in the past and who hope to do great things together in the future.

*The Image of Confederation* (1964).

At times I have to hold my nose while marking the ballot.

Remark made at a Liberal party gathering in 1967, after breaking with the socialist cause and becoming a reluctant Liberal. Quoted by Peter C. Newman in "Frank Underhill" (1970), *Home Country: People, Places, and Power Politics* (1973).

"Underhill gave many years to building the CCF. He found himself on the opposite side from the business community in Toronto on nearly every public question. Yet in a speech in Toronto in 1964, he could in his seventies announce that the liberal hope lies now with the great corporations. This conversion surely shows how consistently he continues to work out the consequences of his thought. He has recognized that the business community in America is no longer the propertied classes of his youth but managers whose ideology is liberal. He is right to believe that corporations and not doctrinaire socialism are the wave of the future." George Grant's *Lament for a Nation: The Defeat of Canadian Nationalism* (1965).

The League for Social Reconstruction is an association of men and women who are working for the establishment in Canada of a social order in which the basic principle regulating production, distribution and service will be the common good rather than private profit.

> From the Manifesto of the L.S.R., founded in Toronto in January of 1932 by F.R. Scott and F.H. Underhill, with J.S. Woodsworth as honorary president. The wording is taken from the Manifesto, reproduced by Walter D. Young in *The Anatomy of a Party: The National CCF 1932-61* (1969).

Emergency measures, however, are of only temporary value, for the present depression is a sign of the mortal sickness of the whole capitalist system, and this sickness cannot be cured by the application of salves. These leave untouched the cancer which is eating at the heart of our society, namely, the economic system in which our natural resources and our principal means of production and distribution are owned, controlled and operated for the private profit of a small proportion of our population.

No C.C.F. Government will rest content until it has eradicated capitalism and put into operation the full programme of socialized planning which will lead to the establishment in Canada of the Co-operative Commonwealth.

> The convention rose as one and cheered when these final paragraphs from the "Regina Manifesto" were read before the founding convention of the CCF, July, 1933. M.J. Coldwell called the last sentence "a millstone around the party's neck." Noted by Walter D. Young in *The Anatomy of a Party: The National CCF 1932-61* (1969).

Canada's greatest need is a moral equivalent of the CPR.

\*

The essential basis of socialism is ethical, not economic.

> Sentiments attributed to Frank Hawkins Underhill, whom F.R. Scott called "the most Shavian of the Fabians."

**Untel, Frère**  See Jean-Paul Desbiens.

**Uvavnuk**
The great sea
Has set me adrift,
It moves me as the weed in a great river,
Earth and the great weather
Move me,
Have carried me away
And move my inward parts with joy.

> Poem by the Iglulik Eskimo woman shaman, Uvavnuk. Knud Rasmussen's *Intellectual Culture of the Iglulik Eskimos: Report of the Fifth Thule Expedition, 1921-24* (1929).

# V

## Valachi, Joseph

Q. The Buffalo family?

A. Buffalo and Canada is all one. When I say Canada, I mean Toronto.

> From the testimony of Joseph Valachi, the convicted heroin trafficker and former member of the Cosa Nostra or Mafia, before a U.S. Senate subcommittee, Washington, 1964.

## Valk, Frederick

And now perhaps when I have done with Shylock, the YMCA will protest. Christianity will be shown up in an unfair light, knocking him out. I toughen him.

\*

I seem to have seen it all—I don't want to see more. Canada appears, looking back, like an antiseptic laboratory and the people like archangels. [Letter written from Tetuan in Spanish Morocco, where the actor was appearing in a film in December, 1955]

> Frederick Valk—Hamburg-born, Prague-trained, London-based—was an actor in the grand tradition. He created Stratford's Shylock in the controversial 1955 production of *The Merchant of Venice*. Quoted by Diana Valk in *Shylock for a Summer: The Story of One Year (1954-5) in the Life of Frederick Valk* (1958).

The Canadian theatre will come quite logically, you can't live on lumbering and industry alone, the muses have to come in.

> "The Theatre in Europe and the Americas" (1955), *Empire Club of Canada: Addresses 1955-56* (1956). See also Tyrone Guthrie.

## Vallières, Pierre

The author of this book is a Québécois, a French Canadian, a proletarian, a colonized man and a baptized son of the Church. Hence, an extremely frustrated individual for whom "freedom" is not a metaphysical question but a very concrete problem.

\*

Making over the face of the Church, like making over the face of the capitalist system, modifies its nature only very superficially! A witch who undergoes plastic surgery to get rid of her warts and her crooked nose still remains a witch.

The Church is the witch of God, and I hope the Québécois of the future will learn to get along without her, just as children today have stopped believing in the boogie-man and take an interest in the real adventure of the astronauts instead.

\*

Instead of submitting to history, perhaps at last the hour had struck to begin making it *ourselves*.

\*

The Canadian Confederation was nothing more than a vast financial transaction carried out by the bourgeoise at the expense of the workers of the country, and more especially the workers of Quebec.

\*

As for me, a Québécois, proletarian, white nigger of America, one of the "wretched of the earth," to take responsibility for our history was, inevitably, to begin by denouncing and exposing the inhuman conditions of our existence, to build up a body of concrete knowledge and orient it entirely in the direction of "the practical results of action," of revolutionary action, of total liberation.

> Vallières's first book was written in the Manhattan House of Detention for Men in 1966 and 1967, when he was twenty-nine and a member of the FLQ. *White Niggers of America* (1971), translated by Joan Pinkham.

The greatest, the purest of uninvolved observers isn't worth the least important of conscious, resolute participants. The only way you can measure your condition is by acting upon it within the cadre of a common, collective enterprise.

*

History unites us, and our unity makes History. . . .

> *Choose!* (1972), translated by Penelope Williams.

Objectivity is the ideology of the status quo.

> Quoted in *Challenge for Change*, Autumn, 1972.

**Vancouver, Captain George**
To describe the beauties of this region will, on some future occasion, be a very grateful task to the pen of a skilled panegyrist. The serenity of the climate, the innumerable pleasing landscapes, and the abundant fertility that unassisted nature puts forth, requires only to be enriched by the industry of man with villages, mansions, cottages, and other buildings to render it the most lovely country that can be imagined; whilst the labour of the inhabitants would be amply rewarded, in the bounties which nature seems ready to bestow on cultivation.

> Spring of 1792, *A Voyage of Discovery to the North Pacific Ocean and Round the World* (1798). A description of the area around Vancouver.

**Van den Bark, Melvin**
See Lester V. Berrey.

**Van Dyke, Henry**
It is good to have a good neighbour, and it is not necessary that all neighbours should always marry.

> "Canada and the United States," *Empire Club of Canada: Addresses Delivered to the Members During the Year 1919* (1920).

**Van Horne, Cornelius**
And after all, why should I go to bed every night? Sleep is only a habit.

> Quoted by C. Lintern Sibley in "Van Horne and His Cuban Railway," *The Canadian Magazine*, September, 1913.

I do not believe that universal peace is either possible or desirable. If it were

possible and could be brought about, I feel sure that it would result in universal rottenness. All the manliness of the civilized world is due to wars or the need of being prepared for wars. All the highest qualities of mankind have been developed by wars or the dangers of wars. Our whole civilization is the outgrowth of wars. Without wars, religion would disappear. All the enterprise of the world has grown out of the aggressive, adventurous, and warlike spirit engendered by centuries of wars. [Letter to S.S. McClure, 1910]

*

Patriotic sentiments have never in the history of the world stood long against the pocket-book. This is an unhappy truth which cannot be escaped.

> Quoted by Walter Vaughan in *The Life and Work of Sir William Van Horne* (1920).

The last spike will be just as good an iron one as there is between Montreal and Vancouver, and anyone who wants to see it driven will have to pay full fare.

*

It was a reference to the familiar lines: "Not until Craigellachie shall move from his firm base, etc." I heard of this when I first became connected with the company, and was much impressed by it, and determined that if I were still with the company when the last spike should be laid, the spot should be marked by a station to be named "Craigellachie."

*

Canada is doing business on a back street. We must put her on a thoroughfare.

*

I have not the least fear of the future. I regard it as certain as sunrise.

*

What this country wants more than anything else is a fool-killer. [1891]

*

Shall we play gosling to the American fox?

*

The greatest men of the past were all Masters of Humbug, and so are the greatest men of today. [1919]

*

Nothing is too small to know, and nothing is too big to attempt. [Said to be his personal maxim]

\*

I don't care why people do things in novels or in real life. Working out motives and lives of thought is about as useful as a signboard on Niagara Falls. Nothing is left to the imagination.

\*

When I think of all I could do, I should like to live for five hundred years.

\*

Tired? Tired? I have only been tired twice in my life.

> Quoted by Walter Vaughan in *Sir William Van Horne* (1926).

Have no means paying wages, pay car can't be sent out, and unless we get immediate relief we must stop. Please inform Premier and Finance Minister. Do not be surprised, or blame me if an immediate and most serious catastrophe happens. [Telegram from Van Horne to Donald Smith, April 15, 1885]

All I can say is that the work has been done well in every way. [Impromptu remark when the "last spike" was driven, Craigellachie, British Columbia, November 7, 1885]

Building that railroad would have made a Canadian out of the German Emperor. [On renouncing his American citizenship, 1880s]

The biggest things are always the easiest to do because there is no competition.

\*

Since we can't export the scenery, we'll import the tourists.

\*

Raise less hell and more wheat! [To a delegation of Manitoba farmers demanding lower freight rates; the remark is also attributed to Mary Lease, the populist leader who ordered it the other way round in the 1880s: "Kansas had better stop raising corn and begin raising hell"]

\*

Family trees are apt to be questionable about the roots.

\*

WISE MEN OF THE EAST, GO WEST BY CPR.

\*

BY THUNDER! (BAY) PASSES THE CPR!

\*

BEATS ALL CREATION, THAT CPR STATION!

\*

"How High We Live," said the Duke to the Prince, "on the Canadian Pacific Railway."

> Slogans devised by Van Horne for the CPR, about 1890. Quoted by Peter C. Newman in *Flame of Power: Intimate Profiles of Canada's Greatest Businessmen* (1959). See also O.D. Skelton.

## Vanier, Georges

I should like to leave a footprint somewhere.

> Quoted by Robert Speaight in *Vanier: Soldier, Diplomat and Governor General: A Biography* (1970).

Canada's vast unoccupied continent to the north constitutes the fiercest challenge and the brightest promise that has ever fallen to one nation's lot in recorded history.

> Quoted by R.A.J. Phillips in *Canada's North* (1967).

Good heavens! I forgot to say something in French.

> Impromptu remark made after the governor general had addressed the Montreal Men's Press Club in the mid-1960s and was taking his seat. See also Jacques Chevrier.

## Vanier, Jean

This is our problem. How are we to break down the barriers of security that we have built around us and open ourselves up to compassion, to tenderness?

> "A World in Violence: Eruption to Hope?" February 11, 1971. *The Empire Club of Canada: Addresses 1970-71* (1971).

We are all sick, all lonely, all in need of love.

> Son of the late governor general, Georges Vanier, and the founder of L'Arche, a home for retarded children in France, quoted in *Time*, June 18, 1973.

## Van Paassen, Pierre

See Paassen, Pierre van.

**Van Stolk, Mary**   See Stolk, Mary Van.

**Van Vogt, A.E.**
As a child I lived in the prairie province of Saskatchewan, and it was there that I ran into the very curious assumption that the world around me was full of common people. This was never said in so many words. It was just understood that greatness or extra value as a human being existed only among the dead, or else it was an attribute of someone far away, whom one never met. I grew up feeling the full weight of my insignificance, and slowly, slowly began to build up my ego. Receiving no help from the environment, I withdrew from it into a world of imagination which was particularly illuminated by fiction stories which I read in the British *Chum* magazine. . . .

> The science-fiction writer was born in Manitoba in 1912 and raised in Saskatchewan. In 1939, he married Edna May Hull, daughter of a Canadian publisher and a writer in her own right, and "early in 1952 achieved the greatest prize of the twentieth century: American citizenship." "Alfred Elton Van Vogt," *Twentieth Century Authors: First Supplement* (1955), edited by Stanley J. Kunitz.

**Varley, F.H.**
The further north you travel in Canada the greater is the quality of nobility you see in the peoples' faces.

\*

When you paint a person well you are not yourself. You empty yourself of all preconceived ideas about the subject. As you look at the sitter you see the truth emerging in the face. All people are beautiful in one way or another.

\*

Trouble is good for mankind. When you are in trouble you get an understanding of life and you find the answers to many questions.

\*

I worship God on my toes. [To Chester Massey, father of Vincent; shortly before his death in 1926, the patriarch asked Varley to join him on his knees in prayer]

> Quoted by McKenzie Porter in *Maclean's Magazine*, November 7, 1959.

**Vaudreuil-Cavagnal, Marquis de**
Quebec is impregnable.

> Vain boast of Pierre de Rigaud, Marquis de Vaudreuil-Cavagnal, the last governor of New France, in 1759, quoted by Christopher Hibbert in *Wolfe at Quebec* (1959).

My firmness is generally applauded. It has penetrated every heart; and each man says aloud: "Canada, our native land, shall bury us under its ruins before we surrender to the English!" This is decidedly my own determination, and I shall hold to it inviolably.

> Letter to the minister of Marines and Colonies in Paris, May 28, 1759, quoted by Francis Parkman in *Montcalm and Wolfe* (1884). Christopher Hibbert in *Wolfe at Quebec* (1959) gives a variant translation: "My enthusiasm is generally applauded. It has penetrated every heart; all men say aloud: 'We shall die in the ruins of Canada, our native land, before we surrender to the English.' "

Everything proves that the grand design of the English has failed.

\*

I have no more anxiety about Quebec. M. Wolfe, I can assure you, will make no progress. Luckily for him, his prudence saved him from the consequences of his mad enterprise, and he contented himself with losing about five hundred of his best soldiers. Deserters say that he will try us again in a few days. That is what we want; he'll find somebody to talk to.

> Letter to François-Charles de Bourlamaque, September 1, 1759, quoted by Francis Parkman in *Montcalm and Wolfe* (1884).

Those English have not got wings—I'll see about it tomorrow.

> Attributed to the governor of New France, dismissing Montcalm's recommendation that a battalion be stationed at Anse au Foulon, September 12, 1759, hours before Wolfe's troops scaled the cliff and took Quebec.

C.P. Stacey, in "The Anse au Foulon, 1759: Montcalm and Vaudreuil," *Canadian Historical Review*, March, 1959, has traced *"nous verrons cela demain"* back to the diary of Father Jean-Félix Récher, published in 1903. About the alleged disagreement, Stacey concludes: "There is, however, little reason to believe that it took place, and considerable evidence to suggest that it did not." See also Louis-Antoine de Bourgainville and Marquis de Montcalm.

## Vaughan, Colin
The suburbs want mobility and the city wants stability.

Editorial, *The Toronto Star*, March 2, 1973.

## Verchères, Madeleine de
Let us fight to the death. We are fighting for our country and our religion. Remember that our father has taught you that gentlemen are born to shed their blood for the service of God and the King.

Fourteen-year-old Madeleine de Verchères rallied the spirits of her two younger brothers and three others when their seigniory on the St. Lawrence River was attacked by Indians on October 22, 1692. Quoted by Francis Parkman in *Count Frontenac and New France Under Louis XIV* (1877).

"O mother of Christ have pity," shrieked the woman in despair,
"This is no time for praying," cried the young Madeleine Verchères,
"Aux armes! aux armes! les Iroquois! quick to your arms and guns,
Fight for your God and country and the lives of the innocent ones."

One of twenty stanzas of "Madeleine Verchères" by William Henry Drummond, *Complete Poems* (1926).

## Verigin, John J.
On the basis of our principles and religious convictions in the faith of Jesus Christ, we consider ourselves to be citizens of the whole universe; Christ is the King of all Kings, therefore we are his citizens. We categorically proclaim that we cannot be automatically citizens of this or any other country.

Protest to Prime Minister Mackenzie King, *The Vancouver Sun*, January 30, 1947. John J. Verigin, grandson of Peter Petrovich Verigin, settled in Canada in 1928. As honorary chairman of the Union of Spiritual Communities of Christ, he was the third Doukhobor leader. Quoted by George Woodcock and Ivan Avakumovic in *The Doukhobors* (1968).

## Verigin, Michael
Michael the Archangel.

During the 1930s the third cousin of Peter Verigin in the female line, a Saskatchewan farmer named Michael Orekoff, assumed the name of Verigin and appointed himself the Doukhobor leader and prophet. Often called "Michael the Archangel," he was rejected by the majority of Doukhobors.

## Verigin, Peter
"You'll be glad to be in a country," said Mr. Moffat, "where there is religious and individual freedom."
"I haven't looked around yet," answered Verigin, through his interpreter, "so I cannot tell whether this is a free country or not."

The first Doukhobor leader of the Sons of Freedom sect, Peter Verigin, or "Peter the Lordly," conversing with the acting commissioner of the police on his arrival at Winnipeg. *The Manitoba Free Press*, December 23, 1902. Quoted by George Woodcock and Ivan Avakumovic in *The Doukhobors* (1968).

## Verigin, Peter Petrovich
Yes, we will take everything of value that Canada has to offer, but we will not give up our Doukhobor souls. [To reporters on his arrival in New York, September 16, 1927]

*

Sons of Freedom cannot be the slaves of corruption. [Characteristic remark]

*

I am Christiakov, I shall divide lies from truth, and light from darkness.

Peter Petrovich Verigin was the second leader of the Doukhobors and the son of Peter Verigin. *Christiakov* is Russian for "the Purger," so he became known as "Peter the Purger." Quoted by George Woodcock and Ivan Avakumovic in *The Doukhobors* (1968).

### Verne, Jules

"But what interest can the [Hudson's Bay] Company have in making a fort on the shore of the Arctic Ocean?"

"A great interest, madame," replied the Captain; "I may say a very great interest, indeed."

*The Fur Country* (1870), translated by Henry Frith, concerns an expedition to establish a most northerly post. At least two of Verne's short stories are set in the Arctic wastes, and "the Canadian" figures in *Twenty Thousand Leagues Under the Sea* (1870).

The French, it is true, were unable to maintain this magnificent American colony; but the population, the great majority of it, did not become less French, but bound itself to ancient Gaul by those ties of blood, that racial identity, those natural instincts that international politics never managed to break.

In reality, the "few acres of ice," as they are so disdainfully dismissed, form a kingdom the surface of which is equal to that of Europe.

Jules Verne's *Famille-sans-nom* has never appeared in English, but a Quebec reprint in 1970 found a wide readership. The novel is a dramatization of the 1837 rebellion in Upper Canada and presents the Anglo-Saxons as the villains. It was published in Paris in the 1890s in a series "*Les Voyages extra-ordinaires.*"

### Vézina, Georges

When the Canadiens get a goalkeeper as good as I am to take my place, then I'll leave you.

The decision of Georges Vézina, one of hockey's greatest goalkeepers, then suffering from tuberculosis and playing against doctors' orders. He finished the 1926 season but died shortly after. The Vézina Memorial Trophy is awarded annually to the NHL goalie with the fewest goals scored against him.

### "The Chicoutimi Cucumber."

Sobriquet of the goalkeeper, derived from his home town and his legendary coolness under pressure. Quoted by Andy O'Brien in *The Jacques Plante Story* (1972).

### Vickers, Jon

Canada is a great school—I should know, all my training was in Canada—but it is in danger of remaining a school.

The opera singer was quoted in *The Globe and Mail*, February 2, 1968.

### Victoria, Queen

That is the place.

Attributed to Queen Victoria when she selected Ottawa from among five contending cities to be the permanent capital of the Province of Canada in 1857. The deciding factor, it is said, was her admiration of a watercolour depicting an Ottawa hill, executed by Lady Julia, the wife of an earlier lieutenant-governor, Sir Francis Bond Head.

"I am commanded by the Queen to inform you that, in the judgment of Her Majesty, the City of *Ottawa* combines greater advantages than any other place in *Canada* for the permanent Seat of the future Government of the Province, and is selected by Her Majesty accordingly."

Letter to Governor General Sir Edmund Walker Head from Henry Labouchère, Downing Street, London, December 31, 1857. Tabled March 16, 1858, in *Journals of the Legislative Assembly of the Province of Canada* (1858).

. . . We, therefore, by and with the advice of Our Privy Council, have thought fit to issue this Our Royal Proclamation, and we do ordain, declare and command that, on and after the first day of July, 1867, the Provinces of Canada, Nova Scotia and New Brunswick, shall form and be One Dominion, under the name of Canada. . . . Given at Our Court at *Windsor Castle*, this twenty-second day of May, in the year of our Lord one thousand and eight hundred and sixty-seven, in the thirtieth year of Our Reign. *God save the Queen.*

> "A Proclamation . . . by the Queen," *Journals of the House of Commons of the Dominion of Canada . . . being the 1st Session of the 1st Parliament of the Dominion of Canada* (1868).

Her Majesty hopes that this new colony on the Pacific may be but one step in the career of steady progress by which Her Majesty's dominions in North America may ultimately be peopled, in an unbroken chain from the Atlantic to the Pacific, by a loyal and industrious population of subjects of the British Crown.

> Address to the British House of Commons in 1871. It was quoted by Alexander Morris in "The Hudson's Bay and Pacific Territories" (1858), *Nova Britannia; or Our New Canadian Dominion Foreshadowed* (1884). See also Alexander Morris.

### Viger, Denis-Benjamin
This tree—the maple—which grows in our valleys . . . at first young and beaten by the storm, pines away, painfully feeding itself from the earth, but it soon springs up, tall and strong, and faces the tempest and triumphs over the wind which cannot shake it any more. The maple is the king of our forest; it is the symbol of the Canadian people.

> Quoted by Amédée Robitaille in "La Société Saint-Jean-Baptiste," in H.-J.-J.-B. Chouinard, *Fête nationale des canadiens-français célébrée à Québec, 1881-84* (1890).

### Vigneault, Gilles
Mon pays ce n'est pas un pays c'est l'hiver
Mon jardin ce n'est pas un jardin c'est la plaine
Mon chemin ce n'est pas un chemin c'est la neige
Mon pays ce n'est pas un pays c'est l'hiver

\*

My country is not a country it's the winter
My garden is not a garden it's the plain
My road is not a road it's the snow
My country is not a country it's the winter

> Refrain from "Mon Pays," *Avec les vieux mots* (1965), with English translation.

My passport is bilingual, though my heart is not.

> Quoted in *Time*, January 24, 1972.

It's not a nationality song. I'm so afraid what men can do with nationality. It's not a flag or an anthem. It's a song seeking identification and finding none. It's a cold song.

> The well-known *chansonnier* discussing his composition "Mon Pays," quoted by Blaik Kirby in *The Globe and Mail*, February 7, 1973.

### Viirlaid, Arved
Man's spirit will grow in victory as well as in defeat, even in humiliation, as long as he defends noble ideals.

> *Year of Storms* (1949).

### Villeneuve, Arthur
If you really want to know what my paintings are about, you have to go inside them, get lost in them.

\*

Our eyes are too wide open for them to be closed.

> Quebec primitive painter quoted by Don Bell in *Weekend Magazine*, April 8, 1972.

### Vining, Charles
Depletion of our forests is even more serious, for we are consuming them at a prodigious rate. A single Sunday issue of *The New York Times*, for example, means some 225 acres of our forest. The tabloid *New York News*, with its huge circulation, is using sixty square miles a year. The Canadian mills, during the last five years of selling newsprint at a loss, have consumed at least four thousand square miles of forest, equivalent to a strip twelve miles wide, stretching from Montreal to Toronto.

> Vining was president of the Newsprint Association of Canada. "The Newsprint

Industry," February 8, 1937, *Addresses Delivered before the Canadian Club of Toronto: Season of 1936-37* (1937).

**Virgin Mary, the Blessed**
See Lucia dos Santos.

**Vizinczey, Stephen**
If our dreams aren't to be fulfilled they should at least be splendid.

\*

We have less control over others and more power over ourselves than we like to think.

\*

All men are powerless against chance, but the defeated know the secret. They live for the present—the future has already betrayed them. They are the children of reality.

\*

There is a new loneliness in the modern world—the *solitude of speed*. We pass by each other on the throughways of our new freedoms.

\*

I wish I could print a leaflet and distribute a few million copies around the suburbs and the slums. The text would be one sentence:

> *The Fontainebleau Manifesto*
> WE NEED A ROYAL REVOLUTION,
> SO THAT ALL MEN MAY LIVE LIKE KINGS.

*The Rules of Chaos* (1969), by the Budapest-born Canadian author. See also George Feyer.

**Vlastos, Gregory**
Human life is human relatedness. No one lives alone. Robinson Crusoe is a feat of literary imagination.

"The Ethical Foundations," *Towards the Christian Revolution* (1936), edited by R.B.Y. Scott and Gregory Vlastos.

**Volkoff, Boris**
A nation's character and soul is typified by its dances.

Favourite adage of "the father of Canadian ballet" in his obituary notice, *The Globe and Mail*, March 12, 1974.

**Voltaire**
We have lost in one day . . . fifteen hundred leagues of ground. These fifteen hundred leagues being frozen deserts, are perhaps not really a loss. Canada has cost much and has brought in very little.

*Précis de Louis XV* (1768), quoted by George F.G. Stanley in *New France: The Last Phase: 1744-1760* (1968).

What a big fuss over a little thing. It's like the war with the English, which started over a few acres of snow.

Undated letter to Charles-Augustin Feriol, Comte d'Argental, quoted by Theodore Besterman in *Voltaire's Correspondence* (1960). The original French: "*Voilà une grande tracasserie pour un mince sujet. Cela ressemble à la guerre des Anglais qui commença pour quatre arpents de neige.*"

You know that these two nations have been at war over a few acres of snow near Canada, and that they are spending on this fine struggle more than Canada itself is worth.

The French cynic made this celebrated observation in Chapter 23 of *Candide, ou L'Optimisme* (1759), which was published the year Quebec fell to the British. The original French runs: "*Vous savez que ces deux nations sont en guerre pour quelques arpents de neige vers le Canada, et qu'elles depensent pour cette belle guerre beaucoup plus que tout le Canada ne vaut.*" (An *arpent* is approximately one and a half acres.) Here is the famous passage in its context, from *Candide, or Optimism* (1966), translated by Robert A. Adams.

"You have been in England; are people as crazy there as in France?"

"It's a different sort of crazy," said Martin. "You know that these two nations have been at war over a few acres of snow near Canada, and that they are spending on this fine struggle more than Canada itself is worth. As for telling you if there are more people in one country or the other who need a strait jacket, that is a judgment too fine for my understanding; I know only that the people we are going to visit are eaten up with melancholy."

If I only dared, I would implore you on

my knees to rid France for ever from the administration of Canada. By losing Canada, you lose nothing; if you want her restored to you, you restore a perpetual source of war and humiliation—no more.

> Letter to Etienne-François, Duc de Choiseul, October 3, 1760. Quoted by Raymond Douville and Jacques Casanova in *Daily Life in Early Canada* (1968), translated by Carola Congreve.

I much prefer peace to Canada; and I believe that France can do very well without Quebec.

> Letter to Etienne-François, Duc de Choiseul, September 6, 1762. The original is in the Public Archives of Canada, Ottawa, and is reproduced in *A Pageant of Canada: The European Contribution to the Iconography of Canadian History* (1967), prepared by Roy Strong. The last part is sometimes translated: "France can be happy without Quebec."

Canada is a few acres of snow and not worth a soldier's bones.

*

It is a sinkhole for money and a sponge for the blood of France.

*

Well, we are well rid of fifteen thousand acres of snow and ice.

> These remarks are popularly attributed to the French cynic and may or may not have historical bases.

**Von Pitts, F.**
What would happen if a teacher tried to teach his pupils that L stands for Love, and would make them write "Love thy neighbour as thyself"? It would probably cause an uproar about bringing religion into schools. So we teach them to love General Motors because it's good for the country.

> Observation made by the director of the Saskatchewan Farm Union, September, 1960.

**Von Schoultz, Nils**
How easily we embarked on this counterfeit cause.

> The Polish-American freedom-fighter was hanged on December 8, 1838, after occupying Windmill Point, near Prescott. Quoted by K.F. Scott in *Prescott's Famous Battle of the Windmill, November 13-18, 1838* (1967).

**Voznesensky, Andrei**
And the City Hall—that skyscraper in Toronto. Its two vertical planes float like two folds of a shell placed at a distance —and it seems that the air between them will hum at any moment.

> *Soviet Union Today*, October, 1971.

Canada is horizontal. Only a comparatively narrow strip above the American border is populated. Like a layer of cream on a jug of milk. Or as in the landscapes of Rerich—a strip of earth and an expanse of sky. The sky is ever-sensed above Canada, untamed nature to the pole—green sky of summer and white of winter.

> "North Country Passing," *Maclean's Magazine*, December, 1971.

# W

## Waddington, Miriam
Poetry is always drawing up new blueprints for reality. It joins two poles: dream and reality.

> Quoted by Merle Shain in *Chatelaine*, October, 1972.

The artist's function in our noisy computerized world is to keep on affirming the existence of stillness and of the kind of reality which can never be reduced to mere fact. Maybe that's love.

> Leading poet quoted in *The Toronto Star*, January 2, 1973.

## Wade, Mason
French and English will never be wholly one in Canada, but they can come to understand one another, and thus avert the recurrence of the crises here chronicled. The problem of Canadian union is merely a special case of the great world problem of our time, for mankind must learn to be equal without being identical, if it is to survive.

> *The French-Canadian Outlook: A Brief Account of the Unknown North Americans* (1946).

Today everything is changing, and there is general agreement that it should change. It seems clear that while French Canada is becoming more North American, it is doing so on its own terms, and that Quebec will remain French and Catholic and devoted to its traditions, in the future as in the past.

> *The French Canadians: 1760-1967* (1968).

## Wales, Prince of
See: Edward Augustus, Edward VII, Edward VIII.

## Walker, Alan
The first duty of a magazine is to be read.

> *The Toronto Telegram*, May 10, 1969.

Meredydd Zzzyhaff.

Walker, a magazine editor, convinced Bell Telephone that this was his real name and thereby managed to secure the last listing in the 1961 Metropolitan Toronto Telephone Directory.

## Walker, Annie Louisa
See Annie Louisa Walker Coghill.

## Walker, Thomas
Behold the Pope of Canada and the English Sot.

> "When the Quebec Act was passed in Montreal, a statue of King George the Third was covered with a papal mitre, the face painted black, a string of potatoes thrown around the neck and, in the outstretched hands, was placed the inscription: *'Voilà le pape du Canada et le sot Anglais.'*" W.A.D. Styles in *Unusual Facts of Canadian History* (1947). The statue in Place d'Armes was defaced on May 1, 1775, supposedly by Thomas Walker, a pro-American merchant.

## Walking Buffalo
The outdoors of the Great Spirit's making has been like a Bible to me—not one written by human hands but by the Great Spirit. Too bad the white man doesn't know more about it. He's a smart fellow in some ways, this white man, but he can't boss or bully Nature. He took the country that did not belong to him and pushed the Indians into some small corners. He killed off the buffalo and then turned to other game animals and forests and grass and soil with the idea of selling them for money. Now he's digging into the heart of the earth to find something else he can sell for cash. And he thinks he can teach the Indians how to live. He's a smart fellow but he should not lose his sanity about money and he should not allow himself to become a stranger in Nature's community. The Indian can still teach him a few things about living. But the white man will not listen.

Walking Buffalo or Tatanga Mani—also known as George McLean—was a Stoney chief who died in 1967. Quoted by J.W. Grant MacEwan in *Portraits from the Plains* (1971).

## Wallace, George
There hasn't been any voluntary integration in Alabama as there hasn't been any voluntary integration of Indians in Canada. There is some hypocrisy among the press here. Before you criticize us you should clean up your own backyard. If you've got any moral crusade to run, you can run it in your own country.

> The governor of Alabama was in Toronto to address a convention of the Lions' International. Quoted by Robert Fulford in *Maclean's Magazine*, August 8, 1964.

## Wallace, Joe
The American way of life:
You can get away with murder
If you use a golden knife.   ["Verse"]
> \*

Ours is a sovereign nation
Bows to no foreign will
But whenever they cough in Washington
They spit on Parliament Hill.
                    ["A Sovereign Nation"]
> \*

He must be a politician's brother:
He talks one way
And he walks another.   ["Verse"]
> \*

There's panic in the papers
Stocks and bonds are cutting capers
Rich men jumping from skyscrapers.

What's the rumpus all about?
Peace broke out.   ["Panic"]

> *A Radiant Sphere* (1964), by the Communist versifier living in Vancouver.

## Wallace, W. Stewart
In the beginning was geography.

> "The Growth of National Feeling," *Canadian Historical Review*, June, 1920.

If students of Canadian history can retain, or recover, the Parkman tradition, they need have no fear for the future.

> "Some Vices of Clio," *Canadian Historical Review*, September, 1926. In prais-

ing Parkman, Wallace continued, "With his scholarship, he preserved also the immemorial art of telling a story. With science he combined imagination."

## Walpole, Horace
You may now give yourself what airs you please. An ambassador is the only man in the world whom bullying becomes. All precedents are on your side: Persians, Greeks, Romans, always insulted their neighbours when they took Quebec. Think how pert the French would have been on such an occasion! What a scene! An army in the night dragging itself up a precipice by stumps of trees to assault a town and attack an enemy strongly entrenched and double in numbers! The King is overwhelmed with addresses on our victories; he will have enough to paper his palace.

> Letter to Sir Horace Mann, ambassador to Florence, quoted by Francis Parkman in *Montcalm and Wolfe* (1884). Horace Walpole, who built Strawberry Hill and wrote *Castle of Otranto* (1764), was a member of the British Parliament.

The incidents of dramatic fiction could not be conducted with more address to lead an audience from despondency to sudden exaltation than accident prepared to excite the passions of a whole people. They despaired, they triumphed, and they wept; for Wolfe had fallen in the hour of victory. Joy, curiosity, astonishment, was painted on every countenance. The more they inquired, the more their admiration rose. Not an incident but was heroic and affecting.

> Quoted by Francis Parkman in *Montcalm and Wolfe* (1884).

Who the deuce was thinking of Quebec? America was like a book one has read and done with. But here we are on a sudden, reading our book backwards.

> The defeat of General James Murray at St. Foy in the spring of 1760 surprised Walpole who thought the conquest of British North America settled with the taking of Quebec in 1759. Quoted by Christopher Hibbert in *Wolfe at Quebec* (1959).

## Walsh, James

I think a commission should have been sent out long ago, but that it has been neglected so long is one reason why it should not be sent at once. What great credit would it be to Canada to kill a few poor Half-breeds who feel they have been neglected? Don't forget that these people have the hearty sympathy of all the white settlers in their district. Do you suppose if the white settlers had the grievances the Half-breeds have, that they would not have made a disturbance? and in case they did, who is the man in Canada who would cry out against sending a commission to treat with them? These people are not rebels, they are but demanding justice.

> Inspector Walsh, who resigned from the North-West Mounted Police in 1883, spoke openly on the Métis. He rejoined in 1897 and became commissioner of the Yukon. Quoted by Charles Pelham Mulvaney in *The History of the North-West Rebellion of 1885* (1885).

## Walsh, W.E.

When an American dies he goes to Paris, but when the fell hand of the iniquitous income-tax strikes down an Englishman in his prime he passes to his reward in V.I. [Vancouver Island] and lives happy ever after, sharing with the simple-hearted Siwash the innocent pleasures of the chase.

> "The Importance of Being English" (1923), *Our Sense of Identity* (1954), edited by Malcolm Ross.

## Walters, Angus J.

The wood of the vessel that will beat the *Bluenose* is still growing!

> The most famous sailing ship of the century was the *Bluenose*, launched at Lunenburg in 1921, the last of the great Nova Scotian clippers. "They didn't beat the *Bluenose*," Captain Walters explained after the ship lost its one and only race. "They beat *me*." It sank off Haiti in 1946. Oland's Brewery built a replica, *Bluenose II*, in 1963, but Captain Walters said, "There'll never be another like her." Quoted by Brian and Phil Backman in *Bluenose* (1965).

## Walz, Jay

The early failure to conquer Canada is not stressed much in American textbooks, perhaps because the story has so many elements that could confuse budding patriots. There was George Washington himself planning a major campaign that did not succeed; Benjamin Franklin failing on a diplomatic mission; and Benedict Arnold, of all people, being the only man to emerge from Canada with his reputation enhanced.

> *

She is not without honour in Canada. Across the country there are Laura Secord candy stores. At one time the face on the candy boxes was Laura's own determined middle-aged visage framed by a stiff bonnet, but American influence has subversively transformed Canada's heroine. Currently a misty-eyed maiden, a gentle immigrant from the Old South, purports to be Laura on the candy boxes.

> *Portrait of Canada* (1970), by Jay and Audrey Walz. Jay Walz was *The New York Times*'s man in Ottawa.

**Wampohama**   See Mother Damnable.

## Ward, Artemus

Gentlemen, I give you *Upper Canada*; because I don't want it myself.

> American humourist's toast, quoted by Stephen Leacock in "Mark Twain in Canada," *Queen's Quarterly*, Spring, 1935.

## Ward, Barbara

It is a truism that one person who wants something is a hundred times stronger than a hundred who want to be left alone. A Canada prepared to pioneer with lucidity and daring the role of the first "international nation" in history would not only have an immense impact on its fellow states. It might also transform its own political life. It could, conceivably, turn the present rather bored citizen acquiescence in modern politics into something more exciting and active, into participation, into enjoyment, into purpose, even into fun.

> "The First International Nation" (1968),

*Canada: A Guide to the Peaceable Kingdom* (1970), edited by William Kilbourn.

## Ward, Mrs. Humphry
"See Canada! What is there to see?"

*Canadian Born* (1908), a novel for young readers.

So, in a swallow's flight from sea to sea, I saw the marvellous land wherein, perhaps, in a far, hidden future, lies the destiny of our race.

Journal of the popular British novelist's trip across Canada in 1908. Quoted by Stanley Baldwin, "To a Canadian Audience," *This Torch of Freedom: Speeches and Addresses* (1935).

## Ward, Samuel Ringgold
A man entrusted with a plan of importance grows with it. If it be the fruit of his own thoughts and one of his own purposes, he is more of a man for having conceived it. If it must be wrought out with his own unaided hands, it improves him to entertain the intention of doing it. If in the way of his resolution—and, still more, in the way of executing it—there stand many mighty obstacles of which he is well aware, but the existence of which appalls him not, he has in him all the elements of your moral or physical hero, or of both.

Now, the slave, intending, planning, determining to escape, is one of that class.

Ward was a Negro preacher living in Toronto. He worked with the Canadian Anti-Slavery Society and wrote *The Autobiography of a Fugitive Slave* (1855).

## Warman, Cy
Come to me, sweet Marie, sweet Marie,
  come to me;
Not because your face is fair, love, to see,
But your soul, so pure and sweet,
Makes my happiness complete,
Makes me falter at your feet, sweet
  Marie.

Chorus of "Sweet Marie," the only song written by Cy Warman, an American-born resident of London, Ontario, who in 1893 wrote these lyrics for his future

wife. Set to music by Raymon Moore, the song was a Broadway hit in Moore's musical comedy *Africa*. Ed Manning in *The London Free Press*, October 29, 1966, claimed the chocolate bar was named after the song. Ralph L. Woods in *A Second Treasury of the Familiar* (1950).

## Warner, Jack L.
I had created enough stars, if I may use the word "create" modestly, to fill the Hollywood skies.

\*

No, no! Jimmy Stewart for governor—Reagan for his best friend!

\*

Voltaire, Voltaire, all these writers want to be Voltaire.

\*

The day you don't enjoy being roasted—you're cooked.

Jack L. Warner, youngest and best-known of the four Warner brothers, was the only one with a Canadian connection. Born in London, Ontario, in 1892, he founded Warner Brothers Pictures with Harry, Albert, and Samuel. Against Harry's objections ("Who the hell wants to hear actors talk?"), he completed the first "all-talking" picture, *The Jazz Singer* (1927). He personally produced *My Fair Lady* and *Camelot* and published *My First Hundred Years in Hollywood* (1965). "Goddammit," Errol Flynn once said, "I refuse to predecease Jack Warner!" It is his brother Harry whom Norman Zierold in *The Moguls* (1969) credits with the immortal line: "We'll make the pictures; let Western Union deliver the messages."

## Warwick, Jack
The presence of a North in man is even more critical than the presence of men in the North.

*The Long Journey: Literary Themes in French Canada* (1968).

## Washington, Booker T.
For no one set of people on this continent can be down without every section of our people living on this continent, whether in the United States or in Can-

ada, feeling the effect of the life of those people who are down.

> "The Work at Tuskegee," February 5, 1906, *Addresses Delivered before the Canadian Club of Toronto: Session 1905-1906* (1906).

My race remembers with most tender gratitude the generosity and kindness manifested on the part of the people of the Dominion of Canada in the dark days of slavery. I remember as a child hearing my parents and the older slaves speak of Canada with such tenderness and faith for what it would do for our race that I had no definite idea that it had any tangible, visible place. I thought it an invisible ideal.

> Booker T. Washington was principal of Tuskegee Normal and Industrial Institute in Alabama and a leading spokesman for the blacks. "The Negro in the Southern States," February 6, 1906, *Addresses Delivered before the Canadian Club of Ottawa: 1903-1909* (1910).

## Washington, George

I charge you, therefore, and the officers and soldiers under your command, as you value your own safety and honour, and the favour and esteem of your country, that you consider yourself as marching not through the country of an enemy, but of our friends and brethren, for such the inhabitants of Canada, and the Indian nations have approved themselves in this unhappy contest between Great Britain and America, and that you check, by every motive of duty and fear of punishment, every attempt to plunder or insult the inhabitants of Canada. Should any American soldier be so base and infamous as to injure any Canadian or Indian in his person or property, I do most earnestly enjoin you to bring him to such severe and exemplary punishment, as the enormity of the crime may require. Should it extend to death itself, it shall not be disproportioned to its guilt, at such a time and in such a cause.

> Letter from General Washington at Cambridge, Massachusetts, September 14, 1775, to Colonel Benedict Arnold

who was soon to lead his army against Canada. Quoted by John Codman II in *Arnold's Expedition to Quebec* (1901).

## Wasserman, Jack

Thoughts while recovering from a hangover: It's better to have a few mornings after than never to have a night before.

*

The stuff that dreams are made of usually comes out of the refrigerator around midnight.

> Popular columnist for *The Vancouver Sun*, 1960s.

## Watkins, Melville H.

One can speculate that the abandonment of economic nationalism and the expanding appetites of the provinces might just create that mixture of competition newly faced and energies newly released that could get us out of our historic rut and on to a broader road to growth.

> "Canadian Economic Policy: A Proposal," *The Prospect of Change: Proposals for Canada's Future* (1965), edited by Abraham Rotstein. (Melville H. Watkins would shortly repudiate this continentalist proposition and adopt a more nationalistic position.)

It would be criminal to stand idly by as spectators applauding the decline of the nation-state. But it would be equally derelict to imagine that nationalism can be an adequate answer to our present discontents. The compelling need for the future is not for national societies in a world community—desirable though such a social system would be today—but rather for a world society fit for a global village.

> "Technology and Nationalism," in *Nationalism in Canada* (1966), edited by Peter Russell.

The extent of foreign control of Canadian industry is unique among the industrialized nations of the world.

> Opening sentence of *Foreign Ownership and the Structure of Canadian Industry: Report of the Task Force on the Structure of Canadian Industry* (1968), commonly called "The Watkins Report."

Economic independence without socialism is a sham.

&ast;

Our aim as democratic socialists is to
build an independent socialist Canada.
Our aim as supporters of the New
Democratic Party is to make it truly a
socialist party. [*The Waffle Manifesto*
(1969)]

&ast;

Continentalism and capitalism have
gone together in the past; independence and socialism must go together in
the future. [Address, Winnipeg Convention of the NDP, 1969]

&ast;

The multinational corporation is like
the man who came to dinner. You welcome him as a guest and then find that
he's making the rules and giving the
orders for the household. [*The Toronto
Star*, January 16, 1970]

> Gordon to Watkins to You—Documen-
> tary: The Battle for Control of Our
> Economy (1970), edited by Dave God-
> frey and Mel Watkins.

It is the commonplace condition of
Canadians that we live in a branch
plant economy and ultimately a branch
plant society. The burden of my argument is that we must take the risk of
struggling to build an independent
socialist Canada.

> "The Multi-National Corporation and
> Canada," *The Star-Spangled Beaver*
> (1971), edited by John H. Redekop.

It was an educational experience, for a
potential nationalist, to get involved at
the top level of government and come
to realize that you weren't going to be
allowed to be a nationalist. In Ottawa,
no less!

> Describing the reception of the Watkins
> Report, "Learning to Move Left," *This
> Magazine Is About Schools*, Spring, 1972.

**Watmough, David**
I'm used to listening to the spoken
word. It's a very Celtic thing, making
songs out of words. And if I ever saw
an accident with one car in it, I'd tell
you it was five cars. Celts aren't very
good at mathematics.

The performer-writer interviewed by
Paul Grescoe in *The Canadian Magazine*, November 18, 1972.

**Watson, Homer**
There is at the bottom of each artistic
conscience a love for the land of their
birth. It is said art knows no country
but belongs to the world. This may be
true of pictures, but great artists are no
more cosmopolitan than great writers,
and no immortal work has been done
which has not as one of its promptings
for its creation a feeling its creator had
of having roots in his native land and
being a product of its soil.

> Quoted by J. Russell Harper in *Paint-
> ing in Canada: A History* (1966). "This
> is my find in America. Mr. Watson is
> the Canadian Constable and Barbizon
> without ever having seen Barbizon."—
> Oscar Wilde introducing Homer Watson
> to James McNeill Whistler at the Chel-
> sea Club in London, England.

**Watson, John**
A university has as its main aim to supplement the weakness of the individual
by the strength of the race.

> Watson was an influential Kant scholar
> and professor of philosophy at Queen's
> University from 1872 to 1924. Quoted
> by John A. Irving in "The Development
> of Philosophy in Central Canada from
> 1850 to 1900," *Canadian Historical Re-
> view*, September, 1950.

**Watson, Patrick**
Alexander wept; there were no more
worlds to conquer. What would make a
Canadian Prime Minister weep?

> *Conspirators in Silence* (1969).

**Watson, Sheila**
. . . when you fish for the glory you catch
the darkness too.

> *The Double Hook* (1959).

**Watson, Wilfred**
See Marshall McLuhan.

**Watson-Watt, Sir Robert**
There must somewhere have been an

ancient Chinese philosopher who said, "The summit of human wisdom is to know the exact shade of grey to wear on any particular occasion."

＊

About three o'clock on an afternoon in October 1954, my wife and I were proceeding from Toronto to Kingston, Ontario, in a Buick *Century* car. I was driving. As we descended the hill leading into Port Hope we heard a police bell and drew into the side of the road. An officer of the Ontario Provincial Police approached and said, "You are charged with driving at an excessive speed in a controlled area." I said, "How did you do it; was it by radar?" He replied with notable stolidarity. "It was not by radar; it was by an electronic speed-meter," to which subtle differentiation my wife answered, "You may be interested to know that King George VI knighted my husband for inventing radar." This exchange of courtesies continued. "I don't know who invented anything, I know you were driving at an excessive speed."

> *Three Steps to Victory: A Personal Account by Radar's Greatest Pioneer* (1957). This event made headlines around the world. Sir Robert lived in Thornhill, Ontario, during the 1950s.

## Watts-Dunton, Theodore

What Wordsworth tried all his life to do, the poets of Canada, of the Australias, of the Cape, have the opportunity of doing.

> Introduction by the British man of letters to *Flint and Feather: The Complete Poems of E. Pauline Johnson* (1912).

## Wayne, Johnny

Support your fellow Canadians. We should buy lousy Canadian novels instead of importing lousy American novels.

> Quoted by H.R.W. Morrison in *Star Week*, April 20, 1968. See also Frank Shuster.

Happiness isn't everything.

> Tongue-in-cheek reply to the question:

"Why do you remain in Canada rather than go to the States?"

Frank Shuster: "Our business is comedy and if you're crazy it's a help." [Interview, 1968]

Johnny Wayne: "What do you say when people congratulate you for staying in your own country? Sometimes I'm tempted to shake my head like a hero and say, 'Lady, it's been hard.' But I can't. It's been great." [Interview, 1967]

Frank Shuster: "It takes two. One to do the work and the other to push him. Some days you don't have it in you but the other guy has. That's the way we work." [Interview, 1958]

See also Frank Shuster.

## Weadick, Guy

Their requests were simple and clear, namely, "make it the greatest thing of its kind in the world; we don't want to lose money, but we would rather lose and have it right, than make money and fail in our objectives." Those were the only orders I ever received from this group of public-spirited old-timers.

> In March, Weadick raised $100,000 for the first Calgary Stampede which opened September 2, 1912. "Origin of the Calgary Stampede," *Alberta Historical Review*, Autumn, 1966.

## Weaver, Robert

Morley Callaghan is not only the first and most important of the modern short-story writers in Canada; he was also for many years almost the only writer of fiction in this country who gave continuing evidence that the spirit of contemporary literature could exist here.

> Introduction, *Canadian Short Stories: Second Series* (1968), edited by Robert Weaver.

## Webb, Beatrice and Sidney

Thus, what is in progress in Canada during the opening years of the twentieth century is not the normal growth of a settled community, but the rapid—almost the sudden—economic appropriation of a new land. To the economist, the discovery of Canada will date, not from Jacques Cartier, or its acquisition from Wolfe, but from the opening of the "C.P.R." (Canadian Pacific Railway) in 1886. The present inhabitants of Canada are a race of conquerors.

> Quoted by Helen MacMurchy in *Third Report on Infant Mortality* (1912). The British socialists visited Canada for the Poor-Law Commission in the summer of 1911 and set forth their findings in their celebrated "Minority Report."

### Webb, Captain Matthew
There is no place in the world like it, and I am trusting to fortune.

> Captain Webb was the first person to swim the English Channel. On July 24, 1883, at the age of thirty-five, he decided to brave the Whirlpool Rapids in the Niagara River below the falls. Before being swept to his death, he was interviewed by *The Globe*. The reporter asked him, "When do you think your difficulties will commence?" He replied: "I don't know; you know just as much about it as I do. There is no place in the world like it, and I am trusting to fortune." His courage was extolled and his death was mourned around the world. Quoted by Edgar Andrew Collard in *Canadian Yesterdays* (1955).

### Webb, Phyllis
My poetry is my only access to truth, the only real thing I have.

*

To contemplate suicide is surely the best exercise of the imagination.

> Quoted by Merle Shain in *Chatelaine*, October, 1972.

### Webster, Daniel
Public opinion, strong or united, is not with you, in your Canadian project. Whether it ought to be or ought not to be, the fact that it is not, should, by this time, be evident to all; and it is the business of practical statesmen, to act upon the state of things as it is, and not to be always attempting to prove what it ought to be. The acquisition of that country is not an object generally desired by the people.

> Address made by the American orator during the War of 1812. *Great Speeches of Daniel Webster* (1879), edited by E.P. Whipple.

She has dotted the whole surface of the globe with her possessions and military posts, whose morning drum-beat, following the sun and keeping company with the hours, encircles the earth with one unbroken strain of the martial airs of England. [Speech in the U.S. Senate, March 7, 1850]

### Webster, Jack
I know where a lot of skeletons are buried and people trust me.

> The Vancouver broadcaster explaining what makes him the country's leading hot-liner. Quoted in *Time*, July 17, 1972.

### Weeks, Edward
In the days to come I believe you will produce a native poet who will break away from the past as sharply as Walt Whitman did; a poet who will never be mistaken for anything but a Canadian, and who will find in the challenging space of your prairies and forests his greatest themes.

> "Books and Canada" (1955), *Empire Club of Canada: Addresses 1955-56* (1956). Weeks was editor of *The Atlantic Monthly*.

"The story of a quarrelsome, love-making family in Canada. It smells of the stable."

> Anonymous reader's report on a manuscript submitted for *The Atlantic Monthly's* $10,000 prize. The manuscript was *Jalna* (1927), by Mazo de la Roche. Quoted by Edward Weeks in *My Green Age* (1974), who concluded: "It is indeed the story of a passionate Canadian family, the Whiteoaks, dwelling and feuding in their country place on the shore of Lake Ontario, protective in their loyalty, downright in what they disliked."

### Wees, Frances Shelley
Canada is bounded on the north by gold; on the west by the East; on the

east by history; and on the south by friends.

> This widely quoted aphorism was coined by the detective-story writer who, born in Oregon, has lived in western and eastern Canada for many years. It comes from a prose poem, "Geography Lesson," which has appeared in textbooks since 1937. See also Dorothy Duncan and Richard M. Nixon.

A person who has fought a cobra is not going to fear a mouse.

> *The Country of the Strangers* (1959).

Life is a gentleman, you know. If you expect bludgeons, he will provide bludgeons. If you wear sack-cloth, he will bring ashes rather than criticize your illusion. But if you wear a diaphanous garment he will be careful with his sword.

> *It Began in Eden* (1936).

Gossip began to accumulate like dregs in vinegar, out of nothing.

> *Under the Quiet Water* (1949).

## Weinzweig, John

Question: What was the most difficult thing you had to learn, as a composer?

Answer: To put down the essential notes and no more.

> Composer interviewed by *Musicanada*, March, 1968.

## Weir, E. Austin

The Golden Age of Radio was also the Golden Age of Music.

> *The Struggle for National Broadcasting in Canada* (1965). The so-called golden age is generally dated from 1940, shortly before the commencement of the national news broadcasts, until 1955, shortly after the advent of television and its stellar costs.

## Weir, R. Stanley

O Canada! Our home and native land!
True patriot-love in all thy sons
    command.
With glowing hearts we see thee rise,
The True North, strong and free,

And stand on guard, O Canada,
We stand on guard for thee.

*O Canada, glorious and free!*
*We stand on guard, we stand on guard*
    *for thee.*
*O Canada, we stand on guard for thee!*

O Canada! Where pines and maples
    grow,
Great prairies spread and lordly rivers
    flow,
How dear to us thy broad domain,
From East to Western Sea,
Thou land of hope, for all who toil!
Thou True North, strong and free!

*O Canada, glorious and free!*
*We stand on guard, we stand on guard*
    *for thee.*
*O Canada, we stand on guard for thee!*

O Canada! Beneath thy shining skies
May stalwart sons and gentle maidens
    rise,
To keep thee steadfast through the
    years
From East to Western Sea,
Our own beloved native land!
Our True North, strong and free!

*O Canada, glorious and free!*
*We stand on guard, we stand on guard*
    *for thee.*
*O Canada, we stand on guard for thee!*

> There are two official anthems: "God Save the King" and "O Canada." The former is the royal anthem, the latter the national anthem. Parliament made this distinction in 1967 but it refused to accept the English words of "O Canada," only the melody. In 1972 it considered a revised version of the lyrics (see below).
>
> "O Canada" was commissioned by Theodore Robitaille, lieutenant-governor of Quebec, for a banquet in Quebec City on June 24, 1880, to be attended by the governor general, the Marquis of Lorne, and H.R.H. Princess Louise. The French lyrics were written by Sir Adolphe-Basile Routhier, a prominent Quebec City lawyer and writer, in the form of a poem, which was set to music by Calixa Lavallée, a composer and teacher. The French song was an immediate hit. Routhier published the lyrics

in *Les Echos* (1882) and went on to become chief justice of Quebec. Lavallée fell on hard times and had to move to Boston to support himself as a musician.

Numerous attempts have been made to translate Routhier's lyrics or to write brand-new ones to accompany Lavallée's stirring melody. The generally accepted English version is by R. Stanley Weir. The Montreal lawyer and sometime judge of the Exchequer Court of Canada prepared the English version for Quebec's tercentenary celebration in 1908, and it was sung at the Diamond Jubilee of Confederation in 1927.

The English words are too martial for many ears. In 1972, Parliament made minor revisions in the Weir version: the last two lines of the first verse were emended to read: "From far and wide, O Canada, / God keep our land glorious and free!"

For the original French lyrics, see Sir Adolphe-Basile Routhier. For "The Maple Leaf Forever," see Alexander Muir. For "Canada, Mon Pays, Mes Amours," see Sir George-Etienne Cartier. For "God Save the King," see Anonymous: Songs.

### Weir, Walter

A premier of Manitoba should be able to kick manure off tractor wheels!

> Observation of the premier of Manitoba in 1967.

### Weld, Isaac

I shall speedily take my departure from this Continent, well pleased at having seen as much of it as I have done; but I shall leave it without a sigh, and without the slightest wish to revisit it.

> *Travels through the States of North America, and The Provinces of Upper and Lower Canada, during the Years 1795, 1796, and 1797* (1799).

### Wellington, Duke of

I have already told you and Lord Bathurst that I feel no objection to going to America, though I don't promise to myself much success there. I believe there are troops enough there for the defence of Canada forever, and even for the accomplishment of any reasonable offensive plan that could be formed from the Canadian frontier. I am quite sure that all the American armies of which I have ever read would not beat out of a field of battle the troops that went from Bordeaux last summer, if common precautions and care were taken of them. That which appears to be wanting in America is not a General, or General Officers and troops, but a naval superiority on the Lakes. Till that superiority is acquired, it is impossible, according to my notion, to maintain an army in such a situation as to keep the enemy out of the whole frontier, much less to make any conquest from the enemy, which with those superior means, might, with reasonable hopes of success, be undertaken. I may be wrong in this opinion, but I think the whole history of the war proves its truth.

> Letter of the Duke of Wellington, ambassador to France, to the prime minister of Great Britain, November 9, 1814. Quoted by J. Mackey Hitsman in *The Incredible War of 1812: A Military History* (1965).

If you lose Upper Canada, you will lose all your colonies, and if you lose them you may as well lose London.

> Hyperbole attributed to "the Iron Duke" and a former prime minister of England concerning the Rebellion of 1837.

### Wells, H.G.

Am I to understand that Plutarch also pirated Miss Deeks' manuscript?

> The occasion was the lawsuit of Florence Amelia Deeks against H.G. Wells in 1931. The Toronto spinster maintained that Wells's *The Outline of History* (1920) plagiarized her unpublished manuscript "The Webb" which she had submitted to Macmillan of Canada. Lower courts found substance in her charge, but upper courts in England ended the amazing case of Deeks *vs.* Wells by vindicating Wells—at his own expense, as Miss Deeks was by this time destitute.
>
> "Miss Deeks was present at these

earlier proceedings, and this was the only occasion that she and Wells saw each other. It is said that the celebrated novelist on this occasion made a humorous sally. A question relating to a passage which he admitted he had taken from Plutarch was being pressed by counsel, when Wells ironically said, 'Am I to understand that Plutarch also pirated Miss Deeks' manuscript?' " Quoted by Hector Charlesworth in *I'm Telling You: Being Further Candid Chronicles* (1937).

If Max gets to Heaven he won't last long. He will be chucked out for trying to pull off a merger between Heaven and Hell . . . after having secured a controlling interest in key subsidiary companies in both places, of course.

> The British author is describing his friend Max Aitken, Lord Beaverbrook, as quoted by A.J.P. Taylor in *Beaverbrook* (1972).

## Wells, Kenneth McNeill
I know two things about the horse
And one of them is rather coarse.
["Anon. (20th Cent.)"]

\*

I think that I shall never see
A skunk with equanimity. ["Old Tattered MSS."]

\*

Our dreams are all we own. [Inscribed on the author's mantle]

> *The Owl Pen* (1947).

## West, Benjamin
The event happened in the year 1759, in a region of the world unknown to the Greeks and Romans, and at a period of time when no warrior who wore such a costume existed. The subject I have to represent is a great battle fought and won and the same truth which gives law to the historian should rule the painter.

> When Benjamin West was officially commissioned to paint "The Death of Wolfe" in 1770, he was visited by Sir Joshua Reynolds who objected to West's plan to depict the soldiers in contemporary garb. Quoted by Oliver Warner in *With Wolfe to Quebec: The Path to*

*Glory* (1972). See also Sir Joshua Reynolds.

## West, Bruce
Although no student of the Bible I know has ever been able to find it for me, my late Grandmother Nancy West used to claim that somewhere in the Good Book it was predicted that the world would grow "wiser, but weaker."

> "The Wilderness Breed: An Affectionate Memoir," *Wilderness Canada* (1970), edited by Borden Spears.

## West, Paul
A community of Irish mystics cut adrift on the Atlantic.

> British writer and one-time instructor at Memorial University giving his reaction to Newfoundland, quoted by Richard Gwyn in *Smallwood: The Unlikely Revolutionary* (1968).

Confronted with, involved with Canada, the coy colossus, poets will have to be ambitious and bold.

> "Ethos and Epic," *Canadian Literature*, Spring, 1960.

## Weston, Garfield
You surely don't think I'm in business to make money, do you?

\*

We make more money out of men than we ever make out of things.

\*

Success in anything is ninety percent inspiration and only ten percent brains.

> The last remark is a lofty version of Thomas Alva Edison's celebrated aphorism, "Genius is one percent inspiration and ninety-nine percent perspiration," from Edison's autobiography published in 1932. Garfield Weston was the largest bread manufacturer in the world. Quoted by Matthew Halton in "Big Dough in Bread," *Maclean's Magazine*, August 15, 1948.

## Wetmore, Andrew R.
"Father, what country do we live in?"

"My dear son, you have no country, for Mr. Tilley has sold us all to the

Canadians for eighty cents a head."

> Imaginary dialogue used in an anti-Con-
> federation address in New Brunswick,
> March, 1865. Quoted by Laurier La
> Pierre in *Genesis of a Nation* (1967). The
> "eighty cents" is a reference to the per
> capita grant the province would receive
> upon entering Confederation.

## Whalley, George

Nothing has stopped the migration of
the Canada Geese. I'm hooked anyway;
a country and its people cannot be
judged by the musical quality of their
national anthem. And some day somebody will find a market for muskeg.

> "Horses and Kings" from Andy Wain-
> wright's *Notes for a Native Land: A
> New Encounter with Canada* (1969).

The best way for a university to fulfill
its obligations to society is to insist upon
being itself, by discovering and fulfilling
the kind of life peculiar to its nature.
Like an artist, a university will always
look a little strange in its self-possession.
But no matter how sensitive it may be
to the needs of society, it will by its
nature behave as though it had no concern beyond its own self-enclosing life.

> "Further Proposals," *A Place of Liberty:
> Essays on the Government of Canadian
> Universities* (1964), edited by George
> Whalley.

## Whalley, Peter    See Eric Nicol.

## Whelan, Patrick James

I don't care a damn. I'll either swing or
go to the penitentiary for life. I shot
that fellow like a dog.

> *

Whisky is the devil. If it was not for
whisky I would not have shot McGee. I
was as drunk as the devil when I did it.

> Quoted by Thomas H. Raddall in "The
> Assassination of D'Arcy McGee," *His-
> toric Headlines* (1967), edited by Pierre
> Berton.

All that sentence, my Lord, cannot make
me guilty.

> To the judge who pronounced him
> guilty. Quoted by W. Stewart Wallace

in "The Death of D'Arcy McGee," in
*Murders and Mysteries: A Canadian
Series* (1931).

They Got To Find Mee Guilty Yet.

> Scratched on his tin jail cup by Whelan
> while awaiting execution for the assas-
> sination of Thomas D'Arcy McGee on
> April 7, 1868. Quoted by T.P. Slattery
> in *They Got to Find Mee Guilty Yet*
> (1972).

## Whitbourne, Richard

Those flies seeme to have a greate power
and authority upon all loytering people
that come to the Newfoundland; for
they have the property, that when they
find any such lying lazily, or sleeping in
the Woods, they will presently bee more
nimble to seize on them, than any
Sargeant will bee to arrest a man for
debt; neither will they leave stinging or
sucking out the blood of such sluggards,
untill like a beadle they bring him to
his Master, where hee should labour; in
which time of loytering those flies will
so brand such idle persons in their faces,
that they may be known from others as
the Turks doe their slaves.

> A reference to mosquitos from *A Dis-
> course and Discovery of New-found-land*
> (1620).

## White, John

I notice this year for the first time we
are setting our thermostat at sixty-nine
degrees instead of seventy-two degrees,
and if one of the youngsters is a little
chilly, the youngster goes and gets a
sweater. You know, this was not undertaken deliberately in our family but I
suspect it is the result of reading almost
daily or hearing almost daily that there
is an energy crisis.

> Ontario Treasurer John White at a
> news conference on the proposed energy
> tax, April 12, 1973. The press simplified
> this to "Everyone can wear sweaters."

We have proven ourselves responsive
and flexible so far as the public well-
being and the public wishes are concerned. I think—acknowledging that the
proposal was intolerable for most of our
citizens—it is not a defeat for me. I think

it is a victory for democracy, personally.

> News conference, April 24, 1973, following the withdrawal of a proposed seven per cent on home-heating fuels.

## White, T.H.
This is an animal called the *Beaver*, none more gentle, and his testicles make a capital medicine. For this reason, so Physiologus says, when he notices that he is being pursued by the hunter, he removes his own testicles with a bite, and casts them before the sportsman, and thus escapes by flight. What is more, if he should again happen to be chased by a second hunter, he lifts himself up and shows his members to him. And the latter, when he perceives the testicles to be missing, leaves the beaver alone. . . . The creature is called a Beaver (Castor) because of the castration.

> *The Bestiary: A Book of Beasts, Being a Translation from a Latin Bestiary of the Twelfth Century Made and Edited by T. H. White* (1954). The English author of *The Sword in the Stone* notes: "The testicles of a beaver are internal and cannot be bitten off."

## Whitehead, Paxton
And when I die, I think more than anything I want people to tell marvellous stories about me. I want people to know who Paxton Whitehead was. What great fun that would be.

> Quoted by Don Rubin in *The Toronto Star*, May 1, 1971. Whitehead founded the Shaw Festival at Niagara-on-the-Lake in 1962.

## Whitehead, Robert
I've been in the business long enough to determine to entertain.

> Montreal-born Broadway producer, married to Zoe Caldwell, quoted in *The Globe and Mail*, May 17, 1958.

## Whitelaw, Marjory   See Derek Patmore.

## Whiteway, Sir William
I find that Newfoundland is said to be celebrated for its codfish, its dogs, its hogs, its fogs and bogs. That is a very erroneous opinion, I assure you.

> Address in London, England, on his retirement as prime minister of Newfoundland, July 5, 1897.

## Whitman, Walt
From Paumanok starting I fly like a
  bird,
A round and around to soar to sing the
  idea of all,
To the north betaking myself to sing
  there arctic songs,
To Kanada till I absorb Kanada in myself, to Michigan then,
To Wisconsin, Iowa, Minnesota, to sing
  their songs. . . .

> "From Paumanok starting I Fly like a Bird," *Drum-Taps* (1865). *Leaves of Grass* (1891-92).

Long ere the second centennial arrives, there will be some forty to fifty great States, among them Canada and Cuba. . . . The Pacific will be ours, and the Atlantic mainly ours. There will be daily electric communication with every part of the globe. What an age! What a land! Where, elsewhere, one so great? The individuality of one nation must then, as always, lead the world. Can there be any doubt who the leader ought to be? [May, 1870; the "second centennial" of the American Revolution would make it 1975]

As we approach Toronto everything looks doubly beautiful, especially the glimpses of blue Ontario's waters, sunlit, yet with a slight haze, through which occasionally a distant sail.

In Toronto at half-past one. I rode up on top of the omnibus with the driver. The city made the impression on me of a lively dashing place. The lake gives it its character.

\*

We are off, off into Toronto Bay (soon the wide expanse and cool breezes of Lake Ontario). As we steam out a mile or so we get a pretty view of Toronto from the blue foreground of the waters, —the whole rising spread of the city, groupings of roofs, spires, trees, hills in the background. Goodbye, Toronto, with your memories of a very lively and agreeable visit.

*

I see, or imagine I see in the future, a race of two million farm-families, ten million people—every farm running down to the water, or at least in sight of it—the best air and drink and sky and scenery of the globe, the sure foundation-nutriment of heroic men and women. The summers, the winters—I have sometimes doubted whether there could be a great race without the hardy influence of winters in due proportion.

> *Walt Whitman's Diary in Canada, with Extracts from Other of His Diaries and Literary Note-Books* (1904), edited by William Sloane Kennedy. The American poet visited Toronto on July 26-27, 1880.

### Whitney, Sir James Pliny
Ontario does not think I am a great man. It does think I am honest. And honest I must be.

> Premier of Ontario, after the election of 1908. Quoted by Sir John Willison in *Reminiscences Political and Personal* (1919).

### Whittaker, Byng
Broadcasting is a business or institution, if you like, which is of my generation.

> "London Tells the World" (1945), *Empire Club of Canada: Addresses Delivered to the Members During the Year 1944-45* (1945).

### Whittaker, Herbert
That is the one commodity common to all branches and members of the Canadian theatre today—hope. The dark days of the century can now be seen to have served an important purpose. Canadians were thrown back on their own resources. Canadians are a people trained to think of themselves as sitting atop the greatest natural resources in the world, smugly wearing the label of The Country with the Greatest Future. In the theatre, as in many other fields of development, that future is upon us now.

> "The Theatre," *The Culture of Contemporary Canada* (1957), edited by Julian Park.

July 13, 1953, was the most exciting night in the history of Canadian theatre. I doubt if there will ever be another night to match it, for me and for a great many others who were at that opening of the first Stratford Festival.

> Introduction to *The Stratford Festival 1953-1957: A Record in Pictures and Text of the Shakespearean Festival in Canada* (1958), with a foreword by Vincent Massey.

Nathan [Cohen] may not be our only dramatic critic, but he is certainly our most dramatic critic.

> Quoted by Alex Barris in *The Pierce-Arrow Showroom Is Leaking: An Insider's View of the CBC* (1969). See also Nathan Cohen.

### Whittier, John Greenleaf
Even so in our mortal journey
   The bitter north-winds blow,
And thus upon life's Red River
   Our hearts, as oarsmen, row.

> Whittier, the poet of rural New England, was intrigued by the Selkirk Settlement, and about 1860 wrote a short poem, "The Red River Voyager," from which the above stanza has been taken.

*

And the prayers of the elders
   Had followed his way,
As homeward he glided,
   Down Pentecost Bay.
O, well sped La Tour!
   For, peril and pain,
His lady kept watch,
   For his coming again.

> "St. John, 1647," a verse on the La Tours and the sacking of Fort La Tour, in present-day New Brunswick. *The Poetical Works of John Greenleaf Whittier* (1895).

### Whitton, Charlotte
Canadian women got the vote as a gift rather than as a reward.

> "Is the Canadian Woman a Flop in Politics?" *Saturday Night*, January 26, 1946.

We remain the most inert, in the consciousness or use of our power, of women in nations the world over.

"Women the World Over," *Chatelaine*, September, 1946.

Conservative. If I could only find the conservative party. [Answering a question about her political allegiance]

*

My mother's a Catholic. My father was an Orangeman. Where does that leave me? Right in the Anglican Church.

Quoted by Eva-Lis Wuorio in *Maclean's Magazine*, March 1, 1951.

Whatever women do they must do twice as well as men to be thought half so good . . . luckily, it's not difficult.

*

Speak up, gentlemen, I am not opposed to male participation in government. [During a noisy council meeting while mayor of Ottawa]

*

Call me anything you like, but don't call me a lady.

Characteristic remarks of the first woman mayor of Ottawa in the 1950s, whom *Reader's Digest* once described as "hell on wheels."

## Wicks, Ben

It's a fact of North American culture that Henry Ford has probably done more to give individuals their start in life than any other single individual. He is more important than even Dr. Spock. Cupid plays a poor second fiddle—takes the back seat, you might say—to Henry Ford.

*Back Seat Driving and Other Things* (1968), with Peter Worthington.

## Wieland, Joyce

There are two kinds of art. Man art and woman art. They are two different kinds of people, so the art comes out differently.

*Women in the Arts in Canada: A Study Prepared for the Royal Commission on the Status of Women in Canada* (1971), by Sandra Gwyn.

## Wilde, Oscar

I am having charming audiences, you will be glad to hear; the Canadians are very appreciative people, but it is a great fight in this commercial age to plead the cause of Art. Still the principles which I represent are so broad, so grand, so noble that I have no fear for the future. [Letter to Mary Anderson from Halifax, October 8, 1882]

*

. . . while as for Canada it was at my feet. [Letter to Mrs. George Lewis from Boston, June 3, 1882]

*

I am just off to the Art Schools and the University. Tonight I lecture as usual, will be home I don't know when. I must go to Japan, and live there with sweet little Japanese girls. [Letter to Norman Forbes-Robertson from Toronto, May 25, 1882]

*The Letters of Oscar Wilde* (1962), edited by Rupert Hart-Davis.

In the Rockies I saw the only rational method of art criticism I have ever come across. Over the piano was printed a notice: "Please do not shoot the pianist: he is doing his best." The mortality among pianists in that place is marvellous.

Quoted by Sean McCann in *The Wit of Oscar Wilde* (1969). See also Homer Watson.

Niagara Falls is simply a vast unnecessary amount of water going the wrong way and then falling over unnecessary rocks. The wonder would be if the water did not fall.

*

Niagara Falls must be the second major disappointment of American married life.

Attributed to the Anglo-Irish playwright at a news conference in New York, 1882.

I was disappointed with Niagara—most people must be disappointed with Niagara. Every American bride is taken there, and the sight of the stupendous waterfall must be one of the earliest, if not the keenest, disappointments in American married life. One sees it under bad conditions, very far away, the point of view not showing the splendour of the water. To appreciate it really one has to see it from underneath the fall, and to do that it is necessary to be dressed in a yellow oil-skin, which is as ugly as a mackintosh—and I hope none of you ever wears one. It is a consolation to know, however, that such an artist as Madame Bernhardt has not only worn that yellow, ugly dress, but has been photographed in it.

> *Impressions of America* (1906), edited by Stuart Mason.

## Wilkie, William

I will go further and say to the magistrates in the name of the people of this province, that we are governed by a set of drivellers, from whom we can expect no remedy, but in *poison*, no relief but in *death*.

> *A Letter to the People of Halifax, Containing Strictures on the Conduct of the Magistrates . . .* (1820), by "A Nova-Scotian." George V.V. Nicholls in "A Forerunner of Joseph Howe," *Canadian Historical Review*, September, 1927, has established the identity of the author of this anonymously published pamphlet.

## Wilkins, Sir George Hubert

Since then I have come to know that Canadians were not as we had painted them in Australia—going out blowing the call of the wild and all working at chopping down little trees in the bush.

> "Sixteen Years of Polar Exploration," March 15, 1937, *Addresses Delivered before the Canadian Club of Toronto: Season of 1936-37* (1937). The famous Antarctic explorer took part in Stefansson's Arctic expedition of 1913-17.

## Wilkinson, Anne

The poet's daily chore
Is my long duty;
To keep and cherish my good lens
For love and war
And wasps about the lilies
And mutiny within.

> Opening verse of "Lens" (1955), *Selected Poems* (1968), edited by A.J.M. Smith.

## Wilkinson, Doug

For Canada to be great, Canada must realize it is a great country and most of it is North. The difference between Canada and Russia is that the Russians look north and Canadians look south.

> Quoted by Nancy Naglin, *The Toronto Star*, January 29, 1972.

## Willan, Healey

If you want to know how to write fugues, write fugues.

> Quoted by John Beckwith in *The Canadian Forum*, December, 1972.

## William IV

Let not these Provinces be lost or given away.

> Attributed to the "Sailor-King" of England who was succeeded by Victoria in 1837. The remark (sometimes given as "Canada must be neither lost nor given away") may date from 1831 when the boundary differences between New Brunswick and Maine were referred to the king of the Netherlands for arbitration. Quoted by James FitzGibbon in *A Few Observations on Canada, and the Other Provinces of British North America* (1849).

## Williams, Daniel ("Nigger Dan")

A Loyal British Subject
Who Objects to be trodden upon
By any man except
Her Gracious Majesty Queen Victoria

> Warning erected by the eccentric Fort St. John settler where the property he squatted on met that of the Hudson's Bay Company, April 12, 1873. Quoted by A.C. Garrioch in *A Hatchet Mark in Duplicate* (1929). Williams was known as "Nigger Dan" and was quite illiterate, so the wording of his sign varies in grammar and spelling from account to account. Peter Freuchen in *The Legend of Daniel Williams* (1956) quotes approvingly an old-timer's estimate of "Nigger Dan": "He only recognized two masters — Queen Victoria and Jesus Christ! He was always writin' notes to one an' prayin' to the other."

## Williams, Harry

It's a long way to Tipperary, it's a long way to go;

It's a long way to Tipperary, to the
sweetest girl I know!
Good-bye Piccadilly, farewell, Leicester
Square,
It's a long, long way to Tipperary, but
my heart's right there!

"Over in England Jack Judge and Harry
H. Williams had written a song called
'It's a Long Way to Tipperary,' which
was to lie on the publisher's shelves for
two years, awaiting a war that would
start British soldiers marching to its
stimulating rhythm." Sigmund Spaeth
in *A History of Popular Music in America* (1948).

The words of this popular marching
song were written by Harry Williams, a
Canadian, and the music by Jack Judge,
a Britisher. The date of composition is
usually given as 1908; the British army
adopted it as a marching song in 1914.
Tipperary is a lovely town in Ireland.

In the shade of the old apple tree,
Where the love in your eyes I could see,
When the voice that I heard,
Like the song of the bird,
Seem'd to whisper sweet music to me;
I could hear the dull buzz of the bee,
In the blossoms as you said to me,
With a heart that is true,
I'll be waiting for you
In the shade of the old apple tree.

Williams also wrote the words to "In
the Shade of the Old Apple Tree," a
hit song in 1905, the chorus of which,
reproduced here, is said to be inspired
by a tree on Glen Edith Drive in Toronto. The melody was composed by an
American, Egbert Van Alstyne, who
teamed up with the twenty-six-year-old
Williams in 1900 to make good on Tin
Pan Alley.

## Williams, Percy

My ideals of the Olympic Games are all
shot. I always imagined it was a game of
heroes. Well, I'm in the semifinals myself so it can't be so hot. [Diary entry,
July 29, 1928, Amsterdam]

\*

I was just like any kid of twenty. I was
simply bewildered by it all. I didn't like
running. Oh, I was so glad to get out of
it all. [Recollections, 1956]

Williams was called "the world's fastest
human" after winning two gold medals
at the Olympic Games in Amsterdam,
July 30, 1928. Quoted by Ray Gardner
in *Maclean's Magazine*, November 24,
1956.

## Williams, Roger Neville

They were not immigrants to Canada,
though Canadian law said they were;
they were American exiles.

*The New Exiles: American War Resis-
ters in Canada* (1971).

## Williamson, Henry

Those who came out with me, are scattered in various parts of Canada. I have
heard from them and they are doing
well. We came like terrapins,—all we
had on our backs.

Williamson was a Maryland slave who
settled in Hamilton. Quoted by Benjamin Drew in *The Refugee: or the Narratives of Fugitive Slaves in Canada*
(1856).

## Willingdon, Lord

Its wealth is endless, its possibilities
boundless, opportunities are here for the
taking. Any man who is not afraid of
hard work can succeed in Canada.

Address of the governor general to the
Canadian Club of Montreal, January,
1927. Quoted by John Cowan in *Canada's Governors-General 1867-1952* (1952).

## Willison, Sir John

. . . women know men better than they
know themselves and better than men
ever suspect. . . .

\*

What is not disclosed by contemporary
writers will never be disclosed. Hence
history can never be a true record, and
the exact relation of public men to the
causes in which they are concerned never
can be determined. If there is reticence
in the present and ignorance in the future, at best we can have only light in
the darkness.

\*

There was the Montreal story of a dispute between a French Roman Catholic
and a Scottish Presbyterian. Finally the

exasperated Scotsman said, "To hell with the Pope." The Frenchman retorted, "You say, to hell wis zee Pope, den I say, to hell wis Harry Lauder."

*Reminiscences Political and Personal* (1919).

This thing they call irresolution is often the very pith and marrow of statesmanship.

*Sir Wilfrid Laurier and the Liberal Party: A Political History* (1926). See also Phillips Thompson.

**Willison, Marjory MacMurchy**
"To make things go well" in a home is an art, and the woman who does this is an artist.

\*

The business woman is not a revolutionary.

*The Woman—Bless Her: Not as Amiable a Book as It Sound*s (1916).

**Wills, Archie**
Caddy, Cadborosaurus.

Nicknames given British Columbia's monstrous sea serpent by the news editor of *The Victoria Daily Times*, October, 1933. At one sighting in the Straits of Georgia, off Cadboro, near Victoria, it was claimed the snake-like monster "shone like aluminum." *In the Wake of the Sea-Serpents* (1968), by Bernard Heuvelmans, translated by Richard Garnett.

**Wilson, Cairine**
You are going to make me the most hated woman in Canada.

To W.L. Mackenzie King in 1930, when he decided to appoint Mrs. Wilson (the daughter of Senator Robert Mackay) the country's first woman senator.

**Wilson, Sir Daniel**
In the application of the term *Prehistoric*—introduced, if I mistake not, for the first time in this work,—it was employed originally in reference to races which I then assigned reasons for believing had preceded the oldest historical ones in Britain and Northern Europe. But since then the term has become identified with a comprehensive range of speculative and inductive research, in which the archaeologist labours hand in hand with the geologist and ethnologist, in solving some of the most deeply interesting problems of modern science.

Credit for the first use of the word "prehistoric" has been granted by *The Oxford English Dictionary* to Sir Daniel Wilson, Scots-born professor of History and English at University College, University of Toronto. The word appeared in the first edition of *Prehistoric Annals of Scotland* (1851). In the preface to the second edition, which was published twelve years later, Sir Daniel made the above reference to his neologism.

**Wilson, Edmund**
In my youth, of the early nineteen-hundreds, we tended to imagine Canada as a kind of vast hunting preserve convenient to the United States.

\*

It is possible, in English Canada, to have reasonable conversations in which people pretty well speak their minds—they listen, I noted, to one another instead of "shooting off their faces" in competition, as we are likely to do—and the Canadians, as I shall show in a moment, now have subjects that stimulate discussion and about which we in the United States are in a state of almost opaque ignorance.

\*

The Canadian Morley Callaghan, at one time well known in the United States, is today perhaps the most unjustly neglected novelist in the English-speaking world.

\*

The reviewer, at the end of this article, after trying to give an account of these books, is now wondering whether the primary reason for the current underestimation of Morley Callaghan may not be simply a general incapacity—apparently shared by his compatriots—for believing that a writer whose work may be mentioned without absurdity in association with Chekhov's and Turgenev's can possibly be functioning in Toronto.

*O Canada: An American's Notes on Canadian Culture* (1965).

The people in Toronto, although no great beauties, seem healthier and better set-up than those in New York and Boston. Not so driven and not so cramped between big buildings and in narrow streets, they seem to be more good-natured, and they probably enjoy themselves more.

*Upstate: Records and Recollections of Northern United States* (1971).

## Wilson, Edward Arthur

I am not a man: I am a glorious power. Ignorant men say, "I am a body and I possess a soul," when in truth it should be: "I am a soul and I possess a body." I cannot sin, so any woman joining with me cannot sin.

\*

At every critical period in world history, certain individuals are born with a distinct mission, born, fully equipped with the knowledge, fully equipped with a plentitude of power, to fulfil that mission. . . . Such a man am I, Brother Twelve, your beloved Guru! My immediate task is the overthrow of those great examples of organized evil, the Jewish world-monopoly of wealth, and the Roman Catholic Hierarchy.

*Canada's False Prophet: The Notorious Brother Twelve* (1967), by Herbert Emmerson Wilson.

## Wilson, Ethel

The only thing in our changing world that we can now regard as being safe and sure is that next Monday will certainly be Monday, next Tuesday will be Tuesday and nothing else, and that Saturday afternoon will always be Saturday afternoon and for this much stability we should be thankful.

*The Innocent Traveller* (1949).

A writer's mind seems to be situated partly in the solar plexus and partly in the head.

\*

I am sure that the business of writing is one of the four or five most private things in the world, excluding the planning of international treaties or crime.

"A Cat Among the Falcons" (1959),

*Masks of Fiction: Canadian Critics on Canadian Prose* (1961), edited by A.J.M. Smith.

## Wilson, Harold

All aid short of help.

"A few years ago Harold Wilson, then president of the Board of Trade, made a tour of Canada; at one point he summed up the Canadian attitude as: 'All aid short of help.' I believe Mr. Wilson made that remark under the impression he was speaking off the record, but it got into the papers and it created a considerable fuss at the time." Quoted by Blair Fraser in "Canada and Britain's Economy," *The Listener*, March 26, 1953. The remark made by the future prime minister of Great Britain recalls F. D. Roosevelt's formula "all aid to Britain short of war."

## Wilson, J. Tuzo

The limit to man's conquest of the inanimate world now clearly depends upon man's power to control himself.

"How International Is Science?" (1961), *Empire Club of Canada: Addresses 1960-61* (1961).

There is one thing Canadians should always remember. In many parts of the world including much of the southern United States people will be uncomfortable if heating fuel is cut off, but in Canada many people would die. We need our energy fuels just to stay alive in our rigorous climate and fuel for our future is essential. We cannot return to the use of wood and coal, and nuclear power has not yet been developed to be an adequate alternative to fossil fuels.

"Selling Today What We'll Need Tomorrow," *Maclean's Magazine*, March, 1973.

## Wilson, Milton

We have often been told of our necessary dullness because we had no Revolutionary War, no French Revolution, no War Between the States. In poetry likewise we had no Renaissance, no Neo-Classicism, no Romanticism. But one of the advantages of a poetry less than a hundred years old is that all the things that couldn't happen when they should have happened keep happening all the time.

\*

I even wonder whether colonialism may not be, in theory at least, the most desirable poetic state. It gives you a catholic sense of the things poetry can do without embarrassing you by telling you what at this particular moment it can't.

"Other Canadians and After" (1958), *Masks of Poetry: Canadian Critics on Canadian Verse* (1962), edited by A.J.M. Smith.

**Winch, E.E.**
Truly the road of a politician has many slippery places whilst that of a socialist is firm, even if hard going at times. Hard going! we don't know what hard going is.

Letter of October 1, 1956, quoted by Dorothy G. Steeves in *The Compassionate Rebel: Ernest E. Winch and His Times* (1960).

**Winch, Harold E.**
It is sometimes said that the reason why we cannot see the future as plainly as the past is because we know too little of the real present.

Foreword to *The Compassionate Rebel: Ernest E. Winch and His Times* (1960), by Dorothy G. Steeves.

**Winchell, Walter**
" 'This is the best place,' the columnist remarked. 'Besides, when I was a hoofer, I was in Canada once and Mexico, too, and I discovered foreigners don't like us.' "

Bob Thomas in *Winchell* (1971).

**Windsor, Duke of**   See Edward VIII.

**Winks, Robin W.**
But of what relation is Uncle Tom to the story of the Canadian Negro? Precisely this: as Canadians came increasingly to assign Tom's role to Henson, as the myths of the North Star, the Underground Railroad, and the Fugitives' haven "under the lion's Paw" grew in the post-Civil War years, when these myths no longer could be tested, Canadians came increasingly to congratulate themselves upon their lack of prejudice and to contrast themselves favourably with the immoral and once slave-ridden United States. . . . If Uncle Tom came to Canada, could conditions need improving?

*The Blacks in Canada: A History* (1971). See also Josiah Henson.

**Winslow, Colonel John**
Gentlemen, I have received from His Excellency, Governor Lawrence, *the King's* instructions, which I hold in my hand. By his orders you are called together to hear His Majesty's resolution . . . His Majesty's instructions and commands . . . are, that your lands and tenements and cattle and live stock of all kinds are forfeited to the Crown, with all your other effects, except money and household goods, and that you yourselves are to be removed from this Province. . . . *The peremptory orders of His Majesty are* that *all* the French inhabitants of these districts be removed. . . .

Summoned "on pain of forfeiting their goods and chattels in default of real estate," the Acadians attended church at Grand Pré on Friday, September 5, 1755, when, at three o'clock in the afternoon, Colonel Winslow read out the order of expulsion. Governor Lawrence was acting on his own orders, not the king's. Winslow wrote in his journal: "Thus ended the memorable 5th of September, a day of great fatigue and trouble." See also Governor Charles Lawrence.

*October 8th.* Began to Embarke the Inhabitants who went of Very Solentarily and unwillingly, the women in Great Distress Carrying off Their children In their arms. Others Carrying their Decript Parents in their Carts and all their Goods Moving in great Confusion & appeard a Sceen of Woe & Distress. . . . the Kings Command was to me absolute & Should be absolutely obeyed & that I Did not Love to use Harsh Means but that the time Did not admit of Parlies and Delays and Then ordered the whole

Troops to fix their Bayonets & advance Towards the French. . . . Thus Ended this Troublesome Jobb, which was Scheen of Sorrow.

> On October 8, 1755, at Minas Basin, Colonel Winslow executed the orders of Charles Lawrence, governor of Nova Scotia, and expelled the Acadian population, dispersing them among the American colonies. "Journal of Colonel John Winslow of the Provincial Troops While Engaged in Removing the Acadian French Inhabitants from Grand Pré . . . 1755," *Collections (1883-84), Nova Scotia Historical Society.*

We are now hatching the noble and great project of banishing the French Neutrals from the Province. . . . If we accomplish this expulsion, it will have been one of the greatest deeds the *English in America* have ever achieved, for among other considerations, the *part of the country which they occupy is one of the best soils in the world*, and, in this event, we might place some good farmers on their homesteads. [Journal, Beauséjour, 1755]

### Winters, Robert H.

You have perhaps heard the story of the four students—British, French, American, Canadian—who were asked to write an essay on elephants. The British student entitled his essay "Elephants and the Empire." The French student called his "Love and the Elephant." The title of the American student's essay was "Bigger and Better Elephants," and the Canadian student called his "Elephants: A Federal or a Provincial Responsibility?"

> Adapted from a businessmen's address delivered by the federal cabinet minister in 1966.

Tell me where the centre is and I'll tell you where I stand.

\*

The more good decisions made in boardrooms . . . the fewer will have to be made in cabinet chambers.

> Quoted by Peter C. Newman in *The Distemper of Our Times: Canadian Politics in Transition: 1963-1968* (1968).

### Withers, Iva

I think there's a little Lorelei in every woman.

> The Winnipeg-born actress and singer succeeded Carol Channing as Lorelei Lee in the Broadway production of *Gentlemen Prefer Blondes*. Quoted in *The Toronto Star*, February 22, 1952.

### Withrow, William

Artists are great survivors.

> *Contemporary Canadian Painting* (1972).

### Wolfe, James

Better be a savage of some use than a gentle, amorous, puppy, obnoxious to all the world.

\*

All that I wish for myself is that I may at all times be ready and firm to meet that fate we cannot shun, and to die gracefully and properly when the hour comes.

\*

"Appointments made for merit, and not through routine and patronage, shocked the Duke of Newcastle, to whom a man like Wolfe was a hopeless enigma; and he told George II that Pitt's new general was mad. 'Mad is he?' returned the old King; 'then I hope he will bite some others of my generals.' " [Wolfe was appointed major-general in 1758]

\*

British colours on every French fort, port, and garrison in America. [Major-General James Wolfe's toast at Louisbourg, June 6, 1759, before setting out to take Quebec]

\*

I will have Quebec if I stay here till the end of November. [Summer of 1759]

\*

My writing to you will convince you that no personal evils worse than defeats and disappointments have fallen upon me. The enemy puts nothing to risk and I can't in conscience put the whole army to risk. My antagonist has wisely shut himself up in inaccessible intrenchments, so that I cannot get at him without spilling a torrent of blood, and that perhaps to little purpose. The Marquis de Montcalm is at the head of a great number of bad soldiers, and I am at the head of a small number of good ones, that wish for nothing so much as to fight him; but the wary old fellow avoids an action, doubtful of the behaviour of his army. People must be of the profession to understand the disadvantages and difficulties we labour under, arising from the uncommon natural strength of the country. [Last letter to his mother, August 31, 1759]

\*

The troops will land where the French seem least to expect it. [From the general orders, September 12, 1759]

> Quoted by Francis Parkman in *Montcalm and Wolfe* (1884).

Gentlemen, I would rather have written those lines than take Quebec tomorrow.

> Major-General James Wolfe was in a poetic mood the day before his attack on Quebec. Late that evening, September 12, 1759, he recited Gray's "Elegy, Written in a Country Churchyard," and then made the above remark. Tradition has it that he lingered over the fourth line of the stanza below:
>
> The boast of heraldry; the pomp of
>    power,
>    And all the beauty, all the wealth
>       e'er gave,
> Await alike th' inevitable hour:
>    The paths of glory lead but to the
>       grave.
>
> Eighteen hours later Wolfe was dead on the Plains of Abraham. Quoted by Francis Parkman in *Montcalm and Wolfe* (1884). See also Thomas Gray.

I would rather have been the author of that piece than beat the French tomorrow.

> The authority for this famous statement derives from the testimony of John Robison who was in the boat with Wolfe at the time. Robison later taught natural philosophy at Edinburgh University and related the remark to a student who was the first to commit it to writing in 1804. W. T. Waugh, in *James Wolfe: Man and Soldier* (1928), notes that "tomorrow" should be "to-

day," as the remark would have been made early the morning of the attack. Waugh, who studied the matter in some detail, admitted that the celebrated utterance was characteristic of the general.

> "Did this really happen? The answer seems to be that the tale has more foundation than most of the Quebec legends, but that the incident did not take place as the boats moved down the river in the early morning of the 13th. Wolfe had issued orders enjoining strict silence. There are cases on record of generals who disobeyed their own orders when it suited them—but hardly in circumstances like these." C.P. Stacey in *Quebec, 1759: The Siege and the Battle* (1959).

"When the Genl. received the Shot I caught hold of him and Carried him off the Field—he walked about one Hundred Yards and then beg'd I would set him down which I did. Then I open'd his Breast and found his Shirt full of blood at which he smiled and when he seen the distress I was in, 'My Dear,' said he, 'Don't grieve for me I shall be happy in a few Minutes take care of Yourself as I see you are Wounded. But tell me O tell me how goes the Battle?'

"Just then came some Officers who told him that the French had given Ground and that our Troops was pursuing them to the Walls of the Town. He was then Lying in my arms just Expiring. That great man whose sole Ambition was his Country's Glory raised Himself upon the News and Smiled in my Face. 'Now' said he 'I die Contented'— from that Instant the Smile never left his Face till he Deided."

> A contemporary account of Wolfe's death from a letter home by James Henderson, a volunteer of the Louisbourg Grenadiers, quoted by Oliver Warner in *With Wolfe to Quebec: The Path to Glory* (1972).

". . . he desired those who were about him to lay him down; being asked if he would have a Surgeon? he replied, 'it is needless; it is all over with me.' One of them then cried out, 'they run, see how they run.' 'Who runs?' demanded our hero, with great earnestness, like a person roused from sleep. The Officer answered, 'The enemy, Sir; Egad, they give way everywhere.' Thereupon the General rejoined, '*Go one of you, my lads, to Colonel Burton—; tell him to march Webb's regiment with all speed to Charles's river, to cut off the retreat of the fugitives from the bridge.*' Then turning on his side, he added, '*Now, God be praised, I will die in peace:*' and thus expired."

A contemporary account of Wolfe's death by Captain John Knox in *An Historical Journal of the Campaigns in North America* (1769), edited by Arthur G. Doughty in 1914.

Wolfe was surprised to find himself lying on the ground, supported by one of his officers.
Someone was singing a nursery rhyme.
*See how they run,*
*See how they run. . . .*
How confusing it was: It all seemed so far off now.

*The Great Fur Opera: Annals of the Hudson's Bay Company 1670-1970*, by Kildare Dobbs and Ronald Searle.

Here Died
WOLFE
Victorious
Sept. 13
1759

Original inscription on Wolfe's Monument. A memorial was erected in 1832 to mark the spot where Wolfe fell on the Plains of Abraham. The inscription above was added in 1849 but later effaced. When the monument was replaced, the word "victorious" was missing. John Charles Dent in *The Canadian Portrait Gallery* (1880-81).

See also: Lord Aylmer, William Cowper, George II, Thomas Gray, Marquis de Montcalm, Sir Joshua Reynolds, Walter Carruthers Sellar, Benjamin West. For a full account of the deaths of Wolfe and Montcalm, see Francis Parkman.

## Wolfe, Thomas
I also went to Canada. Montreal is four-fifths imitation American and one-fifth imitation English—but the beer and ale were splendidly real. Quebec was more interesting: it is entirely French-Canadian, and the people speak little or no English and no French either, so far as I am concerned. But this place too I found disappointing. It is like Dr. Johnson's dog walking on hind legs. "The wonder is not that he walks well, but that he walks at all." People are interested in Quebec only because it is a French town in America, and that means so little to me.

Letter to Henry T. Volkening, August 9, 1929, *The Letters of Thomas Wolfe* (1956), edited by Elizabeth Nowell.

Canada looks like a rich, magnificent country — naturally — but there are not men enough to till the soil. [Letter to Mrs. Julia Elizabeth Wolfe, August 13, 1929]

*

Dear Mama: This is a beautiful little city, and the capitol of British Columbia—Like its name it is Victorian and seems very slow and quaint after the U.S. Tom. [Last postcard to Mrs. Julia Elizabeth Wolfe, July 6, 1938; the American novelist died later that year]

*The Letters of Thomas Wolfe to His Mother* (1968), edited by C. Hugh Holman and Sue Fields Ross.

## Wolfe, Tom
Suppose he is what he sounds like, the most important thinker since Newton, Darwin, Freud, Einstein, and Pavlov—what if he is right?

The New York journalist asked this question about Marshall McLuhan and his media theories in "The New Life Out There" (1965), *McLuhan: Hot & Cool* (1967), edited by Gerald Emmanuel Stearn. McLuhan's reply was characteristic: "I'd rather be wrong." See also Marshall McLuhan.

## Wolfit, Donald
I always had at the back of my mind an intention to visit Canada as soon as it was possible, with a repertoire of Shakespeare. The intervention of six years of war delayed this intention of mine, but

as soon as ocean transport became in any way practical once again, I began to make plans and contacts, though it took over six months of patient plotting, not to mention the twisting, writhing and turning round the buffers of officialdom and bureaucracy, to get here; and all that effort was worth while, if for nothing else than to be able to order two eggs and bacon every morning and to really see them on the plate, thus combining a regular diet of Bacon and Shakespeare.

"Shakespeare in War and Peace" (1947), *Empire Club of Canada: Addresses Delivered to the Members During the Year 1946-47* (1947).

## Wood, Henry Wise

Unless we can reorganize the fabric of civilization, unless we can grasp the true laws of life and learn how to put them into practical operation, unless we can rebuild civilization from the foundation stone up and make a true democracy in which war will be as impossible as peace is today—unless we can do all that, we must face a future absolutely without hope. [December 4, 1918]

\*

The Kingdom of Heaven and perfect democracy are synonymous terms. [December 11, 1918]

\*

The divine right of the money interests has not yet been terminated. [May 21, 1919]

\*

Democracy may be simply defined as the people in action. [July 2, 1919]

\*

Class organization is the only road along which civilization can travel to safety. I believe in that as I believe in God. [November 5, 1919]

\*

Water cannot rise above its source, neither can social progress rise higher than the level of the citizenship of the people. [*Western Independent*, February 18, 1920]

\*

We have lots of time to make everything but mistakes [In answer to the complaint that he was slow, August 14, 1948]

Unless otherwise attributed, these aph-

orisms appeared in the *Grain Growers' Guide*. Henry Wise Wood (who was sometimes called "Wise Old Henry") was president of the United Farmers of Alberta from 1916 to 1931 and chairman of the Alberta Wheat Pool Board from 1923 to 1937. Quoted by William Kirby Rolph in *Henry Wise Wood of Alberta* (1950).

## Wood, Colonel S.T.

I find it still necessary to explain that the motto of the force is *Maintiens le droit*, and not "Get your Man," as some fictional writers would have us believe.

"The R.C.M.P.," *Canada: Reprinted from the Canadian Number of The Times, May 15, 1939* (1939).

## Wood, William

What the camel is to desert tribes, what the horse is to the Arab, what the ship is to the colonizing Briton, what all modern means of locomotion are to the civilized world today, that, and more than that, the canoe was to the Indian who lived beside the innumerable waterways of Canada.

*All Afloat: A Chronicle of Craft and Waterways* (1920).

## Woodcock, George

America's strengths *as a state* are its gravest flaws; Canada's weaknesses *as a state* are its greatest virtues.

"Various Americas" in *The New Romans: Candid Canadian Opinions of the U.S.* (1968), edited by Al Purdy.

I have found, even intellectually and politically, more freedom, more space to move my mind, in Canada than in most of the other places I have known.

\*

The size and emptiness of the land are two facts that are ever present in Canadian minds. Men are few and the solitudes are vast.

\*

There is a Lost World quality about colonial cultures. They preserve, in remoteness and isolation, forms of expression that have often died away in the places of their origin.

*

This is in the true Canadian vein. Heroes impose on others, and Canadians do not like to be imposed on, but they think they are, and hence they are inclined to identify with martyrs, particularly as martyrdom is the kind of fate into which even a moral, rational man can be trapped. What most attracts modern Canadians about Louis Riel is not his micro-patriotism as leader of a few thousand people who called themselves a nation, nor his frenzied chiliasm, but the fact that at his trial he preferred condemnation as a man who acted from reasoned motives to acquittal as an inspired lunatic.

*

In their [the rising generation's] hands Canada will not become a great country, which no Canadian wants, but it may become a humane country; its future not safe or splendid, but as free and audacious as any future can be in this world and time.

> *Canada and the Canadians* (1970).

Complete liberty implies freedom from the tyranny of abstractions as well as from the rule of men.

> "The Tyranny of the Clock" (1944), *The Rejection of Politics and Other Essays on Canada, Canadians, Anarchism and the World* (1972).

## Woodman, Elijah

My dear wife and children, it will be nine years next August since we were all together but I have faith that I will see you all once more, so keep up good courage and think as little as possible of me. I have a mind strong enough to withstand anything the Lord sees fit to put upon me and never murmur.

> Last letter written by Elijah Woodman to his family after being exiled to Van Diemen's Land (Australia), March 1, 1847, for taking part in the Rebellion of 1837. Woodman died before reaching home on June 13, and was buried at sea. Forwarded to his widow were his last words: "Do not any of you mourn my exit. It is but for a short time." The naval officer who took the dictation on June 6, added: "By this time he had

not strength to say more." Quoted by Fred Landon in *An Exile from Canada to Van Diemen's Land: Being the Story of Elijah Woodman Transported Overseas for Participation in the Upper Canada Troubles of 1837-38* (1960).

## Woods, N.A.

Ottawa, as the capital of Canada, seems such a monstrous absurdity, that, like all who have penetrated to it, I can never treat its metropolitan future as anything more than a bad practical joke, in which no one ever saw any meaning, but which, now that the Prince has solemnly laid the foundation stone of "intended Parliament buildings," is considered as having gone rather too far, and is awakening a feeling of almost indignation throughout Canada.

> *The Prince of Wales in Canada and the United States* (1861). See also Edward VII.

## Woodside, Willson

The university must be alert to change.

> *The University Question: Who Should Go? Who Should Pay?* (1958).

## Woodsworth, J.S.

We are thankful for these and all the good things of life. We recognize that they are part of our common heritage and come to us through the efforts of our brothers and sisters the world over. What we desire for ourselves we wish for all. To this end may we take our share in the world's work and the world's struggles.

> Woodsworth's prayer, called "Grace befor Meat," is a product of the merging of religion and unionism. J. S. Woodsworth's *The First Story of the Labour Church* (c. 1920), quoted by Kenneth McNaught in *A Prophet in Politics: A Biography of J.S. Woodsworth* (1959). Woodsworth resigned from the Methodist ministry in 1918 and the same year helped establish the Labour Church, "founded on the Fatherhood of God and the Brotherhood of man" and devoted to the social gospel.

At least in this world, souls are always

incorporated in bodies, and to save a man, you must save him body, soul, and spirit. To really save one man you must transform the community in which he lives. [June 30, 1915]

\*

Last century made the world a neighbourhood; this century must make it a brotherhood. [February, 1917]

\*

The fight is not between hand workers and brain workers. It is not between industrial workers and agricultural workers. The fight is essentially between producers and the parasites. [July 25, 1919]

\*

There have always been those who imagine that "a whiff of grape shot" would stop the cry of the people for justice. There are those in Winnipeg who think the shooting on Saturday taught labour a lesson. But labour did not need the lesson. . . . Labour already knew that two dozen men on horseback, shooting to kill, could disperse a crowd of several thousand unarmed men and women.

> *Records Relating to the Winnipeg General Strike, 1919*, quoted by Margaret Fairley in *Spirit of Canadian Democracy: A Collection of Canadian Writings from the Beginnings to the Present Day* (1945).

I am not afraid of the word "Socialism" which comes from a perfectly good Latin word which means "comradeship," which means that today we as individuals are no longer living isolated lives, that no nation is any longer living an isolated life, but rather that we are living in society in a thousand and one complicated relationships and that we must adapt our political ideals and our political institutions and our political policies to meet the new situation that confronts us.

> From an address made in 1924, quoted by Grace MacInnis in *J.S. Woodsworth: A Man to Remember* (1953).

. . . in any case, I am convinced that we may develop in Canada a distinctive type of Socialism. I refuse to follow slavishly the British model or the American model or the Russian model. We in Canada will solve our problems along our own lines.

> Report of the First National Convention of the CCF, Regina, July, 1933, quoted by Walter D. Young in *The Anatomy of a Party: The National CCF 1932-61* (1969).

The stars in their courses are fighting for the cause of socialism.

> CCF slogan, *New Commonwealth*, April 18, 1936.

I said I wanted to state my conviction. Now you can hammer me as much as you like.

> The leader of the CCF was a convinced pacifist and stood, virtually alone, in opposing the country's entry into the Second World War. House of Commons, September 8, 1939. Quoted by Kenneth McNaught in *A Prophet in Politics: A Biography of J.S. Woodsworth* (1959).

I know a lot of my friends who won't drive a car that is of a model more than two years old. A great many of us have machinery in our heads that is of a model a hundred years old.

> Quoted by F.H. Underhill in *In Search of Canadian Liberalism* (1960).

God has many bests.

\*

What we desire for ourselves, we wish for all.

> Characteristic remarks recalled by his daughter Grace MacInnis. Woodsworth attributed the first aphorism to a friend; see John Mark King. See also William Irvine.

**Wordsworth, William**
In sleep I heard the northern gleams;
The stars, they were among my dreams;
In rustling conflict through the skies,
I heard, I saw the flashes drive,
And yet they are upon my eyes,
And yet I am alive. . . .

> Lines depicting the *aurora borealis* from "The Complaint of a Forsaken Indian Woman." A note published in *Poems Founded on the Affections* (1791) adds: "See that very interesting work *Hearne's*

*Journey* from *Hudson's Bay* to the *Northern Ocean.* In the high northern latitudes, as the same writer informs us, when the northern lights vary their position in the air, they make a rustling and a crackling noise, as alluded to in the following poem."

But when the bleak winds roar
Through the stiff lance-like shoots of
    pollard ash,
Dread swell of sound! loud as the gusts
    that lash
The matted forests of Ontario's shore
By wasteful steel unsmitten—then would
    I
Turn into port; and, reckless of the gale,
Reckless of angry Duddon sweeping by,
While the warm hearth exalts the man-
    tling ale,
Laugh with the generous household
    heartily
At all the merry pranks of Donnerdale.

> Sonnet XIII: "Open Prospect, The River Duddon: A Series of Sonnets" (1820), *The Poetical Works of William Wordsworth* (1910), edited by Edward Dowden. See also Rudyard Kipling.

**Worthington, Peter**   See Ben Wicks.

**Wray, Fay**
Mr. Cooper said to me that he had an idea for a film in mind. The only thing he'd tell me was that I was going to have the tallest, darkest leading man in Hollywood. Naturally, I thought of Clark Gable.

> "What she got was King Kong," added Denis Gifford in *A Pictorial History of Horror Movies* (1973). Merian C. Cooper was co-producer of the imaginative film. *King Kong* was released in 1933. The twenty-six year old Alberta actress was known to be "a great screamer," especially when the delicate Canadian girl was in the grip of the American gorilla.

**Wright, Alonzo**
My opinions are mine, but my vote belongs to my party.

> Attributed to Alonzo Wright, Ottawa County M.P. from 1867 to 1891, known as "King of the Gatineau."

**Wright, Frank Lloyd**
Every graveyard in Canada, if it could speak, would say "amen" to the slab. Well, that's what this building says for Toronto. You've got a headmarker for a grave and future generations will look at it and say: "This marks the spot where Toronto fell."

> The famous American architect did not care for Viljo Revell's plan for Toronto's new City Hall. Quoted by Pierre Berton, *The Toronto Star*, September 29, 1958.

**Wright, William H.**
Don't you worry sometimes, Harry, that this is all a dream, that it never really happened, that you will wake up one day and find yourself squatting over a tin plate of cold beans on some freezing scree in Alaska? I do.

> "I don't," replied Harry Oakes to the English immigrant who made a major gold strike in the Kirkland Lake area in 1911 and founded the Wright-Hargreaves mine. Sir Harry's subsequent discovery nearby, Tough Oakes, dwarfed Wright's bonanza. See also Sir Harry Oakes.

My object in purchasing the *Globe* was not to make money out of it—at least that was not my main object. I thought I could do something for the country by making our mining industries better known. Anything that is of advantage to mining is of advantage to the country as a whole.

> *Mining World*, October 24, 1936. Quoted by Brian J. Young in "C. George McCullagh and the Leadership League," *Canadian Historical Review*, September, 1966.

**Wrong, George M.**
The only person sure of himself is the man who wishes to leave things as they are, and he dreams of an impossibility.

> Remark made in 1921, quoted by Walter Stewart in *Divide and Con: Canadian Politics at Work* (1973).

Under the worst evils of democracy the people are at least equal to exercise their own judgment and to make effective their own decisions.

"Democracy in Canada," *Canadian Historical Review*, December, 1921.

There is in reality no barrier of race to keep the English and French apart in Canada: the two peoples are identical in racial origins.

*The Two Races in Canada, A Lecture Delivered before the Canadian Historical Association* (1925), Montreal, May 21, 1925.

History tends to be partial to the victor.

\*

The historian is both the guardian and the interpreter of the past. He is a treasure-house of human experience.

"The Historian and Society," *Canadian Historical Review*, March, 1933.

What I want is a scholar and a gentleman, and if he knows any history, so much the better. [Wrong's hiring policy]

George M. Wrong occupied the chair of Modern History at the University of Toronto from 1895 to 1927. Quoted by W. Stewart Wallace in "The Life and

Work of George M. Wrong," *Canadian Historical Review*, September, 1948.

Revolution has always brought reaction and this is sadly true even when the revolution has been beneficent in spirit and friendly to liberty.

"Revolution and Reaction," *Canadian Problems as Seen by Twenty Outstanding Men of Canada* (1938), edited by W. R. Herridge and Richard B. Coates.

**Wrong, Hume**
We should not be here at all, as our instructions should be summarized as: say nothing and do nothing unless you can undo something of what was done at Geneva. . . . Dining alone this evening I developed a plan for the perfect representation of Canada at Conferences. Our delegate would have a name, even a photograph; a distinguished record, even an actual secretary—but he would have no corporal existence and no one would ever notice that he was not there.

Reflections of a leading member of the Department of External Affairs, and resident representative to the League of Nations, 1937. Quoted by Vincent Massey in *What's Past Is Prologue* (1963).

# X

**Xisto, Pedro**
Why should the word "freedom" in a poem mean less than the same word scribbled on a wall?

Brazilian concrete poet, resident in Toronto in 1967.

# Y

## Yanovsky, Zalman

My one regret is I didn't save any of the five thousand weekly fan letters we used to get. Some of those mash notes from the groupies might bolster me in my old age.

Zal Yanovsky was lead guitarist in the rock group The Lovin' Spoonful. *Canadian Panorama*, October 14, 1972.

## Yates, A.B.

To err is human; but to wear out the eraser before you wear out the pencil is taking too many liberties.

Director, Northern Economic Development, Department of Indian Affairs and Northern Development, 1960s.

## Yates, J. Michael

How far north will a mind consent? I'm alive because I wonder how far things can go. Anything that survives its original purpose becomes a record. Anything that survives.

\*

The wolves say to the dogs what the madman of me says to the citizen. I need to go fishing until I need to return.

*The Great Bear Lake Meditations* (1970).

## Yat-Sen, Madame Sun

The new China will never forget Dr. Bethune. He was one of those who helped us become free. His work and his memory will remain with us forever.

Preface by Soong Ching-Ling (Madame Sun Yat-Sen) to *The Scalpel, The Sword: The Story of Dr. Norman Bethune* (revised edition, 1973), by Ted Allan and Sydney Gordon.

## Yeatman, Robert Julian

See Walter Carruthers Sellar.

## Yeats, W.B.

I think it was a very good poem. I made it when shut up in a railway train coming from Canada. I think a railroad train a good place to write when the journey is long enough. One will exhaust the scenery in the first two or three hours and the newspaper in the second two or three hours (even an American newspaper), and towards the end of the day one can hardly help oneself, but one has begun to write. Indeed I think that if some benevolent government would only shut one up in the smoking car of a railway train and send one across the world one would really write two or three dozen lyrics in the year.

Letter to Lady Gregory, January 21, 1904, from St. Paul, Minnesota, after a trip to Toronto. *The Letters of W.B. Yeats* (1954), edited by Allan Wade.

I have been lecturing every night for a week, with long journeys in between, and today is Sunday and I am very tired. . . . I am at St. Catherine's, the guest of the hotel proprietor, and described last night the theatre of beauty and I think I puzzled the audience.

Even the Irish poet misspelled St. Catharines. Letter to Lady Gregory, February 13, 1914, quoted by Joseph Hone in *W.B. Yeats: 1865-1939* (1943).

I am thinking of tomorrow, and wondering . . . wondering if there is breakfast on the Boston train.

When Yeats visited Montreal, Stephen Leacock held a dinner party in his honour at the University Club. A guest, noting Yeats's withdrawn air, asked the poet his thoughts. From Yeats's reply, Leacock concluded that even poets must eat. Quoted by Stephen Leacock in "Thinking of Tomorrow," *Too Much College: or Education Eating Up Life* (1939).

## Yeats-Brown, Francis

"Why don't you write about your own experiences as a professional soldier, especially about those seven years served in India?"

Colonel John Bayne MacLean urged Francis Yeats-Brown, the British army officer, to turn to writing when he applied to the colonel for an editorial position on *Maclean's Magazine* in 1923. His successful biography *Lives of a Bengal Lancer* appeared in 1930. Quoted by Floyd S. Chalmers in *A Gentleman of the Press* (1969).

## Yevtushenko, Yevgeny
I say the best Canadian poet is Phil Esposito, and that is not a joke.

The Russian poet was quoted by John Fraser in *The Globe and Mail*, December 6, 1973.

## Yorke, Ritchie
The Americans could not have secured more thorough domination of the Canadian record market if they had deliberately planned it.

*Axes, Chops & Hot Licks: The Canadian Rock Music Scene* (1971).

## Young, Alan
My father put in a full and hard eight hour day at his job in the shipyard. When I was barely in my teens, he saw me open a pay envelope and take out three dollars for my first five-minute performance on radio. He said, "Son, you stick with this talking business. Lips don't sweat."

I don't like to disagree with my father but, thirty years later I must say, "Dad, they do! They *really* do!"

I was blessed with the necessity of having to act to make a living. Any mistakes along the way — and there were many — were carefully noted. I seldom made them again.

\*

There is always room at the top and plenty of room at the bottom. But it gets mighty crowded in the middle.

The Hollywood comedian Alan Young was born Angus Young in Britain in 1919 and raised in British Columbia. After much CBC work he left for American films and radio in 1946. *The Christian Science Monitor*, October 25, 1965.

## Young, Egerton Ryerson
They're thieving and treacherous; to drive these dogs successfully the driver must be able to swear in English, French and Indian.

*Stories from Indian Wigwams and Northern Camp Fires* (1893).

## Young, John H.
A gentleman should never lower the intellectual standard of his conversation in addressing ladies. Pay them the compliments of seeming to consider them capable of an equal understanding with gentlemen. You will, no doubt, be somewhat surprised to find in how many cases the supposition will be grounded on fact, and in the few instances where it is not, the ladies will be pleased rather than offended at the delicate compliment you pay them. When you "come down" to commonplace or small-talk with an intelligent lady, one of the two things is the consequence: she either recognizes the condescension and despises you, or else she accepts it as the highest intellectual effort of which you are capable, and rates you accordingly.

\*

Do not use the word "limb" for "leg." If legs are really improper, then let us on no account mention them. But having found it necessary to mention them, let us by all means give them their appropriate name.

\*

No lady should make use of any feminine substitutes for profanity. The woman who exclaims, "The Dickens," or "Mercy," or "Goodness" when she is annoyed or astonished, is vulgar in spirit.

\*

Tea or coffee should never be poured into a saucer to cool, but sipped from the cup. . . . If a person wishes to be served with more tea or coffee, he should place his spoon in his saucer. If he has had sufficient, let it remain in the cup.

*Our Deportment; Or the Manners, Conduct and Dress of the Most Refined Society* (1883). This book of etiquette was published in Paris, Ontario!

## Young, Neil

I want to do something where I know there's a chance of failing. I don't want next year to be a repeat of last year. I'm not going to put out stuff that comes from a bored mind.

> The singer-guitarist-composer was born in Toronto in 1945, the son of writer Scott Young.

## Young, Scott

As every suburban gardener among you knows, no grass roots grow in ivory towers.

> "The Problem of Stuffed Shirtism" (1957), *Empire Club of Canada: Addresses 1957-58* (1958).

A strange thing to me is to look back at hockey as it has affected me from my corner rink days. There is in hockey something that in more pretentious nations would be called a mystique—and this has always been part of me.

> *The Leafs I Knew* (1966).

## Young, Walter D.

Socialists belong to movements, capitalists support parties.

> *The Anatomy of a Party: The National CCF 1932-61* (1969).

## Younger, J.W.

The fact that developing nations must tailor their policies to big corporations is all to the good. It makes rather irresponsible governments more responsible.

> Secretary and general counsel to the Steel Company of Canada (STELCO), 1972.

# Z

## Zabotin, Nicolai

Now that the Americans have invented it, we must steal it!

*

The less you talk the more they give. You need only to learn to listen when they speak. They will tell you everything.

> Colonel Nicolai Zabotin was the military attaché to the Russian embassy in Ottawa when his cipher clerk Igor Gouzenko defected on September 5, 1945. The espionage agent's opinion of Canadian service officers was not high. Quoted by Igor Gouzenko in *This Was My Choice: Gouzenko's Story* (1948).

Alek handed over to us a platinum with 162 micrograms of Uranium 233 in the form of acid, contained in a thin lamina.

> Coded telegram sent to Moscow, July 9, 1945. It was signed "Grant," for Zabotin; "Alek" was identified by a royal commission as Dr. Allan Nunn May, a British scientist working in Canada. Mort Sahl, the Montreal-born nightclub entertainer, used to say, "If the Russians steal our atomic secrets, they'll be two years behind."

Yesterday our allies, today our neighbours, tomorrow our enemies!

> Zabotin toasting the Americans after securing their uranium samples. Quoted by Andy O'Brien in "My Friend—the Traitor," *My Friend, the Hangman: Dramatic Encounters in Sport, Crime and War* (1970). O'Brien, a sports reporter, had a hand in writing Igor Gouzenko's autobiography.

## Zacks, Samuel

We should expect the artist to reveal something that is original and unique and a private vision of the world.

Toronto millionaire collector, quoted by Kay Kritzwiser, *The Globe and Mail*, April 27, 1970.

## Zangwill, Israel

You cannot speak of such a great space of country as an entity. Neither will I presume to speak of Canada. Many years ago I crossed Niagara Falls and stopped half an hour here and I have not yet written a book about Canada.

\*

As regards Canada I had one or two notes which I cannot find. I have found Canada very hospitable and I was late today because a number of gentlemen were so amiable as not to tell me the hour was passing. Canada figures in several of my books and in *The Master*. The story begins in Nova Scotia. I have never been in Nova Scotia and people sometimes say, "How do you do it?" Well, how did Dante describe hell?

"Some American Experiences," January 28, 1924, *Addresses Delivered before the Canadian Club of Toronto: Season of 1923-24* (1924).

I was not aware that Canada was under Prohibition until two gentlemen offered me bottles of whiskey within fifteen minutes of my arrival here.

Toronto address delivered by the well-known Anglo-Jewish novelist, quoted by Hector Charlesworth in *More Candid Chronicles: Further Leaves from the Note Book of a Canadian Journalist* (1928).

## Zanuck, Darryl F.

He has an accent. So does everyone in Canada.

Comment of the film producer on the casting of the Danish actor Jean Hersholt as Dr. Dafoe in *The Country Doctor*, a film starring the Dionne Quintuplets released in 1936. Quoted by Mel Gussow in *Don't Say Yes Until I Finish Talking* (1971).

## Zavitz, C.A.

The Canadian people in rural life are noted for physical strength, mental power, and moral stability. Surely Canada has before her a bright future.

"Field Crops in Canada," *Handbook of Canada: Issued by the Local Committee on the Occasion of the Meeting of the British Association for the Advancement of Science at Toronto, August 1924* (1924).

I have visited many countries,
    Away beyond the sea,
But this great and prosperous Canada
    Is good enough for me.

"Canadian Agriculture as Applied to Wheat Growing," February 15, 1909, *Addresses Delivered before the Canadian Club of Toronto: Season of 1908-1909* (1909). Zavitz taught at the Ontario Agricultural College in Guelph.

## Zend, Robert

Being a philosopher, I have a problem for every solution.

\*

No matter how rich you are, you cannot use your two bathrooms at the same time.

\*

People have one thing in common: they are all different.

\*

Classless society is a dream of people with no class.

Happiness is when the toothache stops.

\*

In wakefulness we react to events with emotions; in dream we react to emotions with events.

\*

Einstein's truth is relative: there will be a Zweinstein.

\*

Marriage: love gone—woman stays.

\*

I would rather have a hundred smug friends than one friend insecure: every insecure person is a potential Hitler or Stalin.

\*

An editor is blessed with the talent of others.

\*

The opposite of a male is a husband.

\*

I am willing to do anything for money, even work.

\*

There are too many people, and too few human beings.

Robert Zend is the Hungarian-born, Toronto-based author of *From Zero to One* (1973).

### Ziegfeld, Florenz

Go back to Canada and forget the stage.

Advice to Norma Shearer after she auditioned for the Broadway showman just after World War I. The Montreal-born star never did appear on the stage, but after marrying Irving Thalberg of MGM in the 1920s, her film career blossomed. Quoted by Bob Thomas in *Thalberg: Life and Legend* (1969). See also Norma Shearer.

### Zolf, Larry

He looked on Canada as a place where Americans sent people they didn't really want to have *now* but might take in later on, provided that while here they were always on good behaviour. In a sense, he regarded Canada as America's Australia —a temporary penal colony for temporary undesirables. [On his Russian father]

\*

Let the country continue to be a land of unAmerican activities. Boil me no melting pots and dream me no dreams. Worry not, rumour has it that God is Dead. If so, he can't bless America.

"Boil Me No Melting Pots, Dream Me No Dreams" in *The New Romans: Candid Canadian Opinions of the U.S.* (1968), edited by Al Purdy. See also Pierre Elliott Trudeau.

The Humpty Dumpty Canadian federal state had had a slight fall, but all the Trudeau horsemen had put it together again. Henceforth, Canada would be one nation-state, not "two nations warring within the bosom of a single state." The Trudeau Philosopher-Kingdom would be peaceable, not piecemeal. One and indivisible, bilingual and multicultural.

*Dance of the Dialectic: How Pierre Trudeau Went from Philosopher-King to Incorruptible Robespierre to Philosopher-Queen Marie Antoinette to Canada's Generalissimo Ky and Then to Mackenzie King and Even Better* (1973).

### Zolar

If you dream of Canada: You will have good business.

If you dream of seeing Canada on the map: You will have a vigorous mind.

If you dream of going to Canada from abroad: You have many loyal friends.

If you dream of going abroad from Canada: Happiness is assured.

Adapted from *Zolar's Encyclopaedia and Dictionary of Dreams* (1963).

The use of this index is discussed in the Preface. The letter *a* or *b* after the page number indicates the left- or right-hand column.

# A

*Aberhart, William
social credit to Alberta, 83b
only one first, 158a
*Abortion
if men could get pregnant, 518a
*Abraham, Plains of
See Plains of Abraham.
*Abyssinia
Canada ranks with, 88a
*Acadians
decision to expel, 335b
Evangeline, tale of Acadie, 360a
no publicity in France, 432b
marched to Cape Breton, 554b
expulsion of the, 637b
*Accent
a mid-Atlantic, 10a
good French no asset, 43a
the soft Canadian, 77b
lost everything except, 192a
my Canadian M's, 476a
not flow with English, 491b
everyone has an, 649a
*Accomplished
precedent, sir, is fact, 67a
leadership not in what, 475b
*Accomplishment
greatest joy of life, 34a
you can accomplish any, 201a
things I prevented, 307a
someone willing to fight, 334a
*Achievement
I can't do anything, 34a
Klondike experience taught, 52a
admit ability when there's, 178b
life is redeemed by, 233a
never realize the best, 328a
commonplace people do, 338b
do most, dream most, 342a
you lose a little sleep, 374b
missed it again, 394a
crown of his life, 450b
some deals done as well, 466a
live for 500 years, 611a
*Achilles
bound like the shield of, 384a
*Acquisition
Canada matter of marching, 285b
greed is on increase, 379b
of Canada first ambition, 385b
of Canada not an object, 426a
of that country is not, 625a
*Acres
a few a. of snow, 616b
15,000 a. of ice, 617a

*Acting
psychology-probing Method, 122b
pretending led me into, 131b
love a. but not starving, 361a
three-quarters is listening, 495a
not being emotional, 495a
*Action
leading to concerted, 64a
human a. of yesterday, 137a
poetry of a. exists, 161a
travels are dreams in, 167a
in preventing bad, 307b
hockey is all, 456b
man of a. or the poet, 515a
energies are so absorbed, 568a
*Acton, Lord
many people quote, 40b
*Actors
don't have husbands, 8a
every a. has to move, 61b
beautiful nor, 189a
Canadians a race of, 257a
old a. never die, 315a
like a method, 327a
playing one character, 448a
is never established, 479b
lawyers should study, 504a
no future in Canada, 506a
never retire, children, 536b
*Adam
in the will of, 202b
where A. wore the fig, 213b
*Administration
nothing impossible, 269b
*Adult
gulf between child, 355b
child becomes an, 451a
will reform society, 522a
*Adventure
the anvil of high, 91b
that is the great, 164a
arresting a. in spirit, 189a
life is a great, 216a
that life is an, 405a
have a gift for them, 428a
*Adventurers
governor and company of, 107b
*Advertisement
no English need apply, 248b
for sale one coffin, 308a
art a bad a. for country, 467b
no English need apply, 563b
editorial content is, 584b
*Advertising
made in Canada, 61a
baths 50 cents, 70b
decline to sell M.P.s, 149b
pressure comes from, 193a
tell your story to public, 173a
on the American pattern, 183b
religious jingles, 204b
slogan for products, 223b
my stakes are in, 223b
space at bottom prices, 293b

salesmanship in print, 300a
reason why concept, 300a
arresting intelligence, 339a
shop at Honest Ed's, 422a
broadcasting as auxiliary, 471a
instigation to revolution, 545a
deceive with truth, 560b
made in Canada better, 566a
without it's Russia, 566b
radio a billboard, 588a
signs were beautiful, 591a
*Advice
friend helps, 179b
give one bit, 307b
political prisoners, 346b
*Advocacy
events stronger than, 385b
*Affection
without fear, favour, 18a
ceremonies cool, 244a
Ontario English better, 341b
*Affluence
thing I dread is, 34a
private a., public, 211a
the affluent society, 211a
*Afraid
I am a. of the worst, 513b
*Africa
a woman's like, 62b
for a leper colony, 304a
theory of black king, 327a
Eskimos instruct Congo, 342b
living in civilized Congo, 426a
horns in, 564a
Indian, Australian, 579b
do that everyday, 343b
[See also Union of South Africa.]
*Age
I am not old, 8a
not interested in, 26a
after seventy velvet, 35a
when I was 85, 39b
now I'm 60, 40a
a woman interested at 84, 41a
get it in your, 58a
roundness a function of, 58a
as good as new, 80a
don't change as you, 114a
asking a woman her, 114b
burdened with young fogeys, 140a
a kindly old man, 148b
old enough to know better, 178b
when one is getting, 179a
old enough to gratify, 179a
no, only 59, 203b
think young ones fools, 245b
now we are gray, 288b
reached the age of 66, 319a
follow my white plume, 330b
better than being dead, 341a
front line of life, 341b
it's better farther on, 355a
amidst the infirmities, 373b
oldest man, 402b
not a quitter at 80, 437a

useless men above 60, 457b
old enough to die, 473b
lost time I was born, 478a
get defeated in election, 520b
Canada older than U.S., 587a
at 58 not old, 595b
    *Ages
I brought the a. home, 134b
    *Aggression
victim not prepare menu, 316b
    *Agriculture
from plant's point of view, 137b
chief industry not, 238b
fields in Soviet Union, 315a
no cultivating beaver, 343a
National Policy and, 378a
happens to be cultivated, 574b
    *Aid
all a. short of help, 636b
    *Ain't
hit 'em where they, 297b
    *Air
temporary use of, 7a
have given away, 25a
country of the larger, 83b
wholesome in Nfld., 252b
    *Air Canada
my enterprise, 269a
    *Air Force
5BX Plan, 455b
    *Airplane
See Aviation.
    *Aivilik
the A. say simply, 99b
    *Akhoond
The A. is dead, 323b
    *Alabama
voluntary integration, 619a
    *Alaska
Boundary Award, 7a
let his igloo to friends, 17b
or A. Russians, 198a
Labrador another, 258b
longest frontier, 402b
appoint commissioners, 510a
    *Albania
love in, 120b
    *Alberta
feed, clothe, shelter, 1b
eyes of world on, 2a
I'm leaving sunny, 13b
next year country, 14b
A. land, A. land, 24b
so farewell to, 24b
to the A. Highland, 71b
had never heard of, 75b
a social credit to, 83b
a 4,000-acre ranch, 177b
I come from, 186a
next year country, 208b
kindle a world-wide torch, 289b
bow to no one, 316a
shall it be, 361b
land of second chance, 461b
elections renewed faith, 481b
decent guys from, 539b
come to A. and go, 542b
    *Alcohol
prohibit use of, 338a
breathe smells of water, 381b

    *Alderville
family lives at, 569b
    *Alexander the Great
wept, what would Canadian,
    623b
    *Alger, Horatio
never a Canadian hero, 356a
    *Algoma
what's A., vegetable, 137b
    *Algonquins
they have no libraries, 319b
    *Alice in Wonderland
Alicia in Terra Mirabili, 100b
sooner have written, 337b
    *Alienation
a day of mental, 502a
    *Aliens
don't like the word, 232a
no a. need apply, 369a
    *Alive
privilege to be, 48a
    *All
before a. I am a, 101b
a.-and-a-half, 400a
    *All Canadian
nothing more absurd, 599a
    *Allan, Andrew
the great times of, 232a
learned to act from, 400a
    *Allegiance
the oath of, 20b
to give or to refuse, 82a
a nation founded on, 436a
    *Alleluia
either a. or anguish, 572b
    *Alley
can't lick 'em in the, 555a
    *Allies
necessity made us, 300b
loyal does not spy, 559a
    *Almighty
nephew of the, 79a
    *Alouette
gentille A., 23a
    *Always
they a. get their man, 18b
get their man, 254a
    *Amalgamation
competition ever, 48b
    *Amazons
of the great God, 345b
    *Ambition
go farther than, 125a
French have no, 462b
setting a limit, 499b
    *America
A.'s attic, an empty room, 7b
found but a grave, 12a
a woman's like, 62b
belongs to Catholic, 68a
like A. businessman, 78a
map of continent of, 80b
is before us, 164a
God bless, but, 178a
saved us the fate, 209a
whole of French, 237a
owes much to Louis XIV, 464a
A.'s sweetheart, 476a
where else but in, 533a
where A., the Indies, 536a

white nigger of, 609b
like reading a book, 619b
God can't bless, 650b
    *American
ravaged by imperialism, 95a
party strong, 98b
who reads an A. book, 106a
speak French and breathe, 107a
money in industries, 110a
could have enjoyed, 123a
any other word than, 147a
in Canada be a better, 150b
party at work, 183a
more respect in London, 187a
jokes about the, 193b
disaster of history, 199b
Canada taught me how, 205b
pro-Canadian not anti-A., 275b
use A. for conversation, 341b
my A. gift of invention, 346b
I am not anti-A., 369b
statesman covets Canada, 379b
borrowing energy from, 384a
influences on Canadian, 419b
yes, I am a Canadian, 468b
that Canada is, 542b
of un-A. activities, 650a
    *American Revolution
great historical disaster, 199b
in the war of, 455b
    *Americanism
immense sea of saxonizing, 68a
is a reality, 124a
you may perhaps, 181a
find tiresome anti-A., 499a
    *Americans
take Canada for granted, 2a
spacemen up before the, 43a
French as the A. are, 67b
benevolently ignorant, 73a
rape of our country by, 75b
all the faults of the, 78a
Canadians just like, 265a
interested in expansion, 316b
return to virtues, 421b
bought my father's grave, 511b
anyone raced to help, 545b
friends whether we like, 584a
not only neighbours, 600a
    *Amherst
Trotsky held in, 594a
    *Amiens
Vimy Ridge followed by, 555a
    *Amusements
are here necessary, 77a
    *Anarchism
order covers elements, 181a
noted a. Emma Goldman, 222a
quick to exploit, 324b
    *Ancestors
none of my a. stole, 40a
virtues inherited from, 162a
ideal from my illiterate, 166b
not just one or two, 182a
process by which gods, 221b
    *Ancien
régime, 572a
    *Andy Hardy
I was A.H.'s girl friend, 516a

*Anerca
to make poetry, 99b
*Angels
wings of an, 259a
hark the herald, 305a
the sense of, 313b
make a spectacle to, 319b
if I had the wings, 326b
no doubt are socialists, 339b
socialistic commonwealth, 342a
would debauch a, 376b
take turns being, 400a
experience dreaming of, 508a
*Anger
even a. is reaction, 41b
an ecstacy in, 57a
when man wrong 244b
*Anglican
you might hit an, 13a
class distinction, 157a
you will never, 181a
Catholic and A. hold, 222a
by adoption, 303b
right in the A. church, 632a
*Anglo-Americans
Canadians the true, 432b
*Anglo-French
a free Confederacy, 67b
*Anglo-Saxon
dictatorial section of, 181a
encircling A.-S. sea, 236b
ordained to be leader, 392a
*Anglostocracy
first commandment of, 147b
*Anguish
written in French, 571b
alleluia or, 572b
*Angularity
the ideal of, 58a
*Animal
man is a recording, 226b
responsibility for, 234a
flee from a path, 268a
occupied only by, 357b
medicine and man from, 458b
wild things no rights, 534b
*Anna
and the King of Siam, 347b
*Annapolis Royal
A. must be defended, 446b
*Anne of Green Gables
by mistake a girl sent, 428a
*Annexation
territory to this Union, 45a
peaceably if possible, 48a
acquire entire fur trade, 115b
destiny of Canada and, 154b
Dominion to P.E.I., 165b
sleepy Canada ripe for, 183b
resented is not, 208a
to the mother country, 271b
a matter of marching, 285b
of French Canada, 346b
Canada has hesitated, 535a
obsessed by American, 607a
*Annie
Tugboat Annie, 489a
*Anonymous
anonymous section, 9a
*Anse au Foulon

See Wolfe's Cove.
*Answer
mouths of cannon, 206b
when you get around, 269a
Christianity has, 303b
*Anthem
God Save the Queen, 22b
even wrote a national, 366b
humming the national, 394b
O Canada, terre de nos, 514a
O Canada, our home and, 626a
*Anthropology
the male bond, 588b
*Anti-Semitism
anti-Jewish Christian, 187a
*Anticipation
we are rich in, 283b
*Antigonish Movement
no one can walk on him, 590b
*Antiquity
deep reverence for, 368a
*Anxiety
empire's disintegrate, 434a
*Apple
Canada like an, 59a
des vraies Canada, 432b
Canada fall like ripe, 440b
you'll find a rotten, 492a
shade of the old a. tree, 634a
*Apply
no Englishmen need, 9b
no English need, 248b
no aliens need, 369a
no English need, 563b
*Appointment
an a. with destiny, 153b
*Apprehended
insurrection real or, 19b
that a. insurrection, 599a
*April
snow is abominable, 428b
*Arabian
deserts of soul in, 183a
night's entertainment, 459a
horse is to the, 641b
*Arbitrary
measures never advise, 294b
*Archaelogy
Peking Man, 58a
labours hand in hand, 635b
*Architecture
light over an elevator, 27b
bad food and bad, 123a
real fascination lies, 184b
no Parthenons, 227a
richness, variety, 235b
a form of expression, 281b
most tasteless, vulgar, 283a
somewhat gothic, 284a
important religious, 304a
English, American, 406b
backdrop for activity, 432b
Habitat in tradition, 518b
spot where Toronto fell, 644b
no monuments calling 385b
a Gothic pile, 552a
designed by Supreme, 567a
*Archives
gift of one generation, 158a

the a. of universe, 512a
*Arctic
variable imponderable, 14b
express the sum total, 37b
military in the, 92b
bred strange conceits, 141b
fought their way to, 150b
Meta Incognita, 181b
great elements hold, 193a
call of the wild, 222a
from the A. islands, 241a
sleep for six months, 259a
ah, the cold is, 277b
permission from Washington,
    281a
best defence is, 307b
blood be the price of, 309b
all the way around, 325b
some record was left, 369b
land of the great white, 444a
business under horizon, 446b
Indian and polar worlds, 485b
Manhattan through waters, 493a
sleeps no longer, 508b
the A. trails have their, 534b
the friendly, 559b
no prime minister exiled, 560b
dusky husky maiden, 571b
to sing there, 630b
[See also North.]
*Arctic Circle
north to the, 582b
*Arctic Ocean
arguments about life, 560b
fort on shore of, 614a
*Arden, Elizabeth
and one Miss, 106a
*Argentine
another heading was, 160b
*Argument
think it, say it, 442a
*Aristocracy
of virtue and talent, 385b
of wealth, 429a
*Aristotle
man a political animal, 83a
*Arliss, George
play Disraeli, 342b
*Arll
beautiful sea poem, 409b
the piper of, 527a
*Armentières
Mademoiselle from, 496b
*Armistice Day
In Flanders Fields, 373a
*Arms
sleep no more except, 384b
to a., to, 613a
*Army
military in Arctic, 92b
militia can do, 99b
each for all, 130b
my trust in Corps, 135a
think not of the, 135b
a non-Israeli, 142b
at 14 enlist, 159a
divide First Division, 274a
dagger pointed at Berlin, 399b
thousand could stop, 429a
duty to fighting men, 489b

poor for democracy, 601b
*Arnold, Benedict
fly so save his bacon, 21a
reputation enhanced, 620b
consider as marching, 622a
*Arpents
quelques a. de neige, 37a
quelques a. de neige, 616b
*Art
artistic things, 4b
unlearn what learned, 29b
never collect by ear, 33a
vital a. of nation, 34b
buy Old Masters, 41a
pay any price, 51a
children not draw, 61b
of wilderness lakes, 62a
great a. is fostered, 80a
will always disturb, 80b
and a 6B pencil, 88b
less that a. is long, 98b
no word meaning, 99b
only a. avails, 99b
the term creative, 100a
making obvious obvious, 106a
anti-death league, 123a
my aim as artist, 123b
of northern peoples, 123b
in old world voices, 127b
pictures of its own, 139a
positive test of, 142b
pet aversion modern, 197b
white ties and, 200a
dream for awakened, 207a
the hot mush school, 210a
lies in that more, 213a
objects saved solely, 227a
for meaning turn to, 229b
painting not in mainstream,
   231b
not mirror but hammer, 234b
beginning, infinitude, 238a
stimulus to perception, 250a
binds us together, 250a
no Eskimo word for, 268a
make best frames in, 281a
without a country, 282a
immense vitality, 285a
not good, expensive, 285a
better break stones, 296a
woman artist, 303a
Duchamp and Jackson, 313a
no a., no literature, 320b
feeling of generations, 346a
state of post-conscious, 351a
on par with Greece, 351a
awareness, alertness, 356b
choke with brushes, 361a
generalizes while science, 368a
going to get anywhere, 369b
subjective excluded from, 369b
tradition not essential, 372b
support native, 375a
lives in decorative, 375a
can get away with, 396b
entire world a work, 396b
specialist artefacts, 397a
planet a corporate, 397a
we have no, we do, 397b
automatisme, 407a

always be mystery, 417b
adventures in shape, 420b
capacity for aesthetic, 421a
control superb moments, 423a
if it isn't alive, 423a
Raphael a signpainter, 429a
almost criminally fine, 433a
nudes not energetic, 434b
legends could teach, 435b
demanding a great, 446a
printmakers, carvers, 456b
medicine, science, 458b
painter a fisherman, 471b
with great people, 477a
war put us in, 479a
joyfully 10 caribou, 480b
pain and pleasure, 491a
never finished, 492a
no configuration, 503a
drew deer perfectly, 536b
and life enjoyed, 556a
flower not forced, 568a
they will know, 586a
work is what I think, 588b
paintings speak, 591a
collage is medium, 591a
you paint a person, 612a
go inside them, 615b
affirm existence of, 618a
roots in native land, 623b
death of Wolfe, 628a
private vision, 649a
man a. and woman, 632a
plead the cause of, 632b
nightmare from which, 209a
*Arthur, King
in the days of, 201a
that true north, 580b
*Arthur Ellis
official executioner, 182b
*Artist
function to disturb, 54a
creative function, 57b
lives in Toronto, 78b
perceptual window, 105a
first an explorer, 195a
keeps everyone awake, 214a
make truth many, 234b
particular environment, 240b
more than two eyes, 244b
speak in idiom, 285b
unexplored territory, 356a
high calling of, 357b
what and how are, 383a
democracy fatal to, 401a
not produce great, 522b
greatest asset to an, 535b
shall be intellectual, 550a
sways on tightrope, 590b
*Artists
only road of modern, 164b
live apocalypse, 207a
no. a. as Canadians, 226a
to Europe to paint, 281a
Canada Council and, 303b
great survivors, 638b
*Arts
elegant unknown, 77a
state should assist, 115b
poets, painters, 117a

whenever I hear word, 171b
subsidy, raise, spread, 172b
no judgment a. perish, 188a
becoming wealthy, 202b
reveal real society, 208a
divine discontent, 250a
are DEW lines, 297a
at roots of nation, 411a
councils, apple, 602b
*Arvida
Aluminum Company, 188b
*Ascendant
lords of a. at Montreal, 280b
*Ashburton-Webster Treaty
neither lost nor given, 633b
*Asia
a woman's like, 62b
fabrics, products, 228b
difficult to immigrate, 304b
*Assimilation
we may not, 328a
wheat fields, symphonies, 367b
*Assiniboia
renamed Alberta, 361b
*Assiniboine River
justice on banks of, 60a
English settler on, 142b
see the winding, 384b
*Astor, Lady
Jew from Cape Breton, 120b
not merely an, 446a
*Astrology
particular conjunction, 337a
*Astronomy
compassed the world, 485b
*Athabasca
an Eskimo in, 17b
the A. trail, 161a
never support large, 344a
lives on Lake A. or, 348b
*Atheism
Haine haint, 242b
no more be proved, 506b
*Athens
a new A. rising, 77a
*Athletics
Canada's outstanding, 258a
contributes to, 302a
track and swimming, 452a
*Atkinson, Joseph E.
resent called old, 163a
what do you intend, 173b
*Atlantic
North A. Triangle, 10a
mid-A. accent, 10a
*Atlantic Ocean
wild billows of, 74b
no A. seaboard, 208b
on its eastern side, 319a
mournful, misty, 360a
unite the Pacific, 367b
a new nationality, 425a
if known across, 604a
Irish mystics adrift, 628b
*Atlantic Provinces
little ports of, 365a
*Atmospheric
radio an a. billboard, 588a
*Atomic

Mounties vs. invaders, 4a
secret of bomb, 278a
Canadian finger on catch, 469a
not yet developed, 636b
Americans invented, 648a
[See also Nuclear.]
　*Audiences*
hurl themselves, 239a
have an a. in mind, 239a
have been my downfall, 354b
there is where you, 374a
requires to be made, 422b
I puzzled the, 646b
　*Aurora*
the A. speech, 60a
　*Australia*
primer of A. literature, 27a
a woman's like, 62b
expect me to buy farm, 177b
one by from, 195a
from the fate of, 209a
the other foot in, 215b
black sheep exported, 296b
rhyme is of horse, 354b
alliance of Britain, 375b
British Columbia and, 378a
language spoken by, 466a
starfish off reef, 570a
Canadian, A., African, 579b
become people like, 607a
poets of Canada and, 624a
Canada as America's, 650a
as we painted them, 633a
Van Diemen's Land, 640a
　*Austria*
equal in extent to, 81a
late Emperor of, 83b
paid for sin, 313b
　*Author*
tells his story, 139b
when Canadian produces, 305a
can boast three, 498b
without new a. springing, 528a
Shaw said Canada had, 568a
　*Authority*
violence upheld by, 163b
freedom torn from, 193a
to disobedience, 244b
temptation of power, 471b
anything you can, 474a
all ridiculous, 533b
as obedience, 601a
　*Automata*
if we were toy, 64b
　*Automation*
continue in business, 262a
　*Automatisme*
aesthetic term, 407a
　*Automobile*
Canadian a. industry, 81a
buying a used, 114b
first bicycle, then, 156a
mobile Walden Pond, 374a
McLaughlin carriage, 393b
　*Autonomy*
maintenance of cultural, 211a
unity on provincial, 514b
transformed Empire, 554b
　*Autumn*
throughout the a. lands, 95b

most lovely colours, 164b
landscape flamed red, 281a
for joyous production, 320b
out for a late walk, 341a
flaming a. maples, 365a
[See also Fall.]
　*Avalonia*
pro patria et, 94a
　*Avenir*
notre maitre, l', 221a
　*Average*
just an a. Canadian, 153b
　*Aviation*
solitary flights, 36b
first man in air, 44b
Americans can fly, 49b
air age faces man, 57b
God speed you, 57b
hours of boredom, 62b
war in the air, 79a
airplane trip, 111a
Howard Hughes taught, 143a
title of bush pilot, 150b
women get into planes, 172a
how thunder bird stay, 182b
king of pathfinders, 190b
boor flies to Europe, 222a
Avro Arrow, 223b
no part in defence, 274a
history of North before, 298a
flying over Canada saw, 315a
hanging crepe at Malton, 390a
slipped the surly bonds, 403a
never get it off, 442a
The Norseman, 450a
Lester no name for, 468a
to invent airplane, 508a
as long as sex, 597a
[See also Flying.]
　*Avon River*
flow with accents, 491b
　*Awake*
my country, the hour, 504a
　*Awe*
wonder and a. of, 356b
　*Aye*
[See Ready, Aye, Ready.]
　*Ayorama*
that's destiny, 118b


# B


　*Baby*
everything for the, 79b
carols are sung, 116a
they kiss him, 159b
Olympics have deficit, 162a
mothers weaned as, 244a
bonus, allowance, 447b
immigrant not as good, 475a
the b. is fine, 600b
　*Babylon*
-on-the-Humber, 388b
　*Bacall, Lauren*
if you wanted, 499a
　*Bachelors*
don't understand women, 323a
　*Backwoods*

Canada is a vast, 62a
　*Bacon, Francis*
diet of B. and Shakespeare, 641a
　*Badly*
speak English but, 317b
　*Baffin Island*
here white falcons, 42b
took possession of, 51b
down the coast of, 325a
being here the same, 353a
in passing, 440a
　*Bagdad*
polygamy in Toronto, 132a
　*Bahá'í Faith*
'Abdu'l-Bahá, la
　*Bahamian*
I'm a, 576b
　*Balconies*
the more the better, 216a
　*Baldness*
why so many, 158b
　*Baldwin, F. W. (Casey)*
man into the air, 44b
　*Balfour, Arthur*
the B. Declaration, 19b
had explained it, 187a
　*Balinese*
have no art, 397b
　*Ballet*
songs lead to, 34b
mediocrity easiest, 82a
vision makes strong, 110b
going to dance, 252b
do a little more, 374b
daughters to the, 445a
quality, quality, 454b
part of me die, 579b
as Russians hockey, 512b
heart on shoulders, 535b
　*Ballot*
woman asks not, 116a
corrupt way of, 565b
holding my nose, 607b
　*Baltic*
Europe tilted, 528b
　*Baneful domination*
of mother country, 275a
　*Banff*
National Park signs, 13b
　*Bank*
when I go into, 337a
　*Bank of Canada*
vote in favour, 128b
governor is limited, 591a
　*Bankruptcy*
spectre, not of rose, 171b
let creditors take, 180a
　*Banks*
of Newfoundland, 47a
Montreal consists of, 77b
profession robbing, 296b
when I go into a, 337a
a changed man, 516 b
　*Banting, Sir Frederick*
Joe—three dead, 319b
　*Baptiste, Jean*
Jean Baptiste, 51b
　*Bardot, Brigitte*
if Canada so is, 398b

*Bargaining
labour, collective, 155b
ethics, collective, 463b
*Bark
every dog in Quebec, 379a
*Barr, Robert
on booze than books, 568a
*Barrens, The
to the B. floor, 83b
rooms for me in, 160a
land of feast and famine, 266b
intellectual conditions, 320b
the B. ground must be, 521b
*Baseball
hit 'em where they ain't, 297b
trip over polar bears, 562a
*Basketball
tribute from inventor, 443a
*Bastard
term of endearment, 224a
eastern b. is brother, 571b
*Bateau Harbour
in Labrador, 325a
*Batoch
defeated Indians at, 481b
*Battle
how goes the, 639b
*Battleford
meet me at b. on, 419a
give firearms up, 482a
*Bay, The
See Hudson's Bay Company.
*Bay of Fundy
twenty-foot tidal, 485a
*Beamsville
Fred C. Dobbs is, 504a
*Bear
home b. rugs, 5b
vast backwoods, 62a
outgrown b. which, 299a
less dangerous to men, 408b
Nanook, 443b
to hunt the great, 448b
trip over polar, 562a
*Beat
can't beat 'em on ice, 555a
*Beatles
send the B. to Toronto, 160a
*Beats
John A. b. the devil, 265b
John A. b. the, 378b
*Beauceville
lives of our people, 124a
*Beauharnois
power contributions, 48b
*Beauport
always recall Quebec, 520b
*Beautiful
the b. province, 15a
how b. the body, 54b
nature withal so, 83b
rugged grandeur, 429b
no country as, 546a
country in the world, 567a
all people are, 612a
Joe my name is, 525a
*Beauty
a flower, 16a
new b. in its face, 93b
walks unconscious, 165a

girl has a pretty, 179b
does not flaunt its, 210b
things in proper order, 234b
bird seldom sings, 244b
ask an Indian what, 254b
death a name for, 336a
not to keep alive, 357b
what makes adrenalin, 446b
nothing wrong thinking, 451b
alone is bountiful, 488b
the b. of heaven, 521b
I need imperfections, 540a
the b. of strength, 550
*Beaver
and a maple leaf, 62a
good national symbol, 92a
a b. proper, 107a
not found in Tiber, 107b
emblems, b., maple, 142a
b.'s up, 187b
beloved of French, 343a
does everything well, 345a
I shall dream of, 407a
looking for sea of, 413b
are gone forever, 471a
land of b. work, 476a
most respected, 523a
grand bone of, 544b
been well damned, 568a
two races, man and, 582b
removes testicles, 630a
*Beaver Dam
came to me at, 194a
in the neighbourhood, 531a
*Beaverbrook, Lord
will be only one, 4b
is at his very best, 113a
personality cult in N.B., 439a
quite a somebody, 576a
if Max gets to heaven, 628a
*Bed
no one gets, out, 9b
heroes not die in, 82b
not thinking of, 600b
*Bedrooms
States has no place in, 558a
state in b. of nation, 595a
*Beer
do you drink, 54b
Moose Head Ale, 69b
all the b. they want, 97b
forty years without, 151b
we won't hurry out, 223b
somebody give me a, 261b
Canadian Ace, 318b
merely drink whisky, 338a
bought 8 bu. of barley, 424a
betting, b. and bingo, 442a
splendidly real, 640b
*Before
old Frenchman's done it, 83b
all I am a Canadian, 101b
*Begging
bad in Ottawa, 359a
*Behan, Brendan
late Gilbert Harding, 249a
*Belasco, David
what's your name, 476a
*Belfast

like B. after Dublin, 431b
*Belgium
Montreal between B. and, 191b
*Belief
world's b. in living, 57b
only ones left who, 100a
I b. in probably, 190b
safer than b. too little, 245a
Canada's dominance, 333a
*Believe
explain nothing, 29a
I b. in parliament, 165b
impossibility of anything, 284b
most, doubts everything, 303b
in it all, 341a
force one to b. any, 472a
it or not, 503a
*Bell, Max
Thomson or merchant, 435b
*Bell Sir Raymond
wear the Maple Leaf, 213b
*Bell, Thomas M.
this is black Friday, 39a
*Belle
la b. province, 15a
*Belleville
county north of, 486a
*Belongs
20th century b. to, 331b
Canada to the U.S., 333b
*Bennett, Arnold
ask if he, 40b
*Bennett, R.B.
tide in affairs of men, 76b
trouble my friend, 150a
premier of Hottentot, 186a
God in speech of, 259b
send for B. on Bluff, 450a
between B. and Stalin, 452a
*Bennett, W.A.C.
premier called me, 36a
walk a straight line, 292a
*Benson, Edgar
dedicated to poverty, 558a
*Beothuck
are called Red, 102b
Mary March, 405b
*Berceau
la revanche du, 447b
*Bering Strait
we passed through, 325b
*Berlin
or shamlike, 77b
less worried about Wall, 596b
*Bernhardt, Sarah
Canada semi-barbarous, 252a
no poets, no poetry, 568a
yellow ugly dress, 633a
*Bests
God has many, 305a
God has many, 643b
*Bethune, Norman
kind of Communist we, 5b
Chinese visit birth, 268b
not died in China, 522b
mobile operating unit, 603a
new China never forget, 646a
*Biafra
where's, 598a
*Bible

we land, they, 216b
birds fluttered to me, 313b
translating Eskimo, 247a
two Gideon Bibles, 416a
in scripture-astrolabe, 485b
promised land of our, 491b
literature, Shakespeare, 492a
wiser but weaker, 628b
 *Bible Bill
See William Aberhart.
 *Biculturalism
advantages of living, 528b
 *Bidwell, Barnabas
the law, never mind, 566a
 *Bidwell, Marshall Spring
and glorious minority, 55a
and glorious minority, 253b
 *Biggar
New York is big, 13a
 *Bilingual
telephone operators, 46b
the more we become, 106b
fortunately figures are, 200a
a truly b. culture, 288b
my passport, not heart, 615b
one and indivisible, 650b
 *Bilingualism
question is not, 81b
unilingualism narrow, 348b
multilingual brain, 472a
practise telepathy, 487b
way to speak to father, 519b
if it's Tuesday it's, 564b
more expensive but richer, 595a
qu'on lis in English, 599a
forgot to speak French, 611b
 *Billboard
radio an atmospheric, 588a
 *Binks, Sarah
sweet songstress of Sask., 261a
 *Bird
every man favourite, 178b
in a cage of bone, 213a
beautiful seldom sing, 244b
mocking has no voice, 245a
national, grouse, 297b
in hand is, 364a
starling a national, 545b
 *Birds
pigs very unlikely, 10b
fly over border, 174a
3,000 honkers, 198a
spread Miner's fame, 239a
cuckoos never, 290b
Iroquois take flight, 319b
understanding is easy, 421b
most of us are not, 430a
we are not, 501b
 *Birmingham
not squalid like, 77b
 *Birney, Earle
20th century belongs, 334a
 *Bishops
old priests not best, 128a
eat out of my hand, 170a
 *Bison
prairies home of, 247b
 *Bite
mad is he, then, 215b

others of generals, 638b
 *Black
coloured men free, 21b
not cut a b. man's hair, 119b
to purchase negro girl, 131b
coloured people live, 163a
imagine waking up, 233a
white man creates negro, 397a
in b. and writing, 492b
dark days of slavery, 622a
[See also Slavery.]
 *Black Donnellys
killers by their side, 124b
 *Black flies
and the b.f., little, 256b
 *Black Friday
this is b.F., boy, 39a
this is b.F., boy, 46a
 *Black king
British control the, 327a
 *Blackbeard
the Pirate, 578a
 *Blackfoot
Cree and B. tradition, 311a
Treaty, I will sign, 132b
 *Blank cheque
ask parliament for, 306b
 *Blast
a way into markets, 48b
into markets, 259b
 *Bleeding
forget your b. heart, 302b
lot of b. hearts, 598a
 *Bless
God. b. America but, 178a
and Heaven, 439a
 *Blindness
open society's eyes, 31b
half of us are, 457a
 *Blood
not b. but ink, 83a
shed may b. here, 155b
shall be redeemed by, 262b
be price of Arctic, 309b
not a drop, thrill, 319a
never see white, 570b
sponge for France, 617a
 *Blue
hills of old Toronto, 63b
a good standing colour, 375b
hills of old Toronto, 431b
 *Blue Nose
land of the, 51b
Nova Scotian sobriquet, 244a
wood still growing, 620a
 *B.N.A. Act
See British North American Act.
 *Boat Song, Canadian
exiles from fathers' land, 423b
rapids are near and day, 431a
 *Boer War
See War, Boer.
 *Bogart, Humphrey
you had to be American, 499a
 *Bois-Brûlés
sing the glory of, 188b
 *Bold
come all you b. Canadians, 21a
 *Bolters
the seven, 69b

 *Bomb
mad bomber of Parliament, 108a
only way to set fire, 114a
goodbye till 1967, 273a
did it for kicks, 317a
 *Bonaparte, Napoleon
Napoleon would have sold, 67b
the drowning of, 188a
 *Bonavista
from B. to Vancouver, 241a
 *Bond, James
tricks learned in Oshawa, 196b
is Superman legend, 521b
 *Bond
the male, 588b
 *Bonne Entente
the b.e., 10a
expression of, 410b
 *Bonnie Prince Charlie
preserver of, 374b
 *Book
poorest market in world, 36a
this b. belong to, 53b
strange b. titles, 85b
turns up nose at Canadian, 88a
who reads an American, 106a
good b. has no ending, 133b
want to have read a, 139a
review impression made, 142b
read newspapers, 145b
stigma of colonial, 158b
write the b. he likes, 212a
only when it is read, 238b
a mine and a mint, 278a
it doesn't weigh enough, 292b
three in Charlottetown, 305a
owe a good deal of, 341a
hobo and priest fight, 343a
Britannia, Swedenia, 360b
who reads a Canadian, 364b
low-minded to buy, 365a
anyone can write a, 368a
reciprocity in b. trade, 384a
smallest printed, 402b
store not supermarket, 416b
unknown to obscurity, 442a
ruined by a, 444a
a thick or thin, 500a
the dream, wish, 545a
born in a b. shop, 558b
reading a b. backwards, 619b
 *Books
more spent on whisky, 35b
still being written, 54b
those of Henry James, 78b
had a mild impact, 80a
who needed, 85a
Canadians do not buy, 93a
two no literature, 129b
should look different, 137b
we do not censor, 222b
daily companions, 238b
weaken understanding, 245b
some read in parlour, 245b
are very few, 270a
beside us a mountain of, 270b
masterpieces we sell, 305a
mother and child, 371a
McLuhan reads, 398a
critics condemn my, 428b

between men and, 457a
easier to buy than read, 458a
without patients, 459a
unreadable b. about, 499b
where will it sell, 551b
look at back stacks, 552b
American independence, 569a
 *Bootlegging
see you in hell first, 489b
 *Bordeaux
not house of ill-repute, 31b
 *Borden, Sir Robert
crinkled, curly hair, 515a
 *Border
54 40 or fight, 6b
row of forts, 99a
boundaries and science, 117a
frontier misleading, 124b
between Canada and, 174a
to get a drink, 178a
ridiculous boundary line, 183b
thinks of changing, 276a
world's longest undefended,
 291b
invisible, illogical, 298a
an imaginary line, 312a
with American girl on, 364b
a borderline case, 396b
longest continuous, 402b
eliminate fort, 403a
frontier undefended, 410b
Canada Goose flies, 421b
unguarded boundary, 449a
stones thrown across, 450b
it might disappear, 499a
by a surveyor's line, 507a
[See also Forty-ninth Parallel.]
 *Born
a man, died grocer, 15b
a Canadian I was, 153b
not ceased to be French, 185a
in Canada beneath, 290a
and am not dead yet, 313b
on banks of Saskatchewan, 328b
a British subject I was, 380a
in Canada so what, 382b
 *Bosom
two nations warring in, 170b
 *Boston
crook-neck squash from, 587a
theatre different in, 587b
Torontonians healthier, 636a
breakfast on train, 646b
 *Botheration
the B. scheme, 214a
scheme ventilated, 272a
 *Bougainvillaea
Bougainville, 66b
 *Bourassa, Robert
my dear Robert, 324b
 *Bourgeois
image of b. and voyageur, 348b
playing on rivalry, 442b
rich and happy, 511a
Confederation carried, 609b
 *Bourinot's
Rules of Order, 96b
 *Bow, Clara
has it, 220b
 *Bowell, Sir Mackenzie

suppose it is late, 380b
yes, B., I suppose, 381b
Bowells of Compassion, 451b
 *Boxing
nothing as tough, 113
wine, women and, 393a
 *Boy
will become a man, 155b
see his b. as he, 338a
was I a good, 342b
meets girl in Winnipeg, 395a
 *Boy Scouts
our thanks to, 30a
each is expected, 30a
 *Boys
our b. are marching, 22a
land of the Byng, 51b
 *Brains
rust corrodes, 472a
mind dependent on, 472a
million-dollar, 334b
come hard and high, 459a
success is only, 628b
 *Brampton
from the Boyne to, 85b
 *Branch
Conservatives lop the, 49a
 *Branch-plant
ought to be grateful, 495b
economy and society, 623a
 *Brant, Joseph
sold to old Indian, 480a
speaks 12 languages, 530a
 *Brave
push on b. York volunteers, 76a
man laughs at life, 176a
world tomb of men, 490b
 *Brazil
using Eskimo themes, 41b
coffee from teacup, 273b
goals of Nazi war, 314a
 *Bread
cake of the world's, 10b
selling at the price, 54a
with its promise of, 86b
a sermon or, 344b
bullets for you but, 386b
world's b. basket, 542b
buttered your b. now, 584a
 *Brébeuf, Jean de
martyrdom of, 494a
when Lallemant and, 528b
 *Brecht, Bertolt
original of Mahoney, 403b
 *Bretons
cousin of the, 76b
 *Brewery Bay
that name, old, 342a
 *Bribed
no b. into loyalty, 543a
 *Bribery
can buy any government, 33a
become so widespread, 111b
to do greasing, 266b
not single farthing, 377a
gratefulness a factor, 571a
 *Brick
throw without breaking, 604b
 *Bridge

a stupid game, 133b
 *Bright
there was a young lady, 86a
 *Britain
when B. goes we go, 49a
a vaster, 96a
in the Battle of, 110a
unbreakable ties with, 112b
rise original thinkers, 188b
genius and might of, 242a
lost the smaller half, 354b
the B. of the West, 388a
climate I prefer, 389a
when B.'s message came, 415b
from B.'s shore, 439a
 *British
parliament cruel, 26b
connection, 33a
Canada for the, 35b
a damned Britisher, 41b
a B. subject, 46a
not a B. hireling, 54a
I say, B., yes, 68a
once more on B. soil, 112a
born a B. subject, 143b
born a B. colonist, 143b
English at expense of, 171a
the old traditions, 190a
period of domination, 212b
shall be the greater, 228b
more B. than the king, 365a
I am B. to the core, 328b
subject by birth, 330b
a B. subject I was born, 380a
born a B. subject, 438b
government a monster, 569a
more B. than Canadian, 575b
colours on every fort, 638b
 *British Channel
nature created the, 253a
 *British Columbia
aboard for Pacific, 14a
splendor sine occasu, 15a
going to West Coast, 74b
means before Christ, 78a
land of golden promise, 81a
with men from, 91a
revolution now and then, 143b
must lay our head on, 212a
a sea of mountains, 228b
country called Fu Sang, 235a
almighty fact about, 242b
the fiishing boats of, 248b
Liberal Association, 259b
how shall we live, 264b
were I an immigrant, 310b
not worth keeping, 317a
have been born here, 340b
paradoxical place, 366b
until road is built, 377b
interest in Australia, 378a
not limited to, 379b
to far C.s shore, 388a
daddy, what is a, 411b
years to know it, 421a
shooting in Kootenay, 456a
Peace Arch Park, 505b
politics an adventure, 520b
decent guys from, 539b
Fusang, Chinese, 540a

centre of Empire, 589b
beauties of West Coast, 610a
new colony on Pacific, 615a
the capital of, 640b
*British Commonwealth
See Commonwealth of Nations.
*British Empire
autonomous within, 19b
I was chained to, 31a
been a citizen of, 38a
Canada First, then, 48b
and a horse in Toronto, 53a
first, 64b
unity of the, 68b
happiness sacrificed, 71b
Unity of the, 97a
one bright spot in, 110a
unique position in, 112a
Canada worth 1,000, 117b
hangs in the balance, 135a
remain part of, 141b
first use of term, 144a
blessings of relations, 157b
part of a third, 186b
splendidly isolated, 200a
statesmen who built up, 212a
will rejoice in news, 216a
half-way house of, 228a
the harlot of the, 230a
most powerful factor, 233b
link in girdle of, 242a
colonists pariahs of, 244b
but not 15 countries, 257a
sun never sets upon, 270b
interest and authority, 271b
our statesman in councils, 271b
toiled and died, 309b
members of imperial family,
    309b
mighty tentacle of, 326a
a galaxy of nations, 328a
all citizens chew gum, 355b
mightiest world has seen, 379b
Britannic E. of North, 422b
idealist's end of, 434b
we hold a vaster, 435a
we hold a vaster, 439b
first lady magistrate, 441a
Imperial Order Daughters, 441b
one throne, one, 441b
knowledge of in Canada, 450b
sisterhood of British, 509b
Newfoundland, Cinderella, 510b
in absence of mind, 520b
granary of the, 549b
transformed the, 554b
northward course of, 559b
attached by light bond, 572b
bonds that unite, 573a
in this the tone, 580a
who serves Canada, 583b
B.C. center of the, 589b
elephants and the, 638b
*British-Israelites
nephew of Almighty, 79a
*British North America
Canada is not, 93b
a rope of sand, 142a
Nova Scotia normal school, 271a
phenomenal progress, 332a

epoch of progress, 360b
*British North America Act
One Dominion under, 19a
uniting two parishes, 376a
have a rendez-vous with, 528a
Kingdom, Dominion, 588b
shall form and be one, 614b
*Britons
four million not free, 59b
character and freedom, 76a
borrowing power from, 384a
where B. go, 580b
*Broadcasting
greater understanding, 35a
greatest triumphs, 123b
media owners profits, 138a
private broadcasters, 138b
to you to lead radio, 198b
the rest housekeeping, 202a
cultural integrity, 211a
first hockey game, 260a
playwright on radio, 395a
no CBC brass in U.S., 405a
symbol of developing, 441b
national control, 471a
public and national, 557a
Canadian content, 563a
who turns the dial, 588a
know where skeletons, 625b
golden age of radio, 626a
is of my generation, 631a
*Broadcloth
must doff the, 454b
*Broadway
go back to Canada, 650a
*Brock, Sir Isaac
Brave B. looked up, 21a
his dying words, 21a
from B. to Currie, 85b
true martyr, hero, poet, 523b
this is the man, 578a
come, we go, 578a
*Brother André
prayed at tomb of, 104b
*Brother Twelve
such a man am I, 636a
*Brotherhood
let us here lie, 16b
form a nobler, 94b
help of patriotism, 404b
found that hand in, 505b
make the world a, 643a
*Brown, David K.
epitaph of, 16a
*Brown, George
all able men, 266b
been able to beat, 376b
John A. drunk and, 380b
Doukhobor and politics, 551a
*Browns
and the Clearys, 298b
*Buchan, John
not blood but ink, 83a
tradition that includes, 367a
reading Proust in Rideau, 502b
*Buck
a b. is a, 101a
*Buckingham, Duke of
Dominion caused by, 379b
*Buckingham Palace

obeisance to little shrimp, 539a
*Buckskin
the b. curtain, 541a
*Buddha
in this citadel of, 347b
vain that B. taught, 527b
*Budget
who prepared speech, 193b
gain without loss, 492b
*Buffalo
brought home b. rugs, 5b
breath of a b. in winter, 133a
the ass of a big, 259a
a black a b. great, 299a
fled to lands of, 471a
side view better, 545a
white man killed off, 618b
*Builded
better than they knew, 11a
*Bulgaria
Marie Louise of, 111b
too much history, 492a
someone who understands, 460b
*Bullets
ideas more powerful, 155b
for you, not bread, 386b
melt our spoons into, 445b
*Bums
corporate welfare, 352a
*Bundle
the b. of sticks, 245a
not a b. of rods, 551b
*Bureaucracy
business top heavy, 298a
paper has genius, 298b
not objective to be gray, 475a
man into civil service, 523b
*Burns, George
decline of vaudeville, 36a
*Bush
as poetic as grove, 224a
English gentleman not, 429a
the Queen's, 480b
man of education in, 567b
*Bush pilot
proud of b.-pilot, 150b
b.-flying fading, 182b
Hollywood's idea of, 371b
*Business
socialists as hard-nosed as, 36a
turned situation to, 40a
great man of, 40b
manufacturers of enthusiasms,
    56b
support of home industries, 61a
the tyranny of, 159b
make it your b. to get, 165a
government leave alone, 198b
communication needs, 223b
Y.C.D.B.S.O.Y.A., 255b
brass paid as gold, 298a
finest b. history, 304a
most unethical thing, 314b
Canadians very, 315a
politics a question of, 328b
pursue studies of use, 339a
art of losing money, 340b
governments and b. hold hands,
    352a

from beginning of world, 358b
dreamer, son of bitch, 368b
marry a b. girl, 370b
Senate to settle problems, 416a
what community wants, 435b
under sub-Arctic, 446b
I buy then rent, 448b
of people to maintain, 454b
as usual after war, 529a
offices for Ottawa, 551b
get rid of management, 576b
afford to be orthodox, 585a
my family or my, 585b
on a back street, 610b
to make money, 628b
woman not revolutionary, 635a
more decisions made, 638a
you have good, 650b
 *Bust
Pike's peak or, 477a
 *Butler
Remember B., 90b
 *Buxton Settlement
to emancipation, 308a
 *Buy
Canadian, 9b
at a discount, 585b
 *Byng, Lord
land of B. Boys, 51b
don't want any more, 138a

# C

 *C.A.A.E.
See Canadian Association for
   Adult Education.
 *Cabbagetown
largest slum, 213b
 *Cabin
never locked his door, 141a
 *Cabinet
Macdonald, c.-maker, 380b
members poorer, 596b
 *Cabot, John
seek out, discover, 257b
 *Caddy
Cadborosaurus, 635a
 *Caesar, Julius
my village at time of, 78a
scheme as dead as, 272a
we were Caesars, nobody, 488b
 *Cain
land God gave to, 101b
gave Labrador to, 241b
country God gave to, 258b
 *Caisse populaire
credit union founder, 148b
 *Calgary
had 139 inhabitants, 78a
ranch 40 miles south, 117b
over 3,000 feet above, 178b
Mother Melville in, 416b
remember Pearl Miller, 420b
White Russians at, 452a
 *Calgary Bob
See Bob Edwards.
 *Calgary Stampede
not another one, 437b

money is here, 624b
 *California
cars designed for, 81b
hold C. as hostage, 376a
be C. or Canada, 459b
melt like butter, 561b
Jimmy Stewart for, 621b
 *Call
in the members, 101b
us to your councils, 329a
me anything but, 632a
 *Callaghan, Morley
a writer is tough, 213b
he was discovered, 232a
never been broken, 263a
whatever happened to, 524a
not only the first, 624b
most unjustly neglected, 635b
 *Callas, Maria
little C., not me, 566b
 *Cambodia
and Vietnam, 232a
 *Camp, Dalton
attacks on Diefenbaker, 246b
 *Canada
and Quebec must, 3a
good country from, 8b
no meaning, 9b
made in, 9b
Carries On, 10a
was born Dominion of, 11a
we'll go, capture, 22a
Canaday-I-O, 24a
but to breed quarrels, 28a
for the British, 35b
kinship with Russia, 37b
barbaric, picturesque, 43a
I did it for, 45b
slang terms for, 51b
like apple on tree, 59a
I see a Serpent, 60b
Polish labour camps, 65b
nationalist Quebec, 67b
first and forever, 68b
it is this and that, 69b
had crooked teeth, 73a
of ten provinces, 75b
a live country, 77b
of the larger air, 83b
Scotland extended, 84a
to the wilds of, 87b
highlands of, 91b
Miss Canada, 95a
who only C. knows, 96a
what street C. on, 96b
Scotland of America, 99b
O C., mon pays, 101a
even unto, ready way, 102a
diamonds of, 102b
linchpin, English world, 112a
white paper of possible, 115a
conquest of, 115b
loss of C. a gain, 117b
could have enjoyed, 123a
colony dominated, 125b
spiritual adventures, 140a
a vast tract of land, 147b
a C. of the north, 152b
this C. of ours, 164b

this C. of ours, 175b
melting pot, salad, 176a
richer, ruined houses, 183b
smells of resin, 192b
to send Cartier to, 203a
nobody here, 207b
someday graduate from, 209a
entered history, 214b
Ca-na-da, we love thee, 219a
country in plural, 221a
impossibility of, 229a
subconscious and, 234b
boring second fiddle, 235b
the Romance of, 240a
the land of nothing, 243a
still-bitter fruit, 255a
hello C. and hockey, 260a
only needs to be known, 266a
acquisition a matter, 285b
cold, uninviting, 290b
from Monsieur Cane, 293b
no one ideology, 304b
lady of the snows, 309a
risks her own soul, 311b
worth royal commission, 327b
Laurier and the larger, 329b
England advance, recede, 329b
twentieth century shall, 330a
first, last, always, 330a
inspiration of life, 330b
twentieth century belong to,
   331b
belong to twentieth, 332b
dumbest population, 353a
sanctimonious icebox, 353b
destined to disappear, 353b
monstrous, empty, 353b
couldn't live without, 354a
close to America, 359a
must be demolished, 362a
major problems, 365b
a great sandpile, 371a
a sacrifice market, 378a
hard country to govern, 381b
to be a wonderful, 382b
Tuponia and Hochelaga, 386a
Mackenzie from C. by land, 389b
Canada Dry, 393a
champagne of ginger, 393a
a Cree word, 394a
very neat, clean, 394a
means well, 401b
one place same as, 423b
finest country in, 428b
is a bore, 430a
had C. on the brain, 433b
idealist's end of empire, 434b
language Canodeta, 449b
self-made country, 454b
a small canon, 455b
horse manure about, 456b
to the Emperor of, 472b
keeping Guadaloupe, 478a
vertical mosaic, 481a
pertaining to Muses, 481b
restraint, tidiness, 484b
less grand than, 488a
eternal monotonous, 490a
a large country in, 498b
world-famous over, 499a

good neighbourhood, 499b
the Kingdom of, 506b
mid-C. development, 508b
to Peru, Callicuth, 509b
we would take, 510a
Delenda est, 540b
first and foremost, 542a
da, da, 546a
can make it in, 547b
there is a unified, 551a
rich nature, policy poor, 552b
unmilitary community, 557b
made in C., Chicago, 566b
beautiful country, 567a
clean, healthy, young, 570b
at parting of the ways, 572b
whom we love, prize, 579b
ever be True North, 581a
three bywords, 591b
fifty-first state, 592a
good for artisan, 592b
antiseptic laboratory, 609a
die in ruins of, 612b
one dominion under, 614b
cost much, little, 616b
few acres of snow, 616b
much prefer peace, 617a
independent socialist, 623a
bounded on north, 625b
O.C., our home and native,
    626a
the coy colossus, 628b
I absorb Kanada in, 630b
it was at my feet, 632b
lost nor given, 633b
if you dream of, 650b

*Canada: French & English
Anglo-French Confederacy, 67b
Quebec disruptive, 85b
double flight stairs, 109b
hostile divisions, 170b
invidious distinction, 176b
prejudices respected, 181a
preserve existence, 199a
two tribes of men, 253a
marriage, divorce, 288a
long estranged, 330a
across the sea, 331b
presence a guarantee, 349a
separatism and, 351b
like oil and alcohol, 394b
phrase two solitudes, 394b
but not a Canadian, 396b
natural differences, 410b
Montreal 350 miles, 516b
British than Canadian, 575b
identical origins, 645a

*Canada: Great Britain
dictate our politics, 8a
fostered growth, 99a
brother, mother, 99b
forgive much, 103a
buy more goods, 104b
neither pay taxes, 118a
amicable separation, 154b
theatres in Old, 197b
destinies of Canada, 219b
married flirt ready, 252b
quarrel, bread, butter, 253a
annexation to mother, 271b

daughter in my mother's, 308b
call us to councils, 329a
must advance, recede, 329b
when Britain at war, 330b
Britain war, Canada, 331a
countries across sea, 331b
England centre, 375b
loving, loyal colony, 380b
hands holding, 586b

*Canada: Anglo-American
    Relations
North Atlantic Triangle, 10a
linch-pin of peace, 112a
clearer perspective, 187b
powerful factor, 233b
co-operation, 240a
heart and hand, 270b
in losing the U.S., 354b
prevent British, 355a
hands across the sea, 355b
England, U.S., war, 376a
Imperial connection, 385b
to form a hinge, 429a
true Anglo-Americans, 432b
U.S. capital, British, 442b
British to U.S. influence, 469b
pressure, support, 472b
kindred, neighbours, 484a
less British, more, 542a
without prepossession, 569a
we would reply, 605b

*Canada: United States
assume C. bestowed, 2a
integrate two nations, 4a
in national interest, 4a
use of the air, 7a
common purpose, 12b
national mental illness, 28b
rearguard action, 33a
good-will of two, 38b
annexation of that, 45a
country of 80 millions, 67b
American capital, 95a
a C. without the, 97a
absorption by U.S., 98b
day is not distant, 113b
U.S. got hold of, 122a
complementary, not, 124b
an American nation, 137a
coffee poorer, tea, 147a
a better American, 150b
fences necessary, 153a
happy to have us, 166a
destinies interwoven, 172b
distinctive character, 180b
free world co-operation, 180b
American party at work, 183a
half-annexed already, 183b
take without soldiers, 185b
veiled invitation, 198a
don't like American, 199b
like Siamese twins, 202a
20 million prefer, 203b
disappear into larger, 208a
shares continent, 209a
between corporations, 211a
influence of economy, 211b
two rival nations, 223a
Uncle Sam looks, 224b
colonial dependency, 224b

think of the U.S., 229a
peaceful absorption, 231a
marvellous interplay, 232a
close co-operation, 249b
resolved in private, 255b
Canadians stay longer, 256a
U.S. forget about, 265a
publishing takeover, 273b
a United States-er, 273b
3,986.8 miles, 276a
early warning system, 282a
acquisition, marching, 285b
high price to pay, 289a
resist modernization, 289b
Yankee must south of us, 290a
U.S. gets cold and, 295a
boundary invisible, 298a
Washington sneezes, 298b
geography, neighbours, 300b
any aspect of U.S., 312a
absolutely independent, 329a
clouded relationship, 348a
regard marriage, 353a
American politically one, 353b
strategic orbit of, 372a
U.S. statesman covets, 379b
Massachusettize the, 384a
sleep no more except, 384b
on our terms, theirs, 384b
acquisition first, 386a
never been a nation, 395a
great-grandmother's day, 398a
war totally absurd, 399a
means, expectations, 406b
to enjoy influences, 410b
cultural Americana, 411b
not in same boat, 416a
just like Americans, 417a
future with that of, 425a
acquisition no object, 426a
to keep C. wonderful, 432a
demand after demand, 436a
own us outright, 438a
into lap like apple, 440a
as Chrysler to G.M., 443a
friendly differences, 449a
reassess relationship, 450b
take for granted, 453a
blessed thing, 454a
living with wife, 468b
touchy when overlooked, 469a
North American not, 474a
economic swamping, 484b
cautious, assertive, 484b
into traitors, 490a
Manhattan and Macdonald,
    493a
seems to be problem, 495b
yes, we are nicer, 499b
ideals and aims, 508a
American spelling, 509a
not local but global, 513a
against mass culture, 514b
ever-growing, 535a
union, annexation, 552a
indistinguishable from, 558b
smuggling and union, 562a
as Scotland, England, 563b
terrible effect, 566a
no mountains separate, 568b

at parting of ways, 572b
friends whether we like, 584a
fifty-first state, 592a
richer country, poorer, 593b
greater they believe, 594b
sleeping with an elephant, 597a
Americans neighbours, 600a
more willy than nilly, 600a
not foreign countries, 603a
civilization differs, 606b
continental influences, 607a
neighbours not marry, 610a
gosling to American fox, 610b
cough in Washington, 619a
early failure to conquer, 620b
consider yourself marching, 622a
fifty great states, 630b
strengths, weaknesses, 641b
　*Canada Council
some unique features, 115b
not apply for grant, 139b
lunching with Treasury, 172a
ten years of fellowships, 217b
scholars, artists, 303b
intelligences highest, 602b
　*Canada Dry
buy ginger ale, 447a
　*Canada East
form and be one Dominion,
　614b
　*Canada First
then the Empire, 48b
within Empire, C.F., 64b
we should put, 146b
C.F., origin, 175a
but first in what, 180b
our new nationality, 201b
last, always, 330a
　*Canada West
form and be one Dominion,
　614b
　*Canadian
buy, 9b
typically, 34b
still a C., British, 46a
he was now a, 51b
love in a canoe, 53a
they'll discover it's, 94a
before all I am a, 101b
precisely is a, 113b
transcends borders, 125b
having blue eyes, 140a
a C. I was born, 153b
may be a Mountie, 185a
Sunset, 219a
a distinctively C. way, 240b
easy social graces, 256a
drinks Brazilian coffee, 273b
pro-C., not anti-U.S., 275b
no one and nothing, 291b
doesn't play for keeps, 304a
young man, one of ourselves,
　320b
first, last, all time, 330b
someone who keeps asking, 336b
be anyone and be a, 348a
can't tell him much, 350b
not even pro-C., 369b
I was born, I will die, 380b

$10 price of being, 383b
he made the Crown, 411b
going somewhere but, 436b
a C. an American, 468b
North American not, 474a
often a baffled, 484a
puffed hashish but, 499b
the quiet, 562b
Canadian content, 563a
shortcomings excused, 592b
all-C. boy absurd, 599a
　*Canadian Association for
　　Adult Education
slogan vulgar, 302b
　*Canadian Authors'
　　Association
plant native maple, 528a
visited G. B. Shaw, 568a
　*Canadian Boat Song
See Boat Song, Canadian.
　*Canadian Broadcasting
　　Corporation
CBC never learned, 5b
first CBC-TV program, 189b
sail on, O CBC, 191a
the voice of CBC Radio, 286b
no brass in U.S. TV, 405a
　*Canadian Co-operative
　　Federation
See C.C.F.
　*Canadian National Railways
CN insignia, 196a
　*Canadian Pacific Railway
the national dream, 52b
letters C.P.R., 160b
nationalize it, 351b
until completed, 378a
termini are Liverpool, 379b
that be terminus, 390a
born in 1885, 398b
book dedicated to, 456a
take good care of, 536b
to Alberta and go, 542b
passes on the C.P., 547a
stand fast, Craigellachie, 562a
moral equivalent of, 608b
last spike an iron one, 610b
no means paying wages, 611a
Van Horne's slogans, 611a
not Cartier but C.P.R., 625a
　*Canadian Press
independent political, 197b
no soul, no ass, 485b
[See also Journalism.]
　*Canadian Radio-Television
　　Commission
we're trying to breathe, 294b
　*Canadian Wolf
come near at your peril, 23b
　*Canadianism
teach everything but, 136b
diluted with imperialism, 189b
20 million who prefer, 203b
un-C. is C., 265b
true C., moderation, 330b
the word is Gothic, 344a
sound sense of possible, 388b
only definition of, 430b
education's contribution, 603b
　*Canadians

the C. never budge, 5a
come all you bold, 21a
to hold C. captive, 30a
you ever put a mouse, 43a
malevolently informed, 73a
never patronize the, 91a
first, foremost, always, 153a
un-northern temperaments,
　154a
have sought to sunder, 174a
be C. and future is, 204b
lawless, unprincipled, 272b
Europe's sham politeness, 294b
New Canadians, 300a
with equilibrium, 316b
big cocks, dirty, 351a
love country, not, 357a
bumptious provincials, 358b
I call them, 369b
above all let us be, 381a
name any three at all, 451a
least militant minority, 499b
if understand snow, 522a
indistinguishable from, 558b
romantics lost courage, 572a
where Britons go, dare, 580b
we would reply, 605b
Russians north, south, 633b
　*Canadien
un c. errant, 216b
　*Canajan
language of Anglos, 456a
　*Candy
made of sugar, 112b
　*Cane, Monsieur
Canada so called, 293a
　*Cannon
no other reply than, 206b
　*Canoe
making love in a leaky, 18a
mon canot d'écore, 23b
Canadian makes love in, 53a
I done it alone, 189b
give me a good, 234a
poetry of the, 354b
to encounter others, 357b
every man paddle his own, 407a
carry, paddle, walk, 511a
most of great rivers, 596a
purifies you rapidly, 600b
was to the Indian, 641b
　*Canoe Lake
artist, woodsman, guide, 585b
　*Canton
not cramped like, 77b
　*Canuck, Johnny
I'm what you call, 5a
hold Canadians captive, 30a
Canuckland, 51b
post myself in C. airs, 64a
about Yankees and, 273b
　*Cape Bonavista
terra primum vista, 92a
　*Cape Breton
instead of George in, 69b
imagine a Jew from, 120b
toast to taking, 467b
North America is west, 554a
marching by land to, 554b
　*Cape Charles

polar landscape begins, 109b
*Cape Diamond
diamonds of Canada, 192b
*Cape St. Mary's
pays for all, 10b
let me fish off, 298b
*Capital
cities of Canada, 14b
attached to man, 107a
most precious water, 161b
nationalism and, 279a
less to manipulate, 462b
*Capital punishment
degraded society, 38a
pleasure to see hanged, 42a
no execution, 60a
we know how to hang, 66a
he'll never break, 118b
paid on scaffold, 145b
extreme sentence of, 184a
do die instantaneously, 239a
done my duty, 262b
my execution be of use, 361a
rather die in jail, 482a
minister of justice, 488a
hanged by the neck, 498a
Mr. Jarvis, do your, 517a
either finish me or, 530b
public hangings, 547b
*Capitalism
face is fascism, 108b
road to ruin, 127a
rooted like cannibalism, 198b
luxury no longer afford, 198b
my stakes are in, 223b
disguised as idealistic, 289b
call it and kick it, 340b
workers are in jail, 392b
save from capitalists, 454a
paternalistic, 462a
wastes tolerated, 527b
labour and maintenance, 583b
not between socialism, 607b
until eradicated, 608a
continentalism and, 623a
*Capitalists
socialists, hard-nosed, 36a
working man considers, 121b
in the c. empire, 229a
possess as much wealth, 260b
champagne-flavoured, 365b
abuse led to unions, 478b
myself a socialist, 597a
depression a sickness, 608a
support parties, 648b
*Captain Canada
beavers up, 186b
*Captive
to hold Canadians, 30a
sold to a Frenchman, 241b
*Career
you build a, 268a
second should, 472a
*Cares
boy meets girl in, 395a
*Caribbean
See West Indies.
*Caribou
meat grew on bones, 26a
will see c. everywhere, 160a

no idea of comfort, 232b
joyfully I see, 480b
*Carling, Sir John
as honest as you look, 381b
*Caroline
remember the, 163a
cut out the boat, 508a
*Carr, Emily
grave markings, 16b
*Carries
Canada C. On, 10a
*Carthage
Italian states and, 122a
delenda est, 362a
*Cartier, Sir George-Etienne
is French for cashier, 47a
all able men, 266b
*Cartier, Jacques
and St. Lawrence, 69a
tourist who stopped, 163b
to send C. to Canada, 203a
westward sailed, 386b
horse which he rode, 604b
discovery not date, 625a
*Cataraqui River
trace the grand, 431b
*Catechism
most precious book, 12a
*Catholic
or Jewish isn't chic, 26b
pretensions of C. church, 27a
called a dogan, 43a
to all C. America, 68a
a four-dollar mass, 89a
felt to be outside, 141a
shrink with horror, 175a
win over North America, 210b
colonized by Rome, 221a
and Anglican in city, 222a
Irish and French, 225b
Pope Pius IX reported, 232b
defence of our faith, 236b
three publications, 282b
Recollect Roman church, 299b
in doctrine of church, 303b
excommunicated by, 331a
true catholicity of, 384b
more C. than pope, 365a
criminal intercourse, 425b
never builds on back, 540a
no C. co-operatives, 590a
much a Protestant, 597b
Quebec will remain, 618a
my mother's a, 632a
French and Presbyterian, 634b
the Roman C. hierarchy, 636a
*C.B.C.
See Canadian Broadcasting
   Corporation.
*C.C.F.
hear the C.C.F.'ers, 39a
hot air, heifer dust, 437a
Underhill and the, 608a
no government rests, 608a
Regina Manifesto, 608b
[See also New Democratic
   Party.]
*Celts
born optimistic, 76b
aren't good at math, 623a

*Censorship
not send proof-sheets, 143a
we do not censor books, 222b
open, unshackled press, 271a
likes not hair colour, 271b
never subdued by fear, 265b
died in a dung heap, 373b
believe in c. because, 410a
I went to bat for, 529b
*Cent
not a c. for N.S., 192b
a single c. to Tory, 306a
*Centennial
hopes on this C. day, 203b
Canada, a C. Song, 219a
watershed in history, 319b
spirit of courage, 349a
100 years becoming, 447a
to love Toronto, 557b
second c. arrives, 630b
*Centre
liberal, man of the, 469b
where the c. is, 638a
*Century
20th c. belongs to, 331b
only spoke in wheel, 502a
world a neighbourhood, 643a
*Chamberlain, Joseph
think continentally, 197a
*Chambord, Château de
double stairs, 109b
*Champlain, Samuel de
and St. Lawrence, 69a
history from time, 212b
through forest, 422a
New France shadow, 432a
honoured by Republic, 432b
shores and islands, 464a
boats of C. poking, 498a
cab which C. used, 604b
*Chance
stare at c.-taking dead, 186b
always hiding ahead, 334a
land of the Second, 461b
men powerless, 616a
*Change
don't as you grow, 114a
exchanges and, 205b
we don't really, 214a
naught in Quebec, 256b
it's time for a, 349a
to c. his mind, 421b
social c. is law, 434b
too poorly educated, 444b
absurd not to try, 447a
we'll stay home, 471b
hour is great with, 504b
much c. if country, 513a
today everything, 618a
university alert to, 642b
*Chaos
King or, 306b
abyss beyond which, 338b
*Chapdelaine, Maria
daughter of, 188a
*Chaplin, Charles
and Mickey Mouse, 410a
*Character
history encounter, 129b

happiness depends on, 245b
women for complections, 252a
discretion negative, 401b
to challenge the, 407b
what he really is, 421a
important than ideology, 447a
grumpy, growling, 556a
nation's c. in dances, 616a
*Charbonneau, Bishop Joseph
where oh where is, 529a
*Charity
poor in new clothes, 324a
if c. were needle, 485b
*Charles River
speed to cut off, 640a
*Charlesbourg
oldest man born, 402b
*Charlesworth, Hector
Demosthenes of press, 568a
*Charlevoix, P.-F.-X. de
population estimated, 550b
paradise of Hurons, 573b
*Charlie Bonnie Prince
the preserver of, 374b
*Charlottetown
wicked enough for, 11a
Cradle of Confederation, 15a
if I sold 3 copies, 304b
*Charlottetown Conference
builded better than knew, 11a
*Château Frontenac
for Quebec Conference, 281a
two Gideon Bibles, 416b
*Château Laurier
view from window, 32b
house Eskimos in, 430a
*Château St. Louis
the parties excessively, 544a
*Chatham
heartsick of shame, 128a
*Chee-mo
Eskimo Chimo, 9a
*Cheer
Order of Good, 349b
*Cheese
old c.-makers never, 315a
unrivalled queen of, 388b
the C. poet, 388b
*Chekhov, Anton
great dramatists, 140a
French interpreter of, 185a
and Callaghan, 635b
*Chemistry
elements are to, 313b
waiting for reaction, 117b
*Chemophiliac
the c. society, 404a
*Cheque
parliament give a blank, 306b
*Chesapeake
the C. and the Shannon, 21b
appears ready for sea, 76b
and the Shannon, 335b
*Chicago
Edmonton as big as, 13b
rich in or Quebec, 27a
*Chicken
some c., some neck, 112b
*Chicoutimi
lives of our people, 124a

postal clerk English, 199a
the C. cucumber, 614b
*Chief
you call me c. and, 216b
I was Indian, 216b
magistrate taught, 294b
*Chien d'or
the golden dog, 312b
house of the, 514a
*Chilcott, Barbara
what an entrance, 483b
*Child
on Ontario farm, 70b
believes in Santa, 110b
into this land, 285a
rather doesn't like, 345b
woman second only, 339b
rainbow-hued world, 371a
adults imperfect, 451a
strongest memories, 476b
of nations, giant, 504b
*Children
our c. shall understand, 12b
maternal dislike, 94a
creative than grown, 100a
born out of wedlock, 249b
to walk to school, 298a
middle-age spread, 298a
C.'s Aid Society, 299a
believed in Santa, 341a
gulf between world, 355b
not a handicap, 371a
ruin lives, 444b
Confederation good for, 549a
no lobbyists for, 565a
*Chilkoot
scaling perpetual, 52a
*Chimo
chy-mo, chee-mo, 9a
*China
I am going to, 54b
Peking Man, 58a
not end up in, 62b
other than Cathay, 92a
come all way from, 120a
and Canada joined, 135b
called Fu Sang, 235a
even unto Cathay, 242b
intend to come, 268b
passage to Pole, 273a
Emperor's falcons, 479b
Bethune not have died, 523a
settle and build, 549a
never forget Bethune, 646a
*Chinese
person of C. race, 19a
orthodoxy of, 94a
origin in Commons, 152b
learn to lecture, 342a
Ukrainian or, 348a
entremets chinois, 364b
a future for, 591b
Marxists like Quebec, 601b
people's liberation, 603a
ancient philosopher, 624a
*Chinook
its lair the soft, 83b
*Chiropractic
I am originator, 451a
*Choose

to govern is to, 69a
needing to believe, 190b
to govern is, 595b
*Christian
spirit of C. France, 68a
any C. nations left, 68b
duty, as C. men, 103a
wage war on war, 149b
rather a decent, 168a
every C. in Hitler's, 187a
death of Jerusalem, 187b
endeavour to live, 288b
community of, 367b
continue the work of, 575a
*Christianity
revolution needed, 52b
endeavour to maintain, 81a
do-it-yourself, 150a
the main question, 303b
diffusion important, 517a
trade among Indians, 518b
unfair light, 609a
*Christians
you call yourselves, 71b
will be persecuted, 73b
o white, 119b
I suggest for all, 141a
lessons of Marxism, 199a
provinces unknown to, 257b
*Christmas
first Canadian C. card, 72b
armaments are C. tree, 267b
once asked a C. group, 341a
no candle but stars, 398b
*Church
Roman Capitalist, 20a
basic foundation, 68a
Montreal consists, 77b
duty to intervene, 106b
felt like outside, 141a
neither despair in, 187a
most faithful to, 210b
compulsory intervention, 221a
lecture approved, 222b
sermons, monks, 225b
will want me, 267a
place for vulnerability, 303b
press more than pulpit, 323b
Queen's predominate, 340a
always arrives breathless, 359b
outside pillar of, 382a
legislation, damnation, 411b
peeping priest, 426a
anvil vs. hammers, 442a
French never go beyond, 462b
submissive sons of, 462b
of Last Purification, 484b
glory of c. and country, 504a
never built on back, 565a
throw brick without, 604b
built on top of, 604b
baptized son of, 609a
the witch of God, 609b
right in Anglican, 632a
*Churchill, Sir Winston
afraid Communists, 162a
down river with Howe, 269b
removed the cigar, 297a
*Churchill Falls

our waterfall, 548b
*Chymo
Chimo, 9a
*Cinderella
of the Empire, 510b
*Citibank
in at own peril, 224b
proceed at peril, 507b
*Cities
dignity of the, 310b
there was nothing, 311a
be a millionaire, 368a
anywhere but, 415b
from metropolis, 436a
second-largest French, 604a
dreams of living, 607b
wants stability, 613a
*Citizen
died a c. of U.S., 44b
immunities of a nation, 143b
of the world, 245a
with perfect, 342a
vital principle, 364b
anyone a subject and, 436a
making me a Canadian, 443a
of the universe, 613a
*Citizenship
high standard, 126a
for attention, noted, 585b
out of German emperor, 611a
progress no higher, 641a
*Civil liberties
obligation, 242b
at reducing, 598b
Confederation and, 602b
*Civil service
duty to crush him, 523b
*Civil war
bloodless civil bore, 57a
never a major, 78b
*Civilization
and freedom increase, 1a
source of your, 37b
the c. process, 51a
to happiness, 71b
to get away from, 89b
independence in, 100b
care of archives, 158a
non-exploitation, 198b
five taking shape, 221a
modern vs. local, 229a
prairies touched, 247b
powerful directive, 279a
unique, superior, 279a
on outskirts, 320b
provide Eskimo with, 326a
against universal, 344a
build the next, 404a
defend our share, 411a
England no culture, 412b
I collect lost, 442a
treat a foreigner, 460a
pioneers of, 462b
Indian, Spanish, 464a
flourish unimpaired, 509b
pioneer communities, 537a
American form, 542a
person doesn't beat, 582b
Canadian, American, 606b
rebuild c. from, 641a

*Claire
a la c. fontaine, 23a
*Clark Kent
archtypical Canadian, 541b
*Classes
always travel first, 276a
erecting conservatives, 356a
it has no, 480b
Toronto has no social, 523a
organization only road, 641a
dream of people with no, 649b
*Claudel, Paul
I'll quote, 600b
*Clean
these hands are, 46b
hands are, 376b
Canada means, 394a
*Clear Grit
only men who are, 111b
*Clearys
Browns and the, 298b
*Climate
the rigours of the, 81b
elements own land, 135b
more healthy than, 169a
have been in all, 177a
nine months winter, 185a
surely the best, 245a
hockey a symbol of, 302a
as I compare, 389a
one cannot resist, 565a
overcoming rigors, 600a
[See also Weather.]
*Close
the 49th parallel, 289b
*Clothes
grey and goat, 149a
no man can tell, 179b
you wear it, 299b
moccasins and frock, 348b
colour at concerts, 445b
not buy new, 643a
eat in emergency, 560b
*C.N.
corporate symbol, 196a
*C.N.R.
See Canadian National Railways.
*Coats
peasants in sheepskin, 542b
in a sheepskin, 543a
*Cobalt
sing a little sing, 24a
*Cobourg
for my birthplace, 162a
*Cod
done a catching, 15b
point of view of, 46b
sailors gang to fish, 88a
Nehru, my c. to, 549b
Nfld. celebrated, 630a
*Coffee
poorer, tea better, 147a
maturity means another, 206b
real test of, 212b
like weak, 316a
never be poured, 647b
*Cohen, Nathan
most dramatic critic, 631b
*Cold
in northern woods, 3a

a c. kingdom, 7b
don't call this, 17b
it grew wondrous, 122b
8 months intolerable, 259a
the c. is Arctic, 277b
hockey in a land, 302b
we don't call this, 309b
on Canadian hills, 322b
it was c. in Canada, 319a
conquered green things, 483a
hunger and fear, 534b
going to Canada, 586b
*Coldwell, M.J.
protest against, 39a
a millstone, 608b
*Coleridge, Samuel Taylor
imagery for poem, 283a
*Coles
notes, 122a
*Colonial
three centuries of, 68a
miniature scenes, 118a
mentality which, 125b
not for literature, 149b
deadweights we do not, 155a
stigma of printer, 158b
no c. in c. office, 271b
will not be a, 336b
connection, golden, 377b
status of slaves, 417b
victim of c. misrule, 489b
lost world quality, 641b
*Colonialism
reduce culture, 5b
abject political, 137a
what c. is about, 225a
the black king, 327a
transatlantic, 445a
desirable poetic, 637a
*Colonies
most mature of our, 83b
millstone around, 155a
do not cease to be, 155a
encumbrance and, 461b
than solar system, 551b
deformity through, 589a
*Colonists
of well-governed, 122a
die tadpole British, 143b
American respected, 187a
pariahs of Empire, 244b
lands brought, 367b
American free of, 426a
weaken mother, 427a
*Colony
immense fortunes, 52a
of ordinary crown, 117b
so strengthen the, 121a
Canada a pure, 208a
single c. of Empire, 228b
from c. to nation, 279a
a c., yet nation, 329a
independence yet, 329b
of the maple leaf, 354b
must be useful, 362b
French of Canada, 550b
New France not a, 558a
*Colour
like bright, 91b

lovely autumn, 164b
governor likes not, 271b
Indians white if, 345a
gold my favourite, 586a
　*Coloured
See Black.
　*Columbia River
full view of Pacific, 583b
　*Columbus, Christopher
to every mountain, 277a
well-remembered, 474b
　*Combined
united to support, 12b
　*Come
all you bold Canadians, 21a
on the tigers, 50a
let them c., dare, 253b
　*Comfortable
the c. pew, 52b
　*Common
valour game them a, 193b
life, sentiments, aims, 552b
　*Common Market
invite Canada into, 436b
　*Commonwealth of Nations
British Commonwealth, 19b
unswerving fidelity, 112a
Crown a link, 182a
head of the, 182a
British C. of Nations, 186b
socialistic c. of, 342a
Britain confides, 367b
of nations, British, 510b
belonging can help, 550b
　*Communication
speak when heard, 37b
a shouted hit from, 224a
government, bias, 279a
without no society, 557b
　*Communications
radio and TV, 52b
trail-blazers of, 92b
maximizing profits, 138a
media reflect, 139b
TV and end of radio, 147a
really matters, content, 202a
business conflict, 223b
medium is message, 396a
social, psychic changes, 397b
　*Communism
would eliminate, 54a
too far to the right, 65a
and not Red flag, 230a
Lenin congratulated, 347a
Doukhobors practised, 414a
and rheumatism, 441a
Workers' Progressive, 442b
Bennett and Stalin, 452a
save capitalism, 454a
Russian government, 516a
purges, trials, 521b
is Canadian because, 549b
deep seated in, 552a
many went away, 556b
not be afraid, 596a
　*Communist
Bethune the kind, 5b
suppose Norman had been, 6a
soviet party chief, 74a
membership in, 84b

first moral duty, 188a
shares bathroom, 340b
Lenin pro-Communist, 447b
leaders in jail, 566a
learn from Bethune, 603b
when fanatics, 94b
croakings of, 127a
Churchill afraid, 162a
football fans beat, 399a
organize demonstrations, 545a
full of surprises, 568b
　*Community
of radical scholars, 3b
hockey an enterprise, 302a
people build and, 302b
involved in education, 318b
socialism works in, 339b
feeling in Canada, 524b
transform the, 643a
　*Compact
evils which a family, 55a
that this Family, 253b
nation not founded on, 436a
[See also Family Compact.]
　*Competition
amalgamation, never, 48b
　*Complex
national inferiority, 147a
　*Concerted
leading to c. action, 64a
　*Concerts
for wrong reasons, 226a
musical mercantilism, 226a
I never go to, 226a
colours at a, 445b
　*Confederacy
founder of your league, 144b
kinship constitution, 183a
awake, my country, 504a
　*Confederation
genocide without end, 5b
the Fathers of, 9b
long courted, won, 11a
dates of, 14b
cradle of, 15a
I see one vast, 74b
through at six, 80b
of British American, 81a
question of absorption, 98b
laying foundation, 99a
of B.A. provinces, 99a
graveyard of minorities, 106b
opposition sincere, 126b
original object, 129a
agreement 100 years, 182a
are said to be a, 187a
millions for corruption, 192b
wrought well, unfinished, 119a
botheration scheme, 214a
weighty question, 220a
not for Canada, 233b
if Fathers reappeared, 236a
let's have a vote, 264a
goose hissing, 272a
sold for sheepskin, 272b
divorce after century, 288a
rainbow emblem of, 291a
object to consolidate, 330a
whole design balance, 349a
if C. fails, 349b

immence c. of freemen, 375b
yet in gristle, 376b
fought the battle of, 277a
vested interest, 385b
a new C. of North, 385b
we are in rapids, 385b
tow P.E.I. into, 386a
so unemotional, 391b
more elastic union, 422a
to Ottawa for, 424b
greatest work of, 425a
godfather, Hamilton, 440b
like a bra, 447b
provinces railroaded, 447b
is C. a myth, 448a
whether C. was hoax, 460a
pressure, support, 472b
think constitutionally, 512a
complete and, 512a
thing wrong with, 548b
never thought I'd see, 548b
only living father, 549a
good for children, 549a
not bundle or rods, 551b
father was deadlock, 552b
civil liberties, 602b
vast financial, 609b
Mr. Tilley has sold, 628b
[See also British North America
　Act.]
　*Connor, Ralph
read along with, 550a
　*Conquest, The
come to take Canada, 7a
vessel for Bigot, 56b
be prepared, 66b
weakened, degraded, 68a
born French, 185a
held for water, 247a
fateful, dramatic, 260b
God saved us as, 317b
battle between regiments, 349b
no right to be, 427a
suppose enemy have wings, 427b
happier calamity never, 464a
happy, happy day, 478b
happy without Canada, 480a
makes little difference, 480a
king will have peace, 480a
if Wolfe had written, 532b
place to land, 564b
spare the women, 591b
before we surrender, 612b
lost in one day, 616b
few acres of snow, 616b
insult neighbours, 619b
French least expect, 639a
rather have written, 639a
　*Conrad, Joseph
books like those, 78b
in J.C.'s words, 123b
　*Conscience
what mother told you, 110b
free men from their, 148a
freedom for believers, 221a
Quebec is ours, 265b
tells us when neighbours, 368b
the court of my own, 377a
astray according to, 501b

\*Consciousness
cosmic c. a higher form, 84b
of our common nature, 117b
national in literature, 320b
a cliché an act of, 397b
\*Conscription
anti-C. address, 267b
not necessarily c. but, 307a
American of draft, 316b
excommunicated by, 331a
if enforced, die, 335a
scatter our sons from, 417b
first thought, 489b
if necessary but not, 529a
[See also Draft.]
\*Conservation
is pure conversation, 334a
give my pledge to, 372a
\*Conservative
conserve all good, 49a
lops the mouldered, 49a
believe in unity, 68b
I am a continuing, 92b
hyphen in Liberal-C., 104a
is second-hand, 140a
a Macdonald conservative, 199b
belief in moral, 209b
impossibility of, 229a
revolutions, obstinate, 328a
I am a C. Liberal, 338a
not to mean English, 374a
make a decent, 375b
why worry technique, 409b
a c. tradition, 439b
Anglo-Saxon racists, 475b
regard to survival, 513a
university instrument, 542a
what for C. to conserve, 552a
Ontario C. party, 571a
three nation-saving, 591b
turned over on him, 607b
only find the Party, 632a
[See also Tory.]
\*Constitution
of their king and, 76a
creditable document, 80b
of tyranny, 88a
cannot escape the, 91b
parody of our old, 118a
dignity not in safe, 148b
a wonderful c. it, 183a
no semblance of liberty, 202a
change but not man, 245b
of such a country, 384b
so fond of their, 437b
very image, transcript, 544a
\*Consultation
continuous c. leading, 64a
\*Content
matter is program, 202a
Canadian, 563a
\*Contented
now I die, 639b
\*Continent
unanimous voice of, 3a
an economic unit, 174a
float half off, 211b
flee over C.al Divide, 316a
least the scope of, 347a
on a sub-arctic, 353a

\*Continentalism
prepared to accept, 33a
see one vast, 74b
is like an apple, 59a
not who favours, 172b
learn to think, 197a
magic circle of, 535a
excellent states, 535a
destiny on own, 552b
ultimate union, 553a
condition of 20th, 607a
and capitalism, 623a
\*Continuous
consultation leading, 64a
\*Contractor
Liberal and dishonest, 69a
\*Contradict
Caesars, nobody to, 488b
\*Conversation
pure conservation, 334a
use American for, 341b
to trifles in colony, 344a
educated person, 444a
possible in Canada, 635b
\*Conway, John
American Faustian, 584b
\*Coolies
where in your poem, 528b
\*Cooper, Merian C.
had an idea, 644a
\*Co-operation
yes, domination, 47b
not one-way, 170a
importance in free, 180b
leadership in, 249b
\*Co-operatives
industry, 155b
never be without, 318b
no Catholic, 590a
education, action, 590b
\*Copyright
evils traced to, 568b
unprotected by, 605a
\*Corner Brook
songs yet found in, 294b
\*Coronation Gulf
Vancouver not like, 353b
\*Corporate
welfare bums, 352a
the multinational, 408a
no soul, no ass, 485b
global penetration, 513a
multinational, man, 623a
\*Corporations
may have great, 93b
Canada and U.S., 211a
wave of future, 608a
tailor policies, 648b
\*Corridor
mid-Canada development, 508b
\*Corruption
by defeat and, 40b
fortunes in colony, 52a
bad when over 15%, 82b
local legislatures, 96a
so widespread, 111b
more under Liberals, 170a
millions for, 192b
Canadians over Turks, 266b
government and wealthy, 298a

politics is, 370a
another ten thousand, 376b
utter magnificence, 444b
catch them in pockets, 480b
say the others are, 551b
gratefulness a factor, 571a
lack of absolute power, 598b
cannot be slaves of, 613b
\*Cosmic consciousness
a higher form, 84b
\*Councils
call us to your, 329a
\*Country
Next Year, 14b
must be chosen, 28b
Canadians have two, 67b
Canada a live, 77b
life in the, 80a
of the larger air, 83b
without glamour, 83b
scale outside humanity, 84a
Mr. Mother, 86b
last God made, 102b
come too soon to so, 130b
God's, 135b
a hard c. to live in, 139a
170 seats and we'll, 159b
attached to immense, 162a
young, born old, 175b
youthful to outstrip, 177a
uninterested in own, 238b
my c. right or wrong, 257a
for home and, 265b
measures by men, 271b
have art without, 282a
I saw the lady, 310a
I love my, 318a
difficult c. to govern, 330a
immense tree on, 336a
a c. like a woman, 343a
a c. without mythology, 347b
not a c. but winter, 354a
greatest in universe, 375b
get stirred up, 395a
raw material for, 451b
experiment in pride, 473a
awake, my c., hour, 504a
patria not exist, 565a
good for artisan, 592a
own c. and religion, 613a
is not a c., winter, 615a
congratulate for staying, 624b
with greatest future, 631a
not become great, 642a
\*Courage
of early morning, 36b
history gives you, 129b
all your tranquil, 135a
false by laughing, 176a
victory of political, 229b
surest wisdom, 233a
face of meaninglessness, 349a
stand still then, 454a
from eternal rock, 488b
curiosity, taste, 526a
northern people, 567a
romantics who lose, 572b
\*Coureur-de-bois
no life so happy as, 511a
first use in print, 519a

[See also Voyageur.]
*Course
northward c. of empire, 559b
  *Courteau
Johnny C. of the, 163b
  *Courted
long c., won at last, 11a
  *Cow
Morris kills a, 10b
milk is for calves, 79b
slice of c.'s rear, 114b
prosperity follows, 143a
  *Coward, Noël
liked Ed Sullivan or, 553b
  *Cowcatcher
summet to sea on, 374a
  *C.P.
See Canadian Press.
  *C.P.R.
See Canadian Pacific Railway.
  *Cradle
of Confederation, 15a
revenge of the, 236a
hand that rocks, 370b
the revenge of, 447b
cheer the ancient, 504a
  *Craigellachie
Stephen to call, 129a
Stand Fast, 562a
spot be named, 610b
  *Crawford, Joan
can I compete, 538b
  *Crazy
poetry never went, 234b
anyone not c. is, 532a
  *Creation
Eskimo c. myth, 25b
conceive and, 40b
process takes time, 52b
artist in spirit, 54a
whence man grew, 105b
watching c. or end, 109b
interpretive, critical, 123b
disaffiliation, 141a
hymns of praise, 156b
  *Credit
union founder, 148b
care who gets, 201a
money, c. card, 396b
  *Cree
syllabics to print, 186a
Blackfoot tradition, 311a
old C. squaw, 334a
Canada a C. word, 394a
  *Cremation
of Sam McGee, 534a
  *Crestwood Heights
in central Canada, 532a
  *Cricket
English games, 194b
dignified but less, 418a
  *Crime
unmitigated murder, 42a
only was failure, 145b
exist nowhere but, 191a
profession robbing, 296b
inhumanity as a, 356a
index of 4,183.4, 464a
Montreal underworld, 479a

  *Criminal
no c. shall vote, 19b
killers aristocrats, 38b
receiver of stolen, 49a
no woman, idiot, vote, 370b
  *Cripps, Sir Stafford
Toronto, Oxford and, 285a
  *Critic
nostalgia for Paradise, 29b
eunuchs in a harem, 43a
only drama c. in, 120b
can be forever wrong, 164a
inferior colonialism, 383a
condemn my books, 428a
discovers genius, 383a
separate reactions, 540b
our most dramatic, 631b
  *Criticism
not c. you know, 82a
last judgment, 207b
fiercely creative, 123b
live critically in, 229b
goslings are swans, 453a
hopefulness pervades, 460b
sketch of buffalo, 544b
Frye and scientific, 581b
day don't enjoy, 621b
not shoot pianist, 632b
  *Cross, James R.
want C. to live, 68b
guineas have class, 175a
a gift for Mr., 322a
  *Crosses
to crucify us all, 72b
row on row, 372b
  *Crowfoot
no one like him, 317b
  *Crown
and Parliament, 99a
national sovereignty, 182a
freedom wears a, 190a
nations under British, 328a
made the C. Canadian, 411b
Imperial fountain, freed, 416a
unity, diversities, 436a
Republic cannot swallow, 481b
subjects of British, 615a
forfeited to the, 637b
  *C.R.T.C.
See Canadian Radio-Television
  Commission.
  *Crusoe, Robinson
feat of imagination, 616a
  *Cuba
main sugar plantation, 235b
going in a canoe, 596a
fifty great states, 603b
  *Cubism
announced the medium, 396a
  *Cultural
sagging c. economy, 43a
Canada has no c. unity, 67a
question not c. growth, 81b
level of masses, 117a
protectionism, 209a
autonomy, 211a
words in c. history, 313b
for the c. lag, 499b
  *Culture
favour of cultured, 142b

other than American, 147a
whenever I hear word, 171b
identity expressed, 207b
next year country, 208b
local anachronistic, 229a
fruits of science, 278a
to appraise, 279a
weaken or strengthen, 279a
Quebec City not, 282b
noosphere or, 291b
hockey part of, 302a
beauty, richness, 324b
a Canadian renaissance, 353a
American girl on border, 364b
has little at all, 366a
reprimitivization of, 397b
process of dissolution, 398a
France has, no, 412b
suspiciously, 450b
not legislated, 499a
tide against U.S., 514b
special form of, 566a
history of ideas, 581b
  *Curiosity
basis of education, 176a
you a curious fellow, 335a
people stirred by, 477a
H.B.C. shown no, 507a
courage and taste, 526a
  *Curling
we all curl in, 88a
  *Currie, Sir Arthur
from Brock to, 85b
  *Curtain
the buckskin, 541a
  *Cyprus
of Canada, Rhodes, 91b
  *Czechoslovakia
son of C. hath not, 46b

# D

  *Dada
founder of, 606b
  *Dafoe, John W.
words may be used, 557a
  *Damned
by too much government, 96a
I'll be d. if I will, 274a
  *Dan McGrew
sat dangerous, 534a
  *Dance
becoming wealthy, 202b
as long as I live, 252b
wasn't greatest tap, 297b
I'm short for a, 579b
nation's character, 616a
  *Dante
glorified your Rockies, 111a
how did D. describe, 649a
  *Dare
let them come if they, 253b
  *Daughter
father, I love your, 9a
I in my mother's house, 308b
Imperial Order, 441b
  *Davis, Murray and Donald
what an entrance, 483b

*Davis Strait
nor hope of passage, 30b
north of, 30b
*Daws, John
died 1650, 15b
*Dawson City
all cried when left, 318b
*Daylight
Saving Time, 197a
*Days
in d. of yore, 439a
*De Havilland
a Caribou built, 564b
*De la Roche, Mazo
tradition includes, 367a
lives in delightful, 432b
smells of stable, 625b
*Dead
wait until you're, 169a
decorate tombs of, 272a
souls are reborn, 302a
the Akhoond is, 323b
we are the, 372b
Joe—three, 391b
*Dean, John
epitaph of, 16b
*Death
with a glorious, 29b
quickly and gently, 54b
winged peace or winged, 57b
our spiritual life, 84b
drowned running canoe, 100a
when spirit has gone, 100a
in swaying treetop, 122b
wish I could stick, 137a
interrupts all that is, 145b
all kings when we die, 146a
country needs no one's, 148b
courage by laughing, 176a
stare at chance-taking, 186b
valour gave them common, 193b
in the midst of life, 195a
building his nest, 213a
has never repelled, 213a
ashamed at eagerness, 226a
life, tragedy ending, 233a
wordless protest, 238a
an old meaning to, 241a
know not what we, 272a
global truth and, 297b
fear not that slays, 309a
as simple as life, 312a
such discerning auditor, 314b
there is no one like, 317b
risk of resurrection, 327b
is law, supreme, 328b
name for beauty not in, 336a
old age better than, 341a
moving into no man's, 341b
out of public life, 358b
nothing to a Frenchman, 361a
so be my passing, 400a
Canada and d. of him, 419a
why did people die, 423a
question of decently, 436a
sleep, forgetting, 457b
implies possibilities, 506b
some far away places, 548a
I am very near, 553a
chief whose name, 578b

can't take it with, 585b
no relief but in, 633a
but for short time, 642a
*Death penalty
See Capital Punishment.
*Decatur, Stephen
Commodore saying, 122a
*Decide
let Parliament, 305b
*Declaration
inspired by, 112b
of Independence, 583b
*Deeds
not bred by scenery, 69a
better than sonnets, 161a
cast long shadows, 239b
*Deeks, Florence Amelia
Plutarch also pirated, 627b
*Deer
go and shoot wild, 8b
although toothless, 9b
northern grazing country, 559b
*Defeat
worse stings of, 178a
one way out of life, 358b
will of people has, 495a
tired of seeing us, 520b
I was laid off, 549a
enthusiastic majorities, 557a
spirit will grow in, 615b
children of reality, 616a
for me a victory, 629b
*Defence
what is defending it, 38b
men defend destitution, 94b
dumping ground, nuclear, 153a
right to defend them, 167a
joined to U.S., 202a
common d. line at, 300b
and military bands, 303b
in Arctic is Arctic, 307b
our own d. policy, 348a
border undefended, 410b
what we are defending, 410b
Annapolis must be, 446b
U.S. not stand idly by, 509b
draw on rowers, boxers, 537b
without king paying, 574a
determined to d. lands, 578b
*Deficit
Montreal Olympics have a, 162a
*Delenda
est Carthago, 362a
est Canada, 540b
*Democracy
no greater farce than, 68b
the vast American, 113a
women should have it, 116a
ideal temperament for, 123b
majority rule, 207b
that final goal, 256b
most revolting kind, 272b
defeat economist, 278b
black king violated, 327a
public power, 352b
grows, liberty disappears, 401a
fatal to artist, 401a
patronage udder of, 515b
majority rule, minority rights,
    553b

gratefulness to democratic, 571a
first lesson in British, 594a
judged by minority, 597b
position of socialist, 601b
army poor training ground,
    601b
French and English, 601b
French never fought, 601b
not defeat but victory, 630a
people in action, 641a
heaven and perfect, 641a
in which war will be, 641a
under worst evils of, 644b
*Denmark
equal in extent to, 80b
example of king of, 187a
speaking everywhere, 205b
on Danish furniture, 273b
*Dentistry
pink tooth brush, 70a
if it hurts, don't, 430a
ethical practice, 463a
*Depression
best way to survive, 75a
tighten your belt, 159b
wiped me, took me, 282b
not a five-cent piece, 306a
essence of being in, 395b
very bad boom, 430b
sickness of capitalist, 608a
*Derby, Lord
at insistence of, 379b
*Despair
poverty has roots in, 148b
man truly despairs, 229a
ancestors who never, 237a
far side of longing, 303b
mind that wrestles, 316a
*Destiny
use terms of gentlemen, 45a
on the edge of, 57b
reserved for us, 109b
consciousness of common, 117b
ayorama, that's, 118b
promptings of your, 140a
an appointment with, 153b
magnificent d. in store, 165a
be masters of your, 214b
a great separate, 234b
a nation of nobodies, 243b
countries in control of, 365a
philosophers of history, 515b
uncertainty, obscurity, 518a
lies the d. of race, 621a
*Development
mid-Canada d. corridor, 508b
*Devil
Eskimo speaks to, 144a
John A. beats the, 265b
John A. beats the, 378b
*Dew
covers Island like, 11a
*DEW Line
Canada is a, 396b
arts and sciences, 397a
Canada valuable as, 398a
for the rest, 513a
*Dewdney, Edgar
dilatoriness of, 502b
*Diabetes

insulin and control, 33b
all that was written, 34a
*Diamonds
diamants of Canada, 102b
said Quebec diamants, 105b
roses rather than, 222b
*Dickens, C.H. "Punch"
Hollywood's idea of, 371b
*Dickens, Charles
formula for happiness, 224a
Pickwick did more, 338a
have you read, 338b
*Dickey, A.R.
support you whenever, 381a
*Dickson, Lovat
the Whiteoaks books, 145a
*Dictator
only portable, 66a
direct actionists, 117a
you are a d., Mr., 122a
what a d. we have, 268b
we will fall into, 602b
*Did
I d. it for Canada, 45b
*Die
he wants to, 9b
died citizen of U.S., 44b
if England lives, 49a
for my flag I come, 130b
not d. but step into, 135a
cost of living seeing, 190b
I d. famous, 239a
I do not fear to, 262b
in Toronto, Saturday, 278b
going to d. now, 315a
old garagemen never, 315a
to d. in Europe, 335a
insurance agents and, 337a
not afraid to, 357a
you'll never d., John A., 379a
a British subject I will, 380a
with special dash, 400a
guards d., surrender, 452b
right to d. in peace, 472a
old enough, live, 473b
time to learn to, 477b
writing about, 500a
neglected to prepare, 502a
got to d. of something, 540b
gracefully, properly, 638b
now I d. contented, 639b
*Diefenbaker, John G.
inspired Kennedy, 31b
time for a D. government, 95a
I am not worried, 96b
someone has passed away, 108b
the besetting disease, 125b
Dalton Camp's attacks, 246b
don't trust the bunch, 269b
the Chief's friends, 290b
predecessor John, 293b
called him s.o.b., 300b
what is a, 352a
right instincts in him, 446b
why burden sons, 585b
*Dieppe Raid
thousands slaughtered, 162b
what he did at, 226a
responsibility mine, 399b

come on over, 418a
lacked surprise, 504b
*Diet
sensible way to eat, 138a
fat people, lepers, 225a
*Difficult
educates in tight, 60b
Canada a place, 97b
a d. country to govern, 330a
do not crush men, 416a
*Dignity
are to have human, 109a
boundaries lack, 109b
constitution in English, 148b
beings live in, 302b
cities that impressed, 310b
no accepted symbols, 477a
*Dionne Quintuplets
know more about the, 136a
chosen for a miracle, 154b
*Dior, Christian
never darken my, 355a
*Diplomacy
resolve views in private, 255b
perpetual dialogue, 276a
tread softly, 367b
in stream of scotch, 347a
*Directions
rode madly off in all, 337a
*Dirty
the d. thirties, 282b
*Disarmament
in pursuit of, 87b
*Disaster
an unmitigated, 120b
precedes reform, 368b
which do come, 445a
*Discobolus
the D. standeth, 89b
*Discovery
dangerous, pleasant, 53b
European of America, 55a
names begin with c, 248a
Canadians and final, 276a
finding discoverer, 277b
no account encourage, 362b
has been my life, 560a
when European sets foot, 560b
of Canada and C.P.R., 624b
*Disease
small-pox, Indians, 51b
welcome the risk, 53b
periodontal, 70a
health best insurance, 169b
house with cholera, 391a
care for patient, 457a
list of symptoms, 457b
know syphilis, 458a
nature and gall, 458b
twenty drugs for, 458b
without books, 459a
Arabian Nights', 459a
[See also Illness.]
*Disneyland
Hollywood slums of, 202b
*Disraeli, Benjamin
twin brother of Sir John, 154a
since Arliss played, 342b
*Dissolution
P.M. requested, 91b

*Distant Early Warning
System
See DEW Line.
*Diversity
not carried far, 304b
unity of a thousand, 436a
to harness, 473b
*Divide
flee over Continental, 316a
*Divine
right of the Byngs, 91a
can be divined, 388b
yeast works in all, 477a
*Divorce
like an amputation, 28b
more plumbing, 280b
amend marriage, 288a
then remarriage, 288a
geese never apply, 421b
*Dixon, Franklin W.
even a ghost has, 383b
*Doctor
greatest ambition, 33b
key isn't skill, 219b
he could not save, 402b
who treats himself, 457a
educate is duty, 458b
*Documentary
the d. spirit, 123b
first to use term, 234b
*Dog
man's best friend, 9a
three noble, 15b
wonders why other, 133b
pursued by mad, 139b
by snow, Indians, 190a
failure to license, 259b
the golden, 312a
every d. in Quebec, 379a
name is Beautiful Joe, 525a
wolves say to, 646a
thieving, treacherous, 647b
*Dollard des Ormeaux, Adam
arise, D., and live, 236b
*Domain
on Canada's fair, 429a
*Domination
more than economic, 31b
not control but, 40a
co-operation, yes, 47b
baneful d. of mother, 275a
*Dominicans
and Jesuits fighting, 170a
*Dominion
was born the D. of, 11a
shall form and be one, 19a
are autonomous, 19b
the new, 22b
for me Triefste Provinz, 29a
autonomy of the, 68b
be known as the D. of, 98b
begun in Lamentations, 103b
our d. in America, 154b
business to get rid, 165a
we are called a, 187a
experiment failed, 231a
because of geography, 279b
geographical expression, 377b
a geographical expression, 378a
wound the Yankees, 379b

to get rid of the, 539a
shall be from sea to sea, 588b
shall form and be one, 614b
Her Majesty's in North, 615a
 *Dominion Day
if tourists turn up, 14b
 *Dominion Drama Festival
founded on love and whisky, 456b
 *Done
old French's d. it before, 83b
 *Donnellys, Black
See Black Donnellys.
 *Door
never locked his cabin, 141a
 *Dorion, Sir Antoine-Aimé
cut loose from Holton, 375b
 *Dostoyevsky, F.M.
read more D. than Keynes, 597b
 *Douglas, Major C.H.
when could you come, 1b
open a book by, 356a
 *Doukhobors
secure independence, 100b
this is D. country, 182a
confronted by six, 305b
continue to feel, 353b
honest, serious, 413a
form of communism, 414a
peasants in sheepskin coats, 542b
running naked over, 551a
most precious, 590a
automatically citizens, 613a
not given up souls, 613b
 *Draft
call it selective service, 3a
men will not enlist, 94b
every American dodges, 316b
objectors to Sweden, 370a
won't fight, 521a
dodgers, deserters, 584b
not immigrants, exiles, 634b
[See also Conscription.]
 *Drama
must include a, 53a
two great dramatists, 140a
dinghy sailing among, 146b
[See also Dominion Drama
 Festival.]
 *Drawers
hewers of wood and, 217b
 *Dream
you may d. of Niagara, 36b
the nation, 52b
man must have a, 101a
better things to do, 161a
art for awakened minds, 207a
imagine a Canadian, 265b
history before Europeans, 295a
socialism is but a, 338b
who do most d. most, 342a
I love a great, 368b
shall d. of beavers, 407a
live a life apart in, 443b
farmer guardian of, 505a
cannot d. of anything, 542a
the d. book, 545a
men who work cannot, 554b
poetry joins reality, 618a
people with no class, 649b

me no, 650b
of Canada, business, 650b
 *Dreaming
for high d. meant, 96a
go into wilderness, 238a
blind, hopeless, 294b
nationalism, utopia, 348a
businessman and a, 368b
 *Dreams
work to embody obscure, 166b
travels are d. twisted, 167a
are disturbing their, 176a
magnificent, 228b
emotion on fringe of, 241a
real and life sweet, 321b
not material of art, 369b
in d. behold Hebrides, 423b
make our d. our life, 463b
sidelines with our, 478a
become nightmares, 488a
prefer reality close, 491a
Paris a decor in, 506b
a lot of broken, 600b
splendid, fulfilled, 616a
refrigerator around, 622b
are all we own, 628a
 *Dressler, Marie
Dear Miss, 126a
real queen of movies, 508a
 *Drew, George
knows my father, 163a
terse response to, 269a
trouble with you, 454a
 *Drink
moderately, 77a
to get a d. of rye, 178a
a prohibitionist, 178b
make a dead horse, 321b
beaver gives us, 343a
yourself sober, 474a
recovering from, 622b
 *Drinking
and excellent hunters, 387b
no crime but disgrace, 389a
no duty performed, 392a
champagne of ginger, 393b
legislation, damnation, 411b
taking Cape Breton, 467b
 *Droit
maintiens le, 18a
 *Drugs
hair, hostels, hash, 156b
Canadian bouncer, 322a
chemophilic society, 404a
twenty for each disease, 458b
psychedelic coined by, 459b
puffed hashish but, 499b
get high on pot, 598a
 *Druid
no D. claims oaks, 592a
 *Drunk
John A. D., Brown sober, 380b
 *Dublin
like Belfast after, 431b
 *Duchamp, Marcel
and A.Y. Jackson, 313a
 *Duddy Kravitz
man without land is, 499a
 *Dufferin, Lord
saying no history, 212b

address in Greek, 381a
wrote to Tennyson, 580a
 *Dumbells, The
we entertained men at, 479b
 *Dumping
American periodicals, 293b
 *Dunkin, Christopher
was a hair to split, 384b
 *Duplessis, Maurice
portable dictatorship, 66a
thankful for celibacy, 66a
he'll never break me, 118b
not healthy to resist, 232b
can't do anything, 267b
a portable government, 324a
watch this young man, 575b
 *Durbin, Deanna
wears a turban, 25a
 *Durham, Lord
ten years before, 147b
appears then from, 253b
Canada death of, 419a
 *Dutch
origin in Commons, 152b
ambitious D. girl, 264b
Hurons trade with, 519a
[See also Holland.]
 *Duty
a man's chief, 60a
I have done my, 262b
not honourably avoid, 270b
share responsibilities, 329a
disagreeable, 428a
to fighting men, 489b
Mr. Jarvis, do, 517a
what we consider, 520a
live as long as, 605b
 *Dylan, Bob
the Charlebois of America, 107a

# E

 *E
Mari Merces, 15a
 *Eagle Hill
camped at east end, 482a
 *Earl Grey Trophy
for music, drama, 234a
 *Earth
whole habitable, 55b
his table is the, 74a
richest inheritance, 76a
occupy and possess, 84b
meek a time inheriting, 189a
heaven and hell on, 190b
rent for room on this, 233a
rich in Newfoundland, 252b
as men of the planet, 347a
surly bonds of, 403a
 *East
till West is, 308b
her gates both e. and west, 503b
bounded on west by, 625b
 *Eastern
bastard is my brother, 571b
 *Eastern Townships
cry echoing from rock, 377b

*Eastern Canada
hearts eastward, home, 257b
if you write of the, 549b
  *Eat
says et by a wolf, 134b
food known pleasure, 291a
let them e. shit, 598a
  *Eaton's of Canada
masters of consumption, 20a
want to write about, 37a
goods satisfactory or, 173b
together we make, 308b
the top of T. Eaton's, 326b
ruined by catalogue, 444b
read catalogue with, 550a
  *Eclectic
it's e. detachment, 550a
  Ecology
go on as we are, 61b
and ecological conditions, 351a
between man, surroundings,
      463b
  *Economic
government organize its, 1b
worries more than, 31b
has no e. unity, 67a
held in solving problem, 117a
necessity of Yankee blood, 183b
with e. goes political, 225a
political courage over, 229b
purpose of life and, 259b
socialism ethical not, 608b
  *Economic Nationalism
substantial in peace, 73a
parity with Texas, 115a
not desirable for, 137a
the Gray Report, 230b
fight the sale, 442b
ought to be grateful, 495b
if subways owned in, 509b
bought father's grave, 511b
mesmerized by the facts, 513a
with inferiority complex, 596a
abandonment of, 622b
  *Economy
medical and world, 54a
possible to plan an, 159a
triumph of politics, 183a
laissez faire dead, 199a
firmly Keynesian, 211a
the Detroit differential, 211b
to regain control of, 224b
democracy will defeat, 278b
lost unless he learn, 279a
has made us friends, 300b
leap into technology, 303a
statutory bones, 339b
apprehension is business, 342b
more self-sufficient, 348a
art without rewards, 568b
lying in bed not, 600b
discovery to the, 624b
  *Eddy, E.B.
taken at the Eddy, 76b
purchases of matches, 550a
  *Eddy, Nelson
let N.E. live, 14b
and Jeanette MacDonald, 206a
and Jeanette MacDonald, 524b

  *Eden
Upper Canada into a, 567a
  *Edison, Thomas Alva
if it weren't for, 62b
  *Editor
rather be e. of Globe, 81a
never ceased to be, 197b
live e. or dead hero, 270a
country could do with, 466a
against God or the, 584b
with talent of others, 649b
  *Edmonton
as big as Chicago, 13b
industry, integrity, 14b
or scattered like, 77b
go no farther than, 222b
Grads basketball, 443a
tell the people of, 461a
  *Education
of radical scholars, 3b
authorize females to, 14b
preservation of tribe, 57b
do will be ephemeral, 57b
well-rounded student, 58a
God educates people, 60b
not allowed to draw, 61b
Jeannine prayed, 104b
with human life, 116b
man ceased to learn, 117a
go to read novels, 134a
not without love, 148a
ridiculous, not free, 169b
curiosity basis of, 176a
disturbing dreams, 176a
adventure in realm, 189a
of white man's, 216b
principal of high, 238a
Confederation good thing, 264a
every house be school, 270a
normal school, colonies, 271b
folk keep too much, 277b
ceases to be student, 277b
high quality system, 288b
good thing, schoolhouse, 298a
forget bleeding heart, 302b
adult e. all about, 302b
sensitive, tough, 302b
a woman, whole family, 316a
co-operatives and, 318b
head of a school, 335b
examined last time, 337a
send B.A. to uncle, 338b
acquire cultivated, 339a
value of imbecility, 340a
a professor emeritus, 340b
last as long as life, 340b
fitted me for nothing, 342a
owe a lot to teachers, 342b
structuring yourself, 343a
by liberal e. I mean, 343b
not mind but e. lacking, 345a
Quebec's real revolution, 350b
teacher's interests, 359b
physical e., sports, 390b
legislation, damnation, 411b
get all you can then, 421b
concept of educated, 444a
authorities prevent, 444b
political e. my own, 447a
teacher three periods, 457b

place of music in, 472b
anti-British dialect, 509a
common as water, free, 517b
grandfather a savage, 521a
librarians have made me, 523a
students educate the, 532a
second-class students, 546b
expansion, deterioration, 554a
country can afford, 565b
man with e. in bush, 567b
teachers American, 569a
faith uneducated can, 590b
practical, co-operative, 590b
adult e., brains, 590b
to Canadianism, 603b
teach to love G.M., 617b
  *Edward VIII
you can't marry him, 415a
  *Edwards, Bob
all the best criminals, 450a
  *Edwards, Jonathan
has had no, 477a
  *Egypt
using Eskimo themes, 41b
Old Kingdom sculptures, 123a
government like mummy, 271a
art on a par with, 351a
the East but the West, 554a
if an E. from time, 591a
[See also Nile Expedition.]
  *Eh
great monosyllable, 456a
  *Einstein, Albert
truth is relative, 649b
  *Eisenhower, Dwight D.
Mount Eisenhower, 13b
  *Elbow
on the E. with his, 13a
  *Eldorado
Canada somebody's, 79a
  *Election
bribed with it, 47a
I want to win the, 267a
promise a boomerang, 323a
annexation of French at, 346b
like a horse-race, 378b
but to lose twice in one, 473a
politician someone who, 482b
will of people has spoken, 495a
tired seeing us around, 520b
conventions exciting, 447a
not won by prayers alone, 575a
  *Electricity
making her a servant, 41a
electric speech, 46a
[See also Hydro.]
  *Elephant
provincial politics like, 175a
Jumbo the king of the, 294a
can't wait to see, 355a
living next to U.S. like, 597a
nationalities like, 638a
  *Eleventh of November
Armistice Day, 373a
  *Elgin County
the preoccupations of, 167b
breathtaking loveliness, 210b
to listen to grass, 258b
  *Elite
the managerial, 211a

an é. group in charge, 250b
 *Elizabeth II
Her Majesty Queen, 20b
 *Emblems
of Canada, 14b
adoption of rainbow as, 291a
rainbow and Confederation,
  291a
Maple Leaf our e. dear, 439a
put Schenley's on, 471b
 *Emerson, Ralph Waldo
builded better than they, 11a
Twain must sit below, 339b
 *Emigration
let any Englishman, 59a
turn the tide of Europe, 81a
to wilds of Canada, 87b
Dominion ending in, 103b
geniuses of easy virtue go, 139a
not alter character, 205b
save from parochialism, 228a
young folk run off, 243b
keep people together, 316a
of radical elements, 356a
artists go to States, 369b
National Policy and, 378a
that's for them to say, 430a
move to keep whole, 566b
league of fallen leaves, 568a
 *Emotion
aroused by tragedy, 241a
with impermanence, 476b
acting is expressing, 495a
outbursts about matters, 556b
reaction to events, 649b
 *Emperor
to the e. of Canada, 472b
the little, 545a
made a Canadian out of, 611a
 *Empire
what an e. is here, 245a
northward course of, 559b
[See also British Empire.]
 *Empire Day
24th of May, 191b
festival on which, 233b
British sentiment, 511b
 *Employee
every e. tends to, 473b
 *Employment
National Policy and, 378a
every employee tends to, 473b
no English need apply, 563b
 *En roulant
ma boulé, 23b
 *Encyclopaedia
world unreadable as, 156a
Britannica and Alice, 337b
 *Enemy
know who is your, 9a
outlived all my, 35a
what do they look like, 54b
what you think of, 164b
come to find not make, 274b
fever, famine, war, 457a
suppose the e. have wings, 426b
they are ours, ships, 473b
 *Energy Crisis
Eastern bastard is, 571b
everyone wear sweaters, 629b

many would die, 636b
 *England
the Old Country, 28a
country overseas, 37b
who dies if E. lives, 49b
better without Canada, 63a
brethren across water, 271a
final expulsion of, 285b
Churchill image of, 297a
Victoria a piece of, 311a
splendidly isolated, 328b
advance or recede, 329b
18th c. belonged to, 333a
thank you, Mother, 339b
more civilized than, 345a
fear of offending, 358b
civilization no culture, 412b
see E.'s hand holding, 586b
 *English
you play politics, 26a
French as Americans, 67b
kindly looking face, 77b
eye of schoolmaster, 83a
callous shoulders of, 87a
enjoyed E. government, 123a
expense of British, 171a
without any accent, 192a
minority in Quebec, 227a
immigrant not popular, 248b
no E. need apply, 248b
mosquitos bite E. worst, 250b
speak E. but badly, 317b
use E. for literature, 341b
I talk Ontario, 341b
British can't speak, 349b
politics a business, 328b
have no sense, 345a
keep my E. chattels, 346b
can expect from, 361a
let us be E. or French, 381a
scorned the Indian, 464a
distinctive variety, 466a
no E. need apply, 563b
grand design failed, 612b
have not got wings, 612b
and the E. sot, 618b
 *English Canadians
enemies are anglicizers, 68a
two countries, one, 331b
no democracy for others, 601b
 *Englishman
no E. need apply, 9b
apt to be Philistine, 27a
term of anger, 41b
let any emigrant, 59a
who speaks French, 101b
feel the pride of, 177a
asserts from top, 191b
the noble E. will, 253b
found a great many, 286b
social standing depends, 368a
Anglo-Saxon leads way, 392a
raised the Indian up, 403b
duly catalogued, 542a
sets foot on land to, 560b
not be an E. merely, 587a
 *Entente
bonne entente, 10a
 *Entertainment
radio a source of, 147a

world of commercialized, 356b
Arabian Night's, 459a
in business long enough, 630a
 *Enthusiasm
we manufacture, 56b
a crank also, 134a
such capacity for, 154
 *Environment
problem of obliterated, 208a
not passive wrappings, 396b
man's relation to, 463b
is a total system, 463b
Eskimo influenced by, 559b
writer now an, 570a
 *Episcopalian
is chic, 26b
 *Epitaphs
they were broken then, 110a
everyman's friend, 141a
Mon Dieu est ma Roche, 145b
I am yesterday, 191b
that the beggar died, 228b
to the last round-up, 231a
Haine haint, 242b
that deep ideal life, 250a
I was well, 305b
two Canadian memorials, 309a
so be my passing, 400a
[See also Anonymous: Select
  Epitaphs.]
 *Equality
or to seek our, 3a
equal status, Dominions, 64b
the quest for, 125b
British Empire champion, 233b
equal status, 305b
worship of the god, 365a
Jack's as good's his, 392b
I want for women, 400a
men and women are not, 451a
Conservatives don't, 475b
 *Equivalent
moral e. of C.P.R., 608b
 *Erebus
possible survivor of, 203a
 *Errant
un Canadien, 216b
 *Eskimo
an E. in Athabaska, 17b
creation myth, 25b
legend of olden days, 25b
customs from life, 29a
adept at using themes, 41b
presence of several, 51b
vast backwoods, 62a
no word meaning art, 99b
the E. sings of life, 99b
love leads the, 109b
accepts things as, 118b
Esquimaux magicians, 144a
a Canadian may be, 185a
live in the moment, 195a
happiest people I know, 195b
kindly, brave, simple, 195b
soldiers half-breed, 198a
shared tea with, 245b
but make Ookpiks, 247a
translating the Bible, 247a
hidden forces appear, 267a

wisdom they have for, 268a
the carving tradition, 268a
cannot be certain, 277a
splendour of heaven, 279b
food consists of souls, 281b
adapting to money, 286b
sell an icebox to, 292a
distinctive music died, 297a
provide with heating, 326a
to instruct Congolese, 342b
Flaherty lived near, 353b
how mosquitoes came, 404b
found men clothed in, 408b
house E. in Chateau, 430a
be subject and citizen, 436a
shamans do everything, 443b
we believe in dreams, 443b
women become dangerous, 444a
fable of gnat, 445b
dark, I am falling, 448b
people say so much, 451b
to sing, to breathe, 456b
printmakers, carvers, 456b
spirit in the moon, 478a
joy of a singer, 478b
I see 10 caribou, 480b
managers of H.B.C., 485a
repeat what heart, 486a
luck follows, 487b
in need, abundance, 490b
wage struggle for, 490b
may you get to place, 490b
nothing but ice, 512a
happiness produced by, 512b
whether one was Indian, 553b
directly by environment, 559b
something intelligent, 559b
foreigners, friends, 560a
live by golden rule, 560b
the inuit change, 571a
my work is what, 588b
great sea adrift, 608b
 *Esposito, Phil*
best Canadian poet, 647a
 *Estevan*
murdered in Sept., 16b
 *Et*
he's been et by wolf, 134b
 *Eternity*
know the meaning of, 154a
too short to weary, 312b
beyond it is, 341b
union binds us, 406b
 *Ethics*
redefine medical, 54a
science and none at all, 189a
collective bargaining, 463b
basis of socialism is, 608b
 *Ethiopia*
not worth single life, 324b
 *Ethnicity*
cultural traditions of, 211a
each group dream, 221a
New Canadians and, 300a
native, foreign-born, 201b
ghettos of unpasteurized, 304b
just to all men, 385b
unity, diversities, 385b
land of Second Chance, 461b
white, heterosexual, 499b

and social class, 480b
 *Ethnology*
geologist and, 635b
 *Etrog*
the film award, 62b
the Etrog, 185b
 *Etruria*
as Rome by, 122a
 *Eunuchs*
critics like e. in harem, 43a
 *Europe*
a woman's like, 62b
its past glories, 65a
to laud well, 101b
English and French, 109b
proud, happy nations, 112a
historical centers, 161a
is behind us, 164a
can't find on globe, 222a
look upon past, 237b
independence essential, 293b
E.'s sham politeness, 294b
history a dream before, 295a
whose sensibility, 336b
a half-hour in, 353b
about as large as, 354b
stranger to E.'s sham, 534b
striving to remain, 552b
sets foot to dissover, 560b
 *European Economic Community*
See Common Market.
 *Evangeline Country*
New Brunswick's, 360a
 *Events*
stronger than advocacy, 385b
 *Evangeline Country*
refugee of our time, 315b
 *Everything*
for the baby, 79b
good now, 293a
 *Evil*
most scandalous, 97a
Canada shake world for, 233b
a choice between, 368a
whom people speak no, 368b
a basis for unity, 491b
but deliver us from, 502a
transcendence, 515b
 *Evolution*
won independence by, 180b
important thing is, 461a
there has been no, 503a
 *Executive*
thing an e. should, 28b
never do anything, 474a
 *Exile*
less fortunate in my, 109a
a Canadian e. wandered, 217a
condemning me to, 382a
from our father's land, 423b
one lives in orange, 462b
not immigrants but, 634b
 *Expediency*
is our God, 387a
is supreme law, 506a
 *Experience*
now I have, 40b
old enough to know, 178b
theatre good but no, 296b

of innocence, 357b
there are problems, 368a
distance essence of, 392a
seeing much, wisely, 458b
people ripened by, 477a
historian is treasure, 645a
 *Exploitation*
civilization reach, 198b
citizen's resistance, 207b
the state is our, 316a
 *Exploration*
dangerous, pleasant, 53b
sail toward Northwest, 92a
ambition to go far, 125a
camera on our, 195a
the wilderness, 435b
 *Explorer*
first then artist, 195a
supposed to be born, 238b
poet of action, 560b
 *Exodus*
Dominion ending in, 103b
 *Expo 67*
visit/ez Expo, 12a
our success at, 34b
Man and His World, 519b
[See also Habitat.]
 *Expression*
a mere geographical, 377b
more than a geographical, 378a
someone in front, 503a
 *Expulsion*
of the Acadians, 637b
 *External Affairs*
perfect representative, 645b
 *Eye Opener*
such high ideals, 178b
 *Eyebrow*
Marquis on the, 13a

---

# F

 *Fabians*
most Shavian of, 608b
 *Fact*
precedent, sir, is accomplished, 67a
 *Failure*
only crime was, 145b
a state of mind, 293a
man never to fall, 305a
best thing is trying, 428a
sugar of life, 448a
not afraid, I've, 479a
mingled successes, 486b
to give success, 593a
a chance of, 648a
 *Faith*
one law and one, 74b
guts without God, 170a
an expression of, 174b
defender of the, 182a
defence of Catholic, 236b
of ignorant man, 245a
antidote to idolatry, 303b
infuse into history, 322a
nations not civilized, 345a

Canada, supreme act of, 365a
if ye break f. with, 372b
not covetousness, 485b
the weapon of, 496a
agnosticism modest, 560b
have f. in man, 590a
*Falcons*
one catches white, 42b
bred in the north, 479b
*Fall*
spring forward, back, 14b
before f. comees, 166a
three months in, 185a
[See also Autumn.]
*Fame*
is in the song, 98b
privilege of being, 164b
reputation better, 164b
from literary view, 179b
history gave them a, 193b
dreaming of literary, 238b
remember us with no, 321b
everyone wants, 509a
*Family*
the disgrace to the, 180a
educate a woman and, 316a
allowance, baby bonus, 447b
raise large, 575a
choose my business, 585b
trees are questionable, 611a
*Family Compact*
evils which a, 55a
that this, 253b
of Upper Canada, 253b
*Famine*
land of feast and, 266b
things that change, 354a
great destruction, 404b
great enemies, 457a
*Famous*
become very very, 41b
I die, 239a
world-f. in Canada, 499a
to become very, 555b
*Farewell*
to N.S., sea-bound, 23b
this is my final word, 39b
*Farm*
as a boy on a, 211b
deficit into the, 342a
to be born on, 368a
two million families, 631a
*Farmers*
lives of f. all remind, 25a
I have helped the, 41a
cow worth only a, 114b
American millionaires, 128b
ever see him kiss a, 154a
you're not a, 159b
in Manitoba demand, 183b
Canadian may be a, 185a
chased by his bull, 249a
first farming colonist, 255a
the f. is king, 261a
in Sask. interested, 355b
aware yet inarticulate, 356b
remedy farm conditions, 400a
does in spare time, 400a
guardian of western dream,
    505a

you and the plough, 567a
sell the wheat, 596b
for physical strength, 649b
*Farmhouse*
frontier and the, 436a
poetry is like some, 491b
dotted with, 567a
*Farragut, David*
sailing up St. Lawrence, 2b
*Farther*
you go no, 500b
*Fascism*
Madrid the tomb of, 54a
Spain the tomb of, 54a
face of capitalism, 108b
private, public feud, 190b
*Fashion*
keeps the stalls, 244a
wear it, it doesn't, 299b
lipstick, rouge, 524a
*Fat*
See Obesity.
*Fate*
how our f. was changed, 12b
how cruel it can be, 68b
ayorama, destiny, 118b
not create misery, 404a
it is said it is so, 443b
ready and firm to, 638b
we cannot shun, 638b
*Father*
George Drew knew my, 163a
leap from honoured, 270b
doesn't like son, 345b
into the f.-land, 403a
takes sons to hockey, 445a
great f. in France, 480a
U.S. bought f.'s grave, 511b
creates circumstances, 548b
order and discipline, 598a
changed f.-hood, 600b
*Fathers of Confederation*
the F. of C., 9b
wrought well, 199a
if they reappeared, 236a
Harris' painting, 250b
only living, 549a
the father was deadlock, 552b
*Fátima*
our lady of, 523b
*Favour*
without fear, affection, 18a
*Fear*
loosely connected by, 75b
nothing to f. from, 97b
human race scares, 116b
thine own reproach, 135b
was afraid of nothing, 167a
and imagination, 190b
a f.-filled people, 268a
not death that slays, 309a
afraid of the worst, 513b
cold, hunger and, 534b
takes too much time, 598b
going to f. a mouse, 626a
*Feast*
land of f. and famine, 266b
*Federal-provincial relations*
fed up with federalism, 20a
a bit boring, 132b

cement more binding, 201b
a five-cent piece, 306a
assemblage of sovereign, 371b
all feel at home, 595b
foretaste of hindsight, 604b
elephants and, 638a
*Federalism*
clear mandate for, 596a
had a slight fall, 650b
*Federation*
although we are a, 187a
*Feeling*
as young as you feel, 26a
this disastrous, 85b
picture a highway, 250a
French have no, 327b
Englishmen never thinks, 328b
friend with warm, 334b
pictures not felt, 421a
power that drives art, 421a
few of us feel, 457a
*Fellow*
by f. Canadians, 152a
you are a curious, 335a
*Female*
deadly than male, 309a
more feminine than, 357b
*Fenian Brotherhood*
not take Zorra, 12b
let the F.s come, 22a
we are the, 22a
as well as a live, 42a
invaders of 1866, 349a
let the F.s come, 387b
was done for Ireland, 455a
propriety of invading, 455b
*Ferguson, Howard*
two monarchs, 258a
*Ferland, J.-B.-A.*
and Garneau, 129b
*Fertility*
a paradise of, 142b
paradise of, 262b
*Fetched*
their men every time, 254a
*Fifty-four forty*
or fight, 6b
and we didn't fight, 573a
*Fifty-fourth*
the highest floor, 230b
*Fight*
fifty-four forty, 6b
we've had a good, 7a
nothing relaxes boys, 113a
as you have ever, 135a
cut down trees, 148a
then I'll rise and f. again, 153b
for England, France, 331a
willing to f. losing, 334a
write as you, 434b
for God and country, 613a
people, none better, 248a
undrilled man not, 275a
Iroquois come, foxes, 319b
secret is, no hit, 393a
*Fighting Words*
TV panel show, 120b
*Film*
will reach people, 7a

prisoner of Zenda, 56b
a Canadian for you, 62a
English taxpayers, 62a
soon as they say, 85b
seen Topper, 100b
fan club is group, 100b
tall, high-bred, 114a
human race scares, 116b
greatest triumphs, 123b
animation is art, 127a
she can't sing, 143a
no interest in theatre, 159a
trouble, joy, fun, 162b
getting stuck-up, 170b
stay down, last, 171b
earliest exhibitors, 176a
The Etrog, 185b
actors in Canadian, 189a
Faulkner, Mounties, 190a
as Honest John, 192b
knew nothing about, 195a
no thought making, 195a
they try to rush, 198a
Toronto movie industry, 209b
Hollywood press agent, 210b
in a cowboy movies, 214a
money with no strings, 220b
in Hollywood with It, 220b
what is truth, 234b
vastly important, 235b
have your own, 235b
directors prefer TV, 262a
parts in Hollywood, 268a
stage better, 275b
can afford to say, 287a
having them shown, 295b
took Boris out, 296b
I couldn't act, 297b
paid me $10,000, 319a
saw Arliss, Disraeli, 342b
demystify mystique, 343b
genial or shifty, 358b
Canada is okay, 350a
every frame matters, 367a
new-fangled things, 390b
give intellect rest, 393a
animation, movements, 393b
reconcile disparities, 401b
Mickey and Charlie, 410a
stage experience, 410a
public my judges, 414b
up in the mountains, 426a
for casting Englishman, 430b
body opens doors, 432a
Canadians know little, 433a
art that is of use, 447a
one-day pictures, 452b
movie like a novel, 460b
snow scenes detrimental, 467a
exceptional, accident, 470a
America's Sweetheart, 476a
my Metro years, 476b
sidelines with dreams, 478a
industry but finances, 482b
Marie Dressler Queen, 508a
N.F.B. a model, 512b
earned two Oscars, 516a
Andy Hardy's girl, 516a
done with mirrors, 522a

as a boilermaker, 533a
working for M.G.M., 538a
establishment films, 538b
short features, 538b
things work out, 538b
endless Mounted, 539b
invent a name like, 540a
or theatre, same, 540b
say noting, 547b
actress' position, 550b
is a cosmic strip, 555b
man who never smiled, 556a
Mounties vs. Atomic, 559a
wanted to ride, 563a
to Toronto not for, 569b
the I-don't-care, 574a
quota system on, 577b
performance same, 587b
to be a star, 606a
created enough stars, 621b
a great screamer, 644a
crowded in middle, 647a
everyone an accent, 649a
go back to Canada, 650a
*Finance
health more important, 37a
a buck is a buck, 101a
the f. system, 158a
ask the Minister a, 193b
figures are bilingual, 200a
well-designed expenditure, 342a
Montreal the capital, 542b
*Fingers
the law of the five, 56a
million f. in dikes, 275b
*Fire-proof house
we live in a, far, 137b
*Firefly
life is a flash of a, 133a
no lighted lamps, 156b
*First, Canada
See Canada First.
*Fish
catch plenty of, 8b
N.S. surrounded by, 11b
point of view of, 46b
gravest f. is the, 47a
weather for catching, 60a
swim through border, 174a
inexhaustive supply, 218b
oil from oolichan, 235a
swimming in Canadian, 263b
nothing but furs, 290b
let me f. off, 298b
sailors off Nfld., 349b
didn't discover water, 463b
inexhaustible supplies, 465b
halibut by thy name, 467a
*Fishing
steal your lines, 10b
per angler per day, 124a
excuse, near rivers, 242a
too busy to go, 387b
Confederation, f.-rods, 551b
Catholic way of, 590a
I need to go, 646a
*Five
law of the f. fingers, 56a
Nations Confederacy, 144b
f.-cent piece, 306a

5BX Plan, 455b
*Flag
wind that wants a, 7b
no foreign f. shall float, 21a
bore holes in British, 31b
protecting aegis of, 49b
one fleet, one f., one, 64a
protection of British, 81a
procrastination has a, 88b
keep the f. flying, 113a
American f. will float, 113b
the sake of my, 130b
no spirit for distinctive, 136b
the day we acquire a, 138a
British f. never cease, 141b
last hand waves British, 181a
one school, one f., one, 227a
the British f. will, 230a
born beneath the British, 290a
shot my f. to ribbons, 290a
the old, 315b
wherever the British, 330a
strangle Riel with the, 379a
folds of Union Jack, 379b
old f., old policy, 380b
wrapped himself in England's,
    382b
that floats above us, 416a
planted firm Britannia's, 439a
one f., one throne, 441b
British f. floats over, 455b
future does not dishonour, 469a
Manhattan did not fly, 493a
this country hasn't a, 519a
moved a mile, 528b
serving under an alien, 539a
last shot fired by a French
    Canadian, 572a
indifference in Quebec, 594b
[See also Union Jack.]
*Flaherty, Robert
tremendous advantage, 353b
*Flanders
line of defence is, 68a
not in trenches of, 334b
In F. Fields, 372b
battle-ploughed roads, 527b
*Flaubert, Gustave
include Tolstoy and, 367a
*Fleet
one f., one flag, one, 64a
*Fleming, Donald
ought to be on record, 39a
you should know, 269a
*Flies
the little black, 256b
*Flight
In High, 403a
*Flin Flon
the sunless city, 483b
*Floral
wheat elevators out, 69b
*Floral
Canadian f. emblems, 14b
*Florida
Nova Scotia to, 131a
go to F., bask., 343b
*Flowers
trees brilliant as, 164b
women fly and, 172a

water the field or, 172b
savage as well as, 406b
delphiniums sprout, 446b
struck by smallness, 484a
should not mean, but, 530a
scentless bloom, 580b
 *F.L.Q.
the manifesto, 20a
thought about killing, 126b
bad dream end, 132a
created as entity, 242a
goodbye till 1967, 273a
victim, no menu, 316b
did it for kicks, 317a
gift for Mr. Cross, 322a
[See also October Crisis.]
 *Flung
himself from his horse, 377a
 *Flying
Americans on their side, 49b
Hughes taught me to, 143a
I was f. too law, 210a
Phil, minister of, 210a
[See also Aviation.]
 *Flynn, Errol
a real man's man, 226a
I refuse to predecease, 621b
 *Follow
let those f. who can, 41a
my white plume, 330b
 *Follower
if leader strides, 277a
for 33 years I was, 322b
 Fon Sang
See Fusang.
 *Fontainbleau
the F. manifesto, 616a
 *Food
rotting in warehouses, 1b
recipe is a theme, 50a
mirages of heavenly, 54b
Pablum, 79b
killed by cooking, 89b
mouth and stomach, 110a
slice of cow's rear, 114b
and bad architecture, 123a
sensible way to eat, 138a
human f. consists, 218b
pleasure of eating, 291a
Canada, vichyssoise, 297b
ice cream is soft, 298a
buffalo makes f. of, 299a
it's a lump of coal, 301b
beaver gives us, 343a
rest, f., fresh air, 458b
after the riot eat at, 485a
deep apple pie, 528b
largest business, 561b
crook-neck squash, 587a
refrigerator around, 622b
why people lack, 643a
 *Fool
Aberhart's f.-osophy, 2a
gravest man is the, 47a
all the damn f. on my, 158b
can laugh at death, 176a
keep at a distance, 179a
things you try, 179a
not addicted to own, 180a

are purchasers, 244a
forest or palace, 349b
wisdom is f.-ishness, 458b
and his heritage, 506b
wants a f.-killer, 610b
 *Football
to happen to him, 35a
come on after, 71a
when the tape is, 92b
who beat Commies, 399a
back-breaking, 418a
to toss the ball, 473a
homesick, hospital, 493b
lost when think, 588a
 *Force
the silent, 19a
shalt not let down, 360b
not application of, 364b
keep status quo, 509b
 *Forcibly
peaceably if possible, 48a
 *Ford, Henry
history bunkhouse, 447b
more important, 632a
 *Foreign
not regarded as, 198a
all aid short of help, 636b
 *Foreign affairs
poor countries assist, 298a
scope for independent, 348a
majesty of England, 380a
 *Foreign investment
not less Canadian, 63b
ought to be grateful, 495b
wasn't narrow issue, 513a
extent of control, 622b
 *Foreigners
can expect deportation, 230a
test of civilization, 460a
don't like us, 637a
 *Forest Hill
Crestwood Heights, 532a
 *Forests
gave away the, 25a
background of primaeval, 59a
eternal, 63b
exuberant as tropical, 84a
annihilation, 104a
I had died in, 109a
dark gloomy, pine, 283a
red man in pathless, 295b
belonging to himself, 349b
stands the f. primeval, 359b
from the f. and prairies, 360a
too much, 372b
full of harsh, 406b
disdain the dryad, 592a
challenging space, 625b
 *Foretaste
a f. of hindsight, 605b
 *Forrester, A.
ran 100 yards, 503a
 *Forsey, Eugene
in more modest terms, 333a
 *Fort Garry
assembled in Upper, 82a
received visitors at, 348b
 *Fort Macleod
code of rules, 577a

 *Fort Ste. Marie
set fire to it, 489a
 *Fort William
mental hospitals, 88b
feudal state of, 280b
 *Fort William Henry
spare the English, 426b
 *Fortune
leads on to, 76b
immense in colony, 52a
seeking in U.S., 126b
empties chamberpot, 377b
hastening to make, 426b
 *Forty-ninth Parallel
between the, 113b
close down the, 134a
close the 49th, 289b
who live north of, 353b
[See also Border and Frontier.]
 *Founder
the f. of Manitoba, 501b
U.E.L. grand F.s, 581a
 *Fountain
unto a f. clear, 23a
 *Four
million Britons not free, 59b
the f. H's, hair, 156b
strong winds, 606a
 *Fox
Macdonald is as sharp, 322a
hunting the Canadian, 448b
you bite very hard, 500a
 *Foxes
Iroquois come like, 319b
 *France
to the expense of, 52a
surrounded by a little, 63a
King of F. sleeps, 65b
amity and kinship, 67b
spirit of Christian, 68a
under Pétain, 68b
despot who rules, 76a
country as large, 80b
on account of wines, 101b
rather improve old, 108a
councils of allies, 112b
no connection with, 162a
transmitting language, 171a
language, manners, 171a
of police power, 183a
we are French despite, 204b
part fulfilled in, 210b
the substance of, 214a
expects you to do, 214b
not always French, 237a
martyrs for Christ, 260a
political passions, 328a
we may meet again, 350a
couldn't live without, 354a
people, depopulate, 362b
needs you, build, 404a
has culture, but no, 412b
des vraies Canada, 432b
produces emphatic art, 433a
Quebec far away, 442a
shall F. remain here, 464a
St. Pierre and Miquelon, 484b
all round Paris lies, 524b
battle-ploughed roads, 527b

best natural scenery, 564b
Christian civilization, 575a
change in peasantry, 576b
old F. is in Canada, 589b
vive la F. et les, 596a
do well without Que., 617a
*Franchise
person means a male, 19a
men start to vote, 370a
vote by ballot is, 565b
*Franco, Francisco
Spain under, 68b
*Franglais
tongue not French, 460b
*Frank Slide
Ballad of the, 212b
*Frankenstein
not true I was born, 296b
*Franklin, Benjamin
has had no, 477a
on diplomatic mission, 620b
*Franklin, Sir John
record left here, 369b
heroic sailor soul, 579b
*Franklin, District of
Northwest Territories, 15a
*Fraser River
hurray, the R.'s ours, 22a
where the F.R. flows, 261a
*Fraternizing
too much with enemy, 187b
*Frechette, Louis-Honoré
come too soon, 130b
*Fredericton
Fredericopolis silvae, 15a
O snow-washed city, 119b
*Free
where coloured men, 21b
coloured men are, 22a
responsibilities of, 45a
Britons who are not, 59b
defended by f. men, 76a
no f. country can, 87a
as winds of Heaven, 99a
someone pays, 169b
world co-operation, 180b
trade to enrich, 217b
equal and unfettered, 270b
their press not, 271a
do great things, 477b
true north strong and, 626a
trade and national, 604a
*Freedom
and civilization shall, 1a
without f., no name, 2a
the ways of, 12b
who stands if f. fall, 49a
every man enjoys, 49b
fierce desire for, 65a
the home of, 74b
character of Britons, 76a
vives to F.'s name, 94b
absolute, unqualified, 99a
spirit of f. a, 112b
are imprisoned in, 148a
right to be wrong, 152b
stop me from talking, 153a
shed my blood for, 155a
wears a crown, 190a

that must be won, 193a
expression of tolerance, 207b
literary f. lawyers, 209a
air perfumed with, 227a
fearless champion of, 233b
made a man roll, 257b
baneful domination, 275a
reaching a land, 288a
with friendship, 293b
is bred in bone, 301b
star towards which, 330a
under institutions, 330b
wide land of, 361b
single desire for, 384a
have f. of comment, 398a
there is no more, 405b
when abused, 410a
for Hungary, 412b
Crown is Imperial fountain,
416a
who saw it first, 455a
society is anchor, 479b
not a legacy, 541a
none between joining, 558a
gravity interferes, 588b
mother taught me, 597a
just society establishes, 597b
and totalitarianism, 607a
not metaphysical, 609a
religious, individual, 613b
Sons of F. cannot, 613b
throughways of, 616a
space to move my, 641b
tyranny of abstractions, 642a
in poem scribbled, 645a
*Freedonia
this Marx Brothers', 304b
*French
we fight politics, 26a
be F. as Americans, 67b
enjoyed F. culture, 123a
born F., not ceased, 185a
Babel and F. kiss, 188a
are F. despite France, 204b
period of supremacy, 212b
whatever has role, 214b
ideal for future, 221b
a minority in Canada, 227b
distinct F. life, 236b
whole of F. America, 237a
not F. from France, 237a
comes from France, 237a
sending a colony, 290b
keep my F. heritage, 346b
let us be English, 381a
embraced the Indian, 464a
*French Language
good F. accent no, 43a
language used, 51a
enemies of language, 68a
an Englishman who, 101b
speak French and breathe, 107a
understand every word, 153a
understand better, 153b
spoken only by, 295a
Kennedy and Diefenbaker's,
301a
less bad than some, 324a
mangles, learns, 328a

to speak in Ont., 334b
vanishes as one goes, 340a
learning a foreign, 406b
slight Norman accent, 413b
a Canadian accent, 449a
O Montreal, what, 463b
of a province that, 508a
speak, not understand, 605a
essayant à parler, 605a
I forgot to speak, 611b
*French Canada
France's régime, 67b
Canadianism extinguished, 80b
doctor, priest, 109b
quest for equality, 125b
million inhabitants, 157b
role comparable to, 162a
live, love, dream, 166b
nationality destitute, 171a
americanise, anglicise, 181a
conflict in the soul, 185a
mission to fulfil, 210b
annexation of, election, 346b
balanced attitudes, 346b
Quebec political voice, 349b
scatter our sons, 417a
given to nostalgia, 422a
right to separation, 442b
mission to radiate afar, 462b
miracle of survival, 528a
relic of past, 552a
where it is going, 571b
has come from, 571b
apathy for years, 589a
Trois-Rivières second city, 604a
bound to ancient Gaul, 614a
more North American, 618a
*French Canadian
most ignorant, dirty, 35b
deserving of success, 36b
history of nationalism, 63a
common adventure, 74a
bilingualism, paradox, 106b
shalt not criticize, 148a
last hand waves British flag,
181a
advantages, privileges, 193a
make it chic to be, 236a
for one millionaire, 246b
bowlegged cousins, 301b
make the total man, 346b
one in Ottawa, 405b
not become an Astor, 446a
nationalism, defence, 463a
will fire last shot in American
soil, 572a
patriot has hope, 575a
sagacity than English, 575b
opposed to nationalism, 595a
*French Canadians
weakened and degraded, 68a
insert into American spirit, 68a
literary pabulum, 89a
nothing to fear from, 97b
raise the tricolour, 138a
no ambition beyond, 147b
are improved Frenchmen, 169b
English women happy, 191b
against tradition, 229b
submissive in faith, 232b

that little group of, 237b
keep people together, 316a
position of command, 318a
aware of themselves, 324b
belong to one country, 331b
assimilate in Que., 349b
have no ambition, 462b
governed to satisfaction, 478b
speak the French of, 508a
follow is to war, 537a
language of Louis XIV, 561b
simple happiness, 589a
distinct and vivacious, 589b
there at end of story, 591b
coming people, 592a
no belief in democracy, 601b
never for democracy, 601b
  *French River
no moose south of, 134b
  *Frenchman
no more of them, 82b
some old F.'s done it before, 83b
is naturally noisy, 118b
a million F. forgotten, 130a
French Canadians improved,
  169b
death is nothing to a, 361a
borrowing grace from, 384a
sank to Indian's level, 403b
gentlemen and, 555a
  *Freud, Sigmund
God carries less weight, 570a
  *Friday
black F., boy, 39a
this is black, 46a
  *Friend
best is his dog, 9a
who is your, 9a
next to a worthy, 103b
he was everyman's, 141a
an acquaintance, 179b
prefer f. to alien, 232a
hope an unsafe, 244b
warm feelings, 334b
what a f. we have in Jesus. 531a
one f. insecure, 649b
  *Friendly
the f. Arctic, 559b
  *Friends
will take the trouble, 42b
this book belongs to, 53b
don't tell friends, 164b
room for many, 165a
will exaggerate your, 179b
need cheering up, 190b
history has made us, 300b
economics has made us, 300b
no f. in Canada, 366a
Americans f. whether, 584a
bounded on the south, 625a
you have many loyal, 650b
  *Friendship
share warmth of fire, 116b
terminate in peace, 154b
selfishness half the, 244a
seeks its counterparts, 244b
freedom with, 293b
maintain, independent, 329a
more f.s than warships, 421b
like a Red River cart, 572a

  *From
sea to sea, 14b
Canada, by land, 389b
sea to sea, 588b
  *Front de Libération du
    Québec.
See F.L.Q.
  *Frontenac, Comte de
and the St. Lawrence, 69a
  *Frontier
of friendship, 12b
where there is no, 38a
a great line, 38b
two great powers, 47b
that long f. from, 112a
undefended because, 124b
natural f. between, 174a
the country is all, 253a
and the farmstead, 436a
we have our f. land, 560a
[See also Forty-ninth Parallel.]
  *Frost, Jack
gratuitously guards us, 264a
  *Frozen
words f., not heard, 487b
slept at edge of f. sea, 507a
  *Frye, Northrop
and McLuhan at University,
  581b
  *Fu Sang
See Fusang.
  *Fuddle-duddle
origin of, 599b
  *Fuel
if heating is cut, 636b
  *Fuller Brush Company
a good brush could, 209b
  *Fulton, E. Davie
for F. means no more, 39a
  *Fundy
in the Bay of, 86b
  *Funeral
of Montcalm, New France, 427a
Montcalm that of New, 464a
  *Fur Lady, My
Uncle Lou, Uncle Lou, 156b
  *Fur trade
build me a fortune, 28a
not reason coming, 72a
music drama of, 74a
accustomed to women, 97a
nothing to acquire, 115b
distance from Canada, 131a
failed as source of, 152a
sent furs home, 158b
monopoly of land, 220a
Sinbads of the wilderness, 280a
nothing but f., fish, 290b
fondness for beaver, 345a
and love of rum, 387b
or Lebanese fur-trappers, 451a
strip local quadrupeds, 416b
Canada useful for, 480a
Revillon Brothers, 495b
philanthropy not object, 544b
northward course of empire,
  560b
[See also Coureur-de-bois.]
  *Furnace
full f. of this hour, 321a

  *Fusang
country, B.C., 235a
Chinese name for, 540a
  *Future
pioneers of glorious, 18a
there's no, 33b
possession of our own, 50b
no f. for us, 65a
beating out the, 65a
putting in debt, 83a
can feel it too, 103b
long frontier pattern, 112a
be what we make it, 137a
mercy the f. hidden, 199b
be Canadians and f. yours, 204b
I have seen the, 208b
and it doesn't work, 208b
our master the, 221a
question of Canada's, 225a
magnificent dreams, 228b
sense of great, 234b
past, master of, 236a
in America a great, 237b
lost, invented, 264a
common aspirations, 300b
greater looming, 322a
still more hope, 332a
belongs to those who build, 333b
I care about our, 369b
with hope, anxiety, 384a
probable of provinces, 385b
alone with history, 394b
of f. is present, 398a
Trudeau walks into, 447a
greater than past, 460b
flag not dishonour, 469b
with national spirit, 512a
title-deeds to the, 555a
have no remarkable, 560a
scares hell out of me, 561a
is beyond knowing, 584b
find our greatness, 598a
to do great things in, 607b
as certain as sunrise, 610b
betrayed the defeated, 616a
country with greatest, 631a
see the f. plainly, 637a
a f. without hope, 641a
free and audacious, 642a
  *Futureless
makeshifts suit a f. people, 201b

## G

  *Gaelic
blessing, Lord hold, 11b
true to the ear, 386b
Canadian Boat-Song, 423b
  *Galahad
with Machiavelli, 557a
  *Galaxy
Empire a g. of nations, 327b
  *Galbraith, J.K.
greatest modern, 87a
  *Gambling
king of Monte throwers, 66a
only game in town, 96a

*Game
golf not a, 338b
playing a poor hand, 350a
*Games
people play, 51a
*Gananoque
Friendship Bridge, 509b
*Gang
it's the Happy, 467b
*Garbage
everywhere, 27b
New York spends more, 298a
no collection of, 528b
*Garden
of the Gulf, 15a
carve initials here, 89a
spot of the Gulf, 249b
get ourselves to, 422b
*Gardiner, James G.
not a farmer, 159b
*Garneau, F.-X.
and Ferland, 129b
*Gas
shall flow from, 39a
magic in natural, 311a
*Gaspé
Cartier stopped at, 163b
beaver is beloved, 343a
*Gassy Jack
I have done well, 144a
*Gates
traversed the ocean, 125a
wholesome sea is at, 503b
*Gatineau
crucifix in hills, 84a
*Gaulle, Charles de
words shocked and, 469b
*General Motors
masters of consumption, 20a
be riding with, 131a
direct descendant, 394a
teach them to love, 617b
*Generalities
governor-generalities, 83b
*Generation
humiliation against older, 192a
none self-sufficient, 237a
if we fail this, 431a
crooked, perverse, 459a
say we'll stay, 471b
*Genest, Jacques
Montreal, hypertension, 432a
*Genius
never mount high, 77a
render you great, 224a
remoteness, reticence, 250a
fanned by domestic, 270a
permanent popularity, 339b
celebration of 487a
suspicion, distrust, 522b
French not same as, 575b
*Gentlemen
embezzle, not steal, 341b
we g., they burglars, 377a
English g. in bush, 429a
no advantage to poor, 429b
hard for the poor, 592b
born to shed blood, 613a
rather have written, 639a
a scholar and a, 645a

never lower standard, 647b
*Geographical
has no g. unity, 67a
cement more binding, 201b
a mere g. expression, 377b
more than a g. expression, 378a
more than a g. expression, 532a
laid down in g. position, 583a
*Geography
triumph of politics, 183a
lost unless learns, 279a
Dominion emerged because,
    279b
has made us neighbours, 300b
neighbours accident of, 306b
some countries too much, 306b
cannot legislate against, 328b
defied g. to produce, 336b
preferred to Druid, 592a
in the beginning was, 619a
and ethnologist, 635b
*George II
Newcastle told that, 638b
*George III
if we had hated, 391b
behold the pope, 618b
*George V
obeisance to shrimp, 539a
*George VI
goodbye, brother, 234a
Vancouver City Hall, 387a
knighted my husband, 624a
*German
girls bending over, 4a
will never turn out, 5a
enemy not the Boches, 68a
origin in Commons, 152b
see G. in England, 162a
the G. method is, 164b
war upon the world, 248b
in the G. army, 263a
movie in a G. car, 273b
my camera like a, 297a
invented printing, 297a
becoming a wee bit, 326a
worse G. at our gates, 334b
prepared for worst, 358a
be nationalized, 383b
rewards Canada to U.S., 424b
Trotsky in camp for, 594a
won independence, 530a
late lamented Kaiser, 568a
Canadian out of emperor, 611a
*Germany
declare war on, 83b
absence of taste, 204b
travelling now, 256a
where was he born, 313b
and Japan want you, 314a
not more civilized, 345a
*Get their man
always, 18b
their men, 254a
your man, 369a
not, 641b
*Ghibellines
like the Guelphs and, 82b
*Ghosts
our lack of, 57a
Esther Cox, 128a

denied, overcome, 139b
recipe for a real, 320a
no place for, 567b
spirits banished, 592a
*Giant
strength of a, 32a
prepare for warlike, 468b
g.-limbed child, nations, 504b
the people make, 590a
*Ginger Ale
the Champagne of, 393b
*Giotto
the frescoes of, 123a
*Girl
poor little g. of, 24a
looks not virtue, 164a
has pretty face, 179b
the King's, 318a
mistake marrying, 342a
the g. from Toslow, 346a
boy meets girl in Winnipeg,
    395a
nicest marry snakes, 401b
*Girl Guides
thanks to groups, 30a
*Glasgow
sensible Scots pouring, 117b
*Global
village idiots, 174b
image of g. village, 396a
*Globe and Mail, The
rather be editor, 81a
subject truly loyal, 294b
object purchasing, 644b
*Glorious
Bidwell and g. minority, 55a
*Go
you g. no farther, 500b
*God
g.-given right to suffer, 1b
damn the English judge, 8a
bless, 6a
not heard by, 9b
your own g.-damn, 10b
rocks at Labrador, 10b
gone to meet his, 15b
save our gracious Queen, 22b
g.-forsaken Canaday, 24a
the candle of, 60a
by g. and Methodists, 70b
true g. and son, 72a
invoked the g. of nations, 82a
O g., O Montreal, 90a
act of g. to beat us, 92b
land g. gave to Cain, 101b
Labrador lost g. made, 102b
he took arrows, 105b
bring inhabitants to, 105b
stooped to pick up, 110a
French sing g. save king, 112a
is alive, magic afoot, 120a
g.'s country, 135b
chosen for a miracle, 154b
no guts without, 170a
bless America but, 178a
but g. save the king, 178a
nor talk of death of, 187a
praying as g. were all, 190b
fulfil our intention, 203a
ancestors, making, 221b

little seal of, 247a
put him in speech, 259b
white man's willed it, 290a
has many bests, 305a
man never to fall, 305a
used Conquest to save, 317b
I love my, 318a
poet writes for, 336a
a great people, 362a
divine disposer of, 367b
save the king like hell, 382b
he fought for us, 426b
served faithfully, 427a
save our Queen, 439a
without g. no rights, 451a
afterthoughts of, 457a
forget flood interview, 490a
starts nations, 501b
calls the other, 527a
purpose wrought, 527b
spirit of man my, 529b
stones sing g. save, 544b
designed by supreme, 567a
church, witch of, 609b
worship on my toes, 612a
be praised, I die, 640a
has many bests, 643b
can't bless America, 650b
 *Goethe, J.W. von
how many G.s or, 336b
 *Gold
where you find it, 14a
up in Porcupine, 24b
they gave away, 25a
northern Ontario claim, 33b
is a woman, 81b
amid mud of politics, 103a
stones in sun like, 206b
columns rise, 271b
the g. fever in B.C., 317a
dig out in North Ont., 342a
streets paved with, 362b
men who moil for, 534a
my favourite colour, 586a
bounded on north by, 625b
[See also Klondike.]
 *Gold Rush
See Klondike Gold Rush.
 *Golden
the g. dog that gnaws, 312a
was a g. ship, 445a
maison du chien d'or, 513b
the g. age of radio, 626a
 *Golf
spells backwards, 62b
played on Sunday, 338b
 *Gompers, Samuel
can't attend funeral, 393a
 *Good
peace, order, g. gov't., 19a
sound g. will of two, 38b
not much can be done, 60a
still moveth towards, 94b
greatest to greatest, 173b
cheaper than wicked, 179a
man who goes wrong, 179a
success paved with, 179b
be g. to be lucky, 223a
Canada shake world for, 233b
everything g. now, 293a

noblest motive public, 312a
we dream of, 328a
be g. and happy, 334a
order of g. cheer, 349b
Toronto the, 388b
Jack's as g.'s his, 392b
don't believe in, 545b
common good, profit, 608a
 *Goods
satisfactory or money, 173b
 *Goose
to describe a, 230a
youngest in Canada, 239a
hissing at coach, 272a
silly as a, 421b
take only one mate, 421b
nine lives on each, 421b
beaver and Canada, 523a
allusions to Canada, 549b
migration of the, 629a
 *Goose Bay
touched down in, 100b
 *Gooseberries
radishes and, 235b
 *Gordon, General Charles
from G.'s chain, 91a
 *Gordon, Margaret
rose goddess, 98a
 *Gordon, Walter L.
prepared budget speech, 193b
told an accountant, 507b
 *Gothic
motifs of Canadianism, 344a
a G. pile, 552a
 *Gouzenko, Igor
I cannot see him, 519b
 *Govern
to g. is to choose, 69a
a hard country to, 138b
colonial deadweights, 155a
a difficult country to, 330a
not easy to g. a, 365a
a hard country to, 381b
most difficult to, 469b
to their satisfaction, 478b
to g. is to choose, 595b
 *Government
peace, order and good, 19a
in advance of opinion, 32a
I can buy any, 33b
the g. fired me, 36a
the g. of soldiers, 43b
reform means more, 49a
only excuse for, 49b
persecution by the, 61b
entrust g. of country, 64b
ten provinces with, 75b
when people have no, 82a
N.S. does not support, 87a
if votes your way, 91b
reigns 4,000 miles, 94b
time for Diefenbaker, 95a
damned by too much, 96a
institutions challenged, 111a
tolerable, unbearable, 137a
responsible g. at least, 147b
Opposition's duty to turn, 153b
clutches of big, 159b
wise old gardener, 161b
couldn't manage me, 167a

wonderful constitution, 183a
we have ten, 187a
services, aids to business, 199a
legislation in minutes, 201a
industry took over, 218b
Tory only g. for, 244a
patriot no sycophant to, 245b
happiness on character, 245b
stupidly one managed, 263b
ancient Egyptian mummy, 271a
bias of communication, 279a
wealthy afford inefficient, 298a
Duplessis a portable, 324a
fight neglect of, 328b
with perfect citizens, 342a
big business hold hands, 352a
application of force, 364b
with a big surplus, 376b
interest in good, 391a
get things out of, 400a
guess-work, 415b
that is despotic, 427b
peace, order and good, 436a
colonial misgovernment, 445b
maintain people or, 454b
minority g. not easy, 469a
no accepted symbols of, 477a
secular vs. spiritual, 479a
education best security, 517b
know a good picture, 537a
compared with England's, 552b
gratefulness in dealing, 571a
parades itself before, 587a
best were least reminded, 587a
not opposed to males in, 632a
made in boardrooms, 638a
irresponsible g. more, 648b
 *Governor General
cannot escape world, 91b
the G.G.'s Award, 120a
this sea-to-sea Dominion, 124a
wonder if we want more, 137a
not going into history, 149b
Gee Gee, 156b
who had lost Canada, 165a
superintending machinery, 165b
a dubious joke on, 166b
tightrope of platitude, 233b
Rideau Hall saved us, 298b
seignorial rights, 323b
be walking behind, 344b
who didn't buy it, 481b
reading Proust in Rideau, 502b
get rid of the Dominion, 539a
who had lost Canada, 539a
not stay as Duke of, 571a
 *Governor Generalities
must confine himself to, 83b
 *Grace
happiness obstacle to, 220a
Canadians' easy social, 256a
from the Frenchman, 384a
Lord grant us, 483a
were their compass, 485b
before meat, 642b
 *Grain elevator
light in west over a, 27b
pride in theatres, 282a
 *Granary
of the Empire, 549b

*Grand Pré
low tide on, 98b
little village of, 360a
*Grand Trunk
a G.T. of thought, 384a
*Granny's Laddie
composed in Saskatoon, 326a
*Grant, George Monro
this wonderful progeny, 17a
*Grant, George P.
Underhill gave years, 608a
*Grape shot
a whiff of, 155b
a whiff of, 643a
*Grass
will grow, 155b
sea of waving, 247b
listen to g. grow, 258b
please walk on the, 584a
in ivory towers, 648a
*Gratefulness
an important factor, 571a
*Grave
as deep as the, 11a
who find in America, 12a
canoe over my, 23b
paths lead to, 230b
fathers leap from, 270b
old g. was history, 339a
Americans bought, 511b
paths of glory lead, 639a
*Gray, James H.
remember Pearl Miller, 402b
*Gray, Thomas
written G.'s Elegy, 532b
*Gray
not obpective to be, 475a
exact shade of, 624a
*Gray Report
faced squarely, 225a
*Gray's Elegy
recited by Wolfe, 639a
*Great
too near to be, 12b
Island, 15a
the g. lone land, 91a
recognizing greatness, 99a
good to greatest number, 173b
known to be great, 266a
people make country, 312b
men are frauds, 335a
funny and, 339b
this g. country, people, 362a
develop g. men, 604a
*Great Britain
infinite shadows, 38a
amity and friendship, 67b
Upper Canada larger, 81a
too-ordered island, 178a
glories of Mother, 201b
magnificent dreams, 228b
shall be Greater, 228b
struggles for liberties, 270b
size of Vancouver Island, 311a
is at war, Canada also, 331a
records of empire, 367b
is connection with, 380a
ardent good wishes, 425a
acquired her Empire, 520b
constitution very image, 544a

U.K. citizenship, 585b
surface of the globe, 625b
*Great Lakes
armed vessels on, 31a
to Ontario's towers, 71b
they are too big, 78a
another 1,000 miles, 228b
to the G.L. waters, 241a
unite with Ottawa, 328a
people who live north, 353b
of the Northland, 360a
red men scalped each, 369a
five-fold lakes, 384b
arms-limitation clause, 515b
excellent States, 535a
boundless horizon of, 583a
naval superiority, 627b
*Great Slave Lake
north country around, 84a
in Yellowknife, 316a
lives on Lake Athabasca, 348b
*Greece
as large as, 80b
philosophic climate, 119b
as G. by Persia, 122a
sort of vassal, 235b
decline of civilization, 279a
art on a par with, 351a
action is duty, 461b
*Greek
poets on beavers, 108a
music based on, 297a
you don't know, 381a
*Greene, J.J.
enjoy several positions, 557b
*Greenland
along shores of, 238a
in Vineland days, 344b
pygmies, Skraelings, 417a
I saw several, 440a
called Skrellings, 587b
*Grenfell, Wilfred
lives given for mine, 15b
*Grey, Earl
for as he said, 567b
*Grey Cup
superfan comes to, 35a
amateur rugby, 234a
dreaming happily, 607b
*Grimshaw
Alberta and Mile Zero, 316a
*Grip
motto of, 47a
*Grits
want only clear, 111b
truth sounds to, 153b
Gritterdämmerung, 203b
giving the, 378b
who vote G. or Tory, 392b
but dine with, 454a
[See also Liberals.]
*Grocer
born a man, died, 15b
*Grosse Ile
memorial to dead, 12a
*Group of Seven
the hot mush school, 210a
one called Jack Pine, 356b
never going anywhere, 369b
the hot mush school, 375a

bad advertisement, 467b
*Growth
learn to grow, 57a
we fostered their, 99a
Canada not greatly, 203b
growing points, 234b
means never having, 241b
*Guadaloupe
some for keeping, 478a
*Guarantee
goods satisfactory or, 173b
*Guard
die, never surrender, 452b
stand on g. for thee, 626b
*Guelfs
like G. and Ghibellines, 82b
*Guelph
the royal city, 215a
*Guess-work
government, 415b
*Guibord, Joseph
buried by arms, 69a
*Guilty
not g. but don't, 375b
if I thought you were, 513b
got to find me, 629b
*Gulf
Garden of the, 15a
garden spot of the, 249b
*Guns
amid the g. below, 372b
have g. will travel, 406b
never had g. taken, 604b
*Guthrie, Tyrone
proposal an air of, 322b
*Gypsy
all kinds when we die, 146a
oldest living, 343b

# H

*Ha Ha
Saint-Louis-du, 12a
*Habit
of millions, 277b
difficult things a, 360b
tenacious than work, 434a
sleep is only a, 610a
*Habitant
with a pipe, 7b
with a h. tomorrow, 89a
millions are, 277b
wide awake boy, 575b
*Habitat
spontaneous, self-made, 518b
[See also Expo 67.]
*Hair
when I see you, 254b
likes not colour of, 271b
Tribal Love-Rock Musical, 364a
a h. to split, 384b
short-h., long-h., 507a
*Hakluyt, Richard
to say, my dear, 465b
*Half-breed
I am the h.-b. question, 500b

*Half-way
house of the Empire, 228a
*Haliburton, T.C.
witty head of, 322a
*Halifax
E Mari Merces, 15a
Warden of the North, 15a
dog's tail in, 96b
typographical error, 113b
a posting in, 160b
chain of theatres, 197b
bookshelf reaching from, 238b
after H. we visited, 251a
to the Pacific in days, 271b
attack of H. next year, 285b
warden of the honour, 308b
not limited to, 379b
glacier-scraped, 395a
I arrived in, 413b
named in honour of, 488b
introduction to speech, 582b
Trotsky's wife held, 594a
*Hall, Basil
Canada inhabited, 561b
*Hall, Charles Francis
he talks wildly, 605b
*Halves
do nothing by, 529b
*Hamilton, Alexander
godfather of Confederation,
440b
*Hamilton
scaffold in disrepair, 184a
*Hamlet
features of Horatio, 347b
*Hand
changed and by whose, 12b
these h.s are clean, 46b
bishops eat out of, 170a
right out of action, 177b
might be disabled, 178a
last which waves, 181a
infinite number, 255a
whenever I see a, 255b
have h.s across the sea, 355b
a bird in the, 364a
that rocks the cradle, 370b
these h's are clean, 376b
I admire his h.-writing, 381b
never let one know, 529a
*Hanging
the H. Judge, 42b
we know how to, 66a
to a past age, 184a
he shall h. though, 379a
*Hansard
survive horrors of, 76b
official records, 248a
challenge reporter, 599b
*Happiness
to communicate, 60a
civilization for, 71b
of people sacrificed, 71b
in love you manifest, 88a
farthest boundaries, 109b
may be glandular, 140a
on St. Lawrence, 145b
cosmopolitan unhappy, 192a
capacity infinite, 213a

future h. of the world, 220b
formula for misery, 224a
depends on character, 245b
Canada happiest of all, 310b
happiest, I compose poems,
335b
give h. and prosperity, 363a
haven to be place of, 368b
life, liberty and, 436a
renounce the idea of, 444b
lies in some vocation, 457a
by a blue bead, 512b
more to life than, 541a
simple h. contents, 589a
isn't everything, 624a
when toothache stops, 649b
is assured, 650b
*Happy
and glorious, 22b
I have been very, 55a
take off clothes, 62a
God takes no thought, 220a
be good and be, 334a
from proud yoke, 426b
work today and be, 472a
without Canada, 480a
be h. without Quebec, 617a
*Happy Gang
it's the, 467b
*Happy Hooker
make more money, 264b
*Hard
Canada a h. country to, 381b
as No. 1 Manitoba, 398a
*Hardy, Andy
I was A.H.'s friend, 516a
*Hardy Boys
even a ghost has some, 383b
*Harem
critics like eunuchs in, 43a
like Turk in his, 270b
*Harmony Harbour
we give you ships, 257b
*Harris, Frank
memories left me cold, 444b
*Hart House
a very good play, 537b
*Hate
love those we can, 149b
efficiency makes, 179a
most hated woman, 635a
*Hays, Charles
great artists today, 567b
*He shoots
he scores, 260b
*Head, Sir Francis
lark named Charley, 16a
*Head
you get your h. above, 171b
use your bloody, 302b
have your h. in air, 454b
Scots all right in, 358b
*Health
ministry more important, 37a
in h. manifest, 88a
most h. country, 169a
insurance against disease, 169b
not resist Duplessis, 232b
know about mental, 235a
no care more expensive, 246a

right possessed by all, 246a
comprehensive public, 288b
reason for selling, 308a
not come for our, 438a
the quadrangle of, 458b
*Heart
how a h. can pump, 2a
gut but not the, 5b
small roots of her, 9a
your treasury is, 49b
cool the, 55b
let each say his, 69a
sick for something old, 78a
of man in times, 93a
always near my, 105a
proud to wear, 110a
absinthe makes, 131b
dateless calendar, 167b
never while living, 206b
into wilderness of, 238a
mechanism of the, 244b
Quebec the original, 255a
roving h. gathers, 284a
in the h. of people, 290b
forget your bleeding, 302b
thought, harnessed, 313a
my h. is calling, 358a
writer have pores, 371b
as sound as No. 1 hard, 398a
the h. is Highland, 423b
youth dwells forever, 428b
looking into my, 462a
have nothing but my, 502a
mistakes of the, 548b
passport bilingual, 615b
right there, 634a
*Hearts
in the h. and minds, 11a
your h. beat in unison, 33a
there is room for, 165a
turn your h. home, 257b
with ten-cent, 334b
Scots all right in, 458b
worn-out, fun-loving, 547b
philosophy in the, 563a
a lot of bleeding, 598a
with glowing h. we, 626a
our h., as oarsmen, 631b
*Heaven
creator of H. and, 72a
free as winds of, 99a
the white man's, 160a
like Union Nationale, 169b
believe in h. on earth, 190b
Marxism and Kingdom, 199a
as near to h. by sea, 218a
all the splendour of, 279b
is a great land, 302a
see you in Spence Bay, 315a
tired woman rest, 334a
don't need socialism, 342b
sweetest music this side, 359a
where we do things, 368b
ask about this in, 371a
right here on earth, 435a
and h. bless, 439a
which art, halibut, 467a
if h. were haven, 485b
pray for him in, 502a
if h. more beautiful, 521b

future of man my, 529b
love thee in, 579b
if Max gets to, 628a
perfect democracy, 641a
  *Hebrew
prince of the, 79a
yadoa in, 563a
  *Hebrides
in dreams behold the, 423b
  *Hell
talk of h. and paradise, 72a
insignificant, 148b
truth sounds like, 153b
believe in h. on earth, 190b
war h., homesteading, 301b
all h. for a basement, 311b
Canada anteroom of, 325a
already have socialism, 342b
mines like darkness of, 349b
so what the h.'s the use, 382b
in Norway like Toronto, 503b
slavery next thing to, 603b
less h. and more wheat, 611a
merger between heaven and,
  628a
on wheels, 632a
how did Dante describe, 649a
  *Hello
after you say, 51a
Canada and hockey, 260a
  *Hellyer, Paul
going and leaving, 559a
  *Help
friend, acquaintance, 179b
want us to h. you, 329a
for other fellow, 421b
all aid short of, 636b
  *Hemingway, Ernest
danmed short sentences, 113b
not liked Canada, 561a
  *Hémon, Louis
Maria Chapdelaine, 238b
myself as Canadian, 366b
  *Henderson, Alexander
think continentally, 197a
  *Heritage
destroy of solitude, 203b
imbecility or our, 340a
no h. worth preserving, 499a
land to that tribe, 501b
fool and his soon, 506b
  *Hero
Mackenzie was this, 21b
cannot make a h. of, 82b
imagine myself the, 120a
memory of the past, 129b
at Dieppe, quietly, 226a
Dollard with accents, 236b
live editor, dead, 270a
Horatio Alger never, 356a
vanish in a wood of, 347b
Wolfe the dauntless, 439a
true martyr, h., sage, 523b
impose on others, 642a
  *Herodotus
father of lies, 276b
  *Herridge, W.H.
put in the phrase, 150a
  Hewers
of wood and drawers, 217b

  *Hiawatha
should you ask me, 360a
  *High Flight
slipped the surly bonds, 403a
  *High River
ceiling of drugstore, 69b
  *Highlands
the h. of Canada, 91b
the heart is, 423b
peopled by dispossessed, 434b
  *Highwood River
ranch in valley of, 177b
  *Hills
blue h. of old Toronto, 63b
thy pine-clad, 70b
cold on Canadian, 322b
unto the h. around, 362a
  *Hincks, Sir Francis
all able men, 266b
  *Hinge
priceless of pure gold, 428b
  *Hinky-dinky
par-lee-voo, 496b
  *Hirsch, John
used to say that, 492a
  *Historians
record nothing older, 38a
a double task, 322a
substantial definition, 336b
literary ballonists, 375a
guardian of the past, 645a
  *History
your Canadian textbook 12a
no consistency in, 40a
repossession of our, 50b
reading h. one must, 57b
record of stolidity, 58a
psychology, not of, 72b
wrote on margins of, 83a
where h. is bound, 103b
much in 100 years, 118b
jump on Canada's spine, 120a
intellectual like broken, 125b
encounter, character, 129b
sense of courage, 129b
literature not science, 129b
teaching all wrong, 136b
and eternity, 154a
people with no literature, 171a
need not repeat, 179b
them a common fame, 193b
yesterday's news, 203b
coldly scientific, 212a
of Canada as a whole, 212b
is yet to be written, 212b
about time Canada entered,
  214b
has taught us that, 225a
society with least, 229a
which is most alive, 236b
carries virtues of race, 237a
into h. in Europe, 240a
men of the north, 243a
art more than, 250a
can't never finish, 251a
what biography, 266a
pass into legend not, 267b
as dull as ditchwater, 276b
Herodotus father of, 276b

hoped-for appointment, 277a
lost unless learns, 279a
dream before Europeans, 295a
music in any book, 295a
of North and airplane, 298a
has made us friends, 300b
business h., poem, 304a
neighbours an accident, 306b
countries have too much, 306b
in course of human, 307b
word origin cultural, 313b
Algonquins no past, 319b
storms, battles, 325a
modest yet heroic, 332a
old grave was, 339a
bourgeois, voyageur, 348b
meaningless in eyes of, 349a
written in language, 367b
the real h. of Canada, 368b
name mentioned in, 374b
Canadians not written, 375a
alone with h., science, 394b
an unknown thing, 395b
of ideas, of race, 401a
have just enough, 492a
more made than written, 407b
to our h. be faithful, 416a
write, read, make, 422a
and took whisky, 431b
is bunkhouse, 447b
two miracles of, 528a
writing with the gun, 567b
American not British, 569a
of ideas approach, 581b
must stand outside, 584a
no h. associations, 592b
to point liberty, 601a
not impossible, 602b
instead of submitting, 609b
responsibility for our, 610a
unites and makes, 610a
bounded on east by, 626a
never be true record, 634b
partial to victor, 645a
if he knows any, 645a
  *Hit
'em where they ain't, 297b
  *Hitler, Adolf
tyrannies of, 112b
no posthumous victories, 187a
purged by pistol, 313a
and Swastika, Ont., 493a
insecure person, 649b
  *Hiving
the Grits, 378b
  *Hobbes, Thomas
copy the linees, 91a
  *Hochelaga
great river of, 102a
the town of, 102b
send Cartier to, 203a
suitable name for, 386a
[See also Montreal.]
  *Hockey
true Canadian invention, 6a
stick to your league, 43a
defensive play, 44a
in the Metropolitan, 56a
statistics for losers, 70a
a war too dull, 78b

rattlesnake hunt to, 85b
two intermissions, 95b
game you love, 113a
few bodychecks, 128a
beating Russia is, 185a
like scoring goals, 215b
Team Canada and, 217b
a shouted hit him, 224a
democracy all about, 256b
hello Canada and fans, 260a
he shoots, he scores, 260b
giving autographs, 269b
great h. player, 270a
has been good to me, 274b
is a war, 278a
my job is win, 278a
of national culture, 302a
Canadian metaphor, 302a
dance of life, 302b
against Israelis, 313a
play to win, 419a
Canadiens institution, 424a
sons to the game, 445a
Panamanian player, 451a
to World War II, 452a
is all action, 456b
go in myself, 466a
getting shot at, 478b
some suggestions, 487b
size doesn't matter, 497b
some were good, 497b
ballet as Russians, 512b
les Canadiens sont, 532b
players are Canadian, 542a
was never in doubt, 546a
give him a tickle, 546a
can't beat 'em on ice, 555a
the Stanley Cup, 558b
birthplace of, 574b
goalkeeper as good, 614a
called a mystique, 648b
*Hoei Shin
visited B.C., 235a
*Hog's Back Falls
Prince of Wales Falls, 177b
*Hogtown
Toronto the Good, 388b
[See also Toronto.]
*Hold
a vaster empire, 439b
*Holland, Andrew
film exhibitors, 176a
*Holland
like tulip bulbs, 235b
Dutch have their, 290a
crime three times, 464a
[See also Dutch.]
*Hollywood
slums of Disneyland, 202b
ones in H. who have It, 220b
made me a monster, 296b
thing I like about, 357a
enough stars to fill, 621b
*Holton, Luther H.
cut loose from Dorion, 375b
*Home
of the R.C.M.P., 15a
of the Klondike, 15b
bring h. with him, 43a

so you come from, 47b
that encourages, 63b
true woman asks, 116a
wherever we happen, 116b
brought the ages, 134b
Canada, my h. land, 217a
young, strong, 237a
eastward, turn hearts, 257b
for h. and country, 265b
raise to highest, 266a
house, schoolhouse, 270a
don't think I'll come, 339b
can be really at, 351a
build an enduring, 365a
our beloved Canadian, 387b
half of what I have, 426b
our h. and native land, 626a
make things go well, 635a
*Homer
glorified your waves, 111a
*Homestead
the Alberta, 25a
war is hell, but what is, 301b
*Honest Ed's
fun to shop at, 422b
*Honesty
a Liberal contractor, 69a
men are ruined, 426b
*Hong Kong
and Liverpool and, 379b
*Honour
sacrificed everything, 11b
guided by sentiments, 97b
a man of, 111b
the sense of, 166b
acquit themselves, 212a
life, tragedy, field, 233a
eternal to discoverers, 246a
warden of the h. of, 308b
to save our, 309a
single desire for, 384a
any peace is, 535b
the hon. stinker, 597b
*Honours
decorations, damages, 175a
away with tunics, hats, 213b
medals be of silver, 414a
*Hooker
the Happy, 264b
*Hope
nothing to h. from, 97b
for a millennium, 117b
a new hopefulness, 238a
pleasant acquaintance, 244b
beyond hopelessness, 303b
the h.-despair balance, 316b
in the human race, 356a
springs eternal, 416a
Trudeau burdened with, 447a
romantics lost courage, 572b
thou land of h. for, 626b
common to theatre, 631a
*Horatio
wild Hamlet with, 347b
*Horning, L.E.
a questionnaire, 180b
*Horse
treat like a woman, 26b
and jockeys mature, 41b
British Empire and a, 53a

you talk like a, 66b
in Toronto I show a, 78b
dark h. against, 95b
lost, h. dead, 105a
decadence of the, 156a
candidate good h.-man, 205a
great h.s live again, 250b
lead a dead h. to, 321b
his h. and rode madly, 337a
poetry of the, 354b
if you'll be a good, 373b
election like h.-race, 378b
invention had to do, 468a
the h. before cart, 492b
just wanted to ride, 563a
talked only of, 570a
two things about the, 628a
is to Arab, 641b
*Horwood, Harold
name Grenfell meant, 233a
had never seen Toslow, 346a
*Hospitality
lovely, redeeming, 78a
has been such, 249a
Canada a generous, 448b
*Hot
the h. mush school, 210a
the h. mush, vital, 375a
line, war, 469a
*Hotel Fort Macleod
code of rules, 577a
*Hottentot
whether Canadian or, 136b
premier of H. village, 186a
*Hour
is great with change, 504a
*House
when h. is on fire, 66b
open doors of the, 145b
in the h. of words, 151b
richer in ruined, 183b
rest is h.-keeping, 202a
I'm a h. painter, 202b
half-way h. of Empire, 228a
every h. be a school, 270a
h.-holds complicated, 297b
daughter in my mother's, 308b
masters of our own, 349a
not same for a woman, 440b
I am a h.-wife, 519b
is the whole of Canada, 595b
*House of Commons
few speeches inspired, 30b
master of its rules, 39a
always H. of C. man, 153b
[See also Parliament.]
*Howe, C.D.
you can do and Howe, 156b
but a nice fascist, 383a
*Huckleberry Finn
greater than Kant's, 337b
*Hudson, Henry
historical picture, 452b
this dreamer, mote, 482b
*Hudson Bay
adventurers trading, 107b
zeroes through Nfld., 365b
excellent states, 535a
Sinbad never saw, 583a
*Hudson's Bay Company

Home of the Bay, 15a
governor, adventurers, 107b
pro pelle cutem, 158b
evils of monopoly, 220a
and miners in B.C., 317a
strip local quadrupeds, 461b
where Eskimo managers, 485a
slept at frozen sea, 507a
pro pelle cutem, 515b
philanthropy not object, 544b
what interest in fort, 614a
  *Hughes, Howard
taught me to land, 143a
  *Hugo, Victor
the daughter of, 274b
  *Human
enemies of h. race, 54b
tribe is now race, 57b
concern for h. condition, 94a
half the h. race scares, 116b
as if I rejoined, 141a
unilingualism, 348b
only h.s are wild, 421a
awful to be a, 423a
too few h. beings, 650a
  *Humane
Canada may become, 642a
  *Humanity
owe allegiance to, 38a
greatest contributions, 68a
scale outside that, 84a
the love of, 103b
service to France, 162a
electric chair, 184a
real society, 208a
claims of industry, 305a
over all nations, 305a
nations unite to, 307b
you are a part of, 343a
three great enemies, 457a
above all nations, 551b
revolutions devour, 601a
  *Humber River
Babylon-on-the, 388b
  *Humour
awful in its own, 6a
no Mr. Pickwick, 340a
hard, meritorious, 337b
hyperbole and myosis, 337b
he has no sense of, 338a
essentially comforter, 339a
apt to be melancholy, 339a
kindliness, 339b
kindly contemplation, 340a
best definition, 341b
droll situations, 458a
best of Leacock, 484a
not congenitally comic, 533a
surprise, violence, 533a
  *Hungary
when I left, 192a
freedom for, 412b
poet, traveller, 465b
  *Hunting
shoot other game, 8b
like most societies, 268a
brings out fish, 382b
drinkers excellent, 387b
Eskimos desire, 490b
vast h. preserve, 635b

  *Huron, Lake
in a valley near, 70b
  *Hurons
long live the, 3b
if we spoke Iroquois, 130a
Christmas carol, 72b
conflicts with Iroquois, 283b
Jesuit fathers, 309a
obstinacy, 318a
set fire to Huronia, 489a
peace with Iroquois, 518b
paradise of the, 573b
  *Hurry
socialists, liberals in, 520a
  *Husbands
actresses don't have, 8b
ignorance of women, 61a
men, women, wives, 103b
girls at Montreal, 295b
don't understand women, 323a
suspects one other, 445a
opposite of male, 650a
  *Hydro
electricity servant, 41a
nationalization, 350b
public utility, 400a
[See also Electricity.]
  *Hymn
work for the night is, 118b
unto the hills do I, 362a
  *Hyphen
in liberal-conservative, 104a
left at embarkation, 136a
no h.-ated consideration, 152b

# I

  *I don't care
the I-don't-care girl, 574a
  *I Remember
Je me souviens, 15a
  *I'll
never smile again, 364a
  *I'm Alone
see you in hell, 489b
  *Ibsen, Henrik
two dramatists, 140a
  *Ice
mast-high floating, 122b
retreat left Canada, 229b
a new Inferno all, 282b
marine sponge, 486b
nothing but i. there, 512b
that i. is stone, 512b
can't beat 'em on, 555a
  *Ice-breaker
the John A., 493a
  *Ice worms
when the i.w. nest, 571b
  *Icebox
this sanctimonious, 353b
  *Iceland
in Vineland days, 344b
  *Idea
in a dress suit, 34b
not needed for parties, 82b
man of noble, 111b

some transforming, 117a
attacked by mad, 139b
more powerful than, 155b
public afraid of, 238b
maddest to, 250b
rich with one, 244b
French have no, 327b
no new ideas, 337b
just jot down, 342a
bulging briefcase, 367b
born in stables, 392b
history of race, 401a
mission less change, 462b
mental highways, 479a
give the people, 590a
blow the roof, 590b
have hands and feet, 590b
a hundred years old, 643b
  *Idealism
autobiography, 368b
glitter delivers, 423a
  *Ideals
begin and end, 34a
illiterate ancestors, 166b
not abolition of, 220b
constantly strive, 328a
pursuit of abstract, 358a
not become an Astor, 446a
true to creation, 459a
Canada in great, 573a
he defends noble, 615b
  *Identity
separate national, 33a
individuality vanished, 59a
group derives its, 82a
strong political, 85b
know what I am, 126b
what we are, 167a
lack of i. is, 175a
no one is looking, 179a
remain invisible, 203a
do not discover, 203a
uncreated i. of, 207b
distinct from, 289a
taxed for having, 288b
determined for a, 232a
not without interest, 353b
lives without an, 396b
sense of density, 396b
violence quest for, 398a
too much search, 426a
annihilation, 428a
if not ourselves, 431a
British, American, 469b
unity, uniformity, 506b
intellectuals in, 515b
liked Ed Sullivan, 553b
  *Ideology
land of no one, 304b
character more, 447a
not begin in, 481b
basis of socialist, 601b
objectivity is the, 610a
  *Idiot
no i. shall vote, 19b
  *Idly
U.S. not stand by, 509b
  *Igloos
biggest mines among, 474b
  *Ignorance

never tackled, 34a
lot is bad, 179b
may find truth, 277a
more satisfaction, 368b
of Upper Canada, 391a
of Canada in, 450b
  *Ile d'Orleans
on Island of Orleans, 84a
  *Illegitimacy
children born out, 249b
  *Illinois
fifty bullocks from, 38b
  *Illness
moveth towards, 94b
God gives insurance, 169b
mental i. is like, 235a
in my childhood, 313b
[See also Disease and Mental
  Health.]
  *Illusions
part of, truth is, 254a
life's I, 422b
lived under, 450a
  *Image
glamourizer, 301a
very i. and transcript, 544a
  *Imagination
stolidity broken, 58a
with a big enough, 74b
those powers of, 77a
like caged tiger, 93a
men declares he is, 139b
and fear, 190b
loses its power, 207a
society of perverted, 208a
comprehend society, 208a
make sense of, 208a
find meaning, 229b
shadow a little, 244a
tradition a stimulus, 372a
not art material, 369b
primitivism, 404b
great gift of gods, 534a
holy water, 586b
too matter-of-fact, 592b
Crusoe a feat of, 616a
suicide best exercise, 625a
  *Imagism
and the prairies, 275a
  *Immigrant
Irish i.'s prayer, 11b
any young Englishman, 59a
English not popular, 248b
to land in B.C., 310b
good as Canadian baby, 475a
chairman an i. boy, 509a
  *Immigrants
no Englishman need apply, 9b
we are all, 28b
and labour laws, 133b
of well-governed, 122a
but we are, 346b
not i. but exiles, 634b
  *Immigration
you have no rent, 8b
eaten by tigers, 9b
surplus population, 104b
to depopulate, 120b
Canada-Ukraine, 136a

traverse climes, 222b
friendly to people, 227b
disgrace to family, 296b
New Canadians, 300a
difficult for Asians, 304b
build Babylons, 345b
of conservative, 356a
depopulate France, 362b
too many spoons, 392b
Englishman two years, 413b
deterring one family, 429b
organize reverse, 439a
treat a foreigner, 460a
snow scenes and, 467a
Group of Seven and, 467b
mixed interest, 534b
peasants in sheepskin coats,
  542b
country of welcomes, 547a
the King's girls, 574a
penal colony, 650a
  *Imminence
of the natural world, 208b
  *Immorality
not buy books, 222b
man advises behaviour, 444b
  *Immortality
but step into, 135a
small measure of, 238a
  *Imperial
from i. service, 178a
strengthen the connection, 385b
no stronger link, 410a
  *Imperial Order Daughters
    of the Empire
always taking me, 31a
Daughters of the Empire, 441b
  *Imperial Preference
Borden favoured, 311b
  *Imperialism
sentiment, outlook, 50b
Canadian nationalism, 50b
diluted with, 189b
citizen's resistance, 207b
the black king, 327a
foreign-based unions, 356a
  *Imperialist
man who accepts, 48b
the true i. is, 95b
foul i. profits, 261a
not pretend to be, 330b
attacked as an, 330b
nationalist must be an, 504b
  *Imperially
learn to think, 197a
  *Impregnable
Quebec is, 612b
  *In Flanders Fields
the poppies blow, 372b
  *In High Flight
slipped the surly bonds, 403a
  *Incognita
Meta, 181b
  *Income
less than ours, 33a
  *Incompetence
employee tends to rise, 473b
  *Independence
we manufacture spirit, 57a
Doukhobors secure, 100b

is easy, how many, 125b
sovereign, independent, 143b
only desire to see, 145b
won your i. by, 180b
fight for their, 224b
control our economy, 224b
question of Canada's, 225a
baneful domination, 275a
egalité ou, 287b
worthy monuments, 288b
Anglo-Saxon supremacy, 289b
essential to Europe, 293b
maintain friendship, 329a
with dependency, 329b
I die crying, 361a
a step for political, 380a
without cultural, 410b
modified out of, 436a
and socialism must, 623a
economic without, 623a
  *Independent
colonies do not cease, 155a
will not be colonial, 336b
even more dependent, 469a
no young person not, 514a
  *India
turn towards, 92a
rubber, 114a
woods of Hindostan, 118b
British in Forster, 205b
do yeoman service, 376a
from I. to Lapland, 487a
seven years in, 646b
you, Canadian, Indian, 579b
  *Indian
bows and arrows, 5b
male person including, 19a
give 'em new eyes, 39b
field-game of lacrosse, 42a
extinction of title, 60a
shyness mentioning name, 63a
vast I. territories, 81a
confidence in myself, 97a
not a Red I. hunting, 98a
fit into new scheme, 114b
advice given me, 132b
if your heaven is, 160a
man reach people, 186b
I spoke real, 195a
Ojibway snowshoes, 234a
home of red man, 247b
ask what is beauty, 254b
to sing the glories, 290a
red man no longer, 295b
medicines of the white, 296a
Karkakonias saw, 296a
first commandment, 299b
attached to landscape, 304b
mystery, romance, 311a
told me Beaver does, 343a
annual treaty trips, 352b
to get another, 369a
names of braves, 400a
Frenchman married, 403b
every tree were Iroquois, 404a
long as sun shines, 414a
only legends teach, 435b
prophetess Wampohama, 437a
Mohawk language, 439b

can farm and adjust, 461a
Spanish, English, French, 464a
every I. who disappears, 471b
keep covenant, 480a
and polar worlds, 485b
write Brébeuf from I. view, 491a
Spirit made us, 492b
his unique values, 510b
huzza pour le, 511a
first European, 513b
Christianity spread, 518b
mouthpiece, visible, 520b
grandfather a savage, 521a
priest savage or I. priest, 528b
prefer the manners, 530a
what does woman want, 531b
last of the Beothucks, 536b
kemo sabe, 543b
will live here, 547a
everywhere, anywhere, 594b
one was I., Eskimo, 553b
work cannot dream, 554b
reserve is a bottle, 570b
we stand together, 570b
lily of the Mohawks, 579b
our minds to problem, 596b
canoe was to the, 641b
swear in English, 647b
can teach white man, 618b
[See also Anonymous: Indian.]
    *Indian Act
gives Indian the right, 318b
    *Indian Summer
along the line of smoky, 95b
hush of a Quebec, 395b
    *Indians
tomorrow we'll finish, 7a
the spirit walking, 9a
here as brothers lie, 16b
grave markings of, 16b
your escort for, 18b
resignation of the, 50b
must plunder and kill, 55b
law of five fingers, 56a
Spirit was angry, 58b
persecution their custom, 61b
vast backwoods, 62a
red-skinned children, 65b
pity on the poor, 72a
I bury the hatchet, 94a
progress of their dead, 100a
are called red, 102b
believe in one God, 105b
unhappy I. whom, 109a
I, Dekanahwideh, 144a
a dying race, 146a
sold skins for, 152a
sudden rush of savages, 161a
no soldiers, gendarmes, 183a
surrounded by snow, 190a
soldiers half-dead, 198a
did not know names, 204a
safe passage, 204a
farces worthy of savages, 204b
the land, the bibles, 216a
learn language, 219b
appear stupid, 230b
we're different, 266a
we I. own these, 290a
to learn French, 295a

distinctive music, 297a
no one like him, 317b
Jesuit to Huron, 318a
natives brutish, 319a
come like foxes, 319b
nous sommes sauvages, 325b
war of attrition, 344a
mind not lacking, 345a
would be white if, 345a
culture of Northwest, 351a
continue to feel, 353b
scalped each other, 369b
game and fish failed, 404b
defeated at Batoch, 418b
savages of Louisiana, 427a
to see my red children, 434a
do more than say ugh, 455b
local bipeds off, 461b
before white cames, 471a
listen to Spirit, 475a
terms of peace, 482a
tied me to post, 488b
did I call you, 491b
did not murder Son, 492b
martyrdom of Brébeuf, 494a
a king in every, 505b
are very white, 505b
governed themselves, 513b
assimilated by Affairs, 521a
connubial alliances, 544b
Paradise of Hurons, 573b
trinkets and grave, 578b
no voluntary integration, 619a
    *Individual
biography to life, 266a
interests not in, 495a
weakness of, 623b
    *Individualism
possessive, 401a
    *Industry
oligarchy will arise, 66b
Canadian automobile, 81a
American money in, 110a
trade will grow, 110a
labour, co-operative, 155b
results of energy, 177a
took over government, 218b
perseverance, economy, 270b
and humanity, 305a
political, democracy, 326a
give resources back, 360b
north more spiritual, 455a
and enterprise, 567a
wheels of i. turn on, 574b
not to possess, 575a
live on lumbering, 609a
foreign control, 622b
    *Inequality
at a distance, 31b
social and Christ, 530a
    *Inferiority complex
part of folklore, 147a
French, English, Jews, 227b
signs of an i. feeling, 289a
fatal to cherish an, 314b
    *Infinite
art has infinitude, 238a
for our arena, 328a
    *Inflammable materials
fire-proof house far from, 137b

    *Inflation
being a little pregnant, 119b
universal poverty, 416a
money spent abroad, 596b
unemployment side effect, 598a
war against, 599a
has been beaten, 600b
    *Information
instead of virtue, 124a
accessible to all, 364a
more data banks, 397b
loyal ally exchanges, 559a
accumulating since, 599a
    *Inhabitants
a million may seem, 157b
    *Inheritance
politics are an, 40b
alien to best of, 411b
bequeathed splendid, 422a
    *Injure
united to support, 12b
    *Injustice
100 years of, 12a
greatest is economic, 370b
    *Ink
not blood, 83a
small drop, 91b
    *Innocence
synthesis, experience, 357b
honest to God, I'm, 510b
two people know I'm, 603a
    *Insanity
call my pretensions, 501a
    *Insect
superfluity of life, 84a
grandfather gnat, 445b
were terrible, 434b
    *Insignificance
sink into, 375b
vested interest in, 385b
anchored ourselves in, 148b
    *Inspiration
loyalty a fruitful, 153a
Canada, of life, 330b
success is 90%, 628b
    *Institutions
media are human, 138a
supports as a whole, 245b
habits of millions, 277b
of our public life, 320b
we have here no, 385a
nos i., notre langue, 463b
rational, benevolent, 495a
    *Insulin
tie off pancreas, 33b
publications on, 53a
    *Insurance
association of mutual, 137b
best against disease, 169b
I detest agents, 337a
    *Insurrection
real or apprehended, 19b
apprehended exists, 599a
    *Intellect
meaning in other, 299a
films give rest, 393a
    *Intellectual
growing callous, 2b
genuine passion, 58a

life and progress, 82b
history broken record, 125b
two life-styles, 174b
non-conductor, 238b
conditions of people, 320b
Toronto not place for, 353a
conversion and, 522a
I'm an omnibrow, 546a
    *Intellectuals
the hard-hatted, 93b
sink the party, 278b
many colour blind, 451b
heaven protect us, 515b
nation of woodcutters, 544a
new treason of, 601b
    *Intelligence
critical not creative, 123b
especially for living, 148b
advertising arrests, 339a
victims of our own, 410b
sensitivity, taste, 526a
is also required, 550a
is like witchcraft, 565a
coldly let us be, 601a
    *Interests
unless you have nation, 59b
identity not without, 353b
of individuals, 495a
    *Internationalism
stop on way to, 137a
manias we have, 234b
sure basis for, 278b
foreign-based unions, 356a
a British Columbian is, 411b
the spirit of, 603a
the first i. nation, 620b
    *Interpreter
Canada is the, 112b
hacking through forest, 186b
    *Intuition
final discovery by, 276a
    *Inuit
if i. could not change, 751a
    *Invasion
come to protect, not, 274b
president thinks it, 355a
took up arms against, 501a
    *Investigator, The
1,000 years of treason, 540a
    *Investment
foreign direct can act, 230b
wrong place to discuss, 269b
    *I.O.D.E.
See Imperial Order Daughters
    of the Empire.
    *Iona Station
a place as good as this, 211a
    *Ireland
as a boy in, 5b
pestilence and famine, 12a
we're going to fight, 22a
put up a shillelagh, 43a
Upper Canada larger, 81a
richer in ruined houses, 183b
trace it back to, 301b
what Fenians did, 455a
essay upon snakes in, 606b
slightly bigger Ulster, 607a
long way to Tipperary, 633b
    *Irish

immigrant's prayer, 11b
an I. Catholic, 43a
enemies are I. priests, 68a
of Scottish and, 157a
jokes about the, 193b
are the favourites, 248b
nor I.-Canadian, 384b
or Scottish neighbour, 390b
can be subject, 436a
resist being made, 500b
and Canadian languages, 522a
one was I. or Slav, 553b
opposed nationalism, 595a
community of mystics, 628b
    *Iroquois
spoke I. or Huron, 130a
leader Dekanahwideh, 144b
country of the, 72b
conflicts with Hurons, 283b
comes like foxes, 319b
if every tree were an, 404a
Brébeuf from I. view, 491a
took Brébeuf and, 494a
peace with Hurons, 518b
    *Irving, K.C.
let him present, 505b
    *Irving, Washington
will have to make, 96a
    *Island
covers like drew, 11a
the great, 15a
    *Isle aux Coudres
chartered a sloop, 35b
    *Isolated
England splendidly, 328b
    *Isolation
splendid, 200a
    *Isolationism
live in a fire-proof house, 137b
Germans at our gates, 334b
    *Israel
put a matzo ball, 43a
a non-I. army, 142b
criticism suspect, 187a
Jerusalem in hearts, 292b
498-1 against, 313a
Israelis and lovers, 548b
    *It
either have i. or not, 202b
    *Italians
nothing against, 74a
admire skies of, 101b
and the I. states, 122a
choose the commandos, 142b
of origin in Commons, 152b
home from an I. movie, 273b
music written in, 297a
costs $10 to be, 383b
    *Italy
under Mussolini, 68b
heredity of mediaeval, 82b
admire skies of, 101b
Walpole said of, 283b
susceptibilities, 361b
in the war in, 605b
    *Ivory tower
slopes of commitment, 174b
becomes control tower, 397a
no grass roots in, 648a

    *Ivy Lea Bridge
dedication of, 509b


# J


    *Jack
Canuck's country, 51b
Frost guards us, 264a
Pine was one, 356b
as good's his master, 392
clear it with, 475a
    *Jackson, A.Y.
contemporary of Duchamp, 313a
myself his advocate, 353b
    *Jails
made for men, 109a
should put in, 154b
Indian brooms in, 226b
between j. and job, 392b
new ideas brought, 392b
    *Jake
and the Kid, 423a
    *Jalna
was inspired by, 144b
smells of a stable, 625b
    *Jamaica
Canada is behind, 124b
    *James, Henry
like those by, 78b
    *James Bay
the way to Japan, 202b
left his name, 283a
    *James Bond
learned in Oshawa, 196b
Superman legend, 521b
    *Japan
for this is not, 202b
long way from, 263b
by the Pole to, 273a
Germany and J. want, 314a
21st century belongs, 333b
U.S.'s customer, 449a
trading partner, 449b
the empire of, 583a
I must go to, 632b
    *Japanese
nature here is, 78b
Indians, Esquimaux, 198a
soldiers were, 198a
rotsa ruck, 263a
picks up his pen, 273b
naturalization papers, 443a
Canada like J. wife, 443a
    *Jarvis, Sherrif William
do your duty, 517a
    *Je
me souviens, 15a
I remember, 236a
me souviens, 572a
    *Jean Baptiste
Canada personified, 51b
    *Jefferson, Thomas
has had no, 477a
    *Jerusalem
wish the death of, 187b
Toronto's destruction, 246a
been in our hearts, 292b

*Jesuits*
Joques and Lallemant, 109a
and Dominicans fighting, 170a
preached to Hurons, 309a
preach the incarnation, 318a
brother J. in France, 528b
*Jesus Christ*
the Pope hears, 69a
true God and his son, 72a
our true greatness, 72a
your king is born, 72b
Himself is our light, 73b
cousin of the Lord, 79a
name of Christ, 243a
martyrs for Canada, 260a
a life of Christ, 263a
incarnation of, 318a
thirsty for the Son, 345a
Indians did not murder, 492b
change the curiosity, 500b
social structure and, 530a
what a friend we have in, 531a
ministers spread, 569b
King of all kings, 613a
and praying to, 633b
*Jew*
from Cape Breton talking, 120b
Canadian a euphemism, 318b
and Canadian emerge, 499a
I'm a Canadian and a, 499b
freedom to opt out, 510b
*Jewish*
isn't chic, 26b
survivors of holocaust, 187a
governor of Jerusalem, 292b
Edward VIII isn't, 415a
and hung on a J. hill, 483a
Riel with a J. nose, 505a
to J. nationalism, 595a
monopoly of wealth, 636a
*Jews*
Montreal streets, 12a
we don't attack, 26a
boys in the camp are, 47b
no posthumous victories, 187a
survivors of holocaust, 187b
a minority elsewhere, 227b
Israeli hockey players, 313a
like their neighbours, 357b
Ararat, city for, 449b
purges, trials, 521b
awaiting the pogrom, 561a
*Job*
difference between jail, 392b
*Joe*
my name is Beautiful, 525a
Beef, son of the people, 41b
*John A.*
beats the devil, 265b
well, John A. beats, 378b
you'll never die, 379a
Macdonald, icebreaker, 202a
*John Bull*
Uncle Sam, Johnny Canuck, 94b
yea and amen to it, 183b
ready to betray, 252b
*Johnnie Courteau*
of de mountain, 163b
*Johnny Canuck*

I'm what you call, 5a
hold Canadians captive, 30a
John Bull, Uncle Sam or, 94b
*Johnson, Pauline*
don't forget our dear, 571a
*Johnson, Dr. Samuel*
Quebec like his dog, 640b
*Jolliet, Louis*
joyful portages of, 496a
*Jonquière*
workers at the pulp, 188b
*Joques, Isaac*
and Père Lallemant, 109a
heroic death of, 496a
*Joual*
is not sufficient, 148a
not so screechy, 327a
and Canajan, 456a
*Joubert, Pierre*
authenticated age, 402b
*Journalism*
sporting section, 17b
want to write about, 37a
goodly fellows of, 38a
a wonderful story, 41a
The Whitehorse Star, 70b
weapon, silence, 76b
a small drop of ink, 91b
people read headlines, 95b
about j. responsibility, 132a
authority on opinion, 137a
equivalent of the VW, 138b
thought-throwing, 143a
as influential as, 145b
interviewed by, 179b
pressure on papers, 193a
and Canadian Press, 197b
news read out loud, 227b
every person a story, 235a
truth of the west, 262a
too big for breeches, 263a
do not desert, 271a
make j. work, 281a
here are the news, 293a
for an interview, 314a
tricks of the trade, 340b
right to insolence, 346a
better, less popular, 367a
news standards raised, 399b
every bloody one paid, 441b
of five words, 44b
no ignorance of Canada, 450b
it was steady work, 493b
NDP and free enterprise, 526b
who went to the Orient, 545b
why the McGill daily, 549b
works are ephemeral, 552b
two papers better, 556a
N.Y.T. and Spruce, 573b
John Brown went, 583b
editorial content, 584b
make contribution to, 586a
in bedrooms of state, 595a
*Joy*
he has the j. of life, 48a
of being alive, 57b
more than any, 162b
I walk beside a, 213a
write to communicate, 383a

without twinkle, 426b
mingled sorrow, 486b
my inward parts, 608b
*Joyce, James*
why he left the church, 430a
Frye and McLuhan, 581b
*Judge*
God damn the English, 8a
The Hanging, 42a
*Judgment*
our standards of, 88b
the arts perish, 188a
time never affects, 373b
*July 1, 1867*
on and after the day, 614b
*July 22*
by land, 1793, 389b
*Juno*
top award, 231a
*Jury*
no j. but time, 375a
*Just*
price theorem, 158a
the J. Mary stories, 228a
be j. to all, 384a
the j. society, 596b
society freedom would, 597b
*Justice*
morality and, 54a
on banks of the Saskatchewan, 60a
individual, collective, 69a
endeavour to maintain, 81a
not court of law, 146b
a whiff of grape shot, 155b
for the execution of, 184a
law is not, 242b
common concern, 307b
chaste than in France, 318b
important than land, 328a
every man will render, 329a
to my memory, 363a
enforcement of law, 377a
disrespect for law, 402a
ideals of British, 416a
the minister of, 488a
wider ramifications, 500a
established by, 506a
taken to every man's door, 546b
really interests me, 547b
not here to dispense, 578a
making social j. work, 589a
cry of people for, 643a

**K**

*Kamloops*
songs yet found in, 294a
*Kane, Paul*
you must have stood, 545a
*Kant, Immanuel*
Critique of Pure Reason, 338a
*Karloff, Boris*
supposedly insane, 235a
*Karsh, Yousuf*
glamourizer of legends, 301a
*K-K-K-Katy*

beautiful Katy, 453a
*Keewatin
District of, 15a
*Kemo sabe
Tonto's reply, 543b
*Kennedy, John F.
legislation, 31b
exempt Time-Life, 293b
*Kent, Tom
won war on poverty, 153b
*Kent County
couple of K.C. boys, 280a
*Kentucky
the militia of, 115b
between Belgium and, 191b
*Kerosene
discoverer of, 217b
*Keynes, J.M.
firmly Keynesian policy, 211a
read more Stendhal, 597b
*Khan, The
Men of the Northern, 301b
*Khruschev, Nikita
Mt. Khruschev, 13b
*Kid
Jake and the, 423a
*Kidd, Bruce
fleet-footed, 29a
*Kill
as many whites, 55b
sportsman has to, 341b
trait of destructiveness, 548b
*Killaloe Station
ain't the law of, 207a
*Killam
watch for pedestrians, 13b
*Kindness
race of people, 140b
reassertion of natural, 180a
essence of humour, 339b
*King, W.L. Mackenzie
strike a happy medium, 76b
dissolution, 91b
in small change, 129a
and spiritualism, 273b
mystery of a, 276a
or Chaos, 306b
so liberal, 365b
spirit hypothesis, 474a
it is wonderful, 475a
leader prevents, 475b
prime minister because, 607a
Conscription Crisis, 489b
he blunted us, 529b
home with my diary, 596b
philosopher-king to, 600b
*King
to be a poet, 5a
the cause of their, 76a
but God save the, 178a
thrill to the service, 319a
British control, 327a
call the king alleged, 341a
serve God as my, 427a
of England powerless, 479a
obeisance to a little, 539a
stones sing God, 544b
*King's girls
divine right of, 91a

instead of virtue, 164a
against the cold, 318a
Amazons of God, 345b
free of blemish, 574a
*King Kong
tallest darkest, 644a
*Kingdom
a cold k., 8b
have become a, 187a
change of title, 379b
the K. of Canada, 506b
the peaceable, 584b
replaced by Dominion, 588b
*Kings
all k. when we die, 146a
worthy daughter of our, 361b
divine right of, 594b
men may live like, 616a
*Kingston
stone mansion in, 84a
half burnt down, 151a
between Toronto and, 183b
government to, 246a
vivacity conspicuous, 566b
dirtier streets, 573b
proceeding from Toronto, 624a
*Kissing
if it puckers, 31b
husbands on Monday, 61a
osculation sincerest, 131b
ever see him, farmer, 154a
French k. confusion, 188a
she wants to be, 252b
snow in April not, 428b
can't give too many, 595b
*Kitchener, Lord
you have orders, 274a
*K-K-K-Katy
beautiful Katy, 453a
*Klondike Gold Rush
never had a million, 7b
in man's brain, 14a
of all proverbs, 14a
home of the, 15b
the K. experience, 52a
by right of discovery, 98a
ain't the trail, 403b
*Knew
builded better than, 11a
*Knighthood
how could I accept, 136b
*Knowledge
collection of scraps, 57b
woman influenced by, 179a
words are milestones, 314a
but I shall know, 314a
satisfaction, ignorance, 368b
quest for k. Occident, 458b
relation of public men, 634b
*Known
Canada only needs to, 266a
*Kootenay
shooting, hanging, 456a
*Korea
armistice talks, 407b
*Kosygin, Alexei
freedom for Hungary, 412b
*Kravitz, Duddy
man without land, 499a

# L

*Laberge, Lake
on the marge of, 534a
*Labische, Emmeline
original Evangeline, 360a
*Labour
generations of agricultural, 40a
co-operation, yes, 47b
all the beer they want, 97b
where l. is at rest, 104b
even a L. government, 121b
laws in Canada, 133b
sweep to co-operative, 155b
come into its own, 155b
right not to disorganize, 169b
work and wages, 186a
each man dependent, 188a
enact legislation, 201a
neither wholly right, 222a
men of Canada, fight, 223a
gold-headed stick, 248b
physical, moral, 260b
source of wealth, 260b
going to win the day, 261b
one man in Parliament, 295a
state our exploiter, 316a
working man into, 326a
a friend of, 338a
called the division, 340a
degradation of mass, 402a
not such a hardship, 429b
father of l. movement, 452b
composed of humans, 478b
fighting l.'s battles, 527b
true makers of Canada, 532b
hardest is idleness, 552a
takes a lot of, 554a
no Englishman need apply, 563b
maintenance of capitalism, 583b
Canada good for poor, 592b
the L. church, 642b
producers and parasites, 643a
*Labrador
hurled rocks at, 10b
wonderful dreariness, 29a
the land God gave to Cain, 101b
last which God made, 102b
strange magic about, 109b
fitted to endure, 126b
a Labourer's land, 233a
God had Joey, 241b
old-age pension for Nfld., 258b
country Britain gave to Canada, 259b
latent menace of, 278b
Baffin Island and, 325a
call it Markland, 344b
this is our land, 548b
*Lac St. Pierre
can't get drown on, 163b
*Lacrosse
peculiar to country, 42a
dandiest hemstitching, 493b
*Lady
there was a young, 86a
My Fur, 156b

I was no l., I, 222a
our l. of the snows, 309a
that's known as Lou, 534a
don't call me a, 632a
conversation in, 647b
　*Lady Chatterley
I went to bat for, 529b
filthy, obscene, 576a
　*Lake Champlain
arms-limitation clause, 515b
　*Lake Erie
see Canada across, 198a
　*Lake Louise
a lady from near, 17b
　*Lake of the Woods
beauty pervades me, 16a
　*Lake Ontario
four leagues from, 257a
shadows over O.'s bed, 431b
the crippled kids, 517a
and presently on to, 556b
dwelling and feuding, 625b
blue O.'s waters, 630b
　*Lake Superior
Mariposa country, 337b
austerity, 563a
　*Lakes
more than the world, 292a
blessed country with, 358a
　*Lallemant, Gabriel
Père Joques and, 109a
martyrdom of, 494a
when L. and de Brébeuf, 528b
　*Lamentations
Dominion begun in, 103b
　*Lampman, Archibald
failed to appreciate, 515a
　*Land
my own, my native, 11b
gave away the, 25a
the great lone, 91a
always be changing, 93b
one's own is best, 101a
the l. God gave to Cain, 101b
the character of, 103b
where hope matters, 111a
loveless, lifeless, 133a
don't own the, 135b
the l. of desolation, 141b
of little sticks, 160a
broken up, stolen, 167a
glorious, first, 180b
the l. is strong, 182b
monopoly, dangerous, 186a
private ownership, 188a
we l., they bibles, 216a
heaven by the sea as by, 218a
desire to own bit, 238a
this l. is your, 241a
made for you and me, 241a
keep people on your, 242a
plough, labour, 255a
of feast and famine, 266b
we are the, 291b
of true and leal, 301a
keep our people in, 316a
justice more important, 328a
from Canada, by, 389b
important than we, 395b
lay hold of the, 446a

buy l., stopped making, 467b
loving the l. as a, 473b
man without l. nobody, 499a
do you own the, 501b
this l., our l., best, 503b
no l. not loved, 522a
said to be discovered, 560b
leave bones upon, 578b
not a commodity, 583b
in his bones vastness, 601a
size, emptiness, 641b
creator had roots in, 623b
our home and native, 626a
　*Landlady
a parallelogram, 337a
　*Landless
the l. man, manless, 197b
the l. man, 198b
　*Landmarks
to chart old, 397a
become hitching posts, 477a
　*Langevin, Sir Hector-Louis
present at McGill, 381a
　*Language
the French used, 51a
one l. and one law, 74b
dialect of universal, 127b
Canada lacks own, 130a
only points of unity, 130b
primitives have a, 148a
home of meanings, 148a
of discovering the, 164a
Canadian does not, 166a
Ontario bounded by, 167b
retaining peculiar, 171a
learning a second, 176a
French Canadian here, 183b
doesn't speak their, 186b
equal rights, 199a
make those invaders, 219b
slang is present, 221b
one school, one flag, 227a
jargon of Toronto, 236b
defence of French, 236b
French spoken only, 295a
jargon intolerable, 299b
what words are to, 314a
equilibrium and our, 316b
French less bad, 324a
cornerstone of culture, 324b
joual and state, 327a
two l.s, no patois, 334b
two spoken, slang, 341b
Ukrainian, Polish, 348a
soul not in the, 365a
oppress one or, 379b
key to his house, 403b
of mind's growth, 439b
such as Mohawk, 439b
Canajan, 456a
understands Bulgarian, 460a
nos institutions, 463b
distinctive variety, 466a
listen to music in, 471b
French of non-existent, 508a
anti-British dialect, 509a
Irish and Canadian, 522a
is sound as sense, 526a
Brant speaks twelve, 530a
current, Louis XIV, 561b

la communiqué does, 599a
　*L'Anse aux Meadows
site of Vineland, 344b
fine, fruitful, 588a
　*Lapalme Drivers
let them eat shit, 598a
　*Lapland
from India to, 487a
　*Laporte, Pierre
want L. to live, 68b
easy to say he was, 251b
　*Laprairie
wicked road to, 299a
　*Larger
country of l. air, 83b
Laurier and l. Canada, 329b
　*Larks
this l. taken to, 16a
still bravely singing, 372b
student-lark, 458b
　*LaSalle, Sieur de
and St. Lawrence, 69a
pathetic death of, 496a
three balls in head, 590b
　*Last Spike
See Spike, Last.
　*La Tour, Claude & Charles
O well sped, 631b
　*Lauder, Harry
to hell with, 635a
　*Laughter
he who laughs last, 39b
public pay more for, 179a
until you make money, 179a
Ottawa's political, 225a
I'll never laugh again, 364a
cry one minute and, 479b
thinking can't be, 533b
　*Laurendeau, André
felt isolated, 68b
　*Laurentia
separate French and, 237a
　*Laurentian Mountains
after-glow over, 32b
stern L. range, 504b
　*Laurier, Sir Wilfrid
attachments to leaders, 82b
talked to newsboy, 152b
and the larger, 329b
too English for me, 604a
　*Laval University
for progress look, 542a
　*Lavallée, Calixa
O Canada, Magic Flute, 514a
　*Law, Andrew Bonar
get me Bonar, 40b
　*Law
carry out good British, 18b
statute books muddled, 42b
of five fingers, 56a
one language and one, 74b
silent service, 103a
bench like Navy, 103a
people that have no, 105b
charge should read, 108b
we have to break, 109a
must be a lawyer, 109b
judicial institutions, 111a
as civil as you, 121a

Supreme Court not, 136b
bloody, arbitrary, 145b
court of justice not, 146b
no prisons, lawsuits, 183a
extreme sentence, 184a
highest sentence, 184a
maintained in west, 188b
ain't the law of Killaloe, 207a
is not justice, 242b
against section 105, 264b
judged by principles, 271a
like music, property, 288a
keeps police handcuffed, 292b
of peace, work, health, 306b
safety, l., honour, 312a
clutches of advocates, 318b
death the supreme, 328b
Toronto predominates, 340a
forestalls libel, 341a
allows them to do, 352a
privilege of stupidity, 362a
compulsions runs, 362b
loathed or forgotten, 363a
has one unalterable, 371a
enforcement, justice, 377a
order shields privilege, 402a
write the contract, 419a
jury have died, 427b
Mother's Rules of, 436b
first lady magistrate, 441a
indicative of health, 447b
Bennett on Bluff, 450a
shooting in Kootenay, 456a
a hard, queer, 482a
demands an account, 498a
juryman at Riel's, 502b
thought you guilty, 513b
the l. of Yukon, 533b
justice taken to every man's
      door, 546b
right to fair trial, 547b
taken into custody, 547b
judges as stars of, 552b
the law, never mind, 566a
still in statute books, 566a
dispose of case, 578a
of gravity interferes, 588b
damned infernal lie, 592b
state in bedrooms of nation,
      595a
pay abortion bill, 595b
crush l. and order, 597b
at sight of army, 598a
Plutarch pirated, 627b
sentenced, guilty, 629b
magistrates no remedy, 633a
   *Lawrence, Charles
king's instructions, 637b
   *Lawrence, D.H.
left me cold, 444b
went to bat for the, 529b
filthy obscene, 576a
   *Laws
Hurons without, 3b
full power to make, 20a
I'm under British, 21b
sentiment will move, 71a
of Great Britain, 101b
complained, bad, 164a
public learn to obey, 251a

torn my husband, 363a
notre langue, nos, 463b
English l., best, 478b
legislating a few, 587a
   *Lawyers
social workers in politics, 36a
there were too many, 50a
I have an orgasm, 150b
freedom paved with, 209a
old l. never die, 315a
bless also the, 500b
criminal l. actor, 504a
   *Lay
I'll l. me down, rest, 153b
   *Leacock, Stephen
Uncle Stephen spelled, 304b
tradition includes, 367a
shall now read, 383b
amiable nonsense, wit, 484a
even poets, 646b
   *Leadership
we lead, let those, 41a
leading himself, 54b
Dollard, powerful, 236b
hidden from followers, 277a
he leader, I party, 279b
send for Leader of Opposition,
      305b
nation wiser than its, 310a
I must follow, I am, 335a
disbelieve magical, 447a
faith people develop, 590b
the leadership cult, 447a
secret to prevent, 475b
   *Leadership League
I have no politics, 373b
   *League
I, Dekanahwideh, 144b
   *League for Social
      Reconstruction
common good, private, 608a
   *League of Nations
association of mutual insurance,
      137b
no interest in Ethiopia, 324b
undo what was done, 645b
   *Leal
land of true and, 301b
   *Learning
a little, dangerous, 179b
to think continentally, 197a
pursuit of fine living, 302b
from Bethune, 603a
get education, add, 421b
   *Lectures
series to fall back, 205b
sensible people never, 338b
to learn Chinese, 342a
   *Ledge, The
never raised by sheriff, 365b
   *Lee, Canada
generous, warm, 448b
   *Left
rather waffle to the, 75a
I'm not a, 116b
no l.-of-centre party, 159a
what you have l. that, 516a
   *Legends
pass into l., history, 267b
glamourizer of, 301a

whence these, 360a
none of those old, 385b
only l. could teach, 435b
no legendary tales, 592a
   *Léger, Paul-Emile Cardinal
pope tried to move, 162a
one answer might be, 304a
pastor of Montreal, 524a
   *Legislate
cannot l. against geography,
      328b
   *Legislation
inspired Kennedy's, 31b
sober second thought in, 375b
education, salvation, 411b
   *Leicester Square
farewell, 634b
   *Lenin, Nikolai
congratulations to, 347a
the L. School of Espionage, 441a
was L. pro-Communist, 447b
   *Lesage, Jean
minister or president, 447a
six years dealing, 548b
   *Lest
we forget, 16b
   *Let
them come if they dare, 253b
Parliament decide, 305b
   *Letter
never write, destroy, 376b
   *Level
mountain-climbing only, 487b
   *Lévesque, René
not Trudeau's, 551a
   *Lévis
songs yet found in, 294a
hard-up story from, 468a
   *Lewis, Sinclair
what Canada needs, 314b
   *Liar
been et by a wolf is, 134b
Baron Münchausen, 440a
   *Liberace
Welcome L. and P.M., 469a
   *Liberalism
believe in autonomy, 68b
leaven which will, 306b
I have outlived, 331a
not to mean French, 374a
be l. with the, 384a
conservative and l. tradition,
      438b
middle way, extremes, 469b
[See also Whiggery.]
   *Liberals
demonstration of part, 39a
contractor and dishonest, 69a
hyphen in L.-Conservative, 104a
cost more when L. in power,
      170a
nine years of L. rule, 182b
sit as a P.E. Trudeau, 199b
twilight of the Grits, 203b
B.C. L. Association, 259b
a L. government in office, 298b
revolutions, exaggeration, 328a
I am a L. Conservative, 338a
saturated with L. principles,
      365b

in office for mankind, 475b
socialists are L. in hurry, 520a
voter asleep on L. side, 607b
marked ballot, nose, 607b
how long a member of, 468b
Tuesday, bilingualism, 564b
philosophy, simplicity, 601b
[See also Grits.]
    *Liberation
true l. of women, 103b
from the gods, 164a
of individual, 164a
looked on death, 213a
colonized in l. movements, 412a
in an atmosphere of, 469b
revolutionary action, 609b
    *Liberty
enough for present, 31a
breathe atmosphere, 31b
every man enjoys, 49b
the l. of Spain, 60b
exceeds property, 71b
endeavour to, 81a
destroy English, 87a
fantastic thing, 87b
born on St. Lawrence, 145b
we enjoy our, 155b
putting l. to work, 166b
realized in ordered, 188b
totalitarian state and, 191a
spectacle of, 191a
constitution with no, 202a
device of France, 262b
forever, 262b
for l. of world, 270b
British l. in colony, 271a
stay here to conquer, 334b
long live, 361a
ample to govern, 379b
greater than States, 386a
democracy grows against, 401a
ideals of British, 416a
life, l., happiness, 436a
everything lawful when, 452b
all that is good, 480b
tears and taxes, 506a
education security, 517b
American emphasis, 589a
history points out, 601a
tyranny of abstractions, 642a
    *Librarians
have made me, 523a
    *Libraries
Canada needs national, 88a
lacking in modern works, 222b
do not censor, 222b
world like open, 270a
Algonquins no, 319b
reading room and, 338b
bookstore like, 416b
necropolis of immortals, 552b
    *Libre
vive l'univers, 107a
vive le Québec, 214b
vive le, 293b
    *Licence
TV station l. to print, 585a
    *Lick
if you can't l. 'em, 555a

    *Lie
for all you're, 28a
truth, lie's, 104a
only time I tell, 210a
damned infernal, 592b
    *Liechtenstein
put a postage stamp, 43a
    *Lies
telling to a child, 110b
if the world, 120a
violence and more, 207b
Herodotus, father of, 276b
a maker of, 296a
    *Life
is as it is, 29a
Klondike an approximation, 52a
revolution, principle, 54a
little flame of, 54b
amusements necessary, 77a
spiritual, death, 84b
in love manifest, 88a
royal flush in, 98a
little care that l. is, 98b
Eskimo sings of, 99b
your paintings come, 105a
whole armour of, 114a
education coterminus, 116b
ayorama, destiny, 118b
a flash of firefly, 133a
brave man laughs, 176a
in West held sacred, 188b
so close to death, 195a
a great adventure, 216a
beginning, middle, 218b
gave his l. a gift, 226a
like Labrador, 233a
field of honour, 233a
tragedy or field, 233a
new meaning to, 241a
chart, coast, 244b
never be in way, 244b
decencies of, 245a
simple as l. or death, 312a
dreams real, l. sweet, 321b
Canada, inspiration, 330b
knocks poet on head, 336a
humour, incongruities, 340a
education for, 340b
playing a poor hand, 350a
actual passage, 356b
literature fastened, 371b
killing experience, 388b
consider alternative, 296b
till my work done, 402b
is an adventure, 405a
don't know l. at, 422b
liberty, happiness, 436a
whole philosophy, 459a
here to add what, 459a
quite bearable, 462b
span about same, 472a
struggle demands, 488b
being alive, 506b
needs editing, 519a
greater than we, 527b
adaptation, 533a
theatre, home of, 533b
ride's the thing, 556a
and art quietly, 556a
each l. a grade, 559a

intellectual, spirit, 575a
some nasty things, 595b
human relatedness, 616a
is a gentleman, 626a
    *Ligate
pancreatic ducts, 33b
    *Light
that fills the world, 9a
last one left turn, 13a
speed far faster than, 86a
quality of sunlight, 166a
darkness but I see, 492b
    *Lillie, Beatrice
Toronto produced, 106a
    *Lillooet
printed, God willing, 441b
    *Lily
with l., thistle, shamrock, 439a
of the Mohawks, 579b
    *Limericks
one dozen, 17b
    *Linchpin
Canada the l. of peace, 112a
the l. of English, 112a
    *Lincoln, Abraham
was he an accident, 237b
    *Lindsay
first appearance, 162b
    *Link
vital l. in English, 113a
    *Lion
beneath paws, 21b
see it cowers, 22a
make stand still, 297a
will give way, 363a
under l.'s paw, 637a
    *Lions
Iroquois attack like, 319b
    *Lip-stick Liz
was in the biz', 534a
    *Lips
don't sweat, 647a
    *Liquor
why not milk, 400a
keep Indians off, 561b
    *Listening
things to do, 269a
only learn, 648a
lavish producer, 357b
personal serenity, 217b
acting is, 495a
    *Literacy
schizophrenia and, 396a
    *Literature
primer of Canadian, 27a
softening minds, 27a
not only mirror, 28b
put down Canadian, 28b
Barbra Streisand of, 29a
has had none, 80a
from odd moments, 80a
in or of Canada, 88b
salvation of, 88b
if country has no, 93b
behind Jamaica, 124b
from U.S., 128b
history is l., science, 129b
two books no, 129b
if we spoke Huron, 130a
a plank sidewalk, 138a

great prose epic, 139a
countries have to have, 139a
most serious needs, 139b
writers of past, 139b
ideal review is, 142b
colonial position, 149b
poetry pemmican of, 160b
Canadian influence world, 161a
problem of development, 164a
market for Canadian, 167b
with no history, no, 171a
achieved flavour, 175a
solitude, contacts, 175a
fame from, 179b
what Canadian, 180b
conflict, novels, 185a
amused, dismayed, 192b
two dreams, 207a
human apocalypse, 207b
train imagination, 208a
forms are autonomous, 208a
grow up inside, 208b
autonomous world, 208b
is conscious mythology, 208b
just being born, 212b
native tradition, 224a
concerned with truth, 237b
novelists in East, 249a
Imagism and prairies, 275a
Burbank, story, 314a
needs a Sinclair Lewis, 314b
equilibrium and our, 316b
temperament for, 320a
no art and no l. could, 320b
national consciousness, 321a
what everybody knows, 326b
devotion not perfect, 336a
half a pint of, 337b
use English for, 341b
done more for, 366a
ambition to contribute, 366b
light as cobweb, 371b
foreign unfairness, 383a
nationalistic prejudice, 383a
good stick, bad crutch, 403b
we love our, 412a
girl is sent, 428a
in her newspapers, 403a
demanding a great, 446a
may not be glorious, 460b
need great people, 477a
tremendous leap, 477b
some ancestors, 491b
Bible, Shakespeare, 492a
English vocabulary, 522b
intellectuals, woodcutters, 544a
write of far north, 549b
field of distinction, 551b
write under breath, 564a
great artists Shaughnessy, 567b
more clergyman book, 570a
best in English, 571a
poets created climate, 571b
American, in French, 571b
craving for marvellous, 572b
McLuhan and Frye, 581b
spirit of contemporary, 624b
  *Little
too l., too late, 350b
so l. for mind, 444a

  *Little Emperor
Sir George, 545a
  *Little Red Riding Hood
and responsible, 32a
unreasoning fear, 134b
  *Little theatre
See Dominion Drama Festival.
  *Liverpool
and Hong Kong, 379b
  *Living
a year or lives ago, 98b
intelligence for, 148b
like navigation, 148b
seeing others die, 190b
pursuit of learning, 302b
lived too long, 331a
first half ruined, 444b
live in the ward, 458a
old enough to die, 473b
recipe for, 496b
as long as I can, 605b
  *Lobbyists
no l. for children, 565a
  *Loggers
we are only, 317b
  *Lois Lane
never met a girl, 541b
  *London, England
no navy made in, 92b
replace the centre, 134a
Americans respected, 187a
more culture in Toronto, 291b
yearn for the dark of, 382a
to N.Y. or, 467a
C.P.R. offices in, 467a
old Tory capital, 558b
  *London, Ont.
impertinence in itself, 43a
Highway 401, 69b
friendlier than, 251b
  *London Conference
Macdonald is the man, 322b
  *Lone
the great l. land, 91a
  *Loneliness
feeling of fresh, 77b
solitary in woods, 407a
without privacy, 451a
learn passion of, 561a
we all feel, 611b
a new l., solitude, 616a
  *Long
it's a l. way to Tipperary, 633b
  *Long-distance
transmission of voice, 44a
yes, Alec, it is I, 46a
  *Longest
street in the world, 521a
  *Longevity
cultivate an ailment, 457a
  *Longfellow, Henry W.
now L. is gone, 215a
he sat upon the deck, 218a
  *Lord's Prayer
halibut be thy name, 467a
deliver us from evil, 502a
  *Lords
hold you in the, 11b
of ascendant at Montreal, 280b
of lakes and forests, 280b

  *Lorelei
little L. in every, 638b
  *Los Angeles
uptight in, 525b
on the edge, 584b
  *Lose
what have you got to, 96b
  *Losers
statistics are for, 70a
a group of cranky, 93b
  *Lots of luck
rotsa ruck, 263a
  *Lou
lady that's known as, 534a
  *Loud
speak l., look big, 75b
  *Louder
the l. voices, 600b
  *Louis XIV
le grand, 325b
language in Montreal, 561b
faults of, 589a
  *Louis XV
America owes much, 464a
Montcalm is dead, 480a
  *Louis, Uncle
hard to beat, 520a
  *Louisbourg
nor strengthen the French, 335b
see walls of fortress rising, 362b
authentic French, 461a
  *Louisiana
sold to Americans, 67b
deplored occupation, 122a
Louis le grand, 325b
savages of L. want, 427a
  *Lount, Samuel
Mr. Jarvis, do your, 517a
  *Lousy
no longer any place to be, 36b
  *Love
abiding for subject, 3b
comes after marriage, 9a
your daughter, 9a
a jewel that wins, 16a
never can l. forget, 23a
quite something, 41a
Canadian in a canoe, 53a
had to make, 54a
give my everlasting, 55a
make way for, 65a
in l. with idea, 66b
we l. thee, smiling land, 70b
like l. without climax, 85b
in l. you manifest, 88a
maternal dislike, 94a
the l. of humanity, 103b
revolutionary does not, 105a
made me desirous, 105b
better to mourn, 108a
leads the Eskimo, 109b
your first be your last, 114a
chaos that l. can bring, 114b
true woman asks, 116a
have conspired against, 120a
doesn't last long, 134a
reserve and irony, 139b
education requires, 148a
those whom we hate, 149b

fell in l. with Canada, 181b
too horrible to demand, 184b
amour-propre, 188a
single night of, 218a
laughs at locks, 244b
end of love, sigh, 252a
falling in l. spoils, 254a
to l. the state, 327b
power, huzza, 335b
in l. with dimple, 342b
love of self, 346b
their country not each other, 357a
in token of the l. shown, 361b
in the present, 369b
a great dream, 368a
practical definition, 395a
mystery surrounding us, 395b
a golden hook, 401b
with revolt, 404a
an immense purpose, 406b
without an object, 421a
condemned criminal, 429a
joined in l. together, 439a
travel, suffer, read, 444b
on l. and whisky, 456b
I l. my country, 462a
equal amounts of, 496b
race will l. land, 522a
sweet is ridiculous, 533b
money, conquest, 545b
wear l.'s brand, 567b
we all in need of, 611b
to l. G.M., 617b
maybe that's, 618a
and the elephant, 638a
marriage, l. gone, 649b
*Lover
of the universe, 143a
*Loving
be clothed with, 78a
for themselves, 270a
poetry maiden I, 272a
play, not acrobats, 359a
the land as country, 473b
can cost a lot, 535b
*Lower Canada
pass up St. Lawrence, 80b
Montreal capital, 418b
*Loyal
will be l. to Queen, 13b
she began, 15a
Majesty's Opposition, 154a
subject who is truly, 294b
people in Que. still, 437b
educated always, 517b
a British subject, 633b
*Loyalists
See United Empire Loyalists.
*Loyalties
never have too many, 83b
age of jealous, 166b
*Loyalty
created, personal, 82b
to the Crown, 99a
of the Canadians, 118a
fruitful inspiration, 153a
bow down to her ass, 390a
exuberant, sacrifice, 425a
questioned by Senate, 450a

Canada not bribed into, 543a
*L.S.R.
See League for Social Reconstruction.
*Luck
better than long legs, 9a
better lucky, smart, 37a
write a p in front, 178b
to be good, 223a
lots of, 263a
great believer in, 342a
follows misfortune, 487b
luckiest persons, 538a
preparation, opportunity, 595b
*Lumbering
can't live on, 609a
*Lunatic
no l. shall vote, 19b
*Lundrigan, John
let them eat what, 599b
*Lundy's Lane
Queenston Heights or, 580b
*Luxury
capitalism a, 198b
sex l. available, 298a

# M

*McCourt, Edward
not unworthy to, 264b
Saskatoon, Sask., 319a
Service occupies, 534a
*McCrae, John
he wrote on, 6b
*MacDonald, Daniel
epitaph of, 16a
*MacDonald, J.E.H.
artist, woodsman, 586b
*MacDonald, Jeanette
and Nelson Eddy, 206a
Nelson Eddy and, 524b
*Macdonald, Sir John A.
attachments to leaders, 82b
from M. to McGuigan, 85b
grim sphinx-like, 107b
saw from east to, 152b
Disraeli's twin, 154a
gentlemanlike, 155a
a conservative I sit, 199b
John A. beats the devil, 265b
usually Jack, 266b
Italian epitaph, 305b
a sharp fox, 322a
in killing Riel, 417b
father of Confederation, 440b
Sir John, Eh?, 456a
pray for him in, 502a
dilatoriness, 502b
was a juicer, 524a
Orangemen, Papists, 553a
*Macdonald
icebreaker for Manhattan, 202a
Canadian ice-breaker, 493a
*McGee, Sam
I cremated, 534a
*McGee, Thomas D'Arcy
nationalist shot, 189b
do you think of, 375b

two drunkards, 380b
shot fellow like, 629a
*McGill University
attends the sick, 340a
is in Toronto, 340b
distinction is men, 342b
address in Greek, 381a
credit for physics, 516b
why is the daily, 549b
soak M. for twice, 582a
*McGrew, Dan
sat dangerous, 534a
*McGuigan, James C.
from Macdonnell to, 85b
*Machiavelli, Niccolò
and Sir Galahad, 557a
*MacIver, Joanne
life is a grade, 559a
*Mackenzie, Alexander
of a Tory character, 381a
from Canada, by land, 389b
stone-mason still, 551b
*Mackenzie, Sir William
to Robert Flaherty, 195a
*Mackenzie, William Lyon
was this hero called, 21b
I do think if, 27b
red-haired, five, 323a
come again, 343b
if I had Mac along, 363b
King prime minister because, 607a
*Mackenzie, District of
Northwest Territories, 15a
*Mackenzie Highway
is a stone, 316a
*Macks, Alphias
died October 2, 15b
*McLaughlin Buick
a M. reliable carriage, 292b
*Maclean's Magazine
publishes an article, 213b
*MacLennan, Hugh
most authentic song, 256b
*McLuhan, Marshall
greatest modern, 87a
fate of Australia, 209a
difference between, 441b
put his telescope to, 550a
and Frye at, 581b
*Macmillan, Sir Harold
duly noted, 585b
*MacNab, Sir Allan
Drew do you think, 163a
the other MacNab, 399a
*Macpherson, Sir David
dilatoriness of, 502b
*Mad
is he then I hope, 215b
is he, I hope, 638b
*Made
in Canada, 9b
Coca-Cola, 61a
better in Chicago, 566b
*Mademoiselle
from Armentières, 496b
*Madly
rode m. off in all, 337a
*Madrid
centre of gravity of, 54a

tomb of fascism, 54a
    *Mafia
Maritime m. has, 441b
the Buffalo family, 609a
    *Magazines
Playboy and consumer, 138a
totally dependent, 211a
beside us a mountain, 270b
first outlet in, 321a
no m. in Canada, 366a
not consider Time, 366b
provincial, 374b
expense of publication, 390b
time not ripe, 564a
first duty to be, 618a
    *Maggie
when you and I were, 288b
    *Magic
make way for, 65a
is afoot, God is, 120a
among the Eskimo, 144a
Houdini's death, 267c
shamans could do, 443b
    *Magna Charta
inspired by the, 112b
    *Maiden
sweet m. of Passamaquoddy,
    146a
    *Maine
for in M. will find, 146a
    *Maintain
le droit, 18a
the right, 369a
not get your man, 641b
    *Maitre
notre m., l'avenir, 221a
le passé, 236a
chez nous, 349a
a campaign slogan, 350b
    *Majority
tyranny of the, 245b
treats minority, 597b
    *Malamute
in the M. saloon, 533b
    *Malapropisms
got bull by tail, 127b
let's not stop, 321b
black and writing, 492a
lie in your bread, 584a
    *Malaya
monkeys on coast, 118b
    *Male
the m. bond, 588b
opposite of husband, 650a
    *Malton
De Havilland Caribou, 564a
    *Man
born, died grocer, 15b
always get their, 18b
greatest service, 33b
to comprehend, 53a
creative spirit, 54a
infest earth, 55b
candle of God, 60a
no can prophesy, 64b
political animal, 83a
a dull m. indeed, 83b
too many loyalties, 83b
very little spirit, 93a
glory of, 94a

to man or men, 106b
to become a, 134a
have a baby, 162a
an evil old, 163a
bad found out, 179a
old enough to, 179a
next to underwear, 180a
as m. were all, 190b
feel a woman, 220b
deserves man, 221b
a recording animal, 226b
cannot change, 245b
art a voice of, 250a
wins by assault, 252a
always get their, 254a
continues to be, 277b
one becomes, 315b
the old m., flag, 315b
woman second only, 339b
spoken of, 368b
get your, 369a
first then property, 372a
old m., old flag, 380b
wish you were, 400a
knew Pierre as a, 441a
pasting wings on, 454a
medicine, animals, 458b
has two passions, 458b
behind every successful, 470a
approach solitary, 506a
higher destiny, 517b
dark, crooked, 518b
and his world, 519a
this is the, 578a
two races, beaver, 582b
have faith in, 590a
touched the moon, 602b
art and woman art, 632a
    *Mangez
de la merde, 598a
    *Manhattan
U.S. oil tanker, 202a
not fly flag, 493a
    *Manitoba
Arctic climate, 13a
Home of the Bay, 15a
coat of arms, 69b
demand annexation, 183b
prairie province, 247b
School Question, 331a
No. 1 hard M. wheat, 398a
master of life, 437a
half-breeds in, 501a
the founder of, 501b
short-haired men, 507a
bare paper, 515a
mystical people, 561a
farming in, 567a
premier kicks, 627a
    *Manitou
mighty Gitchi, 72a
master of life, 437a
    *Mankind
eternal procession of, 32b
three-quarters of, 85a
for best, worst, 223a
maddest ideas, 250b
future of all, 300b
welfare, progress, 307b

ancient wisdom, 368a
Liberals in office, 475b
transcendence, 515b
    *Manless
landless man, m. land, 197b
to the m. land, 198b
    *Mann, Sir Donald
great artists today, 567b
    *Manners
complained against, 164a
retaining peculiar, 171a
betrayal of bad, 238b
self-respect guarantees, 361b
there are no more, 410a
    *Manufacturers
of enthusiasms, 56b
Canadian M. Assoc., 61a
automobile, 81b
drawers of waters, 217b
    *Manufacturing
slightly higher, 211b
second-rate sector, 288b
suburbs of town, 323a
National Policy, 378a
    *Maple Leaf
emblem of Canada, 14b
a beaver and a, 62a
when leaves are gone, 128a
beaver and, 142a
we'll wear where Adam, 213b
wave proudly, freely, 227b
plant the native, 528a
allusions to, 549b
flash of the sun, 310a
the colony of the, 354b
shade of trees knew, 415b
deserve the symbol, 431a
league of fallen, 568a
king of forest, 615a
where pines and m. grow, 626b
    *Maple Leaf Forever, The
in days of yore, 439a
    *Maple Leaf Gardens
think of opera in, 56a
a shouted hit, 224a
religious building, 304a
    *Maple sugar
immense quantities, 35b
vivid recollections, 459a
    *Maples
where pines and m. grow, 626b
    *Marching
our boys are, 22a
with the workers, 131a
acquisition, matter of, 285b
tramp the boys are, 387b
    *Mari
usque ad mare, 14b
e m. merces, 15a
a m. usque ad, 588b
    *Maria Chapdelaine
the daughter of, 188a
stands one book, 238b
    *Marie
come to me, sweet, 621a
    *Marie Celeste
famous mystery ship, 17a
    *Mariposa
not a real town, 337b

*Maritimes
out to the, 71b
with men from the, 91a
most desperate, 221a
provinces united, 245a
what an empire here, 245a
tumbledown farmhouse, 320a
mafia just scratched, 441b
from classic heroes, 451b
politics a disease, 521a
immense resources of, 604a
*Markets
blast a way into, 48b
*Markland
a name that fits, 344b
*Markle, Fletcher
great times of, 232a
*Marquette, Jacques
joyful portages of, 496a
*Marquis
hit the M. on, 13a
*Marquis Wheat
national Burbank for, 314a
still king, 525a
superior strain, 525b
*Marriage
love comes after, 9a
affair with husband, 114b
to a minister, 168a
forced upon me, 177a
spoils courting, 244b
politics harridan I, 272a
government of bed, 285b
amend the contract, 288a
mistake marrying girl, 342b
a business girl, 370b
gander takes one mate, 421b
nobody should, been, 445a
not just for lunch, 470a
intermarriage has, 510b
being single is, 536a
connubial alliances, 544b
author of married love, 565a
married last spring, 565b
Niagara disappointment, 632b
love gone, woman, 649b
*Martin, Paul
minority not running, 39a
bought a paper, 585a
*Martinique
and St. Domingue, 318a
*Martyrdom
for Christ, France, 260a
made a spectacle, 319b
name of Canadian sung, 363a
Brébeuf and Lallemant, 494a
burning heretics, 528b
to identify with, 642a
*Marx, Karl
carries less weight, 570a
more Tolstoy than, 597b
*Marxists
apply lessons of, 199a
Chinese M., Quebec, 601b
*Mary
the Just M. stories, 228a
*Mary Celeste
See Marie Celeste.
*Mass media
See Communications.

*Massachusettize
the Canadian mind, 384a
*Masses
only the Masseys and, 523a
*Massey, Vincent
bit of a savage, 128b
*Massey Hall
one serious centre, 291b
*Massey-Harris
farm implement, 550a
*Masseys
only the M. and masses, 523a
*Master
our m., the future, 221a
our m., the past, 236a
author produces m.-piece, 305a
Jack's as good's his, 392b
of Life, Manitou, 437a
*Masters
we have no more, 69b
in our own house, 349a
our own house, 350b
in our house we, 595b
*Mathews, Peter
Mr. Jarvis do your, 517a
*Mavor, James
has an advertisement, 248b
*May the 24th
the Queen's birthday, 25a
school day preceding, 511b
*Mayor
of all the people, 474b
*Meaning
language the home of, 148a
hidden m. of all, 164a
other than intellect, 229a
of meaninglessness, 349a
new means, new, 397b
some day they will, 586a
*Mecca
the M.s are elsewhere, 506a
*Medicine
spirit of service, 26a
greatest service, 33b
knowledge of literature, 34a
physiologist believes, 53a
redefine ethics, 54a
a luxury trade, 54a
can operate as well, 54b
cool the heart, 55b
ecstasy in anger, 57a
Pablum, 79b
man to medical man, 85b
must be doctor, 109b
cure, prevent, 110b
make quintuplets, 136a
psychiatrists for nations, 139b
give injunctions, 140b
God gives insurance, 169b
key is patient's will, 219a
must cure himself, 235a
McGill predominates, 340a
mentally defective, 398b
Penfield, Selye, 432a
speck in cornea, 457a
art based on science, 458b
not take medicine, 458b
desire to take medicine, 458b
psychedelic coined by, 459b
chiropractic art, 461a

physician's rule, 472a
in quart of gin, 542a
neurology will have, 546b
age-old confidence, 563b
refuse a woman, 565a
sorcerers, doctors, 574b
epilepsy, dandruff, 579b
Raz-Mah, T-R-C's, 579b
mobile unit, 603a
*Medicine Hat
sophistication in, 50a
all hell for basement, 190a
tending bar up in, 192b
very name asset, 311a
*Mediocrity
easiest thing, 82a
private radio and, 138b
march sluggishly, 272b
please Kansas City, 410a
objective to be gray, 475a
the cult of, 529a
*Medium
strike a happy, 76b
the m. is message, 396a
is message because, 396a
*Melting pot
more tossed salad, 176a
mosaic of cultures, 481a
boil me no, 650b
*Members
call in the, 101b
*Memory
books when he, 85a
do justice to my, 171a
amnesia mother of, 174a
cultivated, praised, 277b
Algonquin library, 319b
destruction time, 373b
*Men
come from Almighty, 71a
comings, goings, 78a
women and wives, 103b
the liberation of, 103b
jails made for, 109a
of Canada, keep both, 167b
of Canada keep, 168a
steady women, 178b
because cheaper, 179a
fraternizing with enemy, 187b
fetched their m. every, 254a
not understand women, 323a
pin-headed women, 371a
dangerous without, 444a
in Eaton's catalogue, 444b
women love weak, 444b
between m. and books, 457a
long-haired m. and, 507a
could get pregnant, 518a
some more perfect, 536a
in groups, 588b
make more money, 628b
do twice as well, 632a
women know, 634b
*Mental health
largest hospital, 88b
about mental illness, 235a
whose is excellent, 242b
supreme goal not, 262a
*Menu

victim not prepare, 316b
*Mercantile Bank*
at our own peril, 224b
proceed at peril, 507b
*Merchandising*
is many rogues, 10b
cannot expect much, 149a
use no deception, 173a
*Mercy killing*
not permitted, 472a
*Merde*
mangez de la, 598a
*Meredith, George*
books like those, 78b
*Mes Amours*
O Canada, mon pays, 101a
*Message*
I have no m. for you, 233a
don't leave showing, 242b
the medium is the, 396a
is the m. because, 396a
*Meta Incognita*
beyond unknown, 181b
*Methodist*
dominated by God, 70b
background, enthusiasm, 303b
no co-operative store, 590a
*Métis*
demands of the, 60a
half-breeds at Batoch, 418b
half-breed problem, 500b
not dare shoot, 530b
kill a few poor, 620a
*Mexico*
war breaks out in, 22a
and immigration, 535a
I was in M. too, 637a
*Michael the Archangel*
Doukhobor leader, 613b
*Michelangelo*
Trudeau and, 85a
*Mickey Mouse*
and Charlie Chaplin, 410a
*Mid-Atlantic*
a m.-A. accent, 10a
*Mid-Canada*
Development Corridor, 508b
*Middle power*
a m.p. such as, 519b
*Midnight sun*
strange things done in, 534a
*Mild*
isn't it, 36b
*Mile*
Zero, like mukluks, 316a
*Military*
have never been, 557b
*Militia*
what Canadian can do, 99b
think not of the, 135b
hands on Union Jack, 168a
every regiment in, 253b
*Milk*
cow's milk is for, 79b
America's Grade A, 265a
if liquor, why not, 400a
I like Mike, 469a
layer of cream, 617b
*Mill, John Stuart*
more Stendhal than, 597b

*Miller, Henry*
no effect on me, 444a
*Miller, Pearl*
remember, 420b
*Millerites*
hiked over to, 273a
*Million*
four m. Britons not free, 59b
what's a, 268
anyone can make a, 541a
*Millionaire*
for one French, 246b
careers of Canadian, 326a
mix good deal, 337a
interested in city, 368a
*Millions*
for corruption, not, 192b
*Millstone*
wretched colonies a, 155a
*Milton, John*
providence their guide, 11a
*Minas Basin*
the Basin of Minas, 360a
I see the, 384b
*Minds*
in the hearts and, 11a
no consistency, 40a
the faculties of, 77a
like caged tiger, 93a
Ontario a state, 167b
detached may watch, 174b
standard of man, 271b
deepest runnels of, 276a
absence of stimulation, 292a
failure a state, 293a
not in winter, 320b
among savages, 345a
can't plough in, 387b
big enough to change, 421b
so little for the, 444a
championship a state, 452b
continues free, 472a
naturally adapts, 604a
writer's situated, 636a
consents to north, 646a
have a vigorous, 650b
*Miner*
pathfinder, pioneer, 141a
never saw sun, 371b
*Minerals*
ore bodies lie, 174a
best in production, 245a
helicopters and, 264a
such as m., bulky, 344a
*Minerva's Owl*
begins its flight, 278b
*Mining*
solid pitchblende, 317a
darkness of hell, 349a
National Policy and, 378a
challenge, romance, 509a
advantage to country, 644b
*Ministry*
of all the talents, 332a
*Minority*
the smug, 52b
Bidwell and glorious, 55a
social history of, 63a
let Ontario m. be, 68a
Confederation graveyard of, 106b

blackmail of a, 111a
power of sword, 157b
tyranny of organized, 207b
French, English, Jews, 227b
traditionally friendly, 227b
autonomous French state, 237b
brothers in groups, 237b
Bidwell and glorious, 253b
the psychology of group, 265b
rights protected, 376a
a unity, diversities, 436b
Canadians least militant, 499b
judged by treatment of, 597b
*Minto, Lord*
don't want any more, 137a
*Misfortune*
sport of historic, 57a
poorer, greater, 134a
the Conquest not a, 317b
luck follows, 487b
*Misrule*
rod of unrelenting, 445a
victim of colonial, 489b
*Mission*
ours to fulfill, 210b
radiating afar hearth, 462b
possess the earth, 575a
*Missionary*
tell 'em they must, 39a
Indian persecution, 61b
a man reach people, 186b
Bible into Eskimo, 247a
Jesuits, Moravians, 284a
brutish natives, 319a
Indians stretch out, 345a
be thou beside me, 476b
like sun-glasses, 569b
*Mississauga*
Lord Thomson of, 585b
*Mississippi River*
boundary of, 152a
*Mister*
Watson, come here, 44a
Mother Country, 86b
Canada, speaker, 193b
*Mistress*
collect old masters, 41a
woman in bedroom, 108a
but m. in my own, 308b
*Moby Dick*
a Canadian version, 28b
*Mock Parliament*
Nellie McClung's, 370a
*Modesty*
is brought forward, 244b
Winnipeg too, 311a
sexual morality, 467a
*Mohammed*
lived and died, 527b
*Mohawk*
a language as, 439b
scriptures into, 530b
kemo sabe, 543b
lily of the, 579b
*Mon*
pays ce n'est, 616a
O Canada, m. pays, mes, 101a
*Monarchy*
Vive Elisabeth . . . Taylor, 12a

allegiance to Her, 20b
free us from, 21b
tribute to principle, 98b
union with ancient, 99a
indifferent to visit, 138b
Britannic Majesty's, 176b
no nobles, kings, 183a
freedom wears crown, 190a
Tory government, 244a
loyally supported, 253b
free and united, 385b
Windsor Castle far, 420b
a benefit or was, 438a
monarchies to America, 462a
republic can't swallow, 481b
editors against, 584b
more good than harm, 595a
    *Money
system destroys food, 1b
cannot circulate, 2a
N.S. m.-lender, 15b
on whisky not books, 35b
first 10,000, 40a
invest in Masters, 41a
Joe wants his coin, 41b
when hasn't any, 46a
admit I took, 47a
penny to invest, 59a
capital no nationality, 63b
politics for, 103b
attention to interests, 107a
larger going out, 133b
lose dollars, 133b
keep m. working, 148b
dollars, silver, 160a
delicate, volatile, 171b
nobody thought, 173a
not enough to, 173a
goods satisfactory or, 173b
laugh until make, 179a
bankruptcy when you, 179b
if m. talks, 179b
figures bilingual, 200a
bring the most, 220b
easier to make, 244b
more vertically, 264b
million unimportant, 269a
Eskimo adapting to, 286b
theatre no, 296b
advertising, mind, 339a
business, art of losing, 340b
corn is green like, 359a
easier to make, 394a
poor's credit card, 396b
dollar bill looks, 405a
found among poor, 450a
and hockey, 456b
talent to bed with, 478a
love, m., conquest, 545b
industry and, 575a
TV station licence to, 585a
I'm a m.-making, 585a
don't like spending, 585b
abroad not inflationary, 596b
a sinkhole for, 617a
in business to make, 628b
more out of men, 628b
divine right of, 641a
anything, even work, 650a
    *Mongolian

person of m. race, 19a
    *Monk, Maria
Catholics shrink, 175a
    *Monroe Doctrine
American continent, 426a
    *Montana
missile bases in, 325a
    *Montcalm, Marquis de
honour to, 29b
and St. Lawrence, 69a
see M. dying, 419b
funeral of New France, 427a
war grave of the, 427a
funeral of M., of, 464a
to see surrender, 465a
king will have peace, 480a
of bad soldiers, 638b
    *Montgomery's Tavern
two lives lost, 27b
    *Montreal
streets spell out, 12a
they may take, 12b
there was a young girl, 17b
I'll be living up, 22a
frighten every butcher, 38b
Joe Beef of, 41b
French accent no asset, 43a
a Saturday city, 45a
treble clef from, 74a
consists of banks, 77b
a true M.-er, 89a
most agreeable, 89b
O God, O Montreal, 90a
at your feet, 115b
preserve the past, 119b
renew my neurotic, 119b
trade with Indians, 131a
case of whoopee, 132a
towards gambling, 154b
the founding of, 156b
Canadians over in, 159a
as much veneration, 161a
next Vatican Council, 162a
Olympics no deficit, 162a
from Ville Marie, 163b
father born in, 181a
Rosemount ward of, 188b
Belgium to Kentucky, 191b
British in Westmount, 205b
my starting point, 205b
French, English, Jews, 227b
commander, Ville-Marie, 236b
ladies in Westmount, 240b
quality of police, 242a
no longer Ville-Marie, 260a
wide open but honest, 267b
by rail to Quebec, 271b
something happened, 272b
offends M. interests, 280a
hospitable magnates, 280b
lords of the ascendant, 280b
the M. Opera Company, 291b
girls of M. displeased, 295b
dirt and discomfort, 299a
Presbyterians of all, 299b
great archdiocese, 304a
fearing no man, 308b
Notre Dame des Neige, 309a
black-frocked priests, 310b
below island of, 328a

on annual visit to, 331b
middle-aged voyageur, 348b
San Francisco hostage, 376a
not limited to, 379b
exotic and Gallic, 388a
Boston of colonies, 390b
second-largest French, 395a
duty to found colony, 404a
surrounded, reporters, 413b
for capital, 418b
Penfield, Selye, 432a
statue of Victoria, 444a
out of M. be born, 451a
O M., what French, 463b
de Gaulle's journey, 469b
lilies reign over, 476b
powerless, underworld, 479a
American luxury, Europe, 484b
cognac, riot, women, 496a
350 miles from Toronto, 516b
drains, abattoirs, 522b
I'm from M., barman, 524b
living with two, 528b
and Hollywood weather, 538a
breakfasted with, 542a
the Macs fill 6 pages, 542b
Westmount Rhodesians, 557a
he enters Mont-Réal, 561b
first, Frenchness, 563a
mountain of churches, 565a
seems one prison, 573b
impossible to walk, 573b
from Wales to, 582a
tin roofs shining, 586b
French revolution, 586b
planks from Toronto, 593b
brick, churchwindow, 604b
Cartier's horse, 604b
iron spikes between, 610b
story of Catholic and, 634b
four-fifths American, 640a
[See also Hochelaga and Ville
    Marie.]
    *Montreal Canadiens
a M.C. sweater, 69b
an institution, 424a
    *Montreal Star
news I want to see in, 227b
    *Monument
posterity a common, 193b
to guide stranger, 347b
    *Moon
secrets in rocks, 189a
20th century and, 334a
spirit in the, 478a
touched the tranquil, 602b
    *Moore, George
and Irish language, 522a
    *Moose
brought home heads, 5b
vast backwoods, 62a
no m. south of, 134b
called l'orignal, 297a
    *Moose Jaw
odd name for, 13a
there was a young man, 17b
sacred Indian city, 355b
went Troy better, 372b
    *Moral
free of outrage, 94a

maintain m. roots, 229a
possession of richness, 237a
shutting out whole, 407a
equivalent of C.P.R., 608b
  *Morality
code of fundamental, 54a
reproduction not, 418b
sexual m., modesty, 467a
  *Morgan, Pierpont
you ain't, 12b
  *Morgan's
masters of consumption, 20a
  *Mormons
Tanner of the church, 304b
where I've laboured, 574b
  *Morrice, James Wilson
distinguished person, 48a
likes living alone, 48a
over hill and dale, 412b
interpreter of Paris, 413a
  *Morris
kills a cow, 10b
  *Morris, James
quarantine station, 12a
rowing song, 91a
demanded Melbourne, 416b
Palmerston said, 461b
eloquent imperialist, 510b
  *Morris, Jan
See James Morris.
  *Mortem
virtus communem, 193b
  *Mortlach
in the M. midden, 372b
  *Mosaic
a juxtaposition, 84b
a red tile in a, 97a
our Canadian, 201b
connection with, 217b
of vast dimensions, 253a
the vertical, 480b
of cultures, 481a
vision, Muses, 481a
  *Moscow
why a M. hireling, 54a
good enough for, 84b
hard heads in, 93b
known in files of, 227a
  *Mosquitoes
in summer ownland, 135b
bite the English, 250b
Eskimo origin of, 404b
ubiquitous, 434b
Sinbad never mentions, 583a
flies seem, 629b
  *Mother
seemed to understand, 43b
Mr. Mother Country, 86b
maternal dislike, 94a
weaned as babies, 244a
baneful domination of, 275a
daughter am I in my, 308b
how many suffered, 363b
hand that rocks, 370b
and child wander, 371a
grandm.'s day, 398a
had a great, 414b
write your m., son, 416b
daughters to ballet, 445a
I am a wife and, 519b

freedom and fantasy, 597a
  *Mottos
of Canada, 14b
slightly higher, 211b
  *Mt. Eisenhower
and Khruschev, 13b
  *Mount Royal
sound of chimes, 71b
called this mountain, 102b
  *Mountains
last of our, 57a
that sea of, 59b
changing colour, 78b
a sea of, 228b
greater height, 238a
B.C.'s almighty, 242b
feel the enormous, 353b
too much, 372b
Canada up in the, 426a
m.-climbing on level, 487b
out of a molehole, 492b
3,000 miles long, 499a
  *Mountbatten, Philip
a prince of men, 75a
water looks good, 474b
  *Mounted Police
See Royal Canadian Mounted
    Police.
  *Mouths
reply from cannon, 206b
nationalism needs more, 264a
as a m. I serve, 335b
  *Mounties
See Royal Canadian Mounted
    Police.
  *Movements
Socialists belong to, 648b
  *Mowat, Sir Oliver
admire his handwriting, 381b
  *Mozart, Wolfgang Amadeus
listen to music by, 383b
O Canada not composed by, 514a
  *Muddy York
See York.
  *Multicultural
one, bilingual, 65b
bilingual and, 650b
  *Multinational
enterprises national, 230b
become cosmocorp, 303a
welfare not for, 352a
the m. firm, 408a
explosion of corporations, 513a
corporation like man, 623a
  *Muni, Paul
in a fur hat, 113b
  *Munsinger, Gerda
participation in, 96b
want bedtime Tory, 291a
cabinet-making, 485a
Star Man Finds, 494b
  *Murder
death penalty glamourized, 38b
crime unmitigated, 42a
Coffin m. case, 118b
appeal of m. and sex, 340b
shot him, dead, 555a
I'm innocent, 603a
get away with, 619a

  *Murderer
murdered by R.C.M.P., 16b
refer to you as, 135a
die like cowards, 184a
an alleged, 340b
as infamous, 361a
  *Murray, James
governor of Quebec, 295a
  *Muses
Canada, work of, 481b
have to come in, 609a
  *Museum
working man's university, 134b
  *Mush
the hot m. school, 210a
of vitality, 375a
  *Music
love for subject, 3b
folk songs lead to, 34b
deplore the boring, 41b
to be a composer, 41b
using Eskimo themes, 41b
orchestra were in, 51a
still being played, 54b
drama of fur post, 74a
unpublished MSS, 74a
we have no Viennas, 74a
inevitable as weather, 74b
ukulele-m., 78b
memory, orchestration, 111a
loves the blues, 116a
history can give, 118b
howlings were, 118b
become a singer, 119b
future of business, 135b
happiest in memory, 136b
Canada have to have, 139a
recording dollar, 188a
know so much, 198b
wealthy parasite, 202b
use of recordings, 205a
luscious melody, 206a
excellent player, 215b
multitude of notes, 225b
don't like performing, 226a
mechanization and, 246b
belongs to masses, 288a
singer named Johnson, 288a
at Massey Hall, 291b
index of history book, 295a
native m. died, 297a
singing voice, 297b
on military bands, 303b
Anjou ballad, refrain, 313b
sounds are to, 314a
of running waters, 334a
repairs instruments, 334b
premiere of Levant's, 350a
write the songs, 354a
sweetest m. this side, 359a
first-class singer, 359a
get an audience, 374a
sends the audience, 394b
as a language, 398a
listening public, 412a
pastels for Debussy, 445b
language listen to, 471b
generation of composers, 472b
ears of the young, 472b
no command performances, 472b

gave me a voice, 487a
distinctive Canadian, 500b
and Paul Robeson, 505b
ear cleaning, 526a
risk everything, 526a
sound as sound, 526a
your difficult lonely, 550a
Canadian musicians, 553b
out of one note, 555b
extends inevitably, 557b
children drumming, 564a
one real friend, 566b
Mon Pays not nationality, 615b
down essential notes, 626a
golden age of, 626a
to write fugues, 633b
those mash notes, 646a
record market, 647a
chance of failing, 648a
[See also Anonymous: Martial
    Airs, Songs, Verses &
    Rhymes.]
    *Musical Ride
commissioner of the, 252a
    *Musk-ox
great m.-o. there, 160a
country in summer, 516b
    *Muskeg
sing, learned dame, 156a
find a market for, 629a
    *Musket
myself shouldered a, 328b
carried my m. in '37, 381a
    *Muskoka
interlude remained, 59a
    *Mussolini, Benito
Italy under reign of, 68b
never know tyrannies, 112b
    *My Fur Lady
Uncle Lou, 156b
    *Mystery
for objective, 65a
most revered of, 156b
there are no, 186b
dark m. that, 238b
of Mackenzie King, 276a
love the, 395b
an overwhelming, 591b
    *Myth
young live mythically, 296b
winter our beautiful, 594b
    *Mythology
in country without, 139b
literature is conscious, 208b
a country without a, 347b
created a new form of, 522a

# N

    *Nahanni River
land of the, 193a
white queen of, 409b
    *Name
without freedom no, 2a
Indian too shy to, 63a
its meaning tells, 143a
Indians not know, 204a

fame remembers with no, 321b
what going to use, 410b
written all over it, 433a
new n.s to the stars, 529b
invent a n. like, 540a
    *Nanook of the North
was dead, 195b
    *Naples
see N. and die, 312b
    *Napoleon
See Bonaparte, Napoleon.
    *Nation
none without patriotism, 67b
there was forged a, 91a
to be great, 122a
build a conservative, 229a
a n. of nobodies, 243b
history to life of, 266a
wise n. preserves, 272a
rich in sanity, 276b
from colony to n. to, 279a
Toronto head of a, 284a
a n. spoke to a, 308b
wiser than leaders, 310a
a colony, yet a, 329a
gradually become, 330a
real, not assemblage, 371b
great new northern, 384b
out-travelled soul, 395b
basis is land, 446a
we were, it was hell, 447a
the n. state, 513a
Ontario might be, 552b
to make, common, 552b
States in bedrooms, 558a
in the bedrooms of the, 595a
decides what state should, 601b
body of people who have, 607b
the first international, 620b
state, two nations, 650b
    *National
the n. dream, 52b
    *National Anthem
O Canada, terre de nos, 514a
O Canada, our home and, 626a
    *National Emblems
beaver and maple, 62a
beaver is a good, 92a
beaver, maple, 142a
    *National Film Board
Canada Carries On, 10a
world's largest, 234b
model to nations, 512b
at NFB symposium, 577b
    *National Gallery
never cost taxpayer, 62a
    *National Hockey League
take half a, 95b
    *National Policy
the old policy, 315b
welfare requires, 378a
what Canada wants is, 604a
    *National Spirit
the ebbing out of, 2b
1000 years to develop, 27b
our n. soul not grown, 34b
necessity of fostering, 59b
unless interests, 59b
cultivation of a, 59b
barely materialized, 77b

not concerned about, 136b
inferiority complex, 147a
landscape, atmosphere, 446b
[See also Spirit.]
    *Nationalism
imperialism one form, 50b
history of French, 63a
substantial is economic, 73a
spontaneous solidarity, 82a
a stury, excellent, 88b
of the third-rate, 94a
may prove too much, 116a
millstone of Canadian, 125b
the reassertion of a, 129b
on way to internationalism,
    127a
a warped, twisted, 153a
more than big mouth, 264a
open Canada to world, 266b
basis for internationalism, 278b
exploited by capital, 279a
narrow, garbage-littered, 289b
with utopian dreams, 348a
better than nihilism, 436b
defence mechanism, 463a
how old-fashioned can, 576b
the old concept of, 591b
blue of n. obsolete, 594b
opposed in all forms, 594b
isolation from alien, 607a
answer to discontents, 622b
    *Nationalist
who is minding store, 93b
I am a Canadian, 199b
must be imperialist, 504b
now allowed to be, 623a
    *Nationality
capital has no, 63b
seek to create new, 157b
young and virile, 165a
destitute of all, 171a
ce petit peuple, 237b
energy, grace, 384a
not French, British, 384b
entitled to a new, 385b
foundation of a new, 424a
creation of a new, 424b
your new n. enters, 425a
concept of a new, 433a
being a lost cause, 552a
Mon Pays not a, 615b
[See also New Nationality.]
    *Nationalize
private power, 350b
the C.P.R., sir, 351b
American unions, 442b
costs $10 to be, 383b
    *Nations
cannot be conquered, 8a
live together or, 63a
character of most, 122a
the quality of small, 166b
two nations warring, 170b
uniting their twin, 214b
over all is humanity, 305a
a galaxy of, 327b
may dissolve, 353b
a light among, 388a
the banquet of, 417b
who starts the, 501b

child of n., giant, 504b
not born in a day, 512a
above all is humanity, 551b
too n. at war over, 616b
  *Native
my own, my n. land, 11b
our home and n. land, 626a
  *NATO
her commitments, 450b
and of U.N., 520a
  *Naturalism
you at the pole of, 103b
  *Nature
and Niagara Falls, 1a
wise n., imprinted, 3b
interference with, 7b
unwillingness to reveal, 53a
is half Japanese, 78b
primaeval forces, 83b
not of a beautiful, 84a
objective thusness, 123b
has joined together, 174a
go paint canals, 181a
imminence of natural world,
  208b
heart like works of, 245a
art a stimulus, 250a
and British Channel, 253a
living in harmony, 268a
so joined, 300b
unpoetical and, 323a
ours perfectible, 328a
and Barren Ground, 521b
rich by n., poor policy, 552b
dare I cut hair, 554b
brother to untamed, 586b
took him to itself, 586b
are so beautiful, 591b
white man bully, 618b
  *Navigation
living is like, 148b
difficulties of internal, 344a
  *Navy
no n. made in London, 92b
the bench like the, 103a
  *Navy Island
self-styled patriots, 151a
  *Nazi
purged by N. pistol, 313a
goals of N. war, 314a
emblem for Swastika, 493a
  *Near
too n. to be great, 12a
as n. to heaven, 218a
  *Neat
Canada means, 394a
  *Nebraska
moved to Lincoln, 159a
  *Necessary
but conscription if, 307a
  *Necessity
has made us allies, 300b
  *Neck
some chicken, some, 112b
  *Need
no Englishman n. apply, 248b
no aliens n. apply, 369a
  *Negro
See Black.

  *Neige
quelques arpents de, 37a
quelques arpents, 616b
  *Neighbourhood
make the world a, 643a
  *Neighbours
tragedies like comedies, 179b
Canada is such a, 289b
geography has made us, 300b
fortunate in, 306b
independent of American, 329a
conscience tells us, 368b
should always marry, 610a
  *Neptune
le Théatre de, 349b
  *Nero
drive from his throne, 363a
  *Nest
a n. of traitors, 69b
  *Neurotic
renew my n. affiliations, 119b
  *Neutral
among the N. nation, 72b
uranium country can't, 76b
  *Never
you'll n. die, John A., 379a
  *New
the n. north, 15a
a n. Canada of north, 152b
and background to, 207a
Canadians, 300a
  *New Brunswick
have compassion, 11b
spem reduxit, 15a
land of blue nose, 51b
sister province of, 80b
do the best for, 280a
no longer in, 280a
Evangeline Country, 360a
N.S., N.B. by rail, 377b
to fish in streams, 414b
Beaverbrook's cult, 439a
decent guys from, 539b
and be one Dominion, 614b
Mr. Tilley sold us, 628b
  *New Canada
the North-West, 300a
  *New Canadians
first use, 300a
  *New Deal
do for them in fact, 259b
  *New Democratic Party
waffle to the left, 75a
no left-of-centre, 159a
free enterprise press, 526b
make it socialist, 623a
[See also C.C.F.]
  *New England
surfeit of liberty, 31a
Canada on back of, 147b
north with River, 293a
was a solitude, 464a
Canadian settlers in, 510a
older than, 576a
  *New France
exploitation of, 105b
improve old France, 108a
to people, 120b
to build Babylons, 345b
funeral of Montcalm, 427a

lengthened shadow of, 432a
funeral that of, 464a
economic venture, 558a
old France is Canada, 589b
  *New Glasgow
sign, MacIsaacs, 251a
  *New Nationality
nor seek to create, 157b
an article entitled, 385b
laid the foundation, 424b
simultaneous creation, 424b
your n.n. enters, 425a
of the north, 433a
[See also Nationality.]
  *New World
discovery of the, 73a
wilderness of the, 109a
wastes of the, 109a
prophet of the, 501a
  *New York
is big but Biggar, 13a
Paris, Vancouver, 25b
or hellish like, 77b
on the back of, 147b
intellectual life, 167b
a shouted hit, 224a
on the 95th floor, 230b
make films as well, 235b
going on in, 282a
more on garbage, 298a
they understood, 354a
come all the way to, 354b
collecting garbage, 405a
earn a living, 414a
to N.Y. or London, 467a
opening night, 476a
publishing books, 499b
behind style-setting, 499b
subways owned in, 509b
uptight in, 524b
nobody hates me, 567a
happen in Chicago, 596b
Torontonians healthier, 636a
  *New York Times, The
paper-making mill, 573b
a single Sunday, 615b
  *New Zealand
police power, 183a
poets of Australias, 624a
  *Newcastle, Duke of
appointments shocked, 638b
  *Newfie
from Newfoundland, 51b
  *Newfoundland
surrounded by fog, 10b
Quaerite prime, 15a
then hurrah for our own, 23b
cod fisheries dispute, 46b
banks are sound, 47a
Newfie, 51b
boarding a N. dog, 56a
sport of historic, 57a
instead of George, 69b
Ode to, 70b
mark that island, 80b
terra primum vista, 92a
pro patria et, 94a
half of St. Domingue, 96b
sell to a contractor, 104b
passed in a fog, 106b

strange magic about, 109a
plunged from status, 117b
million miles away, 123a
fill stage with epic, 125b
circa an. 1494, 143b
my new-found-land, 156b
rough diamond in crown, 169a
could not live there, 252b
found the new isle, 257b
Dominion was murdered, 258b
hockey fans in U.S., 260a
a distinct ethos, 267a
gulch a gully, 267a
pie-in-the-kisser, 298b
we are only loggers, 317b
sighted a N. schooner, 325a
L'Anse aux Meadows, 344b
sailors who fish off, 349b
zeroes through, 364b
too prosperous for, 388a
in a fog near stupid, 424b
Mr. King, wonderful, 475a
no debt and wine was, 484b
Cinderella of the Empire, 510b
Squid-Jiggin' Ground, 525b
last of Beothucks, 536b
wrong with Confederation, 548b
king of my own little, 548b
first Quebec, second, 548b
this poor bald rock, 549a
cold was unbelievable, 582a
as inhabited Wineland, 587b
fruitful country, 588a
of Irish mystics, 628b
mosquitoes, 629b
cod, dogs, hogs, fogs, 630a
[See also Vineland.]
    *Newfoundlanders
crafts but political, 258b
not to continent, 258b
rant and roar like true, 346a
inbred, half-witted, 372a
    *Newman, Cardinal
Lead, Kindly Light, 338a
    *News
hello, what's the, 38b
newspaper survey, 147a
yesterday's, 203b
read out loud, 227b
greatest gamble, 263a
world n. is Canadian, 263a
here are the, 293a
not advertising, 300a
from Swat, 323b
four elements of, 545b
my style of, 545b
what's the, 576a
Edinburgh's idea of, 585b
    *Newspaper
thought-throwing, 143a
no community as dull, 209a
made n. work a quest, 235a
all political opinion, 585a
always bought a, 585b
newsprint in Times, 615b
    *Newspaperman
hide of a dinosaur, 231b
[See also Journalism.]
    *Newspapers
own a lot of little, 39b

selling papers at six, 40a
never read a book, 145a
American pattern, 183b
pressure from advertisers, 193a
beside us a mountain, 270b
standard literature, 430a
in same hands, 435b
in 1812 a luxury, 498b
everywhere in chains, 530a
any n. for sale, 584b
one for each day, 585a
    *Next
Year Country, 14b
    *N.F.B.
See National Film Board.
    *Niagara
shooting, 98a
superb spectacle, 109b
attempt to damn, 155b
stuns with thundering, 222b
waters intermingle, 223a
old N. for ever, 312a
    *Niagara Falls
to equal it, 1a
to descend, 28a
you may dream of, 36b
resignation of Indians, 50b
both go down, 61a
to make this trip, 70a
separate awe, fear, 121a
thank God, over, 177a
grand leap of whale, 203a
has no equal, 257a
the hero of, 261b
it's a sure thing, 261b
border, oratory, 276a
beautiful object, 282b
what disappointment, 284b
always keep my word, 336b
one vast volume, 431b
swimming up, 440a
a fraud really, 448a
first of daredevils, 466a
made me homesick, 468a
Caroline adrift, 508a
marriage licence, 508a
really some waterfall, 518a
if I die, turtle, 558b
is very nice, 561b
did I go over, 576a
a signboard on, 611a
no place like it, 625a
wonder if did not fall, 632b
second disappointment, 632b
stupendous waterfall, 632b
not written a book, 649a
    *Nice
or tiresome like, 77b
    *Nicol, Eric
a gold spike into, 567a
    *Nigeria
Biafra, where's, 598a
    *Nigger
King, editorial, 327a
white n. of America, 609b
Dan, loyal to, 633b
    *Night
work, for the n. is coming, 118b
flash of a firefly in, 133a
single n. of universal, 218a

    *Nightingale
P.E.I. needs only, 102b
    *Nihilism
nationalism better, 436b
    *Nile River
row, my boys, row, 91a
    *Nineteenth Century
of U.S. development, 330a
belonged to U.S., 333a
    *Ninety-eight
Trail of, 15b
    *Nineveh
down this road find, 282a
palaces of N. buried, 341a
mushroom of, 464a
    *No
Englishmen need apply, 9b
English need apply, 248b
aliens need apply, 369a
    *Nobel Prize
will share with, 34a
testimonial speech, 260b
acceptance speech, 468b
    *Nobility
further north, 612a
    *Noble Savage
Adario prototype, 3b
    *Norland
grand old name, 243b
    *Normal school
for B.N.A., 271a
for colonies, 271b
    *Norman, Herbert
suppose a Communist, 6a
    *Normandy
inscription at, 17a
Quebec suggested, 576a
    *Norse
the old mythology, 201b
colony, Vinland, 344b
am I when the snow, 382b
    *Norseman
Prince of the, 2b
died in Ontario, 134b
shapeless mounds, 238a
first bush aircraft, 450a
    *North
frontier of U.S., 4a
Atlantic Triangle, 10a
the N. has got him, 14b
combine unknowns, 14b
Warden of the, 15a
the New, 15a
unknown quantity, 52a
from the frozen, 74b
beyond human scale, 83b
colossal no-man's-land, 84a
reigns 4,000 miles, 94b
where avarice, 152a
a Canada of the, 152b
in N. I discovered, 195a
have our back to, 212a
of greatest concern, 221a
immense n. country, 234a
responsibility for, 234a
mounds erected by, 238a
the men of the, 243a
Jack Frost guards, 264a
land of feast and famine, 266b
and after airplane, 298a

warden of honour of, 308b
exiled Queen flying, 310b
the N. could wait, 317a
Saskatoon, Queen of, 319a
unfitted for civilized, 344a
expedition all through, 352a
profoundly spiritual, 362a
unconquerable vastness, 365a
live far south as possible, 384a
dark, true, tender, 385b
of Norumbega, 421a
development of its, 430a
brooding presence, 430b
Great Britannic Empire, 433b
to call it home, 438a
symbol of sanity, 438b
Nanook of the, 443b
spiritual, industrial, 455a
few caught by magnetism, 474b
sterner laws of, 475a
heterosexual ghetto of, 499b
mid-Canada is largely, 508b
administered in absence, 520b
window to infinite, 542b
if you write of, 549b
with southern fringe, 559b
Russians live n., look, 560b
white n. hath bones, 579b
that true N., whereof, 580a
Canada ever be that true, 581a
common Everest, the, 600a
cult of romanticism, 607b
vast unoccupied, 611b
further n., nobility, 612a
presence of N. in man, 621b
bounded by gold, 625b
a true n., strong and, 626a
Russians n., south, 633b
will a mind consent, 646a
[See also Arctic.]
  *North America
first continent to, 229a
a United States-er, 273b
Acadians dispersed, 335b
I find myself a, 347a
hemisphere remain, 509b
west of Cape Breton, 554a
Her Majesty's dominions, 615a
  *North Atlantic Treaty
    Organization
See NATO.
  *North Bay
where Nugget belongs, 435b
  *North Dakota
immensities north of, 265a
missile bases in, 325a
  *North Pole
between me and, 77b
14th parallel to the, 113b
American possessions to, 113b
ardently to reach, 125a
sovereignty up to, 241a
passage to Japan, 273a
I have the, 470b
I die you go on, 606a
  *North River
Hudson's discovery, 453b
  *North Star
take into consideration, 148b

  *North Wind
the N.W. trail, 83b
  *Northern
we are a N. people, 201b
men of the n. zone, 301b
austere N. dignity, 310b
visions and dreams, 362a
call it a n. nation, 384a
great new n. nation, 384b
have seen queer sights, 534a
strength of will, 567a
  *Northern lights
glorious the, 549b
heard the northern gleams, 643b
  *Northland
the great lakes of the, 360a
  *Northmen
of the new world, 243b
  *Northward
the course of empire, 559b
  *Northwest
that inhospitable, 59b
the people of, 82a
to sail toward the, 92a
forty years, no beer, 151b
transplanted romance, 167b
begot in the, 202a
New Canada known as, 300a
called a blizzard, 326a
government of the, 348b
Coast Indian culture, 351a
Englishmen, Yankees, 376a
our poor brother of, 417b
bound by discovery, 433b
challenges and, 455a
few boyish hearts, 496a
is also my mother, 501a
Prince Rupert's Land, 535a
King Arthur in the, 580b
  *Northwest Company
held a feudal sway, 280a
[See also Nor'wester.]
  *Northwest Mounted Police
See Royal Canadian Mounted
    Police.
  *Northwest Passage
doubtless there is, 30b
there is no, 30b
for discovery of, 144a
oil tanker Manhattan, 202a
my lord, only 53, 203b
straight and short, 242b
eternal honour to, 246a
by North Pole, 273a
all around Arctic, 325b
nobody to meet us, 325b
non-existence by land, 389b
and Baron Münchausen, 440a
dreamer in coat, 482b
Manhattan and Macdonald,
    493a
their personal, 505a
mad north-north-west, 536a
to intellectual world, 563a
  *Northwest Rebellion
See Rebellion, Northwest.
  *Northwest Territories
combine unknowns, 14b
the new north, 15a
demands of Métis, 60a

no one flown over, 150b
capital of the, 316a
  *Norumbega
from the north of, 421a
  *Norway
colours were from, 576a
  *Nor'wester
travels the canoe routes, 348b
[See also Northwest Company.]
  *Nos institutions
notre langue, lois, 463b
  *Nose, Blue
See Blue Nose.
  *Notre
maître, l'avenir, 221a
maître, le passé, 236a
  *Nova Scotia
surrounded by fish, 11b
munit haec, 15a
farewell to N.S., sea-bound, 23b
government of petty, 43b
land of the blue nose, 51b
hospitable shores of, 80b
becoming an island, 86b
ill-thriven, hard, 87a
character of people, 131a
not a cent for, 192b
selects influences, 205b
lands I dread, 212b
country too young, 243b
Mr. Blue Nose, 244a
fishing boats of, 248b
poor man's country, 270b
unshackled press, 271a
normal school for B.N.A., 271a
normal school for colonies, 271b
high does your tide rise, 272a
big field, turnip, 272a
not return to this, 335b
and N.B. by railway, 377b
from N.S.'s misty coast, 388a
not graveyard of race, 395a
north of Norumbega, 421a
horribly marine, 423a
this rocky homeland, 488b
happy with square, 496b
insignificance of our, 604a
form and be one dominion, 614b
wood to beat Bluenose, 620a
did Dante describe hell, 649a
banishing French from, 638a
  *Noue, Charles de la
seigneur de Sainte Marie, 160a
  *Novel
not add to women, 346b
unjustly neglected, 635b
buy lousy Canadian, 624a
  *November the Eleventh
Armistice Day, 373a
  *Nuclear
dumping ground for, 153a
probability of war, 228a
not accept weapons, 450b
[See also Atomic.]
  *Nudes
take off clothes, 62a
six naked Doukhobors, 305b
art not energetic, 434b
  *Number One
hard Manitoba wheat, 398a

# O

*O Canada
mon pays, mes amours, 101a
the boat was sinking, 337b
terre de nos aïeux, 514a
oh can a day go by, 528a
our home and native land, 626a
*O God
O Montreal, 90a
*Oak Island
10 feet below me, 302b
lodged goods and treasures, 303a
I've buried my money, 578a
*Oakes, Sir Harry
no one understands, 406b
I don't, 644b
*Oaks
the Battle of Seven, 188b
*Oath of Allegiance
I swear that I will be, 20b
*Obedience
so much authority as, 601a
*Obesity
fat people today's lepers, 225a
power a tendency to, 243b
described as a world figure, 398b
avoiding, 483a
*Objectivity
ideology of status quo, 610a
*Ocean
traversed o. gates of, 125a
a vast o. separates us, 137b
from o. to o. through, 228b
*Ochs, Adolph Simon
Spruce Falls Power, 573b
*October Crisis
fate in a rare example, 69a
I thought about killing, 126b
six kids and revolution, 132a
I refuse to pass judgment, 251b
my dear Robert, 324b
political prisoners are, 346b
final irony in this drama, 430b
a lot of bleeding hearts, 598b
apprehended insurrection, 599a
violence is no stranger, 599b
[See also F.L.Q. and War
    Measures Act.]
*Oil
drilling regulations, 13b
from the oolichan, 235a
in the Rocky Mountains, 278b
nowhere on a tide of, 436b
uncle with a surfeit of, 448a
Manhattan through Arctic, 493a
eastern bastard is my, 571b
wheels of industry turn on, 574b
*Okanagan
during apple-blossom time, 69b
flee to the O. Valley, 316b
*Old
the o. originals, 18a
grow o. by moments, 38a
get sick for something, 78a
to remember the, 207a
the o. man, the o. flag, 315b

the o. man, the o. flag, 380b
if I were 58 I would not, 595b
shade of the o. apple tree, 634a
*Old Crow
start to make big town, 293a
*Old Tomorrow
nickname for Sir John A., 279b
just the name for, 378b
*Oldest
man in the world, 402b
senator, 148b
*O'Leary, Grattan
not done me any good, 150a
*Olympics
can no more have a deficit, 162a
in the O. of nations, 165a
Barbara Ann Scott, 526b
I did everything in swimming,
    574a
my ideals are all shot, 634a
*On to Ottawa
I move that we go, 185b
*One
shall form and be, 19a
flag, throne, empire, 441b
voice, people, heart, 523a
shall form and be o. dominion,
    614b
*O'Neill, Moira
epitaph of Dr. Drummond, 16a
*Ontar-i-ar-i-ar-io
a place to stand, to grow, 435a
*Ontario
no take Zorra, 12b
ut incepit fidelis, 15a
the old O. strand, 24a
poor little girls of, 24a
no O. patriotism, 67b
let the O. minority be, 68a
spread the wealth of, 69a
stupid things said in, 76b
from Oxford to, 85b
shoulder with men from, 91a
a Norseman died in, 134b
Jalna and traditions of, 144b
Majesty's Loyal, 154a
doesn't yet know what, 167a
state of mind bounded, 167b
squat and uninteresting, 167b
the most advanced, 221a
keep an O. chicken, 240a
leaving villages, 248b
black flies in north, 256b
tumbledown farmhouse in, 320a
branded a traitor to, 330b
right to speak French, 334b
I myself talk O. English, 341b
to dig out gold in North, 342a
such a respectable place, 389a
politics a business, 520b
decent guys from, 539a
it might sell in, 551a
severed from literary, 551b
no common hopes, 552b
by herself a nation, 552b
for Quebec's blackmail, 553a
care of illiterate, 569a
Scots brood a little, 569b
Riel's agony and, 575a
not think I am great, 631a

matted forests of, 644a
*Ookpik
did nothing but make, 247a
happy little Arctic, 555b
*Opera
always loved beautiful, 4b
songs lead to, 34b
in Maple Leaf Gardens, 56a
first Canadian grand, 127b
if it doesn't cost, 215b
singer named Johnson, 288a
Montreal O. Company, 291b
complicated households, 297b
Vienna State's subsidy, 303b
a first-class singer, 359a
from Paris to Canada, 438b
convention with tradition, 445a
feather in my hat, 487a
call the police, 548a
given me a break, 566b
remaining a school, 614b
*Opinion
government in advance, 32a
public o. precious, 191b
his or of your own, 328b
we all have, 164b
Englishman respects, 328b
Quebec, sentiments, 331a
greater freedom, 386a
are mine, my vote, 644a
*Opportunity
air waves represent, 207a
do evil turn twice, 381a
luck, preparation, 595b
*Opposition
be leader of the, 40b
duty to turn out, 153b
Her Majesty's Loyal, 154a
leader of the O. paid, 203a
send for the leader of, 305b
football beats, 399a
alarmism temptation of, 471b
there's only one me, 558a
to accepted opinions, 602b
*Oppression
refuge of oppressed, 74b
of a foreign master, 76a
impossible if tried, 379b
*Optimist
visit Canada and be, 180b
*Orange Lodge
from a rank, 42a
enemies are intriguers, 68a
one school, one flag, 227a
to the master of, 526b
make O. vote Papists, 553a
my father was an, 632a
*Orchestra
spending on bands, 303b
the new o., the sonic, 526a
*Order
peace, o., and good, 19a
Bourinot's Rules of, 96b
of Canada, 175a
how thin the crust, 181a
things in the paper, 234b
of Good Cheer, 349b
peace, o., and good, 436a
father taught me, 597a
*Orderly

decontrol, 529a
*Oregon
boundary question, 6b
*Organization
without principles win, 328b
produce men who reject, 356a
*Orient
highway to the, 254a
one who went to the, 545b
*Orientals
no o. need apply, 14a
no aliens need apply, 369a
*Originals
the old, 18b
*Orillia
old Brewery Bay, 342a
*Oromocto
songs to be found in, 294a
*Oshawa
James Bond's tricks, 196b
*Oswego
where wild O. spreads, 222b
*Ottawa
advance, avant, 14b
run a peanut stand, 50a
line of defence is, 68a
a certain graciousness, 77b
only poet living in, 78a
in September 1939, 83b
the train for, 166b
On to Ottawa trek, 185b
life without laughing, 225a
narrowness of, 225b
least objectionable, 253a
when Washington sneezes, 298b
St. Petersburg-like, 310b
colour the town, 321a
real genius discovered, 322b
millionaires and, 326a
not a handsome city, 328a
richest impersonator, 357a
hardest town to beg, 359a
of the future, 365b
lights will be on, 382a
Vancouver a long way, 387a
one French Canadian, 405b
choice of capital, 418b
for some business, 424b
after Washington, 431b
old canal winds through, 454a
cannot leave, 551b
a cabinet at, 552b
sub-arctic lumber village, 553a
that is the place, 614b
not a nationalist in, 623a
monstrous absurdity, 642b
*Ottawa River
still waters of, 32b
on the bank of, 308a
unites with Great Lakes, 328a
I see the, 384a
Ottawa's tide, 431a
think the Nile's the, 554a
*Our
master, the future, 221a
master, the past, 236a
*Ours
this Canada of, 164b
this Canada of, 175b
brave boys, Quebec is, 428b

*Ourselves
count only on, 109a
*Outlook
with his Elbow and, 13a
*Overalls
and don the, 454b
*Owen, Derwyn T.
from Strachan to, 85b
*Owl
gravest bird is, 47a
should be their emblem, 243b
Ookpik, 247a
Minerva's begins, 278b
the student-owl, 458b
Ookpik, happy little, 555b
*Own
my o., my native land, 11b
*Ownership
plan not own economy, 159b
private o. of land, 188a
we are owners, owers, 193b
pride of o. narrower, 452a
dreams are all we, 628a
*Oxford
I attended, and, 285a

# P

*Pablum
mixed cereal, 79b
*Pacific Ocean
all aboard for the, 14a
to cross P., push, 14a
calmer waters of, 74b
on the edge of, 78a
to the shores of, 81a
smashed, hurled, 107a
China and Canada, 135b
from Halifax to, 271b
unite the P. to the, 367b
until road is built, 377b
new nationality to, 425a
full view of the, 583a
*Pacific Scandal
draw on me for, 1a
these hands are clean, 46b
took the money and, 47a
was nothing wrong, 47a
John A. beats devil, 265b
must have another ten, 376b
throw myself upon, 377a
you should be here, 379a
*Pacifism
state my conviction, 643b
*Paddle
song that my p. sings, 290a
every man p. his canoe, 407a
*Paine, Tom
has had no, 477a
*Painless Parker
showman dentist, 463b
*Painter
every pine tree painted, 127a
I'm a house-p., 202b
paint me as a ruler, 331b
to delineate scenery, 429b
how if I do not, 470b

like a fisherman, 471b
don't feel hesitant, 503a
*Painters Eleven
no manifesto here, 375a
*Painting
nothing in mainstream, 231b
no p. of Canada, 282a
never sold until 50, 356b
refusing to sign, 433a
you are at war, 509b
speak for themselves, 591a
what my p.s are, 615b
*Palliser Hotel
drilling regulations, 13b
*Pancreas
tie off p. ducts, 33b
*Panic
your pants fall, 159b
caught with my, 492b
*Papineau, Louis-Joseph
cannot make a hero, 82b
different opinion, 445b
pour toujours, 516b
*Paradise
a p. of fertility, 142b
where horses go, 250b
a p. of fertility, 262b
I had entered, 288a
not confused with, 304b
O plumage of, be, 313b
some new p. of art, 320b
who pays has a bunk, 365b
by hook or crook, 573b
*Parent
only permanent, state, 398b
ruin first half, 444b
*Paris
New York, Vancouver, 25b
small corner of Canada, 65a
swallowed by earthquake, 124a
can tell Winnipeg's not, 179b
is free, is happy, 246b
was worth a mass, 327b
twentieth century was, 333a
Morrice interpreter, 413a
from P. to Canada, 438b
freeing of P. from, 469b
a decor in dreams, 506b
American dies and, 620a
*Paris, Ontario
book on etiquette, 647b
*Parity
with Texas, 115a
*Parker, Gilbert
seats of the mighty, 468a
*Parkman, Francis
and the St. Lawrence, 96a
retain the tradition, 619a
*Parks
entering Toronto, 503b
please walk on grass, 584a
*Parlez-vous
Mademoiselle from, 496b
*Parliament
genius draw inspiration, 30b
if enough women in, 37a
ceased to function, 39b
lowest moment, 39a
minority not running, 39a
privileges, rights, 59a

the Crown and, 99a
to obtain seat in, 111b
freedom enshrined in, 112b
decline to sell to, 149b
Canadians in Commons, 152b
70 seats and we'll, 159b
wisdom, infallibility, 165a
believe in P. no matter, 165b
a spy in Commons, 227a
woman's place in House, 232b
incorporated F.L.Q., 242a
reputations of members, 259a
blather talked here, 269a
more to do than amuse, 269b
writes to complain, 273b
labour has half a man, 295a
it is for P. to decide, 305b
gain 1000 pipelines, lose, 314b
press more than pulpit, 323b
throw myself upon this, 377a
and sang God Save the King,
    382b
a seat, no place, 437a
very much at home, 449b
mills of P. stop, 465b
let P. decide, later, 529a
conservative element, 551b
turned into arena, 584a
[See also House of Commons
    and Senate.]
*Parliament Buildings
homemade bomb exploded, 108a
Robinson Crusoe's canoe, 225b
image hung in House, 310b
a Gothic pile, 552a
stone of intended, 642b
*Parliament Hill
cough in Washington, spit on,
    619a
*Parnassus
beavers not found in, 107b
censor soared beyond, 373b
*Parry Sound
and Charlie Farquharson, 251a
*Parti Québécois
a taste for Quebec, 351a
opponent is Coca-Cola, 463b
*Parties
capitalists support, 648b
*Parting
get to the place, 490b
of the ways, 572b
*Partnership
Western hemisphere, 449b
*Party
for its own sake, 82b
American p. in Canada, 183a
he leader, I the, 279b
make the 20th century, 332b
by p., with p., for, 377b
we say others corrupt, 551b
no p., but people, 552a
both blondes and brunettes,
    595a
my vote belongs to my, 644a
capitalists support, 648b
*Pass
Canadians, 10b
*Passamaquoddy Bay
sweet maiden of, 146a

*Passchendaele
the Battle of, 64b
Vimy Ridge followed, 555a
*Passé
notre maître le, 236a
*Passion
genuine intellectual, 58a
trying to excite, 285b
political sentiment a, 328a
regenerative principle, 357b
only two primal, 458b
fusing the notion, 529b
reason over, 594b
this self-deluding, 601b
*Passport
Canadian so desirable, 348a
to the whole world, 348a
give up his English, 366b
bilingual, not heart, 615b
*Past
there's no, 33b
no longer anvil, 65a
pay our debt to, 83a
happened elsewhere, 119b
present a thing of, 134a
future of yesterday, 137a
loving great men of, 148a
literary of England, 175b
our master the, 236a
nothing so present as, 236b
in Europe a great, 237b
reference to glories, 272a
common values from, 300b
cherishing tradition, 332a
dream world woven, 422a
future greater than, 460b
flag not dishonour, 469b
is gone, present, 561a
magic atmosphere of, 576b
not be worshipped, 598a
done great things in, 607b
see the future as, 637a
historian is guardian, 645a
*Paternalistic
capitalism, 462a
*Paths
of glory lead but, 230b
of glory lead, 639a
*Patient
must cure himself, 235a
care more for, 457a
*Patria
pro p. et Avalonia, 94a
*Patriot
neither sycophant, 245a
he lived a p. and died, 363b
died as he lived, 412a
true p.-love, 626a
*Patriotism
Ontario, Quebec, 67b
that romantic, 83b
has never been enough, 116a
warm over the flame, 130a
doesn't exclude, 182a
and $5 a month, 211b
all cattle lack, 228a
simplest impulse, 320b
common sense and, 376a
rejects the prefix, 384b
brotherhood with help, 404b

my country first, 462a
never teach him, 601a
against pocketbook, 610b
*Patronage
set-up here, 5b
udder of democracy, 515b
passes on C.P., 547a
Canada Council partner, 602b
*Patronize
never p. the Canadians, 91a
*Paw
under the lion's, 637a
*Pays
mon p. ce n'est pas, 615a
*Peace
research, 5a
the works of, 12b
order and good government, 19a
winged p. or death, 57b
pursuit of stable, 87b
in love you manifest, 88a
I bury the hatchet, 94a
we want social, 106b
Canada linch-pin of, 112a
thus the great p. be, 144b
terminate in friendship, 154b
make as exciting as war, 234b
to Europe to grand, 425b
order and good government,
    436a
no p. in province, 452b
blessed thing, 454a
prepare for p. like pygmies, 468b
you have me, 482a
country offer us, 489b
in p. can wastes, 528a
tedious lasting, 530a
any p. is honourable, 535b
maintain 100 years of, 573a
d'y trouver la paix, 602b
universal rottenness, 610a
prefer p. to Canada, 617a
broke out, 619a
I will die in, 640a
democracy in which war, 641a
*Peace River
drink water of the, 13a
gravestone of 12 Foot, 141a
*Peaceable
Canada the p. kingdom, 584b
*Peaceably
if possible, forcibly, 48a
*Peak
Pike's P. or Bust, 477a
*Pearl Harbour
to hell with, 420b
*Pearson, Lester B.
explosion in washroom, 108b
came to power, 293b
Kennedy said exempt, 293b
asked to introduce, 469a
*Peasants
in eyes of Europe, 238a
in sheepskin coats, 542b
stalwart p., sheepskin, 543a
in a sheepskin coat, 543a
*Peasouper
land of the, 51b
*Pefferlaw

come out in, 62b
*Peking Man
Sinanthropus pekinensis, 58a
*Pelletier, Gérard
sing better than shout, 294a
Trudeau and P. join me, 405b
*Pemmican
poetry, p. of literature, 160b
*Penfield, Wilder
Montreal and maps, 432a
*Pensions
aren't given for, 454a
*People
the p. hired me, 36a
Joe Beef, son of, 41b
indignation of wrong, 47a
cannot do for themselves, 49b
games p. play, 51a
privileges, rights, 59a
could not live apart, 63a
a great p. too, 82b
priceless assets, 83b
without glamour, 83b
just read headlines, 95b
your own blood, 97b
died not knowing, 106b
English-speaking, 113b
versatile spirit, 142a
everyone against me but, 153a
never campaign, visit, 153b
no history, literature, 171a
story from life of, 195a
dissolve all mobs, 207b
its moral richness, 237a
that little group of, 237b
patriot no tyrant to, 245b
will want me, 267a
control by not seeing, 308a
make any country great, 312b
a dull p., rivers, 336a
commonplace, p. do, 338b
left out of histories, 375a
I say trust the, 398a
sound as No. 1 Manitoba, 398a
how do you understand, 421b
unsuitable p. in, 423b
maintain government, 454b
great, ripened, stirred, 477a
not party but the, 552a
the p. make giants, 590a
together a giant, 590b
need to explain p. to, 597b
democracy is p. in action, 641a
one thing in common, 649b
too many, human beings, 650a
*Percé
Cartier not visit, 163b
*Perception
art stimulus to, 250a
sophistication is, 397a
*Peril
come near at your p., Wolfe,
  23b
*Perish
end unemployment or, 48b
*Permafrost
sing, learned dame, of, 156a
*Persia
as Greece by, 122a

*Persons Case
means a male, 19a
word includes, 20a
women were not, 371a
I want to be a, 394b
*Peru
to Callicuth, 509b
*Pessimism
propagandists of, 141a
not life failure, 233a
afraid of the worst, 513b
*Pétain, Henri-Philippe
great at Vichy than, 68b
France under régime, 68b
*Peter Principle
every employee tends, 473b
*Peter the Lordly
Sons of Freedom, 613b
*Peter the Purger
I am Christiakov, 614a
*Peterborough
Little Lake Cemetery, 16a
*Pew
the comfortable, 52b
*Philanthropy
must show gratitude, 522a
not object of our visits, 544b
*Philately
nobody more surprised, 124a
*Philistine
of a hard type, 27a
*Philosopher
long to become a man, 134a
of history search, 515b
whether world exists, 560a
arguments for fish, 560b
no more p.-king, 600b
a great Canadian, 606b
ancient Chinese, 624a
problem for solution, 649b
Trudeau, p-kingdom, 650b
*Philosophy
fool-osophy, 2a
holes in receptacle, 48a
reassess political, 182a
keep doing what, 204b
moral and spiritual, 209b
greater than Kant's, 338a
positivism, surrealism, 369b
success makes a man, 368b
become absurdities, 458b
equal amounts of, 496b
expected to understand, 556a
and hearts of men, 563a
curious eye of natural, 592b
*Phipps, R.W.
if you had a secretary, 140b
*Photography
visual order in, 84b
wait for me, daddy, 149a
tourist by his car, 215b
task to reveal secret, 297a
government know good, 537a
*Physical Fitness
5BX Plan, 455b
bride carries groom, 473a
*Pianist
do not shoot the, 632b
*Piccadilly
goodbye P., farewell, 634a

*Pidgeon, Walter
Canadian-born, 499a
*Pie
in-the-kisser bit, 298b
when introduced, 533b
*Piece
not give a five-cent, 306a
*Pierre
le Canadien, 156a
*Pike's
Peak or Bust, 477a
*Pile
a Gothic, 552a
*Pillar
outside p. of church, 382a
*Pilot
See Bush Pilot.
*Pine
our p.-clad hills, 70b
toss about trees in glee, 165b
child called him Jack, 356b
becomes the palm, 554a
and maples grow, 626b
*Pink
tooth brush, 70a
*Pioneer
of a glorious future, 18a
pathfinder, miner 141a
to live for tomorrow, 191a
every one can be, 216a
attached to landscape, 304b
by grace of being, 365a
no civilization in, 537a
frontier land where, 560a
*Pipeline
there will always be a, 39a
gain a p., lose soul, 314b
*Piper
repeat P. of Arll, 409a
Scottish-born, 498a
the p. of Arll, 527a
*Pirate
Blackbeard the, 578a
*Pitchblende
cobalt-blue and, 45b
it was solid, 317a
*Pitt, William
appointment of Bishop, 437b
the P.'s new general, 638b
*Pittmans
the Ryans and the, 346a
*Place
can a sense of, 134a
Toronto, p. of meeting, 280a
a p. to stand, to grow, 435a
no p. for the state, 595a
*Plains
the Riders of the, 18b
that broke the plough, 139a
wider spaces of, 238a
[See also Prairies.]
*Plains of Abraham
was poorly marked, 4b
towards roof of world, 419b
no right to be there, 427a
government goes out, 587a
*Planet
on which we all adrift, 348a
*Planning
not p. but research, 260a

when schemes are laid, 459a
who shall bend to, 528a
full program socialized, 608a
    *Plant
from p's point of view, 137b
    *Plates
melt our p. into bullets, 445b
    *Plato
was like words, 487b
    *Play
games people, 51a
preach importance of, 120b
a hundred grand, 127b
equal amounts of, 496b
what we like to do, 533a
    *Playboy Magazine
to cite one example, 138a
first Playmate, 224b
    *Playwright
suffering really was, 140a
Canadian seems incongruous,
    451a
from outside Canada, 499a
    *Please
remember me, 90b
who do as they, 179a
walk on the grass, 584a
    *Pleasure
loss by excess, 285b
make a p. out of pain, 313b
poems here to give, 336a
an orgy of, 356b
    *Plenty
poverty in midst, 158a
    *Plough
plain that broke the, 139a
instrument of change, 261a
can't in your mind, 387b
to p. on and on, 567a
    *Plume
follow my white, 330b
    *Plutarch
pirated Miss Deeks, 627b
    *Poem
unexamined p. not, 164b
rather be author of, 231a
happiest when I, 335b
are here to reveal, 336a
an Alka-Seltzer, 336a
as lovely as a tree, 372b
write as spiders, 486a
about drains or, 522b
word freedom in a, 645a
made it coming from, 646a
    *Poet
tried to be a king, 5a
who never wrote a, 38a
Canada's a bloody place, 78a
sing the p.'s call, 101a
sometimes annoying, 115a
reading a dead, 164a
no pay for laureate, 215a
nocturnal emissions, 243b
I am not a great, 321a
sang as birds, pay, 340a
to describe glories, 429b
sort of poltergeist, 491a
dear bad p.s who wrote, 491b
bird that sings, 515a
not taken seriously, 527a

sensitivity to poetic, 535b
eclectic detachment, 550a
on train to N.Y., 568a
danger of laureate, 587a
of Canada and Australia, 624a
will produce native, 625b
have to be ambitious, 628b
daily chore is duty, 633a
best is Esposito, 647a
    *Poetry
anerca, to breathe, 99b
stuff of epic, 111a
made by white paper, 115a
is a verdict, 120a
so many volumes, 126a
pemmican of literature, 160b
great deeds, sonnets, 161a
don't go after, 225a
never went crazy, 234b
my first love, politics, 272a
Imagism and prairies, 275a
business history, poem, 304a
more flowers than fruit, 312a
Anjou ballad, refrain, 313b
greatness of character, 321a
unpoetical, anti-romantic, 323a
of horse, of canoe, 354b
rather turn one verse, 386b
well-springs of stars, 477b
some lonely farm house, 491b
live for p. by prose, 504b
is when words sing, 526a
each verse, universe, 530a
exploring p. of deeds, 560b
blank verse, town sites, 567b
no poets, no, 568a
blueprints for reality, 618a
only access to truth, 625a
had no renaissance, 636b
colonialism desirable, 637a
    *Pogrom
Jews waiting next, 561a
    *Points
growing, 234b
    *Polack
president is a, 509a
    *Poland
Canada and labour camps, 65b
bringing vodka to, 276b
    *Pole
See North Pole.
    *Police
Montreal gambling, 154b
power pushed very far, 183a
often called for me, 222a
investigative quality, 242a
law keeps p. in handcuffs, 292b
give you something free, 548a
break up demonstrations, 545a
charged with driving, 624a
[See also Royal Canadian
    Mounted Police.]
    *Policy
imperialism a sentiment, 50b
someone stealing pajamas, 159b
submit to nothing wrong, 270b
the Old, 315b
the old flag, the old, 380b
only one for Canada, 543a

rich by nature, poor by, 552b
Canada wants national, 604a
    *Polish
or Ukrainian or Chinese, 348a
    *Politeness
know not Europe's sham, 294b
stranger to Europe's, 534b
    *Political
independent types of, 82b
secret of p. success, 95b
views described, 104a
who write p. slogans, 105a
hatreds attest vitality, 143b
nothing I ever do is, 154a
economic control goes, 225a
industrial democracy, 326a
French no p. ideas, 327b
sentiment is a passion, 328a
prisoners infest, 346b
convention in U.S., 372a
    *Political Economy
first question should, 226b
needs to be rewritten, 583b
    *Politicians
artful p. are bane, 16b
survive depression, 75a
create own reality, 115a
share same bunk, 179a
statesman is a dead, 180a
vain attemps to change, 189a
man who says he is no, 391a
conventions, elections, 447a
you find it, take it, 452a
anyone gets elected, 482b
country does something, 484a
slightly ahead, contact, 600b
talks one way, 619a
road has slippery, 637a
    *Politics
to dictate British, 8a
is a battle, 26a
social workers, lawyers, 36a
are for the few, 40b
trackless wastes of, 95a
gold amid mud of, 103a
nobles vocations, 103b
not meeting on stairs, 109b
interesting, fruitful, 132a
compared with religion, 167b
provincial like elephant, 175b
triumph over geography, 183a
paying Opposition, 203a
characters, story line, 206a
makes a man crooked, 243b
the harridan I married, 272a
Canadian is ditchwater, 276b
intellectuals and party, 278b
great thing, avoid, 307b
women less feminine, 319b
question of business, 328b
since Arliss played, 342b
unsettles men, 370a
purifying effect of women, 370b
I have no p., Canadian, 373b
know a little about, 381a
railroads are our, 387a
teaches people to care, 391a
man's best game, 394b
railroads are my, 399a
art of the possible, 399b

independently rich or poor, 405a
skilled use of blunt, 470a
great game to play, 482b
success the god of, 506a
women in hurly-burly, 507a
in B.C. an adventure, 520b
cede place to younger, 534b
ah, p., p., p., always, 551a
meanest of all trades, 552a
Social Credit above, 584a
not into to be insulted, 597b
opposition to accepted, 602b
raising intellectual level, 606b
bored acquiescence, 620b
 *Pollution
would be more, 474b
their own lungs, 598a
 *Polygamy
more in Toronto, 132a
 *Polymer
rubber business volatile, 515b
 *Pompadour, Madame de
America owes much to, 464a
 *Pontiac
famous conspiracy of, 65b
 *Poor
to be p. in society, 3a
man's tuberculosis, 53b
they rob the, 161b
in new clothes, 324a
work, privilege of, 324b
rich and fewer, 376a
or independently rich, 405a
have all the money, 450a
Canada said Virgin Mary, 523b
rich by nature, policy, 552b
 *Pope
the P. hears Our Lord, 69b
if tried to move, 162a
Léger could become, 304a
behold the P. of, 618b
to hell with the, 635a
 *Poppies
in Flanders fields, blow, 372b
 *Popularity
way of transgressor, 179a
what's right, not, 245b
whatever the loss, 329a
proof of genius, 339b
unable to live up, 527a
 *Population
representation by, 80b
2.6 persons per mile, 263b
with at least 60 million, 329b
the North never support, 344a
density and defence, 362b
mobile p. creates few, 372a
to populate waste places, 385a
nation of 50 million, 429a
of Quebec estimated, 550b
 *Porcupine
Gold up in P., everyone, 24b
 *Porcupines
rape among the, 114a
 *Port Arthur
mental hospitals, 88b
 *Port Hope
leading into, 624a
 *Port Moody

not limited to, 379b
 *Portugal
there remain, 69b
equal to the kingdom, 80b
Our Lady of Fátima, 523b
 *Possessive
American dream of, 95a
individualism, 401a
 *Possible
peaceably if p., forcibly, 48a
sound sense of the, 388b
politics the art of the, 399b
 *Posterity
appear plausible to, 133b
a common monument, 193b
appeal to court of, 377a
 *Potatoes
how are you, 11b
a well-hoed ridge of, 429b
république des patates, 596a
 *Poutrincourt, Jean de
the said M. de, 349b
 *Poverty
free ourselves from, 3a
determined to escape, 40a
greatest asset is, 49b
none of ours is poetic, 74a
the poorer a man, 134a·
has roots in despair, 148b
he won his war on, 153b
in the midst of plenty, 158a
poor man's country, 270b
but individual, 314a
live in a rickety house, 392a
no p. where pretence, 401a
inflation is universal, 416a
not without its smile, 429b
planet's a slum, 550b
dedicated to spreading, 558a
 *Powder
keep our p. dry, 383a
 *Power
Bethune didn't seek, 5b
who is corrupted by, 40b
from the wells of, 95a
my trust in earthly, 141b
that immense north, 234a
tendency to corpulency, 243b
you should strive for, 262b
have overstepped our, 269a
whatever the loss, 329a
love, p., the huzza, 335b
nationalization of, 350b
socialism is ownership, 352b
too liberal to take, 365b
from the Briton, 384a
authoritarianism, 471b
healthy irreverence, 495a
determine reality, 495b
a middle p. like, 519b
absolute p. corrupts, 598b
emergence of a parallel, 598b
more p. over ourselves, 616a
women in use of, 631b
 *Prairie
the p. province, 15a
cross the, 71b
sea-wide, sky-skirted, 86a
Manitoba the p. province, 247b
sea of waving grass, 247b

mosaic essayed of, 253a
how could p. change, 261a
immensities north of, 265a
everything wonderful, 310b
too much, 372b
to live anywhere else, 413b
free wild perilous, 415a
alone on the, 423a
Doukhobor running naked, 551a
beauty of geometric, 561a
indifferent universe, 561a
[See also Prairies.]
 *Prairies
are Bach figures, 74b
Virgil have glorified, 111a
Ontario bounded by, 167b
simple life of the, 178a
people from p. retire, 210a
thousand miles rolling, 228b
leaving the farms, 248b
the edge of heaven, 254a
unrelieved immensity, 262b
Imagism inspired by, 275a
colossus of the, 280b
from the forests and, 360a
sunsets and cold of, 365b
one part horizon, 401b
do with some editing, 466a
politics are a cause, 520b
red sails in dust bowl, 605b
challenging space, 625b
great p. spread and, 626b
give food to east, 436b
[See also Plains and Prairie.]
 *Praise
fewer we p. better, 312b
O plumage of paradise, 313b
strangers, of singing, 430a
in all ways, 530a
alleluia or anguish, 572b
 *Pratt, E.J.
wrote business history, 304a
Brébeuf from Iroquois, 491a
where are coolies, 528b
 *Prayers
an Irish immigrant's, 11b
how long did she, 104b
ask of those, 190b
as though God were all, 190b
everything to God in, 531a
that do not mingle, 542b
elections not won by, 575a
no time for, 613a
 *Precedent
is the fait accompli, 67a
the accomplished fact, 67a
mere precedence is, 277a
 *Prefix
patriotism rejects the, 384b
 *Pregnant
if men could get, 518a
 *Prehistoric
word coined by, 635a
 *Prejudice
so white, not cut, 119b
no racial p. in Vancouver, 233a
government wrapped in, 271a
people who are down, 621b
 *Premier
future p. of Quebec, 169b

of a Hottentot village, 186a
there was no other, 549a
of Manitoba should kick, 627a
  *Presbyterianism
the black P. of Protestants, 27a
of Montreal of all, 299b
story of French Catholic, 634b
  *Present
only the, 33b
beating out the, 65a
thing of the past, 134a
of today the future, 137a
pioneer's is rough, 191a
past which is most, 236b
the p. is a gift, 369b
is full of confusion, 561a
too little of real, 637a
is beyond belief, 584b
defeated live for, 616a
  *Preserve
the wilderness, 435b
  *President
Trudeau a, 210a
liked a Queen or, 553b
never been a, 600a
  *Press
goodly fellows of, 38a
success is getting, 95b
their p. is not free, 271a
leave an unshackled, 271a
more than pulpit, 323b
  *Pressure
strongest is friendly, 469a
  *Prevention
things I have, 307a
in preventing bad, 307b
leadership in what was, 475b
  *Price
sold for p. of sheepskin, 272b
  *Pride
we manufacture Canadian, 57a
in myself as an Indian, 97a
in their nation, 153a
nation fosters national, 272a
rightly on men, 312a
even a ghost has some, 383b
our boast and, 439a
country an experiment in, 473a
  *Priest
one must be a, 109b
old p. don't make, 128a
hobo and p. fight, 343a
soldiery and p.-hood, 587a
  *Prime Minister
only if leader of opposition, 40b
first neither English nor, 152b
never if Gallup Polls, 153b
difficult country to govern, 330a
nationalize the C.P.R., 351b
quit politics if women, 370b
of Canada or president, 447a
welcome Liberace, 469a
kid who wants to be, 499b
never exiled to Arctic, 560b
men who want badly, 595a
wonder they want job, 596a
  *Primum
terra p. vista, 92a
  *Prince
of Regiopolis, 571a

  *Prince Albert
so goes the nation, 153b
the chief's friends, 290b
  *Prince Charlie, Bonnie
the preserver of, 374b
  *Prince Edward Island
covers the island, 11a
parva sub ingenti, 15a
on north shore, 69b
needs only nightingale, 102b
Scots pouring out, 117b
band within land, 161b
Dominion annexed, 165b
lands I dread, 212b
garden spot of Gulf, 249b
tow her into St. Lawrence, 386a
peace on the shores, 438b
a happy contentment, 525a
  *Prince of Wales
no one can visit, 181a
  *Prince of Wales Falls
the Hog's Back Falls, 177b
  *Prince Rupert
founded on hope, 14a
  *Prince Valiant
in Days of King Arthur, 201a
  *Principle
go to p. of things, 164b
not of p., of race, 170b
and the voluntary, 262a
without organization, 328b
assassination vs., 386a
the Peter, 473b
  *Print
advertising, salesmanship, 300a
  *Printer
united to support, 12b
an art in decline, 137b
in Cree language, 186a
old p.s never die, 315a
noble who man pays, 365b
  *Prisons
Hurons without, 3b
reforming prisoner, 60a
palaces and, 71b
outside town, not, 345b
political prisoners, 346b
sentencing causes, 369a
Czar's better, 594a
  *Privacy
loneliness without, 451a
opposite of publicity, 522b
no place for state in bedrooms,
  595a
  *Private
affluence, public squalor, 211a
only p. enterprise, 509a
  *Privilege
abusing, being stupid, 362a
order protects, 402a
no rights only p.s, 451a
  *Pro pelle cutem
motto, 158b
pelle cutem, 515b
  *Problems
good neighbours, 289b
are never solved, 365b
hardly, 473a
perhaps our fault, 590a
best brains, worst, 590b

to those who solve, 597b
Canada has solved, 603a
there are two kinds, 604b
  *Procrastination
has a flag, 88b
  *Proctor, Henry
no Brock, 578a
  *Professions
outside these four, 109b
pleasantness, 141a
fights to win, 418b
ethics, bargaining, 463b
not produce great, 522b
  *Profit
to hell with, 195b
more potent than, 201b
without the margin, 224a
foul imperialist, 261a
motive in sport, 302a
something without, 314b
people are p.s, 430b
H.B.C. making, 507a
common good, 609a
  *Program content
only thing that matters, 202a
  *Progress
cease if satisfied, 34a
nail the flag of, 49a
march of social, 52b
political, intellectual, 82b
linch-pin of world, 112a
an end to this, 189a
least history prior, 229a
austere road to, 298a
welfare and p. of, 307b
star towards which, 330a
to p. is to destroy, 503a
secured little, 510b
revolt essential, 527a
due to C.P.R., 625a
than citizenship, 641a
  *Progressive Conservative
See Conservative.
  *Progressive Party
give five-cent piece to, 306a
send for leader of, 306a
  *Prohibition
against on both grounds, 42b
prohibit use of water, 178b
merely drink beer and, 338a
didn't know until, 649a
  *Promises
of yesterday, taxes, 306a
election p. boomerang, 323a
  *Property
without Christ, 530a
  *Prophecy
self-fulfilling, 100a
Canada will be, 110a
Millerites in, 273a
Hitler's death, 313a
Huron prophetess, 436b
out of Montreal, 451a
our lady of Fátima, 523b
  *Prophet
neither p. nor son of, 271b
minor and major, 313a
soil not friendly, 477a
the p. of New World, 501a

I am a glorious power, 636a
*Prose
live for poetry by, 504b
*Prospecting
a saying among, 195a
solid pitchblende, 317a
all a dream, 644b
*Prosperity
nothing to fear from, 97b
follows the cow, 143a
explains bounding, 248a
give happiness and, 363a
man first, afterwards, 372a
represent principle, 376a
single desire for, 384a
good enough for me, 649b
*Prostitute
never wife's enemy, 3b
more money vertically, 364b
remember Pearl, 420b
oldest known in, 534a
*Protection
Kahn-Tineta's going, 266a
come to protect, 274b
spare the English, 426b
*Protectionism
a raging p. government, 149a
talk about cultural, 209a
argue for national, 288b
done so much for me, 378b
tiresome the cultural, 499a
national policy and, 604a
*Protestant
took it much better, 27a
psalm-singing Dissenter, 266b
oldest in Quebec, 299b
excommunicated by, 331a
white, p. heterosexual, 499b
for a Catholic, 597b
of French Catholic, 634b
*Proust, Marcel
read in Rideau Hall, 502b
*Providence
being their guide, 11a
trust, keep powder dry, 383a
mysterious ways of, 518b
*Province
state a British, 6a
la belle, 15a
collection of ten, 75b
governments and, 132a
should be united, 245a
for Quebec, not, 287b
provincial outlook, 289a
reduce that status, 371b
unity, autonomy, 514b
*Proxy
whose are you, 343a
*Psyche
line runs through, 436a
*Psychedelic
neologism coined, 459b
*Psychiatry
ecstasy in anger, 56a
minister to nations, 139b
Quebec, soul-searching, 189b
does not cure patient, 235a
current fad for, 242b
*Psychology
and not of history, 72b

*Public
satisfy the, 38b
sentiment will move, 71a
tell your story to, 173a
pay for laughing, 179a
private affluence, 211a
ignorant, snobbish, 238b
learn to obey laws, 251a
noblest motive, 312a
consists of cattle, 403b
my judges and jury, 414b
humbug in dealing, 458a
*Public life
only excuse for, 49b
reason I went into, 152b
two ways out, 358b
environment alien, 470a
in public interest, 543b
noblest of all callings, 552a
*Public opinion
we have to reform, 60a
journalist authority on, 137a
of those against, 169b
precious for private, 191b
many-headed monster, 386a
full-ripened corn of, 512a
*Public ownership
socialism, of power, 352b
enlargement of idea, 400a
*Publication
self-invasion, 297a
*Publicity
prisoner of Zenda, 56b
seven brothers, 211b
privacy opposite, 522b
*Publisher
colonial p. knows, 158b
whim of a foreign, 477a
somebody looking for someone,
477a
a reformed Toronto, 605a
those sons of up, 605a
*Publishing
founder of Doubleday, 157a
active independent, 211a
American takeover, 273b
books don't weigh, 292b
a turning point, 315a
Toronto houses agencies, 384a
spoke Swahili, 408a
unreadable book on, 499b
thick or thin book, 500a
Ontario severed from, 551b
evil is copyright, 568b
*Pugwash
is right there, 172b
*Pulp and paper
of good Canadian pulp, 121a
paper produced from, 191a
*Punishment
what strokes came, 66a
influenced by fear, 97b
*Purcell, Gillis
as brief as he makes, 543b
*Puritanism
type of life, 27b
touched by orgy, 58a
*Purpose
live in an immense, 406a
must have some, 465b

*Purse
reach for my, 171b
*Push
brave volunteers, 21a
on, brave York volunteers, 76a
brave boys, Quebec is ours, 428b
*Pussy-footing
nobody did anything, 224a
*Pygmalion
I can forgive, 66b
*Pygmies
who dwell in darkness, 268a
here lived, 417a
prepare for peace like, 468b

# Q

*Qu'Appelle River
justice on banks of, 60a
*Quality
what really counts, 454b
*Quebec
Saint-Louis-du-Ha! Ha!, 12a
Je me souviens, 15a
don't call this cold, 17b
long live a free, 20b
is all our own, 20b
shall be taken, 21a
c'est le bon, 25a
a poor priest in, 27a
a very rich country, 34b
way Bennett feels about, 36a
immense fortunes, 52a
we are a small people, 65a
a Q. patriotism, 67b
nationalist movement, 67b
wealth from Ontario, 69a
an existence apart, 72b
not appear disruptive, 85b
men from Q. stood, 91a
the said Q. diamants, 105b
like Turkey, 106a
not for stopping at, 115b
Americanization, 124a
problem of separate, 129a
French government of, 144a
against Canada, 163b
celebrated platform, 164b
our treasure trove, 167b
belong to province, 169b
no difficulty govern, 170a
deadly animosity, 170b
English at expense, 171a
deserts in the soul, 183a
sure of herself, 189b
more stupid, 193a
miracle of fecundity, 214a
five million, 214a
becoming master of, 214b
most in evidence, 221a
surly, conceited, 225b
a frightful country, 225b
author of that poem, 231a
laying a Q. egg, 240a
the Q. police, 242a
the original heart, 255a
nothing has changed, 256a

is our conscience, 265b
Duplessis and Houde, 267a
acquisition of, 285b
not good for other, 287b
homeland where French, 287b
method of writing, 293a
fearing no man, 308b
there was a young man, 309b
don't call this cold, 309b
branded a traitor, 330b
only sentiments, 331a
nor strengthen the, 335b
there was an old man, 342b
failure to understand, 348b
political voice of French, 349b
education real revolution, 350b
I have a taste for, 351a
not the separation of, 354a
in Eastern Townships, 377b
not limited to, 379b
though every dog bark, 379a
a Q. Indian summer, 395b
reconquer the fatherland, 403a
spirit of France moves, 404a
bed of resurrections, 422a
the knaves grow rich, 426b
still loyal in, 437b
far from France, 442b
possession of land, 446a
minister or president, 447a
on same footing as, 460a
independent, dependent, 469a
three wise men from, 471a
a nation unto itself, 477b
from Lower Canada, 501a
Quiet Revolution, 503a
the ancient cradle, 504a
imagine Canada without, 506b
none not militant, 514a
name of a sickness, 526a
in Q.'s icy forests, 534b
Newfoundland first, 548b
choices limited, 550b
no common hopes, 552b
Ontario pays blackmail, 553a
purpose to populate, 574a
Riel's agony and, 575a
beating of heart, 575b
suggested Normandy, 576a
words Canada East, 586b
crook-neck squash, 587a
embarrassed to have, 595a
confine French-speaking, 595b
Chinese Marxist line, 601b
Champlain arrived, 604b
at expense of workers, 609b
anxiety about, 612b
France do well without, 617a
deuce thinking of, 619b
  *Quebec Act of 1774*
instrument of tyranny, 87a
no liberty, 202a
to their satisfaction, 478b
behold the pope, 618b
  *Quebec City*
must be taken, 3a
Don de Dieu, 15a
there once was a boy of, 17b
a tailor, who sailed, 17b
marching down to Old, 20b

take possession of, 26b
stupid things said, 76b
I must venture to, 77a
stands so nobly as, 77b
to see the inside, 88a
from the proud rock, 104a
where Hamlet's ghost, 106b
capital of immense, 152a
future capital of a, 206b
reflects the sacristy, 225b
language as Toronto, 236b
by rail to Montreal, 271b
a city of gossip, 282b
girls get husbands, 295b
dirt and discomfort, 299a
pillars of strength, 311a
see Q. and live, 312b
was history, 388a
best cities of France, 426b
boys, Q. is ours, 428b
marvellous, wonderful, 442b
a gigantic fortress, 448b
live to see surrender, 465a
the Château Frontenac, 468a
de Gaulle's journey, 469b
order to surrender, 474b
siege was decided, 478b
York and Q. are chief, 499a
recall Q. and Beauport, 520b
planks from Montreal, 593b
is impregnable, 612b
insult neighbours, 619b
have Q. if I stay, 638b
than take Q. tomorrow, 639a
I found disappointing, 640b
  *Quebec Conference*
wonderful, 80b
gateway of Canada, 112b
old lady alive, 281a
  *Québec libre*
vive le, 214b
vive le, 293b
  *Québécois*
are not free, 221a
complete ourselves, 351a
freedom is not, 609a
  *Queen*
long live the, 21b
God save our gracious, 22b
24th of May, 25a
be loyal to the, 132b
indifferent to visit, 138b
of Canada and of all, 182a
doubtless some exiled, 310b
of the North, Sask., 319a
each as noble, 364b
dutiful and loyal, 380b
loyal to her ass, 390a
white q. of Nahanni, 409b
anyone a subject, 436a
God save our, 439a
liked a Q. or a, 553b
  *Queen's University*
wear the Q.'s scarlet, 18b
old Ontario strand, 24a
University buries, 340a
  *Queenston*
upon the heights of, 21a
or Lundy's Lane, 580b
  *Question*

most far-reaching, 464a
I am the half-breed, 500b
  *Quiet Canadian*
Sir William, 196b
the Q.C., 562b
  *Quiet Revolution*
existential phenomenon, 324b
associated with Lesage, 349a
into the Q. question, 503a
  *Quintuplets*
See Dionne Quintuplets.
  *Quotation*
to be apt in, 139b
a book never complete, 247b
inaccurate a sin, 537a

---

# R

  *Race*
in act of being born, 84b
populated by Canadians, 97b
not of principles, 170b
blood and skin, 188a
small racial problem, 232b
history and virtues, 237a
ce petit peuple, 237b
free and dominant, 243a
reunion of human, 245a
millions of Saxon, 247b
art more than, 250a
Canadians, actors, 257a
sort of white native, 314a
trodden underfoot, 318a
evolve a r. of, 320a
hope in the human, 356a
become as one, 391a
national existence, 417a
Conservative party racist, 475b
human r. is my, 529b
hearts of two great, 575b
lies the destiny of, 621a
weakness of individual, 623b
French and English, 645a
  *Racine, Jean*
Chekhov's and not, 185a
  *Radar*
inventor ticketed, 624a
  *Radicalism*
citizen's resistance, 207b
brooms for sweeping, 226b
I was well, wanted, 305b
fast approaching, 323a
quick to exploit, 324b
believer in progressive, 338a
make me feel nervous, 350b
emergent institutions, 513a
  *Radio*
CBC never learned, 5b
terrified of dead air, 52b
documentary, 123b
profitability, mediocrity, 138b
TV hasten end of, 147a
actor reads story, 161b
intelligible speech, 191b
jokes I could tell, 193b
to you to lead, 198b
air waves represent, 207a

literate days, 232a
Romance of Canada, 240a
hello Canada and, 260a
listener lavish, 357b
our r. has run down, 366a
this is Canada calling, 392a
native playwright, 395a
The Investigator, 540a
as national trust, 587b
On King, Huskies, 593a
know where skeletons, 625b
Golden Age of, 626a
lips don't sweat, 647a
 *Radio League
with Machiavelli and, 557a
 *Radishes
and gooseberries, 235b
 *Rag
tag and bobtail, 452b
 *Railroads
to be a president, 38b
last spike in line, 129a
formula for happiness, 224a
great highway to Orient, 254a
free tickets on, 266b
Halifax to Pacific, 271b
steam in Rockies, 271b
galvanize B.C., 317b
one direct line, 376b
bound by iron link, 377b
are our politics, 387a
are my politics, 399a
telegraph, iron road, 433b
provinces railroaded, 447b
move ton of freight, 554a
blank verse in iron, 567b
Canadian out of German, 611a
The Underground, 637b
good place to write, 646b
 *Rainbow
adoption as emblem, 291a
 *Rapids
we are in the, 385b
are near and day, 431a
 *Ravenna
the mosaics of, 123a
 *Rawhide
sail on, O CBC, 191a
 *Raynaul, Guillaume
savage, civilized, 404b
 *Raz-Mah
Templeton's TRC's, 579b
 *R.C.M.P.
See Royal Canadian Mounted
 Police.
 *Reader's Digest
exempt from tax, 293b
six-day race, 470b
 *Reading
not much adventure, 93b
of prose rewarding, 161b
unexamined poem, 164b
a r. list, 176a
stuff they haven't, 179b
paragraph in elevator, 209a
about dukes and lords, 238b
Turk in his harem, 270b
Canadians less than, 353a
who reads Canadian book, 365a
travel, suffer, love, 444b

easier to read than, 458a
half an hour's, 459a
all I know is, 492b
 *Ready, Aye, Ready
to be, 200b
British answer to, 331a
we stand by you, 415b
 *Reagan, Ronald
and Vietnam, 499a
 *Reality
consistent man out of touch, 40a
politicians create own, 115a
do highest justice to, 123b
centre wherever one is, 208a
is slightly tilted, 249a
close to dreams, 491a
and fantasy determined, 495a
defeated are children of, 616a
poetry joins dreams, 618a
 *Reason
in irrational world, 207b
why advertising, 300b
Canada voice of, 247b
survive only by, 477a
over passion, 594b
four-legged creature, 525a
the trustees of, 596b
a more r. man, 601a
 *Rebellion
may each rebel swing, 21b
now that's o'er, 21b
rebel not renegade, 41a
no neglect, no, 60a
buried by force, 69a
would naturally be, 587a
 *Rebellion of 1837
Lord free us all, 21b
two lives lost, 27b
holes in British flag, 31b
Bidwell and glorious, 55a
only crime failure, 145b
beautiful girl of 20, 151a
Remember the Caroline, 163a
Edison's father patriot, 176b
un Canadien errant, 217a
come if they dare, 253b
I do not fear to die, 262b
Liberty forever, 262b
can expect from English, 361a
had plans succeeded, 363a
he lived a patriot, 363b
if I had Mac along, 363b
I carried my musket, 381a
died as he lived, patriot, 412a
John Montgomery living, 427b
I am shot, 429a
rod of misrule, 445a
melt spoons into bullets, 445b
agitate, agitate, 452b
one lives in orange, 462b
cut out the Caroline, 508a
Mr. Jarvis, do duty, 517a
nothing I might not, 538a
march back leisurely, 584a
conquered, not dissolved, 589b
you lose Upper Canada, 627b
it will be nine years, 642a
 *Rebellion, Red River
 (1869-70)
people has no government, 82a

please remember me, 90b
you go no farther, 500b
 *Rebellion, Northwest (1885)
no neglect, no rebellion, 60a
show what militia can, 99b
threatened our lives, 167a
utterly defeated half, 418b
send us terms of peace, 482a
rapine, bloodshed, 497b
people would have done, 500b
demanding justice, 620a
 *Recession
tighten his belt, 159b
 *Reciprocity
made in Washington, 92b
no truck nor trade, 200b
hewers of wood and, 217b
her own soul Canada risks, 311b
of tariffs and trade, 378a
at parting of the ways, 572b
vindicated all at once, 573a
 *Recording
man is a r. animal, 226b
 *Records
wise nation preserves, 272a
 *Red
the R. Baron, 79a
Indians are called, 102b
turn red or shoot, 117b
Emma Goldman, 222a
sails in dust bowl, 605b
 *Red River
justice on banks of, 60a
million fingers in dikes, 275b
but one prairie river, 247b
true conception of, 262b
make a R.R. cart go, 572a
thus upon life's, 631b
 *Red River Rebellion
See Rebellion, Red River.
 *Red River Valley
remember the, 24b
paradise of fertility, 142b
paradise of fertility, 262b
 *Reform
means intervention, 49a
complete r. of all, 80b
brooms for sweeping, 226b
Head, a tried reformer, 253a
my husband espoused, 363a
disaster precedes, 368b
of society, young, 522a
what is there to, 552a
 *Refunded
goods satisfactory or, 173b
 *Refus global
global refusal, 65a
 *Régime
ancien, 572a
 *Regina
no one lives here, 1b
floreat, 15a
Riel dropped to, 129a
Sodom and Gomorrah, 372b
prospect improved, 379a
taken to guardroom, 498a
 *Regina Manifesto
no C.C.F. government, 608b
 *Regiopolis
Prince of, 571a

*Relativity
there was a young lady, 86a
*Religion
can't talk r. to, 1b
law of 5 fingers, 56a
denominationalism, 60b
no religious unity, 67a
and heritage, 68a
I hear my curé, 69a
every country its, 72a
Jeannine prayed, 104b
maxims of our, 120b
points of unity, 130b
compared with politics, 167b
people who quarrel, 178b
congregation gone, 186b
in the Old Testament, 189a
advertising jingles, 204b
easier to make infidel, 245a
Christ gave you a, 479a
religious building, 304b
excommunicated, 331a
not only a religious, 462b
to understanding, 492b
regions where our, 509b
religion and consus, 542a
lose sang-froid, 601b
agnosticism modest, 560b
for country and, 613a
in Anglican church, 632a
*Remain
Yankee must south, 290a
*Remember
je me souviens, 15a
Butler, 90b
the Caroline, 163a
fame r. us with no, 312b
little crippled kids, 517a
je me souviens, 572a
*Renfrew
whole town concerned, 140b
*Reply
have no r. to make, 206b
*Representation
by population, 80b
*Republics
America gives to Europe, 462b
can swallow top hat, 481b
des patates frites, 596a
*Research
peace, 5a
*Resources
frontier of U.S. investment, 4a
would have given away, 25a
never safe if unexploited, 66a
the disposition of, 174a
private ownership of, 188a
owners, owers, 193b
annexation an increase, 208a
nations make best use, 333b
produce tanks, bombs, 351b
a nation's manifold, 356b
give industries back, 360b
for wise use of, 372a
conserve by developing, 390b
giant of the Arctic, 508b
material, mind, character, 573a
what right not exploit, 596a
sitting atop greatest, 631a

*Responsibility
of his race and breed, 48b
a lot of talk about, 132a
when everyone is, 211b
doubled in prosperity, 284b
you may have some, 307b
share r. and duties, 329a
Ontario such r. place, 389a
God not accept the, 454b
his boundless sense of, 603b
*Responsible Government
first used, 32a
defined, 32b
Mr. Mother Country, 86b
giving up of, 117b
was at least, 147b
and the voluntary, 262a
*Revenge
of the cradle, 236a
dog that gnaws bone, 312a
of the cradle, 447b
la revanche du berceau, 447b
*Reviewers
the rest are, 120b
holds attention of, 142b
*Revolt
love cannot exist without, 404a
essential to progress, 527a
*Revolution
violent r. needed, 52b
artist preaches, 54a
and wars broke, 65a
and does not make love, 105a
six kids making a, 132a
a little r. now and, 143b
at last I understand, 152a
very fine so long as, 164b
independence won by, 180b
if I have to lead, 255b
caused by Conservative, 328a
demystify mystique of, 343b
the Quiet, 349a
escape to Canada, 352b
failure to have, 356a
only hated George III, 391b
not by temperament, 397b
advertising an instigation, 545a
province needs cultural, 549a
tyranny generates, 601a
total liberation, 609b
we need a royal, 616a
no revolutionary war, 636b
[See also American Revolution
     and Quiet Revolution.]
*Rexdale
bombing computer from, 564b
*Rhodes
of Canada, Cyprus, 91b
all other damn scholars, 269b
scholarships and CPR, 351b
Borden gave the lectures, 515a
*Rhodesia
British in Ian Smith's, 205b
Westmount Rhodesians, 557a
*Rich
Quebec very r. country, 34b
man's tuberculosis, 53b
curse and pestilence, 321b
fewer at the top, 376a
either independently, 405a

formula for becoming, 448a
can't spend yourself, 474a
I grew too, 478a
a r. man in your own, 545b
by nature, policy poor, 552b
upsets you about the, 570a
nothing sinful about, 585a
use two bathrooms, 649b
*Richthofen, Baron von
when we fought, 79a
*Rideau Canal
but a museum piece, 454a
*Rideau Hall
instead of White House, 298b
someone reading Proust, 502b
*Riders
of the plains, 18b
*Ridgeway
lost in Battle of, 349a
*Riding
with General Motors, 131a
*Riel, Louis
body made a wound, 8a
dropped to death, 129a
we are really, 134a
threatened our leader, 167a
born on banks of Sask., 328b
baffling, rebellious, 348b
strangle R. with French flag,
     379a
shall hang though every dog,
     379a
in killing, Sir John, 417b
prisoners of R. and, 418b
died at dawn in land, 420b
with a smile on lips, 440a
news of surrender of, 482a
sneered at Rebellion, 492a
charged with treason, 497b
of the animal in him, 505a
at moment when R. falls, 575a
how many R.s exist, 597b
battle not yet won, 597b
not his micro-patriotism, 642a
*Right
uphold the, 18a
mistaken to be always, 50b
Communism too far, 65a
rather waffle to the, 75a
freedom to be wrong, 152b
he wasn't always, 152b
if r. I do it, 153a
some happen to be, 164b
judge dispute in terms, 222a
for every civil, 242b
what's r. not popular, 245b
but not fifteen, 257a
nothing but what was, 270b
feel I am in the, 329a
maintain the, 369a
anybody support me when, 381a
what if he's, 398a
judged r. or wrong, 416a
please some, astonish, 468b
nothing survives by, 477a
what if he is, 640b
*Righteous
where r. ought to be, 116b
quest for Oriental, 458b
*Rights

share of national, 59b
Indian Act no, 318b
enforcing seignorial, 323b
died for popular, 363b
of minority protected, 376a
without God no, 451a
Conservatives don't, 475b
of the small nation, 501a
man of action fights, 515a
  *Risks
Canada r. her own soul, 311b
  *River
trust r., not brook, 9a
they gave away the, 25a
immense r. pouring, 84a
great r. of Hochelaga, 102a
will reach the sea, 155b
traverse the border, 174a
fishing excuse to be near, 242a
of Canada bounded, 293a
are wide and beautiful, 336a
as long as the r. runs, 434a
very rivière meanders, 587a
and lordly rivers flow, 626b
  *Roberts, Sir Charles G.D.
Orion and Other Poems, 320b
  *Robichaud, Louis J.
So long, Hugh John, 197a
  *Robinson, John Beverley
said Chief Justice, 427b
  *Robinson Crusoe
feat of imagination, 616a
  *Roblin, Sir Rodmond
we'll get you yet, 370a
  *Rochdale College
garbage everywhere, 418a
permitted to happen, 418a
  *Rocky Mountains
work of the Cyclopes, 61a
colossal symphonies, 74b
Dante glorified, 111a
have no majesty, 133a
beauty and grandeur, 177b
great elements sway, 193a
no human should venture, 204a
three great ranges, 228b
Sir Rider Haggard, 242a
terrible majesties of, 265a
whistle of steam engine, 271b
there's oil in the, 278b
image of Arthur's seat, 361b
into colonization, 367b
the peaks of the, 384b
lack urbanity, intelligence, 484b
the rock character, 563a
drove a gold spike, 567a
do not shoot pianist, 632b
  *Rode
madly off in all, 337a
  *Rods
Confederation not bundle, 551b
  *Roi nègre
the black king, 327a
  *Rolf, Dr. John
I do think if, 27b
  *Romania
uncrowned king of, 71a
best natural scenery, 564b
  *Romantic
abolition of r. ideals, 220b

dreams become nightmares, 488a
who lost courage, 572b
we had no romanticism, 636b
  *Rome
by Etruria, 122a
  *Ronald, Lord
rode madly off in all, 337a
  *Roosevelt, F.D.
quarterback D.C. Howe, 269b
  *Roosevelt, Theodore
owe you much, 337a
  *Roots
values sink deep, 166b
for ourselves, 175b
we would remain, 229a
are entirely Canadian, 569b
trees questionable about, 611a
  *Rose
thistle, shamrock, 439a
  *Rose-Marie
a Canadian may be, 185a
oh, R.-M., I love you, 206a
anything but romantic, 366b
  *Rosebery, Lord
not bribed into loyalty, 543a
  *Rothermere, Viscount
and Northcliffe, 40a
  *Rotsa ruck
lots of luck, 263a
  *Roulant
en r. ma boulé, 23b
  *Rowell-Sirois Report
national unity based, 514b
  *Royal Canadian Mounted
    Police
always getting their man, 3a
vs. Atomic Invaders, 4a
brothers, we've had, 7a
home of the, 15a
murdered by the, 16b
got into the, 75b
done my best, 105a
nothing much but, 113b
if had not come, 132b
Susannah of the Mounties, 147a
40 years without beer, 151b
those red-coated fellers, 172a
splendid example of, 181b
Canadian may be a, 185a
efficiency in the West, 188b
St. Roch, 189b
surrounded by snow, 190a
so-called Lost Patrol, 194a
requires 150 volunteers, 205a
a Rose Marie posting, 206a
perhaps spies in the, 227a
land of Northwest M.P., 239b
commissioner of Musical Ride,
    252a
always get their man, 254a
fetched their men, 254a
to quiet a disturbance, 264b
thank you, Redcoats, 357a
shalt not let Force down, 360b
power and ubiquity, 366a
get your man, 369a
civil not a military, 376b
half-breed trapper or, 430b
enforcing of laws, 447b
and David Niven, 448b

have to get their man, 464a
fresh troubles at hand, 470b
Santa Claus, c/o, 474a
half-breed scout, 481b
conquest of old Northwest, 496a
Riel to guardroom at, 498a
cracking wise at the, 533a
flour on mackinaws, 539b
I shot him, dead, 555a
vs. Atomic Invaders, 559a
On King, on you Huskies, 593a
the motto is not, 641b
  *Royal Canadians
sweetest music this side, 359a
  *Royal Commission
Canada worth a, 327b
sitting on a toilet, 383b
  *Royal Northwest Mounted
    Police
See Royal Canadian Mounted
    Police.
  *Royal Visit
my first visit, 177b
more balconies the better, 216a
some of this for you, 267b
how ghastly, 437b
not come for our health, 438a
busy day in Toronto, 474b
  *Rugby
English games, cricket, 194b
  *Rubber
business is volatile, 515b
  *Rule Britannia
French Canadians sing, 112a
  *Rules of Order
Bourinot's Rules, 96b
  *Rum
is inducement, 387b
  *Run
see how they, 640a
  *Rupert's Land
the people of, 82a
sole trade and commerce, 107b
  *Rush-Bagot Agreement
all other armed vessels, 31a
arms-limitation clause, 515b
  *Russia
elementary kinship with, 37b
if R. disappeared, 54a
whole soil of, 81a
second only to, 99a
Canada, R. of New World, 155a
go down to defeat, 162b
beating R. fo rcountry, 185a
more than an American, 228b
immediate deportation, 230a
atomic secrets and, 278a
goals of Nazi war, 314a
defector in Vancouver, 315a
serf of a R. Boyar, 386a
but yet English, 433b
Beaverbrook like Stalin, 439a
Britain's Asiatic, 440a
same government here, 516a
more decidedly one, 544b
we won, didn't we, 546a
gigantic revolution for, 551a
rule without Dukes, 551a
best natural scenery, 564b

without advertising it's, 566b
how much for Pravda, 585b
no lip-service, 589a
common Everest, North, 600a
[See also Soviet Union.]
  *Russian
Canadian or R. winters, 37a
put a spaceman up, 43a
you're not a, 43b
or Alaskan, 198a
traveller Golovin, 223a
Canada lost to the, 279a
technology more lovable, 395b
White R.s at Calgary, 452a
to ballet as R.s to hockey, 512b
diplomatic relations, 519b
live North, look north, 560b
spires which were, 576a
revolutionaries, 594a
look North, Canadians, 633b
no R. model socialism, 643b
steal atomic secrets, 648a
  *Ryans
and the Pittmans, 346a
  *Rye
to get a drink of, 178a

## S

  *Sacrificed
everything save honour, 11b
  *Sacrifices
prepared to make the, 34a
tempered by fires of, 91a
of the past, 272a
loyalty vs. national, 425a
  *Saguenay River
Cartier to lands of, 203a
I see the, 384b
  *Sahara
plough the desert, 32b
burning sands of, 417b
  *Sailing
from all their rage, 15b
songs and tale, 257b
alone around the world, 548a
red sails in the dust, 605b
  *St. Anne de Bellevue
sign our hymn, 431a
  *St. Boniface
Riel, 16 November 1885, 502a
  *St. Catharines
puzzled the audience, 646b
  *St. David's
James Secord of, 194a
  *St. Domingue
Newfoundland and, 96b
and Martinique, 318a
  *St. Foye
thinking of Quebec, 619b
  *St. Ignace
taking village of, 494a
  *St. James Street
will want me, 267a
  *Saint-Jean-Baptiste
La Société, 171a
  *St. John
the Baptist, 171a

  *Saint John
by rail through, 271b
tidal drop, Fundy, 485a
his lady kept watch, 631b
  *St. John River
I see the, 384b
  *St. John's, Nfld.
most easterly city, 15a
at Signal Hill, 405b
  *St. John's, Que.
wicked road to, 299a
  *St. Joseph
his little dog, 8a
  *St. Laurent, Louis
Uncle Lou, 156b
has never overflowed, 170a
  *St. Laurent, Madame de
is of good family, 176b
  *St. Lawrence River
Sherman marching down, 2b
in turbulent turgid, 17b
some fisherman at, 35b
as noted in song as, 69a
pass up to Lower, 80b
tide so swift, grand, 101a
great river of Hochelaga, 102a
banks looked desolate, 106b
wings folded over, 110a
million Frenchmen forgotten,
  130a
liberty born on banks, 145b
white with sails, 161b
dreamed of on banks, 171a
rapids are very pretty, 183b
five million on shores, 214a
travel 1,000 miles up, 228b
there was a Lordship, 301b
yet are one stream, 328a
the River of Canada, 348b
maples in Valley, 365a
I see the, 348b
tow P.E.I. into, 386a
row, stream runs fast, 431a
country of frozen words, 487b
excellent states, 535a
formed Thousand Islands, 556b
on the banks of the, 575a
planks floated to Quebec, 593b
  *St. Lawrence Seaway
stone bears witness, 12b
convicts to build, 538b
  *Saint-Louis
du-Ha! Ha!, 12a
  *Saint-Malo
port on the sea, 23a
in the seaport of, 386b
  *St. Maurice
overflowed St. Laurent, 170a
  *St. Nazaire
never heard of underwear, 497a
  *St. Pierre and Miquelon
Liliputian reproduction, 484b
  *St. Roch
had I done it alone, 189b
  *St. Thomas
Jumbo, elephant king, 294a
  *St. Urbain Street
ghetto area, 12a
  *Saint-Marie
Charles de la Noue, 160a

we beheld it burn, 489a
  *Salesmanship
tell story to public, 173a
advertising is s. in print, 300a
  *Salvation Army
a stranger among you, 63b
what do you say to, 64a
  *Sam McGee
I cremated, 534a
  *San Francisco
hold that city hostage, 376a
  *Sandwich Town
engagement we had, 21a
  *Sanity
nation rich in, 276b
north a vision of, 438b
  *Santa Claus
child who believes in, 110b
electorate believed, 125b
if they believed, 341a
c/o The Mounties, 474a
  *Sarah Binks
sweet songstress, 261a
  *Saskatchewan
Moose Jaw, 13a
Wheat Province, 15a
there's no place like, 24b
bet on you in, 92a
sweet songstress of, 261a
murmurs mysterious word, 265a
bought a little farm, 273a
Depression and, 282b
let there be wheat, 340a
once the desert of, 341a
for social scientist, 355b
silence and solitude, 372b
grievances of halfbreeds, 502b
decent guys from, 539b
country to breed, 561a
greatness not valued, 612a
  *Saskatchewan River
justice on banks of, 60a
sustaining 80 million, 123a
distant S. rolls, 146a
born on the banks of, 328a
  *Saskatoon
in S., Sask., 92a
Queen of the North, 319a
Granny's Laddie composed,
  326b
  *Satisfactory
goods s. or money, 173b
  *Saturday Night
you later read in, 213b
  *Sault Ste. Marie
a boy at, 17b
war memorial in, 309a
  *Savage, Noble
Adario prototype, 3b
  *Savage
faces worthy of s. of, 204b
nous sommes tous, 325b
among this s. people, 347b
be a s. of some use, 638b
  *Saxonizing
immense sea of S. American, 68a
  *Scandal, Pacific
See Pacific Scandal.
  *Scandals
common denominator of, 241b

*Scandinavian
origin in Commons, 152b
are favourites, 248b
*Scarlet
wear the Queen's, 18b
*Scenery
great deeds not bred by, 69a
of Thousand Islands, 104a
best natural s. from, 564b
since we can't export, 611a
of woe and distress, 637b
*Scepticism
vis-à-vis the media, 138a
difficult truth, 190b
*Schenley's
coat of arms instead, 471b
*Schiller, J.C.F. von
how many Goethes and, 336b
*Scholes, Lou
reception to honour, 537b
*School
strokes came my way, 66a
you want, 170a
one s., one flag, 227a
every house a s. house, 270a
Nova Scotia normal s. for, 271a
normal s. for colonies, 271b
good thing about, 298a
head of s. somewhere, 335b
bored, bullied, 444b
never teach patriotism, 601a
*Schweitzer, Albert
and the name Grenfell, 233a
*Science
advance on our limited, 53a
history is literature, 129b
no ethics at all, 189a
reveal real society, 208a
forced to seek meaning, 229a
achieved its mastery, 229a
not planning, research, 260a
fruits of s., culture, 279a
lost unless learns, 279a
art enduring expression, 368a
art generalizes, 368a
alone with history, 394b
arts and s. are DEW, 397a
credit to man who, 458a
medicine an art based, 458b
to McGill belongs credit, 516b
romantic age needs, 553a
*Science-fiction
A.E. Van Vogt, 612a
*Scientific
free of profundity, 51a
middle of 20th c., 117a
only one way, 117a
secrets in moon rocks, 189a
one future s. asserted, 341a
does not produce great, 522b
*Scores
he shoots, he, 260b
*Scotch
Vancouver severely, 133a
as S., not Scots, 210b
use S. for sermons, 341b
in Ontario brood, 569b
*Scotland
on extended scale, 84a
the S. of America, 99b

the majority from, 248a
trace it back to, 301b
Bonnie Prince Charlie, 374b
best natural scenery, 564b
Edinburgh's news, 585b
*Scots
five hundred Highlanders, 87b
the sensible S. are, 117b
I'm a S. resisting, 126b
community, and Irish, 157a
St. Andrews Society, 181a
jokes about the, 193b
Scotsmen are favourites, 248b
Irish or S. neighbours, 390b
the frowning S. elder, 426a
the backbone of Canada, 458b
dourness in Toronto, 485a
Piper Richardson, 498a
the Macs fill 6 pages, 542b
to hell with the pope, 635a
[See also Highlanders.]
*Scott, Barbara Ann
beauy, brains, 525b
*Scott, Duncan Campbell
only poet in Canada, 78a
*Scott, F.R.
anon. is distinguished, 25a
*Scott, Thomas
rope which bound him, 526b
*Scott, Sir Walter
my own, my native, 11b
*Sculler
world's champion, 248a
*Sea
from s. to s., 14b
wealth from the, 15a
farewell, sea-bound coast, 23b
that s. of mountains, 59b
immense saxonizing, 68a
have gone to, 71a
is a sea-son, 85a
resentful s. gods, 124b
to heaven by s. as by, 218a
a s. of mountains, 228b
if always calm, 245b
give you back the, 257b
hands across the, 355b
cowcatcher, summit to, 374a
non-existence of passage, 389b
full of mystery, 409a
the s. 1,000 years, 483a
wholesome s. at her gates, 503b
slept at edge of frozen, 507a
I had studied the, 548a
a mari usque ad mare, 588b
dominion shall be from, 588b
seven s. that run dry, 606a
from East to Western, 626b
serpent, Caddy, 635a
*Seagram's
lot of sentiment in, 77a
*Seaport
the s. of Saint-Malo, 386b
*Seasons
honesty about the, 38a
look up meanings, 85a
four in one day, 266a
*Seaway
See St. Lawrence Seaway.

*Second Chance
land of the, 461b
*Secord, Laura
a-Laura Secord, 25a
Mrs. Secord's walk, 194a
running through woods, 524b
I learned plans, 531a
misty-eyed maiden, 620b
*Secret
many ways to tell, 120a
give me your, 205b
has a woman's, 244a
revealed by photo, 297a
*Secretary
Phipps, if you had a, 140b
*Security
Jack Frost guards, 264a
under British institutions, 330b
break down barriers, 611b
*Selassie, Haile
two absolute monarchs, 258a
*Self
no generation sufficient, 237a
*Self-government
people competent for, 45a
unstinted freedom in, 99a
questionable result of, 104b
difficult art of, 113b
Dominion of Crown, 117b
willing to accept, 126a
*Self-image
how a man views himself, 497b
preoccupation with, 550b
*Self-reliant
no generation is, 237a
meet life's testes, 400a
paddle his own canoe, 407a
no one can walk, 590
practise self-help, 590a
man's power to, 636b
*Selfishness
friendship half time, 244a
saving money is, 244b
*Selkirk, Lord
reap wheat or plough, 32b
*Sell
country for a sheepskin, 244a
discount house, 422b
*Selye, Hans
Montreal and stress, 432a
*Senate
women eligible to sit, 20a
prevents others doing, 103a
convenience, indifference, 142b
the oldest senator, 148b
danger being forgotten, 148b
sit as Trudeau liberal, 199b
how colourless the, 201a
intend to learn a lot, 219b
take a seat in minutes, 338a
bulwark against mob, 362a
the sober second thought, 375b
large property qualification, 367a
with s. listening near, 386b
advance thinking, 416a
seat an aspiration, 416a
blessing, good fate, 454a
no social materials, 551b
speak too fast for, 558a

hated woman in Canada, 635a
[See also Parliament.]
*Sennett, Mack
to go on the stage, 126a
*Sense
man fool for want of, 284a
sound s. of the possible, 388b
*Sensibility
European whose s. modified, 336b
is no longer enough, 550a
intelligence, taste, 526a
*Sentiment
no separation of will, 33a
we manufacture Canadian, 56b
a lot in Seagram, 77a
nourishment from native, 201b
Quebec has no opinions, 331a
*Sentimentalists
who never shed a, 38a
*Separatism
100 years of injustice, 12a
possession of own future, 50b
shouting signpainters, 105a
Canada's independence, 351b
not change the world, 354a
it's all nonsense, 442b
Parti Québécois main, 463b
independent, dependent, 469a
cultural minority, 477b
not stop shouting, 495a
end of a long story, 503a
through violence, 524a
together by consent, 599a
fall into dictatorship, 602b
*Seraut, Georges
canvasses of, 123a
*Sermons
best way to give, 4b
more in a sigh than, 252a
Punch harder than, 338a
use Scotch for, 341b
give them s. or bread, 344b
on the Mount, 583b
*Service, Robert
heart of a Viking, 71a
lives in the Yukon, 74b
*Settlers
difficulties face, 32b
if not Englishmen, 376a
every man first, 385b
divided like a crystal, 437a
not suffragettes, 467a
in New England, 510a
true makers of, 532b
peasants in sheepskin, 542b
come into the west, 559a
*Seven
the s. bolters, 69b
*Seven Oaks
the Battle of, 188b
Fort Douglas not given, 228a
*Seven Up
for a bottle of, 287a
*Seven Years' War
conspiracy of Pontiac, 65b
Treaty of Paris, 67b
know better to deal, 71a
*Sévigny, Pierre
perhaps it's about, 440b

gift of cabinet, 494b
*Sex
puritanism, orgy, 58a
until I have orgasm, 150b
intentions improper, 285b
only once a month, 285b
slip across border, 291b
only luxury available, 298a
appeal of murder and, 340b
reproduction not, 418b
my body opens, 432a
morality, modesty, 467a
orgy moved elsewhere, 500a
orgasms little to do, 536a
flying as long as, 597a
lose their sang-froid, 601b
*Sexes
there are three, 103b
the battle of the, 187b
*Shade
of the old apple tree, 634a
*Shadow
life a little s. that runs, 133a
*Shakespeare, William
abominable pieces of, 204b
pay special tribute, 239b
Richard III in Winnipeg, 251b
literature, Bible and, 492a
regular diet of Bacon, 641a
*Shamrock
thistle, s., rose, 439a
*Shannon
Chesapeake and, 21b
meet the S. with her, 77a
Chesapeake and the, 335b
*Sharp, Mitchell
resigned six months, 557b
*Shaughnessy, Baron
great artists are, 567b
*Shaw, George Bernard
young man wanted to meet, 17b
Canada no authors, 568a
Underhill most Shavian, 608b
stories of Festival, 630a
*Sheepskin
sell country for a, 244a
sold for price of a, 272b
peasants in s. coats, 542b
peasant in a s. coat, 543b
*Sherbrooke, Lord
came to me and said, 165a
*Sherlock Holmes
C.P.R. and, 160b
*Sherman, William
marching down River, 2b
*Shield, Canadian
the s., the Canadian, 156a
portages and lakes of, 365a
too much of it, 372b
like the s. of Archilles, 384a
hankering to paint, 479a
*Shin, Hoei
visited B.C., 235a
*Ship
empty vessels loom, 10b
when I cross the, 40a
vessel for M. Bigot, 55b
coast of steamboat, 134a
don't give up the, 335b
she was a golden, 445a

to the Briton, 641b
*Shipshaw
Aluminum Company, 188b
*Shit
let them eat, 598a
*Shooting
Niagara, 98a
*Shoots
he s., he scores, 260b
*Shore
from Britain's, 439a
*Shot
last fired by French, 572a
a whiff of grape, 643a
*Show business
outlast trends, 8b
places to be lousy, 36b
work I enjoy, 75b
Wayne from Shuster, 192a
precarious profession, 220b
give them good show, 276a
pie-in-the-kisser, 298b
Ottawa-born impersonator, 357a
arrive when left, 405a
make 'em cry one, 479b
tell the truth, 519a
wish I could afford, 521a
it takes two, 624b
enough to entertain, 630a
*Shuster, Frank
Canadians distinguish, 192a
[See also Johnny Wayne.]
*Siam
Canada ranks with, 88a
Anna and the King of, 347b
*Sibelius, Jean
no Sibeliuses around, 226a
*Sickness
See Disease and Illness.
*Sifton, Sir Clifford
encourage peasants, 244a
discerning auditor, 314b
peasants in sheepskin, 542b
*Sigh
end of love is a, 252a
women say more, 252a
*Signal Hill
St. John's, 406b
*Significance
emotional outbursts, 556b
*Silence
nothing but, 37b
strongest weapon, 76b
success in s.s, 98b
give you my, 205b
real presence, 214a
institute a reign of, 327b
and solitude in Sask., 372b
like under the sea, 483a
pocket of possibility, 526a
crisis never avoided, 604b
*Silent
the s. force, 19a
*Silver
where all s. comes, 24a
gave away the, 25a
let medals be of, 414a
*Simpson Company, R.
of consumption, 20a

if there was a Jack, 173a
together we make, 308b
  *Sin
who doesn't, 9b
a poor unfortunate, 11b
turn away from, 39b
none a woman can't, 167b
woman cannot s. with, 636a
  *Sinanthropus pekinensis
Peking Man, 58a
  *Sinbad the Sailor
these S.s of wilderness, 280a
never saw Hudson's Bay, 583a
  *Since
you and I were young, 288b
  *Singer
Canada to world, 124b
made singing nation, 288a
songs public knows, 294a
become first-class, 359a
I'm a s., not star, 391b
my one big dream, 555b
  *Sioux
one night a young, 18a
  *Sioux Lookout
songs to be found in, 294a
  *Siwash
the simple-hearted, 620a
  *Six Nations
I, Dekanahwideh, 144b
  *Size
of country measured by, 271b
exaggerate importance, 372b
bigness should belong to, 476a
square miles, people, 496b
  *Skating
fast s., hockey, 44a
everything's hot, 286a
win title every, 286a
fall once a day, 403a
listings, Scott, 526b
  *Ski-doo
world-famous motor, 62b
  *Skiing
doesn't everyone, 232a
the song of the, 382b
  *Skies
ever-sensed above, 617b
beneath thy shining, 626b
  *Slavery
go to a bad place, 3a
coloured men are free, 21b
spent Fourth of July, 58b
make slaves of mud, 71a
called a convention, 81b
another country in, 87a
turn out the best, 126b
purchase a negro girl, 131b
knaves who made us, 161b
land monopoly enslaves, 186a
sold to Frenchman, 241b
one potato a day, 247a
I was free, 257b
entered a paradise, 288a
Buxton Settlement, 308a
cut capers in chains, 356b
the lion's paw, 366b
glitter delivers us, 423a
who sells himself, 438a
insulted by, 466b

sold to Brant, 480a
labour, capitalism, 583b
next thing to hell, 603b
Sons of Freedom, 613b
now the slave, 621a
invisible ideal, 622a
came like terrapins, 634b
under lion's paw, 637a
[See also Blacks.]
  *Slavic
one was Irish or, 553b
  *Sleep
to s. on the floor, 9b
everybody goes to, 133b
did not fall, 159b
in a farm land we, 309a
we shall not s. though, 372b
all you lose is a little, 374b
no more expect upon arms, 384b
death a s. and a, 457b
edge of frozen sea, 507a
is only a habit, 610a
  *Sleeping
with an elephant, 597a
  *Slept
edge of frozen sea, 507a
  *Slightly
higher in Canada, 211b
  *Slovakia
immigrant boy from, 509a
  *Slums
visit/ez les, 12a
without Disneyland, 202b
Cabbagetown largest, 213b
  *Small, Ambrose
of Toronto disappeared, 199b
  *Smallwood, J.R. (Joey)
God had J.S. in mind, 241b
  *Smart
better be lucky than, 37a
  *Smile
a cloud-burst, 85a
I'll never s. again, 364a
chamberpot on head, 377b
  *Smiling
we love thee, s. land, 70b
man who never, 556a
  *Smith, A.J.M.
stylistic success, 390a
  *Smith, Donald
drove last spike, 129a
  *Smith, Goldwin
long winter evenings, 27b
what Canadian literature, 180b
  *Smith, John
born a man, died, 15b
  *Smoking
seldom without pipe, 7b
polluting lungs, 598a
  *Smug
the s. minority, 52b
  *Smuggling
receivers make, 244b
contraband merchandise, 561b
contraband activity, 562a
  *Snag
brave beautiful name, 69b
  *Snow
to your heels, 10b
an infinity of, 37a

send down as much, 37a
share not only snow, 37b
snowshoeing here, 42a
snowmobile, Ski-doo, 62b
white savannahs, 122b
both mist and, 122b
not after March, 162a
dramatic effect, 180a
white means snow, 195b
they were hipt, 245a
thirty words for, 268a
holes of heaven, 302a
our lady of the, 309a
frozen to his neck, 309b
it can s. yonder, 326b
really a good road, 354a
April is abominable, 428b
land of snow, 435a
films with s. scenes, 467a
marine sponge, 486b
if two Canadians, 522a
left no footmarks on, 536b
my road, it's the, 615b
a few acres of, 616b
over a few acres of, 616b
  *Sober
John A. drunk, Brown, 380b
can't drink yourself, 474a
  *Social Credit
victorious, when, 1b
gets things done, 49b
a s.c. to Alberta, 83b
not have to understand, 96a
A plus B theorem, 158a
world-wide torch, 289b
Alberta elections, 481b
will of the people, 495a
is above politics, 584a
  *Social science
expression of faith, 174b
fundamental problems, 51a
Saskatchewan rewarding, 355b
  *Social security
decent s.s. system, 288b
  *Social work
premiership extension, 36a
lost my innocence, 495a
  *Socialism
proclaimed in London, 54a
plan without owning, 159a
capitalism disguised, 289b
fields in Soviet, 315a
is but a dream, 338b
except in Heaven, 342b
Lenin on Skelton's, 347a
public ownership, 352b
public utilities, 400a
save capitalism, 454a
mountains of dead, 521b
power to pooling, 528a
between s., capitalism, 607a
basis is ethical, 608b
independent and, 623a
economic independence, 623a
not Russian model, 643a
stars fighting for, 643b
  *Socialist
I'm s. hordes, 36a
hard-nosed capitalists, 36a

and capitalism, 127a
barbarians coming, 50a
envious American, 249b
look southward, 266b
sympathy with idea, 338a
angels no doubt are, 339b
shares workroom, 340b
commonwealth of angels, 342a
build the s. society, 351b
no young person, 514a
liberals in a hurry, 520a
creation of s. state, 570a
or capitalist, 597a
ideology to work, 601b
democratic, 601b
two managers, one, 607b
road is firm, 637a
belong to movements, 648b
 *Society
scorn, disrespect, 3b
liberty in ordered, 188b
humanity has done, 208a
the affluent, 211a
family compact of, 253b
reversion of pyramid, 253b
purify the home, 266a
subordination, 272b
no s. in Toronto, 283b
no human s. no, 353a
conservative, 356a
low-necked dresses, 357a
in conventions of, 362b
law of social change, 434b
anchor of freedom, 479b
adjusting to stress, 491a
segment produce, 509a
not whole of man, 517b
reform of, 522a
freedom enriches, 541a
without communication, 557b
like salt water, 567b
man in bush, 567b
the just, 596b
freedom established, 597b
 *Sociology
history a complex, 322a
substantial definition, 336b
God help me, 455b
 *Soil
nobody identifiable with, 226a
from which Lincoln grew, 237b
which they can own, 238a
surely the best in, 245a
to fall on Canadian, 335a
you immigrants, sons of, 346b
to cling to the, 575a
not men enough to till, 640b
 *Soldiers
German girls please, 4a
deliver from government, 43b
not a Canadian s. will, 64b
vote like a wooden, 219b
in plain with three, 291a
and the priesthood, 587a
small number of good, 638b
 *Solitude
this heritage of, 203b
I see nothing but, 218b
destined to eternal, 341a
silence in Sask., 372b

a new loneliness, 616a
and s. are vast, 641b
 *Solitudes, Two
I did not invent, 394b
two s. protect and touch, 502b
 *Solzhenitsyn, Alexander
who smother their, 94a
 *Something to Sing About
This Land of Ours, 71b
 *Songs
disappear in abyss, 50b
fame is in, 98b
how many I know, 198b
sweet songstress of, 261a
that my paddle sings, 290a
the public knows, 294a
yet to be found in, 294a
about where I am, 354a
will nobody write, 402a
sing it, breathe, 456b
Mademoiselle from, 496b
fifty a day, 511a
market for the writer, 583b
 *Sons of Freedom
slaves of corruption, 613b
Peter the Lordly, 613b
 *Sophistication
is perception, 397a
 *Sorrows
year has mingled, 496b
 *Soul
everything had a, 25b
national s., infancy, 34b
artists creative, 54a
room to expand, 78a
longing remains deep, 93a
country that has no, 93a
desert of s. in Que., 183a
not into wilderness, 238a
human food consists, 281b
go on living without, 291a
her own s. Canada risks, 311b
desolation in the, 357b
find their s. in land, 365a
into the hand of God, 440b
some are Hesperides, 523b
grow a thing apart, 527b
I am a, 636a
incorporated in bodies, 643a
 *Sound
can soar on s. higher, 375b
belong to continuous field, 526a
 *Sourdough
city, 15b
 *South
to the glowing, 74b
moccasins, S. Wind, 129a
effeminate, 201b
than live in the, 247a
Yankee must s. of us, 290a
place his heel, 301b
live as far s. as, 384a
bright, fierce, 385b
Russians north, 633b
 *South Africa
See Africa and Union of South
 Africa.
 *South Bay
there was a young man, 17b
 *South Nahanni River

land of the Nahanni, 193a
white queen of, 409b
 *South Porcupine
burned in 1911, 436a
 *Souviens
je me, 236a
je me, 572a
 *Sovereignty
Crown symbol of, 182a
ours a s. nation, 619a
 *Soviet Union
exceeded only by, 292a
see enormous fields, 315a
nyet, nyet, 546a
[See also Russia.]
 *Space
fear of infinite, 37a
on very verge of, 182b
inhuman, native, 185a
problems in terms, 279a
in possession of dirt, 312b
 *Spadina Avenue
heart of constituency, 521a
 *Spain
tomb of fascism, 54a
and China part, 54b
of liberty of, 60b
since restoration, 68b
account of wines, 101b
Spaniard have his, 290a
more civilized than, 345a
crushed the Indian, 464a
brother Jesuits, 528b
hot breath of, 536a
 *Speak
English but badly, 317b
 *Speech
a lot of shortening, 4a
piece of fiction, 4b
first transmission, 44b
trained to talk, 46b
guarded manner of, 58a
middle moves, 76b
exempt from, 91a
quotation ornaments, 139b
joual is not, 148a
intelligible transmitted, 191b
with s. I fight, 216b
of public speaking, 239a
ugliest, most raucous, 240b
from Tory platform, 258a
not so joual, 327a
keep like fish, 411b
given to conceal, 458b
to be said, 478a
rather sad tone, 483b
way I make a, 557b
speaker tonight is, 582b
 *Speed
was far faster than, 86a
the solitude of, 616a
 *Spence Bay
see you in Heaven, 315a
 *Spike, Last
Smith drove home, 129a
a plain iron, 562b
drove a gold spike, 567a
last an iron, 610b
work done well, 611a

*Spirit
man is candle, 60a
writer concerned, 93a
arresting adventure, 189a
distort to catch, 195a
generous flame of, 243a
art a voice of, 250a
the s. that soars, 316a
infuse into history, 322a
no future without, 512a
[See also National Spirit.]
*Spirits
walking in sky, 9b
when has gone, 100a
dryads, 284b
find the great, 475a
white and red children, 492b
in the hands of, 578b
ghosts banished, 592a
outdoors like Bible, 618b
*Spiritual
our life and death, 84b
large s. adventurers, 140a
a s. awakening, 227b
art a s. alertness, 356b
effect of North, 362a
North more, 455a
insensitiveness, 573a
*Splendid
isolation, 200a
England was, 328b
*Spoke
a nation to a nation, 308b
*Spoons
too many for broth, 392b
melt into bullets, 445b
*Sport
of historic misfortune, 57a
*Sports
hit 'em where they, 297b
profit motive in, 302a
get out and kill, 341b
athletic education, 390b
highly commercialized, 407a
an institution, 424a
not race, religion, 515a
nations cultivated, 537b
tobogganning, skating, 581b
*Spring
forward, fall back, 14b
in lap of winter, 114b
landscape roared, 281a
joyous production, 320b
*Springhill Mining Disaster
a wonderful story, 41a
13,000-foot level, 75a
calls for 7 Up, 287a
town of Springhill, 371b
God saved hole, 407b
live on songs, 516a
*Spruce Falls
Power and Paper, 573b
*Spy
rarely looks part, 226b
would I work, 440b
loyalty does not, 559a
*Squalor
private affluence, public, 211a
*Squid-Jiggin' Ground
where fishermen gather, 525b

*Stadacona
lilies reign over, 476b
[See also Montreal.]
*Stalin, Joseph
insecure person, 649b
*Stampede
See Calgary Stampede.
*Stand
we s. on guard for, 626b
fast, Craigellachie, 562a
*Standard of living
third highest, 292a
*Standard Time
the time-keeper, 196b
*Stanfield, Robert
and noblesse oblige, 564b
*Stanley Cup
emotional, winning, 185a
willing to give, 558a
dreaming happily of, 607b
*Stanley Park
dried-up names, 216b
*Star
my only guiding, 165a
rise and follow, 334a
a bold s. will ornament, 363a
difficult to outgrow, 398b
*Stars
Canadian s. are remote, 77b
vainly seek truth in, 277a
holes of heaven called, 302a
enough to fill, 621b
fighting for socialism, 643b
*Starvation
seen no one starving, 163a
not Communism but, 596a
*State
laying foundation of, 99a
assist the arts, 115b
warring in bosom of, 170b
French s. is due, 237b
is our exploiter, 316a
frigid monster, 327b
Canada is no, 354b
basic principle is, 362b
permanent parent, 398b
rights, privileges, 451a
United States no place, 558a
no place for s. in, 595a
bilingual s. richer, 595b
decides what nation, 602b
weakness, virtues, 641b
*Statesman
great s. once said, 68b
a dead politician, 180a
built up empire, 212a
our s. in empire, 271b
making things, 399b
something for country, 484a
irresolution, 635a
no longer do right, 506a
*Statistics
are for losers, 70a
*Stature
cannot add an inch, 40b
measured from shoulders, 506a
*Status
equal between, 64b
equal, 305b

*Status quo
good things flow, 94b
men who do not accept, 356a
use of force to keep, 509b
objectivity ideology, 610a
*Statute
of Westminster, 20a
*Steamers
go down Niagara, 28a
arrive punctually, 134a
wonderful the harp, 588a
*Steel
old s.-makers never die, 315a
*Stein, Gertrude
writes me, 256a
*Steinberg's
masters of consumption, 20a
*Stendhal
read more than Mill, 597b
*Stephen, Sir George
to call Craigellachie, 129a
*Stewart, Walter
nine years Liberal, 182b
*Sticks
land of little, 160a
the bundle of, 245a
*Stocks
slight fall in price, 124a
stop buying mining, 535b
options customary, 574b
*Stone-mason
being a s.-m. still, 551b
*Stop
who would s. us, 268a
*Stork Derby
the Millar will, 419a
*Story
no s. so fantastic, 120a
history essential, 129b
tell your s. to public, 173a
spoil by sticking to, 179b
out of life of people, 195a
every person had a, 234b
ask me whence these, 360a
none of these old, 385b
I, Nuligak, tell, 451b
*Strachan, John
from S. to Owen, 85b
insolent Bishop, 98a
*Strand
on the old Ontario, 24a
*Stratford
promised land of, 491b
*Stratford Festival
the call girl, 111b
to Will Shakespeare, 239b
practical value, 240a
playing S.-on-Avon, 276b
only thing worth, 322b
climbed a pole, 389a
Toronto good for, 426a
a duty, a pleasure, 426a
how nice, 455a
want to start a, 466b
literature, Bible, 491b
now is the winter, 536a
done with Shylock, 609a
exciting night in, 631b
*Strathroy
hell has S. done for, 382a

*Street
longest s. in, 136a
co-operation not a, 170a
longest in world, 521a
*Streisand, Barbra
States no place, 558a
*Strength
have the s. of giant, 32a
you may test your, 57b
no. s., no strain, 272a
this is beauty of, 550a
*Stress
society adjusting to, 491a
nonspecifically induced, 533a
*Strikes
not as Communists, 84b
final resort to, 131a
Relief Camp Workers, 185b
bullets in Vancouver, 386b
[See also Winnipeg General
    Strike.]
*Strong
here lies the, 16a
the land is, 182b
man in world, 258a
true north, s. and, 626a
*Struggle
not of principles, races, 170b
winning of global, 180b
*Student
movement will choose, 192a
whoever ceases to be, 277b
lark or owl, 458b
*Style
1000 years for a, 27b
like your Canadian, 64a
two life-styles, 174b
wait until mud, 551a
*Subject
Britannic Majesty's, 176b
British s. I was born, 380a
anyone can be s. and, 436a
I was born a British, 438b
a loyal British, 633b
*Suburbs
want mobility, 613a
*Subsidy
whenever I hear culture, 171b
annually on bands, 303b
golden apple divided, 602b
*Subways
in N.Y. owned in, 509b
*Success
French-Canadians and, 36b
you make your own, 45b
secret of political, 95b
is in the silences, 98b
paved with good, 179b
I'm an overnight, 246b
real power you get, 287a
state of mind, 293a
due to father, 307a
don't succeed, quit, 338a
requires three, 368b
makes philosophical, 368a
behind every man, 470a
not to seek but deserve, 470a
years have mingled, 486b
god of politics, 506a
God, I wanted, 549a

to learn from, 579b
failure to give, 593a
90% inspiration, 628b
*Sudbury
war memorial, 309a
never try it in, 556a
*Suffer
God-given right to, 1b
not that I fear to, 74b
capacity infinite, 213a
find enough here, 345a
no one understands, 406b
travel, s., love, 444b
decisions that ease, 472a
*Suffrage
before ladies sit, 106a
based on universal, 112b
thank you, gentlemen, 370b
for settlers, not, 467a
opposed by short-haired, 507a
women not using, 507a
forgot justice to women, 553b
*Sugar candy
because we are made, 112b
*Suicide
my mission is, 26a
did try my very best, 79b
dread of political, 189b
truly despairs, 229a
prophecy of Hitler's, 313b
will this never end, 450a
exercise of imagination, 625a
*Sullivan, Ed
or Noël Coward, 553b
*Summer
it is hot, 38a
Indian, 95b
flying low, 98b
mosquitoes own land, 135b
blue with the sky of, 160a
landscape green, 281a
a too long, 316b
for loafing, dreaming, 320b
mid-s. afternoon, 334a
feeling s. in the old, 346a
little lake on a, 358a
have a s. shower, 377b
its s.'s heat, 389a
fades, life short, 401a
*Summit
cowcatcher from s. to sea, 374a
*Sun
gain nothing appearing, 388b
as long as s. shines, 414a
long as s. shines, 434a
looked the s. straight, 529b
done in the midnight, 534a
*Sunday
almost to madness, 321a
golf played on, 338b
week in Toronto, 453a
*Sunrise
world is waiting for, 358a
*Sunset
Canadian, 219a
saw s. glow, 372b
as real as pigstyes, 428b
*Superman
woman possessed by, 522a
first drawn by, 541a

*Support
united to, combined, 12b
we must s. our, 382a
*Surprised
behind every successful, 470a
*Surrealism
French s. poet, 74a
countries real or, 213a
positivism and, 369b
*Surrender
woman's victory due to, 252a
guards die, never, 452b
die in ruins before, 612b
*Survival
a thematic guide, 28b
no one's death for, 148b
mere s. is affliction, 205a
whether they exist, 236a
of human personality, 307a
of the fittest, 371a
two miracles of, 528a
*Susannah
of the Mounties, 147a
*Suspicion
woman influenced by, 179a
*Susskind, David
where do I stand, 138b
*Suzanne
takes you down to, 120a
*Swahili
if Canadians spoke, 408a
*Swastika
idea of twisted cross, 493a
*Swat
the news from, 323b
*Swear
in English, Indian, 647b
woman who exclaims, 647b
*Sweat
lips don't, 647a
*Sweaters
everyone can wear, 629b
*Sweden
developed two, 81a
un-northern, 154a
Americans of draft, 316b
objectors gone to, 370a
*Sweet Marie
come to me, 621a
*Swimming
I did, I finished, 45b
depended on track, 452a
we're going to make, 452b
I'll go in for, 474b
suddenly remembered, 548a
Marilyn Bell's, 516b
I did everything, 574a
the Whirlpool, 625a
*Switzerland
equal in extent to, 80b
between Canadians and, 256a
best scenery, 564b
Canada peaceable, 584b
not even by power, 157b
*Sydney
if you went to, 62b
*Symphonies
assimilation is wheat, 367b

# T

*Tadoussac*
lives of people in, 124a
*Takeover*
American t. of, 166a
U.S. of publishing, 273b
*Talent*
love an indication, 3b
career of own, 5b
Ministry of All, 332a
wasted and wither, 470a
go to bed with money, 478a
of the spirit, 487a
few men of, 498b
editor blessed with, 649b
*Talk*
stop me, freedom, 153a
if money, 179b
people say so much, 277a
nobody wants to, 430a
woman who doesn't, 465b
*Tamburlaine*
pyramid of skulls, 492a
*Taste*
displays of superior, 139a
no disputing, 139b
to gratify his, 179a
deficiencies in colony, 344a
a t. for Quebec, 351a
refuge of noncreative, 397a
desire to improve, 433a
is first refuge, 463b
curiosity, courage, 525b
*Taxes*
scarcely any, 8b
never cost payer, 62a
thank the English, 62a
and never pay, 301b
few performers pay, 303b
promises of yesterday, 306a
power to destroy, 474a
tears the price of, 506a
high-priced lawyers, 600b
strikes an Englishman, 620a
*Taylor, E.P.*
life to integrating, 229a
Pale Tory, 229b
*Taylor, Elizabeth*
Vive Elisabeth, 12a
married Burton in, 88b
*Tea*
pass, don't pour, 4b
coffee poorer, better, 147a
slatternly wife, 168b
emblem of civilization, 246a
another cup of, 528a
never be poured, 647b
*Teach*
authorizing females, 14b
always tell a good, 117a
never start lecture, 133b
of history wrong, 136b
to write not to, 151b
except pass it on, 342a
interests extend, 359b
owe a lot to my, 342b
are American, 569a

*Technology*
instead of grace, 124a
structure within, 221b
range of society, 229a
leap into another's, 303a
real systems, body, 351a
lovable than Russian, 395b
extension of ourselves, 396a
translates into art, 396b
success of American, 493a
is ourselves, 513b
*Tecumseh*
I saw T. stagger, 58b
Dick Johnson killed, 288a
*Teilhard de Chardin, Pierre*
Black a brother, 58b
calls the noosphere, 291b
*Tekahionwake*
Indian name of Johnson, 290a
*Telegraph*
first message, 219a
first wireless, 405b
and iron road, 433b
*Telephone*
invented in Canada, 44a
history of the, 44a
conceived in Brantford, 44b
development of, 44b
largest users in world, 45a
largest users, 45a
electric speech, 46a
yes, Alec, it is I, 46a
operators bilingual, 46b
Quebeckers greatest, 163b
Canada comes first, 239b
can't start a, 469a
Montreal directory, 542b
*Television*
performs in two groups, 45b
no dead air on, 52b
TV by candlelight, 62b
used to do before, 71a
come on after football, 71a
had seen Topper, 100b
documentary programs, 123b
not always Mr. Affable, 141a
hasten radio's end, 147a
Roman could have seen, 189a
viewers and thinkers, 189b
this Ben Cartwright, 232a
overnight success, 246b
directors and live TV, 262a
our strong imports, 263a
have gun will travel, 406b
can make it in Canada, 547b
licence to print money, 585a
*Temperance*
to make t. medals, 168a
*Templeton's T-R-C's*
Raz-Mah, 579b
*Tennyson, Alfred Lord*
two of us left, 215a
written O loyal, 581a
*Terra*
primum vista, 92a
*Terre des Homme*
man and his world, 519a
*Terror*
possible survivor of, 203a

*Texas*
parity with, 115a
*Thailand*
Anna and the King of, 347b
*Thalberg, Irving*
she sleeps with, 538b
*Thames River*
muddy banks of the, 37b
*Theatre*
impresario Belasco, 43b
national drama, 53a
your Canadian style, 64a
diploma or part, 85a
open a play in, 88b
only drama critic, 120b
Canadian feature, 121a
to be methodical, 122b
epic drama, 125b
to go on stage, 126a
Canadian, what, 127b
loneliness, pretending, 131b
two great dramatists, 140a
dinghy sailing among, 146b
actor reads story, 161b
first stage fall, 162b
bankruptcy haunts, 171b
never been actress, 176b
melodrama, realism, 180a
Chekhov not Racine, 185a
chain from Halifax, 197b
farces for savages, 204b
doing what you believe, 204b
active, independent, 211a
dream of my life, 214a
give birth to, 215b
is like fireworks, 215b
strong supporters, 230a
not too isolationist, 240a
where is the, 249a
attitude in Winnipeg. 251b
London is friendlier, 251b
on the way up, 257a
a race of actors, 257a
is my world, 259a
Britain's in your, 260b
in Winnipeg most, 263b
Broadway doesn't, 268a
stage better than, 275b
vodka to Poland, 276b
place of meeting, 280a
pride in grain, 282a
Ibsen's disturbing, 282a
each time first, 282a
at Massey Hall, 291b
success or failure, 293a
experience, no money, 296b
I couldn't act, 297b
superannuated rep, 320a
artistic director, 323b
le t. de Neptune, 349b
audiences downfall, 354b
excitement of the, 354b
get an audience, 374a
playwright on radio, 395a
an actor in, 400a
arrive when left, 405a
little t. movement, 410a
screen needs stage, 410a
Miller play Hamlet, 419b
make audience, 422b

living motion art, 423a
design on the stage, 424a
director scrubs, 430b
playwright seems, 451a
see best right here, 466b
if father had lived, 476a
what an entrance, 483b
story of Moor, 492a
star material, 506a
not horrible enough, 519a
wish I could afford, 521a
is house of life, 533b
Heartbreak House, 537b
like film, 540b
I-don't-care girl, 574a
Toronto and Boston, 587b
Shylock the YMCA, 609a
come quite logically, 609a
spoken word, 623a
commodity, hope, 631a
little of Lorelei, 638b
Bacon and Shakespeare, 641a
forget the stage, 650a
[See also Dominion Drama Festi-
    val and Stratford Festival.]
  *Theory
must be fruitful, 532b
create counterweights, 602b
  *These
hands are clean, 376b
  *Think
and work hard, 34a
makes millions, 91b
no one else, 78a
draw line around, 100a
too late to stop, 143a
original who, 189a
to t. continentally, 197a
in straight lines, 225a
of the U.S., 229a
we reason, 312a
more modest terms, 333a
force mind to, 472a
important since, 640b
  *Thirties
the dirty, 282b
[See also Depression.]
  *This
Land of Ours, 71b
Canada of ours, 164b
  *Thistle
shamrock, rose, 439a
  *Thomson, Roy
or local merchant, 435b
  *Thomson, Tom
remoteness, reticence, 250a
woods in his bones, 382b
  *Thought
by taking t. we, 40b
bred by scenery, 69a
like dew upon, 91b
about love, 134a
tone to Europe, 171a
art a stimulus, 250a
weight of, 313a
keen and clear, 321a
Grand Trunk of, 384a
sober second, 444b
mission is radiating, 462b
  *Thousand Islands

scenery beautiful, 104a
like Victoria, 311a
tree-covered rock, 556b
  *Three Rivers
Mission of Trois Rivières, 163b
second-largest French, 604a
  *Throne
one flag, one fleet, 64a
a t. sent word to a, 308b
one flag, one, 441b
  *Thule
marine sponge, 486a
  *Thunder Bay
once taught at, 88b
feudal state of Fort, 280b
talk at Port, 340a
by Thunder passes, 611a
  *Thunderbird
long stay up in, 182b
like the T. of old, 216b
  *Tiber River
beavers not found, 107b
  *Tidal Bore
20 foot tidal drop, 485a
  *Tide
high does your t. rise, 272a
  *Tie
off pancreas ducts, 33b
  *Tigers
eaten up by the, 9b
come on the, 50a
  *Tilley, Sir Samuel
have sold us all to, 629b
  *Timbuktoo
if orchestra were in, 51a
  *Time
Daylight Saving, 14b
the end of, 37b
to the end, 97b
standard t.-keeper, 196b
seven t. zones, 197a
about t. Canada entered, 214b
distance abridged, 245a
problems in terms, 279a
feels older, 311a
come which is not, 312b
for a change, 349a
searching for better, 354a
no jury but, 375a
myself and t. against, 381b
in East one travels, 392a
century a spoke in, 502a
but mistakes, 641a
  *Time Magazine
exempt from tax, 293b
not consider Canadian, 366b
  Tipperary
it's a long way to, 633b
  *Tisdale
of rape and honey, 13a
  *Titanic
sinking of the, 409b
  *Titles
Thomson of Fleet, 40a
accept a knighthood, 136b
Elizabeth the Second, 182a
wear Maple Leaf, 213b
prove I'm success, 585b
  *Tobogganing
originated here, 42a

awful, wonderful, 581b
  *Tolkien, J.R.
Toronto, Rivendell, 584b
  *Tolpuddle Martyrs
victory certain, 364a
  *Tolstoy, Leo
include Flaubert, 367a
read more than Mill, 597b
  *Tom, Uncle
my name is not, 258a
if U.T. came to, 637a
  *Tomorrow
pioneer learns to live, 191a
yesterday and I know, 191b
opportunity for great, 207a
Old T. nickname, 279b
Old T. would be, 378b
will let you know, 381b
today is the, 421b
I'll see about it, 612b
I am thinking of, 646b
  *Too
near to be great, 12b
little too late, 350b
  *Toronto
they make take, 12b
longest street, 12b
first prize, one week, 13a
industry, intelligence, 15a
long winter evenings, 27b
Bruce Kidd from, 29a
fine town, finished, 43a
horse and Empire, 53a
public amusements, 63b
blue hills of old, 63b
let good people, 67b
against Italians, 74a
difficult describe, 77b
I show a horse, 78b
manicured park in, 84b
soft spot for, 88b
why I lived in, 93a
my tiger city, 93a
don't let anyone, 93b
being stuffy, 106a
joy and peace, 129a
more polygamy, 132a
calculated crime, 133a
Yonge Street, 136a
first prize, one, 148a
full of life, 150b
wild rabid toryism, 151a
little city, big, 157a
beastly place, 157b
we moved to, 159a
send Beatles to, 160a
capital of new, 172b
right hand done in, 177b
and Kingston, 183b
and Ian Fleming, 196b
Ambrose Small, 199b
future-oriented, 209b
unique situation, 209b
movie industry in, 209b
vilest blue-devil, 212a
excellent player, 215b
Catholic and Anglican, 222a
libraries lacking, 222b
make films as well, 235b

horrible jargon of, 236b
ladies in Rosedale, 240b
exceeded Jerusalem, 246a
not good address, 249a
where is theatre, 249a
on Avenue Road car, 256a
reared enchantment, 259a
reminded of farmer, 265a
abroad without signal, 272b
Bay and Richmond Sts., 275b
to die on Saturday, 278b
place of meeting again, 280a
fatigue, heat, 282b
little, ill-built, 283a
is no society in, 283b
worse and better, 284a
make acquaintance of, 286a
we'd buy a mountain, 286a
Admiralty second-rate, 286b
city of reputations, 286b
ah, T., the pope, 287a
cultural activities, 291b
observe change, 292a
Jaguar at vicarage, 303b
Maple Leaf Gardens, 304a
consumingly commercial, 310b
nobody should visit, 321b
inhabitants not fairest, 325a
close ties with Canada, 326a
second time performed, 335a
know McGill in it, 340a
typical Torontonian, 340a
conversation reduced, 344a
desolate city called, 344a
Levant's premiere in, 350a
to be intellectual in, 353a
imagine a Florence, 353a
girl who made bad, 354b
married some poor boy, 354b
wait to see elephants, 355a
a failed Boston, 359b
thousand doors to knock, 375a
Babylon-on-the-Humber, 388a
full-time garbage, 405a
better to run to, 408b
legislation, damnation, 411b
good for Stratford, 426a
blue hills of old, 431b
that delightful city, 432b
hoping T. has message, 433a
marvellous being woman, 444b
a week, one Sunday, 453a
mayor of all the, 474b
I'm Gladys Smith, 476a
little girl in dream, 476b
headquarters of sect, 484b
penetrating gloom, 485a
handsomest town, 496b
York and Quebec, 499a
Hell reminded me of, 503b
350 miles, Montreal, 516b
longest street in, 521a
Spadina the heart, 521a
I remember a, 522b
has no social classes, 523
people say please, 524b
Timbuctoo, Kazan, 524b
cosier niche than, 528b
Crestwood Heights, 532a
dined with family, 542b

palladium of loyalty, 544b
we all hate, 546a
Centennial project to, 557b
born in bookshop in, 558b
made in Canada, 566b
nobody hates me, 567a
location, vocation, 569b
unhealthy streets, 573b
Spruce Falls Power, 573b
march back leisurely, 584a
edge of U.S. history, 584b
theatre in Boston, 587b
hideous Bay Street, 591a
planks in streets, 593b
reformed publisher, 605a
opposite business, 608a
I say Canada I mean, 609a
the New City Hall, 617b
doubly beautiful, 630b
goodbye T., with, 630b
I lecture as usual, 632b
Chekhov, Turgenev, 635b
reckless driving, 636a
no great beauties, 636a
city hall, graveyard, 644b
[See also York.]
  *Toronto, University of
divides up estates, 340a
in University College, 348b
  *Toronto Star
will print what I, 28b
worst influence, 163a
into office of, 460a
finds Gerda, 494b
  *Tory
hear them moaning, 39a
changing leaders, 50a
a T. until I, 50a
wild rabid Toryism, 151a
whatever may say, 171a
E.P. Taylor, Pale, 229b
government suitable, 244a
spoken from platform, 258a
want my bedtime, 291a
not single cent to any, 306a
I was growing a, 323a
every T. editor kept, 328b
success of colonial, 356a
satisfac-Tory character, 381a
who vote Grit or, 392b
curse of civilized, 402a
want my bedtime, 441a
vote with the, 454a
survived last regime, 475b
[See also Conservative.]
  *Toslow
the girls from, 346a
  *Totalitarianism
spectacular appeal, 191a
global truth and, 297b
contemplate era, 461b
freedom and, 607a
  *Toy
we were t. automata, 64b
  *Trade
blast a way into, 48b
you will buy more, 104b
industry will grow, 110a
years from home, 131a
Canada's declining, 140b

trader, pathfinder, 141a
fullest possible, 172b
in movement of, 174a
no truck nor t. with, 200b
Y.C.D.B.S.O.Y.A., 255b
fifth largest, 292a
active interprovincial, 378a
Japan and U.S., 449a
largest partner, 449b
father of t. unionism, 452b
  *Traditions
deep t. of your past, 67b
they have no, 78a
historical, cultural, 82a
we must forego, 175b
British and French, 199a
past without losing, 201b
develop a native, 224a
vague and general, 283b
whence legends, 360a
Tolstoy and Flaubert, 367a
stimulus to imagine, 372a
we have here no, 385a
dissolution of, 397b
let us be faithful, 416a
what you do with, 491a
  Trafalgar, Battle of
Ukrainians think they won, 304a
  *Trail
of '98, 15b
  *Traitors
a nest of, 69b
in Quebec to, 330b
never sold by, 377a
Canadians converted, 490a
  *Tramp
tramp, tramp, tramp, 22a
our boys are, 387b
  *Trans-Canada Airlines
Air Canada, 269a
  *Trans-Canada Highway
longest continuous, 372b
  *Transactional
analysis, 51a
  *Transcript
very image and, 544a
  *Travel
tourists on skis, 14b
between countries, 110a
charioteers, 118b
dreams into action, 167a
very verge of space, 182b
tourist photographed, 215b
expense of t. in, 222b
always first class, 276a
astronaut pleased, 323a
on a passport, 348a
have gun will, 406b
suffer, love, 444b
get to the place, 490b
I'm too late, 500a
import tourists, 611a
what to see, 621a
  *Travellers, The
This Land Is Your, 241a
  *Treason
oppose the veiled, 380a
guilty of high, 427b
Riel charged, 497b

thousand years of, 540b
of the intellectuals, 601b
  *Treasury Board*
whenever I hear word, 171b
  *Treaty*
of Paris, 67b
right to negotiate, 143b
the obnoxious, 329b
privilege of making, 380a
not secretly, 414a
long as sun shines, 434a
  *Trees*
flat, arid Regina, 1b
every damn pine, 127a
uproot tallest, 144b
fight caterpillars, 148a
brilliant flowers, 164b
to be chopped, 210a
feel downfall, 284a
settler hates a, 284b
country an immense, 336a
autocamps instead, 366a
poem as lovely, 372b
every, an Iroquois, 404a
fight themselves, 406b
a century to grow, 446b
and service pole, 463b
trustworthiness, 506a
approach solitary, 506a
only God make a, 556a
shade of the old apple, 634a
  *Triangle*
North Atlantic, 10a
  *Trollope, Anthony*
charming novel, 457b
  *Troy*
rose and fell ten, 372b
  *Troyer, Warner*
how badly do you, 595a
  *Truck*
no t. nor trade with, 200b
  *Trudeau, Pierre Elliott*
if it puckers, 31b
a dilettante, 85a
him kiss a farmer, 154a
not consult cabinet, 159b
in Senate as T. liberal, 199b
call him president, 210a
and Pelletier join, 405b
burdened with hope, 447a
curtain goes up, 454b
no command performances, 473b
Pilon is a good poet, 477b
No. 1 catch of jet, 503b
never get bald, 524b
as agent and victim, 550b
minister is Billy, 557b
most noted words, 564b
very lovely bubble, 594b
all the T. horsemen, 650b
  *True*
land of the leal, 301b
a t. blue at once, 375b
neither clericals, 462a
North we lately heard, 580a
Canada ever be, North, 581a
the t. north, strong, 626a
  *Truro*
art-loving bishop, 17b
  *Trust*

what a t. is ours, 48b
in earthly powers, 141b
that world we won, 309a
withdraw t. placed, 329a
in Providence, 383a
I say t. the people, 398a
George DuPre and, 496a
  *Truth*
who tells the, 9b
lie's lie, 104a
tell the, 153b
difficult to come, 190b
ask to retract, 193a
lie when I tell, 210a
leads to meaninglessness, 229b
many-faceted, 234b
literature concerned, 237b
trial not inquiry, 242b
part is illusions, 254a
hard thing to speak, 266b
ignorance may find, 277a
error has effect of, 277b
artistic than fiction, 285b
day of global, 297b
inject into history, 322a
set out to look, 339a
a half-t., a brick, 339a
earnest search, 347b
set me free, 400a
probably very small, 432b
sort of tell the, 519a
must be telling, 557b
advertising deceives with, 560b
poetry only access, 625a
Einstein's relative, 649b
  *Tugboat Annie*
popular stories, 489a
  *Tundra*
sing, learned dame, of, 156a
too much, 372b
  *Tuponia*
suitable name for, 386a
  *Tupper, Sir Charles*
tell American statesmen, 379b
dispenser of patronage, 547a
  *Turban*
Deanna Durbin wears a, 25a
  *Turgenev, Ivan*
and Callaghan, 635b
  *Turkey*
Quebec like, 106b
to kow-tow to, 235b
and Canada close, 261a
  *Turks*
twilight of his harem, 270b
Canadians more corrupt, 266b
mosquitoes and, 629b
  *Tuxford*
hit the Marquis, 13a
  *T.V.*
See Television.
  *Twain, Mark*
Huckleberry Finn greater, 337b
sit below Aristotle, 339b
I shall now read, 383b
  *Twelve-Foot Davis*
everyman's friend, 141a
  *Twentieth Century*
shall be the c. of Canada, 330a
belongs to Canada, 331b

Canada belongs to, 332b
what a rotten, 333a
of Canada and bathroom, 333a
weary t.c. blues, 333a
only the first quarter, 333b
was indeed Canada's, 333b
not belong to, 333b
did belong to, 333b
to T.-C.-Fox, 334a
belongs to the moon, 334a
is Canada's, 360b
what a rotten, 522a
Canada and bathroom, 522b
  *Twenty-First Century*
one generation away, 333b
belongs to Japan, 333b
  *Twenty-fourth*
of May, 25a
Empire Day, 191b
born in Buffalo on, 200a
school day preceding, 511b
  *Twenty-second*
of July, 1793, 389b
  *Two*
solitudes protect, 502b
nations warring in bosom, 170b
not invent the phrase, 394b
  *Tyranny*
all miseries of, 31a
Nova Scotia scene of, 43b
never known Hitler's, 112b
twisted nationalism, 153a
organized minorities, 207b
thirst the enemy of, 229b
of the majority, 245b
filled to overflowing, 445a
compulsion, anonymous, 513b
generates revolutions, 601a

# U

  *U.E.L.*
See United Empire Loyalists.
  *Ukrainians*
better Canadians for, 83a
the proper place for, 136a
in House of Commons, 152b
think they won Trafalgar, 340a
or Polish or Chinese, 348a
be subject and citizen, 436a
in sheepskin coats, 542b
become slightly bigger, 607a
  *Unanimous*
voice of the continent, 3a
  *Uncle Louis*
to be hard to beat, 520a
  *Uncle Sam*
goodbye, dear, 22b
John Bull, Johnny Canuck, 94b
  *Uncle Tom*
my name is Henson, 258a
came to Canada, 637a
  *Underground*
the u. railroad, 637a
  *Underhill, Frank H.*
from the fate of Australia, 209a
  *Understand*

nobody could u. anything, 187a
neither King nor, 276a
*Understanding*
to bring inter-human, 57b
very powers of the, 77a
if a man u. one woman, 178b
books weaken your, 245b
never a point of view, 397b
pictures not felt, 421a
birds is easy, 421b
Canada the product of, 596b
*Underworld*
king powerless, 479a
*Undeveloped*
world's last great, 292a
if Canada so is B.B., 398b
isn't exactly, 426a
*Unemployment*
I will end u. or perish, 48b
government creating it, 251a
end u. or perish, 259b
not give a five-cent piece, 306a
regrettable side effect, 598a
main problem, 599a
not asking why, 643a
*Uniformity*
unity without, 205a
*Union*
united to support, 12b
privilege of joining, 131a
still the U. grows, 261b
nobody loses status, 287a
organize in foreign, 356a
adhere to the, 375b
for the common weal, 376a
nationalize all American, 442b
the rag, tag, bobtail, 452b
capitalist abuse led to, 478b
Mine, Mill & Smelt, 505b
and not annexation, 552a
*Union Jack*
no foreign flag above, 21a
for beneath the U.J., 22a
keep both hands on, 168a
under the broad folds, 379b
for beneath the, 387b
took off my hat, 448a
[See also Flag.]
*Union Nationale*
c'est moi, 169a
or heaven will help, 169b
*Union of South Africa*
our intention to follow, 66a
ostrich farm, 177b
poets of the Cape, 624a
[See also Africa.]
*Union of the Canadas*
repeal of Union, 418b
*United*
to support, not combined, 12b
provinces should be, 245a
is to be well, 245a
*United Church*
a uniting church, 442a
*United Empire Loyalists*
they sacrificed everything, 11b
U.E., U.E.L., 97a
Unity of the Empire, 97a
their press not free, 271a
peopled by American, 434b

a grand type, 581a
*United Kingdom*
See Great Britain.
*United Nations*
expect to hear Canada, 247b
more spent on garbage, 298a
be there around a table, 407b
and NATO, 519b
*United States of America*
this state British, 6a
died a citizen of the, 44a
first commandment is, 60b
counterpoise to the, 67b
not part of the, 73b
not, like the States, kicking, 77b
untied states, disunited, 113b
Ontario bounded by, 167b
I was twice in the, 218b
to think of the U.S., 229a
with the least history, 229a
kept woman of the, 230a
malaise in your land, 231b
divergent views resolved, 255b
hockey fans in, 260a
open by keeping out, 266b
banner upon our soil, 270b
not a United States-er, 273b
to visit the Arctic, 281b
early warning system, 282a
a cold, pneumonia, 295a
generosity of spirit, 304a
goals of Nazi war, 314a
real hell would be, 325a
friendship, independent, 329a
19th the century of, 332a
more intelligent air, 353a
American-controlled corps., 360b
country which survived, 367a
not far from home in, 390a
civilization nor culture, 412b
land of opportunity, 414b
declined to go to, 430b
Civil War prophesied, 437a
conservatives are rich, 438b
struggle against, 442b
ownership of resources, 447a
Japan biggest customer, 449a
like Americans, not, 466a
paths of glory lead, 479b
will not stand idly by, 509b
no place in bedrooms, 558a
from richer to poorer, 593b
sleeping with an elephant, 597a
remain in Canada, 624b
bounded on the south by, 626a
yesterday our allies, 648b
*Unity*
all Canada has is, 67a
national u. a myth, 67b
of the Empire, 97a
last obstacle to, 193a
without uniformity, 205a
political life to, 329a
sand needing cement, 371a
let us be united, 385b
under the crown, 436a
evil a basis for, 491b
without uniformity, 506b
on provincial autonomy, 514b
national u. the frame, 595a

Canada has achieved, 603a
history unites us, 610a
*Universe*
vive l'u. libre, 107a
you could govern the, 140b
lover of the, 143a
vast spread of the, 183a
calm sea would poison, 245b
ends with one joke, 339b
speculate on the, 356b
alone in the wide, 498b
archives of the, 512a
new orchestra, sonic, 526a
*University*
community of radical, 3b
not yet in being, 75b
reading list for life, 176a
either graduates or, 198a
traditions of college, 199a
appointment at Toronto, 276b
I attended three, 285a
of Canada, 292b
Canada Council, 303b
I were founding a, 338b
set up a college, 340b
academy-prisoned, 383a
a force to divide, 412a
nationhood born in, 532a
potent instrument, 542a
McLuhan and Frye at, 581b
breeding Ph.D.s, 606b
has as its aim, 623b
its self-possession, 629a
alert to change, 642b
scholar, gentleman, 645a
*Unmitigated*
an u. disaster, 120b
*Unrepented*
unrevised and, 416a
*Unrevised*
and unrepented, 416a
*Unto the Hills*
around do I lift up, 362a
*Uphold*
the right, 18a
*Upper Canada*
distant view in, 63b
inhabitants of, 75b
larger than Britain, 80b
great mass of people, 81a
at your feet, 115b
College with its, 194b
and its capital, 418b
very image and transcript, 544a
into a garden of Eden, 567a
I give you, 620b
if you lose, 627b
*Uranium*
cobalt-blue and, 45b
a u.-producing country, 76b
this baby found me, 293a
it was solid pitchblende, 317a
Denison Mines Ltd., 509a
in form of acid, 648a
*Use*
so what the hell's the, 382b
*Useful*
privilege to be, 110b
who are only, 342b

*Usurer*
a bright-eyed, 321b
*Utopia*
similar to Canada, 207b
and nationalism, 348a

# V

*Valcartier*
munitions worker at, 188b
*Valley*
the Red River, 24b
*Valleyfield*
dynamite shipped out, 564b
*Vallières, Pierre*
fellow absolutist, 551a
*Valour*
gave a common death, 193b
*Value*
real and not face, 40b
where common sink, 166b
Indian's sense of, 510b
*Van Diemen's Land*
Australia, 642a
*Van Horne, Sir William*
passes on the CP, 547a
*Vancouver*
there was an old maid, 18a
sparkling diamond, 25b
it barks right in, 98b
no interest to, 133a
Gassy Jack, 144a
speak French in, 199a
retire on the road, 210a
no bias in, 233a
I was free, 315b
flee to V. and, 316b
and we docked in, 325b
exotic like Coronation, 353b
squib in Sun, 366a
strike, bullets, 386b
City Hall of, 387a
far from Ottawa, 387a
had the scenery, 388a
the East Thing, 437b
history is bunkhouse, 447b
the pick of Canada, 537b
iron spikes between, 610b
*Vancouver Island*
from V.I. to the, 71b
from Bonavista to, 241a
treminus of the R.R., 390a
passes to reward, 620a
*Vanderbilt*
not merely become, 446a
*Vanier, Georges*
epitaph for flier, 110a
*Vaster*
a v. Britain, 96a
we hold a v. empire, 435a
hold a v. empire, 439b
*Vegetable*
what's Algoma, 137b
from plant's view, 137b
*Veiled*
oppose the v. treason, 380a
*Verchères, Madeleine*
of Madeleine, 163b

*Verdun*
Pétain greater at, 68b
*Vermont*
this state British, 6a
*Versailles*
if Paris and, 124a
wake one morning in, 362b
*Vertical*
not horizontal, 264b
the v. mosaic, 480b
*Vézina Trophy*
a goalkeeper good, 614a
*Viceroyalty*
to call it a, 98b
*Vichy*
Pétain greater at, 68b
*Victim*
of his strength, 16a
prepare a menu, 316b
our own intelligence, 410b
of colonial misrule, 489b
*Victoria, Queen*
on her birthday, 191b
hurrah for, 215b
told of death, 331b
Mother the Queen, 414a
to see my children, 434a
as a young queen, 444a
illustrious reign, 512a
trodden upon by, 633b
emancipation of, 434a
it is Victorian, 640b
*Victoria*
riot act never read, 14a
semper liber, 15a
chain of theatres, 197b
bookshelf reaching, 238b
well-forged link, 308b
pillars of beauty, 311a
piece of England, 311a
reparation, separation, 324a
not limited to, 379b
smallest book in, 402b
a Queen's name, 565a
*Victorious*
send her, 22b
here died Wolfe, 29b
here died Wolfe, 640a
*Victory*
you shall achieve, 135a
carry on and, 223a
prepare menu for, 316b
our v. is certain, 364a
spirit will grow, 615b
*Vienna*
nobody hates me, 567a
*Vietnam*
Canada both ends, 51b
and Cambodia, 232a
draft-age Americans, 316b
any peace honourable, 535b
we do our part, 564b
ordered LBJ to stop, 469b
my enthusiasm, 499a
*Vigilance*
must sleep no more, 384b
*Vikings*
call it Markland, 344b
fine country, 588a

[See also Norsemen.]
*Village*
global v. idiots, 174b
premier of Hottentot, 186a
image of global, 396a
*Ville-Marie*
commander of old fort, 236b
no longer called, 260a
[See also Montreal.]
*Vimy Ridge*
there they stood, 91a
taking of coveted, 216a
shade of trees, 415b
birth of a nation, 511b
by Passchendaele, 555a
*Vineland*
which is called, 2b
earliest mention, 243a
nature so generous, 344b
earliest mention, 587b
[See also Newfoundland.]
*Violence*
outrageous kinds, 3a
thought about, 126b
decides everything, 163b
of disaffected, 181a
higher measure of, 192a
cannot produce, 207b
a shouted hit, 224a
quest for identity, 398a
Quebec's, 524b
not trustees of, 596b
is no stranger, 599b
*Virgil*
glorified prairies, 111a
*Virginie*
two girls, one, 527a
*Virgins*
tender, delicate, 345b
send fifty, 591b
*Virtue*
woman's riches in, 285b
to our v. always kind, 381b
unendurable than vice, 368b
authority, ridiculous, 533b
*Vision*
not only snow, 37b
a man to see far, 223b
land of no one, 304b
*Vista*
terra primum, 92a
*Vive*
who howl vives, 94b
l'univers libre, 107a
le Québec libre, 214b
le Québec libre, 293b
le Québec libre, 346b
*Vizinczey, Stephen*
true cosmopolitan, 192a
*Voice*
unanimous of continent, 3a
gave me a, 487a
the louder, 600b
*Volkswagen*
journalistic, 138b
*Voltaire*
countryman, Pascal, 37a
not regret loss, 152a
Candide published, 229b
writers want to be, 621b

*Volunteers
push on, brave, 21a
push on, brave York, 76a
*Vote
no woman shall, 19b
not understand, 96b
like wooden soldier, 219b
offends Montreal, 280a
cheered but, 331a
men start to, 370a
no woman, idiot, lunatic, 370b
Grit or Tory, 392b
with the Tories, 454a
nonsense about women, 507a
ballot corrupt way, 565b
women got the, 631b
opinions mine, my, 644a
*Voter
in a deep slumber, 607b
*Votes
government right, 91b
let us know by, 170a
casting more than, 343a
where you grovel, 564b
*Voyageur
image of bourgeois, 348b
expletive commonly, 568b
[See also Coureur-de-bois.]

W

*Wade, Mason
Abbé Groulx became, 237a
*Waffle
call me a, 36a
rather w. to the left, 75a
*Waiting
world is w. for sunrise, 358a
*Wales, Prince of
no one can visit, 180b
*Wales
favourites as Welshmen, 248b
trace it back to, 301b
the way to Montreal, 582a
*Walk
please w. on grass, 584a
*Walker
the w. of the snow, 536b
*Walpole, Horace
said of Italy, 283b
*Walrus
the aggie will come, 443b
*War
the habiliment of, 47b
industries, napalm, 51b
and revolutions, 65a
no-man's-land in, 84a
with all stupidities, 85a
postponed, fought, 104b
no one wins a, 111a
two world-wide, 114a
never want to see any, 135a
never of Canadian origin, 143a
cast all weapons, 144b
wage w. on w. itself, 149b
probability of nuclear, 228a
make peace as exciting, 234b

one million men, 274a
hockey is a, 278a
is Hell, what homesteading, 301b
taught the lesson, 307b
only on western side, 319b
fallout over west, 325a
to take part in, 329a
if you want us to help, 329a
Britain at w., Canada at, 330b
Canada is at war also, 331a
ready, aye, ready, 331a
failure of human wisdom, 335a
of attrition on Indians, 344a
resources for tanks, 351a
things that change, 354a
to invade Canada, 355a
between England and, 376a
lay waste populous, 385a
man's best game, 394b
unthinkable, absurd, 399b
friendships, warships, 421b
grave of Montcalm, 427a
three enemies, 457a
can't be this bad, 468b
prepare for w. like giants, 468b
don't answer phone, 469a
rules for nice safe, 530a
when women have voice, 565b
all manliness due, 610b
democracy, impossible, 641a
*War of 1812
martial airs, 21a
I saw Tecumseh, 58b
awful, eventful, 76a
choose your terms, 77a
reluctant signer, 115b
give up the fort, 131a
take without soldiers, 185b
Mrs. Secord's walk, 194a
Billy the Scout, 231b
York's destruction, 246a
inhabitants of Canada, 274b
Johnson killed Tecumseh, 288a
Chesapeake and Shannon, 335b
no duty performed, 392a
Americans lost it, 447b
met the enemy, ours, 473b
we have met enemy, 473b
Pike's Peak or Bust, 477a
interest of humanity, 490a
occurrences known, 498b
walked nineteen miles, 531a
Tecumseh fell dead, 578b
acquisition not object, 625a
naval superiority, 627b
*War, American Civil
predicted, 437a
*War, Boer
fought, toiled, died, 309b
their guns taken, 604b
*War I, World
Canadians never budge, 5a
an exact description, 6b
Pass, Canadians, 10b
too near to be great, 12b
come on the tigers, 50a
no Canadian soldier, 64b
first line of defence, 68a
war in the air, 79a
never patronize the, 91a

not as murderers, 135a
with God's help, 135a
prefer to do mine, 155b
sweating blood, 195b
like real soldiers, 197b
coveted Vimy Ridge, 216a
men of Canada, fight on, 223a
divide 1st Division, 274a
war is Hell, but what is, 301b
two Canadian memorials, 309a
realize grossness, 311b
you have your orders, 313a
away to Western front, 326b
not Flanders, Ont., 334b
Germans prepared for worst,
    358a
In Flanders Fields, 372b
die with special dash, 400a
Vimy Ridge dedication, 415b
Germany awards Canada, 424b
over Welland Canal, 462a
training with R.F.C., 468a
Mademoiselle from Armentières,
    496b
Battle of the Somme, 498a
birth of nation at Vimy, 511b
tell boys to come out, 514b
soldiers under sod, 514b
battle-ploughed roads, 527b
as pro-German, 537a
under alien flag, 539a
lousy private in army, 539b
title-deeds to future, 555a
*War II, World
German girls and, 4a
combined Chiefs of Staff, 4b
Pass, Canadians, 10b
Normandy inscription, 17a
hot breath of war, 38a
on coast of Normandy, 74a
take to the rear, 74b
declare war on Germany, 83b
men will not enlist, 94b
Battle of Britain, 110a
V-E Day Message, 130b
Wait for Me, Daddy, 149a
slaughtered at Dieppe, 162b
guts without God, 170a
industry and government, 218b
old Canadian boor flies, 222a
he did at Dieppe, 226a
Paris is free, 246b
second time in lifetime, 248b
carry on from Canada, 263b
wartime contracts, 267b
Quebec Conference, 281a
with you to the end, 307a
not necessarily conscription,
    307a
Germans want you, 314a
a night in 1944, 351a
objectors enlist, 370a
lights on in Ottawa, 382a
Army is dagger at Berlin, 399b
Dieppe my responsibility, 399b
slipped the surly bonds, 403a
sighted sub, sank same, 409b
nothing to worry about, 418a
mannish hockey players, 452a
K-K-K-K-P, dirty old, 453a

over Welland Canal, 462a
liberation of Paris, 469b
in touch with Europe, 479a
operation lacked surprise, 504b
will not stand idly by, 509b
certainly come to Canada, 537b
Triquet's company, 593a
Canadians we would reply, 605b
state my conviction, 643b
*War, Vietnam
See Vietnam.
*War Measures Act
cited, 19a
seditious conspiracy, 108b
the F.L.Q. as entity, 242a
there is no more freedom, 405b
lot of bleeding hearts, 598b
apprehended insurrection, 599a
[See also October Crisis.]
*Warden
of the North, 15a
of the honour of, 308b
*Warlike
Canadians are not, 248a
forced to be, 557b
unmilitary people, 558a
*Warring
two nations in the bosom, 170b
*Washington, George
ordered to take Que., 26b
planning campaign, 620b
*Washington
no reciprocity made in, 92b
tribal brothers in, 94a
begging in Ottawa, 359a
after Ottawa, 431b
we will come from, 443a
more sacred than York, 565b
cough in W., spit on Parlia-
    ment, 619a
*W.A.S.P.
See White Anglo-Saxon Protes-
    tant.
*Water
drink of the Peace River, 13a
disturb w.s of tranquillity, 39b
the field or the flower, 172b
hewers of wood, drawers, 217b
hewers of w., haulers, 231b
French willing to drink, 247a
in Nfld. rich, 252b
lead a dead horse to, 321b
hold me up, mighty, 409b
as long as w. flows, 414a
only flush for no. 2, 441b
fish didn't discover, 463b
not object to holy, 586b
canoe to the w.-ways, 641b
*Waterloo
Anglo-French confrontation,
    188a
*Watkins Report
realized for first time, 513a
*Watson
Mr. W., come here, 44a
*Way
it's a long w. to Tipperary, 633b
*Wayne, Johnny
distinguish Shuster, 192a
[See also Frank Shuster.]

*Wealth
from the sea, 15a
of Ont. across country, 69a
members who amassed, 253b
cared less about, 259b
2% possess half, 260b
labour, source of all, 260b
corrupt government, 298a
collectively, future, 314a
let the producers, 364a
not vigilantly cared, 424a
aristocracy of w. bad, 429a
55 men control one-third, 442a
all ridiculous, 533b
we're rich now, ah, 570a
*Weapons
machine guns, keys, 278b
Canadian finger on catch, 469a
to fight, faith, 496a
we do our part too, 564b
*Weather
fair w. to you, 10b
seven months of Arctic, 13a
Mild, isn't it, 36b
no consistency in, 40a
for catching fish, 60a
a foul-w. fiend, 113a
against bad, 164a
wants little below zero, 178b
four seasons, one day, 266a
[See also Climate.]
*Webster-Ashburton Treaty
See Ashburton-Webster Treaty.
*Weightlifting
here lies the strong, 16a
world's heavyweight, 258a
*Welfare
corporate w. bums, 352a
Eskimo w. services, 430a
Eskimo managers on, 485a
*Welland Canal
and Aimee McPherson, 401a
blow up bridge over, 462a
*Welsh
See Wales.
*Wendigo
no expression, 59a
*West
Scotch wine of, 13a
farewell to the, 24b
the W. and the rest, 38a
no riotous youth, 188b
the landless man, 197b
to manless land, 198b
kept like a desert, 220a
newest civilization, 221a
new hopefulness, 238a
have the truth told, 262a
bias of communication, 279b
New Canada is simply, 300a
till W. is East, 308b
waves of fallout, 325a
French vanishes, 340a
foothill, mountain, 365a
the Britain of the, 388a
in the W., spatial, 392a
her gates both east and, 503b
farmer guardian of dream, 505a
American settlers in, 510a

the last best, 542b
world's bread basket, 542b
road it has to travel, 543b
if you write of the, 549b
settlers had come into, 559a
bounded on the w. by 625b
*West Coast
See British Columbia.
*West Indies
New York and, 25b
difficult immigration, 304b
Columbus' voyage, 474b
*Western Canada
vast amounts of capital, 63b
there is W. patriotism, 67b
can feel the history, 103b
administration concerned, 543a
from east to w. sea, 626b
*Westminster, Statute of
extraterritorial laws, 20a
*Westmount
will disappear, 20b
ladies' bad speech, 204b
the W. Rhodesians, 557a
*Whale
couple of white, 35b
grand leap up Niagara, 203a
flowing with blubber, 247a
*What's
a million, 268b
the news, 576a
*Wheat
grain without sowing, 2b
the w. province, 15a
greatest w. market, 32b
how splendid, 86b
speculation never raised, 178b
Canadian w. pool, 280b
endless w.-bearing acres, 314a
to breed Marquis, 314a
not grow on glacier, 323a
Lord said let there be, 340a
assimilation is w. and, 367b
No. 1 hard Manitoba, 398a
prophecy about, 436b
world's bread basket, 542b
why should I sell, 596b
don't throw w. at me, 597b
less hell and more, 611a
*Wheels
hell on, 632a
*Whiff
of grape shot, 155b
a w. of grape, 642a
*Whiggery
exhort him to give, 168a
[See also Liberalism.]
*Whisky
more on w. than books, 35b
we who make w. say, 77a
bad men and w. killing, 132b
healthy, cheap, 169a
prohibit alcohol, 338a
made history and took, 431b
founded on love and, 456b
they like our spirit, 566b
*White
follow my w. plume, 330b
Protestant, heterosexual, 499b
nigger of America, 609b

*White Anglo-Saxon Protes-
 tant
Clark Kent, WASP, 541b
*White House
Rideau Hall saved us, 298b
*Whitehorse
Trail of '98, 15b
the W. Star, 70b
*Whitemud Creek
decided not to fault, 560b
*Whiteoak
Adeline refused to, 145a
passionate family, 625b
*Whither
are we drifting, 47a
*Whitman, Walt
no W. wanted, 57a
break from past, 625b
*Wholesome
sea is at her gates, 503b
*Wife
prostitute not enemy, 3b
dog better than, 9a
suspects all other, 445a
irritating, impossible, 468b
I am a w. and mother, 519b
*Wild
fresh loneliness of, 78a
Indians called, 102b
followed call of the, 222a
where w. Oswego spreads, 222b
only humans are, 421a
humbly, passionately, 586b
*Wilde, Oscar
Mr. Watson, is the, 623b
*Wilderness
mystique still strong, 62a
home is in the, 122b
Ontario bounded by, 167b
10,000 square miles, 234a
dreamers go into, 238a
town in the midst, 259a
these Sinbads of the, 280a
cut umbilical cord, 301a
rink a symbol of, 302a
occupied by animals, 357b
and visitors, 357b
leave whole country, 376a
toiled and suffered, 429b
not without rose, 429b
to explore, preserve, 435b
and the baseline, 436a
semblance of balance, 455a
Caesars of the, 488b
and unexplored, 586b
*Will
is the human inert, 114a
clause seven of, 192a
clause in w. of, 202b
lack of w. to resist, 208a
patient's w. to, 219b
of people spoken, 495a
northern people have, 567a
*Win
doesn't everyone, 232b
I think necessary to, 278a
if you play to, 419a
all you have to do, 546a
*Wind
that wants a flag, 7b

will I give them, 498a
the turn of the, 528a
laws that govern, 548a
mystery of prairie, 561a
four strong w.s, 606a
*Wine
Scotch is w. of west, 13a
a Bordeaux not a house, 31b
on account of, 101b
hogshead of Spanish, 299b
port w. was a, 484b
*Wineland
See Vineland.
*Winged
peace or w. death, 57b
*Wings
the w. of an angel, 326b
suppose enemy have, 427a
no pasting on man, 454a
English not got, 612b
*Winning
you can't beat, 37a
act of God to beat, 92b
when to drop out, 398a
next to trying, 428a
hockey is fun, 479a
has an incentive, 555a
I like only, 576b
*Winnipeg
unum cum virtute, 15a
treble clef, 74a
tell it's not Paris, 179b
become my Waterloo, 222b
mental attitude, 251b
get there by dog sled, 251b
in W. an igloo, 251b
here still listen, 263b
fingers in the dikes, 275b
member for W. North, 279b
things in abundance, 311a
brash and vigorous, 388a
boy meets girl in, 395a
God looked down, 490a
discouraging place, 543a
cooly sunnyness, 563a
no English, 563b
seen real mud, 605a
*Winnipeg, Lake
Indian hunting by, 98a
*Winnipeg General Strike
from a thousand hills, 155b
British flag will, 230a
purge of lawless, 230a
labour's battles, 527b
shooting taught, 643a
*Winter
Canadian or Russian, 37a
it is cold, 38a
session of white, 91b
spring lingered, 114b
is all wrong for, 119b
elements own land, 135b
oxygen of bright, 165b
before fall comes, 166a
climate nine months, 185a
not always in, 232b
sleep for six months, 259a
landscape of snow, 281a
hockey in chill of, 302b
for reading, study, 320b

mind does not mount, 320b
not a country but, 354a
frigid gates, 389a
brown hares to, 453a
whitewashes us, 594b
my country, it's, 615b
hardy influence of, 631a
*Wireless
See Telegraph.
*Wisdom
Arctic sum total, 37b
be wise, persevere, 114b
variable possession, 139b
ceremony invented, 179a
the conventional, 211a
courage surest, 233a
Eskimo words for, 268a
Canada wisest of us, 310b
more w. lies than, 322a
war failure of, 335a
is a silver fish, 401b
wise who forgives, 451a
look wise, say nothing, 458a
experience in seeing, 458b
foolish w. of tomorrow, 458b
exact shade of grey, 624a
*Wish
often slip apart, 478b
the w. book, 545a
for ourselves, all, 642b
*Wit
in hostilities, 164b
great man's reputation, 179b
taste refuge of w.less, 463b
*Witch
Eskimo w.s, 144a
church is w. of God, 609b
*Wives
here I lie between, 16b
expect too much, 61a
women and husband's, 103b
I had twenty, 511a
*Wolf
come near at your peril, 23b
says he's been et, 134b
stepladders dangerous, 134b
and of course a, 366a
say to the dogs, 646a
*Wolfe, James
to his men did say, 20b
how goes the battle, 20b
here died W. victorious, 29b
and the St. Lawrence, 69a
a magnet's force, 128a
mad is he, then I, 215b
was it Wolfe dying, 419b
the dauntless hero came, 439a
who run, 464b
I will die in peace, 464b
death depicted, 496a
written Elegy instead, 532b
spare the women, 591b
find somebody to talk, 612b
in hour of victory, 619b
historian, painter, 628a
*Wolfe's Cove
100 men posted there, 427a
where to land, 564b
*Woman
no w. shall vote, 19b

treat a horse like, 26b
still interested at, 41a
a magnificent old, 48a
get so bored with, 54a
resembles continents, 62b
in Paris I show a, 78a
gold is a, 81b
a real w. knows, 108a
asking her age, 114b
asks not for ballot, 116a
when pursued by mad, 139b
no sin a w. can't, 167b
man understands one, 178b
influenced by suspicion, 179a
man makes me feel a, 202b
kept w. of the U.S., 230a
is the species, 252a
say more in a sigh, 252a
victory to surrender, 252a
tears a man's terrors, 252a
just like a white, 290a
saw the lady herself, 310a
one rather becomes, 315b
when you educate, 316a
a country like a, 343a
no idiot shall vote, 370b
wish you were a man, 400a
she is the house, 440b
he knew me as a, 441a
love weak men, 444b
bottom of troubles, 458a
doesn't want to talk, 465b
behind successful man, 470a
superficial femininity, 476b
seams on her face, 483a
does w. want here, 531b
can't refuse a, 565a
male gaping at bunny, 604a
man art and w. art, 632a
go well at home, 635a
marriage, w. stays, 649b
*Women
few females possess, 14b
enough in Parliament, 37a
love to be loved, 44b
ignorance of ways, 61a
traders accustomed to, 97a
men, w. and wives, 103b
true liberation of, 103b
before ladies sit, 106a
in confessional, 110b
should have democracy, 116a
fly and like flowers, 172a
never study men, 178b
fraternizing with enemy, 187b
among French Canadians, 191b
sparkling toilet bowl, 232b
place is in the House, 232b
ladies wear breeches, 243b
has a w.'s secret, 244a
injuries, never slights, 245b
all w. are rivals, 252a
wooed for complections, 252a
offer their bodies, 254a
were made to labour, 254a
repining, discontented, 284a
riches in virtue, 285b
spectral Cassandras, 294b
talent more human, 303a

less feminine in politics, 319a
bachelors don't understand,
    323a
tired w. could rest, 334a
good w. greatest thing, 339b
no Mrs. Pickwick, 340a
taken over man's 342a
defect in lady society, 344a
tender virgins, 345b
added to knowledge, 346b
ten best-breasted, 349a
sentencing of females, 369a
quit politics if, 370b
call on dad, 370b
set a low value, 370b
economic dependence, 370b
prefer pin-headed, 371a
were not persons, 371a
I am not a nice, 371b
absolute equality, 400a
dangerous no husbands, 444a
being a w. in Toronto, 444b
buried in bungalows, 445a
so full of tact, 458a
more than just me, 503b
opposed by short-haired, 507a
want to vote for, 507a
they have suffrage, 507a
abortion a sacrament, 518a
and orgasms, 536a
merging of the sexes, 539a
forgot justice to, 553b
wars will cease, 565b
Your Highness spare, 591b
got the vote as gift, 631b
twice as well as men, 632a
know men better than, 634b
[See also King's Girls and
    Suffrage.]
*Women's Institutes
home and country, 265b
*Won
we w. didn't we, 546a
elections not by prayers, 575a
*Wonder
the w. of the thing, 93b
no mysteries only w.s, 186b
I shall not w. more, 314a
awe and w. of our, 356b
great people alive to, 477a
through enlargement, 528b
*Wood
paper produced from, 191a
hewers of w. and, 217b
of w. and haulers, 231b
vanish in a w. of heroes, 347b
no shelter but wild, 567b
of vessel to beat Bluenose, 620a
*Woodcutters
intellectuals among, 544a
*Wooden
vote like w. soldier, 219b
*Woods
cold in northern, 3a
secret hid by those, 160a
solitary loneliness, 407a
hoary w. are grand, 423b
life in backw., 429a
sublime solitude of, 429b

sweep of melancholy, 464a
back to the w., muse, 522b
*Woodstock
they may take, 12b
*Words
my final, 39b
spell, rhythms, 57b
so many fine, 87b
are like things, 91b
in the house of, 151b
poetry of w. exists, 161a
all my journeys, 213a
weasel, 269a
object cannot lie, 286a
origin is history, 313b
last as long as sun, 434a
those five never fade, 466b
necessary to live, 477b
frozen and not heard, 487b
have been victorious, 540b
*Wordsworth, William
waiting their, 78a
what W. tried to do, 624a
*Work
we must w. at, 25a
think and w. hard, 34a
cannot carry on, 40b
for the night is coming, 118b
if one w. hard, 126a
learned what means, 173a
holidays interfere, 179a
the future doesn't, 208b
privilege of poor, 324b
harder, luckier, 342a
without job, die, 353b
every man son of his, 385b
reward is more, 394a
till my life is done, 402b
live on little if, 418b
no habit tenacious, 434a
pensions aren't for, 454a
no ambition beyond, 459a
be happy tomorrow, 472a
said it was steady, 493b
equal amounts of, 496b
what we have to do, 533a
except by hard, 543b
accomplish anything, 566b
doesn't want to do, 579b
how many for money, 585a
done well in every, 611a
even w. for money, 650a
*Workers
to communism from, 84b
spineless who groans, 104a
victim of conspiracy, 106b
himself a capitalist, 121b
right to associations, 131a
marching with the, 131a
right not to organize, 169b
secure legislation for, 201a
we are only loggers, 317b
into your confidence, 326a
difficult to find a, 345a
in foreign unions, 356a
nothing to relieve the, 363b
crawl or fight, 392b
under capitalism in jail, 392b
Canada's advantages, 429b

rag, tag and bobtail, 452b
Confederation at expense, 609b
industrial, agricultural, 643a
  *World
eyes are on Alberta, 2a
it is rotten, 16b
drifted far from anchorage, 64b
senseless, unreadable, 156a
embody their obscure, 166b
see w. as it is, 174a
imminence of natural, 208b
smaller it seems, 245a
library open to all, 270a
fiasco of this, 276b
in a damn wicked, 312b
Canadian passport to, 348a
Canada is a, 354b
makes an impersonal, 358a
is waiting for sunrise, 358a
from beginning to, 358b
hand rocks, not rules, 370b
magnificence of corruption, 444b
tomb of brave men, 490b
over Canada famous, 499a
man and his, 519b
is my country, 529b
  *Worms
when the ice w. nest, 571b
  *Worst
Beaverbrook best, 113a
afraid of the, 513b
  *Wounds
these men make the, 54b
  *Wrestling
only thing on level, 487b
  *Write
speak they will, 143a
should be printed, 143a
I w. with an axe, 148a
to w., not teach, 151b
despair does not, 229a
call a Method novel, 327a
anyone can w. a book, 368a
his autobiography, 368b
never w. a letter, 376b
communicate joy, 383a
nobody w. songs, 402a
as you fight, 434b
suffer, love, read, 444b
desire came upon, 546b
  *Writer
nation-wide attack of, 89a
who lives where born, 93a
there are two kinds, 93a
always watching, 93a
best in America, 93b
being a Canadian, 213b
second-string maybe, 336b
not used Canadian, 353b
greatest, successful, 366a
attention to the day, 367a
must have pores, 371b
a ghost has pride, 383b
only estate is name, 418a
unknown, obscure, 442a
rich by writing, 448a
existence ignorant, 498b
all are parochial, 499b
loser's advocate, 500a

no longer a man, 570a
man is situated, 636a
  *Writing
have a good time, 52a
away from typewriter, 52b
single sentences cost, 52b
compulsion to talk, 57a
ink is gunpowder, 74a
with royalties, 85a
damned short sentences, 113b
influential journalism, 145b
imminence of natural, 208b
chief industry not, 238b
unnecessary to invent, 242b
impossible in Canada, 256a
punch in every paragraph, 263a
written but I say, 279a
just odd jobs, 327a
jot down ideas, 342a
bigger the renaissance, 353a
in black and, 492b
it's about dying, 500a
can make it in Canada, 547b
most private things, 636a
rather have written lines, 639a
  *Wrong
anything w. about that, 47a
never on the side of, 152b
freedom the right to, 152b
good man who goes, 179a
judge dispute in terms, 222a
angry when a man is, 244b
but not fifteen, 257a
to submit to nothing, 270b
be w. than recent, 368a
conscience tells us, 368b
support me when I, 381a
I'd rather be, 398a
now judged right or, 416a
certainly I was, 591a

X

  *Xenia
could have enjoyed, 123a

Y

  *Yankee
tight-sphinctered, 95a
I am a Y. by birth, 159a
infusion of Y. blood, 183b
must south of us remain, 290a
  *Yankees
awful black eye, 43a
four and twenty, 178a
about Y. and Canucks, 273b
no truck nor trade with, 200b
wretched who hunger, 376a
Dominion wound us, 379b
no need to pamper us, 438a
  *Yellowknife
multum in parvo, 15a

of Great Slave Lake, 316a
  *Yesterday
I am y. and I know, 191b
today and tomorrow, 421b
  *Yes
Alec, it is I, 46a
  *Yonge Street
longest street, 12b
the longest, 136a
longest in the world, 521a
  *York
push on, brave Y. volunteers,
    76a
vilest blue-devil haunts, 212a
sacred than Washington, 565b
streets are laid, 573b
[See also Toronto.]
  *York Factory
storms, battles, shipwrecks, 325a
  *You
go no farther, 500b
  *You'll
never die, John A., 379a
  *Young
voices of the, 151b
since you and I were, 288b
country where the y. live, 486a
  *Your man
the expression get, 369a
  *Youth
y.'s for an hour, 16a
I once had, 40b
the last of my, 57a
be careful what you wish, 58a
with young fogies, 140a
young enough not to, 178b
think old men fools, 245b
will not reform society, 522a
she has the gift of, 573a
is not a vanished thing, 428b
poorly educated to change, 444b
decisive point is Canada's, 460b
  *Yukon Territory
all Klondike proverbs, 14a
home of the Klondike, 15b
this is the law of the, 533b
challenge of the, 593a

Z

  *Zembla
the Lord knows where, 480b
  *Zenda
the prisoner of, 56b
  *Zero
Mile Z., like mukluks, 316a
value of their z. land, 353b
  *Zolf, Larry
later quipped, 600b
  *Zone
men of the northern, 301b
  *Zorra
they'll no take, 12b
  *Zzzyhaff
Meredydd, 618a